AF658021

A DICTIONARY OF HINDUISM

A DICTIONARY OF HINDUISM

including

Its Mythology, Religion, History, Literature, and Pantheon

compiled and edited by

Subodh Kapoor

COMPILOR AND EDITOR
THE HINDUS. Encyclopaedia of Hinduism,
THE BUDDHISTS. Encyclopaedia of Budhhism,
Encyclopaedia of Indian Heritage, in 90 volumes,
Companion Encyclopaedia of Hindu Philosophy

Cosmo Publications

2004 **New Delhi**

A DICTIONARY OF HINDUISM

First Published by COSMO 2004

This book first appeared with the title, "Encyclopaedic Dictionary of Hinduism", individually as well as an accompanying volume number 5 of "The Hindus. Encyclopaedia of Hinduism".

ISBN 81-7755-874-9

Published by

MRS. RANI KAPOOR
for COSMO PUBLICATIONS
Publishing Division of
GENESIS PUBLISHING PVT. LTD.
24-B, Ansari Road, Darya Ganj,
New Delhi-110 002, INDIA

Composed at

Cosmo Publications

Printed at

Mehra Offset Press

ॐ

OM SRI GANESH

Om Sri Ganeshay Namah
Om Ma Sarasvati Namah
Om Sri Hanumate Namah
Om Sri Guruve Namah

वक्रतुण्ड महाकाय सूर्यकोटिसमप्रभ ।
निर्विघ्नं कुरू में देव शुभकार्यार्थसिद्धये ।।

This humble work is placed at the beautiful lotus feet of

Sri Ganapati

May he continue to bless the Hindus whereever they are in the world

INTRODUCTION

Hinduism is a vast ocean of striking contrast with a magnificent heritage of civilization and diversity in customs and traditions quite unlike any other system of philosophy or human thought. The volume of written material covering all aspects of Hindu history, thought, philosophy, its mythology and pantheon is enormous. Any student of Indian literature, irrespective of deriving his knowledge in the ancient classical tongue, the Sanskrit in which its earliest and original works are written, or has made his acquaintance with it from the modern Indian vernacular , has felt the difficulties that arise from the frequent mention of ancient personages from—Vedas, Puranas and the Epic literature—mythical characters, deities from the vast ocean of Hindu pantheon, places, objects and innumerable other names that he either does not recognise or has very scanty information on to be of any meaningful use.

Significant attempts were made by worthy scholars like John Garrett and John Dowson who bridged this gap in our knowledge. For several decades their books have remained a cornerstone for the study of Indian literature and its proper understanding. It is therefore very obvious that these two dictionaries form the core of the present work. The present work also draws material from established works by eminent Orientalists like William Jones, H. H. Wilson, Colbrooke, Max Muller, Burnof, Princep etc., who had an intimate grasp of the inner life and feelings of the ancient Hindus, and it would have been a hopeless task to impart this knowledge more accurately or more precisely than in their own words. It is for this reason that copious extracts from their established works and findings have been drawn upon.

The present volume is the first to appear in a series of Indological dictionaries to be published. The work on this dictionary was undertaken as a companion volume to the **Hindu Encyclopaedia** which for the first time attempts to satisfy the need for a vast introductory work on as diverse a subject as Hinduism. The work on two other dictionaries is almost complete, titled—"**Sakti. The Dictionary of Female in Hindu Mythology**" and "**A Dictionary of the Ramayana**". These two dictionaries shall be presented to the readers soon. It is hoped that the *Dictionary of Female in Hindu Mythology* will fulfill a long-standing demand for such a work and will make available ready information on the Female aspect of the Divine Nature in Hinduism.

The main object of the present work was to fill the ever-growing popular demand for a comprehensive HINDU DICTIONARY which covers the entire spectrum of Hinduism. It contains an account of all the Hindu deities, all the mythical personages and objects including mythical beings, gods and goddesses, the vehicles (*vahans*) utilised by the deities, and objects. The various terms of Brahmanical and Buddhist theology and ritual, and of all the schools of Indian philosophy including the various systems of thought propounded by sages and saints, will be found briefly explained. The detailed articles on these will ofcourse be found in my *Hindu Encyclopaedia*. All possible authentic information on ancient Indian geography, its history and antiquity as can be obtained has been provided. For the reason that the Hindus attach great importance to the genealogies from the ancient India, the present work contains almost *every name* occurring in ancient books. As the Hindu mythology and its religion are bound up inseparably, both these areas are therefore amply represented in the present work. Lastly, brief descriptions have been included of the most frequently mentioned literary works either in Sanskrit or of ancient India.

Apart from extensively using the two works mentioned above, Garrett's and Dowson's, the editor is also greatly indebted to the timeless and landmark work on *Ancient Sanskrit Texts* by Dr. John Muir. It remains one of the best works compiled on the original history of the people of India, their religion and institutions and therefore is extensively quoted in the present work. We would also like to mention other great works like *The Vishnu Purana* by Prof. Wilson as well as the *Essays on Sanskrit Literature*, and the *Religion of the Hindus*. The translations of *Mahabharata* and *Ramayana* published by Dr. Tolboys Wheeler have been extensively referred to in the present work, including the poetical translation of *Ramayana* by Griffith. The editor would have liked to also utilise the new edition of The Ramayana published by MLBD, New Delhi but it came to the Editor's notice rather late when the work on the present book was nearing completion. However, they deserve praise for a most beautifully published Ramayana which will probably be used for reference in the preparation of my other work—A Dictionary of the Ramayana.

Extensive information was taken from Max Muller's works especially from the *History of the Ancient Sanskrit Literature*, and his *Chips from a German Workshop*. The present work also draws extensively from *Sanskrit Dictionary* by Goldstucker.

Many other works which have added significantly to the present work are Indian *Epic Poetry* by M. Willams, Colbroke's *Essays*, *Indian Wisdom* by M. Williams, *Earlier Hindu India* by Mazumdar, *Medieval Hindu India* by Vaidya, *Agni Purana* by M. N. Dutt, *Garuda Purana* by the same author, *Inspired Writings on Indology* by Goldstucker, *Rigveda Samhita* by H. H. Wilson, *Dharma Shastras* by M. M. Dutta, *Encyclopaedia of Indian Mysticism* by Santideva, *Encyclopaedia of Tantra* by the same author, and many others.

Hindu Mythology and its traditions are so extensive that it would have required more time and extensive labour to harvest fully the knowledge in Sanskrit literature. The aim here has been to condense and to bring together in compact form that information which lies scattered in several volumes. I have worked diligently and honestly, but mistakes no doubt must have been made. I crave reader's indulgence and invite constructive criticism as I will be striving to improve the Dictionary in future editions. The library of illustrations with plates and cut out is being built up and it is hoped that the future edition will fulfill the desire to have a fully illustrated Hindu Dictionary.

As a person not trained for taking on such a work I cannot but feel diffident on presenting this work to the readers. I hope that the work is welcomed not only in the libraries, or by the scholars of Hinduism but also by a common lay educated person with interest in Hindu literature and its traditions.

I would like to dedicate this work, both with pleasure and gratitude, to the memory of my late father Surendra Kapoor from whom I have drawn inspiration for his abiding interest in ancient Hindu traditions. His respect for Hindu traditions and his faith in the Hindu heritage was not ritualistic but profound and deeply spiritual. It is in him that I first saw the image of a true practising Hindu spiritualist. His memory is profoundly cherished even to this day by anyone who came in contact with him throughout his life.

Ganesh Chaturthi **Subodh Kapoor**

GENERAL ABBREVIATIONS AND SYMBOLS

App.	Appendix
AS.	Anglo-Saxon
c.	circa, approximate date
Cal.	Calcutta
cf.	compare
ch.	chapter
col.	column
comp.	compound
ed.	edition, or edited
e.g.	exempli gratia, for example
E. or Eng.	English
et al.	and others
etc.	et cetera
f.	feminine gender
fasc.	fascicule
F. or Fr.	French
G.	German
Goth.	Gothic
Gr.	Greek
Hind.	Hindi
ibid.	ibidem, 'in the same place or book'
IE.	Indo-European
i.e.	id est, 'that is'
Intro.	Introduction
L.	Latin
lit.	literally
m.	masculine gender
MS. or MSS.	manuscript (s)
n.	neuter gender
N.E.	north-east
nom.	nominative case
N.W.	north-west
OE.	Old English
pa.	parvan
Pá.	Páli
priv.	privative
q.v.	quod vide, 'which see'
rev.	revised edition or version
s. or sing.	singular
Sem.	Semitic
seq. or et seq.	sequens, 'following'
Skt. Sl.	Sanskrit
S.W.	south-west
tr.	translation or translated
v.	vide, 'see'
viz.	videlicet, 'namely'

Symbols

=	'equivalent to', 'equal'
( )	parentheses enclosing remarks, descriptions and explanatory statements
[ ]	brackets enclosing words introduced to link portions of a quoted passage

ABBREVIATED TITLES OF WORKS REFERRED TO

The names of Sanskrit and Pali compositions, and of other works quoted from, or cited or referred to; full details of these works are given in the Bibliography.

ABORI	Annals of the Bhandarkar Oriental Research Institute
AGP.	*Agni Purāṇa,* tr. by Manmatha Nath Dutt Shastri, 4 vols. Cosmo
AHI.	*An Advanced History of India,* 2nd edn., R.C. Majumdar , *et al.*
Ait. Br.	*Aitareya Brahmana,* tr. by A.B. Keith *Ancestor Worship. Origin and Development of the Rituals of*
Ancestor Worship,	Dakshina Ranjan Shastri *AOS.* American Oriental Society, New Haven
AR	*Asiatic Researches,* Jones, W. 24 Vols. Cosmo
Aspects.	*Aspects of Early Viṣṇuism,* J. Gonda
AV.	*Atharva'Veda Samhita,* tr. by W. Dwight Whitney, 2 vols
AVB.	*Hymns of the Atharva-Veda,* tr. by M. Bloomfield
BG.	*Bhagavadgitā,* various translations
BH.	*Brahmanism and Hinduism,* M. Monier-Williams
Bhāg. P.	*Bhagavata Purana*
BIP.	*The Beginnings of Indian Philosophy,* F. Edgerton
Br.	*Brāhmana*
Brah. P.	*Brahmāṇḍa Purāṇa,* tr. G.C. Bosch
Bṛhad-Ār. Up.	*Bṛhad-Āraṇyaka Upaniṣad*
Bṛhadd.	*Bṛhad-Devata,* tr. by A.A. Macdonell
BSOAS.	*Bulletin of the School of Oriental and African Studies,* London
CC.	*Change and Continuity in Indian Religion,* J. Gonda
CD.	*Century Dictionary,* ed. by W.D. Whitney
CG.	*Cosmography and Geography in Early Indian Literature,* D.C. Sircar
Chān. Up.	*Chāndogya Upaniṣad*
C. Herit. I.	*The Cultural Heritage of India,* Sri Ramakrishna Centenary Memorial, 3 vols
CHI.	*The Cambridge History of India,* ed. by E.J. Rapson, 6 vols, 1922
CHS.	*Principles of Composition in Hindu Sculpture,* Alice Boner
CI., or *Cycle I.*	*The Cyclopaedia of India,* 3 vols, E. Balfour *Rep Encyclopaedia Asiatica,* in 9 Vols Cosmo
CII.	*Corpus Inscriptionum Indicarum,* 3 vols, 1888-1929
Cults.	*The Cults of the Greek States,* Lewis Richard Farnell
Dev	*Devata. The Hindu Gods,* by a recluse of Vindhyacha
DHA.	*A Dictionary of Hindu Architecture,* Prasanna Kumar Acharya
DHI.	*The Development of Hindu Iconography,* J.N. Banenjea
DS	*Dharam Shastras. Dutt,* M.N. 6 Vols. Cosmo
EB.	*Encyclopaedia of Buddhism,* ed. by G.P. Malalasekera, fasc. 1-

EBS.	*The Early Brahmanical System of Gotra and Pravara,* John Brough
EH	*Early Hindu India,* Majumdar, A.K. 3Vols
EHI.	*Elements of Hindu Iconography,* T.A.G. Rao, 2 vols
EIM	*Encyclopaedia of Indian* Mysticism, Santideva,S. 12 Vols. Cosmo
EM.	*Epic Mythology,* E.W. Hopkins
EPP	*Encyclopaedia of Philosophy and Psychology,* Baldwin, 5 Vols. Cosmo
ERE.	*Encyclopaedia of Religion and Ethics,* ed. by James Hastings, 13 vols
ES.	*Encyclopaedia of Superstitions,* E. and M.A. Radford.
ET	*Encyclopaedia of Tantra,* Santideva, S 5 Vols. Cosmo
EW.	*History of Philosophy: Eastern and Western,* S. Radhakrishnan, 2 vols
GG.	*The Golden Germ,* F.D.K. Boscn
Hariv.	*Harivaṃśa*
HCD. or *HD.*	*A Classical Dictionary of Hindu Mythology and Religion,* John Dowson
HCIP.	*The History and Culture of the Indian People,* ed. by R.C. Majumdar, *et al.,* v ols 1-5
HG	*The Himalayan Gazetteer,* Atkinson,E.T. 3 Vols 6Pts. Cosmo
HIIA.	*A History of Indian and Indonesian Art,* A.K. Coomaraswamy
HIL.	*A History of Indian Literature,* M. Winternitz *HIP. A History of Indian Philosophy,* S. Dasgupta
HMC	*Hindu Manners, Customs and Ceremonies, Dubois, J.A., 2 Vols. Cosmo*
HOS.	Harvard Oriental Series
HP.	*Hindu Polytheism.* A. Daniclou
HW.	*Hindu World,* 2 vols, Benjamin Walker.
I A. or *Ind. Ant.*	*The Indian Antiquary*
IAL.	*A Comparative Dictionary of the Indo-Āryan Languages.* R.L. Turner
IEA	*International Encyclopaedia of Anthropology.* Channa, S. 12 Vols. Cosmo
IHQ.	*Indian Historical Quarterly*
India	*India and World Civilization, D.P.* Singhal
IT	*The Indian Theogony,* Sukumari Bhattacharji
IW	*Indian Wisdom,* M. Monier-Williams
IWP.	*Indian and Western Philosophy,* Betty Heimann
JA.	*Journal Asiatiaue*
JAOS.	*Journal of the American Oriental Society*
JRAS.	*Journal of the Royal Asiatic Society, London*
JRASB.	*Journal of the Royal Asiatic Society of Bengal*
Kauś.	*Kausika Sutra*
Kauṣ	*Kausitaki Upanisad*
Kauṣ. Br.	*Kausilaki Brahmana,* tr. by A.B. Keith
MAN	*Mythology of Aryan ations.* Cox, G. 2 Vols.
Māṇḍ. Up.	*Māṇḍukya Upaniṣad*
Manu	*The Laws of Manu,* tr. by G. Buhler
Mārk. P.	*Mārkaṇḍdeya Purana,* tr. by F.E. Pargiter
Matsya Pur.	*Matsya Purāṇa—A* Study, V.S. Agrewala
MBh.	*Mahābhārata* sponsored by Pratap Chandra Roy, 2nd ed., 12 vols
MBh. Crit. Edn	The Critical Edition of the *Mahabhāata* ed. by V.S. Sukthankar, F. Edgerton, S.K. DC, *et al.*
MBh., EM.	This refer to E.W. Hop-

	kins' references to the Mahābhārata in his Epic Mythology
MDS	*Manav Dharam Shastras, or the Code of Hindu Laws of Manu.* Haughton, G.C. 4 Vols. Cosmo
Muṇḍd Up.	*Muṇḍaka Upaniṣad*
Myths.	*Myths and Symbols in Indian Art and Civilization, H. Zimmer, ed. by J. Campbell Nir. The Nighaṇâu and the Nirukta, tr. by Lakshman Sarup*
Notes	*Notes on Names and She Name of God in Ancient India,* J. Gonda
OHI.	*The Oxford History of India,* V.A. Smith, rev. by Sir Mortimer *Wheeler el al.*
OM.	*The Masks of God,* vol. II, *Oriental Mythology, i.* Campbell
ORC.	*Obscure Religious Cults,* Shashibhusan Dasgupta
OST.	*Original Sanskrit Texts,* 5 vols, J.Muir
P. or *Pur.*	*Purāṇa*
PI.	*The Purāṇa Index,* 3 vols, V.R. Ramachandra Dikshitar
PSPT.	*The Significance of Prefixes in Sanskrit Philosophical Terminology,* Betty Heunann
PTR.	*Pauranic and Taniric Religion, JM.* Banerjea
PTS.	*The Pāli Text Society's Pāli-English Dictionary,* ed. by T.W. Rhys Davids and William Stede
RAA.	*Religion in Art and Archaeology,* J.N. Banerjea
Rām.	*The Rāmāyaṇa.* tr. by Hari Prasad Shastri, 3 vols
RV.	*The Hymns of the Rgveda,* various translations
RVS	*Rigveda Samhita.* Wilson, H.H. 7 Vols. Cosmo
SBE.	*Sacred Books of the East,* ed. by F. Max Müller
ŚBr.	*Śatapatha Brāhmaṇa,* tr. by Julius Eggeling 5 vols, *SBE.*
SED.	*Sanskrit-English Dictionary,.* M. Monier-Williams *Seers. The Seers of the Rgveda,.* V.G. Rahurkar
Sikh	*The Sikhs. Their Religion, Gurus, Sacred Writings and Authors,* Mecoulif, M.A. 6 Vols. Cosmo
Śūnyasaṃmpādane,	3 vols, tr, by S.C. Nandimath, *el al.*
SV.	*Sama Veda,* tr. by R.T. Griffith
Śvet. Up.	*Svetasvara Upanisad Tail. Br. Taittiriya Brahmana*
Tail. Sam.	*The Veda of the Black Yajus School entitled Taittiriya Samhila,* tr. by A.B. Keith
TPU	*Thirteen Principal Upaniṣads* R.E. Hume
TT.	*The Tantric Tradition,* Agehananda Bharati
Up.	*Upaniṣad*
Vāj. Saṃ.	*Vājasaneyi-saṃhitā*
VI.	*Vedic Inde of Names and Subjects,* A.A. Macdonell and A.B. Keith, 2 vols.
VM.	*Vedic Mythology,* A.A. Macdonell
VP	*Viṣṇu Purāṇa,* tr. by H.H. Wilson
VS.	*Viṣṇuism and Śaivism. A Comparison,* J. Gonda
VSM.	*Vaiṣṇavism and Śaivism and Minor Religious Systems,* R.G. Bhandarkar
WI	*The Wonder that was India,* A.L. Basham
Yakṣas.	*Yakṣas,* A.K. Coomaraswamy, 2 vols.
Yoga	*Yoga: Immortality and Freedom,* Mircea Eliade
YV	*Yajur-Veda*

LIST OF ROMANIZED SANSKRIT CHARACTERS IN ENGLISH ALPHABETICAL ORDER, AND THEIR PRONUNCIATION

The transliteration follows that of Monier-Williams's *Sanskrit-English Dictionary*, with a few exceptions. The letter ṛ replaces his *ṛi*, and ṣ his sh; the nasal symbol, called the *anusvāra*, represented by his ṃ or ṇ is here rendered ṁ or ṅ as in *Sāṃkhya* or *Sāṅkhya*. The *SED*. states that 'the *visarga*, as a substitute for final *s*, is a distinctly audible aspirate, so that the *ḥ* at the end of such a word as *devaḥ* must be clearly heard'.

a	Like u as in cut; never as in bat
ā	father
ai	aisle
au	loud
b	bag
bh	abhor
c	church (but in compounds, expressed or implied, like vac, re, etc., changes to k).
ch	church-hill
d	dice
ḍ	drum
dh	adhere
ḍh	red-haired
e	prey
g	gun
gh	log-hut
h	hit
i	lip
ī	police
J	Jet
jh	hedge-hog
k	kit
kh	ink-horn
l	lull
l	label
m	man
n	nut
ṇ	none
ñ	singe
o	so
P	Pat
ph	up-hill
r	rat
ṛ	rich
ṛi	marine
s	sit
ś	hiss
ṣ = sh	sure
t	dot
ṭ	true
th	nut-hook
ṭh	boat-hook
u	full
ū	rude
v	ivy (but pronounced as w after some consonants)
y	yet

Diacritical Marks—These denote family, tribal or national relationship, gender, etc., and determine pronunciation; but consonants with diacritical dots, such as *ṭ*, *ṭh*, ḍ, ḍ*h*, ṛi, do not differ greatly in pronunciation from their unmarked counterparts.

Mutations—These occur when a particular terminal vowel of one word coalesces with the initial vowel of the following word. Thus *a*+*a* merge and become ā; *a*+ā become a as in Ankara and ācārya, which become Śaṅkarācārya. A terminal *u* before an initial *a* changes to v, as in Manu + antara (Manvantara). A terminal *a* followed by an initial *u* coalesce and become o as in Katha Upaniṣad (Kaṭhopaniṣad).

A

AKARA—The first letter in the Sanskrit and all Indian Alphabets. A name claimed by Krishna as the Supreme Being, (*Bhagavat Gita*, Chapter X, verse 33) similar to the name Alpha given in the Book of Revelation to the Lord Jesus Christ.

ABHASARA—The name of the thirteenth heaven of Buddhism.

ABHASVARAS—A class of deities, sixty-four in number, of whose nature little is known.

ABHAYA—(Fearlessness) one of the sons of Dharma, see *Vishnu Purána*, p. 55.

ABHIDHANA CHINTAMANI—A vocabulary of the Jain doctrines written by Hemachandra, and described by Professor Wilson as one of great utility that may be relied on.

ABHIDHANA—A dictionary or vocabulary. There are many such works. One of the oldest of them is the *Abhidhāna-ratnāmlā* of Halāyudha Bhaṭṭa (*circa* seventh century), and one of the best is the *Abhidhāna Cintāmani* of Hemacandra, a Jaina writer of celebrity (thirteenth century). The former has been edited by Aufrecht; the latter by Colebrooke and by Böhtlingk and Rieu.

ABHIDHARMMA—The third class of the sacred books of the Buddhists, which are called in Páli, the language in which they are written, Pittakattyan, from Pittakan, a basket or chest, and táyo, three, the text being divided into three great classes. The Abhidarmma contain instructions which the Buddhists imagine to be addressed to the inhabitants of the celestial worlds. This is accordingly accounted the highest class of sacred books, and the expounders of it are to be held in the highest honor, for it contains *pre-eminent truths*, as the word itself implies. The books of which it consists are not in the form of sermons, but specify terms and doctrines, with definitions and explanations. The work contains seven sections.—*Gardiner.*

ABHIJIT—A Yádava Chief, *V.P.*, p. 436.

ABHIMANA—In Hindu philosophy means 'selfish conviction.' See Colebrooke's *Essays*, Vol. I, p. 242.

ABHIMANI—He was an Agni, the eldest son of Brahmā. By his wife Svāhā he had three sons of unsurpassing brilliancy, Pāvaka, Pavamāna, and Śuci. "They had forty-five sons, who, with the original son of Brahmā and his three descendants, constitute the forty-nine fires." (*see* Agni)

ABHIMANYU—**(1)** A son of Arjúna and Subhadra, renowned for his strength and valour. He was married to Uttarā, the daughter of Rája Viráta. He fought with distinguished valour on the first day of the great war; cutting down the ensign in Bhíshma's chariot. On the second day he slew Lakṣmaṇa the son of Duryódhana, and when attacked by the latter was rescued by Arjúna. On the thirteenth day of the war, he was commanded by Yudhishthira to charge the Kauravas who were drawn up in the form of a spider's web; he drove his chariot into the enemy's ranks and performed prodigies of valoúr, but was finally overpowered by six warriors and slain. His posterity through the line of his son *Paríkshit*, were the royal race of the lunar line at Hastinápura, (old Delhi); **(2)** A son of Chákshusha. *V.P.*, 98.

ABHINAVAGUPTA—A celebrated teacher of Alankára, under whom Kshemendra states that he studied. Abhinayagupta is supposed to have lived at the beginning of the tenth century, A.D., and is cited by various writers as an authority on Alankára.

ABHIRA, ĀBHIRA—A cowherd; according to Manu the offspring of a brāhmaṇa by a woman of the Ambaṣṭha or medical tribe. A people located in the north of India along the Indus. There has been a good deal of misapprehension respecting this people. Hindu writers have described them as living in the north and in the west, the quarter varying according to the locality of the writer, and translators have mixed them up with a neighbouring people, the śudras, sometimes called śuras, with whom they are generally associated, and have called them Sūrābhīras. Their modern representatives are the Ahīrs, and perhaps there is something more than identity of locality in their association with the śūdras. It has been suggested that the country or city of the Abhīras is the *Ophir* of the Bible.

ABHIRĀMA-MAṆI—A drama in seven acts on the history of Rāma, written by Sundara Miśra in AD 1599. "The composition possesses little dramatic interest, although it has some literary merit."—*Wilson.*

ABHIRAS—**(1)** An ancient race of people inhabiting

the North-West of India: they are mentioned in the Mahá Bhárata, the Rámayana, and in the *V.P.*, but nothing is known of their history; **(2)** The name of a dynasty referred to in the *V.P.* supposed to have reigned in Magadha, B.C. 200.

ABHUTARAJASAS—A class of gods of the fifth Manwantara.

ABHYUDAYA—Offerings to the progenitors of an individual and of mankind, which form part of a religious ceremony on an occasion of rejoicing or an accession of prosperity. See VRIDDI SRÁDDA.

ABJA—The father of Vísala who became incarnate as Náráyana.

ABORIGINES—In all the large jungles and hilly tracts of country throughout India there exist thousands of human beings in a state not very different from that of the Germans as described by Tacitus nearly two thousand years ago. These primitive races are the ancient heritors of the whole soil, from all the rich and open parts of which they were expelled by the Hindu.

These non-Aryan races have always been misrepresented and oppressed. The early Sanscrit writers depicted "the forest tribes as black noseless demons, of small stature and inarticulate speech." In the two great epics and in the Puránas they are termed Rákshakas.

"During the struggle between the worn-out Sanscrit civilization and the impetuous prime of Islam, the Hindus discovered the value of the aboriginal races. Many chiefs of noble Áryan blood maintained their independence by such alliances; others founded new kingdoms amongst the forest peoples. To this day some of the tribes exhibit a black original section living side by side with a fair-skinned composite kindred, sprung from the refugees; and the most exalted Hindu princes have to submit to a curious aboriginal rite on their accession to the throne. It was state before the Royal Asiatic Society in 1852 that the investiture of the Rájput Rájah of Nerwar is not complete till one of his purely aboriginal subjects, a Mina, paints a round spot on his forehead with blood freshly drawn from the toe of another Mina. Without this formal recognition his non-Áryan subjects could not be depended upon; when once it has been performed their fidelity has never been known to waver. They form the treasury and palace guards, hold the personal safety of the prince entirely in their hands, and supply the sole escort to whom he entrusts the honor of his daughters when they go abroad. The Ranah of Udayapur, cited by General Briggs as the higgest in rank of all the sovereigns in India, renders the same homage, however ill it may comport with his caste and personal dignity, to the traditions of his aboriginal subjects. Before he ascends the throne his forehead must first be marked with the blood of a Bhíl. The Hinduized chieftains of Central India, receive investiture by the blood of a pure Kol; and so strong a hold has this ceremony on the minds of the people, that amongst the Cheris—once a great tribe, who defended themselves with honor against Shere Shah and the imperial army, now reduced to five or six families,—the head of the little community is still installed under the title of Rájah, with the token of the round spot of warm aboriginal blood.

"But is not the Hindus alone that have proved the loyalty of these neglected races. Scarcely a single administrator has ruled over them for any length of time, without finding his prejudices conquered, and his heart softened, and leaving on record his sorrow for their present condition, and his belief in their capabilities for good.

* * * *

'They are faithful, truthful and attached to their superiors, writes General Briggs, ready at all times to lay down their lives for those they serve, and remarkable for their indomitable courage. These qualities have been always displayed in our service. The aborigines of the Carnatic were the sepoys of Clive and of Coote. A few companies of the same stock joined the former great Captain from Bombay, fought the battle of Plassey in Bengal, and laid the foundation of the Indian empire. They have since distinguished themselves in the corps of Pioneers and Engineers, not only in India, but in Ava and Afghanistan, and in the celebrated defence of Jalalabad. An unjust prejudice has grown up against them in the armies of Madras and Bombay, where they have done best service, produced by the feelings of contempt for them, existing among the Hindu and Mahomedan troops. They have no prejudices themselves, are always ready to serve abroad, and embark on board ship, and I believe no instance of mutiny has ever occurred among them."' (W. W. Hunter, Preface to *Non-Aryan Dictionary*.) Other testimonies are quoted by the same writer from equally high authorities all showing that the truthfulness and fidelity of these despised races are most satisfactorily established.

Their condition, after many centuries of suffering, is now likely to be improved. Their character and claims are beginning to be understood. It is seen too how they may be utilized by being made to take the place of English soldiers. "In interest, in race, in religion, in habits of life, they are cut off from the Hindus and Mussulmans by a gulf of whose breadth the people of Christian States can form no idea; and their ethnical repugnance is kept in a constant glow by the remembrance of ancient wars and recent wrongs." By extensively employing these tribes as a military police and as soldiers, we should not only relieve the English population of a burden, but we should offer a livelihood to brave predatory peoples whom the stern order of British rule has deprived of an important source of subsistence."

ĀCĀRA—'Rule, custom, usage'. The rules of practice of castes, orders, or religion. There are many books of rules which have this word for the first member of their titles, as *Ācāra-candrika*, 'moonlight of customs', on the customs of the sudras; *Ācāradarsā*, 'looking-glass of customs'; Ācāra-dīad lamp of customs', &c.,&c.

ACHARA—A name of Siva. A name of Vishnu. BRAHM, the Supreme BEING, (in this sense it is sometimes *Mas.*) The word also means eternal beatitude, or exemption from further transmigration. Also religious austerity or moral merit. A spiritual teacher or guide. A title of Droṇa, the teacher of the Pāṇḍavas

ACHARYA—The term Achárya sometimes means a priest; but its most usual meaning is a spiritual guide or preceptor, one who invests the student with the sacred thread, and who instructs him in the law of sacrifices, and the mysteries of religion.

ACHYUTA—Krishnánanda Níthi, author of a commentary on the Siddhánta Kalpataru, called Krishnalankára.

ACYUTA—'Unfallen'; a name of Viṣṇu or Kṛṣṇa: meaning "the imperishable." It has been variously interpreted as signifying "he who does not perish with created things", in the *Mahābhārata* as "he who is not distinct from final emancipation", and in the *Skanda Purāṇa* as "he who never declines (or varies) from his proper nature".

ADBHUTA-BRAHMANA—'The *Brāhmaṇa* of miracles.' A *Brāhmaṇa* of the *Samaveda* which treats of auguries and marvels. It has been published by Weber.

ADBHUTA—The Indira of the ninth Manwantara.

ADHARMA—**(1)** Unrighteousness; all behaviour contrary to the Sruti and Smriti, or religious and legal institutions. **(2)** In philosophy, according to the Nyáya and Vaiṣeshika: moral demerit, the result of doing what is forbidden, the peculiar cause of pain, one of the twenty-four qualities united with substance. According to the Sánkhya, one of the changeable dispositions of the mind, which being the efficient cause, makes the soul migrate into an animal, a deer, a bird, a reptile, a vegetable, a mineral. According to the Buddhistic doctrine it is the consequence of upádána or exertion of body or speech. According to the Jains it is that which causes the soul in general to continue embarrassed with body, notwithstanding its capacity for ascent and natural tendency to soar. **(3)** As a personification, Adharma occurs in the Puránas as one of the Prajápatis or mind-born sons of Brahmá; his wife is Hinsá (mischief) on whom he begot Aurita (falsehood) and Nikriti (immorality) or according to others, Mrishá (falsehood) and his children Dambha (hypoerisy) and Máyá (deceit) who were adopted by Nirriti (misfortune). Adharma is also mentioned as one of the eighteen servants of the sun. *V.P.*

ADHIPURUSHA—The presiding spirit of the Universe—descended from Vishnu.

ADHIRATHA—**(1)** A charioteer. The foster-father of Karṇa, who according to some was the king of Aṅga, and according to others the charioteer of King Dhṛtarāṣṭra; perhaps he was both. **(2)** A son of Satyakarman, one of the kings of Anga. He found Karna in a basket on the banks of the Ganges, where he had been exposed by his mother Pritha.

ADHOGATI—The Jains believe that below this world there is a world called *Adhogati*, the Abyss, the nethermost hell, above which there are seven infernal worlds; and above these again are ten *Pavanalokas*, purifying worlds, (Purgatories) above which is this world of earth.

ADHOSIRAS—One of the divisions of the Hindu Hell (or Naraka) in which persons are punished for bribery. *V.P.*

ADHVARYA PRIESTS—The third class of priests at sacrifices, who had to prepare the sacrificial ground, to adjust the vessels, to procure the animals, and other sacrificial oblations, to light the fire, to kill the animal, and do all the manual labor.

ADHVARYU—A priest whose business it is to recite the prayers of the *Yajurveda*.

ADHYAROPA—A technical term used in the *Vedánta* system of Hindu Philosophy, meaning "erroneous imputation"—an allegation that the Unreal is the Real. One of the four Requisites to the study of the Vedánta is, "the discrimination of the eternal substance from the transient." This is the discerning that God is the eternal substance, and that all else is non-eternal. To understand this fully the Adhyáropa or erroneous imputation must be refuted.

ADHYATMA RAMAYANAA--A spiritualized version of the Rámáyana, being an abridgment of the story, the authorship of which is attributed to the mythical Vyása, in which the whole has been spiritualized, and every conflicting incident either explained or omitted, whilst the greatest stress has been laid upon the character of Ráma as a—"saviour and deliverer."—*Wheeler.* (*see* Rāmāyaṇa)

ADHYĀTMAN—The supreme spirit, the soul of the universe.

ADHYATMA—The ministers of the Soul. A technical phrase in the Sánkhya philosophy. Thirteen instruments or ministers of the soul are enumerated, each of which has a "province" and "presiding deity," viz:—

1. Intellect is a minister of the soul, "Whatever is to be understood" is its province; Brahma is its presiding deity.
2. Self-consciousness is a minister of soul; Whatever is to be believed is its province; Rudra is its presiding deity.
3. Mind is a minister of soul; Whatever is to be resolved on is its province; The moon is its presiding deity.
4. The hearing is a minister of soul, Whatever is to be heard is its province; The Ether is its supernatural presiding power.
5. The touch is a minister of soul, Whatever is to be touched is its province; The air is its supernatural presiding power.
6. The sight is a minister of soul, Whatever is to be seen is its province; The sun is its presiding deity.
7. The taste is a minister of soul, Whatever is to be tasted is its province; Varuna (the god of waters) is its presiding deity.
8. The smell is a minister of soul, Whatever is to be smelled is its province; The earth is its supernatural presiding power.
9. The voice is a minister of soul, Whatever is to be uttered is its province; Saraswati (or Fire) is its presiding deity.
10. The hands are ministers of soul, Whatever is to be grasped is their province; Indra is their presiding deity.
11. The feet are ministers of soul, Whatever is to be gone over is their province; Vishnu is their presiding deity.
12. The organ of excretion is a minister of soul, Whatever is to be excreted is its province; Mitra is its presiding deity.
13. The organ of generation is a minister of soul, What is to be enjoyed is its province; Prajápati is its presiding deity.—*Ballantyne.*

ADHYATMIKA—In the Sánkhya philosophy. The pain which arises from any of the *Adhyátma* or instruments of soul.

ADINA—The son of Sahadeva, celebrated in the wars between the demons and the gods.

ĀDI-PURĀṆA—'The first Purāṇa', a title generally conceded to the *Brahmā Purāṇa.*

ADI—The first. A name given to the Bramha Purána, containing ten thousand stanzas.

ADITI—'Free, unbounded'. Infinity; the boundless heaven as compared with the finite earth; or, according to Max Müller, "the visible infinite, visible by the naked eye; the endless expanse beyond the earth, beyond the clouds, beyond the sky". In the *Rgveda* she is frequently implored "for blessings on children and cattle, for protection and for forgiveness". Aditi is called Devamatri, 'mother of the gods', and is represented as being the mother of Dakṣa and the daughter of Dakṣa. On this statement Yāska remarks in the *Nirukta*: "How can this be possible? They may have had the same origin; or, according to the nature of the gods, they may have been born from each other, have derived their substance from one another." "Eight sons were born from the body of Aditi; she approached the gods with seven but cast away the eighth, Mārtaṇḍa (the sun)." These seven were the Ādityas. In the *Yajurveda* Aditi is addressed as "Supporter of the sky, sustainer of the earth, sovereign of this world, wife of Viṣnu"; but in the *Mahābhārata* and *Ramāyana*, as well as in the Purāṇas, Viṣnu is called the son of Aditi. In the Viṣnu *Purana* she is said to be the daughter of Dakṣa and wife of Kasyapa, by whom she was mother of Viṣnu, in his dwarf incarnation (wherefore he is sometimes called Āditya), and also of Indra, and she is called "the mother of the gods" and "the mother of the world". Indra acknowledged her as mother, and Viṣnu, after receiving the adoration of Aditi, addressed her in these words: "Mother, goddess, do thou show favour unto me and grant me thy blessing." According to the *Matsya Purana* a pair of ear-rings was produced at the churning of the ocean, which Indra gave to Aditi, and several of the Purāṇas tell a story of these ear-rings being stolen and carried off to the city of Prāgjyotiṣa by the *asura* king Naraka, from whence they were brought back and restored to her by Rrsna. Devakī, the mother of Kṛṣa, is represented as being a new birth or manifestation of Aditi. *see* Max Müller's *Rgveda*, i. 230; Muir's *Texts*, iv. ll. v.35. "Adití is an object of frequent celebration in the Rigveda, where she is supplicated for blessings on children and cattle, for protection and for forgiveness." (*Muir.*) "Adití, an ancient god or goddess, is in reality the earliest name invented to express the Infinite; not the Infinite as the result of a long process of abstract reasoning, but the visible Infinite, visible by the naked eye, the endless expanse, beyond the earth, beyond the clouds, beyond the sky. If we keep this original conception of Adití clearly before us, the various forms which Adití assumes, even in the hymns of the Védas, will not seem incoherent."—(*Müller.*)

Dr. Muir, in an elaborate article, discusses the following points: "Adití as the mother of the Ádityas." "Is Adití ever identified with the sky?" "Adití seems to be distinguished from the earth." "Adití may be a personification of universal nature." "Adití as a forgiver of sin." "Adití's position sometimes subordinate."

In the two epics, and in the Bhágavata Purána, Adití is described as the wife of Kásyapa, and the mother of Vishnu in his dwarf incarnation: "An older authority however, the Vajsanhitá, gives quite a different account of the relation of Adití to Vishnu, as it represents her to be his wife. In the following passage of the Tattiríya-sanhitá also she is similarly described. "Supporter of the sky, sustainer of the earth, sovereign of this world, wife of Vishnu, may the all-embracing and powerful Adití, filling us with vigour, be auspicious to us (abiding) in her lap."—Muir, *O.S.T.*, *Vol. V*, *p. 53*.

The Vedic goddess of space, *i.e.*, *a* 'not', and *diti* 'limited'. But she is also associated or identified in the *RV.* with other phenomena, such as Earth, Nature, etc. Müller[1] considers that Aditi, in her cosmic character, is the 'Beyond, the unbounded realm beyond the earth, sky, and heaven...[and] though in more general language she may be identified with heaven and earth in their unlimited character', the original significance of her name is retained in these other contexts. Gonda[2] considers her name to signify 'Freedom,' and her nature to be manifested 'in any expansion of phenomenal life'. Thus one passage refers to her as a fertility goddess, the Cosmic Cow;[3] another declares her 'to be all that has been, and is yet to be', in whom all the gods are comprised (*R.V.*, I. 89, 10). Other passages state that Aditi was born of Daksa and that Daksa was born of Aditi,[4] and that existence from non-existence sprang. These enigmatic statements suggests the attempts of the Vedic Irsis to define the abstract nature of existence, as in X.129, when 'there was neither ought nor nought'.

1. *Vedic Hymns*, *SBE.*, Vol. XXXII, pp. 248f.
2. VS., p. 7.
3. Cf. the ancient Egyptian sky-goddess Nut who appears as a great cow with stars on her body; her legs form the four cardinal points (James, *Tree of Life*, p. 177); also the goddess hathor, 'one of the oldest Egyptian deities, worshipped from Gerzean times under the fertility emblem of a cow with a variety of names' (ibid., p. 267).
4. *OST.*, IV. p. 13.

ĀDITYA PURĀṆA—One of the eighteen Upa-puraṇas.

ĀDITYA—In the early Vedic times the Ādityas were six, or more frequently seven, celestial deities, of whom Varuṇa was chief; consequently he was *the* Āditya. They were sons of Aditi, who had eight sons, but she approached the gods with seven, having cast away the eighth, Martaṇḍa (the sun). In after-times the number was increased to twelve, as representing the sun in the twelve months of the year. Āditya is one of the names of the sun. Dr Muir quotes the following from Professor Roth: "There (in the highest heaven) dwell and reign those gods who bear in common the name of Ādityas. We must, however, if we would discover their earliest character, abandon the conceptions which in a later age, and even in that of the heroic poems, were entertained regarding these deities. According to this conception they were twelve sun-gods, bearing evident reference to the twelve months. But for the most ancient period we must hold fast the primary signification of their name. They are the inviolable, imperishable, eternal beings. Aditi, eternity, or the eternal, is the element which sustains or is sustained by them...The eternal and inviolable element in which the Ādityas dwell, and which forms their essence, is the celestial light. The Ādityas, the gods of this light, do not therefore by any means coincide with any of the forms in which light is manifested in the universe. They are neither sun, nor moon, nor stars, nor dawn, but the eternal sustainers of this luminous life, which exists, as it were, behind all these phenomena."

The names of the six Ādityas are Mitra, Aryaman, Bhaga, Varuṇa, Dakṣa, and Aṁśa. Dakṣa is frequently excluded, and Indra, Savitṛ (the sun), and Dhātṛ are added. Those of the twelve Ādityas are variously given, but many of them are names of the sun.

The Sun, called also Súrya, (and Vivaswat) the chief of the gods at a very early period. The twelve solar dynasties, or personifications of the sun under a different name and sign of the zodiac in each month of the year, are called Ádityas. They belong to a period before the time of the Vedas, when the worship of the elements, particularly of the sun, was first enriched and extended by fancy. The name, Ádityas, is a matronymic from Adití. The various stories related of the sun, or of the Ádityas, will be given in connection with the histories of the demi-gods to which they refer. Vishnu is called chief of the Ádityas.

The sons of Aditi. They were first reckoned as seven or eight. In the later Indian literature they are always said to be twelve. Contradictory accounts of them are cited by Dr. Muir (IV, 104). In 'texts from the Mahábhárata the Ádityas, though their names are not always uniformly given, are stated to be twelve in number, except in one case where only eleven are specified. Vishṇu is always named as one of them, and as by the time when these works were written, his dignity had become enhanced in general estimation, he is declared to be the greatest of the twelve. In the *V.P.* and Harivamsha it is stated that those who formerly, in the Chakshusha Manwantara, were called the Tushitas, are known as the twelve Ádityas in the Vaivasvata Manwantara.

Professor Roth, (in the *Journal of the Germ. Or. Soc.* VI, 68) has the following observations on the Ádityas. There (in the highest heaven) dwell and reign those gods who bear in common the name of Ádityas. We must, however, if we would discover their earliest character, abandon the conceptions which in a later age, and even in that of the heroic poems, were entertained regarding these deities. According to this conception they were twelve sun-gods, bearing evident reference to the twelve months. But for the most ancient period we must hold fast the primacy signification of their name. They are the inviolable, imperishable, eternal beings. Aditi, eternity, or the eternal, is the element which sustains them, and is sustained by them. The eternal and inviolable element in which the Ádityas dwell, and which forms their essence, is the celestial light. The Ádityas, the gods of this light, do not therefore by any means coincide with any of the forms in which light is manifested in the universe. They are neither sun, nor moon, nor stars, nor dawn, but the eternal sustainers of this luminous life, which exists, as it were, behind all these phenomena.— *O.S.T., V*, 56.

ADOPTION—If a married brahman is without male issue he is required to procure a son by means of adoption. He must have a son to perform his obsequies, or believes he would be excluded from happiness after death. so prevalent is this notion amongst the Hindus that women who have only daughters will themselves find their husbands a second wife, notwithstanding all the inconveniences involved. "The adopted son wholly renounces all claim on the property of his natural father, and acquires an unlimited right of succession to all that belongs to his adopted father. From him he is entitled to maintenance and education, as if he were his own son; and to receive, through his means, the advantages of the Triple cord, and of being settled in marriage. The adopted son is obliged, on his part, to take care of his acquired parents in their old age, and attend to their funeral when they die. He farther enters into the *Gótra* or lineage of him by whom he is adopted; and is considered as descended from the same ancient stock. When the ceremonies of adoption commence the new parnets perform one which is held to be the most important and essential of any, by tying round the loius of the youth that little string which every male child in India (not an outcast) is ceremoniously invested with at the age of two or three years. If the ceremony has been previously performed by the natural parents, the adopting ones break the cord, in token of dissolving the Gótra from which the child descended; and put in a new one is sign of being called to theirs. On this, as in all other solemn occasions, their first care is to select an auspicious day, by the help of astrology. The child adopted may be a relative or not, but must be of the same caste."—*Dubois.*

ADRIKA—(1) The mother of *Vyása*. "The *muni Parásara*, having occasion to cross over from one side of the Ganges to the other bank, employed a ferry boat, rowed by a fisherman's daughter, towards whom he felt an attraction; the consequence of which was the birth of a son. A Tamil version of the *Bháratam* enigmatizes the matter, by stating that *Vyása* was born from a fish; but the Sanskrit original, not remarkable for fastidiousness, states the case with all simplicity."—*Taylor.* **(2)** The name of a nymph (*apsaras*). By a *brāhmana's* curse she was transformed into a fish and lived in the Yamunā river, where she picked up a leaf dropped by a hawk or eagle (Syena), on which the sperm of King Uparicara had fallen. The fish ate the sperm and was later caught by fishermen who cut it open, when to their amazement a girl and boy emerged. The fishermen took the twins to the king who adopted the boy, who later became the virtuous King Matsya. The girl, who had a strong fishy smell, was given to the fishermen and called Satyavati. After the 'birth' of the twins Adrikā was released from the curse and ascended to the heavens on the path trodden by the *siddhas*, *ṛṣis, etc.* (*MBh.*, Ādi pa., 63).

ADRISYANTI—The wife of Sakti, and mother of Parásara, which see.

ADVAITANANDA—The author of a commentary on the Védánta; and preceptor of Sadánanda who wrote the Védánta Sára. Nothing certain is known as to the time when the lived.

ADVAITA—The name of a school of philosphy and theology, established by Sankarácharya, founder of the monasterium of Sringéri, near the Túmbúdra river. The system regards the Supreme spirit and the human spirit as one; in degradation through ignorance, and re-absorbed on obtaining true wisdom. It regards the world as an illusion; all external objects as different forms of the one deity, besides whom there exists nothing else. As gold is one, though in various forms, as money, ear-rings and other ornaments, so the one sole existent deity is found in all the various forms that appear to exist around us. "The *Vedánta of Vyása*, which considered all existing beings and things to be an evolution of deity, and the deity in and throughout all beings and things, was, by *Sankarácharya*, drawn out to the full consequence; which is, that the soul of man is a part of deity, not different; the body is a temporary prison; on its decease the soul flows into deity, as air in a closed earthern vessel, when this is broken, flows into the common atmosphere. It does not, however, appear that the idea of deity, on this system, philosophically includes personality; but means the supreme universe. It leans towards the female energy system; of matter (or nature) being the great spontaneous mother. *Sankarácharya* discoursed freely of *Siva* and *Párvati*, and wrote hymns to both; maintaining, besides, the onencess of *Bramha*, *Vishnu* and *Siva*." There are many treatises in Tamil, Telugu and Canarese, on the Adwaita philosophy, which seems to have been made a special study in the south more than the north of India.

ADYAS—One of the five classes of gods prevailing in the sixth Manwantars, of which period Chákshusha was the Manu.

AGADA—One of the eight branches into which medical science is divided by the Hindus. Agada treats of the best antidotes to Poisons.

AGAMA—A divine system of doctrine.

AGASTI, AGASTYA—A *ṛṣi*, the reputed author of several hymns in the *Ṛgveda*, and a very celebrated personage in Hindu story. He and Vasiṣtha are said in the *Ṛgveda* to be the offspring of Mitra and Varuṇa, whose seed fell from them at the sight of Urvaśi; and the commentater Sāyaṇa adds that Agastya was born in a water-jar as "a fish of great lustre", hence he was called Kalaśisuta, Kumbhasambhava, and Ghaṭodbhava. From his parentage he was called Maitrā-vāruṇi and Aurvasīya; and as he was very small when he was born, not more than a span in length, he was called Māna. Though he is thus associated in his birth with Vasiṣtha, he is evidently later in date, and he is not one of the Prajāpatis. His name Agastya, is derived by a forced etymology from a fable which represents him as having commanded the Vindhya mountains to prostrate themselves before him, through which they lost their primeval altitude; or rather, perhaps, the fable has been invented to account for his name. This miracle has obtained for him the epithet Vindhyakūṭa; and he acquired another name, Pītābdhi, or Samudraculuka, 'Ocean drinker', from another fable, according to which he drank up the ocean because it had offended him, and because he wished to help the gods in their wars with the *daityas* when the latter had hidden themselves in the waters. He was afterwards made regent of the star Canopus, which bears his name. The Purāṇas represent him as being the son of Pulastya, the sage from whom the *rākṣasas* sprang. He was one of the narrators of the *Brahmā Purāṇa* and also a writer on medicine.

The *Mahābhārata* relates a legend respecting the

creation of his wife. It says that Agastya saw his ancestors suspended by their heels in a pit, and was told by them that they could be rescued only by his begetting a son. Thereupon he formed a girl out of the most graceful parts of different animals and passed her secretly into the palace of the king of Vidarbha. There the child grew up as a daughter of the king, and was demanded in marriage by Agastya. Much against his will the king was constrained to consent, and she became the wife of the sage. She was named Lopāmudrā, because the animals had been subjected to loss (*lopa*) by her engrossing their distinctive beauties, as the eyes of the deer, &c. She was also called Kauśītakī and Varapradā. The same poem also tells a story exhibiting his superhuman power, by which he turned King Nahuṣa into a serpent and afterwards restored him to his proper form. (*see* NAHUṢA)

It is in the *Rāmāyaṇa* that Agastya makes the most distinguished figure. He dwelt in a hermitage on mount Kuñjara, situated in a most beautiful country to the south of the Vindhya mountains, and was chief of the hermits of the south. He kept the *rākṣasas* who infested the south under control, so that the country was "only gazed upon and not possessed by them". His power over them is illustrated by a legend which represents him as eating up a *rākṣasa* named Vātāpi who assumed the form of a ram, and as destroying by a flash of his eye the *rākṣasa's* brother, Ilvala, who attempted to avenge him. (*see* VĀTĀPI.) Rāma in his exile wandered to the hermitage of Agastya with Sītā and Lakṣmaṇa. The sage received him with the greatest kindness, and became his friend, adviser, and protector. He gave him the bow of Viṣṇu; and when Rāma was restored to his kingdom, the sage accompanied him to Ayodhyā.

Ráma, as he viewed the beautiful wilderness, said to his brother Lakshmana:—"The hermitage of Agastya appears in view; this is the abode of that sage who freed the southern quarter from the Rákshasas; at whose command the Vindhya mountain forbore to rise higher in the sky; who drank up the sea abounding in crocodiles and great fishes; who was entreated by the gods, with Indra at their head, to destroy the Dánavas: O Lakshmana, here will I spend the remainder of my exile: Here the perfect men, the great sage, cast off their old bodies, and ascend in new bodies to heaven on chariots as resplendent as the sun."

Agastya presented Ráma with the bow of Vishnu, the arrow of Brahma, two inexhaustible quivers and a scimitar; also with a superb coat of mail which had been given to the sage by Indra.

The Rámáyana gives the following legend of Vátápi and Ilwala who were destroyed by Agastya:—"In former times, two cruel Rákshasas, the devourers of Bráhmans, resided here, and their names were Vátápi and Ilwala, and Ilwala was accustomed to assume the form of a Bráhman, and speak the sacred tongue, and invite the Bráhmans under pretence of solemnizing a Śraddha: Then his brother Vátápi assumed the form of a ram, and was consecrated for the sacrifice by Ilwala; and when the Brahmans had eaten the ram, Ilwala called to his brother to come forth, and Vátápi came forth out of the stomacha of the Bráhmans, bleating like a sheep, and tearing his way through their bodies. Thousands of Bráhmans were thus destroyed, when Agastya came to this spot, and accepted the invitation to a Śráddha; and Agastya had not easten for many years, and he devoured the whole of Vátápi in the form of a ram, and then prayed to Ganga; and the goddess appeared in his alms dish, and he touched the water, and pronounced her divine name: Then when Ilwala called on his brother to come forth, Agastya laughed and said:—'Your brother has been eaten by me in the form of a ram and has now gone to the abode of Yama, and for him there is no coming forth:' Ilwala in a rage began to assail Agastya, but was immediately consumed by the fire which flashed from the eyes of the sage: This hermitage, which formerly belonged to the two Rákshasas, is now inhabited by the brother of Agastya." Goldstrucker writes, "Agastya was the reputed author of several hymns of the Rig Veda. He is represented as of sort stature, and is said by some to have been born in a water jar. He is also mentioned as one of the oldest medical authors, considered as the civilizer of the south and as the regent of the star Canopus."

The name of Agastya holds a great place also in Tamil literature, and he is "venerated in the south as the first teacher of science and literature to the primitive Draviḍian tribes"; so says Dr. Caldwell, who thinks "we shall not greatly err in placing the era of Agastya in the seventh, or at least in the sixth century B.C. "Wilson also had previously testified to the same effect: "The traditions of the south of India ascribe to Agastya a principal share in the formation of the Tamil language and literature, and the general tenor of the legends relating to him denotes his having been instrumental in the introduction of the Hindu religion and literature into the Peninsula."

In a note of Professo Wilson's to the Uttara Rama Charitra (vol. xi, p. 322), there is a legend of Agastya similar to that related of Astika, *q.v.* "Agastya having seen his ancestors suspended by their heels in a pit, *was* told by them that they could only he extricated from their position by his begetting a son. In order to obtain a wife for this purpose he made a girl of the most graceful parts of the animals of the forest, and gave her without his privacy to the king of Vidarbha, to be his daughter. She was named Lopamudra from the distinctive beauties (*mudra*) of animals, as the eyes of deer, &c., being subjected to loss (*lopa*) in her superior charms. When marriageable Agastya demanded her of her father, and although sorely against his will, the king was obliged to consent to her becoming the wife of the sage."—Wilson, *XI*, 322.

AGATHAMMA—One of the tutelary goddesses of Madras.

AGHĀSURA—(Agha the Asura.) An *asura* who was Kaṁśa's general. He assumed the form of a vast serpent, and Kṛṣṇa's companions, the cowherds, entered its mouth, mistaking it for a mountain cavern: but Kṛṣṇa rescued them.

AGHORAHANTA—The Priest of *Chámundá*, a terrific goddess in the drama of Málati and Mádhava.

AGHORI, OR AGHORAPANTHI—The original *Aghorí* worship seems to have been the *Deví* in some of her terrific forms, and to have required even human victims for its performance. In imitation of the formidable aspect under which the goddess was worshipped, the appearance of her votary was rendered as hideous as possible, and his wand and water-pot were a staff set with bones and the upper half of a skull: the practices were of a similar nature, and flesh and spirituous liquors constituted, at will, the diet of the adept.

"The regular worship of this sect has long since been suppressed, and the only traces of it now left are presented by a few disgusting wretches, who, whilst they profess to have adopted its tenets, make them a mere plea for extorting alms. In proof of their indifference to worldly objects, they eat and drink whatever is given to them, even ordure and carrion. They smear their bodies also with excrement, and carry it about with them in a wooden cup, or skull, either to swallow it, if by so doing they can get a few pice; or to throw it upon the persons, or into the houses of those who refuse to comply with their demands. They also for the same purpose inflict gashes on their limbs, that the crime of blood may rest upon the head of the recusants; and they have a variety of similar disgusting devices to extort money from the timid and credulous Hindu. They are fortunately not numerous, and are universally detested and feared."—Wilson, *Vol. I, p. 234.*

AGNĀYI—Wife of Agni. She is seldom alluded to in the Veda and is not of any importance.

ĀGNEYA PURANA—The name of one of the eighteen Puránas. (See AGNI PURĀṆA).

ĀGNEYA—Son of Agni, a name of Kārttikeya or Mārs; also an appellation of the *muni* Agastya and others.

ĀGNEYĀSTRA—'The weapon of fire.' Given by Bharadvāja to Agniveśa, the son of Agni, and by him to Droṇa. A similar weapon was, according to the *Viṣṇu Purāṇa*, given by the sage Aurva to his pupil King Sagara, and with it "he conquered the tribes of barbarians who had invaded his patrimonial possessions".

Fiery arms or rockets, were possibly employed by the Hindus in remote antiquity, as well as in recent times; whence came the notion of certain mysterious weapons framed of the elements, and to be wielded only by deities and demi-gods. These make a great figure in the battle scenes of the Rámáyaṇa and Mahábhárata.

AGNEYI—The wife of Uru, a descendant of Dhruva, and mother of six excellent sons, Anga, Sumanas, Swati, Kratu, Angiras and Śiva.

AGNI—(1) (Nom. Agnis = Ignis.) Fire, one of the most ancient and most sacred objects of Hindu worship. He appears in three phases—in heaven as the sun, in mid-air as lightning, on earth as ordinary fire. Agni is one of the chief deities of the Vedas, and great numbers of the hymns are addressed to him, more indeed than to any other god. He is one of the three great deities—Agni, Vāyu (or Indra), and Sūrya—who respectively preside over earth, air, and sky, and are all equal in dignity. "He is considered as the mediator between men and gods, as protector of men and their homes, and as witness of their actions; hence, his invocation at all solemn occasions, at the nuptial ceremony, &c. Fire has ceased to be an object of worship, but is held in honour for the part it performs in sacrifices." Agni is represented as having seven tongues, each of which has a distinct name, for licking up the butter used in sacrifices. He is guardian of the south-east quarter, being one of the eight *lokapālas* (*q.v.*), and his region is called Purajyotiṣa./In a celebrated hymn of the *Ṛgveda* attributed to Vasiṣṭha, Indra and other gods are called upon to destroy the Kravyāds 'the flesh-eaters', or *rākṣasa* enemies of the gods. Agni himself is also a Kravyād, and as such he takes an entirely different character. He is represented under a form as hideous as the beings he is invoked to devour. He sharpens his two iron tusks, puts his enemies into his mouth and swallows them. He heats the edges of his shafts and sends them into the hearts of the *rākṣasa*

"He appears in the progress of mythological personification as a son of Aṅgiras, as a king of the Pitṛs or Manes, as a Marut, as grandson of Śāṇḍila, as one of the seven sages or rsts, during the reign of Tāmasa the fourth Manu", and as a star. In the *Mahābhārata* Agni is represented as having exhausted his vigour by devouring too many oblations, and desiring to consume the whole Khāṇḍava forest as a means of recruiting his strength. He was prevented by Indra, but having obtained the assistance of Kṛṣṇa and Arjuna, he baffled Indra and accomplished his object. In the *Viṣṇu Purāṇa* he is called Abhimānī, and the eldest son of Brahmā. His wife was Svāhā; by her he had three sons, Pavaka, Pavamana, and Śuchi, and these had forty-five sons; altogether forty-nine persons, identical with the forty-nine fires, which forty-nine fires the *Vāyu Purāṇa* endeavours to discriminate. He is described in the *Harivaṁśa* as clothed in black, having smoke for his standard and head-piece, and carrying a flaming javelin. He has four hands, and is borne in a chariot drawn by red horses, and the seven winds are the wheels of his car. He is accompanied by a ram, and sometimes he is represented riding on that animal. The representations of him vary.

The names and epithets of Agni are many—Vahni, Anala, Pāvaka, Vaiśvānara, son of Viśvānara, the sun; Abjahasta, 'lotus in hand'; Dhūmaketu whose sign is smoke'; Hutāśa or Huta-bhuj, 'devourer of offerings'; Śuci or Śukra, 'the bright'; Rohitāśva, 'having red horses'; Chāgaratha, 'ram rider'; Jātavedas (*q.v.*); Saptajihvā, 'seven-tongued'; Tomaradhara, 'javelin-bearer'. **(2)** "The deity of Fire, one of the most ancient and most sacred objects of Hindu worship. As such, Agni is considered as the mediator between men and gods, as protector of mankind and their home, and as witness of their actions; hence his invocation in all solemn occasions, at the nuptial ceremony, &c. He is one of the eight Lókapálas, or guardian of the world, and especially the Lord of the south-east quarter. He appears in the process of mythological personification as a son of Angiras, as a king of the Pitris or Manes, as a Marut, as a grandson fo Sandila, as one of the seven sages during the reign of Tamasa, or the fourth Manu, as a star, and as a ṛsis or inspired author of several Vaidic hymns." (Goldstücker.)

He is generally described as having two faces, three legs and seven arms, of a red or flame color, and riding on a ram. Before him is a swallow-tailed banner on which a ram is also represented. He is described by others as a corpulent man of a red complexion, with eyes, eyebrows, head and hair, of a tawny color, riding on a goat. From his body issue seven streams of glory, and in his right hand he holds a spear. Agni is the son of Kásyapa and Adití. His consort of Sakti is Swaha, a daughter of Kásyapa. Brahman priests are ordered to maintain a perpetual fire; and in the numerous religious ceremonies of the Hindus Agni is commonly invoked. The god is sometimes figured with a forked representation of fire issuing from his mouth; and sometimes with seven tongues of fire. (See Colebrooke's *Essays*.)

Agni, like Indra, is sometimes addressed as the one great god who makes all things, sometimes as the light which fills the heavens, sometimes as the blazing lightning, or as the clear flame of earthly fire. The poets pass from one application of the word to another with perfect ease, as conscious that in each case they are using a mere name which may denote similar qualities in many objects. There is no rivalry or antagonism between these deities. Agni is greatest, Varuna is greatest, and Indra is greatest: but when the one is so described, the others are for the time unnoticed, or else are placed in a subordinate position. Thus Agni is said to comprehend all other gods within himself, as the circumference of a wheel embraces its spokes;* (Muir.) and not unfrequently Indra is said to be Agni, and Agni is said to be Indra; while both alike are Skambha, the supporter of the world.

Hence the character of the god is almost wholly physical. The blessings which his worhippers pray for are commonly temporal. In the earlier hymns he is generally addressed as the fire, which to mortal men is an indispensable boon; in the more developed ceremonialism of later times he is chiefly concerned with the ordering of the sacrifices.

"As the special guardian and regulator of sacrifices Agni assumes the character of the Hellenic Hestra, and almost attaints the majesty of the Latin Vesta. He is the lord and protector of every house, and the father, mother, brother and son of every one of the worshippers. During life he shields men from harm, and at death he becomes the *Psycho pompos*, as conveying the 'unborn part' of the dead of the unseen world." (Cox, *Mythology of Aryan Nations*.) **(3)** Agni is also the name of a star in the tail of the planetary porpoise.

AGNI PURĀṆA—This Purāṇa derives its name from its having been communicated originally by Agni, the deity of fire, to the *muni* Vasiṣṭha, for the purpose of instructing him in the twofold knowledge of Brahmā. Its contents are variously specified as "sixteen thousand, fifteen thousand and fourteen thousand stanzas". This work is devoted to the glorification of Śiva, but its contents are of a very varied and cyclopaedical character. It has portions on ritual and mystic worship, cosmical descriptions, chapters on the duties of kings and the art of war, which have the appearance of being extracted from some older works, a chapter on law from the textbook of Yājñavalkya, some chapters on medicine from the Suśruta, and some treatises on rhetoric, prosody, and grammar according to the rules of Piṅgala and Pāṇini. Its motley contents "exclude it from any legitimate claims to be regarded as a Purāṇa, and prove that its origin cannot be very remote". The text of this Purāṇa has been in the *Bibliotheca Indica*, published and edited by Rājendra Lāl Mitra.

AGNIBAHU—One of the ten sons of Príyavrata and Kamya, famous for strength and prowess. It is said of him in the *V.P.*, that when he adopted a religous life, he remembered the occurrences of a prior existence, and did not covet dominion, but diligently practised the rites of devotion, wholly disinterested, and looking for no reward.

AGNI-DAGDHAS—Pitṛs, or Manes, who when alive kept up the household flame and presented oblations with fire. Those who did not do so were called *Anagni dagdhas*. (*see* PITṚS)

AGNIHOTRA—A burnt offering, or libation of clarified butter on sacred fire.

AGNIṢVATTAS—(1) *Pitṛs* or Manes of the gods, who when living upon earth did not maintain their domestic fires or offer burnt-sacrifices. According to some authorities they were descendants of Marīci. They are also identified with the seasons, (*see* PITṚS) **(2)** A class of Pitris, a divine race inhabiting celestial regios of their own. This class consists of those house-holders who when alive did not maintain their domestic fires, nor offer burnt sacrifices. Some of the Purânas identify the Agnishwattas with the seasons. *V.P.*, p.239.

AGNISHTOMA—(1). A son of the Manu Chakshusha; **(2)** the name of a sacrifice produced from the eastern mouth of Brahma, along with the Gáyatri, and the Rig Véda. *V.P.*, 42.

AGNIVARCHAS—One of Súta's scholars, who became a celebrated teacher of the Puránas.

AGNIVARNA—A prince whose name occurs in various Puránas; but little more is known of him beyond his being a descendant of Ráma.

AGNIVESA—A sage named in the Mahábhárata, the son of Agni, the deity of fire. He was one of the early teachers of medicine.

AGRASYA—The first day of the Hindu year which falls on the new moon in March. A feast goes on for three days at this period—the new year's day festival.

AHALYĀ—(1) Wife of the *rsi* Gautama, and a very beautiful woman. In the *Rāmāyana* it is stated that she was the first woman made by Brahmā, and that he gave her to Gautama. She was seduced by Indra, who had to suffer for his adultery. One version of the *Rāmāyana* represents her as knowing the god and being flattered by his condescension; but another version states that the god assumed the form of her husband, and so deceived her. Another story is that Indra secured the help of the moon, who assumed the form of a cock and crowed at midnight. This roused Gautama to his morning's devotions, when Indra went in and took his place. Gautama expelled Ahalyā from his hermitage, and deprived her other prerogative of being the most beautiful woman in the world, or, according to another statement, he rendered her invisible. She was restored to her natural state by Rāma and reconciled to her husband. This seduction is explained mythically by Kumārila Bhaṭṭa as Indra (the sun's) carrying away the shades of night—the name Ahalyā, by a strained etymology, being made to signify 'night'. **(2)** The wife of the ṛṣi Gautama, of whom the following legend is relate: One day when the sage was absent from his dwelling, the mighty Indra passed by, and burned with an impure passion for the wife of Gautama; he entered the hut in the disguise of the sage, and began to entreat Ahalyá; and Ahalyá, knowing him to be the rája of the celestials, in the wantonness of her heart yielded to his desires. Then the sovereign of the gods left the hermitage, but at that moment Gautama entered, and he was invincible even to the gods, through the power of his austerities. Perceiving him, Indra was overwhelmed with sadness; and the sage, beholding the profligate lord of gods in his disguise, thus addressed him in words of dreadful anger:—'O depraved wretch, assuming my form you have perpetrated this great crime! Therefore form this moment do you become a eunuch!' The great sage then pronounced this curse upon his wife Ahalyá:—'O sinful wretch, for thousands of years shall you remain in the forest, abandoned by all and invisible to all, until Ráma, the son of Dasaratha, shall enter here, and you from beholding him shall be cleansed from all sin, and again approach me without fear.' With these words the illustrious Gautama abandoned this hermitage, and performed religious austerities on the summit of the Himálaya mountains.

Having heard this holy legend, Ráma entered the hermitage, preceded by Viswámitra; and at that moment, Ahalyá was released from her curse, and became visible to all; and a shower of flowers fell from heaven, and divine music was heard in the sky. Then the illustrious Gautama, beholding with divine eye that his consort was cleansed from all sin, repaired again to his hermitage; and having paid due honors to Ráma, he engaged in sacred austerities with her purified spouse. And Ráma proceeded to Mithilá with his brother and Viswámitra—It is said that Indra means the sun, and Ahalyá, the night; and as the night is seduced and ruined by the sun of the morning therefore is Indra called the paramour of Ahalyá.

Also called Maitreyī. The wife of the *ṛṣi* Gautama[1] whom Indra seduced while her husband was performing his early morning devotions (*SBr.*, III. 3.4, 18). When the *ṛṣi* learned of his wife's infidelity he drove her from the hermitage and cursed her to become invisible. He revenged himself on Indra by inflicting him with a skin complaint that consisted of a thousand marks resembling the female pudenda.[2]

This myth was extended in the *Rāmayana*, and became the basis of various accounts, in one of which Rāma restored Ahalyā to her normal form and reconciled her with Gautama. Indra was punished by the gods who allowed Rāvana to defeat him.

The *Mārkandeya Purana*. (V.1-9) makes use of the myth to denigrate Indra and to glorify Vishnu.

1. Ahalyā was the first woman created by Brahmā who gave her to Gautama (*V.P.*, IV. 19).
2. In a later myth these marks were changed to eyes and Indra became known as Sahasrāksa (Thousand-eyed). Another myth states that on learning of the seduction, Gautama deprived Indra of his genitals (*vrsana*) and substituted those of a goat (*Rāmayana*, 1.48, 16f, *EM.*).

AHANKARA—Consciousness, or Egotism. The sense of Ahankára, says Professor Wilson, cannot be very well rendered by any European term. It means the principle of individual existence, that which appropriates perceptions, and on which depend the notions, I think, I feel, I am. It might be expressed by the proprosition of Descartes reversed. 'Sum, ergo cotigo, sentio,' &c. The equivalent employed by Mr. Colebrooke, egotism, has the advantages of an analogous etymology. In the Sánkya Kárika three varieties of Ahankára are described. From the first kind proceed the senses; from the third the unconscious elements; both kinds being equally inert of themselves, are rendered productive by the co-operation of the second, the energetic modification of Ahankára, which is therefore said to be the origin both of the senses and the elements. Colloquially "Ahankára" is still in common use throughout India in the sense of pride, or great conceit.

AHAR—Day. One of the forms of Bramha during the work of Creatio. *V.P.*, p. 40.

AHAVANIYA—The consecrated fire for oblations. This, with the Gárhapatya and Dakshiṇá form the Tretágni, or triad of sacred fires, in opposition to the Laukíka or merely temporal ones. *See* FIRE, SACRIFICIAL.

AHI—A serpent. A name of Vṛtra, the Vedic demon of drought: but Ahi and Vṛtra are sometimes "distinct, and mean, most probably, differently formed clouds".—*Wilson.*

AHICCHATRA, AHIKSETKA—A city mentioned in the *Mahābhārata* as lying north of the Ganges, and as being the capital of Northern Pañcāla. It is apparently the Adisadra of Ptolemy, and its remains are visible near Rāmnagar.

AHRAT—(1) A king of southern Karnataka who was converted by Rishabha; **(2)** A name of a deified sage among the Jainas.

AINDRAJALIKA—Conjuring; from *Indra*, a deity, and *jála, a* net. The art of magic or necromancy has always been prevalent in India, and attained a degree of perfection that has perhaps not been surpassed in any other country. Even to this day feats are performed which it is difficult for the most acute observers to explain. The apparent production and growth of a mango tree is a performance so cleverly executed as to excite the astonishment of those who have been most determined to discover how the illusion is effected. In the Hindu dramas magicians are described as having a bunch of peacock's feathers in their hands, and this bunch still forms the implement of conjuring, and is carried by mendicants in India who pretend to skill in magic; it is especially used by Jaina-vagrants.

AINDRI—'Son of Indra.' An appellation of Arjuna.

AIRAVATA—(1) 'Afine elephant.'An elephant produced at the churning of the ocean, and appropriated by the god Indra. The derivation of this name is referred to the word Irāvat, signifying 'produced from water'. He is guardian of one of the points of the compass. (*see* LOKA-PĀLA) **(2)** The king of elephants, produced from the churning of the ocean, and taken by Indra, who subsequently used it as his vehicle. The name has been derived from Iravat "watery," and supposed to allude to the north, as the quarter whence rain comes, or to the original idea of a cloud, in which Indra as the king of clouds, is mounted, and therefore called his elephant. Professor Wilson refers it to the fact of his being produced from the watery ocean; **(3)** Airávata is also the name of the north portion of the sun's path among the lunar asterisms; **(4)** The name of a celebrated serpent with m any heads, one of the progeny of Kadru.

AITAREYA BRAHMANAM—of the Rig Veda: this work contains the earliest speculations of the Brahmans on the meaning of the Sacrificial Prayers, and on the origin, performance, and meaning of the Rites of the Vedic Religion. It consists of forty Adyhayas, Translated and edited by Dr. Martin Haug, 2. vols. 12 mo., Bombay, 1963.

AITAREYA—The name of a *Brāhmaṇa*, an *Āraṇyaka*, and an Upaniṣad of the *Ṛgveda*. The *Brāhmaṇa* has been edited and translated by Dr. Haug; the text of the *Āraṇyaka* has been published in the *Bibliotheca Indica* by Rājendra Lāla, and there is another edition. The Upanisad has been translated by Dr. Roer in the same series. "*The Aitareya Āraṇyaka* consists of five books, each of which is called Āranyaka. The second and third books form a separate Upaniṣad, and a still further subdivision here takes place, inasmuch as the four last sections oithe second book, which are particularly consonant with the doctrines of the Vedānta system, pass as the *Aitareyopaniṣad.—Weber.*

AITAREYA-ARANYAKA—A commentary on the beginning of the Rig Veda. It is ascribed to Mahidasu the son of Itará.

AJA—(1) 'Unborn.' An epithet applied to many of the gods. A prince of the Solar race, sometimes said to be the son of Raghu, at others the son of Dilīpa, son of Raghu. He was the husbsand chosen at her *svayamvara* by Indumati, daughter of Rājā of Vidarbha, and was the father of Daśaratha and grandfather of Rāma. The *Raghuvaṁśa* relates how on his way to the *svayaṁvara* he was annoyed by a wild elephant and ordered it to be shot. When the elephant was mortally wounded, a beautiful figure issued from it, which declared itself *agandharva* who had been transformed into a mad elephant for deriding a holy man. The *gandharva* was delivered, as it had been foretold to him, by Aja, and he gave the prince some arrows which enabled him to excel in the contest at the *svayaṁvara.* When Daśaratha grew up, Aja ascended to Indra's heaven. **(2)** The unborn. A name of Bramha; of Siva; of Vishnu; also of Káma, or Cupid. Aja is also the proper name of a mythical prince, the son of Raghu, and father of Dasaratha. This prince forms the subject of the first and longest of Mr. Griffiths' beautiful Idylls from the Sanscrit. The story is taken from the Raghuvansa of Kálidása. (See RAGHU.) The childhood and youth of Aja are described in glowing terms, and in due course he was sent by his father to the Swayamvara of the princess Indumati Dévi, daughter of the Rája of Vidarbha. On his way thither while resting in the heat of the day, the encampment was disturbed by a wild elephant which Aja ordered to be shot. On being pierced by an arrow a figure of great splendour issued from the body of the elephant; and standing in mid-air thus spoke: "Aja Mahárāya, I was formely a gandharva, but for mocking a holy ṛṣi was cursed to be born in an insane elephant; but on my begging for mercy was told I should be released by the son of Raghu Mahárája, called Aja, when on his way to be married." He then gave Aja the arrows used by the grandharvas and instructed him in the use of them.

On arriving at the capital of Vidarbharáya he was treated with great respect, and was selected from amongst all the assembled princes by the fair Indumati Dévi, who intimated here choice by herself plcing the garland on the nec of Aja. In the contests that ensued with the other disappointed suitors Aja obtained a complete victory by means of the arrows received from the gandharva. He then returned to his father's kingdom, with his lovely bride; succeedd to the throne, and reigned wisely and well for many years.

After the birth of his distinguished son Dasaratha (father of Ráma) his beloved wife Indumati Dévi was killed by the fall of Nárada's garland, when asleep in an arbor of the summer palace. On Dasaratha's attaining his majority Aja is said to hav ascended to Indra's paradise, leaving his body between the rivers Ganges and Sarayu

AJAGAVA—The 'primitive bow' of Śiva, which fell from heaven at the birth of Pṛthu, with celestial arrows and panoply from heaven.

AJAKA—**(1)** A descendant of Purúravas, the son of Sumanta (or according to others of Sunaha) and grandson of Jahnu; **(2)** A king of magadha of the line of Pradyota.

AJAMADHA—**(1)** A son of Suhotra and author of vaidic hymns; **(2)** The twenty-sixth king of the lunar dynasty; **(3)** A surname of Yudhishthira, the friend of Aja.

AJAMIDHA—A son of Hastin, the founder of the celebrated city of Hastinápura, finally ruined by the encroachments of the Ganges, but vestiges of which were lately to be traced along the river nearly in a line with Delhi, about 60 miles to the east.

AJAMILA—A brāhmaṇa of Kannauj, who married aslaveandhad children, of whom he was very fond.

AJANTA—A river in the hills below the river Tapti, to the north of Bombay. "In this ravine, somewhere about the first century of our era. Buddhists began to excavate architectural caves. There are twenty-six in all, and of these twenty-two are conventual abodes, whilst the remaining four are Chaitya halls or places of worship." *A. and M. I.*, p. 401. A full description of these caves is given in Fergusson's History of Architecture. It is seen from the costume carefully represented in the pictures at Ajanta, that the Hindus still dress in the fashion that then prevailed; and which was described by the Greeks who accompanied Alexander the Great to India, as consisting of two cloths, one reaching to the middle of the leg, whilst another is folded around the shoulders. The cloth is described as being made from wool which grows in trees.

AJAPASHYA—A surname of Rájivalóchana, the son of Swétakarna; his sides were black like the skin of certain goats, when he was drawn out of the water, after having been found exposed by his mother and purified by two sons of Sravishta.

AJAPAS—Sons of Kardama, Pitris of the Vaisyas, called also Kávyas and Suswadhas.

AJATASATRU—'One whose enemy is unborn'. **(1)** A king of Kāśī, mentioned in the Upaniṣads, who was very learned, and, although a kṣatriya, instructed the brāhmaṇa Gārgyabālāki. **(2)** A name of Siva. **(3)** Of Yudhiṣṭhira. **(4)** A king of Mathurā who reigned in the time of Buddha.

AJAYAPALA—Author of a Sanskṛt vocabulary of some repute.

AJIGARTA—A Rishi mentioned in the Aitareya Brahmana. He lived in the forests with his three sons Sunapuchha, Sunahsepha and Śunolángúla. He sold his son Sunahsepha to be offered as a sacrifice, showing that the Brahmans at that early period were familiar with the idea of human sacrifices. "If we accept the Áryan origin of Ajigarta, the seller and butcher of his own son, it is important to remark how great a difference there must have been between the various Áryan settlers in India. Yet there remains the fact that, with all the vaunted civilization of the higher Áryan classes, there were Áryan people in India to whom not only a young prince could make the offer of buying their children, but where the father offered himself to bind and kill the son whom he had sold for a hundred cows." (Max Müller, A. S. L., p. 415.)

AJIGARTTA—A brāhmaṇa *ṛṣi* who sold his son Śunahaśephas to be a sacrifice.

AJITA—'Unconquered, unexcelled' A title given to Viṣṇu, Śiva, and many others. There were classes of gods bearing this name in several *manvantaras.*

A form of Vishnu. "The unequalled energy of Vishnu combining with the quality of goodness, and effecting the preservation of created things, presides over all the Manwantaras, in the form of a divinity." *V.P.*, p. 264. **(1)** The proper name of several gods and persons, *viz.*, Vishnu, Siva; **(2)** One of the seven Rishis who preside during the reign of the fourteenth Manu; **(3)** A name of Maitreya or a future Buddha; **(4)** The second of the Arhats or Jaina saints of the present Avasarpini; **(5)** The attendant of the ninth Jaina Arhat; **(6)** A descendant of Ikshwáku and a son of Jitasatru by Vijaya.

AJITAS—A class of deities whose history is thus given. In the beginning of the Kalpa twelve gods name Jayas were created by Brahma, as his deputies and assistants in the creation. They, lost in meditation, neglected his commands; on which he cursed them to be repeatedly born in each Manwantara till the seventh. In the first they became Ajitas.

AJÑÀNA—A technical term used in the *Védá*nta system, meaning "ignorance," which the Vedántists declare is a somewhat that is not to be called positively either entity or non-entity—not a mere negation but the opponent of knowledge, consisting of the three fetters. According to the Naiyáyikas *ajnána* is merely the non-existence, or negation, (*abháva*) of jñána. To deny this the writer calls it *bhára*, implying that it is not *abháva*.

AJOBHAGA—The unborn part of man. After death and the cremation of the body, Agni is supplicated to kindle the unborn part with his heat and name, and, assuming his most auspicious form, to convey it to the world of the righteous. Before, however, this unborn part can complete its course from earth to the third heaven, it has to traverse a vast gulf of darkness. Leaving behind on earth all that is evil and imperfect, and proceeding by the paths which the fathers trod, the spirit, invested with a lustre like that of the gods, soars to the realms of eternal light, &c.—*O. S. T; Vol. V, p.* 303.

AKALI—(Immortals). Belonging to the Sikh religion, soldiers of God, who with their blue dress and bracelets of steel, claimed for themselves a direct institution by Govind Singh. They combined warlike activity with the relinquishment of the world, and became the armed guardians of Amritsar. It cost Ranjit Singh much time and trouble to reduce them to order.

AKAMPANA—A king who lived in the Krita Yuga, but who was so far from enjoying the tranquillity generally predicated of that happy time, that he was overcome by his enemies in a battle, in which he lost his son, and suffered in consequence severe affliction.—*O.S.T.*, Vol. I, p. 505.

AKAMPAN—One of the giant-leaders of Rávaṇa's army; it was Akampan who told his king of the strength and invincibility of Ráma.

"No power can check, no might can tame,
Rama, a chief of noblest fame."

He then counselled Rávaṇa to try stratagem to effect his purpose.

"That hero in the wood beguile
And steal his lovely spouse the while."

AKASAVANI—A divine manifestation, in which the deity is heard but not seen.

AKRURA—A Yādava and uncle of Kṛṣṇa. The son of Swaphalka and Gandíní who took charge of the celebrated syamantaka jewel from Satadhanwan, when he was pursued by Krishna; and through the virtue of that gem there was no dearth nor pestilence in the whole country. When Krishna discovered that the precious jewel was in Akrúra's posession he desired him to retain it; Akrúra, thus urged, afterwards wore it publicly round his neck, where it shone with dazzling brightness; and he moved about like the sun, wearing a garland of light. Akrúra conveyed Krishna and Rama, when youths, to Mathura, where Krishna performed some of his great exploits.

AKSAMALA—A name of Arundhati (*q.v.*).

AKSHA—**(1)** The eldest son of Rāvaṇa slain by Hanumān. Aksha was heir to the throne, a youth merely, but who had already made himself a name in the battle field. He entreated his father to allow him to try his strength with Hanuman. When the noble son of the wind saw this new opponent, his heart was filled with compassion. 'This hero is still but a child,' he thought; it were against my will to slay him in an hour v/hen life seems filled with beauty. Accordiugly, the gallant monkey, wishing to spare Aksha, sprang to the ground, overturned the chariot with a blow and killed the horses. But nothing daunted, the brave youth sprang up, and bounded through the air to meet Hanumán, 'well done, valiant Simian !' he shouted, 'hat thou hast not yet triumphed.' When he saw that Aksha's daring only augmented with the combat, "There is no help for it said the magnanimous ape regretfully, 'A fire that increases cannot be despised; I cannot let pity for this hot headed boy imperil my mission !' Thereupon he seized the young warrior by the feet and threw him down head foremost. So Aksha, the lion-hearted, the joy of the city of Lanka, lay cold and dead on the breast of the one mother-earth.—*I. E.*, 233. **(2)** Also a name of Garuda.

AKSHATA—Grains of rice tinged with a reddish hue, placed by the husband on the head of the infant after the ceremony of Arati, and after the women have retired.

AKSHOHINI—An Army consisting of 109,350 infantry; 65,610 cavalry; 21,870 chariots; and 21,870 elephants.

AKULI—The name of one of the priests of the Asuras. It was he who with another priest of the same class called Kiláta, obtained permission from Manu to sacrifice for him, and took for the victim first a bull of Manu's into which an Asura-slaying voice had entered. When it had been slaughtered the voice departed out of it and entered into Manu's wife Manávi. "Wherever they hear her speaking, the Asuras and Rákshasas continue to be destroyed in consequence of her voice. The Asuras said: 'She does us yet more mischief; for the human voice speaks more.' Kiláta and Akuli said, 'Manu is a devout believer: let us make trial of him!' They came and said to him 'Manu, let us sacrifice for thee!' 'With what (victim)?' he asked. 'With this (thy) wife,' they replied 'Be it so,' he answered. When shed had been slaughtered the voice departed out of her and entered into the sacrifices and the sacrificial vessels. Thence they were unable to expel it. This is the Asura-slaying voice which speaks out (when the two stones are struck with the *śamyá*, as a part of the ceremonial). Wretched become the enemies of that man for whom, when he knows this they cause this voice here to reverberate." (Muir's *O.S.T.*, Vol. I, p. 189.)

AKUPĀRA—A tortoise or turtle. The tortoise on which the earth rests.

ĀKUTI—(1) A daughter of Manu Svāyambhuva and Śatarūpā,whom he gave to the patriarch Ruci. She bore twins, Yajña and Dakṣiṇā, who became husband and wife and had twelve sons, the deities called Yāmas. Dr. Muir remarks that the word is found in the Rig Veda with the significance of "will" or "design;" but appears to be personified in a passage of the Taittiríya Bráhmana, where it is said. "Ira was the wife of the creators. Akúti kneaded the oblation." *O.S.T.*, Vol. I, p. 73. **(2)** Also the name of the wife of Chakshush.

ALAKANANDA—One of the four branches of the river Gaṅgā, which flows south to the country of Bhārata. This is said by the Vaiṣṇavas to be the terrestrial Gaṅgā which Śiva received upon his head.

ALAKA—The Himalayan residence of Kubera the god of riches. It is termed in the "Cloud Messenger" the City of the Blessed; and is described as unmatched for lovely girls, who learn to choose the flowers that suit them best.

> "The amaranth, bright glory of the spring:
> The lotus gathered from the summer flood;
> Acacias taught around their brown to cling;
> The jasmine's fragrant white their locks to stud;
> And bursting at thy rain the young Kadamba bud."
> —Griffiths' Translation.

ALAMBANA—The exercise of the Yógi while endeavouring to bring before his thoughts the gross form of the Supreme Being. It also means the silent repetition of prayer.

ALAMBUSA—A great *rākṣasa* worsted by Sātyaki in the great war of the *Mahābhārata*, and finally killed by Ghaṭotkaca. He is said to be a son of Ṛsyaśṛṅga.

ALANKARA—Ornament, decoration, Alankára is frequently mentioned as one of the daily ceremonies to be observed, and means then the putting on of ornaments. Alankára Sástri means Rhetoric, a subject on which various treatises exist, but none of any intrinsic value.

ALAYUDHA—A *rākṣasa* killed after a fierce combat by Ghaṭotkaca in the war of the *Mahābhārata* (*Fauche*, ix. 278).

ALLAMA PRABHU—Among the *Vira Saivas* a lesser incarnation, or form of *Siva*. He appears to have been a Brahman, who acted in close concert with the elder *Basava*; whether as a primary instigator, or subsequent accomplice, is not clear. But he became *Basava's guru* or spiritual adviser, and, as such, was concerned in the revolution at Kalyánapuri, in which the king *Bijala* was slain, and a new religion established. The *Prabhu linga lila* is a popular poem, in Telugu, and composed expressly in order to magnify the great excellencies of *Allamá prabhu* as a form of *Siva*, and especially his chastity, that resisted all the fascinations of the *támasa guna* or evil portion of *Párvati*; which became incarnate as a woman, Máya or Frans, in order to tempt him. "In the *Basava puránam*, *Allamá prabhu* is stated to have travelled about, and especially to *Sri Sailam* in Telingana, performing various wonders, and possessed of a body invulnerable. No record of the manner of his death has been observed."—(*Taylor.*) There is a good abstract of Prabhu-linga líla, by C. P. Brown, in the *Catalogue Raisonné*, vol. 2, p. 838.

ALLOO—A raw hide used by the Rájputs to cover themselves when they assert their claim to a disputed piece of land.

ALUVAR—*Rulers*; twelve heads and original leaders of the *Vaishnava* faith in the Peninsula only. They were born in various places, and lived in different times. To understand their office and importance the reader must be apprized that the *Saiva* system first obtained a hold and influence in the Peninsula; and, in some instances, by exterminating the Buddhists or Jains who preceded them. The Vaishnavas, on their coming, had not only to deal with a rude and savage people, following superstitious customs, some of which continue to the present day, but also had to contend with the astute and powerful Saivas already in possession; and sometimes in the way of public disputation—as at Villiputtúr in the Pandya kingdom, at Uriyur in the Chola kingdom, and at Srí Permattúr in the Tondam-andalam. These, or others, were engaged in translating portions of the Vedas into Tamil poetry, now known as the *Tiru-morhi* or sacred word. Different books exist, containing in all many thousand stanzas, said to indicate the idiom of foreigners. Twelve individuals, distinguished in these or other ways in the first establishment of Vaishnavism, were named Aluvar; and are regarded with high veneration by modern votaries. An approximation towards deification has been assigned, by metaphorically viewing them as incarnations of Vishnú's arms, ornaments, or attendants. Their names in order are—1, Poyálvār; 2, Puthatálvār; 3, Péyálvár; 4, Tirumal Péyálvár; 5, Namálvár; 6, Kulasec'harálvár; 7, Periyálvar; 8, Tirupanálvár; 9, Tirumangayalvár; 10, Tondamálvár; 11, Yempramanár, or Yetirája, or Rāmánujácharya; 12, Kurattálvár.—*Taylor.*

AMARA KOSHA—A celebrated Sanscrit Vocabulary which is found in a more or less perfect state in all Indian languages. Like most other Sanscrit Dictionaries it is arranged in verse to aid the memory. Synonymous words are collected into one or more verses, and placed in fifteen different chapters, which treat of as many different subjects. The sixteenth contains a few homonymous terms arranged alphabetically, in the Indian manner, by the final consonants. The seventeenth chapter is a pretty full catalogue of indeclinables, which European philologists would call adverbs, prepositions, conjunctions, and interjections, but which Sanscrit grammarians consider as indeclinable nouns. The last chapter of the Amara Kósha is a treatise on the gender of nouns. See Colebrooke's *Essay* on the Sanscrit and Prácrit Languages.

This title may be read in two ways—'the immortal vocabulary', or, more appropriately, 'the vocabulary of Amara or Amara Simha'. "The oldest vocabulary hitherto known, and one of the most celebrated vocabularies of the classical Sanskṛt." It has been the subject of a great number of commentaries. The text has been often printed. There is an edition published in India with an English interpretation and annotations by Colebrooke, and the text with a French translation has been printed by Deslongchamps.

AMARA SIMHA—The author of the vocabulary called *Amarakoṣa.* He was one of the nine gems of the court of Vikrama. (*see* Nava-ratna). Wilson inclines to place him in the first century BC Lassen places him about the middle of the third century A.D., and others incline to bring him down later. Unfortunately he held the tenets of a heterodox sect, and his poems perished in the persecutions fomented by intolerant philosophers against the persons and writings of both Jainas and Buddhists

AMARAKANTAKA—'Peak of immortals'. A place of pilgrimage in the table-land east of the Vindhyas.

AMARAVATI—The capital of Indra renowned for its greatness and splendour, built by Visvakarma, the architect of the gods. It is situated somewhere in the vicinity of Meru. It is described as 800 miles in circumference, and 40 miles high. Its pillars are composed of diamonds; its thrones of pure gold; it is surrounded with gardens and fountains, while music and dancing entertain the celestial inhabitants. It is sometimes called Devapura, 'city of the gods', and Pūṣabhāsā, 'sun-splendour'. There is a ruined town called Amarávati on the banks of the river Kistna containing numerous antiquities in the form of sculptures, all of Buddhist origin. Sir Walter Elliot and Mr. Fergusson made considerable explorations there. The ruined Dágoba whence the relics were taken was on a mound of 150 feet diameter, now converted into a tank. It is called Dípaldinna, the Mound of Light.

AMARESVARA—'Lord of the immortals. 'A titleof Viṣṇu, Śiva, and Indra. Name of one of the twelve great *lingas.* (*see* LINGA)

AMARU-SATAKA—A poem consisting of a hundred stanzas written by a king name Amaru, but by some attributed to the philosopher Śaṅkara, who assumed the dead form of that king for the purpose of converṣing with his widow. Theverses are of an erotic character, but, like many others of the same kind, a religious or philosophical interpretation has been found for them. There is a translation in French by Apudy with the text, and a translation in German by Rückert.

AMAVASU—The third of the six sons of Purúravas and Urvasí, and one of the progenitors of the lunar race of kings.

AMAVASYA—The day of 'conjunction,' just before new-moon—a fast day for all brahmans.

AMBA AND AMBIKA—Names of *Párvati*, the *Sakti* of Siva.

AMBĀ—'Mother.' **(1)** A name of Durgā. **(2)** The eldest daughter of a king of Kāśī. She and her sisters Ambikā and Ambālikā were carried off by Bhisma to be the wives of Vicitravīrya. Ambā had been previously betrothed to a Rājā of Śalva, and Bhīṣma sent her to him, but the Rājā rejected her because she had been in another man's house. She retired to the forest and engaged in devotion to obtain revenge on Bhīsma. Śiva favoured her, and promised her the desired vengeance in another birth. Then she ascended the pile and was born again as Śikhandin, who slew Bhīsma. **(3)** In southern Indian languages *amba* becomes *amma* and is frequently affixed to the names of goddesses and females in general.'

AMBALIKA—The younger widow of Vicitravīrya and mother of Pāṇḍu by Vyāsa. (*see* MAHĀBHĀRATA)

AMBAṢṬHA—**(1)** A military people inhabiting a country of the same name in the middle of the Panjāb; **(2)** The medical tribe in Manu.

AMBARISA—**(1)** A king of Ayodhyā, twenty-eighth in descent from Ikṣvāku. (*see* ŚUNAHAŚEPHAS.) **(2)** An appellation of Śiva. **(3)** Name of one of the eighteen hells.

AMBARISHA—**(1)** The son of the great monarch Mándhatri. He had fifty sisters, all of whom were married to the sage Saubhari; **(2)** The name of several other princes mentioned in the Puránic histories.

AMBEA—The mother of the Kurus,—a race of heroes or demi-gods related to the Pándus.

AMBHA MATHA—A Jaina goddess, still worshipped in various parts of India. The ruins of many beautiful temples erected to her may be seen in the high hills of Marwar.

AMBHANSI—A mystic term for the four classes of beings, gods, demons, men and pitris. It means literally 'waters.'

AMBIKĀ—**(1)** A sister of Rudra, but in later times identified with Umā. **(2)** Elder widow of Vicitravīrya and mother of Dhrtarāsṭtra by Vyāsa. (*see* Mahābhārata). **(3)**'Mother.' A nature-goddess around whom many earlier myths gathered.

Ambikā was formed from the energies of all the gods to destroy the buffalo-demon and his army who were attacking the gods. She overcame the demons, but later the gods were again attacked and conquered by the demons Śumbha and Niśumbha. Śumbha greatly desired Ambikā but she rejected him, and in revenge he sent a great army against her under Canda but Kālī defeated this army and received from Ambika the name Cāmunda.

The Jaina *tīrthankara* Nemi has as his messenger the old mother-goddess Ambikā, who 'often figures as the tutelary genius or *sampradaya-devi* of the Jaina religion'.

According to Sayana, Ambika assumed the form of autumn and so destroys beings through fever and other autumnal diseases, and hence she is propitiated at the height of the harvest season. She is also worshipped before the digging of water-tanks (*Matsya P.*, 58, 26, *Pl.*). The *Kālikā P.* (c. 14th cent.) gives directions for human and animal sacrifices to be offered to Candika (Ambikā). 'Gaurī, Kālī and Uma are called Ambikas. 'R. Williams, 'Before Mahāvīra', *JRAS.*, pts 1 and 2, p. 4, 1966). **(4)** Ambikā is also a name applied to the harvest as the most productive season.

AMBIKEYA—A metronymic applicable to Gaṇeśa, Skanda, and Dhṛtarāṣṭra.

AMNAYA—Sacred tradition. The Vedas in the aggregate.

AMOGAVARSHA—The Jain king of Kánchi, or Tondamandalam, at the end of the ninth century of the Christian era. The principal Jain Puránas are supposed to have been written in his reign, by the king's spiritual preceptor Jina Séna Achárya.

AMOGHA SIDDHA—The remover of the ills of the Kali age; a deity in the Buddhist Pantheon to whom prayers are made and offerings addressed.—*Wilson.*

AMRITA—**(1)** Ambrosia. The beverage of immortality. It was produced at the churning of the ocean, a legend with which all Hindus are familiar, and is said to have occurred in the following way; When the gods were overcome by the Dánavas, they fled for refuge to Vishnu and sought his protection and advice. Hari, the creator of the universe, being thus prayed to by the prostrate divinities, smiled, and thus spake with renovated energy, "Oh gods, I will restore your strength. Do you act as I enjoin? Let all the gods, associated with the Asuras, cast all sorts of medicinal herbs into the sea of milk; and then taking the mountain Mandara for the churning-stick, the serpant Vásuki for the rope, churn the ocean together for Ambrosia; depending upon my aid. To secure the assistance of the Daityas, you must be at peace with them, and engage to give them an equal portion of the fruit of your associated toil; promising them that by drinking the Amrita that shall be produced from the agitated ocean, they shall become mighty and immortal. I will take care that the enemies of the gods shall not partake of the precious draught; that they shall share in the labor alone."

"Being thus instructed by the god of gods, the divinities entered into alliance with the demons, and they jointly undertook the acquirement of the beverage of immortality. They collected various kinds of medicinal herbs, and cast them into the sea of milk, the waters of which were radiant as the shining clouds of autumn. They then took the mountain Mandara for the staff; the serpent Vásuki [see Ananta] for the cord; and commenced to churn the ocean for the Amrita. The assembled gods were stationed by Vishnu at the tail of the serpent; the Daityas and Dánavas at its head and neck. Scorched by the flames emitted from his inflated hood, the demons were shorn of their glory; whilst the clouds driven towards his tail by the breath of his mouth, refreshed the gods with revivifying showers. In the midst of the milky sea, Hari himself, in the form of a tortoise; served as a pivot for the mountain, as it was whirled around. The holder of the mace and discus was present in other forms amongst the gods and demons, and assisted to drag the monarch of the serpent race: and in another vast body he sat upon the summit of the mountain. With one portion of his energy, unseen by gods or demons, he sustained the serpent king; and with another infused vigour into the gods.

"From the ocean, thus churned by the gods and dánavas, first uprose the cow Surabha, the fountain of milk, and curds, worshipped by the divinities, and beheld by them and their associates with minds disturbed, and eyes glistening with delight. Then, as the holy Siddhas in the sky wondered what this could be, appeared the goddess Váruní [the deity of wine,] her eyes rolling with intoxication. Next, from the whirlpool of the deep, sprang the celestial Párijáta tree, the delight of the nymphs of heaven, perfuming the world with its blossoms. The troop of Apsarasas, the nymphs of heaven, were then produced, or surprising loveliness, endowed with beauty and with taste. The cool-rayed moon next rose, and was seized by Mahádeéva: and then poison was engendered from the sea, of which the snake gods (Nágas) took possession. Dhanwantari, robed in white, and bearing in his hand the cup of Amrita, next came forth; beholding which, the sons of Diti and of Danu, as well as the Munis, were filled with satisfaction and delight. Then, seated on a full-blown lotus, and holding a water-lily in her hand, the goddess Srí, radiant with beauty, rose from the waves. The great sages, enraptured, hymned her with the song dedicated to her praise. Viswavasu and other heavenly quiristers sang, and Ghirtachí and other celestial nymphs danced before her. Gangá and other holy streams attended for her ablutions; and the elephants of the skies, taking up their pure waters in vases of gold, poured them over the goddess, the queen of the universal world. The sea of milk in person presented her with a wreath of never-fading flowers; and the artist of the gods (Viswakarmá) decorated her person with heavenly ornaments. Thus bathed, attired, and adorned, the goddess, in the view of the celestials, cast herself upon the breast of Hari, and there reclining, turned her eyes upon the deities, who were inspired with rapture by her gaze. Not so the Daityas, who, with Viprachitti at their head, were filled with indignation, as Vishnu turned away from them, and they were abandoned by the goddess of prosperity (Lakshmí)

"The powerful and indignant Daityas then forcibly seized the Amrita-cup that was in the hand of Dhanwantarí: but Vishnu, assuming a female form, fascinated and deluded them; and recovering the Amrita from them, delivered it to the gods. Sakra and the other deities quaffed the Ambrosia. The incensed demons, grasping their weapons, fell upon them; but the gods, into whom the Ambrosial draught had infused new vigour, defeated and put their host to flight, and they fled through the regions of space, and plunged into the subterraneous realms of Pátála The gods thereat greatly rejoiced, did homage to the holder of the discus and mace, and resumed their reign in heaven. The sun shone with renovated splendour, and again discharged his appointed task; and the celestial luminaries again circled, in their respective orbits. Fire once more blazed aloft, beautiful in splendour; and the minds of all beings were animated by devotion. The three worlds again were rendered happy by prosperity; and Indra the chief of the gods, was restored to power." (*V.P.*, p. 77.) The legend as given in the Rámáyana may be found in Carey's Translation, Vol. I, p. 410—and that of the Mahábhárata in Sir C Wilkins' *Bhagavat Gita*—Bangalore edit., p. 105. **(2)** 'Immortal'. A god. The water of life. The term was known to the Vedas, and seems to have been applied to various things offered in sacrifice, but more especially to the soma juice. It is also called Nirjara and Pīyūṣa. In later times it was the water of life produced at the churning of the ocean by the gods and demons, the legend of which is told with some variations in the *Rāmāyaṇa*, the *Mahābhārata*, and the Purāṇas. The gods, feeling their weakness, having been worsted by the demons, and being, according to one authority, under the ban of a holy sage, repaired to Viṣṇu, beseeching him for renewed vigour and the gift of immortality. He directed them to churn the ocean for the *amṛta* and other precious things which had been lost. The story as told in the *Viṣṇu Purāṇa* has been rendered into verse by Professor Williams thus: The gods addressed the mighty Viṣṇu thus—

'Conquered in battle by the evil demons,
We fly to thee for succour, soul of all;
Pity, and by thy might deliver us!'
Hari, the lord, creator of the world,
Thus by the gods implored, all graciously
Replied—'Your strength shall be restored, ye gods;
Only accomplish what I now command.
Unite yourselves in peaceful combination
With these your foes; collect all plants and herbs
Of diverse kinds from every quarter; cast them
Into the sea of milk; take Mandāra,
The mountain, for a churning stick, and Vāsuki,
The serpent, for a rope; together churn
The ocean to produce the beverage—
Source of all strength and immortality—
Then reckon on my aid; I will take care
Your foes shall share your toil, but not partake
In its reward, or drink th' immortal draught'.
Thus by the god of gods advised, the host
United in alliance with the demons.
Straightaway they gathered various herbs and cast them
Into the waters, then they took the mountain
To serve as chuming-staff, and next the snake
To serve as cord, and in the ocean's midst
Hari himself, present in tortoise-form,
Became a pivot for the churning-staff.
Then did they churn the sea of milk; and first
Out of the waters rose the sacred Cow,
God-worshipped Surabhi, eternal fountain
Of milk and offerings of butter; next,
While holy Siddhas wondered at the sight,
With eyes all rolling Vāruṇī uprose,
Goddess of wine. Then from the whirlpool sprang
Fair Pārijāta, tree of Paradise, delight
Of heavenly maidens, with its fragrant blossoms
Perfuming the whole world. Th' Apsarasas,
Troop of celestial nymphs, matchless in grace,
Perfect in loveliness, were next produced.
Then from the sea uprose the cool-rayed moon,
Which Mahādeva seized; terrific poison
Next issued from the waters; this the snake-gods
Claimed as their own. Then, seated on a lotus,
Beauty's bright goddess, peerless Śri, arose
Out of the waves; and with her, robed in white,
Came forth Dhanvantari, the gods' physician.
High in his hand he bore the cup of nectar—
Life-giving draught—longed for by gods and demons.
Then had the demons forcibly borne off
The cup, and drained the precious beverage,
Had not the mighty Viṣṇu interposed.
Bewildering them, he gave it to the gods;
Whereat, incensed, the demon troops assailed
The host of heaven, but they with strength renewed,
Quaffing the draught, struck down their foes, who fell
Headlong through space to lowest depths of hell!

There is an elaborate article on the subject in Goldstücker's *Dictionary.* In after-times, Viṣṇu's bird Garuda is said to have stolen the *amṛta*, but it was recovered by Indra.

ANABHITRA—A proper name of; **(1)** A prince of the solar race, a descendant of Sagara, son of Nighna and brother of Raghu, the fifty-second king of Ayodhyá;

(2) a son of the king Kroshtu or Kroshtri by Gándhári and father of Sini or, according so others, a grandson of Vrishni, son of Sumitra by Mádri and brother to Sini; or, again, a grandson of Dhrishta, son of Sumitra, &c.

ANADHRSTI—A son of Ugrasena and general of the Yādavas.

ANADI-CHITTA-PARA-MESHTI—Eternal intellectual heavenly dweller; the Jain name of the Supreme Being, the Lord of all, who dwells in *Móksha-lóka*, the world of bliss.

ANAGUNDI—Part of the Dekhin, the maps of which are disgracefully defective. The mountain Rishyamúka, and the scenes in its vicinity, alluded to in the Rámáyaṇa, are said to be now known by the same appellations in the neighbourhood of Anagundi.—*Wilson.*

ANAKA-DUNDUBHI—'Drums.' A name of Vasudeva, who was so called because the drums of heaven resounded at his birth.

ANALA—One of the daughters of Daksha, who was married to Kaṣyapa, and became the mother of all fruit trees.

ANANDA GIRI—A Sanscrit author who lived about the 10th century and wrote several works which are still extant and of some value: among them are the Sankara Dig Vijaya, the Life of Sankarácharya, &c.

ANANDA—'Joy, happiness.' An appellation of Śiva, also of Balarāma.

ANANDA-LAHARI—'The wave of joy'. A poem attributed to Śaṅkarācārya. It is a hymn of praise addressed to Pārvatī, consort of Śiva, mixed up with mystical doctrine. It has been translated into French by Troyer as *L'Onde de Beatitude*.

ANANGA—"The bodiless.' A name of Kāma, god of love.

ANANGANU—A name of the Cupid, the Hindu god of love.

ANANTA—**(1)** A name of Vishnu or Krishna; **(2)** a name of Baladeva, the elder brother of Krishna; **(3)** a name of Siva; **(4)** a name of Rudra, in an Upanishad of the Atharvana veda; **(5)** a name of Sésha, the chief of the Nágas or serpent race as described above: the couch and constant attendant of Vishnu; **(6)** a name of Vásuki, another king of the serpents, the brother of the former; **(7)** a name of one of the Viswadevas; **(8)** the name of the fourteenth of the twenty-four Arhats or Jaina deified saints of the present Avasarpini; **(9)** the name of a king of Kashmir; **(10)** a pro per name common to several authors, &c.

Infinite. Called also Sésha or Vásuki. The king of the Nágas, a race of serpents which inhabit Pátála. He belongs purely to the Puránic period, and is described as having a thousand hooded-heads, on the foreheads of which was inscribed the sign called Swastika, the mystic cross which betokens good fortune. He is clothed in purple and wears a white necklace. In one hand he holds a plough, in the other a pestle. At the end of each kalpa he vomits a venomous fire which destroys all creation. He bears the universe on his head and produces earthquakes whenever he yawns. On his body Vishnu reposes, during the intervals of creation, and is sheltered by his hoods which stretch out above him like a canopy. He proved a very useful personage at the churning of the ocean; the gods seizing his tail and the demons his head, they twisted him round Mount Meru, and thus formed a churn on a large scale.—*J. C. Thomson*

ANARANYA—**(1)** A descendant of Ikṣvāku and king of Ayodhyā. According to the *Rāmāyaṇa*, many kings submitted to Rāvaṇa without fighting, but when Anaraṇya was summoned to fight or submit, he preferred to fight. His army was overcome and he was thrown from his chariot. Rāvaṇa triumphed over his prostrate foe, who retorted that he had been beaten by fate, not by Rāvaṇa, and predicted the death of Rāvaṇa at the hands of Rāma, a descendant of Anaranya. **(2)** A venerable patriarch whose daughter Pushkarani, was mother of the Manu Chakshusa.

ANARGHA RAGHAVA—A drama in seven acts by Murāri Miśra, possibly written in the thirteenth or fourteenth century. Rāghava or Rāma is the hero of the piece. "It has no dramatic merit, being deficient in character, action, situation, and interest. As a poem it presents occasionally poetic thoughts, but they are very few, and are lost amid pages of flat commonplace, quaint conceit, hyperbolical extravagance, and obscure mythology."—*Wilson*. It is also called, after its author, *Murāri Nāṭaka*.

AN-ARYA—'Unworthy, vile.' People who were not Āryans, barbarians of other races and religion.

ANASUYA—'Charity.' Wife of the ṛsi Atri. In the *Rāmāyaṇa* she appears living with her husband in a hermitage in the forest south of Citrakūṭa. She was very pious and given to austere devotion, through which she had obtained miraculous powers. When Sītā visited her and her husband, she was very attentive and kind, and gave Sītā an ointment which was to keep her beautiful for ever. She was mother of the irascible sage Durvāsas. A friend of Śakuntalā.

ANDAKATAHA—The shell of the mundane egg. Beyond the sea of resh water is a region of twice its extent, where the land is of gold, and where no living beings reside. Thence extends the Lóká-lóká mountain, which is 10,000 yojanas in breadth, and as many in height; and beyond it perpetual darkness invests the mountain all around; which darkness is again encompassed by the shell of the egg.

ANDHAKA—**(1)**. A demon, son of Kaśyapa and Diti, with a thousand arms and heads, two thousand eyes and feet, and called Andhaka because he walked like a blind man, although he saw very well. He was slain by Śiva when he attempted to carry off the Pārijāta tree from *suarga*. From this feat Śiva obtained the appellation Andhaka-ripu, 'foe of Andhaka'. **(2)** A grandson of Kroṣṭṛ and son of Yudhājit, of the Yadava race, who, together with his brother Vrsni, is the ancestor of the celebrated family of Andhaka-Vṛṣṇis. **(3)** a grandson of Vrishni (the brother of Andhaka), and son of Swaphalka by Gándiní; **(4)** a son of Sattwat, belonging to the same family, by Kausalyá; **(5)** a son of Bhima (of the same family) and father of Revata.

[The foregoing lineage, 2-5, is taken from the Harivansa. In the Linga Purána an Andhaka is a son of Nahusha who, according to other Puránas, is the ancestor of Kroshtri: in the Kúrma Purána an Andhaka is a son of Ausa and father of Sáttwata, while in the Vishnu P. a prince of that name is mentioned as the son of Sáttwata who is apparently the same as the Sáttwat of the Harvi.]; **(6)** The name of a muni (in the Padma Purána.)

ANDHRA DIPACA—An old and very good Dictionary of the Telugu language by Mámidi Veneaya.

ANDHRA KINGS—a dynasty, celebrated in the south of India from a very early period. Professor Wilson makes it commence about 20 years B.C., though they might not have established their authority in Magadhá until the first centuries of the Christian era. They are noticed by Pliny.

ANDHRA, ANDHRA—Name of a country and people in the south of India, the country of Teleṅgānā. It was the seat of a powerful dynasty, and the people were known to Pliny as *gens Andarae.*

ANDHRA-BHRTYA—A dynasty of kings that reigned in Magadha somewhere about the beginning of the Christian era. The name seems to indicate that its founder was a native of Andhra, now Teleṅgānā.

ANDRAJATIAS—The same as Andhras, the Telugu people, or inhabitants of Telingana, formerly called Gentus.

ANGA—**(1)** A name of a minor Dwipa, peopled by Mlechchhas who worship Hindu divinities; **(2)** A country in the neighbourhood of Bhagulpur. It is the scene of several of the legends of the Rámáyana. A dynasty of Buddhist Rajas reigned at Anga about the second century of the Christian era under the name of Karnas; and it is thought that the Brahmanical compilers of the Mahábhárata wished to established a mythical connection between the Karna who fought in the great war, and the Karna Rajas of Anga who flourished at a much later period. **(3)**. A supplement to the Vedas. (*see* VEDĀṄGA)

ANGADA—**(1)** Son of Lakṣmaṇa and king of Āṅgadī, capital of a country near the Himālaya. **(2)** Son of Gada (brother of Kṛṣṇa) by Vṛhatī. **(3)** Son of Bālī, the monkey king of Kiṣkindhā. He was protected by Rāma and fought on his side against Rāvaṇa.

ANGADA—**(1)** A son of Lackshmana, king of Angadi, and brother of Ráma; **(2)** the son of Vali, who was installed Yuvarája of Kishkindha; **(3)** a son of Gada by Vrihati.

ANGAJA—(Lust). A son of Brahma. The virtues and vices are represented as the progeny of Bramha.

ANGANYASA KARANYASA—The *mantras* used in the early morning by Brahmans, with certain motions of their fingers, and touching various parts of their bodies.

ANGARAKA—A Rudra. There are eleven well-known Rudras, lords of the three worlds; but each one of the eleven has many appellations in the different Puranas.

ANGARAS—One of the peoples enumerated in the *V.P.*

ANGAS—There are six Angas, or subsidiary portions of the Vedas, *viz*:—Śiksha, rules for reciting the prayers, the accents and tones to be observed; Kalpa, ritual; Vyákarana, grammar; Nirukta, glossarial comment; Chhandas, metre; and Jyotish, astronomy. The four Vedas, the six Angas, with Mimánsa, theology; Nyáya, logic; Dharma, the institutes of law, and the Purának, constitute the fourteen principal branches of knowledge.

ANGA—The eldest of the six sons of Uru, a descendant of Dhruva, of the farally of Atri. Anga who had by his wife Sunítha, only one son named Vena, whose right arm was rubbed by the *ṛṣis* for the purpose of producigng from it progeny. (See PRITHU.)

ANGIRAS—**(1)** Arst to whom many hymns *of* the *Ṛgveda* are attributed. He was one of the seven *maharṣis* or great *ṛṣis*, and also one of the ten Prajāpatis or progenitors of mankind. In later times Aṅgiras was one of the inspired law-givers, and also a writer on astronomy. As an astronomical personification he is Bṛhaspati, the regent of the planet Jupiter, or the planet itself. He was also called "the priest of the gods", and "the lord of sacrifice". There is much ambiguity about the name. It comes from the same root as *agni*, 'fire', and resembles that word in sound. This may be the reason why the name Aṅgiras is used as an epithet or synonym of Agni. The name is also employed as an epithet for the father of Agni, and it is found more espescially connected with the hymns addressed to Agni, Indra, and the luminous deities. According to one statement, Aṅgiras was the son of Uru by Āgneyī, the daughter of Agni, although as above stated, the name is sometimes given to the father of Agni. Another account represents that he was born from the mouth of Brahmā. His wives were Smṛti, 'memory', daughter of Dakṣa; Śraddhā, 'faith', daughter of Kardama; and Svadhā 'oblation', and Satī, 'truth', two other daughters of Dakṣa. His daughters were the Ṛcās or Vedic hymns, and his sons were the Manes called Haviṣmats. Buthe had other sons and daughters, and among the former were Utathya, Bṛhaspati, and Mārkaṇḍeya. According to the *Bhāgavata Purāṇa* "he begot sons possessing Brahmānical glory on the wife of Rathītara, a kṣatriya who was childless, and these persons were afterwards called descendants of Aṅgiras." **(2)** A Prajápati who married Smriti (memory) one of the daughters of Daksha. He is the reputed author of many vaidic hymns, but is mentioned also in a subsequent period as one of the inspired legislators of India, and as the autor of an astronomical work. "The various legends connected with his life seem to have been occasioned by the word Angiras coming from the same radical as, and its sound recalling that of Agni, fire (*q.v.*) Hence we find Angiras sometimes either as an epithet or as the father of Agni, and the saint himself connected chiefly with such hymns as are addressed to Agni, to Indra or to deities of a kindred description: a portion of the fourth Veda, the Atharvan, reports him also as an expounder of the Bramhavidyá (*q.v.*) or the sacred knowledge that had been imparted to him by Satyavaha, a descendant of Bharadvaja. Though Angiras, as may be concluded from his name being connected with the authorship of a great portion of the sacred Hindu literature, appears to have been one of the oldest civilizers of India, no historical date is to be obtained from the epic or puránic literature where the vaidic legends of his life are merely amplified; there he is named as one of the Prajápatis or progenitors of mankind, engendered, according to some by Manu, according to others by Brahmá himself, either with the female half of his body or from his mòuth, or from the space between his eye-brows. As such he is considered also as one of the seven Rishis who preside over the reign of the first Manu, or Svayambhuva, he is called, besides, the priest of the Gods, the Lord of the Sacrifice, &c. Sometimes he is considered as a son of Uru by Agnéyí, the daughter of Agni. His daughters are the Richas (or vaidik hymns) and also Sasvati, Sinívali, Kuhú, Raka, Anumati; his sons are Samvarta, the manes called Havishmats, Utathaya, Brihaspati, Markandeya; his wives, Smriti (traditional science), two daughters of Daksha, Swadha and Satí, and Sraddha, the daughter of sage Kardama. As an astronomical personification he is Brihaspati himself, or the regent of the planet Jupiter and presides over the sixth year of the cycle of sixty years."—*Goldstücker.*

ANGIRASAS, ANGIRASES—Descendants of Aṅgiras. "They share in the nature of the legends attributed to Aṅgiras. Aṅgiras being the father of Agni, they are considered as descendants of Agni himself, who is also called the first of the Aṅgirasas. Like Aṅgiras, they occur in hymns addressed to the luminous deities, and at a later period, they become for the most part personifications of light, of luminous bodies, of divisions of time, of celestial phenomena, and fires adapted to peculiar occasions, as the full and change of the moon, or to particular rites, as the Aśvamedha, Rājasūya &c."—*Goldstücker.* In the *Śatapatha Brāhmaṇa* they and the Ādityas are said to have descended from Prajāpati, and that "they strove together for the priority in ascending to heaven"./ Some decendants of Aṅgiras by the kṣatriya wife of a childless king are mentioned in the Purāṇas as two tribes of Aṅgirasas who were brāhmaṇas as well as kṣatriyas.

The hymns of the *Atharvaveda* are called Aṅgirasas, and the descendants of Aṅgiras were specially charged with the protection of sacrifices performed in accordance with the *Atharvaveda.* From this cause, or from their being associated with the descendants of Atharvan, they were called distinctively Atharvāṅgirasas.

ANGIRASAS—(1) A class of *Pitṛs* (*q.v.*). **(2)** Warrior priests. These who were kshatryas by birth, the heads of the family of Rathinara, were called Angiṛasas (sons of Angiras) and were brahmans as well as kshatryas. "This affords an instance of a mixture of character, of which several similar cases occur. Kshatryas by birth become brahmans by profession, and such persons are usually considered as Angirasas, descendants or followers of Angiras, who may have founded a school of warrior priests."—*Wilson.*

ANGULIYA-MUDRA—A finger ring-seal. The use of this seal amongst the Hindus at the present day, as amongst the ancients, is not, as with us, to secure an envelope, but to verify letters and documents, in place of a written signature. Amongst the natives of Hindustan, both Mahommedan and Hindu, the seal is engraved with the name of the wearer; and the surface being smeared superficially only with ink, the application of the seal to the paper, leaves the letters which are cut in the stone, white on a black ground. Such also was the manner in which the seals of the Greeks and Romans were applied. Seals or signets of this kind were from the earliest periods commonly used in the East. Ahaseurus takes his signet off his hand, and gives it first to Haman, and again to Mordecai: and Herodotus notices that each of the Babylonians wore a seal-ring. The Greeks and Romans had their rings curiously engraved with devices, and that cast by Polycrates into the sea was the work of an engraver whose name the historian has not thought unworthy of commemoration.—Wilson, Works, *XII*, 163,

ANILA—(1) (Wind) Vasu. The deities called Vasus, because, preceded by fire, they abound in splendour and might, are severally named Apa, Dhruva, Soma, Dhava (fire), Anila (wind), Anala (fire), Pratúsha (day-break) and Prabhása, (eight); **(2)** The son of Tansu and father of Dushyanta; **(3)** A Rákshasa.

ANILAS—*Agaṇa* or class of deities.forty-nine in number, connected with Anila, the wind.

ANIMA—A superhuman faculty, or the possession of a divine influence to be attained by austere devotion; or the faculty of assuming an atomic, subtle, invisible, supreme condition of existence, supposed to be attainable by men through a course of austerities, attended with magical rites, in honor of Śiva and Párvati.

ANIMISHA—One whose eyes do not twinkle; a term applied to a deity. The gods are supposed to be exempt from the momentary elevation and depression of the upper eyelid, to which mortals are subject, and to look with a firm, unintermitted gaze. Various allusions to this attribute occur in poetry. When Indra visits Síta to encourage her, he assumes at her request the marks of divinity—he treads the air, and suspends the motion of the eyelids (*Rámáyana*). When Agni, Varuṇa, and Indra, all assume the form of Nala at the marriage of Damayanti, she distinguishes her mortal lover by the twinkling of his eyes, whilst the gods are *stabdha-lochana*, fixed-eyed, (*Mahábhárata, Nalopakhyána*). And when the *Aswiní-Kumáras* practise the same trick upon the bride of *Chyavana*, she recognizes her husband by this amongst other indications (*Padma-Purána*). The notion is the more deserving of attention, as it is one of those coincidences with classical mythology which can scarcely be accidental. *Heliodorus* says:

"The gods may be known by the eyes looking with a fixed regard, and never closing the eyelids;" and he cites Homer in proof of it. An instance from the Iliad which he has not noticed, may be cited perhaps as an additional confirmation, and the *marble eyes* of Venus, by which Helen knew the goddess, and which the commentators and translators seem to be much perplexed with, are probably the *stabdha-lochana*, the fixed eyes, of the Hindus, full, and unveiled even for an instant, like the eyes of a marble statue. Wilson, *XI*, p. 237. There are other marks which distinguish divine from mortal bodies. They cast no shadow: they are exempt from perspiration; they remain unsoiled by dust; they float on the earth without touching it; and the garlands they wear stand erect, the flowers remaining unwithered.

ANIRUDDHA—'Uncontrolled.' Son of Pradyumna and grandson of Kṛṣṇa. He married his cousin, Subhadrā. A *daitya* princess named Uṣā, daughter of Bāṇa, fell in love with him. Her companion Chitralékha, being endowed with magic power, set off through the air to Dwáraká, and returned bringing Aniruddha along with her to the palace of Bána. The guards discovering him there with Usha reported it to the king, who sent a body of his followers to seize the prince; but the valiant youth slew his assailants, on which Bána advanced against him and endeavoured to kill him. Finding however that Aniruddha was not to be subdued by prowess, he brought his magical faculties into the conflict, by which he succeeded in capturing the Yadu prince and binding him in serpent bonds. When Aniruddha was missed from Dwáraka, and the Yádavas were enquiring of one another whither he had gone, Nárada came to them and told them he was the prisoner of Bána. Krishna immediately summoned Garuda, who came with a wish, and mounting upon him, along with Bala and Pradyumna, he set off for the city of Bána. A great battle then took place in which Krishna with his discuss lopped away the thousand arms of Bána, and would have killed him but for the interference of Siva on his behalf. Krishna then went to the place where Aniruddha was confined. The fetters that bound him were destroyed, being blasted by the breadth of Garuda; and Krishna, placing him, along with his wife usha, on the celestial bird, returned with Pradyumna and Ráma to Dwáraka." *V.P.* Professor Wilson thinks that the legend describes a serious struggle between the Saivas and Vaishnavas in which the latter were victorious. He is also called Jhaṣāṅka and Uṣāpati. He had a son named Vajra.

ANJAKA—One of the Dánavas, a son of Viprachitti, of the families of the Daityas.

ANJANA—(1) The elephant of the west or south-west quarter. **(2)** A serpent with many heads descended from Kadru.

ANJANA—Mother of Hanumat by Vāyu, god of the

wind.

ANJAN—The second elephant of Indra.

ANKALAMMA—A grámadevata extensively worshipped in the south. Her office is to ward off evil, and to expel demons. Like the other goddesses she enjoys a yearly moveable festival lasting about a week, when her image is carried about, morning and evening, with music and dancing.

ANNAPURNA—'Full of food.' A form of Durgā, worshipped for her power of giving food. Cf. the Roman *Anna Perenna.*

ANRITA—Falsehood, son of Adharma, (vice) married to Nikriti, they had two sons, Bhaya (fear) and Naraka (hell), and twins to them two daughters, Máya (deceit) and Vedanú (torture), who became their wives. In the Rámáyana, Anrita is the name of one of the mystical weapons delivered by Ráma to Viswámitra.

ANSA—One of the twelve Ádityás. *V.P.*, p. 122.

ANSAUMTI—A river mentioned in the Rig Veda, on the banks of which Krishna the Dasyu was conquered by Rája Rigiswan.

ANSUMAN—A mythical rája of the solar race, the son of Asamanj, and father of Dilipa. He was the grandson of Sagara, who was sent by him to recover the sacrifical stred. Ansumat having arrived at the place of the great Rishis, Kapila prayed to him and so propitiated him, that the saint gave up the horse and predicted his future greatness. Sagara on recovering the steed completed his sacrifice.

Son of Asamanjas and grandson of Sagara. He brought back to earth the horse which had been carried off from Sagara's *aśvamedha* sacrifice, and he discovered the remains of that king's sixty thousand sons, who had been killed by the fire of the wrath of Kapila.

ANTACHARAS—A class of Border tribes, mentioned in the *V.P.*

ANTAKA—'The ender.' A name of Yama, judge of the dead.

ANTARIKSHA—A Vyasa, son of Kinnara, the arranger of the Védas in the thirteenth Dwápara. The great Rishis are said in the *V.P.* to have arranged the Védas twenty-eight times, a list is given of the twenty-eight Vyásas of the present Manwantara; **(2)** A king of the family of Ikshwáku, a son of Kinnara and father of Suvarna. **(3)** The atmosphere or firmament between heaven and earth, the sphere *of* the *gandharvas*, *apsarases*, and *yakṣas*.

ANTARVEDI—The Doab or country between the Ganges and the Yamuna.

ANU—Son of King Yayāti by his wife Sarmiṣṭhā, *adaitya* princess. He refused to exchange his youthful vigour for the curse of decrepitude passed upon his father, and in consequence his father cursed him that his posterity should not possess dominion. Notwithstanding this, he had a long series of descendants, and among them were Aṅga, Baṅga, Kaliṅga, &c., who gave their names to the countries they dwelt in.

ANUBHAVAMRITA—A *vairágya* treatise, which exists only in the Dravidian languages, and appears to be entirely unknown in other parts of India. Dr. Ballantyne informed the writer in 1852 that none of the pandits in the Benares College knew of the work: it contains a treatise on the Upanishads,—a sort of exposition of Pantheism—shows that the existence of a material world cannot be proved—that all is Máya—recommends retirement from domestic life and meditation, in order to the soul's purification and final beatitude.

ANUGRAHA-SARGA—A technical phrase meaning "Benevolent Nature," one of the Aphorisms of the Sánkhya Philosophy as stated in the Compendium of Principles. "Benevolent creation" it is said consists of the production of external objects from the five subtile elements, *viz.*, of sound, tangibility, colour, savour, odour. Bramha perceiving these (the senses) to be destitute of a sphere of action, created external objects, or "benevolent nature."

ANUGRAHA—The eighth creation, which possesses both the qualities of goodness and darkness. This seems to have been taken from the Sánkya philosophy, and is described in the Padma, Linga, and Matsya Puránas. It is the creation of which we have a notion, or to which we give assent (*anugraha*) in contradiction to organic creation, or that existence of which we have sensible perception.

ANUHLADA—Son of Hiranyakasipur and brother of the wise Práhlada, the augmenter of the Daitya race [Práhlada.]

ANUHTUBH—**(1)** A metre from the northern mouth of Brahma, along with the Sáma Véda, &c., *V.P.*, p. 42; **(2)** A name of Saraswati.

ANUKRAMANIS—Systematic indices to various portions of the ancient Vaidic literature. The most perfect Anukramaní is that of the Sanhita of the Rig Véda. It is ascribed to Kátyáyaná, an author chiefly known by his works in the Yajur Veda and Sáma Veda. Its name is Sarvanukramani, *i.e.*, the index of all things. It gives the first words of each hymn, the number of verses, the name and family of the poets, the names of the deities and the metres of every verse. Max Müller fixes the date of Kátyáyaná's writing in the latter half of the fourth century, B.C.

ANUMATI—One of the four daughters of Angiras; the first day of the moon's wane. The four daughters are the four phases of the moon, *V.P.*, p. 83. The goddess of the day when the moon is in the third and fourth quarters. The moon on its fifteenth day, when just short of its full. In this stage it is personified and worshipped as a goddess.

ANURADHA—A lunar mansion in Járadgaví. For an explanation of the divisions of the celestial sphere, see *V.P.*, p. 226.

ANUSARA—A *rākṣasa* or other demon.

ANUVATSARA—Fourth cyclic year. Fifteen days of thirty Muhúrttas, each is called a Paksha (a lunar fortnight); two of these make a month, two months a solar season, three seasons a northern or southern declination (Ayana); and these two compose a year. Years, made up of four kinds of months, are distinguished into five kinds; and an aggregate of all the varieties of time is termed a Yuga or cycle. The years are severally called Samvatsara, Parivatsara, Idvatsara, Anuvatsara and Vatsara. This is the time called a yuga.

ANUVINDA—A king of Ujjayini'. (*see* VINDA)

ANYADESYA—The name given to words derived from foreign languages.

APAMURTTI—One of the sinless sons of Atri.

APANA—One of the ten winds which brahmans believe to be lodged in the body; this one resides in the region of the navel, and forces out the solid and liquid secretions.

APA—One of the deities called Vasus. (See ANILA.)

APARA—A technical term in the Sánkhya philosophy, denoting that kind of mental acquiescence or indifference which arises from the reflection that sensual objects perish in consequence of enjoyment, and that there is a feeling of pain or trouble when they perish.

APARAGODANA—(In Buddhistic Cosmogony.) One of the four dwípas or continents, in shape like a round mirror, and seven thousand Yojanas in breadth, to the west of the Mahámeru which is in the centre of the earth.

APARAJITA—**(1)** One of the eleven Rudras; **(2)** A name of Siva and of Vishnu; **(3)** A name of Dúrgá.

APARANTA—'On the western border.' A country which is named in the *Viṣṇu Purāṇa* in association with countries in the north; and the *Vāyu Purāṇa* reads the name as Aparita, which Wilson says is a northern nation. The *Harivaṁśa*, however, mentions it as "a country conquered by Paraśurāma from the ocean", and upon this the translator Langlois observes: "Tradition records that Paraśurāma besought Varuṇa, god of the sea, to grant him a land which he might bestow upon the Brahmāns in expiation of the blood of the Kshatriyas. Varuṇa withdrew his waves from the heights of Gokarṇa (near Mangalore) down to Cape Comorin" (*As. Researches*, V.I). This agrees with the traditions concerning Paraśurāma and Malabar, but it is not at all clear how a gift of territory to brāhmaṇas could expiate the slaughter ofthe kṣatriyas by a brāhmaṇa and in behalf of brāhmaṇas.

APARNĀ—According to the *Harivamśa*, the eldest daughter of Himavat and Menā. She and her two sisters, Ekaparnā and Ekapaia, gave themselves up to austerity and practiced extraordinary abstinence (she did not even eat a leaf during her performance of religious austerities.); but while her sisters lived, as their names denote, upon one leaf or on one *pāṭalā* (*Bignonia*) respectively, Aparnā managed to subsist upon nothing, and even lived without a leaf (a-parnā). This so distressed her mother that she cried out in deprecation, 'U-mā', 'Oh, don't'. Aparna thus became the beautiful Umā, the wife of Śiva.

Originally a non-Āryan goddess who was worshipped by the Śabaras, Barbaras, Pulindas, and other tribes. She is said to be the eldest daughter of Himavat and Menā. Aparnā and her sisters Ekaparnā and Ekapalā practised such extreme austerities (*tapas*) and abstinence that two of them were able to exist on one leaf (*parna*) each, but Apanā denied herself even this meagre portion, and hence her name Aparnā (without a leaf). Such extremes of self-denial caused her despairing mother to cry out, 'Uma! Uma!' (lit. 'Desist, desist'), but her pleas were unavailing and Aparna, as the great female ascetic, became the *śakti* of the great male ascetic Śiva and became known as Uma. The goddess Durgá is sometimes described as *Aparna* ('not having even a leaf for a garment').

1. *DHI.*,p.492.

APASPATI—A son of Uttanapada, and brother of

Dhruva, (*q.v.*)

APASTAMBA—An ancient writer on ritual and law, author of sūtras connected with the Black *Yajurveda* and of a *Dharmaśāstra*. He is often quoted in law-books. Two recensions of the *Taittīnya Saṁhitā* are ascribed to him or his school. The *sūtras* have been translated by Bühler, and has been reprinted in the *Sacred Books of the East* by Max Müller.

APAVA—(1) 'Who sports in the waters.' A name of the same import as Nārāyaṇa, and having a similar though not an identical application. According to the *Brahmā Purāṇa* and the *Hariuaṁśa*, Āpava performed the office of the creator Brahmā, and divided himself into two parts, male and female, the former begetting offspring upon the latter. The result was the production of Viṣṇu, who created Virāj, who brought the first man into the world. According to the *Mahābhārata*, Apava is a name of the Prajapati Vasiṣtha. The name of Āpava is of late introduction and has been vaguely used. Wilson says: "According to the commentator, the first stage was the creation of Āpava or Vasiṣtha or Virāj by Viṣṇu, through the agency of Brahmā, and the next was that of the creation of Manu by Virāj." **(2)** A name of the Prajápati Vasishtha, "As" says Professor Wilson, "he perform the office of Brahma, he should be regarded as that divinity, but this is not exactly the case. Apvan becomes two-fold, and in the capacity of his male half begets offspring by the female." *V.P.*, p. 52.

APPAMANA SUBHA—The fifteenth heaven of Buddhism.

APPAMANABHA—The name of the twelfth heaven of Buddhism.

APRATISHT'HA—One of the Narakas or hells, of which twenty-eight are enumerated. They are called the awful provinces of the kingdom of Yama, terrible with instruments of torture.

APSARAS—(1) The Apsarases are the celebrated nymphs oflndra's heaven. The name, which signifies 'moving in the water', has some analogy to that of Aphrodite. They are not prominent in the Vedas, but UrvasI and a few others are mentioned. In Manu they are said to be the creations of the seven Manus. In the epic poems they become prominent, and the *Rāmāyaṇa* and the Purāṇas attribute their origin to the churning of the ocean, (*see* AMRTA) It is said that when they came forth from the waters neither the gods nor the *asuras* would have them for wives, so they became common to all. They have the appellation of Surāṅganās, 'wives of the gods', and Sumadātmajās, 'daughters of pleasure'.

> Then from the agitated deep up sprung
> The legion of Apsarases, so named
> That to the watery element they owed
> Their being. Myriads were they born, and all
> In vesture heavenly clad, and heavenly gems:
> Yet more divine their native semblance, rich
> With all the gifts of grace, of youth and beauty.
> A train innumerous followed; yet thus fair,
> Nor god nor demon sought their wedded love:
> Thus Rāghava! they still remain—their charms
> The common treasure of the host of heaven;
>
> —(*Rāmāyaṇa*) Wilson

In the Purāṇas various *ganas* or classes of them are mentioned with distinctive names. The *Vāyu Purāṇa* enumerates fourteen, the *Harivamśa* seven classes. They are again distinguished as being *daivika*, 'divine', or *laukika*, 'worldly'. The former are said to be ten in number and the latter thirty-four, and these are the heavenly charmers who fascinated heroes, as Urvaśī, and allured austere sages from their devotions and penances, as Menakā and Rambha. The *Kaśikhaṇḍa* says "there are thirty-five millions of them. but only one thousand and sixty are the principal". The Apsarases, then, are fairylike being beautiful and voluptuous. They are the wives or the mistresses of the *gandharvas*, and are not prudish in the dispensation of their favours. Their amours on earth have been numerous, and they are the rewards in Indra's paradise held out to heroes who fall in battle. They have the power of changing their forms; they are fond of dice, and give luck to whom they favour. In the *Atharvaveda* they are not so amiable; they are supposed to produce madness (love's madness?), and so there are charms and incantations for use against them. There is a long and exhaustive article on the Apsarases in Goldstlüker's *Dictionary*, from which much of the above has been adapted. As regards their origin he makes the following speculative observations: "Originally these divinities seem to have been personifications of the vapours which are attracted by the sun and form into mist or clouds; their character may be thus interpreted in the few hymns of the *Ṛgveda* where mention is made of them. At a subsequent period...(their attributes expanding with those of their associates.the gandhiarvas), they became divinities which represent phenomena or objects both of a physical and ethical kind closely associated with that life" (the elementary life of heaven). **(2)** The name given to the nymphs of heaven created by Brahma in the commencement of the Kalpa. They are also said to have been produced from the whirlpoor of the deep, of surprising loveliness. In some of the Puránas they are called the daughters of Kasyapa and Muni. The Apsarasas are of two kinds: Laukíka, "worldly," of whom thirty-four are specified; and Daivika or divine, ten in number; the latter furnish the individuals most frequently engaged in the interruption of the interruption of the penances of holy sages. There are also fourteen Ganas—or troops of Apsarasas, bearing peculiar designations as Ahutas, &c. "Originally these deities seem to have been personifications of the vapours which are attracted by the sun, and form into mist or clouds: their character may be thus interpreted in the few hymns of the Rig Veda where mention is made of them. At a subsequent period when the Gandharva of the Rig Veda, who personifies there especially the fire of the Sun, expanded into the fire of Lightning, the rays of the moon and other attributes fo the elementary life of heaven, as well as into pious acts referring to it, the apsarasas become divinities which represent phenomena or objects both of a physical and ethical kind, closely associated with that life; thus in the Yajurveda sunbeams are called the Apsarasas, associated with the Gandharva who is the sun; Planets are termed the Apsarasas connected with the Gandharva Fire; Constellations are the Apsarasas of the Gandharva Wind, &c., &c. In the last Mythological epoch when the Gandharvas have saved from their elementary nature merely so much as to be musicians in the paradise of Indra, the Apsarasas appear among other subordinate deities which share in the merry life of Indra's heaven, as the wives of the Gandharvas, but more especially as wives of a licentious sort, and they are promised therefore, too, as a reward to heroes fallen in battle when they are received in the paradise of Indra; while, in the Rig Veda, they assist Soma to pour down his floods, they descend in the epic literature on earth merely to shake the virtue of penitent sages, and to deprive them of the power they would otherwise have acquired through unbroken austerities."—*Goldstücker, Sans. Dict.*

'Essence of the waters'; 'moving in the waters or between the waters', *viz.*, the clouds (*R.V.*, X.I 23,5). The name of the seductive celestial nymphs (the mistresses of the *gandharvas*) who dwell in *svarga*, Indra's paradise. They are the dancers of the gods (*Manu*, 1.37), who may have symbolized clouds or the mists drawn up by the sun.' The chief *apsaras* was Urvasi who became the lover of King Pururavas. The hymn *RV.*, X.95, consists of a dialogue between them which contains the germ of a very entertaining story related in the *ŚBr.*, *MBh.* and *Purāṇas*, which forms the plot of Kālidāsa's well-known drama Vikramorvaśī, 'The Hero and the Nymph'.

The *apsaras* can assume any form at will, and often appear as aquatic birds (*ŚBr.*, XI.5.1,4). Warriors who die in battle are taken by the *apsaras in* brilliantly coloured chariots to Indra's paradise (*MBh.*, 8.4,9, etc., *EM.*), a role similar to that of the Teutonic Valkyries.

The parentage of these nymphs is variously given; they and the *gandharvas* sprang from Prajapati's dismembered body (*SBr.*, IX.4.1,2); or they rose from the Churning of the Ocean after the emergence of the wish-fulfilling *pārijāta*, their favourite tree (*V.P.*, 1.9); or they sprang from Bhāsī, the 'mother of birds'; or from Vāc.

The gods often sent *apsaras* to seduce *ṛṣis* and ascetics, and were thus accused of causing madness (*Tait. Sam.*, 111.4,8). Their other characteristics were promiscuity, lack of maternal feelings, and the discarding of their earthly offspring when they wished to return to their celestial abode.

The *A V.* (IV.37) includes a spell to be used against supernatural foes, particularly against *apsaras* whose names represent certain odours. Among these nymphs are Guggulū (bdellium), Naladī (nard), Pramandanī (a pungent-smelling plant), and Auksagandhī (having an ox-smell). But the scent of the Earth mother, which *apsaras* and *gandharvas* shared, was regarded with favour (*AV.*, XII. 1,23). In the same work they are told to go away to the trees, because they have been recognized, recognition of supernatural creatures being said to take away much of their power.

Both the *gandharvas* and the *apsaras* are said to 'stand' on forest trees, or to dwell in them, especially in the *nyagrodha*, *aśvattha* and *udumbara* (*Tait. Sam.*, 111.4,8; *AV.*, IV.37,4) from which the sounds of their cymbals and lutes may be heard. They are besought to bestow their favours on wedding processions and to bring luck at games of dice (*A V.*, IV.38,3; XIV.2,9).

The *Skanda P.* gives the number of the *apsaras* as thirty-five millions, of whom one thousand and sixty are important; but according to the *MBh.* (7.61,7, *EM*) they number 'seven times six thousand...[who]

dance on the point of Dilipa's sacrificial post to the music of Visvavasu'.

Popular Buddhism adopted the nymphs, and the *Mahavastu* states that they wore garlands of flowers and many jewels; they are also described in several of the *Jataka* tales as 'dove-footed' (*kakuta-padiniyo*) and attendant on Sakka (Pa.), *i.e.*, Indra. *EM.*, p. 158. The *SBr.* (XIII.4.3,7-8) states that Varuna's attendants are *gandharvas*, and Soma's *apsaras*. The latter are closely associated with the waters and fertility and were originally of more significance in early than in late literature (Coomaraswamy, *Yakṣas*, pt. ii. p. 33).

See RAMBHĀ; GHRTĀCĪ; ANTARIKSA; TILOTTAMĀ; ASTĀVAKRA; BRAHMALOKA; URVAŚĪ.

APTORYAMA—A sacrifical rite produced from Bramha's northern mouth, *V.P.* "The *Aptoryam* is the seventh or last part of the Jyotishtoma, for the performance of which it is not essentially necessary, but a voluntary sacrifice instituted for the attainment of a specific desire. The literal meaning of the word would be in conformity with the Praudhamanoṛamá 'a sacrifice which procures the attainment of the desired object."'—*Goldstücker.*

ARADHYA—The name of a class of Brahmans who recede somewhat from the extreme tenets of the *Vira Saivas*, and tend somewhat towards the Vaishnavas. Bassava was originally an Aradhya brahman, though in the Purana bearing his name the sect is spoken of very contemptuously.

ARAGA—A Sun. When Vishnu assumes the character of Rudra, the destoryer, and descends to reunite all creatures with himself, he enters into the seven solar rays which dilate into seven suns—the name of the first is Araga.

ARANYAKA—(1) 'Belonging to the forest.' Certain religious and philosophical writings which expound the mystical sense of the ceremonies, discuss the nature of God, &c. They are attached to the brāhmaṇas, and intended for study in the forest by brāhmaṇas who have retired from the distractions of the world. There are four of them extant: (1) *Bṛhad*; (2) *Taittīrya*; (3) *Aitareya*; and (4) *Kauṣītakī Āraṇyaka*. The Āraṇyakas are closely connected with the Upaniṣads, and the names are occasionally used interchangeably: thus the *Bṛhad* is called indifferently *Brhadaranyaka* or *Bṛhadāraṇyaka Upanisad*; it is attached to the *Śatapatha Brāhmaṇa*. TheAitareya *Upaniṣad is* a part of the *Aitareya Brāhmaṇa*, and the *Kauṣītaki Āraṇyaka* consists of three chapters, of which the third is the *Kauṣītaki Upaniṣad*. "Traces of modern ideas (says Max Müller) are not wanting in the Āraṇyakas, and the very fact that they are destined for a class of men who had retired from the world in order to give themselves up to the contemplation of the highest problems, shows an advanced and already declining and decaying society, not unlike the monastic age of the Christian world." "In one sense the Āraṇyakas are old, for they reflect the very dawn of thought; in another they are modem, for they speak of that dawn with all the experience of a past day. There are passages in these works unequalled in any language for grandeur, boldness, and simplicity. These passages are the relics of a better age. But the generation which became chronicler of those Titanic wars of thought was a small race; they were dwarfs, measuring the footsteps of departed giants." **(2)** "The Treatises of the Forest." So named, as Sáyana informs us, because they had to be read in the Forest. "It might almost seem," says Max Müller, "as if they were intended for the Vanaprasthas only, people who, after having performed all the duties of students and householders, retire from the world to the forest, to end their days in the contemplation of the deity." In some instances the Aranyakas form part of the Brahmanas and thus share the authority of Sruti or revelation. Part of one however is ascribed to a human author Asvalanyaka. Another part is quoted by Sáyana as being a Sútra work of Saunakas. The Aranyakas presuppose the existence of the Brahmanas, and may be regarded as an enlargement upon them. The chief interest which they possess at the present moment consists in their philosophy. The philosophical chapters, termed Upanishads, are almost the only portion of Vedic literature extensively read to this day. The Vedánta, the Sánkya, the Vaiséshika, the Nyáya and Yoga philosophers, all appeal to the Upanishads in support of their tenets. "Traces of modern ideas are not wanting in the Aranyakas, and the very fact that they are destined for a class of men who had retired from the world in order to give themselves up to the highest problems, shows an advanced, and an already declining and decaying society, not unlike the monastic age of the Christian world."—*Max Müller*, *A. S. L.*, Chap. II.

ARANYANI—The goddess of forest solitude. Several hymns in the Rig- and Atharva-vedas are addressed to this goddess. See *O.S.T.*, V, 423

ARATI, ALATI—A ceremony on the birth of a brahman

child. The Abbé DuBois thus describes it: "Upon a plate of copper they place a lamp, made of a paste from rice-flour. It is supplied with oil and lighted. The married women, but not widows, for their presence would be unlucky, take hold of the plate with both hands, and raising it as high as the head of the person for whom the ceremony is performed, describe in that position a number of circles with the plate and the burning lamp.

Sometimes, in place of the rice lamp, they fill the plate with water, colored red with a mixture of saffron and other ingredients; and with this describe their circle, raising it as high as the head of the person who is the object of the ceremony.

The intention of this ceremony is to avert fascination by the eye, and to prevent the accidents which arise out of I know not what evil impression occasioned by the jealous looks of certain persons. The credulity of the Hindus respecting this sort of injury is carried to excess: and it is for that reason that the ceremony of the *árati*, which is considered to have the virtue of preventing the effect of those glances, is so common and so universal among the Hindus, and especially among persons of high rank, who, being more observed and having more enemies than private individuals, are more exposed to the evil influence of malevolent or jealous looks. When such persons therefore appear in public, the first thing that is done on their return home, is to perform this ceremony of the árati over them, as an antidote to the ill-designed looks which may have been cast upon them. For the same reason princes have the ceremoy repeated several times in a day.

This sort of superstition or idle observance is by no means peculiar to the Hindus. I have seen cantons in France, (and I suppose it is not different in many other countries,) where the people were sacrcely less infatuated. I have known decent villagers who would not have dared to show their young children to people they did not know, or to persons of bad appearance, lest their invidious or ill-boding look should occasion some mischief to befall them."—*Manners and Customs of the Hindus.*

ARBUDA—A powerful Dasyu, mentioned in the Big-Veda, as having been overcome and trodden under foot by Indra.

ARBUDAS—The people about Mount Abu in Gujarat—called Arbuda in the Purànas.

ARCHISH—(Flame). The wife of Krisáswa, and mother of Dhúmaketu (comet).

ARDHA-NÀRI—'Half-woman.' A form in which Śiva is represented as half-male and half-female, typifying the male and female energies. There are several stories accounting for this form. It is called also Ardhanārīśa and Parāṅgada.

ARDRA—A lunar mansion in Gajavithi. The path of the sun and other planets amongst the lunar asterisms is divided into three portions or Avasthánas, northern, southern and central, called severally Airávata, Jaradgava and Vaiswánara. Each of these again is divided into three parts or Vithis. Each of these Vithis contains three asterisms.

ARGHA—A gift indicating great respect, such as fruit and flowers, or milk and honey, which are offered to an idol, or to a brahman, or to a bridegroom on his wedding day.

ARHAT—A perfect saint, amongst the Jains or Buddhists; one in whom evil desire is entirely destroyed; one entitled to the homage of gods and men.

ARHATAS—A name applied to the Jains, *q.v.*

ARISHTA—**(1)** A *daitya*, and son of Bali who in the form of a savage bull came one evening to the spot where Krishna and the Gopís were dancing together. His color was that of a cloud charged with rain, he had vast horns; and his eves were like two fiery suns, his tail was erect, his dewlap hung low, and he was a terror to the herds. The herdsmen and their women were exceedingly frightened, and called aloud on Krishna, who came to their succour, without any fear. He waited the near approach of the bull, when he seized him by the horns and pressed his sides with his knees. Tearing off one of the horns he beat the fierce demon with it till he died, vomiting blood from his mouth. The herdsmen then praised Krishna; **(2)** A daughter of Daksha, and wife of Kaṣyapa, *V.P.*

ARISHTANEMI—**(1)** A Prájapati, who married four daughters of Daksha; **(2)** A name of Kaṣyapa. His daughter Kesini became the wife of Sagara.

ARJUNA—"White'. The name of the third Pāṇḍu prince. All the five brothers were of divine paternity, and Arjuna's father was Indra, hence he is calledAindri. A brave warrior, high-minded, generous, upright, and handsome, the most prominent and the most amiable and interesting of the five brothers. He was taught the use of arms by Droṇa, and was his favourite pupil. By his skill in arms he won Draupadi at her *svayaṁvara*. For an involuntary transgression he imposed upon himself twelve years' exile from his family, and during that time he visited Paraśurāma, who gave him instruction in the use of arms. He at this period formed a connection with Ulūpī, a Nāga princess, and by her had a son named Irāvat. He also married Citrāṅgadā, the daughter of the king of Maṇipura, by whom he had a son named Babhruvāhana. He visited Kṛṣṇa at Dvārakā, and there he married Subhadrā, the sister of Kṛṣṇa. (*see* SUBHADRĀ) By her he had a son named Abhimanyu. Afterwards he obtained the bow Gāṇḍīva from the god Agni, with which to fight against Indra, and he assisted Agni in burning the Khāṇḍava forest. When Yudhiṣṭhira lost the kingdom by gambling, and the' five brothers went into exile for thirteen years, Arjuna proceeded on a pilgrimage to the Himālayas to propitiate the gods, and to obtain from them celestial weapons for use in the contemplated war against the Kauravas. There he fought with Śiva, who appeared in the guise of a Kirāta or mountaineer; but Arjuna, having found out the true character of his adversary, worshipped him, and Śiva gave him the *pāśupata*, one of his most powerful weapons. Indra, Varuṇa, Yama, and Kubera came to him, and also presented him with their own peculiar weapons. Indra, his father, carried him in his car to his heaven and to his capital Amarāvatī, where Arjuna spent some years in the practice of arms. Indra sent him against the *daityas* of the sea, whom he vanquished, and then returned victorious to Indra, who "presented him with a chain of gold and a diadem, and with a war-shell which sounded like thunder". In the thirteenth year of exile he entered the service of Rājā Virāṭa, disguised as a eunuch, and acted as music and dancing master, but in the end he took a leading part in defeating the king's enemies, the king of Trigarta and the Kaurava princes, many of whose leading warriors he vanquished in single combat. Preparations for the great struggle with the Kauravas now began. Arjuna obtained the personal assistance of Kṛṣṇa, who acted as his charioteer, and, before the great battle began, related to him the *Bhagavad Gītā*. On the tenth day of the battle he mortally wounded Bhīṣma, on the twelfth he defeated Suśarman and his four brothers, on the fourteenth he killed Jayadratha; on the seventeenth, he was so stung by some reproaches of his brother, Yudhiṣṭhira, that he would have killed him had not Kṛṣṇa interposed. On the same day he fought with Karṇa, who had made a vow to slay him. He was near being vanquished when an accident to Karṇa's chariot gave Arjuna the opportunity of killing him. After the defeat of the Kauravas, aśvatthāman, son of Droṇa, and two others, who were the sole survivors, made a night attack on the camp of the Pāṇḍavas, and murdered their children. Arjuna pursued Aśvatthāman, and made him give up the precious jewel which he wore upon his head as an amulet. When the horse intended for Yudhiṣṭhira's *aśvamedha* sacrifice was let loose, Arjuna, with his army, followed it through many cities and countries, and fought with many Rājās. He entered the country of Trigarta, and had to fight his way through. He fought also against Vajradatta, who had a famous elephant, and against the Saindhavas. At the city of Maṇipura he fought with his own son, Babhrūvāhana, and was killed; but he was restored to life by a Nāga charm supplied by his wife Ulūpī. Afterwards he penetrated into the *dakṣiṇa* or south country, and fought with the Niṣādas and Drāviḍians: then went westwards to Gujarāt, and finally conducted the horse back to Hastināpura where the great sacrifice was performed. He was subsequently called to Dvārakā by Kṛṣṇa amid the internecine struggles of the Yādavas, and there he performed the funeral ceremonies of Vasudeva and of Kṛṣṇa. Soon after this he retired from the world to the Himālayas, (*see* MAHĀBHĀRATA) He had a son named Irāvat by the serpent nymph Ulūpī; Babhruvāhana, by the daughter of the king of Maṇipura, became king of that country; Abhimanyu, born of his wife Subhadrā, was killed in the great battle, but the kingdom of Hastināpura desended to his son Parīkṣit.

Arjuna has many appellations: Bībhatsu, Guḍākeśa, Dhanañjaya, Jiṣṇu, Kirīṭin, Pākaśāśasni, Phālguna, Savyasācin, Śvetavāhana, and Pārtha.

ARJUNA—Son of Kṛtavīrya, king of the Haihayas. He is better known under his patronymic Kaṛtavīrya (*q.v.*).

ARSHA MARRIAGE—One of the eight modes of marriages described by Manu; in which a father receives from a bridegroom one pair of kine, (a bull and a cow) or two pairs, for religious purposes, and then gives away his daughter in due form. This is the ceremony of the Rishis and probably prevailed amongst all the Vedic Aryans. It furnishes proof of the distinction between the marriage rite of the Rishis and that of the Brahmans. No religious qualification was required in the bridegroom, and the young man simply obtained a damsel by presenting her father with a pair or two of kine.—*Wheeler.*

ARSHABHU—The first division of the central portion of the lunar mansions.

ARTHA BRAHMANS—According to the *Kerala Ulpatti*, when *Purasu Ráma* had recovered a large strip of territory from the ocean; on the Malayalam coast, he set apart certain fishermen to officiate as *Brahmans* to the rest of the people, and promised to come at their call. They, however, acted so as to displease him; whereupon he disfranchised them, and called in a colony of pure *Brahmans* from *Hai Kshétram*, to whom he delivered charge of the people, in matters of rites and ceremonies. The fishermen had the title of "half-brahmans."—*Taylor*

ART'HANESVARI—A form of *Siva*, and, on the left-hand half, is *Párvati.* This is doubtless an early hieroglyphic to convey a chaste notion of the union of the active deity, with passive matter; whence creation.

ARTHASADHAK—The finance minister of Rája Dasaratha.

ARTHASASTRA—One of the eighteen principal branches of knoweldge, *viz.*, the science of Government as laid down first by Vrihaspati.

ARUGAN—The name given by the Jains to the Supreme Being. The popular name of God is Jinan, or Jainan; hence the appellation Jains. To this God one thousand and eight sacred names are ascribed. The attributes of omnipotence and omniscience, of omnipresence and infinite benevolene, are given to this deity. See JAINS.

ARUNA—**(1)** 'Red, rosy.' The dawn, personified as the charioteer of the sun. This is of later origin than theVedic Uṣas (*q.v.*). He is said to be the son of Kaśyapa and Kadru. He is also called Rumra, 'tawny", and by two epithets of which the meaning is not obvious, Anuru, 'thighless', and Āśmana, 'stony'. **(2)** A celebrated son of Kaṣyapa and Vinata: and brother of Garuda the destroyer of serpents.

ARUNA—The ruddy. The son of the patriarch Kaṣyapa and his wife Vinata; the younger brother of Garuda, the bird vehicle of Vishṇu. This deity has in the classical period taken the place of Ushas, the personification of dawn in the Vedic creed.

ARUNDHATI—**(1)** Daughter of Kardama, wife of Vasistha, evidently an allegorical personification of a religious rite. "One of the Pleiades and generally regarded as the model of wifely excellence;" it is a small star close to the middle one in the tail of *Ursa Major*: and is said to have been the wife of *Vasistha.* A newly-married couple, amongst brahmans, have this star pointed out to them by the Puróhita, or Astrologer, and are directed to pay it obeisance. **(2)** 'Fidelity.' A daughter of Daksa and wife of Dharma. From her were 'born' the divisions of the earth (*V.P.*, 1.15). **(3)** The star Alcor, belonging to the Great Bear, one of its chief Stars, or the common wife of the seven stars called the seven *ṛṣis.* Alcor is invoked in marriage ceremonies and represents conjugal perfection.'

Arundhatī became jealous of the illustrious Vasistha, and as a result she became a tiny star like fire mixed with smoke, which appears intermittently among the seven bright stars (*MBh.*, Ādi pa., 235).

To be unable to see the Pole Star, the Milky Way and Arundhatī indicates that one is 'already with death' (*Sus. Sam.*, I. p. 287), and to see Arundhati and the Pole Star intermittently presages death within a year (*MBh.*, 12.318,9, *EM.*, p. 182). 'Diehl, *Instrument and Purpose*, p. 188. III. The name of a plant used to heal serious wounds (*AV.*, IV. 12). According to Sayana it was used to stop the flow of blood from sword-cuts. It is said to 'arise', from the *aśvatha*, *khadira*, *nyagrodha* and *parna* trees, etc. (*A V.*, V.5,5), and hence it may be some kind of fungus or parasitic plant, but in the ninth verse of the same hymn, it is said to have 'fallen from the horse's mouth', and may refer to saliva possessing soothing and curative properties.' Arundhati also protects cattle from Rudra's 'hurled missile' (lightning?) (*A V.*, VI.59,3). 'Radford, *Encyclopaedia of Superstitions*, p. 54; or it may refer to knowledge (*jñaña*) which is symbolized by the horse. See HAYAGRIVA. **(4)** One of the ten wives of Kala. Others were Vasu, Yami, Lamba, Bhanu, Marutvati, Samkalpa, Muhurta, Sadhya and Visva.

ARUSA, ARUSI—'Red.' 'A red horse.' In the *Ṛgveda* the red horses or mares of the sun or of fire. The rising sun.

ARUSHI—The daughter of Manu and wife of the great sage Chyavana.—*O.S.T., Vol. I, p.* 124.

ARVAN, ARVA—'A horse.' One of the horses of the moon. A fabulous animal, half-horse, half-bird, on which the *daityas* are supposed to ride.

ARVALAN—The son and heir of Rája Kehama, who offered violence to Kaliyal, the beautiful daughter of a peasant in the neighbourhood of the palace, and was felled to the earth and slain by the avenging arm of her father.

ARVARIVAT—One of the seven Rishis of the second

Manwantara. By the seven Rishis we may often understand the constellation, *Ursa Major.*

ARVAVASU—See RAIBHYA.

ARVAVASU—One of the seven principal solar rays, that which supplies heat to the planet Jupiter.

ARYA SIDDHANTA—The system of astronomy founded by Āryabhata in his work bearing this name.

ARYA, ARYAN—'Loyal, faithful.' The name of the immigrant race from which all that is Hindu originated. The name by which the people of the *Ṛgveda* "called men of their own stock and religion, in contradistinction to the *dasyus* (or dāsas), a term by which we either understand hostile demons or the rude aboriginal tribes" of India, who were An-āryas.

ARYABHATA—The earliest known Hindu writer on algebra, and, according to Colebrooke, "if not the inventor, the improver of that analysis", which has made but little advance in India since. He was born, according to his own account, at Kusumapura (Patna), in AD 476, and composed his first astronomical work at the early age of twenty-three. His larger work, the *Ārya Siddhānta*, was produced at a riper age. He is probably the Andubarius (Ardubarius?) of the *Chronichon Paschale*, and the Arjabahr of the Arabs. Two of his works, *the Dasāgītisūtra and Āryāṣatasata*, have been edited by Kern under the title of *Āryabhaṭīya.* See Whitney in *Jour. Amer. Or. Society* for 1860, Dr. Bhau Dājī in *JRAS* for 1865, and Barth in *Revue Critique* for 1875. There is another and later astronomer of the same name, distinguished as Laghu Āryabhaṭa, *i.e.*, Āryabhaṭa the Less.

ARYAKA—A cowherd in the Sanscrit drama of the Toy-cart. He conspired against the weak and unpopular king then upon the throne at Ananti or Ougein. Aryaka is described as a man with 'arms like elephants, vast tusks, his breast and shoulders brawny as the lion's, his eyes a coppery red.' He succeeded in obtaining possession of the throne.

ARYAMAN—'A bosom friend'. **(1)** Chief of the *pitrs.* **(2)** One of the Adityas. **(3)** One of the Visvedevas. **(4)** One of the twelve Áditya in the Manwantara of Vaivaswata.

ARYAN RACE, ARYAN LANGUAGES—Aryavarta was the holy land of the brahmans, the country lying between the Himálaya and the Vindhya mountains, which was the ancient abode of the Hindus. In the north-western part of that region, in countries watered by the Saraswati, the earliest traditions of the brahmans place the ancestors of the Indian race. The name Aryan is now generally used to designated that ethnological division of mankind otherwise called Indo-European or Indo-Germanic. No one now doubts that the brahmans of India belong to the same family, the Aryan or Indo-European family, which civilized the whole of Europe. The Aryan race consists of two branches, an eastern and a western. The western branch comprehends the inhabitants of Europe, with the exception of the Turks, Magyars, and Finns; the eastern comprehends the inhabitants of Armenia, of Persia, of Afghanistan and Hindustan. The evidence on which a family relation has been established among these nations is that of language.

"At the first dawn of traditional history," says Max Müller, "we see these Aryan tribes migrating across the snow of the Himálaya southward toward the 'Seven Rivers' (the Indus, the five rivers of the Punjâb and the Sarasvatî), and ever since India has been called their home. That before that time they had been living in more northern regions, within the same precinets with the ancestors of the Greeks, the Italians, Slavonians, Germans and Celts, is a fact as firmly established as that the Normans of William the Conqueror were the northern of Scandinavia. The evidence of language is irrefragable and it is the only evidence worth listening to with regard to ante-historical periods. It would have been next to impossible to discover any traces of relationship between the swarthy natives of India and their conquerors, whether Alexander or Clive, but for the testimony borne by language. What other evidence could have reached back to times when Greece was not peopled by Greeks, nor India by Hindus? Yet these are the times of which we are speaking. What authority would have been strong enough to persuade the Grecian army, that their gods and their hero ancestors were the same as those of King Porus, or to convince the English soldier that the same blood was running in his veins and in the veins of the dark Bengalese? And yet there is not an English jury now-a-days, which, after examining the hoary documents of language, would reject the claim of a common descent and a legitimate relationship between Hindu, Greek and Teuton. Many words still live in India and in England, that have witnessed the first separation of the northern and southern Aryans, and these are witnesses not to be shaken by cross-examination. The terms for God, for house, for father, mother, son, daughter, for dog and cow, for heart and tears, for axe and tree, identical in all the Indo-European idioms, are like the watchwords of soldiers. We challenge the seeming stranger; and whether he answer with the lips of a Greek, or German, or an Indian, we recognise him as one of ourselves. Though the historian may shake his head, though the physiologist may doubt, and the poet scorn the idea, all must yield before the facts furnished by language. There *was* a time when the ancestors of the Celts, the Germans, the Slavonians, the Greeks and Italians, the Persians and Hindus, were living together within the same fences, separate from the ancestors of the Semitic and Turanian races.

It is more difficult to prove that the Hindu was the last to leave this common home, that he saw his brothers all depart towards the setting sun, and that then, turning towards the south and the east, he started alone in search of a new world. But as in his language and in his grammar he has preserved something of what seems peculiar to each of the northern dialects singly, as he agrees with the Greek and the German where the Greek and the German seem to differ from all the rest, and as no other language has carried off so large a share of the common Aryan heirloom—whether roots, gramar, words, myths, or legends—it is natural to suppose that, though perhaps the eldest brother, the Hindu was the last to leave the central home of the Aryan family.

The Aryan nations who pursued a north-westerly direction, stand before us in history as the principal nations of north-western Asia and Europe. They have been the prominent actors in the great drama of history, and have carried to their fullest growth all the elements of active life with which our nature is endowed. They have perfected society and morals, and we learn from their literature and works of art the elements of science, the laws of art, and the principles of philosophy. In continual struggle with each other and with Semitic and Turanian races, these Aryan nations have become the rulers of history, and its seems to be their mission to link all parts of the world together by the chains of civilization, commerce and religion. In a word, they represent the Aryan man in his historical character.

But while most of the members of the Aryan family followed this glorious path, the southern tribes were slowly migrating towards the mountains which gird the north of India. After crossing the narrow passes of the Hindu kush or the Himálaya, they conquered or drove before them, as it seems without much effort, the aboriginal inhabitants of the Trans-Himálayan countries. They took for their guides the principal rivers of northern India, and were led by them to new homes in their beautiful and fertile valleys. It seems as if the great mountains in the north had afterwards closed for centuries their Cyclopean gates against new immigrations, while, at the same time, the waves of the Indian Ocean kept watch over the southern borders of the peninsula. None of the great conquerors of antiquity—Sesostris, Semiramis, Nebuehadnezzar, or Cyrus, who waged a kind of half-nomadic warfare over Asia, Africa and Europe, and whose names, traced in characters of blood, are still legible on the thrshold of history, disturbed the peaceful seats of these Aryan settlers. Left to themselves in a world of their own, without a past, and without a future before them, they had nothing but themselves to ponder on. Strugglers there must have been in India also. Old dynasties were destroyed, whole families annihilated, and new empires founded. Yet the inward life of the Hindu was not changed by these convulsions. His mind was like the lotus leaf after a shower of rain has passed over it; his character remained the same, passive, meditative, quiet and full of faith."—*A Sanscrit Lit., p. 16.*

ARYAVARTA. 'The land of the Àryas'. The tract between the Himàlaya and the Vindhya ranges, from the eastern to the western sea.—*Manu.*

ARYAYHICHITA—A celebrated Dravida Brahman who lived at Agrahára in the 16th century of Sáliváhana; his contemporaries considered him as an emanation of Śiva, on account of his devotion for this god, and his great learning. He is said to be the author of 84 books on theology, rhetoric and philosophy; he died at Chillumbrum at the age of ninety.

ASAMANJ—The son and successor of Sagara; He was a wild and wicked young man, and was abandoned by his father, but he succeeded him as king, and, according to the *Harivaṁś a*, he was afterwards famous for valour under the name of Pañcajana. He is thus described in the Rámáyana:

"Prince Asamanj brought up with care,
Scourge of his foes was made the heir.
But liegemen's boys he used to cast,
To Sarju's waves that hurried past,
Laughing the while in cruel glee
Their dying agonies to see.
This wicked prince who aye withstood
The counsel of the wise and good,

Who plagued the people in his hate,
His father banished from the State;
His son, kind-spoken, brave and tall,
Was Ansumán, beloved of all." —*Griffiths*.

ASAMPRAJNATA—Contemplation, in which reason is lost sight of; a complete restraint of the action of thought; the last stage of mental abstraction; in which even the reflection of his individual existence is lost sight of, and he is mentally one with the Supreme Being.

ASAMPRICSHANA—The title of the fifth section of the Pancha Tantra; meaning Inconsiderateness.

ASANA—The third stage of Yoga. There are various postures in which the Yogi is directed to sit when he engages in meditation, Asana is that in which he crosses his legs underneath him, and lays hold of his feet on each side with his hands.

ĀSANGA—Author of some verses in the *Ṛgveda*. He was son of Playoga, but was changed into a woman by the curse of the gods. He recovered his male form by repentance and the favour of the *ṛṣi* Medhātithi, to whom he gave abundant wealth, and addressed the verses preserved in the Veda.

ASARA—A *rākṣasa* or other demon.

ASHADHA—The name of a constellation.

ASHAHRA—The name of one of the lunar months in the Vedas.

ASHTAVAKRA—A brahman, who by a long course of religious penance, standing in water, and meditating on the eternal spirit, became a celebrated sage or Muni. He was deformed from his birth, and on one occasion he was laughed at by the Apsarasas, or divine nymphs, on whom in consequence he denounced imprecations. The nymphs then endeavoured to appease him, and so far succeeded that he promised they should finally return to the sphere of the gods.

Ashṭávakra is the hero of a curious legend in the *Máhábhárata*. *Kahoda*, his father, was the pupil of *Uddálaka* and married his preceptor's daughter. He was so much addicted to study that he rather neglected his bride when far advanced in her pregnancy, and was rebuked for his conduct by his son yet unborn. The father indignantly pronounced that he should be born crooked, in punishment of his impertinence, and hence his name *Ashta*, eight limbs), and *Vakra*, carved. *Kahoda* went to the great sacrifice of Janaka, king of Mithilá, soon after the birth of his son. To that festival came a seeming *Bauddha* sage, who, overcoming all his competitors in argument, had them thrown into the river. *Kahoda* venturing to encounter him suffered this fate. When Ashṭávakra was in his twelfth year he first heard of his father's mischance, and to revenge it, set off for the yet unfinished sacrifice, it being one of those already noticed as of twelve years' duration. Although young in age, the saint was mature in wisdom, and overcame his father's conqueror, "When he insisted on his being thrown into the river, the supposed disputant declared himself to be the son of *Varuna*, the god of the same waters, who had commenced a similar sacrifice with that of Janaka, at the same time, and to secure the attendance of learned *Brahmans*, had adopted the expedient of sending his son to defeat them in disputation, and give them a subsequent ducking. The object being effected, they were dismissed with honour, and the parties separated mutually content. Ashâávakra, by his father's instructions, bathed in the *Samangá* river, and by so doing was rendered perfectly straight. (*Mahábhárata*, *Vana-Parvan*)—He was married to the daughter of the sage *Vadánya*, *Dana-Dharma*.)" Wilson, *XI*, *p*. 293.

ASIKNI—**(1)** The Vedic name of the Cināb, and probably the origin of the classic Akesines. **(2)** The daughter of the patriarch Vírana, wife of Daksha, the great father of mankind.

ASIPATRAVANA—Sins punished in one of the Narakas or hells, of which twenty-eight are enumerated.

A-SIRAS—'Headless'. Spirits or beings without heads.

ASIT—The son of Rája Dhruvasandhi, of the solar race; his career is thus described in the Rámáyana:

"Asit had warfare, fierce and hot,
With rival kings in many a spot,
Haihayas, Talajanghas styled,
And sasivaindhus, strong and wild,
Long time he strove, but forced to yield,
Fled from his kingdom and the field.
With his two wives away he fled,
Where high Himálaya lifts his head,
And, all his wealth and glory past,
He paid the dues of Fate at last."

—*Griffiths*.

ASITA—The Indian Simeon. There exists a legendary history in prose and verse of the life of Buddha, the founder of the religion which bears his name, in which it is related that an inspired sage named Asita, who dwelt on the skirts of the Himalaya mountains, having become informed, by a variety of portents, of the birth of the future lawgiver or Saviour, Buddha, as the son of king Suddbodanda in the city of Kapilavasta, in Northern India, went to pay his homage to the infant. Dr. Muir has published a metrical translation of this remarkable legend, from which we make a few extracts.

The word Buddha, we may observe, means "the enlightened," or "the intelligent," and various Buddhas are mentioned in the Buddhist books. The founder of the existing system was also known as Gautama, as Sákyasinha, as Sákyamuni, *i.e.*, the lion, and the devotee, of the tribe of the Sákas to which he belonged. Buddha was charged by a Brahmanical opponent with having said "Let all the evils (or sins) of the Kali age fall upon me; but let the world be redeemed." This passage is thought by some to give the character of a vicarious redeemer to Buddha. Others interpret it to mean that Buddha voluntarily underwent great Bufferings and privations during a long course of probation, in order that. he might attain the truth and teach it to men, and so redeem them from worldly existence. Professor Cowell does not understand the passage as implying any theological notion of vicarious atonement, but rather the enthusiastic utterance of highly strong moral sympathy and charity; and would compare it with St. Paul's words in Romans ix, 3, and explain it in just the game way as, he thinks, Chrysostom does that verse.

We now proceed to the metrical translation of the legend we have thus introduced, and quote a few stanzas.

On Himálaya's lonely steep
There lived of old a holy sage,
Of shrivelled form, and bent with age,
Inured to meditation deep.
He—when great Buddha had been born,
The glory of the Sákya race,
Endowed with every holy grace,
To save the suffering world forlorn—
Beheld strange portents, signs which taught
The wise that that auspicious time
Had witnessed some event sublime,
With universal blessing fraught.
The cause exploring, far and wide
The Sage's vision ranged; with awe
Within a cradle laid he saw
Far off the babe, the Sákya's pride.
With longing seized this child to view
At hand, and clasp, and homage pay,
Athwart the sky he took his way
By magic art, and swan-like flew ,
And came to king Suddhódan's gates,
And entrance craved—"Go, royal page,
And tell thy lord an ancient sage,
To see the king permission waits."

* * * *

"With all due forms, and meet respect,
The king received the holy man,
And bade him sit; and then began—
"Great sage, I do not recollect
"That I thy venerable face
Have ever seen before; allow
That I inquire what brings thee now
From thy far distant dwelling place."
"To see thy babe," the saint replies,
"I come from Himálaya's steeps."
The king rejoined—" My infant sleeps;
A moment wait until he rise."

* * * *

"In every grace complete, thy son
Of truth shall perfect insight gain,
And far sublimer fame attain
Than ewer law-giver has won.
"He such a Wheel* of sacred lore
Shall speed on earth to roll, as yet
Hath never been in motion set
By priest, or sage, or god of yore.
"The world of men and gods to bless,
The way of rest and peace to teach,
A holy law thy son shall preach—
A law of stainless righteousness.
"By him shall suffering men be freed
From weakness, sickness, pain and grief;
From all the ills shall find relief
Which hatred, love, illusion, breed.
"His hand shall loose the chains of all
Who groan in fleshly bonds confined,
With healing touch the wounds shall bind
Of those whom pain's sharp arrows gall.
"His words of powers shall put to flight
The dull array of leaden clouds
Which helpless mortals' vision shrouds,
And clear their intellectual sight.

* "The term thus rendered, *dharmachakra*, expresses a somewhat singular figure. It denotes the "wheel of the law," or the "wheel of

righteonsneas," or the "wheel of religion."—*Muir*.

"By him shall men who, now untaught,
In devious paths of error stray,
Be led to find a perfect way—
The final calm* at last be brought.
"But once, O King, in many years,
The fig tree somewhere flowers perhaps ,
So after countless ages lapse,
A Buddha once on earth appears.
"And now, at length, this blessed time
Has come: for he who cradled lies,
An infant there before thine eyes
Shall be a Buddha in his prime.
"Full, perfect, insight gaining, he
Shall rescue endless myriads tost
On life's rough ocean waves, and lost,
And grant them immortality.

* * * *

"Thee, child, th' immortals worship all,
The great Physician, born to cure
All ills that hapless men endure;
I, too, before thee prostrate fall."

* "The word in the original is *nirvána* a term of which the sense is disputed—some scholars esteeming it to mean absolute annihilation; others explaining it as the extinction of passion, the attainment of perfect dispassion."—*Muir*.

We may observe that while some of the incidents in the legend are similar to portions of the narrative in the Gospel of St. Luke (Chapter II, 25, &c.), Dr. Muir assures us that he has not at all exaggerated the expressions in the text which speak of Buddha as a deliverer, or redeemer, and that he has not assimilated his character more than. was justifiable to the Christian conception of a Saviour, and confidently appeals to any one qualified to examine the original for himself.

ASITANGA—The name of one of the eight Bhairavas, or inferior manifestations of some portion of Siva.

ASLESHA—A lunar mansion in Airávati, the third vithí of the northern Avashtana.

ASMAKA—Son of Madayantī, the wife of Kalmāṣapāda or Saudāsa. (*see* KALMĀṢAPĀDA)

ASMITA—Selfishness, one of the five afflictions of the Pátanjulu philosophy.

ASOKA—**(1)** A celebrated king of the Maurya dynasty of Magadha, and grandson of its founder. Candragupta. "This king is the most celebrated of any in the annals of the Buddhists. In the commencement of his reign he followed the Brahmānical faith, but became a convert to that of Buddha, and a zealous encourager of it. He is said to have maintained in his palace 64,000 Buddhist priests, and to have erected 84,000 columns (or topes) throughout India. A great convocation of Buddhist priests was held in the eighteenth year of his reign, which was followed by missions to Ceylon and other places." He reigned thirty-six years, from about 234 to 198 BC, and exercised authority more or less direct from Afghānistān to Ceylon. This fact is attested by a number of very curious Pāli inscriptions found engraven upon rocks and pillars, all of them of the same purport, and some of them almost identical in words, the variations showing little more than dialectic differences. That found at Kapur-di-giri, in Afghānistān is in the Bactrian Pāli character, written from right to left, all the others are in the India Pāli character, written from left to right. The latter is the oldest known form of the character now in use in India, but the modern letters have departed so far from their prototypes that it required all the acumen and diligence of James Prinsep to decipher the ancient forms. These inscriptions show a great tenderness for animal life, and are Buddhist in their character, but they do not enter upon the distinctive peculiarities of that religion. The name of Aśoka never occurs in them; the king who set them up is called Piyadaśi (Sans. Priyadarśi), 'the beautiful', and he is entitled Devānampiya, 'the beloved of the gods'. Buddhist writings identify this Piyadaśi with Aśoka, and little or no doubt is entertained of the two names representing the same person. One of the most curious passages in these inscriptions refers to the Greek king Antiochus, calling him and three others "Turamāyo, Antakana, Mako, andAlikasunari/' which represent Ptolemy, Antigonus, Magas, and Alexander. "The date of Aśoka is not exactly that of Antiochus the Great, but it is not very far different; and the corrections required to make it correspond are no more than the inexact manner in which both Brahmānical and Buddhist chronology is preserved may well be expected to render necessary." See Wilson's note in the *Viṣṇu Purāṇa*, his article in the *Journal of the Royal Asiatic Society*, vol. XII, Max Müller's *Ancient Sanskṛt Literature*, and an article by Sir E. Perry in vol. III of the *Journal of the Bombay Asiatic Society.* **(2)** The name of one of the most beautiful of Indian trees. Sir W. Jones observes 'the vegetable world scarcely exhibits a richer sight than an Aṣoka tree in fall bloom. It is about as high as an ordinary cherry tree. The flowers are very large and beautifully diversified with tints of orange scarlet, of pale yellow, and of bright orange, which form a variety of shades according to the age of the blossom:' The Aṣoka is sacred to Śiva, and is planted near his temples. It grows abundantly in Ceylon. In Hindu poetry despairing lov-ers very commonly address objects of nature, clouds, elephants, and birds, on the subject of their lost or absent mistresses.

ASOKAVARDDHANA—Another name for Asóka.

ASRAMA—There are four stages in the life of a brāhmaṇa which are called by this name. (*see* BRĀHMAṆA)

A condition of life; "orders;" when the youth has been invested with the sacred thread, he is diligently to prosecute the study of the Vedas in the house of his preceptor, with an attentive spirit and leading a life of continence.

ASRUVINDUMATI—The daughter of Kámadeva, who was sent by Indra, along with her father, to endeavour to excite passion in the breast of Yayáti. In this they succeeded, and in order to become a fit husband for his young bride, the aged king applied to his sons to give him their youth in exchange for his decrepitude. As elsewhere related they all refused, except Púru, the youngest. After a time, however, Yayáti was prevailed upon by the persuasion of his young bride, at the instigation of Indra, to go to heaven, on which he restored his youth to Púru, and proceeded with his subjects to Indra, who sent them to Śiva, and he directed them to Vishṇu, in whose sphere they obtained a final abode.—Wilson's *Works*, *III*, 37.

ASTAVAKRA—A brāhmaṇa, the son of Kahoḍa, whose story is told in the *Mahābhārata*. Kahoḍa married a daughter of his preceptor, Uddālaka, but he was so devoted to study that he neglected his wife. When she was far advanced in her pregnancy, the unborn son was provoked at his father's neglect of her, and rebuked him for it. Kahoḍa was angry at the child's impertinence, and condemned him to be born crooked; so he came forth with his eight (*aṣta*) limbs crooked (*vakra*); hence his name. Kahoḍa went to a great sacrifice at the court of Janaka, king of Mithilā. There was present there a great Buddhist sage, who challenged disputations, upon the understanding that whoever was overcome in argument should be thrown into the river. This was the fate of many, and among them of Kahoḍa, who was drowned. In his twelfth year Aṣṭāvkara learned the manner of his father's death, and set out to avenge him. The lad was possessed of great ability and wisdom. He got the better of the sage who had worsted his father, and insisted that the sage should be thrown into the water. The sage then declared himself to be a son of Varuṇa, god ofthewaters, who had sent him to obtain brāhmaṇas for officiating at a sacrifice by overpowering them in argument and throwing them into the water. When all was explained and set right, Kahoḍa directed his son to bathe in the Samanga river, on doingwhich the lad became perfectly straight. A story is told in the *Viṣṇu Purāṇa* that Aṣṭāvakra was standing in water performing penances when he was seen by some celestial nymphs and worshipped by them. He was pleased, and told them to ask a boon. They asked for the best of men as a husband. He came out of the water and offered himself. When they saw him, ugly and crooked in eight places, they laughed in derision. He was angry, and as he could not recall his blessing, he said that, after obtaining it, they should fall into the hands of thieves.

ASTIKA—An ancient sage, son of Jaratkāru by a sister of the great serpent Vāsuki. He saved the life of the serpent Takṣaka when Janamejaya made his great sacrifice of serpents, and induced that king to forego his persecution of the serpent race.

A brahman whose father had practised great austerities, bathed in all the holy tanks, and abstained from matrimony, with his body dried up by fasting, he wandered hither and thither, till he accidentally came to a hollow place in which he perceived men hanging over an abyss. Their heads were downwards and suspended by a straw at which a rat was gnawing. Inquiring who they were he discovered that they were his own ancestors. These wretched men tell him that they are thus suspended because their posterity, who should have been the means of ensuring their bliss, had perished; and the one living descendant, whose son might have done so, was entirely given up to austerities, and did not marry. The ascetic tells them that *he* is that one descendant. The ancestors entreat him to marry and have a son who would release them. He promises to do what they desire, but will only marry's girl whose parents give her to him willingly. At length in the forest, Vasuki, king of serpents, offered him his sister, a young girl of lovely form. To her he was married, and the child born to them was Astíka. Of him we are told that he had a noble spirit, was well read in the Vedas, and became powerful through austerities. (Mrs. Manning, from

Fragments du Mahábhárata)

ASTI—The wife of Kansa, and daughter of Jarása-ndha, king of Magadha.

ASURA—(1) 'Spiritual, divine'. In the oldest parts of the *Ṛgveda* this term is used for the supreme spirit, and is the same as the Ahura of the Zoroastrians. In the sense of'god' it was applied to several of the chief deities, as to Indra, Agni, and Varuṇa. It afterwards acquired an entirely opposite meaning, and came to signify, as now, a demon or enemy of the gods. The word is found with this signification in the later parts of the *Ṛgveda*, particularly in the last book, and also in the *Atharvaveda*. The brāhmaṇas attach the same meaning to it, and record many contests between the *asuraa* and the gods. According to the *Taittirīya Brāhmaṇa*, the breath (*asu*) of Prajāpati became alive, and "with that breath he created *asuras*". In another part of the same work it is said that Prjāpati "became pregnant. He created *asuras* from his abdomen". The *Śatapatha Brāhmaṇa* accords with the former statement, and states that "he created *asuras* from his lower breath". The *Taittirīya Āraṇyaka* represents that Prajāpati created "gods. men, fathers, *gandharvas*, and *apsarases*" from water, and that the *asuras*, *rākṣasas, and piśācas* sprang from the drops which were spilt. Manu's statement is that they were created by the Prajapatis. According to the *Viṣṇu Purāṇa*, they were produced from the groin of Brahmā (Prajāpati). The account of the *Vāyu Purāṇa* is: "*asuras* were first produced as sons from his (Prajapati's) groin. ASU is declared by brāhmaṇas to mean breath. From it these beings were produced; hence they are *asuras.*" The word has long been used as a general name for the enemies of the gods, including the *daityas* and *dānavas* and other descendants of Kasyapa, but not including the *rākṣasas* descended from Pulastya. In this sense a different derivation has been found for it: the source is no longer *asu*, 'breath', but the initial *a* is taken as the negative prefix, and *a-sura* signifies 'not a god'; hence, according to some, arose the word *sura*, commonlyused for 'a god', (*see* SURA) **(2)** Demons, born from the thigh of Brahma while the quality of darkness pervaded his body. Asura is a general name for all the giants and demons who composed the enemies of the gods, and the inhabitants of Pátála; and a special designation for a class of these of the first order. They belong, in the wider sense, to the Epic; in the more special sense, to the Puránic period. In the latter they are fabled to be sprung from Brahmá's thigh (*Vishnu, P.*, p. 40), and to be the sons of Kaṣyapa, by Diti and Danáyu. As in the earliest period the Suras were personifications of light, so the Asuras were probably those of darkness; and the original idea of the existence of malignant and terrible beings may thus be traced to the fear that man expereinces in darkness, from the conviction that he is surrounded by creatures which he cannot see, in short, ghosts or goblins. "(The word is derived from *a*, privative, or rather negative, and *sura*, 'a deity.') XI, 22."—*J.C. Thompson.*

In the Puránas the aborigines are described under the names of Asuras and Rákshasas; as being giants and cannibals, and of course very repulsive. "The word Asura has a very interesting history. In classical Sanscrit it only means a demon; and this meaning occurs occasionally even in the early books of the Rig Veda, and often in the later tenth. In the Atharva Veda it occurs very often in this sense, and the Brahmanas are never tired of beginning their legends with the phrase '*devásurá va eshu lokeshu samayatanta,*' 'the gods and asuras contended in these worlds.' But generally in the 'Rig Veda' the word has no such evil meaning, and it appears to have been originally derived from *as* 'to be' with the affix *ura* (a-sura), an to have meant 'living', 'spiritual.' But in later times *asura* acquired a malevolent meaning, just as the Greek *saíμων*; and even in the great epics, the Rámáyana and the Mahábharata, we find a new word *sura*, coined to express the good deities. Henceforth *sura* and *asura* play the same parts in the legends which had once been played by *deva* and *asura*; and a new legend is invented for an etymology, the *suras* being those heavenly beings who shared the liquor of immortality, (*sura*) while those who were excluded became the *asuras*."—*Quarterly Review, July* 1870, *p.* 202.

ASURA-MARRIAGE—The fifth mode of marriage mentioned by Manu, in which the bridegroom gives as much wealth as he can afford to the damsel and her kinsmen, and then takes her according to his own pleasure.

ASURI—One of the earliest professors of the Sāṁkhya philosophy.

ASVALAYANA—A distinguished author, who lived about 350 B.C. He was the pupil of Saunaka and the predecessor of Kátyáyana. He was one of the writers of the Kalpa-sutras which teach the mode of performance of sacrifices enjoined by the Vedas; and the author of the Grihya Sutras, or rules for household rites, as well as founder of a *sāknā of* the *Ṛgveda*

ASVAMEDHA—'The sacrifice of a horse.' This is a sacrifice which, in Vedic times, was performed by kings desirous of offspring. The horse was killed with certain ceremonies, and the wives of the king had to pass the night by its carcase. Upon the chief wife fell the duty of going through a revolting formality which can only be hinted at. Subsequently, as in the time *of the Mahābhārata*, the sacrifice obtained a high importance and significance. It was performed only by kings, and implied that he who instituted it was a conqueror and king of kings. It was believed that the performance of one hundred such sacrifices would enable a mortal king to overthrow the throne of Indra, and to become the ruler of the universe and sovereign of the gods. A horse of a particular colour was consecrated by the performance of certain ceremonies, and was then turned loose to wander at will for a year. The king, or his representative, followed the horse with an army, and when the animal entered a foreign country, the ruler of that country was bound either to fight or to submit. If the liberator of the horse succeeded in obtaining or enforcing the submission of all the countries over which it passed, he returned in triumph with the vanquished Rājās in his train; but if he failed, he was disgraced and his pretensions ridiculed. After the successful return a great festival was held, at which the horse was sacrificed either really or figuratively.

ASVA-MUKHA—'Horse-faced.' (*see* KINNARA)

ASVAPATI—(Lord of Horses). 1, The Rája of Kekaya, and father of Maharája Dasaratha's wife Kaikeyi; 2, And ancient rája, the father of Sávitrí, *q.v.*

ASVATTHAMAN—Son of Droṇa and Kṛpā, and one of the generals of the Kauravas. Also called by his patronymic Drauṇāyana. After the last great battle, in which Duryodhana was mortally wounded, Aśvatthāman with two other warriors, Kṛpa and Kṛtavarman, were the sole survivors of the Kaurava host that were left effective. Aśvatthāman was made the commander. He was fierce in his hostility to the Pāṇḍavas, and craved for revenge upon Dhṛṣṭadyumna, who had slain his father, Droṇa. These three surviving Kauravas entered the Pāṇḍava camp at night. They found Dhṛṣṭadyumna asleep, and Aśvatthāman stamped him to death as he lay. He then killed Śikhaṇḍin, the other son of Drupada, and he also killed the five young sons of the Pāṇḍavas and carried their heads to the dying Duryodhana. He killed Pariksit, while yet unborn in the womb of his mother, with his celestial weapon *brahmastra*, by which he incurred the curse of Kṛṣṇa, who restored Parīkṣit to life. On the next morning he and his comrades fled, but Draupadī clamoured for revenge upon the murderer of her children. Yudhiṣṭhira represented that Aśvatthāman was a brāhmaṇa, and pleaded for his life. She then consented to forego her demand for his blood if the precious and protective jewel which he wore on his head were brought to her. Bhīma, Arjuna, and Kṛṣṇa then went in pursuit of him. Arjuna and Kṛṣṇa overtook him, and compelled him to give up the jewel. They carried it to Draupadī, and she gave it to Yudhiṣṭhira, who afterwards wore it on his head.

ASVINI—A lunar asterism in Nagavithi, the first vithi in the northern Avasthána.

ASVINS, ASVINAU (dual), **ASVINI KUMARAS**—'Horsemen.' Dioskouroi. Two Vedic deities, twin sons of the sun or the sky. They are ever young and handsome, bright, and of golden brilliancy, agile, swift as falcons, and possessed of many forms; and they ride in a golden car drawn by horses or birds, as harbingers of Uṣas, the dawn. "They are the earliest bringers of light in the morning sky, who in their chariot hasten onwards before the dawn and prepare the way for her."—*Roth.*

As personifications of the morning twilight, they are said to be children of the sun by a nymph who concealed herself in the form of a mare; hence she was called Aśvini and her sons Aśvins. But inasmuch as they precede the rise of the sun, they are called his parents in his form Pūṣan. Mythically they are the parents of the Pāṇḍu princes Nakula and Sahadeva. Their attributes are numerous, but relate mostly to youth and beauty, light and speed, duality, the curative power, and active benevolence. The number of hymns addressed to them testify to the enthusiastic worship they received. They were the physicians *of svarga*, and in this character are called Dasras and Nāsatyas, Gadāgadau and Svarvaidyau; or one was Dasra and the other Nāsatya. Other of their appellations are Abdhijau.'ocean born'; Puṣkarasrajau, wreathed with lotuses'; Bāḍaveyau, sons of the submarine fire, Bāḍava. Many instances are recorded of their benevolence and their power of healing. They restored the sage Cyavana to youth, and prolonged his life when he had become old and decrepit, and through his instrumentality they were admitted to partake ufthe libations *of soma*, like the other gods, although Indra strongly opposed them. (*see* CYAVANA)

The Aśvins, says Muir, "have been a puzzle to

the oldest commentators", who have differed widely in their explanations. According to different interpretations quoted in the *Nirukta*, they were "heaven and earth", "day and night", "two kings, performers of holy acts".

"It may seem unaccountable that two deities of a character so little defined, and so difficult to identify, as the Aṣvins, should have been the objects of so enthusiastic a worship as appears from the numerous hymns dedicated to them in the Rig Veda, to have been paid to them in ancient times. The reason may have been that they were hailed as the precursors of returning day, after the darkness and dangers of the night. In some passages they are represented as being, like Agni, the chasers away of evil spirits.

"The Aṣvins are said to be young ancient, beautiful, honeyhued, lords of lustre, bright, of a golden brilliancy, agile, fleet as thought, swift as young falcons, possessing many forms, wearing lotus garlands, strong, mighty, terrible, possessed of wondrous powers, and profound in wisdom."—Muir, *O.S.T.*, vol. v., p. 240.

"The following are a few of the modes in which the divine power of the Aṣvins is declared in different hymns to have been manifested for the deliverance of their votaries.

"When the sage Chyavána had grown old and had been forsaken, they divested him of his decrepit body, prolonged his life and restored him to youth./ "In the same way they renewed the youth of Kali after he had grown old; and when Viṣpalá's leg had been cut off in battle like the wing of a brid, the Asvins are said to have given her as iron one instead.

"They restored Parávjir (or an outcast), who was blind and lame, to sight and the power of walking.

"Finally to say nothing of the succours rendered to numerous other persons, the Aṣvins did not confine their benevolence to human beings, but are also celebrated as having rescued from the jaws of a wolf a quail by which they were invoked.

"The Aṣvins are worshipped with uplifted hands, and supplicated for a variety of blessings, for long life, and for deliverance from calamities, for offspring, wealth, victory, destruction of enemies, preservation of the worshippers themselves, of their houses and cattle. No calamity or alarm from any quarter can touch the man whose chariot they place in the van."—*Ibid.*, *p.* 240.

Professor Goldstücker writes, "The myth of the Aṣvins is, in my opinion, one of that class of myths in which two distinct elements, the cosmical and the human or historical, have gradually become blended into one. It seems necessary, therefore, to separate these two elements in order to arrive at an understanding of the myth. The historical or human element in it, I believe, is represented by those legends which refer to the wonderful cures effected by the Aṣvins, and to their performances of a kindred sort; the cosmical element is, that relating to their luminous nature. The link which connects both seems to be the mysteriousness of the nature and effects of the phenomena of light, and of the healing art at a remote antiquity. That there might have been some horsemen or warriors of great renown who inspired their contemporaries with awe by their wonderful deeds, and more especially by their medical skill, appears to have been also the opinion of some old commentators mentioned by Yáska, for some 'legendary writers,' he says, took them for 'two kings, performers of holy act;' and this view seems likewise borne out by the legend in which it is narrated that the gods refused the Aṣvins admittance to a sacrifice on the ground that they had been on too familiar terms with men. It would appear then that these Aṣvins, like the Ribhus, were originally renowned mortals, who, in the course of time, were translated into the companionship of the gods; and it may be a matter of importance to investigate whether, besides this a *priori* view, there are further grounds of a linguistic or grammatical character for assuming that the hymns containing the legends relating to these humans Aṣvins are posterior or otherwise to those descriptive of the cosmical gods of the same name. "The luminous character of the latter can sacrcely be matter of doubt, for the view of some commentators—recorded by Yáska,—according to which they were identified with 'heaven and earth, appears not to be countenanced by any of the passages known to us. Their very name, it would seem, settles this point, since *asva*, the horse, literally, 'the pervader,' is always the symbol of the luminous deities, especially of the sun. The difficulty, however, is to determine their position amongst these deities and to harmonize with it the other myths connected with them. I may here, however, first observe that, though Yáska records opinions which identify the Aṣvins with 'day and night,' and 'sun and moon,' the passage relied upon by Professor Roth to prove that Yáska himself identified them with Indra and Áditya (the sun), does not bear out any such conclusion. For the passage in question, as I understand it, means: 'their time is after the (latter) half of the night when the (spaces) becoming light is resisted (by darkness); for the middlemost Aṣvin (between darkness and light) shares in darkness, whilst (the other), who is of a solar nature (Áditya), shares in light.' There is this verse relating to them: 'In nights,' etc. Nor does Durga, the commentator on Yáska, attribute to the latter the view which Professor Roth ascribes to him. His words, as I interpret them, are: 'their time is after the (latter) half of the night when the (spaces) becoming light is resisted,' (means) when, after the (latter) half of the night, darkness intersected by light makes an effort against light, that is the time of the Aṣvins...Then the nature of the middlemost (between them) is a share in that darkness which penetrates into light; and the solar one (āditya) assumes that nature which is a share in the light penetrating into darkness. These two are the middlemost and the uppermost: this is the teacher's (*i.e.*, Yāska's) own opinion, for, in order to substantiate it, he gives as an instance the verse '*Vasaitishu sma*,' " etc.

"To judge, therefore, from these words, it is the opinion of Yāska that the Aṣvins represent the transition from darkness to light, when the intermingling of both produces that inseparable duality expressed by the twin nature of these deities. And this interpretation, I hold, is the best that can be given of the character of the *cosmical* Aṣvins. It agrees with the epithets by which they are invoked, and with the relationship in which they are placed. They are young, yet also ancient, beautiful bright, swift, etc.; and their negative character—the result of the alliance of light with darkness—is, I believe, expressed by *dasra*, the destoryer, and also by the two negatives in the compound *nasatya* (na+a-*satya*), though their positive character is again redeemed by the ellipsis of "enemies, or diseases, to *dasra*, and by the sense of *nasatya*, and un-true, *i.e.*, truthful. They are the parents of Púshan, the sun; for they precede the rise of the sun; they are the sons of the sky, and again the sons of vivasvat and Saranyu. Vivasvat, I believe, here implies the firmament 'expanding' to the sight through the approaching light; and though Saranyu is to Professor Müller one of the deities which are foced by him to support his dawn-theory, it seems to me that the etymology of the word, and the character of the myths relating to it, rather point to the moving air, or the dark and cool air, heated, and therefore set in motion, by the approach of the rising sun. The Aṣvins are also the husbands or the friends of Suryā, whom I take for the representative of the weakest manifestation of the sun; and I believe that Sāyana is right when, by the sister of the Aṣvins, he understands Ushas, the dawn. The mysterious phenomenon of the intermingling of darkness—which is no longer complete night—and of light—which is not yet dawn—seems to agree with all these conceptions, and with the further details of a cosmical nature, which are so fully given in the preceding paper."—*Ibid, p.*255-7.

ATÀLA—The first of the seven regions of Pátála,—below the earth—ten thousand yojanas in extent—the soil of Atàla is white, and the place is embellished with magnificent palaces.

ATARVA—One of the fifteen teachers of the school of Vajasaneyi or white Yajush.

ATHARVA VEDA—The name of the fourth of the four Vedas, created from the northern mouth of Brahma. It was arranged by Vyása. The illustrious sage Sumanta taught this Veda to his pupil Kabandha, who made it two-fold. The principal subjects of difference in the Sanhitas of the Atharva Veda, are the five Kalpas or ceremonials. "As to the internal character of the Atharva hymns, it may be said of them, as of the tenth book of the Rík, that they are the productions of another and a later period, and the expressions of a different spirit, from that of the earlier hymns in the other Veda. In the latter, the gods are approached with reverential awe, indeed, but with love and confidence also; a worship is paid them that exalts the offerer of it; the demons, embraced under the general name *Rákshasas*, are objects of horror, whom the gods ward off and destroy; the divinities of the Atharva are regarding rather with a kind of cringing fear, as powers whose wrath is to be deprecated and whose favour curried, for it knows a whole host of imps and hobgoblins, in ranks and classes, and addresses itself to them directly, offering them homage to induce them to abstain from doing harm. The *mantra*, prayer, which in the older Veda is the instrument of devotion, is here rather the tool of superstition; it wrings from the unwilling hands of the gods the favours which of old their good-will to men induced them to grant, or by simple magical power obtains the fulfilment of the utterer's wishes. The most prominent characteristic feature of the Atharva is the multitude of incantations which it contains; these are pronounced either by the person who is himself to be benefited, or, more often, by the sorcerer for him, and are directed to the procurring of the greatest variety of desirable ends; most frequently, perhaps, long life, or recovery from grievous sickness, is the object sought; then a talisman, such as a necklace, is sometimes given, or in very numerous cases some plant endowed with marvellous virtues is to be the immediate external means of the cure; farther, the attainment of welath or power is aimed at, the downfall of enemies, success in love or in play, the removal of petty pests, and so on, even down to the growth of hair on a bald pate. There are hymns, too, in which a single rite or ceremony is taken up and exalted, somewhat in the same strain as the Soma in the Pávámanya hymns of the Rík. Others of a speculative mystical character are not wanting; yet their number is not so great as might naturally be expected, considering the development which the Hindu religion received in the periods following after that of the primitive Veda. It seems in the main that the Atharva is of popular rather than of priestly origin; that in making the transition from the Vedic to modern times; it forms an intermediate step, rather to the gross idolatries and supersititions of the ignorant mass, than to the sublimated pantheism of the brahmans."—*Whitney.*

"It has been surmised (Müller's *Ancient Sanscrit Literature*, p. 447, ff.) that the hymns of the Atharva Veda 'formed an additional part of the sacrifice from a very early time, and that they were chiefly intended to counteract the influence of any untoward event that might happen during the sacrifice.' This is possible; but the great importance which the adherents of this Veda themselves attach to it, is founded on other considerations than these. They argue, as appears from the treatise *Atharvanarahasya*, mentioned above, that the three other Vedas enable a man to fulfil the *dharma*, or religious law, but that the Atharva helps him to attain *móksha*, or eternal bliss. This doctrine is laid down, for instance, in the *Chúlika Upanishad* of this Veda, when it says: 'Those Brâhmans and others who know the science of the (neuter) Brâhman continued in the *Brahma Veda*, became merged in Brâhman;' and it is likewise inferred from other passages in the *Sáunaka Brâhmaná*. The name of *Brahma Veda* itself, by which this Veda is also frequently called, is therefore explained by them, not as implying the Veda which belongs to the province of the priest Brahman, but the Veda which contains the mysterious doctrine of Brahman, the supreme spirit, into which the human soul becomes finally absorbed. It is probable, therefore, that the very uselessness of the Atharva Veda for sacrifical purposes, and the reluctance which was felt to base its santity merely on its incantations and spells, invested it, in the mind of its followers, with a spiritual character, which was then fully developed in the numerous Upanishads (*q.v.*) now connected with it."—*Muir.*

Professor Müller, in his *Ancient Sanscrit Literature*, has given the following hymn from the Atharva Veda, of which the *Quarterly Review* says, "we know of no passage in Vedic literature which approaches its simple sublimity:"—

"The Great one who rules over these worlds beholds all as if he were close by. When any one thinks that he cloaks a thing, the Gods know it all.

"They know every one who stands or walks or glides along secretly or withdraws into his house or into any hiding place. Whatever two persons sitting together devise, Varuna the king knows it as the third./ 'This earth too is Varuna the king's and that vast sky whose ends are far off. The two oceans are Varuna's lotus; he resides too in this little pool.

'He who should flee far beyond the sky, would not there escape from Varuna the king; his messengers from heaven traverse this world, thousand-eyed they look beyond this earth.

King Varuna sees all,—What is within and beyond heaven and earth; the winkings of men's eyes are all numbered by him; he moves all these things as a gamester his dice.

'May all thy destructive nooses, O Varuna, which are cast sevenfold and threefold, bind him who speaks falsehood, and pass by him who speaks truth.' "

ATHARVAN—The fourth Veda. (*see* Veda above)

ATHARVAN—(1) Name of a priest mentioned in the *Ṛgveda*, where he is represented as having "drawn forth" fire and to have "offered sacrifice in early times". He is mythologically represented as the eldest son of Brahmā, to whom that god revealed the *Brahmā-vidydā* (knowledge of God), as a Prajāpati, and as the inspired author of the fourth Veda. At a later period he is identified with Aṅgiras. His descendants are called Atharvanas, and are often associated with the Aṅgirasas.

A distinguished sage, the generator of fire, and producer of Agni. Atharvan is mentioned as the earliest institutor of sacrifice. Atharvan was the first who by sacrifices opened up paths; then the friendly Sun, the upholder of ordinances, was produced. (Muir,

O.S.T., vol. I, p. 169.) **(2)** A priest who is considered to have obtained the fire from heaven, and who in the course of Mythological personifications appears as a Prajápati or father of all beings, as the inspired another of the fourth or Atharva Veda, as the eldest son of Brahma to whom Brahma revealed the Brahma vidya, or knowledge of God; and at a later period as the same as Angiras.

ATHARVANGIRASAS—This name belongs to the descendants of Atharvan and Aṅgiras, orto theAngirasas alone who are especially connected with the *Atharva-veda*, and these names are probably given to the hymns of that Veda to confer on them greater authority and holiness.

ATHARVAS—A class or even caste of priests, who had secrets which they were prohibited from divulging; they were the spiritual guides of their nation, and none but the son of a priest could become a priest—a rule which the Parsís still maintain.† († Muir, *O.S.T.*, vol. I, p. 293.)

ATIKAYA—One of the sons of the giant Rávaṇa, who was killed at the siege of Lanka.

ATIRATRA—A form of sacrifice created from the western mouth of Brahma, along with the Sáma Veda. It is a division of the service of the Jyotishtoma, the fifth part, or Somasamtha, and means literally, lasting through the night.

ATIRATRA—One of the ten noble sons of Chakshusha. *V.P.*, p. 98.

ATIT—From *Atita*, passed away; a religious mendicant liberated from worldly cares and feelings.

ATITHIGRA—A name of Divodása (*q.v.*) who iaaaid in the Rig-Veda to have slain Karanja and Parṇaya with his glittering spear.

ATMA—(1) A name of Vishnu, who has many appellations. **(2)** The soul. The principle of life. The supreme soul. **(3)** Soul, living soul, animating nature and existing before it: "the highest object of their religion was to restore that bond by which their own self, (átma) was linked to the eternal self (paramátman); to recover that unity which had been clouded and obscured by the magical illusions of reality; by the so called Máya of creation."—*Max Müller.*

ATMA-BODHA—'Knowledge of the soul.' A short work attributed to Śankarācārya. It has been printed, and a translation of it was published in 1812 by Taylor. There is a French verṣion by Néve and an English translation by Kearns in the *Indian Antiquary*, vol. V.

ATREYA—A patronymic from Atri. A son or descendant of Atri; a people so-called.

ATRI—'An eater.' A *ṛṣi*, and author of many Vedic hymns. "A Maharṣi or great saint, who in the Vedas occurs especially in hymns composed for the praise of Agni, Indra, the Aśvins, and the Viśvadevas. In the epic period he is considered as one of the ten Prajāpatis or lords of creation engendered by Manu for the purpose of creating the universe; at a later period he appears as a mind-born son of Brahmā, and as one of the seven *ṛsis* who preside over the reign of Svāyambhuva, the first Manu, or, accordingto others, of Svārociṣa, the second, or of Vaivasvata, the seventh. He married Anasūyā, daughter of Dakṣa and their son was Durvasas."—*Goldstücker.*

In the *Rāmāyaṇa* an account is given of the visit paid by Rāma and Sītā to Atri and Anasūyā (*q.v.*) in their hermitage south of Citrakūṭa. In the Purāṇas he was also father of Soma, the moon, and the ascetic Dattātreya (*q.v.*) by his wife Anasūyā. As a *ṛṣi* he is one of the stars of the Great Bear.

One of the nine brahmans celebrated in the Puránas. He was married to Anusúya (charity), one of the twenty-four daughters of Daksha (*q.v.*). When Atri was plunged, by the malice and arts of evil spirits, into a gloomy and burning abyss, the Asvins "speedily came to his assistance, mitigrated the heat with cold, and supplied him with nutriment, so that his situation became tolerable, if not agreeable, till they eventually extricated him from his perilous position." (*O.S.T.*, vol. v, p. 247.) The son of Atri was Soma (the moon), whom Brahma installed as the sovereign of plants, of brahmans, and of the stars.

ATTAPA—The name of the nineteenth heaven of Buddhism.

ATYARATI—The unwise man mentioned in the Aitareya Brahmána, who by means of a Rajasuya sacrifice or religious ceremony, subdued the whole earth; but when the brahman who had officiated asked for his reward, Atyaráti replied; "When I conquer Uttara Kuru, thou shalt be king of the earth, holy man, and I will be merely thy general." The brahman replied: "Uttara Kuru is the land of the gods; no mortal can conquer it. Thou hast cheated me, therefore I take all from thee." And Atyaráti, thus deprived of vigour, was slain by king Sushimna. For Atyaráti had not kept his oath.—*A. & M. I, Vol. I, p.* 104.

AURVA—A *ṛṣi*, son of Urva and grandson of Bhṛgu. He is described in the *Mahābhārata* as son of the sage Cyavana by his wife Āruṣī. From his race he is called Bhārgava. The *Mahābhārata* relates that a king named Kṛtavīrya was very liberal to his priests of the race of Bhṛgu, and that they grew rich upon his munificence. After his death, his descendants, who had fallen into poverty, begged help from the Bhṛgus, and met with no liberal response. Some of them buried their money, and when this was discovered the impoverished kṣatriyas were so exasperated that they slew all the Bhṛgus down to the children in the womb. One woman concealed her unborn child in her thigh, and the kṣatriyas being informed of this, sought the child to kill it, but the child "issued forth from its mother's thigh" with lustre and blinded the persecutors. From being produced from the thigh (*uru*), the child received the name of Aurva. The sage's austerities alarmed both gods and men, andhe for a long time refused to mitigate his wrath against the kṣatriyas, but at the persuasion of the *pitṛs*, he cast the fire of his anger into the sea, where it became a being with the face of a horse called Hayaśiras. While he was living in the forest he prevented the wife of King Bāhu from burning herself with her husband's corpse. Thus he saved the life other son, with whom she had been pregnant seven years. When the child was born he was called Sāgara (ocean); Aurva was his preceptor, and bestowed on him the Āgneyāstra, or fiery weapon with which he conquered the barbarians who invaded his country. Aurva had a son named Ṛcīka, who was father of Jamadagni. The *Harivamśa* gives another version of the legend about the offspring of Aurva. The sage was urged by his friends to beget children. He consented, but he foretold that his progeny would live by the destruction of others. Then he produced from his thigh a devouring fire, which cried out with a loud voice, "I am hungry; let me consume the world." The various regions were soon in flames, when Brahmā interfered to save his creation, and promised the son of Aurva a suitable abode and maintenance. The abode was to be at Baḍavāmukha, the mouth of the ocean; for Brahmā was born and rests in the ocean, and he and the newly produced fire were to consume the world together at the end of each age, and at the end of time to devour all things with the gods, *asuras*, and *rākṣasas*. The name Aurva thus signifies, shortly, the submarine fire. It is also called Baḍavānala and Samvarttaka. It is represented as a flame with a horse's head, and is also called Kākadhavaja, from carrying a banner on which there is a crow.

AUSANA, OR AUSANASA PURANA. (See PURĀṆA).

AUTTAMA, OR ATTUMI—The name of the third Manu, a descendant from Priyavrata.

AUTTAMI—The third Manu. (*see* MANU)

AVALOKITA—A disciple of Kamandaki in the drama of the Toy Cart.

AVANTI—The ancient name of Ujjayinī, one of the seven sacred cities in Central India, where the scene is laid of the popular domestic drama named Mrichchhakato, or Toy Cart.

AVANTYAS—One of the five great divisions of the Haikaya tribe. The Avantyas were in Ujein, and preceded the Rajput tribes by whom that country is now occupied. There are still vestiges of them.—Tod's *Rajasthan, I*, 39.

AVARANT—From *Avarana*, screening or surrounding; the name of a division of the sect of *Rámánujas* who prepare their own meals and eat in the strictest privacy: "they must not eat in cotton garments, but having bathed must put on woolen or silk; all the Rámánujas cook for themselves, and should the meal during this process, or whilst they are eating, attract even the looks of a stranger, the operation is instantly stopped and the viands buried in the ground."—*H. H. Wilson, Vol. I, p.* 39. In the Jain system the five Avaranas mean the difficulties in acquiring as many gradations of holy or driven wisdom.

AVASARPINI—The Jains divide time into two cycles or ages, *viz.*, the Utasarpini and the Avasarpini time. The Avasarpini time, has six stages, *viz.*, super-good time, good-time, good-bad time, bad-good time, bad-time, and super-bad time. The stage in which we now live in the fifth, the bad time. Avasarpini means the age of decreases.

AVASTHANAS—The name of the divisions of the sun's course, which are three, *viz.*, Airavata (northern), Jaradgavu (southern), and Vaiswanara (central).

AVATARA—'A descent.' The incarnation of a deity, esnecially of Viṣṇu. The first indication, not of an *avatāra*, but of what subsequently developed into an *avatāra*, is found in the *Ṛgveda* in the "three steps" of "Viṣṇu, the unconquerable preserver", who "strode over this (universe)", and "in three places planted his step". The early commentators understood the "three places" to be the earth, the atmosphere, and the sky; that in the earth Viṣṇu was fire, in the air lightning, and in the sky the solar light. One commentator, Aurṇavābha, whose name deserves mention, took a more philosophical view of the matter, and interpreted "the three steps" as being "the different positions of the sun at his rising, culmination, and setting". Sāyaṇa, the great commentator, who lived in days when the god Viṣṇu had obtained pre-eminence, understood "the three steps" to be "the three steps" taken by that god in his incarnation of Vāmana the dwarf, to be presently noticed. Another reference to "three strides" and to a sort of *avatāra* is made in the *Taittirīya Saṁhitā*, where it is said, "Indra, assuming the form of a she-jackal, stepped all round the earth in three (strides). Thus the gods obtained it."

1. *Matsya*. 'The fish.' This is an appropriation to Viṣṇu of the ancient legend of the fish and the deluge, as related in the *Śatapatha Brāhmaṇa*, and quoted above. The details of this *avatāra* vary slightly in different Purāṇas. The object of the incarnation was to save Vaivasvata, the seventh Manu, and progenitor of the human race, from destruction by a deluge. A small fish came into the hands of Manu and besought his protection. He carefully guarded it, and it grew rapidly until nothing but the ocean could contain it. Manu then recognised its divinity, and worshipped the deity Viṣṇu thus incarnate. The god apprised Manu of the approaching cataclysm, and bade him prepare for it. When it came, Manu embarked in a ship with the ṛṣis, and with the seeds of all existing things. Viṣṇu then appeared as the fish with a most stupendous horn. The ship was bound to this hom with the great serpent as with a rope, and was secured in safety until the waters had subsided. The *Bhāgavata Purāṇa* introduces a new feature. In one of the nights of Brahmā, and during his repose, the earth and the other worlds were submerged in the ocean. Then the demon Hayagrīva drew near, and carried off the Veda which had issued from Brahmā's mouth. To recover the Veda thus lost, Viṣṇu assumed the form of a fish, and saved Manu as related above. But this Purāṇa adds that the fish instructed Manu and the *ṛṣis* in "the true doctrine of the soul of the eternal Brahmā"; and, when Brahmā awoke at the end of this dissolution of the universe, Viṣṇu slew *Hayagrīva* and restored the Veda to Brahmā.

2. *Kūrma*. 'The tortoise.' The germ of this *avatāra is* found in the *Śatapatha Brāhmaṇa*, as above noticed. In its later and developed form, Viṣṇu appeared in the form of a tortoise in *satyayuga*, or first age, to recover some things of value which had been lost in the deluge. In the form of a tortoise he placed himself at the bottom of the sea of milk, and made his back the base or pivot of the mountain Mandāra. The gods and demons twisted the great serpent Vāsuki round the mountain, and, dividing into two parties, each took an end of the snake as a rope, and thus churned the sea until they recovered the desired objects. These were—(1) *amṛta*, the water of life; (2) Dhanvantari, the physician of the gods and bearer of the cup *of amṛta*; (3) Lakṣmī, goddess of fortune and beauty, and consort of Viṣṇu; (4) *surā*, goddess of wine; (5) *candra*, the moon; (6) Rambhā, a nymph, and pattern of a lovely and amiable woman; (7) Ucchaiḥśravas, a wonderful and model horse; (8) Kaustubha, a celebrated jewel; (9) Parijāta, a celestial tree; (10) Surabhi, the cow of plenty; (11) Airāvāta, a wonderful model elephant; (12) *śaṅkha*, a shell, the conch of victory; (13) *dhanus*, a famous bow; and (14)*viṣa*, poison.

3. *Varāha*. 'The boar.' The old legend of the *Brāhmaṇas* concerning the boar which raised the earth from the waters has been appropriated to Viṣṇu. A demon name Hiraṇyākṣa had dragged the earth to the bottom of the sea. To recover it Viṣṇu assumed the form of a boar, and after a contest of a thousand years he slew the demon and raised up the earth.

4. *Narasiṁha, or Nṛsiṁha*. 'The man-lion.'Viṣṇu assumed this form to deliver the world from the tyranny of Hiraṇyakaśipu, a demon who, by the favour of Brahmā, had become invulnerable, and was secure from gods, men, and animals. This demon's son, named Prahlāda, worshipped Viṣṇu, which so incensed his father that he tried to kill him, but his efforts were all in vain. Contending with his son as to the omnipotence and omnipresence of Viṣṇu. Hiraṇyakaśipu demanded to know if Viṣṇu was present in a stone pillar of the hall, and struck it violently. To avenge Prahlāda, and to vindicate his own offended majesty, Viṣṇu came forth from the pillar as the Narasiṁha, half-man and half-lion, and tore the arrogant *daitya* king to pieces.

These four incarnations are supposed to have appeared in the *satyayuga*, or first age of the world.

5. Vāmana. 'The dwarf.' The origin ofthis incarnation iś "the three strides of Viṣṇu", spoken of in the *Ṛgveda*, as before explained. In the *Tretāyuga*, or second age, the *daitya* king Bali had, by his devotions and austerities, acquired the dominion of the three worlds, and the gods were shorn of their power and dignity. To remedy this, Viṣṇu was born as a diminutive son of Kaśyapa and Aditi (*qq.v.*). The dwarf appeared before Bali, and begged of him as much land as he could step over in three paces. The generous monarch complied with the request. Viṣṇu took two strides over heaven and earth; but respecting the virtues of Bali, he then stopped, leaving the dominion of Pātāla (*q.v.*), or the infernal regions, to Bali.

The first five incamatiotis are thus purely mythological; in the next three we have the heroic element, and in the ninth the religious.

6. Paraśurāma. 'Rāma with the axe.' Born in the *tretā*, or second age, as son of the brāhmaṇa Jamadagni, to deliver the brāhmaṇas from the arrogant dominion of the kṣatriyas. (*see* PARAŚURAMA)

7. Rāma or Rāmacandra. 'The moon-like or gentle Rāma', the hero of the *Rāmāyaṇa.* He was the son of Daśaratha, king of Ayodhyā, of the Solar race, and was born in the *tretā yuga*, or second age, for the purpose of destroying the demon Rāvaṇa.

8. *Kṛṣṇa.* 'The black or dark coloured.' This is the most popular of all the later deities, and has obtained such preeminence, that his votaries look upon him not simply as an incarnation, but as a perfect manifestation of Viṣṇu. When Kṛṣṇa is thus exalted to the full godhead, his elder brother, Balarāma takes his place as the eighth *avatāra.* (*see* Kṛṣṇa and Balarāma)

9. Buddha. The great success of Buddha as a religious teacher seems to have induced the brāhmaṇas to adopt him as their own, rather than to recognise him as an adversary. So Viṣṇu is said to have appeared as Buddha to encourage demons and wicked men to despise the Vedas, reject caste, and deny the existence of the gods, and thus to effect their own destruction.

10. Kalkī or Kalkin. 'The white horse.' This incarnation of Viṣṇu is to appear at the end of the *kali* or Iron Age, seated on a white horse, with a drawn sword blazing like a comet, for the final destruction of the wicked, the renovation of creation, and the restoration of purity.

The above are the usually recognised *avatāras*, but the number is sometimes extended, and the *Bhāgavata Purāṇa*, which is the most fervid of all the Purāṇas in its glorification of Viṣṇu, enumerates twenty-two incarnations: (1) Puruṣa, the male, the progenitor; (2) Varāha, the boar; (3) Nārada, the great sage; (4) Nara and Nārāyaṇa (*q.v.*); (5) Kapila, the great sage; (6) Dattātreya, a sage; (7) Yajña, sacrifice; (8) Ṛṣabha, a righteous king, father of Bharata; (9) Pṛthu, a king; (10) Matsya, the fish; (11) Kūrma, the tortoise; (12) and (13) Dhanvantari, the physician of the gods; (14) Narasiṁha, the man-lion; (15) Vāmana, the dwarf; (16) Paraśurāma; (17) Veda-Vyāsa; (18) Rāma; (19) Balarāma; (20) Kṛṣṇa; (21) Buddha; (22) Kalkī. But after this it adds—"The incarnations of Viṣṇu are innumerable; like the rivulets flowing from an inexhaustible lake. *Ṛṣis*, Manus, gods, sons of Manus, Prajāpatis, are all portions of him."

AVATARANA—An abode of the *rākṣasas.*

AVICHI—One of the twenty-eight Narakas or hells enamerated in the *V.P.* They are all said to be situated beneath the earth and beneath the waters.

AVIDYA—Ignorance. One of the five afflictions of the Pátanjala philosophy.

AVVEYAR—In former times, there existed among the Tamil people seen distinguished sages, of whom four were women and three men. Among them Avveyar and Tiruvalluvar were the most celebrated. Respecting the other five, but little is known either of their lives or their writings.

"The particulars given respecting Avveyar too, are so fabulous and so variously related in different books, that it is quite impossible to come to any true and satisfactory results. I shall attempt to state such results as far as I can, and refer the reader for specimens of the native biography to the history of Kabilar, and to the extract translated from the Skanda Puránam as given in the *Asiatic Researches.*

"Avveyar most probably flourished in the reigns of the three celebrated kings, Ukkiraperuvarithi Pándian and the monarchs of the Seran and Sorhan kingdoms who were his contemporaries. In her history as still transmitted by oral tradition, there are many references to these kings, and to the fabulous miracles she performed before them. Her father seems to have been a Brahman and her mother an outcast, who were united to each other without being aware of the wide difference in their cast. Afterwards howver, on finding it out, the Brahman determined as the only condition on which they should live together, that any children who might be born to them should be deserted immediately on their birth. Avveyar was their second female child, and was born, reared, and educated at a village inhabited by Panars. (The business of the Panars was to attend on kings and celebrated their praises. But the race is now almost extinct.)

"If we may judge from her character and writings, Avveyar was educated by a Panar with great care and talent. One thing is very evident, she must have possessed eminent natural abilities. From the numerous fables respecting her, we may gather that she was not only clever but that she exerted herself to do good. The excellent moral maxims she has left, tend for the most part to the promotion of good sentiments and good conduct.

"Her principal productions now extant are as follows: Átthichuvadi Kondre-Vénthan, Muthuréi (or Vakkundán), Nal-Vaḷi, Kalvi-Orluk-kam, Avvé-Kérao, Avvé-Kovḷ, Pilaiyar-Agaval, Ganapathi-Ásiria-Virutham, and a number of detached verses: but probably some of her productions have been lost: she is reputed to have been very clever in chemistry and medicine, and to have discovered the fablest panacea (or *Kalpa*) by eating which she lived to the age of 240 years.

"Her fame became widely spread abroad, and wherever she went, kings and nobles, the learned and the ignorant, alike showed her the highest respect.

"Her productions are universally read. Some of them are not only among the very first reading books put into the hands of children in almost every Tamil school, but are also greatly and deservedly esteemed.'—*Sugden.*

AVYAYA—A name of Purusha or spirit, it means inconsumable.

AWIHA—The name of the eighteenth heaven of Buddhism.

AYANA—A period of six months, two Ayanas compose a year. The southern Ayana is a night and the northern a day of the gods. Twelve thousand divine years, each composed of such days, constitute the period of four Yugas, or ages. The word is also used in the sense of hemisphere; the uttara-ayana is the apparent course of the sun through the northern signs, and the dakshanayana is the southerly course; hence the northern and southern hemispheres appear to correspond with the two ayanas.

AYANAR—(Lord). The chief mate deity among the Grámade vatas. His temples are so numerous that there is one near every village. They are generally small, and have at their entrance two terrible looking stone door-keepers. In the interior Ayanár is represented in a human form in a sitting posture, with his two wives Púranai and Pudkalaí, on his right and left, and round about them seven figures of stone, representing virgins, which however are not worshipped. Ayanár is daily besought to protect his worshippers from evil spirits. The inhabitants of the villages have an annual festival in his honour, usually after the harvest.

AYATAYAMA—Texts of the Yajur-veda, revealed to Yajnawalkya by the sun in the form of a horse: the Texts thus imparted were unknown to Vaisampayana.

AYATI—One of the descendants of the daughters of Daksha who were married to the Rishis. Lakshmi the bride of Vishnu was the daughter of Bhrigu by Káyati. They had also two sons, Dhátri and Vidhátri, who married the two daughters of the illustrious Meru, *Ayati* and Niryati; and had by them each a son named Prana and Mrikanda.

AYODHYA—"The modern Oude, which is situated on the river Sarayu, the modern Gogra, about three hundred and fifty miles to the south-east of Delhi. In the present day the city of Ayodhyá has disappeared, and little is to be seen of the ancient site beyond a shapeless heap of ruins, a mass of rubbish and jungle which stretches along the southern bank of the Gogra river. But in olden time this city was one of the largest and most magnificent in Hindustan, and its memory is still preserved in every quarter of the Indian peninsula. Its geographical position is highly significant of the progress of Aryan invasion between two great epochs, namely, that of the war of Bhárata, and that of the birth of Ráma. In the Mahá Bhárata the Aryans had apparently advanced no further towards the south-east than the neighbourhod of Delhi; but in the Rámáyana they seem to have established a large and substantial Ráj in the very centre of Hindustan, and to have founded a metropolis which must ever be famous in the ancient History of India."—*Wheeler.*

The Rámáyana gives the following description of Ayodhyá: "The city of Ayodhyá was full of people, and every one was healthy and happy, and every one was well fed upon the best of rice; and every merchant in that city had storehouses filled with jewels from every quarter of the earth. The Brahmans constantly kept alive the sacrificial fire, and were deeply read in the Vedas and Vedángas, and were endowed with every excellent quality; they were profusely generous, and were filled with truth, zeal and compassion, equal to the great sages, and their minds and passions were under perfect control. All these Brahman sages had three classes of disciples; first, the youths who served them as servants serve their masters; then the students who were receiving instruction; and then the Brahmácháris who maintained themselves and their preceptors by collecting aims. Next to the Brahmyans were the Kshatriyas, who were all warriors, and were constantly exercised in the practise of arms in the presence of the Mahárája. After these were the Vaisyas, or merchants, who sold goods of every description, and who came from every corner of the earth. Last of all were the Súdras, who were ever engaged in devotion to the gods, and in the service of the Brahmans. Besides these there were jewellers and artificers, singing men and dancing women, charioteers and footmen, potters and smiths, painters and oilmen, sellers of flowers, and sellers of betelnut. In all that city of well-fed and happy people, no man was without learning, or practised a calling that did not belong to his family or caste, or dwelt in a mean habitation, or was without kinsmen. There were no misers, nor liars, nor thieves, nor tale-bearers, nor swindlers, nor boasters; none that were arrogant, malevolent, mean, or who lived at another's expense; and no man who had not abundance of children, or who lived less than a thousand years."

AYOMUKHA—One of the sons of Kaṣyapa by Danu, hence termed a Dánava.

AYOMUKHI—Iron-faced; a huge misshapen giantess who was wounded by Lakshmana in the forest of Krauncha.

AYOUIJA—'Not of woman born,' a name of Drona, in allusion to the legend of his having been born in a bucket.

AYURVEDA—The Veda of life.' A work on medicine, attributed to Dhanvantari, and sometimes regarded as a supplement to the *Atharvaveda.*

AYUS—The eldest son of Vikrams and Urvasi; Vikramorvasi, or the Hero and the Nymphs (Nahuṣa, Kṣattravṛddha, Rambha, Raji, and Anenas), is the title of a second drama attributed to Kálidása. Urvasi was one of the nymphs of heaven, and when love for the king induced her to dwell on earth, she had been warned that so soon as the king should see a son of hers she must return. From fear of this she kept her infant's birth concealed. Ayus was not seen by his father until he had grown up and was brought from the hermitage of the Rishi Chyavana. His inauguration as vice king then took place in circumstances of great splendour. The rite being concuded a chorus was heard without, invoking blessings upon Ayus—

"Son of the monarch the universe filling,
Son of the god of the mist-shedding night,
Son of the sage, whom the great Brahma;
willing,
Called, with creation, to life and to light."

—*A. and M.I.*, p. 205.

AYUTAYUS—A descendant of the Kuru princes: also a king of Magadha, the name of the future kings of Magadha as enumerated in the *V.P.*, p. 465.

B

BABHRU-VAHANA—Son of Arjuna by his wife Citrāṅgadā, daughter of the Rája of Manipura. Arjuna dwelt at Manipura for three years, and then according to previous arrangements took leave of his wife and son. He was adopted as the son of his maternal grandfather, and reigned at Maṇipura as his successor. He dwelt there in a palace of great splendour, surrounded with wealth and signs of power. When Arjuna went to Maṇipura with the horse intended for the *Aśuamedha*, there was a quarrel between Arjuna and King Babhrū-vahana, and the latter killed his father with an arrow. Repenting of his deed, he determined to kill himself, but he obtained from his step-mother, the Nāga princess Ulūpī, a gem which restored Arjuna to life. He returned with his father to Hastināpura. The description of this combat has been translated from the *Mahābhārata* by Troyer in his *Rājātarangini*, tome i, p. 578.

BADARAYANA—A name of Veda-Vyāsa, especially used for him as the reputed author of the Vedānta philosophy. He was the author of the *Brahmā Sūtras*, published in the *Biblictheca Indica.*

BADARI, BADARIKASRAMA—**(1)** A place sacred to Viṣṇu, near the Ganges in the Himālayas, particularly in Viṣṇu's dual form of Nara-Nārāyaṇa. Thus, in the *Mahābhārata*, Śiva addressing Arjuna, says, "Thou wast Nara in a former body, and, with Nārāyaṇa for thy companion, didst perform dreadful austerity at Badarī for many myriads of years." It is now known as Badarī-nātha, though this is properly a title of Viṣṇu as lord of Badarī. **(2)** An extensive forest near Benares, celebrated as the scene of many mythical austerities. Krishna is said to have stood "on the spacious Badari a hundred years with his arms aloft, on one foot, subsisting on air." (*O.S.T.*, Vol. iv)

BADAVA—"A mare, the submarine fire'. In mythology it is a flame with the head of a horse, called also Hayaśiras, 'horse-head', (*see* AURVA)

BADHAS—There are twenty-eight kinds of badhas, which in the Sánkya system mean imperfections or disabilities, as defects of the senses, blindness, deafness, &c., defects of intellect, as incapacity, ignorance, &c., and moral defects, as stubbornness, discontent, &c.

BADRAVATI—A city about fifty miles from Hastinápúr, from which Bhíma forcibly brought away the horse for the great Aswamedha sacrifice (*q.v.*) performed by Yudhishthira, after the great war.

BAHIKAS—People of the Panjāb, so-called in Pāṇini and the *Mahābhārata*. They are spoken of as being impure and out of the law.

BAHKALI, BAHKALA, BASHKALI—One of the arrangers of the Vedas. Paila divided the Rig Veda, and gave the two Sanhitas, or collections of hymns, to Indrapramati and to Bashkali. Bashkali sub-divided his Sanhita into four, which he gave to his disciples Baudha, Agnimáthara, Yajnawalka and Parásara; and they taught these secondary shoots from the primitive branch.

BAHLIKA—The son of Pratípa, brother of Sántanu and grand-uncle of Dhritarashtra. He governed an independent kingdom, which bore the same appellation, and is identifiable with the modern Balkh.

BAHU, BAHUKA—**(1)** A king of Ayodhya, the seventh in descent from Hariṣchandra. He was overcome by the Haihayas and Tálajangas, and compelled to fly with his queens to the forest, where he died. After his death one of his wives gave birth to a son, who received the name of Sagara (*q.v.*) When he had grown up the youth learnt from his mother all that had befallen his father, and vowed to exterminate the enemies who had conquered his paternal kingdom, He acquired great celebrity, and takes a conspicuous place in Hindu history. **(2)** The name of Nala when he was transformed into a dwarf.

BAHUGARA—A descendant of Puru, son of Sudyumna: called Bahuvidha in the Agni and Matsya Puránas.

BAHULA—**(1)** The name of one of the Prajápatis, *V.P.*, p. 50; **(2)** the name of the a Prince killed by Abhimanyu, (Linga Purana); and **(3)** the name of one of the rivers enumerated in the *V.P.*, p. 183.

BAHULAS—The Kṛttikās or Pleiades.

BAHULASWA—The last but one of the kings of Mithilá. His son was Kriti, with whom terminated the family of Janaka.

BAHUPUTRA—A Prajápati who married two daughters of Daksha, their children were the four lightnings, enumerated in Astrological works as brown, red, yellow and white; portending severally, wind, heat, rain, famine.

BAHURUPA—One of the eleven Rudras, or lords of the three worlds.

BAHUSALIN—A name of Bhíma.

BAHVRCA—A priest or theologian of the *Ṛgveda.*

BAHWASWA—Son of Mudgala, and father of Divodasa and Ahálya.

BAIDYANATHA—A celebrated place of pilgrimage situated on the north-western confines of Bengal, about 200 miles from Calcutta, and marked in the maps as Deogurh. It is said that the shrine of Baidyanatha traces its origin to a Santhal. The legend is that in the olden time a tribe of Brahmans settled on the banks of the highland laks near the temple. There was then nothing but forest and mountains amongst which dwelt the black races. The Brahmans placed the symbol of Śiva near the lake, and made sacrifices; the black tribes would not worship the new god, but came as before to the three great stones which their fathers worshipped. In process of time the Brahmans became indolent and neglected the worship of Siva. This excited the wonder of the black tribes, till at last one of them named Byju, a man of great strength and rich in cattle, vowed he would beat the symbol of the Brahman's god Śiva every day, before touching food. This he did; but one day his cows strayed into the forest, and after seeking them all day he came home hungry and weary, bathed in the lake and sat down to supper. Before eating, he remembered his vow, and tired as he was set off and beat the idol with his club. Suddenly a splendid form rose from the waters and said "Behold the man who forgets his hunger and weariness to beat me, while my priests sleep at home and give me neither to eat nor to drink. Let him ask of me what he will and it shall be given." Byju answered I am strong of arm and rich in cattle; I am a leader of my people; what want I more. Thou art called Nath (lord). Let me to be called Lord, and let thy temple go by my name." Amen ! replied the deity; henceforth thou art not Byju but Byjunáth, and my temple shall be called by thy name.* In Mookerja's Magazine there is a description of the temple in which it is said that in the right of the doorway in the verandah lie couchant the figures of four bulls, representing Naṇdi, the *vahana* or vehicle of Śiva. They are of different sizes, but none so large as a calf. In the inmost sanctum it is dark amid the blaze of noon, where the emblem is fixed. Before it burns a lamp day and night, fed with ghee. This helps to make visible a little stone—a phallus, cropping out of the ground, not higher than a span. It is Baidyanatha himself that stands manifest and greets the eye.

*HUNTER'S *Annals of R.B.*

BAJIARANA—One of the eight branches of Medical Science which treats of the use of aphrodisiacs.

BALABHADRA—(*See* BALARĀMA).

BALA-CHAKRAVARTI—A celebrated daitya or giant, who along with Narakasura was slain by Vishṇu, after a terrific combat. The conflict ended as the sun went down, and Vishṇu was thus unable to perform his diurnal ablutions in the day-time, and had to make them at night. In consequence of this the Brahmans once a year at the *Dípavali habba* bathe at night, a nocturnal ceremony of great merit, conducted with solemnity.

BALAGOPALA—The boy Kṛṣṇa.

BALAKHILYAS—Pigmy sages, no bigger than a joint of the thumb, chaste, pious, resplendent as the sun, whose chariot they constantly surround. The wife of the sage Kratu Sannati, brought forty the sixty thousand Bálakhilyas; another account says they were produced from the hair of Brahma. *V.P.*

BALARAMA—(Balabhadra and Baladeva are other forms of this name.) The elder brother of Kṛṣṇa. When Kṛṣṇa is regarded as a full manifestation of Viṣṇu, Balarāma is recognised as the eighth *avatāra* or incarnation in his place. According to this view, which is the favourite one of the Vaiṣṇavas, Kṛṣṇa is a full divinity and Balarāma an incarnation; but the story of their birth as told in the *Mahābhārata* places them more upon an equality. It says that Viṣṇu took two hairs, a white and a black one, and that these became Balarāma and Kṛṣṇa, the children of Devakī. Balarāma was of fair complexion, Kṛṣṇa was very dark. As soon as Barlarama was born, he was carried away to Gokula to preserve his life from the tyrant Kaṁsa, and Nanda there nurtured him as a child of Rohiṇī. He and Kṛṣṇa grew up together, and he took part in many of Kṛṣṇa's boyish freaks and adventures. His earliest exploit was the killing of the great *asura* Dhenuka, who had the form of an ass. This demon attacked him, but Balarāma seized his assailant, whirled him round by his legs till he was dead, and cast his carcass into a tree. Another *asura* attempted to carry off Balarāma on his shoulders, but the boy beat out the demon's brains with his fists. When Kṛṣṇa went to Mathurā, Balarāma accompanied him, and manfully supported him till Kaṁsa was killed. Once, when Balarāma was intoxicated, he called upon the Yamunā river to come to him, that he might bathe; but his command not being heeded, he plunged his ploughshare into the river, and dragged the waters whithersoever he went, until they were obliged to assume a human form and beseech his forgiveness. This action gained for him the title Yamunābhid and Kālindi-karsana, breaker or dragger of the Yamunā. He killed Rukmin in a gambling brawl. When Duryodhana detained Śamba, son of Kṛṣṇa, as a prisoner at Hastināpura, Balarāma demanded his release, and, being refused, he thrust his ploughshare under the ramparts of the city, and drew them towards him, thus compelling the Kauravas to give up their prisoner. Lastly, he killed the great ape Dvivida, who had stolen his weapons and derided him.

Such are some of the chief incidents of the life of Balarāma, as related in the Purāṇas, and as popular among the votaries of Kṛṣṇa. In the *Mahābhārata* he has more of a human character. He taught both Duryodhana and Bhīma the use of the mace. Though inclining to the side of the Pāṇḍavas, he refused to take an active part either with them or the Kauravas. He witnessed the combat between Duryodhana and Bhīma, and beheld the foul blow struck by the latter, which made him so indignant that he seized his weapons, and was with difficulty restrained by Kṛṣṇa from falling upon the Pāṇḍavas. He died just before Kṛṣṇa, as he sat under a Banyan tree in the outskirts of Dvārakā.

Another view is held as to the origin of Balarāma. According to this he was an incarnation of the great serpent Śeṣa, and when he died the serpent is said to have issued from his mouth.

The "wine-loving" Balarāma (Madhupriya or Priyamadhu) was as much addicted to wine as his brother Kṛṣṇa was devoted to the fair sex. He was also irascible in temper, and sometimes quarreled even with Kṛṣṇa: the Purāṇas represent them as having a serious difference about the *syamantaka* jewel. He had but one wife, Revatī, daughter of King Raivata, and was faithful to her. By her he had two sons, Niśaṭha and Ulmuka. He is represented as of fair complexion, and, as Nīlavastra, 'clad in a dark-blue vest'. His especial weapons are a club (*khetaka* or *saunanda*), the ploughshare (*hala*), and the pestle (*mūsala*) from which he is called Phāla and Hāla, also Halāyudha, 'plough-armed'; Halabhṛt, 'plough-bearer'; Lāṅgali and Saṅkarṣana, 'ploughman'; and Mūsalī, 'pestle-holder'. As he has a palm for a banner, he is called Tāladhvaja. Other of his appellations are Guptacara, 'who goes secretly'; Kāmpāla and Samvartaka.

BALA-RAMAYANA—A drama by Rājaśekhara. It has been printed.

BALEYA—A descendant of Bali, a *daitya.*

BALHI—A northern country, Balkh. Said in the *Mahābhārata* to be famous for its horses, as Balkh is to the present time.

BALHIKAS, BAHLIKAS—"Always associated with the people of the north, west, and ultra-Indian provinces, and usually considered to represent the Bactrians or people of Balkh."—*Wilson*

BÀLI, BÀLIN—The monkey king of Kiskindhā, who was slain by Rāma, and whose kingdom was given to his brother Sugrīva, the friend and ally of Rāma. He was supposed to be the son of Indra, and to have been born from the hair (*bāla*) of his mother, whence his name. His wife's name was Tara, and his sons Angada and Tāra.

BALI—**(1)** A celebrated Daitya, the son of Virochana, son of Prahlāda, son of Hiraṇyakaśipu, who rose to such an eminence in power that Indra and the other gods had to apply for the interference of Vishṇu to protect them from the destructive effects of Bali's rule. The Mahábhárata gives the following legend respecting Bali, as related by Viswámitra to the two young princes, Ráma and Lakshmana, when they visited his hermitage:—

> "In ancient days, before the glorious Vishṇu became incarnate as the Dwarf, this was his holy hermitage, and here he practised sacred austerities as an example to all others. And it came to pass that Bali, the mighty Rája of the Asuras, conquered Indra and the gods; and the gods came to this hermitage and prayed to Vishṇu for succour; And Vishṇu was born on earth in the form of a Dwarf, and he assumed the dress of a mendicant, and went to the abode of Bali, and prayed Bali to give him as much earth as he could step over in three steps: And Bali granted his request: then Vishnu took upon himself a might form, and took three steps; and the first step covered the earth, and the second covered the heavens, and the third was on the head of Bali: And Vishṇu bound Bali, and sent him and all his legions to the realms below the earth, and once more restored the universe to the rule of Indra."

The meaning of this myth is not very obvious. It is said to have originated in an obscure Vedic idea that Vishṇu as the Sun took three steps; *viz.* first, on the earth at his rising; secondly, in the heavens at noonday; and thirdly, on the under-world at his setting. (See Wilson's *Rig Veda*, Vol. I, p. 53, *note.*) The legend however is exceedingly popular, probably on account of the successful trick played against the giant; and a festival is still celebrated in memory of the so-called event.

Bali then became the Sovereign of Pátála. He is said to have had a hundred sons. His wife was Vindhyāvalī. **(2)** An oblation; the last portion of the offering of rice, *&c.*, thrown into the air for the spirits of ilī, the *genii locorum.* At the end of the daily ceremony the householder is enjoined by Manu "to throw up his *bali* in the open air to all the gods, to those who walk by day and those who walk by night."

BÀNA—A *daitya*, eldest son of the hundered sons of Bali, who had a thousand arms. He was a friend of Śiva and enemy of Viṣṇu. His daughter Ūṣā fell in love with Aniruddha, the grandson of Kṛṣṇa, and had him conveyed to her by magic art. Kṛṣṇa, Balarāma, and Pradyumna went to the rescue, and were resisted by Bāṇa, who was assisted by Śiva and Skanda, god of war. Śiva was overpowered by Kṛṣṇa; Skanda was wounded; and the many arms of Bāṇa were cut off by the missile weapons of Kṛṣṇa. Śiva then interceded for the life of Bāṇa and Kṛṣṇa granted it. He is called also Vairoci.

BANDDHAS—Those who take nothing upon authority and admit nothing that cannot be proved; or it is explained, those who by argument cast a doubt upon the efficacy of acts of devotion.

BANDHAYANAS—Followers of a branch of the Vajasanciyi, or white Yajush.

BANDHYA—A disciple of Bashkala, who made him a teacher of a portion of the Sanhita of the Rig Véda.

BANGA—Bengal, but not in the modem application. In ancient times Baṅga meant the districts north of the Bhāgīrathī—Jessore, Kṛṣṇagar, &c. (*see* ANU)

BARBARAS—Name of a people.The analogy to 'barbarians' is not in sound only, but in all the authorities these are classed with borders and foriegners and nations not Hindu."—*Wilson.*

BARHISADS—A class of *pitṛs*, who, when alive, kept up the household flame, and presented offerings with fire. Some authorities identify them with the months. Their dwelling is Vaibhrājaloka. (*see* PITṚS)

BASAVA PURANA—The Purána that narrates the life of Basava the founder or restorer of the Jangama sect. Professor H. H. Wilson places the date of the events it records in the early part of the eleventh century./ Basava's parents were both devout worshippers of Śiva. In recompense of their piety, *Nandi*, the bull of Śiva, was born on earth as their son, becoming incarnate by command of Śiva, on his learning from Narada the decline of the *Saiva* faith and prevalence of other less orthodox systems of religion. The child was denominated after the *Basava* or *Basava*, the bull of the deity. On his arriving at the age of investitutre he refused to assume the thread ordinarily worn by brahmans, or to acknowledge any *Guru* except ISWARA or ŚIVA. He then departed to the town of *Kalyán*, the capital of *Bijala* or *Vijala Ráya*, and obtained in marriage *Gangámbá*, the daughter of the *Dandanáyak*, or minister of police. From thence he repaired to *Sangameśvara*, where he received from *Sangameśvara Svámí* initiation in the tenets of the *Vira Saiva* faith. He was invited back from this palace to succeed his father-in-law upon his decease in the office he had held.

After his return to Kalyán, his sister, who was one of his first disciples, was delivered of a son, *Chenna Basava*, who is not unfrequently confounded with his uncle, and regarded, perhaps more correctly, as the founder of the sect.

After recording these events the work enumerates various marvellous actions performed by Basava and several of his disciples, such as converting grains of corn to perals—discovering hidden treasures—feeding multitudes—healing the sick and restoring the dead to life. The following are some of the anecdotes narrated in the *Purána*:

Basava having made himself remarkable for the profuse bounties he bestowed upon the *Jangamas*, helping himself from the Royal Treasury for that purpose, the other ministers reported his conduct to *Bijala*, who called upon him to account for the money in his charge. Basava smiled, and giving the keys of the Treasury to the king, requested him to examine it, which being done, the amount was found wholly undiminished. Bijala thereupon caused it to be proclaimed, that whoever calumniated Basava should have his tongue cut out.

A *Jangama*, who cohabited with a dancing girl, sent a slave for his allowance of rice to the house of Basava, where the messenger saw the wife of the latter, and on his return reported to the dancing girl the magnificence of her attire. The mistress of the Jangama was filled with alonging for a similar dress, and the Jangama having no other means of gratifying her, repaired to Basava, to beg of him his wife's garment. Basava immediately stripped Gangámbá, his wife, and other dresses springing from her body, he gave them all to the Jangama

A person of the name of *Kanapa*, who regularly worshipped the image of EKAMRESVARA, imagining the eyes of the deity were affected, plucked out his own, and placed them in the sockets of the figure. ŚIVA, pleased with his devotion, restored his worshipped his eyes.

A devout *Saiva* named *Mahadevala Macháya*, who engaged to wash for all the *Jangamas*, having killed a child, the Rája ordered Basava to have him secured and punished; but Basava declined undertaking the duty, as it would be unavailing to offer any harm to the worshippers of ŚIVA. *Bijala* persisting,sent his servants to seize and tie him to the legs of an elephant, but *Macháya* caught the elephant by the trunk, and dashed him and his attendants to pieces. He then proceeded to attack the Rája, who being alarmed applied to Basava, and by his advice humbled himself before the offended Jangama. Basava also deprecated his wrath, and *Macháya* being appeased, forgave the king and restored the elephant and the guards to life.

A poor Jangama having solicted alms of *Kinnaráyu*, one of Basava's chief disciples, the latter touched the stones about them with his staff, and converting them into gold, told the Jangama to help himself.

The work is also in many places addressed to the Jainas in the shape of a dialogue between some of the Jangama saints, and the members of that faith, in which the former narrate to the latter instances of the superiority of the *Saiva* religion, and the falsehood of the *Jain* faith, which appears to have been that of *Bijala Ráya* and the great part of the population of *Kalyána.* In order to convert them, *Ekánta Ramáya*, one of the Basava's disciples, cut off his head in their presence, and then marched five days in solemn procession through and round the city, and on the fifth day replaced his head upon his shoulders. The Jain Pagodas were thereupon, it is said, destroyed by the Jangamas. It does not appear, however, that the king was made a convert, or that he approved of the principles and conduct of his minister. He seems, on the contrary, to have incurred his death by attempting to repress the extension of the *Víra Saiva* belief. Different authorities, although they disagree as to the manner in which Bijala was destroyed, concur in stating the fact: the following account of the transaction is from the Basava Purána:—

"In the city of *Kalyána* were two devout worshippers of Śiva, named *Allaya* and *Madhuvaya.* They fixed their faith firmly on the divinity they adored, and assiduously reverenced their spiritual preceptor, attending upon *Basava* whithersoever he went. The king, *Bijala*, well knew their merits, but closed his eyes to their superiority, and listening to the calumnious accusations of their enemies, commanded the eyes of *Allaya* and *Madhuvaya* to be plucked out. The disciples of Basava, as well as himself, were highly indignant at the cruel treatment of these holy men, and leaving to *Jagaddeva* the task of putting *Bijala* to death, and denouncing imprecations upon the city, they departed from *Kalyána*, Basava fixed his residence at *Sangamesvara.*

Macháya, *Bommidevaya*, *Kinnara*, *Kannatha*, *Bommadeva*, *Kakaya*, *Masanaya*, *Kolakila Bommadeva*, *Kesirajaya*, *Mathirajaya*, and others, announced to the people that the fortunes of *Bijala* had passed away, as indicated by portentous signs; and accordingly the crows crowed in the night, jackals howled by day; the sun was eclipsed, storms of wind and rain came on, the earth shook, and darkness overspread the heavens. The inhabitants of *Kalyána* were filled with terror.

When *Jagaddeva* repaired home, his mother met him, and told him that when any injury had been done to a disciple of the *Saiva* faith, his fellow should avenge him or die. When *Daksha* treated Śiva with contumely, Párvatí threw herself into the flames, and so, under the wrong offered to the saints, he should not sit down contented: thus saying, she gave him food at the door of his mansion. Thither also came *Mallaya* and *Bommaya*, two others of the saints, and they partook of *Jagaddeva's* meal. Then smearing their bodies with holy ashes, they took up the spear, and sword, and shield, and marched together against *Bijala.* On their way a bull appeared, whom they knew to be a form of *Basava*, came to their aid, and the bull went first even to the court of the king, goring any one that came in their way, and opening a clear path for them. Thus they reached the court, and put *Bijala* to death in the midst of all his courtiers, and then they danced, and proclaimed the cause why they had put the king to death. *Jagaddeva* on his way back, recalling the words of his mother, stabbed himself. Then arose dissension in the city, and the people fought amongst themselves, and horses with horses, and elephants with elephants, until, agreeably to the curse denounced upon it by Basava and his disciples, *Kalyána* was utterly destroyed.

Basava continued to reside at *Sangamesvara*, conversing with his disciples, and communing with the divine Essence, and he expostulated with Śiva saying: 'By thy command have I, and thy attendant train, come upon earth, and thou hast promised to recall us to thy presence when our task was accomplished.' Then Śiva and Párvatí came forth from the *Sangamesvara Lingam*, and were visible to *Basava*, who fell on the ground before them. They raised him, and led him to the sanctuary, and all three disappeared in the presence of the disciples, and they praised their master, and flowers fell from the sky, and then the disciples spread themselves abroad, and made known the absorption of Basava into the emblem of Śiva."—Mackenzie's *Collect.*, *Vol. 2nd*; Hálakanara *MSS.* [pp. 3-12.]; Wilson's *Works*, Vol. I, p. 225.

BASAVA—The founder of the Lingait sect. He was originally an Aradhya brahman, and evidently a man of great independency of mind and possessed of great moral courage. He was born about the middle of the eleventh century, in a village to the east of Biájpúr in the Collectorate of Kalladighee. "Having become prime minister at the Court of Kaláyana, the capital of a great empire, which then stretched from ocean to ocean, he succeeded gradually in founding a new sect, called the Lingait, from its votaries wearing the Linga, which they consider to be the true symbol of the Creative divine power. This great success may be attributed to two, perhaps three causes, Basava had great power, popularity and influence, from his high station in life. Converts from Jainism to Lingaitism were unduly favored, though Basava's master, king Bajal, still remained a Jain. Basava is said to have connived at the intercourse the king had with a beautiful sister, and had great power over him. Pecuniary assistance was largely given to itinerant priests of the sec who went about preaching to the people. The second cause of Basava's success was that he addressed himself chiefly to the lower classes. These were flattered by the prospect of their social position being improved if they embraced the new religion. And indeed taking the Linga and becoming a Lingait, was according to the ideas of the Hindus, a step in advance. For the great privilege of wearing this sacred symbol on the body had been to that time confined exclusively to the brahmans. In fact Basava at first merely introduced the peculiar Linga worship, as it was performed by the Aradhya brahmans, to whom he himself belonged, among the different classes of Śudras.

"The spread of the sect was wide and rapid, so that even in the neighbouring *Telugu* and *Tamil* countries, many became the worshippers of Basava; and books regarded as sacred, still extant, were written in those tongues in honor of him. The king however disapproved of this great change. He hated and persecuted the Lingaits. This led to his assassination in his own palace, by two fanatic Lingaits, who it is said were encouraged by Basava. A civil war then broke out, and the empire of Kalyána fell to pieces. Basava was thus the cause of great revolutions in the Deccan. It was to be expected that such a man would, after the lapse of sometime, be deified by credulous men, and the real facts of his history obscured by a mass of legendary lore."—*Wöerth.*

BASAVA—The name of a bull in the Canarese and Telugu langauges, and applied to Nandi the vehicle of Śiva.

BASUSI—The serpent who vomited forth poison at the churning of the milk-sea.

BAUDHAYANA—A writer on Dharmaśāstra or law. He was also the author of a Sūtra work,

BBRAHMADATTA—A sage, the son of Anuha. In the Hari Vamsam is a curious legend of the different transmigrations of Brahmadatta and his six companions, who were successively as many brahmans, then forests, then deer, then water fowl, then swans, and finally, brahmans again, when with the king they obtained liberation. According to the Bhágavat, Brahmadatta composed a treatise on the Yôga, a yóga tantra.

BEERBHOOM—Properly *Vir-bhúmi*, the hero-land. On the frontier of Lower Bengal, between the lofty plateau of Central India, and the valley of the Ganges. This country was the theatre of one of the primitive struggles of Indian history. It stood as the outpost of the Sanscrit race, on the west of Lower Bengal, and had to bear the sharp collisions of Aryan civilization, with the ruder types prevailing among the aborigines. On its inhabitants devolved, during three thousand years, the duty of holding the passes between the highlands and the valley of the Ganges. To this day they are a manlier race than their kinsmen of the plains, and from the beginning of history, one of the two kingdoms has borne the name of Mala-bhúmi, the country of the Wrestlers,—the other the appellation of Vir-bhúmi, the Hero-land.—Hunter, *Rural Bengal.*

BENARES—The sacred city of the Hindus. It is called Kási, Váranási, Atimukta. It was once destroyed by the discus of Krishṇa. "The whole of a city that was inaccessible to gods, was wrapped in flames by the discuss of Hari, and was totally destroyed." *V.P.*, Chap. xxiv. "The term Kási, denominating, if not a city, a people and its chieftains, occurs repeatedly in Sanscrit works of all but the highest antiquity...The kingdom of the Kási and its rulers, as is evinced by the frequency of reference to them, enjoyed from distant ages, more or less of notoriety; and this is substantially all that the Hindu memorials teach us. The Puránas specify but one dynasty of Kási kings; a goodly catalogue, beginning in the most authoritative of those works, with the son of Kása. To Kása, by a lapse of perhaps two centuries, succeeded Divodása, in whose reign Buddhism seems still to have been acting on the aggressive. In this synchronism there is no discernible improbability; and with some likelihood it embodies an historic fact. A reflection of actual events may likewise be afforded in the story of the burning of Váranasí by the discus of Vishnu."—*Hall.*

BHADRĀ—Wife of Utathya (*q.v.*). **(1)** 'Auspicious', 'fortunate'. A name of Durgā; of Vaiśravaṇa's wife; of a daughter of Soma and wife of Utathya; and of one of Kṛṣna's queens. **(2)** The name of one of the four branches of the celestial Ganges (*gaṅgā*) which flows from Mount Meru through the land of the Uttarakurus to the northern ocean. The other three branches are the Sītā, Alakanandā and the Cakṣu (*VP.*,II.2). **(3)** Name of a daughter of Rohini and mother of goats and sheep

(*Vāyu. P.*, III. 3.74-5, *PI.*). **(4)** The wife of the fabulous bird Garuda (*Vayu P.*, 69.328, *PI.*). **(5)** The word Bhadra is used as another name of Subhadra, sister of Sri Krisna. **(6)** One of the wives of Kubera. Once Kunti narrated her story to Pancali and urged her to live like Bhadra.

BHADRABAHU—(1) A son of Vasudeva by his wife Róhiní. **(2)** The author of the Kalpa Sútra, the most sacred religious work of the Jainas. He lived in the early part of the fifth century of the Christian era, but nothing is known of his personal history, though his work is held in such reverence.

BHADRACARU—A son of Kṛṣṇa and Rukmiṇī.

BHADRADEAH—A son of Vasudeva by his wife Devaki. He and his five brothes were killed by Kansa.

BHADRAKĀLĪ—(1) Name of a goddess. In modern times it applies to Durgā. **(2)** A Rudra sprung from the anger of Deví, and sent by Śiva to destroy the sacrifice of Daksha (*V.P.*, Chap. viii). Lord Siva, on hearing about the self-immolation in fire of his wife, Sati at the famous yagna conducted by Daksa rushed in all anger to the spot, and beat the earth with his matted locks, and there were born two forces called Virabhadra and Bhadrakali. This Bhadrakali was Sati or Parvati in another form.

She was probably a nature goddess adopted by Saivas. She bestows boons on children when propitiated by human sacrifice, but became enraged when she discovered that the virtuous *brahmana* Bharata was to be the victim (*Bhag*, *P*. v. 9.12-18) P1.). Bhadrākālī fought on the side of Śumbha and Niśumbha in the war of the gods and the *asuras.* **(3)** Name of one of the *Matris* who attended upon Skanda (Kartikeya)

BHADRASANA—(1) The posture in which the Yógi is directed to sit when engaged in meditation: *viz.*, to cross his legs underneath him and to lay hold of his feet on each side with his hands. **(2)** One of the six sons of Vasudeva, who were killed by Kansa.

BHADRASAVA—A country to the east of Meru, and Ketumala on the west; and between these two is the region of Ilavrita. Four great lakes are near, the waters of which are partaken of by the gods. Bhadraswas is one of the eight varshas or countries described as places of perfect enjoyment, where happiness is spontaneous and uninterrupted. In them there is no vicissitude, no dread of decrepitude or death, there is no distinction of virtue or vice, no difference of degree as better or worse, nor any of the effects produced in this region by the revolutions of ages.

BHADRASRENYA—A Yádava prince, the son of Mahishmat. He is said to have had a hundred sons, all of whom but one, Durdama, were slain by Divadása, the Rája of Benares. Durdama was spared, being an infant; and he lived to recover his patrimonial possessions.

BHADRA—(1) The name of one of the many wives of Vasudeva. **(2)** A celebrated horse, son of Uchchaiḥśravas.

BHADRAVINDA—A son of Krishṇa, who is said to have had in all one hundred and eighty thousand.

BHAGA—An Áditya; the fifth of the eight sons of Aditi. His eyes were knocked out by Rudra (Śiva). "Rudra of dreadful power then ran up to the gods, and in his rage knocked out the eyes of Bhaga with a blow, and incensed, assaulted Púshan with his food, and knocked out his teeth as he was eating the puroḍása offering."* See Savitṛi. He is supposed to bestow wealth and to preside over marriage, and he is classed among the Ādityas and Viśvedevas. **(2)** One of the twelve Ádityas; in the Manwantara of Vaivaswata

* Muir, *O.S.T.*, Vol. iv, p. 168.

BHAGANETRA—A Daitya or Titan slain by Śiva.

BHAGA-NETRAGHNA (or **HAN**)—'Destroyer of the eyes of Bhaga.' An appellation of Śiva.

BHAGAVAD GITA—'The song of the Divine One'. A celebrated episode *of the Mahdbharata*, in the form of a metrical dialogue, in which the divine Kṛṣṇa is the chief speaker, and expounds to Arjuna his philosophical doctrines. The author of the work is unknown, but he "was probably a brāhmaṇa, and nominally a Vaiṣṇava, but really a philosopher and thinker, whose mind was cast in a broad mould". This poem has been interpolated in the *Mahābhārata*, for it is of much later date than the body of that epic; it is later also than the six Darśanas or philosophical schools, for it has received inspiration from them all, especially from the Sāṃkhya, Yoga, and Vedānta. The second or third century AD has been proposed as the probable time of its appearance. Kṛṣṇa, as a god, is a manifestation of Viṣṇu; but in this song, and in the other places, he is held to be the supreme being. As man, he was related to both the Pāṇḍavas and the Kauravas, and in the great war between these two families he refused to take up arms on either side. But he consented to act as the Pāṇḍava Arjuna's charioteer. When the opposing hosts were drawn up in the array against each other, Arjuna, touched with compunction for the approaching slaughter of kindred and friends, appeals to Kṛṣṇa for guidance. This gives the occasion for the philosophical teaching. "The poem is divided into three sections, each containing six chapters, the philosophical teaching in each being somewhat distinct", but "undoubtedly the main design of the poem, the sentiments expressed in which have exerted a powerful influence throughout India for the last 1600 years, is to inculcate the doctrine *of bhakti* (faith), and to exalt the duties of caste above all other obligations, including those of friendship and kindred". So Arjuna is told to do his duty as a soldier without heeding the slaughter of friends. "In the second division of the poem the Pantheistic doctrines of the Vedānta are more directly inculcated than in the other sections. Kṛṣṇa here, in the plainest language, claims adoration as one with the great universal spirit pervading and constituting the universe." The language of this poem is exceedingly beautiful, and its tone and sentiment of a very lofty character, so that they have a striking effect even in the prose translation. It was one of the earliest Sanskṛt works translated into English by Wilkins; but a much more perfect translation, with an excellent introduction, has since been published by Mr. J. Cockburn Thompson, from which much of the above has been borrowed. There are several other translations in French, German, &c.

BHAGAVATA PURANA—The Purāṇa "in which ample details of duty are described, and which opens with (an extract from) the Gāyatrī; that in which the death of the *asura* Vṛtra is told, and in which the mortals and immortals of the Sārapvata Kalpa, with the events that then happened to them in the world, are related, that is celebrated as the Bhāgavata, and consists of 18,000 verses". Such is the Hindu description of this work. "The Bhāgavata," says Wilson, "is a work of great celebrity in India, and exercises a more direct and powerful influence upon the opinions and feelings of the people than perhaps any other of the Purāṇas. It is placed fifth in all the lists, but the Padma ranks it as the eighteenth, as the extracted substance of all the rest. According to the usual specification, it consists of 18,000 *ślokas*, distributed amongst 332 chapters, divided into twelve *skandhas* or books. It is named Bhāgavata from its being dedicated to the glorification of Bhāgavata or Viṣṇu." The most popular and characteristic part of this. Purāṇa is the tenth book, which narrates in detail the history of Kṛṣṇa, and has been translated into perhaps all the vernacular languages of India. Colebrooke concurs in the opinion of many learned Hindus that this Purāṇa is the composition of the grammarian Vopadeva, who lived about six or seven centuries ago at the court of Hemādri, Rājā of Devagiri (Deogurh or Daulatābād), and Wilson sees no reason for calling in question the tradition which assigns the work to this writer. This Purāṇa has been translated into French by Burnouf, and has been published with the text in three volumes folio, and in other forms.

BHAGAVAT—Vishṇu. The Supreme Being. The letter *Bh* implies the cherisher and supporter of the universe. By *ga* is understood the leader, impeller, or creator. The dissyllable Bhaga indicates the six properties, dominion, might, glory, splendour, wisdom and dispassion. The purport of the letter *va* is, that elemental spirit in which all beings exist, and which exists in all beings. And thus this great word Bhagavat is the name of the Vasudeva, who is one with the Supreme Brahma, and of no one else. *V.P.*, Book vi, Chapter 5.

BHAGIRATHA—The son of Rája Dilípa, who spent a thousand years in severe austerities upon a mountain, by which he propitiated Brahma and Śiva, and brought the Ganges to the earth; and with it watered the ashes of the sixty thousand sons of Sagara, who were at once restored to life, purified by the sacred water from all their sins, and ascended to heaven.

"Soon as the flood their dust bedewed,
Their spirits gained beatitude,
And all in heavenly bodies dressed,
Rose to the skies' eternal rest.

"Then thus to king Bhagírath said,
Brahma, when, coming at the head
of all his bright celestial train,
He saw those spirits freed from stain;
'Well done! great Prince of men, well done!
Thy kinsmen bliss and heaven have won.'
The sons of Sagar mighty-souled,
Are with the Blest, as Gods, enrolled."

—Griffiths' *Rámáyana.*

"The saintly king Bhagíratha, in his chariot of gold and ivory, put himself at the head of the Gangá to direct and guide her footsteps. Singing, and dancing, and laughing, and scattering jewels on all sides, the obedient Gangá followed, kissing the trace of his chariot, and babbling words of endearment. Bhagíratha directing his steps to the sea, the docile Gangá followed. From thence he led her into the bowels of the earth, into the gloomy regions of Tartarus. There having performed the ceremony of lustrous waters in honour of his sixty thousand ancestors, he beheld the illustrious Sagarides, clothed in ethereal purity, ascend with rapturous joy to the home of the deathless gods."

BHAGIRATHI—The Ganges. The name is derived from Bhagīratha, a descendant of Sagara, whose austerities induced Śiva to allow the sacred river to descend to the earth for the purpose of bathing the ashes of Sagara's sons, who had been consumed by the wrath of the sage Kapila. Bhagīratha named the river Sāgara, and after leading it over the earth to the sea, he conducted it to Pātāla, where the ashes of his ancestors were laved with its waters and purified.

BHAIMYEKADASI—The eleventh lunar day of the light half other Mágha (10th February.) This is also a festival of traditional origin, said to have been first observed by Bhíma, one of the Pándu princes, in honor of Vishṇu, according to the instructions of Vasudeva. Every eleventh lunar day, it may be observed, is held in extravagant veneration by the Hindus, but more particularly by the Vaishnávas. Fasting on the eleventh is declared to be equally efficacious with a thousand a Śwamedhas, and eating during its continuance as heinous a sin as parricide, or the murder of a spiritual teacher. This extravagance demonstrates its sectarian character, and consequently its more modern origin. The notion may have grown, however, out of particular appropriations of the lunar day, when the eleventh was set apart, as in the present case, to the adoration of Vishṇu.—*Wilson.*

BHAIRAVA (mas.), **BHAIRAVI** (fem.)—'The terrible.' Name of Śiva and his wife Devī. The Bhairavas are eight inferior forms or manifestations of Śiva, all of them of a terrible character—(1) Asitāṅga, black limbed; (2) Saṁhāra, destruction; (3) Ruru, a dog; (4) Kālā, black; (5) Krodha, anger; (6) Tāmracūḍā, red crested; (7) Candracūḍā, moon crested; (8) Mahā, great. Other names are met with as variants: Kapāla, Rudra, Bhīṣaṇa,Unmatta, Ku-pati, &c. In these forms Śiva often rides upon a dog, wherefore he is called Śvāśva, 'whose horse is a dog'.

BHAJAMANA—A son of Andhaka, according to all the best authorities; the Agni makes him the son of Babhru.

BHAJINA—A son of Satwata.

BHAKTI—Faith; this is regarded by a sect of the Vaishnava, that founded by Chaitanya, as infinitely more efficacious than abstraction; than knowledge of the divine nature—as enjoined by the philosophical systems—than the subjugation of the passions, than the practice of the Yoga, than charity, virtue, or anything deemed most meritorious. A consequence resulting from this doctrine is, that all castes become by such faith equally pure, and therefore that all castes are admissible into the sect; that all are at liberty to sink their social differences in the condition of ascetics, in which character they may live with each other without regard to former distinctions, and that all members of the sect are equally entitled to the food which has been previously presented to the deity. The *Bhakti*, or faith, comprehends five stages: quietism, as that of sages; servitude, which every votary takes upon himself; friendship for the deity, such as is felt by Bhíma and others honoured with his acquaintance; tender affection for the deity, of the same nature as love of parents for their children; and the highest degree of affection, such passionate attachment as the Gopis felt for their beloved Krishṇa.—*Wilson.*

BHALANDANA—A son of Nábhága, who had carried off and married the daughter of a Vaisya, in consequence of which he was degarded to the same caste, and deprived of his share of the patrimonial sovereignty, which his son and successor, Bhalandana, afterwards recovered.

BHALLADA, BHALLAKA, BHALLATTA—A king of Hastinápura, the last of the race of Hastin, who had founded the city; which was destroyed by the encroachments of the Ganges.

BHAMAHA—The commentator on the oldest extant grammarian Vararuchi. His commentary is called Manoramá.

BHAMATI—A gloss on Śaṅkara's commentary upon the *Brahmā Sutras* by Vacaspati Miśra. It has been published in the *Bibliotheca Indica.*

BHANA—In dramatic compositions a monologue in one act, in which the performer narrates dramatically a variety of occurrences as happening either to himself or others. Love, war, fraud, intrigue, and imposition, are appropriate topics, and the narrator may enliven his recitation by a suppositions dialogue with an imaginary interlocutor. The language must be polished, and music and singing should precede and close the performance. It is not improbable that ventriloquism assisted to give effect to the imaginary dialogue, as the art is not unknown in India.—Wilson. *Works*, *XI*, *p*. 28.

BHANU—(1) A son of Krishṇa and Satyabháma. **(2)** The daughter of Daksha, wife of Kaṣyapa, who became one of the ten wives of Dharma.

BHANUMAT—A prince, the son of Kusadhwaja, king of Kási or Benaras; or according to the Rámáyana of Sankasya.

BHANUMATI—(Bhánumati), Daughter of Bhānu, a Yādava chief, who was abducted from her home in Dvārakā, during the absence of her father, by the demon Nikumbha. The wife of Duryodhana. During the great war she is said to have had a dream in which she saw a Nakula or mungoose destroy a hundred snakes. This was considered ominous, Nakula being the name of one of the Páṇḍava princes, and the sons of Kuru amounting to a hundred. Duryodhana was at first disposed to be alarmed by it, but afterwards determined to disregard it.

BHANUS—The sons of Bhanu, who became suns, and deities presiding over moments of Muhúrtta.

BHARADVAJA—(1) A *ṛṣi* to whom many Vedic hymns are attributed. He was the son of Bṛhaspati and father of Droṇa, the preceptor of the Pāṇḍavas. The *Taittirīya Brāhmaṇa* says that "he lived through three lives" (probably meaning a life of great length), and that "he became immortal and ascended to the heavenly world, to union with the sun". In the *Mahābhārata* he is represented as living at Haridvār; in the *Rāmāyaṇa* he received Rāma and Sītā is his hermitage at Prayāga, which was then and afterwards much celebrated. According to some of the Purāṇas and *the Harivamśa*, he became by gift or adoption the son of King Bharata, and an absurd story is told about his birth to account for his name: His mother, the wife of Utathya, was pregnant by her husband and by Bṛhaspati. Dīrghatamas, the son by her husband, kicked his half-brother out of the womb before his time, when Bṛhaspati said to his mother, 'Bharadvājam', 'Cherish this child of two fathers'. **(2)** One of the eight celebrated Rishis, the reputed father of Dróna. His hermitage was at Prayága, the modern Allahabad; he is said to have dwelt there surrounded by a band of Brahman disciples, 'who lead the ideal life of austerity, sacrifice, and devotion, which is so frequently described and lauded by Brahmanical bards.' He received Ráma and Síta when they set forth on their exile, and recommended the hill Chitra-kúta as a residence. The Rámáyana says, 'the great Bhara-dwája commanded Bharata to bring his whole army to the hermitage that he might feast them.

'Bring all thy host,' the hermit cried,
And Bharat, to his joy, complied.
Then to the chapel went he sire,
Where ever burnt the sacred fire,
And first, in order due, with sips
Of water purified his lips:
To Viṣvakarmá then he prayed,
His hospitable feast to aid:
Let Viṣvakarmá hear my call,
The God who forms and fashions all:
A mighty banquet I provide,
Be all my wants this day supplied.
Lord Indra at their head, the three
Who guard the worlds I call to me:
A mighty host this day I feed,
Be now supplied me every need.
Let all the streams that eastward go,
And those whose waters westering flow,
Both on the earth and in the sky,
Flow hither and my wants supply.
Be some with ardent liquor filled,
And some with wine from flowers distilled,
While some their fresh cool streams retain
Sweet as the juice of sugar-cane.
I call the Gods, I call the band
Of minstrels that around them stand:
I call the Háhá and Huhú,
I call the sweet Viṣvávasu.
I call the heavenly wives of these
With all the bright Apsarases,
Alambushá of beauty rare,
The charmer of the tangled hair,
Ghritáchi and Viṣváchí fair,
Hemá and Bhimá sweet to view,
And lovely Nágadantá too,
And all the sweetest nymphs who stand
By Indra or by Brahmá's hand—
summon these with all their train
And Tumburu to lead the strain.

* * *

The troops of Bharat saw amazed
What Visvakarmá's art had raised,
On every side, five leagues around,
All smooth and level lay the ground,
With fresh green grass that charmed the sight
Like sapphires blent with lazulite.
There the Wood-apple hung its load,

The Mango and the Citron glowed,
The Bel and scented Jak were there,
And Anolá with fruitage fair.
There, brought from Northern Kuru, stood,
Rich in delights, the glorious wood,
And many a stream was seen to glide
With flowering trees along its side.
There mansions rose with four wide halls,
And elephants and chargers' stalls,
And many a house of royal state,
Triumphal are and bannered gate.
With noble doorways, sought the sky,
Like a pale cloud, a palace high,
Which far and wide rare fragrance shed,
With wreaths of white en-garlanded.
Square was its shape, its halls were wide,
With many a seat and couch supplied,
Drink of all kinds, and every meat
Such as celestial Gods might eat.

—Griffiths' *Rámáyana.*

In some of the vernacular versions of the Rámáyana the sage is represented as having provided a similar entertainment for the great army of monkeys and bears. **(3)** Droṇa. **(4)** Any descendant of Bharadvāja or follower of his teaching. **(5)** Name of a grammarian and author of Sūtras.

BHARADWAJAS—Inhabitants of the northern regions according to the Váyu, but Professor Wilson says they might be thought to be religious fraternities from the sage Atri and Bharadwája.

BHARADWAJI—A deep river in Malwa, included in the *V.P.* list.

BHARANI—A lunar asterism in Nagavithi, the first Vithi in Airávatha, or the northern Avasthána.

BHARATA—(1) A hero and king from whom the warlike people called Bhāratas, frequently mentioned in the *Ṛgveda*, were descended. The name is mixed up with that of Viśvāmitra. Bharata's sons were called Viśvāmitras and Viśvāmitra's sons were called Bharatas. **(2)** An ancient king of the first *manvantara.* He was devoted to Viṣṇu, and abdicated his throne that he might continue constant in meditation upon him. While at his hermitage, he went to bathe in the river, and there saw a doe big with young frightened by a lion. Her fawn, which was brought forth suddenly, fell into the water, and the sage rescued it. He brought the animal up, and becoming excessively fond of it, his abstraction was interrupted. "In the course of time he died, watched by the deer with tears in its eyes, like a son mourning for his father; and he himself, as he expired, cast his eyes upon the deer and thought of nothing else, being wholly occupied with one idea." For this misapplied devotion he was born again as a deer with the faculty of recollecting his former life. In this form he lived an austere retired life, and having atoned for his former error, was born again as a brāhmaṇa. But his person was ungainly, and he looked like a crazy idiot. He discharged servile offices, and was a palankin bearer; but he had true wisdom, and discoursed deeply upon philosophy and the power of Viṣṇu. Finally he obtained exemption from future birth. This legend is "a sectarial graft upon a Paurāṇik stem". **(3)** Son of Daśaratha by his wife Kaikeyī, and half-brother of Rāmacandra. He was educated by his mother's father, Aś vapati, king of Kekaya, and married Māṇḍavi, the cousin of Sītā. His mother, through maternal fondness, brought about the exile of Rāma, and endeavoured to secure her own son's succession to the throne, but Bharata refused to supplant his elder brother. On the death of his father Bharata performed the funeral rites, and went after Rāma with a complete army to bring him back to Ayodhya and place him on the throne. He found Rāma at Citrakūṭa, and there was a generous contention between them as to which should reign. Rāma refused to return until the period of his exile was completed, and Bharata declined to be king; but he returned to Ayodha as Rāma's representative, and setting up a pair of Rāma's shoes as a mark of his authority Bharata ruled the country in his brother's name. "He destroyed thirty millions of terrible *Gandharvas*" and made himself master of their country. **(4)** A prince of the Puru branch of the Lunar race. Bharata was son of Duṣyanta and Śakuntalā. Ninth in descent from him came Kuru, and fourteenth from Kuru came Śantanu. This king had a son named Vicitravīrya, who died childless, leaving two widows. Kṛṣṇa Dvaipāyana was natural brother to Vichitravīrya. Under the law he raised up seed to his brother from the widows, whose sons were Dhṛtarāṣtra and Pāṇḍu, between whose decendants, the Kauravas and Pāṇḍavas, the great war of the *Mahābhārata* was fought. Through their descent from Bharata, these princes, but more especially the Pāṇḍavas, were called Bhāratas.

"There is no reliable information as to the extent of the Kingdom of Bharata, but his wonderful doings and the greatness of his empire, have been set forth in the most extravagant terms. To this day, India is known to the Hindus by the name of Bharatavarshạ, or the country of Bharata. The Kshatriya bards declared that the Rájas of Bharata were descended from the moon, and that one of their number conquered Indra, the ruler of the gods." All that is really known is that an Aryan empire was established by Bharata amidst an aboriginal population. The original seat of the empire was at the site now occupied by the ruins of Takh-i-Bahi, in the country of the Yusufzais to the northward of Pesháwar. **(5)** A sage who is the reputed inventor of dramatic entertainments. **(6)** A name borne by several others of less note than the above. **(7)** In the Bhagavat Gíta a patronymic from Bharata, applied to Arjuna as his descendant. Arjuna is also called Prince of the Bharatas, and best of the Bharatas. **(8)** The eldest of the hundred sons of Rishabha, prince of Himahwa. Rishabha having ruled with equity and wisdom, and celebrated many sacrificial rites, resigned the sovereignty of the earth to the heroic Bharata. Bharata having religiously discharged the duties of his station, resigned the kingdom to his son Samati, a most virtuous prince; and abandoned his life at the holy place Sálagráma to become an ascetic. His thoughts were now wholly on God; his conduct was distinguished by kindness, and he effected in the highest degree the entire control over his mind.

On one occasion while bathing, a doe, being frightened by a lion, suddenly brought forth a fawn, and fell into the river. Bharata took the fawn to his hermitage and tended it with great care. His affection for it became so strong that it distracted his mind and interrupted his devotions. He at last died watched by the deer, with tears in its eyes. He was afterwards born again as a deer with the faculty of recollecting his former life; this gave him a distaste for the world and he again repassed to the holy place Sálagráma. Upon his death he was next born as a brahman, still retaining the memory of his prior existence. Possessed of all true wisdom he beheld soul as contra-distinguished from matter, (Prakriti) he beheld the gods and all other beings as the same in reality. This led him to disregard all castes and distinctions, and his conduct was so extraordinary that he was thought to be idiotic, and was treated with neglect or contempt: he worked in the fields, and on one occasion was pressed as a palankeen bearer for the Rája of Sauvira: being rebuked for his awkwardness, he replied and entered into a dialogue with the king, who soon discovered his merits. Bharata then expounded the nature of existence, the aim and object of life, and the identification of individual with universal spirit. The king then opened his eyes to truth and abandoned the notion of distinct existence. Bharata also obtained exemption from future birth. *V.P.*

BHARATAVARSA—India, as having been the kingdom of Bharata. It is divided into nine *khaṇḍas* or parts; Indradvīpa, Kaśerumat, Tāmravarṇa, Gabhastimat, Nāgadvīpa, Saumya, Gāndharva, Vāruṇa.

BHARATI—A name of Sarasvatī.

BHARGA—A prince, the son of Vainahótra, descended from Alarka.

BHARGABHUMI—The son of Bharga, the prince who is said to have promulgated the four rules of caste.

BHARGAS, BHARGAVAS—A people of the east subdued by Bhíma.

BHARGAVA—A descendant of Bhṛgu, as Cyavana, Śaunaka, Jamadagni, but more especially used for the latter and Paraśurama.

BHARIKA—A son of Krishṇa and Satyabháma.

BHARTRHARI—A celebrated poet and grammarian, who is said to have been the brother of Vikramāditya. He wrote three *Śatakas* or Centuries of verses, called—(1) *Sṛngāra-śataka*, on amatory matters; (2) *Nīti-śataka*, on polity and ethics; (3) *Vairāgya-śataka*, on religious austerity. These maxims are said to have been written when he had taken to a religious life after a licentious youth. He was also author of a grammatical work of high repute called *Vākyapadīya*, and the poem *called Bhaṭṭikāvya* is by some attributed to him. The moral verses were translated into French so long ago as 1670. A note at the end of that translation says, "Trad. par le Brahmine Padmanaba en flamand et du flamand en francais par Th. La Grue." The text with a Latin translation was printed by Schiefner and Weber. There is a translation in German by Bohlen and Schütz, in French by Fauche, and of the erotic verses by Regnaud; in English by Professor Tawney in the *Indian Antiquary.*

BHASAKARNA—A distinguished warrior of Rávaṇa's, who attacked Hanumán armed with a lance, after several of his companions had perished by the superhuman strength of the indomitable Ape. Bhásakarna rushed on him uttering cries for vengeance; accompanied by Praghasa armed with an axe, Hanumán though severely wounded himself waited for them to come near, when he seized a huge rock and buried it at his adversaries with such force that they were both crushed beneath its weight

BHASA-PARICCHEDA—An exposition of the Nyāya philosophy. There are several editions.

BHASI—One of the six illustrious daughters of Támra, the wife of Kaṣyapa. Bhasi gave birth to kites.

BHASKARACARYA (Bhāskara + Ācārya.)—A celebrated mathematician and astronomer, who was born early in the eleventh century AD. He was author *of the Bīja-gaṇita* on arithmetic, the *Līlāvatī* on algebra under date S. S. 1036 (A.D. 1114), and the *Siddhānta Śiromaṇi* (head jewel of accuracy) on astronomy published S. S. 1050 (A.D. 1128). It has been claimed for Bhāskara that he "was fully acquainted with the principle of the Differential Calculus". This claim Dr. Spottiswoode considers to be overstated, but he observes of Bhāskara: "It must be admitted that the penetration shown by Bhāskara in his analysis is in the highest degree remarkable; that the formula which he establishes, and his method of establishing it, bear more than a mere resemblance—they bear a strong analogy—to the corresponding process in modern astronomy; and that the majority of scientific persons will learn with surprise the existence of such a method in the writings of so distant a period and so distant a region."—*Jour RAS*, 1859. It has been said by some that Bhaskara was fully acquainted with the principle of the differential calculus, which was only discovered in Europe during the last century. In 1859 Professor Wilson wrote to Mr. Spottiswoode on this subject, and that gentleman replied to the inquiry in the following terms:—

"I have read Bâpû Deva Sâstrin's letter on Bhâskarâchârya's mode of determining the instantaneous motion of a planet, with great interest, and think that we are much indebted to him for calling our attention to so important an element in the old Indian methods of calculation. It stiil, however, seems to me, that he has over-stated the case, in saying that "Bhâskarâchârya was fully acquainted with the principle of the differential calculus." He has undoubtedly conceived the idea of comparing the successive positions of a planet in its path, and of regarding its motion as constant during the interval; and he may be said to have had some rudimentary notion of representing the are of a curve by means of auxiliary straight lines. But on the other hand, in the method here given, he makes no allusion to one of the most essential features of the differential calculus, *viz.*, the infinitestimal magnitude of the intervals of time and space therein employed. Nor, indeed, in anything specifically said about the fact, that the method is an approximate one.

Nevertheless, with these reservations it must be admitted, that the penetration shown by Bhâskara in his analysis, is in the highest degree remarkable; that the formula which he establishers,...and his methods of establishing it, bear more than a mere resemblance,—they bear a strong analogy,—to the corresponding process in mdoern mathematical astronomy; and that the majority of scientific persons will learn with surprise, the existence of such a method in the writings of so distant a period and so remote a region."—*Wilson.*

BHATTA MURTI—A distinguished Telugu poet, one of "the eight elephants," so styled of *Krishnaraya's* Court. He wrote the *Narasa* Bhúpāliyam during his patron's life; but his chief poem, the *Vasu Charitramu*, after that patron's death. It contains florid descriptions of scenery and love affairs, in recondite versification, much esteemed. Bhaṭṭa Múrti ranks high as a poet.—*Taylor.*

BHATTA—Bhaṭṭa. An honorary title given to learned brahmans who commit one of the Vedas to memory so as to be able to recite the whole without book.

BHATTACHARYAS—The name of the those Hindu scholas who not only learn, as the Bhaṭṭas do, one of the vedas completely by heart, but who study the meaning of each verse and word, so as to be able to give orally the explanation of any passage required. The number of this class of scholars, who represent the doctors of Hindu theology, is now very small. There are three or four, it is said at Benares. They are highly respected, and as incarnations of Vrihaspati (the Pandit of the gods,) at certain occasions regularly worshipped.—*Haug.*

BHATTI KAVYA—An epic poem composed in the Silver age of Sanskrit literature, for the purpose of illustrating, by every variety of example, the rules of grammar, poesy, and its sister rhetoric. Valuable as the work is to a student of the language in which it is written, for its copious illustration of the grammatical treatises of Pánini and Vopadeva, and curious as a portion of it is as an 'Art of Poetry,' teaching by example only—it has additional claims upon our consideration, in its comparative antiquity of composition, and its classic purity and eloquence of style, nor is the poem without passages of great descriptive power and general poetical merit. It narrates the oft-told adventures of 'the subject of all verse,' the beloved Man-God Ráma; his birth and life, his sufferings and triumphs, are celebrated at full length, and in language and style not unworthy of the inspiring theme.—*Griffith.* (*Specimens of Old Indian Poetry.*)

BHAṬṬOJI DIKSHITA—A grammarian, the son of a Brahman, and born in the Mahratta country. He applied to study; but, his own country ranking low in literature, he went to Benares studying Sanscrit and philosphy. He is now chiefly known by his celebrated work on grammar, entitled *Siddánta Kaumudi* (moonlight of accuracy), *Pánini's* old sutras obtained three commentators, *Vara ruchi*, *Bhattoji*, and *Patanjali*; the latter is the most diffuse and perfect; but the *Siddánta Kaumudi*, holding a medium place, has always been in wide and approved use. The author lived a studious and contemplative life; and died at Benares, aged fifty-six—*Taylor.*

BHAUMA—(1) 'Mars,' whose splendid car is of gold, drawn by eight horses of a ruby-red, sprung from fire. **(2)** Son of Bhūmi (the earth). A metronymic of the *daitya* Naraka.

BHAUTYA—The son of Bhuti, the Manu of the fourteenth Manwantara. (*see* MANU)

BHAVA—(1) Śiva, a Muni or Rudra, the husband of Sati, (Truth) who abandoned her corporeal existence in consequence of the displeasure of Daksha. She was afterwards the daughter of Himavat, (the snowy mountains) by Mena; and in that character, as the only Umá, the mighty Bhava again married her. *V.P.*, p. 59; **(2)** The name of a son of Pratiharttá, one of the descendants of Bharata; also **(3)** of a son of Viloman.

BHAVABHUTI—A celebrated dramatist, the author of three of the best extant Sanskṛt dramas, the *Māhavīra Carita*, *Uttara-Rāma Carita*, and *Mālatī Mādhava.* He was also known as Śrīkaṇṭha, or 'throat of eloquence'. He was a brāhmaṇa, and was a native either of Bedar or Berar, but Ujjayinī or its neighbourhood would seem, from his vivid descriptions of the scenery, to have been the place of his residence. The eighth century is the period at which he flourished. His three plays have been translated by Wilson in blank verse, who says *of Mālatī Mādhava*, "The author is fond of an unreasonable display of learning, and occasionally substitutes the phraseology of logic or metaphysics for the language of poetry and nature. At the same time the beauties predominate over the defects, and the language of the drama is in general of extraordinary beauty and power."

BHAVANA—The mental impression or apprehension following upon knowledge. The formation of a fixed idea of the object of contemplation. It is also termed Bháva-bhávaná, apprehension of the being, the existence or substantially of the object; the thing contemplated.

BHAVANI—One of the names of the wife of Śiva. (*see* DEVĪ)

BHAVANMANYA—The son of Vithatha, and grandson of Bharata.

BHAVISHYOTTARA PURANA—This is also a sort of manual of religious offices, the greater portion being appropriated to vratas, and the remainder to the forms with which gifts are to be presented.

BHAVISYA PURANA—"This Purāṇa, as its name implies, should be a book of prophecies foretelling what will be." The copies discovered contain about 7000 stanzas. The work is far from agreeingwith the declared character of a Purāṇa, and is principally a manual of rites and ceremonies. Its deity is Śiva. There is another work, containing also about 7000 verses, called the *Bhaviṣyottara Purāṇa*, a name which would imply that "it was a continuation or supplement of the former," and its contents are of a similar character.— *Wilson.*

One of the eighteen Puránas. "The Purána in which Brahma, having described the greatness of the sun, explained to Manu the existence of the world and the characters of all created beings in the course of the Aghóra Kalpa." This Purána as its name implies should be a book of prophecies. Dr. Wilson says: "It should be rather regarded as a manual of religious rites and ceremonies, in which a few legends enliven the series of precepts."

BHAVISYOTTARA PURANA—(See BHAVISYA PURĀṆA)

BHAVYA—(1) A king mentioned in the Rig Veda,who dwelt on the banks of the Sindhu or Indus. **(2)** One of the ten sons of Priyavrats, who became king of Sakadwipa. Also the name of one of the sons of Dhruva, by his wife Sámbha.

BHAVYAS—One of the five classes of demi-gods of the sixth Manwantars, when Chakshusha was the Manu of the period, and Manojava was the Indra.

BHAYA—(Fear). Son of Auriti (falsehood), and Nikriti (immorality).

BHAYADA—A prince, the son of Manasya, one of the descendants of Puru.

BHELA—An ancient sage who wrote upon medicine.

BHIKSU—A mendicant. The brāhmaṇa in the fourth and last stage of his religious life. (*see* BRĀHMAṆA)

Any mendicant, especially, in its Pāli form, Bhikkhu, a Buddhist mendicant. He is to forego the three objects of human existence (pleasure, wealth and virtue)—to be constantly occupied with devotion, and abstain from all wrong-doing. He is to reside but for one night in a village, and not more than five nights at a time in a city: for the support of existence he is to apply for alms at the houses of the three first castes, when the fires have been extinguished and people have eaten. The mendicant is to call nothing his own, and to suppress desire, anger, pride and covetousness.

BHILS—A tribe of Aborigines who still occupy the hill tracts of Rájputána and Central India, and in ancient times seem to have dwelt in nearly the same localities; having Rájas or Chieftains of their own, but acknowledging or dreading the supremacy of the Kshatriyas. In the Mahábhárata they appear to the south of the Yamuna, and in the immediate neighbourhood of the Ráj of Bharata; whilst in the Rámáyana they make their appearance further to the east, near the junction of the Yamuna and Ganges. They have preserved their rude habits to the present day, and are known as cattle-lifters, robbers, hunters like Nimrod and Esau, capable of almost any outrage, yet imbued with a sense of truth and honour strangely contrasting with their external character.—*Wheeler, Vol. I, p.* 83.

BHIMA SANKARA, BHIMESVARA—Name of one of the twelve great *lingas.* (*see* LIṄGAS)

BHIMA, BHIMASENA—'The terrible.' The second of the five Pāṇḍu princes, and mythically son of Vāyu 'the god of the wind'. He was a man of vast size, and had great strength. He was wrathful in temper, and given to abuse, a brave warrior, but a fierce and cruel foe, coarse in taste and manners, and a great feeder, so that he was called Vṛkodara 'wolfs belly'. Half of the food of the family was allotted to him, and the other half sufficed for his four brothers and their mother. The weapon he generally used was a club, which suited his gigantic strength, and he had been trained in the use of it by Droṇa and Balarāma. His great strength excited the envy of his cousin Duryodhana, who poisoned him and threw his body into the Ganges; but it sank to the realm of the serpents, where it was restored to health and vigour, and Bhīma returned to Hastināpura. At the passage of arms at Hastināpura, he and Duryodhana engaged each other with clubs; but the mimic combat soon turned into a fierce personal conflict, which Droṇa had to put an end to by force. It was at this same meeting that he reviled Karṇa, and heaped contempt upon him, increasing and converting into bitter hatred the enmity which Kaṇra had previously entertained against the Pāṇḍavas. When he and his brothers were in exile, and an attempt was made, at the instigation of Duryodhana, to bum them in their house, it was he who barricaded the house of Purocana, the director of the plot, and burnt him as he had intended to burn them. Soon after this he met the *asura* Hiḍimba, whom he killed, and then married his sister Hiḍimbā. He also slew another *asura* named Vaka, whom he seized by the legs and tore asunder; afterwards he killed his brother, Kirmīra, and other *asuras.* This brought the *asuras* to submission, and they engaged to refrain from molesting mankind. After the Pāṇḍu princes were established at Indraprastha, Bhīma fought in single combat with Jarāsandha, king of Magadha, who had refused to recognise their supremacy. As 'son of the wind', Bhīma was brother of Hanumān, and was able to fly with great speed. By this power of flight, and with the help of Hanumān, he made his way to Kubera's heaven, high up in the Himālayas. When Jayadratha failed in his attempt to carry off Draupadī, he was pursued by Arjuna and Bhīma. The latter overtook him, dragged him by the hair from his chariot to the ground, and kicked him till he became senseless. At Arjuna's remonstrance Bhīma refrained from killing him; but he cut off all his hair except five locks, and compelled him to acknowledge publicly that he was the slave of the Pāṇḍavas. Bhīma refused to listen to his brother's plea for Jayadratha's release, but at Draupadī's intercession he let him go free. In the second exile of the Pāṇḍavas, they went to the Rājā of Virāṭa, whose service they entered. Bhīma, holding a ladle in one hand and a sword in the other, undertook the duties of cook; but he soon exhibited his prowess by fighting with and killing a famous wrestler named Jīmūta. Draupadī had entered into the service of the queen as a waiting-maid, and attracted the admiration of the king's brother-in-law, Kīcaka. When she rejected his advances, he insulted and brutally assaulted her. Her husbands did not seem disposed to avenge her, so she appealed to Bhīma, as she was wont when she sought revenge. Draupadī made an assignation with Kīcaka, which Bhīma kept, and after a sharp struggle with the disappointed gallant, he broke his bones to atoms, and made his body into a large ball of flesh, so that no one could tell how he had been killed or who had killed him. Draupadī was judged to have had a share in his death, and was condemned to be burnt alive; but Bhīma drew his hair over his face, so that no one could recognise him, and, tearing up a large tree for a club, he rushed to the rescue. He was taken for a mighty Gandharva, the crowd fled, and Draupadī was released. Kīcaka had been the general of the forces of Virāṭa and the mainstay of the king. After his death, Suśarman, king ofTrigartta, aided and abetted by the Kauravas and others, determined to attack Virāṭa. The Rājā of Virāṭa was defeated and made prisoner, but Bhīma pursued Suśarman and overcame him, rescued the prisoner, and made the conqueror captive. In the great battle between the Kauravas and Pāṇḍavas, Bhīma took a very prominent part. On the first day he fought against Bhisma; on the second he slew the two sons of the Rājā of Magadha, and after them their father, killing him and his elephant at a single blow. In the night between the fourteenth and fifteenth day of the battle, Bhīma fought with Droṇa until the rising of the sun; but that redoubted warrior fell by the hand of Dhṛṣṭadyumna, who continued the combat till noonday. On the seventeenth day he killed Duḥṣāsana, and drank his blood, as he had long before vowed to do, in retaliation of the insults Duḥśāsana had offered to Draupadī. On the eighteenth and last day of the battle Duryodhana fled and hid himself in a lake. When he was discovered, he would not come out until he had received a promise that he should not have to fight with more than one man at a time. Even then he delayed until he was irritated by the abuse and the taunts of the Pāṇḍavas. Bhīma and Duryodhana fought as usual with clubs. The battle was long and furious; the parties were equally matched, and Bhīma was getting the worst of it, when he struck an unfair blow which smashed Duryodhana's thigh, and brought him to the ground. Thus he fulfilled his vow and avenged Draupadī. In this fury Bhīma kicked his prostrate foe on the head, and acted so brutally that his brother Yudhiṣṭhira struck him in the face with his fist, and directed Arjuna to take him away. Balarāma was greatly incensed at the foul play to which Bhīma had resorted, and would have attacked the Pāṇḍavas had he not been mollified by Kṛṣṇa. He declared that Bhīma should thenceforward be called Jihmayodhin, 'the unfair fighter'. After the conclusion of the war, the old king, Dhṛtarāṣtra, asked that Bhīma might be brought to him. Kṛṣṇa, who knew the blind old man's sorrow for his son, whom Bhīma had killed, and suspecting his intention placed before him an iron statue, which Dhṛtarāṣṭra crushed in his embrace. Dhṛtarpāṣṭra never forgave Bhīma, and he returned the ill feeling with insults, which ended in the old king's retiring into the forest. Bhīma's last public feat was the slaughter of the horse in the sacrifice which followed Yudhiṣṭhira's access on to the throne. Apart from his mythological attributes, the character of Bhīma is natural and distinct. He was a man of burly form, prodigious strength, and great animal courage, with coarse tastes, a gluttonous appetite, and an irascible temper: jovial and jocular when in good humour, but abusive, truculent, and brutal when his passions were roused. His repartees were forcible though coarse, and he held his own even against Kṛṣṇa when the latter made personal remarks upon him. (*see* MAHĀBHĀRATA)

By his asura wife Hiḍimbā he had a son named Ghaṭotkaca; and by his wife Balandharā, princess of Kasī, also he had a son named Sarvatraga or Sarvaga. Other appellations of Bhīma are Bhīmasena, Bāhūsalin, 'the large armed', Jarāsandhajit, 'vanquisher of Jarāsandha'.

"Bhíma is the Hercules or Orlando of the mythological poetry of the Hindus; his uncommon strength was a supernatural endowment. In his youth he was the great plague of the Kuru princes, beating them in every sport and contest. They therefore plotted to get rid of him, and at a juvenile party at one of the water palaces of the king, administered a poisonous drug to him, and took advantage of his slumber to push him into the Ganges. He fell into the region of the sub-terrene snakes, by whom he was bitten; one poison was the antidote of the other, and Bhíma, recovering from his sleep, soon beat off his antagonists; they fled to their king Vásuki who was induced by their report to see the wonderful boy, and went to meet him. In his train was Aryaka, the maternal great great grandfather of Bhíma, who recognised, and welcomed his descendant,. Aryaka being a great favourite with the king of the Nágas, Vásuki offered to give his relation any treasure or gems he could desire, but Aryaka asked permission for him to quaff the invigorating beverage, of which one bowl contained the stren-gth of a thousand Nágas; permission being granted, Bhíma drained this bowl eight times at as many draughts, and then went quietly to sleep for eight days: on his waking he was feasted by the Nágas and then restored to his sorrowing mother and brethren. From this period, dates his miraculous strength. Many of these incidents find parallels in Western Romance. The lady of the Lake inhabits the depths of the water, and is called by Merlin the "white serpent;" the Fata Morgana resided beneath a lake while caressing one of her lovers as a serpent. She is also styled the Fairy of Riches: her treasures were spread over a plain to which Orlando arrived by falling in a conflict with Arridano to the bottom of an enchanted lake: Manto, the protecting fairy of Mantua [Ori. Fur. 43, 74.] being saved by Adonis when pursued in the form of a snake, proffers him anything he may desire. The account she gives of herself makes her to be a regular Nága Kanyá, or Ophite Maiden. The feat of Bhíma may be paralleled by a similar one of Orlando, and many others, of the preux chevaliers of chivalry."—Wilson's *Works*, III, 337.

BHIMA—(1) Name of the father of Damayantī. A name of Rudra or of one of his personifications, (*see* Rudra) **(2)** The fifth of the eight Rudras, to whom was assigned the charge of fire: also the name of a son of Amávasa. **(3)** The Rája of Vidarbha (Berar), and father of Damayanti.

BHIMARATHA—Son of Ketumat and grandson of Dhanwantari, the author of Medical Science. He was the father of Divodasa, of whom many curious legends are narrated.

BHIMARATHI—The ancient name of the river Bhíma.

BHIRAS—The people about Surat; called Phauni or Phryni, by Strabo.

BHISHMAKA—The king of Vidarbha (now Berar) who resided at Kundina. He had a son named Rukmin, and a beautiful daughter named Rukminí. Krishṇa fell in love with the latter and solicited her in marriage; but her brother would not assent to the espousals. At the suggestion of Jarásandha, the powerful sovereign, Bhíshmaka affianced Rukminí to Siṣupála. Krishṇa went to witness the wedding and contrived to carry off the princess. Rukmin, with a large force, pursued and overtook Krishṇa, who with his discus destroyed the host of Rukmin, and would have slain him, but was withheld by the entreaties of Rukminí.

BHISHMASHTAMI—The twenty-third of Mágha, and eighth lunar day of the light half (7th February). This is a festival which, at first sight, appears to be of special and traditional origin, but which has, probably, its source in the primitive institutes of the Hindus, of which the worship of the Pitris, the patriarchs or progenitors, the Dii Manes, constituted an important element. According to the Tithi Tattwa, this day is dedicated to Bhíshma, the son of Gangá, and great uncle of the Pándava and Kaurava princes; who was killed in the course of the great war, and dying childless left no descendant in the direct line, on whom it was incumbent to offer him obsequial honors. In order to supply this defect, persons in general are enjoined to make libations of water on this day to his spirit, and to offer him sesamum seeds and boiled rice. The act expiates the sins of a whole year: one of its peculiarities is, that it is to be observed by persons of all the four original castes, according to a text of Dhavala, an ancient lawgiver, quoted by Raghunandana, "Oh twice-born! persons of all the Varnas should on the eighth lunar day offer water, sesamum seeds and rice, to Bhíshma. If a Brahman, or man of any other caste, omit to make such offerings, the merit of his good deeds during the preceding year is annulled." According to a different reading of the text, however, it should be rendered: "Let all the twice-born castes make the oblations." This excludes Súdras, but extends the duty to the Kshatriyas and Vaisyas as well as Brahmans. The intention of the rite, as now understood, is expressed in the formulæ uttered at the time of presenting the offerings: "I present this water to the childless hero Bhíshma, of the race of Vyághrapada, the chief of the house of Sankṛiti. May Bhíshma, the son of Sántanu, the speaker of truth and subjugator of his passions, obtain by this water the oblations due by sons and grandsons." The simple nature of the offerings which are sufficient on such occasions, water and sesamum seeds, justifies the remark made by Ovid on the Feralia, that the manes are easily satisfied.

BHISMA—'The terrible.' Son of King Śantanu by the holy river goddess Gaṅgā, and hence called Śantanava, Gāṅgeya, and Nadija, 'the river-bom'. When King Śantanu was very old he desired to marry a young and beautiful wife. His son Śantanava or Bhiṣma found a suitable damsel, but her parents objected to the marriage because Bhisma was heir to the throne, and if she bore sons they could not succeed. To gratify his father's desires, he made a vow to the girl's parents that he would never accept the throne, nor marry a wife, nor become the father of children. Śāntanu then married the damsel, whose name was Satyavatī, and she bore him two sons. At the death of his father, Bhisma placed the elder son upon the throne, but he was headstrong and was soon killed in battle. The other son, named Vicitravīrya, then succeeded, and Bhisma acted as his protector and adviser. By force of arms Bhisma obtained two daughters of the king of

Kāśī and married them to Vicitravīrya, and when that prince died young and childless, Bhisma acted as guardian of his widows. By Bhisma's arrangement, Kṛṣṇa Dvaipāyana, who was born of Satyavatī before her marriage, raised up seed to his half-brother. The two children were Pāṇḍu and Dhṛtarāṣṭra. Bhisma brought them up and acted for them as regent of Hastināpura. He also directed the training of their respective children, the Pāṇḍavas and Kauravas. On the rupture taking place between the rival families, Bhisma counselled moderation and peace. When the war began he took the side of the Kauravas, the sons of Dhṛtarāṣṭra, and he was made commander-in-chief of their army. He laid down some rules for mitigating the horrors of war, and he stipulated that he should not be called upon to fight against Arjuna. Goaded by the reproaches of Duryodhana, he attacked Arjuna on the tenth day of the battle. He was unfairly wounded by Śikhaṇḍin, and was pierced with innumerable arrows from the hands of Arjuna, so that there was not a space of two fingers' breadth left unwounded in his whole body, and when he fell from his chariot he was upheld from the ground by the arrows and lay as on a couch of darts. He was mortally wounded, but he had obtained the power of fixing the period of his death, so he survived fifty-eight days, and delivered several long didactic discourses. Bhisma exhibited throughout his life a self-denial, devotion, and fidelity which remained unsullied to the last. He is also known by the appellation Tarpaṇecchu, and as Tālaketu, 'palm banner'. (*see* MAHĀBHĀRATA)

BHISMAKA—**(1)** An appellation of Śiva. **(2)** King of Vidarbha, father of Rukmin and of Rukmiṇī, the chief wife of Kṛṣṇa.

BHOGAVATI—**(1)** 'The voluptuous'. The subterranean capital of the Nāgas in the Nāgaloka portion of Pātāla. Another name is Pūtkārī. **(2)** The capital of Vásuki in Rasátala, one of the seven regions of Pátáḷa.

BHOJA RAJA—A prince of Dhára; or Dhar, in Malwa; supposed to be the same as Vikrama. There is some uncertainty as to the exact time of Bhoja's reign; the "nine gems" are said to have flourished during his reign and that of Vikrama. The period is designated the golden age of Hindu literature, Dr. E. F. Hall says it is high time to give up speaking of this prince as a great patron of literature. His pretensions to be so considered rest on the frailest foundation possible.— H. H. Wilson's *Works*, Vol. v., *p.* 171.

BHOJA—**(1)** A name borne by many kings. Most conspicuous among them was Bhoja or Bhojadeva, king of Dhār, who is said to have been a great patron of literature, and probably died before AD 1082. **(2)** Aprince of the Yādava race who reigned at Mṛttikavatī on the Parṇāśa river in Mālwa; he is also called Mahābhoja. **(3)** A tribe living in the Vindhya mountains. **(4)** A country; the modern Bhojpur, Bhāgalpur, &c.

BHOJAKATA—The city near the Narmada, founded by Rukmin, after his defeat by Krishṇa, as he had vowed never to return to Kundani but as victor.

BHOJA-PRABANDHA—A collection of literary anecdotes relating to King Bhoja of Dhār, written by Ballāla. The text has been lithographed by Pavie.

BHOJAS—Inhabitants of the country near the Vindhya range of mountains; a branch of the yadavas. A Bhoja Rája is amongst the warriors of the Mahábhárata.

BHRAJA—The name of one of the seven suns into which the seven solar rays dilate at the consummation of all things when their radiance is to set the three worlds and Pátáḷa on fire.

BHRAJIRAS—One of the five classes of demi-gods on the fourteenth Manwantras.

BHRAMI—(Revolving.) The daughter of Sisumara (the sphere) wife of Dhruva, according to the Bhágavata, which converts the family of Dhruva into personifications of divisions of time and of day and night.

BHRGU—A Vedic sage. He is one of the Prajāpatis and great *ṛṣis*, and is regarded as the founder of the race of the Bhṛgus or Bhārgavas, in which was born Jamadagni and Paraśurāma. Manu calls him son, and says that he confides to him his Institutes. According to the *Mahābhārata* he officiated at Dakṣa's celebrated sacrifice, and had his beard pulled out by Śiva. The same authority also tells the following story: It is related of Bhṛgu that he rescued the sage Agastya from the tyranny of King Nahuṣa, who had obtained superhuman power. Bhṛgu crept into Agastya's hair to avoid the potent glance of Nahuṣa, and when that tyrant attached Agastya to his chariot and kicked him on the head to make him move, Bhṛgu cursed Nahuṣa, and he was turned into a serpent. Bhṛgu, on Nahusa's supplication, limited the duration of his curse.

In the *Padma Purāṇa* it is related that the ṛsis, assembled at a sacrifice, disputed as to which deity was best entitled to the homage of a brāhmaṇa. Being unable to agree, they resolved to send Bhṛgu to test the characters of the various gods, and he accordingly went. He could not obtain access to Śiva because that deity was engaged with his wife; "finding him, therefore, to consist of the property of darkness, Bhṛgu sentenced him to take the form of the *linga*, and pronounced that he should have no offerings presented to him, nor receive the worship of the pious and respectable. His next visit was to Brahmā, whom he beheld surrounded by sages, and so much inflated with his own importance as to treat Bhṛgu with great inattention, betraying his being made up of foulness. The *muni* therefore excluded him from the worship of the brāhmaṇas. Repairing next to Viṣṇu, he found the deity asleep, and, indignant at his seeming sloth, Bhṛgu stamped upon his breast with his left foot and awoke him; instead of being offended, Viṣṇu gently pressed the brāhmaṇa's foot and expressed himself honoured and made happy by its contact; and Bhṛgu, highly pleased by his humility, and satisfied of his being impersonated goodness, proclaimed Viṣṇu as the only being to be worshipped by men or gods, in which decision the *munis*, upon Bhṛgu's report, concurred."—*Wilson.*

In the Puránic period he is called the husband of Khyáti, or fame, the daughter of Daksha, by Prasúti.—*Vishnu Purána, pp.* 49, 284.

BHRGUS—'Roasters, consumers.' "A class of mythical beings who belonged to the middle or aerial class of gods."—*Roth.* They are connected with Agni, and are spoken of as producers and nourishers of fire, and as makers of chariots. They are associated with the Aṅgirasas, the Atharvans, Ṛbhus, &c.

BHRIHASPATI—See Vṛihaspati. This is not only the name of the puróhita of the gods, but is also used in the ancient Sanscrit hymns as the name of the One Eternal.

BHU, BHUMI—The earth, (*see* PṚTHIVĪ)

BHUDEVI—A name of the earth, and fabled to be married to *Prithu*; the first king who taught the mode of cultivating the ground. Hence the earth is named *Prit'hivi.* One of the *Puránas* was delivered to *Bhudévi*, by *Vishnu*, as *Varáha Swámi.* Bhū-devi, or *Bhumidevi*, is the secondary wife of Vishnu.

BHUJYU—The son of Tugra, who was abandoned by his malevolent companions in the middle of the sea, and rescued by the Aṣvins, who are said to have conveyed Bhujyu out of the liquid ocean with their headlong flying horses. Another account states "Tugra abandoned Bhujyu on the water-cloud, as any dead man leaves his property. Ye, Aṣvins, bore him in animated water-tight ships, which traversed the air. Three nights and three days did ye convey him in three flying cars, with a hundred feet and six horses, which crossed over to the dry land beyond the liquid ocean."—*O.S.T.*, v., p. 244.

BHUMIMITRA—A Kanwa prince, whose father Devabhuti, the last Sunga king, was murdered by his minister.

BHUR—(*See* VYĀHRTI.)

BHURI—A son of Sómadatta, one fo the descendants of Kuru.

BHURISHENA—The third son of the holy age Chyavana,according to the Bhāğavata; the *V.P.* only mentions one son Anartta.

BHURISRAVAS—**(1)** A prince of the Bālhīkas and an ally of the Kauravas, who was killed in the great battle of the Mahabharata. **(2)** A name of Vishṇu, with reference to his becoming incarnate to relieve the earth of her burthen.

BHURLOKA—The sphere of the earth comprehending its oceans, mountains and rivers, and extending as far as it is illuminated by the rays of the sun and moon. (*See* LOKA)

BHUTA—**(1)** A ghost, imp, goblin. Malignant spirits which haunt cemeteries, lurk in trees, animate dead bodies, and delude and devour human beings. According to the *Viṣṇu Purāṇa* they are "fierce beings and eaters of flesh", who were created by the Creator when he was incensed. In the *Vāyu Purāṇa* their mother is said to have been Krodhā, 'anger' and their father, Kaṣyapa. The *bhūtas* are attendants of Śiva, and he is held to be their lord. **(2)** A son of Vasudeva by his wife Róhiṇi.

BHUTADI—The third variety of Ahankars, *q.v.*

BHUTASANTAPANA—A powerful Daitya, the son of Hiranyáksha. The descendants of Hiranyaksha are said in the Padma-purána to have extended to seventy-seven crores, or seven hundred and seventy millions.

BHUTATMA—An appellation of Vishṇu, meaning one with created things.

BHUTAVIDYA—That branch of medicine which treats of the restoration of the faculties from a disorganised state induced by demoniacal possession. This art has vanished before the diffusion of knowledge, but it formed a very important part of medical practice, through all the schools, Greek, Arabic and European, and descended to days very near to our own, as a reference to Burton's Anatomy of Melancholy may prove to general readers.—*Wilson*.

BHUTAVIDYA—The fourth branch of Medical Science, treating of maladies referred to demoniac possession.

BHUTESA, BHUTESVARA—'Lord of beings or of created things'. A name applied to Viṣṇu, Brahmā, and Kṛṣṇa; as 'lord of the Bhūtas or goblins', it is applied to Śiva.

BHUTESA—A name of Vishṇu, meaning lord of the elements, or of created things.

BHUTI—A sage, the son of Angiras, whose pupil Santi, having suffered the holy fire to go out in his master's absence, prayed to Agni, and so propitiated him, that he not only re-lighted the flame, but desired Santi to demand a further boon. Santi accordingly solicited a son for his Guru, which son was Bhúti, the father of the Manu Bhautya. Also the name of a goddess, wife of Kavi.

BHUVANA—The name of one of the eleven Rudras, according to the Váyu Purána list.

BHUVANESVARA—A ruined city in Orissa, sacred to the worship of Śiva, and containing the remains of several temples. It was formerly called Ekāmrakānana.

BHUVAR—(*See* VYĀHṚTI.)

BHUVAR-LOKA—The sphere of the sky, both in diameter and circumference, as far upwards as to the planetary sphere, or Swarlóka. (*See* LOKA.)

BIBHATSU—'Loathing.' An appellation of Arjuna.

BIJALA RAJA—A Jaina king of *Kalyánapura*, otherwise *Silpagiri*, who had the celebrated *Basava*, for his minister of state. He was charged with wasting the state funds, in gathering around himself adherents to a new form of the *Saiva* religion. When called to account, he made up the deficiency in appearance; but soon after caused the king to be assassinated by three men, in his own palace. Thereupon, the *Jainas* were massacred. The exact date is not known; but Professor Wilson places it in the early part of the eleventh century. See BASAVA.

BIKYA—The daughter of the minister of the Rája of Kutuwal in the Dekhan, who was married to Chandrahása, the fortunate boy (*q.v.*).

BINDUMATI—The daughter of Śasabindu, who was married to the celebrated king Mándhatṛi, and became the mother of three sons and fifty daughters.

BINDUSARA—The son and successor of Candragupta.

BIRAPPA—The demon god of the Kurubaru, or shepherd caste in Mysore. At the annual festival of this god it is the custom for the priest to sit on his hands and knees before the idol, with his eyes shut, holding out his shaven head, his body being naked except a cloth round the waist. Four men stand near the priest, to whom the elders hand the cocoanuts which the people have brought, and these are broken on the bare head of the priest who sits without uttering a sound until great heaps of cocoanut fragments are piled upon both aides of him.

BISHESWAR—A name of Śiva, whose-image is the linga, a plain conical stone set on end. Bisheswar is the reigning deity of Benares, and, in the opinion of the people, holds the position of king over all the other deities, as well as over all the inhabitants.

BODHA—(Understanding). A son of Dharma, by one of the Daksha's daughters, Buddhi.

BODHANA—A mountain to the east of Ramghur.

BODHAS—One of the tribes of Central India, according to the Váyu Purána; it is also read Bahyas.

BRAHADARANYAKA, BRHAD UPANISAD—The *Bṛhadāraṇyaka Upaniṣad* belongs to the *Śatapatha Brāhmaṇa*, and is ascribed to the sage Yājñavalkya. It has been translated by Dr. Roer, and published in the *Bibliotheca Indica*. (*see* ĀRAṆYAKA and YĀJÑAVALKYA)

BRAHAD-DEVATA—An ancientworkin *slokas* by the sage Śaunaka, which enumerates and describes the deity or deities to which each hymn and verse of the *Ṛgveda* is addressed. It frequently recites legends in support of its attributions.

BRAHADRATHA—The tenth and last king of Maurya dynasty, founded by Candragupta.

BRAHAT-KATHA—A large collection of tales, the original of the *Kathā-sarit-sāgara* (*q.v.*).

BRAHMA (masculine)—**(1)** The first member of the Hindu triad; the supreme spirit manifested as the active creator of the universe. He sprang from the mundane egg deposited by the supreme first cause, and is the Prajāpati, or lord and father of all creatures, and in the first place of the ṛṣis or Prajapatis (*q.v.*).

When Brahmā has created the world it remains

unaltered for one of his days, a period of 2,160,000,000 years. The world and all that is therein is then consumed by fire, but the sages, gods, and elements survive. When he awakes—he again restores creation, and this process is repeated until his existence of a hundred years is brought to a close, a period which it requires fifteen figures to express. When this period is ended he himself expires, and he and all gods and sages, and the whole universe are resolved into their constituent elements. His name is invoked in religious services, but Puṣkara (*hodie* Pokhar), near Ājmīr, is the only place where he receives worship, though Professor Williams states that he has heard of homage being paid to him at Īdar.

Brahmā is said to be of a red colour. He has four heads; originally he had five, but one was burnt off by the fire of Śiva's central eye because he had spoken disrespectfully. Hence he is called Caturānana or Caturmukha, 'four-faced', and Aṣṭakarṇa, 'eight-eared'. He has four arms; and in his hands he holds his sceptre, or a spoon, or a string of beads, or his bow Parivīta, or a water jug, and the Veda. His consort is Sarasvatī, goddess of learning, also called Brahmi. His vehicle is a swan or goose, from which he is called Hansavāhana. His residence is called Brahmā-vṛndā.

The name Brahmā is not found in the Vedas *and Brāhmaṇas*, in which the active creator is known as Hiraṇyagarbha, Prajāpati, &c.; but there is a curious passage in the *Śatapatha Brāhmaṇa* which says: "He (Brahmā, neuter) created the gods. Having created the gods, he placed them in these worlds: in this world Agni, Vāyu in the atmosphere, and Sūrya in the sky." The points connected with Brahmā are remarkable. As the father of men he performs the work of procreation by incestuous intercourse with his own daughter, variously named Vāca or Sarasvatī (speech), Sandhyā (twilight), Śatarūpā (the hundred-formed), &c. Secondly, his powers as creator have been arrogated to the other gods Viṣṇu and Śiva, while Brahmā has been thrown into the shade. In the *Aitareya Brāhmaṇa* it is said that Prajāpati was in the form of a buck and his daughter was Rohit, a deer. According to the *Śatapatha Brāhmaṇa* and Manu, the supreme soul, the self-existent lord, created the waters and deposited in them a seed, which seed became a golden egg, in which he himself was born as Brahmā, the progenitor of all the worlds. As the waters (*nara*) were "the place of his movement, he (Brahmā) was called Nārāyaṇa" Here the name Nārāyaṇa is referred distinctly to Brahmā, but it afterwards became the name of Viṣṇu. The account of the *Rāmāyaṇa* is that "all was water only, in which the earth was formed. Thence arose Brahmā, the self-existent, with the deities. He then, becoming a boar, raised up the earth and created the whole world with the saints, his sons. Brahmā, eternal and perpetually undecaying, sprang from the ether; from him was descended Marīci; the son of Marīci was Kaśyapa. From Kaśyapa sprang Vivasvat, and Manu is declared to have been Vivasvat's son." A later recension of this poem alters this passage so as to make Brahmā a mere manifestation of Viṣṇu. Instead of "Brahmā, the self-existent, with the deities", it substitutes for the last three words, "the imperishable Viṣṇu". The *Viṣṇu Purāṇa* says that the "divine Brahmā called Nārāyaṇa created all beings", that Prajāpat "had formerly, at the commencement ofthe (previous) *kalpas*, taken the shape of afish, a tortoise, &c., (so now), entering the body of a boar, the lord of creatures entered the water". But this "lord of creatures" is clearly shown to be Viṣṇu, and these three forms, the fish, the tortoise, and the boar, are now counted among the *avatāras* of Viṣṇu. (*see* Avatāra) This attribution of the form of a boar to Brahmā (Prajāpati) had been made before by the *Śatapatha Brāhmaṇa*, which also says, "Having assumed the form of a tortoise, Prajāpati created *offspring*." *Tine Liṅga Purāṇa* is quite exceptional among the later works in ascribing the boar form to Brahmā. The *Mahābhārata* represents Brahmā as springing from the navel of Viṣṇu or from a lotus which grew thereout; hence he is called Nābhija, "navel-born; Kañja, 'the lotus'; Sarojin, 'having a lotus'; Abja-ja, Abja-yoni, and Kañja-ja, 'lotus-born'. This is, of course, the view taken by the Vaiṣṇavas. The same statement appears in the *Rāmāyaṇa*, although this poem gives Brahmā a more prominent place than usual. It represents Brahmā as informing Rāma of his divinity, and of his calling him to heaven in "the golry of Viṣṇu". He bestowed boons on Rāma while that hero was on earth, and he extended his favours also to Rāvaṇa and other *rākṣasas* who were descendants of his son Pulastya. In the Purāṇas also he appears as a patron of the enemies of the gods, and it was by his favour that the *daitya* King Bali obtained that almost universal dominion which required the incarnation of Viṣṇu as the dwarf to repress. He is further represented in the *Rāmāyaṇa* as the creator of the beautiful Ahalyā, whom he gave as wife to the sage Gautama. Brahmā, being thus inferior to Viṣṇu, is represented as giving homage and praise to Viṣṇu himself and to his form Kṛṣṇa, but the Vaiṣṇava authorities make him superior to Rudra, who, they say, sprang from his forehead. The Śaiva authorities make Mahādeva or Rudra to be the creator of Brahmā, and represent Brahmā as worshipping the *linga* and as acting as the charioteer of Rudra.

Brahmā was the father of Dakṣa, who is said to have sprung from his thumb, and he was present at the sacrifice of that patriarch, which was rudely disturbed by Rudra. Then he had to humbly submit and appease the offended god. The four Kumāras, the chief of whom was called Sanatkumāra or by the patronymic Vaidhātra, were later creations or sons of Brahmā.

Brahmā is also called Vidhi, Vedhās, Druhiṇa, and Sraṣṭṛ, 'creator'; Dhātṛ and Vidhātṛ, 'sustainer'; Pitāmaha, 'the great father'; Lokeś'a, 'lord of the world'; Parameṣṭa, 'supreme in heaven'; Sanat, 'the ancient'; Ādi-kavi, 'the first poet'; and Drū-ghaṇa, 'the axe or mallet'. **(2)** The first deity of the Hindu triad; the creator of the world; the great father and lord of all; the supporter of all: yet described as born in the lotus which sprung from the navel of Vishṇu; and as born from the golden egg. The Vishṇu Purána says, the one only god Janárdana, takes the designation of Brahma, Vishṇu and Śiva, accordingly as he creates, preserves or destroys . Mr. Cockburn Thompson says: "In the ante-mythological age this was probably nothing but a name for the sun, considered as producer, vivifier and pervader. He afterwards replaced Súrya in the triad of elementary gods, and was coupled with Vishṇu and Śiva, who were substituted for Varuna and Váyu, the other components of that triad. In the earliest mythological period, Brahma (always masculine) is then first person of the triad, Brahma, Vishṇu and Śiva; and when later the unity of these personages was established by referring them to one Supreme Being, Brahma was that being in his character of creator and enlivener, Vishṇu in that of preserver, and Śiva in that of destoryer. Thus in the Puránas (Vishṇu P., p. 22,) Brahma is said to live 100 of his own years, each of which consits of 360′ days and nights. The days are called Kalpas, and consist of 4,320,000,000 years of mortals, during which the universe exists. During his nights the universe ceases to exist, and is reproduced at the commencement of the next day or Kalpa. He is described in the Puránas as having four faces, and as being produced from the cup of a lotus, which sprang from the navel of Vishṇu. In this mythological character of creator of the universe, he is mentioned in the Bhagavat Gíta and Vishṇu Purána. When, after the period of superstitious mythology, the idea of one Supreme Being was again brought forward, Brahma was considered the chief of the existing trinity, and was at first identified with that idea of an unknown god; and though afterwards Śiva and Vishṇu were each in turn identified with the Supreme Being by their respective followers, the Śaivas and Vaishnavas, the name Brahma, *in the neuter*, was still retained in the language of philosopy to designate the universal Supreme One. In this sense the word occurs throughout the Bhagavat Gíta with the exception of a few places where it is masculine; and once where it occurs in the neuter, but no longer signifies the Supreme Being in his complete character of the essence of both spirit and matter; but merely that portion of him which is the essence of all matter, the universal vital energy. We have thus:—'Ist, Brahma, *masculine*, the mythological personage, first person of the mythological triad, and personification of the creative power, considered as a mortal and material deity; 2nd, Brahma, *neuter*, a name used to designate the Supreme Being in philosophic languge; and 3rd, Brahma, neuter, the personification, in later philosophical language, of the material portion of the Supreme Being. (The word has never been satisfactorily derived, though commonly supposed to come from the root *vrih*, to grow or increase.'"—*Thompson.* Dr. Muir in the 5th Vol. of his *Original Sanscrit Texts*, translates a text which he says, 'is interesting not merely as introducing Brahma but as containing what is probably one of the oldest extant expositions of the conceptions of nāma and rūpa (name and form) as comprehending the whole of the phenominal universe.'

"1. In the beginning Brahma was this [universe.] He created gods. Having created gods, he placed them in these worlds, *viz.*, in this world Agni, in the atmosphere Vāyu, and in the sky Sūrya; (2) And in the worlds which were yet higher he placed the gods who are still higher. Such as are these visible worlds and these gods,—even such were those (higher) visible worlds in which he placed those (higher) gods, and such were those gods themselves; (3) Then Brahma proceeded to the higher sphere (parārddha—explained by the commentator to mean the Satyaloka, the most excellent, and the limit of all the worlds.) Having gone to that higher sphere, he considered 'how now can I pervade all these worlds?' He then pervaded them with two things—with form and with name. Whatever has a name, that is name. And then that which has no name—that which he knows by its form, that 'such is its form'—that is form. This [universe] is so much as is (*i.e.*, is co-extensive with) form and name; (4) These are the two great magnitudes (*abhve*) of Brahma. He who knows these two great magnitudes of Brahma becomes himself a great magnitude; (5) These are the two great manifestations of Brahma. He who knows these two great manifestations of Brahma becomes himself a great manifestations. Of these two, one is the greater, *viz.*, form; for whatever is name is also form. He who knows the greater of these two, becomes greater than him than whom he wishes to become greater; (6) The gods were originally mortal, but when they were pervaded by Brahma they became immortal. By that which he send-s forth from his mind (mind is form; for by mind he knows, 'This is form')—by that, I say, he obtains form. And by that which he sends out from his voice (voice is name; for by voice he seizes name)—by that, I say, he obtains mean. This universe is so much as is (*i.e.*, is co-extensive with) form and name. All that he obtains. Now that all is undecaying. Hence he obtains undecaying merit, and an undecaying world."

"The deity who is described in the later hymns of the Rig Veda, and in the Atharva Veda, under the different titles of Viṣvakarman, Hiranyagarbha and Prajápati, appears to correspond with the Brahma of the more modern legendary books. Though this god was originally unconnected with Vishṇu and Rudra, while at a subsequent period he came to be regarded in systematic mythology as the first person in the triad of which they formed the second and third members, yet the general idea entertained of his character has been less modified in the course of his history than is the case in regard to the other two deities."

"Brahma was from the beginning considered as the Creator, and he continued to be regarded as fulfilling the same function even after he had sunk into a subordinate position, and had come to be represented by the votaries of Vishṇu and Mahádeva respectively, as the mere creature and agent of one or other of these two gods. In later times Brahma has had few special worshippers; the only spot where he is periodically adored being at Pushkara in Rajputana. Two of the acts which the earlier legends ascribe to him, the assumption of the forms of a tortoise and of a boar are in later works transferred to Vishnu."

In the fourth Volume of Muir's *Original Sanscrit Texts*, from which the above extract has been taken, the reader will find the life, character and attributes of Brahma fully illustrated. In some of the Texts translated it is maintained that Brahma, Vishnu and Śiva, are three manifestations of the same divinity. "I shall declare to thee that form composed of Hari and Hara (Vishṇu and Mahádeva) combined, which is without beginning, middle, or end, imperishable, undecaying. He who is Vishṇu is Rudra; he who is Rudra is Pitámaha (Brahma); the substance is one, the gods are three, Rudra, Vishṇu and Pitámaha." (*O.S.T.*, Vol. IV, p. 237.)

BRAHMA BODHYA—A river mentioned in the Vishṇu Purána, but not identified.

BRAHMA PURANA—In all the lists of the Purāṇas the *Brahmā* stands first, for which reason it is sometimes entitled the Ādi or "First" *Purāṇa*. It was repeated by Brahmā to Marīci, and is said to contain 10,000 stanzas, but the actual number is between 7000 and 8000. It is also called the *Saura Purāṇa* because "it is, in great part, appropriated to the worship of Sūrya, the sun". "The early chapters give a description of the creation, an account of the *manvantaras*, and the history of the Solar and Lunar dynasties to the time of Kṛṣṇa in a summary manner, and in words which are common, to it and several other Purāṇas. A brief description of the universe succeeds; and then come a number of chapters relating to the holiness of Orissa, with its temples and sacred groves, dedicated tothesun, toŚiva,andJagannātha,the latter especially. These chapters are characteristic of this Purāṇa, and show its main object to be the promotion of the worship of Kṛṣṇa as Jagannātha. To these particulars succeeds a life of Kṛṣṇa, which is word for word the same as that of the *Viṣṇu Purāṇa*; and the compilation terminates with a particular detail of the mode in which Yoga or contemplative devotion, the object of which is still Viṣṇu, is to be performed. There is little in this which corresponds with the definition of *as Pañcalakṣaṇa Purāṇa*, and the mention of the temples of Orissa, the date of the original construction of which is recorded, shows that it could not have been compiled earlier than the thirteenth or fourteenth century." This *Purāṇa* has "a supplementary or concluding section called the *Brahmottara Purāṇa*, which contains about 3000 stanzas. This bears still more entirely the character of a *māhātmya* or local legend, being intended to celebrate the sanctity of the Balajā river, conjectured to be the same as the Banās in Marwar. There is no clue to its date, but it is clearly modern, grafting personages and fictions of its own invention on a few hints from older authorities."—*Wilson.*

BRAHMA SUTRAS—Aphorisms of the Vedānta philosophy by Bādarāyaṇa or Vyāsa. They are also called *Brahmā Mīmāṁsā Sūtras*. They have been translated by the Rev. K.M. Banerjea in the *Bibliotheca Indica*.

BRAHMA, BRAHMAN (neuter). The supreme soul of the universe, self-existent, absolute, and eternal, from which all things emanate, and to which all return. This divine essence is incorporeal, immaterial, invisible, unborn, uncreated, without beginning and without end, illimitable, and inappreciable by the sense until the film of mortal blindness is removed. It is all-pervading and infinite in its manifestations, in all nature, animate and inanimate, in the highest god and in the meanest creature. This supreme soul receives no worship, but it is the object of that abstract meditation which Hindu sages practise in order to obtain absorption into it. It is sometimes called Kalahaṁsa.

There is a passage in the *Śatapatha Brāhmaṇa* which represents Brahmā (neut.) as the active creator, (*see* Brahmā)

The Veda is sometimes called Brahmā.

BRAHMABALI—A disciple of Devaderṣa and teacher of the Sámaveda.

BRAHMABHUTA—To become identified with the Supreme Spirit: to have the conviction that spirit is one, universal and the same.

BRAHMACHARI—A religious student who has been invested with the sacred thread; he is to prosecute the study of the Vedas in the house of his preceptor: and to wait on him constantly; in the morning he is to salute the sun, in the evening fire; and then to address his preceptor with respect. He must stand when his preceptor is standing; move when he is walking, and sit beneath him when he is seated: he must never sit, nor walk, nor stand, when his teacher does the reverse. He is to read the Veda attentively, placed before his preceptor; and to eat the food he has collected as alms, when permitted by his teacher. He is to bathe in water which has first been used for his preceptor's ablutions; and every morning bring fuel and water, and whatever else may be required. *V.P.*

One of the hymns translated by Dr. Muir in his Original Sanscrit Texts ascribes "very astonishing powers to the Brahmachārin or religious student." Dr. Muir says: "Some parts of it are obscure, but the translation I give, though imperfect, will convey some idea of the contents."

"The Brahmachārin works, quickening both worlds. The gods are joyful in him. He has established the earth and the sky. He satisfies his āchārya (religious teacher) by tapas; 2, The Fathers, the heavenly hosts, all the gods separately, follow after him, with the 6,333 Gandharvas. He satisfies all the gods by tapas; 3, The āchārya, adopting him as a disciple, makes him a Brahmachārin even in the womb, and supports him in the belly for three nights. When he is born the gods assemble to see him; 4, This piece of fuel is the earth (compare verse 9), the second is the sky, and he satisfies the air with fuel. The Brahmachārin satisfies the worlds with fuel, with a girdle, with exertion, with tapas; 5, Born before Brahma, the Brahmachārin arose through tapas, clothed with heat. From him was produced divine knowlege (brāmaṇa), the highest Brahma, and all the gods, together with immortality; 6, The Brahmachārin advances, lighted up by fuel, clothed in a black antelope's skin, consecrated, long-bearded. He moves straightway from the eastern to the northern ocean, compressing the worlds, and again expanding them; 7, The Brahmachārin, generating divine science, the waters, the world. Prajāpati, Parameshṭhin, Virāj, having become an embryo in the womb of immortality, having become Indra, crushed the Asuras; 8, The Áchāryas has constructed both these spheres, broad and deep, the earth and the sky. The Brahmachārin preserves them by tapas. In him the gods are joyful; 9, It was the Brahmachārin who first produced this broad earth and the sky as an alms. Making them two pieces of fuel (compare verse 4) he worships. In them all creatures are contained; 10, The two receptacles of divine knowledge are secretly deposited, the one on this side, the other beyond the surface of the sky. The Brahmachārin guards them by tapas. Wise, he appropriates that divine knowledge as his exclusive portion; 16, The Brahmachārin is the Áchārya, the Brahmachārin is Prajāpati; Prajāpati shines (*virājati*); the shining (*Viráj*) became Indra, the powerful; 17, Through self-restraint and tapas a king protects his dominions. Through self-restraint an Áchārya seeks after a Brahmachārin; 18, By self-restraint a damsel obtains a young man as her husband. By self-restraint as ox and a horse seek to gain fodder; 19, By self-restraint and tapas the gods destroyed death. By self-restraint Indra acquired heaven from [or for] the gods; 20, Plants, whatever has been, whatever shall be, day and night, trees, the year, with the seasons, have been produced from the Brahmachārin; 21, Terrestrial and celestial beings, beasts, both wild and tame, creatures without wings and winged, have been produced from the brahmachārin; 22, All creatures which have sprung from Prajāpati have breath separately in themselves; all of these are preserved by divine separately in themselves; all of these are preserved by divine knowledge (Brahma), which is produced in the Brahmachārin...; 26, These things the Brahmachārin formed; on the surface of the water he stood performing tapas in the sea."

BRAHMADIKAS—The Prajāpatis (*q.v.*).

BRAHMAGUPTA—An astronomer who composed *the Brahmāgupta Siddhānta* in AD 628.

BRAHMAJÀÑA—Sacred Study, that which communicates to soul the knowledge of good and evil: one of the five great sacrifices or obligations of the Brahmachári.

BRAHMÁKETU—A prince, the son of Visvaketu, king of Drávida, who was doomed to die in his sixteenth year, but who, by advice of Angiras, went to Benares, and lay down in the path of Yama, when on a visit to Śiva. Yama who never deviates from a straight path, and even an equal step, and could therefore neither walk round Brahmáketu nor stride over him, at last, to induce him to rise, promised to allow him to live a century, which accordingly happened. There is an underplot of Brahmáketu's marrying ihe daughter of the king of Kámpilya, in lieu of the hunchbacked son of the king of Kekaya, which has some resemblance to a story in the Arabian Nights.—Wilson's *Works*, III, 44.

BRAHMALOKA—The highest heaven, the world of infinite wisdom and truth, the inhabitants of which never again know death. (*See* LOKA)

BRAHMANA—'Belonging to brāhmaṇas.' Works composed by and for brāhmaṇas. That part of the Veda which was intended for the use and guidance of brāhmaṇas in the use of the hymns of the *mantra*, and therefore of later production; but the *Brāhmaṇa*, equally with the *mantra*, is held to be Śruti or revealed word. Excepting its claim to revelation, it is a Hindu Talmud. The *Brāhmaṇa* collectively is made up of the different brāhmaṇas, which are ritualistic and liturgical writings in prose. They contain the details of the Vedic ceremonies, with long explanations of their origin and meaning; they give instructions as to the use of particular verses and metres; and they abound with curious legends, divine and human, in illustration. In them are found "the oldest rituals we have, the oldest linguistic explanations, the oldest traditional narratives, and the oldest philosophical speculations". As literary productions they are not of a high order, but some "striking thoughts, bold expressions, sound reasoning, and curious traditions are found among the mass of pedantry and grandiloquence". Each of the Saṁhitās or collection of hymns has its *Brāhmaṇas*, and these generally maintain the essential character of the Veda to which they belong. Thus the *Brāhmaṇas* of the Ṛg are specially devoted to the duties of the Hotṛ, who recites the *ṛcās* or verses, those of the *Yajur* to the performance of the sacrifices by the Adhvaryu, and those of the *sāmara* to the chanting by the Udgātṛ. The Ṛg has the *Aitareya Brāhmaṇa*, which is perhaps the oldest, and may date as far back as the seventh century BC. This is sometimes called Āś valāyana. It has another called Kauṣītaki or Śānkhāyana.The *Taittirīya Saṁhitā* of the *Yajurveda* has the *Taittirīya Brāhmaṇa*, andthe *Vājasaneyī Saṁhitā* has the *Śatapatha Brāhmaṇa*, one of the most important of all the *Brāhmaṇas*. The *Samaveda* has eight *Brāhmaṇas*, of which the best known are the *Prauḍha* or *Pañcaviṁśa*, the *Tāṇḍya*, and the *Saḍviṁśa*. The *Atharva* has only one, the *Gopatha Brāhmaṇa*. In their fullest extent the *Brāhmaṇas* embrace also the treatises called Āraṇyakas and Upaniṣads.

BRAHMANA—The first of the four castes; the sacerdotal class, the members of which may be, but are not necessarily, priests. A brāhmaṇa is the chief of all created beings; his person is inviolate; he is entitled to all honour, and enjoys many rights and privileges. The *Śatapatha Brāhmaṇa* declares that "there are two kinds of gods; first the gods, then those who are brāhmaṇas, and have learnt the Veda and repeat it: they are human gods". The chief duty of a brāhmaṇa is the study and teaching of the Vedas, and the performance of sacrifices and other religious ceremonies; but in modern times many brāhmaṇas entirely neglect these duties, and they engage in most of the occupations of secular life. Under the law of Manu, the life of a brāhmaṇa was divided into four *āśramas* or stages:

1. *Brahmācārī*—The student, whose duty was to pass his days in humble and obedient attendance upon his spiritual preceptor in the study of the Vedas.
2. *Gṛhastha*—The householder; the married man living with his wife as head of a family engaged in the ordinary duties of a brāhmaṇa, reading and teaching the Vedas, sacrificing and assisting to sacrifice, bestowing alms and receiving alms.

3. *Vānaprastha*—The anchorite, or "dweller in the woods", who, having discharged his duties as a man of the world, has retired into the forest to devote himself to self-denial in food and raiment, to mortifications of various kinds, to religious meditation, and to the strict performance of all ceremonial duties.

4. *Saṁnyāsī*.—The religious mendicant, who, freed from all forms and observances, wanders about and subsists on alms, practising or striving for that condition of mind which, heedless of the joys and pains, cares and troubles of the flesh, is intent only upon the deity and final absorption.

The divisions and subdivisions of the brāhmaṇa caste are almost innumerable. It must suffice here to notice the great divisions of north and south, the Pañca Gauḍa and Pañca Drāviḍa. The five divisions of Gauḍa, or Bengal, are the brāhmaṇas of—(1) Kānyakubja, Kannauj; (2) Sārasvata, the north-west, about the Sarasvatī or Sarsūti river; (3) Gauḍa; (4) Mithilā, North Bihar; (5) Utkala, Orissa. The Pañca Drāviḍa are the brāhmaṇas of—(1) Mahārāṣṭra, the Mahratta country; (2) Teliṅga, the Telugu country; (3) Drāviḍa, the Tamil country; (4) Karnāṭa, the Canarese country; (5) Gūrjjara, Gujarat.

BRAHMANAS—The portions of the Vedas which comprise precepts inculcating religious duties, maxims which explain these precepts, and arguments which relate to theology. "The Brâhmanas represent no doubt a most interesting phrase in the history of the Indian mind, but judged by themselves, as literary productions, they are most disappointing. No one would have supposed that at so early a period, and in so primitive a state of society, there could have risen up a literature which for pedantry and downright absurdity can hardly be matched anywhere. There is no lack of striking thoughts, of bold expressions, of sound reasoning and curious traditions in these collections. But these are only like the fragments of a *torso*, like precious gems set in brass and lead. The general character of these works is marked by shallow and insipid grandiloquence, by priestly conceit and antiquarian pedantry. It is most important to the historian that he should know how soon the fresh and healthy growth of a nation can be blighted by priestcraft and superstition. It is most important that we should know that nations are liable to those epidemics in their youth as well as in their dotage. These works deserve to be studied as the physician studies the twaddle of idiots, and the raving of madmen. They will disclose to a thoughtful eye the ruins of faded grandeur, the memories of noble aspirations. But let us only try to translate these works into our own language, and we shall feel astonished that human language and human thought should ever have been used for such purposes."*

The Brahmana of all tribes, according to Hindu writings and traditions, are originally descended from seven Rishis, or sages, held by Hindus universally in profound veneration as semi-deities of great sanctity and wisdom. These, as given by the Nirni Sindhu, and also by the Dharma Sindhu, are as follows:—

1. Brighu.
2. Angirá.
3. Atri.
4. Vishwamitra.
5. Kaṣyapa.
6. Vasishṭha.
7. Agastí.

Each of these Rishis stands at the head of a great division, the various members of which are further sub-divided into sections, termed *gotras* or classes. These gotras are found more or less in all the Brahmanical tribes.

In their ceremonies the Brahmans follow the rituals or instructions of one or other of the four Vedas. Five of the principal gotras observe the Sama Veda; five others, the Rig Veda; five others, the Yajur Veda; and five, the Atharva Veda. The rest of the Brahmans of all gotras follow the Yajur Veda.

Great and important distinctions subsist between the various tribes of Brahmans. Some are given to learning; some to agriculture; some to politics; some to trade.

But all are classed under two great divisions, named Gaur and Drávira, each of which consists of five tribes. These are mostly separated by geographical boundaries. Speaking somewhat generally, the Gaur tribes are found in Northern India, and the Drávida tribes in the Deccan or Southern India. The river Narmada in Central India is commonly regarded as a rough geographical line of demarcation between the Gaura and Drávidas. Yet there is an important distinction between them which ought to be always borne in mind, that the former are of greater antiquity than the latter, the Southern Brahmans having in fact originally migrated from the tribes in the North. In addition to the ten well-known principal tribes, there are several supplementary tribes, which, although not usually reckoned amongst them, are doubtless of Brahmanical origin

DIVISIONS OF BRAHMANS

The Gaur, or Northern Division, consisting of five Tribes.

I. Kanyakubja or Kanoujiya.
II. Sáraswat.
III. Gaur.
IV. Maithila.
V. Utkala.

The Drávida, or Southern Division, consisting of Five Tribes.

I.Maháráshtra.
II. Tailanga.
III. Drávira.
IV. Karnáta.
V. Gurjar.

Besides these there are twenty-five supplementary tribes.

The Kányakubja Brahmans belong to the old kingdom of Kanouj, and are found dispersed over a large portion of the North-Western Provinces, as far as Benares, where they are very numerous, especially that branch of them known as Sarwaria or Sárjupári, which is scattered over the country from the northern bank of the Sarju, on the confines of Ondh, its original home, to Benares, and beyond. The Sáraswat Brahmans are in the North-west of India; the Gaurs are found in the vicinity of Delhi, and in Bengal; the Maithilas inhabit the northern part of Behar; and the Utkalas have their home in Orissa, The five Dravira tribes may be separated, like the five Gaurs, by geographical boundaries. The Maháráshtras belong to the Mahratta country; the Tailangas, to Telingáná; the Dráviras, to the Tamil-speaking districts; the Karnátas, to the Karnatic; and the Gujars, to Gujerat. Of the subordinate or supplementary tribes, the Máthurs are found in the city of Mathura and its neighbourhood; the Sákádwípís, in the old Magadh country; the Málwá Brahmans, in Málwá; the Kurmáchalís, in Kumaon; the Naipális, in Nepal; the Káshmírís, in Cashmere; the Sapt-Shati Brahmans, in Bengal; the Shenevi Brahmans, in the Mahratta country; the Palashe Brahmans in Southern India. The remainder are found in various places, chiefly in Northern India, and are of little weight or importance.

It is important to observe, as a distinguishing caste characteristic of all these tribes, that, although some of them may partake of cooked food together, yet they do not intermarry. The five Gaur tribes are entirely distinct from one another, both in regard to marriage and eating food; and are likewise, in these respects, distinct from the five tribes of Southern Brahmans. Yet the five Dráviras are not quite so exclusive in their relations to one another. None of them intermarry; nevertheless, four out of the five can eat together. These are the Maháráshtra, the Tailanga, the Drávira, and the Karnáta. None of them, however, eats with the Gurjar tribe, owing to certain peculiarities in this tribe not found in the rest. The supplementary tribes keep themselves aloof from one another and from all other tribes.—Sherring, *T.C.I.*

* Max Müller.

BRAHMANASPATI—A Vedic equivalent of the name Bṛhaspati.

BRAHMANDA PURANA—"That which has declared, in 12,200 verses, the magnificence of the egg of Brahmā, and in which an account of the future *kalpas* is contained, is called the *Brahmāṇḍa Purāṇa*, and was revealed by Brahmā." This Purāṇa, like the *Skanda*, is "no longer procurable in a collective body", but is represented by a variety *of khaṇḍas* and *māhātmyas* professing to be derived from it. The *Adhyātma Rāmāyaṇa*, a very popular work, is considered to be a part of this Purāṇa.

BRAHMANI—The female form, or the daughter of Brahmā, also called Satarūpā (*q.v.*).

BRAHMAPURA—The city of Brahmā. The heaven of Brahmā, on the summit of Mount Meru, and enclosed by the river Gaṅgā.

BRAHMA-PURANA—The, gives a description of the creation, an account of the Manwantaras, and the history of the solar and lunar dynasties to the time of Krishṇa. It also sets forth the sanctity of Orissa, with its temples and sacred groves, dedicated to the sun, to Śiva and Jagganath. Its object seems to be the promotion of the worship of Krishṇa as Jagganath.

BRAHMARSI-DESA—"Kurukṣetra, the Matsyas, the Pañcālas, and-the Surasenas. This land, which comes to Brahmāvarta, is the land of Brahmārṣis."—*Manu.*

BRAHMAS OR BRAHMARISHIS—According to the *V.P.* the names of the nine Brahmans, or Brahmarishis, are Brighu, Pulastya, Pulaha, Kratu, Angiras, Marichi,

Daksha, Atri and Vasishta. They are also called Prajápatis and Brahmaputras. Considerable variety prevails in the lists of them in the different books: but the variations are of the nature of additions made to an apparently original enumeration of but seven, whose names generally recur. In the *V.P.* they are termed the mind-engendered progeny of Brahma: born from his continued meditations. In the South of India they are usually termed the Seven Penitents. Two it is said were not originally brahmans, but they practised so long and severe a penance that they obtained the remarkable favor of being raised to that rank by the ceremony of the cord. From penitent Rájas they became penitent brahmans: their rise was from a still lower rank according to the philosophical poet Vernana. These Rishis existed prior to the Vedas, in which they are often mentioned. The Abbe Dubois thinks they were the seven sons of Japhet.

BRAHMÁKETU—A prince, the son of Visvaketu, king of Drávida, who was doomed to die in his sixteenth year, but who, by advice of Angiras, went to Benares, and lay down in the path of Yama, when on a visit to Śiva. Yama who never deviates from a straight path, and even an equal step, and could therefore neither walk round Brahmáketu nor stride over him, at last, to induce him to rise, promised to allow him to live a century, which accordingly happened. There is an underplot of Brahmáketu's marrying ihe daughter of the king of Kámpilya, in lieu of the hunchbacked son of the king of Kekaya, which has some resemblance to a story in the Arabian Nights.—Wilson's *Works*, III, 44.

BRAHMA-SAVARNI—The tenth Manu. (*see* MANU)

BRAHMAVAIVARTA PURANA—"That Purāṇa which is related by Sāvarṇi to Nārada, and contains the account of the greatness of Kṛṣṇa, with the occurrences of the Rathantara-kalpa, where also the story of Brahmāvarāha is repeatedly told, is called the *Brahmāvaivarta Purāṇa*, and contains 18,000 stanzas." The copies known rather exceed the number of stanzas, but the contents do not answer to this description. "The character of the work is so decidedly sectarial, and the sect to which it belongs so distinctly marked—that of the worshippers of the juvenile Kṛṣṇa and Rādhā, a form of belief of known modem origin"—that it must be a production of a comparatively late date. A specimen of the text and translation has been published by Stenzler.

BRAHMAVARTTA—"Between the two divine rivers, Sarasvatī and Dṛsadvatī, lies the tract of land which the sages have named Brahmāvārtta, because it was frequented by the gods."—*Manu*, II, 17.

BRAHMAVEDA—A name given to the *Atharvan* or fourth Veda, the Veda of prayers and charms.

BRAHMA-YUGA—'The age of Brahmāns'. The first or *Kṛta-yuga*. (*see* YUGA)

BRAHMI—One of the eight Śaktis, or hideous goddesses, who attend upon Śiva as Bhairava, the terrific and destructive deity, who is propitiated by offerings of wine and flesh.

BRAHMOTTARA PURANA—(*see* BRAHMĀ PURĀṆA)

BRAMHARSHIS—Descendants of the five patriarchs who were the founders of races or Gotras of brahmans, or Kaṣyapa, Vasishtha, Angiras, Atri and Brighu. The Brahmarshis dwell in the sphere of Brahma.

BRAMMEDHYA—The name of a river in the Vishṇu Purána not yet identified.

BRHANNARADIYA PURANA—(*see* NĀRADA PURĀṆA)

BṚHASPATI—In the *Ṛgveda* the names Bṛhaspati and Brahmāṇaspati alternate, and are equivalent to each other. They are names "of a deity in whom the action of the worshipper upon the gods is personified. He is the suppliant, the sacrificer, the priest, who intercedes with gods on behalf of men and protects mankind against the wicked. Hence he appears as the prototype of the priests and priestly order; and is also designated as the *purohita* (family priest) of the divine community. He is called in one place 'the father of the gods', and a widely extended creative power is ascribed to him. He is also designated as 'the shining' and 'the gold-coloured', and as 'having the thunder for his voice."

In later times he is a *ṛṣi.* He is also regent of the planet Jupiter, and the name is commonly used for the planet itself. In this character his car is called Nītighoṣa and is drawn by eight pale horses. He was son of the rsi Aṅgiras, and he bears the patronymic Āṅgirasa. As preceptor of the gods he is called Animiṣācārya, Cakṣas, Ijya, and Indrejya. His wife, Tārā, was carried off by Soma, the moon, and this gave rise to a war called the Tārakāmaya. Soma was aided by Uśanas, Rudra, and all the *daityas* and *dānavas*, while Indra and the gods took the part of Bṛhaspati. "Earth, shaken to her centre", appealed to Brahmā, who interposed and restored Tārā to her husband. She was delivered of a son which Bṛhaspati and Soma both claimed, but Tārā, at the command of Brahmā to tell the truth, declared Soma to be the father, and the child was named Budha. There is an extraordinary story in *theMatsya* and *Bhāgavata Purāṇas* of the ṛṣis having milked the earth through Bṛhaspati. (*see Viṣṇu Purāṇa*, i, pp. 188,190) Bṛhaspati was father of Bharadvaja by Manatā, wife of Utathya. (*see* Bharadvāja) An ancient code of law bears the name of Bṛhaspati, and he is also represented as being the Vyāsa of the "fourth, *dvāpara* age". There was a *ṛṣi* of the name in the second *manvantara*, and one who was founder of an heretical sect. Other epithets of Bṛhaspati are Jīva, 'the living', Dīdivis, 'the bright', Dhiṣaṇa, 'the intelligent', and, for his eloquence, Gīṣpati, 'lord of speech'.

BṚHAT-SAMHITA—A celebrated work on astronomy by Varāhamihira. It has been printed by Kern in the *Bibliotheca Indica*, who has also published a translation *Jour. RAS* for 1870 and following years.

BUDDHA—Gautama Buddha, the founder of Buddhism. Viṣṇu's ninth incarnation, (*see* AVATĀRA)

BUDDHI—Understanding, synonyme of Mahat; also the name of a daughter of Daksha who became the wife of Dharma.

BUDHA—(Mercury). The son of Soma, the moon, by Rohiṇī, or by Tārā, wife of Bṛhaspati. (*see* BṚHASPATI) *Budha* married *Ilā*, daughter of Manu Vaisvata Vaivasvata, and by her had a son, Purūravas; whose sex had been changed by Śiva. Thence the lunar, as distinguished from the solar, line of kings; and to that point is to be referred many important opinions and results, very widely disseminated. See ILĀ.

There exists a doubt whether the names of planetary bodies were given to early men, or whether the planets were named after distinguished men of the earliest age. The purānas give a brief legend, which has been deemed astronomical, but of a doubtful school; such as reduced Abraham to a constellation. This legend is that *Chandra* (the moon) was placed in the house of *Vrihaspati* (Jupiter) as his pupil, and that Tárá (the lunar path of 27 asterisms) fell in love with *Chandra*, and seduced him while *Vrihaspati* was away at a sacrifice made by Indra (the firmament); the result was the birth of *Budha* (Mercury). If there *be* any astronomical meaning, it would imply that the old Chaldeans thought that the moon in some part of its orbit attracted a satellite of Jupiter, detached it from that planet, and was the occasion of its finding an orbit around the sun, as a primary planet. However, this interpretation has great improbabilities.

The poets, and especially Telugu poets, have paraphrased the legend in their own way; and very freely too. If the parties were men on earth we get at one of the earliest known wars. For, the claim to the parentage and right of *Budha* by Vrihaspati and Chandra, led to a fierce war, dividing gods and men into two parties.

From his parents he is called Saumya and Rauhineya. He is also called Praharṣaṇa, Rodhana, Tuṅga, and Śyāmāṅga, 'black-bodied'. The intrigue of Soma with Tārā was the cause of a great quarrel, in which the gods and the *asuras* fought against each other. Brahmā compelled Soma to give up Tārā, and when she returned to her husband she was pregnant. A son was born, who was so beautiful that Bṛhaspati and Soma both claimed him. Tārā for a long time refused to tell his paternity, and so excited the wrath and nearly incurred the curse other son. At length, upon the command of Brahmā, she declared Soma to be the father, and he gave the boy the name of Budha. This name is distinct from Buddha.

BURA PENNOU—The deity worshipped by the Khonds; he is called the god of light and source of good; while his consort Tari-Pennou is the source of evil in the world.

BYROBA—A demi-god of the herdsmen; worshipped wherever a few of the pastoral tribes are settled.

CASTE—The term Caste, derived from the Portuguese *Casta*, expressive of the Indian word Játi, has been universally adopted by Europeans to denote the different classes or tribes into which the people of India are divided. "The permanent division of the community into classes, with hereditary professions assigned to each, is one of the most remarkable institutions of Hindustan. There are four great divisions. The most distinguished of all is that of Brahmana or Brahmans, who are said to have come from the mouth of Braham: the second in rank is that of Kshatriya or Rájas, from the arm of Brahma; the third of Vaisya, or merchants, from the thigh of Brahma; the fourth the Sudras, or workmen, from his foot: all with their females. Each of these four tribes is subdividied into several more; the Sudras especially have an almost endless number of distinctions; such as herdmen who keep the cows; shepherds who tend the sheep; weavers; five castes of Artizans, *viz.*, carpenters, goldsmiths, blacksmiths, stone-cutters, founders. The several castes of cultivators take precedence of other Sudras, and look with contempt on tradesmen and labourers. There is a Caste of Kaḷḷaru, or robbers, who consider their profession as no way discreditable to themselves or their tribe. Each caste exhibits some particular and local varieties of its own by which it is discriminated from the rest: Some distinguish themselves by the cut and colour of their clothes; some by the manner in which they put them on. But however extravagant their modes and customs are, they never excite from castes of the most opposite habits and fashions the least appearance of contempt or dislike. Upon this point there seems to be the most perfect toleration.

In the South of India there is another division of the different tribes still more general than those which have been yet mentioned. It is that of Right-hand and Left-hand Castes. The greater number of Hindus castes belong either to the Right-hand or the Left. The Brahmans, the Pariahs (or outcastes) and several tribes of the Sudras, are considered neutral, and enjoying all the privileges and honors attached to both hands, they take no part with either. These neutral castes are frequently called upon to arbitrate in the fierce disputes that occur between the Right and Left-hand parties. Both parties lay claim to certain privileges; and when any encroachment is made by either it is followed by tumults that spread through a district, accompained with every excess; and generally with bloody contests. The Hindu, usually so gentle and timid, seems to change his nature. There is no danger he fears to encounter in maintaining these rights."—*Dubois*

Dr. Muir in the first volume of his *O.S.Texts*, has very fully investigated the mythical accounts of the creation of man and of the origin of the four castes. He says "it will be seen from the texts adduced that from a very early period the Indian writers have propounded a great variety of speculations regarding the origin of mankind, and of the classes or castes into which they found their own community divided. The most commonly received of these explanations is the fable which represents the Brahmans, Kshatriyas, Vaisyas and Sudras, to have been separately created from the head, the breast or arms, the thighs, and the feet of the Creator. Of this mythical account no trace is to be found in any of the hymns of the Rig Veda, except one, the Purusha Sūkta."

Dr. Muir is of opinion that this hymn belongs to the most recent portion of the Rig Veda. Mr. Colebrook, Professors Max Müller and Weber concur on this view; which however is controverted by Dr. Haug.

After quoting a great number of texts from the oldest authorities, Dr. Muir remarks. "When we discover in the most ancient Indian writings such different and even discrepant accounts of the origin of man, all put forth with equal positiveness, it is impossible to imagine that any uniform explanation of the diversity of castes could have been received at the period when they were composed, or to regard any of the texts which have been cited as more orthodox and authoritative than the rest. Even, therefore, if we should suppose that the author of the Purusha Sūkha meant to represent the four castes as having literally sprung from separate parts of Purusha's body, it is evident that the same idea was not always or even generally adopted by those who followed him, as a revealed truth in which they were bound to acquiesce. In fact, nothing is clearer than that in all these cosmogonies, the writers, while generally assuming certain prevalent ideas as the basis of their descriptions, gave the freest scope to their individual fancy in the invention of details. In such circumstances, perfect coincidence cannot be expected in the narratives."

The following are the results of Dr. Muir's careful investigation of all the Texts bearing on the subject:—

"The details which I have supplied in the course of this chapter must have rendered it abundantly evident that the sacred books of the Hindus contain no unifrom or consistent account of the origin of castes; but, on the contrary, present the greatest varieties of speculation on this subject. Explanations mystical, mythical, and rationalistic, are all offered in turn; and the freest scope is given by the individual writers to fanciful and arbitrary conjecture.

First: we have the set of accounts in which the four castes are said to have sprung from progenitors who were separately created; but in regard to the manner of their creation we find the greatest diversity of statement. The most common story is that the castes issued from the mouth, arms, thighs, and feet of Purusha, or Brahma. The oldest extant passage in which this idea occurs, and from which all the later myths of a similar tenor have no doubt been borrowed,is, as we have seen, to be found in the Purusha Sūkta; but it is doubtful whether, in the form in which it is there presented, this representation is anything more than an allergory. In some of the texts which I have quoted from the Bhágavata Purána, traces of the same allegorical character may be perceived; but in Manu and the Puránas the mystical import of the Vedic text disappears, and the figurative narrative is hardened into a literal statement of fact. In other passages, where a separate origin is assigned to the castes they are variously said to have sprung from the words Būh, Bhuvah, Svàh; from different Vedas; from different sets of prayers; from the gods, and the asuras; from nonentity, and from the imperishable, the perishable, and other principles. In the chapters of the Vishṇu, Váyu, and Márkanḍeya Puránas, where castes are described as coeval with the creation, and as having been naturally distinguished by different gunas, or qualities, involving varieties of moral character, we are nevertheless allowd to infer that those qualities exerted no influence on the classes in whom they were inherent, as the condition of the whole race during the Kṛita age is described as one of uniform perfection and happiness; while the actual separation into castes did not take place according to the Váyu Purána, until men had become deteriorated in the Treta age.

Second: in various passages from the Bráhmanas, Epic poems, and Puránas, the creation of mankind is, as we have seen, described without the least allusion to any separate production of the progenitors of the four castes. And whilst in the chapters where they relate the distinct formation of the castes, the Puránas, as has been observed, assign different natural dispositions to each class, they elsewhere represent all mankind as being at the creation uniformly distinguished by the quality of passion. In one of the texts I have quoted, men are said to be the offspring of Vivasvat; in another his son Manu is said to be their progenitor; whilst in a third they are said to be descended from a female of the same name. The passage which declares Manu to have been the father of the human race explicitly affirms that men of all the four castes were descended from him. In another remarkable text the Mahábhárata categorically asserts that originally there was no distinction of classes, the existing distribution having arisen out of differences of character and occupation. Similarly, the Bhágavata Purána in one place informs us that in the Kṛita age there was but one caste; and this view appears also to be taken in some passages which I have adduced from the Epic poems./ In these circumstances we may fairly conclude that the separate origination of the four castes was far from being an article of belief universally received by *Indian Antiquary*."—Vol. I, p. 160.

"There is one peculiarity observable in all the castes in modern days, not to be found in any one of them in primitive ages. The facility for intermarriages has given place to rigid exclusiveness, so that it is now absolutely impossible for the pure castes to intermarry with the mixed, or for the mixed to intermarry with one another. Yet all such intermarriages were permitted in early Hindu times...It is common to speak of the castes of India in their relation to the Hindu religion; and in that light they may very properly be regarded. Yet they sustain another highly important relation. Ethnologically they are so many tribes and clans, with separate histories and customs. The members of a caste are, doubtless, united together by peculiar sacred and social ties. In addition they hear a tribal relation to one another of great significance. Each caste, in virtue of its distinctiveness, and of its holding no marriage connection with other castes, either in its neighbourhood or elsewhere, is in fact a tribe governed by laws of the most imperious character. The races of men, whether in ancient or modem times, have seldom, in any country, been divided into separate tribes and clans by such sharply defined boundaries, over which it is impossible for one to pass to another, as we find separating the various castes of India. Indeed so absolute and tyrannical is this spirit of exclusiveness that the castes are taught to believe that there is a natural distinction subsisting between them, which utterly forbids their union."—Sherring. *T.C.I.*

CHAIDYAS—A race of kings, descendants of Chedi, amongst whom were Damagosha and Śisupála.

CHAITANYA-CANDRODAYA—'The rise of the moon of Caitanya.' A drama in ten acts by Kavikarṇa-pura. It is published in the *Bibliotheca Indica*. Caitanya was a modern Vaiṣṇava reformer, accounted an incarnation of Kṛṣṇa.

CHAITRARATHA—The grove or forest of Kubera on Mandāra, one of the spurs of Meru; it is so-called from its being cultivated by the *gandharva* Citraratha.

CHAITRA—The name of the third lunar month (Feb.-March).

CHAITYAKA—The modern Mount Sonár; the fifth and largest of the five mountains of Rájgir; forming a portion of a rocky mountain chain stretching nearly thirty miles from the neighbourhood of Gaya, north-west as far as Giryak in Bihar. Their sides are rugged and precipitous, and are mostly covered with an impenetrable jungle, broken only by irregular pathways overgrown with brushwood, which are yearly trodden by hundreds of Jaina pilgrims from Murshidábád, Benares and even Bombay, who throng to Rájgir during the cold and dry seasons to do homage to the sacred *ckaranas* or 'foot-prints' of their saints, enshrined in the temples which crown the mountain tops.—*I. A.*

CHAKORA—(1) A kind of partridge. A fabulous bird, supposed to live upon the beams of the moon.

(2) One of the thirty Andhrabhritya kings; he only reigned six months.

CHAKRA— The discus of Vishnu; a sharp-edged quoit; Arjuna performed wonderful feats with his chakra. It was with this weapon that Krishṇa slew Śiṣupála. It is always seen in one of the four hands of Vishṇu. The Chakra has also been converted into the prayer wheel of the Buddhists.

CHAKRAS—A race of people who about the commencement of our era, extended along the West of India, from the Hindu Kosh to the mouths of the Indus.

CHAKRAVAKA—A Brahmani goose: the name of a wise counsellor in the Pancha Tantra; Hiranyagarbha, the king of the water-fowl, was anxious to make war, when his minister, Chakraváka, made many speeches to prevent it, suggesting that victory was ever doubtful, &c.

The ruddy goose, (Anas Casarca) commonly called the Brahmany duck or goose. These birds are always observed, to fly in pairs daring the day, but are supposed to remain separate during the night. "The Chakravákí," in the poetry of the Hindus, is their turtle-dove for constancy and connubial affection; with the singular circumstance of the pair being doomed for ever to nocturnal separation, for having offended one of the Hindu *Munis*, or sages. If we believe popular tradition and assertions, the cause is so far confirmed by the effect observable in the conduct of these birds to the present day, who are said to occupy the opposite banks of a water or stream regularly every evening, and exclaim the live-long night to each other, thus:

> "Say shall I come my love to thee ?
> Ah no, indeed, that cannot be,—
> But may I wing my love to you ?
> Nay, chuck, alas! this will not do."—*Wilson*

CHAKRAVARTI—A universal emperor, described by the *Viṣṇu Purāṇa* as one who is born with the mark of Viṣṇu's discus visible in his hand; but, Wilson observes, "the grammatical etymology is, 'He who abides in or rules over an extensive territory called a Cakra'." On the death of such an emperor it was the custom to collect and deposit the ashes of the body, after burning, in a pyramidal monument.—*Wilson.*

CHAKSHU—(1) A prince, the son of Purujánu, one of the descendants of Dwimídha.

(2) One of the four great rivers, made by the division of the Ganges, and which is said in the *V.P.* to flow into the sea after traversing all the western mountains, and passing through the country of Ketumala.

CHAKSHUPA—A prince renowned for his valour, the son of Khanitra, one of the descendants of Nediṣhta.

CHAKSHUSHAS—The first of the five classes of gods in the fourteenth Manwantara.

CHAKSHUSHA—The Manu of the sixth Manwantara, son of Ripu by Vrihati. The Márkandeya has a legend of his birth as a son of Kshatriya; of his being exchanged at his birth for the son of Visranta Rája, and being brought up by the prince as his own; of his revealing the business when a man, and propitiating Brahma by his devotions, in consequence of which he became a Manu; In his former birth he was born from the eye of Brahma; whence his name from Chakshush 'the eye.'

CHAMPA, CAMPAVATI, CAMPAMALINI, CAMPAPURI—(1) The capital city of the country of Aṅga. Traces of it still remain in the neighbourhood of Bhāgalpur. It was also called Mālini, from its being surrounded with *campaka* trees as with a garland (*mālā*). It is said to have derived its name from Campa, its founder, but the abundant *campaka* trees may assert a claim to its designation. **(2)** A town on the Ganges in which is a Vihára, or Buddhist convent. It is described in the Dasukumáru as notoriously abounding in rogues. **(3)** The son of Pritulaksha, a descendant of Anu, who founded the city of Champápuri, a city of which traces still remain in the vicinity of Bhaghulpur. Champa is everywhere recognised as the capital of Anga.

CHAMPA—Son of Pṛthulākṣa, a descendant of Yayāti, through his fourth son, Anu, and founder of the city of Campā.

CHAMUNDA—An emanation of the goddess Durgā, sent forth from her forehead to encounter the demons Caṇḍa and Muṇḍa. She is thus described in the *Mārkaṇḍeya Purāṇa*—"From the forehead of Ambikā (Durgā), contracted with wrathful frowns, sprang swiftly forth a goddess of black and formidable aspect, armed with a scimitar and noose, bearing a ponderous mace, decorated with a garland of dead corpses, robed in the hide of an elephant, dry and withered and hideous, with yawning mouth, and lolling tongue, and bloodshot eyes, and filling the regions with her shouts." When she had killed the two demons, she bore their heads to Durgā, who told her that she should henceforth be known, by a contraction of their names, as Cāmuṇḍā.

CHANAKKO or CHANAKYA—A brahman of the city of Takkasila (Taxila) who lived about 330 B.C. He is said to have achieved the knowledge of the three Vedas; could rehearse the *mantra*; was skilful in stratagems, and dexterous in intrigue as well as policy. After his father's death he became celebrated as the filial protector of his mother. A long legend is told of the way in which he brought up Chandragupta and ultimately placed him on the throne about 315 B.C. When Chandragupta was a wandering adventurer, the ambitious intriguing brahman became his ardent friend, and promised to open for him a pathway to the throne. Nine brothers, called the nine Nandas, then reigned at Magadha. "Chandragupta was looked upon as their half-brother by a Sudra mother. He is called a Takshaka, or descendant of the great snake Seshanága.

Feeling unsafe amongst his relatives in Behar he had wandered forth to seek his fortune elsewhere." It was then he met with Chánakya, who in pursuance of his intention to place Chandragupta on the thone "contrived to give dire offence to the nine Nandas." He entered their dining-room unannounced, and with the cool assumption of a powerful brahman, took possession of the place of honour. The kings, having the remonstrances of their wise minister, they dragged him from his seat with score.

"Then Chánakaya, blind with indignation, stood up in the centre of the hall, loosened the knot of hair on the top of his head, and thus vowed the destruction of the Nanda race.

'Until I have exterminated these haughty and ignorant Nandas, who have not known my worth, I will not again tie up these hairs.' Having thus declared war he sought out the discontented Chandragupta.

"In the meantime, Rákshasa, who was the prime minister of the Nandas, did all for his princes that could be done either by valour or sagacity. But all in vain, the Nandas 'perished like mother in the flame of Chánakya's revenge.' "

The drama entitled "Mudra Rákshasa," attributed to Visákhadatta, is founded on this story of Chánakya.—*Hindu Theatre. Mrs. Manning*; *A. & M. I.*, Vol. II, p. 221.

CHANDA, CHANDI—The goddess Durgā, especially in the form she assumed for the destruction of the *asura* called Mahiṣa.

CHANDA—A demon servant of the demon chief Śumbha, who was killed by the goddess Umá, who ultimately slew his master also. The Kálipúja festival is in commemoration of the victory of Umá over Cháṇḍa and Muṇḍa.

CHANDALA—An outcaste or pariah; one of the lowest of the mixed tribes descended from a Śudra mother and a Brahman father.

CHANDANA DASA—A banker and intimate friend of Rákshasa in the drama of the "Signet of the Minister." He was condemned and dressed for execution, bearing the stake upon his shoulder, followed by his wife and child; when he was rescued, pardoned and made provost of the merchants.

CHANDANA—A river in Bhalgulpúr.

CHANDANODAKADUNDHUBI—A Yádava chief called also Bhava, a freind of the Gandharba Tumburu.

CHANDAS, CHANDO—Metre. One of the Vedāṅgas. The oldest known work on the subject is "the *Chandaḥśāstra*, ascribed to Piṅgala, which may be as old as the second century BC". It is published in the *Bibliotheca Indica.* The subject is one to which great attention has been given by the Hindus from the earliest times.

CHANDI OR CHANDIKA—A form of Parvati. Human sacrifices are believed to have been formerly made to this goddess. Blood drawn from the offerer's own body is looked upon as a proper oblation to the goddess Chaṇḍika. "By human flesh Chaṇḍika is pleased one thousand years. An oblation of blood, which has been rendered pure by holy texts, is equal to ambrosia; the head and flesh also afford much delight to the goddess Chaṇḍika."—*Asiatic Researches*, Vol. V, Art. XX III.

CHANDI-MAHATMYA, CHANDIKA-MAHATMYA—The same as the *Caṇḍīpāṭha.*

CHANDIPAT, CANDIPATHA—A poem of 700 verses, forming an episode of the *Mārkaṇḍeya Purāṇa.* It celebrates Durgā's victories over the *asuras*, and is read daily in the temples of that goddess. The work is also called *Devī-māhātmya.* It has been translated by Poley and by Burnouf.

CHANDOGA—A priest or chanter of the *Sāmaveda.*

CHANDOGYA—Name of a Upaniṣad of the *Sāmaveda.* (*see* UPANIṢAD) It has been printed by Dr. Roer, and it has been translated into English by Rājendra Lāl, and published in the *Bibliotheca Indica.* There is also another printed edition of the text. The *Chāndogya Upaniṣad* consists of eight out of ten chapters of the *Chāndogya Brāhmaṇa*; the first two chapters are yet wanting. This work is particularly distinguished by its rich store of legends regarding the gradual development of Brāhmaṇical theology.

CHANDO—The name of the bull that protected Chandragupta in infancy.

CHANDRA—The moon, either as a planet or a deity, (*see* SOMA)

CHANDRABHAGA—The name of a river, that takes its rise in the Himálayás and which Professor Wilson identifies as the Chinab.

CHANDRAGIRI—A prince descended from Kusa, the son of Ráma.

CHANDRAGUPTA—This name was identified by Sir W. Jones with the Sandracottus or Sandrocyptus mentioned by Arrian and the other classical historians of Alexander's campaign; and somewhat later on as having entered into a treaty with Seleucus Nicator through the ambassador Megasthénes. The identification has been contested, but chief writers on Indian antiquities have admitted it as an established fact, and have added confirmatory evidence from various sources, so that the identity admits of no reasonable doubt. This identification is of the utmost importance to Indian chronology; it is the only link by which Indian history is connected with that of Greece, and everything in Indian chronology depends upon the date of Candragupta as ascertained from that assigned to Sandracottus by the classical writers. His date, as thus discovered, shows that he began to reign in 315 BC and as he reigned twenty-four years, his reign ended in 291 BC. Candragupta is a prominent name in both Brāhmaṇical and Buddhist writings, and his accession to the throne is the subject of the drama *Mudrārākṣasa.*

When Alexander was in India, he learned that a king named Xandrames reigned over the Prasi (Prācyas) at the city of Palibothra, situated at the confluence of the Ganges and another river called Erranaboas (the Sone). At this time, Sandracottus was young, but he waged war against Alexander's captains, and he raised bands of robbers, with whose help he succeeded in establishing freedom in India.

Hindu and Buddhist writers are entirely silent as to Alexander's appearance in India, but they show that Candragupta overthrew the dynasty of the Nandas, which reigned over Magadha, and "established freedom in India by the help of bands of robbers". He established himself at Pāṭaliputra, the capital of the Nandas, which is identical with the Greek Palibothra, and this has been shown to be the modern Patna. That town does not now stand at the confluence of two rivers, but the rivers in the alluvial plains of Bengal frequently change their courses, and a change in the channel of the Sone has been established by direct geographical evidence. There is a difficulty about Xandrames. This is no doubt the Sanskṛt Candramas, which some consider to be only a shorter form of the name Candragupta, while others point out that the Greek references indicate that Xandrames was the predecessor of Sandracottus, rather than Sandracottus himself.

The dynasty of the Nandas that reigned over Magadha are frequently spoken of as the "nine Nandas", meaning apparently nine descents; but according to some authorities the last Nanda, named Mahāpadma, and his eight sons, are intended. Mahāpadma Nanda was the son of a śūdra, and so by law he was a śūdra himself. He was powerful and ambitious, cruel and avaricious. His people were disaffected; but his fall is represented as having been brought about by the brāhmaṇa Cāṇakya. Chandragupta was then raised to the throne and he founded the Mauryan dynasty, the third king of which was the great Aśoka, grandson of Candragupta. The brāhmaṇas and Buddhists are widely at variance as to the origin of the Maurya family. The drama *Mudrārākṣasa* represents Candragupta as being related to Mahāpadma Nanda, and the commentator on the *Viṣṇu Purāṇa* says that he was a son of Nanda by a woman of low caste named Murā, wherefore he and his descendants were called Mauryas. This looks very like an etymological invention, and is inconsistent with the representation that the low caste of Nanda was one cause of his deposition; for were it true, the low-caste king would have been supplanted by one of still lower degree. On the other hand, the Buddhists contend that the Mauryas belonged to the same family as Buddha, who was of the royal family of the Śākyas. The question of the identification of Sandracottus and Candragupta has been discussed at length by Wilson in the preface to the *Mudrārākṣasa* in his *Hindu Theatre*, and in the *Viṣṇu Purāṇa*, vol. I*V.P.* 185; also by Max Müller in his *History of Ancient Sanskrit Literature.*

"The relative positions of Chandragupta, Vidmisára, or Bimbisára, and Ajátaśtru, serve to confirm the indentification, Sákya was contemporary with both the latter, dying in the eighth year of Ajátaśatru's reign. The Maháwanśo says he reigned twenty-four years afterwards; but the Váyu makes his whole reign but twenty-five years, which would place the close of it B.C. 526. The rest of the Saiśunága dynasty, according to the Váyu and Matsya, reigned 143 or 140 years; bringing their close to B.C. 383. Another century being deducted for the duration of the Nandas, would place the accession of Chandragupta B.C. 283. Chandragupta was the contemporary of Seleucus Nicator, who began his reign B.C. 310, and concluded a treaty with him B.C. 305. Although therefore his date may not be made out quite correctly from the Paurânic premises, yet the error cannot be more than twenty or thirty years. The result is much nearer the truth than that furnished by the Buddhist authorities. According to the Maháwanśo a hundred years had elapsed from the death of Buddha to the tenth year of the reign of Kálásoko (p. 15). He reigned other ten years, and his sons forty-four, making a total of 154 years between the death of Ś ákya and the accession of Chandragupta which is consequently placed B.C. 389, or above seventy years too early. According to the Buddhist authorities, Chan-ta-kutta or Chandragupta, commenced his reign 396 B.C. Burmese Table; Prinsep's *Useful Tables*. Mr. Turnor, in his Introduction, giving to Kálásoko eighteen years subsequent to the century after Buddhas, places Chandragupta's accession B.C. 381, which, he observes, is sixty years too soon; dating, however, the accession of Chandragupta from 323 B.C. or immediately upon Alexander's death, a period too early by eight or ten years at least. The discrepancy of dates, Mr. Turnover is disposed to think, proceeds from some intentional perversion of the Buddhistical chronology." *V.P.—Wilson*

CHANDRAHASA—(1) In the farthest extremity of the Dekhan there lived a Rája who was doomed to the severest adversity. He had a son born at a propitious period, but was himself soon after slain in battle, and his Ráni perished in the funeral pile. The nurse fled away with the infant to Kutuwal, but died herself in three years without having made known the secret of the child's birth. The boy was now quite destitute and suffered much; but one day happening to go to the house of the prime minister, the astrologers present declared that the boy's face had all the signs of royalty. The minister hearing this, determined that the lad should be assassinated. But the men employed for the purpose took compassion on him and resolved not to kill him. He was found in the jungle and adopted by a certain dependant of the Minister, who called the boy Chandrahása because when he laughed it was said his face resembled the moon.

As Chandrahása grew up he was distinguished for his skill and courage, and his achievements came to the ears of the Rája. The Minister became jealous and determined to visit the Zamindar who had adopted Chandrahása, when he discovered that the young man was the very boy he had sent into the jungle to be murdered. Still bent on the youth's destruction he wrote a letter to his son Madan and requested Chandrahása to carry it to the city; the letter was as follows:—

> "May my son eat the fruits of youth, and know that this same Chandrahása is my enemy, and that he is eager to get possession of all my property: Look not you to his youth of comeliness, nor trouble yourself as to whose son he is, or whether he be a man of rank or learning or abilities, but give him *poison.*"

As he approached the city he enetered a pleasant garden belonging to the Minister, and being very weary, he tied his horse to a tree, laid down in the shade and fell asleep. That very morning the Minister's daughter Bikya, with the Princess and her maids, had come to amuse themselves in the garden. Bikya, wandering away from the others, saw a young man asleep with such a charming face that her heart burnt towards him. Seeing a letter falling from his bosom and perceiving that it was in her father's handwriting, and addressed to her brother, she opened and read it. Having compassion on the youth she determined to alter the letter, and as the word signifying enemy was such that by taking away a single letter she could turn it into a word meaning friend, she did no. The word signifying poison was Bikya, which, as the young man was very good-looking, she altered into her own name of Bikya; and re-sealing the letter placed it again on the youth's bosom, and returned to her companions.

Soon after Chandrahása rose from his sleep, found his way to the house of the Minister, and gave the letter to his son. Madan read the letter with great surprise, but saw that the orders were very positive and that he must obey them without delay.

Chandrahása who was more confounded than any one, was presented with a bridegroom's dress, and directed to prepare himself to be married that evening to the beautiful daughter of the Minister. There was the usual distribution of presents, and great rejoicing throughout the city.

The Minister on his return home was congratulated by every one he met, and "entered his house in a state bordering on madness," when he found what had occurred. His own letter was produced, and as he could not discover the alterations that had been made, he "could only wonder at the greatness of his own blunder." Early next morning he hired some assassins to secrete themselves in the temple of the goddess Durga which was outside the city, and murder the man who should come at evening time to present a golden-pot of incense to the goddess. He then told Chandrahása it was the fixed rule for every man who married into his family to offer a golden-cup of incense at the temple of Durga, and Chandrahása readily promised to comply with the custom that same evening.

But that very day, the Rája, in consequences of a dream, determined to raign his kingly authority, and not knowing of the minister's return sent for Madan, to whom he communicated his intention, and his determination to make Chandrahása his successor. He desired Madan to bring his new brother-in-law to the palace with all speed. Madan gladly set out in search of Chandrahása and found him in the road to the temple of Durga with the golden-cup in his hand; and having briefly explained to him the urgent necessity for his immediate presence at the palace, he took the cup from his hand and promised to present it himself to the goddess. Madan thus sent back Chandrahása to the palace of the Rája and proceeded alone with the golden-cup to the temple of Durga. On entering it he was cut down by the swords of the assassins and killed on the spot. Chandrahása on arriving at the palace, was crowned by the Rája himself. The minister on hearing how his plot had been again defeated, and his own son killed, destroyed himself in the same temple.—*Wheeler's Mah*ábhárata. **(2)** Ravana's famous sword. Ravana , in the course of his trimphal tour after receiving the boons from Brahma, subjucated kings, and marching northward reached the valleys of Mount Kailash. But Nandi stopped him there, and Ravana threatening to move even Siva along-with Kailash, put all of his twenty hands under the the mountain. Siva did not allow the mountain to be moved by putting the waight of his foot on the ground. This crushed the hands of Ravana. Ravana not able to remove his hands from under the mountain remained there for a thousand years and sang the praise of Lord Siva. At last Siva was pleased with him and presented him with the sward called Chandrahasa. It was this sward which Ravana used to win all his wars with the Devas.

CHANDRAKANTA—(Chandrakánta), the moon-gem, which is supposed to absorb the rays of the moon, and to emit them again in the form of pure and cool moisture. It is supposed to exercise a cooling influence. So in the *Meghadūta* —

> "The moon's white rays the smiling night illume,
> And on the moon-gem concentrated fall,
> That hangs in woven nets in every hall;
> Whence cooling dews upon the fair descend,
> And life renewed to languid nature lend."

It is also called Maṇicaka.

CHANDRAKETU—(1) A son of Lakṣmaṇa. and king of Chandravaktra, a country near the Himálaya. **(2)** A king of the city of Cakora. **(3)** A country near the Himālayas.

CHANDRAMA—A river mentioned in the *V.P.*, but which has not been identified.

CHANDRASRI—One of the thirty Andhrabhritya kings, who reigned three years. *V.P.*

CHANDRASUKTA—One of the islands into which the Varsha of Bharata is divided, as enumerated in the Bhágavata and Padma. It has not been identified.

CHANDRASWA—One of the three sons of Dhundhumára, who survived the conflict with the demon Dhundu. Dhundu hid himself beneath a sea of sand which king Kuvalayaswa, aided by twenty-one thousand sons, dug up, undeterred by the flames which checked their progress and finally destroyed all but three of them. Kuvalayaswa was hence called Dhundumára. Professor Wilson thinks that the legend originates probably in the occurrence of some physical phenomena, as an earthquake or volcano.

CHANDRA—The moon; who is fabled to have been married to the twenty-seven daughters of the patriarch *Daksha*, who are in fact personifications of the lunar asterisms. His favourite amongst them was Rohiṇí, to whom he so wholly devoted himself as to neglect the rest. They complained to their father, and Daksha repeatedly interposed, till, finding his remonstrances vain, he denounced a curse upon his son-in-law, in consequence of which he remained childless and became affected by consumption. The wives of Chandra having interceded on his behalf with their father, Daksha modified an imprecation which he could not recall, and pronounced that the decay should be periodical only, not permanent, and that it should alternate with periods of recovery. Hence the successive wane and increase of the moon. (*Padma-Purána, Swarga Khanda*, Sec. II.) *Rohiní* in astronomy is the fourth lunar mansion, containing five stars, the principal of which is Aldebaran.

CHANDRAVALOKA—A prince descended from Kusa, the son of Ráma.

CHANDRA-VAMSA—The Lunar race. The lineage or race which claims descent from the moon. It is divided into two great branches, the Yādavas and Pauravas, respectively descended from Yadu and Puru. Kṛṣṇa belonged to the line of Yadu, and Duṣyanta with the Kuru and Pāṇḍu princes to the line of Puru. The following is a list of the Lunar race as given in the *Viṣṇu Purāṇa*, but the authorities vary—

2 THE LUNAR RACE

Atri, the *ṛṣi*
Soma, the Moon
Buddha; Mercury
Pururavas
Āyu, Āyus

Nahuṣa (and 3 others)
Yayāti (and 5 others)

Yādavas	*Pauravas*	*Kings of Kāśī*
Yadu, eldest	Puru, youngest (and 3 others)	Kṣatravṛddha
Kroṣṭu (and 3 others)		Suhotra
Vṛjinīvat	Janamejaya	Kasa
Svāhi	Pracinvat	Kāśirāja
Ruṣadgu	Pravīra	Dīrghatamas
Citraratha	Manasyu	Dhanvantari
Śasabindu	Abhayada	Ketumat
Pṛthuśravas (one of a million sons)	Sudyumna	Bhīmaratha
	Bahugava	Divodāsa
Tamas	Samyāti	Pratardana
Uśanas	Ahamyati	Dyumat
Śiteyus	Raudrāśva	Śatrujit
Rukmakavaca or Rucaka	Ṛteyu (and 9 others)	Vatsa.
	Rantināra	Ṛtadhvaja or Kuvalayāśva
	Taṁśu	
Paravrt	Anila	Alarka
Jyāmagha	Duṣyanta	Sannati,
Vidarbha	Bharata	
Kratha	Bharadvaja	
Kuntī	or } adopted	Santati.
Vrsni	Vitatha	Sunītha
Nirvṛtti	Bhavanmanyu	Suketu
Daśārha	Bṛhatkṣatra (and many others)	Satyaketu
Vyoman		Vibhu
Jimūta	Suhotra	Suvibhu
Vikṛti	Hastin (of Hastina-	
pura)	Sukumāra	
Bhīmaratha	Ajamīḍha (and 2 others)	Dhṛṣṭaketu
Navaratha		
Daśaratha	Ṛkṣa (and others)	Vainahotra
Śakuni	Samvaraṇa	Bhārga
Karambhī	Kuru	Bhārga-bhūmi
Devarata	Jahnu (and many others)	
Devakṣattra		
Madhu	Suratha	
Anavaratha	Vidūratha	
Kuruvatsa	Sārvabhauma	
Anuratha	Jayasena	
Puruhotra	Ārāvin	
Aṁśu	Ayutāyus	
Satvata	Akrodhana	
Andhaka (and 6 others)	Devātithi	
Bhajamāna	Ṛkṣa	
Vidūratha	Dilīpa	
Śūra	Pratīpa	
Śāmin	Śāntanu (and 2 others)	
Pratikṣattra	Pāṇḍu *	
Svayambhoja	Dhṛtarāṣṭra	
Hṛdika	Yudhiṣṭhira	
Devamīḍhuṣa	Parīkṣit	
Śūra	Janamejaya	
Vasudeva (and 9 others)	Śatānīka	
	Aśvamedhadatta	
Kṛṣṇa and Balarama	Adhisīmakrsna	
	Nicakru.	
Uṣṇa		
(Extinct)	Citraratha	

Vṛṣṇimat
Suṣena
Sunītha
Ṛca
Nṛcakṣuṣ
Sukhābala
Pariplava
Sunaya
Medhāvin
Nṛpañjaya
Mṛdu
Tigma
Bṛhadratha
Vasudāna
Śatānika
Udayana
Ahīnara
Khaṇḍapāṇī
Niramitra
Kṣemaka

See Table under MAHĀBHĀRATA.

CHANDRAYANA—Penances, which, according to the Vedánta, cause, not the acquisition of any thing positive, but merely the removal of sin. They are regulated by the moon's age; and consist in diminishing the daily consumption of food every day, by one mouthful, for the dark half of the month, beginning with fifteen at the full moon, until it is reduced to one at the new moon; and then increasing in like manner during the fortnight of the moon's increase: there are other forms of this penance.

CHANURA—A demon who was killed by Krishṇa, after a very severe contest, in which Chanúra was whirled round a hundred times, until his breath was expended in the air, and Krishṇa dashed him on the ground with such violence as to smash his body into a hundred fragments, and strew the earth with a hundred pools of gory more. *V.P.*

CHARAKA—A writer on medicine who lived in Vedic times. According to his own statement, he received the materials of his work from Agniveśa, to whom they were delivered by Ātreya. A legend represents him as an incarnation of the serpent Śeṣa. The work was translated into Arabic before the end of the eighth century. The text has been printed in India.

CHARAKA—One of the chief schools of the *Yajurveda.*

CHARAKA—A renowned medical writer of great antiquity. "Charaka appears to have been a person of varied thought and culture, and to have had an earnest desire to teach men so to manage their bodies, as not only to avoid all unnecessary pain on earth; but so as to ensure happiness after death. Charaka states that originally the contents or material of his work was communicated by Atreya to Agnivesa. By Agnivesa it was taught to Charaka, and by him condensed "where it was too prolix and expanded where it seemed too brief." The result of Charaka's labour was a work of considerable extent, no less than one hundred and twenty chapters in eight divisions.—Mrs. Manning; *A. and M. I.*, vol. I, p. 342, where the reader will find an abstract of Charaka's work; made from the Sanskrit manuscripts of the India Office Library.

CHARAKA-BRAHMANA—A Brāhmaṇa of the Black *Yajurveda.*

CHARAKAS—The students of a Sákhá so denominated from its teacher Charaka.

CHARANA—A Vedic school or society. It is explained by a commentator as "a number of men who are pledged to the reading of a certain *śākhā* of the Veda, and who have in this manner become one body."

CHARANAS—Inferior demi-gods, or heavenly spirits, who are often introduced into Hindu dramas, and represented as mingling freely with human beings, to the extent of intermarrying with mortals, and even electing earthly princes and heroes to be their leaders and rulers. It is difficult to describe accurately the persons, character and offices, of the various inferior races of divinities, being as *Wilson* says "very ill-defined in the heavenly polity of the Hindus."

CHARANAVYAHA—The name of a 'Parisishta' work, which is considered to have been composed later than the Sutras, and representing a distinct period of Hindu literature. See PARISISHTA.

CHARIOT—The sun, moon and planets are all represented in the Puránas as having chariots or ears. That of the sun is stated in the *V.P.* to be nine thousand leagues in length, and the pole of twice that longitude: that of the moon has three wheels and is drawn by ten white horses.

CHARISHNU—A son of the sage Kirttimat.

CHARMAMANDALAS—A northern people, living in the district of Mandala or Khanda of Charma. Pliny mentions a king of a people so called, Charmaru rex.

CHARMANVATI—The name of a river, the Chambal.

CHARU HASINI—'Sweet smiler.' This epithet is used for Rukmiṇī and for Lakṣmaṇa, and perhaps for other wives of Kṛṣṇa.

CHARU, CHARUDEHA, CHARUDESHNA, CHARUGUPTA, CHARUVINDA—Five sons of Krishṇa by Rukmini, one is termed in the *V.P.* the mighty Cháru.

CHARUDATTA—An impoverished brahman who is one of the principal characters in the drama of the Toy Cart, *Mṛcchakaṭika*. . On one occasion Chárudatta says:—

My friend,
The happiness that follows close on sorrow,
Shows like a lamp that breaks upon the night,
But he that falls from affluence to poverty,
May wear the human semblance, but exists
A lifeless form alone.

On being further questioned, Chárudatta declares that he would much prefer death to poverty.

"To die, is transient suffering, to be poor
Interminable anguish."

And he further explains that he does not grieve for the lost wealth:

"But that the quest no longer seeks the dwelling
Whence wealth has vanished.

* * *

And then with poverty comes disrespect;
From disrespect does self-dependence fail;
Then scorn and sorrow following, overwhelm
The intellect; and when the judgment fails
The being perishes. And thus from poverty
Each ill that pains humanity proceeds."

—*A. and M. I.*, vol. 2, p. 157.

CHARUGUPTA—Son of Sri Krishna by Rukmini. Pradyumna, Charudesna, Sudesana, Charudeha, Sucharu, Charugupta, Bhadracharu, Charuchandra, Aticharu and Charu were the ten sons of Rukmini. The Mahabharata gives three more names of the sons of Rumini, *viz.*, Charuyasas, Charuvesa and Charusravas.

CHARUMATI—A daughter of Krishṇa by Rukmini.

CHARVAKA—**(1)** A *rākṣasa*, and friend of Duryodhana, who disguised himself as a brāhmaṇa and reproached Yudhiṣṭhira for his crimes, when he entered Hastināpura in triumph after the great battle. The brāhmaṇas discovered the imposture and reduced Cārvāka to ashes with the fire of their eyes. **(2)** A sceptical. A philosopher who about the third century, founded a new school of undisguised materialism—maintaining that perception is the one only source of knowledge and means of proof: that while there is body there is thought and sense of pleasure and pain; none when body is not; and hence, as well as from self-consiousness, it is concluded that self and body are identical. In the Vedánta Sára there is a refutation of no less than four followers of Chárváka, who assert his doctrine under various modifications; one maintaining that the gross corporal frame is identical with soul; another that the corporeal organs constitute the soul; a third affirming that the vital functions do so; and the fourth insisting that the mind and the soul are the same.

CHATAKAS—Pupils of Vaisampáyana (*q.v.*). The Váyu states that they were styled Chátakas from chát 'to divide,' because they shared amongst them their master's guilt. Those pupils of Vaisampáyana were called Chátakas by whom the crime of Brahmanicide was shared.

CHATURMASYA—Sacrifices every four months.

CHATURUNGA—A Prince, the son of Romapáda, one of the descendants of Anu.

CHATUR-VARNA—The four castes, (*see* VARṆA)

CHAYA—'Shade.' Ahandmaid of the sun. Saṁjñā, wife of the sun, being unable to bear the fervour of her lord, put her handmaid Chāyā in her place. The sun, believing Chāyā to be his wife, had three children by her: Śani, the planet Saturn; the Manu Sāvarṇi; and a daughter, the Tapatī river. As mother of Saturn, Chāyā is known as Śaniprasū. The partiality which she showed for these children provoked Yama, the son of Saṁjñā, and he lilted his foot to kick her. She cursed him to have his leg affected with sores and worms. This made it clear that she was not Saṁjñā and mother of Yama, so the sun went in search of Saṁjñā and brought her back. According to one Purāṇa, Chāyā was a daughter of Viśvakarmā, and sister of Saṁjñā, the wife of the sun.

CHEDI—Name of a people and of their country, the modern Chandail and Bundelkhand. The capital was Śuktimatī, and among the kings of this country were Damaghoṣa and Śiśu-pāla.

CHEDYAS—The inhabitants of Chedi, which is usually considered as Chandail, on the west of the Jungle mehals, towards Nagpore. It is known in times subsequent to the Puránas as Ranastambha.

CHEKITANA—A son of Dhṛṣṭaketu, Rājā of the Kekayas, and an ally of the Pāṇḍavas.

CHERA—A kingdom in the south of the peninsula, which was absorbed by its rival the Cola kingdom.

CHHALA—A Prince, the son of Dala, one of the descendants of Kusa.

CHHANDAJAS—The Vasus and similar divinities. They have the epithet Chhandajá as born in different Manwantaras of their own will.

CHHANDAS—An Aṇga of the four Vedas, the one which relates to metre.

CHHANDOGA-BRAHMANA—In the Brâhmaṇa of the Chhandogas it is evident that, after the principal collection was finished (called the prauḍha or Panchavinśa—brâhmana, *i.e.*, consisting of twenty-five sections,) a twenty-sixth Brâhmaṇa was added which is known by the name of Shadvinśa-brâhmaṇa. This Brâhmaṇa together with the Adbhuta-brâhmaṇa must be of very modern date. It mentions not only temples (Devâyatanâni,) but images of gods (daivata-pratimâ) which are said to laugh, to cry, to sing, to dance, to burst, to sweat and to twinkle. These two have long been supposed to be the only Brâhmanas of the Chhandogas, and they constitute, no doubt, the most important part of that class of literature. It is curious, however, that whenever the Brâhmṇas of the Chhandogas are quoted, their number is invariably fixed at eight. Kumârila Bhaṭṭa says, "in the eight Brâhmaṇas, together with the Upanishads, which the Chhandogas read, no single accent is fixed."—*A.S.L.*

CHHANDOGA-PRIESTS—The second class of priests at sacrifices.

CHIKITSA—One of the eight branches of mediveal science; that which treats of the administration of medicines, or medical treatment in general.

CHINTAMANI—An Epic poem in Tamil, of considerable merit, and regarded as the highest classical authority in that language. It contains the heroic story of a king named Jivagan, and is probably founded on a similař story found in the Mahá Purána, a sacred work of the Jains written in Sanscrit.

Chintámani is a compound of two Sanscrit words *Chintá*, thought or reflection, and *mani* a jewel. It is generally applied to a fabulous gem which is supposed to yield its possessor whatever may be required. 'The wish-gem'. A jewel which is supposed to have the power of granting all desires. The philosopher's stone. It is said to have belonged to Brahmā, who is himself called by this name. It is also called *divya-ratna.* This diamond was begotten at the time of cherning of the mythical ocean by the Devas and danavas (Asuras).

CHIRAJIVIN—'Long-lived'. Gods or deified mortals, who live for long periods.

CHITAR—A chief mentioned in the Rig Veda as living with other chiefs near the Sarasvatí.

CHITI—Synonyme of Mahat, "is that by which the consequences of acts and species of knowledge are selected for the use of soul."—Wilson, *V.P.*, p. 15.

CHITRABAHA—A Purána river, not identified.

CHITRAGUPTA—The Registrar of Yama; all that die appear before Yama, and are confronted with Chitragupta by whom their actions have been recorded. "Chitragupta is described in the following tasteless and extravagant style in the Vṛihannáradíya Purána. 'The dreadful Chitragupta with a voice like that issuing from the clouds at the mundane dissolution, gleaming like a mountain of collyrium, terrible with lightning-like weapons having thirty-two arms, as big as three yojanas, red-eyed, long-nosed, his face furnished with grinders and projecting teeth, his eyes resembling oblong ponds, bearing death and disease.' " *O.S.T.*, Vol. v., p. 302.

CHITRAKA—A prince, the son of Prisni, a descendant of Siní.

CHITRAKETU—A son of Vasishtha, the great sage, according to the list in the Bhágavata.

CHITRAKUTA—An isolated hill situated on a river called the Pisani, fifty miles south-east of the town of Banda in Bundelkund. It is a sacred spot crowded with temples, and shrines of Ráma and Lakshmaṇa; celebrated too as the seat of Valmíki, the sage and poet, who became famous in after years as the author of the Rámáyana.

"We have often looked on that green hill: it is the holiest spot of that sect of the Hindu faith who devote themselves to this incarnation of Vishṇu. The whole neighbourhood is Ráma's country. Every headland has some legend, every cavern is connected with his name; some of the wild fruits are still called *Sítaphal*, being the reputed food of the exiles. Thousands and thousands annually visit the spot, and round the hill is a raised foot-path, on which the devotee, with naked feet, treads full of pious awe."—*Calcutta Review, Vol. XXIII*

The following extracts from Mr. Griffith's translation of the Rámáyana will serve to show how this sacred character has been acquired:—

"Then, as he saw the morning break,

In answer Bharadvája spake,
'Go forth to Chitrakúṭa's hill,
Where berries grow, and sweets distil:
Full well, I deem, that home will suit
Thee, Ráma, strong and resolute.
Go forth, and Chitrakúṭa seek,
Famed mountain of the Varied Peak.
In the wild woods that gird him round,
All creatures of the chase are found:
Thou in the glades shalt see appear
Vast herds of elephants and deer.
With Sítá there shalt thou delight
To gaze upon the woody height;
There with expanding heart to look
On river, table-land, and brook,
And see the foaming torrent rave
Impetuous from the mountain cave.
Auspicious hill ! where all day long
The lapwing's cry, the Koil's song
Make all who listen gay:
Where all is fresh and fair to see,
Where elephants and deer roam free,
There, as a hermit, stay."
"Then on from wood to wood they strayed,
O'er many a stream, through constant shade,
As Bharadvája bade them, till
They came to Chitrakúṭa hill.
And Ráma there, with Lakshmaṇ's aid,
A pleasant little cottage made,
And spent his days with Sítá, dressed
In coat of bark and deerskin vest.
And Chitrakúṭa grew to be
As bright with those illustrious three
As Meru's sacred peaks that shine
With glory, when the gods recline
Beneath them: śiva's self between
The Lord of Gold and Beauty's Queen."

CHITRALEKHA—The companion and friend of the princess Usha, to whom Usha related her dream, and who by her magic power brought Aniruddha to the palace.

CHITRANGADA—(1) The daughter of the Rája of Manipura who was married to Arjuna in his travels, but remained in her own city with her son Babhruváhana, when Arjuna returned to Hastinápur.

(2) The son of Sántanu by his wife Satyavati. He was killed when young, in a conflict with a Gandarvá, who was also named Chitrangada.

(3) Daughter of King Critravāhana of Maṇipura, , wife of Arjuna and mother of Babhrūvāhana.

Chitraratha was also the name of the son of Rushadru and father of Saṣavinda who was lord of the fourteen great gems. There was another Chitraratha, son of the Dharmaratha, who drank the Soma juice along with Indra. A fourth Chitraratha is mentioned in the *V.P.* as the son of Ushṇa, a descendant of Paríkshit.

CHITRARATHA, CHITRASENA, CHITRO-PALA—The names of three rivers in the *V.P.* which have not been yet identified.

CHITRARATHA—The king of the celestial choristers;

"On Chitraratha, true and dear
My tuneful bard and charioteer
Gems, robes, and plenteous wealth confer
Mine against friend and minister."

—Griffith's *Rámáyana.*

CHITRASENA—(1) One of the hundred sons of Dhṛtarāṣtra.

(2) A chief of the Yakṣas.

CHITRA—The name of a lunar mansion in Govithi, in the Central Avasthana.

CHITRAVARNA—The name of the peacock king in the Panchatantra stories.

CHITRA-YAJÑA—A modern drama in five acts upon the legend of Dakṣa. It is the work of a Paṇḍit named Vaidyanātha Vācaspati.

CHOLAS—The inhabitants of the lower part of the Coromandel coast; so called after them Chólamandala.

CHRONOLOGY—The *Vishṇu Purána* says, "Time is a form of Vishṇu: hear how it is applied to measure the duration of Brahma, and of all other sentient beings. Fifteen twinklings of the eye make a Kásh'thá; thirty Kásh'thás, one Kalá; and thirty Kalás, one Muhúrtta. Thirty Muhúrattas constitute a day and night of mortals: thirty such days make a month, divided into two half-months: six months form an Ayana (the period of the sun's progress north or south of the ecliptic:) and two Ayanas compose a year. The southern Ayana is a night, and the norther a day, of the gods. Twelve thousand divine years, each composed of (three hundred and sixty) such days, constitute the period of the four Yugas, or ages. They are thus distributed: the Krita age has four thousand divine years; the Tretá three thousand; the Dwápara, two thousand; and the Kali age, one thousand: so those acquainted with antiquity have declared." The period that precedes a Yuga is called a Sandhyá, and it is of as many hundred years as there are thousands in the Yuga; and the period that follows a Yuga, termed the Sandhyánsa, is of similar duration. The interval between the Sandhyá and the Sandhyánsa is the Yuga, denominated Krita, Tretá, &c. The Krita, Tretá, Dwápara and Kali, constitute a great age, or aggregate of four ages: a thousand such aggregates are a day of Brahma, and fourteen Manus reign within that term. Hear the division of time which they measure.

Seven Rishis, certain (secondary) divinities, Indra, Manu, and the kings his sons, are created and perish at one period; and the interval, called a Manwantara, is equal to seventy-one times the number of years contained in the four Yugas, with some additional years: this is the duration of the Manu, the (attendant) divinities, and the rest, which is equal to 8,52,000 divine years, or to 3,06,720,000 years of mortals, independent of the additional period. Fourteen times this period constitutes a Brahma day, that is, a day of Brahma; the term (Brahma) being the derivative form. At the end of this day a dissolution of the universe occurs, when all the three worlds, earth, and the regions of space, are consumed with fire. The dwellers of Maharioks (the region inhabited by the saints who survive the world,) distressed by the heat, repair then to Janaloka (the region of holy men after their decease.) When the three worlds are but one might ocean, Brahma, who is one with Náráyans, satiate with the demolition of the universe, sleeps upon his serpent-bed—contemplated, the lotus born, by the ascetic inhabitants of the Janaloka—for a night of equal duration with his day; at the close of which he creates anew. Of such days and nights is a year of Brahama composed; and a hundred such years constitute his whole life. One Parárddha, or half his existence, has expired, terminating with the Mahá Váráha is the first of the second period of Brahma's existence."

CHUNCHU—A prince, the son of Harita, a descendant of Harischandra.

CHYAVANA, CYAVANA—A sage, son of sage Bhṛgu, and author of some hymns.

In the *Ṛgveda* it is said that when "Cyavana had grown old and had been forsaken, the Aśvins divested him of his decrepit body, prolonged his life, and restored him to youth, making him acceptable to his wife, and the husband of maidens." This storyis thus amplified in the *Śatapatha Brāhmaṇa*: The sage Cyavana assumed a shrivelled form and lay as if abandoned. The sons of Śaryāta, a descendant of Manu, found this body, and pelted it with clods. Cyavana was greatly incensed, and to appease him Śaryāta yoked his chariot, and taking with him his daughter Sukanyā, presented her to Cyavana. The Aśvins endeavoured to seduce her, but she remained faithful to her shrivelled husband, and under his direction she taunted them with being incomplete and imperfect, and consented to tell them in what respect they were deficient, if they would make her husband young again. They directed that he should bathe in a certain pond, and having done so, he came forth with the age that he desired. She then informed them that they were imperfect because they were excluded from a sacrifice the other gods were performing. They departed and succeeded in getting admitted to join the other gods.

According to the *Mahābhārata*, Cyavana besought Indra to allow the Aśvins to partake of the libations of Soma. Indra replied that the other gods might do as they pleased, but he would not consent. Cyavana then commenced a sacrifice to the Aśvins; the other gods were subdued, but Indra, in a rage, rushed with a mountain in one hand and his thunderbolt in another to crush Cyavana. The sage having sprinkled him with water and stopped him, "created a fearful open-mouthed monster called Mada, having teeth and grinders of portentous length, and jaws one of which enclosed the earth, the other the sky; and the gods, including Indra, are said to have been at the root of his tongue like fishes in the mouth of a sea monster." In this predicament "Indra granted the demand of Cyavana, who was thus the cause of the Aśvins becoming drinkers of the *soma*".

In another part of the *Mahābhārata* he is represented as exacting many menial offices from King Kuśika and his wife, but he afterwards rewarded them by "creating a magical golden palace", and predicted the birth of "a grandson of great beauty and heroism (Paraśurāma)".

The *Mahābhārata*, interpreting his name as signifying 'the fallen', accounts for it by a legend which represents his mother, Pulomā, wife of Bhṛgu, as having been carried off by the demon Puloman. She was pregnant, and in her fright the child fell from her womb. The demon was softened, and let the mother depart with her infant.

The verṣion of the story as told in the *Mahābhārata* and Purāṇas is that Cyavana was so absorbed in penance on the banks of the Narmada that white ants constructed their nests round his body and left only his eyes visible. Sukanyā, daughter of King Śaryāta, seeing two bright eyes in what seemed to be an ant-hill, poked them with a stick. The sage visited the offence of Śaryāta, and was appeased only by the promise of the king to give him Sukanyā in marriage. Subsequently the Aśvins, coming to his hermitage, compassionated her union with so old and ugly a husband as Cyavana, and tried to induce her to take one of them in his place. When their persuasions failed, they told her they were the physicians of the gods, and would restore her husband to youth and beauty, when she could make her choice between him and one of them. Accordingly the three bathed in a pond and came forth of like celestial beauty. Each one asked her to be his bride, and she recognised and chose her own husband. Cyavana, in gratitude, compelled Indra to admit the Asvins to a participation of the soma ceremonial. Indra at first objected, because the Aśvins wandered about among men as physicians and changed their forms at will. But Cyavana was not to be refused; he stayed the arm of Indra as he was about to launch a thunderbolt, and he created a terrific demon who was on the point of devouring the king of the gods when he submitted.

According to the *Mahābhārata*, Cyavana was husband of Āruṣī or Sukanya and father of Aurva. He is also considered to be the father of Hārīta.

The name is Cyavana in the *Ṛgveda*, but Cyavana in the *Brāhmaṇa* and later writings.

CLEPSYDRA—A water-clock, is thus described in an extract from a commentary, given in a note to the Vishṇu Purána. "A vessel made of twelve Palas and a half of copper, and holding a Prastha, Magadha measure, of water, broad at top, and having at bottom a tube of gold, of four Máshas weight, four fingers long, is placed in water, and the time in which the vessel is filled by the hole in the bottom, is called a Nádika. The common measure of Nádi is a think shallow brass-cup, with a small hole in the bottom. It is placed in the surface of water, in a large vessel, where nothing can disturb it, and where the water gradually fills the cup and sinks it."

CLOUDS—Clouds, in the Puránas, are of three classes:—1, Ágneya, originating from fire or heat, or in other words evaporation: they are charged with wind and rain and are of various orders; 2, Brahmaja, born from the breath of Brahma; these are the clouds whence thunder and lightning proceed; and 3, Pakshaja, or clouds which were originally the wings of the mountains, and which were cut off by Indra; these are the largest of all, and are those which at the end of the Kalpas and Yugas, pour down the waters of the deluge. The shell of the egg of Brahma, or of the universe, is formed of the primitive clouds. The Vishṇu Purána states that "during eight months of the year the sun attracts the waters and then pours them upon earth as rain." Consequently the Linga Purána observes there is no waste of water in the universe as it is in constant circulation. The Vishṇu Purána adds, "The water that the sun has drawn up from the Ganga of the skies he quickly pours down with his rays, and without a cloud; and men who are touched by this pure rain are cleansed from the soil of sin and never see hell; this is termed celestial ablution." "The water which the clouds shed upon the earth is the Ambrosia of living beings, for it gives fertility to the plants which are the support of their existence. By this, all vegetables grow and are matured, and become the means of maintaining life."

COBRA—"Next to the Rakshasas the Cobra, or deadly-hooded snake, plays the most important part in the legends, as a supernatural personage. This is only one of the many traces still extant of that serpent-worship formerly so general in western India...Serpent-worship, as it still exists is something more active than a mere popular superstition. The Cobra unless disturbed, rarely goes far from home, and is supposed to watch jealously over a hidden treasure. He is, in the estimation of the lower classes, invested with supernatural powers, and according to the treatment he receives, he builds up or destroys the fortunes of the house to which he belongs. No native will willingly kill him if he can get rid of him in any other way; and the poorer classes always after he is killed, give him all the honours of a regular cremation, assuring him, with many protestations, as the pile burns, 'that they are guiltless of his blood; that they slew him by order of their master;' or 'that they had no other way to prevent his biting the children or the chickens.' *Sir B. Frere.* (*Introduction to Old Deccan Days*.)

D

DABHASAYANA—A placed between Rameshwara and Cape Comorin, where Ráma, reclining on a couch of sacred grass, prayed to the sea for a passage.

DABHITI—Aking mentioned in the Rig Veda who was saved by Indra from being carried off by the Asuras or Dasyus. "Indra burnt all their weapons in a kindled fire, and enriched Dabhiti with their cattle, horses and chariots."

DADHICHA—One of the nineteen Bhrigus, composers of hymns.—*O.S.T.*, Vol. I, p 279.

DADHIKRA—The name given in the Rig Veda to a divine horse, described as the straight-going, the graceful-moving, the resplendent, the rapid, the destroyer of enemies like a heroic prince. In a second hymn the Rishi says, "May Aditi, consentient with Mitra and Varuna, render him free from sin who has performed the worship of the steed Dadhikra, when the fire has been kindled at the opening of the dawn."

DADHIVIDARCHAS, DAHAS—Two tribes of people mentioned in the Vishṇu Purána but not identified.

DADHYAÑC, DADHICA—(Dadhīca is a later form.) AVedic ṛṣi, son of Atharvan, whose name frequently occurs. The legend about him, as it appears in the *Ṛgveda*, is that Indra taught him certain sciences, but threatened to cut off his head if he taught them to any one else. The Aśvins prevailed upon Dadhyañc to communicate his knowledge to them, and, to preserve him from the wrath of Indra, they took off his own head and replaced it with that of a horse. When Indra struck off the sage's equine head the Aśvins restored his own to him. A verse of the *Ṛgveda* says, "Indra, with the bones of Dadhyici, slew ninety times nine Vrtras"; and the story told by the scholiast in explanation is, that while Dadhyañc was living on earth the *asuras* were controlled and tranquillised by his appearance; but when he had gone to heaven, they overspread the whole earth. Indra inquired for Dadhyañc, or any relic of him. He was told of the horse's head, and when this was found in a lake near Kurukṣetra, Indra used the bones as Weapons, and with them slew the *asuras*, or, as the words of the Vedic verse are explained, he "foiled the nine times ninety stratagems of the *asuras* or Vṛtras". The story as afterwards told in the *Mahabhrarata* and Purāṇas is that the sage devoted himself to death that Indra and the gods might be armed with his bones as more effective weapons than thunderbolts for the destruction of Vṛtra and the *asuras*. According to one account he was instrumental in bring about the destruction of "Dakṣa's sacrifice". (*see* DAKṢA)

DADHYAUCH—One of the ancient great sages, the son of Atharvan.

DADU—The founder of a Vaishnava sect, who taught that Bhakti, or implicit faith, was more efficacious than subjugation of the passions, charity, or knowledge. Dádú was originally a cotton-cleaner at Ajmír.

DADU-PANTHIS—The designation of the disciples of followers of the above. One of the Vaishnava sects in Hindustan. It had its origin from Dadu, a cotton-cleaner by profession, who, having been admonished by a voice from heaven to devote himself to a religious life, retired with that view to the Baherana mountain, where, after some time, he disappeared, and no traces of him could be found. His followers believed him to have been absorbed into the Deity. He is supposed to have flourished about A.D. 1600. The followers of Dádú wear no peculiar mark on the forehead, but carry a rosary, and are further distinguished by a round white cap according to some; but, according to others, one with four corners, and a flap hanging down.

DAGOBA—A conical erection surmounting relics among the Buddhists. The name is said by Mr. Hardy to be derived from dá, dátu, or dhátu, an osseous relic, and geba or garbha, the womb. These buildings, are sometimes of immense height, of circular form, and composed of stone or brick, faced with stone or stucco. They are built upon a platform, which again rests upon a natural or artificial elevation, which is usually reached by a flight of steps. The utmost respect is felt for d ágobas among the Buddhists, chiefly because they contain relics of different kinds. Professor Wilson, in his 'Ariana Antiqua,' thus describes the ordinary contents of a dágoba: "The most conspicuous objects are, in general, vessels of stone or metal; they are of various shapes and sizes; some of them have been fabricated on a lathe. They commonly cotain a silver box or casket, and within that, or sometimes by itself, a casket of gold. This is sometimes curiously wrought. One found by Mr. Masson at Deh Bimaran is chased with a double series of four figures, representing Gautama in the act of preaching; a mendicant is on his right, a lay-follower on his left, and behind the latter a female disciple; they stand under arched niches resting on pillars, and between the arches is a bird; a row of rubies is set round the upper and lower edge of the vessel, and the bottom is also chased with the leaves of the lotus: the vase had no cover. Within these vessels, or sometimes in the cell in which they are placed, are found small pearls, gold buttons, gold ornaments and rings, beads, pieces of white and coloured glass and crystals, pieces of clay or stone with impressions of figures, bits of bone, and teeth of animals of the ass and goat species, pieces of cloth, and folds of Tuz or Burj leaf, or rather the bark of a kind of birch on which the Hindus formerley wrote; and these pieces bear sometimes characters which may be termed Bactrian; but they are in too fragile and decayed a state to admit of being unfolded or read. Similar characters are also found superficially scratched upon the stone, or dotted upon the metal vessels. In one instance they were found traced upon the stone with ink. Within some of the vessels was also found a liquid, which upon exposure rapidly evaporated, leaving a brown sediment, which was analysed by Mr. Prinsep, and offered some traces of animal and vegetable matters."

The principal dágobas in Ceylon, as we learn from Mr. Hardy, are at Anurádhapura, and it would appear that it was accounted a ceremony of great importance among the ancient ascetics to walk round one of these sacred structures. It is regarded by the Hindu Brahmans as a most meritorious walk to circumambulate a temple, raising the person who performs this pious act to a place in the heaven of the god or goddess to whom the temple belongs. The Nepaulese also account it one of the most devout employments in which a Buddhist can be engaged to march round a dágoba, repeating mental prayers, and holding in his right hand a small cylinder fixed upon the upper end of a short staff or handle, which he keeps in perpetual revolution. The reverence in which these structures are held is thus noticed by Mr. Hardy, in his valuable work, entitled 'Eastern Monachism:' "Any mark of disrespect to the dágoba is regarded as being highly criminal, whilst a contrary course is equally deserving of reward. When Elaro, one of the Malabar sovereigns, who reigned in Ceylon B.C. 205, was one day riding in his chariot, the yoke-bar accidentally struck one of these edifices, and displaced some of the stones. The priests in attendance reproached him for the act; but the monarch immediately descendend to the ground, and prostrating himself in the street, said that they might take off his head with the wheel of his carriage. But the priests replied, 'Great king! our divine teacher delights not in torture; repair the dágoba.' For the purpose of replacing the fifteen stones that had been dislodged, Elaro bestowed 15,000 of the silver coins called kahapana. Two women who had worked for hire at the erection of the great dágoba by Dutugamini were for this meritorious act born in Tawntisa. The legend informs us that on a subsequent occasion they went to worship at the same place, when the radiance emanating from their persons was so great that it filled the whole of Ceylon."

The grond on which a dágoba is held in so high estimation is simply because it contains relics which have from remote times been worshipped by the Buddhists. As far back as the fourth century, Fa Hian, a Chinese traveller, mentions such a practice as then prevailing. "The bones of Gautama, the garments he used, the utensils he used, and the ladder by which he visited heaven, were worshipped by numbers of devout pilgrims; and happy did the country consider itself that retained one of these precious remains." The most celebrated relic which is still to be found among the worshippers of Gautama Buddha is the DALADÁ (which see). To make a present or offering to a dágoba is viewed as an act of the highest virtue, which will be rewarded both in this world and the next, and will lead to the attainment of *Nirwana* and *annihilation.* Budha himself declared while on earth, "Though neither flowers nor anything else whoudl be offered, yet if any one will look with a pleasant mind at a dágoba or the court of the bó-tree, he will undoubtedly be born in a DEVA-LOKA (which see); it is unnecessary to say that he who sweeps these sacred places, or makes offerings to them, will have an equal reward; furthermore, should any one die on his way to make an offering to a dágoba, he also will receive the blessedness of the DEVA-LOKAS." Some dágobas are alleged to have the power of working miracles, but this privilege is almost exclusively confined to those which have been built in honor of the *rahats*, or beings who are free from all evil desire, and possess supernatural powers.

"It was not till the year 1837 in which Mr. Jas. Prinsep deciphered the written character of king Asoka's edicts, that anything was known of the Buddhism of ancient India. Then first was it understood when and by whom, and for what purpose, these dágobas were erected."—*A. and M. I.*

DAHANA—The name of one of the eleven Rudras, according to the enumeration in the Matsya Purána.

DAHRAGNI—A name of the sage Agastya.

DAITYAS—Demons. The Daityas are thought to have been, in the epic period, personifications of the Aborigines of India, more particularly of the southern part of the Peninsula; who, to increase the glories of the heroes who conquered them, were represented as giants and demons. They are associated with the Danavas, who bear the same character. In the Puránic period they play a very important part, as the enemies who are constantly at war with the deities for the sake of obtaining the sovereignty of heaven. They are there considered as the descendants of Kaṣyana and Diti (from whom the name Daitya is called a matronymic). At the churning of the ocean they attempted to seize the cup of Amrita or Ambrosia which was then produced, and was in the hand of Dhanwantari, but Vishṇu, assuming a female form, fascinated and deluded them; and recovering the Amrita from them delivered it to the gods. Sakra and the other deities quaffed the Ambrosia. The incensed demons, grasping their weapons, fell upon them; but the gods, into whom the ambrosial draught had infused new vigour, defeated and put their host to flight; they then fled through the regions of space, and plunged into the subterraneous realms of Pátáḷa. The gods thereat greatly rejoiced, did homage to the holder of the discus and mace, and resumed their reign in heaven. The Daityas then inhabited Pátáḷa. Hiranyakaṣipu was their king, but when deposed by Vishṇu, his illustrious son Prahláda received the sovereignty. The Vishṇu Purána relates other legends of the Daityas obtaining the sovereignty of the earth, and being deluded from the tenets of the Vedas were easily conquered.

DAKINI—A kind of female imp or fiend attendant upon Kālī and feeding on human flesh. The Ḍākinīs are also called Aśrapas, 'blood drinkers'.

DAKṢIṆĀ—A present made to brāhmaṇas; the honorarium for the performance of a sacrifice. This is personified as a goddess, to whom various origins are assigned.

DAKṢA—'Able, competent, intelligent'. This name generally carries with it the idea of creative power. Dakṣa is a son of Brahmā; he is one of the Prajāpatis, and is sometimes regarded as their chief. There is a great deal of doubt and confusion about him, which of old the sage Parāśara could only account for by saying that "in every age Dakṣa and the rest are born and are again destroyed". In the *Ṛgveda* it is said that "Dakṣa sprang from Aditi, and Aditi from Dakṣa". Upon this marvellous mutual generation Yaṣka in the *Nirukta* remarks, "How can this be possible? They may have had the same origin; or, according to the nature of the gods, they may have born from each other, and have derived their substance from each other." Roth's view is that Aditi is eternity, and that Dakṣa (spiritual power) is the male energy which generates the gods in eternity. In the *Śatapatha Brāhmaṇa*, Dakṣa is identified with Prajāpati, the creator. As son of Aditi, he is one of the Ādityas, and he is also reckoned among the Viśvedevas.

According to *the Mahābhārata*, Dakṣa sprang from the right thumb of Brahmā, and his wife from that deity's left thumb. The Purāṇas adopt this view of his origin, but state that he married Prasūti, daughter of *Priyavrata*, and granddaughter of Manu. By her he had, according to various statements, twenty-four, fifty, or sixty daughters. The *Rāmāyaṇa* and *Mahābhārata* agree in the larger number; and according to Manu and the *Mahābhārata* he gave ten of his daughters to Dharma and thirteen to Kaśyapa, who became the mothers of gods and demons, men, birds, serpents, and all living things. Twenty-seven were given in marriage to Soma, the moon, and these became the twenty-seven Nakṣatras or lunar mansions. One of the daughters, named Sati, married Śiva, and killed herself in consequence of a quarrel between her husband and father. The *Kāśi-Khaṇḍa* represents that she became a *satī* and burnt herself.

Another legend of the *Mahābhārata* and Purāṇas represents Dakṣa as being born a second time, in another *manvantara*, as son of the Pracetasas and Māriṣā, and that he had seven sons, "the allegorical persons Krodha, Tamas, Dama, Vikṛta, Aṅgiras, Kardama, and Aśva". This second birth is said to have happened through his having been cursed to it by his son-in-law Śiva. Dakṣa was in a certain way, by his mother Māriṣā, an emanation of Soma, the moon; and as twenty-seven of his daughters were married to that luminary, Dakṣa is sometimes referred to as being both the father and the offspring of the moon, thus reiterating the duality of his nature.

In the *Harivaṁśa* Dakṣa appears in another variety of his character. According to this authority, Viṣṇu himself became Dakṣa, and formed numerous creatures, or, in other words, he became the creator. Dakṣa, the first of males, by virtue of yoga, himself took the form of a beautiful woman, by whom he had many fair daughters, whom he disposed of in marriage in the manner related by Manu and above stated.

An important event in the life of Dakṣa, and very frequently referred to, is "Dakṣa's sacrifice", which was violently interrupted and broken up by Śiva. The germ of this story is found in the *Taittirīya Saṁhitā*, where it is related that the gods, having excluded Rudra from a sacrifice, he pierced the sacrifice with an arrow, and that Pūṣan, attempting to eat a portion of the oblation, broke his teeth. The story is found both in the *Rāmāyaṇa* and *Mahābhārata*. According to the latter, Dakṣa was engaged in sacrifice, when Śiva in a rage, and shouting loudly, pierced the offering with an arrow. The gods and *asuras* were alarmed and the whole universe quaked. Therṣis endeavoured to appease the angry god, but in vain. "He ran up to the gods, and in his rage knocked out the eyes of Bhaga with a blow, and, incensed, assaulted Pūṣan with his foot and knocked out his teeth as he was eating the offering." The gods and ṛṣis humbly propitiated him, and when he was appeased "they apportioned to him a distinguished share in the sacrifice, and through fear resorted to him as their refuge". In another part of the same work the story is again told with considerable variation. Dakṣa instituted a sacrifice and apportioned no share to Rudra (Śiva). Instigated by the sage Dadhīci, the god hurled his blazing trident, which destroyed the sacrifice of Dakṣa and fell with great violence on the breast of Nārāyaṇa (Viṣṇu). It was hurled back with violence to its owner, and a furious battle ensued between the 'two gods, which was not intermitted till Brahmā prevailed upon Rudra to propitiate Nārāyaṇa. That god was gratified, and said to Rudra, "He who knows thee knows me; he who loves thee loves me."

The Váyu Purána contains a full account of the great sacrifice offered by Daksha. One of his daughters, Sati, was married to Śiva; but neither she nor her husband were invited to the sacrifice, as Daksha had been offended with Śiva not long before. Sati, however, attended, and on being affronted threw herself into the flames of the sacrifice and perished.* Śiva exasperated, tore off a lock of his hair and cast it with violence to the ground. It started up in the shape of Víra Bhadra with a thousand hands, whom Śiva sent to destory the sacrifice. He did so, and according to some accounts cut off Daksha's head. According to the Vishṇu Purána, viíra Bhadra, was created from Śiva's mouth a being like the fire of fate, a divine being with a thousand heads, a thousand feet, &c., &c. It is only the Kási Khanda, however, that makes Sati throw herself into the fire, and Professor Wilson thinks this an improvement indicative of a later age. In other legends she is represented as killing herself on account of a quarrel with her father. The conduct of Víra Bhadra in interfering with and destroying the sacrifice, displeased the gods who were present, and they complained of it to Brahma; whereupon he with them proceeded to Śiva, interceding on behalf of Daksha. Śiva then went personally to the scene of disorder, and having resuscitated Daksha, whose head could not be found, replaced it by the head of a ram. The exploits of the Rudras on the occasion are particularly specified in the Kurma and Bhágavata Puránas. Indra is knocked down and trampled on; Yama has his staff broken; Saraswati and the Mátris have their noses cut off. Mitra or Bhaga has his eyes pulled out: Púsha has his teeth knocked down his throat; Chandra is pummelled; Vahni's hands are cut off; Bhrigu loses his beard; the Brahmans are pelted with stones; the Prajápatis are beaten; and the gods and demi-gods are run through with swords or stuck with arrows. Other accounts state that Daksha himself propitiated the mighty god, the holder of the trident, Maheshwara." V.P

The story is reproduced in the Purāṇas with many embellishments. Dakṣa instituted a sacrifice to Viṣṇu, and many of the gods repaired to it, but Śiva was not invited, because the gods had conspired to deprive him of sacrificial offerings. The wife of Śiva, the mountain goddess Umā, perceived what was going on. Umā was a second birth of Sati, daughter of Dakṣa, who had deprived herself of life in consequence of her father's quarrel with herself and her husband, Śiva. Umā urged her husband to display his power and assert his rights. So he created Vīrabhadra, "a being like the fire of fate", and of most terrific appearance and powers. He also sent with him hundreds and thousands of powerful demigods whom he called into existence. A terrible catastrophe followed: "the mountains tottered, the earth shook, the winds roared, and the depths of the sea were disturbed". The sacrifice is broken up, and, in the words of Wilson, "Indra is knocked down and trampled on, Yama has his staff broken, Sarasvatī and the Mātṛs have their noses cut off, Mitra or Bhaga has his eyes pulled out, Pūṣan has his teeth knocked down his throat, Candra (the moon) is pummelled, Vahni's (fire's) hands are cut off, Bhṛgu loses his beard, the brāhmaṇas are pelted with stones, the Prajāpatis are beaten, and the gods and demigods are run through with swords or stuck with arrows." Dakṣa then, in great terror, propitiated the wrathful deity and acknowledged his supremacy. According to some versions, Dakṣa himself was decapitated and his head thrown into the fire. Śiva subsequently restored him and the other dead to life, and as Dakṣa's head could not be found, it was replaced by that of a goat or ram. The *Harivaṁśa*, in its glorification of Viṣṇu, gives a different finish to the story. The sacrifice was destroyed and the gods fled in dismay, till Viṣṇu intervened, and seizing Śiva by the throat, compelled him to desist and acknowledge his master.

"This," says Wilson, "is a legend of some interest, as it is obviously intended to intimate a struggle between the worshippers of Śiva and Viṣṇu, in which at first the latter, but finally the former, acquired the ascendancy."

Dakṣa was a law-giver, and is reckoned among the eighteen writers of Dharmaśāstras.

The name Dakṣa was borne by several other persons.

Daksa Prajapati begot sisty beautiful daughters by his wife Asikni. Ten of these girls were married to Dharmadeva, thirteen of them to Kashyapa, twenty-seven of them to Soma (Chandra–Moon), and four of them to Aristhenemi. Of the rest two were given to Bahuputra, two to Angiras and twi to the wise Krsasva. The names of the wifes of each are given here – (1) Kashyapa. Aditi, Diti, Danu, Aristi, Surasa, Khasa, Surabhi, Vinata, Tamra, krodhasava, Ira, Kadru, Muni. (2) Dharmadeva. Arundhati, vasu, Yami, Lamba, Bhanu, Marutvati, Sankalpa, Mahurata, Sadhya, Visva. (3) Soma. Asvayuk, Bharani, Krttika, Rohini, Mrgasiras, Tarakam (Ardra), Punarvasu, Pusyam, aslesam, Janakam, Phalguni, Uttarphalgunam, Hastam, Citra, Svati, Vishakham, Anuradha, Jyestha, Mulam, Puruasadham, Uttarasadham, Srona, Sravistha, Prachetas, Purvaprosthapadam, Uttaraprosapadam, Revati. The names of the wives given to Angiras, Aristhanemi, Bahuputra and Krsasva are not mentioned anywhere. Besides these, twentyfour daughters were born to Daksa of his wife Prasuti who was the sister of Uttanapada. Dharmadeva married thirteen of them also, named Sraddha, Laksmi, Dhriti, Tusti, Medha, Pusti, Kriya, Buddhi, Lajja, Vapus, Santi, Siddhi, Kirti. Of the rest, Khyati was given to Brghu, Sati to Siva, Sambhuti to Marici, Smriti to Angiras, Priti to Puastaya, Ksama to Pulaha, Santati to Kratu, Anusuya to Atri, Urja to Vasistha, Svaha to Agideva Svadha to the Manes.

The other name of Daksa is "Kan".

(* Hence a widow consenting to be bound with the corpse of her husband is called a *Sati.* The common word *suttee* is not the act of burning, but the female burnt.)

DAKṢA-SAVARNA—The ninth Manu. (*see* MANU)

DAKṢAYANA—Connected with Dakṣa. A son or descendant of that sage.

DAKṢAYANI—A name of Aditi as daughter of Dakṣa.

DAKṢHA-SAVARNI—The name of the Manu of the Ninth Manwantara; described in the Váyu as one of the mind-engendered sons of a daughter of Dakṣa, by himself and the three gods Brahma, Dharma and Rudra, to whom he presented here on Mount Meru.

DAKSHAYANA—One of the names of the goddes Párvati. It is also the name of a lunar asterism in general. The grammarian Vyádi, author of the Sangraha, is sometimes called Dákshâyana.

DAKSHINA—**(1)** A fire for sacrifices placed to the south of the household fire and fire for oblations. The sacred fire of the Hindus, which was originally one, is said to have been made threefold by Purúravas. **(2)** One of the twin daughters of Ruchi and Akúti. These descendants of the first pair are evidently allegorical: thus Yajni (the name of the other twin daughter) is 'sacrifice;' and Dakshiná, 'donation' to brahmans. See *V.P.*, Chap. VIII. The first Manu, Svayambhuva, son of Brahma, accepted his sister Satarupa as his wife. Satarupa gave birth to two sons Priyavrata and Uttanapada, and two daughters, Prasuti and Akuti. Prasuti was given to Daksa in marriage and Akuti to Prajapati Ruci. Akuti gave birth to twins, a son named Yagna and a daughter named Daksina.

The same Daksina was reborn as Susila in Gokula when she was a cowherd women and a friend of Radha. She was also very close to Sri Krisna. She was once sitting in the lap of Krisna in an amorous posture and was seen by Radha who cursed her to turn into ashes. On getting down from the lap of Krisna Susila felt quite ashamed of her conduct and started immediately on a penance upon Mahalaksmi. Pleased with her steadfast penance Mahalaksmi absorbed her into her own being. The disappearance of Susila, being the reincarnate of Daksina (donation), soon, made the sacrifice of the devas fruitless. The devas worried about this went to Brahma for a remedy, and he meditated upon Visnu for a solution to this serious problem. Pleased with Brahma and to save the devas, Visnu got back Daksina from Mahalaksmi and gave her to Brahma, who in turn gifted her to Yagnapurusa (the Lord of Sacrifices), so that the sacrifices of the devas should bear fruit once again. The union of the two resulted in the birth of a child named Pṛhalada. It is the three of them, Daksina, Yagñapuruṣa and Pṛhalada, who divide the fruits of actions among the men.

DAKSHINACHARIS—A leading division of the sect of Sáktas, the followers of the right-hand ritual; often popularly caled the right-hand caste; the followers of the left-hand ritual being temed Vámáchais.

DAKSHI—The name of the mother of the celebrated Sanscrit grammarian Pánini.

DAKSINACARIS—Followers of the right-hand form of Śākta worship, (*see* TANTRA)

DALA—A prince, the son of Kusa, a descendant of Ráma.

DALADA—The left canine tooth of *Buddha*, the most highly venerated relic among the Buddhists, particularly in Ceylon. To preserve this, the only portion which remains of the body of the holy sage, a temple has been erected, in which it is deposited, being placed in a small chamber, enshrined in six cases, the largest of them being upwards of five feet in height and formed of silver. All the cases are constructed in the conical shape of a dágoba, and two of them are inlaid with rubies and precious stones. The outer case is ornamented with gold and jewels, which have been offered by devotees. Mr. Hardy describes the relic itself as 'a piece of discoloured ivory or bone, slightly curved, nearly two inches in length, and one in diameter at the base; and from thence to the other extremity, which is rounded and blunt, it considerably decreases in size.' The vihára or temple which contains the sanctuary of this relic, is attached to the palace of the former kings of Kandy. From a work composed on the subject of Buddha's tooth, dating as far back as A.D. 310, it is said that one of the disciples of the sage procured his left canine tooth when his relics were distributed. This much-valued treasure he conveyed to Dantapura, the chief city of Kalinga, where it reminded for 800 years. It subsequent history we quote from Mr. Hardy's 'Eastern Monarchism:' "The Brahmans informed Pándu, the lord paramount of India, who resided at Pátaliputra, that his vassal, Guhasiwa worshipped a piece of bone. The monarch, enraged at this intelligence, sent an army to arrest the king of Kálinga, and secure the bone he worshipped. This commission was executed, but the general and all his army were converted to the faith of Buddhism. Pándu commanded the relic to be thrown into a furnace of burning charcoal, but a lotus arose from the flame, and the tooth appeared on the surface of the flower. An attempt was then made to crush it upon an anvil, but it remained embedded in the iron, resisting all the means employed to take it therefrom, until Subaddha, a Buddhist, succeeded in its extraction. It was next thrown into the common sewer; but in an instant this receptacle of filth became sweet as a celestial garden, and was mantled with flowers. Other wonders were performed, by which Pándu also became a convert to Buddhism. The relic was returned to Dantapura; but an attempt being made by the princes of Sewet to take it away by force, it was brought to Ceylon, and deposited in the city of Anurádhapura. In the fourteenth century it was again taken to the continent, but was rescued by Prákrama Bahú, IV. The Portuguese say that it was captured by Constantine de Braganza, in 1560, and destoryed; but the native authorities assert that it was concealed at this time at a village in Saffragam. In 1815, it came into the possession of the British Government; and although surreptitiously taken away in the rebellion of 1818, it was subsequently found in the possession of a priest, and restored to its former sanctuary. From this time the keys of the shrine in which it was deposited were kept in the custody of the British agent for the Kandian provinces, and at night a soldier belonging to the Ceylon Rifle Regiment mounted guard in the temple, there being from time to time public exhibitions of the pretended tooth, under the sanction of the British authorities. The relic has since been returned to the native chiefs and priests, by a decree from the Secretary of State for the Colonies."

The Daladá is worshipped with great reverence by all Buddhists, but the inhabitants of Kandy more especially attach the highest importance to the possession of the sacred relic, regarding it as in fact the very glory and security of their country.

DALAKI—One of the four pupils of Sákapúrni, and

teacher of the Rig Veda.

DAMA—A son, or, according to the *Viṣṇu Purāṇa*, a grandson of King Marutta of the Solar race. He rescued his bride Sumanā from his rivals, and one of them, named Vapuṣmat, subsequently killed Marutta, who had retired into the woods after relinquishing his crown to his son. Dama in retaliation killed Vapuṣmat and offered his blood in the funeral rites of Marutta, while he made an oblation of part of the flesh, and with the rest fed the *brāhmaṇas* who were of *aksasa* descent. *Vishṇu Purána*, Book IV.

DAMAGHOSA—King of Cedi and father of Śiśupāla.

DAMALIPTAS, OR TAMALIPTAS—The people at the western mouth of the Ganges, in Medinipur and Tamluk. Tamralipti was a celebrated seaport in the fourth century and retained its character in the ninth and twelfth.

DAMANA—A great sage who visited the court of king Bhíma at Vidarbha, where he was so kindly and hospitably received by the childless king and his royal consort, that he bestowed on them a boon—that they should have children—as he knew it was for children they had long pined. In due course the promise was fulfilled; and there were born to the happy parents:—

> "One gweet girl, the pearl of maidens,—and three fair and noble sons,
>
> Damayantí, Dama, Dánta—and illustrious Damana;
>
> Richly gifted with all virtues—mighty, fearful in their might.
>
> Damayantí with her beauty—with her brilliance, brightness, grace,
>
> Through the worlds, unrivalled glory—won the slender-waisted maid."*
>
> The four children being all named in honour of the sage who had conferred the boon.

(*Milman's Translation of the *Story of Nala and Damayantí*.)

DAMANAKA—The name of the one of the jackals in the Panchatantra.

DAMA—The eldest son of Bhíma, king of Vidarbha; and brother of Damayantí.

DAMAYANTI—The daughter of Bhíma, Rája of Vidarbha. The name is already familiar to many English readers through Dr. Milman's metrical translation of the story, "Nala and Damayanti"—and a translation in blank verse by Mr. Chas. Bruce, which appeared in *Fraser's Magazine* a few years ago. The story itself is referred to the Vedic period of Hindu history. Damayanti was famous amongst all the Rájas for her radiant charms and exceeding grace. Nala, the Rája of Nishadha, had so often heard of the exquisite loveliness of Damayanti, the pearl of maidens, that he was enamoured without having seen her; and the soul-disturbing Damayantí had in like manner, so often been told of the god-like comeliness and virtues of the hero Nala, that she secretly desired to become his bride. Nala one day wandering in a grove, caught a swan of golden plumage; the bird cried out, 'Slay me not O gentle Rája, and I will so praise thee to Damayantí that she shall think of no other man but thee. So Nala set it free, and the bird flew away with its companions and entered the garden of Rája Bhíma. It took an opportunity of saying to Damayantí, 'O Damayantí, thou art the loveliest of maidens, and Nala is the handsomest of heroes; if the peerless wed the peerless how happy will be the union.' Then the royal maiden whispered, 'Say the same words to Nala.' And the bird flew away to Nishadha and told all to Nala.

Meantime the beautiful maiden grew pale and dejected. She could not sleep, she often wept, she found no joy in banquets or in conversation. The father saw that she must be married, and at the proclamation of her Swayamvara all the Rájas assembled. Nala repairs as a suitor to Vidarbha; but Indra and three other gods become incarnate for the same purpose, and, meeting Nala in the way, they beg him to be the bearer of their message of love. He remonstrates, but at last consents. He delivers it, but Damayantí declares that, even in the presence of the gods, she shall select the noble Nala. The assembly meets, and all the royal suitors are in array; but Damayantí discovers, to her dismay, five Nalas, each of the deities having assumed the form, features, and dress of the king of Nishadha. She utters a supplicatory prayer to the gods to reveal to her the true object of her choice. They are moved with compassion, and stand confessed, their spiritual bodies being distinguished from that of the human hero by their casting no shadow, nor touching the ground, and otherwise. Damayantí throws the wreath of flowers around the neck of the real Nala in token of her choice. The assembly breaks up amid the applause of the gods, and the lamentations of the disappointed suitors. The nuptials are celebrated and Nala and his bride are blessed with two lovely children.

Nala, the model of virtue, and piety, and learning, at length performs the Aśwameda, or sacrifice of a horse, the height of Indian devotion. In the course of time, however, Nala is induced by an evil spirit to play at dice with his brother, *Pushkara*, and loses his kingdom, his wealth, his very clothes. One stake only remains,—Damayantí herself. This Pushkara proposes, but Nala refuses. The ill-fated pair are driven together into the wilderness all but naked. Nala persuades his wife to leave him, and return to her father's court, but she will not forsake him. The frantic man, however, resolves to abandon her while asleep. He does so. Each passes through a series of strange and stormy adventrues, ending in Nala becoming master of the horse to the King of Ayodhya (Oude,) and Damayantí returning to her father's house. After some time, Damayantí in order to discover the retreat of Nala, proclaims her intention to hold another *Swayamvara*, and to form a second marriage, though forbidden by the laws of Manu. Rituparṇa, the King of Oude, resolves to become a suitor, and sets forth with his charioteer—the disguised Nala. As they enter the city of Bhíma, Damayantí recognises the sound of her husband's trampling steeds, his driving could not be mistaken by her ear. She employs every artifice to discover her lord; she suspects the charioteer; she procures some of his food, and recognises the flavour of her husband's cookery; she sends her children to him. Nala can conceal himself no longer; but the jealous thought that his wife was about to take a second husband, rankles in his heart, and he rebukes her with sternness. Damayantí solemnly denies any such design, declaring that she had only employed the artifice to win back her lord. Nala re-assumes his proper form and character—wins backs his wife and all that he had lost to his unprincipled brother, and re-ascending his ancestral throne, recommences a reign of piety, justice and felicity.—Mrs. Manning, *A. & M. I.*

DAMBHA—Hypocrisy. The son of Adharma (vice,) and Hinsa (violence.)

DAMBHODBHAVA—A king whose story is related in the *Mahabharata* as an antidote to pride. He had an overweening conceit of his own prowess, and when told by his brāhmaṇas that he was no match for Nara and Nārāyaṇa, who were living as ascetics on the Gandhamādana mountain, he proceeded thither with his army and challenged them. They endeavoured to dissuade him, but he insisted on fighting. Nara then took a handful of straws, and using them as missiles, they whitened all the air, and penetrated the eyes, ears, and noses of the assailants, until Dambhodbhava fell at Nara's feet and begged for peace.

DAMINS—The name of brahmans in Kusa-dwípa.

DAMODARA—A name given to Kṛṣṇa because his foster-mother tried to tie him up with a rope (*dāma*) round his belly (*udara*).

DAMODAS—The name of one of the nine divisions of the Atharva Veda.

DANAVAS—Enemies of the gods, who, "incapable of steadiness and animated by ambition, put forth their strength against the gods. They were the descendants of Kaṣyapa by his wife Danu, hence their name. They wee a class of mythological giants; in the Epic period they were probably personifications of the Aborigines of India; in the Puranic period they are regarded as the inhabitant of Pátáḷa and enemies of the gods. —*Thomson.* See DAITYAS.

DANDA—**(1)** A measure of time—sixty Vikalás. Sixty Daṇḍas make one siderial day. **(2)** The name of a son of Dharma by Kriya. Also the name of one of the hundred sons of Ikshwáku. Professor Wilson thinks that by these sons of Ikshwáku we are to understand colonies or settlers in various parts of India. In the Padma P., and the Uttara Khanda of the Rámáyana, there is a detailed narrative of Daṇḍa, whose country was laid waste by an imprecation of Bhárgava, whose daughter Daṇḍa had violated. His kingdom became in consequence the Daṇḍaka forest. The Hari Vansa states that Daṇḍa was killed by Sudhyumna.

DANDADHARA—'The rod-bearer'. A title of Yama, the god of death.

DANDAKA—**(1)** "A class of metre in Sanskrit which admits an inordinate length of the verse, which may consist of any number of syllables from twenty-seven to nine hundred and ninety-nine; and the specific name varies accordingly. The construction of the metre requires that the first six syllables be short, and the remainder of the versebe composed of cretic feet, or the bacchus. These two kinds of metre are distinguished by different names. A verse consisting of any number of anapæsts within the limitation above mentioned, is also comprehended under this general designation; as are verses of similar length consisting exclusively of iambic or trochaic feet. They have their peculiar denominations." **(2)** An extensive forest near the Godavary, frequently mentioned in the Rámáyana as the scene of Ráma's wanderings. Ráma was living in a hermitage in this forest when Rávaṇa carried off Síta. The river which the unhappy Síta loved was a tributary to the Godavery, running through the dense forests and wild districts not yet entirely explored, which lie to the north of Bombay and stretch away towards Orissa. The plash of the water-fowl bathing in the bright waters of the Godavery is the most cheerful feature of the scene; but, unlike the Gogra, it is skirted by sea-bright hills, with flashing torrents, but hemmed in by the weary woods of "the pathless Daṇḍaka;" where twining creeper plants, hanging and climbing from bough to bough, alone relieve the "forest gloom." The country is said to be still the "pathless Daṇḍaka." *A. and M. I.*, vol. II, p. 22.

DANḌIS—One of the Vaishnava or Saiva sects among the Hindus, and a legitimate representative of the fourth Asrama or mendicant life, into which the Hindu is believed to enter after passing through the previous stages of student, householder, and hermit. A Brahman, however, does not require to pass through the previous stages, but is allowed to enter at once into the fourth order. The Daṇḍi is distinguished by carrying a small dand or wand, with several projections from it, and a piece of cloth dyed with red ochre, in which the Brahmanical cord is supposed to be enshrined, attached to it; he shaves his hair and beard, wears only a cloth around the loins, and subsists upon food obtained ready-dressed from the houses of the Brahmans once a day only, which he deposits in the small clay-pot that he always carries with him. He should live alone, and near to, but not within a city; but this rule is rarely observed, and, in general, the Daṇḍis are found in cities, collected like other mendicants in *Maths*. The Daṇḍi has no particular time or mode of worship, but employs himself chiefly in mediatation and in the study of the Vedánta works. He reverences *Siva* and his incarnations in preferences to the other members of the Hindu Triad, and hence the Daṇḍis are reckoned among the Śaivas. They bear the Śiva mark upon the forehead, smearing it with the *Tripundra*, that is, a triple transverse line formed with the ashes of fire made with burnt cow-dung. This mark, beginning between the eyebrows and carrying it to their extremity, is made with the thumb reverted between the middle and third fingers. The genuine Daṇḍi, however, is not necessarily of the Śiva or any other sect, and in their establishments they are usually found to adore *Nirguna* or *Niranjana*, the deity devoid of attribute or passion. The Daṇḍis have usually great influence and authority among the Śiva Brahmans of the North of India, and they are the Sanyasis or monastic portion of the Smarta sect of Brahmans in the north.

It is not so much the speculative as the practical Daṇḍis that are worshippers of Śiva, and the form in which they adore him is that of *Bhairava* (which see), or Lord of Terror. In the case of those who thus worship Śiva, part of the ceremony of initiation consists in inflicting a small incision on the inner part of the knee, and drawing the blood of the novice as an acceptable offering to the god. The Daṇḍis of every description differe from the great mass of Hindus in their treatment of the dead, as they put them into some sacred stream. Hindus of all castes are occasionally found assuming the life and emblems of the order of Daṇḍis. There are even Brahmans who, without connecting themselves with any community, take upon them the character of this class of mendicants. There is, however, a sect of Daṇḍis termed Dasnamis (which see), which admit none but Brahmans into their order.—*Wilson.*

DANSHTRINAS—The progeny of Krodavasá, carnivorous animals, brids and fishes—all sharp-toothed monsters.

DANTA—The youngest of the three sons of Bhíma, rája of Vidarbha; and brother of Damayantí.

DANTAVAKTRA—A *dānava* king of Karūṣa and son of Vṛddha-śarma. He took a side against Rrsna, and was eventually killed by him.

DANU—(1) A *dānava.* Also The daughter of Daksha and the mother of the *dānavas.* The demon Kabandha (*q.v.*). According to the Mahabharata (*Adi Parva*) one hundred sons were born to Danu from her marriage with Kasyapaprajapati. From these *danavas* the important are

Vipracitti	Namici
Sibara	Puloma
Asiloma	Asvagrivan
Kesi	Suksma
Durjaya	Tuhunda
Ayassiras	Ekapada
Asvasiras	Ekacakra
Asvasanku	Virupaksa
Garga	Harihara
Amurdha	Nichandra
Vehavan	Nikumbha
Ketuman	Kapata
Svarabhanu	Sarabha
Asva	Salabha
Asvapati	Surya
Vrsaparvan	Chandra

Ajaka

Ten families of Danavas rose from the above named *asuras*. All the danavas belong to one of these families. The founders of the ten families are:

Ekaksa	Tapana
Amrtapa	Sara
Pralamba	Mahahanu
Naraka	Garvistha
Vatapi	Dirghajihva

(2) The mother of Vrittra who was slain by Indra, along with her son, and when slaughtered, lay over him like a cow over her calf. *O.S.T.* Vol. v., p. 95. **(3)** A fallen demi-god who was restored by Ráma. Danu was the son of Lakshmi; but was brought by a curse to the state of a demon, and reduced to a headless trunk by the weapons of Indra; but on meeting with Ráma his miraculous recovery is said to have been instantaneous. Danu then counselled Ráma and his brother to go to Rishyamúka; for said he there dwells an eminent monkey named Sugríva who will give you tidings of your lovely Síta. Danu had previously been employed by Mályaván to mar the forest in order to ruin Ráma.

DANUS—Another name for Danavas, the sons of Dánu.

DANUSHA—An unerring bow;—one of the fourteen gems obtained at the churning of the milk sea in the second or Kúrma Avatar of Vishnu.

DAPPLE-SKIN—The name of the wonderful cow of plenty belonging to the great sage Vasishtha, and which Rája Viswámitra took away by force.

DARADA—A country in the Hindu Kush, bordering on Kaśmir. The people of that country, "the Durds, are still where they were at the date of the text (of the *Viṣṇu Purāṇa*) and in the days of Strabo and Ptolemy; not exactly, indeed, at the sources of the Indus, but along its course above the Himālaya, just before it descends to India."—*Wilson.*

DARDURA—Name of a mountain in the south; it is associated with the Malaya mountain in the *Mahābhārata.*

DARPA—(Pride). The name of the one of the sons of Dharma.

DARRAS—'Tearers'. *Raksasas* and other destructive demons.

DARSANA—'Demonstration'. The *ṣaḍ-darśanas* or six demonstrations, *i.e.*, the six schools of Hindu philosophy. All these schools have one starting-point *ex nihilo nihil fit*; and all have one and the same final object, the emancipation of the soul from future birth and existence, and its absorption into the supreme soul of the universe. These schools are:

1. *Nyāya*, founded by the sage Gotama. The word *nyāya* means propriety or fitness, the proper method of arriving at a conclusion by analysis. This school has been called the Logical School, but the term is applicable to its method rather than to its aims. It is also said to represent "the sensational aspect of Hindu Philosophy", because it has "a more pointed regard to the fact of the five senses than the others have, and treats the external more frankly as a solid reality". It is the exoteric school, as the Vedānta is the esoteric.

2. *Vaiśeṣika*, founded by a sage named Kaṇāda, who lived about the same time as Gotama. It is supplementary to the Nyāya, and these two schools are classed together. It is called the Atomic School, because it teaches the existence of a transient world composed of aggregations of eternal atoms.

   Both the Nyāya and Vaiśeṣika recognise a Supreme Being.

3. *Sāṁkhya.* The Sāṁkhya and Yoga are classed together because they have much in common, but the Samkhya is atheistical, while the Yoga is theistical. The Sāṁkhya was founded by the sage Kapila, and takes its name from its numeral or discriminative tendencies. The *Sāṁkhya-Kārikā*, the textbook of this school, has been translated by Colebrooke and Wilson, and part of the aphorisms of Kapila were translated for the *Bibliotheca Indica* by the late Dr. Ballantyne.

4. *Yoga.* This school was founded by Patañjali, and from his name is also called Pātañjala. It pursues the method of the Sāṁkhya and holds with many of its dogmas, but it asserts the existence not only of individual souls, but of one all-pervading spirit, which is free from the influences which affect other souls.

5. *Pūrva Mīmāṁsā.*

6. *Uttara Mīṁaṁsā*: The prior and later Mīmāṁsās. These are both included in the general term Vedānta, but the Pūrva Mīmāṃsā is commonly known as the Mīmāṁsā and the Uttara Mīmāṁsā

as the Vedānta, 'the end or object of the Vedas'. The Pūrva Mīmāṁsā was founded by Jaimini, and the Uttara Mīmāṁsā is attributed to Vyāsa, the arranger of the Vedas. "The object of both these schools is to teach the art of reasoning with the express purpose of aiding the interpretation of the Vedas, not only in the speculative but the practical portion." The principal doctrines of the Vedānta (Uttara) are that "God is the omniscient and omnipotent cause of the existence, continuance, and dissolution of the universe. Creation is an act of his will; he is both the efficient and the material cause of the world." At the consummation of all things all are resolved into him. He is "the sole-existent and universal soul", and besides him there is no second principle; he is Advaita 'without a second'. Śaṅkarācārya was the great apostle of this school.

The period of the rise of these schools of philosophy is uncertain, and is entirely a matter of inference, but they are probably later than the fifth century BC. The Vedanta (Uttara Mīmāṁsā) is apparently the latest, and is supposed to have been evoked by the teachings of the Buddhists. This would bring it to within three or four centuries BC. The other schools are to all appearance older than the Vedānta, but it is considered by some that all the schools show traces of Buddhist influences, and if so, the dates of all must be later. It is a question whether Hindu philosophy is or is not indebted to Greek teaching, and the later the date of the origin of these schools the greater is the possibility of Greek influence. Mr. Colebrooke, the highest authority on the subject, is of opinion that "the Hindus were in this instance the teachers, not the learners".

Besides the six schools, there is yet a later system known as the Paurāṇik and the Eclectic school. The doctrines of this school are expounded in the *Bhagavad Gītā* (*q.v.*).

The merits of the various schools have been thus summed up: "When we consider the six Darśanas, we shall find that one of them, the Uttara Mīmāṁsā, bears no title to be ranked by the side of the others, and is really little more than a mystical explanation of the practical injunctions of the Vedas. We shall also admit that the earlier Vedānta, very different from the school of Nihilists now existing under that name, was chiefly a controverṣial essay, seeking to support the theology of sacred writ, but borrowing all its philosophical portions from the Yoga school, the most popular at the time of its composition. Lastly, the Nyāya is little more than a treatise on logic, introducing the doctrines of the theistic Sāmkhya; while the Vaiśeṣika is an essay on physics, with, itis true, the theory ofatoms as its distinguishing mark, though even to this we feel inclined to refuse the imputation of novelty, since we find some idea of it lurking obscurely in the theory of subtile elements which is brought forward in Kapila's Sāṁkhya. In short, the basis of all Indian philosophy, if indeed we may not say the only system of philosophy really discovered in India, is the Samkhya, and this forms the basis of the doctrines expounded in the *Bhagavad Gītā*."—*Cockburn Thomson.*

Colebrooke's *Essays* are the great authorities on Hindu philosophy. Ballantyne has translated many of the Original aphorisms, and he, Cockburn Thomson, Hall, Banerjea, and others have written on the subject.

DARSAPAURNAMASA—**(1)** One of the five great sacrificial ceremonies: *viz.*, new and full-moon, those at which four priests officiate. **(2)** The small festivals held at the new moon and full moon. "In the beginning of the Darsapurnamása sacrifice, the Adhivarya priest having called the cows and calves together, touches the calves with a branch, and says, 'You are like the winds.'"—*Max Müller.*

DARUKA—The charioteer of Krishṇa. He was sent to apprise Arjuna of Krishṇa's approaching end, when he was about to quit the body, and "unite himself to his own pure, spiritual, inexhaustible, imperishable and universal spirit—to become Nirguṇa, devoid of all qualities.

DARUNA—The name of the one of the Narakas, or hells, described in the Puránas.

DARVAN—The son of Uṣínara, one of the descendants of Anu.

DASA-BALA—Ten powers or modes of wisdom possessed by BUDDHA. Mr. Spence Hardy, to whose excellent works we are indebted for our information on the principles and rites of the BUDDHISTS, thus enumerates the Dasabala, in his 'Manual of Buddhism:'—"1, The wisdom that understands what knowledge is necessary for the right fulfilment of any particular duty, in whatsoever situation; 2, That which knows the result or consequences of karma, or moral action; 3, That which knows the way to the attainment of nirwána or annihilation; 4, That which seems the various sakwalas or systems of worlds; 5, That which knows the thoughts of other beings; 6, that which knows that the organs of sense are not the self; 7, That which knows the purity produced by the exercise of the dhyánas or abstract meditation; 8, That which knows where any one was born in all his former births; 9, That which knows where any one will be born in all future births; 10, That which knows how the results proceeding from karma, or moral action, may be overcome."

DASA-DANDU—Ten prohibitions which are enjoined upon the Buddhist monks to be studied during their noviciate. Mr. Hardy, in his 'Eastern Monarchism,' thus describes them—"1, The easting of food after mid-day; 2. The seeing of dances or the hearing of music or singing; 3, The use of ornaments or perfumes; 4, The use of a seat or couch more than a cubit high; 5, The receiving of gold, silver, or money; 6, Practising some deception to prevent another priest from receiving that to which he is entitled; 7, Practising some deception to injure another priest, or bring him into danger; 8, Practising some deception in order to cause another priest to be expelled from the community; 9, Speaking evil of another priest; 10, Uttering slanders, in order to excite dissension among the priests of the same community. The first five of these crimes may be forgiven, if the priest bring sand and sprinkle it in the court-yard of the vihára, and the second five may be forgiven after temporary expulsion."

DASAGRIVA—A name of Rávana, meaning the ten necked.

DASAKHANDARA—A name of Rávaṇa, the ten-headed sovereign of Lanka.

DASA-KUMARA-CARITA—'Tales of the ten princes', by Śrī Daṇḍī. It is one of the few Sanskṛt works written in prose, but its style is so studied and elaborate that it is classed as a *kāvya* or poem. The tales are stories of common life, and display a low condition of morals and a corrupt state of society. The text has been printed with a long analytical introduction by H. H. Wilson, and again in Bombay by Bühler. There is an abridged translation by Jacobs, also a translation in French by Fauche, and a longer analysis in vol. IV of Wilson's works.

DASANANA—'Ten-faced', A name of Rāvaṇa.

DASARA—An Annual Festival, called in the north of India the Durga Pújá. It is the most popular, splendid and expensive of any of the Hindu festivals, and takes place in the mouth *Aswiya*, (the end of September or beginning of October). The preliminary ceremonies occupy several days previous to the three days of worship. "During the whole of this period all business, in many parts of the country, is suspended, and pleasure and festivity prevail...The artisans and labourers offers sacrifices to the tools and implements which they use in their daily work. The labourer brings his plough, hoe, and other instruments, piles them together, and offers to them a sacrifice consisting of incense, flowers, fruits, rice, and similar articles; after which he prostrates himself before them, and then returns them to their places. The mason offers the same adoration and sacrifices to his trowel, his rule, and other instruments. The carpenter is no less pious with regard to his hatchet, his adze, and his plane. The barber, too, collects his razors in a heap, and worships them with similar rites. The writing-master or copyist sacrifices to the iron pencil or style with which he writes; the tailor to his needles; the weaver to his loom; the butcher to his cleaver. The women, at the same time, heap together their baskets, the rice mill, the wooden cylinder with which they bruise the rice, and the other household implements; and fall down before them after having offered the sacrifices above described. In short, every person adores the instrument or tool which he principally uses in gaining his livelihood. The tools are now considered as so many deities; to whom they present their supplications that they would continue propitious, and furnish them still with the means of living. The festival is concluded by erecting a shapeless statue in each village, composed to paste from grain. It is intended to represent the goddess Párvati; and, being placed under a sort of canopy, is carried about and receives the homage of the inhabitants, who flock to render it their adorations."

Many other usages prevail at this festival in different parts of the country. Amongst the Mahrattas, sheep and buffaloes are sacrificed. The chiefs often give money to enable their soldiers to buy sheep to perform sacrifices, which from furnishing them with a good dinner, are by many considered as the most essential ceremonies of the Dasara. The cannon belonging to the army are planted, praised, invoked, and propitiated by several species of offering. Sir John Malcolm states that on the morning of the tenth day, the Péshwa with all his officers and soldiers, used to move out to the camp in the vicinity of the city, each mounted on his best horse, drest in his finest clothes, and with his arms highly polished. Horses, elephants, and camels were all arranged in their gayest trappings, and every crops spread its gaudiest flags and banners. The whole population of the capital, either as actors or spectators, joined in this grand procession, which moved towards the sacred tree, the object of adoration. After the offerings and prayers the Péshwa plucked some leaves of the tree, in which all the cannon and musketry commenced firing. The Péshwa then plucked from a field, purchased for the occasion, a stalk of jowri, on which the whole crowd fired off their arms or shot arrows, and rushing to the field, tore up all the stalks, each person securing some share of the spoil, which he carried home with joy.

DASARATHA—A prince of the Solar race, son of Aja, a descendant of Ikṣvāku, and king of Ayodhyā. He had three wives, but being childless, he performed the sacrifice of a horse, and, according to the *Rāmāyaṇa*, the chief queen, Kauśalyā, remained in close contact with the slaughtered horse for a night, and the other two queens beside her. Four sons were then born to him from his three wives. Kauśalyā bore Rāma, Kaikeyī gave birth to Bharata, and Sumitra bore Lakṣmaṇa and Śatrughna. Rāma partook of half the nature of Viṣṇu, Bharata of a quarter, and the other two shared the remaining fourth. The *Rāmāyaṇa*, in explanation of this manifestation of Viṣṇu, says that he had promised the gods to become incarnate as man for the destruction of Rāvaṇa. He chose Daśaratha for his human parent; and when that king was performing a second sacrifice to obtain progeny, he came to him out of the fire as a glorious being, and gave him a vessel full of nectar to administer to his wives. Daśaratha gave half of it to Kauśalyā, and a fourth each to Sumitrā and Kaikeyī. They all in consequence became pregnant, and their offspring partook of the divine nature according to the portion of the nectar each had drunk. There were several others of the name. (*see* Rāmacandra) He was a descendant from Surya, and one of his ancestors, Raghu, had conquered the seven dwípas or the whole earth.

"There reigued a king of name revered,
To country and to town endeared,
Great Daṣaratha good and sage
Well read in Scripture's holy page;
Upon his kingdom's weal intent,
Mighty and brave and provident:
The pride of old Ikshváku's seed
For lofty thought and righteous ded.
Peer of the saints for virtues famed,
For foes subdued and passinos tamed;
A rival in his wealth untold
Of Indra and the Lord of Gold.
Like Manu first of kings, he reigned,
And worthily his state maintained.
For firm and just and ever true,
Love, duty, gain he kept in view;
And ruled his city rich and free,
Like Indra's Amarávatí."

—Griffith's *Ramayanaa.*

Another Daṣaratha was the son of Múlaka; a third, the son of Navaratha; a fourth, the son of Suyaṣas. The name of Daṣaratha, in a similar ancient character to that of Piyadai's inscriptions, has been found at Gaya amongst Buddhist remains, and like them deciphered by Mr. Prinsep. *V.P.*

DASARHA, DASARHA—**(1)** Prince of the Daśārhas, a title of Kṛṣṇa. The Daśārhas were a tribe of Yādavas. **(2)** A Prince, the son of Nirvriti. In the Linga Purána it is said that Dasárha was the destroyer of the host of copper (faced) foes.

DASARNA—**(1)** A place mentioned in Kálidása's *Cloud Messenger*, "Darárna's fields await the coming shower." Dr. F. E. Hall says it was situated to the east of Chandeyru. Vidisá is described as the capital of the District. Dasárna is said to be derived from Dasa, ten; and Riṇa, a stronghold or Durga. the Droog of the Peninsula, and means the District of the ten citadels.—*Wilson*. **(2)** A river mentioned in the Puránas, and identified in the Dhosaun in Bundlekund.

DASARUPAKA—An ancient and valuable treatise on dramatic literature. It is a description of the ten kinds of theatrical composition of which the term *Rúpaka*, (that which has a form) is the proper designation. The work consists of a Text and a Gloss, with examples. The text is the composition of Dhananjaya the son of Vishṇu, who styles Munja, his patron, and who consequently wrote in the eleventh century. The Gloss might be thought to be by the same hand as the Text, the author being Dhanika the son of Vishṇu; agreeing in the patronymic and differing little in the name. But the date of the Gloss remains undetermined, though it is no doubt of some antiquity.—*Wilson*.

DASAS—'Slaves.' Tribes and people of India who opposed the progress of the intrusive Āryans.

DASA-SIL—*Dasasikha*, *Dasa-pariji*, *Dasa-nasanu*, *Dasa-dandu*, *Dasa-sil*, the ten obligations binding on the Buddhist priest—to abstain from murder, theft, sexual intercourse, falsehood, intoxicating drink, eating after mid-day, dancing, perfumes, luxury, receiving of gold or silver. The other Dasas relate to the same rules with slight modifications. The Dasa-dandu forbid deceiving or speaking evil of other priests.

DASNAMI DAṆḌIS—The primitive members of the order of Daṇḍis. They are said to refer their origin to Sankara Achárya, a remarkable individual who acted a conspicuous part in the religious history of Hindustan. The word Dasnami means ten-named, there, being ten classes of mendicants descended from this remarkable man, only three of them, however, having so far retained their purity as to entitle them to be called Sankara's Daṇḍis. These are numerous, especially in and about Benares. The chief Vedántist writers belong to this sect. The most sturdy beggars, as we learn from Professor Wilson, are members of this order, although their contributions are levied particularly upon the Brahmanical class, as whenever a feast is given to the Brahmans, the Daṇḍis of this description present themselves, though unbidden guests, and can only be got rid of by bestowing upon them a share of the viands. Many of them practise the Yoga, and profess to work miracles. The author of the 'Dabistan' speaks of one who could keep his breath suspended for three hours, bring milk from his veins, cut bones with hair, and put eggs into a narrow-mouthed bottle without breaking them.

The remaining members of the Dasnami class, though they have degenerated from the purity of the practice necessary to the original Daṇḍis, are still religious characters, only they have given up the staff or wand, the use of the clothes, money, and ornaments; they prepare their own food, and admit members from any order of Hindus. These Atíts, as they are often called, are frequently collected in *Maths*, as well as the Daṇḍis, but they mix freely in the business of the world; they carry on trade, and often accumulate property, and some of the them even enter into the married state, when they receive the name of Samyogi."—*Wilson, vol. I, p.* 204.

DASRAS—'Beautiful'. The elder of the two Asvins, or in the dual (Dasrau), the two Aśvins.

DASYUS—In the Vedas they are evil beings, enemies of the god and men. They are represented as being of a dark colour, and probably were the natives of India who contended with the immigrant Āryans. It has, however, been maintained that they were hermits and ascetics of Āryan race. In later times they are barbarians, robbers, outcasts, who, according to some authorities, descended from Viśvāmitra.

There is no doubt that in many passages of the Rig-Veda, the words Dasyu and Dása are applied to demons of different orders, or goblins, (Asuras, Rákshasas, &c.) but it is tolerably evident from the nature of the case, that in all, or at least most of the texts, we are to understand the barbarous aboriginal tribes of India as intended by these terms. This is yet more clearly established by the sense in which the word Dasyu is used (*i.e.*, for men and not for demons) in the Aitareya Bráhmana, in Manu, and in the Mahábhárata."—*Muir*, II, 68.

Professor Roth, in his *Lexicon*, defines Dasyu as denoting 1, "a class of superhuman beings, who are maliciously disposed both to gods and men, and are overcome by Indra and Agni in particular. 2, the word is an approbrious designation of hostile, wicked, or barbarous men." Professor Müller remarks, "Dasyu simply means enemy; for instance when Indra is praised because he destroyed the Dasyus and protected the Arian colour." Dr. Muir quotes some passages in which the Dasyus are spoken of as monsters.

DAṬṬAKA-CANDRIKA—A treatise on the law of adoption by Devana Bhaṭṭa. Translated by Sutherland.

DATTAKA-MIMAMSA—A treatise on the law of adoption by Nanda Paṇḍita. Translated by Sutherland.

DATTAKA-SIROMANI—A digest of the principal treatises on the law of adoption.

DATTATREYA—Son of Atri and Anasūyā. A brāhmaṇa saint in whom a portion of Brahmā, Viṣṇu, and Śiva, or more particularly Viṣṇu, was incarnate. He had three sons, Soma, Datta, and Durvāsas, to whom also a portion of the divine essence was transmitted. He was the patron of Kārtavīrya, and gave him a thousand arms.

DATTDI—A name of Agastya, in a previous Manwantara.

DAYABHAGA—A celebrated Sanscrit treatise on the Hindu Law of Inheritance. Mr. Colebrooke first published a translation of this work, in 1810; and a new edition, with valuable notes, was published in 1865 by Mr. Whitley Stokes.

DAYA-KRAMA-SAMAGRHA—A treatise on the law of inheritance as current in Bengal, by Śrī Kṛṣṇa Tarkālaṁkāra. Translated by Wynch.

DAYA-TATVA—A treatise on the law of inheritance as current in Bengal, by Raghunandana Bhaṭṭācārya.

DEMONS—A belief in demons is found to prevail all over India. Every Hindu work containing allusions to native life, and the Dictionaries of all the Hindu dialects, prove the general prevalence of a belief in the existence of malicious or mischievous demons, in demoniacal inflictions and possessions, and in the power of exorcisms. The majority of the demons are supposed to have been originally human beings; and the class of persons most frequently supposed to have been transformed into demons are those who had met with a sudden or violent death, especially if they had made themselves, dreaded in their life-time. Demons may in consequence be either male or female, of low or high caste, of Hindu or foreign lineage. Their character and mode of life seem to be little if at all modified by differences of this nature. All are powerful, malicious, and interfering; and all are desirous of bloody sacrifices and frantic dances.

In every part of India innumerable legends respecting goblins and their malice are current; but scarcely any trace of their worship in the proper sense of the term, much less of their exclusive worship, can be discovered beyond the districts in which the Shánárs, or other primitive illiterate tribes, are found. This superstition respecting demons, in whatever form and under whatever modifications it may appear, is found to be productive of evil; but it was reserved for the Shánárs and a few other illiterate tribes to exemplify the debasing effect of it in its fullest extent by their worship of demons, a degradation beneath which the human mind cannot descend.

In all Brahmanical myths the demons are represented as being the ancient enemies of the gods, as warring against the gods, and sometimes gaining the upper hand; and as the inventors and special patrons of bloody sacrifices. Every new deity gains prodigious victories over the demons, and yet somehow they never are thoroughly conquered.

In all Brahmanical books and legends in which the state of the original inhabitants of Peninsular India is described, we are referred to a period when demons ruled in the primeval jungles, and when those jungles were inhabited solely by vile sinners who ate flesh and offered bloody sacrifices. In like manner the Buddhists represent Ceylon, prior to the advent of Buddhism, as having been overrun with serpent gods and demons.*

Mr. Caldwell shows conclusively that a high antiquity must be assigned to demon-worship, that it was established in the arid plains of Tinnevelly and amongst the Travancore jungles, long anterior to the influx of the Brahmans and their civilization of the primitive Tamil tribes. (* *The Tinnevelly Shánárs*, by Rev. R. Caldwell.)

DEVA—**(1)** (Nom. Devas = *Deus*, from the root *div*, to shine.) God. A deity. The gods are spoken of as thirty-three in number, eleven for each of the three worlds. **(2)** A divine being, whether resident upon earth or in a deva-loka. Deva is also a divine epithet variously applied but rarely to the superior deities if alone. Maha deva is sometimes met with. The most frequent use of the term is in the plural, and may be translated "Celestials." The Hindu books say there are thirty-three crores of them; that is, three hundred and thirty millions of celestials; but this is probably only a figurative expression to denote a great number. They are not demi-gods, as has been stated; but deified human heroes. Rama or Krishṇa is not one of them, but of higher order. The *devatas* people the paradise of Vishṇu; but they especially belong to the *Svarga*, the paradise of Indra. They are usually ranged under eight divisions, with a *vasu*, as leader, at the head of each division.

DEVABHAGA—The son of Sura and one of the nine brothers of Vasudeva.

DEVABHUTI—The last Sunga prince, the dynasty moving consisted of ten, who governed the kingdom for a hundred and twleve years. Devabhúti being addicted to immoral practices, was murdered by his minister, the Kanwa named Vasudeva, who usurped the kingdom.

DEVADARSA—A teacher of the Atharva-Veda, a pupil of Kahandha. He had four disciples who taught this veda.

DEVADATTA—One of the five sons of a brahman named Govindadatta who lived on the banks of the Ganges. The sons were of goodly persons, but rude manners and uncultivated minds. A brahman of great learning having on one occasion, when the father was abroad, demanded the rites of hospitality, was treated with disrespect by the youths, and was about to depart in wrath when the father arrived. The severity with which he rebuked the lads pacified the brahman and he was induced to remain. The anger of his parent produced a favourable impression on Devadatta, who, repenting of his idle habits, set off to Badarikáṣrama to propitiate Śiva. The rigour of his austerities engaged the approbation of the god. Śiva appeared to him and promised that he should become possessed of learning, for which purpose he directed him to go to Pátaliputra, and study under Vedakhumba. He afterwards repaired to Pratisbthana, where he studied with diligence and success under another teacher of repute.

He there beheld the daughter of the king Suṣarma at a balcony of the palace. She also noticed him, and the attraction was mutual. After they had interchanged glances she beckoned to him to approach. He obeyed; on which she took a flower, and having touched her teeth with it, threw it to him, and then disappeared. Devadatta taking the flower returned home. The flame that preyed on his heart soon betrayed itself to the experience of his preceptor, and he quickly drew from him the secret of his passion. He explained the story of the flower to signify an assignation on the part of the princess to meet Devadatta at a temple called Pushpa, (a flower.) The youth was charmed with this explanation, and set off to the temple to await the coming of the princess. On her arrival in due course she enquired how he had so readily apprehended her meaning; but when he confessed he was indebted to his preceptor's sagacity, rather than to his own, she was highly offended with his lack of discernment and left him in displeasure.

Devadatta was now more wretched than ever, when Śambhu, commisserating his condition, sent one of his attendants, Panchisikha, to console and assist him. Panchisikha male the youth put on a female garb, whilst he assumed the appearance of an aged brahman. Thus changed, they repaired to the palace, when the supposed brahman thus addressed the monarch: "King, I am an old man, without connections in your capital. I sent my only son on family affairs some time ago to a distant country, and he does not return. I am weary of expecting him, and fear some evil may have befallen him. I will therefore go forth in quest of him; but how can I dispose of my daughter-in-law in the meantime? I leave her, king, as a sacred deposit in your charge." The monarch, afraid of the brahman's malediction, reluctantly accepted the trust, and the supposed brahman departed. The daughter was transferred to the interior of the palace, where, revealing himself to the princess, Devadatta succeeded in pacifying her indignation, and recovering her regard. She listened to his suit with complacency, and they pledged their troth to each other by the ritual that unites in wedlock the inferior spirits of heaven.

When it became no longer possible to conceal their secret intercourse, the friendly spirit was summoned by a wish to their assistance—he appeared, and conveyed Devadatta out of the palace by night. The next morning he made the youth discard his female habiliments, and accompany him, again metamorphosed to a venerable brahman, to the palace, in the character of the son of whom he had been in search. He came, he said, to claim his daughter-in-law, and the king ordered her to be sent for; but all parties were struck with real, or seeming consternation, when it was announced that she was nowhere to be found. The king, at a loss to comprehend the possibility of her evasion, and recollecting old legends, suspected that the brahman was not what he seemed to be, and, apprehensive of incurring his displeasure, professed himself willing to submit to any conditions he should impose. These were readily arranged, and the princess was given to the brahman's supposed son, in exchange for the bride that he pretended to have lost. The princess bore a son, who was named Mahídhara. When the king was advanced in years, he retired to the forests, resigning his sovereignty to his grandson; and after witnessing the glory of Mahídhara, his parents also withdrew from the world to the silence of the hermitage: devoting all their thoughts to Śambhu, they obtained his favour; and when released from this mortal coil, they were elevated to the rank of spirits, attendant on the god and his celestial consort, as Pushpadanta and his wife Jayá, the same whose indiscreet curiosity had lately been punished by their temporary return to the infirmities of human nature.—Wilson's *Works*, III, 185.

DEVAGIRI—Deogur or Ellors; the mountain of the gods; the Apocopie are said by Ptolemy to be also called mountains of the gods.

DEVAHUTI—A third daughter, according to the Bhágavata of the Manu Swáyambhuva. She was married to the Rishi Kardama, and was mother of the sage Kapila.

DEVAKA—**(1)** Father of Devakī and brother of Ugrasena. **(2)** One of the sons of Ahuka. Also the name of one of the sons of Yudhishthira, the Pándava.

DEVAKI—Wife of Vasudeva, mother of Kṛṣṇa and cousin of Kaṁsa. She is sometimes called an incarnation of Aditi, and is said to have been born again as Pṛśnī, the wife of King Sutapas. No person could bear to gaze upon Devaki, from the light that invested her;

the gods, invisible to mortals, celebrated her praises continually from the time that Vishṇu was contained in her person. Before the birth of Krishna "the quarters of the horizon were irradiate with joy as if moonlight was diffused over the whole earth. The virtuous experienced new delight, the strong winds were hushed, and the rivers glided tranquilly, when Janárdana was about to be born. The infant was brought forth and conveyed to a place of safety, to escape from the enraged Kansa who had voewed his destruction. Kansa made unavailing search for the child, and ordered that every boy in whom there were signs of unusual vigour should be slain without remorse." See KRISHṆA.

DEVAKSHATRA—A prince, the son of Devrata, one of the descendants of Jyamagha.

DEVALA—**(1)** A Vedic ṛṣi, to whom some hymns are attributed. There are several men of this name; one was author of a code of law, another was an astronomer, and one the grandfather of Pāṇini. **(2)** Music, personified as a female.

DEVALOKA—The world of the gods, *i.e., svarga*, Indra's heaven. The six celestial worlds between the earth and the Brahma lokas.

DEVA-MATṚ—'Mother of the gods'. An appellation of Aditi (*q.v.*).

DEVAMIDHA—An ancient Rája of the solar race, one of the ancestors of king Janaka.

DEVAMIDHUSHA—The son of Vrishni; also the name of a son of Hridika.

DEVAMITRA—Also called Sákalya, a teacher of the Rig Veda. He died in consequence of his being defeated by Yajnavalkya in a disputation at a sacrifice celebrated by Janaka.

DEVANAMPRIYA-TISHYA—A king of Ceylon from 307 to 267 B.C. He adopted Buddhism and made it, like Asoka, with whom he was contemporary, the State religion of the island.

DEVANIKA—A prince, the son of Kshemadhanawan, one of the descendants of Kusa.

DEVANTAKA—One of the sons of the giant Rávaṇa, who was killed at the siege of Lanka.

DEVAPI—The son of Pratipa, who abdicated the throne and adopted in childhood a forest life; while an ascetic in the forst he was perverted from the doctrines of the Vedas. The Vishṇu Purána states that he is still in existence.

DEVARAKSHITA—The daughter of Devaka, sister of Devaki and aunt of Krishṇa; also the name of a prince who reigned in a city on the sea-shore over the Kosalas and Tamraliptas.

DEVARATA—**(1)** A royal sage of the solar race, the name given to Sunaṣepha when he was adopted by Viswámitra. Sunasépha refused to return home with his father Ajigartha, who had offered for 300 cows, to sacrifice him (See SUNAṢEPHA) and was afterwards enrolled as the adopted son of Viswámitra by the name of Devaráta (Theodotus); **(2)** Also a son of Rája Śuketu; **(3)** The name of a son of Karambhi, one of the descendants of Jyámagha; **(4)** also a name of Bhíshma.

DEVARSIS (Deva-ṛṣis.)—Rsts or saints of the celestial class, who dwell in the regions of the gods, such as Nārada. Sages who have attained perfection upon earth and have been exalted as demigods to heaven.

DEVASARMAN—The name of a brahman who figures in the Panchatantra; he had no child and his wife was very unhappy in consequence: at length by some mantram the promise of a son was obtained; the child when born proved to be a snake. It was proposed that the monster should be destoryed, but maternal affection prevailed, and it was reared with tenderness. At the proper age it was married to a brahman girl, and one night was changed into a man, intending to resume its serpent form next morning; but the girl's father discovering the deserted skin threw it into the fire, and the son-in-law ever after remained in the figure of a man.

DEVASAVARNI—The thirteenth Manu according to the Bhágavata, which differs from the other Puránas in the enumeration.

DEVASRAVAS—One of the sons of Sura, and brother of Vasudeva.

DEVATA—A divine being or god. The name *devatās* includes the gods in general, or, as most frequently used, the whole body of inferior gods.

DEVATADHYAYA-BRAHMANA—The fifth *Brāhmaṇa* of the *Sāmaveda*. The text has been edited by Burnell.

DÉVATITHI—A Kuru prince, one of the sons of Akrodhana.

DEVAVAT—A son of Akrura, also a son of Devaka.

DEVAVRIDDHA—One of the sons of Satwata, said in the vishṇu Purána to be equal to the gods.

DEVAYANI—The ambitious only daughter of the Bhārgava priest Śukra, the *purohita* of Yayāti, paramount ruler of several native and as yet not fully brahmanized kingdoms, one of whose vassals was King Vṛṣaparvan, father of a very attractive daughter Śarm-iṣṭhā. These five—and Kaca, Śukra's pupil—comprise the *dramatis personae* of a closely woven succession of stories (MBh., Adi, pa., 76-83), which include myth, folklore, magic, social customs, feminine psychology, and genealogy.

The first story concerns the mythical origin of fire (*agni*) brought to earth by the ancient fire-priest Bhrgu, who passed on the magical element to his descendants, the Bhārgavas. Agni, alone of the gods to possess immortality, thus aroused their envy, so they deputed Kaca, Bṛhaspati's son, to become a pupil of the Bhārgava Śukra and by devious means obtain the secret of immortality.

Kaca made several attempts, each of which might have cost him his life but for Devayānī, whose motive in rescuing him was her determination that he should marry her. This was an unforeseen complication, which was aggravated by his refusal and his explanation, that as her father's pupil his relationship to her was that of a brother, and that therefore their marriage would be incestuous. That problem was resolved by Kaca's discovery of Sukra's secret and his return to the delighted gods.

The next episode is concerned with the peculiarly feminine quarrel of Devayani and Śarmiṣṭhā. She fell in love with her father's pupil Kanju, and finding her advances rejected, became soured in temper and vindictive in character. One day when out in the jungle with Sarmishta, daughter of the Rája of the Daityas and a number of other young damsels, on reaching a pleasant pool they all threw off their garments and went into the water to bathe, when it so happened that Váyu the god of the wind passed by, and seeing their clothes upon the bank he mingled them up together. Then when the damsels came out of the water, Devayáni and Sarmishta by mistake put on each other's clothes and quarreled. At last Sarmishta pushed Devayáni into a well and left her there. A Rája named Yayáti, who was hunting in the forest discovered her in the well and extricated her from it. Devayáni, on meeting her maid, said she would never enter the city again. Her father Sukra went to the Rája of the Daityas to obtain an apology from him for his daughter's conduct. Devayáni said to the Rája, "I shall be satisfied upon one condition, that when my father shall give me to a husband, your daughter who pushed me into a well, shall be given to me as a servant." To this the Rája assented, and Devayáni had afterwards the daily attendance of Sarmishta and her maids. One day the whole party was surprised by the Rája Yayáti, who in hot pursuit of a stag burst in upon the damsels. The sight of so much loveliness almost deprived Yayáti of his senses; but the adventure terminated in Devayáni proposing that he should espouse her, which, on obtaining her father's consent, he did.

With her potential rival removed, Devāyanī took the first opportunity of letting Yayati know that she would not prove an unwilling bride. The king reminded her that she was the daughter of a priest, and he of a lower social order, saying, 'Even your father cannot bestow you on a king, however great.'[1] But finally he agreed, provided she obtained her father's consent. Despite the sin of contracting a *pratiloma* marriage and creating a mixed caste Sukra consented, provided that the king remained faithful to Devāyanī. At her insistence Sukra added that Sarmistha should be given a separate establishment and thus not be a possible rival. During the ensuing years Devāyanī bore two sons, Yadu and Turvasu, and Yayāti added to his dominions. But Sarmistha, tired of her banishment, and realizing that her youth was slipping away, arranged a secret meeting with Yayati, and made it clear that she wished to become his second wife.[2] She said that she had been unjustly made the slave of Devāyanī and that as he was Devayānī's lord and master, therefore he must be hers also. Unable to resist her appeal, Yayāti consented.

When Śarmiṣṭhā subsequently bore a son, Devayānī, though at first suspicious, was given an explanation that allayed her doubts of her husband's fidelity. Śarmiṣṭhā was more circumspect about the births of her second and third sons, but Devayānī finally learned of them and implored her father to avenge her, adding what rankled most with her: 'father, here is Śarmiṣṭhā with three sons, while I have only two!'

Yayati, pressed for an explanation by Sukra, replied, 'O *brahmana*, what I did was from no selfish motive. When solicited by a woman in certain circumstances, a man may not lawfully reject her.' Sukra's reply was to curse Yayāti that he should immediately become old and decrepit. Aware of the irrevocability of a *brahmana*'s curse, Yayāti nonetheless pleaded for its mitigation. Finally Sukra declared that his youth would be restored only if one of his sons accepted the curse. The youngest, Śarmiṣṭhā's son Puru, alone agreed to do so. The intention in the subsequent account of his life appears to be merely to link it with the genealogy of the Pandavas and Kauravas.

Two or three years afterwards Sarmishta obtained her revenge by stealing away Yayáti's affections, and Devayáni left him and returned to her father's house.—(Wheeler's *Mahábhárata*). In the *V.P.* an entirely different account is given.

1. Such a marriage between two classes was forbidden.
2. *i.e.*, after three monthly periods have passed, a maiden (who is free to marry) may 'unite herself, of her own will, to a blameless man' (*Gautama Dharmasastra*, XVIII.20).

DEVA-YONI—'Of divine birth.' A general name for the inferior gods, the Ādityas, Vasus, Viśvadevas, and others.

DEVI BHAGAVATA PURANA—A Śaiva Purāṇa, which is by some placed among the eighteen Purāṇas instead of the Śrī Bhāgavata, which is devoted to Viṣṇu. This is devoted to the worship of the Śaktis.

DEVĪ—(1) Puranas hold the opinion that Devi is without a biggening and provides a detailed description of her manifestation in a form, which could be understood, and worshiped by humans. "While Visnu was lying on a fig leaf contemplating about his own origin Devi appeared before him attended by all her attributes Rati (the erotic), Bhuti (Prosperity), Buddhi (Intelligence), Mati (Intillect), Kirti (Reputation or Fame), Dhṛti (Understanding), Smṛti (Remembrance), Sṛddha (Attention), Medha (Intellect), Svadha (Thirst), Nidra (Sleep), Daya (Compassion), Gati (Movement), Tusti (Pleasure), Pusti (Growth), Ksama (Forgiveness), Lajja (Sense of Shame) and Tandra (Laziness). She requested Visnu to start the process of generation and creation of the world with the help of Brahma who was to take birth from the navel of Visnu as that is the place where reside gentle attributes (*sattvaguna*), and Rudra to take shape from the centre of the brows where reside the destructive and regenerative powers (*rajoguna*). The world was thus created according to the will of Devi."

Devi Bhagvata says that all forces of nature are but manifestations of Devi to help Devas. She assumes different forms attended by respective attributes shapes and weapons at various times to restore the balance of nature in favour of the devas and her followers. She is therefore addressed by different names. The primordial nature incarnated as Visnu and his female aspect manifested in five forms as Durga, Laksmi, Sarasvati, Savitri and Radha, also known as Pancadevis.

Durga is the mother of Ganesa and consort of Siva. She is the basis and root cause of everything. She is eternal and manifests to uphold Dharma. She provides salvation to her devotees and blesses with happiness, joy and welfare.

Laksmi is the subtle form of the Devi. She is all wealth and riches personified and is the seat of beauty, compassion, welfare, peace and prosperity. She is the consort of Visnu

Sarasvati is the presiding deity of knowledge and education, intellect and arts, reason and logic. She is the goddess of learning and language.

Savitri is the mother of the four varnas (castes), Vedangas and the Tantric sciences. She manifests in the form of Mantras and provides the Vedic knowledge and its attendant secrets.

Radha, the fifth of the *Pancaprakritis*, is the presiding deity of the five *pranas*. She took birth as the consort of Krisna in Vrindavana for the express purpose to give the divine quality of *bhakti* (devotion) to the humans and her worshippers. Her manifested shape in the form as it appears in Vrindavana is only available to her devotees and not even to the devas. Brahma, in the Puranas, as stated to have performed penance for a period of sixty thousand years to have a glimpse of Radha's lotus feet but without any success.

These above mentioned are Devi's complete forms. There are some partial manifestations also (*Amsarupas*), by which she is known These are Ganga, Tulasi, Manasadevi, Devasena, Manglacandika, Bhumi, Amsakaladevi, Svaha, Daksinadevi, Diksa, Svadha, Svasti, Pusti, Tusti, Sampatti, Dhṛti, Sati, Daya, Praishta, Siddha, Kirti. Kriyadevi, Mithya, Santi, Lajja, Buddhi, Murti, Sridevi, Nidra, Ratri, Visappu, Prabhadevi, Mrtyu or Jara, Tandra and Sradha or Bhakti. **(2)** 'The goddess', or Mahādevī, 'the great goddess', wife of the god Śiva, and daughter of Himavat, *i.e.*, the Himālaya mountains. She is mentioned in the *Mahābhārata* under a variety of names, and with several other characteristics, but she owes her great distinction to the Purāṇas and later works. As the Śakti or female energy of Śiva she has two characters, one mild, the other fierce; and it is under the latter that she is especially worshipped. She has a great variety of names, referable to her various forms, attributes, and actions, but these names are not always used accurately and distinctively. In her milder form she is Umā, 'light', and a type of beauty; Gaurī, 'the yellow or brilliant'; Pārvatī, 'the mountaineer'; and Haimavatī, from her parentage; Jaganmātā, 'the mother of the world'; and Bhavānī. In her terrible form she is Durgā, 'the inaccessible', Kālī and Śyāmā, 'the black'; Caṇḍī and Caṇḍikā, 'the fierce'; and Bhairavī, 'the terrible'. It is in this character that bloody sacrifices are offered to her, that the festivities of the *Durgā -pūjā* and *Carak-pūjā* are performed in her honour, and that the sacrifices and worship of the Tāntrikas are held to propitiate her favours and celebrate her powers. She has ten arms, and in most of her hands there are weapons. As Durgā she is a beautiful yellow woman, riding on a tiger in a fierce and menacing attitude. As Kālī or Kālikā, 'the black', "she is represented with a black skin, a terrible countenance, dripping with blood, encircled with snakes, hung round with skulls and human heads, and in all respects resembling a fury rather than a goddess." As Vindhyavāsinī, 'the dweller in the Vindhyas', she is worshipped at a place of that name where the Vindhyas approach the Ganges, near Mirzapur, and it is said that there the blood before her image is never allowed to get dry. As Mahāmāyā she is the great illusion.

The *Caṇḍi-māhātmya*, which celebrates the victories of this goddess over the *asuras*, speaks of her under the following names: (1) Durgā, when she received the messengers of the *asuras*. (2) Daśabhujā, 'Ten-armed', when she destroyed part of their army. (3) Siṁhavāhinī 'Riding on a lion', when she fought with the *asura* general Raktabīja. (4) Mahiṣamardinī, 'Destroyer of Mahiṣa,' an *asura* in the form of a buffalo. (5) Jagaddhātṛ, 'Fosterer of the world', when she again defeated the asura army. (6) Kālī, 'The black'. She killed Raktabīja. (7) Muktakeśī, 'With disheveled hair'. Again defeats the *asuras*. (8) Tārā. 'Star'. She killed Śumbha. (9) Chinnamastakā. 'Decapitated', the headless form in which she killed Niśumbha. (10) Jagadgaurī, 'World's fair one', as lauded by the gods for her triumphs. The names which *devī* obtains from her husband are: Babhravī (Babhru), Bhagavatī, Īśānī, Īśvarī, Kālānjarī, Kapālinī, Kauśikī, Kirātī, Maheśvarī, Mṛḍā, Mṛḍānī, Rudrāṇī, Śarvāṇī, Śivā, and Tryambakī. From her origin she is called Adrijā and Girijā, 'mountain-born'; Kujā, 'earth-born'; Dakṣajā, 'sprung from Dakṣa'. She is Kanyā, 'the virgin'; Kanyākumārī, 'the youthful virgin'; and Ambikā, 'the mother'; Avarā, 'the youngest'; Anantā and Nityā, 'the everlasting'; Āryā 'the revered'; Vijayā, 'victorious'; Ṛddhi, 'the rich'; Satī, 'virtuous'; Dakṣiṇā, 'right-handed'; Piṅglā, 'tawny, dark'; Karburī, 'spotted'; Bhramarī, 'the bee'; Koṭarī 'the naked'; Karṇamoti, 'pearl-eared'; Padma lochaṇā, 'distinguished by a lotus'; Sarvamaṅgalā, 'always auspicious'; Śākambharī, 'nourisher of herbs'; Śivadūtī, 'Śiva's messenger'; Siṁharathī, 'riding on a lion'. As addicted to austerities she is Aparṇā and Kātyāyanī. As Bhūtanāyakī she is chief or leader of the goblins, and as Gaṇanāyakī, the leader of the *gaṇas*. She is Kāmākṣī, 'wanton-eyed'; and Kāmākhyā, 'called by the name of Kāma, desire'. Other names, most of them applicable to her terrible forms, are Bhadrakālī, Bhīmadevī, Chāmuṇḍā, Mahākālī, Mahāmārī, Mahāsurī, Mātaṅgī, Rājāsī, 'the fierce'; and Raktadantī, 'red or bloody toothed'.

The general term for a goddess; the feminine form of *dew*, a god or celestial power. The *RV.* frequently refers to the *devis* as wives of the gods, or to parts of religious worship personified as goddesses, such as Hotrā, Bharatī and Ilā (11.1,11, etc.).

Dawn (Usas) and Night (Rātrī) are similarly personified (VIII. 10,2; etc.), as also are sacred rivers, including; Gaṅgā, Yamunā, Sutudrī, Vipās, Paruṣṇī and Sarasvatī (III.33,l;X.75,5;etc.).

But it is not until the post-Vedic period that the term *devī* becomes Devi, *the* Goddess, or Mahadevi, Supreme Goddess, and is identified with Cosmic Energy (*sakti*), the dynamic aspect of Śiva. Such a significant notion represents a long period of philosophical speculation and the absorption of many local goddesses into the Saiva pantheon, though many still retain a pseudo- individuality in popular festivals.[1] They comprise a great number, and include such familiar names as Pārvatī, Durgā, Kālī, Umā, Gaurī, Jagan-mātā. But as such distinctions are apparent rather than real; each is Devī and Devī is each of them and the sum of all that they represent.[2]

Historically the notion of *devi* is the culmination of long process that began with the worship of the fertility or mother-goddess, and local nature-goddesses, a common feature of most early mythologies. Thus it is not 'unreasonable to conclude that the early Indus Valley ringstones and female figurines along with the circular discs and tiny nude female figures of the historic period collectively establish the long continued existence of the worship of the female principle in anionic and iconic forms'.[3]

Ultimately Devi became associated with the *trimūrti*, and homage paid to her is counted as homage to the three deities comprising it, since they are believed to have been born from her qualities.[4] Thus when the joint power of Brahma, Visnu and Siva is combined in the form of Īśvara 'it becomes the Supreme-Goddess (Bhagavati), the Resplendent-One (Devi)'.[5] Devi is all things, as is indicated by her numerous epithets. Thus she is Ambika (the Mother), Kanyā (the Virgin), Satī (Virtuous), Kāmākṣī (Wanton-eyed), etc. On *aduhkhanavami*, the ninth day of the first fortnight of bhadrapada, women worship Devi to avert evil during the coming year.

1. Such as 'the present-day *numpatrikā-prawśa* ceremony in the autumnal worship of Durga in Bengal which is based on much earlier authority' (*PTR.*, p. 126). 2. Cf. the Sumerian goddess Innina (Ishtar) who gradually absorbs 'into herself the attributes of most of the other female divinities, and is known as the goddess *par excellence'* (Hooke, *Babylonian and Assyrian Religion*, p. 30). 3. *PTR.*, p. 111. 4. Appropriation of Śiva's attributes by Devi', *BSOAS.*, 1955, xvii. 5. *HP., p.* 253.

DEVIKA—The name of a river, the Déva or Goggra.

DEVIKOTA—A Puranic city, usually considered to be the modern Devicottah in the Carnatic, which is commonly believed to be the scene the Báṇa's defeat.

DEVI-MAHATMYA—'The greatness of Devī'. A poem of 700 verses, which celebrates the triumphs of *devī* over various *asuras*. It is the textbook of the worshippers of *devī*, and is read daily in her temples. It is an episode of the *Mārkaṇḍeya Purāṇa*, and is also called *Caṇḍipāṭha* (*q.v.*).

DEVIPITHA—These are the power centres where the several organs and pieces from the body of Sati fell on earth. Daksa, Sati's father, organised a sacrifice (*yagna*) where he invited all the devas and gods but did not send an invitation to Siva. Sati could not hold herself back from visiting her father on the occasion and went there inspite of Siva's will to the contrary. Siva's insult at the festivities led to Sati jumping into the sacrificial pit and burning herself. When the news was broken to Siva of Sati's sacrifice he became furious. He first sent his messengers to destroy the sacrifice and later visited the place himself. In this condition of distress he lifted the burnt body of Sati on his shoulder and carried it all over the place. While he was going around in all directions pieces from Sati's body started falling on the ground. Where they fell the place became the centres of power and worship and were known as Devipithas.

These are 108 in number and are known by a different name of the Devi. Some of the important Devipithas are:

Varanasi	Visalaksi
Prayaga	Lingadharini
Gandhamadana	Kumuda
Daksina Kailasa	Kumuda
Uttara Kailasa	Kumuda
Puskara	Puruhuta
Gokarna	Bhadrakarika
Salagrama	Mahadevi
Mayapuri	Kumari
Gaya	Mangala
Ramatiratha	Ramana
Yamunatiratha	Mrgavati
Sivakunda	Subhananda
Vrndavana	Radha
Mathura	Devaki
Patala	Parmeshavari
Citrakuta	Sita
Vindhya	Vindhyavasini
Karavira	Mahalaksmi
Vinayaka	Umadevi
Amarakantaka	Candika
Somesvara	Vararoha
Sarasvati	Devamata
Jalandhara	Visvamukhi
Jivasarira	Sakti

According to the Puranas it was at the request of the *devas* that Visnu shot arrows at Sati on the shoulder of Siva in order to make the dead body fall off and put an end to Siva's sorrow. After this was accomplished Siva went to Kailash and went straight into penance (*samadhi*). The detailed list of all the 108 Devipithas is provided in my bigger work on Hinduism. These are centers of great worship and reverence.

DHAMAJAYA—A Vyása, the arranger of the Vedas in the sixteenth Dwápara.

DHANADA—'Giver of wealth.' Kubera, the god of riches.

DHANAKA—A prince, the son of Durdama, a descendant of Yadu.

DHANAMITRA—The name of a wealthy merchant in Kálidása's drama of *Sakuntala*; the merchant, trading by sea, was lost in a shipwreck; and as he was childless, the whole of his property became by law forfeited to the king. The king ascertained that the merchant's widow was expecting to give birth to a child, and declared that the unborn child had a title to his father's property; a proclamation which was received with acclamations of joy.

DHANA-NANDO—The youngest son of Kálásoka, king of Pátaliputra. The nine sons succeeded their father in the order of their seniority. The youngest was called Dhana-nando from his being addicted to hoarding treasure. He collected money to the amount of eighty Kotís; and to keep it securely he diverted the Ganges from its course, by constructing a dam across it: and in a rock in the bed of the river having caused a deep excavation to be made, he buried the treasure there. Over this cave he laid a layer of stones, and to prevent the admission of water poured molten lead in it. Repeating this process, which made it like a solid rock he restored the river to its former course. This prince was afterwards killed by the brahman Chánakko, who raised Chandragupta to the throne in his stead. As everything in India Chronology depends on the date of Chandragupta, great pains have been taken by Wilson, Max Müller, and others, to determine it accurately.

DHANAÑJAYA—(1) 'Conqueror of riches.' A title of Arjuna and of several others. **(2)** A fierce and venomous many-headed serpent, one of the progeny of Kadru.

DHANAÑJAYA-VIJAYA—'Victories of Dhanañjaya' (Arjuna). A drama in one act, the subject of which is taken from the Viráṭa Parvan of the Mahábhárata, and describes the recovery of the cattle of the Rája Viráṭa by Arjuna, after they had been carried off by Karna and the Kuru princes. The different chiefs appear and threaten each other, and praise themselves very much in the strain of Homer's heroes. The battle is thrown into narrative, being described in a conversation between Indra and some of his attendants as they contemplate it from the clouds. The drama belongs to the class termed Vyáyoga.

DHANAPATI—'Lord of wealth,' *i.e.*, Kubera.

DHANḌANITI—Policy; one of the four branches of royal knowledge; originally written by Vishnugupta in six thousand stanzas for the use of the Maurya kings.

DHANESVARA—'Lord of wealth', *i.e.*, Kubera.

DHANEYU—A prince; one of the ten sons of Raudraswa, a descendant of Puru.

DHANISHTA—An asterism, or lunar mansion, in Migravithi, in the southern Avashtána.

DHANUR-VEDA—The science of archery or arms, taught by Bhrigu.

DHANVANTARI—(1) Name of a Vedic deity to whom offerings at twilight were made in the north-east quarter. **(2)** The physician of the gods, who was produced at the churning of the ocean. He was a teacher of medical science, and the *Āyurveda* is attributed to him. In another birth he was son of Dīrghatamas, and his "nature was exempt from human infirmities, and in every existence he had been master of universal knowledge". He is called also Sudhāpāṇi, 'carrying nectar in his hands', and *amṛta*, 'the immortal'. Other physicians seem to have had the name applied to them, as Bhela, Divodāsa, and Pālakāpya. **(3)** A celebrated physician, who was one of "the nine gems" of the court of Vikrama. (*see* NAVA-RATNA)

DHANWANTARA—A sage produced from the churning of the ocean, robed in white, and bearing in his hand the cup of Amrita, which was afterwards seized by the Daityas. He is called the physician of the gods. In a second birth he was the son of Dirghatamas, and taught the Ayur Veda, or medical science. He was exempt from human infirmity, and master of universal knowledge. The only work at present existing under the title of Ayar Veda is said to have been revealed by Dhanwantari to his pupil Susruta; Dhanwantari having himself, as he declares, received it from Bramha.

DHANYAS—The designation of Vaisyas in Krauncha Dwípa.

DHARA—A city to the south of the river Godavari, where the celebrated Rája Vikrama resided.

DHARANA—Steady thought; retention or holding of the image or idea formed in the mind by contemplation; one of the eight stage by which "Yoga" must be accomplished. See YOGA.

DHARANI— The earth. The wife of Paraśurāma. A daughter of the Pitris, and wife of Meru. In the Vishṇ Purána she is said to have been well acquainted with theological truth; addicted to religious meditation; accomplished in perfect wisdom, and adorned with all estimable qualities.

DHARBAGA—The son of Ajatasatru, king of Maghada, one of the ten Saiṣunágas, the aggregate of whose united reigns amounted to three hundred and sixty-two years.

DHARMA RAJA—A name of the eldest of the five Pándavas, Yudhishthira, (*q.v.*) son of the Kunti Devi, by *Yama*; Pándu, the nominal father, being impotent.

DHARMA SASTRA—A law-book or code of laws. This term includes the whole body of Hindu law, but it is more especially applicable to the laws of Manu, Yājñavalkya, and other inspired sages who first recorded the Smṛti or "recollections" of what they had received from a divine source. These works are generally in three parts: (1) *Ācāra*, rules of conduct and practice; (2) *Vyavahāra*, judicature; (3) *Prāyaścitta*, penance.

The inspired law-givers are spoken of as being eighteen in number, but the names of forty-two old authorities are mentioned. Manu and Yājñavalkya stand apart by themselves at the head of these writers. After them the eighteen other inspired sages are recognised as the great authorities on law, and the works ascribed to them are still extant, either wholly or partially or in an abridged form: (1) Atri; (2) Viṣṇu; (3) Hārīta; (4) Uśanas; (5) Aṅgirasa; (6) Yama; (7) Āpastamba; (8) Samvarta; (9) Kātyāyana; (10) Bṛhaspati; (11) Parāśara; (12) Vyāsa; (13) and (1 4) Saṅkha and Likhita, whose joint treatise is frequently quoted; (15) Dakṣa; (16) Gotama; (17) Śātātapa; (18) Vasiṣṭha. But there are others who are more frequently cited than many of these, as Nārada, Bhṛgu, Marīci, Kaśyapa, Viśvāmitra, and Baudhāyana. Other names that are met with are Pulastya, Gārgya, Paiṭhīnasī, Sumantu, Lokākṣī, Kuthumi, and Dhaumya. The writing of some of these lawgivers have appeared in different forms, and are referred to with the descriptive epithets of Vṛddha, 'old'; Bṛhat, 'great'; and Laghu, 'light or small'.

A general collection of the Smṛtis or Dharmaśāstras has been printed in Calcutta under the title of *Dharmaśāstra-saṁgraha*, by Jīvānanda.

DHARMA—An ancient sage, sometimes classed among the Prajāpatis. He married thirteen (or ten) of the daughters of Dakṣa, and had a numerous progeny; but all his children"are manifestly allegorical, being personifications of intelligences and virtues and religious rites, and being therefore appropriately wedded to the probable authors of the Hindu code of religion and morals, or the equally allegorical representation of that code, *dharma*, moral and religious duty".—*Wilson.*

DHARMADHRIS—One of the sons of Swaphalka, a descendant of Sini.

DHARMADHWAJA—**(1)** A king of Mithila,—who is also called Janaka; **(2)** The name of a king of Burdwan, mentioned in the Belata Panchavinsati, as having restored Brahmanism, which had been put aside for the Jaina religion.

DHARMAKETU—A prince, the son of Suketana, (according to the Bhágavata list) a descendant of Alarka. In the Vishṇu Purána he is made the son of Sukumára, and in the Agni he appears as the son of Alarka himself.

DHARMANETRA—The son of Haihaya, a descendant of Yadu—the tribe in which Krishṇa was born.

DHARMAPAL—One of the ministers of justice of Mahárája Dasaratha.

DHARMA-PUTRA—'Son of Dharma.' A name of Yudhiṣṭhira.

DHARMARANYA—A sacred grove. **(1)** A forest in Madhyadeśa into which Dharma retired. **(2)** A city mentioned in the *Rāmāyaṇa* as founded by Amurtarajas, son of Kuśa. **(3)** A Puránic city in the mountainous part of Magadha, the residence of Amurtarajas. **(4)** Is also the name of the wood to which the god of justice is said to have fled through fear of Sóma the moon-god.

DHARMARATHA—A prince, the son of Divaratha. He is said to have drank of Sóma juice along with Indra.

DHARMARAYA HABBA—An annual festival in honor of the five Páṇḍava princes, the eldest of whom Yudhishthira, is also called Dharmaráya. The festival is a very popular one amongst the Śúdras, though Brahmans take no part in it. The *pújári* or priest who officiates is a Śúdra. In the morning ablutions are performed in tanks; daring the day buffaloes and sheep are sacrificed; and in the evening a car is drawn through the principal streets.

DHARMA-SAVARNI—The Manu of the eleventh Manwantara. One of the mind-engendered sons of a daughter of Daksha, by himself and the three gods Brahma, Dharma, and Rudra, to whom he presented her on Mount Meru. (*see* MANU)

DHARMA-SUTRAS—The *Sāmayācārika Sūtras* are so-called because they had among them maxims of a legal nature.

DHARMA—**(1)** The god of justice; the Hindu Pluto. See YAMA. **(2)** Virtue, religion, duty, law, moral and religious truth according to the law and the Vedas. Any peculiar or prescribed practice or duty; thus giving alms, &c., is the *dharma* of a householder: administering justice is the *dharma* of a king; piety is the *dharma* of a brahman; courage is the *dharma* of a kshatriya, &c.

DHARMA-VYADHA—'The pious huntsman.' This man is represented in the *Mahābhārata* as living by selling the flesh of boars and buffaloes, and yet as being learned in the Vedas and in all the knowledge of a brāhmaṇa. This is accounted for by his having been a brāhmaṇa in a former birth, and cursed to this vile occupation for having wounded a brāhmaṇa when hunting.

DHARSHTAKAS—The race of Kshatriyas, some of whom obtained brahmanhood upon earth. *V.P.*

DHATA—A Rudra, the son of Bhrigu by Khyati.

DHATAKI—A prince, the son of Savaṇa, king of Pushkara—an island without mountains or rivers in which men live a thousand years without sickness or sorrow. *V.P.*

DHÀTṚ—'Maker, creator.' In the later hymns of the *Ṛgveda*, Dhātṛ is a deity of no very defined powers and functions, but he is described as operating in the production of life and the preservation of health. He promotes generation, brings about matrimony, presides over domestic life, cures diseases, heals broken bones, &c. He is said to "have formed the sun, moon, sky, earth, "air, and heaven as *before*". He appears also as one of the Ādityas, and this character he still retains. In the later mythology he is identified with Prajāpati or Brahmā the creator; and in this sense of'maker' the term is used as an epithet of Viṣṇu and Kṛṣṇa. Sometimes he is a son of Brahmā.

DHATRI—A son of Viṣṇu and Lakshmi, married to Ayati, daughter of Meru.

DHATU—A linguistic root. In European languages if grammar attempts to reduce a word to its last limit, it calls such a limit its 'root,' and a root in grammar thus answers to an element in chemistry, representing the farthest result of analysis attainable by the analyser; but in Sanskrit grammar,—dhátu, though generally translated root, does not imply that which is expressed by the European term. The former designates that theoretical form, from which, by conjugational affixes, verbal bases, and by krit affixes nominal bases may be derived. Yet as such derivations may not only be made from those forms which have been collected in lists called Dhátupátha, and may be called primary Dhátus, but also from those derivative forms,—the passives, intensives, causals, desideratives, and denominatives;—even these derivative forms are, to the Hindu grammarian *Dhátus*. To his mind therefore a *dhátu* is not an absolutely last linguistic element; but even a primary dhátu, or that form from which passive and other secondary dhátus could be derived, is to him only that form which, to the *popular* understanding, appeared to be a last limit of derivation." (Mrs. Manning, *A. and M. I.*)

DHATU-PARAYANA—A celebrated commentary on Dhátus, written by Hemachandra.

DHAUMYA—**(1)** The younger brother of Devala and family priest of the Pāṇḍavas. He also officiated as Hótri and cooked the sacrifice when it was offered. He accompanied the Páṇḍavas on their exile; and on their return performed the inauguratory ceremonies for Rája Yudhishthira; and at the great Aswamedha squeezed milk out of the horse's ear. There are several others of the same name. **(2)** Author of a work on law. **(3)** great sage who is said to have had iron teeth.

DHAVA—(Fire). A deity of the class termed Vasu; because they are always present in light or luminous irradiation.

DHENUKA—A demon killed by Balarāma. Kṛṣṇa and Balarāma, as boys, picked some fruit in a grove belonging to Dhenuka, when he took the form of an ass, and running to the spot began to kick Balarāma. The young hero seized him by the heels, whirled him round till he was dead, and cast his carcase on to the top of a palm-tree. Several of his companions who ran to his assistance were treated in the same way, so that "the trees were laden with dead asses".

DHIMAT—One of the six sons of Purúravas; the name also of the valiant son of Virat.

DHISHANA—A princess of the race of Agni, and wife of Havirdhána.

DHISHNYAS—The seven little circles extending in a straight line from the Marjála to the Agnidhra fire.—*Ait. Brah.*

DHI—The wife of the Rudra Manyu.

DHOTI OR DHOTRA—The cloth wrapped round the loins, and universally worn by Hindus. It is spoken of by Nearchus as reaching to the middle of the leg. It is from 2½ to 3½ yards long by 2 to 3 feet broad. "Native sepoys march thirty or forty miles a day in dhótis without fatigue." "In the frescoes on the caves of Ajanta this costume is carefully represented."—*Edin. Rev., Jan.* 1868.

DHRIDHASWA—One of the three sons of Kuvaláyaswa, who escaped from the conflict with the demon Dhundu.

DHRISHTADYUMNA—A prince, the son of Rája Drupada, in whose reign the possessions of the Pánchálas were divided. Dhrishtadyumna was the brother of Draupadi, who proclaimed the terms of her Swayamvara.

"The gallant Dhrishtadyumna on the plain
Descended, and his father's will proclaimed;—
Princes, this bow behold ! You mark—these shafts—
Who'er with dextrous hand at once directs
Five arrows to their aim; and be his race,
His person, and his deeds, equivalent
To such exalted union,—He obtains
My sister for his bride. My words are truth.
Thus said, he to the Princess next described
Each royal suitor by his name and lineage,
And martial deeds; and bade her give the wreath
To him whose prowess best deserved the boon.

Arjuna was the successful suitor, and Draupadi became the wife of the five Pándu brothers. Dhrishtadyumna followed the brothers home, and ascertained that they were not brahmans but Kshatriyas of the royal house of Hastinápura, and soon acquainted his father with the tidings. At the beginning of the great war Dhrishtadyumna was elected commander-in-chief; after several days' fighting, Rája Drupada was slain by Drona, and Dhrishtadyumna vowed that he would be revenged for his father's death by killing Drona. This he did the following day, aided by Bhíma. He was afterwards surprised by Aswatthámа, the son of drona, while sleeping in the tents of the Páṇḍavas and was barbarously murdered. See DRUPADA.

DHRISHTAKETU—**(1)** The son of Dhrishtadyumna, he commanded the troops of Chedi and Malwa in the great war; **(2)** The name of a son of Satyadhriti or Sudhriti, king of Mithila, who was celebrated for his piety, and received the designation of "royal saint." **(3)** A son of Suketu, a descendant of Alarka. **(4)** King of Cedi, and an ally of the Pāṇḍavas. **(5)** A king of the Kekayas, also an ally of the Pāṇḍavas. **(6)** Son of Satyadhṛti. **(7)** Son of Nṛga.

DHRISHTA—One of the sons of the Manu Vaivaswata. Before their birth the Manu, being desirous of sons offered a sacrifice for that purpose to Mitra and Varuṇa; but the rite being deranged through an irregularity of the ministering priest, a daughter, Ila, was produced. (See ILA and MANU). From Drishta sprang the Kshatriya race of Dharshtakas.

DHRISHTASARMAN—A prince, one of the sons of Swaphalka, of the family of Anamitru.

DHRISHTI—The war minister of Mahárája Dasaratha.

DHRITA—A prince, the son of Dharma.

DHRITAMATI—A river among those enumerated in the Vishṇu Purána as one of the rivers of Bharata.

DHRITARASHTRA—**(1)** The elder son of Kuru and the widow of Vichitravírya (see Bhíshma), king of Hastinápura, and father of Duryodhana and his ninety-nine brothers. Being blind from birth, he eventually delivered his sceptre to Duryodhana, at whose suggestion he banished the Páṇḍava princes, his own nephews, from his kingdom. It is to him that his charioteer and bard (*súta*), Sanjaya, relates the Bhagavat Gíta, or dialogue between Krishṇa and Arjuna, having received, as he says, from the Vyása, the mystic power of being present while it was carried on. His wife's name was Gándhári, and the chief of her hundred sons were Duryodhana, Duhṣásana, Vikarṇa, and Chitrasena. (Dhritaráshtra is derived from *dhrita*, 'held firm;' and *ráshtra*, a 'kingdom,' 'who tenaciously maintains the sovereignty.' The name, Schlegel observes, may have arisen from his remaining on the throne in spite of his blindness.) (*J.C.Thomson.*) On the death of Duryodhana, who was killed by Bhíma, he meditated revenge, and caused an instrument of strongly constrictive power to be made, which he wore on his person; and then expressed a strong desire to embrace Bhíma, his nephew, before he died. Krishna a being aware of the device (the hug as of a bear) caused a stone image to be substituted; and as the blind king could not distinguish the difference, he was deceived, and Bhíma escaped. **(2)** Dhritaráshtra was also the name of a powerful many-headed serpent, of immeasurable might; one of the progeny of Kadru.

DHRITARASHTRI—The daughter of Kaṣyapa, one of the wives of Garuda and mother of geese, ducks, teal and other water-fowl.

DHRITAVRATA—One of the eleven Rudras. Also the name of a prince, one of the descendants of Anu.

DHRITIMAT—A celebrated sage, the son of Kirthimat, by his wife Dhenuka. Also the name of a son of Yavinara.

DHRITI—Steadiness. One of the twenty-four daughters of the patriarch Daksha, married to Dharma (righteousness), their son was Niyama (precept). *Dhriti* was also the name of several princes—of a son of Vethavya, king of Mithila; of a son of Babhru; and of a son of Vijaya. The wife of Manu, one of the eleven Rudras, was named Dhriti.

DHRUVA SANDHI—One of the sons of Rája Tresandhi, king of Ayódhya, and father of Bharata. A prince, the son Pushya, a descendant of Ráma.

DHRUVA—The polar star, the pivot of the atmosphere; on it rests the seven great planets, and on them depend the clouds: the rains are suspended in the clouds and fall for the support of created beings. This source of rain is termed the sacred station of Vishṇu, and the support of the three worlds. Vishṇu Purána, Ch. VIII,. From it proceeds the stream that washes away all sin, the river Gunga, embrowned with the unguents of the nymphs of heaven, who have sported in her waters. Having her source in the nail of the great toe of Vishṇu's left foot, Dhruva receives her and sustains her day and night devoutly on his head. *V.P.*

As Dhruva revolves it causes the moon, sun and stars to turn round also; and the lunar asterisms follow in its circular path, for all the celestial luminaries are bound to the polar star by ærial cords. The rain is evolved by the sun; the sun is sustained by Dhruva; and Dhruva is supported by the celestial porpoise-shaped sphere, which is one with Náráyaṇa. Náráyaṇa, the primeval existent, and eternally enduring, seated in the heart of the stellar sphere, is the supporter of all beings. *V.P.*, Ch. IX.

Dhruva was the son of Uttánapáda and Suníti; when a child he observed his half-brother Uttama in the lap of his father as he was seated on his throne, and was desirous of ascending to the same place. He was reproved for this by the mother of Uttama, Suruchi, the favorite wife of his father. The boy being angry went to the apartment of his own mother, who took him on her lap and asked what had vexed him. Suníti, distressed by the narrative of the boy, said, Suruchi has rightly spoken; thine, child, is an unhappy fate; those who are born to fortune are not liable to the insults of their rivals. Yet be not afflicted my child. That the king favors Suruchi is the reward of her merits in a former existence. It is not proper for you to grieve; a wise man will be contented with that degree which appertains to him; be amiable, be pious, be friendly, be assiduous in benevolence to all living creatures; for prosperity descends upon modest worth as water flows towards low ground.

Dhruva answered: "Mother, the words that you have addressed to me for my consolation, find no place in a heart that contumely has broken. I will exert myself to attain such elevated rank that it shall be revered by the whole world." The youth then went forth from his mother's dwelling and applied to seven Munis, whom he found sitting in an adjoining thicket. By their advice he devoted himself entirely to the service of Vishṇu, concentrating his whole mind on this one object. He commenced a course of religious austerities; resisted all the attempts made to change his purpose; and was finally elevated by Vishṇu to the skies as the pole-star. *V.P.*

DHRUYU—The eldest son of king Yayáti, by his wife Sarmishta; called in some of the Puránas, the handmaid of his first wife Devayáni. Dhruyu became king of the western part of his father's dominions.

DHUMAKETU—(Comet). An allegorical personage, the son of Kriṣáswa, by his wife Archish (flame). The deified weapons of the gods were the progeny of Kriṣáswa. Dhumaketu is also the name of one of the sons of Trinavindu by the celestial nymph Alambushá, who became enamoured of Trinavindu.

DHUMRAVARNA—(1) 'Smoke coloured'. One of the One Thousand names of Sri Ganesh. **(2)** A king of the serpents. A legend in the Harivaṁśa relates that Yadu, the founder of the Yādava family, went for a trip of pleasure on the sea, where he was carried off by Dhūmavarṇa to the capital of the serpents. Dhūmavarṇa married his five daughters to him, and from them sprang seven distinct families of people. (For the complete listing of the One Thousand Names of Sri Ganesh please see my *Hindu Encyclopaedia*)

DHUMRAKSHA—One of Rávaṇa's generals who was killed at the siege of Lanka.

DHUMRAKESA—One of the five sons of the celebrated Prithu, the universal emperor or Chakra-vertti.

DHUMRASWA—The son of Suchandra and king of Vaiṣáli—the city founded by Vaiṣáli, son of Trinavinda. The Buddhists consider Vaiṣ áli to be Prayága, or Alláhabad. Among them it is celebrated as a chief seat of the labours of Sakhya and his first disciples.

DHUNDHU—An *asura* who harassed the sage Uttanka in his devotions. The demon hid himself beneath a sea of sand, but was dug out and killed by king Kuvalayāśva and his 21,000 sons, who were undeterred by the flames which checked their progress, and were all killed but three. This legend probably originated from a volcano or some similar phenomenon. From this exploit Kuvalayāśva got the name of Dhundhumāra, 'slayer of Dhundhu'.

DHUNDUMERA—The name of Kuvalayáswa, after

the conflict above described. In the Rámáyana he is termed the son of Trisanku. (*see* DHUNDHU and KUVALAYĀŚVA)

DHURJATI—'Having heavy matted locks.' A name of Rudra or Śiva.

DHURTA-NAKTAKA—'The rogue actors.' A farce in two parts by Śāma Rājā Dīkṣita. "The chief object of this piece is the ridicule of the Śaiva ascetics."

DHURTA-SAMAGAMA—'Assemblage of rogues'. A comedy by Śekhara or Jyotir Īśvar. "It is somewhat indelicate, but not devoid of humour." It has been translated into French by Schoebel.

DHUTI—One of the twelve Ádityas who in a former Manwantara were deities called Tushitas; they entered the womb of Aditi, daughter of Daksha, and were born as the sons of Kaṣyapa, and named the twelve Ádityas.

DHYANA—Profound meditation on Vishṇu. When the image (of Vishṇu) never departs from the mind of the sage, whether he be going or standing, or be engaged in any other voluntary act, then he may believe his retention to be perfect. There are six stages in the attainment of this object: 1, *Yama* acts of restraint and obligation; 2, *Asana* sitting in particular postures; 3, *Praṇáyáma*, modes of breathing; 4, *Pratyáhára*, exclusion of all external ideas; 5, *Bhavana*, apprehension of internal ideas; 6, *Dhárana*, fixation or retention of those ideas. Those who thus devote themselves to meditation, must divest their minds of all sensual desire, and have their attention abstracted from every external object, and absorbed with every sense in the prescribed subject of meditation. Patanjali says, 'Restraint of the body, retention of the mind, and meditation, which thence is exclusively confined to one object, is Dhyána.' See *V.P.*, p. 657.

DIGAMBARA—**(1)** 'Clothed with space.' A naked mendicant. A title of Śiva. **(2)** A naked ascetic, or gymnosophist. The Jains are divided into two principal divisions, Diagambaras and Śvetambaras; the former of which appears to have the best pretensions to antiquity, and to have been most widely diffused. The discriminating difference is implied in these terms, the former meaning the sky-clad, that is, naked; and the latter the white-robed, the teachers being so dressed. In the present day, however, the Digambara ascetics do not go naked, but wear coloured garments; they confine the disuse of clothes to the period of their meals, throwing aside their wrapper when they receive the food given them by their disciples.—*Wilson.*

DIGGAJAS—The elephants who protect the eight points of the compass: (1) Airāvata; (2) Puṇḍarīka; (3) Vāmana; (4) Kumuda; (5) Añjana; (6) Puspadanta; (7) Sarvabhauma; (8) Supratīka.

DIGVIJAYA—'Conquest of the regions (of the world)'. **(1)** A part of the *Mahābhārata* which commemorates the conquests effected by the four younger Pāṇḍava princes, and in virtue of which Yudhiṣṭhira maintained his claim to universal sovereignty. **(2)** A work by Śaṅkarācārya in support of the Vedānta philosophy, generally distinguished as Śaṅkara Digvijaya.

DIKPALA—'Supporters of the regions.' The supporters of the eight points of the compass, (*see* DIGGAJAS)

DIKSHA—**(1)** Certain ceremonies preliminary to a sacrifice. It also means a new birth—and a rite of initiation. **(2)** The wife of Ugra, one of the eight Rudras or manifestations of Brahma; or according to the Bhágavata, the wife of Vámadeva, another Rudra.

DIKSHANIYA ISHTI—A curious sacrificial ceremony, apparently suggested by "a feeling nearly akin to belief in original sin. The gods, and especially Vishṇu and Agni, are invoked to come to the offering with the Díksha. 'Grant the Díksha to the sacrifice. Agni as fire, and Vishṇu as the sun, are invoked to elcanse the sacrificer, by the combination of their rays, from all gross and material dross. The worshipper is then covered up in a cloth, on the outside of which is placed the skin of a black antelope; and, after a certain time has elapsed, and specified prayers have been recited, the coverings are removed, the new birth is considered to have been accomplished, and the regenerated man descends to bathe."* (* Mrs. Manning, *A. and M. I.*)

DIKSHAVISARJANE—A religious ceremony amongst brahmans; it is customary for a man to allow his hair to grow for six months after his marriage, and then go to his father-in-law's house to have his head shaved; this act, and the observances which accompany it, is termed Díkshavisarjane.

DILIPA—The son of Ansuman and father of Bhagíratha who brought Ganga down to the earth.

> Ansuman's son, Dilípa famed,
> Begot a son Bhagírath named,
> From him the great Kakutstha rose;
> From him came Raghu feared by foes.

Dilípa is described in the Raghuvansa as a grand ideal of what a king should be.

"Tall and broad-shouldered, stout and strong of limb,
Valour incarnate fixed her throne in him,
Matchless in beauty and heroic might,
He towers like Meru in his lofty height.
Meet for his god-like form, his noble mind
To worthy studies in his youth inclined.
Thence great designs inspired his generous soul,
And mighty deeds with glory crowned the whole."

This monarch was the delight of his subjects, who followed him as their guide, and thereby obeyed the laws of Manu.

"And well they knew the tax they gladly paid,
For their advantage on the realm was laid.
The bounteous sun delights to drink the lakes,
But gives ten thousand-fold the wealth he takes."

Just as the earth and water, fire and ether, were given by the good Creator for the benefit of all mankind; so was the king, Dilípa, sent to bless his subjects, and find his own happines in that of others. Theft was unknown in his dominions,and

"He ruled the earth, from rival sceptre free,
Like one vast city girdled by the sea."

But one boon was wanting. He had a lovely queen, but no son.

"Oh ! how he longed, that childlees king, to see
A royal infant smiling on her knee;
With his dear mother's eyes and face divine,—
Asecond self to ornament his line !"

In the hope of attaining this boon he resolves to seek his holy guide, the renowned Vasistha, who now lived far away in a secluded hermitage. His queen goes forth with him, and they travel in a car, which "tells his coming with the music of its bells."

"Fresh on their cheeks the soft wind gently blows,
Wafting the perfume of the woodland rose:
And, heavy with the dust of rifled flowers,
Waves the young branches of the mango bowers.
They hear the peacock's joyous cry; his head
Lifted in wonder at the courser's tread.
They watch the cranes in jubilant armies fly,
Crowning, like flowers, the portals of the sky.
From shady coverts by the way, the deer
Throw startled glances when the car is near.

* * *

Through towns they pass, and many a hamlet fair, Founded and cherished by their royal care."

Peasants bring them curds and milk;...the king calls attention to the varied beauties of the woodland scene; and, lost in delight, they reach the end of their journey quite unexpectedly.

"Evening is come, and, weary of the road,
The horses rest before the saints' abode."

The hermitage reminds one of that described in Kalidâsa's play, Sakuntalâ. Hermits from the neighbouring forest have come for grass and fuel; playful fawna are waiting to be fed with rice; young girls are watering the roots of trees, &c.

The king and the queen are most kindly receivd. After "food and rest," the sage inquires of the king his wishes, and having heard that

"Mother earth, whom tears nor prayers have won.
Is still ungracious, and denies a son,"

and that "the spirits of his fathers pine," seeing no hope of funeral offerings,...the great Vasishtha falls into profound meditation, and, after a few minutes, announces the cause of the misfortune. The king, Dilípa, had once, thoughtlessly and unconsciously, omitted to pay reverence to "to holy cow," which was lying under a celestial tree near the falls of the Ganges...Therefore, by way of penance, he and his queen must tend a cow, called Nandiní, in the sacred woods close by; and when they have gained the love of this descendant of the affronted cow, the curse will be removed. The attendance is given faithfully: the queen worships the cow, by walking round her and scattering grain; and the king cannot be persuaded, even by illusive phantoms, to desert his trust. He hastens to the queen:

"And though she read at once his looks aright,
He told her all again with new delight.
Then, at the bidding of the saint, he quaffed
Of Nandinî's pure milk a precious draught,
As though, with thirst that rises from the soul,
He drank eternal glory from the bowl."

At the dawn of day,

"Swift towards their home the eager horses bound;
The car makes music o'er the grassy ground.
They reach the city, where the people wait,
Longing to meet their monarch, at the gate.
Dim are his eyes, his cheek is pale, his brow
Still bears deep traces of his weary vow."

In due time a son was born.

"There was a glory round the infant's head;
And e'en the unlit torches seemed to shine
As in a picture, with that light divine."

And, when all rites had been duly performed,—

"Still greater glory crowned Dilípa's son."

—*A. and M. I.*, vol. II, pp. 99-101.

Kálidása in the Raghuvansa makes Raghu the son of Dilípa and great grandfather of Ráma.

He was of the Solar race and ancestor of Rāma. On one occasion he failed to pay due respect to Surabhi, the 'cow of fortune', and she passed a curse upon him that he should have no offspring until he and his wife Sudakṣiṇā had carefully tended Surabhi s daughter Nandinī. They obediently waited on this calf Nandinī, and Dilīpa once offered his own life to save hers from the lion of Śiva. In due time the curse was removed, and a son, Raghu, was born to them. This story is told in the *Raghuvaṁśa.* There was another prince of the name. (*see* KHAṬVĀṄGA)

DINA-CHARIYAWA—The daily observances of Buddhist priests. These are very numerous, and are prescribed with minute detail. At the conclusion it is said the priest must maintain a course of good behaviour, he must keep under the five senses, with matured wisdom, and without any haughtiness of either body, speech or mind.

DIPAKARNI—An ancient monarch, whose wife, named Śakti-mati, more dear to him than his existence, whilst reposing in a bower in the garden, was bitten by a snake, and died. The king, overcome with grief for her loss, made a vow to observe perpetual continence—a vow to which he rigidly adhered, although the want of a son to succeed him in the kingdom was a subject of profound affliction to him. Whilst thus distressed, he was directed by Śiva, in a dream, in what manner to obtain a son and successor, without violating his faith to his departed wife. For the remainder of the legend, see Sátaváhana.

DIPAKA—The Illumination. A figure of poetical rhetoric throwing "a quickening ray of light upon the colouring of the poet's pictures; for its power it is indebted to arrangement in general, especially to the connection of the single verb, which (to use the expression of the commentator) lights up the whole description."—*Colebrooke.*

DIPAVALI-HABBA—A festival instituted in memory of two celebrated giants, Bala-chakravarti and Narakasura. The latter had become the scourage of the human race and infested the earth with his crimes. Vishṇu at length delivered both gods and men from the terror of this monster, whom he slew after a dreadful combat. The contest ended but with the day. Thus Vishṇu not having it in his power to make his diurnal ablutions before the setting of the sun, had to perform them in the night. The Brahmans in commemoration of this great event, put off their ablutions to the night; and this is the only occasion, in the course of the year, in which they can transgress the ordinance of never bathing after sunset. But this exception of the noeturnal bathing, possesses a high degree of merit, and is conducted with solemnity.

The word *Dipavali-habba* signifies the Feast of Lamps; and the Hindus actually light a great number of lamps round the door of their houses. They make paper lanterns also, which they hang in the streets. The husbandmen celebrate this festival in a different way. Being then the harvest time for grain they assemble in the rági fields and offer prayers or sacrifices. Some sacrifice to the dunghill which is afterwards to enrich the ground. The offerings consist of burning lamps, fruits, or flowers which are deposited in the mass of ordure.—*Abbé Dubois.*

DIPTIMAT—One of the sons of Krishṇa by Rohiṇí. The Vishṇu Purána says that Krishṇa had one hundred and eighty thousand sons, but the names of only a few are given.

DIRGHABAHU—A prince, the son of Khatwánga.

DIRGHAMUKHA—A crane that figures in the *Panchatantra*; the name means "long bill."

DIRGHASRAVAS—Son of Dīrghatamas, and therefore a *ṛṣi*, but as in a time of famine he took to trade for a livelihood, the *Ṛgveda* calls him "the merchant".

DIRGHATAMAS, DIRGHATAPAS—'Long darkness.' A son of Kāśī-rāja, according to the *Mahābhārata*; of Ucāthya, according to the *Ṛgveda*; and of Utathya and Mamatā in the Purāṇas. His appellations of Aucathya and Māmateya favour the latter parentage. He was born blind, but is said to have obtained sight by worshipping Agni (*ṚV* III. 128). He was father of Kakṣīvat and Dhanvantari; and he is said (in the *VP*) to have had five children by Sudeṣṇā, wife of Bali, *viz.*, the countries Aṅga, Baṅga, Kaliṅga, Puṇḍra, and Suhma.

DISA—The wife of Bhíma, one of the eight Rudras.

DISHTA—One of the sons of Manu Vaivaswata, the son of the celestial luminary.

DIS—Space, which is said in the Bhágavata to be the deity which presides over the ear. Dis is also the name of a river in the Vishṇu Purána.

DITI—A goddess or personification in the Vedas who is associated with Aditi, and seems to be intended as an antithesis or as a complement to her.

In the *Rāmāyaṇa* and in the Purāṇas she is daughter of Dakṣa, wife of Kaśyapa, and mother of the *daityas*. The *Viṣṇu Purāṇa* relates that having lost her children, she begged of Kaśyapa a son of irresistible prowess, who should destroy Indra. The boon was granted, but with this condition: "If, with thoughts wholly pious and person entirely pure, you carefully carry the babe in your womb for a hundred years." She assiduously observed the condition; but Indra knew what was preparing for him. So he went to Diti and attended upon her with the utmost humility, watching his opportunity. In the last year of the century, Diti retired one night to rest without washing her feet. Indra then with his thunderbolt divided the embryo in her womb into seven portions. Thus mutilated, the child cried bitterly, and Indra being unable to pacify it, became angry, and divided each of the seven portions into seven, thus forming the swift-moving deities called Maruts, from the words, 'Mā-rodiḥ', 'weep not', which Indra used to quiet them.

DIVAKARA—A prince, the son of Prativyoman, of the family of Ikshwáku (*q.v.*).

DIVARATHA—A prince, the son of Para, a descendant of Anu.

DIVASPATI—The Indra of the thirteenth Manwantara.

DIVIJATA—One of the sons of Purúravas, according to the list in the Mataya.

DIVODASA—**(1)** A pious liberal king mentioned in the *Ṛgveda*, for whom it is said that Indra demolished a hundred impregnable cities of the black-skinned Sambara. Indra hurled Sambara from the mountain; he destroyed ninety-nine cities and gave the hundredth to Divodása, meaning perhaps the mythological aerial cities of the *asuras*. **(2)** A brāhmaṇa who was the twin-brother of Ahalyā. He is represented in the Veda as a "very liberal sacrificer", and as being delivered by the gods from the oppressor Śambara. He is also called Atithigva. 'he to who guests should go'. **(3)** A king of Kāśī, son of Bhīmaratha and father of Pratardana. He was attacked by the sons of King Vītahavya and all his sons were slain. His son Pratardana (*q.v.*) was bom to him through a sacrifice performed by Bharadvāja. He was celebrated as a physician and was called Dhanvantari.

DIVYA—One of the sons of Satwata.

DOLA YATRA OR DOLOTSAVA—The swinging festival; as commemorated in Bengal, this festival begins on the fourteenth day of the light half of Phálguna (about the middle of March.) The head of the family fasts during that day. In the evening fire-worship is performed; after which the officiating Brahman sprinkles upon an image of Krishṇa, consecrated for the occasion, a little red powder, and distributes a quantity of the same among the persons present. [HOLI.] A bonfire is made on a spot previously prepared, and a sort of Guy-Fawkes-like effigy, termed Holiká, made of bamboo laths and straw is formally carried to it and committed to the flames. In many cases musicians and singers are in attendance. The day is then spent in merriment and feasting, with many of the sports practised during the Holi (*q.v.*).

DOSHA—The wife of Kalpa, the son of Dhruva.

DRAGONS—These are represented in the Vishṇu Purána to be the progeny of Surasá; one of the Daityas.

DRAMA—It is said by Professor Wilson that the invention of dramatic entertainments is usually ascribed by Hindu writers to a *Muni* or inspired sage, named Bharata. The dramatic representations originally were of three kinds, *Nátya*, *Nritya*, and *Nritta*; and were exhibited before the gods by the Gandharbas and Apsarasas, the musicians and nymphs of Indra's heaven, who were trained by Bharata to the exhibition.

Of these different modes of representation the Nátya is the only one strictly dramatic, being defined to be gesticulation with language. The Nritya is merely pantomime, and the Nritta, simple dancing. The other two modes of performance termed *Tándava* and *Lasya* are merely styles of dancing.

An intimate connexion between the idea of dancing and dramatic representation may be observed, and this no doubt subsisted in the classical drama. The dances of the Chorus were no less important than their songs, and the arrangement of the ballet was as much the task of the author as the invention of the plot.

Bharata was probably one of the earliest writers by whom the art was reduced to a system. His *Sutras*, or aphorisms, are constantly cited by commentators on different plays, and suggest the doctrines which are taught by later authors. One of the best and earliest existing treatises on dramatic literature, as the *Dasa-Rúpaka*, or description of the ten kinds of theatrical composition, of which the term Rúpaka is the most appropriate designation. This work is exclusively devoted to dramatic criticism. An account of other works treating of poetical or rhetorical composition will be found under their respective titles. For the different kinds of dramatic entertainments cousult Rúpaka, Nátaka, Prakarana, &c.

"The plays of the Hindus are not numerous; they were only acted on special occasions, and the subject of the plot is with predilection borrowed from the legendary literature of ancient India. Hindu dramatists have little regard for unity of time, place and action; and with the exception of Kálidása, they must be considered as inferior in poetical worth to the renowned dramatic writers of ancient Greece and of modern Europe. Besides the reasons to be sought for in the religious, mystical and metaphysical tendencies of the Hindu mind, a free development of the Hindu drama was probably also impeded by the heavy and artificial canon which weighed upon Hindu dramaturgy, and which, ascribed to sacred sources, and looked upon as a law not to be transgressed by any dramatic poet, did not allow much scope for poetical imagination, and would keep down any free movement upon which it might have ventured. The various kinds of dramatic performances, the number of their acts, the characters of the plays, the conduct of the plot, the sentiments to be represented and even the modes of diction—all these were strictly regulpted; so much so, that in spite of the differences which must exist between different authors and plays, there is still a kind of uniformity which pervades the whole Hindu drama and must strike any one unacquainted with this elaborate dramatical canon."—*Goldstucker*.

DRAUNAYANI—The son of Drona, a patronymic of Aswatthâman (*q.v.*).

DRAUNI—The Vyása of the Dwápara which immediately follows the twenty-eight Dwáparas enumerated in the Vishṇu Purána.

DRAUPADI—Daughter of Drupada, king of Pañcāla, and wife of the five Pāṇḍu princes. Draupadī was a damsel of dark complexion but of great beauty, "as radiant and graceful as if she had descended from the city of the gods". Her hand was sought by many princes, and so her father determined to hold a *svayaṁvara* (*q.v.*) and allow her to exercise her own choice in the selection of a husband. The *svayaṁvara* was proclaimed, and princes assembled from all parts to contend in the lists for the hand of the princess; for although in such contests the lady was entitled to exercise her *svayaṁvara* or own choice, it generally followed that the champion of the arena became her husband. Most astonishing feats of arms were performed, but Arjuna outshone all by his marvellous use of the bow, and he became the selected bridegroom. A roar of acclamation arose from the vast assembly; the beautiful Draupadí was filled with joy and wonder at the youth and grace of the hero; as commanded by her brother she came forward and threw the garland round the neck of Arjuna, and permitted him to lead her away according to the rule of the Swayamvara. In the works of H.H. Wilson, Vol. iii, pp. 328-335, the following poetical version of the account of the Swayamvara is given

In Panchála's spacious realm
The powerful monarch Drupada observes
A solemn feast; attending princes wait
With throbbing hearts, his beauteous daughter's choice;
The royal Draupadí, whose charms surpass
All praise, as far as her mild excellence
And mind transcend the beauties of her person.

* * *

And now the day of festival drew nigh;
When Drupada, whose anxious hopes desired
A son of Páṇḍu for his daughter's lord,
And who had sent his messengers to search
The banished chiefs, still sought by them in vain,
Devised a test—no other force but theirs
He deemed could undergo, to win the bride.
A ponderous bow with magic skill he framed,
Unyielding but to more than mortal strength.
And for a mark he hung a metal plate
Suspended on its axle, swift revolving
Struck by a shaft that from the centre strayed.
This done he bade proclaim—that he whose hand
Should wing the arrow to its destined aim,
Should win the Princess by his archery.

Before the day appointed, tropping came
Princes and chiefs innumerous 'midst the throng
Duryodhana and all the hundred sons
Of Dhṛitaráshṭra, with the gallent Karṇa,
In haughty cohort at the court appeared.
With hospitable act the king received

His royal guests and fitting welcome gave.
Between the North and East without the gates
There lay a spacious plain; a fosse profound
And lofty walls enclosed its ample circuit,
And towering gates and trophied arches rose,
And tall pavilions glittered round its borders:
Here ere the day of trial came, the sports

Were held: and loud as ocean's boisterous waves,
And thick as stars that gem the Dolphin's brow,
The might city here her myriads poured.
Around the monarch's throne on lofty seats
Of gold with gems emblazoned sat the kings,
Each lowering stern defiance on the rest.
Without the barriers pressed the countless crowd
Or clambering upon scaffolds clustering hung.
Skirting the distance multitudes beheld
The field from golden lattices, or thronged
The high house-tops, whose towering summits touched
The clouds, and like the mountain of the gods
With sparkling peaks streamed radiant through the air.
A thousand trumpets brayed, and slow the breeze
With incense laden wafted perfume round.
Whilst games of strength and skill—the graceful dance,
The strains of music, or dramatic art,
Awoke the gazer's wonder and applause.

Thus sixteen days were passed, and every chief
Of note was present—and the king no more
Could with fair plea his daughter's choice delay.
Then came the Princess forth in royal garb
Arrayed and costly ornaments adorned:
A garland interwove with gems and gold
Her delicate hands sustained—from the pure bath
With heightened loveliness she tardy came,
And blushing in the princely presence stood.
Next in the ring the reverend Priest appeared
And strewed the holy grass and poured the oil,
An offering to the God of Fire, with prayer
Appropriate, and with pious blessings crowned.
Then bade the king the trumpets' clangor cease
And hush the buzzing crowd—while his brave son
The gallant Dhrishṭadyumna on the plain
Descended and his father's will proclaimed.

"Princes, this bow behold—you mark—these shafts—
Whoe'er with dexterous hand at once directs
Five arrows to their aim, and be his race,
His person and his deeds equivalent
To such exalted union, He obtains
My sister for his bride—my words are truth."
Thus said, he to the Princess next described
Each royal suitor by his name and lineage
And martial deeds, and bade her give the wreath
To him whose prowess best deserved the boon.
Quick from their gorgeous thrones the kings uprose,
Descending to the conflict, and around
The lovely Draupadí contending pressed;
Like the bright gods round Śiva's mountain bride.
Love lodged his viewless arrows in their hearts,
And jealous hatred swelled their haughty minds;
Each on his rivals bent a lowering glance,
And friends till now, they met as deadliest foes.
Alone the kindred bands remained aloof
Who owned Janárdana their glorious chief.
He and the mighty Haláyudha curbed
Their emulous zeal,—and tranquil they beheld
Like furious elephants the monarchs meet;
Their rage by courteous seeming ill represt
Like fire amidst the smouldering embers glowing.

And now in turn the Princes to the trial
Succeeding past, in turn to be disgraced—
No hand the stubborn bow could bend—they strained
Fruitless each nerve, and many on the field
Recumbent fell, whilst laughter pealed around.
In vain they cast aside their royal robes
And diamond chains and glittering diadems,
And with unfettered arm and ample chest
Put forth their fullest strength—the bow defied
Each chief nor left the hope he might succeed.
Karṇa alone the yielding bowstring drew
And ponderous shafts applied, and all admired.
The timid Draupadí in terror cried,
I wed not with the base-born—Karṇa smiled
In bitterness and upwards turned his eyes
To his great Sire the Sun—then cast to earth
The bow and shafts and sternly stalked away.

Thus foiled the Princes, through the murmuring crowd
Amazement spread—then Arjuna from where
He and his brethren with the Brahmans placed
Had viewed the scene, advanced to prove his skill—
The priestly bands with wonder struck beheld
Who seemed a student of their tribe aspire
To triumph where the mightiest chiefs had failed—
They deemed the like disgrace would shame the attempt,
And ridicule their race and name assail,
And many a venerable elder strove
To turn the stripling from the hopeless task:
They strove in vain—nor did they all despair—
For many marked his elephantine strength,
His lion port and self-collected soul;
And fancied that they saw revived in him
The son of Jamadagni: to o'erthrow
Once more the haughty Kshatriya's power and pride.
Unheeding praise or censure, Arjuna
Passed to the field: with reverential steps

He round the weapon circled, next addressed
A silent prayer, to Mahadeo, and last
With faith inflexible on Krishṇa dwelt.
One hand the bow up bore, the other drew
The sturdy cord, and placed the pointed
shafts—
They flew—the mark was hit—and sudden
shouts
Burst from the crowd long silent: flattering
waved
The Brahman scarfs, and drum and trumpet
brayed,
And Bard and Herald sung the hero's triumph.

When the five brothers returned to the house where their mother, Kuntī, was staying, they told her that they had made a great acquisition, and she told them to share it among them. These words raised a great difficulty, for if they could not be adroitly evaded they must be obeyed. The sage Vyāsa settled the matter by saying, "The destiny of Draupadī has already been declared by the gods; let her become the wife of all the brethren." So she became their common wife, and it was arranged that she should stay successively two days in the house of each, and that no one of them but the master of the house should enter it while she was there. Arjuna was her favourite, and she showed her jealousy when he married Subhadrā. In the great gambling match which the eldest brother, Yudhiṣthira, played at Hastināpura against his cousins, the Kauravas, he lost his all—his kingdom, his brothers, himself, and their wife Draupadī. So she became a slave, and Duryodhana called her to come and sweep the room. She refused, and then Duḥśāsana dragged her by the hair into the pavilion before all the chieftains, and tauntingly told her that she was a slave girl, and had no right to complain of being touched by men. He also abused her and tore off her veil and dress, while Duryodhana invited her to sit on his thigh. Kṛṣṇa took compassion upon her, and restored her garments as fast as they were torn. She called vehemently upon her husbands to save her, but they were restrained by Yudhiṣthira. Bhīma was in a rage of passion; he was prevented from action; but he vowed in loud words that he would drink the blood of Duḥśāsana and smash the thigh of Duryodhana in retaliation of these outrages, which vows he eventually fulfilled. Draupadī vowed that her hair should remain dishevelled until Bhīma should tie it up with hands dripping with the blood of Duḥśāsana. The result of the gambling match was that the Pāṇḍavas, with Draupadī, went into exile for twelve years, and were to dwell quite incognito during another year. The period of thirteen years being successfully completed, they were at liberty to return. Twelve years of exile were passed in the jungle, and in the course of this period Jayadratha, king of Sindhu, came to the house of the Pāṇḍavas while they were out hunting. He was courteously received by Draupadī, and was fascinated by her charms. He tried to induce her to elope with him, and when he was scornfully repulsed, he dragged her to his chariot and drove off with her. When the Pāṇḍavas returned and heard of the rape, they pursued Jayadratha, and pressed him so close that he put down Draupadī, and endeavoured to escape alone. Bhīma resolved to overtake and punish him; and although Yudhiṣthira pleaded that Jayadratha was a kinsman, and ought not to be killed, Draupadī called aloud for vengeance, so Bhīma and Arjuna continued the pursuit. Bhīma dragged Jayadratha from his car, kicked and beat him till he was senseless, but spared his life. He cut off all Jayadratha's hair except five locks, and made him publicly acknowledge that he was a slave. Draupadī's revenge was then slaked, and Jayadratha was released at her intercession. In the thirteenth year, in which her husbands and she were to live undiscovered, they entered the service of the king of Virāṭa, and she, without acknowledging any connection with them, became a waiting-maid to the queen. She stipulated that she should not be required to wash feet or to eat food left by others, and she quieted the jealous fears which her beauty excited in the queen's mind by representing that she was guarded by five *gandharvas*, who would prevent any improper advances. She lived a quiet life for a while, but her beauty excited the passions of Kīcaka, the queen's brother, who was commander-in-chief, and the leading man in the kingdom. His importunities and insults greatly annoyed her, but she met with no protection from the queen, and was rebuked for her complaints and petulance by Yudhiṣthira. Her spirit of revenge was roused, and she appealed as usual to Bhīma, whose fiery passions she well knew how to kindle. She complained of her menial position, of the insults she had received, of the indifference other husbands, and of the base offices they were content to occupy. Bhīma promised revenge. An assignation was made with Kīcaka which Bhīma kept, and he so mangled the unfortunate gallant that all his flesh and bones were rolled into a ball, and no one could discover the manner of his death. The murder was attributed to Draupadī's *gandharvas*, and she was condemned to be burnt on Kīcaka's funeral pile. Then Bhīma disguised himself, and tearing up a tree for a club, went to her rescue. He was supposed to be the *gandharva*, and every one fled before him. He released Draupadī, and they returned to the city by different ways. After the term of exile was over, and the Pāṇḍavas and she were at liberty to return, she was more ambitious than her husbands, and complained to Kṛṣṇa of the humility and want of resolution shown by Yudhṣṭhira. She had five sons, one by each husband—Prativindhya, son of Yudhiṣṭhira; Śrutasoma, son of Bhīma; Śrutakīrtti, son of Arjuna; Śatānīka, son of Nakula; and Śrutakarmań, son of Sahadeva. She with these five sons was present in camp on the eighteenth and last night of the great battle, while her victorious husbands were in the camp of the defeated enemy. Aśvatthāman with two companions entered the camp of the Pāṇḍavas, cut down these five youths, and all whom they found. Draupadī called for vengeance upon Aśvatthāman. Yudhiṣṭhira endeavoured to moderate her anger, but she appealed to Bhīma. Arjuna pursued Aśvatthāman, and overtook him, but he spared his life after taking from him a celebrated jewel which he wore as an amulet. Arjuna gave this jewel to Bhīma for presentation to Draupadī. On receiving it she was consoled, and presented the jewel to Yudhisṭhira as the head of the family. When her husbands retired from the world and went on their journey towards the Himālayas and Indra's heaven, she accompanied them, and was the first to fall on the journey, (see Mahābhārata)

Draupadī's real name was Kṛṣṇā. She was called Draupadī and Yājñasenī, from her father; Pārṣatī, from her grandfather Pṛṣata; Pāncālī, from her country; Sairindhri, 'the maid-servant' of the queen of Virāṭa; Pañcami, 'having five husbands'; and Nitayauvanī, 'the ever-young'.

DRAVIDA—The country in which the Tamil language is spoken, extendingfrom Madras to Cape Comorin. According to Manu, the people of this country were originally kṣatriyas, but sank to the condition of śūdras from the extinction of sacred rites and the absence of brāhmaṇas. As applied to the classification of brāhmaṇas it has a much wider application, embracing Gujarāt, Mahāraṣtra, and all the south.

DRAVIDIAN—The term applied to designate the five languages of Southern India, *viz*—the Tamil, the Telugu, the Canarese, the Malayálim, and the Toulava. South India was formerly called the Drávida country. The Tamil is the most cultivated of the Dravidian tongues; it contains the largest portion and the richest variety of undoubtedly ancient forms, and the smallest infusion of Sanskrit terms. It is the vernacular of about 12 millions of people. The Telugu ranks next to the Tamil in respect of culture and copiousness; in point of euphonse sweetness it ranks in the first place. It is the vernacular of about 14 millions. The Canarese occupies the third place. Sanskrit words have been extensively introduced into the modern dialect, and during the reigns of Hyder and Tippu in Mysore, Hindustani words became common; but the ancient dialect, spoken from about 800 to 1500 A.D. was free from any admixture of foreign terms. It is the vernacular of about 10 millions. The Malayálim ranks next in order and is spoken along the Malabar Coast from Cannanore to Trevandrum by about 3 millions of people. The Toulava is the least important of the five, and is spoken by the smallest number of people.

DRAVINA—One of the sons of Prithu, the universal emperor. Also the name of one of the sons of the sage Dhava.

DRAVIRAS—The people of the Coromandel Coast, from Madras southwards; those by whom the Tamil langauge is spoken.

DRAVYA—Substance; thing; the receptacle or substratum of properties, one of the six *Padárthas*, or categories, into which Kanáda distributes the contents of the universe.

DRIDHADHANAṢH—A prince, the son of Senajit, of the family of Hastin.

DRIDHANETRA—The youngest of the four sons of Viṣwámitra, born when he had retired to the jungles of the south to practice austerities.

> And in that solitary spot,
> Four virtuous sons the king begot,
> Havishyand from the offering named,
> And Madhushyand for sweetness famed,
> Mahárath, chariot-borne in fight,
> And Dridhanétra, strong of sight." —*Griffiths.*

DRIDHASONA—A king of Maghada, the son of Susam; he reigned 48 years.

DRIDHAYAS—One of the sons of Purúravas, according to the Matsya list.

DRISHADWATI—A river of considerable importance in the history of the Hindus, although no traces of its ancient name exist. *V.P.*, p. 181.

This river is also called Himavat, and is said to be the mother of Prasenajit.

DRISHTANTA—An illustration, example, for familiar instance; in the Nyáya system of Gautama, it is a topic on which in controversy both disputants consent; or "that on regard to which, a man of an ordinary and a man of a superior intellect, entertain the same opinion."

DRISHTEDYUMNA—The son of Rája Drupada and brother of Draupadí. Their birth was remarkable and occurred under the following circumstances: King Drupada, after his disgrace and the dismemberment of his kingdom, burning with resentment, had recourse to supernatural agency to procure the birth of a son, who should one day avenge his defeat and accomplish the death of Dróṇa. After some difficulty he prevailed on two learned Brahmane, named Yája and Upayája, who performed a sacrifice for this purpose, and at the proper period summoned the Queen of Drupada to assist at the rite. Her Majesty was engaged at her toilet, and delaying her arrival with true feminine want of punctuality, the ceremony was completed without her. Two children, one male, one female, arose from out of the sacrificial fire. The former was Dhrisht-adyumna, who appeared with a diadem on his head, armed in full mail, and bearing a bow and arrow in his hand. The latter was Krishná, so named from her black complexion, though of exceeding beauty. She is better known by her patronymic Draupadí, the daughter of Drupada. Dhrishṭadyumna proclaimed the terms of her Swayamvara.—*F. Johnson*. (*Selections from the Mahábhárata*.)

DRONA—'A bucket.' A brāhmaṇa so named from his having been generated by his father, Bharadvāja, in a bucket. He married Kṛpā, half-sister of Bhīṣma, and by her was father of Aśvatthāman. He was *āc ārya*, or teacher of the military art, both to the Kaurava and Pāṇḍava princes, and so he was called Droṇācārya. By birth a Brahman, but acquainted with military science, which he received as a gift from Parasuráma (see RÁMA.). "Droṇa was not ascetic, and having in childhood shared the lessons and sports of the royal heir of the neighbouring kingdom of Panchála, he felt inclined to live again at that court, now that his old playfellow had become king. Never doubting of a hearty welcome, he presented himself to king Drupada quite unceremoniously, merely saying, 'Behold in me your friend.' His reception however was totally different to what he anticipated.

> ..."the monarch sternly viewed
> The sage, and bent his brows, and with disdain
> His eyeballs reddened; silent awhile he sat,
> Then arrogantly spoke: Brahman, methinks
> Thou showest little wisdom, or the sense
> Of what is fitting, when thou call'st me friend.
> What friendship, weak of judgment, can subsist
> Between a luckless pauper and a king ?"

"The King of Panchála stares at the idea of friendship between a learned brahman and one to whom the Vedas are a mystery, or between a warrior and one who cannot guide a chariot through the ranks of war; and continues—

> ... he to whose high mandate nations bow,
> Disdains to stoop to friends beneath the throne.
> Hence then with idle dreams; dismiss the
> memory
> Of other days and thoughts; I know thee not."

Droṇa was too much astonished to speak, but he instantly withdrew from Panchála to Hastinápura, where he was most reverentially welcomed, and was at once entrusted with the instruction of the five young Pándu and the hundred young Kuru princes." Droṇa had in youth been equally instructed in wisdom and in arms; and he taught the young princes to rein the steed, to guide the elephant, to drive the chariot, launch the javelin, hurl the dark, wield the battle-axe, and whirl the mace."*

In the *Vishṇu Purána*, p. 454, Droṇa is called the husband of Kripí, and father of Aswattháma; afterwards king of the north part of the Panchála country, and a general in the Kuru army. After Bhíshma had been mortally wounded, Droṇa was elected to the command of the army. He promised Duryodhana that he would take Yudhishthira prisoner, but he could not do so as Krishṇa and Arjuna were ever on the alert to prevent it. On the fourth day of his command he killed Viráta and Drupada. Dhrishṭadyumna then vowed to slay Droṇa in revenge for the death of his father Drupada. A combat took place; but it was not till Droṇa was falsely told that his son Aswattháma was dead, that he laid down his arms, and Dhrishṭdyumna rushed upon him and severed his head from his body. Droṇa was also called Kūṭaja. The common meaning of Kūṭa is 'mountain-top', but one of its many other meanings is 'water-jar'. His patronymic is Bhāradvāja. (* Mrs. Manning, Professor Wilson, *Oriental Mag*., Vol. iii.)

DRONAKAS—A term by which, in the Puránas, the inhabitants of valleys, are designated.

DRSADVATI—A common female name. **(1)** The wife of King Divodāsa. **(2)** A river forming one of the boundaries of Brahmā-vartta, perhaps the Kāgar before its junction with the Sarsuti.

DRUHYU—Son of Yayāti, by Sarmisṭhā, daughter of the *daitya* king Vṛṣaparvan. He refused to exchange his youth for the curse of decrepitude passed upon his father, and in consequence Yayāti cursed him that his posterity should not possess dominion. His father gave him a part of his kingdom, but his descendants became "princes of the lawless barbarians of the north".

DRUPADA—King of Pañcāla and son of Pṛṣata. Also called Yajñasena. He was schoolfellow of Droṇa, the preceptor of the Kaurava and Pāṇḍava princes, and he mortally offended his former friend by repudiating his acquaintance. Droṇa, in payment of his services as preceptor, required his pupils to make Drupada prisoner. The Kauravas attacked him and failed, but the Pāṇḍavas took Drupada captive and occupied his territory. Droṇa spared his life and restored the southern half of his kingdom to him. Drupada returned home burning for revenge, and, to procure it, he prevailed upon two brāhmaṇas to perform a sacrifice, by the efficacy of which he obtained two children, a son and a daughter, who were called "the altar-born", because they came forth from the sacrificial fire. These children were named Dhrsṭadyumna and Kṛṣṇa, but the latter is better known by her patronymic Draupadī. After she had chosen Arjuna for her husband at her *svayamvara*, and she had become, with Drupada's consent, the wife of the five Pāṇḍavas, he naturally became the ally of his sons-in-law. He took an active part in the great battle, and on the fourteenth day he was killed and beheaded by Droṇa, who on the following day was killed by Dhṛṣṭadyumna, the son whom Drupada had obtained for wreaking his vengeance on Droṇa. Besides the two children mentioned, Drupada had a younger son named śikhandin and a daughter Sikhandini.

DUHSALA—The only daughter of Dhrtarastra and wife of Jayadratha, Rája of Sindhu

DUHSASANA—One of the chief of the hundred sons of Dhritaráshtra. He took part in the great war. It was he who dragged Draupadi into the gambling pavilion by the hair, and insulted her before the assembly. Bhíma vowed to drink his blood; and on the sixteenth day of the great war, after a deadly conflit, Bhíma slew Duhsásana and fulfilled his vow.

DUKHA—Pain. The son of Naraka and Vedana.

DUNDHUBI—A huge giant slain by Báli. When Sugríva wished Ráma to destroy Báli, in order to convince him of the great strength of the latter he showed Ráma the dead body of Dundhubi:—

"The prostrate corse of mountain size
Seemed nothing in the hero's eyes
He lightly kicked it as it lay
And cast it twenty leagues away."

DURADARSIN—Far-seeing; the name of a Vulture in the Panchatántra, who was the chief minister of the peacock king Chitravarna.

DURDAMA—The son of Bhadrasrenya, who recovered his father's kingdom from Divodása (*q.v.*)

DURDHARSHA—One of the Rávaṇa's five renowned warriors who were sent against Hanumán. He aimed an arrow that struck the undaunted Ape in the neck and then lashed his steeds nearer; but when he was close to the doorway, Hanumán with a sudden cry, let himself fall upon the chariot; it was shivered into fragments, and the Rákshasa hurled from it lifeless.—*I. E.*, 232.

DURGÀ—'Inaccessible. The Śakti or wife of the god Śiva, and the goddess of destruction; she is described as terrible in form and irascible in temper. She was the daughter of Himálaya, the sovereign of the snowy mountains. Durgá is often called Káli. In her amiable form she is termed Bhaváni. "The adoration of Káli, or Durgá, is however particularly prevalent in Bengal, and is cultivated with practices scarcely known in most other provinces. Her great festival, the Daṣará, is in the West of India, marked by no particular honors, whilst its celebration in Bengal occupies ten days of prodigal expenditure. This festival, the Durgá Pújá, is now well known, as is the extensive and popular establishment near Calcutta, the temple of Kálí at Kálí Ghát."

"That human offerings to the dark forms of Śiva and Durgá were sometimes perpetrated in later times, we know from various original sources, particularly from that very effective scene in the drama of Mádhava and Málatí, in which Aghoraghanṭa is represented as about to sacrifice Málatí to Chámuṇḍá, when she is rescued by her lover. No such divinities, however, neither Siva nor Durgá, much less any of their terrific forms, are even named, so far as we know, in the Vedas, and therefore these works could not be authority for their sanguinary worship. That the practice is enjoined on particular occasions by the Tantras and some of the Puráṇas connected with this branch of the Hindu faith, is, no doubt, true; but these are works of a much later date."*

"Durgá combines the characteristics of Minerva, Pallas and Juno. Her original name was Párvatí, but having, by a display of extraordinary valour, defeated a giant named Durgá, she was thenceforth dignified with the name of her conquered foe. This monster is by some supposed to be a personification of vice, and Durgá of virtue, while the struggle typified the action and reaction of good and evil in the world."—*G. Small.* (See Aparṇā, Devī, Kālī, Karālī, Pārvatī, Sati, Yoganidrā.). (see DEVI)

A composite goddess embodying a number of local divinities and demonesses associated with mountains, vegetation and fire. This assimilation began about the end of the Vedic period[1] and culminated in the Śākta cult. Many factors, now unknown, must have contributed to the development of these cults, but there is little doubt that early Indian folk-religion exerted 'a great influence in moulding the notion of the "motherly divinities".'[2] Thus there is some justification for assuming a connection between these 'mother-goddesses', like Uma, Durga, Parvati, Laksmi, etc., and the fertility goddesses like Sarasvati, Puramdhi, Aditi, etc.,[3] although 'maternal' is not the most fitting description either of the *asaklis* or of some village mother-goddesses of South India, whose cults[4] have persisted with only minor modifications to the present day.

Durgā is portrayed in the Purāṇas and the Epic as a notable female warrior, the bloodthirsty destroyer of giant *asuras.* This has probably a historical basis, recalling the warfare between the Indo-Aryans and native tribes. The warrior Durga assumes ten forms: 1. As Durgā she received the messengers of the giant Sumbha; 2. As Dasabhuja she destroyed Sumbha's army commanded by Dhumalocana; 3. As Simha-vahini she rides a lion, the latter symbolizing her warlike nature and invincibility; 4. As Mahisa-suramardini (the slayer of Mahisa) she slew Sumbha in his buffalo form; 5. As Jagaddhatri (mother of the world) she destroyed another army of giants; 6. As Kālī or Kālī Mā, she fought the army of the giant Raktavija who, realizing that his men were no match for her, attacked the goddess in person. Kālī wounded him repeatedly, but from every drop of blood that flowed from his wounds a thousand giants arose. She retaliated by materializing Caṇḍi,[5] another of her forms. While Candi continued the fight Kali drank the giants' blood until only Raktavija was left, whereupon Caṇḍi slew him with a single blow; 7. As Muktakesi she destroyed more of the giant's troops; 8. As Tara she slew Sumbha; 9. As Chinnamasta she slew Nisumbha; 10. As Jagadgauri (the Yellow Woman) she is praised by gods and men for delivering them from demons.

In her fierce aspect she may represent fire and its cathartic properties. Her epithets Kālī and Karali are also the names of two of Agni's tongues (*i.e.*, flames) (*Mund. Up.*, 1.2,4); another of her names is Jatavedasi (the feminine form of one of Agni's epithets). Durga's connection with vegetation is shown by the *navapalrika* or ceremony of the Nine Plants, and her identification with Sakambhari, the nourisher of herbs; as Vindhya-vasini she is associated with the Vindhyas where she dwells, and as Parvati she is the goddess of the Himalaya. Her beneficent aspect is also indicated in Yudhisthira's hymn to her: 'Thou art called Durga by all because thou savest men from difficulty...Thou art the sole refuge of men.'[6] Her primitive side can be seen in the human and animal sacrifices offered to her, the use of intoxicants, and her epithet Chinnamasta (the Headless).[7] In Durga's principal temple in Calcutta, seven to eight hundred goats are slaughtered during the Durga *puja* in the autumn, their heads being placed in piles before her image. Pigs, fowls, sheep and water buffaloes are also immolated. Until 1835 when the British Government, with the help of some enlightened Indians, suppressed human sacrifice, a boy was beheaded every Friday before the altar. In 1830 a Raja sacrificed twenty-five men to Durga.[8]

As the *sakti* of Siva the great ascetic[9] (also a composite god embodying several local *devas*) Durga became the goddess of yogins; but to the masses she remains the great Mother-goddess. Banerjea considers that some concepts of Durga stem from prehistoric times,[10] and Campbell suggests affinities with the village cults of Melanesia and New Guinea as well as with 'Near Eastern matrices of civilization'.[11] **(2)** A commentator on the *Nirukta.* **(3)** The name of a river flowing from the Vindhya.

1. Her name appears in the *Bṛhadd.* (11.77), but Macdonell considers it an interpolation, although an early one.
2. *S.* Kumar Das, *Sakti or Divine Power*, p. 41.
3. *Ibid.*, p. 42.
4. The rites connected with these cults are described by H. Whitehead, *Village Gods of South India*, pp. 71 ff.

5. In this myth the disparate elements in Durga can be seen, as both Kali and Candi emanate from her, and do the actual killing of demons..
6. Arthur Avalon, *Hymns to the Goddess*, pp. 70f.
7. The *Kdlika Pur.* gives minute details of the correct method of offering a human victim to Kali. Human ! blood is said to satisfy her for a thousand years (Wilson, *Selected Works*, II, p. 268). Since the Middle Ages, animals are 'decapitated before the sacred icon, in such a way that some of the blood fell on it. The ritual slaughter of animals was justified by the doctrine that the soul of the victim went straight to heaven...its survival in Bengal and elsewhere is a matter of shame to most modern Hindus' (*WI.*, p. 336).
8. E.A. Gait, 'Human Sacrifice (Indian)', *ERE.*
9. Siva's vegetal form is that of the *bilwa* tree (Aegte marmelos) (*AIA.*, I, p. 165).
10. *DHL*, pp. 173, 490. E.A. Payne considers the name Durgā to be aboriginal (*The Saktas.*, p. 6.).
11. Oriental Mythology, *Masks of God*, II, p. 171.

* H.H.Wilson's *Works*, vol. ii.

DURGADASA—A distinguished commentator on the Sanskrit Grammar of Vopadeva.

DURGAMA—Durmada. Two sons of Vasudeva by his wife Rohini.

DURGAS—Strongholds. There are four kinds; three of which are natural from their situation in mountains, amidst water, or in other inaccessible spots; the fourth is the artificial defences of a village hamlet or city.

DURJAYANTA—A mountain in the Vishṇu Purána not yet identified.

DURMUKHA—'Bad face.'A name of one of Dhrtarastra's sons. Also of one of Rāma's monkey allies, and of several others.

DURVASAS—'Ill-clothed'. A sage, the son of Atri and Anasuya, but, according to some authorities, he was a son or emanation of Śiva. He was noted for his irascible temper, and many fell under his curse. It was he who cursed Sakuntala for keeping him waiting at the door, and so caused the separation between her and King Dusyanta. But it was he who blessed Kunti, so that she became a mother by the Sun. In the *Viṣṇu Purāṇa* he is represented as cursing Indra for treating with disrespect a garland which the sage presented to him. The curse was that "his sovereignty over the three worlds should be subverted", and under it Indra and the gods grew weak and were overpowered by the *asuras*. In their extremity they resorted to Viṣṇu, who directed them to churn the ocean of milk for the production of the *amrta* (water of life) and other precious things. In the *Mahābhārata* it is stated that on one occasion Kṛṣṇa entertained him hospitably, but omitted to wipe the fragments of food from the foot of the sage. At this the latter grew angry and foretold how Kṛṣṇa should be killed. The *Viṣṇu Purāṇa* states that Kṛṣṇa fell according to "the imprecation of Durvasas", and in the same work Durvasas is made to describe himself as one "whose nature is stranger to remorse".

DURVASAS PURANA—One of the eighteen Upa Purāṇas. (see Pur ana)

DURYAMAN—A prince, the son of Dhrita, a descendant of Druhyu.

DURYODHANA—'Hard to conquer.' "Difficult to be fought with." The eldest of the Kurus. The eldest of the hundred sons of Dhritaráshtra, and one of the principal actors, among the Kauravas, in the great war...Pándu was the younger brother of Dhritaráshtra, but Yudhishthira his eldest son was born before Duryodhana, and according to the customs of those times had in consequence a prior right to the throne of Hastinápura. This led to constant rivalry between Yudhishthira and Duryodhana for the post of Yuvarája. As the five Pándavas had, on the death of Pándu, come under the guardianship of their uncle Dhritaráshtra, the cousins were brought up together in the old palace of Hastinápura. It is stated in the Mahábhárata that "about this time Duryodhana the eldest of the Kauravas, became very jealous of the strength of Bhíma, and resolved to work evil against him. He attempted to take his life by poison, and throwing him into a lake while stupified from its effect. Bhíma was not however killed but appeared again to play an important part in the struggles of their lives."

"The jealousy and hatred of the Kurus towards the Pándavas increased as they all attained manhood. The father of the Kurus being blind, required a vice king, or Yuvarâjá, *i.e.*, "Little Rája." In this office Yudhishthira was installed, he being entitled to it as eldest son of the late king Pándu. But Duryodhana was highly discontented at this arrangement, and at length persuaded his blind father to send away the Pándavas to the city of Váranávṛta (the modern Allah-abad). Here a splendid house was prepared for them; but hemp, resin, and other combustible substances, were secreted within; for the wicked Duryodhana plotted that the house should be set on fire, and the five Pándavas and their mother burnt to death. Warning, however, was given to these intended victims before they left Hastinápura; and, on taking possession of their splendid new habitation, they had an underground passage made, by which, when the expected fire took place, they all escaped."

Among the poor people whom Kunti had been feasting was a Bhíl woman, with five sons, who, according to the practice of their tribe, drank deeply of intoxicating liquor, and then lay down and slept heavily. The next morning their bodies were found amid the ruins of the conflagration; and it was believed in Hastinápura that the Pándavas had perished, and Duryodhana pretended to mourn their death.

After the Pándavas (*q.v.*) had conquered their misfortunes "the very splendour of their success revived the dark jealousy of Duryodhana; for he and his brother Duhsásana, and one or two others, plot to deprive the newly-inaugurated king of his territories. They first secure the co-operation of a relative, named Sakuni, who was a noted gambler, and then induce the blind old Mahárája to invite the Pándavas to a gambling festival at Hastinápura. Yudhishthira accepts the invitation, with secret misgiving; for "he was not very skilful in throwing the dice," and he knows that "Sakuni is dwelling in Hastinápura." Of Sakuni, it is said that "he is very skilful in throwing dice, and in playing with dice that were loaded; insomuch, that whenever he played he always won the game." Nevertheless, Yudhishthira feels compelled to go; for "no true Kshatriya can refuse a challenge to war or play." The game they played at seems to have resembled backgammon, "pieces on a board being directed by the throwing of dice." Certain seeds or nuts served as dice; and dice of this description were used for the guidance of a portion of the religious sacrifice. So that, to throw dice, was not deemed objectionable; and only when a passion, or the stake immoderate, was it esteemed a vice. It was, of course, contrived that Yudhishthira should be led on to stake and to lose all that he possessed.*

Then the Pándavas returned from their second exile it was chiefly owing to Duryodhana that the great war was fought. He rejected all Krishṇa's proposals for peace, though Bhíshma and Drona, as well as his aged father, were anxious that he should accept them...The war commenced.

"The Kuru host entrusted to his care.
The son of Bharadwája marshals; first
The chiefs of Sindhu, and Kalinga's king,
With the young prince Vikarna on the right
He stations, by Gândhára's martial chivalry;
With glittering lances armed and led by Sakuni,
Their sovereign's son, supported. On his left
Duhsásana and other chiefs of fame
Commanded the array: around them rode
Kámboja's horse, Sakas and Yavanas,
On rapid coursers, mighty in the field,
The nations of the north, and east, and south,
Composed his main battalions: in the rear
Secure the monarch marched; whilst in the van
The gallant Karna led his faithful bands,
Exulting in their sovereign's stately stature,
High raised upon his elephant of war,
And gorgeous shining as the rising sun.
His warriors deemed the gods themselves were weak,
With Indra at their head, to stem his prowess,
And each to each their thoughts revealed, they moved,
Secure of victory, to meet the foe."

—Wilson's *Works* (vol. iii, p. 291.)

On the last day of the war Bhíma fought Duryodhana in single combat with clubs, and killed him. It is said that he then fulfilled the vow he made to avenge the insult which Duryodhana had offered to Draupadi. Duryodhana was called also Suyodhana, 'good fighter'. (* *A. and M. I.*)

DUSANA—A *rākṣasa* who fought as one of the generals of Rāvaṇa, and was killed by Rama. He was generally associated with Rāvaṇa's brother, Khara.

DUSHYANTA—The eldest son of Anila, and father of the emperor Bharata. The Mahábhárata relates the following legend of this king. "Once upon a time the valiant Rája Dushyanta was hunting in the forest, when he beheld the beautiful Sakuntalá, the adopted daughter of Kanwa the sage; and he prevailed on the damsel to become his wife by a Gandharva marriage, and gave her his ring as the pledge of his troth. Then Dushyanta returned to his own city, whilst Sakuntalá, remained in the hermitage of her father. After this Durvásas the sage visited the hermitage of Kanwa, but the thoughts of Sakuntalá were fixed upon her husband, and she heard not the approach of the sage. And Durvásas cursed the damsel, that she should be forgotten by the man the loved; but after a while he relented, and promised that the curse should be removed as soon as Dushyanta saw the ring. When Sakuntalá found that she was with child, she set off for the palace of her husband; but on her way she bathed in a sacred pool, and the ring dropped from her finger and was lost beneath the waters. When she reached the palace of the Rája, his memory had departed from him, and he would not own her to be his wife; and her mother came and carried her away to the jungle, and there she gave birth to a son, who was named Bharata. And it so happened that a large fish was caught by a fisherman, and the ring of Dushyanta was found in the belly of the fish, and carried to the Rája; and Dushyanta saw the ring, and he remembered the beautiful Sakuntalá, who had become his wife by a Gandharva marriage. And the Rája went into the jungle and saw the boy Bharata sporting with young lions and setting at nought the lioness that gave them suck; and his heart burned towards the lad; and presently he beheld the sorrowing Sakuntalá, and he knew that Sakuntalá was his wife, and that Bharata was his son. So Rája Dushyanta took Sakuntalá and Bharata to his own city; and he made Sakuntalá his chief Ráni, and appointed Bharata to succeed him in the Raj:" The story of Sakuntalá is the subject of the beautiful drama of Kalidása, "The Lost Ring."

DUTAṄGADA—'The ambassador Aṅgada.' A short play founded on the mission of Aṅgada to demand from Rāvaṇa the restoration of Sītā. It is attributed to a poet named Subhaṭa.

DŪTÀS—Messengers. The Gananátas or Dútas are divided into three classes;

1. Siva-dútas, who are represented as red, short, and thick like the Bhúta. Their hair-locks twisted together, rest on their heads like a cap, and from their mouths project two great lion's teeth. They have four hands in which they hold, respectively, a snake, a cord, a trident, and a wine-jug; whilst their body is adorned with various ornaments. By means of these messeugers Isvara fetches the souls of his devotees at their death to his seat of bliss, called Kailāsa, and that in a Pushpakavimāna, *i.e.*, a self moving chariot.
2. The Vishṇu-dútas have their hair dressed like the Śiva-dútas, and also like them a lion's teeth, but otherwise they resemble Vishṇu, being of a blue color, and wearing the Tirunāma on their forehead, arms, and breasts; and round their necks a rosary of Tulasimani; whilst they hold in their four hands, respectively, a Sankha, a Chakra, a battle-axe, and a club. Through these messengers Vishṇu fetches .the souls of his faithful devotees into his abode of bliss called Vaikuntha.
3. The Yama-dútas, the messengers of Yama, the king of death and hell, are painted quite black, like demons, with horrible faces and great teeth. In their four hands they carry a trident, a club and many ropes; and in their girdles, daggers. Their business consiate in carrging the souls of the wicked into Naraka or hell; but they are not allowed to lay hold on any one before his fixed life-time is elapsed, and the souls of the pious they cannot touch at all, When, however, such die as are neither virtuous nor wicked; then it happens that the messengers of Yama and those of Śiva or Vishṇu come into conflict with each other, each party claiming the indifferent souls:"

DVAIPAYANA—(*see* VYĀSA)

DVAPARAYUGA—The third age of the world, extending to 860,000 years, (*see* YUGA)

DVARAKA, DVARAVATI—'The city of gates.' Kṛṣṇa's capital, in Gujarat, which is said to have been submerged by the ocean seven days after his death. It is one of the seven sacred cities .Also called Abdhinagarī.

DVIJARṢIS—(*see* BRAHMĀRṢIS).

DVIPA—An insular continent. The Dvīpas stretch out from the mountain Meru as their common centre, like the leaves of a lotus, and are separated from each other by distinct circumambient oceans. They are generally given as seven in number: (1) Jambu, (2) Plakṣa or Gomedaka, (3) Śālmala, (4) Kuśa, (5) Krauñca, (6) Śāka, (7) Puṣkara; and the seas which surround them are: (1) Lavaṇa, salt water; (2) Ikṣu, sugar-cane juice; (3) Surā, wine; (4) Sarpis or Ghṛta, clarified butter; (5) Dadhi, curds; (6) Dugdha or Kṣira, milk; (7) Jala, fresh water. In the *Mahābhārata* four *dvīpas* are named: (1) Bhadrāśva, (2) Ketumāla, (3) Jambudvīpa, (4) Uttara Kuru. Jambudvīpa has nine *varṣas* or subdivisions: (1) Bhārata, (2) Kiṁpuruṣa, Kinnara, (3) Harivarṣa, (4) Ilāvṛta, which contains Meru; (5) Ramyaka, (6) Hiraṇmaya, (7) Uttara Kuru, (8) Bhadrāśva, (9) Ketumāla. According to the *Viṣṇu Purāṇa*, Bhāratavarṣa or India is divided into nine *dvīpas* or portions: (1) Indradvīpa, (2) Kaś'erumat, (3) Tāmravarṇa, (4) Gabhastimat, (5) Nāgadvīpa, (6) Saumya, (7) Gāndharva, (8) Vāruṇa; (9) is generally left without a name in the books, but Bhāskara Ācārya calls it Kumāraka.

DVIVIDA—**(1)** An *asura* in the form of a great ape, who was an implacable foe of the gods. He stole Balarāma's ploughshare weapon and derided him. This was the beginning of a terrific fight, in which Dvivida was felled to the earth, and "the crest of the mountain on which he fell was splintered into a hundred pieces by the weight of his body, as if the Thunderer had shivered it with his thunderbolt." **(2)** A monkey ally of Rāma.

DWAPARA—The third Yuga or age, which lasts 2,400 divine years; these are converted into years of mortals by multiplying them by 360, a year of men being a day of the gods—thus 2,400 x 360 = 864,000 mortal years, the duration of the Dwápara or third Yuga. The predominant duties of the four Yugas are said to be austere fervour on the Kṛita age, knowledgo in the Tretá, sacrifice in the Dwápara, and liberality alone in the Kali Yuga. *O.S.T.*, vol. i, p. 39

DWARAKA—The city of Krishṇa; after he had conquered many difficulties in his position, he solicited a space of twelve furlongs from the ocean, and there he built the city of Dwáraka; defended by high ramparts, and beautiful with gardens and reservoirs of water, crowded with houses and buildings, aud splendid as the capital of Indra, Amarávati. After Krishṇa abandoned his mortal body, Arjuna conducted his many wives and all the people from Dwáraka, with tenderness and care. The ocean then rose and submerged the whole of Dwáraka except the dwelling of Krishṇa. The Vishṇu Purána says the sea has never been able to wash that temple away, as Krishṇa still abides there. The Mahábhárata declares that the sea did not spare any part whatever. "It is clear therefore;" says Professor Wilson, "that when the latter was compiled the temple was not standing, and that it was erected between the date of the compilation and the two Puránas. The present shrine, which is held in great repute, stands at the extremity of the peninsula of Guzerat: It is still an object of pilgrimage; it was so in the reign of Akbar; and has been no doubt, from a remote period."

DWESHA—Hatred; one of the five affictions of the Pátanjali philosophy.

DWIJA—Twice-born; a brahman, whose investiture with the sacred thread constitutes, religiously and metaphorically, their second birth. In this sense it may be applied to the Kshatriya and Vaishya.

DWIMIDHA—One of the sons of Hastin, founder of Hastinápura.

DWIMURDDHA—One of the Danavas, a son of Kaṣyapa by Danu.

DWIPA—Insular continents, of which there are seven chief, and with the seven seas are supposed to form alternate concentric; circles, *viz*: l, Jambu Dwípa, surrounded by a salt sea (Lavaṇa); 2, Plaksha, by a sea of sngar-cane juice, (Ikshu); 3, Sálmali, by a sea of wine, (Surá); 4; Kusa, by a sea of clarified butter, or ghee, (Sarpi); 5; Krauncha, by a sea of curds, (Dugdha); 7, Pushkara, by a sea of fresh water. The whole is surrounded by a circular mountain designated Chakravaligiri. An account of the kings, divisions, inhabitants, &c., of these Dwípas will he found in the *Vishṇu Purána*, Chap. IV, Book I. The geography of the Puránas, says Prof. Wilson, cccurs in most of these works; and in all the main features, the seven Dwípas, seven seas, the divisions of Jambudwípa, the situation and eztent of Meru, and the sub-division of Bharata, is the same. It has been stated that the first rudiments and general outline of this fiction, including the circular mountain, are rabbinical, and may be found in the Talmud.

DWIVIDA—**(1)** An Asura, the foe of the friends of the gods, which in the form of an ape, committed great devastation. "The whole world, disordered by this iniquitous monkey; was deprived of sacred study and religious rites, and was greatly afflicted." (*V.P.*) On one occasion, when Bala Ráma was enjoying himself in the groves of Raivata, the monkey Dwivida csme there, threw over the wine and groaned at the company. An encounter followed, in which the monkey struck the Yádava on the breast with his paws. Bala Ráma replied with a blow of his fist upon the forehead of Dwivida, which felled him lifeless to the earth. The crest of the mountain on which he fell was splintered into a hundred pieces by the weight of his body, as if the thnnderer had shivered it with his thunderbolt. *V.P.*, &c. **(2)** One of the sons of the Aṣvins, famed for his beauty.

DYAUS and PRITHIVI—Heaven and Earth, seemed to have been very ancient Aryan divinities, and are in many passages of the Rig Veda described as the parents of the other gods. There are several hymns specielly devoted to their honour. In the hymns, Heaven and Earth are characterized by a profusion of epithets, not only such as are suggested by their varions physical characteristics, as vastless, breadth, profundity, productiveness, unchangeableness, but also by such as are of a moral or spiritual nature, as innocuous or beneficent, wise promoters of righteousness.

While Heaven and Earth are described as the universal parents, they are spoken of in other places as themselves created Thus it is said in the Rig Veda that 'he who produced heaven and earth must have been the most skilful artizan of all the gods.' Indra also is described as their creator; as having beautifully fashioned them by his power and skill; as having bestowed them on his worshippers; as sustaining and upholding them, &c.

"In other passages we encounter various speculations about their origin. In one hymn the perplexed poet inquires which of these two was the first? and which the last ? How have they been produced? Sages who knows? In another hymn the creation of heaven and earth is ascribed to the sole agency of the god Viṣvakarman. Some are of opinion that the functions which in the older Indian Mythology were assigned to Dyaus, were at a later period transferred to Indra. *O.S.T.*, vol. v., pp. 21-34.

DYUMAT—One of the sons of the Rishi Vasishtha, according to the list in the Bhágavata, which differs altogether from that in the Vishṇu Purána.

DYUTIMAT—One of the ten sons of Priyavrata: three of them adopted a religious life: Priyavrata having divided the earth into seven continents, gave them respectively to his other seven sone. Dyutimat was king of Krauncha-dwipa, where the inhabitants resided without apprehension, associating with the bands of divinities.

DYUTIRNAN—The king of Krauncha Dwípa.

E—This sound means Devi.

EAR-RINGS—Among the various articles produced at the churning of the ocean, ear-rings are enumerated; these were taken by Indra and given to Aditi; the daughter of Daksha and wife of Kaṣyapa. The ear-rings were stolen by Naraka, son of the Earth, and conveyed by him to Prágjyotisha, "an impregnable, formidable and unassailable city of the Asuras." Krishṇa attacked the place, overcame all opposition; slew Naraka, recovered the jewelled ear-rings, and returning to the heaven of the gods, restored them to Aditi, who praised Krishṇa in verses which contain some remarkable sentiments. They will be found in the *V.P.*, 584-5.

EARTH—The Earth, considered as one of the ancient 'elements' occupies nearly the same place in all the Puránas. The order is, ether, (ákás) air, (váyu) fire, (tejas) water and earth. The order of Empedocles was ether, fire, earth, water, air. The Puránas describe the earth as having been raised from the lowest regions on the ample tusks of the Varáha (boar) avatar. The Bhágavata states that, when the earth, oppressed by the weight of the mountains, sunk down into the waters, Vishṇu was seen in the sub-terrene regions, or Rasátala, by Hiranyáksha, in the act of carrying it off. The demon claimed the Earth, and defied Vishṇu to combat: and a conflict took place in which Hiranyáksha was slain. There are legends which relate the subjugation of the Earth by the mighty Prithu, when he was invested with universal dominion. Prithu levelled or uprooted mountains; defined boundaries on the irregular surface of the Earth; introduced cultivation, pasture, highways, commerce, in a word, civilization. The Vishṇu Purána states, "This Earth, the mother, the nurse, the receptacle, and nourisher of all existent things, was produced from the sole of the foot of Vishṇu: And thus was born the mighty Prithu, the heroic son of Vena, who was the lord of the Earth, and who, from conciliating the affections of the people, was the first ruler to whom the title of Rája was ascribed.

Five chapters in the Vishṇu-Purána are devoted to a description of the Earth; its people and countries. Jambu-dwípa is placed in the centre of the seven great insular continents (see Dwipas) and in the centre of Jambu-dwípa is the golden mountain Meru—the shape of which is variously described in the different Puránas; though all represent it as if enormous size and great beauty. The apples of the Jamba-tree are as large as elephants; from their expressed juice is formed the Jamba river, the waters of which are drunk by the inhabitants; and in consequence of drinking of that stream they pass their days in content and health, neither exposed to decrepitude or decay. Ample details of the Varshas or countries, are given in most of the Puránas, but they are all of an equally fanciful and extravagant character.

The Vishṇu Purána says, "Sesha bears the entire world like a diadem, upon his head when Ananta, his eyes rolling with intoxication, yawns, then Earth, with all her woods and seas, and mountains, and rivers, trembles." In another place, "At the end of a thousand periods of four ages the Earth is for the most part exhausted. A total dearth then ensues which lasts a hundred years: and in consequence of the failure of food all beings become languid, and at last entirely perish. The eternal Vishṇu then assumes the character of Rudra the destroyer, and descends to re-unite all his creatures with himself. He enters into the seven rays of the sun; drinks up all the waters of the globe, and causes all moisture to evaporate, thus drying up the whole earth.

The destroyer of all things, Hari, in the form of Rudra, becomes the scorching breadth of the serpent Sésha, and thereby reduces Pátáḷa to ashes. The great fire, when it has burnt all the divisions of Pátála proceeds to the earth, and consumes it also." *V.P.*, 632.

ECLIPSE—The popular notion of the cause of an Eclipse current among the Hindus is founded on the following mythological legend. When the gods had obtained Amrita, (*q.v.*) or ambrosia, by the churning of the ocean of milk, one of the giants stole and drank some portion of it secretly. The sun and moon however observed the theft and informed Vishṇu of it, who upon this got very angry and severed the head of the giant from his trunk; but because the giant had tasted Amrita, both parts remained alive invisible in the sky; they are regarded as the eighth and ninth planets named Ketu and Rahu, and are said every now and then to take revenge on the sun and moon by swallowing them for a short time, thus causing eclipses.

EGG OF THE WORLD—In the Rig Veda the Supreme Spirit is represented as producing an egg, and from the egg is evolved a world. At a later period, Brahma is set forth as depositing in the primordial waters an egg shining like gold. The Purànas all contain accounts of the first aggregation of the elements in the form of an egg. The Vishṇu Purána says, "This vast egg, compounded of the elements, and resting on the waters, was the excellent natural abode of Vishṇu in the form of Brahmá; and there Vishṇu, the lord of the universe, whose essence is inscrutable; assumed a perceptible form, and even he himself abided in it in the character of Brahmá. "Its womb, vast as the mountain Meru, was composed of the mountains; and the mighty oceans were the waters that filled its cavity. In that egg, O Brahman, were the continents and seas and mountains, the planets and divisions of the universe, the gods, the demons, and mankind. And this egg was externally invested by seven natural envelopes, or by water, air, fire, ether, and Ahankára the origin of the elements, each tenfold the extent of that which it invested; next came the principle of intelligence; and, finally, the whole was surrounded by the indiscreet principle: resembling thus the cocoanut, filled interiorly with pulp, and exteriorly covered by husk and rind."

"It seems impossible," says Professor Wilson, "not to refer this notion to the same origin as the widely diffused opinion of antiquity, of the first manifestation of the world in the form of an egg." "It seems" says Bryant, "to have been a favourite symbol, and very ancient, and we find it adopted among many nations." Traces of it occur among the Syrians, Persians and Egyptians; and besides the Orphic egg amongst the Greeks, and that described by Aristophanes, part of the ceremony in the Dionysiaca and other mysteries, consisted of the consecration of an egg, by which, according to Porphyry, was signified the world:'/ "The shell of the mundane egg is said to be outside of the seven spheres of which this system is composed: In the *V.P.* ii, 7, 19 it is said.

"These seven spheres have been described by me; and there are also seven Pátálas; this is the extent of Brahmá's egg. The whole is surrounded by the shell of the egg at the sides, above and below, just as the seed of the wood apple is covered by the rind."

This system, however, it appears is only a very small part of the whole of the universe; in verse 24 it is added.

"There are thousands and ten thousands of thousands of such mundane eggs; may hundreds of millions of millions:"

"Indian mythology, when striving after sublimity, and seeking to excite astonishment, often displays an extravagant and puerile facility in the fabrication of large nnmbers. But in the sentence last quoted, its conjectures are substantially in unison with the discoveries of modern astronomy; or rather they are inadequate representations of the simple truth, as no figures can express the contents of infinite space."' Muir, *O.S.T.*, vol. i, p. 504.

EKA—"The one:" a synonym of Mahat, from its singleness. See MAHAT.

EKA-CAKRA—**(1)** A city in the country of the Kīcakas, where, by advice of Vyāsa, the Pāṇḍavas dwelt for a time during their exile. General Cunningham has identified it with the modern Ara or Arrah. **(2)**

One of the renowned Danavas, son of Danu and Kaṣyapa. **(3)** The city in which Bhíma and his mother and brethren were advised by tho sage Vyása to reside; they dwelt there for a long time in the house of a brahman. It was in this city that Bhíma destroyed the cannibal Vaka. "In the neighbourhood there lived a giant,—the same sort of being as the modern earth-goddess of Orissa; that is a demon who feeds on human beings." One day, it is said, the Páṇdavas heard a great noise in the house in which they were dwelling, and enquiring into its cause, were told that the demon compelled the king of Ekachakra every day to send him a great quantity of provisions; and that Vaka daily devoured the man as well as the provisions; and that on that very day the family of the brahman was required to supply the man. While reposing in an inner apartment the Páṇdavas overheard the father, the mother, and the daughter, each urging a separate claim to be allowed to suffer for the rest.

The father commences, saying, that never would he be so base as to give a victim from his house and consent himself to live; but still he expresses anxiety at not knowing how to provide a place of refuge for his wife, daughter, and little son, after his removal. He cannot, he says, surrender his faithful wife,—the sweet friend given to him by the gods; nor his daughter,—whom Brahma made to be a bride, and the mother of heroes; not yet his son:...but if he offer himself; sorrow will pursue him in the world to come, and his abandoned wife and children will be unable to live without him.

The wife next speaks, and chides her husband for yielding to grief, like one of lowly caste; for, whoever knows the Vedas, must know that—

"Fate, inevitable, orders;—all must yield to death in turn.
Hence the doom, th' irrevocable,—it beseems not thee to mourn.
Man hath wife, and son, and daughter,—for the joy of his own heart;
Wherefore, wisely check thy sorrow,—it is I must hence depart.
'Tis the wife's most holy duty,—law on earth without repeal,—
That her life she offer freely,—when demands her husband's weal."

She goes on to argue, that he can support and guard the children when she is gone, but that she would have no power to guard and support them without him. Deprived of his protection, "rude and reckless men," she says, would come seeking their blameless daughter; and helpless, and beset on every side, she would be unable to check the suit of Sudra lovers...She concludes, by saying, that her honored husband will find another wife, to whom he will be as gentle and kind as he has been to her.

"Hearing thus his wife, the husband fondly clasp'd her to his breast:
And their tears they pour'd together—by their mutual grief oppress'd."

When the daughter overheard the troubled discourse of her parents, she put in her claim to be the offered victim; for, if they died before her, she would sink to bitterest misery: but, if she died to preserve them, she would "then become immortal, and partake of bliss divine."

Whilst they were all thus weeping, the little son opened wide his eyes, and lisped out in broken accepts:

"Weep not, father, weep not, mother; oh, my sister, weep not so
First to one, and then to th' other, —smiling went he to and fro.
Then a blade of spear-grass lifting, thus in bolder glee he said:
With this spear-grass will I kill him—this man-eating giant—dead.'
Though o'erpowered with bitterest sorrow, as they heard their prattling boy,
Stole into the parents' bosom-mute and inexpressive joy."

Happily the child's chivalry was not required. After some discussion the brahman reluctantly consented that Bhíma should go himself to the Asura, and he set out with the ordained quantity of provisions, and went on until he came to the banyan tree under which Vaka was accustomed to eat his meals. Bhíma then ate up all the victuals that were in the waggon and refilled it with dirt. Vaka then came forward ravenous with hunger, and finding nothing but dirt, struck Bhíma in a great rage. They then tore up large trees by the roots and fought together until not a tree was left. They then fought with their fists until the Asura was spent; when Bhíma seized him by the legs and rent him asunder. The date of the story is fixed in the age of Buddhism. Ekachakra has been identified ae the modern Arrah. It was occupied by Brahmans who may be regarded as the later representatives of the Aryan population, while the jungle was evidently in the possession of the Asuras or Aborigines. (Mrs. Manning. *A. & M. I.*)

EKADANTA—'Having one tusk.' A name of Gaṇeśa.

EKADASI—Ekádaṣí is also the eleventh day after the new and full moon, observed by the Vaishnavas as a fast day. The fast kept on this day is known as Ekadasi Vrata.This vrata provides salvation who are looking for it. Those who observe the Ekadasi vrata should be on a regulated diet excluding meat and should avoid sexual acts on the last, the *Dasami* day. The vrata is not observed on a day which combines Dasami with Ekadasi / A ceremony performed on the eleventh day after the death of a relative. During the previous ten days the relatives are supposed to be mourning, and in a state of *asaucha* or impurities, so that no one can communicate with them. When Ekádaṣí is performed the period of uncleanness ceases.

EKALAVYA—**(1)** Grandson of Devaśravas, the brother of Vasudeva. He was brother of Śatrughna. He was exposed in infancy, and was brought up among the Niṣādas, of whom he became king. He assisted in a night attack upon Dvārakā, and was eventually killed by Kṛṣṇa, who hurled a rock at him. **(2)** The king of the Nishádas; he was regarded as invincible by mortals but was attacked and slain by Krishṇa.

EKAMRA, EKAMRA KANANA—A forest in Utkala or Orissa, which was the favourite haunt of Śiva, and became a great seat of his worship as the city of Bhuvaneśvara, where some very fine temples sacred to him still remain. They have been described by Bābū Rājendra Lāla in his great work on Orissa.

EKAPADA—'One-footed.' A fabulous race of men spoken of in the Purāṇas.

EKAPADAKAS—A nickname or term of derision, found in the geographical accounts of the Puránas; it means one-footed or rather, one-slippered, aud is probably an exaggeration of national ugliness, or allusion to some peculiar custom, in the people to whom the term is applied. Professor Wilson thinks that such terms, of which there are many in the Puránas, may have furnished the Mandevilles of ancient and modern times, with some of their monsters.

EKAPARNA, EKAPATALA—These, with their sister Aparṇā, were, according to the *Harivaṁśa*, daughters of Himavat and Menā. They performed austerities surpassing the powers of gods and *dānavas*, and alarmed both worlds. Ekaparṇā took only one leaf for food, and Ekapāṭalā only one *pāṭalā* (Bignonia). Aparṇā took no sustenance at all and lived *a-parṇa*, 'without a leaf. Her mother being distressed at her abstinence, exclaimed in her anxiety, "U-mā"—"Oh don't". Through this she became manifest as the lovely goddess Umā, the wife of Śiva.

EKASHTAKA—The daughter of Prajápati, who through practising austere-fervour, became the mother of the glorious Indra, and of Soma. According to other authorities, Indra is one of the sons of Kaṣyapa and Dakshâyani. *O.S.T.*, vol. v, p. 80.

EKASTAKA—A deity mentioned in the *Atharvaveda* as having practised austere devotion, and being the daughter of Prajāpati and mother of Indra and Soma.

EKAVINSA—The name of the collection of hymns created fiom the northern mouth of Brahma.

EKODDISHTA-SRADDA—Obsequial offerings on account of a kinsman recently deceased. These are performed monthly. The proper period of mourning is ten days, on each of which offerings of cakes and libations of water are to be made to the deceased, augmenting the number of cakes each day, so that in the last day, ten cakes are presented.

ELAPATRA—One of the progeny of Kadru, a powerful serpent, with many heads.

ELEPHANTA—"A small island about 7 miles in circumference, situated between the island of Bombay and the Mahratta shore, from which it is distant 5 miles, and 7 miles from the castle of Bombay. Its name among the natives is Gorapori; that by which it is known to Europeans was derived from the figure of an elephant twice the size of life cut out of the solid black rock on the acclivity of a hill about 250 yards from the landing-place. This figure is now completely dilapidated. At a short distance from the elephant stands the figure of a horse, also cut out of the rock. On this island is a remarkable temple-cave. The entrance to this cave, or temple, occurs about half way up the steep ascent of the mountain or rock out of which it is excavated. Its length, measuring from the entrance, which is on the north side, is 130 feet, and its breadth 123 feet; the floor not being level the height varies from 15 to 17½ feet. The roof was supported by 26 pillars and 8 pilasters, disposed in four rows; but several of the pillars are broken. Each column stands upon a square pedestal and is fluted, but instead of being cylindrical is gradually enlarged towards the middle. Above the tops of the columns a kind of ridge has been cut to resemble a beam about 12 inches square, and this is richly carved. Along the sides of the temple are carved between 40 and 50 colossal figures varying in height from 12 to 15 feet; none of them are entirely detached from the wall. On the south side, facing the main entrance, is an enormous bust with three faces, which is supposed to represent the triple deity, Brahma, Vishṇu, and Śiva. The centre face is 5 feet in length. At the west side of the temple is a recess, 20 feet square, having in the centre an altar. The entrance to this recess is guarded by eight naked figures, each 13½ feet high, sculptured in a superior manner. The origin of this cave is quite unknown: it is frequently visited by devotees for the purpose of offering prayers and oblations.—*English Encyclopædia.*

ELLAMMA—One of the grámadévatas in Southern India—identified with Renuká, wife of Jamadagni, mother of Parasuráma, Ellammá is represented in a sitting posture, with a red skin, a fiery face, and four arms and hands. If any one is bitten by a poisonous serpent he calls on Ellamma for aid. Fishermen when in danger call on Ellamma and make vows to her.

ELLORA—A town in the province of Aurangabad, and near to the city of Dowlatabad. In one instance, about a mile to the eastward of the village the side of a great mountain has been excavated, so as to give a level floor 250 feet wide by 370 feet in length. In the centre stands the rock-cut temple called Kailâs, similar in form to the Pagoda at Tanjore. It is between 80 and 90 feet high, and is preceded by a large square porch, supported by sixteen columns. In the front of this stands a detached porch, reached by a bridge; and again, in front of the whole, a gateway, connected with the last porch by a rock-cut bridge, and flanked on either side by pillars or deepdans (which word is literally lamp-post.) Two elephants, the site of life, are also mentioned; and all around the court are cloisters, with cells. And the whole,—pillars, cloisters, halls, bridges, and vimâna,—are sculptured out of the rock.—Mrs. Manning. *A. and M. I.*, Vol. 1, p. 420.

ELU—A dialect of the ancient Singhalese, which differs from the colloquial Singhalese, rather in style than in stracture, having been liberally enriched by incorporation from Sanskrit and Pali. Mr. Spence Hardy mentions a number of Buddhist works which are written in Elu.

The word in Malyalam means "Seven". The figure of Seven has a special significance in the Puranas as there are:

1. Seven Qualities described for man – Dhairya (courage), Sama (forebearence), Dama (control of the senses), Shtiva (cleanliness), Daya (compassion), Mrduvak (Geniality of speech), and Ahimsa (non-violence)
2. Seven Chiranjivies (beings with perrinial life span) – Aswathama, Bali, Vyasa, Hanuman, Vibhisana, Kṛpa, and Parsurama
3. Seven Rivers – Ganga, Yamuna, Godavari, Sarasvati, Narmada, Sindhu and Kaveri.
4. Seven Nadis – Ida, Pingla, Susumna, Musa, Alambusa, Asthijihva and Gandhari.
5. Seven Wives of Vasudeva – Devaki, Srutadeva, Yasoda, Srutisravas, Upadeva and Surupa
6. Seven Mountains – Himavan, Nisadha, Vindhya, Malyavan, Pariyatra, Gandhamadana and Hemakuta.
7. Seven Patalas – Atala, Vitala, Sutala, Nitala, Talatala, Rasatala and Mahatala.
8. Seven Holy Places – Ayodhya, Mathura, Gaya, Kasi, Kanchi, Avanti, and Dvaravati.
9. Seven Maruts – Avaha, Samvaha, Pravaha, Udvaha, Vivaha, Parivaha, and paravaha.
10. Seven Forests – Kamyaka, Aditi, Vyasa, Phalki, Surya, Madhu and Sita.
11. Seven Defects (*Dosasa*) – Laziness, Arrogance, Ignorance, Profligacy, Hauteur, Pride and Selfishness.
12. Seven Vices – Hunting, dice, womenising, drinking, squandering, harshness of speech and cruality.
13. Seven Seas – Lavana, Iksu, Sura, Sarpis, Dadhi, Ksira and Suddhodaka.
14. Seven Notes in Music – Sadja, rsabha, Gandhara, Madhyama, Panchama, Dhaivata and Nisada.

EMUSA—In the *Brāhmaṇa*, a boar which raised up the earth, represented as black and with a hundred arms. This is probably the germ of the Varāha or boar incarnation, (*see* Avatāra). "Formerly this earth was only so large, of the size of a span. A boar called Emúsha, raised her up. Her lord Prajápati, therefore, prospers him with (the gift of) this pair, the object of his desire, and makes him complete." *O.S.T.*, vol. i, p. 53.

ERANNOBOAS—The ancient name of the river Sone. The ancient city of Palibothra stood at the confluence of the Ganges and Erannoboas. "The capital of Chandragupta, Pátaliputra, was no doubt the same as the Palibothra of Sandracottus, the modern Patna. But exception was taken on the ground that Patna was not situated near the confluence of the Ganges and Sone, or Erannoboas, where Palibothra stood. This, however, has been explained by a change in the bed of the river Sone, which is established on the best geographical evidences." (Max Müller, *A.S.L.*, p. 280.)

EREENIA—The benevolent Glendoveer (Gandharba) in Southey's poem "the curse of Kehama."

ETTAIA—A place in the North-west of India, said to be the scene of a conflict between Krishṇa and Kali; where some fine ruins still exist.

EXPIATION—The Vishṇu Purána says that "suitable acts of expiation have been enjoined by the great sages for every kind of crime. Arduous penances for great sins, trifling ones for minor offences, have been propounded by Swápambhuva and others: but reliance upon Krishṇa is far better than any such expiatory acts, as religious austerity or the like. Let any one who repents of the sin of which he may have been culpable, have recourse to this best of all expiations, remembrance of Hari; by addressing his thoughts to Nárayaṇa at dawn, at night, at sunset, and midday, a man shall be quickly cleansed from all guilt: the whole heap of worldly sorrows is dispersed by meditating on Hari; and his worshipper, looking upon heavenly fruition as an impediment to felicity, obtains final emancipation."

FAITH—The paramount efficacy of faith is a tenet of the Vedánta school; particularly that branch of it which follows the authority of the Bhagavat Gíta. In that work, and in many of the Puránas, passages relating to faith constantly recur.

FAKIR—The word Fakír is derived from an Arabic term signifying "poor people," and belongs strictly to those who profess Mahomedanism, not to Hindus. But the word is sometimes used by Europeans to designate all classes of monks, who subject themselves to austerities and mortifications. Some of them vow to preserve a standing posture during their whole lives, supported only by a stick or rope under their armpits. Some mangle their bodies with scourges or knives. Others wander about in companies, telling fortunes, and in other ways imposing on the people. Some go aboat as mendicants asking alms in the name of God. *See* SANYASI.

FERINGAHI—A name of Párvati or Devi.

FEVER—In the Vishṇu Purána, Fever is personified, as an emanation from Maheṣwara, having three feet and three heads, (alluding, says Dr. Wilson, to the three stages of febrile paroxysms, or to the recurrence of tertian ague). Fever fought desperately with Vishṇu in defence of the city of Báṇa. Baladeva, upon whom his ashes were scattered, was seized with burning heat, and his eyelids trembled: but he obtained relief by clinging to the body of Krishṇa. The fever emanating from Śiva was quickly expelled from the person of Krishṇa by fever which he himself engendered. Brahma beholding the impersonated malady, bewildered by the beating inflicted by the arms of the deity, entreated the latter to desist; and the foe of Madhu refrained, and absorbed into himself the fever he had created. The rival fever then departed, saying to Krishṇa, "Those men who call to memory the combat between us shall be for ever exempt from terrible disease."

FIRES—According to the Vishṇu Purána there are forty-nine fires. The Agni named Abhimání, who is the eldest born of Brahmá, had, by Swáhá, three sons of surpassing brilliancy, Pávaka Pavámana, and Suchi, who drinks up water: they had forty-five sons, who, with the original son of Brahmá and his three descendants, constitute the forty-nine fires. According to the Vaya Purána, Pávaka is electric, or Vaidyuta fire; Pavamána is that produced by friction, or Nirmathyaya, and Suchi is solar, or Saura fire. The Bhágavata explains these different fires to be so many appellations of fire employed in the invocations with which different oblations to fire are offered in the ritual of the Vedas.

FIRE-SACRIFICIAL—The ceremony of consecrating the fire and hallowing the sacrificial implements is the groundwork of all religious acts amongst the Hindus, and may therefore be particularly described—"First, the priest smears with cow-dung a level piece of ground four cubits square, free from all impurities and sheltered by a shed. Having bathed and sipped water, he sits down with his face towards the east, and places a vessel of water with *kuśa* grass on his left; then, dropping his right knee, and resting on the span of his left hand, he draws with a root of *kuśa* grass a line, one span or twelve fingers long, and directed towards the east. From the nearest extremity of this line he draws another at right angles to it, twenty-one fingers long, and directed towards the north. Upon this line he draws three others, parallel to the first, equal to it in length, and distant seven fingers from each other. The first line is really, or figuratively, made a yellow line, and is sacred to the earth; the second is red, and sacred to fire; the third black, and sacred to *Brahma* the creator; the fourth blue, and sacred to *Indra*, the regent of the firmament; the fifth white, and sacred to Sóma. He next gathers up the dust from the edges of these lines, and throws it away towards the north-east, saying, "What was [herein] bad, is cast away:" and he concludes by sprinkling water on the several lines.

Having thus prepared the ground for the reception of the sacrificial fire, he takes a lighted ember out of the covered vessel which contains the fire, and throws it away, saying, "I dismiss far 'away carnivorous fire; may it go to the realm of *Yama*, bearing "sin [hence]." He then places the fire before him, saying, "Earth! Sky ! Heaven !" and adding, "this other [harmless] fire "alone remains here; well knowing [its office], may it convey my "oblation to the gods." He then denominates the fire according to the purpose for which he prepares it, saying, "Fire ! thou art named so and so;" and he concludes this part of the ceremony by silently burning a log of wood, one span long and smeared with clarified butter.

He next proceeds to place the *Brahman* or superintending priest. Upon very solemn occasions, a learned *Brahman* does actually discharge the functions of superintending priest; but, in general, a bundle containing fifty blades of *kuśa* grass is placed to represent the *Brahman*. The officiating priest takes up the vessel of water, and walks round the fire keeping his right side turned towards it: he then pours water near it, directing the stream towards the east; he spreads *kuśa* grass thereon; and crossing his right knee over his left without sitting down, he takes up a single blade of grass between the thumb and ring finger of his left hand, and throws it away towards the south-west corner of the shed, saying, "What was herein bad, is cast away." Next, touching the water, resting the sole of his right foot on his left ankle, and sprinkling the grass with water, he places the *Brahman* on it, saying, "Sit on [this] seat until [thy] fee [be paid thee]." The officiating priest then returns by the same road by which he went round the fire; and sitting down again with his face towards the east, names the earth inaudibly.

If any profane word have been spoken during the preceding ceremony, atonement must be now made by pronouncing this text: "Thrice did *Vishnu* step, and at three strides traversed the "universe: happily was his foot placed on the dusty [earth]." "The meaning is, since the earth has been purified by the contact of *Vishnu's* foot, may she (the earth so purified) atone for any profane word spoken during this ceremony.

If it be intended to make oblations of rice mixed with milk, curds, and butter, this too is the proper time for mixing them; and the priest afterwards proceeds to name the earth in the following prayer, which he pronounces with downcast look, resting both hands on the ground: "We adore this earth, this auspicious and most excellent earth: do thou, O fire I resist [our] enemies. Thon dost take [on thee] the power [and office] of other [deities]."

With blades of *kuśa* grass held in his right hand, he must next strew lea:.es of the same grass on three sides of the fire, arranging them regularly, so that the tip of one row shall cover the roote of the other. He begins with the eastern side, and at three times strews grass there, to cover the whole space from north to south; and in like manner distributes grass on the southern and western sides. He then blesses the ten regions of space; and rising a little, puts gome wood on the fire with a ladle-full of clarified butter, while he meditates in silence on Brahma, the lord of creatures.

The priest then takes up two leaves of *kuśa* grass, and with another blade of the same grass cuts off the length of a span, saying, "Pure leaves ! be sacred to Vishṇu;" and throws them into a vessel of copper or other metal. Again he takes two leaves of grass, and holding the tips between the thumb and ring finger of his right hand, and the roots between the thumb and ring finger of his left, and crossing his right hand over his left, he takes up clarified butter on the curvature of the grass, and thus silently casts some into the fire three several times. He then sprinkles both the leaves with water, and throws them away. He afterwards sprinkles with water the vessel containing clarified butter, and puts it on the fire, and takes it off again, three times, and thus concludes the ceremony of hallowing the butter; during the course of which, while be holds the leaves of grass in both hands, he recites this prayer: "May the divine generator [*Vishṇu*] purify thee by means of [this] faultless pure leaf; and may the sun do so, by means of [his] rays of light: be this oblation efficacious."

The priest must next hallow the wooden ladle by thrice turning therein his four-finger and thumb, describing with their tips the figure of 7 in the inside, and the figure of 9 on the outside of the bowl of the ladle. Then dropping his right knee, he sprinkles water from the palms of his hands on the whole southern side of the fire, from west to east, saying, "*Aditi!* [mother of the gods !] grant me thy approbation." He does the same on the whole western side, from south to north, saying, "*Anumati!* grant me thy approbation;" and on the northern side, saying, "*Saraswati !* grant me thy approbation." And lastly he sprinkles water all round the fire, while he pronounces this text, "Generous sun! approve this rite; approve the performer of it, that he may share its reward. May the celestial luminary, which purifies the intellectual soul, purify our minds. May the lord speech make our prayers acceptable."

Holding *kuśa* grass in both hands, he then recites an expiatory prayer; and throwing away the grass, he thus finishes the hallowing of the sacrificial implements: a ceremony which necessarily precedes all other religious rites.

He next makes oblations to fire, with such ceremonies, and in such form as are adapted to the religious rite which is intended to to be subsequently performed. The sacrifice, with the three mysterious words, usually precedes and follows the particular sacrifice which is suited to the occasion; being most generally practised, it will be the most proper specimen of the form in which oblations are made.

Having silently burnt a log of wood smeared with clarified butter, the priest mates three oblations, by pouring each time a ladle-full of butter on the fire, saying, "Earth ! be this oblation efficacious:" "Sky! be this oblation efficacious:" "Heaven ! be this oblation efficacious." On some occasions he makes a fourth offering in a similar mode, saying, "Earth ! Sky ! Heaven ! be this oblation efficacious." If it be requisite to offer a mixture of rice, milk, curds and butter, this is now done; and the oblations, accompanied with the names of the three worlds, are repeated.

There are five fires, which were overcome and demolished by Vishṇu. Their names are the Áhavaniya, Gárhapatya, Dakshins, Sabhya and Ávasathya; of which the three first have a religious, and the other two a secular character. The first is a fire prepared for oblations at an occasional sacrifice: the second is the household fire, to be perpetually maintained: the third is a sacrificial fire, in the centre of the other two, and placed to the south: the Sabhya is a fire lighted to warm a party: and the Ávasathya, the common domestic or culinary fire. *Mann*, iii, 100, 185, and Kullúka Bhatta's explanation.

Brahmans who devote themselves to the priesthood have to maintain a perpetual fire. They have also to worship fire, making an oblation to it with this prayer: Fire ! seven are thy fuels; seven thy tongues; seven thy holy sages; seven thy beloved abodes; seven ways do seven sacrifices worship thee. Thy sources are seven. Be content with this clarified butter. May this oblation be efficacious.

The seven tongues of fire are enumerated *Pravaha*, *Avaha*, *Udvaha*, *Samvaha*, *Vivaha*, *Parivaha*, *Nivaha*, all of which imply the power of conveying oblations, to the deities to whom offerings are made. Fire, like the sun itself, is supposed to emit seven rays; this perhaps may account for the number seven being so often repeated."—Colebrooke's *Essays, vol. I, p.* 153.

FREE-WILL—The *Mimánsa* philosophy in effect denies the doctrine of free-will; but endeavours to reconcile the existence of moral evil under the government of an all-wise, all-powerful and benevolent Providence, with the absence of free-will, by assuming the past eternity of the universe, and the infinite renewals of worlds, into which every individual being has brought the pre-dispositions contracted by him in earlier states, and so retrospectively, without beginning or limit.

G—The letter G means Vinayaka and also Gandharvas.

GABHASTIMAT—One of the nine divisions of Bharata varsha. Also the name of one of the divisions of Patála.

GACHCHAS—One of the peoples enumerated in the Vishnu Purána, but not identified.

GADA—**(1)** A son of Vasudeva by Bhadra; **(2)** The name of Bhíma's formidable weapon. **(3)** A younger brother of Kṛṣṇa.

GADHI, GATHIN—A king of the Kuśika race, and father of Viśwāmitra. He was son of Kuśāmba, or, according to the *Viṣṇu Purāṇa*, he was Indra, who took upon himself that form.

An incarnation of Indra, born as the son of Rája Kusámba. Kusámba being desirous of a son, engaged in devout penance to obtain ore who should be equal to Indra. Observing the intensity of his devotions, Indra was alarmed, lest a prince of power like his own should be engendered, and determined therefore to take upon himself the character of Ku[s.]ámba's son, Gádhi, the father of Viswámitra.

GAHVARAS—Dwellers in mountain caves. The mountains from Cabal to Bamian furnish numerous instances of cavern habitations.

GAJASURA—A Titan or Asura in the form of an elephant, who was killed by Śiva. Part of the scanty raiment worn by Śiva consists of the skin of the above elephant.

GAJAVITHI—The second division (or Vithi) of the lunar mansions, in the northern Avashtána.

GALAVA—A pupil of Viśvāmitra. It is related in the *Mahābhārata* that at the conclusion of his studies he importuned his master to say what present he should make him. Viśvāmitra was annoyed, and told him to bring 800 white horses, each having one black ear. In his perplexity Gālava applied to Garuḍa, who took him to king Yayāti at Pratiṣṭhāna. The king was unable to provide the horses, but he gave to Gālava his daughter Mādhavi. Gālava gave her in marriage successively to Haryaśva, king of Ayodhyā, Divodāsa, king of Kāśī, and Uśinara, king of Bhoja, receiving from each of them 200 of the horses he was in quest of, upon the birth of a son to each from Mādhavī. Notwithstanding her triple marriage and maternity, Mādhavī, by a special boon, remained a virgin. Gālava presented her and the horses to Viśvāmitra.The sage accepted them, and had a son by Mādhavī, who was named Aṣṭaka. When Viśvāmitra retired to the woods, he resigned his hermitage and his horses to Aṣṭaka, and Gālava having taken Mādhavi back to her father, himself retired to the forest as his preceptor had done. The horses were first obtained by the brāhmaṇa Ṛcīka from the god Varuṇa. They were originally 1000 in number, but his descendants sold 600 of them, and gave the rest away to brāhmaṇas.

According to the *Harivaṁśa*, Gālava was son of Viśvāmitra, and that sage in a time of great distress tied a cord round his waist and offered him for sale. Prince Satyavrata (*q.v.*) gave him liberty and restored him to his father. From his having been bound with a cord (*gala*) he was called Gālava.

There was a teacher of the White *Yajurveda* named Gālava, and also an old grammarian named by Pāṇini.

GAMES—There are many public games described in the various Puránas; and an account of each will be found under its native name.

GANA-DEVATAS—'Troops of deities.' Deities who generally appear, or are spoken of, in classes. Nine such classes are mentioned: (1) Ādityas; (2) Viśvas or Viśvedevas; (3) Vasus; (4) Tuṣitas; (5) Ābhāsvaras; (6)Anilas; (7) Mahārājikas; (8) Sādhyas; (9) Rudras. These inferior deities are attendant upon Śiva, and under the command of Gaṇeśa. They dwell on Gaṇaparvata, *i.e.*, Kailāsa.

GANANATHAS—Messengers of the gods. Sec Dútas.

GANA-PATI—(*see* GAṆEŚA)

GANAPATYA—A small sect who worship Gaṇapati or Gaṇeśa as their chief deity. The worshippers of Ganésa, or Ganapati; all the Hindus in fact, worship this deity as the obviator of impediments, and never set off on a journey without invoking his protection.

GANAS—(*see* GAṆA-DEVATĀS)

GANDAKI—The river Gaṇḍak (vulg. Gunduk), in Oude.

GANDAKI—A large river in Oude.

GANDHAKALI—An Apsara, who had been condemned by a sage, whose reflections had been disturbed by her beauty, to wear the form of a crocodile, and was released by Hanumán who slew the crocodile in the lake of Gandhamádana.

GANDHAMADANA—'Intoxicating with fragrance.' **(1)** A mountain and forest in Ilāvṛta, the central region of- the world, which contains the mountain Meru. The authorities are not agreed as to its relative position with Meru. **(2)** One of the generals in Rama's army at the siege of Lanka; he was wounded by the magical weapons of Indrajit and left on the field for dead, but was restored to life by the medicinal herbs brought by Hanuman from the golden hill Rishaba, on the crest of Kailása. Although he is represented as being a large and powerful monkey, he is said to have been the son of Kuvera, the god of wealth

"Of Gandhamádan brave and bold. The father was the Lord of gold."

GANDHAMOJAVAHA—A son of Swaphalka, by his wife Gándiní.

GANDHARA, GANDHARA—(1) A country and city on the west bank of the Indus about Attock. Mahomedan geographers call it Kandahār, but it must not be confounded with the modern town of that name. It is the Gandaritis of the ancients, and its people are the Gandarii of Herodotus. The *Vāyu Purāṇa* says it was famous for its breed of horses.

According to ancient Indian geography this land stretched from the shores of river Sindhu to Kabul. According to the Agni Purana there is a relationship between the Gandharas and dravidas In descending order from Visnu were Candra – Budha – Pururvas – Ayus – Nahusa – Yayati – Turvasu. In order from Turvasu were Varga – Gobhanu – Traisani – Karandhama – Marutta – Dusyanta – Varutha – Gandhira – Gandhara. From the Gandharas arose the famous amd pewerful dynasties of Colas, Pandyas, Kolas and Keralas. **(2)** A prince, the son of Aradwat, a descendant of Druhyu.

GANDHARBA LOKA—The region of celestial spirits, the sphere or lóka above the earth to which Súdras are elevated after death.

GANDHARBA MARRIAGE—A form of wedlock requiring no public ceremony, but which is nevertheless, recognised in ancient Hindu law as legal for kings and warriors.

GANDHARBA VEDA—The drama, and the arts of music, dancing, etc., of which the Muni Bhárata was the author; and the Artha Sastrum, or Science of Government, as laid down first by Vrihaspati.

GANDHARBA—One of the nine divisions, or dwípas, of Bharata Varsha.

GANDHARBAS or GANDHARVAS—(1) (Southey's Glendoveer's.) A race born from Bramhá, described in the Vishnu Purána as "born imbibing melody; drinking of the goddess of speech they were born, and thence their appellation." (Gam dhayantah). They are a species of demi-gods or angels, the musicians of heaven, inhabiting Indra loka, the paradise of the deities, and witnesses of the actions of men. They form the orchestra at the banquet of the gods. In the creation of the second Manwantara they are called the illustrious Gandharbas, the children of Arishtá and Kasyapa. In the Vishnu Purána it is said, "in the regions below the earth, the Gandharbas, called Maneyas (or sons of the Muni Kasyapa) who were sixty millions in number, had defeated the tribes of the Nágas or snake-gods, and seized upon their most precious jewels, and usurped their dominion." Narmadá, the personified Nerbudda river, was the sister of the Nágas, and on her aid being solicited, she went to Purukutsa, and conducted him to the regions below the earth, where, being filled with the might of the deity, he destroyed the Gandharbas. They originally belong to the latter Epic period, but figure more prominently in the Puránas.

"The Gandharvas or heavenly bards had originally a warlike character, but were afterwards reduced to the office of celestial musicians cheering the banquets of the gods. Dr. Kuhn has shown their identity with the Centaurs in name, origin, and attributes."—*Gorresio.* **(2)** The 'heavenly *gandharva*' of the Veda was a deity who knew and revealed the secrets of heaven and divine truths in general. He is thought by Goldstücker to have been a personification of the fire of the sun. The *gandharvas* generally had their dwelling in the sky or atmosphere, and one of their offices was to prepare the heavenly *soma* juice for the gods. They had a great partiality for women, and had a mystic power over them. The *Atharvaveda* speaks of "the 6333 *gandharvas*". The *gandharvas* of later times are similar in character; they have charge of the *soma*, are skilled in medicine, regulate the asterisms and are fond of women. Those of Indra's heaven are generally intended by the term, and they are singers and musicians who attend the banquets of the gods. The Purāṇas give contradictory accounts of the origin of the *gandharvas.* The *Viṣṇu Purāṇa* says, in one place, that they were born Brahmā, "imbibing melody. Drinking of the goddess of speech (*gām dhayantaḥ*), they were horn, and thence their appellation." Later on it says that they were the offspring of Kaśyapa and his wife Ariṣta. The *Harivaṁśa* states that they sprang from Brahmā's nose, and also that they were descended from Muni, another of Kaśyapa's wives. Chitrarathawas chief of the *gandharvas*; and the *apsarases* were their wives or mistresses. The "cities of the *gandharvas*" are often referred to as being very splendid. The *Viṣṇu Purāṇa* has a legend of the *gandharvas* fighting with the Nāgas in the infernal regions, whose dominions they seized and whose treasures they plundered. The

Nāga chiefs appealed to Viṣṇu for relief, and he promised to appear in the person of Purukutsa to help them. Thereupon the Nāgas sent their sister Narmadā (the Nerbudda river) to this Purukutsa, and she conducted him to the regions below, where he destroyed the *gandharvas.* They are sometimes called Gātus and Pulakas. In the *Mahābhārata*, apparently, a race of people dwelling in the hills and wilds is so-called.

GANDHARBI—The daughter of Surabhi, and parent of horses.

GANDHARI—Princess of Gandhāra. The daughter of Subala, king of Gandhāra, wife of Dhṛtarāṣṭra, and mother of his hundred sons. Her husband was blind, so she always wore a bandage over her eyes to be like him. Her husband and she, in their old age, both perished in a forest fire. She is also called by the patronymics Saubalī and Saubaleyī. She is said to have owed her hundred sons to the blessing of Vyāsa, who, in acknowledgement of her kind hospitality, offered her a boon. She asked for a hundred sons. Then she became pregnant, and continued so for two years, at the end of which time she was delivered of a lump of flesh. Vyāsa took the shapeless mass and divided it into 101 pieces, which he placed in as many jars. In due time Duryodhana was produced, but with such accompanying fearful portents that Dhṛtarāṣṭra was besought, though in vain, to abandon him. A month afterwards ninety-nine other sons came forth, and an only daughter, Duḥśalā.

GANDHARVALOKA—(*see* LOKA)

GANDHARVAVEDA—The science of music and song, which is-considered to include the drama and dancing. It is an appendix of the *Sāmaveda*, and its invention is ascribed to the muni Bharata.

GANDINI—**(1)** Daughter of Kāśirāja: the following legend of her birth is told in the *V.P.*, "when the time of delivery arrived the child issued not from the womb, twelve years passed away and still the girl was unborn. Then Kásirája spoke to the child 'Daughter, why is your birth thus delayed ? come forth. I desire to behold you; why do you inflict this protracted suffering upon your mother ? Thus addressed, the infant answered, if, father, you will present a cow every day to the brahmans I shall at the end of three years more be born.' The king accordingly presented daily a cow to the brahmans, and at the end of three years the damsel came into the world. Her father called her Gándiní, and he subsequently gave her to Swaphalka when he came to his palace. Gándiní as long as she lived, gave a cow to the brahmans every day." **(2)** The Gaṅgā or Ganges.

GANDIVA—It was Brahma who made this bow which was enough to fight a hundred thousand opponents at the same time. Brahma kept the bow for a 1000 years. For the next 1000 years it was kept by Prajapati, who gave it to Indra. Indra kept the bow for 3585 years, and gave it to Chandra who kept it for 500 years with him. He gave it Varuna who kept it for 100 years. Arjuna was the final receipint of the bow who used it in the great Bharata war and kept it for 65 years. It was returned to Agni at the shores of the Red Sea when the Pandavas, after installing Parikshit as the monarch, were on their great final journey.

GANDUSHA—One of the ten sons of Súra, and brother of Vásudeva.

GANESA (GAṆA + ĪŚA), GAṆAPATI—Lord of the *gaṇas* or troops of inferior deities, especially those attendant upon Śiva. Son of Śiva and Pārvatī, or of Pārvatī only. One legend represents that he sprang from the scurf of Pārvatī's body. He is the god of wisdom and remover of obstacles; hence he is invariably propitiated at the beginning of any important undertaking, and is invoked at the commencement of books. He is said to have written down the *Mahābhārata* from the dictation of Vyāsa. He is represented as a short fat man of a yellow colour, with a protuberant belly, four hands, and the head of an elephant, which has only one tusk. In one hand he holds a shell, in another a discus, in the third a club or goad, and in the fourth a water-lily. Sometimes he is depicted riding upon a rat or attended by one; hence his appellation Akhuratha. His temples are very numerous in the Dakhin. There is a variety of legends accounting for his elephant head. One is that his mother Pārvatī, proud of her offspring, asked Śani (Saturn) to look at him, forgetful of the effects of Śani's glance. Śani looked and the child's head was burnt to ashes. Brahmā told Pārvatī in her distress to replace the head with the first she could find, and that was an elephant's. Another story is that Pārvatī went to her bath and told her son to keep the door. Śiva wished to enter and was opposed, so he cut off Genesa's head. To pacify Pārvatī he replaced it with an elephant's, the first that came to hand. Another version is that his mother formed him so to suit her own fancy, and a further explanation is that Śiva slew Āditya the sun, but restored him to life again. For this violence Kaśyapa doomed Śiva's son to lose his head; and when he did lose it, the head of Indra's elephant was used to replace it. The loss of one tusk is accounted for by a legend which represents Paraśurāma as coming to Kailāsa on a visit to Śiva. The god was asleep and Gaṇeśa opposed the entrance of the visitor to the inner apartmentrs. A wrangle ensued, which ended in a fight. "Gaṇeśa had at first the advantage, seizing Paraśurāma with his trunk and giving him a twirl that left him sick and senseless. On recovering, Paraśurāma threw his axe at Gaṇeśa, who, recognising it as his father's weapon (Śiva having given it to Paraśurāma), received it with all humility on one of his tusks, which it immediately severed; hence Gaṇeśa has but one tusk, and is known by the name of Ekadanta or Ekadaṁṣṭra (the single-tusked). These legends are narrated at length in the *Brahma Vaivartta Purāṇa.*/ Gaṇeśais also called Gajānana, Gajavadana, and Karimukha, 'elephant-faced'; Heramba'; 'boastfal'; Lambakarṇa, 'long-eared'; Lambodara, 'pendant-bellied;' Dvideha, 'double bodied'; Vighneśa, Vighnhāri, 'remover of obstacles'. A peculiar appellation is Dvaimātura, 'having two mothers', in allusion, it is said, to his birth from the scurf of Pārvatī's body.

GANESA PURANA—An Upa Purāṇa having especial reference to the glory and greatness of Gaṇeśa.

GANESA—A distinguished Hindu mathematician and astronomer who lived in A. D. 1520.

GANESA-GITA—The *Bhagavad Gītā*, but with the name of Gaṇeśa substituted for that of Kṛṣṇa. It is used by the the Gāṇaptyas or worshippers of Gaṇeśa.

GANGA—The sacred river Ganges. It is said to be mentioned only twice-in the *Ṛgveda*. The Purāṇas represent the Viyadgaṅgā, or heavenly Ganges, to flow from the toe of Viṣṇu, and to have been brought down from heaven, by the prayers of the saint Bhagīratha, to purify the ashes of the sixty thousand sons of King Sagara, who had been burnt by the angry glance of the sage Kapila. Ságara king of Ayódhya had by one of his wives sixty thousand sons. Whilst performing the horse sacrifice, the horse was stolen. He commanded his sons to go and search for it. Not finding it on the earth, they dug down to Pátála, where they found the horse feeding, and Kapila Muní near it in profound meditation. On being charged with the theft, he by one glance reduced them all to ashes. On account of their long absence, Ságara sent his grandson, Ansumat, to seek for them. He found their ashes, and *the* horse feeding near them. Unable to find water to pour on the ashes, he was directed by Kapila (who was a minor incarnation of Vishnu,) not to pour common water upon them, but now to take the horse and complete his grandfather's sacrifice; and be assured that his (Ansumat's) grandson should obtain for their ashes the heavenly Ganges. Ságara reigned 30,000 years; Ansumat 32,000; his son Dilípa 30,000; his grandson Bhagíratha intent, as his ancestors had been, on bringing down the Ganges, persevered in a long course of austerities. After 1000 years Brahma signified bis pleasure by commanding him to ask a boon. He begged that the sons of Ságara might obtain water for their funeral rites; that, their ashes being wetted by the celestial Ganges, they might ascend to heaven. Brahma granted his request on condition that he prevailed on Siva to break the fall of the waters; else the earth would be washed away. From this earthly parent the river is called Bhāgīrathī. Gaṅgā was angry at being brought down from heaven, and Śiva, to save the earth from the shock of her fall, caught the river on his brow, and checked its course with his matted locks. From this action he is called Gaṅgādhara, 'upholder of the Ganges'. The river descended from Śiva's brow in several streams, four according to some, and ten according to others, but the number generally accepted is seven, being the Sapta-sindhava, the seven *sindhus* or rivers. The Ganges proper is one of the number. The descent of the Ganges disturbed the sage Jahnu as he was performing a sacrifice, and in his anger he drank up the waters, but he relented and allowed the river to flow from his ear, hence, the Ganges has the name of Jāhnavi. Personified as a goddess, Gaṅgā is the eldest daughter of Himavat and Menā, and her sister was Umā. She became the wife of King Śāntanu and bore a son, Bhīṣma; who is also known by the metronymic Gāṅgeya. Being also, in a peculiar way, the mother of Kārttikeya (*q.v.*), she is called Kumārasū. Gold, according to the *Mahābhārata*, was borne by the goddess Gaṅgā to Agni, by whom she had been impregnated. Other names and titles of the Ganges are Bhadrasomā, Gāndinī, Kirātī, Devabhūti, 'produced in heaven'; Haraśekharā, 'crest of Śiva'; Khāpagā, 'flowing from heaven'; Mandākinī, 'gently flowing'; Tripathagā or Triśrotāḥ, 'triple flowing', running in heaven, earth, and hell.

GANGADHARA—A name of Śiva. (*see* GAṄGĀ)

GANGADVARA—The gate of the Ganges. The opening in the Himālaya mountains through which the river descends into the plains, now known as Haridvāra.

GANGA-DWARA—The portal of Gangá, is the opening

in the Himálaya mountains by which the Ganges descends into the plain of Hindustan. It is celebrated as the scene of Daksha's great sacrifice. It is now more usually known by the name of Hardwár; properly Haridwára, the gate of Vishṇu, or Śiva; appellations bestowed upon it probably in times more recent than the composition of the Mahábhárata, when the Hindus were first ranged under the different and sometimes contending sects of Vaishnavas and Saivas.

GANGAMMA—A river goddess among the hill tribes; she is supposed to be present at every stream. On the Nílagiris it was formerly the practice for every owner of cattle to throw a quarter of a rupee into the rivers before crossing them, as the cattle were sometimes carried away by the torrent. It is enumerated amongst the great sins of the hill tribes at their funerals that they had crossed a stream without paying due adoration to Gangamma.

GANGASAGARA—The mouth of the Ganges, a holy bathing-place sacred to Viṣṇu.

GANGEYA—**(1)** A name of Bhīṣma, from his reputed mother, the river goddess Gaṅgā. **(2)** Also of Kārttikeya.

GARA—One of the five sons of Usínara, a descendant of Anu.

GARDDHABAS, GARDDBABBINS—A race of kings in the west of India, but not yet satisfactorily identified, though many learned conjectures have been made respecting them.

GARGA—An ancient sage, and one of the oldest writers on astronomy. He was a son of Vitatha. The *Viṣṇu Purāṇa* says, "From Garga sprang Śiṅga (or Śini); from them were descended the Gārgyas and Śainyas, brāhmaṇas of kṣatriya race." The statement of the *Bhāgavata* is, "From Garga sprang Śina; from them Gārgya, who from a kṣatriya became a brāhmaṇa." There were many Gargas; one was a priest of Kṛṣṇa and the Yādavas. The initiatory rites of Krishna and Rama were performed by the sage Garga, who was sent to Gokula by Vasudeva for that purpose. In the Bhágavata Garga describes himself as the Purohita or family priest of the Yádavas. Garga was also the name of one of the sons of Bhavanmanyu.

GARGABHUMI, GARGYA—Two of the descendants of Alarka, according to the list in the Váyu Purána.

GARGAS, GARGYAS—Descendants of Garga, who, "although kṣatriyas by birth, became brāhmanas and great *ṛsis*". Professor Wilson says that all the authorities concur in this statement; thus furnishing an additional instance of one caste proceeding from another

GARGYA, GARGYA BALAKI—Son of Bālāki. He was a brāhmaṇa, renowned as a teacher and a grammarian, who dealt especially with etymology, and was well read in the Veda, but still submitted to receive instruction from the kṣatriya Ajātaśatru.

GARGYA—**(1)** A disciple of Bashkali, and teacher of the Rig Veda; also a Brahman, who, through arduous penance, living upon iron sand for twelve years, became the father of the hero Kálayavana. **(2)** An etymologist and grammarian of much celebrity in Sanscrit Literature.

GARHAPATYA—Perpetual household fire, which is to be always burning; and, in the event of becoming extinct, can be renewed only by igniting certain consecrated sticks by attrition. The household fire ia never to be used for domestic or culinary purposes. It is the pure vestal flame, the emblem of eternal light, and is maintained solely for religious offices. *See* FIRE-SACRIFICIAL.

GARMANAS—Hindu or Buddhist priests mentioned by the geographer Strabo. They are represented as feeding on fruits, and wearing only a covering made of the bark of a tree.

GARUDA PURANA—Professor Wilson doubts whether a genuine Garuda Purána exists. The one he examined contained no account of the birth of Garuda. Only a brief notice of the creation; and the greater part being occupied with a description of Vratas, or religious observances, of holidays, of sacred places, &c. It contained also treatises on astrology, palmistry, precious stones, and medicine.

The description given of this Purāṇa is, "That which Viṣṇu recited in the Gāruḍa Kalpa, relating chiefly to the birth of Garuḍa from Vinatā, is called the *Garuḍa Purāṇa*, and in it there are read 19,000 stanzas." The works bearing this name which were examined by Wilson did not correspond in any respect with this description, and he considered it doubtful if a genuine *Garuḍa Purāṇa* is in existence.

GARUDA—The king of the feathered tribes and the remorseless enemy of the serpent race. He was the son of Kasyapa and Vinatá. Garuda is always represented as the bird on which Vishnu is carried and described as something between a man and a bird. Garuda is the vehicle of Krishna, appearing whenever he is wanted, and conveying his master with incredible speed to the most distant localities. When Krishna recovered the jewel mountain, he placed it, with the umbrella of Varuna, upon Garuda, and mounting him himself, he set off to the heaven of the gods to restore the ear-rings of Aditi. Garuda is represented as a large white-necked kite or eagle. On the walls of many Vaishnava temples he is represented by the figure of a young man seated, with the palms of the hands closed, and fingers pointed upwards, denoting reverence. "He may be compared with the Símurgh of the Persians, the Anka of the Arabs, the Griffin of chivalry, the Phoenix of Egypt, and the bird that sits upon the ash Yggdrasil of the Edda."—*Griffiths.*

A mythical bird or vulture, half-man, half-bird, on which Viṣṇu rides. He is the king of birds, and descended from Kaśyapa and Vinatā, one of the daughters of Dakṣa. He is the great enemy of serpents, having inherited his hatred from his mother, who had quarrelled with her co-wife and superior, Kadru, the mother of serpents. His lustre was so brilliant that soon after his birth the gods mistook him for Agni and worshipped him. He is represented as having the head, wings, talons, and beak of an eagle, and the body and limbs of a man. His face is white, his wings red, and his body golden. He had a son named Sampāti, and his wife was Unnati or Vināyakā. According to the *Mahābhārata*, his parents gave him liberty to devour bad men, but he was not to touch brāhmanas. Once, however, he swallowed a brāhmaṇa and his wife, but the brāhmaṇa so burnt his throat that he was glad to disgorge them both.

Grauḍa is said to have stolen the *amṛta* from the gods in order to purchase with it the freedom of his mother from Kadru. Indra discovered the theft and fought a fierce battle with Garuḍa. The *amṛta* was recovered, but Indra was worsted in the fight, and his thunderbolt was smashed.

Garuḍa has many names and epithets. From his parents he is called Kāśyapi and Vainateya. He is the Suparṇa and the Garutmān, or chief of birds. He is also called Dakṣāya, Śālmālin, Tārkṣya, and Vināyaka, and among his epithets are the following: Sitānana, 'white-faced'; Raktapakṣa, 'red-winged'; Śvetarohita, 'the white and red'; Suvarṇakaya, 'golden bodied'; Gaganeśvara, 'lord of the sky'; Khagesvara, 'king of birds'; Nāgāntaka, and Pannaga-nāśana, 'destroyer of serpents'; Sarpārāti, 'enemy of serpents'; Tarasvin, 'the swift'; Rasāyana, 'who moves like quicksilver'; Kāmacārin, 'who goes where he will'; Kāmāyus, 'who lives at pleasure'; Chirād, 'eating long'; Viṣṇuratha, 'vehicle of Viṣṇu'; Amṛtāharaṇa and Sudhāhara, 'stealer of the *amṛta*'; Surendra-it, 'vanquisher of Indra'; Vajrajit, 'subduer of the thunderbolt', &c.

GARUTWANTA—A name of Garuda.

GATHĀ—A song, a verse. A religious verse, but one not taken from the Vedas. Verses interspersed in the Sanskṛt Buddhist work caled *Lalitavistara*, which are composed in a dialect between the Sanskṛt and the Prākṛt, and have given their name to this the *Gāthā* dialect. The Zend hymns of the Zoroastrians are also called *Gāthās.*

GATHIN—The same as Gádhi, (*q.v.*)

GATI—(Movement.) An allegorical personage, one of the daughters of Devahúti, and wife of Pulaka.

GATRA—One of the seven pure sages, a son of Vasishta.

GATRAVAT—A son of Krishna by Lakshmaná.

GATU—A singer, a Gandharva.

GAUPAYANAS—Sons or descendants of Gopa. Four ṛṣis, who were the authors of four remarkable hymns in the *Ṛgveda.* One of them, named Subandhu, was killed and miraculously brought to life again. The hymns have been translated by Max Müller in the *Journal RAS*, vol. II 1866.

GAURI—The 'yellow' or 'brilliant', a name of the consort of Śiva. (*see* DEVĪ) Varuṇa's wife also is called Gaurī.

GAUTAMA SAKYA SIÑHA—See BUDDHA.

GAUTAMA—(1) A name of the sage Śaradvat, as son of Gotama. The founder of the Nyáya school of philosophy. Little is known of his personal history. He was born at Himalaya about the same time as Rama. He married Ahalyá the daughter of Bramha, and lived as a very austere ascetic, the Rámáyana states, for thousands of years, in a holy hermitage adorned with fruits and flowers, daily performing religious austerities.

One day when the sage was absent from bis dwelling, the mighty Indra passed by, and burned with an impure passion for the wife of Gautama; and he entered the hut in the disguise of the sage, and began to entreat Ahalyá: and she, knowing him to be king of heaven, in the wantonness of her heart yielded to his desires. As he was leaving the hermitage Gautama entered, and he wax invincible even to the gods through the power of his austerities. Indra was overwhelmed with sadness; and the sage beholding the profligate celestial, addressed him thus; O depraved wretch, assuming my form you have perpetrated this great crime! therefore from this moment you become a eunuch! The sage then pronounced this curse upon his wife Ahalyá; O sinful wretch, for thousands of years shall you remain in this forest, abandoned by all and invisible to all, until Ráma the son of Dasaratha, shall enter here, and you from beholding him shall be cleansed from all sin and again approach me without fear. These words of the illustrious Gautama were all fulfilled. Rámáyana 49. For an account of Gautama's philosophical system, see NYÁYA.

Kumárila says: 'In the same manner, if it is said that Indra was the seducer of Ahalyá, this does not imply that the God Indra committed such a crime, but Indra means the sun, and Ahalyá (from ahan and lí) the night; and as the night is seduced and ruined by the sun of the morning, therefore is Indra called the paramour of Ahalyá.'—Max Müller, *A. S. L.*, *p.* 530. The legend is thus versified by Mr. Griffiths:

"This was the grove—most lovely then—
Of Gautam, O thou best of men.
Like heaven itself, most honoured by
The Gods who dwell above the sky.
Here with Ahalyá at his side
His fervid task the ascetic plied.
Years fled in thousands. On a day
It chanced the saint had gone away,
When Town-destroying Indra came,
And saw the beauty of the dame.
The sage's form the God endued,
And thus the fair Ahalyá wooed:
Love, sweet! should brook no dull delay,
But snatch the moments when be may.'
She knew him in the saint's disguise,
Lord Indra of the Thousand eyes,
But touched by love's unholy fire,
She yielded to the God's desire
'Now, Lord of Gods!' she whispered, 'flee,
From Gautam save thyself and me.'
Trembling with doubt and wild with dread
Lord Indra from the cottage fled:
But fleeing in the grove he met
The home-returning anchoret,
Whose wrath the Gods and fiends would shun,
Such power his fervent rites had won.
Fresh from the lustral flood he came,
In splendour like the burning flame,
With fuel for his sacred rites,
And grass, the best of eremites.
The Lord of Gods was sad on heer
To see the mighty saint so near,
And when the holy hermit spied
In hermit's garb the Thousand-eyed,
He knew the whole, his fury broke
Forth on the sinner as he spoke:
'Because my form thou hast assumed,
And wrought this folly, thou art doomed.
For this my curse to thee shall cling,
Henceforth a sad and sexless thing.'

No empty threat that sentence came,
It chilled his soul and marred his frame,
His might and god-like vigour fled,
And every nerve was cold and dead,

Then on his wife his fury burst,
And thus the guilty dame he cursed:
For countless years, disloyal spouse,
Devoted to severest vows,
Thy bed the ashes, air thy food,
Here shalt thou live in solitude.
This lonely grove thy home shall be,
And not an eye thy form shall see.
When Ráma, Dasaratha's child,
Shall seek these shades then drear and wild,
His coming shall remove thy stain,
And make the sinner pure again."

(2) Author of a Dharmaśástra, which has been edited by Stenzler. **(3)** A Prajápati; one of the seven Rishis of the seventh Manwantara.

GAUTAMESA—'Lord of Gautama'. Name of one of the twelve great *liṅgas.* (*see* LINGA)

GAUTAMI—(1) An epithet of Durgā.

(2) Name of fierce *rākṣasī* or female demon.

GAVAKSHA—One of the monkey chiefs of Sugríva's army, who at the first sight of the giant Kumbhakarna threw down his weapons and fled, but was recalled to his post by Angada.

GAVYA—All that is derived from the cow; milk and all preparations of or from milk; these are proper to be offered as food to deceased ancestors. The sacrifice of a cow or calf formed part of the ancient [S']ráddha. It then became typical, or a bull was turned loose, instead of being slaughtered.

GAYA—(1) A city in Bihār. It is one of the seven sacred cities, and is still a place of pilgrimage, though its glory has departed. **(2)** A son of Havirdhána by Dishaná. a princess of the race of Agni; also the name of a prince the son of Nahta, descended from Bharata; also of one of the sons of Sudyumna, after his transformation from Ila to a man.

GAYATRI—A most sacred verse of the *Rgveda*, which it is the duty of every brāhmaṇa to repeat mentally in his morning and evening devotions. It is addressed to the sun as Savitṛ, the generator, and so it is called also Sāvitrī. Personified as a goddess, Sāvitrī is the wife of Brahmā, mother of the four Vedas, and also of the twice-born or three superior castes. Colebrooke's translation of the Gāyatrī is " Earth, sky, heaven. Let us meditate on (these, and on) the most excellent light and power of that generous, sportive, and resplendent sun, (praying that) it may guide our intellects." Wilson's version is, in his translation of the *Ṛgveda*, "We meditate on that desirable light of the divine Savitṛ who influences our pious rites." In the *Viṣṇu Purāṇa* he had before given a somewhat different version, "We meditate on that excellent light of the divine sun: may he illuminate our minds." A later version by Benfey is, "May we receive the glorious brightness of this, the generator, of the god who shall prosper our works."

Wilson observes of it: "The commentators admit some variety of interpretation; but it probably meant, in its original use, a simple invocation of the sun to shed a benignant influence upon the customary offices of worship; and it is still employed by the unphilosophical Hindus with merely that signification. Later notions, and especially those of the Vedānta, have operated to attach to the text an import it did not at first possess, and have converted it into a mystical propitiation of the spiritual origin and essence of existence, or Brahmā." It is considered so holy that copyists often refrain from transcribing it.

The name given to Śatarūpā (*q.v.*), Brahmā's famale half, daughter, and consort, as "the declarer of sacred knowledge". It is also applied to the consort of Śiva in the *Harivaṁśa*.

"We meditate on that excellent light of the divine sun; may he illuminate our minds." Such is the fear entertained of profaning this text, that copyists of the Vedas not unfrequently refrain from transcribing it, both in the Sanhita and Bháshya. Pious brahmans every morning at sunrise scatter water, purified by the mystical Omkara and consecrated by the Gáyatri; and by this water as by a thunderbolt the foul fiends are scattered.

GENTOOS—The name formerly applied by Europeans to the Hindus, especially to the Telugu people.

GETHU—The associate of Raghu in the theft of the nectar, and also one of the constellations.

GHATAKARPARA—A poet, who was one of the "nine gems" of the court of Vikramāditya. There is a short artificial poem, descriptive of the rainy season, bearing this name, which has been translated into German by Dursch. The words mean 'potsherds', and form probably an assumed literary name.

GHATASRINJAYAS—A people from the north-west, amongst the warriors of the Mahábhárata.

GHATOTKACHA—The son of Bhíma by a Rákshasí, or female fiend, Hidimbá, whose brother he slew. The scene of these transactions was on the east of the Ganges, and the Rákshasí may therefore mean a princess of some of the bordering tribes east of Hindustan, or between Bhote and Ava; all of whom eating meat, and following other impure practices, might well be considered Rákshasas or cannibals, by the Hindus. Heramba is in fact applied geographically to designate the western portion of Asam. Ghatotkacha was slain by Kama with the javelin he had received from Indra. *See* KAMA.—Wilson's *Works*, Vol. III, p. 297.

GHOṢĀ—It is said in the Veda that the Aśvins "bestowed a husband upon Ghoṣā growing old", and the explanatory legend is that she was a daughter of Kakṣivat, but being a leper, was incapable of marriage. When she was advanced in years the Aśvins gave her health, youth, and beauty, so that she obtained a husband.

GHORATA—Terror. One of the properties assigned to perceptible objects by the Sánkya philosophy.

GHOSHAVASU—A prince, the son of Palindaka; one of the ten Sungas, who governed the earth for a hundred and twelve years.

GHRITACHI—A celestial nymph, one of those frequently engaged in the interruption of the penances of holy sages.

GHRITACHI—The wife of Rája Kusanábha and queen of Magadha: the mother of a hundred daughters, all of whom Váyu the god of wind, wished to "forsake their mortal lot, and accompany him to the sky," and on their refusal.

"He heard the answer they returned
And mighty rage within him burned,
On each fair maid a blast he sent
Each-stately form he bowed and bent."

They were afterwards married to Bramhadatta, Rája of Kámpilí, and by this means recovered their strength and beauty.

"Soon as the hand of each young maid
In Bramhadatta's palm was laid,
Deformity and cares away
She shone in beauty bright and gay."

—*Griffiths.*

An *apsaras* or celestial nymph. She had many amours with great sages and mortal men. She was mother often sons by Raudrāśva or Kūśanābha, a descendant of Puru, and the *Brahmā Vaivartta Purāṇa* attributes the origin of some of the mixed castes to her issue by the sage Viśvakarman. The *Harivaṁśa* asserts that she had ten daughters as well as ten sons by Raudrāśva. Another legend represents her as mother by Kuśanābha of a hundred daughters, whom Vāyu wished to accompany him to the sky. They refused, and in his rage he cursed them to become deformed; but they recovered their natural shape and beauty, and were married to Brahmadatta, king of Kāmpila.

GHRITAPRISHTHA—One of the ten sons of Priyavrata, according to the list in the Bhágavata; which says that Priyavrata drove his chariot seven times round the earth, and the ruts left by the wheels became the beds of the oceans, separating it into seven Dwípas; it is uncertain which of them was given to Ghritaprishtha.

GHRITASAMADA—A son of Suhótra, and father of Saunaka who first established the distinctions of the four castes. *V.P.* 406.

GHRITEYA—A prince, one of the sons of Randraswa, a descendant of Puru.

GIRIGAHVARAS—A race who lived in caves; probably between Cabul and Bamian, but their cavern habitations have not been satisfactorily identified.

GIRIJA—The mountain-born; a name of Párvatí. She was originally Sati, the daughter of Daksha; was born again as the daughter of the mountain Himálaya, and was again married to Śiva. From this, her second birth, she is called Párvatí the mountaineer, or Girijá the mountain-born. (*see* DEVĪ)

GIRI—One of the sons of Swaphalka by his wife Gándiní.

GIRIVRAJA—A royal city in Magadha, identified with Rājagṛha in Bihār.

GIRIVRAJA—**(1)** A city in the mountainous part of Magadha near the wood of Dharmaranya. **(2)** The city of Rája Aswapati to which Bharata and Satrughna were sent. The Rájá was the grandfather of the young princes and they were sent to him that they might be out of the way when it was resolved that Ráma should be appointed Yuvarája at Ayódhya.

GITA GOVINDA—The Song of the Divine Herdsman, a beautiful little pastoral drama, furnishing a specimen of that mystical or emblematical theology, "that figurative mode of expressing the fervour of devotion, or the ardent love of created spirits towards their beneficent Creator, which has prevailed from time immemorial in Asia."* "On the Mystical Poetry of the Hindus."

Under the figure of the love, quarrels, and reconciliation of the incarnate Deity.dwelling like the Grecian Apollo, amongst the flocks and herds, under the name of Krishṇa, with the beautiful shepherdess Rádhá, it shadows forth the reciprocal attachment which exists between the human soul and Divine Beauty, goodness, and knowledge. As Krishṇa, faithless for a time, discovers the vanity of all other loves, and returns with sorrow and longing to his own darling Rádhá, so the human soul, after a brief and frantic attachment to objects of sense, burns to return to the God from whence it came—"from its original instinct it vergeth towards him as its centre, and can have no rest till it be fixed on him...He doth cherish and encourage our love by sweetest influences and most consoling embraces;" and "in that mysterious union of spirit whereby we do closely adhere to, and are, as it were inserted in him,...we cannot but feel very pleasant transports."**

With respect to the date of the composition nothing certain is known, but it seems now to be generally believed that the author, Jayadeva, flourished at least as late as the twelfth century of our era." Mr. Griffith, from whose *Specimens of old Indian Poetry* the above has been taken, has translated a few stanzas, but says "the exquisite melody of the verse can only be appreciated by those who can enjoy the original."

A lyrical poem by Jayadeva on the early life of Kṛṣṇa as Govinda the cowherd. It is an erotic work, and sings the loves of Kṛṣṇa with Rādhā, and other of the cowherd damsels, but a mystical interpretation has been put upon it. The poems are supposed to have been written about the twelfth or thirteenth century. There are some translations in the *Asiatic Researches* by Sir W. Jones, and a small volume of translations has been lately published by Mr. Edwin Arnold. There is also an edition of the text, with a Latin translation and notes, by Lassen, and there are some others.

* Sir W. JONES.

** These passages are extracted from one of Barrow's *Sermons*, quoted by Sir W. Jones, in his *Essay on the Mystical Poetry of the Hindus*.

GITA—The *Bhagavad Gitā* (*q.v.*).

GOBHANA—A son of Vahni, and grandson of Turvasu, whose line failed and merged into that of Puru, in consequence of the malediction denounced on his son by Yayáti, for refusing to take his father's infirmities on him.

GOBHILA—An ancient writer of the sūtra period. He was author of some *Gṛhya Sūtras*, and of some *sūtras* on grammar. The *Gṛhya Sūtras* have been published in the *Bibliotheca Indica*.

GODAVERI—The river which still bears that name; it is so called in all the Puránas.

GOGHUATAS—A people who formerly resided in Gumanta, part of the Konkan about Goa.

GOHAMUKHA—A mountain mentioned in the Vishnu Purána, but not identified.

GOKALASHTAMI—A festival to celebrate the birthday of Krishṇa. It is customary in the South of India for all Brahmans to fast until midnight, and then, after worship, to partake of food.

GOKARNA—**(1)** 'Cow's ear.' A place of pilgrimage sacred to Śiva, on the west coast, near Mangalore. **(2)** A famous and venerated region near the Malabar Coast; celebrated as the scene of Rája Bhagírath's austerities

"The good Bhagirath, royal sage,
Had no fair son to cheer his age.
He, great in glory, pure in will,
Longing for sons was childless still.
Then on one wish, one thought intent,
Planning the heavenly stream's descent,
Leaving his ministers the care
And burden of his state to bear,
Dwelling in far Gokarna he
Engaged in long austerity."

GOKULA—The village in which the cowherd Nanda resided, when Krishna and Balaráma were entrusted to his care, to be brought up as his own children, in order to escape the vengeance of Kansa. It was at Gokula that the female fiend Pútana attempted the life of the child Krishna, by giving him her breast to suck; the infant Krishna sucked it with such violence that he drained it of the life and she expired.

GOLAKA—A disciple of Sákalya, and teacher of the Rig Veda.

GOLOKA—The highest world of all, and the residence of Krishna; represented as indestructible while all else is subject to annihilation. Professor Wilson thinks this is an addition to the original system of seven worlds, in which we have probably some relation to the seven climates of the ancients, the seven stages or degrees of the earth of the Arabs, and the seven heavens of the Mahomedans, if not to the seven Amshaspends of the Parsis. Seven, suggested originally perhaps by the seven planets, seems to have been a favourite number with various nations of antiquity. Amongst the Hindus it was applied to a variety of sacred or mythological objects, which are enumerated in a verse in the Hanumáns Nátaka. Ráma is described there as piercing seven palm-trees with an arrow, in which other groups of seven take fright, as the seven steeds of the sun, the seven spheres, the seven Munis, the seven seas, the seven continents and the seven mothers of the gods.

GO-MANTA—A great mountain in the Western Ghāṭs. According to the *Harivaṁśa* it was the scene of a defeat of Jarāsandha by Kṛṣṇa.

GOMATIPUTRA—One of the Ándhra kings, the son of Sivaswáti, who reigned 21 years.

GOMATI—The Gūmtī river in Ayódhya or Oude; but there are others which bore the name. One fell into the Sindhu or Indus.

GONDS, or KHONDA—One of the aboriginal or non-aryan tribes of India who now inhabit part of Orissa. They have partially preserved what may be regarded as the primitive religion of Hindustan—a religion that has been designated devil worship, *is* they sacrifice only to demons or malignant deities.

GONIKA—The mother of Patanjali ,the grammarian.

GOPALA, GOVINDA—'Cow-keeper.' A name of the youthful Kṛṣṇa, who lived among the cowherds in Vṛndāvana.

GOPALA-KAKSHAS—Tribes of eastern India.

GOPALA-TAPANI—An Upaniṣad in honour of Kṛṣṇa. Printed in the *Bibliotheca Indica*.

GOPARASHTRA—The district of cowherds, that is of Nomadic tribes Gova or Kuva is an ancient name of the southern Konkan.

GOPAS—Herdsman; the designation of the inhabitants of Gokula, where Krishna spent his early days; they afterwards emigrated to Vrindávana and were the associates of Krishna and Balaráma, who joined heartily in whatever sports amused the sons of the herdsmen.

GOPATHABRAHMANA—The Brāhmaṇa of the *Atharva* or fourth Veda. It has been published by Rājendra Lāla in the *Bibliotheca Indica*.

GOPATI-ṚSABHA—'Chief of herdsmen.' **(1)** A title of Śiva. **(2)** A demon mentioned in the *Mahābhārata*

as slain by Kṛṣṇa.

GOPICHANDANA—A magnesian or calcareous clay, forming the white earth used by the Vaishnavas to make the sectarial streaks on their faces, breasts, and arms. The purest description is brought from Dwáraká, being said to be the soil of a pool at that place in which the Gopís drowned themselves when they heard of Krishṇa's death. The Rámánujas mark two perpendicular white lines, drawn from the root of the hair to the commencement of each eyebrow, and a transverse-streak connecting them across the root of the nose; they have also patches of Gopichandana, with a central red streak, on the breast and each upper arm.

GOPIS—The cowherd damsels and wives with whom Kṛṣṇa sported in his youth. Their sports with Krishna are narrated in detail in the Vishnu Purána, as also in the Bhágavata, &c. The Gopis are said to have wept bitterly when he left Gokula for Mathura.

GOSAIN—Any devotee is called a Gosain, whether he lives a life of celibacy or not, whether he roams about the country collecting alms, or resides in a house like the rest of the people, whether he leads an idle existence, or employs himself in trade. The mark however, that distinguishes all who bear this name is, that they are devoted to a religious life. Some besmear their bodies with ashes, wear their hair dishevelled and uncombed, and, in some instances, coiled round the head like a snake or rope. These formerly went naked, but being prohibited by the Government to appear in this fashion in public, bid defiance to decency nevertheless by the. scantiness of their apparel. They roam about the country in. every direction, visiting especially spots of reputed sanctity, and as a class are the pests of society and incorrigible rogues. They matter sacred texts or mantras and are notably fond of uttering the names of certain favourite deities. Some of them can read and a few may be learned; but for the most part they are stolidly ignorant. Others, of a much higher grade, reside in *maths*, or monasteries, where they lead a life of contemplation and asceticism. Yet they quit their homes occasionally, and, like the first named, undertake tours for the purpose of begging, and also proceed on pilgrimage to remote places. Most of them wear a yellowish cloth, by which they make themselves conspicuous.

Fakirs or devotees of both of these classes, usually wear several garlands of beads suspended from their necks and hanging low down in front; and carry a short one in the hand which by the action of a thumb and finger, they revolve perpetually, but slowly, keeping time with the low utterances proceeding from their lips. They also bear upon their foreheads, and frequently on other parts of their bodies, particularly the arms and chest, sacred marks or symbols, in honour of their gods.

In addition there is a considerable number of Gosains, not however separated from the rest by any caste distinctions, who although by profession belonging to this religious, class, apply themselves, nevertheless to commerce and trade. As merchants, bankers, tradesmen, they hold a very respectable position. Some carry on their transactions on a large scale.

One of the chief peculiarities of this caste is, that besides its natural increase from within, it is constantly adding to its numbers from without. Brahmans, Kshatriyas, Vaisyas, and Sudras, the two former especially, may if they choose, become Gosains; but if they do so, they are cut off for ever from their own tribes. It is this circumstance which constitutes the Gosains a distinct and legitimate caste, and not merely a religious order.—*Sherring*, p. 256.

GOSWALA—One of the five disciples of Sákalya, and teacher of the Rig Veda.

GOTAMA—One of the twenty-eight Vyásas. The founder of the Nyāya school of philosophy. He is called also Śatānanda, and is author of a Dharmaśāstra or law-book, which has been edited by Stenzler. He is frequently called Gautama.

GOTRAS—Families or tribes of brahmans. The names of the Gótras were liable to confusion, particularly in later times, when their number had become very considerable. But the respect which the brahmans from the very earliest time paid to their ancestors, and the strictness with which they prohibited marriages between members of the same family, lead us to suppose that the genealogical lists, even at the present day, furnish in their general outlines, a correct account of the priestly families of India. All Brahmanic families who keep the sacred fires are supposed to descend from the seven Rishis. These are—*Bhrigu, Angiras, Visvâmitra, Vasistha, Kasyapa, Atri, Agastya.* The real ancestors, however, are eight in number:—*Jamadagni, Gautama*, and *Bharadvâja, Visvâmitra, Vasishta, Kasyapa, Atri, Agastya.* The eight Gótras, which descend from these Rishis, are again subdivided into forty-nine Gótras, and these forty-nine branch off into a still larger number of families. The names gótra, vansa, varga, paksha, and gana, are all used in the same sense, to express the larger as well as the smaller families, descended from the eight Rishis.

A Brahman, who keeps the sacrificial fire, is obliged by law to know to which of the forty-nine Gótras his own family belongs, and in consecrating his own fire he must invoke the ancestors who founded the Gótra to which he belongs. Each of the forty-nine Gótras claims one, or two, or three, or five ancestors, and the names of these ancestors constitute the distinctive character of each Gótra. Max Müller. *A.S.L.*, p. 80.

GOUDA, GAURA—The ancient name of Central Bengal; also the name of the capital of the country, the ruins of which city are still visible. The great northern nation of brāhmaṇas. (*see* BRĀHMAṆA)

GOVA—An ancient name of the Southern Konkan , it may imply the district of cowherds, that is of Nomadic tribes.

GOVARDHANA—A mountain in Vṛndāvana near Mathura. The Vishnu Purána states that Krishna thus addressed the Gopas: Cattle and mountains are our gods. Brahmans offer worship with prayer; cultivators of the earth adore their landmarks, but we, who tend our herds in the forests and mountains, should worship them and our kine. Let prayers and offerings then be addressed to the mountain Govardhana, and kill a victim in due form." Accordingly the inhabitants of Vraja worshipped the mountain, presenting to it curds and milk and flesh: and they fed thousands of brahmana who came to the ceremony. Indra, offended by the loss of his offerings, caused a heavy rain to deluge Gokula. Krishna then to calm the troubled cowherds held up the mountain Govardhana as a largo umbrella to shelter them and their cattle. For seven days and nights it rained incessantly at Gokula, but the inhabitants were protected by the elevation of the mountain. The threats of Indra having been fruitless, Krishna restored the great mountain to its original site. Professor Wilson says that it seems not unlikely that this legend has some reference to the caves or cavern temples in various parts of India. A remarkable representation of it occurs upon the sculptured rocks of Mahabalipur.

GOVARDHANA-DHARA—'Upholder of Govardhana.' A title of Kṛṣṇa.

GOVINDA—'Cow-keeper.' A name of Krishna, given to him by Indra after having preserved the cattle by raising the mountain Govardhana. Govinda is he who knows, finds, or tends cattle. As the Indra of the cows he was called Govinda. Pilgrims invoke Govinda when travelling to Tirupati, &c.

GOVINDADATTA—A brahman who lived on the banks of the Ganges; he had five sons, one of whom was Devadatta, (*q.v.*) whose subsequent celebrity conferred distinction on the father.

GOVITHI—A division of the lunar mansions: in the Central or Járadgava Avasthána.

GRAHA—'Seizing.' **(1)** The power that seizes and obscures the sun and moon, causing eclipses; the ascending node, Rāhu. **(2)** Evil spirits with which people, especially children, are possessed, and which cause sickness and death. They are supposed to be amenable to medicine and exorcism.

GRĀMADEVATĀ(S)—Minor powers or tutelary goddesses (*devatās*) of villages (*grāmas*). The *grāmadevatās* can certainly be assigned to an archaic period, even pre-Dravidian, according to Eliade. 'Their association with the water-jar or pot (a symbol of the womb) indicates a close association with the ubiquitous fertility cult. Thus they are often represented by a jar or pot.'

Among the rural communities of southern India religion revolves round the *grāmadevatās*, whose shrines, like those of *yakṣas*, are often situated near trees,4 a further confirmation of their vegetal connection. They are sometimes represented by a platform under a tree, or by a stone slab on which is carved a crude figure of a woman, who may have two, four, six or eight arms, or none at all. But their usual icons are 'simple stone images of the female organ of generation (*yoni*).

Among the animals sacrificed to these goddesses are sheep, goats and buffaloes, their blood being sprinkled on the worshippers, on lintels and doorposts of houses, cowsheds and boundary stones, or mixed with rice and scattered in the streets or around the village boundary.

Whitehead stresses that the *grāmadevatās 'symbolize only the facts of village life*. They are related, not to great world forces, but to such simple facts as cholera, smallpox, and cattle-disease'. Some of them are said actually to 'possess' their devotees.

These goddesses are also worshipped by fishermen' and those whose livelihood is connected with lakes and rivers. The great goddess Mahādevī or Mahāgramadevata, is said to have been born 'in the waters, within the sea', thus possibly connecting her with maritime communities. With very few exceptions the village deities are feminine. The outstanding exception is Iyenar, the name is said to be a corruption of Hari-Hara (Visnu-Siva). lyenar is concerned with the guardianship of the fields, crops and herds and is the nightwatchman of the village, and large and small clay figures of horses are offered to him. On these horses he if supposed to ride round the village at night driving off a demons.

GRAMANIS—The seven attendants on the sun's car; the agents in the distribution of cold, heat, and rain at their respective season. They are also called Yákshas.

GRAMMAR—The Hindus and the Greeks are the only two nations in the whole history of the world which have conceived independently, and without any suggestions from others, the two sciences of Logic and Grammar. Carefully collecting the facts brought to light by critical and pains-taking observation, they have elaborated a system of Grammar, of gigantic dimensions, far surpassing anything that has ever been effected, in this branch of study, in any country or age of the world. Their greatest and most brilliant champion, in this science, is Pánini: yet many other grammarians helped to rear the stupendous fabric which now excites the admiration of mankind. And while they emulated the genius of the Greeks in generalising upon the results of their observations, they far outshine them in the correctness and extent of their investigations. *See* PÁNINI.

GRANTHA—In the later literature of India, Grantha was used for a volume, and in *granthakuti*, a library, we see clearly that it has that meaning. But in the early literature, *grantha* does not mean *pustaka*, or book; it means simply a composition as opposed to a traditional work.

GRHYA SUTRAS—Rules for the conduct of domestic rites and the personal sacraments, extending from the birth to the marriage of a man (*see* SŪTRA) The *Gṛhya Sūtras* of Āśvalāyana have been printed in the *Bibliotheca Indica.*

GRIDHRIKA—A daughter of Kasyapa and his wife Tamra, the parent of vultures.

GRIHA-DEVATA—Household gods. No house is supposed to be without its tutelary divinity, but the notion attached to this character is now rattier vague. The *Kula-devata* is always one of the leading personages of the Hindu mythology; but the Griha-devata rarely bears any distinct appellation. In Bengal the domestic god is sometimes the Sálagrama stone; sometimes the *tulasi* plant; sometimes a basket with a little rice on it, sometimes a water-jar to either of which a brief adoration is addressed, most usually by the females of the family. Occasionally small images of Lakshmi or Chaṇḍí fulfil the office, or should a snake appear, he is venerated as the guardian of the dwelling. In general, however, in former times, the household deities were regarded as the unseen spirits of ill, the ghosts and goblins who hovered about every spot, and claimed some particular sites as their own. Offerings were made to them in the open air, by scattering a little rice with a short formula, at the close of all ceremonies, to keep them in good humour. In this light the household gods correspond better with the *genii locorum*, than with the *lares or penates* of antiquity.—Wilson, *Works, XI, p.* 21.

GRIHASTHA—A householder; his duties are thus defined in the Vishnu Purána. "When the scriptural studies appropriate to the student have been completed, and he has received dismissal from his Guru, let the regenerate man enter into the order of the householder; and taking unto himself, with lawful ceremonies, house, wife, and wealth, discharge to the best of his ability the duties of his station; satisfying the manes with funeral cakes; the gods with oblations; guests with hospitality; the sages with holy study; the progenitors of mankind with progeny; the spirits with the residue of oblations; and all the world with words of truth. A householder secures heaven by the faithful discharge of these obligations. There are those who subsist upon alms, and lead an erratic life of self-denial, at the end of the term during which they have kept house. They wander over the world to see the earth, and perform their ablutions, with rites enjoined by the Vedas, at sacred shrines: houseless, and without food, and resting for the night at the dwelling at which they arrive in the evening, The householder is to them a constant refuge and parent: it is his duty to give them a welcome, and to address them with kindness; and to provide them, whenever they come to his house, with a bed, a seat, and food. A guest disappointed by a householder, who turns away from his door, transfers to the latter all his own misdeeds, and bears away his religious merit. In the house of a good man, contumely, arrogance, hypocrisy, repining, contradiction, and violence are annihilated: and the householder who fully performs this his chief duty of hospitality is released from every kind of bondage, and obtains the highest of stations after death."

GRTSAMADA—The reputed *ṛṣi* of many hymns in the second Maṇḍala of the *Ṛgveda.* According to the *Viṣṇu Purāṇa* he was a kṣatriya and son of Śunahotra, being descended from Purūravas of the Lunar race. From him sprang Śaunaka, the eminent sage versed in the *Ṛgveda* "who originated the system of four castes". The *Vāyu Purāṇa* makes Śunaka to be the son of Gṛtsamada, and Śaunaka the son of Śunaka: this seems probable. "It is related of him by Sāyaṇa that he was first a member of the family of Angiras, being the son of Śunahotra. He was carried off by the *asuras*, whilst performing a sacrifice, but was rescued by Indra, under whose authority he was henceforth designated as Gṛtsamada, the son of Śunaka or Śaunaka of the race of Bhṛgu. Thus the Anukramaṇikā says of him: He who was an Āṅgirasa, the son of Śunahotra, became Śaunaka of the race of Bhṛgu." According to the *Mahābhārata*, he was son of Vītahavya, a king of the Haihayas, a kṣatriya, who became a brāhmaṇa. (*see* Vītahavya) The *Mahābhārata* alludes to a legend of his having assumed the semblance of Indra, and so enabled that deity to escape from the *asuras*, who were lying in wait to destroy him. There are several versions of the story, but they all agree that after Indra had escaped Gṛtsamada saved himself by reciting a hymn in which he showed that Indra was a different person.

GUDAKESA—'Whose hair is in tufts.' An epithet of Arjuna.

GUDARAS—A class of mendicants, deriving their name from a pan of metal, which they carry about with them, containing fire for burning scented woods at the house of those from whom they receive alms. They do not solicit alms directly, but repeat the word Alakh, "invisible" expressive of the indescribable nature of the deity.

GUHA—'Secret'. **(1)** A name of the god of war. (*see* KĀRTTIKEYA) **(2)** A king of the Niṣādas or Bhīls, who was a friend of Rāma. After entertaining Ráma with great liberality, the Rája provided a well-furnished boat in which his distinguished guest crossed the Ganges. He also afforded great assistance to Bharata when proceeding to the hermitage of Bharadwája in search of Ráma. **(3)** A people near Kaliṅga, who possibly got their name from him.

GUHAS—The kings of Kalinga and Mahendra; some parts of Orissa and Berar.

GUHYAKAS—'Hidden beings.' Inferior divinities attendant upon Kubera, and guardians of his hidden treasures.

GUHYAS—The name of a class of demigods who attend on Kuvera the god of wealth, and whose city is Alákapura.

GUNA—Quality, virtue, excellence. A property of all created beings; three are particularized, the

1. *Satwa*, principles of truth or existence.
2. *Rája*, passion or foulness.
3. *Tamas*, darkness or ignorance.

GUNADHYA—The human name of MálYaván, when he was condemned to return to the infirmities of human nature. He was born at Pratishṭhána, the capital of Sáliváhana, supposed, to be the same as Pattan or Pyetan on the Godáveri.—*Wilson*.

GUPTA—A name said in the Vishnu Purána to be suited to Vaisyas and Sudras.

GUPTAS—A race of kings who reigned in Magadha. They were Rájas of the Vaisya caste. Of the existence and power of the Guptas we have recently had ample proofs from inscriptions and coins, as in the Chandragupta and Samudragupta of the Allahabad column, etc., in all which the legends are written in a character prior to the use of the modern Devanágiri and was current probably about the 5th century of our era. *Vishṇu Purána*, p. 480.

GURJJARA—The country of Gujarat.

GURU—"A spiritual preceptor occupying in some measure the place of the confessor of the middle ages. He is regarded as a representative and vehicle of divine power, and therefore entitled to receive the most implicit obedience from his disciples. The Gurus are a class of priests carefully to be distinguished from the Puróhita, who is a sort of domestic chaplain and *must* be married. The Gurus generally live in celibacy, though some are married. Each caste and sect has its particular Guru, who may be either a Brahman or a Súdra, and who exercises great authority and influence. He superintends those under his jurisdiction and enforces the observance of the rules and customs of the sect. He can expel from caste, and some Gurus can restore those who have been expelled. All Gurus do not possess equal authority. There is a gradation amongst them and the inferior Gurus frequently derive their power from the superior, and are sometimes deposed by them and others appointed.

When the people come into the presence of the

Guru, they make the Sashtanga, *i.e.*; prostration of the eight members, and this, when followed by the Guru's Asirvada, *i.e*; benediction, is effectual for the remission of all sins. The look even of a Guru has the same efficacy. The Prasada, *i.e.*, the present which the Guru confers upon his disciples consists in things otherwise of small value, such as a portion of cow-dung ashes, to beautify the forehead, flowers that were previously offered up to idols, the crumbs from his meals, or the water in which he had washed his feet, which is preserved and sometimes drunk by those who receive it. These and other things of like nature coming from their holy hands, possess the virtue of purifying body and soul from all uncleanness.

But if the benediction of the Guru and the other little tokens of his favour, which he bestows on his disciples, have so wonderful an influence in attracting the respect and reverence of the populace, his *curse* is thought to be not less powerful, and fills them with terror and awe. The Hindus are persuaded that it never fails to take effect, whether justly or unjustly incurred. Their books are full of stories which seem to have been invented for the express purpose of inspiring this belief; and, to add greater force to it, the attendants of the Guru, who are interested in the success of the impostor's game, do not fail to recount many marvellous stories respecting him, of which they pretend to have been eye-witnesses; and to avoid any possibility of detection, they lay the scene of the miracles in some distant country.

The Gurus, in general, rank as the first and most distinguished order of society. Those who are elevated to this great dignity, receive, in most cases, marks of reverence or rather of adoration which are hardly rendered to the gods themselves. But this is not surprising when it is understood that the power of controlling the gods is generally attributed to them, by which it is supposed they have the means of obtaining whatsoever the deities can bestow.

As a role, the Gurus reside in a kind of monasteries or insulated hermitages, named Matas. The place of residence of the principal Gurus is commonly called Simhasana, *i.e.*, throne, and that of the inferior ones Pitha, *i.e*; seat.

The great Gurus never appear in public except with great pomp; but it is when they proceed to a visitation of their district that they are seen surrounded with their whole splendour. They commonly make the procession on the back of an elephant, or seated in a rich palanquin. Some of them have a guard of horse, and are surrounded with troops both cavalry and infantry, armed with pikes and other weapons. Several bands of musicians precede them playing on all the instruments of the country. Flags in all the varieties of colour wave round them, adorned with the pictures of their gods. Some of their officers take the lead, singing odes in their praise, or admonishing the spectators to be prepared to pay the mighty Guru, as he comes up, the honor and reverence which are due to him. Incense and other perfumes are burnt in profusion; new cloths are spread before him on the road. Boughs of trees, forming triumphal arches, are expanded in many places on the way through which he passes. Bands of young women, the dancing girls of the temples, relieve each other, and keep up with the procession, enlivening it with lewd songs and lascivious dances.

During the visitation, their principal object is to amass money. Besides the fines which are levied from persons guilty of offences or any breaches of the ceremonies of the caste or sect, they often rigorously exact from their adherents a tribute to the utmost extent of their means. This is called Pada-kanika, *i.e*; feet offering. There is no affront or indignity which the Gurus are not disposed to inflict on any disciple, who fails, either from inability or unwillingness, to produce the sum at which he is rated, and in the last resort, they threaten to inflict the *curse.* And such is the credulity of the Hindu, and such is the dread of the evils he supposes to spring from the malediction of a Guru, that this extreme denunciation seldom fails to exact the payment.

The dignity of Guru descends, among the married, from father to son; but upon the death of one who has lived single, a successor is appointed by some one of the grand Gurus, who, in the exercise of this power, generally nominates one of his own dependants."—*Abbe Dubois.*

H

HAIHAYA—This name is supposed to be derived from *haya*, 'a horse'. **(1)** A prince of the Lunar race, and great-grandson of Yadu. **(2)** A race of tribe of people to whom a Scythian origin has been ascribed. The

Viṣṇu Purāṇa represents them as descendants of Haihaya of the Yadu race, but they are generally associated with borderers and outlying tribes. In the *Vāyu* and other Purāṇas, five great divisions of the tribe are named: Tālajaṅghas, Vītihotras, Avantis, Tuṇḍikeras, and Jātas, or rather Sujātas. They conquered Bāhu or Bāhuka, a descendant of King Hariścandra, and were in their turn conquered, along with many other barbarian tribes, by King Sagara, son of Bāhu. According to the *Mahābhārata*, they were descended from Śaryāti, a son of Manu. They made incursions into the Doāb, and they took the city of Kāśī (Benares), which had been fortified against them by King Divodāsa; but the grandson of this king Pratardana by name, destroyed the Haihayas, and re-established the kingdom of Kāśī. Arjuna-Kārtavīrya, of a thousand arms, was king of the Haihayas, and he was defeated and had his arms cut off by Paraśurāma.

The Vindhya mountains would seem to have been the home of these tribes; and according to Colonel Todd, a tribe of Haihayas still exists "near the very top of the valley of Sohagpoor, in Bhagelkhand, aware of their ancient lineage, and, though few in number, still celebrated for their valour".

HAITAKAS—Causalists; either the followers of the Nyáya or logical philosophy, or Bauddhas, those who take nothing upon authority, and admit nothing that cannot be proved; or it is explained, those who by argument cast a doubt upon the efficacv of acts of devotion.

HALA—A prince, the son of Arishtakarman, one of the thirty Andhrabhritya kings, whose united reigns amounted to four-hundred and fifty-six years.

HALABHRITA (HALABHṚT)—A name of Balaráma, implying his use of a ploughshare as a weapon. He is represented of a white colour, clothed in a dark blue vest.

HALAYUDHA—'Who has a ploughshare for his weapon', *i.e.*, Balarāma.

HAMSA—**(1)** This, according to the *Bhāgavata Purāṇa*, was the name of the "one caste", when, in olden times, there was only "one Veda, one God, and one caste". **(2)** A name used in the *Mahābhārata* for Kṛṣṇa. **(3)** A mountain in the north of Meru; projecting from its base like a filament from the root of the lotus. *V.P.*

HAMSA—Haṁsa and Dimbhaka were two great warrior brothers mentioned in the *Mahābhārata* as friends of Jarāsandha. A certain king also named Haṁsa was killed by Balarāma. Hearing that "Haṁsa was killed", Dimbhaka, unable to live without him, committed suicide, and when Haṁsa heard of this he drowned himself in the Yamunā.

HANUMAN, HANUMAT, HANŪMAT—A celebrated monkey chief. He was son of Pavana, 'the wind', by Añjanā, wife of a monkey named Kesarī. He was able to fly, and is a conspicuous figure in the *Rāmāyaṇa*. He is called Hanumán of the broken jaw. When he was a child in his mother's arms, the ruddy sun laughed down into his face; and he, thinking it was some splendid blossom, sprang from his mother's arms five yojanas into the air in his eagerness to clutch the radiant thing. In the fall that happened to him then he broke his jaw. He and the other monkeys who assisted Rāma in his war against Rāvaṇa were of divine origin, and their powers were superhuman. Hanumān jumped from India to Ceylon in one bound; he tore up trees, carried away the Himālayas, seized the clouds, and performed many other wonderful expolits. (*see* SURASĀ) His form is "as vast as a mountain and as tall as a gigantic tower. His complexion is yellow and glowing like molten gold. His face is as red as the brightest ruby; while his enormous tail spreads out to an interminable length. He stands on a lofty rock and roars like thunder. He leaps into the air, and flies among the clouds with a rushing noise, whilst the ocean waves are roaring and splashing below." In one of his fights with Rāvaṇa and the *rākṣasas*, they greased his tail and set it on fire, but to their own great injury, for with it he burnt down their capital city, Laṅkā. This exploit obtained for him the name Lankādāhi. His services to Rāma were great and many. He acted as his spy, and fought most valiantly. He flew to the Himālayas, from whence he brought medicinal herbs with which he restored the wounded, and he killed the monster Kālanemi, and thousands of Gandharvas who assailed him. He accompanied Rāma on his return to Ayodhyā, and there he received from him the reward of perpetual life and youth. The exploits of Hanumān are favourite topics among Hindus from childhood to age, and paintings of them are common. He is called Marutputra, and he has the patronymics Ānili, Māruti, &c., and the metronymic Āñjaneya. He is also Yogacara, from his power in magic or in the healing art, and Rajatadyuti, 'the brilliant'. Among his other accomplishments, Hanumatwas a grammarian; and the *Rāmāyaṇa* says, "The chief of monkeys is perfect; no one equals him in the *śāstras*, in learning, and in ascertaining the sense of the scriptures [or in moving at will]. In all sciences, in the rules of austerity, he rivals the preceptor of the gods...It is well known that Hanumat was the ninth author of grammar."—*Muir*, IV. 490.

1. The son of the wind, or as he is sometimes represented, an incarnation of Váyu the god of the wind. He was the chief general of the monkey king Sugríva, who assisted Rama in his war with the giant Ráva[n.]a. When Rama was in distress at the loss of his wife Síta, Hanumán was employed as a spy; and, after many researches discovered that Síta was kept a close prisoner in Lanka. Four armies of monkeys and bears were dispatched, but only that to the south, uuder the command of Hanumán, met with any success, and brought back tidings of the lost Síta. The story of Hanumán's adventures in Lanka is one of the best sustained efforts of pure imagination to be found in the Rámáyana. The exploits of the vast monkey hero, who could swell himself to the size of a mountain, or dwarf himself to the size of a man's thumb; are narrated in a Baron Munchausen style, sometimes ludicrous, sometimes almost sublime. The following incidents may be mentioned:

2. When Hanumán arrived at the sea-shore, opposite Ceylon, several of his companions offered to leap across, but Hanumán alone was equal to so great a leap.

> "Then by Sampati's counsel led
> Brave Hanumán who mocked at dread,
> Sprang at one wild tremendous leap,
> Two hundred leagues across the deep."

Having discovered Síta in a grove of Asoka trees attached to Rávana's palace, he gave proofs of his supernatural strength, and was then conducted into the presence of the king, where he announced himself as the ambassador of his master, king Sugríva, who demanded the restoration of Síta on behalf of Ráma. This so irritated Rávana that he ordered Hanumán to be put to death, but Vibhíshana, Rávana's brother, reminded him that the life of an ambassador was always sacred. It was therefore decided that he should be punished by having his tail set on fire. Hanumán then escaped from his guards, jumped on the house-tops with his burning tail, and set the whole city on fire. After having satisfied himself that Síta had not perished in the conflagration, and exhorted her to maintain her spirits and firmness, he bade her adieu, and sprang from a mountain which staggered under the shock and sank into the earth. He then darted through the air, rejoined his. companions on the opposite coast, and recounted to them the narrative of his adventures. When the monkeys returned to Sugríva, Ráma learnt the hiding-place of Síta. Hanumán described his interview with her, and to attest the truth of his story, gave Síta's token to Ráma, who praised the monkey general, enquired about the fortifications of Lanka, and soon marched southwards, attended by Hanumán and the monkey army, to fight for Síta's deliverance.

In the course of the battle when Indrajit the bravest of the sons of Rávana, had, by means of magical weapons, inflicted terrible wounds on all the leaders of Ráma's army, Hanumat flew to the Himálaya mountains for four medicinal herbs by which the dead and wounded might be restored; but the divine plants suspected his object, and rendered themselves invisible. Upon this the irritated monkey chief tore up the mountain peak and carried it with all its contents into the camp of Ráma and Lakshmana; who with all the dead and wounded generals were instantly restored by the exhalations issuing from the healing plants.

When Lakshmana was dangerously wounded, the physician Sushena said that a celebrated medicinal plant (mahaushadi), growing on the northern mountain Gandha-mádana, would cure him, Hanumán undertook to fetch it and accordingly flew there. As he passed over Ayodhya and Nandigramu he was observed by Bharata, who seeing a strange object in the sky prepared to shoot it; but Hanumán descended, and arresting the arrow, gave Bharata tidings of his brothers. On reaching the mountain Gandha-mádana, he was attacked by a terrible Rákshasa named Kála-nemi, who had been sent by Rávana to kill Hanumán. This demon first took the. form of an anchorite, and persuaded Hanumán to drink some water out of a lake where there was a monstrous crocodile. Hanumán, however, killed both the crocodile and Kála-nemi, and afterwards destroyed 30,000 gandharvas who attacked him. He then looked about for the plant, and not finding it, took up the whole mountain bodily in his arms, and deposited it, with its rocks, metals, forests, lions, elephants, and tigers, at the feet of Sushena, who knew well where to look for the plant, gathered it, and made Lakshmana breathe its healing exhalations. Hanumán then restored the mountain to its place, killing with his feet and tail more Rákshasas who attacked him on his way while he carried the mountain, and was unable to use his hands.

When Rávana was at last killed Hanumán was sent by Ráma with a message to Síta, and subsequently sent to announce his return to Bharata.*

"Hanumán, best of monkey kind,
Was son of him who breathes the wind,
Like thunderbolt in frame was he,
And swift as Garud's self could flee."

The dangers to which Hanumán was exposed in crossing the ocean to Lanka may be seen by referring to the articles SURASA, and SINHIKA. See also MAINAKÁ, for the supernatural help he received on the same journey. Arriving at Lanka he reduced his size to that of a cat; and when night had let down shadow on the town, he sprang into the ramparts, and crouching down surveyed the position from thence. As the sky is adorned by its constellations so was Lanka embellished by its glorious palaces. Hanumán examined every dwelling and saw some strange and memorable sights.

After he had discovered Síta in the Asoka grove and received her message to Ráma about the red *tilaka*** that he might know that Hanumán had really seen his beloved; the brave monkey said to himself, 'shall I quit this isle of Lanka' and do no damage to this Rávaṇa, who has dared to menace the peerless bride of Ráma? So he set about tearing up the trees in the grove, and to defacing the monuments and grottoes it contained. Eight thousand warriors rushed forth, by command of Rávaṇa, against Hanumant. The agile SON of the wind sprang out of them, and bounding on to the roof of a lofty palace, he uprooted a huge column of marble, exclaiming, 'I am Hanumán, the messenger of Ráma; death to Rávaṇa'; then hurling the pillar amongst them he crushed the whole army of Rákshasas. Other heroes and warriors were then sent against him, who though wounded several times, succeeded in killing all who came against him. (*See* JAMBUMÁLIN, DURDHARSHA, PRAGHASA, AKSHA, &c.) At last Indrajit was sent by Rávaṇa to capture or slay the monkey hero. Indrajit shot a miraculous arrow he had received from Brahma, which was received by Hanuman on his huge body with full respect to the weapon bearing the name of Brahma himself. The gigantic Hamuman was thus fettered with iron chains by officious Rákshasas. But Indrajit drew forth the miraculous arrow and motioned Hanumán to follow him into the presence of Rávaṇa. The incensed king ordered his execution but Vibhíshaṇa, Rávaṇa's brother, reminded him that the life of an ambassador was always sacred. Rávaṇa, however, ordered his servants to set tire to the tail of Hanumán; but Síta prayed to the Fire, and the fire, leaping up in a bright golden flame played around the tail as though it were performing a *pradakshina*, and did not burn it. And thus it answered the gentle princess: I am good to Hanumán. The maruti then reduced his size to that of a grasshopper and stepped out of his bonds; swiftly resuming his gigantic proportions, he sprang to the roof of the nearest dwelling, and lashing his tail, round which the fire still played, from side to side, soon set the palace in a blaze.—*I.P.*, p 240.

Hanumán is now regarded as a demi-god, and his whole race as sacred; and because of this monkeys are allowed to multiply indefinitely, and commit mischief of every kind, no one being willing to interfere with them.

* Williams; *Indian Epic Poetry*.

** Tilaka, a mark on the forehead and between the brows, either as an ornament or a sectarial distinction.—*Wilson*.

HANUMAN NATAKA—A play, the subject of which is the story of the Rámáyaṇa; it is often emphatically termed the Maha, or great, Náṭaka. It is said to be originally the work of Hanumán who engraved or wrote it on the rocks. Valmíki saw it and anticipated that the greater beauty of its style would throw his Rámáy-aṇa into the shade. When he complained to Hanuman, the latter had so little of the author about him, that he told the bard to cast the verses into the sea. Valmíki obeyed the injunction and the Maha-Náṭaka remained for ages under the waves. At last a portions were discovered and brought to Raja Bhoja, by whose command Damodara Misra arranged the fragments, filled up the chasms, and formed the whole into an entire work. There is no reason to doubt so much of this story as is credible, or that the fragments of an ancient drama were connected in the manner described. Some of the ideas are poetical and the sentiments just and forcible; the language is in general very harmonious; but the patchwork is very clumsily put together.

The date of the play is established by the mention of Bhoja, to be a work of the tenth or eleventh century; and it is in part corroborative of the correctness of the assertion, that the drama was the wotk of Damodara Misra, that the poet is named in the Bhoja Prabandhu *as* one of the many writers patronised by that monarch. That work also records the anecdote of some verses attributed to Hanumán being discovered by a merchant in Bhoja's reign, engraved upon some rocks on the sea shore; the merchant brings a copy of the first two stanzas of one verse, and Bhoja travels to the spot to obtain the other two.—*Wilson*.

HARA—One of the eleven Rudras. Also a name of Siva, meaning the supremely powerful.

HARI VANSA—The last portion of the Mahabharata, and believed to be a comparatively recent addition to that work. It is chiefly occupied with the adventures of Krishna, but, as introductory to his era it records particulars of the creation of the world, and of the patriarchal and regal dynasties; done, says Professor Wilson, with much carelessness and inaccuracy of compilation.

HARI—A name which commonly designates Viṣṇu, but it is exceptionally used for other gods.

HARIDVARA—'The gate of Hari.' The modern Hardvār. The place where the Ganges finally breaks through the moutains into the plains of Hindustan. It is a great place of pilgrimage.

HARIHARA—A combination of the names of Viṣṇu and Śiva, and representing the union of the two deities in one, a combination which is differently accounted for.

HARI-HARA-PUTRA—Vishnu, Siva's son, because he is said to owe his origin to the union of Siva and Vishnu in a female form, called Mohini. A name of Ayenár, the chief male deity among the Gramadévatas. See AYENÁR.

HARIKESA—The name of one of the seven solar rays.

HARIS—A class of deities in successive Manwantaras.

HARISCANDRA—Twenty-eighth Hindu king of the Solar race, and son of Triśaṅku, a descendant of Ikshwáku, and a prominent person in the legendary history of ancient India. He was celebrated for his piety and justice. There are several legends about him. The *Aitareya Brāhmaṇa* tells the story of his purchasing Śunaḥśephas to be offered up as a vicarious sacrifice for his own son. (*see* ŚUNAHŚEPHAS) The *Mahābhārata* relates that he was raised to the heaven of Indra for his performance of the *rājasūya* sacrifice and for his unbounded liberality. The *Mārkaṇḍeya Purāṇa* expands the story at considerable length. One day while Hariścandra was hunting he heard female lamentations, which proceeded "from the Sciences, who were being mastered by the austerely fervid sage Viśvāmitra, and were crying out in alarm at his superiority". Hariścandra, as defender of the distressed, went to the rescue, but Viśvāmitra was so provoked by his interference that the Sciences instantly perished, and Hariścandra was reduced to a state of abject helplessness. Viśvāmitra demanded the sacrificial gift due to him as a brāhmaṇa, and the king offered him whatever he might choose to ask, "gold, his own son, wife, body, life, kingdom, good fortune", whatever was dearest. Viśvāmitra stripped him of wealth and kingdom, leaving him nothing but a garment of bark and his wife and son. In a state of destitution he left his kingdom and Viśvāmitra struck Śaibyā, the queen, with his staff to hasten her reluctant departure. To escape from his oppressor he proceeded to the holy city of Benares, but the relentless sage was waiting for him and demanded the completion of the gift. With bitter grief wife and child were sold, and there remained only himself. Dharma, the god of justice, appeared in the form of a hideous and offensive *cāṇḍāla*, and offered to buy him. Notwithstanding the exile's repugnance and horror, Viśvāmitra insisted upon the sale, and Hariścandra was carried off "bound, beaten, confused, and afflicted", to the abode of the *cāṇḍāla*. He was sent by his master to steal grave-clothes from a cemetery. In this horrid place and degrading work he spent twelve months. His wife then came to the cemetery to perform the obsequies of her son, who had died from the bite of a serpent. They recognised each other, and Hariścandra and his wife resolved to die upon the funeral pyre of their son, though he hesitated to take away his own life without the consent of his master. After all was prepared, he gave himself up to meditation on Viṣṇu. The gods then arrived, headed by Dharma and accompanied by Viśvāmitra. Dharma entreated him to refrain from his intention, and Indra informed him "that he, his wife, and son, had conquered heaven by their good works." Hariścandra declared that he could not go to heaven without the permission of his master the *cāṇḍāla*. Dharma then revealed himself. When this difficulty was removed, Hariścandra objected to go to heaven without his faithful subjects. "This request was granted by Indra, and after Viśvāmitra had inaugurated Rohitāśva, the king's son, to be his successor Hariścandra, his friends, and followers, all ascended in company to heaven." There he was induced by the sage Nārada to boast of his merits, and this led to his expulsion from heaven. As he was falling he repented of his fault and was forgiven. His downward course was arrested, and he and his followers dwell in an aerial city, which, according to popular belief, is still visible occasionally in mid-air.

In the Aitareya Brahmana he is described as a king without a sou, though he had a hundred wives.

In his house lived, Parvata and Nárada. He asked Nárada 'Tell me what do people gain by a son whom they all wish for ?'

Being asked by one verse, Nárada replied in ten verses:

'If a father sees the face of a son, born alive, he pays a debt in him, and goes to immortality.

'The pleasure which a father has in his son is greater than all the pleasures that are from the earth, from the fire, and from the waters.

'Always Lave the fathers overcome the great darkness by a son; for a self is born from his self; it (the new-born self, the son) is like a ship, full of food, to carry him over.

'What is the flesh ? What is the skin ? What are the hairs What the heat ? Try to get a BOD, you Brahmans; he is undoubtedly the world.

'Food is life for men, clothing is protection, gold is beauty, cattle is strength. His wife is a friend, his daughter is a pity; but the son is his light in the highest world.

As husband he embraces a wife, who becomes his mother, when he becomes her child. Having been renewed in her, he is born in the tenth month.

'A wife is a wife (jâyâ) because man is born (jâyate) again in her. She is a mother (âbhûti) because she brings forth (âbhûti); a germ is hidden in her,

'The gods and the old ages brought great light unto her. The gods said to men: "In her you will be born again."

'There is no life for him who has no son, this the animals also know.

'The path which those follow who have sons and no sorrows, is widely praised and happy. Beasts and birds know it, and they have young ones everywhere.'

Having thus spoken, he said to him: 'Go to Varuna the king, and say: May a son be born to me, and I shall sacrifice him to you.' The king assented, he went to Varuna the king, and said;

'May a son be born to me and I shall sacrifice him to you.' Varuna said, 'Yes.' A son was born to him, called Rohita. Then Varuna said to Harischandra: 'A son is born to thee, sacrifice him to me.' Harischandra said: 'When an animal is more than ten days old, it can be sacrificed. May he be older than ten days and I shall sacrifice him to you.'

Varuna assented. The boy was more than ten days old, and Varuna said: 'He is older now than ten days, sacrifice him to me.' Harischandra said: 'When an animal's teeth come, then it can be sacrificed. May his teeth now come, and I shall sacrifice him to you.'

Varuna assented. His teeth came. and Varuna said: His teeth have come, sacrifice him tc me.' Harischandra said: 'When an animal's teeth fall out, then it can be sacrificed. May his teeth fall out, and I shall sacrifice him to you.'

Varuna assented; his teeth fell out, and Varuna said: 'His teeth have fallen out, sacrifice him to me.' Harischandra replied:

'When an animal's teeth come again, then it can be sacrificed. May his teeth come again, and I shall sacrifice him to you.'

Varuna assented: His teeth came again, and Varuna said: "His teeth have come again, sacrifice him to me.' Harischandra said:

'When a warrior (kshatriya) is girt with his armour, then he can be sacrificed. May he be girt, and I shall sacrifice him to you.'

Varuna assented. He was girt, and Varuna said: 'He has been girt, let him be sacrificed to me.'

Harischandra assented. He addressed his son and said:' Child, he gave you to me; Death ! that I sacrifice you to him.' The son said,' No !' took his bow, and went to the forest, and lived there for a year.

And Varuna seized Harischandra, and his belly swelled. This Rohita heard and went from the forest to the village (grama). Indra, in the form of a man, went round him, and said: 'For a man who does not travel about there is no happiness, thus we have heard, O Rohita ! A good man who stays at home is a bad man. Indra is the friend of him who travels. Travel.'

Rohita thought, a Brahman has told me to travel, and thus he travelled a second year in the forest. When he went from the forest to the village, Indra, in the form of a man, went round him, and said:

'A traveller's legs are like blossoming branches, he himself grows and gathers the fruit. All his wrongs vanish, destroyed by his exertion on the road. Travel.'

Rohita thought, a Brahman has told me to travel, and thus he travelled a third year in the forest. When be went from the forest to the town, Indra, in the form of a man, went round him, and said:

'The fortune of a man who sits, sits also; it rises, when he rises; it sleep, when he sleeps; it moves well when he moves. Travel!'

Rohita thought, a Brahman has told me to travel, and thus he travelled a fourth year in the forest. When he went from the forest to the town, Indra, in the form of a man, went round him, and said:

'A man who sleeps is like the Kali age; a man who awakes is like the Dvâpara age; a man who rises is like the Trêta age; a man who travels is like the Krita age. Travel!'

Rohita thought, a Brahman has told me to travel, and thus he travelled a fifth year in the forest. When he went from the forest to the town, Indra, in the form of a man, went round him, and said:

'A traveller finds honey, a traveller finds sweet figs. Look at the happiness of the sun, who travelling never tires. Travel!'

Rohita thought, a Brahman has told me to travel, and thus he travelled a sixth year. He met in the forest a starving Rishi, *Ajîgarta*, the son of *Sûyavasa*. He had three sons, *Sunahpuccha*, *Sunahsepha*, and *Sunolângûla*. Rohita said to him: 'Rishi, I give you a hundred cows, I ransom myself with one of these thy sons.' The father embraced the eldest son, and said: 'Not him.' 'Nor him,' said the mother, embracing the youngest. And the parents bargained to give Sunahsepha, the middle son. Rohita gave a hundred, took him, and went from the forest to the village. And he came to his father, and said: 'Father, Death ! I ransom myself by him.' The father went to Varuna, and said': 'I shall sacrifice this man to you.' Varuna said, 'Yes, for a Brahman is better than a Kshatriya.' And he told him to perform a Râjasûya sacrifice. Harischandra took him to be the victim for (he day, when the Soma is spent to the gods.

Visvamitra was his Hotri priest, *Jamadagni* his Adhvaryu priest, *Vasishtha*, the Brahman, *Ayâsyu*, the Adyâtri priest. When Sunahsepha had been prepared, they found nobody to bind him to the sacrificial post. And Ajîgarta, the son of Sûyavasa said: 'Give me another hundred, and I shall bind him.' They gave him another hundred, and he bound him. When he had been prepared and bound, when the Aprî hymns had been Bung, and he had been led round the fire, they found nobody to kill him. And Ajîgarta, the son of Sûyavasa said: 'Give me another hundred, and I shall kill him.' They gave him another hundred, and he came whetting his sword. Then Sunahsepha thought, 'They will really kill me, as if I was not a man. Death ! I shall pray to the gods.' He went with a hymn to *Prajápati* (Lord of the world), the first of gods. Prajâpati said to him: 'Agni (fire) is the nearest of gods, go to him. He went with a hymn to Agni, and Agni said to him: '*Savitri* (the progenitor) rules all creatures, go to him.' He went with a hymn to Savitri, and Savitri said to him: 'Thou art bound for Varuna the king,' and Varuna said to him: '*Agni is* the mouth of the gods, the kindest god, praise him, and we shall set thee free.' Thus he praised Agni, and Agni said to him: Praise the Visve Devâh, and we shall set thee free.' Thus he praised the Visve Devâh, and they said to him: 'Indra is the greatest, mightiest, strongest, and friendliest of the gods, praise him, and we shall set thee free.' Thus he praised Indra, and Indra was pleased, and gave him in his mind a golden car, which Sunahsepha acknowledged by another verse. Indra said to him: 'Praise the *Asvinau*, and we shall set thee free.' Thus he praised the Asvinau, and they said to him: 'Praise *Ushas* (dawn), and we shall set thee free.' Thus he praised Ushas with three verses. While each verse was delivered, his fetters were loosed, and Harischandra's belly grew smaller, and when the last verse was said, his fetters were loosed, and Harischandra well again." *A.S.L.*, p. 408-414.

Harischandra is represented in all the legends as a king of great uprightness. The following story illustrates this. Once when all the gods and Rishis were assembled in Dévéndra's audience chamber, the latter asked Vasishtha, whether he knew of any one among men on earth who did never lust after another's wife, nor speak a lie; to which the Rishi replied: "Yes, there is a disciple of mine, king Harischandra, he never spoke a lie." On hearing this Visvamitra called out: "Harischandra is a deceiver and liar." Then said Vasishtha: "If Harischandra is found to speak the least untruth, I will cease to be a Rishi and to come into this assembly." "Well," answered Visvámitra, "if I find him altogether truthful, I will give him all the merit of my penance; but I am afraid, you will at once tell him that I am about to try him." Upon this Vasishtha took an oath, that he would not at all go near the king till the matter was settled; and Visvámitra went to Harischandra and tempted him in different ways, more especially through women, to speak an untruth; but the king did not swerve from the truth. At last the

Rishi asked him far a large sum of money, and having received it, he returned it to him with the request to take care of it till he would require it. After a very long time Visvamitra came and desired all the money, together with compound interest, which amounted to a sum exceeding the value of his kingdom; but Harischandra, in order to pay the sum, sold all he had, and also himself together with his wife and son. Subsequently he was separated from his wife Satyavati, and employed to burn corpses. Then, behold, one day, there comes a woman to have her dead child burnt, and he recognizes her as his wife by her Tali (the marriage-badge); which he requires of her as his wages for burning the child, and which she will not give away. While they yet talk, there come messengers to seize the woman, because she was suspected of having kidnapped a royal prince who happened to be very similar to her child. Being found guilty, she is condemned to death, and Harischandra is ordered to behead her; and he is ready to obey: but, behold, suddenly the sword is turned into flowers, the child becomes alive, and the royal couple are restored to their former glory."

In consequence he was elevated with his subjects to heaven, from whence, having been insidiously led by Nárada to boast of his merits, he was again precipitated. His repentance of his pride, however, arrested his downwards descent, and he and his train paused in mid-air. The city of Harischandra is popularly believed to be at times still visible in the skies. The indignation of Vasishtha at Viswámitra's insatiableness produced a quarrel, in which their mutual imprecations changed them to two birds, the Saráli, a sort of Turdus, and the Baka, or Crane. In these forms they fought for a considerable term, until Brahma interposed, and reconciled them. The Bhágavata alludes to this story, in its notice of Harischandra; but the Váyu refers the conflict to the reign of a different prince: According to the Siva Purána, Harischandra was an especial worshipper of that deity; and his wife Satyavatí was a form of Jayá, one of Durga's handmaids.

HARISRAVA—A river mentioned in the Vishnu Purána but not identified.

HARITA, HĀRĪTA—**(1)** A son of Yuvanāśva of the Solar race, descended from Ikṣvāku. From him descended the Hārita Aṅgirasas. In the *Liṅga Purāṇa* it is said, "The son of Yuvanāśva was Harita, of whom the Hāritas were sons. They were, on the side of Aṅgiras, twice-born men (brāhmanas) of kṣatriya lineage"; or according to the *vāyu*, "they were the sons of Angiras, twice-bore men (brāhmaṇas), of kṣatriya race", possibly meaning that they were sons raised up to Harita by Aṅgiras. According to some he was a son of Cyavana. **(2)** Author of a Dharmaśāstra or law-book.

HĀRĪTA-ĀṄGIRASES—(*see* HARITA)

HARITAS—**(1)** A class of gods in the twelfth Manwantara; one of the tribes of Aborigines, who occupy the hills and jungles. **(2)** The descendants of Harita, the son of Yuvanáswa. They were brahmans with the properties of Kshatriyas. **(3)** 'Green'. In the *Ṛgveda* the horses, or rather mares, of the sun, seven or ten in number, and typical of his rays. "The prototype of the Grecian Charites."—*Max Müller.*

HARITASWA—A son of Sudyumna after his transformation from Ilá into a man.

HARITS, HARITAS. HARIVAMŚA—The genealogy of Hari or Viṣṇu, a long poem of 16,374 verses. It purports to be a part of the *Mahābhārata*, but it is of much later date, and "may more accurately be ranked with the Paurāṇik compilations of least authenticity and latest date." It is in three parts; the first is introductory, and gives particulars of the creation and of the patriarchal and regal dynasties; the second contains the life and adventures of Kṛṣṇa; and the last and the third treats of the future of the world and the corruptions of the *kali age*. It contains many indications of its having been written in the south of India.

HARI-VARSHA—A country to the north of Hemakuta and south of Nishádha. Also, the name of the nine sons of Agnióthra, king of Nishádha.

HARSANA—A deity who presides over the *śraddha* offerings.

HARSBAVARDDHANA—A prince, the son of Yajnakrit, one of the descendants of Kshattravriddha.

HARSHA DEVA—A king of Kashmir who reigned between A. D. 1113 and 1125, and the reputed author of the play called "Ratnavali, or the necklace," translated by Wilson, in the *Hindu Theatre*.

HARSHA—(Joy). A son of Kama (Love) by his wife Nandi (delight).

HARYAKSHA—One of the five sons of Prithu, according to the Bhágavata enumeration.

HARYANGA—A prince, the son of Champa one of

the descendants of Anu. Champa was the founder of Champapuri, a city of which traces still remain in the vicinity of Bhágulpúr.

HARYASVA—A grandson of the Kuvalayāśva who killed the demon Dhundhu. The country of Pañcāla is said to have been named from his five (*pañca*) sons. There were several others of this name.

HARYASVAS—Five thousand sons of the patriarch Dakṣa, begotten by him for the purpose of peopling the earth. The sage Nārada dissuaded them from producing offspring, and they "dispersed themselves through the regions and have not returned".

In the Vishnu Purána it is stated that Daksha, being commanded by Bramha, created living creatures. The creation and disappearance of the Haryaswas is thus described. "In the first place he willed into existence the deities, the Rishis, the quiristers of heaven, the Titans, and the snake-gods. Finding that his will-born progeny did not multiply themselves, he determined, in order to secure their increase, to establish sexual intercourse as the means of multiplication. For this purpose he espoused Asikní, the daughter of the patriarch Vírana, a damsel addicted to devout practices, the eminent supportress of the world. By her the great father of mankind begot five thousand mighty sons, through whom he expected the world should be peopled, Nárada, the divine Rishi, observing them desirous to multiply posterity, approached them, and addressed them in a friendly tone: Illustrious Haryaswas, it is evident that your intention is to beget posterity; but first consider this: why should you, who, like fools, know not the middle, the height, and depth of the world, propagate offspring ? When your intellect is no more obstructed by interval, height, or depth, then how, fools, shall ye not all behold the term of the universe?' Having heard the words of Nárada, the sons of Daksha dispersed themselves through the regions, and to the present day have not returned; as rivers that lose themselves in the ocean come back no more."

HARYASWA—The son and successor of Dridhaswa. Dridhaswa was one of the three sons of Kuvalayáswa who survived the conflict with the Asura Dhundu, all the others, to the extent of twenty thousand nine hundred and ninety-seven, having perished.

Haryaswa was also the name of a son of Prishadaswa; of a son of Drishtakétu; and of a son of Chakshu.

HARYATMA—Called also Uttama, the Vyasa of the twenty-first Dwápara."

HASTA—A lunar mansion in Govithi, in the Central Avashthána.

HASTINAPURA—The capital city of the Kauravas, for which the great war of the Mahābhārata was waged. It was founded by Hastin, son of the first Bharata, and hence, as some say, its name; but the *Mahābhārata* and the *Viṣṇu Purāṇa* call it the "elephant city", from *hastin*, an elephant. The ruins are traceable near an old bed of the Ganges, about 57 miles N.E. of Delhi, and local tradition has preserved the name. It is said to have been washed away by the Ganges, and is placed by Lassen, in his map to the *Indische Alterthuns Kunde*, about 78° long, and 28° 50' lat.

HASTIN—The son of Suhótra and founder of the city of Hastinápura.

HASTI-SIKSHA—The management of elephants; an accomplishment curiously characteristic of national manners. The proficiency of the Indians in this art early attracted the attention of Alexander's successors; and natives of India were so long exclusively employed in this service, that the term Indian was applied to every elephant driver, to whatever country he might belong.—*Schlegel.*

HASTISIMA—A river mentioned in the Vishnu Purána list, but not identified.

HASYARNAVA—'Ocean of laughter.' A modern comic piece in two acts, by a Paṇḍit named Jagadiśa. "It is a severe but grossly indelicate satire upon the licentiousness of brāhmaṇas assuming the character of religious mendicants."—*Wilson.*

HAVIRBHA—(Oblation-born). The wife of the Rishi Pulastya, and mother of Agastya.

HAVIRBHUJ, HAVIṢMATA—*Pitṛs* or Manes of the kṣatriyas, and inhabitants of the solar sphere, (*see* PITṚS)

HAVIRDHANA—The son of Antarddhána by his wife Sikhandini.

HAVISHMANTAS—A class of Pitris, of the corporeal order, living in the solar sphere, sons of Angiras, and Pitris of Kshatriyas. See PITRIS.

HAVYA—According to the Váyu Purána, one of the five sons of Atri after his penance.

HAVYAVAHANA—The fire of the gods, the *son* of Suchi.

HAYAGRIVA—'Horse-necked.' According to one legend,

a *daitya* who stole the Veda as it slipped out of the mouth of Brahmā while he was sleeping at the end of a *kalpa*, and was killed by Viṣṇu in the fish *avatāra*. According to another, Viṣṇu himself, who assumed this form to recover the Veda, which had been carried off by two *daityas*.

HAYAMUKHI—The horses head; one of the Rákshasí guardians of Síta when a captive in Lanka. She told Síta that youth and beauty were capricious gifts, and recommended her to respond to Rávaṇa before grief and fasting bad impaired her charms.

HAYASIRAS, HAYAŚĪRṢA—**(1)** 'Horse-head.' In the *Mahābhārata* it is recorded that the sage Aurva (*q.v.*) "cast the fire of his anger into the sea", and that it there "became the great Hayaśiras, known to those acquainted with the Veda, which vomits forth that fire and drinks up the waters". A form of Viṣṇu.

In the *Bhāgavata Purāṇa* Brahmā is represented as saying, "In my sascrifice Bhagavat himself was Hayaśirṣa, the male of the sacrifice, whose colour is that of gold, of whom the Vedas and the sacrifices are the substance and the gods the soul, when he respired, charming words came forth from his nostrils." **(2)** The daughter of Vrishaparvan, the renowned Danava, and wife of Kratu.

HEMACHANDRA—**(1)** The king of Vaisali, a place celebrated amongst the Buddhists as the chief seat of the labours of Sákhya and his first disciples—now Allahabad; **(2)** A zealous and able propagator of the Jain doctrines in the twelfth century. He was well versed in the peculiarity of the system which he taught, and may be regarded as a safe guide. He was the author of a useful vocabulary termed the *Abhidana Chintamani*, and of a life of *Maha* Víra. Wilson.

HEMĀDRI—"The golden mountain', *i.e.*, Meru.

HEMAKUTA—'Golden peak.' A chain of mountains represented as lying north of the Himālayas, between them and Mount Meru.

HEMA—The son of Ushadratha, a descendant of Yayáti. Also the name of a river in the Vishnu Purána.

HERMIT—See VÁNAPRASTHA.

HETI—A Rákshas, that always resides in the sun's car during the month of Madha or Chaitra, us one of its seven guardians.

HIDIMBA—A hideous Asura and cannibal, with yellow eyes and a horrible aspect, but possessed of. great strength. He lived in the jungle south of Váranávata, and attacked the Pándavas on their march, but was killed by Bhíma after a severe contest.

HIDIMBI—The sister of the above who is described as beautiful, and was afterwards married to Bhíma.

HIMACALA, HIMĀDRI—The Himālaya mountains.

HIMAPANDURA—One of the four elephants by whom the earth is believed to be supported. The sublime Himapándura has the eastern quarter assigned to him. *See* VIRUPÁKSHA.

HIMAVAT—The personification of the Himālaya mountains, husband of Menā or Menakā, and father of Umā and Gaṅgā.

The king of mountains. Part of the snowy range. The well-known range of mountains now called the Himálaya, forming the northern barrier of the Indian peninsula, containing the highest elevations in the world. The Imüs or Emodus of classical writers. In Mythology Himavat is husband of the Air-nymph Menaka; father of the river Ganga and of Durga or Uma, in her descent as Parvati to captivate Siva, and seduce him from the austerities which he practiced in those mountains. In this personification the name belongs to the Puranic; as a mountain only, to the Epic.

On account of the majestic height of this mountain range, and the apparent impossibility of reaching its summit, the imagination of the ancient Hindus invested it with the most mysterious properties, and connected it with the history of some of their deities. In the Puránas, Himavat is placed to the south of the fabulous mountain Meru, which stands in the centre of the world, and described as the king of the mountains, who was inaugurated as such when Prithu was installed in the government of the earth. As the abode of Siva, he is the goal of penitent pilgrims, who repair to his summit in order to win the favours of this terrific god. His wife was Menâ, whom the Pitris or demigods Vairâjas, engendered by the mere power of their thought.

HINDI—One of the tongues of India; it abounds in Sanskrit words, and has many dialects. Speaking generally the tongues spoken in the whole of upper India, including the Punjab, from the Himálayan to the Vindhyan range, may be said to be Hindi. Also the languages of Kamaon and Garhwal, all along the Sub-Himalayan range as far as the Gogra river; the impure dialect of the Gorkhas; the Brij-Bhasha (or Baka as it is pronounced on the Ganges,) the Panjabi, Multani,

Sindi, Jataki, Haruti, Marwari and it is said Konkani. The Bengali is a form of Hindi, but so highly polished as to be classed as a distinct tongue.

HINDUS—"The great bulk of the people known by this appellation are the descendants of Scythian and Aryan immigrants, who in bye-gone days, as conquerors, in search of a milder clime, left the cold regions of the north, some off-shoote moving westward and others to the south. Remnants of Scythian languages are found in Beluchistan, and the seat of the great Sanskrit speaking people was long in Kashmir, proving that one great highway to the south, had been along the valley of the Indus, through Kashmir, and the Panjab. But between the valley of the Indus, and that of the Brahmaputra, there are twenty or thirty other passes in the Himalayas, through which the northern races could stream to the genial south. Amongst the first of these immigrants seemingly were the Tamil races, belonging to the Turanian or Tartar family of mankind, a body of whom seem to have followed the course of the Indus and spread themselves over the peninsula. As to the date of their advent, however, history is silent; but there seems no doubt that great branches of the Scythic stock were occupants of India, at the time that it was invaded, and to a considerable extent conquered, by the Sanskrit speaking tribes of the Aryan family. In the north, the subjugation or ousting of the Tamilians from all rank and power was so complete that Sanskrit forms of speech became the language of the country, and the Kashmiri, the Panjabi, the Sindi, the Guzerathi, the Hindustani and the Bengali, all of them with a large admixture of Sanskrit, are sister tongues known as forms of Hindi. South of the Nerbudda, however, it is otherwise. Throughout the peninsula, the languages differ from the Sanskrit in grammar, and only admit Sanskrit words, in the same way that the Anglo-Saxon admitted terms of law and civilization from the Norman French. At the present day, the south of India more largely represents the Tartar, and the north, the Aryan race. But the fair, yellow colored Aryans are to be met with south even to Cape Comorin, and though mixing with the various Tamil nations, races and tribes, for at least two thousand years, in physical form, complexion, intellect and manners, the Brahmanical and other Aryan families are as distinct as when their forefathers first came conquering from the north. The great Aryan migration, however, which seems to have received its first check south of the Aravali, took place between the fourteenth and eighth centuries before out-era. Major Cunningham in his learned work on the Bhilsa topes (p. 15) uses the term Aryan in allusion to "the race of Aryya, whose emigrations are recorded in the Zendavesta, who starting from Ericene Vijo, gradually spread to the south-east, over Aryavartha or Arya-desa, the northern plains of India, and to the south-west, over Iran or Persia: he adds that the Medas are called Apìtol by Herodotus. The original meaning of the word is also said to have been equivalent to Upper Noble. It has also, however, been suggested that as the Aryans were originally and essentially an agricultural and therefore a peasant race, they may have derived their name from their plough. The Aryans seem to have brought with them a servile race, or to have had amongst them a social distinction between the noble and the common people which has ever continued. As they conquered southwards, amongst the Tartar races whom they found in the country, they reduced them everywhere to a state of slavery. They named them in fierce contempt Dása or slave, and these formed the true servile race of Manu and other writers. Where the races who had preceded them retained their independence, these proud immigrants styled them M'hlechhas, a term which even to the present day, is intended to comprise every thing that is hateful or vile. In Vedic times, along the western coast of Hindustan dwelt other races, different alike from the Scythic tribes and from the Aryans of the Vedas—earlier colonizers or emigrants, most probably from Assyria and the west,—who had a civilization of their own. Mr. Wheeler divides the history of the Hindus into four great epochs corresponding with the four great changes in their religious belief:—

1. The Vedic age, which was characterised by the worship of the elementary deities, such as Agni and Indra, and appears to have prevailed in the Panjab prior to the disappearance of the Saraswati river in the sand.
2. The Brahmanic age, which was characterised by the worship of Brahma, and appears to have prevailed between the disappearance of the Saraswati in the sand, and the advent of Sakya Muni about B. C. 600.
3. The Buddhist age, which was characterised by the pursuit of Nirvána, and appears to have prevailed from about B.C. 600 to A.D. 800 or 1000.
4. The Brahmanical revival, which was characterised by the worship of incarnations of deities, and appears to have prevailed from about A. D. 800

to the present time."

Professor Wilson writes "The circumstances that are told of the first princes have evident relation to the colonization of India, and the gradual extension of the authority of new races over an uninhabited or uncivilized region. It is commonly admitted, that the Brahmanical religion and civilization were brought into India from without. Certainly, there are tribes on the borders, and in the heart of the country, who are still not. Hindus; and passages in the Rámáyána, and Mahábharata, and Manu, and the uniform traditions of the people themselves, point to a period when Bengal, Orissa, and the whole of the Dakhin were inhabited by degraded or outcaste, that is, by barbarous tribes. The traditions of the Puránas confirm these views: but they lend no assistance to the determination of the question whence the Hindus came; whether from a central Asiatic nation, as Sir William Jones supposed, or from the Caucasian mountains, the plains of Babylonia, or the borders of the Caspian, as conjectured by Klaproth, Vans Kennedy, and Schlegel. The affinities of the Sanskrit language prove a common origin of the now widely scattered nations amongst whose dialects they are traceable, and render it unquestionable that they must all have spread abroad from some centrical spot in that part of the globe first inhabited by mankind, according to the inspired record. Whether any indication of such an event be discoverable in the Vedas, remains to be determined; but it would have been obviously incompatible with the Pauránik system to have referred the origin of Indian princes and principalities to other than native sources. We need not therefore, expect, from them, any information as to the foreign derivation of the Hindus.

We have, then, wholly insufficient means for arriving at any information concerning the ante-Indian period of Hindu history, beyond the general conclusion derivable from the actual presence of barbarous and apparently, aboriginal tribes—from the admitted progressive extension of Hinduism into parts of India where it did not prevail when the code of Manu was compiled—from the general use of dialects in India, more or less copious, which are different from Sanskrit—and from the affinities of that language with forms of speech current in the western world—that a people who spoke Sanskrit, and followed the religion of the Vedas, came into India, in some very distant age, from lands west of the Indus. Whether the date and circumstances of their immigration will ever be ascertained, is extremely doubtful: but it is not difficult to form a plausible outline of their early site and progressive colonization.

The earliest seat of the Hindus, within the confines of Hindusthan, was, undoubtedly, the eastern confines of the Panjab. The holy land of Manu and the Puránas lies between the Drishadwati and Saraswati rivers,—the Gaggar and Saraswati of our maps. Various adventures of the first princes and most famous sages occur in this vicinity; and the Ashramas or religious domiciles of several of the latter are placed on the banks of the Saraswati. According to some authorities it was the abode of Vyása, the compiler of the Vedas and Puránas; and agreeably to another, when on one occasion, the Vedas had fallen into disuse and been forgotten, the Brahmans were again instructed in them by Saraswata, the son of Saraswati.

One of the moat distinguished of the tribes of the Brahmans is known as the Saraswata; and the same word is employed by Mr. Colebrooke, to denote that modification of Sanskrit which is termed generally Prakrit, and which in this case, he supposes to have been the language of the Saraswata nation, 'which occupied the banks of the river Saraswati.' The river itself receives its appellation from Saraswati, the goddess of learning, under whose auspices the sacred literature of the Hindus assumed shape and authority. These indications render it certain, that, whatever seeds were imported from without, it was in the country adjacent to the Saraswati river that they were first planted, and cultivated and reared, in Hindusthan.

The tract of land thus assigned for the first establishment of Hinduism in India, is of very circumscribed extent and could not have been the site of any numerous tribe or nation. The traditions that evidence the early settlement of the Hindus in this quarter, ascribe to the settlers more of a philosophical and religious, than of a secular character, and combine, with the very narrow bounds of the holy land; to render it possible, that the earliest emigrants were the members, not of a political, so much as of a religious community; that they were a colony of priests, not in the restricted sense in which we use the term, but in that in which it still applies in India, to an Agrahara, a village or hamlet of Brahmans, who although married, and having families, and engaging in tillage, in domestic duties and in the conduct of secular interests affecting the community, are, still, supposed to devote their principal attention to sacred study and religious offices. A society of this description with its artificers and servants, and, perhaps, with a body of martial followers, might have found a home in the Brahmavarta of Manu, the land which, thence, was entitled 'the holy,' or, more literally, 'the Brahman region,' and may have communicated to the rude, uncivilized, unlettered, aborigines the rudiments of social organization, literature, and religion; partly in all probability, brought along with them, and partly devised and fashioned, by degrees, for the growing necessities of new conditions of society. Those with whom this civilization commenced would have had ample inducements to prosecute their successful work; and in the course of time, the improvement which germinated on the banks of the Saraswati was extended beyond the borders of the Jumna and the Ganges.—*Preface to V.P.*

HIRANMAYA—A mountainous country lying between the Sevéta and Srinji ranges; to the north of mount Meru.

HIRANVAT—The king of Sweta, installed by his father, the pious king Agnídhra, before he retired to a life of penence at Sálagráma.

HIRANYAGARBHA—'Golden egg' or 'golden womb'. In the *Ṛgveda* Hiraṇyagarbha "is said to have arisen in the beginning, the one lord of all beings, who upholds heaven and earth, who gives life and breath, whose command even the gods obey, who is the god over all gods, and the one animating principle of their being'.' According to Manu, Hiraṇyagarbha was Brahmā, the first male, formed by the undiscemible eternal First Cause in a golden egg resplendent as the sun. "Having continued a year in the egg, Brahmā divided it into two parts by his mere thought, and with these two shells he formed the heavens and the earth; and in the middle he placed the sky, the eight regions, and the eternal abode of the waters." (*see* BRAHMĀ)

HIRANYAHASTA—The son given by the Asvins to the wise Vadhrimati, in answer to her prayers. *O.S.T.* v., p. 247.

HIRANYAKASIPU—'Golden dress.' A *daitya* who, according to the *Mahābhārata* and the Purāṇas, obtained from Śiva the sovereignty of the three worlds for a million of years, and persecuted his son Prahlāda for worshipping Viṣṇu. He was slain by Viṣṇu in the Narasiṁha, or man-lion incarnation. He and Hiraṇyākṣa were twin-brothers and chiefs of the *daityas*.

A son of Kasyapa and Diti, who became king of the Daityas, and usurped the authority or Indra, and exercised of himself the functions of the sun, of the air, of the waters, of fire, and of the moon. Having conquered the three worlds he was inflated with pride, and enjoyed whatever he desired. "He obtained the sovereignty of all the immortals for a hundred million years." (*O.S.T.*, iv, 159.) Prahláda, his son, remained devoted to Vishnu, and when ordered by his father to be put to death, Vishnu appeared as his deliverer. Hiranyakasipu was reconciled to his son, but was notwithstanding put to death by Vishnu as Narasimha (the man-lion) and Prahláda became the sovereign of the Daityas.

HIRANYAKSHA—'Golden eye.' The twin-brother of Hiranyakasipu, termed "the invincible." He was the *daitya* who dragged the earth to the depths of the ocean and was destroyed by Vishnu in his boar incarnation. In the Padma Purána it is said that this occurred in the first, or Matsya avatara: that Vishnu in the form of a fish entered the ocean and destroyed Hiranyaksha.—Wilson's *Works*, *Vol. III.*, *p.* 58.

HIRANYANABHA—One of the descendants of Ráma, a pupil of Jaimini, and teacher of the Sama Veda. He had a large number of disciples who were termed the northern and eastern chaunters of the Śáman, and founders of schools.

HIRANYARETAS—One of the ten sons of Priyavrata, according to the enumeration in the Bhágavata.

HIRANYAROMAN—A Lókapála, regent of the North, son of Parjanya and Maríchi.

HITOPADESA—'Good advice.' The well-known collection of ethical tales and fables compiled from the larger and older work called *Pañcatantra.* It has been often printed, and there are several translations; among them is an edition by Johnson of text, vocabulary, and translation.

HLADA—One of the four mighty sons of Hiranyakasipu.

HLADINI—The Gladdener; the name of one of the seven rivers mentioned in the Rámáyana, in connection with the descent of Ganga. Only two, the Ganges and Indus, are known to geographers.

HOLI—A vernal festival originally designed to typify the genial influence of Spring upon both the inanimate and animated creation, and to express the passionate feelings inspired by the season, and the delight which the revival of nature diffused. The primitive institution was the adoration of the personified Spring as the friend and associate of the deity of Love. In the South of India the festival is in honour of Kamadeva, whose effigy is committed to the flames;* though, as Professor Wilson remarks, the amusement of the Hóḷí and the style of the Charak púja, but ill express the sympathy which man, in all countries, feels with the vernal season, and has little in common with the worship that might be supposed acceptable to Káma and his lovely bride, and which it would appear they formerly enjoyed. The time for the celebration of the Hóḷí (15th day of Phálguna) is the season of Spring, when the foliation of trees, the budding of the grass, and the pairing of birds are observed. The festival is considered to be especially promotive of the multiplication of offspring, and preservative of the health and life of children. But though traces of the original purport of the festival are palpable enough, yet Love and Spring have been almost universally deposed from the rites over which they once presided, and have been superseded by new and less agreeable mythological creations; new legends have also been invented to account for the origin and object of the celebration, having little or no obvious relation to the practices which are pursued.—*Wilson*.

The festival in Bengal is observed by the worship of the juvenile Krishṇa. But in every part of India it is customary for the lower orders to sally forth into the streets and throw a red powder† over passers by, or a red liquid is squirted over them through a syringe, the operators often using immodest language. "In the villages the men generally take part in the mischief, and persons of respectability and females are encountered with gross expressions, or sometimes with rough usage, and rarely, therefore, trust themselves out of their houses whilst the license continues." Where there is no police to interfere an open spot in the vicinity of the village is selected, and the materials of a bonfire brought together; useful articles, if not vigilantly guarded, being often appropriated for this purpose, and if once added to the pile the owner can not retain them. "During the whole period the people go about scattering the powder and red liquid over each other, singing and dancing, and annoying passengers by mischievous tricks, practical jokes, coarse witticisms, and vulgar language." The bonfire is consecrated and lighted up by a Brahman, and when the flames break forth, the spectators crowd round it to warm themselves, an act that is supposed to avert ill-luck for the rest of the year; they engage also in rough gambols, and as the blaze declines jump over and toss about the burning embers.

According to Colonel Tod the utmost license prevails amongst the Rájpúts; the lower classes regale in stimulating confections and intoxicating liquors, and even respectable persons roam about the streets like bacchanals, vociferating songs in praise of the powers of nature. A characteristic mode of keeping the festival is playing the Hóḷí on horseback, when the riders pelt each other with balls of the red powder enclosed in thin plates of talc which break when they strike.

Of the songs which are sung at this season the character is generally said to be highly exceptionable. Professor Wilson states that all he had an opportunity of seeing were characterized by little else than insipidity. They were either praises of the mouth, or allusions to the juvenile Krishṇa in connexion with the festival, and supposed to be uttered by the female companions of his boyish frolics at Vṛindávana.

The practices of the carnival as now observed in Italy have been trimmed of their excesses, but even in them there remain vestiges which denote their community of origin with the Hóḷí of the Hindus. The time properly embraces the whole period from the beginning of the year, but as in tlic festival of Phálguna, the last few days are those in which the principal demonstrations take place, and in the license which is permitted both in speech and conduct, the wearing of masks and disguixes, the reciprocal pelting with real or with mock comfits, and in some places sprinkling with water or throwing powder over each other, obvious analogies exist. There is another practice which presents also a parallel, the extinguishing of the carnival. This in Italy is refined into frolicsome attempts to blow out each others lighted candles; but the notion appears to be the same as the burning of the Hóḷí, the lighting and extinction of the bonfire, and scattering of the ashes.

There is another of the usages of the Hóḷí which finds a parallel in modern times, although at a somewhat later period. One subject of diversion during the Hóḷí, is to send people on errands and expeditions that are to end in disappointment, and raise a laugh at the expense of the person sent. The identity of this practice with making April Fools is noticed by Maurice, who remarks 'that the boundless hilarity and jocund sports, prevalent on the first of April in England and during the Hóḷí festival in India, have their origin in the ancient practice of celebrating, with festival rites, the period of the vernal equinox, when the new year of Persia anciently began.'

There was a Festum Stultorum about this period amongst the Romans; some antiquaries have supposed that it constituted the originals of the festivals of the Roman Church, the extravagances of the Abbot of Unreason, and the sleeveless errands of All Fools, or April Fool Day. The identity of designation and similarity of practice, render it not unlikely that the day of All Fools had originally something in common with the Festum Stultorum and with the Hóḷí.**

* This is supposed to commemorate the legend of Káma's having been consumed by the flames which flashed indignant from the eye of Siva, when the archer-god presumed to direct his shaft against the stern deity, and inflame his breast with passion for Párvatí.—WILSON.

† This powder termed Phalgu, or Abíra is made chiefly of the dried and pounded root of the Curcuma Zerumbet, or of the wood of the Cæsalpinia Sappan, which are of a red colour, or in some places the yellow powder of turmeric is substituted,—WILSON.

**WILSON, *Works*, II, 243. Reference is made to Brand's Popular Antiquities and various other works for still more striking coincidences between the Hólí and the other above-mentioned festivals.

HOMA—A sort of burnt offering which can be made by Brahmans only. It is only made on special occasions, such as the celebration of a festival, the investiture of a young brahman with the sacred thread, marriages, and funerals. The method of making it is as follows: During the utterance of Mantras, five species of consecrated wood, together with the Dharba grass, rice and butter, are kindled and burnt; and the fire is then kept burning as long as the festival or ceremony lasts. Great efficacy is ascribed to this rite.

HOTRI, HOTṚ—The priest who recites the hymns from the *Ṛgveda at* the performance of sacrificial rites.

HRASWARMAN—One of the kings of Mithila, the son of Suvarnarman; sometimes called Hrasvaroma.

HRI—'Modesty,' An allegorical personage represented as one of the daughters of Daksha, and wife of Dharma.

HRIDIKA—A Yádava prince, the son of Swayambhoja, and father of Súra, in whose family Vishnu took a human form.

HṚISHIKESA—A name of Vishnu, meaning 'lord of the senses.'

HUNAS—According to Wilson, "the White Huns or Indo-Scythians, who were established in the Panjāb and along the Indus at the commencement of our era, as we know from Arrian, Strabo, and Ptolemy, confirmed by recent discoveries of their coins", and since still further confirmed by inscriptions and additional coins. Dr. Fitzedward Hall says, "I am not prepared to deny that the ancient Hindus, when they spoke of the Hūṇas, intended the Huns. In the Middle Ages, however, it is certain that a race called Hūṇa was understood by the learned of India to form a divison of the ksatriyas."—*VP.*, II.134.

HUN-DESA—The country round Lake Mānasarovara.

HUSKA, HUVIṢKA—A Tuṣkara or Turki king, whose name is mentioned in the *Rājataranginī* as Huṣka, which has been found in inscriptions as Huviṣka, and upon the corrupt Greek coins as Oerki. He is supposed to have reigned just at the commencement of the Christian era. (*see* KANIṢKA)

HUTASANA—The god of flame.

I

IDA—One of the daughters of Daksha who was married to Kasyapa.

In the *Ṛgveda* Iḍā is primarily food, refreshment, or a libation of milk; thence a stream of praise, personified as the goddess of speech. She is called the instructress of Manu, and frequent passages ascribe to her the first institution of the rules of performing sacrifices. According to Sāyaṇa, she is the goddess presiding over the earth. A legend in the *Śatapatha Brāhmaṇa* represents her as springing from a sacrifice which Manu performed for the purpose of obtaining offspring. She was claimed by Mitra-Varuṇa, but remained faithful to him who had produced her. Manu lived with her, and praying and fasting to obtain offspring, he begot upon her the race of Manu. In the Purāṇas she is daughter of the Manu Vaivasvata, wife of Buddha (Mercury), and mother of Purūravas. The Manu Vaivasvata, before he had sons, instituted a sacrifice to Mitra and Varuṇa for the purpose of obtaining one; but the officiating priest mismanaged the performance, and the result was the birth of a daughter, Ida or Ilā. Through the favour of the two deities her sex was changed, and she became a man, Sudyumna. Under the malediction of Śiva, Sudyumna was again turned into a woman, and, as Ilā, married Buddha or Mercury. After she had given birth to Purūravas, she, under the favour of Viṣṇu, once more became Sudyumna, and was the father of three sons. According to another version of the legend, the Manu's eldest son was named Ilā. He having trespassed on a grove sacred to Pārvatī, was changed into a female, Ilā. Upon the supplications and prayers of Ilā's friends, Śiva and his consort conceded that the offender should be a male one month and female another. There are other variations in the story which is apparently ancient.

IDAVIDA—Daughter of Tṛṇabindu and the apsaras Alambuṣā. There are different statements in the Purāṇas as regards her. She is represented to be the wife of Viśravas and mother of Kubera, or the wife of Pulastya and mother of Viśravas.

IDHMAJIHWA—One of the ten sons of Priyavrata according to the Bhágavata.

IDVATSARA—The name of the third cycle or Yuga, of which five are enumerated, each cycle comprehending sixty-one solar months or 1,830 days.

IJIKAS, ALSO ITIKAS—A people of the South of India.

IKSHULA IKSHUMATI—The name of a river mentioned in the Rámáyana and Vishnu Purána, but not identified.

IKSVAKU—Son of the lawgiver Manu Vaivasvat, who was son of Vivasvat, the sun. "He was born from the nostril of the Manu as he happened to sneeze." Ikṣvāku was founder of the Solar race of kings, and reigned in Ayodhyā at the beginning of the second *yuga* or age. He had a hundred sons, of whom the eldest was Vikukṣi. Another son, named Nimi, founded the Mithilā dynasty. According to Max Müller the name is mentioned once, and only once, in the *Ṛgveda*. Respecting this he adds: "I take it, not as the name of a king, but as the name of a people, probably the people who inhabited Bhājeratha, the country washed by the northern Gaṅgā or Bhāgirathī." Others place the Ikṣvākus in the north-west.

"Ikshwáku was the son of Manu, the first king of Kosala, and founder of the solar dynasty or family of the children of the Sun, the god of that luminary being the father of Manu.

The following extract from the Rámáyana gives the line of kings from Ikswaku to Bharata.

"From viewless nature Brahma rose,
No change, no end, no waste, he knows.
A son had he, Maríchi styled,
And Kasyap was Maríchi's child.
From him Vivaswat sprang; from him
Manu whose fame shall ne'er be dim.
Manu, who life to mortals gave,
Begot Ikshváku good and brave.
First of Ayodhyá's kings was he,
Pride of her famous dynasty.
From him the glorious Kukshi sprang,
Whose fame through all the regions rang.
Rival of Kukshi's ancient fame,
His heir, the great Vikukshi came.
His son was Vana, lord of might,
His Anaranya, strong to fight.
His son was Prithu, glorious name,
From him the good Trisanku came.
He left a son renowned afar,
Known by the name of Dhundumár.
His son who drove the mighty car
Was Yuvanaswa fear'd in war.
He passed away. Him followed then
His son Mándhátá, king of men,
His son was blest on high
emprise Susandhi fortunate and wise.
Two noble sons had he, to wit,
Dhruvasandhi and Prasenajit
Bharat was Dhruvasandhi's son,
And glorious fame that monarch won."

—*Griffiths.*

ILA, ILĀ—(*see* Iḍā)

ILA—Before the birth of the sons mentioned above, the Manu, being desirous of sons, offered a sacrifice for that purpose to Mitra and Varuna; but the rite being deranged through an irregularity of the ministering priest, a daughter, Ilá was produced. Through the favour of the two divinities, however her sex was changed, and she became a man named Sudyumna, (*q.v.*)

ILĀVILĀ—(*see* Iḍāvidā)

ILAVILA—One of the sons of Dasaratha, who does not appear however to have achieved any distinction.' The daughter of Trinavinda, became the wife of Visravas, and mother of Kubera the god of wealth.

ILAVRITA—One of the nine sons of Agnídhra, king of Jamba-dwípa. The region in the centre of which Mount Meru is situated was conferred on Ilávrita.

ILWALA—A celebrated demon, the son of Hláda. He is the hero of various legends in the Puránas. He had a cousin of the same name, the son of Viprachitti, who was also distinguished amongst the Danavas. One legend of Ilwala is that he was accustomed to assume the form of a Brahman, and in conjunction with his brother Vátápi, lure many of them to destruction, as related in the account of AGASTYA, (*q.v.*) the sage by whom Ilwala was destroyed. (*see* VĀTPĀPI)

INDIA—"Is bounded on the north and the east by the Himalaya mountains, on the west by the Indus, and on the south by the sea. Its length from Kashmere to Cape Comorin is 1,900 miles; its breadth from the Rann of Kutch to Sudiya, in Assam, 1,500 miles. The superficial contents are 1,287,000 miles, and the population, under the then British and native rule, was estimated at 200,000,000, and has now crossed over a billion souls. It is crossed from east to west by a chain of mountains called the Vindya, at the base of which flows the Narmada. The country to the north of this river is generally designated Hindustan, and that to the south of it the Deccan. Hindustan is composed of the basin of the Indus on one side, and of the Ganges on the other, with the great sandy desert on the west, and an elevated tract now called, from its position, Central India. The Deccan has on its northern boundary a chain of mountains running parallel with the Vindya, to the south of which stretches a table land of triangular form, terminating at Cape Comorin, with the western Ghats, on the western coast, and the eastern Ghats, of minor altitude, on the opposite coast. Between the Ghats and the sea lies a narrow belt of land which runs round the whole peninsula.

Of the ancient history or chronology of the Hindus there are no credible memorials. The history was compiled by poets, who drew on their imagination for their facts, and the chronology was computed by astronomers, who have made the successive ages of the world to correspond with the conjunctions of the heavenly bodies. The age of the world is thus divided into four periods: the *satya yuga* extending to 1,728,000, and the second, or *treta yuga*, to 1,296,000 years; the third, or the *dwápara yuga*, comprises 864,000 years; and the fourth, or *kali yuga* is predicted to last 432,000 years. A *kalpa*, or a day of Brahma, is composed of a thousand such periods, or 4,320,000,000 years. Extravagant as these calculations may appear, they are outdone by the Burmese, who affirm that the lives of the ancient inhabitants extended to a period equal to the sum of every drop of rain which falls on the surface of the globe in three years. The dates given for the first three ages must, therefore, be rejected as altogether imaginary, while the commencement of the fourth, or present age, which corresponds, to a certain degree, with the authentic eras of other nations, may be received as generally correct.

India is designated by native writers Bharata Varsha, from king Bharat, who is said to have reigned over the whole country. That he did not enjoy universal monarchy in India is certain, though he was doubtless one of the earliest and most renowned of its rulers; but this fact loses all historical value when we are told in the shastras that he reigned ten thousand years, and on his death was transformed into a deer. Thus do we plod our way through darkness and mystery, at every step fact is confounded with fable, and our entire research end only in conjecture. The original settlers are identified with the various tribes of Bhíls, Koles, Gonds, Mínas, and Chúars, still living in a state almost of nature, in the forests of the Soane, the Nerbudda, and the Mahanuddi, and in the hills of Surgúja and Chota Nagpore. Their languages have no affinity with the Sanskrit, and their religion diners from Hinduism. In those fastnesses, amidst al! the revolutions which have convulsed India, they have continued to maintain, unchanged, their original simplicity of habits, creed, and speech. They were apparently driven from the plains by fresh colonies of emigrants; and these were in their turn conquered by the Hindus, who brought their religion and language with them from regions beyond the Indus, and, having reduced the inhabitants to a servile condition, branded them with the name of súdras. Of the four Hindu castes, three are designated the twice born, which seems to indicate that they all belonged to the conquering race, although the term is now applied exclusively to brahmans. In the Institutes of Manu reference is also made to cities governed by súdras, which the twice-born were forbidden to enter, and the allusion evidently applies to súdra chiefs, who continued to maintain their independence after the Hindu invasion.

The Hindus who originally crossed the Indus took possession of a small tract of land, 100 miles north-west of Delhi, about 65 miles by 30, which was considered the residence of gods and holy sages, while the brahmans appear to have subsequently occupied the country north of the Yamuna and the Ganges, stretching to the confines of north Behar. The India of the Vedas, of Manu, and the earliest writers was exclusively confined to the region north of the Nerbudda, and comprised but a small portion even of that limited quarter. It was in the north that the four places of greatest sanctity were situated during the early ages, though the Deccan now contains many places of distinguished merit. The north was also the seat of the solar and lunar races, the scene of chivalrous adventures, and the abode of all those who are celebrated in the legends, the mythology, and the philosophy of the Hindus. Even in the polished age in which the Rámáyan and the Mahábharat were composed, the south was the land of fable, the dwelling of bears and monkeys, and it was not till a very late period that these apes and goblins and monsters were transformed into orthodox Hindus. It must, therefore, be distinctly borne in mind that the revolutions described in the sacred books of the Hindus belong to Hindustan and not to the Deccan." (Marshman's *History of India*, vol. 1.)

INDRA—The god of the firmament, the personified atmosphere. In the Vedas he stands in the first rank among the gods, but he is not uncreate, and is represented as having a father and mother: "a vigorous god begot him; a heroic female brought him forth". He is described as being of a ruddy or golden colour, and as having arms of enormous length; "but his forms are endless, and he can assume any shape at will". He rides in a bright golden car, drawn by two tawny or ruddy horses with flowing manes and tails. His weapon is the thunderbolt, which he carries in his right hand; he also uses arrows, a great hook, and a net, in which he is said to entangle his foes. The *soma* juice is his especial delight; he takes enormous draughts of it, and, stimulated by its exhilarating qualities, he goes forth to war against his foes, and to perform his other duties. As deity of the atmosphere, he governs the weather and dispenses the rain; he sends forth his lightnings and thunder, and he is continually at war with Vṛtra or Ahi, the demon of drought and inclement weather, whom he overcomes with his thunderbolts, and compels to pour down the rain. Strabo describes the Indians as worshipping Jupiter Pluvius, no doubt meaning Indra, and he has also been compared to Jupiter Tonans. One myth is that of his discovering and rescuing the cows of the priests or of the gods, which had been stolen by an *asura* named Paṇi or Vala, whom he killed, and he is hence called Valabhid. He is frequently represented as destroying the "stone-built cities" of the *asuras* or atmospheric demons, and of the *dasyus* or aborigines of India. In his warfare he is sometimes represented as escorted by troops of Maruts, and attended by his comrade Viṣṇu. More hymns are addressed to Indra than to any other deity in the Vedas, with the exception of Agni. For he was reverenced in his beneficent character as the bestower of rain and the cause of fertility, and he was feared as the awful ruler of the storm and director of the lightning and thunder. In many places of the *Ṛgveda* the highest divine functions and attributes are ascribed to him. There was a triad of gods —Agni, Vāyu, and Sūrya—which held a pre-eminence above the rest, and Indra frequently took the place of Vāyu. In some parts of the Veda, as Dr. Muir remarks, the ideas expressed of Indra are grand and lofty; at other times he is treated with familiarity, and his devotion to the *soma* juice is dilated upon, though nothing debasing is perceived in his sensuality. Indra is mentioned as having a wife, and the name of Indrāṇi or Aindrī is invoked among the goddesses. In the *Śatapatha Brāhmaṇa* she is called Indra's beloved wife.

In the later mythology Indra has fallen into the second rank. He is inferior to the triad, but he is the chief of all the other gods. He is the regent of the atmosphere and of the east quarter of the compass, and he reigns over *svarga*, the heaven of the gods and of beatified spirits, which is a region of great magnificence and splendour. He retains many of his Vedic characteristics, and some of them are intensified. He sends the lightning and hurls the thunderbolt, and the rainbow is his bow. He is frequently at war with the *asuras*, of whom he lives in constant dread, and by whom he is often worsted. But he slew the demon Vṛtra, who, being regarded as a brāhmaṇa, Indra had to conceal himself and make sacrifice until his guilt was purged away. His continued love for the soma juice is shown by a legend in the *Mahābhārata*, which represents him as being compelled by the sage Cyavana to allow the Aśvins to partake of the *soma* libations, and his sensuality has now developed into an extreme lasciviousness. Many instances are recorded of his incontinence and adultery, and his example is frequently referred to as an excuse in cases of gallantry, as by King Nahuṣa when he tried to obtain Indra's wife while the latter was hiding in fear for having killed the brāhmaṇa in the person of the demon Vṛtra. According to the *Mahābhārata* he seduced, or endeavoured to seduce, Ahalyā, the wife of the sage Gautama, and that sage's curse impressed upon him a thousand marks resembling the female organ, so he was called Sayoni; but these marks were afterwards changed to eyes, and he is hence called Netrayoni, and Sahasrākṣa "the thousand-eyed". In the *Rāmayana* it is related that Rāvaṇa the *rākṣasa* king of Laṅkā or Ceylon, warred against Indra in his own heaven, and that Indra was defeated and carried off to Laṅkā by Rāvaṇa's son Meghanāda, who for this exploit received the title of Indrajit (*q.v.*), 'conqueror of Indra'. Brahmā and the gods had to sue for the release of Indra, and to purchase it with the boon of immortality to the victor. Brahmā then told the humiliated god that his defeat was a punishment for the seduction of Ahalyā. The *Taittirīya Brāhmaṇa* states that he chose Indrāṇi to be his wife in preference to other goddesses because of her voluptuous attractions, and later authorities say that he ravished her and slew her father, the *daitya* Puloman, to escape his curse. Mythologically he was father of Arjuna (*q.v.*), and for him he cheated Karṇa of his divine coat of mail, but gave Karṇa in recompense a javelin of deadly effect. His libertine character is also shown by his frequently sending celestial nymphs to excite the passions of holy men, and to beguile them from the potent penance which he dreaded.

In the Purāṇas many stories are told of him, and he appears especially in rivalry with Kṛṣṇa. He incurred the wrath of the choleric sage Durvāsas by slighting a garland of flowers which that sage presented to him, and so brought upon himself the curse that his whole dominion should be whelmed in ruin. He was utterly defeated by the *daityas*, or rather by their ally, Raja, son of Āyus, and grandson of Purūravas, and he was reduced to such a forlorn condition that he, "the god of a hundred sacrifices", was compelled to beg for a little sacrificial butter. Puffed up by their victory, his conquerors neglected their duties, and so they became the easy prey of Indra, who recovered his dominion. The *Bhāgavata Purāṇa* represents him as having killed a brāhmaṇa, and of being haunted by that crime, personified as a Cāṇḍāli.

Indra had been an object of worship among the pastoral people of Vraja, but Kṛṣṇa persuaded them to cease this worship. Indra was greatly enraged at this, and sent a deluge of rain to overwhelm them; but Kṛṣṇa lifted up the mountain Govardhana on his finger to shelter them, and so held it for seven days, till Indra was baffled and rendered homage to Kṛṣṇa. Again, when Kṛṣṇa went to visit *svarga*, and was about to carry off the *pārjāta* tree, Indra resented its removal, and a fierce fight ensued, in which Indra was worsted, and the tree was carried off. Among the deeds of Indra recorded in the Purāṇas is that of the destruction of the offspring of Diti in her womb, and the production therefrom of the Maruts (*see* DITI); and there is a story of his cutting off the wings of the mountains with his thunderbolts, because they were refractory and troublesome. Indra is represented as a fair man riding on a white horse or an elephant, and bearing the *vajra* or thunderbolt in his hand. His son is named Jayanta. Indra is not the object of direct worship, but he receives incidental adoration, and there is a festival kept in his honour called Śakradhvajotthāna, 'the raising of the standard of Indra'.

The king of heaven; the king of the Devas; is represented with four arms and hands, with two he holds a lance, in the third one the thunderbolt (Vajrayudha) and the fourth one is empty. Sometimes he is drawn as a white man sitting on an elephant, with the thunderbolt in his right hand and a bow in his left. His reign is to continue one hundred years of the gods, after which another individual from among the gods, the giants, or men, by his own merit, raises himself to this eminence. The sacrifice of a horse one hundred times will, it is said, raise a person to the rank of Indra. The Purának relate many stories of Indra, who is described as very jealous lest any person should, by sacred austerities or sacrifices, excel him in religious merit, and thus obtain his kingdom. To prevent these devotees from succeeding in their object, he generally sends one of the celestial nymphs to draw away their minds, and thus bring them from then' religious observances, induce them to return to a life of sensual gratification. It was Indra who stole the horse consecrated by king Sagara, who was about to perform for the hundredth time the sacrifice of that animal.

"Indra plays an important part in each of the three periods of Indian mythology. In the earliest age he seems to have been the unknown mysterious being who inhabited the sky, the firmament between earth and the sun, who rode upon the clouds, who poured forth the rain, hurled the forked lightning upon earth, and spoke in the awful thunder. His character was at once beneficent as giving rain and shade; and awful and powerful in the storm. He is the original of the Jupiter Tonans of the west, and the Thor of the north, and like them rose in the earliest ages to the first place, and the sovereignty among the gods. Fear, a stronger motive among men than gratitude, raised him above the elementary triad. In the Epic period he is the first person of the pure mythological triad, Indra, Agni, and Yama. In the Puránic age, when the powers of a Supreme Being were personified in the superior triad of Brahmá, Vishnu, and siva, Indra's star declines. He is no longer the principal divinity, but only the chief of the inferior deities; and, as such, is at constant war with the giants and demons, by whom ho is for a time deposed. A curse from the Rishi

Durvása causes his power and that of the deities subject to him gradually to decline; and he is defeated by Krishna in a fight for the Párijáta tree, which had been produced at the churning of the ocean, and planted by Indra in his own garden. An amusing account of this battle is given in the Vishnu-Purána, p. 687. His wife's name is sachí. He is lord of the eight Vasus. The sage Gautama pronounced upon him the curse of wearing one thousand disgraceful marks which he afterwards turned to eyes. He ravished the daughter of Puloman, whom he slew to avoid his curse. He is borne on a white horse. The rain-bow is supposed to be his bow bent for the destruction of his foes, and thunderbolts are his weapons. The heaven over which he rules, and which the other secondary deities inhabit, is, in the Epic age, called Swarga, and later, Indralóka, or Devalóka. His horse is Uchchhaihshravas; his elephant, Airávata; his city, Amarávati; his palace, Vaijayanta. These details belong to the Puránic age."—*Thomson*.

Dr. Muir writes "Indra and Agni are said to be twin brothers. A variety of vague and general epithets are lavished upon Indra. He is distinguished as youthful, ancient, strong, agile, martial, heroic, bright, undecaying, all-conquering, lord of unbounded wisdom and irresistible power and prowess, wielder of the thunderbolt, &c. He has vigour in his body, strength in his arms, a thunderbolt in his hand, and wisdom in his head. The thunderbolt of Indra is generally described as having been fashioned for him by the Indian Hephaistos, Tvashtri, the artificer of the gods. Another instrument of warfare, a net, is assigned to Indra. 'This world was the great net of the great Sakra. With this net of Indra I envelope them all in darkness.'

"Invoked by his mortal worshippers Indra obeys the summons, and speedily arrives in his chariot to receive their offerings. He finds food provided for his horses, and large libations of soma juice are poured out for himself to quaff. He becomes exhilarated by these libations, which are also frequently described as stimulating his warlike dispositions and energies, and fitting him for his other functions, even for supporting the earth and sky. He is said to have drunk at one draught thirty bowls of soma." Thus exhilarated by soma juice, "Indra hurries off escorted by troops of Maruts, and sometimes attended by his faithful comrade Vishnu, to encounter the hostile powers in the atmosphere, who malevolently shut up the watery treasures in the clouds. These demons of drought, called by a variety of names, as Vrittra, Ahi, sushna, Namuchi, Pipru, Sambara, Urana, &c., armed on their side also, with every variety of celestial artillery, attempt, but in vain, to resist the onset of the gods. Heaven and earth quake with affright at the crash of Indra's thunder. The enemies of Indra are speedily pierced and shattered by the discharge of his iron shafts. The waters, released from their imprisonment, descend in torrents to the earth, fill all the rivers and roll along to the ocean. The gloom, which had overspread the sky, is dispersed, and the sun is restored to his position in the heavens. Constant allusions to these elemental conflicts occur in nearly every part of the Rig Veda; and the descriptions are sometimes embellished with a certain variety of imagery. The clouds are represented as mountains, or as cities or fortresses of the Asuras, or atmospheric demons, which Indra overthrows."

Dr. Muir selects a great variety of passages as specimens of the language in which Indra is most commonly celebrated in the hymns. He adds, "it will be observed that the attributes which are ascribed to him are chiefly those of physical superiority, and of dominion over the external world. In fact he is not generally represented as possessing the spiritual elevation and moral grandeur with which Varuna is so often invested." Vol. v., p. 103.

"Thou Indra art a friend, a brother
A kinsman dear, a father, mother.
Though thou hast troops of friends, yet we,
Can boast no other friend but thee.

With faith we claim thine aid divine,
For thou art ours *and* we are thine.
Thou art not deaf; though far away,
Thou nearest all, whate'er we pray.

Preserve us friend, dispel our fears,
And let us live a hundred years
And when our earthly course we've run,
And gained the region of the sun,
Then let us live in ceaseless glee,
Sweet nectar quaffing there with thee."

O.S.T., Vol. v., p. 139.

Indra's names are many, as Mahendra, Śakra, Maghavān, Ṛbhukṣa, Vāsava, Arha, Datteya. His epithets or titles also are numerous. He is Vṛtrahan, 'the destroyer of Vṛtra'; Vajrapāṇi, 'of the thunderbolt hand'; Meghavāhana, 'home upon the clouds'; Pākaśāsana, 'the subduer of Pāka'; Śatakratu, 'of a hundred sacrifices'; Devapati and Surādhipa, 'chief of the gods'; Divas-pati, 'ruler of the atmosphere'; Marutvān, 'lord of the winds'; Svargapati, 'lord of paradise'; Jiṣṇu, 'leader of the celestial host'; Purandara, 'destroyer of cities'; Ulūka, 'the owl'; Ugradhanvan, 'of the terrible bow', and many others. The heaven of Indra is *svarga*; its capital is Amarāvatī; his palace, Vaijyanta; his garden, Nandana, Kandasāra, or Pāruṣya; his elephant is Airāvata; his horse, Ucchaiḥśravas; his chariot, Vimāna; his charioteer, Mātali; his bow, the rainbow, Śakradhanus; and his sword, Parañja.

INDRA-DWIPA—One of the nine portions of the Varsha of Bharata.

INDRADYUMNA—Son of Sumati and grandson of Bharata. There were several of the name, among them a king of Avantī, by whom the temple of Viṣṇu was built, and the image of Jagannātha was set up in Orissa.

INDRAJIT—Meghanāda, the bravest and most powerful of the sons of Rāvaṇa. When Ravaṇa went against Indra's forces in *svarga*, his son Meghanāda accompanied him, and fought most valiantly. Indra himself was obliged to interfere, when Meghanāda, availing himself of the magical power of becoming invisible, which he had obtained from Śiva, bound Indra and carried him off to Laṅkā. The gods, headed by Brahmā, went thither to obtain the release of Indra, and Brahmā gave to Meghanāda the name Indrajīt, 'conqueror of Indra'. Still the victor refused to release his prisoner for anything less than the boon of immortality. Brahmā refused, but Indrajit persisted in his demand and achieved his object. One version of the *Rāmāyaṇa* states that Indrajit was killed and had his head cut off by Lakṣmaṇa, who surprised him while he was engaged in a sacrifice.

He was skilled in magic, could render himself invisible, possessed enchanted weapons, described as a kind of rope, which when thrown at an enemy became transformed into a serpent, and retained him in its folds. By means of these magical weapons he pierced a great number of warriors and inflicted terrible wounds on all the leaders of Ráma's army; *viz.*, Sugríva, Angada, Níla, Jámbavat, Nala, Tára, Sarabha, Sushena, Panasa, Gandha-madana, Dwivida, Kesarí, Sampáti, Binata, Rishabha; as well as on Ráma and Lakshmána, leaving them for dead. They were all restored by the exhalations issuing from the healing plants brought by Hanumán from Kailasa. All this occurred after Hanumán had destroyed the great army of Rákshasas sent against him by Rávana, the latter being filled with dismay, ordered his son Aksha to go forth, and he was also slain. Then Rávana filled with grief sent for his famous son Indrajit, and said go you and conquer this evil Monkey. Indrajit then ascended his chariot drawn by four tigers, and went out at the head of a vast army to fight against the Monkey chief. The combat commenced, bat Indrajit could not conquer until he bound Hanumán in the irresistible noose of Brahma. Afterwards Indrajit performed three sacrifices to Agni, and confined Ráma and Lakshmána in his noose, and successfully charged the army of Monkeys. He was ultimately killed by Lakahmána, with an arrow given to him by Indra at the hermitage of Agastya.

INDRAKILA—The mountain Mandāra of the Vishnu Purána but not identified.

INDRA-LOKA—Amarávati, the heaven of Indra and Kshatriyas, called also Swarga. It was built by Visvakarma, the architect of the gods, a son of Brahma. It is described as eight hundred miles in circumference, and forty miles high. Its pillars are composed of diamonds; all its thrones, beds, etc., of pure gold, as also its palaces. It *is* surrounded by beauteous gardens and pleasure grounds, interspersed with pools, fountains, etc., while music, dancing, and every sort of festivity entertain the celestial inhabitants. The audience chamber is so large that it accommodates all the three hundred and thirty millions of celestials, together with the forty-eight thousand Rishis, and the multitude of attendants. (*see* LOKA)

INDRANI—Wife of Indra, and mother of Jayanta and Jayantī. She is also called Śaci and Aindrī. She is mentioned a few times in the *Ṛgveda*, and is said to be the most fortunate of females, "for her husband shall never die of old age". The *Taittirīya Brāhmaṇa* states that Indra chose her for his wife from a number of competing goddesses, because she surpassed them all in voluptuous attractions. In the *Rāmāyaṇa* and Purāṇas she appears as the daughter of the *daitya* Puloman, from whom she has the patronymic Paulomī. She was ravished by Indra, who killed her father to escape his curse. According to the *Mahābhārata*, King Nahuṣa became enamoured of her, and she escaped from him with difficulty. Indrāṇī has never been held in very high esteem as a goddess.

The wife of Indra (called also Sáchi) is represented as an ever-blooming virgin, and whilst the dignity of the king of the gods passes from one to another, she remains the wife of each succeeding Devéndra. Indráni, never a mother herself, had a son, Chitraputra, born unto her of a cow, as a reward for the austerities which she practised in honour of Iswara, to the end that he might grant her a son. When Chitraputra was born from the cow, Indráni felt like a woman in travail, and her breasts became full, so that she could nurse the child.

In the Rig Veda one speaker says "I have heard that among all these females Indráni is the most fortunate , for her husband shall never at any future time die of old age." The Aitareya Brahmana alludes to a wife of Indra, called Prásahá. The Satap. Br. says "Indráni is Indra's beloved wife, and she has a head dress of all forms." *O.S.T.*, Vol. v., p. 82.

INDRA-PRAMATI—An early teacher of the *Ṛgveda*, who received one Saṁhitā direct from Paila. Indrapramita imparted his Sanhita to his son Mandakeyu, and it thence descended through successive generations as well as disciples.

INDRA-PRASTHA—The city of the Pándavas situated between Delhi and the Kútub. "The pilgrim who wends his way from the modern city of Delhi to pay a visit to the strange relics of the ancient world which surround the mysterious Kútub, will find on either side of his road a number of desolate heaps, the *debris* of thousands of years, the remains of successive Capitals which date back to the very dawn of history; and local tradition still points to these sepulchres of departed ages as the sole remains of the Raj of the sons of Pándu, and their once famous city of Indra-prastha." The Mahábhárata contains a poetical description of the flourishing state of the kingdom under the rule of Rája Yudhishthira. When he resolved on retiring from the world he gave the Ráj of Hastinápur to Paríkshit the son of Abhímanyu, and the Ráj of Indra-prastha to Yuyutsa, the only surviving son of Maharaja Dritaráshtra. The name is still known, and is used for a part of the city of Delhi.

INDRAS OF THE MANWANTARA—Each Manwantara has its own Indra. The Indra of the second Manwantara was Vipaschil; of the third, Susanti, of the fourth Siva (also named Satakrata, as he obtained the honour by his performance of a hundred sacrifices,) of the fifth Vibha, of the sixth, Manojava; of the seventh, Purandara; of the eighth, Bali; of the ninth, Avbhuta; of the tenth, Sánti; of the eleventh, Vrisha; of the twelfth, Rithudáma; of the thirteenth, Divaspati; of the fourteenth, Suchí.

INDRASAVARNI—The Manu of the fourteenth Manwantara, according to the Bhágavata.

INDRASENA (mas.), **INDRASENĀ** (fem)—**(1)** Names of the son and daughter of Nala and Damayanti. **(2)** The charioteer of Yudhishthira.

INDRIYATMA—"One with the senses;" a name of Vishnu, who is described by *five* appellations.

1. Bhutátma, One with created things.
2. Pradhanátam, One with crude nature.
3. Indriyátma, One with the senses.
4. Paramátma, Supreme spirit.
5. Átma, Soul, living soul animating nature and existing before it.

INDU—The moon. (*see* SOMA)

INDUMANI—The moon gem. (*see* CANDRAKĀNTA)

INDUMATI DEVI—**(1)** The daughter of the Rája of Vidarbha and wife of Aja. [See AJA.] **(2)** Sister of Bhoja, king of Vidarbha, who chose Prince Aja for her husband at her *svayaṁvara*. She was killed by Nārada's garland falling upon her while asleep in an arbour.

IRAVAT—A son of Arjuna by his Nāga wife Ulūpi.

IRAVATI—**(1)** The river Rāvī or Hydraotes. **(2)** The wife of the Rudra Bhava according to the Bhágavata. **(3)** The mother of Airávata the elephant of Indra which is elsewhere said to have been produced at the churning of the milk sea.

ISA—**(1)** 'Lord'. A title of Śiva. Name of a Upaniṣad (*q.v.*) which has been translated by Dr. Roer in the *Bibliotheca Indica*. **(2)** A name of a month occurring in the Vedas, and belonging to a system now obsolete. It is one of the months according to the Vishnu Purána in which the sun is in his southern declination.

ISANA—A name of Śiva or Rudra, or of one of his manifestations. (*see* RUDRA) He is guardian of the north-east quarter.

ISTI-PASAS—'Stealers of offerings.' *Rākṣasas* and other enemies of the gods, who steal the oblations.

ISVARA—'Lord'. A title given to Śiva.

ISVARAKRSNA—Author of the philosophical treatise called *Sāṁkhya Kārikā*.

ISWARA—Brahma in the neuter form is abstract supreme spirit: and Iswara is the Deity in his active nature, he who is able to do, or leave undone, or to do anything in any other manner than that in which it is done. Iswara is that which knows all things as if they were present. Mahat is also called Iswara from its exercising supremacy over all things. In Southern India Iswara is identical with Siva. All who profess the Siva mata (the religion of Siva) regard Iswara as the highest god in whose honour they have everywhere built pagodas, and celebrate many festivals. Iswara is also the name of one of the Rudras in the Váyu list.

ITIHASA—Historical tradition taught by Vyása. It is usually supposed that by the Itihása the Mahábhárata is meant.

IVILAKA—One of the Andhra kings, the son of Lambódara.

J

JABALAS—Students of a branch of the Vájasaneyi, or white Yajush.

JABALA—The mother of Satyakáma, who could not tell her son who was his father and to what gotra he belonged; the son had consequently the utmost difficulty in obtáining permission to become a Brahmá chárin. *See* SATYAKÁMA.

JABALI, JAVAU—A brāhmaṇa who was priest of King Daśaratha, and held skeptical philosophical opinions. He is represented in the *Rāmāyaṇa* as enforcing his views upon Rāma, who decidedly repudiated them. Thereupon he asserted that his atheistic arguments had been used only for a purpose, and that he was really imbued with sentiments of piety and religion. He is said to have been a logician, so probably he belonged to the Nyāya School.

JAGADDHATAṚ (DHĀTṚ)—'Sustainer of the world.' An epithet given to both Sarasvatī and Durgā.

JAGANMATṚ (MĀTṚ). 'Mother of the world.' One of the names of Śiva's wife. (*see* DEVI)

JAGANNATHA—'Lord of the world.' A particular form of Viṣṇu, or rather of Kṛṣṇa. He is worshipped in Bengal and other parts of India, but Puri, near the town of Cuttack, in Orissa, is the great seat of his worship, and multitudes of pilgrims resort thither from all parts, especially to the two great festivals of the *Snānayātrā* and *Rathayātrā*, in the months of Jyesṭha and Āṣāḍha. The first of these is when the image is bathed, and in the second, or car festival, the image is brought out upon a car with the images of his brother Balarāma and sister Subhadrā, and is drawn by the devotees. The legend of the origin of Jagannātha is peculiar. Kṛṣṇa was killed by a hunter, and his body was left to rot under a tree, but some pious persons found the bones and placed them in a box. A devout king named Indradyumna was directed by Viṣṇu to form an image of Jagannātha and to place the bones of Kṛṣṇa inside it. Viśvakarmā, the architect of the gods, undertook to make the image, on condition of being left quite undisturbed till the work was complete. After fifteen days the king was impatient and went to Viśvakarmā, who was angry, and left off work before he had made either hands or feet, so that the image has only stumps. Indradyumna prayed to Brahmā, who promised to make the image famous, and he did so by giving to it eyes and a soul, and by acting as high priest at its consecration.

This is perhaps the most famous form of Krishna. The image has no legs, and only stumps of arms. The head and legs are very large. At the festivals, the Brahmans adorn him with silver or golden hands.

Krishna having been accidentally killed by Jará, a hunter, he left the body to rot under a tree. Some pious persons, however, collected the bones of Krishna and placed them in a box. There they remained till King Indradyumna (a great ascetic) was directed by Vishnu to form the image of Jaggannátha, and put into its belly these bones of Krishna. Visvakarma (the architect of the gods) undertook to prepare it, on condition that he should be left undisturbed till its completion. The impatient king, however, after fifteen days, went to the spot; on which Visvakarma desisted from his work, and left the god without hands or feet. The king was much disconcerted, but on praying to Brahmá, he promised to make the image famous in its present shape. Indradyumna then invited all the gods to be present at the setting up of this image. Brahma himself acted as high priest, and gave eyes and a soul to the god, which completely established the fame of Jaggannátha. This image is said to lie in a pool, near the famous temple at Jaggannátha-kshetra (*i.e.* Jagganath's field), near the town of Purí in Orissa, commonly called by the English, Jaggernath's Pagoda.

There are many other temples to Jaggannátha in Bengal and other parts of India, besides that in Orissa, built by rich men as works of merit, and endowed with lands, villages, and money, at which the worship of the god is performed every morning and evening.

There are two great annual festivals in honour of the god, *viz.*, the Snán-yátrá in the month Jyaistha

(May, June) and the Bath yathra in the following month Ásárha. These are everywhere most numerously attended; but especially those celebrated at the great temple at Purí. Thither pilgrims from the remotest corners of India flock to pay their adoration at the hallowed shrine. Between two and three thousand persons, it is computed, used to lose their lives on the annual pilgrimages to this temple, and not less than 200,000 worshippers were present at the festivals, from which the Brahmáns draw immense revenue. Since the withdrawal of the large annual grant, however, which the British Government of India, till very recently, made to the Orissa Temple, the numbers attending these festivals have very greatly diminished. All the land within twenty miles round the "Pagoda" is considered holy; but the most sacred spot is an area of about six hundred and fifty feet square, which contains fifty temples, the most conspicuous of which is a lofty tower, about one hundred and eighty-four feet in height, and about twenty-eight feet square inside, in which the idol, with his brother Bala-Ráma, and his sister Subhadra, is lodged. Adjoining are two pyramidical buildings. In one, about forty square, the idol is worshipped, and in the other, the food prepared for the pilgrims is distributed. These buildings were erected in A.D. 1198. The walls are covered with statues, many of which are in highly indecent postures. The grand entrance is on the eastern side, and close to the outer wall stands an elegant stone column, thirty-five feet in height, the shaft of which is formed of a single block of basalt, presenting sixteen sides. The pedestal is richly ornamented. The column is surrounded by a finely sculptured statue of Hanumán, the monkey chief of the Rámáyana. The establishment of priests and others belonging to the temple has been slated to consist of three thousand nine hundred families, for whom the daily provision is enormous. The holy food is presented to the idol three times a day His meal lasts about an hour, during which time the dancing girls, the Devadasi, belonging to the temple, exhibit their professional skill in an adjoining building. "At the Snán-yátra (or bathing festival) the god is bathed by pouring water on his head during the reading of incantations. At the Rath-yátrá (or car festival) the devotees, by means of a hawser, for some distance draw the carriage, containing the three images (which has sixteen wheels and two wooden horses). On this occasion many cast themselves beneath the ponderous wheels and are crushed to death."—Small, *H.S.L.*, p. 157.

JAHNAVI—The Ganges, as the daughter of Jahnu (*see* JAHNU)

JAHNU—A sage descended from Purūravas. He was disturbed in his devotions by the passage of the river Gaṅgā, and consequently drank up its waters. He afterwards relented, and allowed the Stream to issue from his ear, hence Gaṅgā is called Jāhnavi, daughter of Jahnu. (*see* GAṄGĀ)

The son of Suhotra. This prince whilst performing a sacrifice, saw the whole of the place overflowed by the waters of the Ganges; being highly offended at this intrusion, he united the spirit of sacrifice with himself by the power of his devotion, and drank up the river. The gods and sages upon this came to him and appeased his indignation, and re-obtained Gangá from him in the capacity of his daughter.

"It chanced that Jahnu, great and good
Engaged with holy offerings stood.
The river spread her waves around
Flooding his sacrificial ground.
The saint in anger marked her pride,
And at one draught her stream he dried.
Then god and sage and bard afraid,
To noble high-souled Jahnu prayed.
And begged that he would kindly deem
His own dear child that holy stream.
Moved by their suit, he soothed their fears,
And loosed her waters from his ears.
Hence Gangá through the world is styled
Both Jahnaví and Jahnu's child." —*Griffiths.*

Jahnu is also the name of a son of Kuru. *V.P.*

JAIMINI—A pupil of Vyása, and teacher of the Sáma Veda. Also the name of a celebrated author in the South of India, who lived about the thirteenth century. He wrote a free translation from the Sanskrit of the Áswamedhika Parva of the Mahābhárata, detailing the horse sacrifice. This work *is* acknowledged by all sects to be the finest specimen of Canarese poetry in existence. 'He has read Jaimini' is a proverbial saying, equivalent to 'be is an accomplished man.'

JAIMINIYA-NYAYA-MALA-VISTARA—A work on philosophy by Mādhava. It has been edited by Goldstücker and Cowell.

JAINAS—The Jainas were a very numerous and important sect in the eighth and ninth centuries of the Christian era. The founder of the system was Rishabadeva, a Hindu, but the system itself was an off-shoot or after-growth of Buddhism with which it has many leading doctrines in common, but is distinguished from it by its recognition of a divine personal Ruler of all, and by its political leaning towards Brahmanism. The Jainas have left many monuments of their skill and power in the fine temples built in different parts of the Deccan, as well as in the provinces of Mewar and Marwar, which have been designated the cradle of their system. The literature of the Jainas is very extensive, including, besides Puránas of their own, various works in grammar, astronomy, mathematical science, medicine, &c. They were the first who reduced the Canarese language to writing, and cultivated it to a high degree of perfection. The best Epic poem in the Tamil language, the Chintámani, is the work of a Jaina.

"The leading tenets of the Jainas and those which chiefly distinguish them from the rest of the Hindus, are, first, the denial of the divine origin and infallible authority of the Vedas: secondly, the reverence of certain holy mortals, now termed Tirthankara, or saints, who acquired by practices of self-denial and mortification a station superior to that of the gods; and thirdly, extreme and even ludicrous tenderness for animal life.

"The Jainas are still found in most of the; provinces of Upper Hindustan; in the cities along the Ganges, in Calcutta, but more especially to the westward. They are also numerous in Guzerat, in the upper part of the Malabar Coast, and are scattered throughout the Peninsula. They still form a large and important division of the population of India. The name of the sect means a follower of Jina, the latter being one of the denominations of their deified saints; and as another name of these saints is Arhát, the Jainas are also called Arhattas.—*Wilson*

Munshi Sastram Aiyar wrote the following account of Jainism in Tamil.* "The Jainas verily believe that their system alone was the primeval system of the world; that all other systems were derived from it; that some of the learned professors of their system, by the fault of the time in which they lived, formed various other systems; that Móksha [bliss] can be obtained in this system and in no other; that this alone is the true system; and that all other systems believe falsehood to be truth.

"The Jainas positively affirm that the world exists from all eternity, and that it will exist for ever, without being destroyed, and that it was not created by God, Or by any other person. They moreover affirm that this world is divided into three parts, namely, the lower world, the middle world, and the upper world; and that below this world, there *is* a world called Adhogati [abyss, the nethermost hell], above which there are seven infernal worlds; and above those again are ten Pavanalokas, purifying worlds [Purgatories], above which is this world of earth; above this again is the Jotiloka, world of light [starry world]; and that in this our world, of earth there are two worlds included, namely, the Vyantraloka, world of demons [devils], and the Vidyadharaloka, world of demi-gods; and again above these are sixteen different kinds of Devalokas, worlds of the gods, over which is the Ahamindraloka, world of Indra; and above that again is the Mokshaloka, world of bliss; where dwells the Lord of all these worlds, the Supreme Being, called the Anadi-chitta-para-meshti [Eternal-intellectual-heavenly-dweller.]

"They believe that this earth is sixteen cords high, and seven cords broad; but this measurement is not within the comprehension of men; it is known only to the wise. The seas and islands that are situated on the earth cannot be perceived and estimated by man's understanding. They affirm that in the midst of the earth is the great mountain Meru, and that to the South of it is situated the Bharata region, and to the North the Airavata region, and to the East and West is the Videha region. They also affirm that on both sides of Mount Meru are situated the three kinds of Bhogabhumi, fruitful, or felicitous regions; and that the natives of these regions attain to great age and size; that they cannot interchange places; and that while it is day in one of the lands, it is night in the other. The people of Videha also attain to great age and stature.

"The Jainas consider Arugan to be their principal god, and worship him. The popular name of this god is Jinan; and from this the appellation Jainas is derived. To this god one thousand and eight sacred names are ascribed. His greatness is such that the three worlds worship and adore him. His knowledge is so great that it extends simultaneously to all things sentient and unsentient, to things that have been conceived and that will be conceived, to worlds and to worldless spaces. He is powerful to impart the knowledge of his doctrines simultaneously to all kinds of living beings, in their respective language, without the aid of mind, word, or body; and this he does of pure grace, and not from any selfish motives. He does not possess the power [act] of creating anything, or of preserving anything. He is not "subject to birth or death. He manifests great grace, and love, and mercy, to all sentient beings. He is of infinite wisdom, of infinite intelligence, of infinite power, and of infinite bliss. It is he that in the beginning, with a view of causing happiness to all living beings, made known the twelve primeval Vedas. He is the possessor of the triple-umbrella. He is without beginning and without end. He is the possessor of the three wheels of justice. He is represented with four holy faces, and as seated in the shade of the Ashóka tree. He has forsaken the one hundred and forty-eight actions of life. He has declared that the Veda, the World, Time, Souls, Action, and Virtue are, like himself, imperishable and eternal objects.

"The god Arugan has declared that there is no other god besides himself; that all who worship and adore him will obtain bliss, and that those who do not worship him will not obtain bliss; that all living beings will enjoy the fruits of their good or evil actions; that by preponderance of evil, souls enter hell, and by preponderance of good, they enter the world of the gods; but when good and evil are equally balanced, they are born *as* human beings; when evil alone exists, they are born as irrational animals; and when both good and evil are destroyed, then they are liberated. Since Arugan has declared these things, the Jains firmly believe them to be true doctrines, and since certain persons have intermediately introduced all other systems, they positively affirm them all to be false systems.

"As Time is considered to be eternal, it is indestructible in its nature, and is divided into two sorts, *viz.*, the Utsarpini and the Avasarpini time. The Avasarpini time has six stages, *viz.*, good-good time, good time, good-bad time, bad-good time, bad time, and bad-bad time. In like manner the Utsarpini time has six stages, only that it begins at the bottom of the list with bad-bad time and goes backwards. In the Utsarpini time, beginning from bad-bad time, the age and stature of men increase, as that of the waxing moon. But in the Avasarpini time, beginning from the good-good time, the age and stature of men decrease, as that of the waxing moon. The increase and decrease of stature is up to six thousand Vils [bows], and down to a cubit. The increase and decrease of age will be from three pallams, to fifteen years. This account of pallams is not to be understood by men. In the above specified six divisions of time, the first consists of four krores of krores of oceans of years. The second consists of three krores of krores of oceans of years. The third consists of two krores of krores of oceans of years. The fourth, one krore of krores of oceans of years, save forty-two thousand years. The fifth consists of twenty thousand years. The sixth also consists of twenty thousand years. This account of oceans is not to be understood by men. The stage in which we now live is the fifth, *viz.*, the bad time. When the two sorts of time, Tie, the Utsarpini and Avasarpini times run out, it is said to be a Yugam. Utsarpini means the age of increase, and Avasarpani means the age of decrease.

"As the present is the Avasarpini time, we must infer that the three good stages of time have already passed by, and that the Bharata region, and the Airavata region have both been Bhogabhumis, fruitful lands. The people of those times, as before stated, had stature of body, and length of age adequate to the times. The people of those times forty-five days after their birth, became perfect men, and were well up in all sciences, and attained all knowledge by themselves, simply from the plastic power of the time. Moreover in these three stages of time there was no light of the sun or of the moon; but day and night were formed from the reflection and non-reflection of the Kalpaka trees. Those people at death entered the world of the gods, and did not go to hell and they were not subject to the ordinary physical evils connected with disease, the discharges of the body, &c.

"Thus after the existence of the Bhogabhumi, when yet there was one eighth of time, in the third stage, fourteen Manus were born. It was in the time of these Manus that the sun and moon, the stars and clouds appeared; division of time into years and months, the equinoctical or solstitial course, the lunar half-month or fortnight, the six seasons, the day of twenty-four hours, and the day as distinguished from night, were instituted, means of warding off the evils arising from wild beasts were discovered; river, tanks, reservoirs, mountains, and a variety of means of livelihood were brought into use. Of the above mentioned Manus, the fourteenth is said to have been Nabhi Mahárájah. In the reign of this Manu, as the people were born with the umbilical cord, the name Nabhi was given. In his reign clouds appeared, and it rained. Then appeared trees and various kinds of corn. By this Manu men were taught to eat fruit and grain, and the way of preparing food; and he also pointed out the way of weaving cloths from cotton, and of wearing them; and the use of flowers, garlands, perfumes, and ornaments, to adorn the person, came into vogue.

"This Nabhi Mahárájah is said by some to be

Brahma. His consort was Murudeviammal. In his reign was born the first incarnated personage named Vrishabha Tirthankara. After him were born twenty-three Tirthankaras, equal to himself. In their days, the twelve Chakravartis, the nine Baladevas, the nine Vasudevas, and the nine Prativasudevas were all born in the fourth stage. These sixty-three persona were called Salaka purushas, divine personages.

"The twenty-four Tirthankaras, without the instruction of a Guru, were skilled in the circle of the sciences, knew the five Kaliyanas or ceremonies of the gods, were worshipped by the four classes of the gods, and at their very birth were endued with the three kinds of knowledge; they also had the fourth kind of knowledge, by the exercise of which they were cognizant of the thoughts of all living beings, and they also possessed the fifth kind of knowledge called Kevalajnanam [spiritual knowledge,] by which they were instantaneously cognizant of all things done in all the worlds. They sat exalted on the throne in the temple called Sambbavasaranam, constructed by the Devendras. They were the possessors of the triple-umbrella and the Ashoka tree; they were believed in as gods over gods, as omniscient, as lords of the three worlds, as removers of sin and bestowers of heavenly bliss, as persons praised by all living beings, as possessors of divine attributes, as bearing the one thousand and eight divine appellations, as having the one thousand and eight divine marks on their sacred bodies, and as manifesting abundant grace, love, and mercy to all living beings, and pre-eminent in imparting instruction in their respective languages to the inhabitants of the celestial and the terrestrial worlds, to those of the Nagaloka, Vaiyantriloka, and Jotiloka, and also to irrational animals, and inculcating the virtues, such as not killing, *&c.*, prescribed in the twelve Vedas. As these twenty-four Tirthankaras are incarnations of wisdom, and are divine personages who appeared in the world and attained the enjoyment of heavenly bliss, the Jainas consider them to be Swamis equal to the divine-natured Arugan, who exists in this Avasarpini time. And accordingly they build temples in honour of these Tirthankaras, and make images like them of stone, wood, gold, and precious gems, and considering these idols as the god Arugan himself, they perform daily and special pujas [worship], and observe fasts, and celebrate festivals, in their honour

"They moreover say that in the time of Vrishaba Tirthankara, and in the reign of Baradeswara, the first Chakravarti, the four castes, namely, the Brahman, the Kshatriya, the Vaisya, and the Sudra, were instituted in connection with this system.

"They moreover allege that in the time of Vrishaba Swami, who was the first Tirthankara, the Saiva system was first introduced; and about the same period, by the fault of the time, one hundred and six heterodox sects were established by Marichi, a Prajapati [Patriarch]; and that from the time of Vimalaswami, the 13th Tirthankara, the Vaishnava system was introduced; and that in the time of Paraswanatha, the 20th Tirthankara, Mahomedanism was established. They also say that there are three hundred and thirty-six false systems of religion.

"They moreover affirm that during the period of the 20th Tirthankara, by the fault of the time, Yagam, animal sacrifice, was first introduced by an Asura named Mahakalesuran; and after the introduction of thaw Yagams, temples were built for Siva and Vishnu.

"Moreover, as it is declared in the Jaina Vedas that all the gods worshipped by the various Hindu Sects, namely, Siva, Brahma, Vishnu, Ganapati, Subramaniyan, and others, were devoted adherents of the above mentioned Tirthankaras, the Jainas therefore do not consider them as unworthy of their worship; but as they are servants of Arugan, they consider them to be deities of their system, and accordingly perform certain pujas in honour of them, and worship them also.

"As Jaina temples and idols are to be seen in all villages and countries, and in some places even underground, it is evident that the Jaina system, as declared in their Vedas, was the primeval system of the Hindus. As moreover, when the Jaina Vedas are carefully examined, there will be found in them many things calculated to benefit mankind; and since Jaina idols are to be found in all countries; and as the deities worshipped by others are believed to be devotees of Arugan; and as all the precepts of Arugan point only to what is good to all sentient beings; and by the great doctrine that no sentient being whatever, even a tree, should be destroyed; and as there are many things in the system beyond the reach of man's understanding, and which can by no means whatever be comprehended; and as it is evident from their Vedas as well as from experience, that all other systems originated among themselves through the fault of the time, from misunderstanding, and from a variety of other causes; it is evident that this system was the primeval one.

"The Jainas are divided into two parties, the

Swetambaras, and Digambaras. Though both parties have the same Veda, they disagree in a few things. The Swetambaras have many internal divisions, and the Digambaras also appear to have a few internal divisions.

"The Jainas are prevalent in the North. Their tenets and observances are the following: They believe that not to kill any sentient being is the greatest virtue; not to tell lies, not to steal other men's goods, not to covet other men's wives, and to desire moderately such things as money, grain, house, garden, land, vehicle, clothing, &c.; these four ordinances they consider of equal importance with the injunction *not to kill*,

"Moreover, not to eat at night, and to drink water strained, are held to be high virtues, And not to drink toddy, or honey, or arrack, are also believed to be important injunctions. They are also forbidden to eat figs, the fruit of the banian, the peepul, the koli and the jujube,—well as the snake-vegetable, the calabash, gunjah (bhang), opium, onions, assafætida, garlic, radish, mushroom, &c. Such articles, and others which have much seed in them, they will not go much as think of eating even in an emergency where death is imminent on such abstinence; and any kind of flesh meat they will not even inadvertently touch with the hand

"These and similar observances are enjoined on those who live in the domestic state; and if we were to write largely upon them many books would be required; we shall, therefore, abridge what we have to say. They have in fact twelve thousand injunctions to observe. But regarding those who live in the ascetic state, as much time will be required both to write and to read, we have not ventured to describe them. However, it is necessary to know that they firmly believe that there is no final liberation [bliss] in the domestic, but only in the ascetic state; nor is liberation to be attained by females, irrational animals, or Sudras, nor by celestial, nor infernal beings; and they moreover hazard the assertion that during the fifth and sixth stages of time there is no liberation for any one; and they show that *Time* alone is the cause of this evil. They also affirm that there are always three less nine krores of Munis [ascetics] on earth.

"The Jainas hold that the function [act, work] of the Divine Being is to exercise love and mercy to all living beings, and reveal to them the Vedas, in order that they may walk according to the precepts enjoined in them; and that the function [act, work] of all living beings is either to do good or evil, and have fruition of their deeds; and that the attainment of heaven or hell is also their own act, and that it is in their own power to renounce sin, and to obtain merit. This they consider to be true doctrine."

According to Mr. Max Müller the Nirwána of the Buddhists is absolute and total annihilation; but the Jainas certainly do not attach any such meaning to the term; it is with them a more denned state of existence than the Moksha of the Hindus. "The Jainas not only affirm that there is such a state, but they define the size of the emancipated souls, the place where they live, their tangible qualities, the duration of their existence, the distance at which they are from one another, their parts, natures and numbers. Those who attain to this nirwána, this extinction of action, this final liberation, do not return to a wordly state, and there is no interruption to their bliss. They have perfect vision and knowledge, and do not depend on works. (Rev. J. Stevenson. *The Kaipa Sutra*.)

As noticed in the extract given above from Munshi Sastram, the Jainas are divided into two principal divisions, Digambaras and Swetambaras. The former word means 'sky-clad,' or naked, but in the present day, ascetics of this division wear coloured garments, and confine the disuse of clothes to the period of their meals. Swetambara means 'one who wears white garments;' but the points of difference between these two divisions are far from being restricted to that of dress: it is said to comprehend a list of seven hundred topics, of which eighty-four are considered to be of paramount importance. Amongst the latter are mentioned the practice of the Swetambaras to decorate the images of their saints with earrings, necklaces, armlets, and tiaras of gold and jewels; whereas the Digambaras leave their images without ornaments. Again, the Swetambaras assert that there are twelve heavens and sixty-four Indras; whereas the Digambaras maintain that there are sixteen heavens and one hundred Indras. In the south of India, the Jainas are divided into two castes; in Upper Hindustan, they are all of one caste. It is remarkable, however, that amongst themselves they recognise a number of families between which' no intermarriage can take place, and that they resemble, in this respect also, the ancient Brahmanical Hindus, who established similar restrictions in their religious codes.

As regards the pantheon of the Jaina creed, it is

still more fantastical than that of the Brahmanical sects, whence it is borrowed to a great extent, but without any of the poetical and philosophical interest which inheres in the gods of the Vedic time. The highest rank amongst their numberless hosts of divine beings—divided by them into four classes, with various sub-divisions—they assign to the deified saints, which they call Jina, or Arhat, or Tirthankara, besides a variety of other generic names. The Jainas enumerate twenty-four Tirthankaras of their past age, twenty-four of the present, and twenty-four of the age to come; and they invest these holy personages with thirty-six superhuman attributes of the most extravagant character. Notwithstanding the sameness of these attributes, they distinguish the twenty-four Jainas of the present age from each other in colour, stature, and longevity. Two of them are red, two white, two blue, two black; the rest are of a golden hue, or a yellowish brown. The other two peculiarities are regulated by them with equal precision, and according to a system of decrement, from Rishabha, the first Jina, who was five hundred poles in stature, and lived 8,400,000 great years, down to Mahâvîra, the 24th, who had degenerated to the size of a man, and was no more than forty years on earth; the age of his predecessor, Pârswanatha, not exceeding one hundred years. The present worship is almost restricted to the two last Tirthankaras; and as the stature and years of these personages have a reasonable possibility, H.T.Colebrooke inferred that they alone are to be considered as historical personages. As, moreover, amongst the disciples of Mahávîra there is one, Indrabhuti, who is called Gautama, and as Gautama is also a name of the founder of the Buddha faith, the same distinguished scholar concluded that, if the identity between these names could be assumed, it would lead to the further surmise that both these sects are branches of the same stock. But against this view, which would assign to the Jaina religion an antiquity even higher than 543 before Christ—the date which is commonly ascribed to the apotheosis of Gautama Buddha—several reasons are alleged by Professor Wilson. As to the real date, however, of the origin of the Jaina faith, as the same scholar justly observes, it is immersed in the same obscurity which invests all remote history amongst the Hindus. We can only infer from the existing Jaina literature, and from the doctrines it inculcates, that it came later into existence than Buddhism

* From the *Chintámani*. By the Rev. H. Bower. Madras, 1868.

JAITRA—The name of the chariot of Krishṇa.

JAJALI—A brāhmaṇa mentioned in the *Mahābhārata* as having by asceticism acquired a supernatural power of locomotion, of which he was so proud that he deemed himself perfect in virtue and superior to all men. A voice from the sky told him that he was inferior to Tulādhāra, a vaiśya and a trader. He went to this Tulādhāra and learnt wisdom from him.

A pupil of Pathya, and teacher of the Atharva Veda.

JALARUPA—The fish or the *makara* on the banner of Kāma.

JALASAYIN—'Sleeping on the waters.' An appellation of Viṣṇu, as he is supposed to sleep upon his serpent couch on the waters during the rainy season, or during the submersion of the world.

JALEYU—One of the ten sons of Raudraswa, a descendant of Puru.

JAMABVATI—One of the wives of Krishṇa obtained as related in the preceding article.

JAMADAGNI—(1) A brāhmaṇa and a descendant of Bhṛgu. He was the son of Ṛcika and Satyavati, and was the father of five sons, the youngest and most renowned of whom was Paraśurāma. Jamadagni's mother, Satyavati, was daughter of King Gādhi, a kṣatriya (*q.v.*). The *Viṣṇu Purāṇa* relates that when Satyavatī was pregnant, her brāhmaṇa husband, Ṛcika, prepared a mess for her to eat for the purpose of securing that her son should be born with the qualities of a brāhmaṇa. He also gave another mess to her mother that she might bear a son with the character of warrior. The women changed the messes, and so Jamadagni, the son of Ṛcīka, was born as a warrior-brāhmaṇa, and Viśvāmitra, son of the kṣatriya Gādhi, was born as a priest. The *Mahabhārata* relates that Jamadagni engaged deeply in study and "obtained entire possession of the Vedas". He went to King Reṇu or Prasenajit of the Solar race and demanded of him his daughter Reṇukā. The king gave her to him, and he retired with her to his hermitage, where the princess shared in his ascetic life. She bore him five sons, Rumaṇvat, Suṣena, Vasu, Viśvāvasu, and Paraśurāma, and she was exact in the performance of all her duties. One day she went out to bathe and beheld a loving pair sporting and dallying in the water. Their pleasure made her feel envious, so she was "defiled by unworthy thoughts, and returned wetted but not purified by the stream". Her husband beheld her "fallen from perfection and shorn of the lustre of her sanctity". So he reproved her and was exceeding wroth. His sons came into the hermitage in the order of their birth, and he commanded each of them in succession to kill his mother. Influenced by natural affection, four of them held their peace and did nothing. Their father cursed them and they became idiots bereft of all understanding. When Paraśurāma entered, he obeyed his father's order and struck off his mother's head with his axe. The deed assuaged the father's anger, and he desired his son to make a request. Paraśurāma begged that his mother might be restored to life in purity, and that his brothers might regain their natural condition. All this the father granted.

The mighty Kārtavirya, king of the Haihayas (*q.v.*), who had a thousand arms, paid a visit to the hermitage of Jamadagni. The sage and his sons were out but his wife treated her guest with all proper respect. Unmindful of the hospitality he had received, Kārtavirya threw down the trees round the hermitage, and carried off the calf of the sacred cow, Surabhi, which Jamadagni had acquired by penance. Paraśurāma returned and discovered what had happened, he then pursued Kārtavīrya, cut off his thousand arms with arrows, and killed him. The sons of Kārtavīrya went in revenge to the hermitage of Jamadagni, and in the absence of Paraśurāma slew the pious sage without pity. When Paraśurāma found the lifeless body of his father, he laid it on a funeral pile, and vowed that he would extirpate the whole kṣatriya race. He slew all the sons of Kārtavīrya, and "thrice seven times" he cleared the earth of the kṣatriya caste. **(2)** The son of Richíka, was a pious sage, who by the fervour of his devotions, whilst engaged in holy study, obtained entire possession of the Vedas, Having gone to king Prasenajit, he demanded in marriage his daughter Reṇuká, and the king gave her unto him. The descendant of Bhṛigu conducted the princess to his hermitage, and dwelt with her there, and she was contented to partake in his ascetic life. They had four sons, and then a fifth, who was Jámadagnya, (Ráma) the last but not the least of the brethren. Once when her sons were all absent, to gather the fruits on which they fed, Reṇuká, who was exact in the discharge of all her duties, went forth to bathe. On her way to the stream she beheld Chitraratha, the prince of Mrittiká-vatí, with a garland of lotuses on his neck, sporting with his queen in the water, and she felt envious of their felicity. Defiled by unworthy thoughts, wetted but not purified by the stream, she returned disquieted to the hermitage, and her husband perceived her agitation. Beholding her fallen from perfection, and shorn of the lustre of her sanctity, Jamadagni reproved her, and was exceeding wrath. Upon this there came her sons from the wood, first the eldest, Rumanwat, then Sushena, then Vasu, and then Viśwávasu; and each, as he entered, was successively commanded by his father to put his mother to death; but amazed, and influenced by natural affection, none of them made any reply: therefore Jamadagni was angry, and cursed them, and they became as idiots, and lost all understanding, and were like unto beasts or birds. Lastly, Rama returned to the hermitage, when the mighty and holy Jamadagni said unto him, 'Kill thy mother, who has sinned; and do it, son, without repining.' Ráma accordingly took up his axe, and struck off his mother's head; whereupon the wrath of the illustrious and mighty Jamadagni was assuaged, and he was pleased with his son, and said, 'Since thou hast obeyed my commands, and done what was hard to be performed, demand from me whatever blessings thou wilt, and thy desires shall be all fulfilled.' Then Ráma begged of his father these boons the restoration of his mother to life, with forgetfulness of her having been slain, and purification from all defilement; the return of his brothers to their natural condition; and, for himself, invincibility in single combat, and length of days; and all these did his father bestow.

"It happened on one occasion, that, during the absence of the Rishi's sons, the mighty monarch Kárttavírya, the sovereign of the Haihaya tribe, endowed by the favour of Dattátreya with a thousand anna, and a golden chariot that went wheresoever he willed it to go, came to the hermitage of Jamadagni, where the wife of the sage received him with all proper respect. The king, inflated with the pride of valour, made no return to her hospitality, but carried off with him by violence the calf of the milch cow of the sacred oblation, and cast down the tall trees surrounding the hermitage. When Rama returned, his father told him what had chanced, and he saw the cow in affliction, and he was filled with wrath. Taking up his splendid bow, Bhárgava, the slayer of hostile heroes, he assailed Kárttavírya, who had now become subject to the power of death, and overthrew him in battle. With sharp arrows Ráma cut off his thousand arms, and the king perished, The sons of Kárttavírya, to revenge his death, attacked the hermitage of Jamadagni, when Rama was away, and slew the pious and unresisting sage, who called repeatedly, but fruitlessly upon his valiant son. They then departed; and when Ráma returned, bearing fuel from the thickets, he found his father lifeless. *V.P.* See Ráma. **(3)** The patronymic of Paraśurāma (*q.v.*).

JAMBAVAT—King of the bears. A celebrated gem called *syamantaka* had been given by the Sun to Satrājit. He, fearing that Kṛṣṇa would take it from him, gave it to his brother, Prasena. One property of this jewel was to protect its wearer when good, to ruin him when bad. Prasena was wicked and was killed by a lion, which was carrying off the gem in its mouth, when he was encountered and slain by Jāmbavat. After Prasena's disappearance, Kṛṣṇa was suspected of having killed him for the sake of the jewel. Kṛṣṇa with a large party tracked the steps of Prasena, till it was ascertained that a lion had killed him, and that a bear had killed the lion. Kṛṣṇa then tracked the bear, Jāmbavat, into his cavern, and a great fight ensued between them. After waiting outside seven or eight days, Kṛṣṇa's followers went home and performed his funeral ceremonies. On the twenty-first day of the fight, Jāmbavat submitted to his adversary, gave up the gem, and presented to him his daughter, Jāmbavatī, as an offering suitable to a guest. Jāmbavat with his army of bears aided Rāma in his invasion of Laṅkā, and always acted the part of a sage counsellor.

JAMBAVATI—Daughter of Jāmbavat, king of the bears, wife of Kṛṣṇa, and mother of Sāmba.

JAMBHA—Name of several demons. Of one who fought against the gods and was slain by Indra, who for this deed was called Jambha-bhedin. Also of one who fought against Arjuna and was killed by Kṛṣna.

JAMBU RIVER—The apples of the Jambu tree are as large as elephants; when they are rotten they fall upon the crest of the mountain, and from their expressed juice is formed the Jambu-river, the waters of which are drunk by the inhabitants; and in consequence of drinking of that stream they pass their days in content and health, being subject neither to perspiration, to foul odours, to decrepitude, nor organic decay. *V.P.*

JAMBUDVIPA—One of the seven islands or continents of which the world is made up. The great mountain, Meru, stands in its centre, and Bhāratavarṣa or India is its best part. Its *varṣas* or divisions are nine in number: (1) Bhārata, south of Himālayas and southernmost of all, (2) Kiṁpuruṣa, (3) Harivarṣa, (4) Ilāvṛta, containing Meru, (5) Ramyaka, (6) Hiraṇmaya, (7) Uttara-Kuru, each to the north of the preceding one, (8) Bhadrāśva and (9) Ketumāla lie respectively to the east and west of Ilāvṛta, the central region.

JAMBUMALI—A formidable Rákshasa the son of Prahasta, who was sent by Rávaṇa against Hanumán, with orders not to return until he had slain the boasting monkey. After a severe contest in which Hanumán was wounded on the cheek and breast, he seized a marble pillar and dashing it down on Jambumáli, the tiger amongst warriors, he crushed the gigantic Rákshasa into a formless mass. —*I.E.*, 280.

JAMBUNADA—The soil in the banks of the river Jambu, absorbing the Jambu juice, and being dried by gentle breezes becomes the gold termed Jambunáda, of which the ornaments of the Siddhas are fabricated.

JAMBU—The name of the rose-apple tree on Mount Gandha-mádana, the southern buttress of Mount Meru. From the Jambu-tree the insular continent, Jambudwípa derives its appellation; the apples are said to be as large as elephants. *V.P.*

JANAKA—(1) King of Mithilā (the modern Tirhoot), of the Solar race. When Nimi, his predecessor, died without leaving a successor, the sages subjected the body of Nimi to attrition, and produced from it a prince "who was called Janaka, from being born without a progenitor". He was the first Janaka, and twenty generations earlier than Janaka the father of Sītā. **(2)** King of Videha and father of Sītā, remarkable for his great knowledge and good works and sanctity. He is called Śīradhvaja, 'he of the plough banner', because his daughter Sītā sprang up ready formed from the furrow when he was ploughing the ground and preparing for a sacrifice to obtain offspring. The sage Yājñavalkya was his priest and adviser. The *Brāhmaṇas* relate that he "refused to submit to the hierarchical pretensions of the brāhmaṇas, and asserted his right of performing sacrifices without the intervention of priests". He succeeded in his contention, for it is said that through his pure and righteous life he became a brāhmaṇa and one of the *rājarṣis*. He and his priest Yājñavalkya are thought to have prepared the way for Buddha.

JANAKI—A patronymic of Sītā (*q.v.*).

JANAKPUR—A ruined city in the northern skirts of the Mithila district (Tirhút) and supposed to indicate the site of a city founded by one of the princes of that name.

JANA-LOKA—The heaven of saints where Sanandana and other pure-minded sons of Brahma reside, situated twenty millions of leagues above Dhruva. During a *pralaya* or general conflagration of all things at the end of a Kalpa, Jana-loka is beyond the reach of the all-devouring flame; and the saints who dwell in Mahar-loka, when the heat of the flames that destroy the world, is felt by them, repair to Jana-loka in thin subtle forms, destined to become re-embodied, in similar capacities as their former, when the world is renewed at the beginning of the succeeding Kalpa. *V.P.*

JANAMEJAYA—**(1)** The king of Vaiṣáli, whose father Sómadatta celebrated ten times the sacrifice of a horse; **(2)** A son of Puranjaya, a descendant of Ana; **(3)** A son of Paríkshit, the son of Kuru; **(4)** The son of Paríkshit who was grandson of Arjuna, and with whose reign the Kaliyuga commenced just after the death of Krishṇa. There is a copper grant still in existence belonging to the Gowja Agrabár, Anantapura Taluq, Mysore, which was executed in the reign of this king. The language is a mixture of Sanskrit and Canarese. It begins as follows: "Emperor Janamėjaya, the refuge of the whole universe; the master of the earth, the king of kings; the Paraméswara of rulers; the great Mahárája; the sovereign of Hastinápura, the flower of cities; the bestower of widowhood on the wives of the hostile kings of Aróha, and Bhagadatta; the son of the lotus of the Páṇḍava race; most skilled in warfare; whose bow resembled the Kálinga serpent; the unassisted hero; the dauntless in battle; the slayer of Asvapatiráya, Disápata and Gajapatiráya; the smiter on the head of Narapatiráya; the most accomplished equestrian; the terror of the 14 States of Konkana, Rékha Révanta, Sámanta, Mrigachamara, &c.; the ever brilliant; the son of other's wives; the bearer of the flag with the emblem of the golden boar; the most glorious of Rájas; the adorned; the descendant of the great lunar race; the son of Emperor Paríkshit; was reigning at Hastinápura, (diverted) by happy historic amusements."

JANARDANA—'The adored of mankind.' A name of Kṛṣṇa, but other derivations are offered as 'extirpator of the wicked', by Śaṅkarācārya.

JANASRUTI—A king mentioned in the Chhándogya-Upanishad, described as charitably-disposed, the giver of large *gifts*, and the preparer of much food; who built houses everywhere that people from all sides might come and feast therein.

JANASTHANA—A place in the Daṇḍaka forest where Rāma sojourned for a while in his exile.

An extensive forest inhabited by Rákshasas,
Of Janasthan I need not tell,
Where Súrpanakhá, Khára, dwell
And Dúshan with the arm of might
And Trisiras, the fierce in fight,
Who feeds on human flesh and gore;
And many noble giants more,
Who roam in dark of midnight through
The forest, brave and strong and true.
By my command they live at ease,
And slaughter saints and devotees.

—Griffith's *Rámáyana* (vol. iii, p. 165.)

JANGALAS—One of the aboriginal tribes, dwellers in thickets and jungles. Many of the aborigines were driven into the forests by the Aryan invaders.

JANGAMS, OR LINGAYATS—One of the forms in which the Linga worship appears, is that of the Lingáyats, Lingawants, or Jangams, the essential characteristic of which is wearing the emblem on some part of the dress or person. The type is of a small size, made of copper or silver, and is commonly worn, suspended in a case, round the neck, or sometimes tied in the turban. In common with the Saivas generally, the Jangamas smear their foreheads with *Vibhúti* (ashes), wear necklaces, and carry rosaries made of the Rudráksha seed. The clerical members of the sect usually stain their garments with red ochre. They are not numerous in upper India, and are rarely encountered except as mendicants, leading about a bull, the living type of Nandi, the bull of Siva, decorated with housings of various colours and strings of kauri shells. The conductor carries a bell in his hand, and, thus accompanied goes about from place to place, subsisting upon alms. In the South of India the Lingáyats are very numerous, and the officiating priests of the *Saiva* shrines are commonly of this sect, when they bear the designations of *Arádhya* and *Pandáram.* The sect is also there known by the name of *Víra Saiva.* The restorer if not the founder of this faith, was Basava whose history is given in the Basava Purána, (*q.v.*)—*H. H. Wilson, Vol. I, p. 224.*

JANIWARA—(Janiwára). The Brahmanical cord or thread with which children of Brahmans are invested when they attain the age of seven or nine years. It costs something considerable and Brahmans who are poor are, in order to acquire it, obliged to ask contributions from their friends; and Hindus of all castes believe they perform a meritorious act in contributing to the charges of the ceremony. The cord has to be made with much care, and with many observances. The cotton with which it is formed ought to be gathered from the plant by the hands of Brahmana only, in order to avoid pollution. For the same reason it should be corded, spun, and twisted, by persons of the tribe, and be always kept exceedingly pure. The ceremony of investiture with the cord is termed UPANAYANA, and to the article under that head the reader is referred for a description of the procedure adopted on the occasion.

JANMA—A birth; a state of existence; nativity, one of the branches of the study included in the Brihat-Sanhita.

JANTU—The eldest of the hundred sons of Sómaka. Also the name of a son of Sudanwan.

JARA—An allegorical personage signifying 'old age" decay'—mentioned in the Vishṇu Purána as the name of the hunter by whom Krishna was slain. He mistook the foot of Krishna for part of a deer, and shooting his arrow lodged it in the side. He then said, 'Have pity on me; I have done this unwittingly, Krishṇa forgave him and sent him to heaven in his own car. Jará was also the name of the female fiend who united the two parts of Jarasandha.

JARADGAVA—The southern portion or Avashthána of the planetary sphere or path of the sun and planets amongst the lunar asterisms.

JARADGAVI—A division of the lunar mansions, occurring in the Central or Vaiswánara Avasthána.

JARAS—'Old age.' The hunter who unwittingly killed Kṛṣṇa.

JARÀSANDHA—Son of Bṛhadratha, and king of Magadha. Bṛhadratha had two wives, who after being long barren brought forth two halves of a boy. These abortions were regarded with horror and thrown away. A female man-eating demon named Jarā picked them up and put them together to carry them off. On their coming in contact a boy was formed, who cried out so lustily that he brought out the king and his two queens. The *rākṣasi* explained what had happened, resigned the child, and retired. The father gave the boy the name of Jarāsandha, because he had been put together by Jarā. Future greatness was prophesied for the boy, and he became an ardent worshipper of Śiva. Through the favour of this god he prevailed over many kings, and he especially fought against Kṛṣṇa, who had killed Kaṁsa, the husband of two of Jarāsandha's daughters. He besieged Mathurā, and attacked Kṛṣṇa eighteen times, and was as often defeated; but Kṛṣṇa was so weakened that he retired to Dvārakā. Jarāsandha had many kings in captivity, and when Kṛṣṇa returned from Dvārakā, he, with Bhīma and Arjuna, went to Jarāsandha's capital for the purpose of slaying their enemy and liberating the kings. Jarāsandha refused to release the kings, and accepted the alternative of a combat, in which he was killed by Bhīma.

JARATKARU—An ancient sage who married a sister of the great serpent Vāsukī, and was father of the sage Āstīka. The Vyasa of the twenty-seventh Dwápara.

JARITÀ—A certain female bird of the species called Śārṅgikā, whose story is told in the *Mahābhārata*. The saint Mandapāla, who returned from the shades because he had no son, assumed the form of a male bird, and by her had four sons. He then abandoned her. In the conflagration of the Khāṇḍava forest she showed great devotion in the protection other children, and they were eventually saved through the influence of Mandapāla over the god of fire. Their names were Jaritāri, Sārisṛkta, Stambamitra, and Droṇa. They were "interpreters of the Vedas"; and there are hymns of the *Ṛgveda* bearing the names of the second and third.

JARUDHI—One of the mountain ridges which project from the base of Mount Meru, on the western side.

JATAKA—A birth; a state of existence; the title of one of the sacred books of the Buddhists, containing an account of Gautama Buddha in 550 different births.

JATAS—One of the five great divisions of the Haiháya tribe.

JATASUR—A *rākṣasa* who disguised himself as brāhmaṇa and carried off Yudhiṣṭhira, Sahadeva, Nakula, and Draupadī. He was overtaken and killed by Bhīma.

JATAVEDAS—A Vedic epithet for fire. "The meaning is explained in five ways: (1) Knowing all created beings; (2) Possessing all creatures or everything existent; (3) Known by created beings; (4) Possessing Vedas, riches; (5) Possessing Vedas, wisdom. Other derivations and explanations are found in the *Brāhmaṇas*, but the exact sense of the word seems to have been very early lost, and of the five explanations given, only the first two would seem to be admissible for the Vedic texts. In one passage a form, Jātaveda, seems to occur."—*Williams.*

This form of the term, and the statement of Manu that the Vedas were milked out from fire, air, and the sun, may perhaps justify the explanation, 'producer of the Vedas'.

JATAYU, JATAYUS—According to the *Rāmāyaṇa*, a semi-divine bird who was son of Viṣṇu's bird Garuḍa, and king of the vultures. Others say he was a son of Aruṇa. He became an ally of Rāma, and he fought furiously against Rāvaṇa to prevent the carrying away of Sītā. Rāvaṇa overpowered him and left him mortally wounded. Rāma found him in time to hear his dying words and to learn what had become of Sītā. Rāma and Lakṣmaṇa performed his funeral rites to "secure his soul in the enjoyments of heaven", whither he ascended in a chariot of fire. In the Purāṇas he is the friend of Daśaratha. When that king went to the ecliptic to recover Sītā from Śani (Saturn), his carriage was consumed by a glance from the eye of the latter, but Jaṭāyu caught the falling king and saved him. The *Padma Purāṇa* says Daśaratha assailed Saturn because of a dearth, and when he and his car were hurled from heaven, Jaṭāyu caught him.

JATHARA—A range of mountains running north and south, and connecting the two chains of Nishadha and Níla.

JATHARAGNI—The name in a previous birth of the Muni Agastya.

JATHARAS—A tribe of aborigines inhabiting the mountain range termed Jathara.

JATILA—A daughter of Gotama, who is mentioned in the *Mahābhārata* as a virtuous woman and the wife of seven husbands.

JAUGHIRA—An interesting and picturesque place of pilgrimage between Bhagulpúr and Monghír. In the middle of the river there is a romantic rock, with a temple surmounting it sacred to Śiva; while in the mainland, and close to the small town, there is another hill of the same kind, on which temples have been built, some of them of great antiquity. The place has long enjoyed the reputation of being the residence of holy devotees; Mussalman as well as Hindu.

JAVALI—**(1)** A renowned logician who at Chitra Kúta endeavoured to persuade Ráma that it was his duty to accept the Ráj when Bharata himself offered it. Ráma regarded his arguments as atheistical and wanting in respect for his deceased father the Mahárája. Javáli ultimately recants. Mr. Wheeler regards the incident as an interpolation to bring forward Buddhism and Atheism for the sake of refuting them.

JAYA—**(1)** A name of Arjuna; a bold metonymy: not merely Victor, but Victory. **(2)** One of the kings of Mithila, the son of Gusruta.

JAYADEVA—A poet, author of the *Gītā-Govinda* (*q.v.*).

JAYADHWAJA—The king of Avanti; one of chief of the hundred sons of Kárttavírya.

JAYADRATHA—A prince of the Lunar race, son of Bṛhamanas. He was king of Sindhu, and was "indifferently termed Rājā of the Sindhus or Saindhavas, and Rājā of the Sauvīras, or sometimes in concert Sindhusauvīras", the Saindhavas and Sauvīras both being tribes living along the Indus. Jayadratha married Duḥśalā, daughter of Dhṛtarāṣṭra, and was an ally of the Kauravas. When the Pāṇḍavas were in exile he called at their forest abode while they were out hunting and Draupadī was at home alone. He had with him six brothers and a large retinue, but the resources of the Pāṇḍavas were equal to the occasion, and Draupadī was able to supply five hundred deer with accompaniments for breakfast. This is explained by the statement that Yudhiṣṭhira, having worshipped the sun, obtained from that luminary an inexhaustible cauldron which was to supply all and every viand that might be required by the Pāṇḍavas in their exile. Jayadratha was captivated by the charms of Draupadī, and tried to induce her to elope with him. When he was indignantly repulsed he carried her off by force. On the return of the Pāṇḍavas they pursued the ravisher, defeated his forces, and made him prisoner. His life was spared by command of Yudhiṣṭhira, but Bhīma kicked and beat him terribly, cut off his hair, and made him go before the assembled Pāṇḍavas and acknowledge himself to be their slave. At the intercession of Draupadī he was allowed to depart. Arjuna killed him, after a desperate conflict, on the fourteenth day of the great battle.

A descendant of Anu and son of Vrihanmanas. Also the name of a son of Vrihatkarman, a descendant of Hastin. **(2)** The Rája of the Sindhu-Sauvíras, sometimes termed the Rája of the Sindhus, or Saindhavas; whether the same as the dwellers on the Indus, or a kindred tribe, must have occupied much the fame territory—the western and southern portion of the Panjab. Jayadratha, accompanied by six brothers and many followers, joined the Páṇḍavas before the great war. In the Mahábhárata it is stated that they had on some occasion five hundred deer, &c., for breakfast! "Whence was Draupadí to procure all this good cheer? The mystery is explained by reference to a passage in the beginning of the Vana Parva. When the Páṇḍavas repaired to the forest they were followed by a number of Brahmans who adhered to their party. Yudhishṭhira endeavoured to persuade them to return, alleging the impossibility of his feeding them, and the sin he should incur if they were starved. As they persisted in their purpose Yudhishṭhira was advised by Dhaumya to have recourse to the Sun as the source of all sustenance. He accordingly worshipped Súrya, who appeared to him, and gave him a copper cauldron, which he told the prince should be filled with fruits, roots, potherbs, and even flesh, ready dressed, whenever food was wanted, until the exile of the Páṇḍavas should terminate. With such an inexhaustible larder, Draupadí was able to entertain the followers of Jayadratha.—*Wilson*.

JAYANTA—**(1)** Son of Indra, also called Jaya. **(2)** A name applied to one of the Rudras. The Puranic writers apply to the Rudras different appellations of the common prototype, or synonyms of Rudra and Śiva, selected at random from his thousand and eight names.

JAYANTI—Daughter of Indra. She is called also Jayanī, Devasenā, and Tāviṣī.

JAYANTPURA—A city founded by Nimi, near the Aṣrama of Gautama.

JAYASENA—The son of Adína; one of the descendants of Kuru, Sarvabhauma had a son also named Jayasena.

JAYAS—In the beginning of the Kalpa twelve gods, named Jayas, were created by Bramha as his deputies and assistants in the creation. They, lost in meditation, neglected his commands, on which he sentenced them to be repeatedly born in each Manwantara till the seventh. They were accordingly in the several successive Manwantaras, Ajitas, Treshitas, Satyas, Haris, Vaikunthas, Sadyas, and Ádityas.

JAYATI—The metre created from the western mouth of Bramha along with the Sáma Véda, the collection of hymns termed Saptadása and the Aitarátra sacrifice.

JHAJHARA—A daitya of great prowess, the son of Hiraṇyaksha.

JILLIKAS—one of the aboriginal or Non-Aryan tribes mentioned in the *V.P.*

JIMUTA—**(1)** A great wrestler, who was overcome and killed by Bhīma at the court of Virāṭa. **(2)** A prince, son of Vyoman, a descendant of Jyámagha.

JIMUTAVAHANA—**(1)** 'Whose vehicle is the clouds.' A title of Indra. A name borne by several persons, and among them by the author of the Dāyabhāga. **(2)** The son of Jimútaketn, and prince of the Vidyá-dbaras; he is the hero of the Nágánanda, (*q.v.*).

JISNU—A name of Arjuna.

JIVATA—Man's individual spirit; it is an error to attribute the spirit of life (or man's individual spirit, *jívata*,) to the Supreme Spirit, just as it is an error to take a post for a man. When once the true nature *of jívata* has been recognised jívata itself disappears." *Atma Bodha*, quoted in *A*.and *M. I*, p. 214.

JIVA—The soul; "Spirit cannot change; intelligence has no knowledge; the soul (*jíva*) knowing things in excess is subject to illusion, and says, 'I act, I see.' If spirit falls into the error of supposing the individual soul, *jíva*, to be itself, as one might suppose a rope to be a snake, it becomes frightened; but so soon as it perceives I am not *jíva*, but the Supreme spirit, (*parmátman*) it is released from all fear." *Alma Bodha*, quoted in *A* and *M. I.*, Vol. I, *p*. 212.

JÑÀNA—"Wisdom," the various epithets applied to it in the Yoga philosophy are that it "requires no exercise," "without the practice of abstract contemplation;" "not to be taught," "not capable of being enjoined" "internally diffused," etc., "of all means knowledge alone is able to effect emancipation; as without fire there can be no cooking, so without *jnana*, science, there can be no final deliverance." *Atma Sodha*, *A* and *M.I.*, Vol. I, *p*. 210.

JOGI—A class of devotees of which there are many kinds. Some are prognosticators of future events; others lead about animals of monstrous formation in order to excite religious wonder and curiosity; others have their ears split and wear in them a kind of earring for sacred purposes. Persons of all castes can now enter the order; but this was not the rule originally. Jogis are not particular on the subject of marriage, and some of them take to themselves wives. At death their bodies are buried; and their tombs, termed *Samádh*, are held in sacred estimation and are often visited by pilgrims for idolatrous purposes.

The term Jogí or Yogí is properly applicable, says Mr. Wilson, to the followers of the Yoga or Patanjala school of philosophy, which, amongst other tenets, maintained the practicability of acquiring, even in life, entire command over elementary matter by means of certain ascetic practices.—*Sherring*. See Yogi.

JRIMBHAKA—A celestial or magical weapon, which causes drowsiness. These weapons are of a very unintelligible character. Some of them are occasionally wielded as missiles, but in general they appear to be mystical powers exercised by the individual; such as those of paralysing an enemy, or locking his senses fast in sleep, or bringing down storm and rain and fire from heaven. There is a list of one hundred of these weapons given in the first book of the Rámáyana.—*Wilson*, XI, 297.

JRIMBHIKA—"Yawning," a form or manifestation of Brahma. *V.P.* 40.

JUMNOTRI—A sacred spot in the Himálaya Mountains, near a junction of three streams. From the bed of the torrent the mountain rises at once to its height, apparently without any very extensive irregularities, and the steepness of the declivity at this point may in some degree be estimated, when it is understood that here, though at the foot of this upper region of the mountain, the very peaks arc seen towering above as ready to overwhelm the gazer with the snow from their summit, and, in fact, the avalanches from above fall into the channel of the river. The particular spot which obtains the name of Jumnotri is very little below the place where the various small streams formed on the mountain brow, by the melting of many masses of snow, unite in one, and fall into a basin below. Balfour's *Encyclopaedia Asiatica*.

JUSKA—A Turuṣka or Turki king, who ruled in Kaśmïr and in Northern India, (*see* KANIṢKA)

JVALAMUKHI—'Mouth of fire.' A volcano. A celebrated place of pilgrimage in the Lower Himālayas, north of the Panjāb, where fire issues from the ground. According to the legend, it is the fire which Satī, the wife of Śiva, created, and in which she burnt herself.

JYAMAGHA—A king of the Lunar race, celebrated for his devotion to his wife. "Of all the husbands submissive to their wives, who have been or who will be, the most eminent is the king Jyámagha, who was the husband of Saivyá, who was barren: but Jyámagha was so much afraid of her, that he did not take any other wife. On one occasion the king, after a desperate conflict with elephants and horse, defeated a powerful foe, who abandoning wife, children, kin, army, treasure, and dominion, fled. When the enemy was pat to flight, Jyámagha beheld a lovely princess left alone, and exclaiming, "Save me, father! Save me, brother!" as her large eyes rolled wildly with affright. The king was struck by her beauty, and penetrated with affection for her, and said to himself, "This is fortunate; I have no children, and am the husband of a sterile bride: this maiden has fallen into my hands to rear up posterity: I will espouse her; but first I will take her in my car, and convey her to my palace, where I must request the concurrence of the queen in these nuptials." Accordingly he took the princess into his chariot, and returned to his own capital.

When Jyámagha's approach was announced, Śaivyá came to the palace gate, attended by the ministers, the courtiers and the citizens, to welcome the victorious monarch; but when she beheld the maiden standing on the left hand of the king, her lips swelled and slightly quivered with resentment, and she said to Jyámagha, "Who is this light-hearted damsel that is with you in the chariot?" The king unprepared with a reply, made answer precipitately, through fear of his queen; this is my daughter-in-law." "I have never had a son," rejoined Saivyá, "and you have no other children. Of what son of yours then is this girl the wife?" The king disconcerted by the jealousy and anger which the words of Śaivyá displayed, made this reply to her in order to prevent further contention; "She is the young bride of the future son whom thou shalt bring forth." Hearing this, Śaivyá smiled gently, and said, "So be it;" and the king entered into his great palace. *V.P.*

JYESHTA—A lunar month corresponding to May. The goddess of misfortune; produced at the churning of the ocean according to the enumeration in the Uttara Khaṇda of the Padma-Purána. Also the name of a lunar mansion in Járadgavi in the Central Avashtána.

JYOTANA—"Dawn"—a form or manifestation of Brahma.

JYOTIRATHA—The name of a river mentioned in the Puránas, but not identified

JYOTISHA—"Astronomy;" an anga of the Vedas, or subsidiary portion of the Vedas. "New moon festivals, and full moon festivals, were integral elements in early Hindu worship, and each veda appears to have had a calendar, called jyotisha; but whether any original copies of these calendars still exist, seems doubtful. They are interesting as being first steps in astronomy, although constructed solely with a view to the regulation of religious ceremonies.

The Súrya Siddhánta, one of the most important of Sanscrit works on Astronomy, has been attacked and defended and explained by competent European scholars."

"M. Biot believed that the Hindus derived their system of nakshatras, or moon stations, from the

Chinese; and Professor Whitney shows that the Hindu nakshatra does not mean the same thing as the Chinese *slew. Slew* means a single star, whereas nakshatra generally expresses a group of stars, or rather a certain portion of the starry heavens.

The Arab *manázil*, and the signs of the lunar zodiac, bear a marked resemblance to the Hindu nakshatras, being groups of stars marking out the ecliptic into twelve nearly equal divisions. Such a system, Professor Whitney observes, is as well suited as any that could be devised for a people seeking to define the daily stages of the moon's revolution, without the aid of instruments.

"The path of the moon was in fact marked by twenty-seven stations believed by Hindu observers to be equi-distant. But when a 'new and more exact astronomy had been brought in from the West,' the moon was reduced in significance* to one of a class of planetary bodies all whose movements were capable of being predicted, and their places at any given time determined, and their conjunctions calculated by an elaborate system of rules. Then first the lesser planets were mentioned by Hindu astronomers, and then first was an observation made by aid of the junction stare, which yielded a trustworthy date. That this must have been not far from A. D. 500 is, Professor Whitney considers, proved.

"The results of this one grand effort, never repeated and sever rivalled, are recorded with occasional slight and unexplained modifications, by every succeeding author from century to century. The date coincides with that of the Hindu Astronomer Aryabhata; and Aryabhata we understand, 'availed himself largely of the progress which the Greeks, (especially Hipp-archus) had made in astronomy; and 'not only improved upon their new theories and inventions, but added also the results of his own independent investigations.'

"The beginning of the sixth century stands out, therefore, as an important era in the history of astronomy in India; and every fragment of intelligence concerning Aryabhata and his works becomes invested with peculiar importance. (See ARYABHATA). His idea of the roundness of the earth is thus expressed:—

'The terrestrial globe, a compound of earth, water, fire and air, entirely round, encompassed by a girdle (*the equator*) stands in the air, in the centre of the stellar sphere. Like as a ball formed by the blossoms of the nuclei kadamba is on every side beset with flowerets, so is the earth-globe with all creatures, terrestrial and aquatic.'

"And this globe he believed to have a daily revolution. 'Aryabhata' says Dr. Kern, 'for aught we know was the first, and remained almost the sole astronomer among his countrymen, who affirmed the daily revolution of the earth on its own axis.' He gives the following quotation from one of Aryabhata's works:—

'As a person in a vessel while moving forward, sees an immovable object moving backwards; in the same manner do the stars, however immovable, seem to move daily.'

Thus showing it is the earth not the stars that move:—

"On another occasion Aryabhata says, 'the sphere of the stars is stationary; and the earth, making a revolution, produces the daily rising and setting of stars and planets.'

"Mr. Colebrooke states that 'Aryabhata affirmed the diurnal revolution of the earth on its axis;' that he accounted for it by a wind or current of aerial fluid, the extent of which, according to the orbit assigned to it by him, corresponds to an elevation of little more than a hundred miles from the surface of the earth; that he possessed the true theory of lunar and solar eclipses, and disregarded the imaginary dark planets of the mythologists and astrologers,—affirming the moon and primary planets (and even the stars) to be essentially dark, and only illumined by the sun. "But after attaining this excellence, astronomy in India appears to have drifted away from science, for no second correct determination of polar longitude and polar latitude is recorded; and writers subsequent to Aryabhata confuse astronomy with astrology."

The popular notion even at the present day is that an eclipse is caused by Ráhu, the demon, attempting to devour a portion of the sun or moon. See Ráhu. (* Mrs. Manning. *A.*and *M.I.*, vol. I, p. 367.) *See* BHÁSKARACHÁRYA, VARÁHAMIHIRA, &c.

JYOTISHMAT—The youngest of the ten sons of Priyavrata,—installed by his father king of Kúsa-dwipa. Jyotishmat had seven sons, after whom the seven portions or varshas of the island were named. At the end of all things the seven solar rays dilate to seven suns, one of which is termed Jyotishmat.—*Vishnu Purána.*

JYOTISHTOMA—One of the great sacrifices, in which especially the juice of the soma plant is offered for the purpose of obtaining Swarga or heaven.

K

KA—The interrogative pronoun "who?" This word has been raised to the position of a deity, In the words of Max Müller, "The authors of the Brāhmaṇas had so completely broken with the past, that, forgetful of the poetical character of the hymns (of the Veda) and the yearning of the poets after the unknown god, they exalted the interrogative pronoun itself into a deity, and acknowledged a god Ka or Who? In the *Taittiriya Brāhmaṇa*, in the *Kauṣītaki Brāhmaṇa*, in the *Tāṇḍya Brāhmaṇa*, and in the *Śatapatha Brāhmaṇa*, wherever interrogative verses occur, the author states that Ka is Prajāpati, or the lord of creatures. Nor did they stop here. Some of the hymns in which the interrogative pronoun occurred were called Kadvat, *i.e.*, having *kad* or *quid*. But soon a new adjective was formed, and not only the hymns but the sacrifice also offered to the god were called Kāya or Who-ish...At the time of Pāṇini, this word had acquired such legitimacy as to call for a separate rule explaining its formation. The commentator here explains Ka by Brahmān. After this we can hardly wonder that in the later Sanskrt literature of the Purāṇas Ka appears as a recognised god, as a supreme god, with a genealogy-of his own, perhaps even with a wife; and that in the laws of Manu one of the recognised forms of marriage, generally known by the name of the Prajāpati marriage, occurs under the monstrous title of Kaya." The *Mahābhārata* identifies Ka with Dakṣa, and the *Bhāgavata Purāṇa*, applies the term to Kaśyapa, no doubt in consequence of their great generative powers and similarity to Prajāpati.

KA—**(1)** A name of Prajápati, the creator of the universe; "Ka is Prajápati; to him let us offer our oblations;" **(2)** A name given to Daksha; **(3)** The name of the divinity who presides over the excretory and generative organs.

KABANDHA—**(1)** A disciple of Sumantu, the earliest teacher of the *Atharvaveda.* **(2)** A monstrous *rākṣasa* slain by Rāma. He is said to have been a son of the goddess Śri. He is described as "covered with hair, vast as a mountain, without head or neck, having a mouth armed with immense teeth in the middle of his belly, arms a league long, and one enormous eye in his breast". He was originally a Gandharva, and his hideous deformity arose, according to one account, from a quarrel with Indra, whom he challenged, and who struck him with his thunderbolt, and drove his head and thighs into his body. According to another statement, his deformity arose from the curse of a sage. When mortally wounded, he requested Rāma to bum his body, and when that was done he came out of the fire in his real shape as a *gandharva*, and counselled Rāma as to the conduct of the war against Rāvaṇa. He was also called Danu. The story is thus translated by Mr. Griffiths.

"A hideous giant then he saw,
Kabandha named, a shape of awe.
The monstrous fiend he smote and slew,
And in the name the body threw;
When straight from out the funeral flame
In lovely form Kabandha came,
And bade him seek in his distress
A wise and holy hermitess.
By counsel of this saintly dame
To Pampá's pleasant flood he came,
And there the steadfast friendship won
Of Hanumán the Wind-God's son.
Counselled by him he told his grief
To great Sugríva, Vánar chief,
Who, knowing all the tale, before
The sacred flame alliance swore.'

KABIR—The most celebrated of the twelve disciples of the Hindu reformer Rámánand. He produced a great effect in the state of popular belief; assailing the whole system of idolatrous worship, and ridiculing the learning of the Paṇdits and doctrines of the Śastras, in a style peculiarly suited to the genius of his countrymen. Kabír lived at the beginning of the 15th century. The Bhakta Málá gives an account of his birth and life. The doctrines taught by Kabír are contained in the *Sukh Nidán*, and do not differ much from those of the Vaishnavas. The moral code is short but favorable to morality.—Wilson's *Works*, *Vol. I*, *p.* 153.

KACA—A son of Brhaspati. According to the *Mahābhārata* he became a disciple of Śukra or Uśanas, the priest of the asuras, with the object of obtaining from him the mystic power of restoring the dead to life, a charm which Śukra alone possessed. To prevent this the *asuras* killed Kaca again and again, but on both occasions he was restored to life by the sage at the intercession of Devayāṇī, his daughter, who had fallen in love with Kaca. They killed him a third time, burnt his body, and mixed his ashes with Śukra's wine, but Devayāṇī again implored her father to bring back the young man. Unable to resist his daughter's importunity, Śukra once more performed the charm, and to his surprise heard the voice of Kaca come out from his own belly. To save his own life, Śukra taught his pupil the great charm. He then allowed himself to be ripped open, and Kaca, upon coming out, performed the charm, and restored his master to life. This incident is said to have caused Śukra to prohibit the use of wine to brāhmaṇas. Kaca resisted the proposals of Devayāṇi, and refused to make her his wife. She then cursed him, that the charms he had learnt from her father should be powerless, and he in return condemned her to be sought by no brāhmaṇa, and to become the wife of a kṣatriya.

KACHCHAS—An aboriginal tribe, the name of which implies that the people dwelt in districts contiguous to water and in marshy spots: such as the province still called Cutch.

KACHHAPA—One of the sons of Viṣvámitra.

KAṆḌU—A sage who was beguiled from long and severe austerities by Pramlocā, a nymph sent from heaven by Indra for this purpose. He lived with her some hundreds of years, which seemed to him only as a day, but he at length repudiated her and "went to the region of Viṣṇu". Pramlocā gave birth, in an extraordinary manner, to his daughter Māriṣā (*q.v.*).

KADAMBARI—A daughter of Citraratha and Madirā. Her name has been given to a well-known prose work, a kind of novel, written by Vāṇa or Bāṇabhaṭṭa, in the seventh century. The work has been printed at Bombay.

KADAMBA—The name of the tree that grows on Mount Mandara, the flowers of which are said to yield a spirit on distillation, whence Kádambarí is one of the synonyms of wine or spirituous liquor.

KADRU—A daughter of Dakṣa and one of the thirteen that were married to Kaśyapa. She was mother of "a thousand powerful many-headed serpents, the chief amongst whom were Śeṣa, Vāsuki,...and many other fierce and venomous serpents". The *Viṣṇu Purāṇa*, from which this is taken, names twelve, the *Vāyu Purāṇa* forty. Her offspring bear the metronymic Kādraveya.

KAHLANABHA—One of the many sons of Hiranyaksha; also the name of a son of Viprachitti.

KAHODA—A learned brāhmaṇa, father of Aṣṭāvakra. He with many others was overcome in argument at the court of Janaka by a Buddhist sage, and as a penalty was thrown into the river. Some years afterwards he was recovered by his son, who overcame the supposed Buddhist sage, and thus brought about a restoration. (*see* AṢṬĀVAKRA)

KAIKASI—One of the daughters of Sumáli and Ketumati; Sumáli with his family lived for a long time in Pátáḷa; and once happening to visit the earth he desired his daughter Kaikasi to go and woo Viṣravas, who received her graciously, and she became the mother of the dreadful Rávaṇa, the huge Kumbhakarna, and the two younger brothers, who all grew up in the forest. *Muir*, IV, 487, 488.

KAIKEYA—(1) Name of a country and of its king. He was father-in-law of Kṛṣṇa, and his five sons were allies of the Pāṇḍavas. His real name appears to have been Dhṛṣṭaketu. **(2)** One of the four sons of Śiví, who has given a name to a province and people in the northwest of India.

KAIKEYAS, KEKAYAS—The people of Kaikeya, one of the chief nations in the war of the *Mahābhārata*. The *Rāmāyaṇa* places them in the west, beyond the Sarasvatī and Byās.

KAIKEYAS—The five sons of Dhristakétu, rajah of Kaikeya, are termed the Kaikeyas.

KAIKEYI—One of the queens of Mahárája Dasaratha, and mother of Bharata. When it was proposed to instal Ráma, the son of Queen Kausalya, as heir apparent, Kaikeyi was pleased, and offered a reward to her slave woman Manthara who brought her the news, saying

> "I joy that Ráma gains the throne,
> Kausalya's son is as mine own."

But the old hag Manthara, who disliked Ráma, excited the jealousy of Kaikeyi by representing the degradation and ruin that would come to Bharata and herself.

> "When Ráma's hand has once begun
> Ayódhya's realm to sway."

This roused her to action and she ran to the chamber of displeasure, sulky and angry. The Mahárája afterwards sought her, and finding her in this state of affliction, protested his love and affection, but she remained silent; at last in a critical moment she extorted a promise from him and then with "a woman's obstinacy compelled him to keep his word." "He had made the promise and she insisted upon its fulfilment. To all he could urge she had but one answer 'Unless Ráma is exiled and Bharata is installed, you will be stigmatized as a liar and I will take poison.' "

"The monarch as Kaikeyi pressed
With cruel words her due request,
Stood for a time absorbed in thought,
While anguish in his bosom wrought."

The result was the exile of Ráma; and when her own son Bharata returned from Girivraja he strongly reproached his mother for what she had done. She lived, however, to rejoice in Ráma's return to his kingdom. (*see* DAŚARATHA, RĀMA)

KAILAKILA YAVANAS—A race of kings, who lived when the Greek princes or their Indo-Scythic successors, following the course of the Indus, spread to the upper part of the western coast of the peninsula. From an inscription which has been found dated *A.* D. 1058, Kilakila, or Kilagila as it is there termed, is called the capital of Márasinha Deva, king of the Konkan.

KAILASA—A mountain situated like Meru, in the lofty regions to the north of the Himálaya, and celebrated in the traditions and myths of India. "Meru and Kailása are the two Indian Olympi. Perhaps they were held in such veneration because the Sanskrit-speaking Indians remembered the ancient home where they dwelt with the other primitive peoples of their family before they descended to occupy the vast plains which extend between the Indus and the Ganges."—*Gorresio.*

In the Puránas Kailása is a fabulous mountain several yójanas in breadth, to the west of Meru. Kailása is described as a mountain of pure silver, brilliantly white, and as the residence of Śiva. In former ages it is said all the mountains had wings; but their flights were productive of so much mischief and danger, that Indra struck off their wings with his thunderbolts, and fixed them in their present position. Kailása is often mentioned in the Rámáynna, as the region of the sacred lakes, near the northern heights of the Himálayas.

KAISIKA—One of the sons of Vidarbha, (*q.v.*) and grandson of Jyámagha.

KAITABHA—Kaiṭabha and Madhu were two horrible demons, who, according to the *Mahābhārata* and the Purāṇas, sprang from the ear of Viṣṇu while he was asleep at the end of a *kalpa*, and were about to kill Brahmā, who was lying on the lotus springing from Viṣṇu's navel. Viṣṇu killed them, and hence he obtained the names of Kaiṭabhajit and Madhusūdana. The *Mārkaṇḍeya Purāṇa* attributes the death of Kaiṭabha to Umā, and she bears the title of Kaiṭabhā. The *Harivaṃśa* states that the earth received its name of Medini from the marrow (*medas*) of these demons. In one passage it says that their bodies, being thrown into the sea, produced an immense quantity of marrow or fat, which Nārāyaṇa used in forming the earth. In another place it says that the *medas* quite covered the earth, and so gave it the name of Medinī. This is another of the many etymological inventions. *O.S.T.*, Vol. IV., p. 371.

KAIVALYA—The fourth chapter of the Yoga Sutras, being a treatise on the extatic abstraction or isolation of the soul. The state of emancipation that may be obtained even during life: it is termed jivanmukti; and is the highest state of Yóga before the soul is actually re-absorbed into the Supreme Being. The body still exists, and of course the soul exists within it; but its connection with it is supposed to be entirely broken, and the soul can consequently quit and re-enter the body, and wander about where and as it lists.—*J.C. Thomson.*

KAJNGHAS—An aboriginal tribe mentioned in the Purána lists, but not satisfactorily identified.

KAKAMUKHAS—A nickname or term of derision, meaning crow-faced, applied to designate some of the aboriginal tribes.

KAKAS—A tribe of aborigines, dwelling on the banks of the Indus, as it leaves the mountains.

KAKAVARNA—One of the kings of Magadha, who reigned for thirty-six years; he was the son of Siṣunaga.

KAKNATA, KARṆĀṬAKA—The country where the Canarese language is spoken, in the central districts of the Peninsula, including Mysore. The name "Carnatic" is derived from this.

KAKSHAS—The same as Kachchas.

KAKSHEYA—One of the *ten* sons of Raudraswa, a descendant of Puru.

KAKSIVAT, KAKṢĪVĀN—A Vedic sage, particularly connected with worship of the Aśvins. He was the son of Dirghatamas and Uśiij (*q.v.*), and is author of several hymns in the *Ṛgveda.* He was also called Pajriya, because he was of the race of Pajra. In one of his hymns he lauds the liberality of King Svanaya. The following legend, in explanation, is given by the commentator Sāyaṇa and the Nītimañjara: Kakṣīvat, having finished his course of study, took leave of his preceptor and departed homewards. As he journeyed night came on, and he fell asleep by the roadside. In the morning he was aroused by Rājā Svanaya, who, being pleased with his appearance, treated him cordially and took him home. After ascertaining his worthiness, he married him to his ten daughters, presenting him at the same time with a hundred *niṣkas* of gold, ahundred horses, ahundred bulls, a thousand and sixty cows, and eleven chariots, one for each of his ten wives, and one for himself, each drawn by four horses. With these he returned home to his father, and recited the hymn in praise of the munificence of Svanaya.

KAKUBHA—A mountain in Orissa.

KAKUDMIN—A name of Raivata (*q.v.*).

KAKUDMIN—A name of Raivata, the prince who went to the heaven of Brahma to consult the god where a bridegroom fit for his lovely daughter should be found.

KAKUD—One of the daughters of Daksha who was married to Dharma.

KAKUTSTHA—In the Treta age a violent war broke out between the gods and the Asúras, in which the former were vanquished. They consequently had recourse to Vishṇu for assistance and propitiated him by their adorations. Náráyana had compassion on them and said, there is an illustrious prince named Puranjaya, the son of a royal sage, into his person I will infuse a portion of myself, and by him subdue all your enemies. Acknowledging with reverence the kindness of the deity, the immortals quitted his presence, and repaired to Puranjaya to solicit his alliance.

The prince replied, "Let this your Indra, the monarch of the spheres, the god of a hundred sacrifices, consent to carry me upon his shoulders, and I will wage battle with your adversaries as your ally." The gods and Indra readily answered, "So be it;" and the latter assuming the shape of a bull, the prince mounted upon his shoulder. Being then filled with delight, and invigorated by the power of the eternal ruler of all movable and immovable things, he destroyed in the battle that ensued all the enemies of the gods; and because he annihilated the demon host whilst seated upon the shoulder (or the hump, Kakud) of the bull, he thence obtained the appellation Kakutstha (seated on the hump). *V.P.* (*see* PURAÑJAYA)

KALA—(Kála) The name of one of the eleven Rudras according to the Bhágavata; the son of Vasu Dhruva was named Kála. One of the daughters of Daksha, who was married to Kaṣyapa was named Kála.

KALA—(Kála) Thirty Káshtas make one Kála; fifteen twinklings of the eye make a Káshta. Kála or Time, is thus computed:

15 Nimishas	= 1 Káshta
30 Káshtas	= 1 Kála
30 Kálas	= 1 Kshana
12 Kshanas	= 1 Muhúrtta,
30 Muhúrttas	= 1 day and night.

KALA—(Kalá.) A gradation or manifestation of the Múla Prakriti; the principal Kalás are Swáhá, Swadhá, Dakshiná, Swasti, Pushti, Tushti, and others, most of which are allegorical personifications as Dhriti, fortitude, Pratishta, fame, and Adharma, wickedness, the bride of Mrityu, or death. Aditi the mother of the gods, and Diti, the mother of the demons, are also Kalás of Prakriti. The list includes all the secondary goddesses.—Wilson's *Works*, *Vol. I*, *p.* 246.

KALA—(Kála.) **(1)** Time. A form of Vishṇu. "The deity as Time is without beginning and his end is not known: and from him the revolutions of creation, continuance, and dissolution, unintermittingly succeed; for when, in the latter season the equilibrium of the qualities (Pradhána) exists, and spirit (Pumán) is detached from matter, then the form of Vishṇu, which is Time abides." *V.P.*, p. 12.

"This being the case it is asked what should sustain matter and spirit whilst separate, or renew their combination so as to renovate creation ? It is answered. Time, which is when every thing else is not; and which, at the end of a certain interval, unites Matter, Pradhána, and Purusha, and produces creation. Conceptions of this kind are evidently comprised in the Orphic triad, or the ancient notion of the co-operation of three such principles in creation, as Phanes or Eros, which is the Hindu spirit or Purusha; Chaos, matter or Pradhána; and Chronos, or Kála, Time." (Professor Wilson). Kála is also a name of Yama, the Hindu Pluto. "In two remarkable hymns in the Rig Veda we find an altogether new doctrine; Kála or Time is there described as the source and ruler of all things." *O.S.T.*, Vol. v., p. 407. **(2)** 'Time'. A name of Yama, the judge of the dead. In the. *Atharvaveda* Time is addressed as the source and ruler of all things. "It is he who drew forth the worlds and encompassed them. Being their father, he became their son. There is no other power superior to him." The *Viṣṇu*, *Bhāgavata*, and *Padma Purāṇas* state that Brahmā existed in the form of Time, "but the Purāṇas do not generally recognise Time as an element of the first cause".

KALA—In the Vishṇu Purána the moon's surface is

said to be divided into sixteen Kalás or phases; the moon is also apportioned as a receptable of nectar, into fifteen Kálas or digits, corresponding to the fifteen lunations on the fourteen of which during the wane, the gods drink the amrita, and in the fifteenth of which the Pitris, exhaust the remaining portion. Professor Wilson remarks on the indistinctness of this account, but states that none of the other Puránas make it any clearer. Colonel Warren explains Kála, in one of its acceptations, 'the phases of the moon, of which the Hindus count sixteen.'

KALAJOSHAKAS—One of the aboriginal races mentioned in the Puránas.

KALAKA—One of the daughters of Daksha who was married to Kaṣyapa. According to the *Rāmāyaṇa* and *Mahābhārata* she was a daughter of Dakṣa, but the *Viṣṇu Purāṇa* states that she and her sister Pulomā were daughters of the *dānava* Vaiśvanara, "who were both married to Kaśyapa, and bore him 60,000 distinguished *dānavas*, called Paulomas and Kālakañjas, who were powerful, ferocious, and cruel". The *Mahābhārata* states that she obtained from the deity, in reward for her severe devotion and penance, the privilege of bringing forth children without pain. The giants or *dānavas* were called after her Kālakeyas.

KALAKANJAS, KĀLAKEYAS—Sons of Kaśyapa by his wife Kālakā. There were many thousands of them, and they were "distinguished *dānavas*, who were powerful, ferocious, and cruel".

KALAKAS, KALAKANJAS, KALAKEYAS—The names applied to a claw of Danavas who were powerful, ferocious, and cruel.

KALAMUKHAS—'Black faces.' People who sprang from men and *räkṣasa* females.

KALANARA—A prince, the son of Sabhánara, one of the descendants of Anu.

KALANAS—(Kalyāṇa.) A brāhmaṇa who yielded to the inducements of Alexander the Great and left his native country to accompany the court of the conqueror. He afterwards repented of what he had done and burnt himself at Pasargada.

KALANEMI—**(1)** In the *Rāmāyaṇa* a *rākṣasa*, uncle of Rāvaṇa. At the solicitation of Rāvaṇa, and with the promise of half his kingdom, he endeavoured to kill Hanumān. Assuming the form of a hermit-devotee, he went to the Gandhamādana mountain, and when Hanumān proceeded thither in search of medicinal herbs, the disguised *rākṣasa* invited him to his hermitage and offered him food. Hanumān refused, but went to bathe in a neighbouring pond. Upon his placing his foot in the water it was seized by a crocodile, but he dragged the creature out and killed it. From the dead body there arose a lovely *apsaras*, who had been cursed by Dakṣa to live as a crocodile till she should be released by Hanumān. She told her deliverer to be beware of Kālanemi; so Hanumān went back to that deceiver, told him that he knew him, and, taking him by the feet, sent him whirling through the air to Laṅkā, where he fell before the throne of Rāvaṇa in the council-room. **(2)** In the Purāṇas a great *asura*, son of Virocana, the grandson of Hiraṇyakaśipu. He was killed by Viṣṇu, but was said to live again in Kaṁsa and in Kāliya.

KALANJARA—A fabulous mountain, is placed in the Puránas to the north of Meru.

KALANSA—A sub-division of the more important Kalis, or manifestations of Prakriti; the Kalánsas are all womankind, who are distinguished as good, middling, or bad, according as they derive their being from the parts of their great original in which the Satya, Rajas, and Tamo Guna, or property of goodness, passion and vice predominate.

KALAPA—The name of the fabulous village in which Maru, ft descendant of Kusa, has lived for a long period, through the power of devotion, that in a future age he may be the restorer of the Khshatriya race in the solar dynasty. *V.P.*

KALASUTRA—One of the Narakas, or hells, enumerated in the Vishṇu *Purána*, and described as one of the awful provinces in the kingdom of Yama, terrible with instruments of torture.

KALAVAS—One of the aboriginal races mentioned in the Puranas.

KÀLAYAVANA—(Lit. 'Black Yavana', Yavana meaning a Greek or foreigner.) AYavana or foreign king who led an army of barbarians to Mathurā against Kṛṣṇa. That hero lured him into the cave of the mighty Mucukunda, who being disturbed from sleep by a kick from Kālayavana, cast a fiery glance upon him and reduced him to ashes. This legend appears to indicate an invasion from the Himālayas. According to the *Viṣṇu Purāṇa* and *Harivaṁśa*, Kālayavana was the son of a brāhmaṇa named Garga, who had an especial spite against the Yādavas, and was begotten by him on the wife of a childless Yavana king. Professor Wilson thinks the story may have originated in some knowledge of the power and position of the Greek Bactrian princes, or their Scythian successors, mixed up with allusions to the first Mahomedan aggressions.

KALAYAVI—A disciple of Báshkali and teacher of the Rig Veda.

KALHANA PANDIT—Author of the *Rājataranginị̄*, a history of Kaśmīr. He is supposed to have lived about AD 1148.

KALI YUGA—The last age. It consists of 1,200 years of the gods, a year of men being a day of the gods; these divine years may, therefore, be converted into years of mortals by multiplying them by 360, which makes the duration of the Kali Yuga 432,000 years. The date of its commencement is fixed in the thirteenth or fourteenth century B.C., when Vishṇu returned to heaven after his incarnation as Krishṇa. During this age all things will decline, and the deterioration of mankind will be general. The Vedas will be disregarded. The minds of men will be wholly occupied in acquiring wealth; and wealth will be spent solely on selfish gratifications. Women will follow their inclinations and be fond of pleasure. Men of all degrees will consider themselves equal to Brahmans. Cows will be held in esteem only as they supply milk. These are a few of the evils, selected from the long catalogue of them contained in the Vishṇu Purána which are to prevail in the Kali age. A few redeeming properties of the age are, however, mentioned. The efficacy of devotion to Vishnu is more strikingly manifested. The least moral merit obtains in this age, the greatest reward; and is by all classes most easily displayed. The Kali Yuga is to be followed by the Kṛita Yuga.

KÁLI—(Káli.) The Moloch of Indian Mythology. A form of Parvati, called Káli, or Mahá-Káli, the consort of Śiva, in bis destroying character of Time. As such, she is painted of a black or dark blue complexion. In Calcutta, her images are usually seen of the last-mentioned colour. In plates, she is shown as trampling (as the personification of Eternity) on the body of Śiva (Time) In one hand she holds the exterminating sword, in another a human head; a third points downward, indicating, according to some, the destruction which surrounds her, and the other is raised upwards, in allusion to the figure of regeneration of nature by a new creation. Mr. Ward, however, is of an opinion, which he has expressed respecting others of the deities, but which appears to be much at variance with the character of Káli, who is here annihilating Time itself, *viz*; that of the two last mentioned hands, one is bestowing a blessing, the other forbidding fear. Whatever her gestures may import, the image of this goddess is truly horrid, as are the devotional rites performed in honor of her. Her wild dishevelled hair reaching to her feet, her necklace of human heads, the wildness of her countenance, the tongue protruded from her distorted mouth, her cincture of blood-stained hands, and her position on the body of Śiva, altogether convey in blended colours so powerful a personification of that dark character she is intended to pourtray, that whatever we may think of their tastes, we cannot deny to the Hindus our full credit for the possession of most extraordinary and fertile powers of imagination. A model of this goddess has the body of a dark blue, the insides of the hands are red, as is also the circlet of hands round the waist. The heads which form the necklace have a ghastly appearance. Her tongue is protruded from her mouth, the sides of which are marked with blood. Her head-dress and other ornaments are splendidly adorned with gems of various kinds. The body of Śiva is white. Káli is also called the goddess of cemeteries, under which form she is described dancing with the infant Śiva in her arms, surrounded by ghosts and goblins (likewise dancing) in a cemetery amongst the dead. A paragraph appeared sometime ago in a Calcutta paper, which stated, that her images, under this form, were now worshipped by the Hindus as a propitiation against the destructive ravages of the cholera. To this ferocious goddess sanguinary sacrifices are made. The *Kalika Purána* which details, in due order and with much precision, the different descriptions of animals that are to be sacrificed, and the length of time by which this insatiate lady will be gratified and kept in good humour by each, ordains that one man (or a lion) will please her for a thousand years, but that by the immolation of *three* men she will graciously condescend to be pleased one hundred thousand years. The sacrificer must repeat the name Kali and pay her the compliment of saying "Hrang, bring, Kali, Kali! O horrid-toothed goddess ! cat, cut, destroy all the malignant, cut with this axe; bind, bind, seize, seize, drink blood, spring, secure, secure, salutation to Kali!" Immense sums of money are annually spent in the worship of this terrific deity. There is a celebrated temple dedicated to her at Kali-ghat in the vicinity of Calcutta, or the city of Kali, and sacrifices are offered to it.—Coleman. *Myth, Hind.* p. 94.

KĀLĪ—'The black'. In Vedic days this name was associated with Agni (fire), who had seven flickering tongues of flame for devouring oblations of butter. Of these seven, Kālī was the black or terrific tongue. This meaning of the word is now lost, but it has developed into the goddess Kālī, the fierce and bloody consort of Śiva. (*see* Devī)

KALI—The *kali yuga*, personified as the spirit of evil. In playing dice *kali* is the ace and so is a personification of ill luck.

KÁLI—A male personification of the Kali age, or the fourth and last age through which the world is now passing. He wished to obtain Damayantí in marriage, and when he found that she had chosen Nala, he was greatly enraged and determined to be revenged. One evening when Nala failed in some ceremonial observance Kali seized the opportunity and straightway entered into him and possessed his inmost soul. Nala had a brother named Pushkara, and Kali said to Pushkara, go you and play at dice with Nala, and I will make you the winner of his Raj. Pushkara challenged Nala to a game at dice, and they sat down to play in the presence of Damayantí. They played for gold and jewels and raiment, for chariots and horses, but Nala was worsted at every throw, for Dwápara embodied the dice, and Kali had mastered him body and soul. Then the faithful friends of Nala prayed him to throw no longer, but he was maddened with the love of play, and shut his ears to all they said. He staked his Raj, and the vestments which he wore, and he lost all to Pushkara. Then followed his exile, see Nala. Kali after this induced Nala to desert Damayantí in the jungle, and this completed his revenge.

KÁLIDASA—The greatest poet and dramatist of India. He was one of "the nine gems" that adorned the court of King Vikramāditya at Ujjayinī. Wilson inclines to the belief that this was the Vikramā-ditya whose era begins in 56 BC, but Dr. Bhāu Dājī argues in favour of Harṣa Vikramāditya who lived in the middle of the sixth century, so the date of Kālīdāsa is unsettled. Williams thinks that Kālidāsa wrote about the beginning of the third century. Lassen places him half a century earlier. Some believe that there was more than one poet who bore this name as an honorary title. Kālidāsa was author of the dramas *Śakuntalā* and *Vikramorvaśi*, and a third drama *Mālavikāgnimitra* is attributed to him. *Śakuntalā* was translated by Sir W. Jones, and first brought Sanskṛt literature to the notice of Europe. Wilson has translated *Vikramorvasī*, and given a sketch of *Mālavikāgnimitra* The following poems are ascribed to Kālidāsa: *Raghuvaṁśa*, *Kumārasambhava*,*Meghadūta*,*Ṛtusaṁhāra*,*Nalodaya*, by this authorship of all these, especially of the last, may well be doubted. He was also author of the *Śrutabodha*, a work on prosody. The merits of Kālidāsa as a poet are well attested by his great popularity in India, as well as by the great favour with which *Śakuntalā* was received in Europe, and the praise it elicited from Goethe:

> "Willst du die Blüthe des frühen, die Früchte des späteren Jahres,
> Willst du, was reizt und entzückt, willst du, was sättigt und nährt,
> Willst du den Himmel, die Erde, mit einem Namen begreifen,
> Nenn' ich Śakuntalā dich, und so ist Alles gesagt."
> "Wouldst thou the young year's blossoms and the fruits of its decline,
> And all by which the soul is charmed, enraptured, feasted, fed? Wouldst thou the earth and heaven itself in one sole name combine?
> I name thee, O Śakuntalā! and all at once is said."

Lassen in his *Indische Alterthumskunde* says, "Kālidāsa may be considered as the brightest star in the firmament of Hindu artificial poetry. He deserves this praise on account of the mastery with which he wields the language, and on account of the consummate tact with which he imparts to it a more simple or more artificial form, according to the requirements of the subjects treated by him, without falling into the artificial diction of later poets or over-stepping the limits of good taste; on account of the variety of his creations, his ingenious conceptions, and his happy choice of subjects; and not less on account of the complete manner in which he attains his poetical ends, the beauty of his narrative, the delicacy of his sentiment, and the fertility of his imagination." Many of his works have been translated, and there is a French translation of the whole by Fauche.

KÁLIKA PURANA—One of the eighteen Upa-Purāṇas. "It contains about 9000 stanzas in 98 chapters, and is the only work of the series dedicated to recommend the worship of the bride of Śiva, in one or other of her manifold forms as Girijā, Devī, Bhadrakāli, Kālī, Mahāmāyā. It belongs, therefore, to the Śākta modification of Hindu belief, or the worship of the female powers of the deities. The influence of this worship shows itself in the very first pages of the work, which relate the incestuous passion of Brahmā for his daughter, Sandhyā, in a strain that has nothing analogous to it in the *Vāyu*, *Liṅga*, or *Śiva Purāṇas*. The marriage of

Śiva and Pārvatī is a subject early described, with the sacrifice of Dakṣa and the death of Satī. And this work is authority for Śiva's carrying the dead body about the world, and the origin of the Pīṭhasthānas, or places where the different members of it were scattered, and where *liṅgas* were consequently erected. A legend follows of the births of Bhairava and Vetāla, whose devotion to the different forms of Devī furnishes occasion to describe, in great detail, the rites and formulae of which her worship consists, including the chapters on sanguinary sacrifices translated in the *Asiatic Researches* (vol. v). Another peculiarity in this work is afforded by very prolix descriptions of a number of rivers and mountains at Kāmarūpa Tīrtha, in Assam, and rendered holy ground by the celebrated temple of Durgā in that country, a Kāmākṣī or Kāmākhyā. It is a singular and yet uninvestigated circumstance, that Assam, or at least the north-east of Bengal, seems to have been, in a great degree, the source from which the Tāntrika and Śākta corruptions of the religion of the Vedas and Purāṇas proceeded."—*Wilson.*

KÁLIKA—(1) The goddess Kālī. **(2)** One of the daughters of Vaiswánara, the wife of Kaṣyapa and mother of the ferocious and cruel Danavas.

KÁLIKÁMUKHA—A distinguished Rákshasa chief, the son of Sumali and Retumatí; he was the uncle of the great giant Rávana, and took part in the mythical battles with the gods.

KALINDAS—One of the tribes of Kshatriyas who from seeing no brahmans became outcasts. *O.S.T.*, Vol. I, p. 482.

KALINDI—A name of the river Yamunā, as daughter of Kalinda (the sun)

KALINDI—(1) One of the wives of Krishṇa, the daughter of the Sun, whom Krishna met on one of his visits to Indraprastha, and who claimed him as the reward of her penance; **(2)** The goddess of the Yamuna, as daughter of Kalinda; **(3)** One of the widows of king Asit, and mother of Sagara;

There came the other widowed queen
With lotus eyes and beauteous mien
Longing a noble son to bear,
And wooed the saint with earnest prayer.
When thus Kálindí fairest dame,
With reverent supplication came,
To her the holy sage replied;
'Born with the poison from thy side,
O happy queen shall spring ere long
An infant fortunate and strong
Then weep no more and check thy sighs
Sweet lady of the lotus eyes.'

—Griffiths' *Rámáyana.*

(4) The daughter of the king of the Asuras, who after her father's death offered her kingdom and herself, twin wives, to Mátanga (*q.v.*) who readily assented, married the damsel, and became king of Pátāḷa.

KALINGA—One of the five sons of Bali. Kalinga is the name of the sea coast west of the mouths of the Ganges, with the upper part of the Coromandel Coast. The inhabitants are called Kalingas.

KÁLIYA—A serpent king who had five heads, and dwelt in a deep pool of the Yamunā, with numerous attendant serpents. His mouths vomited fire and smoke, and he laid waste all the country round. Kṛṣṇa, while yet a child, jumped into his pool, when he was quickly laced and entwined in the coils of the snakes. His companions and friends were horrified, but Balarāma called upon him to exercise his divine power. He did so, and the serpents were soon overcome. Placing his foot on the middle head of Kāliya, he compelled him and his followers to implore mercy. He spared them, but bade Kāliya and his followers to free the earth from their presence, and to remove to the ocean. The *asura* Kālanemi is said to have been animate in him.

KALIYAL—The beautiful daughter of the peasant Ladurlad whose violation was attempted by Arvalan, the son of Rája Kehama. Arvalan was slain in consequence by Ladurlad, upon whom was afterwards pronounced the doom which gives the title to Southey's poem. Kaliyal afterwards joined her "father, and often soothed him under the withering effects of Kehama's curse, and Ladurlad is often able to extricate his daughter from great dangers of fire and flood.

KÁLKI—'The white horse.' Viṣṇu's tenth incarnation. An Avatára of Vishṇu to be born near the close of the Kali age, when all whose minds are devoted to iniquity shall be destroyed, and righteousness be established on earth; and the minds of those who live at the end of the Kali age shall be awakened and be as pellucid as crystal. (*see* AVATĀRA)

KALMÁṢAPÁDA—A king of the Solar race, son of Sudāsa (hence, he is called Saudāsa), and a descendant of Ikṣvāku. His legend, as told in the *Mahābhārata*, relates that while hunting in the forest he encountered Śaktri, the eldest son of Visiṣṭha, and as this sage refused to get out of his way, he struck him with his whip. The incensed sage cursed him to become a cannibal. This curse was heard by Viśvāmitra, the rival of Vasiṣṭha, and he so contrived that the body of the king became possessed by a man-eating *rākṣasa*. In this condition he caused human flesh to be served up to a brāhmaṇa named Mitrasaha, who discovered what it was, and intensified the curse of Śaktri by a new imprecation. One of Kalmāṣapāda's first victims was Śaktri himself, and all the hundred sons of Vasiṣṭha fell a prey to his disordered appetite. After remaining twelve years in this state, he was restored to his natural condition by Vasiṣṭha. The *Viṣṇu Purāṇa* tells the story differently. The king went out to hunt and found two destructive tigers. He killed one of them, but as it expired it was changed into a *rākṣasa*. The other tiger disappeared threatening vengeance. Kalmāṣapāda celebrated a sacrifice at which Vasiṣṭha officiated. When it was over and Vasiṣṭha went out, the *rākṣasa* assumed his appearance, and proposed that food should be served. Then the *rakṣasa* transformed himself into a cook, and, preparing human flesh, he served it to Visistha on his return. The indignant sage cursed the king that henceforth his appetite should be excited only by similar food. A wrangle ensued, and Vasiṣṭha having found out the truth, limited the duration of his curse to twelve years. The angry king took water in his hands to pronounce, in his turn, a curse upon Vasiṣṭha, but was dissuaded from his purpose by his wife, Madayantī. "Unwilling to cast the water on the ground, lest it should wither up the grain, and equally reluctant to throw it up into the air, lest it should blast the clouds and dry up their contents, he threw it upon his own feet", and they were so scalded by it that they became black and white, and so gained for him the name of Kalmāṣapāda, 'spotted feet'. Everyday for twelve years, at the sixth watch of the day, he gave way to his cannibal appetite, "and devoured multitudes of men". On one occasion he devoured a brāhmaṇa in the midst of his connubial happiness, and the brāhmaṇa's wife passed upon him a curse that he should die whenever he associated with his wife. At the expiration of Vasiṣṭha's curse, the king returned home, but, mindful of the Brāhmaṇī's imprecation, he abstained from conjugal intercourse. By the interposition of Vasiṣṭha, his wife, Madayantī, became pregnant, and bore a child in her womb for seven years, when she performed the Caesarean operation with a sharp stone, and a child came forth who was called Aśmaka (from Aśman, 'a stone').

KALPA—A period of time: a great mundane age; a day of Brahmá. The most simple calculation of a Kalpa is its being 1,000 great ages or ages of the gods. Thus 4,320,000 years or a divine age, multiplied by 1,000 is equal to 4,320,000,000 years, or a day or night of Brahma.

One year of mortals is equal to one day of the gods. 12,000 divine years are equal to a period of four Yugas which is thus made up, *viz.*:—

Kṛita Yuga, with its	mornings and	evenings	4,800	divine years.
Tretá Yuga,	,,	,,	3,600	,,
Dvápara Yuga	,,	,,	2,400	,,
Kali Yuga,	,,	,,	1,200	,,
making			12,000	

As a day of the gods is = to one year of mortals, the 12,000 divine years must be multiplied by 360, the assumed number of days in a year, to give the number of the years of mortals in this great period of four Yugas, thus: 12,000 divine years x 360 = 4,320,000 years of mortals. 1,000 of these periods of 12,000 divine, or 4,320,000 human years—*i e.*, 4,320,000,000 human years, are = 1 day of Brahma, and his night is of the same duration. Within that period of a day of Brahmá, 14 Manus reign, and a Manwantara, or period of Manu, is consequently = the 14th part of a day of Brahmá. In the present Kalpa (= a day of Brahmá) six Manus, of whom Svayambhuva was the first, have already passed away, the present Manu being Vaivasvata. In each Manwantara seven Rishis, certain deities, an Indra, a Manu, and the kings, his sons, are created and perish. A thousand of the systems of four Yugas, as has been before explained, occur coincidently with these 14 Manwantaras; and consequently about 71 systems of 4 Yugas elapse during each Manwantara, and measure the lives of the Manu and the deities of the period. At the close of this day of Brahma a collapse of the universe takes place, which lasts through a night of Brahma, equal in duration to his day, during which period the three worlds are converted into one great ocean, when the lotus born god, expanded by his deglutition of the universe, and contemplated by the yogis and gods in Janaloka, sleeps on the serpent Śesha. At the end of that night he awakes and creates anew.—*Wilson.*

KALPA-SUTRAS—Aphorisms regarding the performance of sacrifices enjoined by the vedas; written by human authors, and therefore not considered as Śruti or revelation, are yet regarded as of very high authority. Ceremonial; one of the Vedāṅgas.

KALPA—The name of a son of Dhruva; also an Anga of the Vedas, containing the Ritual: the ceremonials of the Atharva-Vedas are called the five Kalpas.

KAMA, KĀMADEVA—The god of love. Eros, Cupid. In the *Ṛgveda* (x. 129) desire is said to have been the first movement that arose in the One after it had come into life through the power of fervour or abstraction. "Desire first arose in It, which was the primal germ of mind; (and which) sages, searching with their intellect, have discovered in their heart to be the bond which connects entity with non-entity." "It is well known," observes Dr. Muir, "that Greek mythology connected Eros, the god of love, with the creation of the universe somewhat in the same way." "This Kāma or desire, not of sexual enjoyment, but of good in general, is celebrated in a curious hymn *Atharvaveda* ", which exalts Kāma into a supreme God and Creator: "Kāma was born the first. Him neither gods, nor fathers, nor men have equalled. Thou art superior to these and for ever great." In another part of the same Veda Kāma appears to be first desire, then the power which gratifies the desire. Kāma is also in the same Veda often identified with Agni, and when " distinguished from each other, Kāma may be looked upon as a superior form of the other deity". According to the *Taittirīya Brāhmaṇa*, he is the son of Dharma, the god of justice, by Śraddhā, the goddess of faith; but according to the *Harivaṁśa* he is son of Lakṣmī. Another account represents him as springing from the heart of Brahmā. A fourth view is that he was bom from water, wherefore he is called Irāja, 'the water-born'; a fifth is that he is Ātmabhū, 'self-existent', and therefore he is called, like other of the gods, Aja, 'unborn', or An-anya-ja, 'born of no other'. In the Purāṇas his wife is Rati or Revā, the goddess of desire. He inspired Śiva with amorous thoughts of Pārvatī while he was engaged in penitential devotion, and for this offence the angry god reduced him to ashes by fire from his central eye. Śiva afterwards relented and allowed Kāma to be born again as Pradyumna, son of Kṛṣṇa and Rukmiṇī or Māyā, 'delusion'. He has a son named Aniruddha, and a daughter, Tṛṣā. He is lord of the apsarases or heavenly nymphs. He is armed with a bow and arrows: the bow is of sugar-cane, the bowstring a line of bees, and each arrow is tipped with a distinct flower. He is usually represented as a handsome youth riding on a parrot and attended by nymphs, one of whom bears his banner displaying the *makara*, *or* a fish on a red ground.

The mysterious origin of Kāma and the universal operation of the passion he inspires have accumulated úpon him a great variety of names and epithets Among his names are Iṣma, Kañjana and Kiṅkira, Mada, Rāma or Rāmaṇa and Smara. As produced in the mind or heart he is Bhavaja and Manoja. As Pradyumna, son of Kṛṣṇa, he is Kārṣṇī, and as son of Lakṣmī he is Māyī or Māyāsuta and Śrīnandana. As reduced to ashes by Śiva he is Anaṅga, 'the bodiless'. He is Abhirūpa, 'the beautiful'; Darpaka and Dīpaka, 'the inflamer;' Gadayitnu, Gṛdhu, and Gṛtsa, 'lustful or sharp'; Kamana and Kharu, 'esirous'; Kandarpa, 'the inflamer of Brahmā'; Kantu, 'the happy'; Kalākeli, 'the gay or wanton'; Māra, 'destroyer'; Māyī, 'deluder'; Madhudīpa, 'the lamp of honey or of spring'; Muhira, 'the bewilderer'; Murmura, 'the crackling fire'; Rāgavṛnta, 'the stalk of passion'; Rūpāstra, 'the weapon of beauty'; Ratanārīcha, 'the voluptuary'; Samāntaka, 'destroyer of peace'; Sansāra-guru, 'teacher of the world'; Smara, 'remembrance'; Śṛṅgārayoni, 'source of love'; Titha, 'fire'; Vāma, 'the handsome'. From his bow and arrows he is called Kusumāyudha, 'armed with flowers'; Puṣpa-dhanuṣ, 'whose bow is flowers'; and Puṣpaśara, 'whose arrows are flowers'. From his banner he is known as Makaraketu; and from the flower he carries in his hand he is Puṣpaketana.

KĀMADHENU—The cow which grants desires, belonging to the sage Vasiṣṭha. She was produced at the churning of the ocean. Among the examples of her supernatural powers was the creation of a host of warriors who aided Vasiṣṭha against Kārtavīrya. The sacred cow of the Muni Jamadagni, which was stolen by Rájá Kártavírya, and afterwards recovered by the Muni's son Paraṣaráma, who slew the robber king. She is called also Kāmaduh, Śavalā, and Surabhi.

KAMAGAMAS—A class of deities of the eleventh Manwantara.

KAMAKHYA, KAMAKSHI—The name of a form of Dúrga in the north-east of Bengal. There are some celebrated temples in Assam dedicated to the goddess under this form. (*see* KĀLIKĀ PURĀṆA)

KAMALASNA—A name of Brahmá, as the soul of the universe, contained in the Egg of the world.

KAMANDAKI—Author of a work known by his name on "The Elements of Polity". The text has been printed in the *Bibliotheca Indica* by Rājendra Lāla Mittra.

KAMARUPA—The north-eastern part of Bengal and the western portion of Assam. The name still survives as Kāmrūp.

KAMBALA—One of the many-headed serpent kings, of the progeny of Kádru.

KAMBALAVARHISH—One of the four sons of Andhaka.

KAMBOJAS—A north-western tribe famous for their horses, of which they appear to have possessed a remarkably fine breed. They were conquered by Sagara, who would have destroyed them utterly, but at the request of Vaśisht'ha contented himself with imposing on ail the vanquished tribes peculiar distinguishing marks, such as shaving their heads, letting their beards grow, &c.

KAMERI—The Indian cuckoo, or bird of Káma, whose emblems are peculiarly appropriate, being a bow and arrow composed of roses and jessamine, and other flowers in which no thorns ever lark. Colonel Tod says "the Kámeri poured forth its monotonous but pleasing notes, from an embrageous peepul, amidst the stillness of a lovely scene, where the last tints of sunset illuminated the dark hues of the surrounding woods."

KAMPILYA—One of the five sons of Haryaswa. Their father said these my five (*pancha*) sons are able (*alam*) to protect the countries; hence they were called the Pánchálas. Pánchála was at first the country north and west of Delhi, between the foot of the Himálaya and the Chambal. It was afterwards divided into northern and southern Pánchála separated by the Ganges. Kampilya was the name also given to part of the country, and was called Kampil by the early Mahommedan invaders. Kampilya was the city of Rája Drupada. It corresponds with the Kāmpita of modern times, situated in the Doāb on the old Ganges, between Badāūn and Farrukhābād.

KAṀSA—A tyrannical king of Mathurā, son of Ugrasena and cousin of Devakī the mother of Kṛṣṇa; so he was the cousin, not the uncle, of Kṛṣṇa, as he is often called. He married two daughters of Jarāsandha, king of Magadha. He deposed his father. It was foretold that a son born of Devakī should kill him, so he endeavoured to destroy all her children. But Balarāma, her seventh son, was smuggled away to Gokula, and was brought up by Rohiṇī. When Kṛṣṇa the eighth was born his parents fled with him. The tyrant then gave orders for a general massacre of all vigorous male infants. Kaṁsa became the great persecutor of Kṛṣṇa, but was eventually killed by him. Kaṁsa is also called Kalāṅkura, 'crane'. He is looked upon as an *asura*, and is in some way identified with the *asura* Kālanemi.

KAṀSA-BADHA—A drama in seven acts upon the destruction of Kaṁsa by Kṛṣṇa. The author is called Kṛṣṇa Kavi, and the play was probably written about two centuries ago. It is weak as a drama, but "the language is in general good, although highly elaborate". —*Wilson.*

KAMYA—Daughter of Kardam who was married to Priyavrata.

KAMYAKA—An extensive forest on the banks of the Saraswati, to which the Pándavas retired, on the occasions of their second exile.

KANADA—The sagewho founded the Vaiśeṣika school of philosophy. (*see* DARŚANA)

KANAKAS—Inhabitants of Múshika, or the country of thieves, a name applied to the pirate coast of Konkan. Professor Wilson thinks it may also designate Malabar where polyandry then as now prevailed.

KANAKHALA—The name of the village according to the Linga Purána, where the great sacrifice of Daksha took place. Gangadwára, the place where the Ganges descends to the plains,—or Haridwar, as it is more usually termed, is commonly specified as the scene of action.

KANCHANA—The sou of Bhíma, a descendant of Pururavas.

KANCHI—One of the seven sacred cities, *hodie* Conjeveram.

KANDARPA—The Hindu Cupid, (*see* KĀMA)

KANDARSI—A *ṛṣi* who teaches one particular *kāṇḍa* or part of the Vedas.

KANDU—An eminent sage, who practised pious austerities on the lovely borders of the Gomati river. Indra sent the nymph Pramlochá to disturb his penance, and the sweet-smiling damsel diverted the sage from his devotions. They lived together in the valley of Mandura for a hundred and fifty years, wholly given up to enjoyment. Then the nymph requested permission to return to heaven; but the sage still fondly attached to her, prevailed upon her to remain for some time longer; and the graceful damsel continued to reside for another hundred years and delight the great sage by her fascinations. Then she again wished to return to the abodes of the gods, and again the Muni desired her to remain. Similar scenes occurred several times.

"On one occasion the sage was going forth from their cottage in a great hurry. The nymph asked him where he was going. 'The day,' he replied, 'is drawing fast to a close; I must perform the Sandhyá worship, or a duty will be neglected.' The nymph smiled mirthfully as she rejoined, 'Why do you talk, grave air, of this day drawing to a close: your day is a day of many years, a day that must be a marvel to all: explain what this means.' The Muni said, 'Fair damsel, you came to the riverside at dawn; I beheld you then, and you then entered my hermitage. It is now the revolution of evening, and the day is gone. What is the meaning of this laughter ? Tell me the truth.' Pramlochá answered, 'you sáy rightly,' venerable Brahman,' that I came hither at morning dawn, but several hundred years have passed since the time of my arrival. This is the truth.' The Muni, on hearing this, was seized with astonishment, and asked her how long he had enjoyed her society; to which the nymph replied, that they had lived together nine hundred and seven years, six months, and three days. The Muni asked her if she spoke the truth, or if she was in jest; for it appeared to him that they had spent but one day together: to which Pramlochá replied, that she should not dare at any time to tell him who lived in the path of piety an untruth, but particularly when she had been enjoined by him to inform him what had passed.

"When the Muni, princes, had heard these words, and knew that it was the truth, he began to reproach himself bitterly, exclaiming, 'Fie, fie upon me; my penance has been interrupted; the treasure of the learned and the pious has been stolen from me: my judgment has been blinded: this woman has been created by some one to beguile me: Brahmá is beyond the reach of those agitated by the waves of infirmity. I had subdued my passions, and was about to attain divine knowledge. This was foreseen by him by whom this girl has been sent hither. Fie on the passion that has obstructed my devotions. All the austerities that would have led to acquisition of the wisdom of the Vedas have been rendered of no avail by passion that is the road to hell.' The pious sage, having thus reviled himself, turned to the nymph, who wag sitting nigh, and said to her, 'Go, deceitful girl, whither thou wilt: thou hast performed the office assigned thee by the monarch of the gods, of disturbing my penance by thy fascinations. I will not reduce thee to ashes by the fire of my wrath. Seven paces together is sufficient for the friendship of the virtuous, but thou and I have dwelt together. And in truth what fault hast thou committed ? why should I be wrath with thee ? The sin is wholly mine, in that I could not subdue my passions: yet fie upon thee, who, to gain favour with Indra, hast disturbed my devotions; vile bundle of delusion.'

"Thus spoken to by the Muni, Pramlochá stood trembling, whilst big drops of perspiration started from every pore; till he angrily cried to her, 'Depart, begone.' She then, reproached by him, went forth from his dwelling, and, passing through the air, wiped the perspiration from her person with the leaves of the trees. The nymph went from tree to tree, and as with the dusky shoots that crowned their summits she dried her limbs, which were covered with moisture, the child she had conceived by the Rishi came forth from the pores of her skin in drops of perspiration. The trees received the living dews, and the winds collected them into one mass. "This," said Soma, "I matured by my rays, and gradually it increased in size, till the exhalation that had rested on the tree tops became the lovely girl named Márishá " *V.P.*

KANISHTAS—A class of deities of the fourteenth Manwantara.

KANISKA—"Huṣka, Juṣka, Kaniṣka". These are the names recorded in the *Rāja Tarangiṇī* of three great Turuṣka, that is Turk or Tatar, kings, who were of the Buddhist religion. It may, perhaps, be taken for granted that Huṣka and Juṣka come in their natural succession, for the names might be transposed without detriment to the metre; but the short syllable of the name Kaniṣka is required where it stands by the rules of prosody, so that the position of the name in the verse is not decisive of his place in the succession of kings. Nothing is known of Juṣka beyond the simple recital of his name as above quoted, but the names of Kaniṣka and Huṣka (or Huviṣka) have been found in inscriptions and upon coins, showing that their dominions were of considerable extent in northern India, and that they were, as the *Rājatarangiṇī* represents, great supporters of the Buddhist religion. The name of Kaniṣka has been found in inscriptions at Mathurā, Manikyāla, Bhāwalpur, and Zeda, while his name appears on the corrupt Greek coins as Kanerki. Huviṣka's name has been found at Mathurā and on a metal vase from Wardak in Afghanistan; on the coins his name is represented as Oerki. Kaniṣka preceded Huviṣka, and it is certain that their reigns covered a period of fifty-one years, and probably more. The time at which they reigned seems to have been just before the Christian era. A Roman coin of the date 33 BC was found in the tope of Manikyāla, which was built by Kaniṣka.

KANKA—One of the sons of Ugraséna.

KANOUJ—A city on the banks of the river Sone. The Rámáyana contains an extraordinary legend of its foundation. The Rája Kusanábha had a hundred beautiful daughters to whom Váyu the god of wind made some amorous proposals which they rejected, declaring that they would only accept such husband as their father might give them. Váyu then rendered them hunchbacked. Subsequently they were all married to a young Rája, Brahmadatta, who cured them by a touch, and the city in which they dwelt was henceforth called Kanyákubja, the hunch-backed, and still goes by the name of Kanouj.—*See* GRITÁCHÍ, KUSANÁBHA.

KANSA, KANSAVATI, KANKI—Daughters of Ugraséns.

KANSA—Rajah of Mathura; he deposed his father Ugraséna; and threatened to slay his cousin Devaki on her wedding day. Vasudeva engaged to deliver up her children to him. He was warned before the birth of Krishṇa, that the latter would take away his life. He accordingly attempted to destroy Krishṇa as soon as he was born; failing in this he ordered that all the worshippers of Vishṇu, young and old, should be slain; and he commanded his warriors to make search for all young children throughout that country, and to slay every male child. He afterwards employed demons to find and kill Krishṇa, and sent Akrúra to bring him to Mathura. Public games were celebrated with great splendour; there was a severe contest in which Krishṇa slew the powerful demon Cháṇúra, and afterwards killed king Kansa himself.

KANVAS—The descendants or followers of Kaṇva.

KANWA—**(1)** A teacher of the white Yajush, and founder of several schools for the purpose; **(2)** The name of a son of Aprati-ratha from whom the Kaṇwáyana brahmans descended; **(3)** A son of Ajamídha, a descendant of Hastin. **(4)** Name of a *ṛsi* to whom some hymns of the *Ṛgveda* are ascribed; he is sometimes counted as one of the seven great *ṛsis*. **(5)** The sage who brought up Śakuntalā as his daughter. There are several others of the same name

KANYA—(*see* ŚATAPATHA BRĀHMAṆA)

KANYAKAGUNAS—A race of Aborigines.

KANYAKUBJA—The modern form of the name is Kannauj or Kinnauj, spelt in a variety of ways. **(1)** An ancient city of Hindustan on the Kālī-nadī, an affluent of the Ganges, and lying a little to the west of the latter. It was once the capital of a powerful dynasty. It was known to classical geographers as "Canogyza". The name means "humpbacked damsel", and refers to a legend relating to the hundred daughters of King Kuśanābha, who were all made crooked by Vāyu for refusing to comply with his licentious desires. **(2)** A great national division of the brāhmaṇa caste, (see Brāhmaṇa)

KANYA-KUMARI—'The virgin-damsel'. A name of Durgā. Her worship extended to the southernmost extremity of India in the days of Pliny, and 'Kumāri' still appears in the name Cape Comorin.

KAPALI, KAPARDDI—Two of the eleven Rudras according to the Vishṇu Purána.

KAPALIKA—The following description of the *Kápalika* is *from* the *Sankara Vijaya* of *Ánandagiri*:

"His body is smeared with ashes from a funeral pile, around his neck hangs a string of human skulls, his forehead is streaked with a black line, his hair is wove into the malted braid, his loins are clothed with a tiger's skin, a hollow skull is in his left hand (for a cup), and in his right he carries a bell, which he rings incessantly, exclaiming aloud, ho, *Sambhu, Bhairava*—. ho, lord of Káli."

KAPARDIN—'Wearing the *kaparda*', a peculiar braid or knot of hair. This epithet is applied to Śiva, to one of the Rudras, and some others.

KAPI—A prince, the son of Urukshaya, who afterwards became a brahman. *V.P.*, p. 451.

KAPIDHVAJA—An epithet of Arjuna, because he bore an ape (*kapi*) on his standard (*dhvaja*).

KAPILA PURANA—(*see* PURĀṆA)

KAPILA, KAPILAVASTU—A town on the river Rohiṇī, an affluent of the Rāptī, which was the capital of Śuddhodana, the father of Gotama Buddha.

KAPILA—**(1)** A great Rishi, who destroyed the sons of Sagara. When the latter commenced the performance of the solemn sacrifice of a horse, it was guarded by his own sons; nevertheless some one stole the animal, and carried it off into a chasm in the earth. Sagara commanded his sons to search for the steed. They at last found it freely wandering about in Pátála, and at no great distance saw the Rishi Kapila sitting, absorbed in profound meditation, and illuminating the surrounding space with radiance as bright as the splendour of the autumnal sun, shining in an unclouded sky. Exclaiming "This is the villain who has interrupted our sacrifice and stolen the horses, kill him; kill him; they ran towards him with uplifted weapons. The Muni slowly raised his eyes and for an instant looked upon them, and they were reduced to ashes by the sacred name that darted from bis person. Kapila wae the founder of the Śankya school of philosophy. A work said to be written by him, called the Śánkya-Praváchana, or Preface to the Śankya Philosophy, is still extant, and was printed at Serampore in 1821. The great reverence in which Kapila was held, may be presumed from the fact that he is sometimes considered as an incarnation of the god Agni; and sometimes of Vishṇu himself. He seems to belong only to the Puránic period. See Śánkya. **(2)** A renowned Danava. **(3)** One of the serpent kings of the progeny of Kadru. **(4)** The name of a mountain in the west of Meru. **(5)** One of the Puránic rivers. **(6)** A city mentioned in the Puránas.

KAPILASRAMA—The name of the hermitage of Kapila, on the shore of the island of Sagara, which is still the scene of an annual pilgrimage.

KAPILASWA—One of the three sons of Kuvalayáswa, who survived the great conflict with the demon Dhunda.

KAPISA—Mother of the Piśācas, who bear the metronymic Kāpiśeya.

KAPOTOROMAN—The son of Vrishta, a descendant of Sini.

KARABHANJIKAS—An aboriginal mountain tribe of the north.

KARAKAS, KARATAS—Aboriginal tribes enumerated in the Puránas.

KARALI—'Dreadful, terrible.' In Vedic times one of the seven tongues of Agni (fire), but in later days a name of the terrible consort of Śiva. (*see* DEVĪ) *O.S.T.*, Vol. IV, p. 364.

KARAMBHI—A prince, the son of Sakuni of the race of Jyámagha.

KARANDHAMA—The powerful, wealthy, and valiant son of Khaninetra, who when besieged by revolted tributaries is said to have created an army by breathing in his hands; hence his name.

KARARI—Is the worshipper of Devi in her terrific forms, the representative of the *Aghora Ghanta* and *Kápálika*, who as lately as only seven or eight centuries ago, there is reason to suppose, sacrificed human victims to KALI, CHAMUNDA, and other hideous personifications of the Śakti of Śiva.—Wilson's *Works*, Vol. I, p. 264.

KARDAMA—(1) According to the *Mahābhārata* and *Rāmāyaṇa*, he is one of the Prajāpatis who sprang from Brahmā. who was married to one of the daughters of Daksha named Devahúti. **(2)** According to other authorities, he, or another sage of the same name, was a son of Dakṣa or a son of Pulaha.

KARISHAKAS, KARITIS—Aboriginal tribes enumerated in the Puránas.

KARKKOTTA—One of the serpent kings of the progeny of Kadru.

KARLI—Is situated about half way between Poona and Bombay, and is celebrated for the numerous inscriptions in its caves in the Pali language; of a date estimated at 543 B.C. to 176 A.D. The religion, or divinities or sages mentioned are Buddhist; the invocation is to the Triad; no doubt meaning Buddha, Dharma, Sanga. The kings or princes mentioned, Dr. Wilson says, are, Vijara, but Dr. Stevenson, Arodhana, lord of India. Garga, ruler of the Śakas. Of the numerous Buddhist inscriptions in the cave temple at Karli, Drs. Wilson and Stevenson are not quite agreed about the reading. Garga, the "ruler of the Śakas" (Sakya, Buddha's tribe), is mentioned.

The cave temples, in the southern part of India, are classed by Mr. Fergusson into

(a) the Vihara or monastery caves, which consist of (1) natural caverns or caves slightly improved by art. These are the most ancient, and are found appropriated to religious purposes in Behar and Cuttack; next (2) a verandah, opening behind into cells for the abode of priests, as in Cuttack and in the oldest Vihara at Ajanta; the third (3) has an enlarged hall supported on pillars: the most splendid of these caves are those of Ajanta;. though the Dherwarra at Ellora is also fine, and there are same good specimens at Salsette and Junir.

(b) Buddhist Chetya caves form the *second* class. These are the temples or churches of the series and one or more of them is attached to every set of caves in western India, though none exist on the eastern side. Unlike the Viharas, all these caves have the same plan and arrangement, and the

Karli cave is the most perfect in India. All these consist of an external porch or music gallery, an internal gallery over the entrance; a central aisle, which may be called a nave, roofed by a plain waggon vault, and a semi-dome terminating the nave, under the centre of which always stands a Dagoba or Chaitya. In the oldest temples, the Dagoba consists of a plain central drum surmounted by a hemispherical dome crowned by a Tee, which supported the umbrella of state, of wood or stone.

These two classes comprehend all the Buddhist caves in India.

The *third* class consists of brahmanical caves, properly so called. The finest specimens are at Ellora and Elephanta though some good ones exist also on the island of Salsette and at Mahabalipur.

In form, many of them are copies of, and a good deal resemble the Buddhist Vihara. But they have not been appropriated from the Buddhists, as the arrangement of the pillars and position of the sanctuary are different.

The *Fourth* class consists of rock cut models of structural Brahmanical temples. To this class belong the far famed Kylas at Ellora, the Sivite temple at Doomnar, and the Ruths at Mahabalípur. This last is cut out of isolated blocks of granite, but the rest stand in pits.

The *Fifth* or true Jaina caves occur at Khandagiri in Cuttack and in the southern parts of India, but are few and insignificant. In that in the rock of Gwalior fort, there are cut in the rock a number of rude colossal figures, from 30 to 40 feet high, of one of the Thirtankaras, some sitting and some. standing.

The Ajanta, are the most complete series of Buddhist caves in India, without any mixture of Brahmanism, and contain types of all the rest; they are in a ravine or small valley in the ghát south of the Taptee. At Baug in a ravine or small valley in the ghát, on the north side of the valley of the Taptee, are three ancient Buddhistical caves.

The Salsette or Kannari caves in the island of Salsette, are also purely Buddhist, but very inferior to the former. The Kannari caves are excavated in a hill situated in the midst of an immense tract of forest country, and Mr. Fergusson supposes their date about the 9th or 10th century of the Christian era.

Dhumnar, about 40 miles S.E. from Neemuch but close to Chundwassa, contains Buddhist caves with a Brahmanical rock temple behind.

The Ellora caves are excavated in a porphyritic green stone or amygdaloid.

The Elephanta caves are cut in a harder rock than those of Ellora. Those of Dhumnar and Ellora contain a strong admixture of Brahmanism, and those of Elephanta are entirely Brahmanical, though perhaps of the same age as those of Ellora.—Balfour's *Encyclopaedia Asiatica*.

KARMA—According to the doctrines of Buddhism the power that controls the universe is Karma, literally Action; consisting of kusala and akusala, or merit and demerit. There is no such monad as an immaterial spirit, but at the death of any being, the aggregate of his merit and demerit is transferred to some other being, which new being is caused by the karma of the previous being, and receives from that karma all the circumstances of its existence. Thus, if the karma be good, the circumstances are favourable, producing happiness, but if it be bad, they are unfavourable, producing misery.

The manner in which being first commenced cannot now be ascertained. The cause of the *continuance* of existence is ignorance, from which merit and demerit are produced, whence comes consciousness, then body and mind, and afterwards the six organs of sense. Again, from the organs of sense comes contact; from contact, desire; from desire, sensation; from sensation, the cleaving to existing objects; from this cleaving, reproduction; and from reproduction, disease, decay, and death. Thus, like the revolutions of a wheel, there is a regular succession of death and birth, the moral cause of which is the cleaving to existing objects, whilst the instrumental cause is karma. It is, therefore, the great object of all beings who would be released from the sorrows of successive birth to seek the destruction of the moral cause of continued existence, that is to say, the cleaving to existing objects, or evil desire. It is possible to accomplish this destruction, by attending to a prescribed course of discipline, which results in an entrance to one of the four paths, with their fruition, that lead, by different modes, to the attainment of nirwána. They in whom evil desire is entirely destroyed are called arhats. The freedom from evil desire ensures the possession of a miraculous ene-rgy. At his death the arhat invariably attains nirwána, or ceases to exist.—*Spence Hardy*.

KARMA-MĪMĀṀSĀ—The Pūrva Mīmāṁsā. (*see* DARŚANA)

KARMA-MĪMĀṀSA-SŪTRA—A work on the Vedānta philosophy, ascribed to Jaimini.

KARMOSA—The eldest sou of the Patriarch Pulaka. In the Bhágavata he is designated Karmaṣreshta.

KARNA—Son of Pṛthā or Kuntī by Sūrya, the sun, before her marriage to Pāṇḍu. Kama was thus half-brother of the Pāṇḍavas, but this relationship was not known to them till after his death. Kuntī, on one occasion, paid such attention to the sage Durvāsas, that he gave her a charm by virtue of which she might have a child by any god she preferred to invoke. She chose the sun, and the result was Karṇa, who was bom equipped with arms and armour. Afraid of censure and disgrace, Kuntī exposed the child on the banks of the Yamunā, where it was found by Nandana or Adhiratha, the *sūta* or charioteer of Dhṛtarāṣṭra. The charioteer and his wife, Rādhā, brought him up as their own, and the child passed as such. When he grew up, Indra disguised himself as a brāhmaṇa, and cajoled him out of his divine cuirass. He gave him in return great strength and a javelin charged with certain death to whomsoever it was hurled against. Karṇa became king of Aṅga or Bengal. Some authorities represent his foster-father as having been ruler of that country, but others say that Karṇa was made king of Aṅga by Duryodhana, in order to qualify him to fight in the passage of arms at the *svayaṁvara* of Draupadī. This princess haughtily rejected him, saying, "I wed not with the base-born". Kama knew that he was half-brother of the Pāṇḍavas, but he took the side of their cousins, the Kauravas, and he had especial rivalry and animosity against Arjuna, whom he vowed to kill. In the great battle he killed Ghaṭotkaca, the son of Bhīma, with Indra's javelin. Afterwards there was a terrific combat between him and Arjuna, in which the latter was nearly overpowered, but he killed Karṇa with a crescent-shaped arrow. After Karṇa's death his relationship to the Pāṇḍavas became known to them, and they showed their regret for his loss by great kindness to his widows, children, and dependants. From his father, Vikarttana (the sun), Karṇa was called Vaikarttana; from his foster-parents, Vāsusena; from his foster-father's profession, Ādhirathi and Sūta; and from his foster-mother, Rādheya. He was also called Aṅgarāja, 'king of Aṅga'; Campādhipa, 'king of Campā'; and Kānīna, 'the bastard'.

KARNA-PRĀVARAṆAS—Men whose ears served them for coverings. They are mentioned in the *Mahābhārata*, *Rāmāyaṇa*, and other works.

KARNAPRAVARANAS—A nickname applied in the Purānas to some of the aboriginal tribes, meaning those who wrap themselves up in their cars.

KARNATAKAS—The Canarese people; the inhabitants of the centre of the peninsula, the proper Karnata, or Carnatic.

KARTAVIRYA—Son of Kṛtavīrya, king of the Kaikaya tribe. This is his patronymic, by which he is best known; his real name was Arjuna. "Having worshipped a portion of the divine being called Dattātreya, sprung from the race of Atri, he sought and obtained these boons, *viz.*, a thousand arms and a golden chariot that went wheresoever he willed it to go; the power of restraining wrong by justice; the conquest of the earth and the disposition to rule it righteously; invincibility by enemies, and death at the hands of a man renowned over the whole world. By him this earth was perfectly governed", and of him it is said: "No other king shall ever equal Kārtavīrya in regard to sacrifices, liberality, austerities, courtesy, and self-restraint." "Thus he ruled for 85,000 years with unbroken health, prosperity, strength, and valour." —*VP.*

He visited the hermitage of Jamadagni, and was received by that sage's wife with all respect; but he made an ill return for her hospitality, and carried off by violence "the calf of the milch-cow of the sacred oblation". For this outrage Paraśurāma cut off his thousand arms and killed him. In another place a different character is given to him, and more in accordance with his behaviour at Jamadagni's hut. "He oppressed both men and gods", so that the latter appealed to Viṣṇu for succour. That god then came down to the earth as Paraśurāma for the especial purpose of killing him. Kārtavīrya was the contemporary of Rāvaṇa, and when that demon monarch came "in the course of his campaign of conquest to Mahiṣmatī (the capital of Kārtavīrya), he was captured without difficulty, and was confined like a wild beast in a corner of his city." The statement of the *Vāyu Purāṇa is* that Kārtavīrya invaded Laṅkā, and there took Rāvaṇa prisoner.

KARTIKA—The name of one of the lunar months, corresponding to October.

KARTIKEYA—The Hindu Mars, or god of war, generated from the vivifying principle of Śiva cast into Agni, or Fire, who unable to retain it, cast it into Ganga, or the Ganges. On the banks of this river was born the beautiful boy who was destined to lead the armies of the gods, and to be the destroyer of Táraka, and Súra, a demon who by his austerities, had alarmed both gods and men, and gained the dominion of the universe. When born Kártikeya was nursed by six nymphs called the Krittikáș, or Pleiades, who each called him her son, and offering her breast, the child assumed to himself six mouths and received nurture from each. He is considered to bo the brother of Gaṇésa who was the reputed eldest son of Śiva and Párvatí. Ho is represented riding on a peacock; sometimes with one (ace, sometimes with six faces and twelve arms. One account of his birth is as follows: Śiva emitted from his eyes sparks of fire, which being thrown into the lake Saravana, became six infants, who were nursed by the wives of the Rishis who are to be seen in the sky as the Pleiades. When Párvatí saw the children she was so transported with their beauty, and embraced all of them together so forcibly, that their six bodies became one, while their six heads and twelve arms remained. Kártikeya is better known in the south of India as Subramanya, and Tuesday is the weekly day of his devotees. The Skauda Purána gives the fullest account of Subiamanya, containing his war with Śura, and relates how he was sent by his father to frustrate the sacrifice of Daksha, and, at the instigation of the latter, was delayed in Ilia way by beautiful damsels, who entertained him with song and music. Hence it is the practice still for the dancing girls who serve in the pagodas, to be betrothed and married to him, and then not allowed to marry men though they may prostitute themselves.—*John Garrett*

The god of war is also called Skanda. He is said in the *Mahābhārata* and *Rāmāyaṇa* to be the son of Śiva or Rudra, and to have been produced without the intervention of a woman. Śiva cast his seed into fire, and it was afterwards received by the Ganges: Kārttikeya was the result; hence, he is called Agnibhū and Gaṅgāja. He was fostered by the Pleiades (Kṛttikā), and hence he has six heads and the name Kārttikeya. His paternity is sometimes assigned to Agni (fire); Gaṅgā (the Ganges) and Pārvatī are variously represented to be his mother. He was born for the purpose of destroying Tāraka, a *daitya* whose austerities had made him formidable to the gods. He is represented riding on a peacock called Paravāṇi, holding a bow in one hand and an arrow in the other. His wife is Kaumārī or Senā.

He has many titles: as a warrior he is called Mahāsena, Senāpati; Siddhasena, 'leader of the Siddhas'; and Yudharaṅga; also Kumāra, the boy; Guha, 'the mysterious one'; Śaktidhara 'spear-holder'; and in the south he is called Subrahmaṇya. He is Gaṅgāputra, 'son of the Ganges'; Śarabhū, 'born in the thicket'; Tārakajit, 'vanquisher of Tāraka;' Dvādaśakara and Dvādaśākṣa, 'twelve-handed' and 'twelve-eyed'; Ṛjukāya, 'straight-bodied'. (*see* KRAUÑCA)—*John Dowson*

KARUNDHAKA—One of the ten sons of Súra and brother of Vásudeva, in whose family Krishṇa was born.

KARUSAS—A people of Mālwa, inhabiting the back of the Vindhya mountains. They are said to be deceased from Karuṣa, one of the sons of the Manu Vaivasvata.

KARUSHA—One of the sons of the Manu Vaiwaswata, from whom descended the celebrated warriors termed Kárúshas, who lived in the Paripátra or Vindhya mountains.

KASA—The son of Suhotra of the family of Áyus, and king of Kásí.

KASERAMAT—One of the nine divisions of the Varsha of Bhárata.

KASHTHA—Fifteen twinklings of the eye, or Nimishas; five Kshanas.

KASHTHA—One of the daughters of Daksha and wife of Kaṣyapa; she was the mother of beasts with uncloven hoofs.

KASI KHANDA—A long poem, forming a part of the *Skanda Purāṇa*. It gives a very minute description of the temples of Śiva in and around Benares, and is presumably anterior to the Mahomedan conquest, (*see* SKANDA PURĀṆA)

KASI, or VARANASI—Benares, (*q.v.*) the sacred city of the Hindus, which they believe to have descended from the *gods* originally.

KASINA—An ascetic rite among the Buddhists, by which it is supposed that a miraculous energy may be received. There *are* ten descriptions of this rite,

1. Prathawi .... earth.
2. Apo......... .... water.
3. Tejo......... .... fire.
4. Váyu......... .... wind.
5. Nila......... .... blue.
6. Pita......... .... golden.

7. Lohita.........	blood red.
8. Odata.........	white.
9. Alaka.........	light.
10. Akása.........	space.

There are various ceremonies prescribed for the performance of these different kinds of Kasina, and from its practice in any one of its forms, a Buddhist priest expects to derive many advantages. See Hardy's Manual of Buddhism.

KASIRAJA—One of the kings of Kási—the son of Kása, an ally of the Pándavas.

KASIS—The people of the Benares district, and that opposite.

KASMIRAS—The people of Kashmir.

KASYA—A prince, the son of Senajlt, one of the descendants of Hastin.

KASYAPA—A sage, the son of Maríchi, the sou of Brahma, and one of the Prajápatis or progenitors of created things. He married thirteen of the daughters of Daksha; from whom descended tho twelve Ádityas; the nymphs of the lunar constellations; the Daityas and Danavas; many classes of animals, etc., etc. His share in creation was thus no unimportant one, as he was the father of the gods and demons, man, beasts, and reptiles. Kaṣyapa was the father of Vivasvat, and he again of Manu. "Righteous wax this wise Manu on whom a race was founded. Hence this family of men became known as the race of Manu. Brahmans, Kshatriyas, and other men sprang from this Manu." (*O.S.T.*, Vol. I, p. 125.) "The Chhándogya Upanishad agrees with the above passage from the Mahábhárata, in recognising Manu as the progenitor of the brahmans as well as the other castes." (p.196.) "Having assumed the form of a tortoise Prajápati created offspring. That which he created, he made; hence the word *kúrma.* Kaṣyapa means tortoise; hence men say all creatures are descendants of Kasyapa. This tortoise is the same as Ádityas." (Vol. IV, p. 23.)

The Mahábhárata states: "From Kaṣyapa, who was the son of Maríchi, were produced the deities and the Asuras; and he was the source from which all beings sprang. Aditi had twelve sons, beginning with Śakra. The youngest of them was Vishṇu, on whom the worlds are supported." "Ansa, Bhaga, Mitra, Varuna, lord of the waters, Dhátri, Aryaman, Jayanta, Bháskara, Tvashtri, Púshan, Indra, and Vishçu, who is called the twelfth; these are the twelve Ádityas, the sons of Kaṣyapa, according to tradition (or the veda *sruti.*)" In another passage Vivasvat and Savitûi occur instead of Jayanta and Bháskara; Tvashtri is placed the eleventh in order, and it adds "the twelfth is called Vishnu, who though the latest born, surpasses all the Ádityas in his attributes." (Vol. IV, p. 103,104.)

In the Rámáyana the following passage occurs; Visvámitra speaks:—"At this period O Ráma, the divine Kaṣyapa, luminous as fire, glowing, as it were, with splendour, attended by the goddess Aditi, having completed an act of austerity which had lasted for a thousand years of the gods, celebrated thus the praises of the boon-bestowing Madhusúdana. 'Through intense austerity I behold thee the Supreme Spirit, whose essence is austerity, who art a congeries of austerity, the impersonation of austerity, whose wealth is austerity. In thy body, lord, I behold this whole universe; thou art unbeginning, and ineffable; to thee I have resorted as my refuge.' Then Hari, gratified, whose taint of sin had been purged away; 'Ask a boon; may good attend thee, thou art regarded by me as deserving a boon.' Hearing them words of his, Kaṣyapa, the son of Maríchi, replied; 'Sinless lord, become the son of Aditi and myself. Slayer of the Asuraa become the younger brother of Śukra. (Indra.) Thou oughtest to succour the gods who are oppressed with grief, Vishçu, of mighty energy, was accordingly born of Aditi, shaded by an umbrella, in the form of a mendicant, resplendent with a drinking gourd, and a lock of hair on his crown." (*Ibid*, p. 116.)

Kaṣyapa is supposed by some modern writers to be a personification of the remains of the antediluvian race, who took refuge in the central Asiatic chain, in which traces of his name so plentifully abound, as in the Koh-i-Kas or Caucasus, the Kaspian, and Kashmir. It is asserted that the thirteen Gotras or families of Brahmans owe their origin to as many divine sages called after their names. Kasyapa is one of the number. The Asvaláyana Sútra of the Rig Veda contains the enumeration of the Gotras and their sub-divisions, but in a very involved and unintelligible *style.* The popular enumeration of them, however, is now wholly confined to the South of India, where several of the reputed representatives of these tribes yet exist; especially about Gooty and Gondavir. Nandavaram, it is said, was a grant to the thirteen Gotras by the sovereign of India, Nanda, in the year of Kali 980; but if there be any foundation for the grant, it is of much more recent date, Nanda having lived in the fourth century before the Christian era.—*Hindu Theatre*, Vol. II, p. 11.

KASYATA—A son of Paurnamáṣa, a descendant of one of the (laughters of Daksha who was married to one of the Rishis.

KATANTRA—A Sanskṛt grammar by Sarvavarman. Edited by Eggeling for the *Bibliotheca Indica*.

KATAPRU—'Worm.' A class of beings similar to or identical with the Vidyādharas.

KATHA—Name of a Upaniṣad (*q.v.*). It has been translated by Dr. Roer in the *Bibliotheca Indica*.

KATHAKA—A school or recension of the *Yajurveda*, occupying a position between the Black and the White. It is supposed to be lost.

KATHARNAVA—'Sea of stories.' A compilation of miscellaneous stories in four books; the first two are the originals of the Hindī *Baitāla Pacīsī* and *Singhāsana Battīsī*.

KATHA-SARIT-SAGARA—'The ocean of the rivers of stories.' A collection of popular stories by Somadeva Bhaṭṭa of Kaśmīr, made about the beginning of the twelfth century AD. It is drawn from a larger work called *Bṛthatkathā*. The text has been printed and in part translated by Brockhaus.

KATYAYANA—An ancient writer of great celebrity, who came after Pāṇini, whose grammar he completed and corrected in what he called Vārttikas, 'supplementary rules and annotations'. He is generally identified with Vararuci, the author of the *Prākṛta Prakāśa*. Max Müller places him in the second half of the fourth century BC; Goldstücker in the first half of the second century BC; Weber about twenty-five years BC. Besides his additions to Pāṇini's Grammar, he was the author of the *Śrauta-sūtras* which bear his name, and of the *Yajurveda Prātiśākhya*. His *sūtras* have been edited by Weber. Professor Goldstücker, in his *Pánini*, &c., *his Place in Sanscrit Literature* (London, 1861) has shewn that he cannot have. been a contemporary of Pánini, as was generally assumed; and in a paper recently read by him before the Royal Asiatic Society (February, 1863,) he has proved that this Kátyáyana lived at the same time as the great grammarian Pátanjali, whose date he had previously fixed between 140 and 120 before the Christian era. A story in the *Kathā-sarit-sāgara* makes him the incarnation of a demigod named Puṣpadanta. A Kātyāyana was author also of a Dharmaśāstra.

KATYAYANI A name of Durgā. (*see* DEVĪ)

KAUṬILYA—Another name of Cāṇakya, the minister of Candragupta. (*see* CĀṆAKYA)

KAUKUNDAKAS, KAUKATTAKAS, KAUNKANAS— Aboriginal tribes inhabiting the mountainous districts of the Konkan and its neighbourhood.

KAUMARA CREATION—The creation of Rudra or Nílalóhita, a form of Śiva, by Bramhá, and of certain other mind-born sons of Brahmá, termed Sanatkumára, &c., who declining to create progeny remained, as the name implies, ever boys, kumáras, that is ever pure and innocent; whence their creation is called the Kaumára. Sanatkumára and his brethren are described in the Śaiva Puránas as Yógis. The Linga Purána has "Being ever as he was born he is called a youth; and hence his name is well known as Sanatkumára."

KAUMARABHRITYA—One of the eight branches of medical science embracing midwifery and the management of children. *Vishṇu Purána*, p. 407.

KAUMODAKI—The mace of Kṛṣṇa, presented to him by Agni when engaged with him in fighting against Indra and burning the Khāṇḍava forest.

KAUNDINYA—An ancient sage and grammarian. He offended Śiva, but was saved from that god's wrath by Viṣṇu: he was hence called Viṣṇugupta, 'saved by Viṣṇu'.

KAUNTEYA—Son of Kuntī. A metronymic applicable to Yudhiṣṭhira, Bhīma, and Arjuna, but commonly applied to Arjuna.

KAURAVAS—The sons of the Mahárája Dhritaráshtra and his wife Gándhári. At an early period they became jealous of their cousins, the Páṇḍavas, who were brought up with them in their father's court. Duryodhana, the eldest of the Kauravas, attempted to take the life of his cousin Bhíma. The chief incidents of their lives are related under their respective names, *q.v.* (*see* MAHĀBHĀRATA)

KAUŚALYA—(mas.), **KAUSALYĀ** (fem.). Belonging to the Kosala nation. There are several women known by this name. The wife of Puru and mother of Janamejaya. The wife of Daśaratha and mother of Rāma. (*see* Daśaratha) The mother of Dhṛtarāṣṭra and the mother of Pāṇḍu both were known by this name, being daughters of a king of Kāśī.

KAUSAMBI—An ancient city of Hindustan, which appears as the capital of Vatsa. According to the Rámáyana, it was built by Kusamba, the son of Kusa, a descendant of Ráma. Buchanan, upon the authority of the Bhágavata, ascribes its foundation to Chakra, a descendant of Arjuna; but neither the Bhágavata nor Vishṇu Purána state that Nimichakra built Kausambi. They only say that when Hastinápura shall be washed away by the Ganges, Nimichakra will reside at Kausambi. From which it is to be inferred, that Kausambi existed at the time that Hastinápura was destroyed. The site of Kausambi, Buchanan supposes to have been that of the ruins ascribed to Hastinápura, but it was most probably lower down in the Doab, bordering upon Magadha on one side, and Koṣala on the other. In the Hindu drama Ratnávali the scene is laid in the palace of King Vatsa at Kauṣámbí.—*Wilson, H.T.*

KAUSHARAVI—A name of Maitreya, a disciple of Parásara, who related the *V.P.* to him.

KAUSIKA—(1) A devotee mentioned in the *Mahābhārata* as having gone to a hell of torment for having pointed out to robbers a road by which they pursued and killed some persons who fled from them.

(2) One of the sons of Vasudeva by his wife Vaisali: the half-brother of Krishṇa.

KAUSIKAS—The descendants of Viswámitra. The Gotras, the families or tribes of the Kausika brahmans are given in the *V.P.* (p.40.5) *and* are said to have been multiplied by intermarriages with other tribes, who were originally of the regal cast, like Viswámitra; but like him, obtainedd Brahmanhood through devotion. As these Gotras partook more of the character of schools of doctrine, in which teachers and scholars became one family by intermarrying, it shows the interference of the Kshatriya caste, with the Brahmanical monopoly of religious instruction and composition.

KAUSIKI—(1) A character in the Hindu Drama Agnimitra and Málaviká; the sister of the Rajá's minister Sumati. On one occasion when her brother bad to convey the princess Málaviká, she accompanied them, and on their way through the Vindhya mountains they were attacked by foresters, and in the affray Sumati was slain and Málaviká was lost. Kausikí left alone committed her brother's body to the flames, and resumed her journey. Kausikí soon found out Málaviká but forbore to discover herself, confiding in the prophecy of a sage, who had foretold that the princess, after passing through a period of servitude would meet with a suitable match. **(2)** The name of the river into which Satyavatí was transformed for following her husband in death. It is now called the Kosi, which rising in Nepal, flows through Puraniya into the Ganges, nearly opposite to Rájamahal.

KAUSITAKI—(1) A *śākhā* of the *Ṛgveda.*

(2) (Kauṣītaki) the name of a *Brāhmaṇa*, and Āraṇyaka, and an Upaniṣad. (*see* those terms) The *Brāhmaṇa* has been published with a translation by Professor Cowell in the *Bibliotheca Indica.*

KAUSTABHA—The jewel worn by Vishṇu, and which was one of the articles produced at the churning of the ocean.

> "And Kaustabha the beat
> Of gems, that burns with living light,
> Upon Lord Vishṇu's breast"
> "And Kaustabha the gem
> Whose ever beaming lustre glows
> In Vishṇu's diadem."

KAUTILYA—A name of the brahman Chánakya, through whose agency the Nandas were destroyed, and Chandragupta raised to the throne of Palibothra.

KAUTSA—A rationalistic philosopher, who lived before the days of Yāska the author of the *Nirukta.* He regarded "the Veda as devoid of meaning, and the *Brāhmaṇas* as false interpretations" Yāska replied to his objections.

KAUTUKA-SARVASVA—A modern farce, in two acts, by a Paṇḍit named Gopīnātha. "It is a satire upon princes who addict themselves to idleness and sensuality, and fail to patronise the Brāhmaṇas."—*Wilson.*

KAVASA, KAVAṢA-AILŪṢA—Son of Ilūṣa by a slave girl. He was author of several hymns in the tenth book of the *Ṛgveda.* The *Aitareya Brāhmaṇa* relates that the *ṛsis* were performing a sacrifice on the Sarasvati, and that Kavaṣa was with them; but they drove him from among them because he was the son of a slave, and therefore unworthy to drink the water of the Sarasvatī. When he was alone in the desert, a prayer was revealed to him by which he prevailed over the Sarasvatī, and its waters came and surrounded him. The *ṛsis* saw this, and knowing that it was by the special favour of the gods, they admitted him to their society.

KAVERI—A river which takes its rise in Coorg, runs through the south of India, and empties itself in the Bay of Bengal. It seems always to have borne the same appellation, being the Chaberis of Ptolemy.

KAVI—(1) One of the sons of the Manu Chakshusha;

(2) The name of one of the sons of Priyavrata according to the Bhágavata; (3) A son of the Kshatriya Urukshaya, who afterwards became a Brahman.

KAVIRAJA—The author of the curious poem entitled Raghava-Pándaviya, a remarkable specimen of "studied ambiguity," as it may, at the option of the reader, be interpreted as relating the history of Ráma and the other descendants of Dasaratha,—or that of Yudhishthira and the other sons of Páṇḍu.—*Colebrooke.*

KAVYA-DARSA—'Mirror of poetry'. A work on the Ars Poetica by Śrī Daṇḍī. It has been printed in the *Bibliotheca Indica.*

KAVYA-PRAKASA—A work on poetry and rhetoric by Mammaṭa Bhaṭṭa of Kaśmīr. It has been printed at Calcutta.

KAVYAS, KĀVYAS—A class of *pitṛs*; according to some they are the Manes of men of the third caste.

KAVYAS—**(1)** The name given to the descendants of Kavi, as a race of brahmans; **(2)** One of thę classes of Pitris, or progenitors, identified with the cyclic years

KAYAVYA—The son of a kṣatriya by a Niṣāda female, who is related in the *Mahābhārata* to have risen by virtue, knowledge, and devotion from the state *of a dasyu* to perfection.

KEDARESA, KEDĀRANĀTHA—A name of Śiva. Name of one of the twelve great *liṅgaa.* It is a shapeless mass of stone at Kedāranātha in the Himālayas, (*see* LIṄGA)

KEHAMA—The name of the mythical Rája who is the principal figure in Southey's poem "The Curse of Kehama." By a long course of penances and austerities he acquired supreme power over the world, and caused the gods themselves to tremble for their independence. His son Arvalan, the heir apparent to all his power and wickedness, was slain with a stake by a peasant whose daughter he was attempting to violate. The incensed Rája pronounced on the peasant, Ladurlad, the doom which gives name to the poem.

KEKAYA—An ancient city supposed to have been in the Panjáb. The king Aṣvapati, (lord of horses) was the father of Rája Daṣaratha's wife Kaikeyi.

KELIKILA—A demigod attendant upon Śiva.

KENA, KENOPANIṢAD—Name of an Upaniṣad (*q.v.*) translated by Dr. Roer for the *Bibliotheca Indica.*

KERAKAS—One-footed men who live in forests, according to the *Mahābhārata.*

KERALA—The country of Malabar proper on the western coast.

KERARI—A sect who worshipped Párvatí in her terific forms, and used to oner up human sacrifices. They used to inflict upon themselves bodily tortures, and pierce their flesh with hooks, &c. Such things are now made a criminal offence.

KESAVA—'Having much or fine hair'. A name of Viṣṇu or Kṛṣṇa.

KESIDHWAJA—The celebrated son of Kritadhwaja. He had a cousin named Kháṇḍíkya, who was renowned for religious rites, and the importance he attached to them; while Kesidhwaja regarded spiritual knowledge as the great object of pursuit. The quarrel became so serious that Kháṇḍíkya was expelled from his dominions by Kesidhwaja. The latter, on an occasion of great perplexity, was informed by his counsellors, that none but his enemy Kháṇḍíkya could give him the information he wished to obtain. The desired interview took place, and Kesidhwaja's difficulties were all removed. He, anxious to reward his preceptor, wished him to name the remuneration that would be most pleasing to himself. His friends recommended him to require his whole kingdom to be restored to him. But Kháṇḍíkya, addressing Kesidhwaja said "As it is known that you are learned in the spiritual learning that teaches the doctrine of the soul, if you will communicate that knowledge to me, you will have discharged your debt. Declare to me what acts are efficacious for the alleviation of human affliction." Then Kesidhwaja delivered a discourse on the nature of ignorance and the benefits of the Yoga or contemplative devotion. See *V.P.*, pp. 649-659.

KESIN—A powerful demon, who was ordered by Kansa to destroy Krishṇa. He assumed the form of a horse "spurning the earth with his hoofs, scattering the clouds with his mane, and springing in his paces beyond the orbits of the sun and moon." The formidable demon, however, soon had "his mouth rent open by the arm of Krishna, and fell down, torn asunder like a tree struck by lightning; thus he lay separated into two portions, each having two legs, half a back, half a tail, one ear, one eye, and one nostril." Krishna was afterwards called Keṣava in honour of this exploit. *V.P.*, p. 540.

KESINI—**(1)** One of the wives of Sagara, who being childless, solicited the aid of the sage Aurva, and the Muni pronounced this boon, that one wife should bear one sou, and the other sixty-thousand; and he left it to them to make their election. Kesiní chose to have the single son; **(2)** Wife of Viśravas and mother of Rāvaṇa; also called Kaikasī **(3)** The fair-haired maid servant of Damayanti, who was sent with a message to Nala, and in the interview perceived his divine powers, and reported accordingly to Damayanti.

KETU—The descending node in astronomy, represented by a dragon's tail; also a comet or meteor, and the ninth of the planets. He is said to be a *dānava*, and son of Vipracitti and Siṁhikā. He is also called Akaca, "hairless'; Aśleṣābhava, 'cut off; Muṇḍa, 'bald', (*see* Rāhu)

KETUMALA—One of the eons of king Agnídhra, and sovereign of Gandhamádana. Also the name of a Varsha or country,

KETUMATI—The wife of Sumali, the great Rákshasa chief.

KETUMTA—**(1)** A Lókapála, the son of Rajas, regent of the west; **(2)** The name of the son of Dhanwantari.

KEVALA—**(1)** A prince, the son of Nara; **(2)** The name of one of the Puránic countries.

KHAKIS—One of the Vaishnava sects of Hindus, of modern origin. Many of them go nearly naked, smearing their bodies with ashes and earth. They add the worship of Hanumán to that of Vishṇu.

KHANDAPANI—A prince, the son of Ahínara, of the race of Puru.

KHANDAS—**(1)** The name applied to the divisions or portions of the Skanda and Padma Puránas: **(2)** The divisions of the Bhárata Varsha.

KHANDAS—The elements of sentient existence among the Buddhists, of which there are five constituents.

1. The organized body, or the whole of being apart from mental processes.
2. Sensation.
3. Perception.
4. Discrimination.
5. Consciousness.

The four last *Khandas* arc results or properties of the first, which must be understood as including the soul as well as the body. At death the Buddhists believe the Khandas entirely vanish. Gautama says that none of the Khandas, taken separately, are the Ego; and that taken conjointly they are not the Ego. Yet there is no such thing as an Ego apart from the five Khandas.

KHANDAVA, KHĀṆḌAVA-PRASTHA—A forest and country on the banks of the Yamunā, which the Pāṇḍavas received as their moiety when Dhṛtarāṣṭra divided his kingdom. In it they built the city of Indraprastha and made it their capital. The forest was consumed with fire by the god Agni assisted by Kṛṣṇa and Arjuna.

KHANDIKYA—A son of Amitadhwaja, who taught his cousin Kesidhwaja the expiation of a sin, and was by him instructed in the Yóga doctrine.

KHARA—A man-eating *rākṣasa*, the younger brother of Rāvaṇa. He was killed by Rāmacandra.

KHARVA—A dwarf, (*see* VĀLAKHILYA)

KHASA—A daughter of Dakṣa, wife of Kaśyapa, and mother of the *yakṣas* and *rākṣasas*, called after her Khaśātmajas.

KHASAS, KHAŚĀKAS, KHAŚĪKAS—An outlying or border people classed with the Śakas and other northern tribes. Professor Wilson thought that traces of them might be sought among the barbarous tribes on the north-east of Bengal, the Khasiyas.

KHASIKAS, KHASIRAS—Non-Aryan or Aboriginal tribes in the north-east of Bengal; or it has been thought that they may be referred to the situation of Kashgar.

KHASRIMA—A chief of the Danavas, one of the sons of Vipra-chitti.

KHATVANGA (also called Dilīpa)—**(1)** A prince of the Solar race. In a battle between the gods and the demons he rendered great assistance to the former, who desired him to ask a boon. He begged that he might know the duration of his life, and the answer was, "Only an hour". He hastened to the world of mortals, and by earnest prayer he became united with the supreme being, Viṣṇu. "Like unto Khaṭvāṅga will there be no one upon earth, who, having come from heaven and dwelt an hour amongst men, became united with the three worlds by his liberality and knowledge of truth."—*VP.* **(2)** A club; the club of Śiva; it is also called Khiṅkhira and Pānśula.

KHONDS—A non-aryan or aboriginal tribe in Orissa, Their condition is in many respects peculiar. They have come less into contact with civilization, and evince greater wildness of deportment, than most of the other non-aryan tribes. "Their religion is very peculiar, and in its whole features entirely distinct from Hinduism. Their supreme god is called Bura-Pennou the god of light, who created for himself a consort, the earth-goddess called *Tari-Pennou*, the source of evil in the world. The god of light arrested the action of physical evil, while he left man at perfect liberty to reject or receive moral evil. They who rejected it were deified, while the great mass of mankind who received it were condemned to all kinds of physical suffering, with death, besides being deprived of the immediate care of the Creator, and doomed to the lowest state of moral degradation. Bura-Pennou and his consort, meanwhile, contended for superiority, and thus the elements of good and evil came to be in constant collision both in the heart of man and in the world around him. At this point the Khonds diverge into two sects, which are thus described by Major MacPherson in an interesting memoir read before the Asiatic Society, and inserted in their Journal:—"One sect," says he, holds that the god of light completely conquered the earth-goddess, and employs her, still the active principle of evil, as the instrument of his moral rule. That he resolved to provide a partial remedy for the consequences of the introduction of evil, by enabling man to attain to a state of moderate enjoyment upon earth, and to partial restoration to communion with the Creator after death. And that, to effect this purpose, he created those classes of subordinate deities, and assigned to them the office—first, of instructing man in the arts of life, and regulating the powers of nature for his use, upon the condition of his paying to them due worship; secondly, of administering a system of retributive justice through subjection to which, and through the practice of virtue daring successive lives upon earth, the soul of man might attain to beatification. The other sect hold, upon the other hand, that the earth-goddess remains unconqnered; that the god of light could not, in opposition to her will, carry out his purpose with respect to man's temporal lot; and that man, therefore, owes his elevation from the state of physical suffering into which he fell through the reception of evil, to the direct exercise of her power to confer blessings, or to her permitting him to receive the good which flows from the god of light, through the inferior gods, to all who worship them. With respect to man's destiny after death, they believe that the god of light carried out his purpose. And they believe that the worship of the earth-goddess by human sacrifice, is the indispensable condition on which these blessings have been granted, and their continuance may be hoped for; the virtue of the rite availing not only for those who practice it, but for all mankind.

"In addition to these human sacrifices, which still continue to be offered annually, in order to appease the wrath of Tari, and propitiate her in favour of agriculture, there is a fearful amount of infanticide among the Khond people. It exists in some of the tribes of the sect of Boora to such an extent, that no female infant is spared, except when a woman's first child is female; and that villages containing a hundred houses may be seen without a female child."

The revolting rites of human sacrifice and female infanticide have prevailed from time immemorial among these barbarous people. The Britisli government, however, was succeessful in almost completely abolishing these bloody rites. Many children, who had been stolen from their parents, and sold to the Khonds for sacrifice, have been rescued from a cruel death, and put into asylums for Christian education and training. The manner in which the revolting human sacrifices were conducted by the Khonds is thus described by Mr. Fry, a government agent, who has rescued numbers from the sacrificial knife:—"The victim," he inform us, "is surrounded by a crowd of half-intoxicated Khonds, and is dragged around some open space, when the savages, with loud shouts, rush on the victim, cutting the living flesh piecemeal from the bones, till nothing remains but the head and bowels, which are left untouched. Death has by this time released the unhappy victim from his torture; the head and bowels are burnt, and the ashes mixed with grain." These Meriah sacrifices, as they are called, are almost abolished.

KHUMBANDAS—An order of beings among the Buddhists who are believed to be the attendants of *Virádha* who is one of the four guardian Devas. They are of great size and disgusting form, have blue garments, hold a sword in one hand, and ride on blue horses. They form one of the thirteen orders of intelligence, exclusive of the supreme Buddhas.

KHYATI—'Celebrity,' a young and bright-eyed daughter of Daksha married to the Muni Bhrigu. Khyáti is also the faculty of discriminating objects by appropriate designations; or the means of individual fruition.—Wilson's Notes to *Vishnu Purána*.

KICAKA—Brother-in-law of the king of Virāṭa, who was commander of the forces and general director of the affairs of the kingdom. He insulted Draupadi, and on her complaining to the Rája, followed her to the Council hall, where his influence was so great that the Rája refused to interfere. Draupadi then professed to receive his offers and engaged to meet him at midnight in the dancing room. On his arrival he was seized by Bhíma, who, after a fight, slew him and rolled the body into a ball.

KIKATA—A country inhabited by people who were not Āryans; it is identified with Magadha or South Bihār.

KILAKILA—See KAILAKILA.

KILATAKULI—(Kilata + Akuli.) Two priests of the *asuras*, who according to the *Śatapatha Brāhmaṇa*, exercised a special influence between Manu and an "*asura*-slaying voice".

KIMPURUSA—'What man?' An indescribable man; one of a low type, partaking of the nature and appearance of animals. In later times it is synonymous with Kinnara. Name of a region between Himavat and Hemakūṭa. (*see* JAMBUDVĪPA) Also of a king of the latter region.

KIMPURUSHAS—Demigods, attached to the service of Kuvera, the god of wealth, celestial musicians, represented like centaurs reversed, with human figures and horses' heads.

KINNARAS—'What men?' Mythical beings with the form of a man and the head of a horse. They are celestial choristers and musicians, dwelling in the paradise of Kubera on Kailāsa. They sprang from the toe of Brahmā with the *yakṣas*, but, according to others, they are sons of Kaśyapa. They are also called Aśvamukhas Turaṅgavaktras, 'horse-faced', and Mayus.

KINNARU—A prince, the son of Sunakshatra, of the family of Ikshwáku.

KIRATAKJUNIYA—A poem descriptive of the combat between Śiva in the guise of a Kirāta or mountaineer and the Pāṇḍu prince Arjuna. The story is first told in the *Mahābhārata*, and has been worked up in this artificial poem of eighteen cantos by Bhāravi. Part of it has been translated into German by Schütz. There are several editions of the text. (*see* ARJUNA)

KIRATAS—Foresters and mountaineers living in the mountains east of Hindustan. (There is a tribe in the Central Himālayas called Kirāntis.) They are described in the *Rāmāyaṇa* as "islanders, who eat raw fish, live in the waters, and are mentigers" (men below and tigers above, according to the commentator). Their females are described as "gold-coloured and pleasant to behold", and as having "sharp-pointed hair-knots". They are perhaps the Cirrhadae placed on the-Coromandel coast by classic writers.

KIRITIN—'Crowned with a diadem.' A title of Indra and also of Arjuna.

KIRMĪRA—A monster *rākṣasa*, brother of Vaka. He opposed the entrance of the Pāṇḍavas into Kāmyaka forest, and threatened that he would eat Bhīma. A furious combat ensued, in which Bhīma and he hurled large trees at each other, but the demon was at length strangled and had all his bones broken by Bhīma.

KIRTARATHA—The sou of Rája Pratíndhak, and thirteenth ill descent from Mahárája Janaka.

KIRTIRAT—The great grandson of the above;

> "Mahandhrak's son of boundless might,
> Was Kírtirát who loved the right."

KIRTTI—"Fame." A daughter of Daksha, married to Dharma.

KIRTTIMAT—**(1)** A son of the patriarch Angiras. **(2)** A *son* of the Mann Uttánapáda. **(3)** A son of Vasudeva and Devaki, who was killed by Kansa.

KISKINDHA—A country in the peninsula, thought to be in the Mysore, which was taken by Rāma from the monkey king Bālī, and given back to his brother Sugrīva, the friend and ally of Rāma. The capital city was Kiṣkindhā.

KLEṢA—In the Patanjala philosophy Kleṣa is the terra employed to designate the five afflictions of the soul, *viz.*, Ignorance, Selfishness, Love, Hatred, Dread of temporal suffering.

KṢAPAṆAKA—An author who was one of "the nine gems" at the court of Vikramāditya. (*see* NAVA-RATNA)

KODAGU—Steep mountains; the name of the country which has been anglicised into Coorg: a country formed by the summits and eastern declivities of the Western Ghauts; about 60 miles in length and 40 in breadth. It comprises 1,585 square miles: covered by forest, save here and there where the clearing of a coffee plantation, or ragi patch, or the park like open glades with their beautiful green sward and varied foliage, afford a charming variety to the landscape. The Koḍagus or Coorgs are supposed to belong to the Dravidian family; and not to have descended from the Pándavas as some have argued, but for which no evidence has been adduced. The Coorgs were probably connected with the Pándya kingdom which flourished in the South of India perhaps in the fifth century before Christ; but the Mahábhárata Pándavas have nothing to do with this Pándyan kingdom, whose rulers were not Kshatriyas but belonged to the agricultural class.—Richter's *Manual of Coorg*, 1870.

KOHALA—An ancient sage, to whom the invention of the drama is attributed; also a writer on music.

KOKANAKAS, KOKARAKAS—The names of aboriginal tribes enumerated in the Vishṇu Purána.

KOLARIA—The ancient name for India. In the modem map of India we find indications of the same name in every province from Burmah to Malabar, *viz.*, the Kols of Central India; the Kolas of Katwar; See Dr. Keith Johnston's Index to his Map of India from the Royal Atlas, for a full confirmation of this view, as stated in Mr, W. Hunter's Dissertation in his Dictionary of Non-Aryan Languages.

KOLIKOD—The ancient and present native name of Calicut.

KOṢALA—The Rámáyana contains the following description of Koṣala: "In ancient times there was a great country named Koṣala; and that country was happy and joyous, and abounded in cattle, and grain, and riches. And in that country on the banks of the river Sarayú, was a famous city named Ayodhyá; and there all the houses were large and beautifully arranged, and the streets were always watered, and there were very many temples richly decorated, and stately palaces with domes like the tops of mountains, with pleasant gardens full of birds and flowers, and shady groves of trees loaded with delicious fruits, and above all there were the sacred and resplendent chariots of the gods. And the tanks in that city were magnificent beyond all description, and covered with the white lotus; and the bees thirsted for the honey, and the wind drove the white lotuses from the bees as modesty drives away the coy bride from her husband. And the ducks and the geese swam upon the surface of the tanks, or dived under the clear waters; and the brilliant kingfishers, wroth as they beheld their own reflection in the bright wave, and under pretence of catching the fish, they beat the water with their wings. And the plantain trees round the tanks were bending with the weight of the fruit, like reverential pupils bowing at the feet of their preceptors. The whole city was adorned with gems, so that it resembled a mine of jewels, and it was like unto Amarávati, the city of Indra. It was perfumed with flowers and incense, and decked out with gorgeous banners; and it was ever filled with the sweet sound of music, the sharp twanging of bows, and the holy chaunting of Vedic hymns. The city was encompassed round about with very lofty walls, which were set in with variously-coloured jewels; and all round the walls was a moat filled with water, deep and impassable; and the city gates were strongly barred, and the porticoes of the gates and the towers on the walls were filled with archers, and stored with weapons of every description. Every quarter of the city was guarded by mighty heroes, who were as strong as the eight gods who rule the eight points of the universe, and as vigilant as the many-headed serpents who watch at the entrance of the regions below."

> "On Sarju's bank of ample size,
> The happy realm of Koṣal lies,
> With fertile length of fair champaign
> And flocks and herds and wealth of grain,
> There, famous in her old renown
> Ayódhya* stands, the royal town
> In bygone ages built and planned
> By sainted Manu's princely hand.
> Imperial seat! her walls extend
> Twelve measured leagues from end to end.
> And three in width from side to side,
> With square and palace beautified.
> Her gates at even distance stand;
> Her ample roads are wisely planned.
> Right glorious is her royal street,
> Where streams allay the dust and heat.
> On level ground in even row,
> Her houses rise in goodly show:
> Terrace and palace, arch and gate,
> The queenly city decorate.
> High are her ramparts, strong and vast,
> By ways at even distance passed,
> With circling moat both deep and wide,
> And store of weapons fortified."
>
> —*Griffiths.*

The name Kosala is variously applied. Its earliest and most celebrated application is that given above, to the country on the banks of the Sarayú, the kingdom of Ráma, of which Ayodha was the capital. In the Mahabhárata we have one Koṣala in the east, and another in the south; besides the Prak-kosalas and Uttara-koṣalas in the east and north. The Puránas place the Koṣalas in the back of Vindhya; and it would appear from the Váyu, that Kusa, the son of Ráma, transferred his kingdom to a more central position; he ruled over Koṣala at his capital of Kusasthali, or Kusávati, built upon the Vindhyan precipices. In later times the country of Koṣala lay south of Oude, for in the Ratnávaḷí the general of Vatsa surrounds the king of Koṣala in the Vindhyan mountains: Ptolemy has a Kouta Koṣala in the south, probably one of the Koṣalas of the Hindus. Wilson's Notes to *Vishṇu Purána* and *Hindu Theatre*, Vol. II.

*"The ruins of the ancient capital of Rama and the children of the sun, may still be traced in the present Ayodhya near Faizabad. Ayodhya is the Jerusalem or Mecca of the Hindus.'—*Griffiths*.

KOTAVI—An eighth portion of Rudrání, and the tutelary goddess of the Daityas, composed of incantations. The Vishṇu Purána states that as Krishna was in the act of casting his discus, to kill Báṇa, the mystical goddess Koṭaví, the magic lore of the demons, stood naked before him, in order to prevent him. The name is sometimes applied to Durgā.

KOUTSYA—A mythical sage, the disciple of Maharishi Varatanta, who rewarded his tutor with fourteen crores of rupees for the fourteen branches of study completed under him. For the way in which the money was obtained, see RAGHU.

KRAMA-PĀṬHA—(*see* PĀṬHA)

KRATHA—The son of Vidarbha; and grandson of Jyámagha (*q.v.*).

KRATU—**(1)** A Prajápati, or one of the mind-born sons of Brahmá and one of the seven glorious spirits who abide in the orb of the sun, scattering light throughout the universe, married to Sansati, daughter of Daksha; The *Viṣṇu Purāṇa* says that his wife Samnati brought forth the 60,000 Vālikhilyas pigmy sages no bigger than a joint of the thumb. **(2)** A son of Uru, of the race of Dhruva.

KRATUSTHALA—The celestial nymph who resides in the car of the sun during the month Chaitra, as one its seven guardians.

KRAUNCA—**(1)** A pass situated somewhere in the Himālayas, said to have been opened by Paraśurāma with his arrows to make a passage from Kailāsa to the southwards. The *Vāyu Purāṇa* attributes the splitting of the mountain to Kārttikeya. Indra and Kārttikeya had a dispute about their respective powers, and agreed to decide it by running a race round the mountain. They disagreed as to the result, and therefore appealed to the mountain, who untruly decided in favour of Indra. "Kārttikeya hurled his lance at the mountain and pierced it at once and the demon Mahiṣa." **(2)** A confederate of the demon Tāraka, against whom Kārttikeya led the gods and triumphed. **(3)** One of the seven Dvīpas. (*see* DVĪPA) The fifth of the seven great insular continents, or dwípas; the king of this Dwipa was Dyutirnán: it had seven boundary mountains, each in succession twice as lofty as the one preceding it; the inhabitants resided there without apprehension, associating with the bands of divinities; the Brahmans were called Pushkaras; the Kshatriyas, Pushkalas; the Vaisyas were termed Dhanyas; and the Sudras, Trishyas.

KRAVYAD—'A flesh-eater'. A *rākṣasa* or any carnivorous animal. In the Veda, Agni is in one place called a Kravyād of terrible power. Fire is also a Kravyād in consuming bodies on the funeral pile. (*see* AGNI).

KRIASWA—**(1)** A sage, who was married to two of the daughters of Daksha: and the deified weapons of the gods were the progeny of Kriáswa. These are also called the Sastra devatas, gods of the divine weapons; a hundred are enumerated in the Rámáyana, and they are there termed the sons of Kriáṣwa by Jayá and Vijayá, daughters of the Prajápati, that is of Daksha; **(2)** A son of Sahadeva;

KRIKANA, OR KRIMI—The son of Bhajamána Krimi; also the name of a son of Uśinara, a descendant of Anu.

KRIMIBHOJANA, KRIMISA—The names of the two of the hells or divisions of Naraka below Pátaḷa. The specific punishments of each are described in the Vishṇu Purána, p. 207-9.

KṚIPA, KṚIPI—Wife of Droṇa and mother of Aśvatthānan. The sage Śāradvata or Gautama so alarmed Indra by his austerities that the god sent a nymph to tempt him. Though she was unsuccessful, two children were found born to the sage in a tuft of grass. King Śāntanu found them and brought them up out of compassion (*kṛpā*), whence their names, Kṛpa and Kṛpā. The children passed as Śāntanu's own. Droṇa was a brāhmaṇa and Śāntanu a kṣatriya: the myth makes Kṛpī a brāhmaṇī, and so accounts for her being the wife of Droṇa. The *Viṣṇu Purāṇa* represents them as children of Satyadhṛti, grandson of Śāradvata by the nymph Urvaśī, and as being exposed in a clump of long grass.

Son of the sage Śaradvat, and the adopted son of King Śāntanu. He became one of the privy council at Hastināpura, and was one of the three surviving Kuru warriors who made the murderous night attack upon the camp of the Pāṇḍavas. He was also called Gautama and Śāradvata. (*see* KṚPĀ and MAHĀBHĀRATA)

KRISANU—An archer mentioned in the Rig Veda.

KRISHNA MISRA—The author of Prabodha-Chandrodaya; or Rising of the Moon of Awakened Intellect. This is a theological and philosophical drama, supposed to have been written about the twelfth century, with the object of establishing the Vedánta doctrine. What others have assailed by reason and argument Krishṇa Misra combats by ridicule. His work is praised by Professor Lassen, who calls it peculiarly Indian, and unlike anything in the literature of other countries.—*Mrs. Manning.*

KRISHNA—(1) One of the sons of Havirdhána, a descendant of Prithu; **(2)** One of the Andhra kings who reigned 10 years.

KRISHNA—(1) The name of one of the Narakas, in which those who live by fraud, &c., are punished; **(2)** The name of the Krish-ṇavéṇa river of the Dakhin, meaning the dark river.

KRISHNA—An Asura or Dasyu mentioned in the Rig Veda, who was slain together with his wives that none of his posterity might survive. "Krishṇa means black, and the name may, on this occasion. Professor Wilson thinks, allude to the dark com-plexioned aborigines. But there is another Krishṇa, even in the Big Veda, and he and his son Viswaka are members of the Angirasa family, who may be called Rig Veda aristocrats of good-old family descent; and both father and son appear among the Rishis of the hymns."—Mrs. Manning, *A & M.I.*, Vol. I, *p.* 65.

KRISHNA—The Indian Hercules and Apollo combined. The most renowned demigod of Indian mythology, and most celebrated hero of Indian history, is the eighth Avatára or incarnation of Vishṇu. "Vishṇu was born as Kṛishṇa for the destruction of Kansa, an oppressive monarch, and, in fact, an incarnate Daitya or Titan, the natural enemy of the gods. Kansa being forewarned of his fate seeing to anticipate his destroyer; but Kṛishṇa is conveyed secretly away from Mathurá, the capital of Kansa, and is brought up as the child of a cowherd at Vṛindávan, a pastoral district near Mathurá. It is whilst thus circumstanced that he has been exalted into an object of adoration, and the mischievous follies of the child, the boy, and the lad, are the subject of popular delight and wonder. His male companions are not very prominent in the tale of his youth; but the females, the deified dairy maids, play a more important part in the. drama. Amongst the most conspicuous is Rádhá, and she receives scarcely less universal homage than Kṛishṇa himself."*

Kṛishṇa cannot be said to belong really to the Epic age, but almost exclusively to the Puránic. When the story of his life is divested of the marvellous, he will be found to be an historical personage, belonging to that epoch when the Áryan race, leaving the north-western corner of the peninsula, began to make their way by gradual conquests towards the interior and the east. The enemies whom he attacks and subdues are the aborigines of the interior, who, to heighten the glory of the hero, are called giants and demons, Daityas and Dánavas. The Aryans were still a nomad people, pasturing their herds of cattle at the foot of the Himálaya range and in the plains of the Panjáb; and the legend would further lead us to believe that the primitive elementary worship now yielded to the more systematic religion of Bráhmanism and the institutions of caste. His identification with Vishṇu would follow as a natural apotheosis of a monarch and warrior of such fame; but the very legend itself, even as it is given in the Puránas, seems to show "that he existed long before the mythological triad of Brahmá, Vishṇu, and Śiva had ever been dreamed of. The following is a curtailed account of his birth and actions, borrowed partly from the Puranas, and partly from Monier Williams' *Eng.-Sanskrit Dictionary*.

The king of the Daityas or aborignes, Áhuka, had two sons, Devaka and Ugrasena. The former had a daughter named Devakí, the latter a son called Kamsa. Devaki was married to a nobleman of the Áryan race named Vasudeva (or Anakadundubhi), the son of Śúra, a descendant of Yadu, and by him had eight sous. Vasudeva had also another wife named Rohini. Kansa, the cousin of Devaki, was informed by the saint and prophet Nárada, that his cousin would bear a son, who would kill him and overthrow his kingdom. Kansa was king of Mathurá, and he captured Vasudeva and his wife Devaki, imprisoned them in his own palace, set guards over them, and slew the six children whom Devaki had already borne. She was now about to give birth to the seventh, who was Bala Ráma, the play fellow of Kṛishṇa, and, like him, supposed to be an incarnation of Vishṇu (see Ráma); but by divine agency, the child was transferred before birth to the womb of Vasudeva's other wife, Rohini, who was still at liberty, and was thus saved. Her eighth child was Kṛishṇa, who was born at midnight, with a very black skin (the name Kṛishṇa, as an adjective, means 'black,') and a peculiar curl of hair called the *Skrívatsa*, resembling a Saint Andrew's cross, on his breast. The gods now interposed to preserve the life of this favoured baby from Kansa's vigilance, and accordingly lulled the guards of the palace to sleep with the Yoga-nidra, or mysterious slumber. Taking the infant, its father Vasudeva stole out undiscovered as far as Yamuná, or Jumna river, which seems to have been the boundary between the Áryans and the aborigines. This he crossed, and on the other side found the cart and team of a nomad Aryan cowherd, called Nanda, whose wife, Yaṣodá, had by strange coincidence just been delivered of a female child. Vasudeva, warned of this by divine admonition, stole to her bedside, and placing Kṛishṇa by her, re-crossed the river, and re-entered the palace, with the female baby of Yaṣodá in his arms, and thus substituted it for his own SON. When Kansa discovered the cheat, be for a while gave up the affair, and set the prisoners at liberty, but ordered all male children to be put to death. Vasudeva then entrusted Kṛishṇa to the care of Nanda, the cowherd, who took him to the village of Gokula, or Vraja, and there brought him up.

Here Kṛishṇa, and his elder brother Bala Ráma, who joined him, wandered about together as children, and evinced their divine character by many unruly pranks of surprising strength, such as kicking over the cart, which served as conveyance and domicile to Nanda and his family. The female Daitya Pútaná was sent to suckle him, but the refractory baby discovering the trick, showed his gratitude by slaying her. Later in life he vanquished the serpent Káliya in the middle of the Yamuná (Jumna) river. A demon, Arishṭa, assuming the form of a bull; another, Keshin that of a horse; and a third, Kálanemi, all undertook to destroy the boy, but each fell victims to his superhuman strength. Kṛishṇa now incited Nanda and the cowherds to abandon the worship of Indra, and to adopt that of the cows, which supported them, and the mountains, which afforded them pasturage. Indra, incensed at the loss of his offerings, opened the gates of heaven upon the whole race, and would have deluged them, had not our hero plucked up the mountain Govarddhana, and held it as a substantial umbrella above the land. He soon took to repose from his labours, and amused himself with the Gopis, or shepherdesses, of whom he married seven or eight, among whom Rádhá was the favourite, and to whom he taught the round dance called *Rása, or Mandala-nrityam*. Meanwhile Kansa had not forgotten the prophecies of Nárada. He invited the two boys, Kṛishṇa an Balaráma, to stay with him at Mathurá; they accepte and went. At the gates, Kansa's washerman insulte Kṛishṇa, who slew him, and dressed himself in hi yellow clothes. He afterwards slew Kansa himsel and placed his father Ugrasena on the throne. A for eign king of the Kala-yavana (Indo-Scythian) race soo invaded the Yadu, or Áryan, territory, whereupo Kṛishṇa built and fortified the town of Dwáraka, i Guzerat, and thither transferred the inhabitants o Mathurá. He afterwards married Satyabhámá, daughter of Satrájit, and carried off Rukmiṇi, daughter o Bhíshmaka. His harem numbered sixty thousan wives, but his progeny was limited to eighteen thousand sons. When afterwards on a visit to Indra's heaven be behaved, at the persuasion of his wife, Satyabhámá in a manner very unbecoming a guest, by stealing th famous parijáṭa tree, which had been produced at th churning of the ocean, and was then thriving in Indra' garden. A contest ensued, in which Kṛishṇa defeate the gods, and carried off the sacred tree. At anothe time, a female Daitya, Ushá, daughter of Bána, carrie off Kṛishṇa's grandson, Aniruddha. His grandfather accompanied by Ráma, went to the rescue, and though Bána was defended by Śiva and Skanda, proved victorious. Pauṇḍraka, one of Vasudeva's family, afterwards assumed his title and insignia, supported by the king of Benares. Kṛishṇa hurled his flaming discus (*chakra*) at this city, and thus destroyed it. He afterwards exterminated his own tribe, the Yádavas. He himself was killed by a chance shot from a hunter. He is described as having curly black hair, as wearing a club or mace, a sword, a flaming discus, a jewel, a conch, and a garland. His charioteer is Sátyaki; his city, Dwáraka; his heaven, Goloka." (*Thomson*).

Kṛishṇa is the principal speaker in the Bhágavat Gita; where he expounds the Sánkya system of philosophy to Arjuna. In the great war he took part with the Pánḍvas, and it was mainly owing to his powerful assistance that the opposite party were vanquished.

Kṛishṇa is known in the Mahábhárata by the following names:—Vásudeva, Keṣava, Govinda, Janárdana, Dámodara, Dáṣára, Naráyana, Hṛishikeṣa, Purushottama, Mádhava, Madhusúdana and Achyuta.

This name occurs in the *Ṛgveda*, but without any relation to the great deity of later times. The earliest mention of Kṛṣṇa, the son of Devakī, is in the *Chāndogya Upaniṣad*, where he appears as a scholar. There was a *ṛṣi* of the name who was a son of Viśvaka.

here was also a great *asura so* named, who with 0,000 followers committed fearful devastation, until e was defeated and skinned by Indra. In another Vedic ymn, 50,000 Kṛṣṇas are said to have been slain, and is added in another that his pregnant wives were lain with him that he might leave so posterity. This , supposed to have reference to the *rākṣasas* or to ne dark-coloured aborigines of India. (* Wilson's *Vorks*, vol. II, *pp.* 66, 67.)

KRISHNAVENI—The river now called the Krishṇa r Kistna.

KRITA—(1) A prince, the sou of Kritaratha, king of Mithila; **(2)** A son of Sannatimat, to whom Hiraṇyanábha taught the philosophy of the Yoga, and who compiled twenty-four Sanhitas for the use of the Eastern Brahmans who study the Sáma Veda.

KRITADHWAJA—The son of Dharmadhwaja; the Vishṇu Purána says of him that he was a king ever intent upon existent supreme spirit.

KRITAGNI, KRITAVARMAN, KRITAVIRYA—Three princes, the sons of Dhanaka, of the Yadava race.

KRITAKA—(1) One of the sons of Vasudeva by his wife Madirá; **(2)** One of the kings of Magadha.

KRITAMALA—A river that takes its rise in the Malaya hills.

KRITANJAYA—(1) The Vyása of the seventeenth Dwápara; **(2)** A prince, the son of Dharman, of the family of Ikshváku.

KRITANTA-DUTARU—Yama's officers; frequently represented as hovering, in a frightful shape, over the beds of the dying, to carry off the departing spirit to Pátáḷa.

KRITANTA—The destroyer; a name of Yama, the Hindu Pluto.

KRITARATHA—One of the kings of Mithila, the son of Prati bhandaka.

KṚITA—The first Yuga or age; consisting of four thousand eight hundred divine years, thus:

Kṛita Yuga	4000
Sandhyá	400
Sandhyásana	400
	4800

If these divine years be converted into years of mortals, by multiplying them by 360, a year of men being a day of the gods, we obtain one million seven hundred and twenty-eight thousand, (1,728,000) ordinary years, the duration of the Kṛita Yuga, according to the Hindu books.

KṚITAVARMAN—One of the three warriors on the Kaurava side who survived at the end of the great war; the three visited the wounded Duryodhana on the plain of Kurukshetra. He was ultimately slain by Sátyaki at Prabhása.

KṚITI—The son of Bahuláṣwa, and the last of the kings of Mithila, in whom terminated the family of Janaka.

KṚITIRATA—One of the kings of Mithila, the son of Mahádriti.

KṚITTIKA—A lunar mansion in Nágavithi in the Northern Avashtána; when the sun is in the first degree of the lunar mansion, Kṛittika, and the moon is in the fourth of Viṣákha, it is the great equinox, or holy equinoctial season.

KṚITWI—The wife of Anaha, one of the descendants of Hastin.

KRIYA—(1) 'Devotion', a daughter of Daksha married to Dharma: an allegorical personification of religious rite married to the equally allegorical representation of the Hindu Code, *viz.*, Dharma, moral and religious duty. Wilson's notes to *V.P.*, p. 55; **(2)** A magical creation, represented in the Vishṇu Purána as a vast and formidable female springing from the southern fire, blazing with ruddy light, and with fiery radiance streaming amidst her hair.

KRIYA-YOGA-SARA—A portion of the *Padma Purāṇa* treating of rites and ceremonies, (*see* PADMA PURĀṆA)

KRODHA. KRODHA-VAŚA—One of the many daughters of Dakṣa and sister-wives of Kaśyapa. She was the mother "of all sharp-toothed monsters, whether on the earth, amongst the birds, or in the waters, that were devourers of flesh".

KṚODHA—(1) 'Passion,' represented as a son of Brahmá: one of the allegorical personages occurring in the list of Brahmá's progeny amongst the scries of 'virtues and vices;' **(2)** 'Wrath', a son of Mritha; called in the Vishṇu Purána an inflictor of misery, and one of the progeny of vice; also, as a terrific form of Vishṇu, operating as a cause of the destruction of this world.

KṚODHAGHARA—The chamber of displeasure; an institution still in vogue in Hindu families, wives resorting to it when. discontented or angry with their husbands.

KṚOSHTU—A son of Yadu, the family in which Krishṇa was born.

KṚṢNA DVAIPAYANA—(*see* VYĀSA)

KṚSNĀ—The personal name of Draupadī.

KṚTA YUGA—The first age of the world, a period of 1,728,000 years, (*see* YUGA)

KṚTANTA—A name of Yama, the god of death.

KṚTAVARMAN—A Kuru warrior, one of the last surviving three who made the murderous night attack upon the camp of the Pāṇḍavas. (*see* MAHĀBHĀRATA) He was killed in a drunken brawl at Dvārakā. He was also called Bhoja.

KṚTAVIRYA—Son of Dhanaka and father of the Arjuna who is better known by his patronymic Kārtavīrya. Kṛtavīrya was a great patron of the Bhṛgus, and according to the Purāṇas, "he ruled over the whole earth with might and justice, and offered 10,000 sacrifices. Of him this verse is still recited, 'The kings of the earth will assuredly never pursue his steps in sacrifice, in munificence, in devotion, in courtesy, and in self-control.'"

KṚTTIKAS—The Pleiades. The six nurses of the god of war, Kārttikeya. They were daughters of a king according to one legend, wives of *ṛṣis* according to another.

KṢANADA-CARA—'Nightwalkers.' Ghosts of evil character, goblins, *rākṣasas*.

KṢATRIYA—The second or regal and warrior caste, (*see* VARṆA).

KṢATTRI—A name by which Vidura was familiarly called. The term, as explained in Manu, means the son of a śūdra father and brāhmaṇa mother, but Vidura's father was a brāhmaṇa and his mother a slave girl.

KṢEMAKA—Son of Niramitra or Nimi, and the last prince of the Lunar race. There is a memorial verse quoted in the *Viṣṇu Purāṇa* which says, "The race which gave origin to brāhmaṇas and kṣatriyas, and which was purified by regal sages,terminated with Kṣemaka in the Kali age."

KṢEMA-VṚDDHI—A general of the Śālvas who had a command in the army which attacked Dvārakā, and was defeated by Kṛṣṇa's son, Śāmba.

KṢHAMA—'Patience.' One of the daughters of Daksha who was married to the Muni Pulaka.

KṢHANA—A measure of time, said in the Vishṇu Purána to be equal to thirty kalas; it is often used to express a very minute portion of time, a moment, an instant.

KSHATRADHARMAN—A prince, the son of Sankriti, a descendant of Raji.

KSHATRANJAS—A king of Magadha, the sou of Kshemadarman.

KSHATRAVRIDDHA—One of the five sons of Áyus, from whose family many names of celebrity proceeded.

KSHATRIYAS—The second of the four castes, said to have been produced from the breast, some authorities say the arms, of Brahmá; their duty being to protect the earth, the cattle, and brahmans. Kings, governors, and all intrusted with civil and military affairs, in general belong to the Kshatriya caste. Parasuráma vowed that he would extirpate the whole Kshatriya race, and thrice seven times, says the Vishṇu Purána, he cleared the earth of them: a legend, says Professor Wilson, which intimates a violent and protracted struggle between the Brahmans and Kshatriyas for domination in India.

KSHEMA—'Prosperity.' A son of Dharma by his wife Śantí.

KSHEMADHANWAN—A prince, the son of Pundaríka, a descend-ant of Kusa.

KSHEMAKA—The last prince of the race of Puru: "the race which gave origin to Brahmans and Kshatriyas, and which was purified by regal sages, terminated with Kshemaka in the Káli age."

KSHEMYA—**(1)** A prince, the son of Ugráyudha, descendant of Dwimídha; **(2)** A son of Suchi, king of Magadhá.

KSHETRAJÑA—"Embodied spirit," or that which knows the Kshetra, 'body'; a form of Vishṇu, implying the combination of spirit with form or matter, for the purpose of creating.

KSHUDRAKA—A prince, the son of Prasenajit, of the line of Ikshváku.

KUBERA—In the Vedas, a chief of the evil beings or spirits living in the shades: a sort of Pluto, and called by his patronymic Vaiśravaṇa. Later he is Pluto in another sense, as god of wealth and chief of the Yakṣas and Guhyakas. He was son of Viśravas by Iḍāviḍā, but he is sometimes called son of Pulastya, who was father of Viśravas. This is explained by the *Mahābhārata*, according to which Kubera was son of

Pulastya, but that sage being offended with Kubera for his adulation of Brahmā, "reproduced the half of himself in the form of Viśravas", and had Rāvaṇa and other children, (*see* Viśravas) Kubera's city is Alakā (also called Prabhā, Vasudharā, and Vasusthalī) in the Himālayas, and his garden Caitraratha on Mandāra, one of the spurs of Mount Meru, where he is waited upon by the Kinnaras. Some authorities place his abode on Mount Kailāsa in a palace built by Viśvakarmā. He was half-brother of Rāvaṇa, and, according to the *Rāmāyaṇa* and *Mahābhārata*, he once had possession of the city of Laṅkā in Ceylon, which was also built by Viśvakarmā, and from which he was expelled by Rāvaṇa. The same authority states that he performed austerities for thousands of years, and obtained the boon from Brahmā that he should be immortal, one of the guardian deities of the world, and the god of wealth. So he is regent of the north, and the keeper of gold and silver, jewels and pearls, and all the treasures of the earth, besides nine particular Nidhis, or treasures, the nature of which is not well understood. Brahmā also gave him the great self-moving aerial car Puṣpaka (*q.v.*). His wife is Yakṣī, Cārvī, or Kauverī, daughter of the *dānava* Mura. His sons are Maṇigriva or Varṇakavi and Nalakūbara or Mayurāja, and his daughter Mīnākṣī (fish-eyed). He is represented as a white man deformed in body, and having three legs and only eight teeth. His body is covered with ornaments. He receives no worship. The name Kubera, as also the variant Kutanu, signifies 'vile body", referring to his ugliness. He is also called Dhanapati, 'lord of wealth'; Icchāvasu, 'who has wealth at will'; Yakṣarāja, 'chief of the Yakṣas'; Mayurāja, 'king of the Kinnaras'; Rākṣasendra, 'chief of the Rākṣasas'; Ratnagarbha, 'belly of jewels'; Rājarāja, 'king of kings'; and Nararāja, 'king of men' (in allusion to the power of riches). From his parentage he is called Vaiśravaṇa, Paulastya, and Aiḍaviḍa or Ailavila. As an especial friend of Śiva he is called Īśasakhī, &c.

KUBJA—A deformed young female servant of Kansa. Meeting her in the high road carrying a pot of unguent, Krishṇa addressed her sportively, and said 'For whom are you carrying that unguent, tell me lovely maiden, tell me truly.' Kubja, smitten by his appearance, and well disposed towards Hari, replied mirthfully, 'Know you not beloved, that I am the servant of Kansa, and appointed, crooked as I am. to prepare his perfumes.' Krishna asked her for some of it, and she gave him and Balaráma as much of the unguent as was sufficient for their persons; and they smeared their bodies with it, till they looked like two clouds, one white and one black, decorated by the many-tinted bow of Indra. Then Krishna made her perfectly straight; and when she was thus relieved from her deformity, she was a most beautiful woman; and from gratitude invited Govinda to her house. He promised to go some other time. *V.P.*

KUHU—**(1)** A daughter of Angiras. The name means the last day of the moon's wane. The four daughters of Angiras designated phases of the moon; **(2)** The name of a river in the Himálaya.

KUKKURA—A prince, the son of Andhaka. Kukuras, and Kukkuras, are given in the Vishṇu Purána as names of tribes of Bhárata.

KUKSHI—One of the daughters of Priyavrata, the grea progenitor.

KUKSHI—The son and successor of Ikshváku, king of Ayodhya; the second of the solar line of kings.

> "Manu who life to mortals gave,
> Begot Ikshváku good and brave,
> First of Ayodhyá's kings was he,
>
> Pride of her famous dynasty.
> From him the glorious Kukshi sprang
> Whose fame through all the regions rang."
>
> —*Griffiths.*

KULADEVATA—The deity who is the object of hereditary and family worship, and is always one of the leading personages of Hindu mythology, as Śiva, Vishṇu, or Durgá. No house is supposed to be without its tutelary divinity, but the notion attached to this character is now very far from precise.

KULA-PARVATAS—'Family mountains.' A series or system of seven chains of mountains in southern India. They are Mahendra, Malaya, Sahya, Śuktimat, Ṛkṣa (for which Gandhamādana is sometimes substituted), Vindhya and Pāripātra. Mahendra is the Orissa chain; Malaya, the hills of Malabar proper, the south part of the Western Ghāṭs; Sahya, the northern parts of the Western Ghāṭs; Śuktimat is doubtful; Ṛkṣa, the mountains of Gonḍwānā; Vindhya is here applied to the eastern division of the Vindhya mountains; and Pāripātra, or Pāriyātra as it is frequently written, applies to the northern and western portions of the same range. The classification seems to have been known to Ptolemy, for he specifies seven ranges of mountains, but his names are not in accord.

KULAPAVATUS—Mountain-ranges in Central India: sometimes termed family mountains or systems; embracing the various chains described under Mahendra, Malaya, Riksha, Vindhya, &c.

KULATTHAS—Aboriginal mountain tribes, described in the Vishṇu Purána as 'ferocious and uncivilized races.'

KULIKA—One of the eight serpent kings, described as of a dusky brown colour and having a half-moon on his head.

KULINDAS, KULINDAPALYAKAS, KULUTAS—Tribes enumerated in the *V.P.* but not identified.

KULINDAS—A people living in the north-west.

KULLŪKABHAṬṬA—The famous commentator on Manu, whose gloss was used by Sir W. Jones in making the translation of Manu.

KUMADVATI—A rıver that rises in the Vindhya mountains.

KUMARA—(1) A name of Skanda, god of war. In the *Brāhmaṇas* the term is applied to Agni. **(2)** A Prajápati, of whom there appear to have been twenty-one; the Vayu Purána states that they are numerous.

KUMARAS—Mind-bom sons of Brahmā, who, declining to create progeny, remained ever boys and ever pure and innocent. There were four of them, Sanatkumāra, Sananda, Sanaka, and Sanātana; a fifth, Ṛbhu, is sometimes added, (*see* VIṢNU PURĀṆA)

KUMARA-SAMBHAVA—"The birth of the war god (Kumāra).' A poem by Kālidāsa. The complete work consists of sixteen cantos, but only seven are usually given, and these have been translated into Latin by Stenzler. Parts have been rendered into English verse hy Griffiths. There are several editions of the text.

KUMARI—(1) 'The damsel.' An epithet of Sītā, also of Durgā. Cape Comorin. **(2)** A river that rises in the Sáktimat mountains.

KUMARILA-BHATTA, KUMĀRILA-SWĀMĪ—A celebrated teacher of the Mīmāṁsā philosophy and opponent of the Buddhists, whom he is said to have extirpated by argument and by force. He was prior to Śaṅkarācārya, in whose presence he is recorded to have burnt himself.

KUMBHAKA—A suspension of breath by the closing of both nostrils: being part of the brahmanical ritual for obtaining control of the external senses.

KUMBHAKARNA—A Rákshasa, the son of Viṣravas, and brother of Rávaṇa. He was brought up in the forest with his brothers, and went about eating Rishis. When Brahmá, had granted boons to Rávaṇa and Vibhíshaṇa, and was about to confer one as Kumbhakarna, the gods interposed, saying he had eaten seven Apsarases and ten followers of Indra, besides Rishis and men; and begged that under the guise of a boon stupefaction might be inflicted on him. Brahmá thought on Sarasvatí, who arrived, and by Brahmá's command entered into Kumbhakarna's mouth, to speak for him. Under this influence he asked that he might receive the boon of sleeping for many years, which was granted to him. *O.S.T.*, Vol. IV, p. 416.

The description given of Kumbhakarna in the Rámáyana is ridiculously extravagant and exaggerated. At the siege of Lanka when Rávaṇa decided to avail himself of the services of his gigantic brother, the difficulty was to know how to awake him, as he was buried in sleep for six months together, and then only awoke for a short time to gorge himself with enormous quantities of food. The messengers tried to enter his room but were blown away from the door by the wind caused by the deep breathing of the sleeping monster. At last, after violent efforts, they forced an entrance; and ten thousand Rákshasas made every sort of din in his ears by beating drums, &c. Then they hammered his limbs with mallets, danced upon him, caused a thousand elephants to walk over his body, piled heaps of food under his very nose, all without effect. Nothing availed but the touch of some beautiful women who eventually succeeded in rousing him. Kumbhakarna consented to go out to battle, and displayed extraordinary valour, routing, wounding, and even devouring thousands of the monkey army, but was ultimately conquered and killed by Ráma. The figure of Kumbbakarna is a favourite one in village representations of the siege of Lanka, and he is generally exhibited asleep. *I.E.P.*

KUMUDA—(1) 'A lotus'. A Nāga or serpent king whose sister, Kumudvatī, married Kuśa, son of Rāma. **(2)** One of the six minor Dwípas, situated beyond the sea; **(3)** A mountain forming the northern buttress of Mount Meru.

KUMUDALI—A pupil of Pathya and teacher of the Atharva Veda.

KUMUDVATI—A Nāga or serpent princess whose marriage to Kuśa, son of Rāma, is described in the *Raghuvaṁśa.*

KUNDAKA—A prince, the son of Kshudraka, and grandfather of Sumitra, who was the last of the kings of the family of Ikshváku.

UNDINAPUR—The capital of Vidarbha, a country f considerable extent and power at various periods. he name remains in Bedar, which may have been the ncient capital; but the kingdom seems to have corre-ponded with the great part of Berar and Kandesh. It ; mentioned in the Ramayanaa amongst the countries f the south.

KUNDOBA—A deified hero of the shepherds, who, mongst the pastoral tribes supersedes all other popular dols.

KUNJARA—An old parrot mentioned in the Pádma ’urána. When the sage Chyavana was wandering over he world in pilgrimage, he came to the south bank of he Narmadá, where a linga called Omkára was erected; nd having worshipped it, he sat under an Indian fig ree where he overheard a conversation between Kun-ara and his four sons, in which the latter related to he former what they had beheld in their flight during he day. Several stories were related the moral of which was the same, the good effects of venerating holy men, and meditating upon Vishṇu. Kunjara then re-ated to Chyavana an account of the preceding births of his sons and himself.—Wilson’s *Works*, Vol. Ill, p. 37.

KUNTALA, KUNTHAKAS—Kuntala is in one place one of the central countries; in another one of the southern; the name is applied in inscriptions to the province in which Kurgode is situated; part of the Adoni district: and consistently with this position it *is* placed amongst the dependant or allied states of Vidarbha, in the Dasa Kumára.

KUNTI—(also called Pṛthā and Pārṣṇī)—**(1)** Daugh-ter of the Yādava prince Śūra and Marisha, king of the Śūrasenas, whose capital was Mathurā on the Yamunā. She was sister of Vasudeva, and was given by her father to his childless cousin Kuntibhoja, by whom she was brought up. In her maidenhood she showed such respectful devotion to the the sage Durvāsas, that he gave her a charm by means of which she might have a child by any god she pleased to invoke. She called upon the sun, and by him had a son named Karṇa, but without any detriment to her virginity; still, to keep the affair secret, the child was exposed on the banks of the Yamunā. Subsequently she married Pāṇḍu, whom she chose at a *svayaṁuara*, and bore three sons, Yudhiṣṭhira, Bhīma, and Arjuna, who were called Pāṇḍavas although they were said to be the sons of the gods Dharma, Vāyu, and Indra respectively. This may have happened, as is stated, from the potency of the old charm, but if so, it is strange that Mādri, the second wife of Pāṇḍu, should have enjoyed the same privilege, and have borne twin children to the Aśvins. This difficulty, however, is got over by a statement that Kuntī imparted to her the charm. Kuntī was a discreet and devoted mother, and although rather jealous of Mādrī, she was a kind mother to her children after Mādrī was burnt on her husband’s pyre. After the end of the great war she retired into the forest with Dhṛtarāṣṭra and his wife Gāndhārī, and there they all perished in a forest fire. **(2)** Name of a people and country in Upper India. **(3)** Kunti was also the name of a son of Dharmanetra of the *Yádava* race; and of a son of Kratha, of the family of Jyámagha.

KUNTIBHOJA—King of the people called Kuntis. The adoptive father of Kuntī.

KURMA or TORTOISE AVATARA—The second of the ten Avatáras of Vishṇu. The legend is that at a very remote period when the gods felt their powers weakened, and were desirous of obtaining Amrita (*q.v.*) the beverage of immortality, Vishṇu directed them to churn, together with the demons, the milk-sea by tak-ing the mountain *Mandara* for their staff, and his ser-pent Vâsuki for their cord, the gods to stand at the tail, and the demons at the head of the serpent; while he himself consented to support the mountain on his back, after having assumed the shape of a gigantic tortoise. The result of this churning of the sea of milk, was, besides the ultimate recovery of the Amrita, the appearance of a variety of miraculous things and beings; but it also led to a violent contest between the gods and demons, in which the latter were defeated. The idea of the lord of creation assuming the shape of a tortoise, and that of sacrificial liquids, especially clarified butter, becoming tortoise-shaped (*Karna*, the word for tortoise, meaning literally, ‘badly or slowly going’), occurs also in the Yajurveda; but the legend on which the tortoise-Avatára of Vishṇu is based seems to belong entirely to the post-Vedic period of Hindu-ism.

KURMA PURANA—“That in which Janārdana (Viṣṇu), in the form of a tortoise, in the regions under the earth, explained the objects of life—duty, wealth, pleasure, and liberation,—in communication with Indra-dyumna and the *ṛṣis* in the proximity of Śakra, which refers to Lakṣmi *kalpa*, and contains 17,000 stanzas, is the *Kūrma Purāṇa*.” The account which the Purāṇa gives of itself and its actual contents do not agree with this description. "The name being that of an *avatāra* of Viṣṇu, might lead us to expect a Vaiṣṇava work; but it is always and correctly classed with the Śaiva Purāṇas, the greater portion of it inculcating the worship of Śiva and Durgā. The date of this Purāna cannot be very remote."—*Wilson.*

KURMIS—Semi-aboriginal cultivators to the south of the Rajputa and Jats.

KURU—**(1)** One of the sons of Agníd'hra, to whom his father gave the country north of the Sweta mountains, bounded by the Srinagavan range; **(2)** An ancient king, the son of Samvarṇa, who gave his name to the district Kurukshetra. He was the ancestor of Vichitravírya, the grandfather of the Kurus and Páṇḍavas. Kuru, it is usually supposed, is the prince who gives the designation to Duryodhana and his brothers, thence called Kauravas, in opposition to their cousins the sons of Páṇḍu, termed Páṇḍavas, Kuru being a remote ancestor of both. The Mahábhárata however gives a different account, and derives the term Kaurava from the country, Kuru-jángala, or Kurukshetra (Lassen, *Ind. Alt.* I, p. 593,) which was subject to the family of Duryodhana, the upper part of die Panjáb beyond Delhi, or Panniput, which is still commonly called by the Hindus Kurukhetr. Kuru, the prince, was descended from Nahusha, the great grandson of Soma, or the moon, by his grandson Puru. The thirteenth descendant of Kuru was Sántanu, who had four sons, Bhíshma, Chitrángada, Vichitravírya, and Vyása. Of these Bhíshma aud Vyása lived unmarried, and the other two died without offspring; on which, to prevent the extinction of the family, and conformably to the ancient Hindu law, Vyása had children by his brother's widows. The sons were Dhritaráshtra and Páṇḍu, who became the founders of the two families of the Kauravas and Páṇḍavas. Wilson's *Works*, Vol. III, p. 290.

KURU-JANGALA—A forest country in the upper part of the Doāb.

KURUKSHETRA—The plain of the Kurus. A tract of land to the east of the Yamuna or Jumna river, in the upper part of the Doab, near the city of Delhi, and the river Saraswati. Hastiná-pura was its capital.

"The Sarasvati is an insignificant stream flowing through Sirhind, between the Yamuna and the Shatadru. It eventually loses itself in the sand of the desert, and is, on that account, fabled by the Hindus to flow underground into the ocean. It is held, however, as one of the most sacred streams of India. Lassen cal the Doab the Belgium of India. It is the gateway o the peninsula, where the eastern and western race have always met in battle. Here in later days wa fought the battle of Panipat; and here was laid th scene of that war which transferred the sovereignt of middle India from the Kurus to the Páṇḍavas. As i was the gate of India so does it in all probabilit derive its sacred name from being the first seat of th Áryan race, whence it worked its way from the Indu to the Ganges, and from being retained in their memor with all the respect due to a fatherland."—*J. C Thomson.*

KURUMBAS—The aboriginal cultivators of Sout Kanara.

KURUS—A very ancient people, who seem to hav been originally situated in Central and Northern Asia as the Vishṇu Purána says they inhabited the middl districts of Bhárata. They probably entered India with the Aryans or were a tribe of that great race, and settled in Kurukshetra. With this meaning the name applies to both Kurus and Páṇḍavas—hence Arjuna is called the best of the Kurus. In its particular and exclusive sense the name is given only to that party which adhered to Duryodhana, and opposed the Páṇḍavas. Both names belong to the Epic period.

KURUVARNAKAS—The aboriginal people of the forests in the upper part of the Doab.

KURUVATSA—A prince, the son of Anavaratha, a descendant of Jyámagha.

KUŚA STHALI—**(1)** A city identical with or standing on the same spot as Dvārakā. It was built by Raivata, and was the capital of his kingdom called Ānarta. When Raivata went on a visit to the region of Brahmā, his city was destroyed by Puṇyajanas, *i.e.*, *yakṣas* or *rākṣasas*. The capital of Ánartta, which was part of Kutch of Gujarat. The Vishṇu Purána says, "that city Kusasthali which was formerly your capital, and rivalled the city of the immortals, is now known as Dwáraka; and there reigns a portion of Vishnu in the person of Baladeva," &c.; **(2)** A city built by Kuśa, son of Rāma, on the brow of the Vindhyas. It was the capital of Southern Kosala. Also called Kuśavatī.

KUṢA—**(1)** A son of Ráma "Kuṣa and Lava were the twin sons of Ráma and Síta, born after Ráma had repudiated Síta, and brought up in the hermitage of Valmíki. As they were the first rhapso-dists the combined name Kusilava signifies a reciter of poems, or an improvisatore, even to the present day." (*Griffiths.*) Kuṣa built Kuśasthali, on the brow of the Vindhya, the capital of Koṣalá; the Ragha Vansa describes Kuṣa as returning from Kuṣavati to Ayodhya, after his father's death; but it seems not unlikely that the extending power of the princes of the Doab, of the lunar family, compelled Ráma's posterity to retire more to the west and south; **(2)** A son of Valákáṣwa, a descendant of Pururavas. **(3)** Sacrificial grass; which, on occasion of offerings made to the gods, is placed upon the ground as a seat for them, having its tips towards the east; **(4)** The name of the fourth of the great insular continents, or Dwípas; so named from a clump of Kuṣa grass (Poa) growing there. There reside mankind along with Daityas and Danavas, as well as with spirits of heaven and gods.

KUSADHVAJA—(1) A brother of Janaka, king of Mithilā, and consequently uncle of Sītā. His two daughters, Māṇḍavī and Śrutakīrtti, were married to Bharata and Śatrughna, the sons of Daśaratha. Some make him king of Sānkāśyā, and others king of Kāśī, and there are differences also as to his genealogy. **(2)** A rishi, the father of Vedavati. He was slain by Śambhu, king of the Daityas.

KUSAGRA—The son of Vrihadratha, one of the ancient kings of Kurukshetra.

KUSAMBA—The eldest son of Kuṣa, aud founder of Kausambi, afterwards Kanouj, and descendant of Purūravas. He engaged in devout penance to obtain a son equal to Indra, and that god was so alarmed at his austerities, that he himself became incarnate as Gādhi, son of Kuśāmba.

KUSANABHA—The second son of Kuṣa, who also took part in building Kausámbi.

KUSAVATI—The capital of Southern Kosala, built upon the Vindhyas by Kuśa, son of Rāma.

KUSHIDI—A pupil of Paushyinji, and teacher of the Śama veda.

KUSHMANDAS—A class of deities mentioned in the Viṣhnu Purána and other Puránas. They are described as taking counsel with Indra how best to interrupt the devout exercises of Dhruva, when, as a child, he commenced the rigorous penance that caused alarm in the celestial regions.

KUŚIKA—A king who, according to some, was the father of Viśvāmitra, or, according to others, the first of the race of Kuśikas from whom Gādhi, the father of Viśvamitra, descended.

KUSMANDAS—'Gourds.' A class of demigods or demons in the service of Śiva.

KUSUMAPURA—The city of flowers.' Pāṭaliputra or Patna.

KUSUMĀYUDHA—A name of Kāma, or Cupid as the bearer of the bow (*āyudha*) of flowers (*kusuma*).

KUSUMAYUDHA—A name of Kámadeva, the Hindu Cupid. The word means. "He whose weapons are flowers." *O.S.T.*, Vol. I, p. 112.

KUTHUMI—A pupil of Paushyinji and teacher of the Śama Veda.

KUTSA—A Vedic *ṛsi* and author of hymns. He is represented as being persecuted by Indra, but on one occasion he was defended by that god against the demon Śuṣṇa. It is oaid that Indra took him to his palace, and that they were so much alike that Śacī Puṣpotkaṭā, Indra's wife, did not know which was her husband.

KUVALASVA, KUVALAYĀŚVA—A prince of the Solar race, who, according to the *Viṣṇu Purāṇa*, had 21,000 sons, but the *Hari-vaṁśa* numbers them only as 100. Attended by his sons, he attacked the great *asura*, Dhundhu, who lived in a sea of sand, and harassed the devotions of the pious sage Uttaṅka. They unearthed the demon and slew him, from which exploit Kuvalāśva got the title of Dhundhumāra, slayer of Dhundhu; but all his sons except three perished by the fiery breath of the monster.

KUVALAYAPIDA—An immense elephant, or a demon in elephantine form, belonging to Kaṁsa, and employed by him to trample the boys Kṛṣṇa and Balarāma to death. The attempt failed and the elephant was killed.

LAGHU—A measure of time equal to fifteen Káshtas.

LAGHU-KAUMUDI—A modern and very much simplified edition of Pāṇini's Grammar by Varadarāja. It has been edited and translated by Dr. Ballantyne.

LAJJA—Modesty. One of the daughters of Daksha, who was married to Dharma.

LAKSHMANA—**(1)** Son of king Daśaratha by his wife Sumitrā. He was the twin brother of Śatrughna, and the half-brother and especial friend of Rāmacandra. Under the peculiar circumstances of his birth, one-eighth part of the divinity of Viṣṇu became manifest in him. (*see* DAŚARATHA)

Then Lakshman's truth was nobly shown,
Then were his love and courage know,
When for his brother's sake he dared
All perils, and his exile shared.

But according to the *Adhyātma Rāmāyaṇa*, he was an incarnation of Śeṣa. When Rāma left his father's court to go to the hermitage of Viśvāmitra, Lakṣmaṇa accompanied him, and afterwards attended him in his exile and in all his wanderings. He was also very attached to Rāma's wife Sītā, which gave rise to the reproach that the two brothers were husbands of one wife. On one occasion, indeed, Sītā reproached Lakṣmaṇa that he did not hasten to rescue Rāma from danger, because he wished to obtain herself. His own wife was Urmilā, the sister of Sītā, and he had two sons, Aṅgada and Candraketu. While Rāma and Lakṣmaṇa were living in the wilderness, a *rākṣasī* named Śūrpanakhā, sister of Rāvaṇa, fell in love with Rāma and made advances to him. He jestingly referred her to Lakṣmaṇa, who in like manner sent her back to Rama. When she was again repulsed she attacked Sītā, whom Rāma was obliged to defend. Rāma then called upon Lakṣmaṇa to disfigure the *rākṣasī*, and accordingly he cut off her nose and ears. The mutilated female called upon her brother to avenge her, and a fierce war ensued. When Sītā was carried off by Rāvaṇa, Lakṣmaṇa accompanied Rāma in his search, and he ably and bravely supported him in his war against Rāvaṇa.

In Dr. Muir's *O.S.T.*, Vol. IV, p. 107, the following legend of Lakshmana's death occurs: Time, in the form of an ascetic came to the palace gate of Ráma; and asked as the messenger of Brahmá, to see Ráma. He was admitted and received with honour, but stated that his message must be delivered in private, and that any one who witnessed the interview would lose his life. Ráma informed Lakshmana of this and desired him to stand outside.

Soon after the irritable Rishi Durvásas came, and insisted on seeing Ráma immediately, under a threat, if refused, of cursing Ráma and all his family. Lakshmana, preferring to save his kinsmen, though knowing that his own death must be the consequence of interrupting the interview of Ráma with Time, entered the palace and reported the Rishi's message to Ráma. Ráma came out, and when Durvásas had got the food he wished and departed, Ráma reflected with great distress on the words of Time, which required that Lakshmana should die. Lakshmana, however, exhorted Ráma not to grieve but to abandon him, and not break his own promise. The counsellors concurring in this advice Ráma abandoned Lakshmana, who went to the river Sarayú, suppressed all his senses, and was conveyed bodily by Indra to heaven. **(2)** A son of Duryodhana, killed by Abhimanyu. **(3)** One of the wives of Krishṇa.

LAKSHMI—"Prosperity." The daughter of Brighu, and bride or Sakti of Vishṇu. The goddess of fortune, wealth and prosperity. She is also represented as the counterpart of Vishṇu. Vishṇu is meaning; she is speech. Vishṇu is understanding; she is intellect. He is righteousness; she is devotion. He is the Creator; she is creation, &c. &c...in a word Vishṇu is all that is called male; Lakshmi is all that is termed female; there is nothing else than they. *V.P.*, p. 61. She is represented as having been born from the churning of the ocean, 'rising from the waves, radiant with beauty.' Indra recited a hymn to her praise, calling her the mother of all beings.

Mr. Griffiths thus translates the story of her birth from the Ramáyána and adds a note from Schlegel.

At length when many a year had fled,
Up floated, on her lotus bed,
A maiden fair and under-eyed,
In the young flush of beauty's pride.
She shone with pearl and golden sheen,
And seals of glory stamped her queen
On each round arm glowed many a gem,
On her smooth brows, a diadem.
Rolling in waves beneath her crown
The glory of her hair flowed down.
Pearls on her neck of price untold,
The lady shone like burnisht gold.
Queen of the Gods, she leapt to land,
A lotus in her perfect hand,
And fondly, of the lotus sprang,
To lotus-bearing Vishṇu clung.
Her, Gods above and men below
As beauty's Queen and Fortune know.

'That this story of the birth of Lakshmi is of considerable antiquity is evident from one of her names *Kshírábdhi-tanayá*, daughter of the Milky Sea, which is found in *Amarasinha*, the most ancient of Indian lexicographers. The similarity to the Greek myth of Venus being born from the foam of the sea is remarkable.'

'In this description of Lakshmí one thing only offends me, that she is said to have four arms. Each of Vishṇu's arms, single as far as the elbow there branches into two; but Lakshmí in all the brass seals that I possess or remember to have seen has two arms only. Nor does this deformity of redundant limbs suit the pattern of perfect beauty.' (*Schlegel.*)

Mr. Griffith has omitted the offensive epithet four-armed. In a passage quoted by Dr. Muir it is said that when Vishṇu was incarnate as Ráma then Lakshmí became Síta; and that when he was born as Krishṇa she became Rukminí. *O.S.T.*, Vol. IV, p. 392.

"Lakshmí is not found in the Rig Veda in the sense which the word bears in the later mythology, of a goddess personifying good fortune, though the word itself occurs in a kindred signification." *O.S.T.*, Vol. V, p. 348.

The beautiful goddess is also said to have been produced at the churning of the ocean. In the Brahmá. Vaivartta Purána, Lakshmí is said to be a portion of Prakriti; and in another place is made to issue from the mind of Krishṇa; in a different part of the work she is described as one of two goddesses into which the first Sarasvati was divided, the two being Sarasvati proper, and Kamala or Lakshmí.—Wilson's *Works*. Vol. III, p. 102. **(2)** The name of a daughter of Daksha who was married to Dharma.

The word occurs in the *Ṛgveda* with the sense of good fortune, and in the *Atharvaveda* the idea has become personified in females both of a lucky and unlucky character. The *Taittirīya Saṁhitā*, as explained by the commentator, makes Lakṣmī and Śri to be two wives of Āditya, and the *Śatapatha Brāhmaṇa* describes Śrī as issuing forth from Prajāpati.

Lakṣmī or Śrī in later times is the goddess of fortune, wife of Viṣṇu, and mother of Kāma. The origin ascribed to her by the *Rāmāyaṇa* is the one commonly received. According to this legend she sprang, like Aphrodite, from the froth of the ocean, in full beauty with a lotus in her hand, when it was churned by the gods and the asuras. Another legend represents her as floating on the flower of a lotus at the creation. With reference to this origin, one of her names is Kṣīrābdhitanayā, 'daughter of the sea of milk'. From her connection with the lotus she is called Padmā. According to the Purāṇas, she was the daughter of Bhṛgu and Khyāti. The *Viṣṇu Purāṇa* says, "Her first birth was the daughter of Bhṛgu by Khyāti. It was at a subsequent period that she was produced from the sea at the churning of the ocean.... When Hari was born as a dwarf, Lakṣmī appeared from a lotus (as Padmā or Kamalā). When he was born as Rāma of the race of Bhṛgu (or Paraśurāma), she was Dharaṇī. When he was Rāghava (Rāmacandra), she was Sītā. And when he was Kṛṣṇa she became Rukmiṇī In the other descents of Viṣṇu she is his associate." One version of the *Rāmāyaṇa* also affirms that "Lakṣmī, the mistress of the worlds, was born by her own will, in a beautiful field opened up by the plough", and received from Janaka the name of Sītā.

Lakṣmī is said to have four arms, but she is the type of beauty, and is generally depicted as having only two. In one hand she holds a lotus. "She has no temples, but being goddess of abundance and fortune, she continues to be assiduously courted, and is not likely to fall into neglect." Other names of Lakṣmī are Hīrā, Indirā, Jaladhijā, 'ocean born'; Cancalā or Lolā, 'the fickle', as goddess of fortune; Lokamātā, 'mother of the world'. (*John Dowson*)

LALABAKSHA—One of the Narakas, that in which those are punished who eat their meals without, offering food to the gods, to the manes, or to guests. *V.P.*, p. 208.

LALITA—A distinguished name of the personified female energy. See SAKTI.

LALITAVISTARA—A work in Sanskṛt verse on the life and doctrines of Buddha. It has been printed in the *Bibliotheca Indica*.

LAMBA—One of the daughters of Daksha and wife of Dharma.

LAMBODARA—One of the Andhra kings who reigned eighteen years: he was the son of Sálakarni the 2nd.

LANGALAS—One of the aboriginal tribes who dwelt in jungles and forests.

LANGALI—**(1)** 'Armed with a ploughshare.' Balarāma. **(2)** A pupil of Paushyinji and teacher of the Sáma Veda.

LANGALINI—A river that has its source in Mahendra.

LANKA—**(1)** The island of Ceylon or its capital city. The city is described in the *Rāmāyaṇa* as of vast extent and of great magnificence, with seven broad moats and seven stupendous walls of stone and metal. It is said to have been built of gold by Viśvakarmā for the residence of Kubera, from whom it was taken by Rāvaṇa. The *Bhāgavata Purāṇa* represents that the island was originally the summit of mount Meru, which was broken off by the god of the wind and hurled into the sea. **(2)** Name of one of the Śākinīs or evil spirits attendant on Śiva and Devī.

LASYA—(Lásya), a mode of dramatic performance or rather style of dancing, taught by Páryatí to the princess Ushá, who instructed the Gopís of Dwáraka, the residence of her husband, in the art; by them it was communicated to the women of Surúshtra, and from them it passed to the females of various regions. —*Wilson*.

LATA—A country comprising Khandesh and part of Guzerat about the Mhye river. It is also called Lār.

LATAYANA—Author of a *sūtra* work. It has been printed in the *Bibliotheca Indica.*

LAUHITYA—An ancient river mentioned in the Puránas, now part of the Brahmaputra.

LAUKIKA—"Worldly," the opposite to Daivika or "Divine's —e. g.. The Apsarasas are thus distinguished, thirty-four of them being specified as Laukíka, and ten as Daivika.

LAVANA—(1) A *rākṣasa*, son of Madhu by Kumbhīnasī, the sister of Rāvaṇa and daughter of Viśravas. He inherited from his father an invincible trident which had been presented to him by Śiva. He was surprised without his weapon and killed by Śatrughna. Lavaṇa was king of Mathurā and Śatrughna succeeded him. **(2)** One of the Narakas, (the salt) in which those are punished who associate with women in. a prohibited degree.

LAVA—The younger of the twin sons of Ráma by Síta, and king of Sráwasti, in northern Koṣala, by which a part of Oude is commonly understood. He was trained up by his mother in the hermitage of Válmíki, and appears to hare become a strong muscular man; having also acquired great skill in archery. When Ráma sent off a horse, previous to its sacrifice, Kusa and Lava seized it, and maintained their hold till Ráma himself came and recognised his two sons. He reigned at Śrāvastī. (*see* RĀMA)

LEKHAS—A class of deities of the sixth Manwantara.

LESA—A son of Suhotra, of the line of the kings of Kási.

LIBATIONS—To be offered to the gods, sages, and progenitors, with the parts of the hand severally sacred to each. The offerer is first to bathe, dress in clean clothes, and scatter water thrice to gratify the gods; as many times to please the Rishis; and once to propitiate Prajápati; he must also make three libations to satisfy the progenitors. For full details see *V.P.*, pp. 302, 303.

LIGHT, OR FIRE—See TEJAS.

LIKHITA—Author of a Dharmaśāstra or code of law.

LILA—A pastime; but mythologically used of certain libidinous amusements of gods among mortals on earth. Krishna's adventures with the Gopis and Šiva's pastimes at Madura, are termed Lílas in Sanskrit books.

LILAVATI—'Charming.' The fanciful title of that chapter of Bhāskara's *Siddhānta-śiromaṇi* which treats of arithmetic and geometry. Colebrooke and Dr. Taylor have translated it, and the text has been printed.

LIṄGA PURANA—"Where Maheśvara (Śiva), present in the Agni *liṅga*, explained (the objects of life), virtue, wealth, pleasure, and final liberation, at the end of the Agni *kalpa*, that Purāṇa, consisting of 11,000 stanzas, was called the *liṅga* by Brahmā himself." The work conforms accurately enough to this description. "Although the *liṅga* holds a prominent place in this Purāṇa, the spirit of the worship is as little influenced by the character of the type as can well be imagined. There is nothing like the phallic orgies of antiquity: it is all mystical and spiritual. The work has preserved, apparently, some Śaiva legends of an early date, but the greater part is ritual and mysticism of comparatively recent introduction."—*Wilson.* It is not likely that this Purāṇa is earlier than the eighth or ninth century. This Purāṇa has been lithographed in Bombay.

LINGA, LIṄGAM—The male organ. The phallus. The symbol under which Śiva is universally worshipped. It is of comparatively modem introduction and is unknown to the Vedas, but it receives distinct notice in the *Mahābhārata.* "The emblem—a plain column of stone, or sometimes a cone of plastic mud—suggests no offensive ideas. The people call it Śiva or Mahādeva, and there's an end." In the *Śiva Purāṇa*, and in the *Nandi Upapurāṇa*, Śiva is made to say, "I am omnipresent, but I am especially in twelve forms and places." These are the twelve great *liṅgas*, which are as follow:

1. *Somanātha*: 'Lord of the moon.' At Somnāth Pattan, a city which still remains in Guzerat. This was the celebrated "idol" destroyed by

Mahmūd of Ghaznī.

2. *Mallikārjuna* or *Srīśaila*. 'The mountain of Śrī.' On a mountain near the river Kṛṣṇa.
3. *Mahākāla*, *Mahākāleśvara*: At Ujjain. Upon the capture of Ujjain in the reign of Altamsh, AD 1231, this deity of stone was carried to Delhi and there it was broken up.
4. *Oṁkāra*: This is also said to have been at Ujjain, but it is probably the shrine of Mahādeva at Oṁkāra Māndhāttā, on the Narmadā.
5. *Amareśvara*: 'God of gods.' This is also placed at Ujjain.
6. *Vaidyanātha*: 'Lord of physicians'. At Deogarh in Bengal. The temple is still in being, and is a celebrated place of pilgrimage.
7. *Rāmeśa* or *Rāmeśvara*: 'Lord of Rāma.' On the island of Ramisseram, between the continent and Ceylon. This *Liṅgam*, whose name signifies 'Rāma's lord', is fabled to have been set up by Rāma. The temple is still in tolerable repair, and is one of the most magnificent in India.
8. *Bhīma Śaṅkara*: In Ḍākinī. This is in all probability the same with Bhīmeśvara, a *Liṅgam* worshipped at Dracharam, in the Rājamahendrī (Rajahmundry) district, and there venerated as one of the twelve.
9. *Viśvesvara*: 'Lord of all.' At Benares. It has been for many centuries the chief object of worship at Benares. Also called Jyotir-liṅgam.
10. *Tryambaka*, *Tryakṣa*: 'Tri-ocular'. On the banks of the Gomatī.
11. *Gautameśa*: 'Lord of Gautama.'
12. *Kedāreśa*, *Kedāranātha*: In the Himālaya. The deity is represented as a shapeless mass of rock.

Nāganātha or Nāganātheśa and Vāmeśvara are other names, probably of No. 6 and No. 11.

LINGADHTRI—One who wears a small lingam on his person, usually in a little silver box, hanging on his breast from a string round the neck; or sometimes fastened to his right arm.

LINGADIKARIES—(Lingadikáries), a sect of the Badagas who wear the lingam. The division was occasioned by the act of a headman of the Adikaries, who, to appease the cravings of hunger, ventured to eat a little meat. His descendants are not allowed to wear the lingam, and can only intermarry with common Badagas.

LINGAYITS—A caste who carry the "Linga" or emblem of Śiva tied round their necks: some keep it in a gold or silver case, and others tie it up in a cloth; but in all instances it is worn round the neck. They are for the most part traders in grain and spices. The Lingayits consist of many clans who do not intermarry, but can eat together. They are very stationary in their habits; are respected by other castes, but regarded as exceedingly stubborn, especially when irritated. They inter the remains of their guru or priest in a mosque, after the Mussulman fashion, and their devotion to the worship of the tomb cannot be surpassed. They bury their dead, and it is their custom to assemble round a corpse and partake of food before interring it. They universally abstain from animal food and intoxicating liquors. The women are very good looking.

LOBHA—"Covetousness," a son of Brahmá—being one of his progeny of virtues and vices as enumerated in the Vishṇu Purána. In another part of the same Purána, Lobha is described as the son of Dharma by one of the daughters of Daksha; also as the son of Adharma (vice) and it states that he was married to Nikriti, and their progeny was Krodha, Hinsa, &c.

LOHA-MUKHAS—'Iron-faced men.' Described in the *Mahābhārata* as swift, one-footed, undecaying, strong men-eaters.

LOHITAS—A class of deities in the twelfth Manwantara.

LOKA PALAKA—World-protector, an epithet constantly given by Hindu writers to a rajah.

LOKA—A world, a division of the universe. In general the *triloka* or three worlds are heaven, earth, and hell. Another classification enumerates seven, exclusive of the infernal regions, also seven in number, which are classed under Pātāla. The upper worlds are: (1) *Bhurloka*, the earth, (2) *Bhuvarloka*, the space between the earth and the sun, the region of the *munis*, *siddhas*, &c., (3) *Svarga-loka*, the heaven of Indra, between the sun and the polar star. (4) *Maharloka*, the usual abode of Bhṛgu and other saints, who are supposed to be coexistent with Brahmā. During the conflagration of these lower worlds the saints ascend to the next, (5) *Janaloka*, which is described as the abode of Brahmā's sons, Sanaka, Sānanda, and Sanatkumāra. Above this is the (6) *Taparloka*, where the deities called Vairāgis reside. (7) *Satyaloka* or *Brahmāloka* is the abode of Brahmā, and translation to this world exempts beings from further birth. The first three worlds are destroyed at the end of each *kalpa*, or day of Brahmā; the last three at the end of his life, or of a hundred of his years; the fourth *loka is* equally permanent, but is uninhabitable from heat at the time the first three are burning. Another enumeration calls the seven worlds earth, sky, heaven, middle region, place of birth, mansion of the blest, and abode of truth; placing the sons of Brahmā in the sixth division, and stating the fifth, or *Janaloka*, to be that where animals destroyed in the general conflagration are born again. The Sāṁkhya and Vedānta schools of philosophy recognise eight *lokas* or regions of material existence: (1) *Brahmāloka*, the world of the superior deities; (2) *Pitṛloka*, that of the *pitṛs,ṛṣis*, and Prajāpatis; (3) *Somaloka*, of the moon and planets; (4) *Indraloka*, of the inferior deities; (5) *Gandharvaloka*, of heavenly spirits; (6) *Rākṣasaloka*, of the *rākṣasas*; (7) *Yakṣaloka*, of the *yakṣas*; (8) *Piśācaloka*, of the *piśācas* or imps and fiends.

For a full account of these lokas, see the Vishnu Purána, pp. 212-215. In the Brahmá Vaivartta Purána another Loka is mentioned as the residence of Krishna denominated Goloka; it is far above the three worlds, and has, at five hundred millions of yojanas below it, the separate Lokas of Vishnu and Šiva, Vaikuntha and Kailash. This region is indestructible, while all else is subject to annihilation, and in the centre of it abides Krishna, of the colour of a dark cloud, in the bloom of youth, clad in yellow raiment, splendidly adorned with celestial gems, and holding a flute. He is exempt from Máya and all qualities, eternal, alone, and the Paramátma, or supreme soul of the world.

LOKAKSHI—One of the pupils of Paushvinji, and a teacher of the Sáma Véda.

LOKALOKA—'A world and no world'. A fabulous belt of mountains bounding the outermost of the seven seas and dividing the visible world from the regions of darkness. It is "ten thousand *yojanas* in breadth, and as many in height, and beyond it perpetual darkness invests the mountains all around, which darkness is again encompassed by the shell of an egg". It is called also Cakravāḍa or Cakravāla. The mountain range encircling the world is termed Lokáloka, because the world is separated by it from that which is not world. The Mahommedan legends of Koh Kaf, 'the stony girdle that surrounds the world,' are evidently connected with the Lokáloka of the Hindus. According to the Śiva Tantra, the Eldorado, at the foot of the Lokáloka Mountains, is the playground of the gods. *V.P.*, p.202

LOKAPALAS—Supporters or guardians of the world. The guardian deities who preside over the eight points of the compass, *i.e.*, the four cardinal and four intermediate points of the compass: (1) Indra, east; (2) Agni, south-east; (3) Yama, south; (4) Sūrya, south-west; (5) Varuṇa, west; (6) Vāyu, north-west; (7) Kubera, north; (8) Soma, north-east. Nirṛti is by some substituted for No. 4, and Pṛthivī or Śiva, especially in his form Īśāna, for No.8. Each of these guardian deities has an elephant that takes part in the defence and protection of the quarter, and these eight elephants are themselves called *lokapālas*: (1) Indra's elephant at the east is Airāvata. He is also called Abhramātaṅga, 'elephant of the clouds'; Arkasodara, 'brother of the sun'; Nāgamalla, 'the fighting elephant'; Sadādāna, 'always in rut'; Madāmbara, 'covered with ichor'. His wife's name is Abhramu. (2) Agni's elephant at the south-east is Puṇḍarīka and his female Kapilā. (3) Yama's at the south is Vāmana and his female Piṅgalā. (4) Sūrya's at the south-west is Kumuda and his female is Anupamā. (5) Varuṇa's at the west is Añjana, whose female is Añjanāvatī. (6) Vāyu's at the north-west is Puṣpadanta, whose female is Śubhadantī. (7) Kubera's at the north is Sārvabhauma; and (8) Soma's elephant at the north-east is Supratīka. The two other females are Añjanā and Tāmrakarṇī, whose spouses are doubtful. Añjanāvati is sometimes assigned to Supratīka. In the *Rāmāyaṇa* (1) Indra's eastern elephant is called Virūpākṣa; (2) Varuṇa's elephant at the west, Saumanasa; (3) Yama's at the south is Mahāpadma, and (4) Kubera's at the north is Himapāṇḍara.

LOMAHARSANA (or Romaharṣaṇa). A bard or panegyrist who first gave forth the Purāṇas.

LOMAHARSHANA—A name of Súta.

LOMAPADA—A king of the Angas in whose reign there was a great dearth for want of rain. "The sufferings of the earth-mother were shared by all living creatures; the gasping land was too feeble to bring forth fruit or herb, so the animals died and the men grew wan from hunger." Lomapáda, after in vain supplicating Víshṇu, called his councillors together, and was advised to allure Rishyasringa from his father's hermitage in the forest, as the youth was destined to be the achiever of noble deeds; and that in return the grateful clouds would pour their treasures of rain on the thirsty laud. *See* RISHYASRINGA.

LOPAMUDRA—A girl whom the sage Agastya formed from the most graceful parts of different animals and secretly introduced into the palace of the king of Vidarbha, where the child was believed to be the daughter of the king. Agastya had made this girl with the object of having a wife after his own heart, and when she was marriageable he demanded her hand. The king was loath to consent, but was obliged to yield, and she became the wife of Agastya. Her name is explained as signifying that the animals suffered loss (*lopa*) by her engrossing their distinctive beauties (*mudrā*), as the eyes of the deer, &c. She is also called Kauṣītakī and Varapradā. A hymn in the *Ṛgveda* is attributed to her.—*Wilson*, XI, 322.

LYRIC POETRY—There are several works of this class in Sanskrit literature, of which the principal are the following: the Ritusanhara, of a description of the Seasons, attributed to Kálidása; the Meghaduta or cloud messenger, also by Kálidása,—a poem in which a demi god, separated by fate from his wife, is imagined to make a cloud, the messenger to her of his woes, and incidentally as it were describes his course over a large tract of India, the *Amarúsataka*, or hundred stanzas of Amaru, on amatory feelings and scenes, the natural sense of which commentators have twisted into a mystical character, so as to make them appear less objectionable, especially as they were supposed by some to have been composed by the celebrated theologian Sankara, when be had animated the dead body of king Amaru; these stanzas have an epigrammatic character, and share in this respect the style of the first Sataka, or hundred. Verses on love by Bhartrihari; the *Bkaminivilasa* by Jaganatha Panditarája, in four books, the second of which is connected with amatory subjects, while the third is a beautiful elegy on the death of the poet's wife; the Gita Govinda by Jayadeva, who probably lived in the 12th century, which in ten sections describes the amours of Krishṇa with the cowherdesses, his separation from his wife Radha, and his ultimate reconciliation with her, and which like the Amarastaka has also been explained in a mystical sense, (see GITA GOVINDA) Krishna then being represented as the soul, which for a time becomes estranged from the supreme soul, but finally returns to it. This poem differs from those mentioned before in being intended for singing, and for representation at a festival held in honour of Vishṇu; it combines the lyric and melodramatic character."—*Goldstucker*. (Chamber's *Encyclopaedia*, vol. VIII, p. 476.)

MABALI—A name of Bali, *q.v.*

MABALIPURAM—A sacred place 34 miles north of Madras called the Seven Pagodas.

MADA—(1) 'Intoxication.' Described in the *Mahābhārata* as "a fearful open-mouthed monster, created by the sage Cyavana, having teeth and grinders of portentous length, and jaws one of which enclosed the earth and the other the sky", who got Indra and the other gods into jaws "like fishes in the mouth of a sea monster". **(2)** Insanity. One of the progeny of Brahmá, Vishṇu Purána, p. 50.

MADAYANTI—Wife of King Saudāsa or Kalmāṣapada. She was allowed to consort with the sage Vasiṣṭha. According to some this was a meritorious act on the king's part and a favour to Vasiṣṭha; according to others it was for the sake of obtaining progeny, (*see* KALMĀṢAPADA)

MADHAVA, MĀDHAVĀCĀRYA—A celebrated scholar and religious teacher. He was a native of Tuluva, and became Prime Minister of Vīra Bukka Rāya, king of the great Hindu State of Vijayanagara. He was brother of Sāyaṇa, the author of the great commentary on the Veda, in which work Mādhava himself is believed to have shared. Wilson observes, "Both the brothers are celebrated as scholars, and many important works are attributed to them; not only scholia on the Saṁhitās and *Brāhmaṇas* of the Vedas, but original works on grammar and law; the fact no doubt being, that they availed themselves of those means which their situation and influence secured them, and employed the most learned brāhmanas they could attract to Vijayanagara upon the works which bear their names, and to which they contributed their own labour and learning; their works were therefore compiled under peculiar advantages, and are deservedly held in the highest estimation." Among the works of Mādhava are the *Sarvadarśana-saṁgraha* and the *Sankṣepa Śaṅkaravijaya*. Mādhava was a worshipper of Viṣṇu, and as a religious philosopher he held the doctrine of *dvaita* or dualism, according to which the supreme soul of the universe and the human souls are distinct. Thus he was opposed to the teaching of Śaṅkarācārya, who was a follower of Śiva, and upheld the Vedānta doctrine *of a-dvaita*, "no duality", according to which God and soul, spirit and matter, are all one.

MADHAVA—A name of Krishṇa, which may be either derived as a patronymic from Matha, who is mentioned among his ancestors, or be considered equivalent to Madhusúdana, 'Slayer of Madhu.'

MADHAVA-MADHU—The names of two of the months as they occur in the Vedas, and belonging to a system now obsolete; corresponding to the lunar months Mágha and Pálguṇa, or December and January.

MADHAVAS—The same of a tribe, descendants of Madhu the son of Vrisha.

MADHAVI—A name of Lakṣmī.

MADHU—**(1)** One of the sons of Kárttavírya; **(2)** A son of Vrisha; **(3)** A son of Devakshatra. All the above are of the race of Yádu to whose family, the Yádavas, Krishṇa belonged; **(4)** The name of a formidable Rákshasa chief, termed a great demon, probably one of the aborigines, who was killed by Krishṇa. **(5)** Another, or the same demon, said to have been killed by Śatrughna.

MADHU-CHANDAS—A son of Viśvāmitra, who had fifty sons older and fifty younger than this one; but they are spoken of as "a hundred sons". He is the reputed author of some hymns of the *Ṛgveda*.

MADHUKASA—Described in the *Atharvaveda* as "the brilliant granddaughter of the Maruts, the mother of the Ādityas, the daughter of the Vasus, the life of creatures, and the centre of immortality". She "sprang from the sky, the earth, the air, the sea, fire, and wind"; and it is added, "all creatures, worshipping her who dwells in immortality, rejoice in their hearts"

MADHURANIRUDHA—A drama in eight acts by Śayani Candra Śekhara. It is quite a modern work. "The subject is the secret loves of Ūṣā, daughter of the *asura* Bāṇa and Aniruddha, grandson of Kṛṣṇa. The piece abounds too much with description to be a good play; the style has considerable merit."—*Wilson.*

MADHUSUDANA—'Slayer of Madhu.' A name of Kṛṣṇa.

MADHUVANA—The grove of Madhu, the demon referred to above. After his death Satrughna founded a city on the spot, which was called Mathura: this became celebrated as a holy shrine, and it was here that Dhruva performed penance.

MADHYADESA—The middle country described by Manu as "the tract situated between the Himavat and the Vindhya ranges to the east of Vināsana and to the west of Prayāga (Allahabad)" Another authority makes it the Doāb.

MADHYANDINA—**(1)** A Vedic school, a subdivision of the Vājasaneyī school, and connected with the *Śatapatha Brāhmaṇa.* It had also its own system of astronomy, and obtained its name from making noon (*madhya-dina*) the starting-point of the planetary movements. **(2)** A teacher of the white Yájur.

MADIRA—**(1)** A name of Vāruṇī, wife of Varuṇa, and goddess of wine. **(2)** One of the wives of Vasudeva.

MADRA—**(1)** Name of a country and people to the north-west of Hindustan. Its capital was Śakala, and the territory extended from the Biyās to the Cināb, or, according to others, as far as the Jhelam. **(2)** One of the four sons of Sivi; who has given a name to a province and tribe in the north of India; **(3)** The name of a river that rises in the Vindhya mountains.

MADRABHUJINGAS, MADRAS, MADREYAS—Tribes of people mentioned in the Puránas but not yet satisfactorily identified.

MADRI—A sister of the king of the Madras, and second wife of Pāṇḍu, to whom she bore twin-sons, Nakula and Sahadeva; but the Aśvins are alleged to have been their real father. She became a *satī* on the funeral pile other husband.

MAGADHA—**(1)** The bard and herald of the Hindus, being attached to the state of all men of rank to chant their praises, celebrate their actions, and commemorate their ancestry. *Wilson.* The name of a herald, a bard who was produced at the sacrifice performed by Brahmá at the birth of Prithu. **(2)** The country of South Bihar, where the Pàli language was spoken. A celebrated country in the Puránas, which furnish lists of the kings who reigned over it.

MAGHA—**(1)** A lunar mansion in Ásharbhí, in the Central Avasthána. **(2)** A poet, son of Dattaka, and author of one of the great artificial poems called, from its subject, Śiśupala-badha, or, from its author, Māghakāvya. **(3)** The name of one of the lunar months corresponding to December.

MAGHAVAT, MAGHAVĀN—A name of Indra.

MAHĀBALI—A title of the dwarf Bali, whose city is call Mahābalipura, which name is applied to the Tamil "Māmallaipura", or Seven Pagodas near Madras, (*see* BALI)

IAHABHADRA—One of the four great lakes, the aters of which are partaken of by the gods. The hágavata calls it a lake of honey.

IAHABHARATA—'The great (war of the) Bhāratas'. he great epic poem of the Hindus, probably the longest the world. It is divided into eighteen *parvas* or ooks, and contains about 220,000 lines. The poem as been subjected to much modification and has ceived numerous comparatively modern additions, ut many of its legends and stories are of Vedic charcter and of great antiquity. They seem to have long xisted in a scattered state, and to have been brought ogether at different times. Upon them have been ounded many of the poems and dramas of later days, nd among them is the story of Rāma, upon which ne *Rāmāyaṇa* itself may have been based. According o Hindu authorities, they were finally arranged and educed to writing by a brāhmaṇa or brāhmaṇas. There s a good deal of mystery about this, for the poem is attributed to a divine source. The reputed author was Kṛṣṇa Dvaipāyana, the Vyāsa, or arranger, of the Vedas. He is said to have taught the poem to his pupil Vaiśampāyana, who afterwards recited it at a festival o King Janamejaya. The leading subject of the poem s the great war between the Kauravas and Pāṇḍavas, who were descendants, through Bhārata, from Puru, he great ancestor of one branch of the Lunar race. The object of the great struggle was the kingdom whose capital was Hastināpura (elephant city), the ruins of which are traceable fifty-seven miles north-east of Delhi, on an old bed of the Ganges.

Kṛṣṇa Dvaipāyana Vyāsa is not only the author of the poem, but the source from whom the chief actors sprung. He was the son of the *ṛṣi* Parāśara by a nymph named Satyavatī, who, although she had given birth to a son, remained a virgin. There was a king, a descendant of Bharata, named Śantanu, who had a son called Śāntavana, better known as Bhīṣma. In his old age Śāntanu wished to marry again, but the hereditary rights of Bhīṣma were an obstacle to his obtaining a desirable match. To gratify his father's desire, Bhīṣma divested himself of all rights of succession, and Śāntanu then married Satyavatī. She bore him two sons, the elder of whom, Citrāṅgada, succeeded to the throne, but was soon killed in battle by a Gandharva king who bore the same name. Vicitravīrya, the younger, succeeded, but died childless, leaving two widows, named Ambikā and Ambālikā, daughters of a king of Kāśī. Satyavatī then called on Kṛṣṇa Dvaipāyan Vyāsa to fulfil the law, and raise up seed to his half-brother. Vyāsa had lived the life of an anchorite in the woods, and his severe austerities had made him terrible in appearance. The two widows were so frightened at him that the elder one closed her eyes, and so gave birth to a blind son, who received the name of Dhṛtarāṣṭra; and the younger turned so pale that her son was called Pāṇḍu, 'the pale'. Satyavatī wished for a child without blemish, but the elder widow shrank from a second association with Vyāsa, and made a slave girl take her place. From this girl was born a son who was named Vidura. These children were brought up by their uncle Bhīṣma, who acted as regent. When they became of age, Dhṛtarāṣṭra was deemed incapable of reigning in consequence of his blindness, and Pāṇḍu came to the throne. The name Pāṇḍu has suggested a suspicion of leprosy, and either through that, or in consequence of a curse, as the poem states, he retired to the forest, and Dhṛtarāṣṭra then became king.

Pāṇḍu had two wives, Kuntī or Pṛthā, daughter of Śūra, king of the Śūrasenas, and Mādrī, sister of the king of the Madras; but either through disease or the curse passed upon him, he did not consort with his wives. He retired into solitude in the Himālaya mountains, and there he died; his wives, who accompanied him having borne him five sons. The paternity of these children is attributed to different gods, but Pāṇḍu acknowledged them, and they received the patronymic of Pāṇḍava. Kuntī was the mother of the three elder sons, and Mādrī of the two younger. Yudhiṣṭhira (firm in fight), the eldest, was son of Dharma, the judge of the dead, and is considered a pattern of manly firmness, justice, and integrity. Bhīma or Bhīma-sena (the terrible), the second, was son of Vāyu, the god of the wind. He was noted for his strength, daring, and brute courage; but he was coarse, choleric, and given to vaunting. He was such a great eater that he was called Vṛkodara, 'wolfs belly'. Arjuna (the bright or silvery), the third, was son of Indra, the god of the sky. He is the most prominent character, if not the hero, of the poem. He was brave as the bravest, high-minded, generous, tender-hearted, and chivalric in his notions of honour. Nakula and Sahadeva, the fourth and fifth sons, were the twin children of Mādrī by the Aśvinī Kumāras, the twin sons of Sūrya, the sun. They were brave, spirited, and amiable, but they do not occupy such prominent positions as their elder brothers.

Dhṛtarāṣṭra, who reigned at Hastināpura, was

blind. By his wife Gāndhāri he had a hundred sons, and one daughter named Duḥśalā. This numerous offspring was owing to a blessing from Vyāsa, and was produced in a marvelous way. (*see* GĀNDHĀRĪ) From their ancestor Kuru these princes were known as the Kauravas. The eldest of them, Duryodhana (hard to subdue), was their leader, and was a bold, crafty, malicious man, an embodiment of all that is bad in a prince. While the Pāṇḍu princes were yet children, they on the death of their father were brought to Dhṛtarāṣṭra, and presented to him as his nephews. He took charge of them, showed them great kindness, and had them educated with his own sons. Differences and dislikes soon arose, and the juvenile emulation and rivalry of the princes ripened into bitter hatred on the part of the Kauravas. This broke into an open flame when Dhṛtarāṣṭra nominated Yuḍhiṣṭhira as his *yuvarāja* or heir apparent. The jealousy and the opposition of his sons to this act was so great that Dhṛtarāṣṭra sent the Pāṇḍavas away to Vārnāvata, where they dwelt in retirement. While they were living there Duryodhana plotted to destroy his cousins by setting fire to their house, which he had caused to be made very combustible. All the five brothers were for a time supposed to have perished in the fire, but they had received timely warning from Vidura, and they escaped to the forest, where they dressed and lived in disguise as brāhmaṇas upon alms.

While the Pāṇḍavas were living in the forest they heard that Draupada, king of the Pāñcālas, had proclaimed a *svayaṁvara*, at which his daughter Draupadī was to select her husband from among the princely and warlike suitors. They went there, still disguised as brāhmaṇas. Arjuna bent the mighty bow which had defied the strength of the Kauravas and all other competitors, and the Pāṇḍavas were victorious over every opponent. They threw off their disguise, and Draupadī was won by Arjuna. The brothers then conducted Draupadī to their home. On their arrival they told their mother Kuntī that they had made a great acquisition, and she unwittingly directed them to share it among them. The mother's command could not be evaded, and Vyāsa confirmed her direction; so Draupadī became the wife in common of the five brothers, and it was arranged that she should dwell for two days in the house of each of the five brothers in succession. This marriage has been justified by a piece of special pleading, which contends that the five princes were all portions of one deity, and therefore, only one distinct person, to whom a woman might lawfully be married.

This public appearance made known the exi ence of the Pāṇḍavas. Their uncle Dhṛtarāṣṭra recall them to his court and divided his kingdom betwe his own sons and them. His sons received Hastināpu and the chief city given to his nephews was Indr prastha on the river Yamunā, close to the modern Del where the name still survives. The close proximity Hastināpura and Indraprastha shows that the ter tory of Dhṛtarāṣṭra must have been of very modera extent. The reign of Yudhiṣṭira was a pattern of ju tice and wisdom. Having conquered many countrie he announced his intention of performing the *rājasū* sacrifice, thus setting up a claim to universal domi ion, or at least to be a king over kings. This excite still more the hatred and envy of the sons of Dhṛtarāṣṭr who induced their father to invite the Pāṇḍavas Hastināpura. The Kauravas had laid their plot, an insidiously prevailed upon Yudhiṣṭhira to gamble. H opponent was Śakuni, maternal uncle of the Kaura princes, a great gambler and a cheat. Yudhiṣṭhira lo his all: his wealth, his palace, his kingdom, his brot ers, himself, and, last of all, their wife. Draupadī w brought into the assembly as a slave, and when sh rushed out she was dragged back again by her hair b Duḥśāsana, an insult for which Bhīma vowed to drin his blood. Duryodhana also insulted her by seatin her upon his thigh, and Bhīma vowed that he woul smash that thigh. Both these vows he afterwards pe formed. Through the interference and commands Dhṛtarāṣṭra the possessions of Yudhiṣṭhira were re stored to him. But he was once more tempted to pla upon the condition that if he lost he and his brother should pass twelve years in the forest, and shoul remain incognito during the thirteenth year. He wa again the loser, and retired with his brothers and wi into exile. In the thirteenth year they entered the se vice of the king of Virāṭa in disguise—Yudhiṣṭhira as brāhmaṇa skilful as a gamester; Bhīma as cook Arjuna as a eunuch and teacher of music and dancing Nakula as a horse-trainer; and Sahadeva as a herds man. Draupadī also took service as attendant an needlewoman of the queen, Sudeṣṇā. The five prince each assumed two names, one for use among them selves and one for public use. Yudhiṣṭhira was Jaya i private, Kaṅka in public; Bhīma was Jayanta an Ballava; Arjuna was Vijaya and Bṛhannalā; Nakula wa Jayasena and Granthika; Sahadeva was Jayadbala an Ariṣṭanemi, a vaiśya. The beauty of Draupadī attracte Kīcaka, brother of the queen, and the chief man in th ngdom. He endeavoured to seduce her, and Bhīma lled him. The relatives of Kīcaka were about to burn raupadī on his funeral pile, but Bhīma appeared as a ild *gandharva* and rescued her. The brothers grew favour, and rendered great assistance to the king in pelling the attacks of the king of Trigartta and auravas. The time of exile being expired, the princes ade themselves known, and Abhimanyu, son of rjuna, received Uttarā, the king's daughter, in marage.

The Pāṇḍavas now determined to attempt the covery of their kingdom. The king of Virāṭa became ieir firm ally, and preparations for the war began. llies were sought on all sides. Kṛṣṇa and Balarāma, eing relatives of both parties, were reluctant to fight. Kṛṣṇa conceded to Arjuna and Duryodhana the choice f himself unarmed or of a large army. Arjuna chose Kṛṣṇa and Duryodhana joyfully accepted the army. Kṛṣṇa agreed to act as charioteer of his especial friend Arjuna. It was in this capacity that he is represented o have spoken the divine song *Bhagavad Gītā*, when he rival armies were drawn up for battle at Kurukṣetra, a plain north of Delhi. Many battles follow. The army of Duryodhana is commanded in succession by his great-uncle Bhīṣma, Droṇa his military preceptor, Karṇa, king of Aṅga, and Śalya, king of Madra and brother of Mādrī. Bhīṣma was wounded by Arjuna, but survived for a time. All the others fell in succession, and at length only three of the Kuru warriors—Kṛpa, Aśvathāman, and Kṛtavarma—were left alive with Duryodhana. Bhīma and Duryodhana fought in single combat with maces, and Duryodhana had his thigh broken and was mortally wounded. The three surviving Kauravas fell by night upon the camp of the Pāṇḍavas and destroyed five children of the Pāṇḍavas, and all the army except the five brothers themselves. These five boys were sons of Draupadī, one by each of the five brothers. Yudhiṣṭhira's son was Prartivindhya, Bhīma's was Śrutasoma, Arjuna's was Śrutakīrtti, Nakula's was Śatānīka, and Sahadeva's was Śruta-karman. Yuidhiṣṭhira and his brothers then went to Hastināpura, and after a reconciliation with Dhṛtarāṣṭra, Yudhiṣṭhira was crowned there. But he was greatly depressed and troubled at the loss of kindred and friends. Soon after he was seated on the throne, the *aśvamedha* sacrifice was performed with great ceremony, and the Pāṇḍavas lived in peace and prosperity.

The old blind king Dhṛtarāṣṭra could not forget or forgive the loss of his sons, and mourned especially for Duryodhana. Bitter reproaches and taunts passed between him and Bhīma; at length he, with his wife Gāndhārī, with Kuntī, mother of the Pāṇḍavas, and with some of his ministers, retired to a hermitage in the woods, where, after two years' residence, they perished in a forest fire. Deep sorrow and remorse seized upon the Pāṇḍavas, and after a while Yudhiṣṭhira abdicated his throne and departed with his brothers to the Himālayas, in order to reach the heaven of Indra on mount Meru. A dog followed them from Hastināpura. The story of this journey is full of grandeur and tenderness, and has been most effectively rendered into English by Professor Goldstücker. Sins and moral defects now prove fatal to the pilgrims. First fell Draupadī: "too great was her love for Arjuna". Next Sahadeva: "he esteemed none equal to himself". Then Nakula: "ever was the thought in his heart, there is none equal in beauty to me". Arjuna's turn came next: "In one day I could destroy all my enemies". "Such was Arjuna's boast, and he falls for he fulfilled it not." When Bhīma fell he inquired the reason of his fall, and he was told, "When thou gazedst on thy foe, thou hast cursed him with thy breath; therefore thou fallest to-day." Yudhiṣṭhira went on alone with the dog until he reached the gate of heaven. He was invited by Indra to enter, but he refused unless his brothers and Draupadī were also received. "Not even into thy heaven would I enter if they were not there." He is assured that they are already there, and is again told to enter "wearing his body of flesh". He again refuses unless, in the words of Pope, "admitted to that equal sky, his faithful dog shall bear him company". Indra expostulates in vain. "Never, come weal or come woe, will I abandon you faithful dog." He is at length admitted, but to his dismay he finds there Duryodhana and his enemies, but not his brothers or Draupadī. He refuses to remain in heaven without them, and is conducted to the jaws of hell, where he beholds terrific sights and hears wailings of grief and anguish. He recoils, but well-known voices implore him to remain and assuage their sufferings. He triumphs in this crowning trial, and resolves to share the fate of his friends in hell rather than abide with their foes in heaven. Having endured this supreme test, the whole scene is shown to be the effect of *māyā* or illusion, and he and his brothers and friends dwell with Indra in full content of heart forever.

Such is the leading story of the *Mahābhārata*, which no doubt had a basis of fact in the old Hindu traditions. Different poets of different ages have added to it and embellished it by the powers of their imagination. Great additions have been made in later times. The *Bhagavad Gītā* and the episode of Nala, with some others, are the productions of later writers; the *Harivaṁśa*, which effects to be a part of the *Mahābhārata*, is of still later date, and besides these, it cannot be doubted that numerous interpolations, from single verses to long passages, have been made to uphold and further the religious opinions of sects and individuals. To use the words of Max Müller, "The epic character of the story has throughout been changed and almost obliterated by the didactic tendencies of the latest editors, who were clearly brāhmaṇas brought up in the strict school of the laws of Manu."

The date of the *Mahābhārata* is very uncertain, and is at best a matter of conjecture and deduction. As a compiled work it is generally considered to be about a century later in date than the *Rāmāyaṇa*, though there can be no doubt that the general thread of the story, and the incidents directly connected with it, belong to a period of time anterior to the story and scenes of that epic. The fact that the scene of the *Mahābhārata* is in Upper India, while that of the *Rāmāyana* is in the Dakhin and Ceylon, is of itself sufficient to raise a strong presumption in favour of the superior antiquity of the former. Weber shows that the *Mahābhārata* was known to Dion Chrysostom in the second half of the first century A.D.; and as Megasthenes, who was in India about 315 B.C., says nothing about the epic, Weber's hypothesis is that the date of the *Mahābhārata* is between the two. Professor Williams believes that "the earliest or prebrāhmaṇical composition of both epics took place at a period not later than the fifth century B.C.", but that "the first orderly completion of the two poems in their Brāhmaṇised form may have taken place in the case of the *Rāmāyaṇa* about the beginning of the third century B.C. and in the case of *Mahābhārata* still later". Lassen thinks that three distinct arrangements of the *Mahābhārata* are distinctly traceable. The varied contents of the *Mahābhārata* and their disjoined arrangement afford some warrant for these opinions, and although the *Rāmāyaṇa* is a compact, continuous, and complete poem, the professed work of one author, there are several recensions extant which differ considerably from each other. Taking a wide interval, but none too wide for a matter of such great uncertainty, the two poems may be considered as having assumed a complete form at some period in the six centuries preceding the Christian era, and that the *Rāmāyaṇa* had the priority. The complete text of the *Mahābhāra* has been twice printed in India, and a complete tran lation in French by Fauche has been interrupted b his death. But M. Fauche's translations are not much repute. This particular one, says Weber, "ca only pass for a translation in a very qualified sense Many episodes and portions of the poem have bee printed and translated. The following is a short epiton of the eighteen books of the *Mahābhārata*:

(*1*) *Ādi-parva*, 'Introductory book'. Describes th genealogy of the two families, the birth and na ture of Dhṛtarāṣṭra and Pāṇḍu, their marriage the births of the hundred sons of the former an the five of the latter, the enmity and rivalry be tween the young princes of the two branche and the winning of Draupadī at the *svayaṁvara*

(*2*) *Sabhā-parva*, 'Assembly book'. The assembl of the princes at Hastināpura when Yudhiṣṭir lost his kingdom and the Pāṇḍavas had to retir into exile.

(*3*) *Vana-parva*, 'Forest chapter.' The life of th Pāṇḍavas in the Kāmyaka forest. This book i one of the longest and contains many episodes among them the story of Nala, and an outline o the story of the *Rāmāyaṇa*.

(*4*) *Virāṭa-parva*, 'Virāṭa chapter'. Adventures of th Pāṇḍavas in the thirteenth year of their exile, whil they were in the service of King Virāṭa.

(*5*) *Udyoga-parva*, 'Effort book'. The preparation of both sides for war.

(*6*) *Bhīṣma-parva*, 'Book of Bhīṣma'. The battle fought while Bhīṣma commanded the Kaurava army.

(*7*) *Droṇa-parva*, 'Book of Droṇa'. Droṇa's command of the Kaurava army.

(*8*) *Karṇa-parva*, "The Book of Karṇa'. Karṇa's command and his death at the hands of Arjuna.

(*9*) *Śalya-parva*, 'Book of Śalya'. Śalya's command, in which Duryodhana is mortally wounded and only three Kauravas are left alive.

(*10*) *Sauptika-parva*, 'Nocturnal book'. The night attack of the three surviving Kauravas on the Pāṇḍava camp.

(*11*) *Strī-parva*, 'Book of the women'. The lamentations of Queen Gāndharī and the women over the slain.

(12) *Śānti-parva*, 'Book of consolation'. A long and diffuse didactic discourse by Bhīṣma on the mor-

als and duties of kings, intended to assuage the grief of Yudhiṣṭhira.

(*13*) *Anuśāsana-parya*, 'Book of precepts'. A continuation of Bhīṣma's discourses and his death.

(*14*) *Asvamedhika-parva*, 'Book of the Aśvamedha'. Yudhisthira's performance of the horse sacrifice.

(*15*) *Āśrama-parva*, 'Book of the hermitage'. The retirement of Dhṛtarāṣṭra, Gāndhārī, and Kuntī to a hermitage in the woods, and their death in a forest fire.

(*16*) *Mūsala-parva*, 'Book of the clubs'. The death of Kṛṣṇa and Balarāma, the submersion of Dwārakā by the sea, and the mutual destruction of the Yādavas in a fight with clubs (*mūsala*) of miraculous origin.

(*17*) *Mahāprasthānika-parva*, 'Book of the great journey'. Yudhiṣṭhira's abdication of the throne, and his departure with his brothers towards the Himālayas on their way to Indra's heaven on mount Meru.

(*18*) *Svargārohaṇa-parva*, 'Book of the ascent to heaven'. Entrance into heaven of Yudhiṣṭhira and his brothers, and of their wife Draupadī.

The *Harivaṁśa* (*q.v.*), detailing the genealogy, birth, and life of Kṛṣṇa at great length, is a supplement of much later date.

GENEALOGY OF THE KAURAVAS AND PĀṆḌAVAS.

Atri, the *rsi*
Soma (Candra or Indu), the Moon
Budha
Āyu
Nahuṣa
Devayāṇī + Yayāti + Śarmiṣṭhā
Yādavas Puru (and two other sons)

Yadu (and another son)	*Pauravas*
Vṛṣṇi	Duṣyanta + Śakuntalā
Devarāta	Bharata
Andhaka	Hastin
Śūra	Kuru

Vasudeva Kuntī Gaṅgā+Śāntanu+Satyavatī
Bhīṣma

Kṛṣṇa	Balarāma
Citrāṅgada	Vicitravīrya (Line extinct)

Vyāsa + the two widows of Vicitravīrya

Ambika (widow)	Ambālikā (widow)
Dhṛtarāṣṭra + Gāndhārī	Kuntī + Pāṇḍu + Mādrī
Duryodhana and 99 other sons	Karṇa
	Yudhiṣṭhira
	Bhīma
	Arjuna
	Nakula
	Sahadeva
	Abhimanyu
	Parikṣit
	Janamejaya

(*See* CANDRAVAṀŚA for the intervening names)

MAHABHOJA—A pious prince, the son of Sátwatu. The name is sometimes read Mahabhága. (*see* BHOJA)

MAHADEVA—**(1)** A Rudra—the name of the eighth manifestation of the Rudra—an account which Wilson says is grounded apparently on Saiva or Yogi mysticism; **(2)** A name of Śiva.

MAHADEVI—'The great goddess'. A name of Devī, the wife of Śiva. (*see* DEVĪ)

MAHAJWALA—The name of one of the Narakas, in which the crime of incest is punished.

MAHAKĀLA—'Great time'. **(1)** A name of Śiva in his destructive character, (*see* ŚIVA) **(2)** One of the twelve great *liṅgas*. (*see* LIṄGA) **(3)** In the caves of Elephanta this form of Śiva is represented with eight arms. In one hand he holds a human figure; in another, a sword or sacrificial axe; in a third, a basin of blood; in a fourth, the sacrificial bell; with two he is drawing behind him the veil which extinguishes the sun; and two are broken off. **(4)** Chief of the *gaṇas* or attendants of Śiva.

MAHA-KAVYAS—'Great poems'. Six are classified under this title: (1) *Raghuvaṁśa*; (2) *Kumārasambhava*; (3) *Meghadūta*; (4) *Kirātārjunlya*; (5) *Śiśupāla-vadha*; (6) *Naiṣadhacaritra*.

MAHAMAGHA—The occurrence of the full moon in or about the asterism Magha, with other astronomical incidents, which occur once in twelve years, and which time is auspicious for bathing. At Khumbakhonam there is a large tank, the water of which is supposed to rise once in twelve years, on the above occasion, and when people in great numbers assemble from distant places to bathe and obtain remission of sins.

MAHAMAYA—(*see* MĀYĀ) The king of Atala, the first of the seven regions of Pátáḷa.

MAHAMOHA—"Extreme illusion," causing addiction to the enjoyments of sense; one of the five kinds of obstruction to the soul's liberation'; or as they are called in the Patanjala philosophy, one of the five afflictions—the 'five-fold Ignorance' of the Vishṇu Purána.

MAHANABHA—A daitya of great prowess, one of the sons of Hiranyáksha.

MAHANADA—A river in Orissa.

MAHANANDI—One of the ten Saiṣunága kings of Magadha, the son of Nandivarddhana.

MAHANATAKA—'The great drama.' The *Hanumān-nāṭaka* (*q.v.*).

MAHANILA—A powerful many-headed serpent. One of the progeny of Kadru.

MAHAN—One of the eleven Rudras.

MAHANTU—A prince, the son of Dhímat; he lived during the Swáyambhuva Manwantara.

MAHAPADMA NANDA—The last of the Nanda dynasty, (*see* CANDRAGUPTA)

MAHAPADMA—**(1)** A prince, the son of Mahananda; his name was Nanda, but he was remarkably avaricious. He was born of a Súdra woman, and after him the kings of the earth were to be all Súdras. Like Parasurama he endeavoured to annihilate the Kshatriya race, and brought the whole earth under one umbrella. He and his descendants, termed the nine Nandas, reigned a hundred years; when the dynasty was overturned by the Brahman Kautilya (also called Chánakya and Chanaki) who placed Chandragupta on the throne. (See the *Mudra Rakshasa*; *Hindu Theatre*, Vol. 2.) **(2)** The name of one of the progeny of Kadru, a powerful many-headed serpent.

MAHAPRALAYA—A total dissolution of the universe at the end of a *kalpa*, when the seven *lokas* and their inhabitants, men, saints, gods, and Brahmā himself, are annihilated. Called also Jahānaka, Kṣiti, and Saṁhāra.

MAHA-PURANAS—' The great Purāṇas.' The *Viṣṇu* and the *Bhāgavata*, the two great Purāṇas of the Vaiṣṇavas.

MAHAPURUSHA—Great or supreme spirit; purusha meaning that which abides or is quiescent in body; incorporated spirit. It is a name applied to Vishṇu; who is any form of spiritual being acknowledged by different philosophical systems: he is the Brahmá of the Vedanta, the Iswara of the Patanjala, and the Purusha of the Sánkhya school.

MAHAR—(*see* VYĀHṚTI)

MAHARAJIKAS—*Agaṇa* or class of inferior deities, 236 or 220 in number.

MAHARASTRA—The land of the Maharattas.

MAHAR-LOKA—The heaven of celestial spirits, the sphere of saints, situated at the distance of ten million leagues above Dhruva: the inhabitants dwell in it throughout a Kalpa or day of Brahmá. Those who are distinguished for piety, abide, at the time of dissolution, in Mahar-loka, with the Pitris, the Manus, the seven Rishis, the various orders of celestial spirits, and the gods. Then at the end of a Kalpa, when the heat of the flames that destroy the world reaches to Mahar-loka, the inhabitants repair to Janaloka, within subtle forms, destined to become re-embodied, in similar capacities as their former, when the world is renewed at the beginning of the succeeding Kalpa. This continues throughout the life of Brahmá; at the expiration of his life all are destroyed; but those who have thus attained a residence in the Brahma-loka by having identified themselves in spirit with the Supreme, are finally resolved into the sole existing Brahmá. See Wilson's *Notes* to *V.P.*, p. 633. (*See* LOKA).

MAHAROMAN—One of the kings of Mithila, the son of Kritaráta.

MAHARSIS—(Mahārṣis). 'Great *ṛsis*.' The great *ṛ*ṣis or Prajāpatis. (*see* ṚṢI)

MAHASENA—'The great captain.' A name of Kārttikeya, god of war.

MAHASWAT—A prince, the son of Amarsha, a descendant of Ráma.

MAHATALA—The fifth of the seven divisions of Pátāḷa, with a sandy soil, embellished with magnificent palaces, in which dwell numerous Dánavas, Daityas Yakshas and the great snake-gods.

MAHAT—Intellect; the first product of Pradhána, sensible to divine, though not to merely human organs, is, both according to the Sánkhya and Purána doctrines, the principle called Mahat literally the Great, explained as 'the production of the manifestation of the qualities:' Mahat, the Great principle, is so termed from being the first of the created principles, and from its extension being greater than that of the rest. Mahat is also called Iswara, from its exercising supremacy over all things. The Puránas generally attribute to Mahat, or Intelligence, the act of creating. Mahat is therefore the divine mind in creative operation; an ordering and disposing mind, which was the cause of all things. See Wilson's *Notes* to *V.P.*, p. 15.

MAHATMAYA—'Magnanimity.' A legend of a shrine or other holy place. A legendary and local description of the greatness or holiness of particular temples, or individual divinities. A chapter taken from some Purána, descriptive of the virtues of some place or person, is termed a Mahátmya.—*Wilson*.

MAHAVICHI—The name of one of the Narakas beneath the earth.

MAHAVIRA CARITA—'The exploits of the great hero (Rāma)'. A drama by Bhavabhūti, translated into English by Pickford. There are several editions of the text. "The situations and sentiments of this drama are of a stirring and martial description, and the language is adapted with singular felicity to the subject from which it springs."—*Wilson*.

MAHAVIRA—**(1)** One of the sons of Priyavrata, according to the Bhágavata; the one who had Krauncha-dwípa assigned to him; **(2)** A son of Savana, king of the seventh dwípa; **(3)** The name of a division of Pushkara dwípa. **(4)** The twenty-fourth Tírthankara of the Jains. His first birth, which occurred at a period indefinitely remote, was as Nayasára, headman of a village in the country of Vijáya. His piety and humanity elevated him next to the heaven called Saudharma, where he enjoyed happiness for some oceans of years. He was next born as Marichi, the grandson of the first Tírthankara Rishaba, thence transferred to the Brahmaloka, whence he returned to earth as a worldly-minded and sensual brahman, the consequence of which was his repeated births in the same caste, each birth being separated by an interval passed in one of the Jain heavens, and each period of life extending to many lakhs of years. He then became Viṣvabhuta, prince of Rajagṛiha, and next a Vásudeva named Triprishta (*q.v.*) then a chakravartti Priyamitra (*q.v.*) then a Nandana leading a life of devotion.

On the return of the spirit of Nandana to earth it first animated the womb of the wife of a brahman, but Mahendra, disapproving of the receptacle as of low caste, transferred it to the womb of Triṣalá the wife of Siddhárta, of the family of Iksváku, and prince of Ravana, in Bharatakshetra. Mahavira was born on the thirteenth of the light fortnight of Chaitra: the fifty-six nymphs of the universe assisted at his birth, and his consecration was performed by Śakra and the other sixty-three Indras. The name given by his father was Varddhamána, as causing increase of riches and prosperity, but Śakra gave him also the appellation of Mahávíra as significant of his power and supremacy over men and gods.

Mahávíra married Yaṣodá, daughter of the prince Samaravíra. By her he had a daughter Priyadarṣana, who was married to Jamali, a prince, one of the saint's pupils, and founder of a schism. Siddhartha and his wife died when their son was twenty-eight years old, on which Mahavíra adopted an ascetic life, the government devolving on his elder brother Nandívarddhana. After ten years of abstinence and self-denial at home he commenced an erratic life, and the attainment of the degree of a Jina.

During the first six years of his peregrinations, Mahávíra observed frequent fasts of several month's duration, during each of which he kept his eyes fixed upon the tip of his nose, and maintained perpetual silence. He was invisibly attended by a Yaksha named Siddhártha, who, at the command of Indra watched over his personal security, and where speech was necessary acted as spokesman. In his travels he acquired a singular follower named Goṣála, a man of low caste who acted as a sort of buffoon,

It is not the duty of a Jain ascetic to inflict tortures on himself: his course of penance is one of self-denial, fasting, and silence; and pain, however meritorious its endurance, must be inflicted by others, not himself. Mahávíra voluntarily exposed himself to maltreatment at the hands of various savage tribes, offering no resistance, but rather rejoicing in his sufferings. At the end of the ninth year he relinquished his silence in answer to a question put by Goṣála, but continued engaged in the practice of mortification and in an erratic life.

In the course of twelve years and six months he attained the *Kevala*, or *only knowledge*. This occurred under a Sál tree, on the north bank of the Rijupalika. Indra instantly hastened to the spot accompanied by thousands of deities, who all did homage to the saint. He commenced his instructions on a stage erected for the purpose by the deities, a model of which is not uncommonly represented in Jain temples. The following is the introductory lecture ascribed to Mahávíra by his biographer.

"The world is without bounds like a formidable ocean; its cause is action (*Karma*) which is as the seed of the tree. The being, (*Jíva*) invested with body, but devoid of judgment, goes like a well-sinker ever downwards, by the acts it performs, whilst the embodied being which has attained purity goes ever upwards by its own acts, like the builder of a palace. Let not any one injure life, whilst bound in the bonds of action; but be as assiduous in cherishing the life of another as his own. Never let any one speak falsehood, but always speak the truth. Let every one who has a bodily form avoid giving pain to others as much as to himself. Let no one take property not given to him, for wealth is like the external life of men, and he who takes away such wealth commits as it were murder. Associate not with women, for it is the destruction of life; let the wise observe continence, which binds them to the Supreme. Be not encumbered with a family, for by the anxiety it involves the person separated from it falls like an ox too heavily laden. If it be not in their power to shun these more subtle destroyers of life, let these who desire so to do avoid at least the commission of all gross offences."

When Mahávíra's fame began to be widely diffused, it attracted the notice of the brahmans of Magadha, and several of their most eminent teachers undertook to rewrite his doctrines. Instead of effecting their purpose, however, they became converts, and constituted his Gaṇadharas, heads of schools, the disciples of Mahávíra, and teachers of his doctrines, both orally and scripturally.

The period of his liberation having arrived, Mahávíra resigned his breath, and his body was burned by Śakra and other deities, who divided amongst them such parts as were not consumed by the flames, as the teeth and bones, which they preserved as relics; the ashes of the pile were distributed amongst the assistants; the gods erected a splendid monument on the spot, and then returned to their respective heavens.—Wilson's *Works*, Vol. I, p. 304

MAHAVIRYA—(1) A prince, the son of Vrihaduktha, one of the kings of Mithila; **(2)** A son of Bhavanmanyu, a descendant of Bharata.

MAHAVISHUBA—The great equinox when the sun is in the third degree of Viṣakhá and the moon is in the head of Krittiká. At this time offerings are to be presented to the gods and to the manes, and gifts are to be made to the Brahmana by serious persons. Liberality at the equinoxes is always advantageous to the donor. *V.P.*, p.225.

MAHAYAJNAS—The great Sacrifices, the great obligations, or as Sir W. Jones terms them sacraments, are but five: *viz*:

1. Bramhayajna, sacred study;
2. Pitriyajna, libations to the manes;
3. Devayajna, burnt offerings to the gods;
4. Baliyajna, offerings to all creatures;
5. Uriyajna, hospitality.

The Prajápatiyajna, or propagation of offspring, and Satyajna, observance of truth, are apparently later additions.—Wilson's *Notes* to *V.P.*

MAHAYOGI—'The great ascetic'. A name of Śiva.

MAHAYUGA—The aggregate of four Yugas or ages: *viz.*:—

Kṛiti Yuga	4000	
Sandhya	400	
Sandhyánsa	400	
		=4800
Tretá Yuga	3000	
Sandhya	300	
Sandhyánsa	300	
		=3600
Dwápara Yuga	2000	
Sandhya	200	
Sandhyánsa	200	
		=2400
Kali Yuga	1000	
Sandhya	100	
Sandhyánsa	100	
		=1200

If these divine years are converted into years of mortals, by multiplying them by 360, a year of men being a day of the gods we obtain the years of which the Yugas of mortals are respectively said to consist:

4800 × 360 =	1,728,000
3600 × 360 =	1,296,000
2400 × 360 =	864,000
1200 × 360 =	432,000
A Maháyuga =	4,320,000

So that these periods resolve themselves into very simple elements; the notion of four ages is a deteriorating series expressed by descending arithmetical progression, as 4, 3, 2, 1: the conversion of units into thousands; and the mythological fiction that these were divine years, each composed of 360 years of men.

It does not seem necessary to refer the invention to any astronomical computations, or to any attempt to represent actual chronology.—Wilson's *Notes* to *V.P.*

MAHENDRA—(1) One of the seven main chains of mountains in Bhárata. Mahendra is the chain of hills that extends from Orissa and the northern Circars to Gondwána, part of which, near Ganjam, is still called Mahendra Malei, or hills of Mahendra; **(2)** The name of a star in the tail of the celestial porpoise; **(3)** The name of a river mentioned in the Puránas. **(4)** A name of Indra. One of the seven mountain ranges of India; the hills which run from Goṇḍvānā to Orissa and the Northern Circars. (*see* KULAPARVATAS)

MAHESVARA PURANA—(*see* PURĀṆA)

MAHESWARA—A name of Śiva, 'the great Lord.'

MAHEYAS—People living near the Mahi river.

MAHI—A river, the Mahy of Western Malwa.

MAHIKAS, OR MAHISHAS—Supposed to be the ancient name for the inhabitants of Mysore.

MAHINASA—One of the eleven *Rudras*.

MAHISA, MAHIṢĀSURA—(1) The great *asura* or demon killed by Skanda in the *Mahābhārata*. (*see* KRAUÑCA) **(2)** Also a demon killed by Candā or Durgā.

MAHISHAKAS—An ancient name of the people of Mysore.

MAHISHMAT—A prince of the Yadava race, the son of Sahanji.

MAHISMATI, MĀHIṢMATĪ—The capital of Kārtavirya, king of the Tālajaṅghas, who had a thousand arms. Colonel Tod has identified it with the village of Chuli Maheśvar, which, according to him, is still called "the village of the thousand-armed".

A city on the road to the south (Mahábhárata, Udyoga Parva) which is commonly identified with Chuli Maheṣwar, on the Narmada.

MAHODAYA—A name of the city of Kannauj.

MAHORAGA (Mahā + uraga). 'Great serpent.' The serpent Śeṣa, or any other great serpent.

MAHYUTTARAS—A people to the north of the river Mahí.

MAINAKA—A mountain stated in the *Mahābhārata* to be north of Kailāsa; so-called as being the son of Himavat and Menakā. When, as the poets sing, Indra clipped the wings of the mountains, this is said to have been the only one that escaped. This mountain, according to some, stands in Central India, and, according to others, near the extremity of the Peninsula.

A son of Himávat and Mená; the brother of Ganga and Párvatí.

MAITREYA—(1) A disciple of Paráṣara, to whom the Vishṇu Purána is related in reply to his inquiries; he is also one of the chief interlocutors in the Bhágavata, and is introduced in the Mahábhárata, (Vana Parva, S. 10) as a great Rishi, or sage, who denounces Duryo-dhana's death. In the Bhágavata he is also termed Kausharavi: **(2)** A son of Mítráyu, from whom the Maítreya Brahmans were descended. **(3)** A *ṛṣi*, son of Kuśarava, and disciple of Parāśara. He is one of the interlocutors in the *Viṣṇu* and *Bhāgavata Purāṇas*.

MAITREYAS—A tribe of Brahmans descended from Mitráyu.

MAITREYI—Wife of the *ṛṣi* Yajñavalkya, who was indoctrinated by her husband in the mysteries of religion and philosophy.

MAITRI, MAITRĀYAṆĪ—An Upaniṣad of the Black *Yajurveda*. It has been edited and translated by Professor Cowell for the *Bibliotheca Indica*.

MAITRI—Friendship, daughter of Daksha, wife of Dharma.

MAKANDI—The capital of Southern Páncháła, the country north of the Ganges as far as to the Chambal.

MAKARA—A huge sea animal, which has been taken to be the crocodile, the shark, the dolphin, &c., but is probably a fabulous animal. It represents the sign Capriconus in the Hindu zodiac, and is depicted with the head and forelegs of an antelope and the body and tail of a fish. It is the vehicle of Varuṇa, the god of the ocean, and its figure is borne on the banner of Kāmadeva, god of love. It is also called Kaṇṭaka, Asitadaṃṣṭra, 'black teeth', and Jalarūpa, 'water form'. It is now the name of a shark in many parts of India.

MAKARAS—The five *m*'s. (*see* TANTRA)

MAKHAVAT—A name of Indra.

MALADAS, MALAJAS, MALAS—Tribes of people enumerated in the Puránas, but not satisfactorily identified.

MALATI-MADHAVA (Mālatī and Mādhava)—A drama by Bhava-bhūti, translated by Wilson. "This drama," says the translator, "offers nothing to offend the most fastidious delicacy, and may be compared in this respect advantageously with many of the dramas of modern Europe which treat of the passion (of love) that constitutes its subject."

MALAVA—The country of Mālwa.

MALAVAS—An aboriginal tribe dwelling along the Páripátra mountains.

MALAVIKAGNIMITBA—(Mālavika and Agni-mitra). A drama ascribed to Kālidāsa, and although inferior to his other productions, it is probably his work. The text, with a translation, has been published by Tullberg. There is a German translation by Weber, an English one by Tawney, and a French one by Foucaux. The text has been printed at Bombay and Calcutta.

MALAYA—1. The country of Malabar proper; the mountains bordering Malabar. (*see* KULAPARVATAS). 2. One of the seven chief chains of mountains in Bhárata; the southern portion of the Western Ghauts.

MALAYAS—The aboriginal tribes of the Southern Ghauts.

MALINA-MUKHA—'Black faced'. *Rākṣasas* and other demons, represented as having black faces.

MALINA—The son of Tansu, a descendant of Puru.

MALINI—'Surrounded with a garland (*mālā*)' of *campä* trees. A name of the city of Campā.

MALLARASHTRA—A name given in the Purȧnas to the Mahratta country.

MALLAS—In Bhíma's Dig-Vijaya we have two people of this name, both in the east, one along the foot of the Himálaya, and the other more to the south.

MALLIKARJUNA—A name of Śiva. One of the twelve great *liṅgas.* (*see* LIṄGA)

MALLINATHA—A poet, the author of commentaries of great repute on several of the great poems, as the *Raghuvaṁśa*, *Meghadūta*, *Śiśupāl-vadha*, &c.

MALYAVAN—A mountain at the base of Meru, to the east.

MALYAVAN—One of Śiva's principal attendants, who for interceding for one of his fellow-servants Pushpadanta (*q.v.*) was sentenced to a similar punishment—namely, to leave the paradise of Kailása and be born as a human being. After a due interval Málvaván was born at Pratishta, under the name of Gunádhya.—Wilson's *Works*, Vol. III, p. 152.

MANASA, MANASĀ-DEVĪ—Sister of the serpent king Śeṣa, and the wife of the sage Jaratkāru. She is also called Jagadgaurī, Nityā (eternal), and Padmāvatī. She had special power in counteracting the venom of serpents, and was, hence, called Viṣaharā.

MANASA, MĀNASA-SAROVARA—The lake Mānasa in the Himālayas. In the *Vāyu Purāṇa it is* stated that when the ocean fell from heaven upon mount Meru, it ran four times round the mountain, then it divided into four rivers which ran down the mountain and formed four great lakes, Aruṇoda on the east, Sitoda on the west, Mahābhadra in the north, and Mānasa on the south. According to the mythological account, the river Ganges flows out of it, but in reality no river issues from this lake, though the river Sutlej flows from another and larger lake called Rāvaṇahrāda, which lies, close to the west of Mānasa.

MANASA—**(1)** A form of Vishṇu, when he was born of Sambhúti, along with the gods Abhútarajasas, in the Rawala Manwantara; **(2)** 'The intellectual.' A name of the Supreme Being. Thus defined in the *Mahābhārata*: "The primeval god, without beginning or dissolution, invisible, undecaying, and immortal, who is known and called by great ṛ*ṣis* Mānasa."

MANAS—Mind; that which considers the consequences of acts to all creatures, and provides for their happiness. It is sometimes used as a synonym of Mahat.

MANASOTTARA—A prodigious range of mountains, running in a circular direction (forming an outer and an inner circle,) situated in Pushkara, the seventh Dwípa. The mountains are represented as 50,000 leagues high, and on the eastern face of the summit, the city of Indra is situated; that of Yama in the southern face; that of Varuna in the west, and that of Soma in the north.

MANAS-PUTRAS—'Mind (born) sons'. The seven or ten mind-born sons of Brahmā, (*see* Prajāpati)

MANAS-TALA—The lion on which Devī rides.

MANASWINI—The wife of Mikrȧnda, the great Muni.

MANASYA—A prince, the son of Mahȧnta, who reigned over India in the first, or Swayambhuva Manwantara.

MANAVA DHARMA-SASTRA—The code of Manu. (*see* MANU SAṢHITĀ)

MANAVA KALPA-SŪTRA—Manu's work on *vaidik* rites. Part of it has been published in facsimile of Goldstücker.

MANAVA PURANA—(*see* Purāṇa)

MANAVI—The wife of Manu. ALSO called Manāyī.

MANCHA—A raised platform, with a floor and a roof, ascended by a ladder. *V.P.*, p. 553.

MANDAHARA—A minor Dwípa; the Bhágavata and Pádma name eight such islands, peopled for the most part by Mlechchhas, but who worship Hindu divinities.

MANDAKARNI—A sage who dwelt in the Daṇḍaka forest, and is said in the *Rāmāyaṇa* to have formed a lake which was known by his name. His austerities alarmed the gods, and Indra sent five apsaras to beguile him from his penance of "standing in a pool and feeding on nothing but air for 10,000 years". They succeeded, and became his wives, and inhabited a house concealed in the lake, which, from them, was called *pañcāpsaras.*

MANDAKINI—The heavenly Ganges. The Ganges. An arm of the Ganges which flows through Kedāranātha. A river near the mountain Citrakūṭa (*q.v.*) in Bundelkhand. It was near the abode of Rāma and Sītā, and is mentioned both in the *Rāmāyaṇa* and *Mahābhārata.* It would seem to be the modern Piṣuni. Ráma thus points out to Síta, some of the beauties of the river.

"My life in fair Ayodhya's town
Was not so sweet to me,
As gazing on this lovely flood,
That glorious hill and thee.
Bathe in the gentle stream, to her
With friendly love repair,
And pluck her lilies in thy play,
And twine them in thy hair.
This mount, with all its savage life,
Ayodhya'a city deem,
And on this beauteous river look
As our own Sarju's stream.
O Síta, I am wild with joy,
So rare a lot is mine,
Cheered by a duteous brother's care,
And loved with love like thine."
—Griffith. *Scenes from the Rámáyana.*

MANDALA—'A circle, orb.' A circuit or territorial division, as Colamaṇḍala, *i.e.*, Coromandel. According to one arrangement, the Saṁhitā of the *Ṛgveda* is divided into ten *maṇḍalas.*

MANDALA-NRTYA—A circular dance. The dance of the Gopis round Kṛṣṇa and Rādhā.

MANDAPALA—A childless saint, who, according to the *Mahābhārata*, after long perseverance in devotion and asceticism, died and went to the abode of Yama. His desires being still unsatisfied, he inquired the cause, and was told that all his devotions had failed because he had no son, *onputra* (*put*, 'hell', *tra*, 'drawer'), to save him from hell. He then assumed the form of a species of bird called Śarṅgikā, and by a female of that species, who was Jaritā, he had four sons.

MANDARA—The great mountain which the gods used for the churning of the ocean. It is supposed to be the mountain so named in Bhāgalpur, which is held sacred, (*see* KŪRMĀVATĀRA, under AVATĀRA)

MANDAVI—Daughter of Kuśadhvaja, cousin of Sītā, and wife of Rāma's brother Bharata.

MANDEHAS—Terrific fiends, *rākṣasas*, who attempt every night to devour the sun. The night is called Usha, and the day is denominated Vyushta, and the interval, between them is called Sandhyá. On the occurrence of the awful Sandhyá, the Mándehas do their utmost to devour the sun; for Brahmá, denounced this curse upon these terrific fiends, that without the power to perish they should die every day (and revive by night,) and therefore a fierce contest occurs daily between them and the sun. *V.P.* The Váyu says the Mandehas are three crores in number. Professor Wilson says the story seems to be an ancient legend imperfectly preserved in some of the Puránas.

MANDGA—A teacher of the Sáma Veda, and disciple of Devadersa.

MANDHATṚ—A king, son of Yuvanāśva, of the race of Ikṣvāku, and author of a hymn in the *Ṛgveda.* The *Harivaṁśa* and some of the Purāṇas make Māndhātṛ to have been born in a natural way from his mother Gaurī, but the *Viṣṇu* and *Bhāgavata Purāṇas* tell an extraordinary story about his birth, which is probably based upon a forced derivation of his name. Yuvanāśva had no son, which grieved him much. Some holy sages near whom he lived instituted a religious rite to procure progeny for him. One night they placed a consecrated vessel of water upon an altar as part of their ceremony, and the water became endowed with prolific energy. Yuvanāśva woke up in the night thirsty, and finding the water, he drank it. So he conceived, and in due time a child came forth from his right side. The sages then asked who would suckle the child, whereupon Indra appeared, gave his finger for the child to suck, and said, "He shall suck me", *mām ayam dhāsyati.* These words were contracted, and the boy was named Māndhātṛ. When he grew up he had three sons and fifty daughters. An old sage named Saubhari came to Māndhātṛ and asked that one might be given him to wife. Unwilling to give one to so old and emaciated a man, but yet afraid to refuse, the king temporised, but at length yielded to the sage's request that the matter might be left to the choice of the girls. Saubhari then assumed a handsome form, and there was such a contention for him that he had to marry the whole fifty, and he provided for them a row of crystal palaces in a most beautiful garden.

MANDODARI—Rāvaṇa's favourite wife and the mother of Indrajīt.

MANDUKEYA—A teacher of the Rig Veda, the son of Indra- pramati who imparted his Sanhita to his son, and it thence descended through successive generations as well as disciples.

MANDUKYA—Name of an Upaniṣad translated by Dr. Roer in the *Bibliotheca Indica.*

MANGALA—The planet Mars, identified with Kārttikeya, the god of war. He was son of Śiva and the Earth, and as son of the Earth is called Aṅgāraka, Bhauma, Bhūmiputra, Mahīsuta. He is also called Śivagharmaja, 'born of the sweat of Śiva'; Gaganolmuka, the torch of the sky'; Lohita, 'the red'; Navārci, 'the nine-rayed'; Cara, the spy'; Ṛnāntaka, 'ender of debts, patron of debtors'. (*see* KĀRTIKEYA)

MANI—A powerful serpent, one of the progeny of Kadru.

MANIBHADRA—The chief of the *yakṣas* and guardian of travellers.

MANIDHANGA—The king of a tract of country near the Vindhya mountains.

MANIMAT—A *rākṣasa* slain by Bhīma.

MANIPURA—A city on the seacoast of Kaliṅga, where Babhru-vāhana, the son of Arjuna, dwelt. Wheeler identifies it with the modem Munnipur or Muneepore, east of Bengal; but this is very questionable.

MANMATHA—A name of the Indian Cupid, the son of Vishṇu, called also Káma, *q.v.* He is represented as the cause of sensual love both in mortals and celestials, but more especially in the female sex: whilst his wife, Rati, inflames the fire in the male sex—like Venus of old.

MANOJAVA—**(1)** The son of the Rudra Isána; **(2)** Hanumán. The son of the Vasu Anila (Wind). Manojava means 'swift as thought;' **(3)** The Indra of the sixth Manwantara was called Manojava.

MANTHARA—An ugly deformed slave, nurse of Queen Kaikeyī, who stirred up her mistress's jealousy against Rāmacandra, and led her to persuade King Daśaratha to banish Rāma from court. Śatrughna beat her and threatened to kill her, but his brother Bharata saved her.

MANTRA—A hymn of invocation or form of prayer in the Sanskrit language. Mantras are used in the performance of every religious rite. They are of various sorts, invocatory, evocatory, deprecatory, conservatory. They are beneficent or hurtful, salutary or pernicious. By means of them it is believed that great and various effects may be produced. Some are for casting out evil spirits; some for inspiring love or hatred, for curing diseases or bringing them on, for causing death or averting it. Some are of a contrary nature to others, and counteract their effect: the stronger overcoming the influence of the weaker. Some are potent enough, it is said, to occasion the destruction of a whole army: while there are others which the gods themselves are constrained to obey.

The Puróhitas, or domestic chaplains, of all Hindus, understand them best. They are indispensably necessary to them for accompanying the ceremonies which it is their office to conduct. But Brahmáns generally are conversant with these formulæ; and when rallied upon the present state of their Mantras, wholly divested as they are of their boasted efficacy and power, they answer that tills loss of their influence is to be attributed to the Kali yuga; the age of the world in which we now live, the iron age, the time of evil and misfortune in which everything has degenerated. See Dubois.

MANU—(From the root *man*, to think.) 'The man.' This name belongs to fourteen mythological progenitors of mankind and rulers of the earth, each of whom holds sway for the period called a Manvantara (*manu-antara*), the age of a Manu, *i.e.*, a period of no less than 4,320,000 years. The first of these Manus was Svāyambhuva, who sprang from Svayambhū, the self-existent. The self-existent, as identified with Brahmā the creator, divided himself into two persons, male and female. From this pair was produced the male Virāj, and from him sprang the Manu Svāyambhuva. As the acting creator, this Manu produced the ten Prajāpatis or progenitors of mankind, called also *maharṣis* (*mahā-ṛṣis*). According to another account, this Manu sprang from the incestuous intercourse of Brahmā with his daughter and wife, Satarūpā. Brahmā created himself Manu, "born of and identical with his original self, and the female portion of himself he constituted Śatarūpā", whom Manu took to wife. The law-book commonly known as Manu is ascribed to this Manu, and so also is a *sūtra* work on ritual bearing the same name. The Manu of the present age is the seventh, named Vaivasvata, 'sun-born', who was the son of Vivasvat, the sun, and he is a kṣatriya by race. He is also called Satyavrata. There are various legends about his having been saved from a great flood by Viṣṇu or Brahmā. The names of the fourteen Manus are: (1) Svāyambhuva, (2) Svārociṣa, (3)Auttami, (4) Tāmasa, (5) Raivata, (6) Cākṣuṣa, (7) Vaivasvata or Satyavrata, (8) Sāvarṇa, (9) Dakṣasāvarṇa, (10) Brahmāsāvarṇa, (11) Dharmasāvarṇa, (12) Sāvarṇa or Rudrasāvarṇa, (13) Raucya, (14) Bhautya.

The sons of Manu Vaivasvata were—Ikṣvāku, Nabhaga or Nṛga, Dhṛṣṭa, Śaryāti, Naraiṣyanta, Prāṁśu, Nābhāganediṣṭa or Nābhānediṣṭa, Karūṣa, and Pṛṣadhra. But there is some variety in the names.

With the seventh Manu, Vaivasvata, is connected the very curious and interesting legend of the deluge. The first account of this is found in the *Śatapatha Brāhmana*, of which the following is a summary: One morning, in the water which was brought to Manu for washing his hands, he caught a fish which spoke, and said, "Take care of me and I will preserve thee." Manu asked, "From what wilt thou preserve me?" The fish answered, "A flood will carry away all living beings; I will save thee from that." The fish desired Manu to keep him alive in an earthen vessel, to remove him to a dyke as he grew larger, and eventually to the ocean, "so that he might be beyond the risk of destruction". The fish grew rapidly, and again addressed Manu, saying, "After so many years the deluge will take place; then construct a ship and pay me homage, and when the waters rise, go into the ship and I will rescue thee." Manu did as he was desired, he built the ship, conveyed the fish to the ocean, and did him homage. The flood rose, and Manu fastened the cable of the ship to the fish's horn. Thus he passed over the northern mountain (the Himālaya, as the commentator explains). The fish then desired Manu to fasten the ship to a tree, and to go down with the subsiding waters. He did so, and found that the flood had swept away all living creatures. He alone was left. Desirous of offspring, he offered sacrifice and engaged in devotion. A woman was produced, who came to Manu and declared herself his daughter, "With her he lived, worshipping and toiling in arduous religious rites, desirous of offspring. With her he begot the offspring which is the offspring of Manu."

The story as told in the *Mahābhārata* represents Manu as engaged in devotion by the side of a river, and the fish craving his protection from the bigger fish. Manu placed the fish in a glass vase, but it grew larger and larger till the ocean alone could contain it. Then it warned Manu of the coming flood, and directed him to build a ship and to embark with the seven *ṛṣis*. He did so, and fastened his ship to the horn of the fish. Then, according to the rendering of Professor Williams—

> Along the ocean in that stately ship was borne the lord of men, and through
> Its dancing, tumbling billows and its roaring waters;
> and the bark,
> Tossed to and fro by violent winds, reeled on the surface of the deep,
> Staggering and trembling like a drunken woman: land was seen no more,
> Nor far horizon, nor the space between; for everywhere around.
> Spread the wild waste of waters, reeking atmosphere, and boundless sky.
> And now, when all the world was deluged, nought appeared above the waves
> But Manu and the seven sages, and the fish that drew the bark.
> Unwearied thus for years on years that fish pulled on the ship across
> The heaped-up waters, till at length it bore the vessel to the peak
> Of Himavān; then, softly smiling, thus the fish addressed the sage:
> 'Haste now to bind thy ship to this high crag. Know me, the lord of all,
> The great creator Brahmā, mightier than all might, omnipotent.
> By me, in fish-like shape, have you been saved in dire emergency.
> From Manu all creation, gods, Asuras, men, must be produced;
> By him the world must be created, that which moves and moveth not.'

The commentators on this legend of the *Mahābhārata* give a metaphysical turn to the legend, and endeavour to illustrate it by philosophical and allegorical intepretations. The same story is reproduced with variations in the *Matsya*, *Bhāgavata*, and *Agni Purāṇas*, and Muir has given translations of the passages in vol. I of his *Sanskrit Texts.*

In the *Rāmāyaṇa* mention is made of a female Manu, and it appears that the word is sometimes used for "the wife of Manu"

The great Hindu law-giver who lived about 800 B.C. The institutes of Manu, or code of laws still extant, is sometimes attributed to Swayambhuva the first Manu. The Manu of the present period is sometimes considered the author of the Dharma-shastra, the code that bears his name. "The name belongs to the Epic and Puranic periods. In the former we may trace in it the remains of the tradition of a first man, alike progenitor, or even creator, like Prometheus, of his descendants, and law-giver. We should conceive its historical value to be the allusion to some legendary personage, such as every nation can boast of, who first wakes his country-men from barbarism and a wild life, to the light of civilization and systematic government." *Thomson.* Manu was "a legislator and saint, a son of Brahmá, or a personification of Brahmá himself, the creator of the world and progenitor of mankind. Derived from the root *man* to think, the word means originally *man*, the thinker, and is found in this sense in the Rig Veda.

"Manu as a legislator is identified with the Cretan Minos; as progenitor of mankind with the German Mannua: 'Celebrant carminibus antiquie, quod unum apud illos memoriæ et annalium genus est, Tuisconem deum terra editum, et filium Mannum, originem gentis conditoresque. TACITUS, Germania, Cap. II."—*Griffiths*

The head or ruler of an extensive period of time, termed a Manwantara. Each Kalpa, or creation of the world, is divided into fourteen Manwantaras or intervals, over which a Manu presides. Six of these periods have passed; the first Manu was Swáyambhuva; the second Swarochisa, the third Auttami; the fourth Tamasa; the fifth Raivata; the sixth Chakshnsha; these six Manus have passed away; the Manu who presides over the seventh, which is the present period, is Vaivaswata, the son of the sun, the wise lord of obsequies. The Vishṇu Purána contains an account of the Manwantaras yet to come , and the names of the Manus who will preside over each. The Jainas have also fourteen Manus to whom they give names different to those in the Hindu Puránas.

The Noah of the Hindus. The Śatapatha Brahmana contains an important legend of the deluge, but speaks of Manu simply, without assigning to him any patronymic, such as Vaivaswata, so that it is uncertain which Manu is referred to. *O.S.T.*, Vol. I, p- 217.

Monier Williams writes of him as the seventh Manu, or Manu of the present period, called Vaivaswata, and regarded as one of the progenitors of the human race. He is represented as conciliating the favour of the Supreme in an age of universal depravity. Dr. Muir gives a translation of the legend in his *Orig. Sans. Texts*, Vol. I, p. 182; Prof. Max Müller has also translated it on his *An. Sans. Lit.*, p. 425. The following translation is from Prof. M. Williams' *Indian Epic Poetry.*

"It happened one morning that they brought water to Manu, as usual, for washing his hands. As he was washing a fish came into his hands. It spoke to him thus: 'Take care of me and I will preserve thee.' Manu asked, 'From what wilt thou preserve me.' The fish answered, 'A flood will carry away all living beings; I will save thee from that.' He said, 'How is thy preservation to be accomplished' ? The fish replied, 'while we are small, we are liable to constant destruction, and even one fish devours another; thou must first preserve me in an earthen vessel; when I grow too large for that dig a trench, and keep me in that. When I grow too large for that, thou must convey me to the ocean; I shall then be beyond the risk of destruction.' So saying, it rapidly became a great fish, and still grew larger and larger. Then it said, 'After so many years the deluge will take place; then construct a ship, and pay me homage, and when the waters rise, go into the ship, and I will rescue thee.' Manu therefore, after preserving the fish—as he was directed, bore it to the ocean; and at the very time the fish had declared he built a ship and did homage to the fish. When the flood rose he embarked in the ship and the fish swam towards him, and he fastened the ship's cable to its horn. By its means he passed beyond this northern mountain. The fish then said 'I have preserved thee; now do thou fasten the ship to a tree. But let not the water sink from under thee while thou art on the mountain. As fast as it sinks do thou go down with it'. He therefore so descended; and this was the manner of Manu's descent from the northern mountain. The flood had carried away all living creatures. Manu alone was left. Wishing for offspring he diligently performed a sacrifice. In a year's time a female was produced. She came to Manu. He said to her, 'Who art thou ?' She answered, 'Thy daughter.' He asked, 'How lady art thou my daughter ?' She replied, 'The oblations which thou didst offer in the waters, *viz.*, clarified butter, thick milk, whey and curds; from these hast thou begotten me. I can confer blessings.' With her he laboriously performed another sacrifice, desirous of children. By her he bad offspring, called the offspring of Manu; and whatever blessings he prayed for were all granted to him."

"From this interesting legend we learn that, according to its author's belief, Manu was not the creator of mankind, as some later accounts considered him to have been, but himself belonged to an earlier race of living beings, which was entirely destroyed by the deluge which is described. The legend regards him as a representative of his generation, who for some reason, perhaps his superior wisdom, or sanctity, or position, was selected out, of the crowd of ordinary mortals to be rescued from the impending destruction. That he was regarded as a mere man, and not as a being of a superior order, is shown by the fact of his requiring the aid of a higher power to preserve him. A supernatural fish, apparently some divine person, conceived as taking the form of a creature which would be perfectly secure and at home in the midst of the raging waters, undertook to deliver him, and guided the ship on which he was directed to embark, through all dangers to its destined haven. No one but Manu took refuge in the ship, for he alone, the story expressly records, was preserved, while all the other living beings were overwhelmed. Finding himself the sole survivor when the waters subsided, he became desirous of progeny; and with intense devotion performed certain religious rites in the hope of realizing his wish through their efficacy. As a result of his oblations, a woman arose from the waters into which they had been cast. A male and a female now existed, the destined parents of a new race of men who sprang from their union,—a union the fruitfulness of which was assured by their assiduous practice of sacred ceremonies. From Manu and Iḍá, we are expressly told, the race known as that of Manu, *i.e.*, the race of men, was produced. The legend says nothing whatever of this race being originally characterized by any distinction of castes, or about four sons, the ancestors of Brahmans, Kshatriyas, Vaisyas, and Sudras being born to Manu and Iḍá. We must therefore suppose that the author of the legend intends to represent the early race of mankind, or at least the first inhabitants of Bharatavarsha, as descended from one common progenitor without any original varieties of caste, however different the professions and social position of their descendants afterwards became. We are consequently entitled to regard this legend of the Śatapatha Brahmana as at variance with the common fable regarding the separate origin of the Brahmans, Kshatriyas, Vaisyas and Sudras."—Muir. *O.S.T., Vol. I, p.* 185.

MANU-SAMHITA—The well-known law-book, the Code of Manu, or Institutes of Manu. It is attributed to the first Manu, Svāyambhuva, who existed nearly thirty millions of years ago, but it bears the marks of being the production of more than one mind. This is the first and chief of the works classified as Smṛti, and is a collection or digest of current laws and creeds rather than a planned systematic code. It is the foundation of Hindu law, and is held in the highest reverence. The work belongs to a period later than that of the Vedas, when the brāhmaṇas had obtained the ascendancy, but its deities are those of the Vedic rather than the Epic or Purāṇic age. It is apparently anterior to the philosophical schools. The fifth century BC is supposed to be about the time when it was composed, but the rules and precepts it contains had probably existed as traditions long before. It is commonly called the Code of Manu, and was current among the Mānavas, a class or school of brāhmaṇas who were followers of the Black *Yajurveda*; but it deals with many subjects besides law, and is a most important record of old Hindu society. It is said to have consisted originally of 100,000 verses, arranged in twenty-four chapters; that Nārada shortened the work to 12,000 verses; and that Sumati made a second abridgement, reducing it to 4000, but only 2685 are extant. It is evident that there was more than one redaction of the laws of the Mānavas, for a Bṛham or Vṛhan Manu, 'great Manu', and Vṛddha Manu, 'old Manu', are often referred to. Sir W. Jones's translation, edited by Haughton, is excellent, and is the basis of all others in French, German, &c. The text has often been printed.

MANVANTARA (Manu-antara). The life or period of a Manu, 4,320,000 years.

A period equal to seventy-one times the number of years contained in the four Yugas, with some additional years: this is the duration of the Manu, the (attendant) divinities, and the rest, which is equal to 852,000 divine years, or to 306,720,000 years of mortals, independent of the additional period. Fourteen times this period constitutes a Brahmá, day, that is a day of Brahmá, or a Kalpa.

MARGASHIRSHA—The month which comprises the latter half of November and the former half of December. "It is otherwise called *Agraháyana* "the commencement of the year," and although the Hindus now begin their year in the month *Vaisháka* (April, May) we find in Prinsep's *Useful Tables*, part II, p. 18, that in Bentley's opinion, this month would have begun the year, before the use of a fixed calendar in India, between B.C. 693 and 451.

MARIC(H)A—(1) A *rākṣasa*, son of Tārakā. According to the *Rāmāyaṇa* he interfered with a sacrifice which was being performed by Viśvāmitra, but was encountered by Rāma, who discharged a weapon at him, which drove him one hundred *yojanas* out to sea. He was afterwards the minister of Rāvaṇa, and accompanied him to the hermitage where Rāma and Sītā were dwelling. There, to inveigle Rama, he assumed the shape of a golden deer, which Rāma pursued and killed. On receiving his death-wound he resumed a *rākṣasa* form and spoke, and Rāma discovered whom he had killed. In the meanwhile Rāvaṇa had carried off Sītā. **(2)** A Daitya, the son of Sunda.

MARICHI—(1) A Prajápati, (*see* Prajāpati) one of the nine Brahmá rishis, or mind-born sons of Brahmá; he was married to Sambhúti (fitness) one of the daughters of Daksha. Their son, Kaṣyapa, and one of the seven great *ṛṣis*. (*see* Ṛṣi) had an extensive posterity; **(2)** The chief of the Maruts, or personified winds.

MARICHIGARBHAS—A class of deities belonging to the ninth Manwantara.

MARISA—Daughter of the sage Kaṇḍu, and wife of the Pracetasas, but from the mode of her birth she is called "the nursling of the trees, and daughter of the wind and the moon" She was mother of Dakṣa. Her mother was a celestial nymph named Pramlocā, who beguiled the sage Kaṇḍu from his devotions and lived with him for a long time. When the sage awoke from his voluptuous delusion, he drove her from his presence. "She, passing through the air, wiped the perspiration from her with the leaves of the trees", and "the child she had conceived by the *ṛṣi* came forth from the pores other skin in drops of perspiration. The trees received the living dews, and the winds collected them into one mass. Soma matured this by his rays, and gradually it increased in size till the exhalations that had rested on the tree-tops became the lovely girl named Māriṣā."—*Viṣṇu Purāṇa*. According to the same authority Māriṣā had been in a former birth the childless widow of a king. Her devotion to Viṣṇu gained his favour, and he desired her to ask a boon. She bewailed her childless state, and prayed that in succeeding births she might have "honourable husbands and a son equal to patriarch". She received the promise that she should be of marvelous birth, should be very beautiful, and should have ten husbands of mighty prowess, and a son whose posterity should fill the universe. This legend is no doubt an addition of later date, invented to account for the marvelous origin of Māriṣā.

MARKANDEYA PURANA—"That Purāṇa in which, commencing with the story of the birds that were acquainted with right and wrong, everything is narrated fully by Mārkaṇḍeya as it was explained by holy sages in reply to the question of the *muni*, is called the Mārkaṇḍeya, containing 9000 verses." This Purāṇa is narrated in the first place by Mārkaṇḍeya, and in the second by certain fabulous birds profoundly versed in the Vedas, who relate their knowledge in answer to the questions of the sage Jaimini. "It has a character different from all the other Purāṇas. It has nothing of a sectarial spirit, little of a religious tone; rarely inserting prayers and invocations to any deity, and such as are inserted are brief and moderate. It deals little in precepts, ceremonial or moral. Its leading feature is narrative, and it presents an uninterrupted succession of legends, most of which, when ancient, are embellished with new circumstances, and, when new, partake so far of the spirit of the old, that they are disinterested creations of the imagination, having no particular motive, being designed to recommend no special doctrine or observance. Whether they are derived from any other source, or whether they are original inventions, it is not possible to ascertain. They are most probably, for the greater part at least, original; and the whole has been narrated in the compiler's own manner, a manner superior to that of the Purāṇas in general, with exception of the Bhāgavata.'

The popular *Durgā Māhātmya* or *Chaṇḍipāṭha* is an episode of this Purāṇa. In the absence of any guide to a positive conclusion as to the date, it may conjecturally be placed in the ninth or tenth century. Professor Banerjea places it in the eighth century. This Purāṇa has been published in the *Bibliotheca Indica*, and translated by the Professor K.M. Banerjea.

MARKANDEYA—A sage, the son of Mṛkaṇḍa, and reputed author of the *Mārkaṇḍeya Purāṇa*. He was remarkable for his austerities and great age, and is called Dīrghāyus, 'the long-lived'.

MARRIAGE—The forms of marriage are eight, the Brahmá, Daiva, the Ársha, Prájápatya, Asura, Gandharva, Rakshasa and Paiṣacha. These different modes of marriage are described by Manu III, 27, &c. The Vishṇu Purána describes the kind of maiden that should be selected by the man who has finished his studies, and proposes to enter into the married state. She should be a third of his own age; one who has not too much hair, but is not without any; one who is not very black nor yellow complexioned, and who is not from birth a cripple or deformed: he must not marry a girl who is vicious or unhealthy, of low origin or labouring under disease; one who has been ill brought up; one who talks improperly; one who inherits some malady from father or mother; one who has a beard, or is of a masculine appearance; one who speaks thick or thin, or croaks like a raven; one who keeps her eyes shut, or has the eyes very prominent; one who has hairy legs, or thick ankles; or one who has dimples in her cheeks when she laughs;* let not a wise and prudent man marry a girl of such a description; nor let a considerate man wed a girl of a harsh skin; or one with white nails; or one with red eyes; or with very fat hands and feet; or one who is a dwarf, or who is very tall; or one whose eyebrows meet, or whose teeth are far apart and resemble tusks. (* For the credit of Hindu taste it is to be noticed that the commentator observes the hemistich in which this clause occurs is not found in all copies of the text).—*Wilson*.

MARSHTI, MARSHTIMAT—Two of the sons of Śarana of the family of Vasudeva.

MARTTANDA—In the Vedas the sun or sun god.

MARTTIKAVATAS—Princes of Mrittikavatí.

MARTYA-MUKHA—'Human-faced.' Any being in which the figures of a man and animal are combined.

MARU—(1) The son of Síghra, a descendant of Ráma. In the Vishṇu Purána it is stated that Maru is, through the power of devotion, (Yóga) still living in the village called Kalápa, and in a future age will be the restorer of the Kshatriya race in the solar dynasty; **(2)** The name of the son of Hariyaṣwa, king of Mithila.

MARUBHAUMAS—The inhabitants of Marubhúmi, the desert; an aboriginal tribe occupying the sandy deserts of Sindh.

MARUDEVA—A prince, the son of Supratítha, a descendant of Ikshváku.

MARUT-LOKA—The heaven of the winds and Vaisyas.

MARUTI—A name of Hanumán, the offspring of Marut, a name of Pávana or Váyu, all meaning wind.

MARUTS—(1) The storm gods, who hold a very prominent place in the Vedas, and are represented as friends and allies of Indra. Various origins are assigned to them. They are sons of Rudra, sons and brothers of Indra, sons of the ocean, sons of heaven, sons of earth. They are armed with lightnings and thunderbolts, and "ride on the whirlwind and direct the storm". The number of them is said in one place to be thrice sixty, and in another only twenty-seven. In the *Rāmāyaṇa* they are represented to have their origin in an unborn son of Diti, whom Indra dashed into forty-nine pieces with his thunderbolt, and in compassion converted into Maruts. This is also the story told p the Purāṇas, and they are said to have obtained their name from the words *mā rodīḥ*, 'weep not', which Indra addressed to them. A scholiast on the Veda says, that after their birth from Diti, as above told, Śiva and Pārvatī beheld them in great affliction, and the latter asked Śiva to transform the lumps of flesh into boys; he accordingly made them boys of like form, like age, and similarly accoutred, and gave them to Pārvatī as her sons, whence they are called the sons of Rudra. Other legends are, that Pārvatī, hearing the lamentations of Diti, entreated Śiva to give forms to the shapeless births, telling them not to weep (*mā rodīḥ*); and another, that he actually begot them in the form of a bull on Pṛthivī, the earth, as a cow. (*see* Diti) All these legends have manifestly been invented to explain those passages of the Vedas that make the Maruts the sons of Rudra. The world of the Maruts, called Māruta, is the appointed heaven of vaiśyas.

(The complete episode is like this: The sons of Diti, who having lost her children prayed for a son of irresistible prowess who should destroy Indra. The Muni Kaṣyapa granted his wife the great boon she solicited, but with one condition; that she should be pregnant a hundred years, and maintain a rigid observance of all religious rites during the whole period. Indra watched for an opportunity of frustrating her intentions, and in the last year of the century, an opportunity occurred. Diti retired one night to rest without performing the prescribed ablution of her feet, and fell asleep: on which Indra divided the embryo in her womb into seven portions. The child, thus mutilated, cried bitterly. Indra failing to silence it again divided each of the seven portions into seven, and thus formed the swift-moving deities called Marutas (winds.) They derived this appellation from the words with which Indra had addressed them (*Marodih*, weep not,) and they became forty-nine subordinate divinities, the associates of the wielder of the thunderbolt. *V.P.* This legend, says Professor Wilson, occurs in all the Puránas in which the account of Kaşyapa's family is related. The Vishņu Purána in another place, says the winds were the children of Marutwatí. The Maruts are said to have given Bharata a son named Dharadwája. *q.v.* Among the lesser gods, an important share of adoration is enjoyed by a group avowedly subordinate to Indra,—involving an obvious allegory,—the Maruts, or Winds, who are naturally associated with the firmament. We have, indeed, a god of the wind, in Váyu; but little is said of him, and that chiefly in association with Indra, with whom he is identified by scholiasts on the Veda. The Maruts, on the contrary, are frequently addressed as the attendants and allies of Indra, confederated with him in the battle with Vŗitra, and aiding and encouraging his exertions. They are called the sons of Pŗişni, or the earth, and also Rudras, or sons of Rudra: the meaning of which affiliations is not very clear, although, no doubt, it is allegorical. They are also associated, on some occasions, with Agni; an obvious metaphor, expressing the action of wind upon fire. It is also intimated that they were, originally, mortal, and became immortal in consequence of worshipping Agni, which is also easy of explanation. Their share in the production of rain, and their fierce and impetuous nature, are figurative representations of physical phenomena.—*Wilson.* **(2)** The god of the wind, and regent of the north-west quarter.

MARUTTA—(1) A descendant of Manu Vaivasvata. He was a Cakravartī, or universal monarch, and performed a celebrated sacrifice. "Never," says the *Vișņu Purāņa*, "was beheld on earth a sacrifice equal to the sacrifice of Marutta. All the implements and utensils were made of gold. Indra was intoxicated with the libations of *soma* juice, and the brāhmaņas were enraptured with the magnificent donations they received. The winds of heaven encompassed the rite as guards, and the assembled gods attended to behold it." According to the *Vāyu Purāņa*, Marutta was taken to heaven with his kindred and friends by Saṁvarta, the officiating priest at this sacrifice. But the *Mārkaņḍeya Purāņa* says he was killed after he had laid down his crown and retired to the woods. **(2)** A king of the Solar race, who was killed by Vapușmat, and fearfully avenged by his son Dama (*q.v.*). **(3)** A son of Karandhama, a descendant of Turvasa.

MARUTWATI—One of the daughters of Daksha, who was married to Dharma.

MATALI—The charioteer of Indra. It was he who was sent to convey Yayáti to heaven, when Indra invited him thither. The Padma Purána relates a philosophical conversation that took place between the king and Mátali, in which the imperfection of all corporeal existence, and the incomplete felicity of every condition of life are discussed. These attributes belong, it is said, even to the gods themselves, for they are affected with disease, subject to death, disgraced by the passions of lust and anger, and are consequently instances of imperfection and of misery. Various degrees of vice are then described, and their prevention or expiation are declared to be the worship of Śiva or Vishņu, between whom there is no difference; they are but one, as is the case indeed with Brahmá also for 'Brahmá, Vishņu, and Maheşwara are one form though three gods; there is no difference between the three: the difference is that of attributes alone.' *See* YAYÁTI.

MATANGA—'An elephant.' A man who was brought up as a brāhmaņa but was the son of a cāņḍāla. His story, as told in the *Mahābhārata*, relates that he was mercilessly goading an ass's foal, which he was driving. The mother ass, seeing this, tells her foal that she could expect no better, for her driver was no brāhmaņa but a cāņḍāla. Matańga, addressing the ass as "most intelligent", begged to know how this was, and was informed that his mother when intoxicated had received the embraces of a low-born barber, and that he, the offspring, was a cāņḍāla and no brāhmaņa. In order to obtain elevation to the position of a brāhmaņa he went through such a curse of austerities as alarmed the gods. Indra refused to admit him. He persevered again for a hundred years, but still Indra persistently refused such an impossible request, and advised him to seek some other boon. Nothing daunted, he went on a thousand years longer, with the same result. Though dejected he did not despair, but proceeded to balance himself on his great toe. He continued to do this for a hundred years, when he was reduced to mere skin and bone, and was on the point of falling. Indra went to support him, but inexorably refused his request, and, when, further importuned, "gave him the power of moving about like a bird, and changing his shape at will, and of being honoured and renowned". In the *Rāmāyaņa*, Rāma and Sītā visited the hermitage of Matańga near Ŗsyamūka mountain.

A brahman mentioned in the Daşakumára who was killed while trying to preserve the life of another brahman. On reaching the city of souls, Yama said to

Chandragupta 'This man's hour is not yet come. He died in defence of a brahman. That one virtuous act effaces all his former sins. Let him behold the penalty paid to the wicked, and then restore him to his former body.' Returning to life his adventures were still more remarkable. Aided by a prince whom he met in the forest he penetrated the path to Pátála. On arriving near the city, he cast himself into the flames of a fire he had prepared and rose again in an angelic form. A damsel richly arrayed and numerously attended, who said her name was Kálindí, daughter of the king of Asuras, and that she had come with the concurrence of her council to offer the kingdom and herself, twin wives, to his espousal. Mátanga married her and became king of Pátāla.—Wilson's *Works*, Vol. IV, p. 174.

MATARISVAN—An aerial being who is represented in the *Ṛgveda* as bringing down or producing Agni (fire) for the Bhṛgus. By some supposed to be the wind.

MATHURA—An ancient and celebrated city on the right bank of the Yamunā, surviving in the modern Muttra. It was the birthplace of Kṛṣṇa and one of the seven sacred cities. The *Viṣṇu Purāṇa* states that it was originally called Madhu or Madhuvana, from the demon Madhu, who reigned there, but that when Lavaṇa, his son and successor, was killed by Śatrughna, the conqueror set up his own rule there and built a city which he called Madhurā or Mathurā.

MATINARA—The son of Rikska, the fifteenth in descent from Puru. *V.P.*

MATI—Understanding—that which discriminates and distinguishes objects preparatory to their fruition by the soul. It is often used to signify mind, intelligence, knowledge, and wisdom.

MATṚS—'Mothers.' The divine mothers. These appear to have been originally the female energies of the great gods, as Brahmāṇī of Brahmā, Maheśvarī of Śiva, Vaiṣṇavī of Viṣṇu, Indrāṇī or Aindrī of Indra, &c. The number of them was seven or eight or sixteen, but in the later mythology they have increased out of number. They are connected with the Tantra worship, and are represented as worshipping Śiva and attending upon his son Kārttikeya.

MATSYA PURANA—This Purána, after the usual prologue of Súta and the Rishis, opens with the account of the Matsya or 'fish' Avatára of Vishṇu, in which he preserves a king named Manu, with the seeds of all things, in an ark, from the waters of that inundation which in the season of a Pralaya overspreads the world. Whilst the ark floats fastened to the fish (Vishṇu) Manu enters into conversation with him, and his questions, and the replies of Vishnu, forms the main substance of the compilation. The first subject is the creation, which is that of Brahmá and the patriarchs; the regal dynasties are next described; and then follow chapters on the duties of the different orders, &c. The account of the universe is given in the usual strain. Saiva legends ensue; as the destruction of Triparásura; the war of the gods with Taraka and the Daityas, and the consequent birth of Kartikeya, with the various circumstances of Uma's birth and marriage, the burning of Kamadeva; the destruction of the Asuras Maya and Andhaka; interspersed with the Vaishnava legends of the Avatáras. There are also chapters on law and morals, and one which furnishes directions for building houses and making images. See Vishṇu Purána, Preface. It consists of between 14,000 and 15,000 stanzas. This work "is a miscellaneous compilation, but includes in its contents the elements of a genuine Purāṇa".

MATSYA, or FISH AVATARA—The first of the ten Avataras of Vishṇu. When, at the end of the last mundane age, the Bhágavata Purána relates, Brahmá, the first god of the Trimúrti, had fallen asleep, a powerful demon, *Hayagríva*, stole the Vedas which had issued from the mouth of Brahmá, and lay by his side. About that time, a royal saint, *Satyavrata*, had by his penance attained the rank of a Manu, and Vishṇu, who had witnessed .the deed of Hayagrîva, and intended to slay him, assumed for this purpose the form of a very small fish, and glided into the hands of the saint when the latter made his daily ablutions in the river. Manu, about to release the little fish, was addressed and asked by it not to expose it to the danger that might arise to it from the larger fish in the river, but to place it in his water-jar. The saint complied with its wish; but in one night the fish grew so large, that at its request he had to transfer it to a pond. Yet soon the pond also becoming insufficient to contain the fish, Manu had to choose a larger pond for its abode; and, after successive other changes, he took it to the ocean. Satyavrata now understood that the fish was no other than *Náráyana*. or Vishṇu, and, after he had paid his adoration to the god, the latter revealed to him the imminence of a deluge which would destroy the world, and told him that a large vessel would appear to him, in which he was to embark together with the seven Rishis, taking with him all the plants and all the seeds of created things. Manu obeyed the behest of the god: and when the water covered the surface of the earth, Vishṇu again appeared to him in the shape of a, golden fish with a single horn, 10,000 miles long; and to this horn Manu attached the vessel, by means of Vishṇu's serpent serving as a cord. While thus floating in the vessel, Manu was instructed by the fish-god in the philosophical doctrines and the science of the supreme spirit; and after the deluge had subsided, the fish-god killed Hayagrîva, restored the Vedas to Brahmá, and taught them to the Manu Satyavrata, who in the present mundane age was born under the name of *Srâddhadeva*, as the son of Vivasvat. A fuller account of this Avatâra is given in the *Matsya-Purána*, where the instruction imparted to Manu by the fish-god includes all the usual detail contained in a Purána (*q.v.*,) that relating to creation, the patriarchs, progenitors, regal dynasties, the duties of the different orders, and so forth. In the Mahábhárata, where the same legend occurs, but without either that portion concerning Hayagrîva, or the instruction imparted by the fish, there is, besides minor variations, that imp-ortant difference between its story and that of the Puránas, that the fish is not a personification of Vishṇu, but of Brahmá, and that the deluge occurs in the present mundane age, under the reign itself of the Manu, who is the son of Vivasvat. The origin of this Avatára is probably a kindred legend, which occurs in the *Sathapatha bráhmana*, of the White Yajurveda; but there the fish does not represent any special deity, and the purpose of the legend itself is merely to account for the performance of certain sacrificial ceremonies".—[MANU.]

MATSYA—(1) The name of one of the Minor Dwípas; **(2)** A teacher of the Rig Veda, a disciple of Vedamitra. **(3)** Name of a country. Wilson says, "Dinajpoor, Rungpoor, and Cooch Behar", but there was more than one country of this name, and one would appear to have been situated in northern India. Manu places Matsya in *brahmarṣi*. According to the *Mahābhārata*, King Virāṭa's capital was called Matsya, his people also were called Matsyas, and he himself was styled Matsya. General Cunningham finds it in the neighbourhood of Jaypur, and says that the town of Virāṭ or Bairāṭ, 105 miles south of Delhi, was its capital.

MATSYAS—The people of Dinajpur, Rangpur, and Cooch Behar. There are, however, two Matsyas, one of which according to the Yantra Samrát, is identifiable with Jaipur. In the Digvijaya of Nakula the Matsyas are placed farther to the west or in Gujarat.

MAUDGALYAS—A class of Brahmans descended from Mudgala: they, as well as the Kanwas, were all followers or partisans of Angiras.

MAUNAS—A dynasty of kings, consisting of eleven sovereigns; and forming part of the seventy-nine princes mentioned in the Vishṇu Purána as to reign over the earth for one thousand three hundred and ninety years.

MAUNEYAS—A class of *gandharvas*, sons of Kaśyapa, who dwelt beneath the earth, and were sixty millions in number. They overpowered the Nāgas, and compelled them to flee to Viṣṇu for assistance, and he sent Purukutsa against them, who destroyed them.

MAURYA—The dynasty founded by Candragupta at Pāṭaliputra (Patna) in Magadha. According to the *Viṣṇu Purāṇa*, the Maurya kings were ten in number and reigned 137 years. Their names were—(1) Candragupta, (2) Bindusāra, (3) Aśokavardhana, (4) Suyaśas, (5) Daśaratha, (6) Sangata, (7) Śāliśūka, (8) Soma śarman, (9) Śaśadharman, (10) Bṛhadratha. The names vary in other Purāṇas. (*see* CANDRAGUPTA)

MAYA—'Illusion, deception.' **(1)** Illusion personified as a female form of celestial origin, created for the purpose of beguiling some individual. Sometimes identified with Durgā as the source of spells, or as a personification of the unreality of worldly things. In this character she is called Māyādevī or Mahāmāyā. **(2)** A name of Gayā, one of the seven sacred cities. **(3)** A *daitya* who was the architect and artificer of the *asuras*, as Viśvakarmā was the artificer of the *suras* or gods. He was son of Vipracitti and father of Vajrakāmā and Mandodarī, wife of Rāvaṇa. He dwelt in the Devagiri mountains not very far from Delhi, and his chief works were in the neighbourhood of that city, where he worked for men as well as *daityas*. The *Mahābhārata* speaks of a palace he built for the Pāṇḍavas. In the *Hariva-ṁśa* he appears frequently both as victor and vanquished in contests with the gods. **(4)** A daughter of Adharma (vice); **(5)** A daughter of Anrita (falsehood).

MAYADEVI, MĀYĀVATĪ—Wife of the demon Śambara. She brought up Pradyumna, the son of Kṛṣṇa, and subsequently married him. Pradyumna is represented as being a revived embodiment of Kāma, the god of love; and in accordance with this legend Māyāvatī is identified with his wife Rati, the Hindu Venus, (*see* MĀYĀ)

MAYODAYA—The ancient name of the city of Kanouj,

q.v.

MAYU—'Bleater, bellower.' The *kinnaras* are called Māyus.

MEDATITHI—One of the sons of Priyavrata who became king of Plaksba dwípa, He had seven sons, and the Dwipa was divided amongst them, each division being named after the prince to whom it was subject, the people enjoyed uninterrupted felicity, being sinless, *V.P.*, p. 197.

MEDHA—'Intelligence'; **(1)** One of the three sons of Priyavrata who adopted a religious life; remembering the occurrences of a prior existence they did not covet dominion, but diligently practised the rites of devotion, in due season, wholly disinterested, and looking for no reward. *V.P.* **(2)** A daughter of Daksha who was married to Dharma.

MEDHATITHI—Name of a Kāṇva who was a Vedic *ṛsi*. There is a legend in one of the Upaniṣads that he was carried up to heaven by Indra in the form of a ram, because the god had been pleased with his austerities.

MEDHAVIN—A prince, the son of Sunaya, of the race of Puru.

MEDINI, MEDINĪ-KOṢA—A well-known Sanskrit vocabulary. There are printed editions.

MEDINI—The earth, (*see* KAIṬABHA)

MEGHADUTA—'Cloud messenger. A celebrated poem by Kālidāsa, in which a banished Yakṣa implores a cloud to convey tidings of him to his wife. It has been translated into English verse by Wilson, and there are versions in French and German. Johnson has printed the text with a vocabulary.

MEGHANADA—A son of Rāvaṇa, (*see* INDRAJIT)

MEKALA--Name of a mountain from which the Narmadā river is said to rise, and from which it is called Mekalā and Mekalakanyā, 'daughter of Mekala'. There were a people of this name, who probably lived in the vicinity of this mountain. Their kings were also called Mekalas, and there appears to have been a city Mekalā.

MEKALAS—A tribe which according to the Purǻnas live in the Vindhya mountains: this locality is confirmed by mythological personations. The Rámáyana places the Mekalas amongst the Southern tribes.

MENA, MENAKĀ—**(1)** In the *Ṛgveda*, a daughter of Vṛṣanaśva, A *Brāhmaṇa* tells a strange story of Indra having assumed the form of Menā and then fallen in love with her. In the Purāṇas, wife of Himavat and mother of Umā and Gaṅgā, and of a son named Maināka. **(2)** An apsara sent to seduce the sage Viśvāmitra from his devotions, and succeeding in this object, she became the mother of the nymph Śakuntalā. **(3)** A river.

MENDICANT—See Vánaprastha.

MERUBHUTAS—See Marubhaumas.

MERU—In the earlier Epic period this is probably the name given to the high table-land of Tartary, to the north of the Himálaya range, from the neighbourhood of which the Aryan race may originally have pushed their way southwards into the peninsula, and thus have preserved the name in their traditions as a relic of the old mountain worship. In the Puránas it is described as the golden mountain in the centre of Jambu-dwípa. Its height is eighty-four thousand Yójanas; and its depth below the surface of the earth sixteen thousand. Its diameter at the summit is thirty-two thousand Yójanas; (the yojana is nine miles) and at its base sixteen thousand; so that this mountain is like the seed cup of the lotus of the earth.—*V.P.*

Prof. Wilson in a note states "the shape of Meru according to this description, is that of an inverted cone; and by the comparison to the seed cup its form should be circular: but there seems to be some uncertainty upon. this subject amongst the Pauránics. The Pádma compares its form to the bell-shaped flower of the Dhatura. The Váyu. represents it has having four sides of different colours , or white on the east, yellow on the south, black on the west, and red on the north: but notices also various opinions of the outline of the mountain, which, according to Atri, had a hundred angles: to Bhrigu a thousand; Savarni calls it octangular; Bhaguri quadrangular; and Varsháyani says it has a thousand angles: Gálana makes it saucer-shaped; Garga, twisted, like braided hair: and others maintain that it is circular. The Linga makes its eastern face of the colour of ruby; its southern, that of the lotus; its western, golden; and its southern coral. The Matsya has the same colours as the Váyu and both contain this line 'Four-coloured, golden, four cornered, lofty: but the Váyu compares its summit in one place to a saucer; and observes that its circumference must be thrice its diameter. The Matsya also says the measurement is that of a circular form but it is considered quadrangular. According to the Buddhists of Ceylon, Meru is said to be of the same diameter throughout.

Those of Nepal consider it to be shaped like a drum."

On the summit of Meru is the vast city of Brahmá, extending fourteen thousand leagues and renowned in heaven; and around it in the cardinal points and the intermediate quarters; are situated the stately cities of Indra and the other regents of the spheres. Mount Meru is in short the Olympus of India.

MERUMANDARA—A mountain to the south of Meru with a large Pípal tree on its summit.

MERU-SAVARNAS—The ninth, tenth, eleventh, and twelfth Manus, said to be the "mind-engendered sons of a daughter of Dakṣa by himself and the three gods Brahmā, Dharma, and Rudra, to whom he presented her on Mount Meru". The signification of the appellation Meru is obvious; that of Sāvarṇa or Sāvarṇi signifies that they were all of one caste (*varṇa*).

The Manus from the ninth to the twelfth Manwantaras; described in the Váyu as the mind-engendered sons of a daughter of Daksha, by himself and the three gods Brahmá, Dharma, and Rudra, to whom he presented her on Mount Meru; whence they are called Meru-sávarṇis. They are termed Sávarṇis from their being of one family.

MIMAMSA—A school of philosophy, (*see* DARŚANA)

MIMAMSA-VARTTIKA—A work on the Mīmāṁsā philosophy by Kumārila Bhaṭṭa.

MIMANSA DARSANA—"The founder of the Mímánsá School was *Jaimini*, of whose history very little is known. He is described as a short young man, of light complexion, wearing the dress of a mendicant, and living at Nílavata-Múla. He was born at Dwaitavana. His father, Śakatayana, was author of a Sanskrit dictionary, and his son, Krití, wrote certain verses in the Deví-Bhágavata.

There are about twenty-six works extant, illustrating the Mímánsá system, the chief of which are the Sútras of Jaimini; the Bháshya, by Shávara (and comments thereon by Bhatta, Váchaspati Mishra and Ránaka); the Satíka-Śástra-Dípiká, by Sóma-Nátha; the Dharma-Dípiká; the Mímánsá-Súra; and the Mímánsá Sangraha.

From the three last-named works chiefly we gather the following abridgment of the system of Jaimini. He taught that God is to be worshipped only through the incantations of the Vedas: that the Vedas were uncreated, and contained in themselves the proofs of their own divinity, the very words of which were unchangeable. His reasoning on the nature of material things was similar to those of Gautama, insisting that truth is capable of the clearest demonstration, without the possibility of mistake. Creation, preservation, and destruction, he represented as regulated by the merit and demerit of works; while he rejected the doctrine of the total destruction of the universe. He maintained that the images of the gods were not real representations of these beings, but only given to assist the mind of the worshipper; that the mere forms of worship had neither merit nor demerit in them; and that the promises of the Sástra to persons who presented so many offerings, so many prayers, &c., were only given as allurements to duty.

He directed the person, who sought final emancipation, to cherish a firm belief in the Vedas, as well as persuasion of the benefits of religion, and the desire of being engaged in the service of the gods; and then, by entering upon the duties of religion, and by degrees ascending through the states of a student, a secular, and a hermit, he would be sure to obtain final absorption in Brahmá.

Of the three divisions of the Veda, the first, called the *Karma Kánda*, or "practical part," relates to religious *ceremonies* (including moral and religious obligations.) This portion Jaimini has attempted to explain in his *Sûtras*, and in the *Púrva* Mímánsá (*i.e*; *former* "Mímánsá," which is commonly referred to when the term "*Mímánsá'* simply is used,) so called in distinction from the *Uttara* (or latter) Mímánsá ascribed to Vyása, which is the same as the Vedánta, and is founded on the *Juána Kánda* (or theological part) of the Vedas, treating of the *spiritual* worship of the Supreme Being or soul of the Universe.

Sound, says Jaimini, in opposition to the Nyaiyikas, who deny this, is *uncreated* and *eternal*, and is of two kinds, *viz.*, *simple* sound, or that which is produced by an impression on the air without requiring an agent, as the name of God; and *compound* (symbolized or audible) sound. Thus, the state of the sea, in a perfect calm, represents simple, uncreated sound; but the sea, in a state of agitation, illustrates sound as made known by an agent.

Symbols, of sounds, or letters, are eternal and uncreated; as is also the meaning of sounds. For instance, when a person has pronounced *ka*, however long he may continue to utter *ka*, *ka*, it is the same sound, sometimes present and sometimes absent; but sound is never new. Its manifestation alone is new by an impression made upon the air. Therefore *sound is God* (Brahmá), and the *world* is nothing but *name.*

The Veda has no human origin, but contains in itself the evidence of divine authorship, find comeing forth as the command of a monarch. It is incumbent on men to receive also, as divine, those works (of the sages) which are found to agree with the Veda, to contain clear definitions of duty, and to be free from contradictions.

What is religion ? That which secures happiness. And it is the duty of man to attend to the duties of religion, not only on this account, but also in obedience to the commands of God. The divine law is called *Vidhi.*

Should any one say, then I have nothing to do with other kinds of instruction, since this alone is divine. To that it is replied, that forms of praise, motives to duty, and religious observances, are auxiliaries to the divine law, and have, therefore, a relative sanctity and obligation.

There are five modes of ascertaining the commands of God, *viz.*: (1), the subject to be discussed is brought forward; (2), questions respecting it are stated; (3), objections are started; (4), replies to these objections are given; and (5), the question is decided. He who acts in religion according to the decision thus come to, does well; and so does he who rejects what will not bear this examination; but he who follows rules which have been hereby condemned, labours in vain.

Those actions from which future happiness will arise are called religious, or good, because productive of happiness; and those which tend to future misery are called evil, on account of their evil fruits. Hence, according to Jaimini, actions of themselves have in them neither good nor evil. Their nature can only be inferred from the declarations of the Veda respecting them, or from future consequences. The Hindús appear to have no just idea of *moral evil.*

Of all the works on the Civil and Canon Law, that of *Manu* is to be held in the greatest reverence, for Manu composed his work after a personal study of the Veda. Other sages have composed theirs from mere comments.

From the evidence of things which God has afforded, especially the evidence of the senses, mistakes cannot arise either respecting secular or religious affairs. When there may exist error in this evidence, it will diminish, but cannot destroy the nature of things.

If there be an imperfection in seed, the production may be imperfect, but its nature will not be changed. The seat of error and inattention is to be found in this reasoning faculty, and not in the senses; error arising from the confused union of present ideas (*anubhava*) with recollection.

Some affirm that ideas are received into the understanding separately, and never two at the same instant. This is incorrect; for it must be admitted, that while one idea is retained, there is an opening left in the understanding for the admission of another. Thus, in arithmetical calculations, "one added to one makes two."

The Veda has, in some parts, forbidden all injury to sentient beings, and in others has prescribed the offering of bloody sacrifices Jaimini explains this apparent contradiction by observing that some commands are general, and others particular: that the former must give way to the latter, as a second knot always loosens, in a degree, the first. So, when it is said that Saraswatí is altogether white, it is to be understood, not literally, but generally, for the hair and eyebrows of the goddess are not white. Therefore, in cases where general commands are given, they must be observed with those limitations which are found in the *Sástra.*

The promises of reward contained in the *Sástra* upon a minute attention to the different parts of duty, have been given rather as an incitement to its performance than with the intention of entire fulfillment. He who has begun a ceremony, but has, by circumstances, been unable to finish it, shall yet not be unrewarded.

The benefits resulting from the due performance of civil and social duties are confined to this life. Those connected with the performance of religious duties are to be enjoyed in a future state, while some meritorious actions, or virtues, reap their reward both in the present and the future life.

Works give birth to invisible consequences—either propitious or otherwise—according to their nature; and, besides works, there is no other sovereign or judge. These consequences, ever accompanying the individual, as the shadow the body, appear in the next birth, in accordance with the time and manner in which those actions were performed in the preceding birth. "Works rule, and men by them are led or driven, as the ox with a hook in its nose."

The progress of all actions, whether they originate in the commands of the Śástras, or in the customs of a country, are as follows:—First, the act is considered and resolved on in the mind; then it is pursued by means of words; and, lastly, it is accomplished by executing the different constituent parts of the action. Hence it follows that religion and irreligion refer to thoughts, words, and actions. Some actions, however, are purely those of the mind, or of the voice, or of the body. The virtue or vice of all actions depends on the state of the heart.

The doctrine that, at a certain period, the whole universe will be destroyed at once, is incorrect. The world had no beginning, and will have no end. As long as there are works, there must be birth, as well as a world like the present, to form a theatre on which they may be performed, and their consequences either enjoyed or endured.

One of the sages of the Mímámsá school thus expresses himself:—'God is simple sound. To assist the pious in their forms of meditation (or incantations). He is represented as light; but the power of liberation lies in the sound 'God—God.' When the repeater is perfect, the incantation, or name repeated, appears to him in the form of simple light or glory.

The objects of worship, which are within the cognizance of the senses, are to be received; for without *faith* religious actions are destitute of fruit. Therefore, let no one treat an incantation as a mere form of alphabetic signs, nor an image as composed of the inanimate material, lest he should be guilty of a serious crime.'—Small, *H. S. L.*

MINARATHA—A prince, the son of Anenas, a king of Mithila, of the family of Janaka.

MIÑJIKA (mas.) and **MIÑJIKĀ** (fem.)—Two beings that, according to the *Mahābhārata*, sprang from the seed of Rudra which was spilt upon a mountain. They are to be worshipped by those who desire the welfare of children.

MIRITTIKAVATI—A city in Malwa, near the Parnáśá river, whose sovereigns were the Bhojas, descendants of Satwata.

MISRAKESI—One of the Apsaras, a Laukíka nymph.

MITAKSARA—A commentary by Vijñāneśvara on the Smṛti or textbook of Yēuñavalkya. The authority of this book is admitted all over India, with the exception of Bengal proper. The portion on inheritance has been translated by Colebrooke, and into French by Orianne. The text has been printed in India.

MITHI—A prince, the son of Nimi, the legend of whose birth is thus related in the Vishṇu Purána. As Nimi left no successor, the Munis, apprehensive of the consequences of the earth being without a ruler, agitated the embalmed body of Nimi, and produced from it a prince who was called Janaka, from being born without a progenitor. In consequence of being produced by agitation. (Mathana) he was further termed Mithi. The Rámáyana places a prince named Mithi between Nimi and Janaka, whence comes the name Mithila.

MITHILA—A city, the capital of Videha or North Bihār, which corresponds to the modem Tirhut and Puraniya, between the Gaṇḍakī and Kośi rivers. It has given its name to one of the five northern nations of brāhmaṇas (*see* Brāhmaṇa), and to a school of law. It was the country of King Janaka, and the name of his capital, Janakapura, still survives in "Janakpoor", on the northern frontier. The modern Tirhoot.

MITRA—(1) Probably connected with the Persian Mithra. A form of the sun. In the Vedas he is generally associated with Varuṇa, he being the ruler of the day and Varuṇa the ruler of the night. They together uphold and rule the earth and sky, guard the world, encourage religion, and chastise sin. He is one of the Ādityas or sons of Āditi. **(2)** A sage, one of the seven sons of Vasishtha. *V.P. Mitra* is the god of the day. Mitra is said to represent the sun by day, and Varnna the setting luminary. "Mitra re-appears in the Zendavesta as the well-known Mithra, who is the angel presiding over and directing the course of the sun."—*Quarterly Review*, July 1870.

MITRASAHA—A prince, the son of Sudása. Having gone into the woods to hunt, he fell in with two tigers by which the forest had been cleared of the deer. The prince slew one of these tigers with an arrow. At the moment of expiring the form of the animal was changed, and it became that of a fiend of a fearful figure and hideous aspect. Its companion, threatening the prince with its vengeance, disappeared. After some interval Saudása celebrated a sacrifice which was conducted by Vasishtha. At the close of the rite Vasishtha went out; when the Rákshasa, the fellow of the one that had been killed in the figure of a tiger, assumed the semblance of Vasishtha, and came and said to the king "now that the sacrifice is ended, you must give me flesh to eat; let it be cooked and I will presently return. Having said this he withdrew, and transforming himself into the shape of the cook, dressed some human flesh which he brought to the king, who, receiving it on a plate of gold, awaited the re-appearance of Vasishtha; as soon as the Muni returned the king offered to him the dish. Vasishtha knowing it to be human flesh was surprised at such an insult, and in his anger denounced a curse upon the Rája, transforming him into a cannibal. "It was yourself replied the Rája to the indignant sage, who commanded this food to be prepared." Vasishtha, having recourse to meditation then detected the whole truth: but though the curse was partially withdrawn, the Rája became a cannibal every sixth watch of the day for twelve years, and in that state wandered through the forests and devoured multitudes of men. On one occasion he met with a brahman and his wife: seizing the husband, and regardless of the wife's reiterated supplications, he ate the brahman as a tiger devours a deer. He returned to his wife Madayanti at the expiration of the period of his curse, but suffered from the imprecation of the brahman's wife. *V.P.*

A king called also Kalmāṣapāda (*q.v.*).

MITṚAVRINDA—One of the seven beautiful wives of Krishṇa.

MITRAYA—**(1)** A scholar of Súta's and teacher of the Puránas and legendary lore: he was also a composer of one of the Sanhitas afterwards collected into the Vishṇu Purána; **(2)** The son of Divodáṣa, from whom the Maítreya brahmans were descended.

MLECCHAS—Foreigners, barbarians, people not of Āryan race. Outcastes. The Vishṇu Purána states that Sagara degraded various Kshatriya races, by being deprived of established usage and the study of the Vedas; and thus separated from religious rites, and abandoned by the brahmans, these different tribes became Mlechchas.

MOHA—'Dulness' or 'Stupefaction,' a property of sensible objects; a kind of ignorance; or illusion produced by the notion of property or possession, and consequent attachment to objects, as children and the like, as being one's own. Moha also occurs in the Bhágavata and Matsya Purána amongst a series of Brahma's progeny, or virtues and vices; Moha is there translated by Wilson to mean Infatuation.

MOHA-MUDGARA—'Hammers for ignorance.' A poem in explanation of the Vedānta philosophy. It has been printed and translated by Nēve.

MOHINI—Vishṇu in a female form. The product of Śiva's union with Móhini was Ayenar, the only male among the Gráma-dévatas (*q.v.*).

MOKSHA—Absorption into the Deity. The Hindu idea of supreme blessedness. It is only those who attain to a fall knowledge of the nature of the deity, the soul, the intellect, &c., derived from meditation, the teaching of the guru, experience, penance, &c.. or the exalted ascetic, who, by austerities is said to have annihilated his passions, and freed his soul from earthly desire, that is considered ripe for this final emancipation or Móksha.

MONOTHEISM—In the Vishṇu Purána it is said, 'the only one God, Janárddana takes the designation of Brahmá, Vishṇu, and Śiva, accordingly as he creates, preserves or destroys. This, says Professor Wilson, is the invariable doctrine of the Puránas, diversified only according to the individual divinity to which they ascribe identity with Paramátmá or Parameswara. In the Vishṇu Purána this is Vishṇu; in the Saiva Puránas, as in the Linga, it is Śiva; in the Brahmá-vaivartta it is Krishṇa. The identification of one of the hypotheses with the common source, the triad, was an incongruity not unknown to the other theogonies; for Cneph amongst the Egyptians, appears on the one hand to have been identified with the Supreme Being, the indivisible unity, whilst on the other he is confounded with both Eureph and Ptha, the second and third persons of the triad of hypostases. *Cudworth*, Vol. I, p. 4-18.

MOON—The Vishṇu, Váyu, and Pádma Puránas all relate in detail the legend of the churning of the ocean, and state that the cool-rayed moon was one of the products of the operation; it was seized by Mahádeva. The Vishṇu Purána says that the chariot of the moon has three wheels, and is drawn by ten horses, of the whiteness of the jasmine, five in the right half of the yoke and five in the left. The horses drag the car for a whole Kalpa. During the dark half of the month nectar and ambrosia are accumulated in the moon, and these are drunk by thirty-six thousand divinities during the light fortnight; the Pitris are nourished by it in the dark fortnight; vegetables with the cool nectary aqueous atoms it sheds on them; and through their development it sustains men, animals and insects; at the same time gratifying them with its radiance. *V.P.*, p. 239. The orb of the Moon, according to the Linga Purána is only congealed water.

MṚCCHAKATI—'The toy-cart.' A drama in ten acts

by King Śūdraka, supposed to be the oldest Sanskṛt drama extant, and to have been written in the first or second century AD The country over which Śūdraka reigned is not known. This play, says Wilson, its translator, "is a curious and interesting picture of national manners...free from all exterior influence or adulteration. It is a portrait purely Indian. It represents a state of society sufficiently advanced in civilization to be luxurious and corrupt, and is certainly very far from offering a flattering similitude, although not without some attractive features." Williams observes, "The dexterity with which the plot is arranged, the ingenuity with which the incidents are connected, the skill with which the characters are delineated and contrasted, the boldness and felicity of the diction, are scarcely unworthy of our own great dramatists." There are translations in French and several editions of the text.

MṚGANKA-LEKHA—A play in four acts, written by Viśvanātha at Benares. The piece takes its name from the heroine, a princess of Kāmarūpa. It is a comparatively modem work.

MṚIDA—A prince, the son of Nripanjaya, of the race of Puru.

MṚIGASIRAS—A lunar mansion, in Gajavithi of the northern Avashtána.

MṚIGAVITHI—A division of the lunar mansions, in the southern Avashtána.

MṚIGAVYADHA—One of the eleven Rudras, according to the enumeration in the Matsya Purána.

MṚIKANDA—The son of Vidhátri and Niryati, descendants of the daughters of Daksha who were married to the Rishis.

MṚITYA—**(1)** 'Death,' one of the progeny of Brahmá; he is also represented in the same work, the Vishṇu Purána, as the son of Bhaya and Maya; and his children are thus given Vyadḥi (disease), Jará (decay), Soka (sorrow), Trishna (greediness), and Krodha (wrath); **(2)** The name of one of the eleven Rudras, in the Váyu list; **(3)** A Vyasa in the sixth Dwápara age.

MUCHUKUNDA—One of the sons of Mándhátri, called the 'king of men,' who in a battle between the gods and demons, had contributed to the defeat of the latter; and being overcome with sleep he solicited of the gods as a boon, that he should enjoy a long repose. 'Sleep long and soundly, said the gods, and whoever disturbs you shall be instantly burnt to ashes by fire emanating from your body.' The black king, Kályavana, met with this fate, by a stratagem of Krishṇa; and Muchukunda having fallen down and worshipped Krishṇa as the undecaying, illimitable and imperishable being, departed to Gandhamádana to perform penance, and obtain emancipation from all existence. Another account states that "Muchukunda carried on war against the Buddhists till he was too weary to fight any longer; whereupon he sought the grateful seclusion of the Guttikonda cave. In this peaceful and salubrious spot he fell asleep; it was a sleep of the greatest profundity, and lasted for some centuries. In an evil moment for the Buddhists they enetered the cave in pursuit of Krishṇa, and disturbed the placid slumbers of Muchukunda. After a nap of some hundreds of years, he was not a man to be trifled with; so he rose up in the exuberance of his renovated energies and extirpated the obnoxious Buddhists." *A. & M. I.*

MUDA—'Pleasure,' a son of dharma by one of the daughters of Daksha, Santósha (Joy).

MUDGALA—**(1)** A Vedic *ṛṣi* from whom the Maudgalya brāhmaṇas sprang. There were several other brāhmaṇas named Mudgala. A sage of this name is recorded in the *Mahābhārata* to have "lived a life of poverty, piety, and self-restraint, offering hospitality to thousands of brahmanas, according to his humble means, with the grain which he gleaned like a pigeon, and which (like the widow of Zarephath's oil) never underwent diminution, or rather increased again, when it was required". The choleric sage Durvāsas went to test the patience of Mudgala, and six times devoured all the food which his host possessed without ruffling his temper. Durvāsas in his admiration declared that Mudgala would go bodily to heaven, and the messenger of the gods arrived with his heavenly car. The sage, before accepting the invitation, desired to be informed of the joys and ills of heaven. After hearing a full explanation, he found that the enjoyments of heaven must come to a close, so he declared that he "had no desire for heaven, and would seek only that eternal abode where there is no sorrow, nor distress, nor change". He dismissed the messenger of the gods, and began to practice ascetic virtues, becoming indifferent to praise and blame, regarding clods, gold, stones, and gold as alike. Pure knowledge led to fixed contemplation; and that again imparted strength and complete comprehension, whereby he obtained supreme eternal perfection in the nature of quietude (*nirvāṇa*). **(2)** A teacher of the Rig Veda; **(3)** One of the five sons of Hariyaswa, king of Panchála.

MUDITA—One of the five kinds of BHAVANA or meditation, in which the Buddhist priests are required to engage. The *mudita* is the meditation of joy, but it is not the joy arising from earthly possessions. It feels indifferent to individuals, and refers to all sentient beings. In the exercise of this mode of meditation, the priest must express the wish, "May the good fortune of the prosperous never pass away; may each one receive his own appointed reward."

MUDRA-RAKSASA—'The signet of the minister.' A drama by Viśākhadatta. This play has a historical interest, for Candragupta, the Sandracottus of Greek writers, is a leading character in it. The date of its production is apparently the eleventh or twelfth century A.D. It is one of the dramas translated by Wilson, who says, "The author was not a poet of the sphere of Bhavabhūti or Kālidāsa. His imagination rises not to their level, and there is scarcely a brilliant or beautiful thought in the play. As some equivalent for the want of imagination, he has a vigorous perception of character and a manly strain of sentiment, that are inferior only to elevated conception and delicate feeling. He is the Massinger of the Hindus. The language of the original partakes of the general character of the play; it is rarely beautiful or delicate, but always vigorous, and occasionally splendid."

MUGDHA-BODHA A standard Grammar by Vopadeva, written towards the end of the thirteenth century. It has been edited by Böhtlingk, and there are several Indian editions.

MUHURTTA—(1) A measure of time, thirty Kalás, according to the Vishṇu Purána. Other Puránas say that a Muhurtta is twelve kshanas, and that one kshana contains thirty kalás. The Bhágavata states that two Narikas make one Muhurtta; **(2)** The name of a daughter of Daksha.

MUKA—A *dānava*, son of Upasunda. He assumed the form of a wild boar in order to kill Arjuna, but was himself killed by Śiva in his form of the Kirāta or mountaineer.

MUKHAGNI—'Fiery-faced.' Spirits or goblins with faces of fire, perhaps meteors.

MUKHYAS—A class of deities to come in the ensuing or eighth Manwantara.

MULAKA—The son of Aṣmaka. The Vishṇu Purána states that when the warrior tribe was extirpated upon earth, he was surrounded and concealed by a number of females; whence he was denominated Nári-kavacha (having women for armour.) Múlaka, or 'the root' refers also to his being the stem whence the Kshatriya races again proceeded. *V.P.* and note, p. 383.

MULA—The nineteenth lunar mansion, in Ajavíthi, of the Southern Avashthána.

MUMMIES—The Vishṇu Purána states that the corpse of Nimi was preserved from decay by being embalmed with fragrant oils and resins, and it remained entire as if it were immortal. This, says Professor Wilson, shows that the Hindus were not unacquainted with the Egyptian art of embalming dead bodies, though such a practice would be thought impure in the present day.

MUNDA—'Bald'. An appellation of Ketu. A demon servant of the demon ruler Niṣumbha, who was killed by Umá (Durga). The goddess ultimately slew his master also. The Kálipúja festival in Bengal is held annually in commemoration of the victory of Umá over Cháṇḍa and Muṇḍa.

MUNDAKA—Name of an Upaniṣad (*q.v.*) translated by Dr. Roer in the *Bibliotheca Indica* and by Rammohun Roy. There are several editions of the text.

MUNDAS—A dynasty of kings, consisting of thirteen, who are said in the Vishṇu Purána to be sovereigns of the earth for upwards of two hundred years; Wilford regards them as Huns, the Morunda of Ptolemy. Notes to Vishṇu Purána.

MUNI—(1) "A holy sage, a pious and learned person, endowed with more or less of a divine nature, or having attained to it by rigid abstraction and mortification. The title is applied to the rsis, and to a great number of persons distinguished for their writings considered as inspired, as Pāṇini, Vyāsa." Their superhuman powers over gods and men have been often displayed in blessings, but more frequently in curses. **(2)** The name of a daughter of Daksha who was married to Kaṣyapa.

MUNJAKESA—A teacher of the Atharva Veda, and founder of a school. Sometimes Munjakeṣa is regarded as another name for Babhra.

MURA, MURU—A great demon who had seven thousand sons. He was an ally of the demon Naraka, who ruled over Prāgjyotiṣa, and assisted him in the defense of that city against Kṛṣṇa. He placed in the environs of the city "nooses the edges of which were as sharp as razors", but Kṛṣṇa cut them to pieces with his discus, slew Muni, "and burnt his seven thousand sons like moths with the flame of the edge of his discus".

MURARI—'The foe of Mura'. An appellation of Kṛṣṇa.

MURARIMISRA—Author of the drama *Murāri Nāṭaka* or *Anargha Rāghava* (*q.v.*).

MURDHABHISHIKTA—An anointed Rájah. Hindu rájahs were formerly consecrated by having water from a sacred stream mixed with honey, ghee, and spirituous liquor, as well as two sorts of grass and the spirits of corn, poured on their heads while seated on a throne prepared for the purpose. The term applies to the *Kshatriya* as the caste from which kings are taken.

MURTTI—'Form' a daughter of Daksha, married to Dharma.

MURUNDAS—See Mundas.

MUSALA—**(1)** The pestle-shaped club carried by Balarāma. It was named Saunanda. **(2)** A club, born of Sambu for the destruction of the Yadavas. Ugrasena had the club, which was of iron, ground to dust, and thrown into the sea; but the particles of dust there became rushes (eraká). There was one part of the iron club which was like the blade of a lance, and which the Andhakas could not break; this, when thrown into the sea, was swallowed by a fish; the fish was caught, the iron spike was extracted from its belly, and was taken by a hunter named Jará, by whom Krishṇa was subsequently killed.

MUSALADHABA, MŪSALĀYUDHA, MŪSALIN—'Armed with a pestle.' An appellation of Balarāma.

MUSHTIKA—A demon celebrated as a great wrestler. At the games of Mathura, when Kansa hoped to destroy Krishṇa, Balabhadra wrestled with Mushtika and at last killed him.

N

NABASWATI—The wife of Antarddhána, a descendant of Pritha.

NABHA—A powerful Danava, the son of Viprachitti by Sinhika, the sister of Hiraṇyakasipu.

NABHAGA—**(1)** The son of the preceding; he became a Vaisya through carrying off and marrying the daughter of a Vaisya; it appears from this that a race of Vaisya princes was recognised by early traditions; **(2)** A son of Sruta, a descendant of Sagara; **(3)** A son of Yayáti.

NABHAGA-NEDISHTA—One of the sons of the Manu Vaivaswata; his name means 'no share,' and in the Aitareya Brahmana he is said to have been excluded from all share of his inheritance on the plea of his being wholly devoted to a religious life. The Bhágavata says that having protracted his period of study beyond the usual age, his brothers appropriated his share of the patrimony. On his applying for his portion they consigned their father to him, by whose advice he assisted the descendants of Angiras in a sacrifice, and they presented him with all the wealth that was left at its termination. Rudra claimed it as his; and Nabhaga acquiescing, the god confirmed the gift, by which he became possessed of an equivalent for the loss of territory.

NABHAS, NABHASYA—**(1)** A name of the months, Srávana and Bhádra, corresponding to July and August, the names occur in the Vedas and belong to a system now obsolete; **(2)** The son of Nala, a descendant of Kusa.

NABHI—One of the nine sons of Agnídhra, to whom the country of Hímahwa was assigned.

NACHIKETAS—A philosopher, the son of Gautama, mentioned in the Katha Upanishad, of whom Dr. Roer says, "the enthusiasm and intimate conviction which Nachiketas shows about the infinite superiority of what is good to the pleasures of the world, and the firmness which he maintains amidst all the allurements which are placed before him, bears some resemblance to the energy of mind with which Plato, in the first and second books of his 'Republic,' shows that justice has an incomparable worth, and ought to be preserved under any circumstances."* In an interview with Yama, who promised Nachiketas any boon, the latter requested to be instructed in the nature of the soul, Yama objected saysing, even gods have doubted and disputed on this subject, for it is not easy to understand it. But Nachiketas could not be persuaded to think any other boon worth asking for.†

The story of Naciketas is told in the *Taittirīya Brāmaṇa* and *Kaṭha Upaniṣad.* Vājaśravasa or Aruni, the father of Naciketas, desirous of attaining heaven, performed great sacrifices, and was profuse in his gifts to the priests. The son told him that he had not given all, for that he, his son, was left, and said, "To whom shall I be given?" On repeating the question, the father angrily replied, "To death". So the son departed to the abodes of death, and, after staying there three nights, Yama was constrained to offer him a boon. He prayed to see his father again and he reconciled. This boon was granted and another offered. All kinds of blessings were proposed, but the youth refused to be contented with anything but a true knowledge of the soul. Yama then proceeded to instruct him. The story has been done into verse by Muir (*Texts*, vol. V, p. 329). (* *Bibliotheca Indica*, Vol. xv, p. 91.) († *A. and M. I*, p. 136.)

NADICHAKRA—(Náḍichakra), the heart, as the centre of the circle of the different organs and tubular vessels, along which the vital air or spirit is conveyed, and this spirit being one with Śiva (*sarvam Sivamáyam*) his form or nature (rúpa) may be said to be seated in the heart. The six organs are the ear, the navel, the heart, the throat, the palate, and the eyebrow. The *Nádis*, or tubes, are one hundred and one in number, but ten are principal, *Ila*, *Pingala*, *Sushumna*, *Gandhári*, *Hastijihwa*, *Púshá*, *Aruná*, *Alambushá*, *Guha*, *Sankini:* these all unite in the heart. These notions belong to the *Yoga*. According to other doctrines there are sixteen principal *Nádis*. To those who have thus discovered the actual presence of divine spirit in themselves, the deity Śiva gives the eight Siddhis, *q.v.*

NAGA—**(1)** A snake, especially the cobra-capella. A mythical semi-divine being, having a human face with the tail of a serpent, and the expanded neck of the cobra. The race of Nāgas is said to be a thousand in number, and to have sprung from Kadru, the wife of Kaśyapa, for the purpose of peopling Pātāla, or the regions below the earth, where they reign in great splendour. From the name of their mother they are called Kādraveyas. Their mother is sometimes called Surasā. This dominion was taken from them by the *gandharvas*, but they recovered it through their sister, the Narmadā river, who induced Viṣṇu to send Pratardana to their assistance. Their females were handsome, and some of them intermarried with men, as Ulupī with Arjuna.

The Nāgas, or a people bearingthe same name, are historical, and have left many traces behind them. There were mountains so-called, and Nāgadvīpa was one of the seven divisions of Bhāratavarṣa. Kings of this race reigned at Mathurā, Padmāvatī, &c., and the name survives in the modem Nāgpur. There are various speculations as to who and what they were, but it seems clear they were a race distinct from the Hindus. The mythological accounts are probably based upon the historical, but they have been mixed up together and confused. The favourite theory is that they were a Scythic race, and probably obtained their name from worshipping serpents or holding them in awe and reverence. **(2)** A mountainous ridge in the north of Meru; **(3)** A serpent, one of the progeny of Kadru; **(4)** Originally the Cobracapella, or Colubernaga. **(5)** "The *Saiva Sannyâsis* who go naked are distinguished by this term. They smear their bodies with ashes, allow their hair, beards, and whiskers to grow, and wear the projecting braid of hair, called the *Játá*; like the *Vairáji Nágas*, they carry arms, and wander about in troops, soliciting alms, or levying contributions. The *Saiva Nágas* are chiefly the refuse of the *Dandi* and *Atít* orders, or men who have no inclination for a life of study or business: when weary of the vagrant and violent habits of the *Nága*, they re-enter the better disposed classes, which they had first quitted. The *Saiva Nágas* are very numerous in many parts of India."—*Wilson*. **(6)** The designation of nine kings who reigned in Padmávati.

NAGADWIPA—A division of Bhárata Varsha.

NAGA-LOKA—Pātāla, the residence of the Nāgas.

NAGA-NANDANA—A Buddhist drama in five acts by Śrī Harṣa Deva. It has been translated by Boyd. The text has been printed.

NAGAPASA—(Nágapása), the name of the arrow presented by Brahma to Indrájit, and with which the latter cast Ráma and Lakshmana senseless on the ground at the siege of Lanka.

NAGARA—A city. There are seven sacred cities which confer eternal happiness—(1) Ayodhyā, (2) Mathurā, (3) Māyā (Gayā), (4) Kāśī (Benares), (5) Kāñcī (Conjeveram), (6) Avantī or Avantikā (Ujjayinī), (7) Dvārakā or Dvārāvatī.

NAGAVITHI—**(1)** A division of the lunar mansions in the Northern Avashthána; **(2)** The milky way, daughter of Yámí (night).

NAGNA—A Jain mendicant; a naked ascetic.

NAGNAJITI—One of the wives of Krishṇa, termed in the Vishṇu Purána the virtuous Nagnajití.

NAGNAS—Apostates. The Rig, Yajur, and Sáma Vedas, constitute the triple covering of the several castes, and the sinner who throws this off is said to be naked or apostate. The three Vedas are the raiment of all orders of men, and when that is discarded they are left bare. (*V.P.*) Wilson in his notes, adds, ascetics whether of the Buddha or Digambara order of Jains, are literally Nagnas, "going naked." The qualified application of it, however, was rendered necessary by the same practice being familiar to ascetics of the orthodox faith. To go naked was not necessarily the sign of a heretic, and therefore his nudity was undertood to be rejecting the raiment of holy writ. Thus the Váyu Purána extends the word to all ascetics, including naked brahmans, who practice austerities fruitlessly, that is heretically or hypocritically.

NAHUSA—(1) Son of Āyus the eldest son of Purūravas, and father of Yayāti. This king is mentioned by Manu as having come into conflict with the brāhmaṇas, and his story is repeated several times with variations in different parts of the *Mahābhārata* as well as in the Purāṇas, the aim and object of it evidently being to exhibit the retribution awaiting any man who derogates from the power of brahmanas and the respect due to them. "By sacrifices, austere fervour, sacred study, self-restraint, and valour, Nahuṣa acquired the undisturbed sovereignty of the three worlds ... Through want of virtuous humility the great king Nahuṣa was utterly ruined."—*Manu.*

One version of the story says that he aspired to the possession of Indrāṇī, wife of Indra, when that god had concealed himself for having killed a brāhmaṇa. A thousand great *ṛṣis* bore the car of Nahuṣa through the air, and on one occasion he touched with his foot the great Agastya, who was carrying him. The sage in his anger cried out, "Fall, thou serpent", and Nahuṣa fell from his glorious car and became a serpent. Agastya, at the supplication of Nahuṣa, put a limit to the curse; and according to one version, the doomed man was released from it by the instrumentality of Yudhiṣṭhira, when he threw off "his huge reptile form, became clothed in a celestial body, and ascended to heaven". **(2)** The son of Ambarísha; **(3)** The eldest of the five sons of Áyus, who having attained the rank of Indra, compelled the Rishis to bear his litter, and was cursed by them to fall from his state and re-appear upon earth as a serpent. From this form he was set free by philosophical discussions with Yudhishtira, and received final liberation; **(4)** The name of one of the progeny of Kadru, a powerful many-headed serpent.

NAIGAMA—A teacher of the Rig Veda, a pupil of Sákapúrṇi.

NAIGAMEYA—One of the sons of Kumára.

NAIKAPRISHTAS—An aboriginal tribe mentioned in the Puránas, so termed probably in derision; it means having more than one back.

NAIKASEYAS—Carnivorous imps descended from Nikaṣā, mother of Rāvaṇa. They are called also Nikaṣātmajas.

NAIMISA, NAIMIṢĀRAṆYA—A forest (*araṇya*) near the Gomatī (Gūmtī) river, in which the *Mahābhārata* was rehearsed by Sauti to the assembled *ṛṣis*.

NAIRṚTA—Belonging to the south-west quarter; the regent of that quarter. An imp, goblin, or *rākṣasa.*

NAISADHA-CARITA, NAIṢADHĪYA—A poem on the life on Nala, king of Niṣadha, by Śrī Harṣa, a great sceptical philosopher who lived in the eleventh or twelfth century A.D. It is one of the six *mahākāvyas.* There are several printed editions.

NAISHADHA—A tract of country near the Vindhya mountains.

NAKHIS—Religious mendicants who practice various austerities, never cut their finger nails, and wear the *Saiva* marks.

NAKSATBAS—Mansions of the moon, lunar asterisms. At first they were twenty-seven in number, but they were increased to twenty-eight. They are said to be daughters of Dakṣa who were married to the moon. (*see* DAKṢA)

NAKSHATRA-MALA—(Nakshatra-Málá), a garland of twenty-seven pearls, the number of the Nakshatras or lunar mansions. This "starry garland" is worn on the brow of a princess at the time of the marriage ceremony. Garlands made part of the bridal as well as sacrificial ornaments among the Greeks.

NAKSHATRAS—The Nakshatras are regarded by Hindu astrologers as heavenly bodies which have great influence on mankind, not only at the time of their birth, but during the whole course of their life on earth. They are also said to constitute the twelve signs of the zodiac, two and-a-quarter Nakshatras forming one sign. Again, they are spoken of as quasi-deities, whose favour needs to be propitiated, and whose frown is fatal to health and life. There is no question that the Nakshatras are a source of infinite terror to Hindus of all castes, and of vast emolument to the Brahmans. They are consulted at births and marriages, and in all times of difficulty, of sickness, and of anxiety. Journeys are commenced under their direction; and according to their decision, days and events become lucky or unlacky. The consultation of the Nakshatras is a part of the Hindu's life, and is as important in his eyes as the institution of caste or the worship of the gods.

The Nakshatras are twenty-seven in number. In the following list it will be observed that the word '*shánti*' is affixed to several names. It means 'rest' or 'quiet' and shows that the ill-natured deity, to whom it refers, requires a ceremony of pacification to be performed in the event of a child being born at the time of her appearance in the heavens, in order that calamities and dangers which she threatens to send upon the child, or its parents, or other relatives, or on its friends, or on its caste, may be averted. Wherever the word '*shánti*' is added, the particular danger, and the object of it, are likewise stated.

The Twenty-seven Nakshatras.

1. Ashwani-Shánti. Danger is threatened to the parents of the child.
2. Bharaní.
3. Kritiká.
4. Rohiní.
5. Mṛigashirá.
6. Argrá.
7. Punarvasú.
8. Puahya-Shánti. Danger is threatened to parents and other relatives.
9. Ashlesá or Ashya-lekhá-Shánti. Out of sixty hours during which she is dominant, only the last four are fraught with danger. If a child be born in the last of these, evil may happen to its father; if in the third, to its mother; if in the second, to itself; and if in the first, to its parents, to its brother, to its caste, and to wealth, if it has any.
10. Maghá-Shánti. Danger is threatened to parents and other relatives.
11. Purváphálguni.
12. Uttaraphálguni.
13. Hasta.
14. Chitrá-Shánti. Danger is threatened to parents, and to the men of the same *gotra* or branch of families.
15. Swáti.
16. Visháká-Shánti. Danger is threatened to the younger child of the father's brother, if a daughter; and if a son, the danger will pass to the younger sister of his wife.
17. Anurádhá.
18. Jeishthá-Shánti. The sixty hours of its dominance are dangerous, as follows: the first six, to the maternal grand-mother of the child; the second six, to its mother's father; the third six, to its mother's brother; the fourth six, to its mother; the fifth six, to the child itself; the sixth six, to all the members of the same *gotra*; the seventh six, to its own family; the eighth six, to its brother; the ninth six, to its father-in-law; the tenth six. to all its relatives.
19. Múl-Shánti. If a child is born during the first fifty-six hours of her dominance, danger impends over the entire family; if in the fifty-seventh, danger threatens the father only; if in the fifty-eighth, the mother only; if in the fifty-ninth, itself. The last hour, or the sixtieth, is devoid of danger, but nevertheless, requires *Shánti.*
20. Purváshárá.
21. Uttaráshárá.
22. Sravan.
23. Dhanishta-Shánti. Danger is threatened both to its father and itself.
24. Shatatáraka.
25. Purvábhádrápadá.
26. Uttarábhádrápadá.
27. Revatí-Shánti. Danger is threatened both to its parents and itself.

NAKSHATRA-YOGINIS—The chief stars of the lunar mansions, or asterisms in the moon's path: these are fabled to have been the twenty-seven daughters of Daksha, who became the virtuous wives of the moon.

There are twenty-seven divisions of the lunar orbit; each marking the motion of the moon in one lunar day. Such is their simple references, astronomically; but the Hindu astrologers make them of great practical consequence, from their assumed good or evil influence. They reckon from the first degree of Aries, in the old Astronomy.

1.	Asvini, the ram's head	good.
2.	Bharini	bad.
3.	Critica, Pleiades	very bad.
4.	Rohini, hyades	good.
5.	Mrigasiras, a triple star	good.
6.	Ardra, one star	bad.
7.	Punar vasu, four stars.	good.
8.	Pushya, nebula in Cancer	good.
9.	Aslesha, five stars	bad.
10.	Magha, cor leonis	good.
11.	Purvap'halguni, two stars	medium.
12.	Uttara P'halguni, two stars	medium.

13. Hasta, five stars good.
14. Chitra, one star bad.
15. Swati, one star good.
16. Visáka, four stars bad.
17. Anuradha, four stars good.
18. Jyeshṭa, three stars bad.
19. Mula, eleven stars, cor scorpionis very bad.
20. Purvashadha, four stars medium.
21. Uttara shadha, three stars good.
22. Sravana, three stars good.
23. Dhanishta, four stars bad.
24. Satabhisha, a hundred stars bad.
25. Purva bhadrapada, two stars medium.
26. Uttara bhadrapada, two stars medium.
27. Revati, thirty-two stars good.

These influences refer principally to marriages. The Nakshatras are classified as *deva*, divine; *manushya*, human; *rakshasa*, savage; if the two parties to be married are born in the same class, it is well: if one asterism be divine, the other human, it may pass; but divine and savage is a cross that may not be permitted.

An intercalary *abhijit*, one-fourth of a Nakshatra, is sometimes introduced between 21 and 22 for astrological purposes, or to make up a complete cycle of the moon's motion.—*Taylor.*

NAKTA—A prince, the son of Prithu, who reigned over one of the divisions of Bharatavarsha in the first or Swáyambhuva Manwantara.

NAKULA—The fourth of the Pāṇḍu princes. He was the twin son of Mādrī, the second wife of Pāṇḍu, but mythologically he was son of the Aśvins, or more specifically of the Aśvin Nāsatya. He was taught the art of training and managing horses by Droṇa, and when he entered the service of the king of Virāṭa he was master of the horse. He had a son named Niramitra by his wife Kareṇumatī, a princess of Cedi. (*see* MAHĀBHĀRATA)

NALA—(1) King of Niṣadha and husband of Damayantī. The story of Nala and Damayantī is one of the episodes of the *Mahābhārata*, and is well-known from having been translated into Latin by Bopp and into English verse by Dean Milman. Damayantī was the only daughter of Bhīma, king of Vidarbha (Birar), and was very lovely and accomplished. Nala was brave and handsome, virtuous, and learned in the Vedas, skilled in arms and in the management of horses, but addicted to the vice of gambling. They loved each other upon the mere fame of their respective virtues and beauty, and Damayantī pined for the presence of her unknown lover. Bhīma determined that his daughter should hold a *svayaṁvara*. Rājās flocked to it in crowds, and among them Nala. Four gods, Indra, Agni, Varuṇa, and Yama, also attended. Nala met them on the way, and reverently promised to do their will. They bade him enter the palace and inform Damayantī that they would present themselves among the candidates, and that she must choose one of them. Nala reluctantly performed his task, but his presence perfected his conquest, and the maiden announced her resolve to pay due homage to the gods, but to choose him for her lord. Each of the four gods assumed the form of Nala, but the lover's eye distinguished the real one, and she made her choice. They married and lived for sometime in great happiness, a son and a daughter, named Indrasena and Indrasenā, being born to them. Kali, a personification of the *kali* or iron age, arrived too late for the *svayaṁvara*. He resolved to be revenged, and he employed his peculiar powers to ruin Nala through his love of gambling. At. his instigation, Puṣkara, Nala's younger brother, proposed a game of dice. Kali charmed the dice, and Nala went on losing; but he was infatuated; the entreaties of friends and ministers, wife and children,were of no avail; he went on till he had lost his all, even to his clothes. His rival Puṣkara became king, and proclaimed that no one was to give food or shelter to Nala, so the ruined monarch wandered forth into the forest with his wife, and suffered great privations. Some birds flew away with his only garment. He resolved to abandon his wife in the hope that she would return to her father's court, so he divided her sole remaining garment while she slept and left her. Thus left alone, Damayantī wandered about in great distress. She did not go home, but she at length found service and protection with the princess of Cedi. Nala fell in with the king of serpents, who was under a curse from which Nala was to deliver him. The serpent bit Nala, and told him that the poison should work upon him till the evil spirit was gone out of him, and that he should then be restored to all he loved. Through the effects of the bite he was transformed into a misshapen dwarf. In this form he entered the service of Ṛtuparṇa, king of Ayodhyā, as a trainer of horses and an accomplished cook, under the name of Bahuka. Damayantī was discovered and conducted to her father's home, where she found her children. Great search was made for Nala, but in vain, for no one knew him in his altered form. One brāhmṇa, however, suspected him, and informed Damayantī. She resolved to test his feelings by announcing her intention of holding a second *svayaṁvara.* King Ṛtuparṇa determined to attend, and took Nala with him as driver of his chariot. Ṛtuparṇa was skilled in numbers and the rules of chances. On their journey he gave a wonderful proof of this, and he instructed Nala in the science. When Nala had acquired this knowledge the evil spirit went out of him, but still he retained his deformity. Damayantī half penetrated his disguise, and was at length convinced that he was her husband by the flavour of a dish which he had cooked. They met, and, after some loving reproaches and the interference of the gods, they became reconciled, and Nala resumed his form. He again played with Puṣkara, and staked his wife against the kingdom. Profiting by the knowledge he had obtained from Ṛtuparṇa, he won back all and again became king. Puṣkara then humbled himself, and Nala not only forgave him, but sent him home to his own city enriched with many gifts. The text of this poem has been often printed, and there are translations in various languages. **(2)** A monkey chief, said to be a son of Viśvakarmā. According to the *Rāmāyaṇa*, he had the power of making stones float in water. He was in Rāma's army and built the bridge of stone called Rama-setu, or Nala-setu, from the continent to Ceylon, over which Rāma passed with his army.

NALAKANAKAS—A people mentioned in the Puránic lists but not identified.

NALAKUBERA—A son of Kubera.

NALINI—The name of one of the five streams formed by the Ganges after it escaped from Śiva.

NALODAYA (Nala + udaya). 'The rise of Nala.' A poem describing the restoration to power of King Nala after he had lost his all. It is ascribed to a Kālidāsa, but the composition is very artificial, and the ascription to the great Kālidāsa may well be doubted. The text has been printed, and there is a metrical translation by Yates.

NALOPAKHYANA—The story of Nala, an episode of the *Mahābhārata.* (*see* NALA)

NAMA—Literally name: the term applied to the tridental mark which the Vaishnavas wear on their forehead, the mark, or figure, is called Tirunáma, 'holy name' it is an imitation of Vishṇu's trident almost like the Hebrew character shin. It consists of two white lines, extending from the hair to the eyebrows, and then leading to the nose where they meet, and a red perpendicular line between them from the nose to the hair.

NAMASIVAYA—The principal Mantra of the Saivas, called Pancháksharа five characters, and means 'O Śiva, be praised:' or 'Adoration to Śiva.'

NAMASKARA—(Namaskára), a mode of salutation or obeisance, made by joining the hands together, and raising them to the forehead. This is the ordinary salutation or recognition amongst Hindus.

NAMUCHI—A powerful Danava, one of the sons of Viprachitti. This Asura was a friend of Indra; and taking advantage of his friend's confidence, he drank up Indra's strength along with a draught of wine and soma. Indra then told the Aṣvins and Sarasvatí that Namuchi had drunk up his strength. The Aṣvins and Saraswati, in consequence gave Indra a thunderbolt in the form of a foam, with which he smote off the head of Namuchi. The Aṣvins then drank the soma mixed with blood and wine, from the belly of Namuchi and transferred it pure to Indra; and by transferring it they delivered Indra. *O.S.T.*, Vol. v, p. 94.

A demon slain by Indra with the foam of water. The legend of Namuci first appears in the *Ṛgveda*, where it is said that Indra ground "the head of the slave Namuci like a sounding and rolling cloud", but it is amplified by the commentator and also in the *Śatapatha Brāhmaṇa* and *Mahābhārata.* When Indra conquered the *asuras* there was one Namuci who resisted so strongly that he overpowered Indra and held him. Namuci offered to let Indra go on promise not to kill him by day or by night, with wet or with dry. Indra gave the promise and was released, but he cut off Namuci's head at twilight, between day and night, and with foam of water, which was, according to the authorities, neither wet nor dry. The *Mahābhārata* adds that the dissevered head followed Indra calling out "O wicked slayer of thy friend."

NANDA—**(1)** The chief of the cowherds, and brother of Radha. He was the foster father of Krishṇa, as it was to his care the infant Krishṇa was committed when Kansa sought to destroy the child; **(2)** One of the sons of Vasudeva; **(3)** The son of Mahananda, and sometimes called Mahapadma, because he was avaricious. He brought the whole earth under one umbrella, and had eight sons, or descendants rather, according to Professor Wilson, who governed for a hundred years; when the brahman Kautilya overthrew the dynasty and placed Chandragupta on the throne. The Mudra Rakshasa (*q.v.*) illustrates this affair.

NANDAKA—One of the hundred sons of

Dhritaráshtra. Duryodhana was the eldest, but as the legend of their birth was not given in the article under his name, it may be recited here. One day the sage Vyása was hospitably entertained by the queen Gándhári, and in return he granted her a boon. She choose to be the mother of a hundred sons, and soon afterwards became pregnant. After two years gestation she produced a mass of flesh which was divided by Vyása into a hundred and one pieces, (as big as the joint of a thumb) and placed in jars. In due time the eldest son Duryodhana was born, but not till after the birth of Pritha's son Yudhishthira. In another month the remaining ninety-nine sons were born from the remaining jars, and one daughter, called Duhṣalá (afterwards married to Jayadratha.) The hundred names are all given in the Mahábhárata; it will be sufficient here to mention the principal ones:—Duryodhana, Durvishaha, Durmukha, Dushpradarṣana, Vivinsati, Vikarna, Duhṣaṣana, Virochana, Kundaka, Nandaka, &c.—Williams. *I.E.P.*

NANDANA—The grove of Indra, lying to the north of Meru.

NANDAYANIA—A pupil of Báshkali and teacher of the Rig Veda.

NANDI—(1) The bull of Śiva. The *Vāyu Purāṇa* makes him the son of Kaśyapa and Surabhi. His image, of a milky white colour, is always conspicuous before the temples of Śiva. He is the chamberlain of Śiva, chief of his personal attendants (*gaṇas*), and carries a staff of office. He is guardian of all quadrupeds. He is also called Śālánkāyana, and he has the appellations of Nādideha and Tāṇḍavatālika, because he accompanies with music the *tāṇḍava* dance of his master. **(2)** Delight,' the wife of Dharma and mother of Hersha (joy.) **(3)** That which is the cause of gratification to men and gods; a sort of benedictory formula, at the commencement of a drama, invoking the protection of some deity in favour of the audience. This benediction may consist of one, two, or three stanzas. The recitation of the Nándí is always considered indispensable; and after it there usually follows some account of the author of the piece about to be acted. It may consist in the eulogium of a king or praise of a deity, recited in benedictory verses at the commencement of a religious ceremony or at the opening of a drama. "Every Sanskrit play opens with one or more Nándís, or benedictions, in which the blessing of some deity is invoked on the audience." The Nágánanda furnishes "the only instance in Sanskrit literature in which the power thus invoked is Buddha."—*Boyd*.

NANDIMUKHAS—A class of Pitris: there seems to be some uncertainty about the character of the Nándímukhas; and they are addressed both as Pitris and gods; being in the former case either the ancestors prior to the great grand-father, ancestors collectively, or a certain class of them; and in the latter being identified with the Viṣwadevas. The term Nándímukha is also applied to the rite itself, or to the Vriddhi Śrádda, and to one addressed to maternal ancestors. See Wilson's Notes to Vishṇu Purána, p. 315.

NANDINI—The cow of plenty belonging to the sage Vasiṣṭha, said to have been born of Surabhi, the cow of plenty that was produced at the churning of the ocean.

NANDI-PURANA—(*see* PURĀṆA)

NANDISA, NANDĪŚVARA—'Lord of Nandi.' A title of Śiva. It is related in the *Rāmāyaṇa* that Rāvaṇa went to the Śara-vana, the birthplace of Kārttikeya, and on his way through the mountains he beheld "a formidable, dark, tawny-coloured dwarf called Nandīśvara, who was a follower of Mahādeva, or rather that deity himself in another body. This being desired Rāvaṇa to halt, as Śiva was sporting in the mountain, and no one, not even a god, could pass. Rāvaṇa asked derisively who Śiva was, and laughed contemptuously at Nandīśvara, who had the face of a monkey. Nandīśvara retorted that monkeys having the same shape as himself and of similar energy should be produced to destroy Rāvaṇa's race. In reply to this menace, Rāvaṇa threatened to pull up the mountain by its roots and let Śiva know his own danger. So he threw his arms round the mountain and lifted it up, which made the hosts of Śiva tremble and Pārvatī quake and cling to her husband. Śiva then pressed down the mountain with his great toe, and crushed and held fast the arms of Rāvaṇa, who uttered a loud cry which shook all creation. Rāvaṇa's friends counselled him to propitiate Śiva, and he did so for a thousand years with hymns and weeping. Śiva then released him, and said that his name should be Rāvaṇa from the cry (*rāva*) which he had uttered. The origin of this story is sufficiently manifest, it has been built up on the name Rāvaṇa, to the glory of Śiva, by a zealous partisan of that deity.

NANDIVARDHANA—(1) The son of Urdávasu, king of Mithila; **(2)** The son of Janaka, king of Magadha; The son of Udayaṣwa, king of Magadha.

NARA—**(1)** 'Bodily forms' in which spirit in enshrined; and of which the waters, with Vishṇu resting upon them, are a type. Waters, the first product of Nara. Vishṇu Purána, p. 28. **(2)** A pious sage, the son of Dharma by Múrtti; **(3)** A prince, the son of Gaya; **(4)** A prince, the son of Sudhriti; **(5)** One of the sons of Bhavanmanyas of the royal family of Bharata.

NARADA PANCARATRA—A ritualistic work of the Vaiṣṇavas. It has been printed in the *Bibliotheca Indica.*

NARADA PURANA, NĀRADĪYA PURĀṆA—"Where Nārada has described the duties which were observed in the Bṛhat Kalpa, that is called the Nāradīya, having 25,000 stanzas." But the only copy that Wilson analysed contained not more than 3000 stanzas. There is another work called the Bṛhan or Great Nāradīya, but this extends only to 3500 verses. These Purāṇas, says Wilson, bear "no conformity to the definition of a Purāṇa; both are sectarial and modern compilations, intended to support the doctrine of *Bhakti* or faith in Viṣṇu". They are modern compositions, possibly even of so late a date as the sixteenth or seventeenth century. One of them refers to the "killers of cows" and "contemners of the gods", meaning, no doubt, the Mohammedans, so that the passage would seem to have been written after India was in their hands.

This Purána is related by Nárada and gives an account of the Vrihas Kalpa. It is communicated to the Rishis at Naimisháraṇya, on the Gamati river. Professor Wilson regards it as a sectarial and modern compilation intended to support the doctrine of Bhakti, or faith in Vishṇu. It contains a number of prayers addressed to one or other form of that divinity; a variety of observances and holidays connected with his adoration; and different legends, some perhaps of an early, others of a more recent date, illustrative of the efficacy of devotion to Hari. There are the stories of Dhruva and Prahláda, the latter told in the words of the Vishṇu Purána; whilst the second portion of it is occupied with a legend of Mohiní, the will-born daughter of a king called Rukmángada; beguiled by whom the king offers to perform for her whatever she may desire. She calls upon him either to violate the rule of fasting on the eleventh day of the fortnight, a day sacred to Vishṇu, or to put his son to death; and he kills his son, as the lesser sin of the two. This shews the spirit of the work. Its date may also be inferred from its tenor, as such monstrous extravagancies in praise of Bhakti are certainly of modern origin. One limits it furnishes itself, for it refers to Śuka and Paríkshit, the interlocutors of the Bhágavata, and it is consequently subsequent to the date of that Purána: it is probably considerably later, for it affords evidence that it was written after India was in the hands of the Mohammedans. In the concluding passage it is said, "Let not this Purána be repeated in the presence of the 'killers of cows' and contemners of the gods." It is possibly a compilation of the sixteenth or seventeenth century. *Vishṇu Purána. Preface.*

NARADA—A *ṛṣi* to whom some hymns of the *Ṛgveda* are ascribed. He is one of the Prajāpatis, and also one of the seven great *ṛṣis.* The various notices of him are somewhat inconsistent. The *Ṛgveda* describes him as "of the Kaṇva family". Another authority states that he sprang from the forehead of *Brahmā*, and the *Viṣṇu Purāṇa* makes him a son of Kaśyapa and one of Dakṣa's daughters. The *Mahābhārata* and some Purāṇas state that he frustrated the scheme which Dakṣa had formed for peopling the earth, and consequently incurred that patriarch's curse to enter again the womb of a woman and be born. Dakṣa, however, relented at the solicitation of Brahmā, and consented that Nārada should be born again of Brahmā and one of Dakṣa's daughters; he was hence called Brahmā and Devabrahmā. In some respects he bears a resmblance to Orpheus. He is the inventor of the *vīṇā* (lute), and was chief of the *gandharvas* or heavenly musicians. He also went down to the infernal regions (*pātāla*), and was delighted with what he saw there. In later times he is connected with the legend of Kṛṣṇa. He warned Kaṁsa of the imminent incarnation of Viṣṇu, and he afterwards became the friend and associate of Kṛṣṇa.

The *Nārada-pañcarātra* relates that Brahmā advised his son Nārada to marry, but Nārada censured his father as a false teacher, because devotion to Kṛṣṇa was the only true means of felicity. Brahmā then cursed Nārada to lead a life of sensuality, in subjection to women, and Nārada retorted the curse, condemning Brahmā to lust after his own daughter, and to be an object unworthy of adoration. Nārada has the appellations, Kalikāraka, 'strife-maker'; Kapivaktra, 'monkey-faced'; Piśuna, 'messenger or spy'.

Nārada was also one of great writers upon law. His textbook, called *Nāradīya Dharmaśāstra*, has been translated into English by Dr. Jolly.

A Prajápati or divine Rishi, born from the hip of Brahmá; the invention of the véna, or Indian lyre, is attributed to Nárada; also a code of laws, and one of the eighteen Puránas entitled Náradiya Purána. In the Brahmá Purána he is called the smooth-speaking Nárada, and his likeness to Orpheus is carried still further by a descent which he made from heaven to visit Pátáḷa, the nether regions. In Manu and in the Vishṇu Purána he is called a Prajápati, in the Mahábhárata he is one of the Gandharvas. It was he who dissuaded the sons of Daksha from multiplying their race; they accordingly scattered themselves through the regions of the universe to ascertain its extent, &c., and the patriarch Daksha finding that all his sons had vanished was incensed and denounced an imprecation of Nárada. It was Nárada who informed Kansa that the supporter of the earth Vishṇu, was going to become incarnate as the eighth child of Devaki. When Nárada visited Krishṇa he presented him with the flower Párijáta from the world of the gods. Krishṇa gave it to Rúkmini, which so excited the jealousy of one of his favourite mistresses Satyabháma, that in order to appease her, Krishṇa went to the heaven of the gods and brought away the tree itself that bore the flower. In mythology Nárada is often described as bearing a resemblance to Hermes or Mercury, being engaged in conveying messages and causing discord among the gods and men. He is usually represented as sitting in a fire, having his hands folded, over his head, and stretching his legs also towards his head, his arms and legs being tied together with a girdle. (*John Garrett*)

NARAKA—(1) An *asura*, son of the Earth. In the *Mahābhārata* and *Viṣṇu Purāṇa* he is said to have carried off the ear-rings of Aditi to the impregnable castle of Prāgjyotisa, but Kṛṣṇa, at the request of the gods, went there and killed him and recovered the jewels. In the *Harivaṁśa* the legend differs. According to this, Naraka, king of Prāgjyotiṣa, was an implacable enemy of the gods. He assumed the form of an elephant, and having carried off the daughter of Viśvakarmā, he subjected her to violation. He seized the daughters of the *gandharvas*, and of gods and of men, as well as the apsarasas themselves, and had more then 16,000 women, for whom he built a splendid residence. He also appropriated to himself jewels, garments, and valuables of all sorts, and no *asura* before him had ever been so horrible in his actions. **(2)** Hell; a place of torture to which the souls of the wicked are sent. Manu enumerates twenty-one hells: Tāmisra, Andha-tāmisra, Mahāraurava, Raurava, Naraka, Kālasūtra, Mahānaraka, Sañjivana, Mahāvīci, Tapana, Sampratāpana, Saṁhāta, Sakākola, Kuḍmala, Pūtimṛttika, Lokaśaṅku, Ṛjiṣa, Panthāna, Śālmali, Asipatravana, and Lohadāraka. Other authorities vary greatly as to the numbers and names of the hells, (*see Viṣṇu, Purāṇa*, II. 214). **(3)** A son of Anrita (falsehood) and Nikriti (immorality); **(4)** A Danava, one of the sons of Viprachitti.

NARAKASURA—A formidable giant or daitya who had become the scourge of the human race and the terror of the three worlds. The monster was at length slain by Vishṇu, after a severe conflict that it is said lasted through the entire day. And as Vishṇu was unable to go through his diurnal ablutions before sunset, he had to perform them in the night. The Brahmans to celebrate this great event, put off their ablutions to the night—the only occasion in the course of the year in which they bathe after sunset. This is termed the festival of *Dípavali kabba*, *q.v.*

NARA-NARAYANA—Two ancient *ṛṣis*, sons of Dharma and Ahiṁsa. The names are sometimes applied to Kṛṣṇa and to Kṛṣṇa and Arjuna. The *Vāmana Purāṇa* has a legend about them which is alluded to in the drama of *Vikramorvaśī*. Their penances and austerities alarmed the gods, so Indra sent nymphs to inspire them with passion and disturb their devotions. Nārāyaṇa took a flower and placed it on his thigh. Immediately there sprung from it a beautiful nymph whose charms far excelled those of celestial nymphs, and made them return to heaven filled with shame and vexation. Nārāyaṇa sent this nymph to Indra with them, and from her having been produced from the thigh (*uru*) of the sage, she was called Urvaśī.

NARANTAKA—One of the sons of the giant Rávaṇa who was killed at the seige of Lanka.

NARA—Paramátma: the waters it is said were the progeny of Nara; that is they were the first productions of God in creation.

NARAS—'Centaurs,' or beings with the limbs of horses and human bodies, created by Brahmá along with Kinnaras, Rakshasas, &c. *V.P.*, p. 42.

NARASIMHA PURANA—(*see* PURĀṆA)

NÁRASIMHA AVATARA—The fourth incarnation of Vishṇu, in the form of a man-lion (*nara* a man, and *Sinha* a lion). One of the two doorkeepers of Vishṇu's paradise, (see *Varaha*) came down to earth as a monarch, named Hiranyakasipu. He was cruel, tyrannical, unjust; particularly so towards his son named Prahláda. But he had obtained from Brahmá, by severe penance, the boon that he should not be slain by any created being; in consequence of which he became very proud, and required all persons to honor him by saying. "Om Hiranya" (Adoration to Hiranya); and those who would not say so he ordered to be punished. His son Prahláda, who was a devout worshipper of Vishṇu, would not obey his father's order, but continued to say "Om namah" (meaning by Om Vishṇu). Hiranya remonstrated with him because of this, but in vain. Then he attempted to punish and kill him, but in vain: Prahláda was struck heavily but did not feel the strokes; he was cast into the fire, but was not burnt: he was trampled on by elephants, but continuing to think of Vishṇu he was not hurt: he was thrown fettered into the sea, but a fish carried him safely to shore. At last, when Prahláda did not cease praising Vishṇu, and asserted that he was everywhere and in everything, Hiranya retorted. "If so why dost thou not show him unto me?" Upon this Prahláda rose and struck a column of the hall in which they were assembled; and behold, there issued from it Vishṇu, in a form which was half-man and half-lion, and tore Hiranya to pieces. *V.P.*

NARA-VISVANA—'A man-devourer'; a *rākṣasa* or other malignant being.

NARAYANA—(1) The son of Nara, the original man, and often identified or coupled with Nara. (2) The creator Brahmā, who, according to Manu, was so-called because the waters (*nara*) were his first *ayaṇa* or place of motion. The name is found for the first time in the *Śatapatha Brāhmaṇa.* The name as commonly used applies to Viṣṇu, and is that under which he was first worshipped. **(2)** A sage, the son of Dharma by Murtti; **(3)** A prince, the son of Bhumimitra, of the Káṇwa dynasty.

NARIKA—A measure of time, fifteen *laghus.*

NARIKAVACHA—A name of Múlaka, *q.v.*

NARISHYANTA—(1) One of the sons of the Manu Vaivaswata; **(2)** The son of Marutta, the fourteenth of the posterity of Dishṭa.

NARMADA—The Narmada river, which is esteemed holy. The personified river is variously represented as being daughter of *ṛṣi* named Mekala (from whom she is called Mekalā and Mekala-kanyā), as a daughter of the moon, as a 'mind-born daughter' of the Somapas, and as sister of the Nāgas. It was she who brought Purukutsa to the aid of the Nāgas against the *gandharvas*, and the grateful snake-gods made her name a charm against the venom of snakes. According to the *Viṣṇu Purāṇa*, she had a son by Purukutsa who was named Trasadasyu. The *Matsya Purāṇa* gives Duḥsaha as the name of her husband. The *Harivaṁśa* is inconsistent with itself. In one place it makes her wife of Purukutsa and mother of Trasadasyu; in another it makes her the wife of Trasadasyu. She is also called Revā and Pūrvagaṅgā, and, as a daughter of the moon, Indujā and Somodbhavā.

NARSIMHA PURANA—(*see* PURĀṆA)

NARSIMHA TAPANI—An Upaniṣad in which Viṣṇu is worshipped under his form Nṛsiṁha. Published with the commentary of Śaṅkarācārya in the *Bibliotheca Indica.*

NARSIMHA—The Narasiṁha or man-lion incarnation. (*see* AVATĀRA)

NARTTAKA—A dancer, who also performs extraordinary feats of strength and agility.

NASATYA—Name of one of the Aśvins. It is also used in the plural for both of them.

NATA—An actor; in popular acceptation it comprehends jugglers, buffoons, and persons practicing sleight of hand, and exhibiting feats of agility.—*Wilson.*

NATAKA—The Play *par excellence*, which comprises all the elements of a dramatic composition. The subject should always be celebrated and important. Like the Greek tragedy the *Nátaka* is to represent worthy or exalted personages only; and the hero must be a monarch, as Dushyanta; a demi-god, as Ráma; or a divinity, as Krishṇa. The action, or more properly the passion, should be but one, as love or heroism. The plot should be simple, the incidents consistent; the business should spring direct from the story as a plant from its seed, and should be free from episodical and prolix interruptions. The time should not be protracted, and the duration of an act, according to the elder authority should not exceed one day: but the *Sáhitya Darpana* extends it to a few days or even to one year. The diction should be perspicuous and polished. The piece should consist of not fewer than five acts, and not more than ten.

In many of these characteristics, the Náṭaka presents an obvious analogy to the tragedy of the Greeks, which was 'the imitation of a solemn and perfect action, of adequate importance, told in pleasing language, exhibiting the several elements of dramatic composition in its different parts, represented through the instrumentality of agents, not by narration, and purifying the affections of human nature by the influence of pity and terror.'

An important difference from the classical drama,

and from that of most countries, is the total absence of the distinction between Tragedy and Comedy. The Hindu plays confine themselves neither to the crimes nor to the absurdities of mankind; neither to the momentous changes nor lighter vicissitudes of life; neither to the terrors of distress nor the gaieties of prosperity. In this respect they may be classed with much of the Spanish and English drama, to which, as Schlegel observes, 'the terms Tragedy and Comedy are wholly inapplicable, in the sense in which they were employed by the ancients.' They are invariable of a mingled web, and blend seriousness and sorrow with levity and laughter. They never offer, however, a calamitous conclusion, which as Johnson remarks, was enough to constitute a Tragedy in Shakespear's days; and although they propose to excite all the emotions of the human breast, terror and pity included, they never effect this object by leaving a painful impression in the mind of the spectator. The Hindus, in fact, have no Tragedy; a defect that subverts the theory that Tragedy necessarily preceded Comedy, because in the infancy of society the stronger passions predominated, and it was not till social intercourse was complicated and refined, that the follies and frivolities of mankind afforded material for satire ... The absence of tragic catastrophe in the Hindu dramas is not merely an unconscious omission; such catastrophe is prohibited by a positive rule, and the death of either the hero or the heroine is never to be announced. With that regard indeed for decorum, which even Voltaire thought might be sometimes dispensed with, it is not allowed in any manner '*ensanglanter la scéne,*' and death must invariably be inflicted out of the view of the spectators.—Wilson, *Works*, XI, p. xxvii.

NAVALA—The daughter of the patriarch Vairája, and wife of the Manu Chakshusha.

NAVARATHA—A prince, the son of Bhímaratha.

NAVA-RATNA—The nine gems: pearl, ruby, topaz, diamond, emerald, lapis lazuli, coral, sapphire, and one not identified called Gomeda. The nine gems of the court of Vikrama, probably meaning Vikramāditya, whose era the *Saṁvat* begins in 56 B.C. A verse gives their names as Dhanvantari, Kṣapaṇaka, Amara Siṁha, Śanku, Vetālabhaṭṭa, Ghaṭakarpara, Kālidāsa, Varāhamihira, Vararuci. The date of Vikramāditya is by no means settled. Bhau Dājī endeavours to identify Vikrama with Harṣa Vikramāditya, who lived in the middle of the sixth century.

NAYA—(Polity) a son of Dharma by Kriya.

NEDISHTA—One of the sons of the Manu Vaivaswata.

NICHAKRA—A prince, the son of Asíma Krishṇa, who when Hastinápura was washed away by the Ganges, removed the capital to Kauṣámbí.

NIDAGHA—A son of Pulastya and disciple of Ribhu; to him Ribhu willingly communicated perfect knowledge. The residence of Pulastya was at Víranagara, on the banks of the Devíká river. "In a beautiful grove adjoining to the stream, the pupil of Ribhu, Nidágha, conversant with devotional practices, abode. When a thousand divine years had elapsed, Ribhu went to the city of Pulastya, to visit his disciple. Standing at the doorway, at the end of a sacrifice to the ViŚwadevas, he was seen by his scholar, was hastened to present him the usual offering, or Arghya, and conducted him into the house; and when his hands and feet were washed, and he was seated, Nídágha invited him respectfully to eat, (when the following dialogue ensued):—

"*Rihu.* 'Tell me, illustrious Brahman, what food there is in in your house; for I am not fond of indifferent vlands.'

"*Nidágha.* 'There are cakes of meal, rice, barley, and pulse in the house; partake, venerable sir, of whichever best pleases you.'

"*Ribhu.* 'None of these do I like; give me rice boiled with sugar, wheaten cakes, and milk with curds and molasses.'

"*Nidágha.* 'Ho dame, be quick, and prepare whatever is most delicate and sweet in the house, to feed our guest.'

"Having thus spoken, the wife of Nidágha, in obedience to her husband's commands, prepared sweet and savoury food, and set it before the Brahman; and Nidágha, having stood before him until he had eaten of the meal which he had desired, thus reverentially addressed him:—

"*Nidágha.* Have you eaten sufficiently, and with pleasure, great Brahman? and has your mind received contentment from your food? Where is your present residence? Whither do you purpose going? and whence, holy sir, have you now come?

"*Ribhu.* 'A hungry man, Brahman, must needs be satisfied when he has finished his meal. Why should you inquire if my hunger has been appeased? When the earthly element is parched by fire, then hunger is engendered; and thirst is produced when the moisture f the body has been absorbed (by internal or digestive heat.) Hunger and thirst are the functions of the body, and satisfaction must always be afforded me by that by which they are removed; for when hunger is no longer sensible, pleasure and contentment of mind are faculties of the intellect; ask their condition of the mind then, for man is not affected by them. For your three other questions, Where I dwell? Whither I go? and whence I come? hear this reply. Man, (the soul of man) goes everywhere, and penetrates everywhere, like the ether; and is it rational to inquire where it is? or whence or whither thou goest? I neither am going nor coming, nor is my dwelling in any one place; nor art thou, thou; nor are others, others; nor am I, I. If you wonder what reply I should make to your inquiry why I made any distinction between sweetened and unsweetened food, you shall bear my explanation. What is there that is really sweet or not sweet to one eating a meal? That which is sweet, is no longer so when it occasions the sense of repletion; and that which is not sweet, becomes sweet when a man (being very hungry) fancies that it is so. What food is there that first, middle, and last is equally grateful. As a house built of clay is strengthened by fresh plaster, so is this earthly body supported by earthly particles; and barley, wheat, pulse, butter, oil, milk, curds, treacle, fruits, and the like, are composed of atoms of earth. This therefore is to be understood by you, that the mind which properly judges of what is or is not sweet is impressed with the notion of identity, and that this effect of identity tends to liberation,'

"Having heard these words, conveying the substance of ultimate truth, Nigágha fell at the feet of his visitor, and said, 'Shew favour unto me, illustrious Brahman, and tell me who it is that for my good has come hither, and by whose words the infatuation of my mind is dissipated.' To this, Ribhu answered, 'I am ribhu, your preceptor, come hither to communicate to you true wisdom; and having declared to you what that is, I shall depart. Know this whole universe to be the one undivided nature of the supreme spirit, entitled Vásudeva.' Thus having spoken, and receiving the prostrate homage of Nidágha, rendered with fervent faith, Ribhu went his way," *V.P.*, p. 53-55.

NIDANA-SUTRA—An old work upon the metres of the Vedas.

NIDHI—'A treasure.' Nine treasures belonging to the god of wealth Kubera. Each of them is personified or has a guardian spirit, which is an object of worship among the *tāntrikas*. The nature of these Nidhis is not clearly understood. See a note by Wilson on verse 534 of the Meghadūta, *Collected Works*, IV, 379. Their names are Kacchapa, Mukunda, Nanda (or Kunda), Kharba, Makara, Nīla, Śaṅkha, Padma, and Mahāpadma. The Nidhis are called also Nidhāna, Nikara, and Śevadhi.

NIDRA—'Sleep.' Sometimes said to be a female form of Brahmā, at others to have been produced at the churning of the ocean.

NIGHANTU, NIGHAṆṬUKA—A glossary, especially of synonyms and obsolete and obscure Vedic terms. There was at least one work of this kind before the days of Yāska. (*see* NIRUKTA)

NIGHNA—The son of Anamitra, and father of Satrájit, to whom the divine Áditya, the sun, presented the Syamantaka gem.

NIKASA—A female demon, the mother of Rāvaṇa. The mother of the carnivorous imps called Piśitāśanas, or by their metronymic Naikuṣeyas and Nikaṣātmajas.

NIKRITI—(Immorality.) Adaughter of Adharma (vice.)

NIKUMBHA—**(1)** A *rākṣasa* who fought against Rāma. He was son of Kumbhakarṇa. **(2)** An *asura* who, according to the *Harivaṁśa*, received the boon from Brahmā that he should die only by the hands of Viṣṇu. He was king of Ṣaṭpura and had great magical powers, so that he could multiply himself into many forms, though he commonly assumed only three. He carried off the daughters of Brahmādatta, the friend of Kṛṣṇa, and that hero attacked him and killed him under different arms more than once, but he was eventually slain outright by Kṛṣṇa, and his city of Ṣaṭpura was given to Brahmāda-tta. **(3)** A prince, the son of Haryyasva.

NILA—'Blue.' **(1)** A mythic range of mountains north of Meru. **(2)** A mountain range in Orissa. **(3)** A monkey ally of Rāma. **(4)** A Pāṇḍava warrior killed by Aśvatthāman. **(5)** A son of Yadu; **(6)** A son of Ajamídha.

NILAKANTHA—'Blue throat'. An epithet of Śiva. (*see* Śiva); the god with a dark blue throat. The colour was the effect of the poison generated at the churning of the ocean, and which Śiva swallowed.

NILALOHITA—A name of Rudra, from the Vaishnava Purānas, which give only one original form, instead of eight as in the Vishṇu Purána, and to which the name of Nílalohita, the blue and red or purple complexioned, is assigned.

NILINI—The wife of Ajamídha.

NIMI—One of the three distinguished sons of Ikshváku. He instituted a sacrifice that was to endure a thousand years, and applied to Vasishtha to offer the oblations. Vasishtha in answer said, that he had been pre-engaged by Indra for five hundred years, but that if the Rája would wait for some time, he would come and officiate as superintending priest. The king made no answer, and Vasishtha went away, supposing that he had assented. When the sage had completed the performance of the ceremonies he had conducted for Indra, he returned with all speed of Nimi, purposing to render him the like office. When he arrived, however, and found that Nimi had retained Gautama and other priests to minister at his sacrifice, he was much displeased and pronounced upon the king, who was then asleep, a curse to this effect, that since he had not intimated his intention, but transferred to Gautama the duty he had first entrusted to himself, Vasishtha, Nimi should thenceforth cease to exist in a corporeal form. When Nimi woke, and knew what had happened, he in return denounced as an imprecation upon his unjust preceptor, that he also should lose his bodily existence, as the punishment of uttering a curse upon him without previously communicating with him. Nimi then abandoned his bodily condition. The spirit of Vasishtha also leaving his body, was united with the spirits of Mitra and Varuna for a season, until, through their passion for the nymph Urvasí, the sage was born again in a different shape. The corpse of Nimi was preserved from decay by being embalmed with fragrant oils and resins, and it remained as entire as if it were immortal. When the sacrifice was conluded, the priests applied to the gods, who had come to receive their portions, that they would confer a blessing upon the author of the sacrifice. The gods were willing to restore him to bodily life, but Nimi declined its acceptance, saying, "O deities, who are the alleviators of all worldly suffering, there is not in the world a deeper cause of distress than the separation of soul and body: it is therefore my wish to dwell in the eyes of all beings, but never more to resume a corporeal shape !" To this desire the gods assented, and Nimi was placed by them in the eyes of all living creatures; in consequence of which their eyelids are ever opening and shutting. *V.P.*

NIMISHA—A measure of time—a twinkle of the eye—a second; according to the Bhágavata, three Lavas.

NIPA—A prince, the son of Para, a descendant of Hastin.

NIRAMITRA—**(1)** One of the Páṇḍavas, the son of Nakulá; **(2)** The son of Khaṇḍapáni; **(3)** The son of Ayutáyus.

NIRMALAS—One of the divisions of the Sikhs who profess to dedicate themselves exclusively to a religious life. They lead a life of celibacy, and disregard their personal appearance, often going nearly naked. They do not assemble together in colleges, nor do they observe any particular form of Divine service, but confine their devotion to speculative meditation on the perusal of the writings of Nának, Kábír, and other unitarian teachers. They are always solitary, supported by their disciples, or wealthy persons who may happen to favour the sect. The *Nirmalas* are known as able expounders of the *Vedanta philosophy*, in which Brahmans do not disdain to accept of their instructions. They are not a very numerous body on the whole; but a few are almost always to be found at the principal seats of Hindu wealth, and particularly at Benares.—Wilson's *Works*, Vol. I.

NIRMALI—(Nirmáli), a sect of Vaishnavas who devote all their time to the one purpose of keeping themselves clean. They bathe many times and wash their hands one hundred and eight times daily. While they do not separate themselves from their families, they refrain from touching even their children, lest they should be defiled. They are very careful not to take the life of any creature. Women as well as men may belong to this sect.—*Sherring*.

NIRMANARATIS—A class of deities who belong to the eleventh Manwantara.

NIRNAYA-SINDHU—A work on religious ceremonies and law by Kamalākara. It has been printed at Bombay and Benares.

NIRRITA—One of the eleven Rudras, according to the Váyu list.

NIRRTI—'Death, decay.' Death personified as a goddess; sometimes regarded as the wife and sometimes as the daughter of A-dharma. One of the Rudras.

NIRUKTA—**(1)** 'Etymology, glossary.' One of the Vedāṅgas. The *Nirukta is* devoted to the explanation of difficult Vedic words. The only work of the kind now known to us is that of Yāska, who was a predecessor of Pāṇini; but such works were no doubt numerous, and the names of seventeen writers of *Niruktas* are mentioned as having preceded Yāska. The *Nirukta* consists of three parts: (1) Naighaṇṭuka, a collection of synonymous words; **(2)** Naigama, a collection of words peculiar to the Vedas; **(3)** Daivata, words relating to deities and sacrifices. These are mere lists of words, and are of themselves of little value. They may have been compiled by Yāska himself, or he may have found them ready to his hand. The real *Nirukta*, the valuable portion of the work, is Yāska's commentary which follows. In this he explains the meaning of words, enters into etymological investigations, and quotes passages of the Vedas in illustration. These are valuable from their acknowledged antiquity, and as being the oldest known examples of a Vedic gloss. They also throw a light upon the scientific and religious condition of their times, but the extreme brevity of their style makes them obscure and difficult to understand. The text of the *Nirukta* has been published by Roth.

NIRUKTAKRIT—The name of the pupil to whom Sákapúrṇi gave his glossary (Nirukta) of the Rig Veda.

NIRUTA—A giant; a regent or guardian of the southwest point of the world. He is represented as of a green colour, and is said to have been raised to the dignity he enjoys in consequences of his severe penance. On his head he wears a crown, and on his forehead Śiva's sign of sacred ashes. Of his four hands one is empty, and in the other three he holds respectively a banner with the sign of a fish, a ring, and a wine jug: his vehicle is a crocodile.

NIRVRITTI—A prince, the son of Vrsni, a descendant of Jyámagha.

NIRWANA—The blowing out. Extinction. The summum-bonum of Buddhism. It was long thought that Nirwána simply meant final beatitude, the emancipation of the soul from the body: its exemption from further transmigration, and re-union with the deity. Some still maintain this view, and regard Nirwána as synonymous with Móksha; the absorption of the individual soul into the divine essence; which the Hindus represent as the highest goal of their religion and philosophy. But it has been shown by Mr. Spence Hardy, Mr. Max Müller, and other high authorities, that Nirwána means utter annihilation, or the destruction of all elements which constitute existence. There are four paths, an entrance into any of which secures either immediately, or more remotely, the attainment of *Nirwána*. They are; (1) *Sowán*, which is divided into twenty-four sections, and after it has been entered there can be only seven more births between that period and the attainment of *Nirw*ána, which may be in any world but the four hells; (2,) *Sakradágámi*, into which he who enters will receive one more birth. He may enter this path in the world of men, and afterwards be born in *déva-lóka*; or he may enter it in a *déva-lóka*, and afterwards be born in the world of men. It is divided into twelve sections; (3.) *Anágámi*,into which he who enters will not again be born in a *káma-lóka*; he may, by the apparitional birth, enter into a *brahma-lóka*, and from that world attain *Nirwána.* This path is divided into forty-eight sections; (4,) *Arya* or *Aryahat*, into which he who enters has overcome or destroyed all evil desire. It is divided into twelve sections.

Those who have entered into any of the paths can discern the thoughts of all in the same, or preceding paths. Each path is divided into two grades; 1, The perception of the path; 2, Its fruition or enjoyment. The mode in which Nirwána, or the destruction of all the elements of existence, may be reached, is thus pointed out by Mr. Spence Hardy, in his 'Eastern Monachism:' "The unwise being who has not yet arrived at a state of purity, or who is subject to future birth, overcome by the excess of evil desire, rejoices in the organs of sense, Ayatana, and their relative objects and commends them. The Áyatanas therefore become to him like a rapid stream to carry him onward toward the sea of repeated existence; they are not released from old age, decay, deaths, sorrow, &c. But the being who is purified, perceiving the evils arising from the sensual organs and their relative objects, does not rejoice therein, nor does he commend them, or allow himself to be swallowed up by them. By the destruction of the 108 modes of evil desire he has released himself from birth, as from the jaws of an alligator; he has overcome all attachment to outward objects; he does not regard the unauthorized precepts, nor is he a sceptic; and he knows that there is no ego, no self. By overcoming these four errors, he has released himself from the cleaving to existing objects he is released from birth, whether as a brahmá, man, or any other being. By the destruction of birth he is released from old age, decay, death, sorrow, &c. All the afflictions connected with the repetition of existence are overcome. Thus all the principles of existence are annihilated, and that annihilation is Nirwána."

NISADA—A mountain tribe dwelling in the Vindhya mountains, said to have been produced from the thigh of Vena; the Bhils or foresters, and barbarians in general, (*see* Veṇa) Any outcast, especially the offspring of a brāhmaṇa father and sūdra mother.

NISADHA—**(1)** A mythic range of mountains lying south of Meru, but sometimes described as on the east. It is north of the Himālaya. **(2)** The country of Nala, probably the Bhīl country.

NISAKARA—A great sage mentioned in the Rámáyaṇa whose hermitage was at the foot of the Vindhya mountains; at evening he used to be lovingly escorted to his abode by a troop of wild animals, lions, tigers, leopards, bears, *&c.* When Sampáti lost his wings he consulted the sage, and asked "of what good is life to a bird who has no wings." 'Of what *pleasure* thou would'st say,' answered Nisákara gravely. "Were thy life of no good the Lord of creatures had not left it thee. But I understand that it seems hard to thee; thou art but one of the younger sons of Brahm, and even his eldest-born, Man, frets often at the fact that his own happiness is not the object of his being. Know then for thy comfort thou shall have thy wings given back to thee some day."—*I.E.*, p. 192.

NISATHA—A son of Balaráma by his wife Revati.

NISCHARA—One of the seven Rishis in the second Manwantara.

NISHADAS—Inhabitants of the Vindhya mountains—barbarians, Nishadha was the country of Nala, and has consequently attained celebrity, but its situation has not been certainly determined; it was not far from Vidarbha (Berar) as that was the country of Damayanti.

NISHADHA—**(1)** A range of mountains to the south of Meru; one of the central ranges, next to Meru, running east and west, and extending one hundred thousand Yojanas; **(2)** A prince, the son of Atithi, and grandson of Kusa.

NISITHA—A son of Kalpa; the name means 'the middle of night.'

NISTIGRI—In the *Ṛgveda*, the mother of Indra.

NISUMBHA—An *àsura* killed by Durgā. (*see* Śumbha). A demon ruler of prodigious strength and power who was destroyed by the goddess Umá. The Devimahátmya narrates this as one of her chief martial exploits.

NISUNDA—A Daitya, the son of Hláda.

NITALA—One of the seven regions of Pátála.

NITI-MAÑJARI—A work on ethics by Dyā-Dviveda, exemplified by stories and legends with special reference to the Vedas. Some specimens are given in the *Indian Antiquary*, vol.v.

NITI-SASTRAS—Works on morals and polity, consisting either of proverbs and wise maxims in verse, or of stories and fables inculcating some moral precept and illustrating its effects. These fables are generally in prose interspersed with pithy maxims in verse.

NIVATA-KAVACAS—'Clothed in impenetrable armour.' A class of *daityas* descended from Prahlāda, "whose spirits were purified by rigid austerity". According to the *Mahābhārata* they were 30,000,000 in number, and dwelt in the depths of the sea. They were destroyed by Arjuna.

NIYAMA—**(1)** Precept. A son of Dharma by one of the daughters of Daksha. **(2)** The second stage of Yoga, being self-restraint, of which five kinds are specified **(3)** The second stage of Yoga, being self-restraint, of which five kinds are specified:—

1. Purity of mind and body
2. Cheerfulness under all circumstances
3. Religious austerity
4. The repetition of incantations
5. The association of all religious ceremonies with the Supreme Being.

These are also designated five duties or obligations, namely purity, contentment, devotion, study of the Vedas, and adoration of the Supreme.

NIYATI—The daughter of Meru who was married to Vidhátri.

NIYAT—The wife of Mahán one of the eleven Rudras.

NIYODHAKA—A prize-fighter, either as a wrestler or boxer or a swordsman—in some parts of India he also fights with gauntlets armed with steel spikes.—*Wilson.*

NRICHAKSHA—A prince, the son of Richa, of the race of Puru.

NRIGA—A son of the Manu Vaivaswata; the Linga Purána relates his transformation to a lizard by the curse of a brahman.

NRIPANJAYA—**(1)** A prince, the son of Suvíra; **(2)** The son of Medhavin of the race of Puru.

NRIYAJNA—One of the five great obligations or sacrifices, *viz.*, that of hospitality; a duty on which great stress is laid.

NYAGRODHA—One of the sons of Ugrasena.

NYASA—A form of gesticulation made with a short and mystic prayer to the heart, the head, the crown of the head, and the eye; as *Om sírase namalí, Om*; salutation to the head; with the addition of the *kavacha*, the armour or syllable *phat*, and the *astra*, the weapon or syllable *hum*. The entire *mantra*, the prayer or incantation, is then "*Om ṣírase namalí, hum, phat.*"—Wilson, *Works*, XI I, 53.

NYAYA—Logic. One of the six schools or systems of Philosophy of the Hindus.

The Nyáya system was originally taught by Gautama, of whose personal history, however, but little is known. From the Rámáyana and the Puránas, we learn that he was born at Himálaya, about the same time as Ráma, *i.e.*, at the commencement of the *Treta* Yuga (or second age of the world); that he married Ahalya, the daughter of Brahmá (*q.v.*). He is said to have lived as a very austere ascetic, first at Pryága (now Allahabad), then in a forest at Mithilá and latterly (after the repudiation of his wife) in the Himálayan mountains. His son, Satánanda, was priest to Janaka, king of Mithilá the father of Sítá, the wife of Ráma. From the above statements we may see how little reliance can be placed on the historical veracity of the Puránas. These works assure us that Gautama, though he lived in the second or silver age, married a daughter of Brahmá; but they meet the anachronism by affirming that all the sages live through the four Yugas (the Satya, Treta, Dwápas, and Kalí,) into which the Hindus divide the whole course of the world's existence.

"The *Nyáya* offers the sensational aspect of Hindu Philosophy. In saying this, it is not meant that Nyáya confines itself to sensation, excluding emotion and intellection; nor that the other systems ignore the fact of sensation; but that the arrangement of this system has a more pointed regard to the fact of the five senses than the others have, and treats the external more frankly as a solid reality.

"The word Nyáya means 'propriety or fitness,' and the system undertakes to declare the *proper method* of arriving at that knowledge of the truth, the fruit of which, it promises, is the chief and of man. The name is also used, in a more limited application, to denominate the proper method of setting forth *argument*. This has led to the practice of calling the Nyáya the '*Hindu Logic*,' a name which suggests a very inadequate conception of the scope of the system. The Nyáya system was delivered by Gautama in a set of aphorisms, so very concise, that they must, from the first, have been accompanied by a commentary, oral or written. The aphorisms of the several Hindu systems, in fact, appear designed, not so much to *communicate* the doctrine of the particular schools, as to *aid*, by the briefest possible suggestions, the memory of him to whom the doctrine shall have been *already* communicated. To this end they are in general admirably adapted. The sixty aphorisms, for example, which constitute the first of Gautama's Five Lectures, presents a methodical summary of the whole system, while the first aphorism, again, of the sixty, presents a summary of these sixty. The first aphorism is as follows:—From knowledge of the truth in regard to evidence, the ascertainable, doubt, motive, example, dogma, confutation, ascertainment, disquisition, controversy, cavil, fallacy, perversion, futility, and occasion for rebuke,—there is the attainment of the *summun-bonum.*

"In the next aphorism, it is declared how knowledge operates mediately in producing this result. 'Pain, birth, activity, fault, false notions,—since, on the successive departure of these in turn, there is the departure of the antecedent one, there is Beatitude.' That is to say, when *knowledge of the truth* is attained to, '*false notions*' depart; on their departure, the '*fault*' of concerning one's self about any external object ceases; thereupon the enlightened sage ceases to 'act;' then, there being no *actions* that all for either reward or punishment, there is no occasion, after his death, for his being *born again* to receive reward or punishment; then, not being born again, so as to be liable to pain, there is no room for '*pain*,' and the absence of pain is the Nyáya conception of the *summum-bonum.*"

As to the instruments adapted to the acquisition of a knowledge of the truth, Gautama teaches that "proofs" *i.e.*, (instruments of right knowledge,) "are the senses, the recognition of signs, the recognition of likenesses, and speech (or testimony.")

The *objects* in regard to which we have to obtain right knowledge, by means of the appropriate instruments, he enumerates as follows:—"Soul, body, sense, sense-object, knowledge, the mind, activity, fault, transmigration, fruit, pain, and beatitude,—these are the objects regarding which we are to seek for right knowledge." Here it is to be carefully observed that the *soul* is spoken of as an entirely different entity from the *mind*. Dugald Stewart tells us that the mind can attend to only one thought at a time. Gautama, recognising the same fact, but speaking of the *known* invariably as the *soul*, accounts for the fact in question by assuming that there is an *instrument*, or internal organ, termed the *mind*, through which alone knowledge can reach the soul, and which, admitting only *one thought at a time*, the Naiyáyika inferred must be no larger than an *atom*.

"Pleasure, pain, desire, aversion, volition, and knowledge," says Gautama, "are that whereby we recognise the (*átman*);" and, again, "the sign" (whereby we infer the existence) "of the mind" (manas) "is the not arising of cognitions" (in the soul) "simultaneously." Thus the *soul* may be practically regarded as corresponding to the thinking principle, and the *mind* (manas) to the faculty of attending to one, and only one, thing at a time; it being further kept in remembrance that the Naiyáyika reckons the mind to be a *substance* and not a *faculty*.

In the list of the objects regarding which right knowledge is to be obtained, the next after *mind*, is activity. This is defined as 'that which originates the [utterance of the] voice, the [cognitions of the] understanding, and the [gestures of the] body.' This activity, we have seen under Aph. II, Gautama regards with an evil eye, as the cause of birth, which is the cause of pain, which it is the *summum- bonum* to get permanently rid of.

He further holds that is through our own '*fault* that we are active; and he tells us that faults (or fallings have this characteristic, that they cause 'activity'. These faults are classed under the heads of affection, aversion, and stolidity or delusion, each of which he regards as a fault or defect, inasmuch as it leads to actions, the recompense of which, whether good or evil, must be received in some birth, or state of mundane existence, to the postponement of the great end of entire emancipation."

The immediate obstacle to "emancipation" *mokshá*, or *apavarga*, namely, "transmigration" *pretyabháva*, he next defines as "the arising again" *punarutpatti*. "Pain," *dukkha*, he defines as "that which is characterised by uneasiness," and absolute deliverance therefrom is "emancipation." This *summum- bonam* is to be obtained by an abnegation of all action, good or bad."—Small, *H.S.L.*

O—This sound signifies Brahma.

OBLATIONS—The householder after pouring libations to the gods, sages, and progenitors, is to offer oblations with fire, not preceded by any other rite, to Brahmá. Oblations are made with such ceremonies, and in such form, as are adapted to the religious rite which is intended to be subsequently performed. The residue of oblations to be offered to Indra, Yama, Varuna, and Soma, at the four cardinal parts of his dwelling; and in the north-east quarter it is to be presented to Dhanwantari. See *V.P.*, p. 304.

OBSEQUIES—See SRÁDDHA.

OCEAN—*Churning of.* See AMṚTA.

ODRA—The country of Orissa. A man of that country.

OGHAVATI—The name of a river in the Puránas, that has not been identified. According to the Puranas there are seven Sarasvati rivers in the world. These are Suprabha, Kancanaksi, Visali, Manorma, Sarasvati, Oghavati and Surenu. In the Mahabharata war it is this Oghavati that is invoked and brought to Kurukshetra. Bhisma fell on the bed of arrows on the banks of Oghavati.

OM or OMKARA—A combination of letters invested by Hindu mysticism with particular sanctity. In the Vedas it is said to comprehend all the gods; and in the Puránas it is directed to be prefixed to many sacred formulas. The syllable Om, says the Pádma Purána is the leader of all prayers; and to be employed in the beginning of all prayers. According to the same authority one of the mystical imports of the term is the collective enunciation of Vishṇu expressed by A, of Srí, his bride, intimated by U, and of their joint worshipper designated by M. A whole chapter of the Váyu Purána is devoted to this term. It is said to typify the three spheres of the world, the three holy fires, the three steps of Vishṇu, & c. It is identified with the supreme undefinable deity, or Brahmá. In the Bhágavat Gíta it is said "Repeating Om, the monosyllable, which is Brahmá, and calling me to mind;" The form or sensible type of Vasudeva, is considered to be the monosyllable Om. Mr. J.C. Thomson says, a more probable origin of the word is that it is composed of the initials of the three personifications of the triad of elements, which is a much more ancient trinity than that of Brahmá, Vishṇu and Śiva. The A would then represent Agni, or fire; the U Varuna, water;

and the M Marut, wind or air. The reverence attached to this monosyllable may be inferred from the fact that some transcribers of MSS. have been afraid to write the word itself, and have substituted some other. (A more complete treatment of the word is to be found in the main entries of my *The Hindus. Encyclopaedia of Hinduism*) (Also see *The Vedic Philosophy*)

ORDEAL—The judgment by ordeal is a leading feature of Hindu jurisprudence. There are four principal kinds of ordeals; *viz.*, by the balance, by fire, by water, and by poison.—*T.M.L.S.*, p. 108.

The gods themselves are represented as having often had recourse to it to establish the truth of dubious facts. The ordeal by fire was the must common amongst them.

Special seasons are fixed for the trial by ordeal, and various solemn ceremonies performed on the occasion. Brahmana always officiate; and the person who is to pass through the ordeal must prepare for it by fasts and ablutions.

There are also a number of private ordeals which do not require so much solemnity; such as that of compelling the suspected person to sink his arm to the elbow into a vase filled with boiling oil, with which cow-dung baa been mixed in order to increase its ardour; that of enclosing a snake, Cobra Copella, in a basket, into which a ring or a piece of money is cast, and the accused compelled to fetch the ring or piece of money after having been blindfolded; and many others. If in the first instance, he does not experience the effects of the boiling oil, and if he is not bitten by the snake in the second, he is reputed not guilty; and guilty if the reverse happens.

The ordeals are recurred to in dubious cases, not only by public magistrates, but also oftener by private persons, to ascertain a fact which interests them. A housekeeper, or the chief of a village in the houses of which any article of value has been stolen, will frequently compel the inhabitants to undergo the ordeal, in order to find out the thief. Jealous husbands often have recourse to it in order to ascertain the virtue of their wives.

These ordeals have sometimes the advantage of intimidating the persons against whom they are directed, who when they perceive they cannot escape them, confess their guilt. But this advantage is far from compensating for the real and serious evils which in most cases result from them, by causing the condemnation of innocent persons. [See an account of the Ordeals prevailing among the Hindus, by the Abbe Dubois]

ORISSA—The holy land of the Hindus. It has been so regarded for two thousand years. Its Sanskrit name Utkala-desa, the glorious country, accords with the many texts and describes it as "the realm established by the gods", and "the land that taketh away sin". An ancient sage in explaining the various places of pilgrimage to his pupil, says, "Of all the regions of the earth India is the noblest; and of all the countries of India Utkala boasts the highest renown. From end to end it is one vast region of pilgrimage. Its happy inhabitants live secure of the reception into the world of spirits; and even those who visit it, and bathe in its sacred rivers, obtain remission of their sins, though they my weigh like mountains. Who shall adequately describe its sacred streams, its temples, its holy places, its fragnent flowers, and exquisite fruits? Who shall estimate the soul's gain from a sojourn in such a land? But what need for enlarging on the praises of a realm in which the gods themselves delight to dwell?*

"Orissa is divided into four great regions of pilgrimage. From the moment the pilgrim passes the Vaitarani river, on the high road forty miles north-east of Cuttack, he treads on holy ground. Behind him lies the secular world, with its cares for the things of this life; before him is the promised land, which he has been taught to regard as a place pf preparation for the heaven. On the southern side of the river rises shrine after shrine to Lord Siva, the all-Destroyer. On its very bank he beholds the house of Yama, the king of the dead; and as he crosses over, the priest whispers into his ear the last texrt that is breathed over the dying Hindu at the moment the spirits takes its flight: "In the dread gloom of Yama's halls is the tepid Baitaraní River.' On leaving the stream he enters Jájpur, literally the City of Sacrifice, the head-quarters of the regien of pilgrimage, sacred to Párvatí, the -wife of the All-Destroyer. To the south-east is the region of pilgrimage sacred to the sun, now scarcely visited, with its matchless ruins looking down in desolate beauty across the Bay of Bengal. To the south-west is the region of pilgrimage dedicated to Śiva, with its city of temples, which once clustered, according to native tradition, to the number of seven thousand, around the sacred lake. Beyond this, nearly due south, is the region of pilgrimage beloved of Vishṇu, known to every hamlet throughout India, and to every civilized nation on earth, as the abode of Jagannáth, the Lord of the World." (Hunter's *Orissa.*)

OSADHI-PRASTHA—'The place of medicinal herbs.' A city in the Himālaya mentioned in the *Kumāra-sambhava.*

OSHTA-KARNAKAS—A nickname or term of derision, or derived from some exaggeration of national ugliness, applied to some of the oborigines of India. It means having lips extending to their ears.

OXYDRACÆ—The Sudra people of the west, or noth-west, towards the Indus. Pliny has Sudraci for the people who formed the limit of Alexander's eastern conquests, or those hitherto inaccurately called Oxydracæ.

P

PADA—The *pada* text of the Vedas, or of any other work, is one in which each word (*pada*) stands separate and distinct, not joined with the next according to the rules of *sandhi* (coalition), (*see* PĀṬHA)

PADMA PURÁNA—A very voluminous work containing fifty-five thousand slokas. These are divided amongst five books or Khandas; (1) The Srishti Khanda, or section on Creation; (2) the Bhumi Khanda, a description of the Earth; (3) the Swarga Khanda, a chapter on Heaven; (4) Pátāḷa Khanda, a chapter on the regions below the earth; and (5) Uttara Khanda, the last or supplementary chapter. There is also current a sixth divison, the Kriyá Yoga Sára, a treatise on the practice of devotion. The denominations of these divisions of the Pádma Purána convey but an imperfect and partial notion of their contents. In the first, or section which treats of creation, the narrator is Ugrasravas the Súta, the son of Lomaharshaṇa, who is sent by his father to the Rishis at Naimishárāṇya to communicate to them the Purána, which, from its containing an account of the lotus (padma), in which Brahmá appeared at creation, is termed the Padma or Pádma Purána. The Súta repeats what was originally communicated by Brahmá to Pulastya and by him to Bhíshma. The early chapters narrate the cosmogony, and the genealogy of the patriarchal families, much in the same style, and often in the same words, as the Vishṇu; and short accounts of the Manwantaras and regal dynasties: but these, which are legitimate Pauráṇik matters, soon make way for new and unauthentic inventions, illustrative of the virtues of the lake of Pushkara, or Pokher in Ajmir, as a place of pilgrimage.

The Bhúmi Kándha, or section of the earth, defers any description of the earth until near its close, filling up one hundred and twenty-seven chapters with legends of a very mixed description, some ancient and common to other Purános, but the greater part peculiar to itself, illustrative of Tírthas, either figuratively so termed—as a wife, a parent, or a guru, considered as a sacred object—or places to which actual pilgrimage should be performed.

The Swarga Khánda describes in the first chapters the relative positions of the Lokas or spheres above the earth, placing above all Vaikuntha, the sphere of Vishṇu; an addition which is not warranted by what appears to be the oldest cosmology. Miscellaneous notices of some of the most celebrated princes then succeed, conformably to the usual narratives; and these are followed by rules of conduct for the several castes, and at different stages of life. The rest of the book is occupied by legends of a diversified description, introduced without much method or contrivance; a few of which, as Daksha'a sacrifice, are of ancient date, but of which the most are original and modern.

The Pátāḷa Khánda devotes a brief introduction to the description of Pátāḷa, the regions of snake-gods; but the name of Ráma having been mentioned Śesha, who has succeeded Pulastya as spokesman, proceeds to narrate the history of Ráma, his descent and his posterity; in which the compiler seems to have taken the poem of Kálidása, the Raghu Vansa, for his chief authority. An originality of addition may be suspected, however, in the adventures of the horse destined by Ráma for an Aswamedha, which form the subject of great many chapters. When about to be sacrificed, the horse turns out to be a Brahman, condemned by an imprecation of Durvásas, a sage, to assume the equine nature, and who, by having been sanctified by connection with Ráma, is released from his metamorphosis, and dispatched as a spirit of light to heaven. This piece of Vaishnava fiction is followed by praises of the Śrí Bhágavata, an account of Krishṇa's juvenility, and the merits of worshipping Vishṇu. These accounts are communicated through machinery borrowed from the Tantras: Sadásiva tells them to Párvati, the ordinary interlocutors of Tantrika compositions.

The Uttara Khánda is a most voluminous aggregation of very heterogeneous matters, but it is consistent in adopting a decidedly Vaishnava tone, and admitting no compromise with any other form of faith. The chief subjects are first discussed in a dialogue between king Dilípa and the Muni Vasishtha; such as the merits of bathing in the month of Mágha, and the potency of the Mantra or prayer addressed to Lakshmi Náráyana. But the nature of Bhakti, faith in Vishṇu—the use of Vaishnava marks on the body—the legends of Vishṇu's Avatáras, and especially of Ráma—and the construction of images of Vishṇu—are too important to be left to mortal discretion: they are explained by Śiva to Párvati, and wound up by the adoration of Vishṇu by those divinities. The dialogue then reverts to the king and the sage; and the latter states why Vishṇu is the only one of the triad entitled to respect; Śiva being licentious, Brahmá, arrogant, and Vishṇu alone pure. Vasishtha then repeats, after Śiva, the Mahátmya of the Bhagavat Gíta; the merit of each book of which is illustrated by legends of the good consequences to individuals from perusing or hearing it. Other Vaishnava Mahátmyas occupy considerable portions of this Khánda, especially the Kártika Mahátmya, or holiness of the month Kártíka, illustrated as usual by stories, a few of which are of an early origin, but the great part modern, and peculiar to this Purána.

The Kriyá Yoga Sára is repeated by Súta to the Rishis, after Vyása's communication of its to Jaimini, in answers to an inquiry how religious merit might be secured in the Kalí age, in which men have become incapable of the penance and abstraction by which final liberation was formerly o be attained. The answer is, of course, that which is intimated in the last book of the Vishṇu Purána—personal devotion to Vishṇu: thinking of his, repeating his names, wearing his marks, worshipping in his temples, are a full substitute for all other acts of moral or devotional or contemplative merit.

The different portions of the Pádma Purána are in all probability as many different works, neither of which approaches to the original definition of a Purána. There may be some connection between the three first portions, at least as to time; but there is no reason to consider them as of high antiquity. They specify the Jains both by name and practices; they talk of Mlechchhas, 'barbarians,' flourishing in India; they commend the use of the frontal and other Vaishnava marks; and they notice other subjects which like these, are of no remote origin. The Pátáḷa Khánda dwells copiously upon the Bhágavata, and is consequently posterior to it. The Uttara Khánda is intolerantly Vaishnava, and is therefore unquestionably modern. It enjoins the veneration of the Sálagram stone and Tulasí plant, the use of the Tapta-mudra, or stamping with a hot iron the name of Vishṇu on the skin, and a variety of practices and observances undoubtedly no part of the original system. It speaks of the shrines of Srí-rangam and Venkatádri in the Dekhin, temples that have no pretension to remote antiquity; and it names Haripur on the Tungabhadra, which is in all likelihood the city of Vijayanagar, founded in the middle of the fourteenth century. The Kriyá Yoga Sára is equally a modern, and apparently a Bengali composition. No portion of the Pádma Purána is probably older than the twelfth century, and the last parts may be as recent as the fifteenth or sixteenth.—*Wilson*.

PADMAKALPA—A Maha Kalpa, a day of Brahmá already expired.

PADMANÁBHA—Lotus-navel; with the addition of Svámi, a name of Náráyana in the Malayalam country. One of the titles of the Travancore rajah was 'the slave of Padmanábha.'

PADMAVATI—**(1)** A titular name which may be understood of *Lakshmi*, as seated on a lotus-flower (padma) it is commonly used to designate a goddess of the Jainas; especially at some shrines of the eastern and western Chalukyas; corresponding with the eastern and western Chalukyas; corresponding with the northern part of Telingána and the southern Mahratta provinces. **(2)** Name of a city. It would seem, from the mention made of it in the drama *Mālatī-Mādhava*, to lie in the Vindhya mountains.

PAHLAVA—Name of a people. Manu places the Pahlavas among the northern nations, and perhaps the name is connected with the word pahlavi, *i.e.*, Persian. They let their beards grow by command of King Sagara. According to Manu, they were kṣatriyas who had become outcasts, but the *Mahābhārata* says they were created from the tail of Vasiṣṭha's cow of fortune; and the *Rāmāyaṇa* states that they sprang from her breath. They are also called Pahnavas.

A northern or north-western nation, often mentioned in Hindu writings, in Manu, the Rámáyana, the Puránas, &c. They were not a Hindu people, and may have been some of the tribes between India and Persia.

PAIJAVANA—A name of the King Sdās, his patronymic as son of Pījavana.

PAILA—The compiler of the Rig-Veda; a disciple or co-adjutor of Vyása in arranging the Vedas. Professor Wilson thinks the tradition records the first establishment of a school, of which the Vyása was the head, and Paila and the other persons named were the teachers.

PAIVATA—**(1)** Son of Reva or Revata. Also called Kakudmin. He had a very lovely daughter named Revatī, and not deeming any mortal worthy other, he went to Brahmā to consult him. At the command of that god he bestowed her upon Balarāma. He was king of Ānarta, and built the city of Kuśasthali or Dvārakā in Gujarat, which he made his capital. **(2)** One of the Manus (the fifth).

PAKA—(Páka), a fierce demon slain by Indra.

PAKASAANA—A name of Indra, and of Arjuna as descended from Indra.

PAKAYAJNA—A sacrifice, in which food is offered; one that may be made by a Súdra. It implies either the worship of the Viśwadevas, the rites of hospitality, or occasional oblations, as building a house, the birth of a child, or any occasion of rejoicing.

PAKSHA—A lunar fortnight; fifteen days of thirty Muhúrttas each.

PAKSHAJA—One of the three classes of clouds; those which were originally the wings of the mountains, and which were cut off by Indra.

PÁLAKA—A protector or ruler; *loka palaka* is an epithet applied to a king. *Dik-palaka* is a regent of one of the eight points of the heavens: each point being supported by one of the *ashta dik gajas*, or elephant caryatides. The names of the *dik-palakas* are Indra, E.; Varuna, W.; Kubera, N.; Yama, S.; Isáni, N.E.; Niruta, S.W.; Váyu, N.W.; Agni, S.E.

PALAKA—The son of Pradyóta, king of Magadhá. There were five kings of the house of Pradyóta, who reigned for a hundred and thirty-eight years.

PALAKAPYA—An ancient sage who wrote upon medicine, and is supposed to have been an incarnation of Dhanvantri.

PALASINI—A river from the eastern portion of the Himálaya, a feeder of the Mahánadi.

PALIN—One of the sons of Prithu.

PALITA—A prince, the son of Parávrit: he was the brother of Jyámagha, and ruled over Videha.

PAMPA—A river which rises in the Ṛsyamūka mountain and falls into the Tuṅgabhadra below Anagundi. Also a lake in the same locality.

PAÑCACUDA—A name of Rambhā.

PĀÑCAJANYA—Kṛṣṇa's conch formed from the shell of the sea-demon Pañcajana. It was made of the bones of the giant Panchajana. When Krishṇa was getting up his military acquirements, the son of his áchárya, or tutor, Sandípani, was drowned in the sea of Prabhása, and carried down to the bottom by the said giant. Krishṇa plunged in, dived down, slew the giant, brought up his bones to make a coach of, and restored his son to the grieving tutor. **(2)** A name of Asamañjas (*q.v.*).

PAÑCALA—Name of a country. From the *Mahābhārata* it would seem to have occupied the Lower Doab; Manu places it near Kannauj. It has sometimes been identified with the Panjāb, and with "a little territory in the more immediate neighbourhood of Hastināpura". Wilson says, "A country extending north and west from Delhi, from the foot of the Himālayas to the Chambal." It was divided into Northern and Southern Pañcālas, and the Ganges separated them. Cunningham considers North Pañcāla to be Rohilkhand, and South Pañcāla the Gangetic Doāb. The capital of the former was Ahichatra, whose ruins are found near Rāmnagar, and of the latter Kāmpilya, identical with the modern Kāmpila, on the old Ganges between Badāūn and Furrukhābād. The name is derived from the five (pánchá) sons of Hariyaswa, who were able (alam) to protect the countries; and hence they were termed the Pánchálas.

PAÑCA-LAKSANA—The five distinguishing characteristics of Purāṇa. (*see* PURĀṆA) An epithet applied to the Puránas, meaning 'that which has five characteristic topics;' these are (1) primary creation, or cosmogony; (2) secondary creation, or the destruction and renovation of worlds; including chronology; (3) Genealogy of gods and patriarchs; (4) Reigns of the Manus, or periods called Manwantaras; and, (5) History, or such particulars as have been preserved of the princes of the solar and lunar races, and of their descendants to modern times.

PAÑCALI—Draupadī as princess of Pañcāla.

PAÑCANANA—'Five-faced.' An epithet applied to Śiva.

PAÑCAPSARAS—Name of a lake. (*see* MANDAKARṆI)

PAÑCAŚIKHA—(1) One of the earliest professors of the Sāṁkhya philosophy. **(2)** One of Śiva's attendants who was sent down to earth to console and assist Devadatta, when his course of true love did not seem likely to run smooth.

PAÑCAVIṀŚĀ—(*see* PRAUḌHA BRĀHMAṆA)

PAÑCAVṚKSA—'Five trees.' The five trees of *svarga*, named Mandāra, Pārijātaka, Santāna, Kalpavṛkṣa, and Haricandana.

PANCHA SARADIYA SAVA—A sacrifice and festival that is supposed to have held the same position in ancient India as the Dúrga-púja does now. It was celebrated successively for five years, the length of the ceremony being limited to five days on each occasion, and beginning with the new moon. The chief sacrifices consisted of seventeen five-year old humpless dwarf bulls, and the same number of dwarf heifers under three years.

The former were simply consecrated and then get free; and the latter, after various invocations and religious observances, were immolated, three on each day, excepting the last, when five were sacrificed.(*Journal of the Asiatic Society of Bengal*. Part I, No. 2, 1872.)

PANCHATANTRA—The collection of Fables and stories termed Panchatantra or Panchopákhyána, is one of the oldest in the world. It was translated from Sanskrit into Persian in the sixth century; and from Persian into Arabic in the ninth century; it was afterwards rendered into Hebrew, Greek, Latin and Syriac; from these versions successive translations were made into all the languages of modern Europe, until it became universally known as Pilpay's *Fables*.

The narrator of the stories is in the Arabic version called Bidpai; in the Sanscrit original no name similar to this occurs; but it is certain that the name Pilpay, by which the work is known in Europe, is a corruption of Bidpai.

The Arabic translation of the Panchatantra is called Kalila wa Damna; it is thus designated in allusion to two jackals which act a conspicuous part in the first story of the Arabic version, and which we recognise in the Sanskrit and Canarese under the forms Karataka and Damanaka.

The most admired Persian translation is not that which was first made, but the one written at the beginning of the sixteenth century, and known under the title of Anwár-i-soheili; which was afterwards rendered into Turkish with the designation of Humáyun Námeh.

With the exception of the Bible and the Pilgrim's progress, there is probably no work that has been translated into so many languages as the Pancha Tantra. In India it has retained its popularity to the present time, and is found in some form in all the spoken dialects of the country.

The Sanskrit epitome of the Panchatantra is termed the "Hitópadésa," or "Salutary Instruction." This has been translated into English by Sir William Jones and by Sir Charles Wilkins.

"Its popularity" says Professor Johnson, "through so many ages, amidst such various nations, is evidence of intrinsic merit; and the pictures of domestic manners and human nature which it presents, however tinctured by national peculiarities, must have been recognised as universally true, as well as diverting; or they would not have been naturalized in the west as well as in the east. In the maxims also which the tales serve to illustrate, there must have been much which secured the acquiescence of all mankind, or the remarks would have been left to enlighten the moralists of India alone. These merits, however, were such as admitted of transfusion into other languages; the merits of its composition are those which have chiefly recommended its preservation by the Press, and its circulation amongst the cultivators of Sanskrit literature."

There is a great diversity in the manuscript copies of the Pancha Tantra. Many differences occur in the various stories. In some versions the residence of the king is in Mahilaropya, a city in the south of India, which Professor Wilson identifies with St. Thomé. The Canarese version of the Pancha Tantra follows the Hitópadésa in making the residence of the king in Pátaliputra on the Ganges.

The king had three sons who were deficient in ability and application. He made this known to his counsellors and sought their advice; asking them "of what use is a son who has neither knowledge nor virtue? Of what use is a cow that has no milk with her calf, &c.? A learned brahman who was present offered to relieve the king of his anxiety by taking the princes to his house and instructing them perfectly. He then composed in their benefit these five chapters; Mitra Bhéda, Dissension of friends; Mitra Prápti, acquisition of friends; Kakolukíya, inveterate enmity; Labda Mashta, loss of advantage; Asamprekshya karitwa, inconsiderateness. Through reading these the princes became in six months highly accomplished, and the five tantras were famous throughout the world.

An analytical account of the Panchatantra is contained in the *Works* of H. H. Wilson, Vol. IV.

PANCHADASA HYMNS—A collection of hymns, created along with the Yajur Veda from the southern mouth of Brahmá.

PANCHAKARYA—The five products derived from the cow, *viz.*, milk, curds, clarified butter, urine and dung. When any one is near death the purohitá pours a little of this mixture into the mouth of the sick man and by the virtue of that nauseous draught the body is perfectly purified. See PRÁYASCHITA.

PANCHANGA—The Hindu Calendar, Panchanga means five members. It contains five principal heads, namely, the days of the month, the sign in which the moon is each day to be found, the day of the week, the eclipses, and the place of the planets. It likewise marks the good days and the evil; those on which one may journey towards any of the four cardinal points; for each point of the compass has its lucky and unlucky days; and a person who might to-day travel very successfully towards the north, would expose himself to some grievous danger if he took a southward course. It farther contains a vast number of predictions of all sorts which would be too tedious for this place.

PANCHAPSARAS—(Panchápsaras), the lake of the five nymphs. The nymphs were sent from heaven by Agni and the gods to lure away the sage Máṇḍakarṇi, (*q.v.*) from his severe austerities. In this they were successful—

And he for his beloved's sake,
Formed a fair palace 'neath the lake.
Under the flood the ladies live,
To joy and ease their days they give.
And lap in bliss the hermit wooed
From penance rites, to youth renewed.

—Griffith's *Ramayana*, vol. III.

PANCHAVATI—A charming valley in the heart of the dark forest Danḍaka; it abounds in fruit trees and limpid waters, like Nandana the garden of Indra. By the advice of the sage Agastya, this blooming valley was selected by Ráma and Lakshmana for their hermitage when in exile: it was here that Lakshmana constructed a graceful cabin, built by branches and thatched with leaves; "and over it a neem tree extended its kindly arms, and whispered something amidst its rustling foliage, which was surely a blessing." "When she saw their new dwelling Síta clapped her hands together for joy." It was from this hermitage that Rávaṇa afterwards carried off Síta.

Panchavati is near Nasik on the Godavary. A letter from a native friend in 1865 describes the locality with great vividness as if the events for which it is celebrated were quite of recent occurrence. The residence of Ráma is pointed out; and the *Sitágumphá*, where Síta used to sit, and from whence Rávaṇa is said to have carried her off; the Tapóvana, where the Munis resided; and the place where Lakshmana cut off the nose and care of *Súrpanakha*.

PAÑCOPAKHYANA—The *Pañcatantra*.

PANDAVAS—The five sons of the *Rája* Páṇḍu. After their father's death they returned to Hastinápur, and were kindly received by their uncle Dritaráshtra; they were brought up with their cousins the Kauravas, in the old palace of Hastinápur; but from the days of their early youth the sons of Dritaráshtra were ever jealous of the sons of Páṇḍu. Dúryodhana, the eldest of the Kauravas, attempted to take the life of Bhíma. Soon after, a famous Brahman preceptor, named Drona, arrived at the city of Hastinápur. Their Uncle Bhíshma engaged him to instruct the Kauravas and Páṇḍavas in arms and sciences. Drona took great pains in teaching all the young men, but especially in teaching the Páṇḍavas. To Yudhishthir he imparted the use of the spear, but that young prince became more renowned for wisdom and goodness than for deeds of arms. To Arjuna he taught the use of the bow, and Arjuna became the most famous archer of his time. To Bhíma he taught the use of the club, for Bhíma was a young man of great appetite and enormous strength, and could wield the club right lustily. To Nakula he taught the whole art of taming and managing horses, and to Sahadeva Astronomy and the use of the sword. Drona instructed the Kauravas in like manner, as well as his own son Aswattháma. But of all his pupils the most beloved was Arjuna, for he was the most perfect of all; and thus, while Duryodhana, the eldest of the Kauravas was jealous of all the Páṇḍavas, he was the most jealous of Arjuna.

This feeling increased and led to many quarrels; ultimately to the exile of the Páṇḍavas, who were sent by Dritaráshtra to the city of Varanávata. Here

Duryodhana plotted their destruction by having them invited to a house built of combustible materials, with the intention of setting it on fire at night when they were all asleep. A retainer of his, Purochana, was the agent sent to effect this. The plot was discovered; au underground passage was dug through which they might escape; and Bhíma set on fire the house of Purochana; the flames reached the house of the Páṇḍavas, who were conducted by Bhíma through the passage underground, and went into the jungle with their mother Kuntí. They afterwards lived as mendicant brahmans in the city of Ekachakra (*q.v.*) Their subsequent history embraces the events that led to the Great War in the plain of Kurukshetra; the details of which will be found under the names of the various actors in it. The brothers at last assumed the garb of devotees, and after passing through many lands, they reached the Himálaya mountains, and there died one after the other, and were transported to the heaven of Indra. The fine description of the renunciation of their kingdom by the five brothers, and their journey towards Indra'a heaven has been well translated by Monier Williams:—

> When the four brothers know the high resolve of king Yudhishthtra,
> Forthwith with Draupadi they issued forth, and after them a dog
> Followed; the king himself went out the seventh from the royal city,
> And all the citizens and women of the palace walked behind;
> But none could find it in their heart to say unto the king,' Return.'
> And so at length the train of citizens went back, bidding adieu.
> Then the high-minded sons of Pándu and the noble Draupadí
> Roamed onwards, fasting with their faces towards the cast; their hearts
> Yearning for union with the Infinite; bent on abandonment
> Of worldly things. They wandered on to many countries, many a sea
> And river. Yudhishthira walked in front, and next to him came Bhíma,
> And Arjuna came after him, and then, in order, the twin brothers.
> And last of all came Draupadi, with her dark skin and lotus-eyes—
> The faithful Draupadí, loveliest of woman, best of wives—
> Behind them walked the only living thing that shared their pilgrimage,
> The dog—And by degrees they reached the briny sea. There Arjuna
> Cast in the waves his bow and quivers. Then with souls well disciplined
> They reached the northern region, and beheld with heaven-aspiring hearts
> The mighty mountain Himavat. Beyond its lofty peak they passed
> Towards the sea of sand, and saw at last the rocky Meru, king
> Of mountains. As with eager steps they hastened on, their souls intent
> On union with the Eternal, Draupadí lost hold of her high hope,
> And faltering fell upon the earth.

"One by one the others also drop, till only Bhíma, Yudhishthira, and the dog are left. Still Yudhishthira walks steadily in front, calm and unmoved, looking neither to the right hand nor to the left, and gathering up his soul in inflexible resolution. Bhíma, shocked at the fall of his companions, and unable to understand how beings so apparently guileless should be struck down by fate, appeals to his brother, who without looking back explains that death is the consequence of sinful thoughts and too great attachment to worldly objects; and that Draupadí's fall was owing to her excessive affection for Arjuna; Sahadeva's (who is supposed to be the most humble-minded of the five brothers) to his pride in his own knowledge; Nakula's (who is very handsome) to feelings of personal vanity; and Arjuna's to a boastful confidence in his power to destroy hit foes. Bhíma then feels himself falling, and is told that he suffers death for his selfishness, pride, and too great love of enjoyment. The sole survivor is now Yudhishthira, who still walks steadily forward, followed only by the dog.

> When with a sudden sound that rang through earth and heaven, came the god
> Towards him in a chariot, and he cried, "Ascend, O resolute prince."
> Then did the king look back upon his fallen brothers, and address'd
> These words unto the Thousand-eyed, in anguish—"Let my brothers here
> Come with me. Without them, O God of Gods, I would not wish to enter
> E'en heaven; and yonder tender princess Draupadí, the faithful wife,
> Worthy of happiness, let her too come. In mercy hear my prayer."

Upon this, Indra informs him that the spirits of Draupadí and his brothers are already in heaven, and that he alone is permitted to ascend there in bodily form. Yudhishthira now stipulates that his dog shall be admitted with him. Indra says sternly, "Heaven has no place for those who are accompanied by dogs (Śwavatám);" but Yudhishthira is unshaken in his resolution, and declines abandoning the faithful animal. Indra remonstrates—"You have abandoned your brothers and Draupadí; why not forsake the dog?" To this Yudhishthira haughtily replies, "I had no power to bring them back to life; how can there be abandonment of those who no longer live?"

The dog, it appears, was his own father Dharma in disguise (Mahaprasthánika-parva.) Reassuming now his proper form he praises Yudhishthira for his constancy, and they enter heaven together. There, to his surprise, he finds Duryodhana and his cousins, but not his brothers or Draupadi. Hereupon he declines remaining in heaven without them. An angel is then sent to conduct him across the Indian Sntyx (Vaitariṇí) to the hell where they are supposed to be. The scene which now follows may be compared to the Necyomanteia in the eleventh book of the Odyssey, or to parts of Dante.

"The particular hell to which Yudhishthira is taken is a dense wood, whose leaves are sharp swords, and its ground paved with razors. The way to it is strewed with foul and mutilated corpses. Hideous shapes flit across the air and hover over him. Here there is a horror of palpable darkness. There the wicked are burning in flames of blazing fire. Suddenly he hears the voices of his brothers and companions imploring him to assuage their torments, and not desert them. - His resolution is shaken. Deeply affected, he bids the angel leave him to share their miseries. This is his last trial. The whole scene now vanishes. It was a mere illusion, to test his constancy to the utmost. He is now directed to bathe in the heavenly Ganges; and having plunged into the sacred stream, he enters the real heaven, where at length, in company with Draupadí and his brothers, he finds that rest and happiness which were unattainable on earth." **(2)** Patronymic from Panḍu, applied first to his five sons, and then generally to their party or army. Also to Arjuna in particular. (* *Indian Epic Poetry*, p. 29 to 31.)

PANDU or PRANA—A son of Dhatrí and Áyatí, who was married to Pundaríka, and was the ancestor of Uṣanas the preceptor of the Daityas.

PANDU—The second son of the Vyása, Krishṇa Dwaipáyana and Ambáliká one of the widows of Raja Vichitravirya,—the Pale, was the half-brother of Dhritáráshtṛa who was blind. "The reason given for these defects is curious. Ambiká, (the mother of Dhritáráshtṛa) was so terrified by the swarthy complexion and shaggy aspect of the sage Vyása, that when he visited her she closed her eyes, and did not venture to open them while he was with her. In consequence of this assumed blindness her child was born blind. Ambáliká, on the other hand, though she kept her eyes open, became so colourless with fright that her son was born with a pale complexion. Páṇḍu seems in other respects to have been good looking."* He was the father of the five Páṇḍava princes Yudhishthira, Bhíma, Arjuna, Nakula, and Sahadeva. He married Kunti, or Pritha, and sometime afterwards his uncle Bhíshma, wishing him to take a second wife, "made an expedition to Śalya, king of Madra, and prevailed upon him to bestow his sister Mádri upon Páṇḍu, in exchange for vast sums of money and jewels."** But as Páṇḍu had incurred a curse from a deer which he shot, he was prevented from having progeny himself, and the Páṇḍava princes were therefore begotten respectively by the gods Dharma, Vayu, Indra, and the twin Aswinas.

Páṇḍu was carefully educated by his uncle Bhíshma, who afterwards installed him as Rája of Bhárata. The Rája Páṇḍu was a great warrior, and is said to have undertaken a campaign which would have extended his empire over all Hindustan, from the Punjab to Bengal, and from the slopes of the Himálayas to the Vindhya mountains. But he was addicted to hunting, and he went with his two wives to the Himálaya Mountains; but his life there is filled with mythical details that may be passed over. While the five princes were still children, Páṇḍu, forgetting the curse of the sage whom he had killed in the form of a deer, ventured one day to embrace his wife Mádri, and died in her arms. She and Kunti then had a dispute for the honour of becoming a sati (suttee) which ended with Mádri burning herself with her husband's corpse.† (* *Indian Epic Poetry*, p. 92. ** *Ibid*. † *Ibid*.)

PANDYA—Pāṇḍya, Cola and Cera were three kingdoms in the south of the Peninsula for some centuries before and after the Christian era. Pāṇḍya was well known to the Romans as the kingdom of King Pandion, who is said to have sent ambassadors on two different occasions to Augustus Caesar. Its capital was Madurā, the Southern Mathurā. Pāṇḍya seems to have fallen under the ascendancy of the Cola kings in the seventh or eighth century.

PANINI—"The greatest known grammarian of ancient India, whose work on the Sanskrit language has up to the present day remained the standard of Sanskrit grammar. Its merits are so great, that Páṇini was ranked among the Rishis, or inspired seers, and at a later period of Sanskrit literature, was supposed to have received the fundamental rules of his work from the god Śiva himself. Of the personal history of Páṇini nothing positive is known, except that he was a native of the village Salâtura, situated north-west of Attock, on the Indus—whence he is also surnamed Sálaturíya—and that his mother was called Dâkehî, wherefore, on his mother's side, he must have been a descendant of the celebrated family of Daksha. A talebook, the *Kathâsa-ritsâgara* (*i. e*, the ocean for the rivers of tales,) gives, indeed, some circumstantial account of the life and death of Páṇini; but its narrative is so absurd, and the work itself of so modern a date—it was written in Cashmere, at the beginning of the twelfth century—that no credit whatever can be attached to the facts related by it, or to the inferences which modern scholars have drawn from them. According to the views expressed by Goldstücker (*Pánini, his place in Sanskrit Literature:* London, 1861,) it is probable that Páṇini lived before Sâkyamuni, the founder of the Buddhist religion, whose death took place about 543 B. C., but that a more definite date of the great grammarian has but little chance of ascertainment in the actual condition of Sanskrit philosophy. The grammar of Páṇini consists of eight Adhyâyas, or books, each book comprising four Pádas, or chapters, and each chapter a number of Sûtras (*q.v.*) or aphoristical rules. The latter amount in the whole to 3996; but three, perhaps four, of them did not originally belong to the work of Páṇini. The arrangement of these rules differs completely from what a European would expect in a grammatical work, for it is based on the principle of tracing linguistic *phenomena*, and not concerned in the classification of the linguistic *material*, according to the so-called parts of speech. A chapter, for instance, treating of a prolongation of vowels, will deal with such a fact whenever it occurs, be it in the formation of bases, or in conjugation, declension, composition, &c. The rules of conjugation, declension, &c, are, for the same reason, not to be met with in the same chapter or in the same order in which European grammars would teach them; nor would any single book or chapter, however apparently more systematically arranged—from a European point of view—such as the chapters on affixes or composition, suffice by itself to convey the full linguistic material concerned in it, apart from the rest of the work. In a general manner, Páṇini's work may therefore be called a natural history of the Sanskrit language, in the sense that it has the strict tendency of giving an accurate description of facts, instead of making such a description subservient to the theories according to which the linguistic material is usually distributed by European grammarians. Whatever objections may be raised against such an arrangement, the very fact of its differing from that in our grammars makes it peculiarly instructive to the European student, as it accustoms his mind to survey language from another point of view than that usually presented to him, and as it must induce him, too, to question the soundness of many linguistic theories now looked upon as axiomatic truths. As the method of Páṇini requires in a student the power of combining many rules scattered all over the work, and of combining, also, many inferences to be drawn from these rules, it exercises, moreover, on the mind of the student an effect analogous to that which is supposed to be the peculiar advantage of the study of mathematics. The rules of Páṇini were criticised and completed by Kátyáyana, who, according to all probability, was the teacher, and therefore the contemporary of Patanjali; and he, in his turn, was criticised by Patanjali, (*q.v.*,) who sides frequently with Páṇini. These three authors are the canonical triad of the grammarians of India; and their works are, in truth, so remarkable in their own department, that they exceed in literary merit nearly all, if not all, grammatical productions of other nations, so far as the two classes are comparable.

The rules of Páṇini were commented on by many authors. The best existing commentary on them is that called the *Kasikavritti*, by Vámana Jayáditya, which follows these rules in their original order. At a later period, attempts were made to arrange the rules of Páṇini in a manner that approaches more to the European method; the chief work of this category is the *Siddhánta Kaumutí*, by Bhaṭṭóji-díkshita. Páṇini mentions, in his Sútras, several grammarians who preceded him, amongst others, Sákatayana. Manuscripts of a grammar ascribed to a grammarian of this name exist in the Library of the India Office in London, and in the Library of the Board of Examiners at Madras. On the ground of a few pages only of the latter an attempt has been very recently made to prove that this grammar is the one referred to by Páṇini, and therefore older than the work of the latter. But the facts adduced in proof of this hypothesis are so ludicrously weak, and the reasoning upon them so feeble and inconclusive, whereas the evidence in favour of the comparatively recent date of this work is so strong, that no value whatever can be attached to this hasty hypothesis. For the present, therefore, Páṇini's work still remains the oldest existing grammatical work of India, and probably of the human race. The Sútras of Páṇini with a modern commentary by two native pandits, and with extracts from the *Vârttikas* of Kâtyâyana and the *Mahâbhâshya of* Patanjali, were edited at Calcutta in 1809. This edition, together with the modern commentary, but with garbled extracts from the extracts mentioned, was re-printed at Bonn in 1839-1840 by Dr. O. Bochtlingk, who added to it remarks of his own and some indices. For the literature connected with Páṇini, see Colebrooke's preface to his *Grammar of the Sanskrit Language* (Calc. 1805,) and Goldstücker's *Páṇini*, &c., as mentioned above."—Chambers' *Encyclopœdia*, VII, 231.

PANIS—'Niggards.' In the *Ṛgveda*, "the senseless, false, evil-speaking, unbelieving, unpraising, unworshipping Paṇis were *dasyus* or envious demons who used to steal cows and hide them in caverns". They are said to have stolen the cows recovered by Śaramā. (*q.v.*).

PANLOMI—The wife of Brighu, a descendant of the daughters of Daksha.

PANNAGA—A serpent, snake, (*see* NĀGA)

PANNAGARI—A teacher of the Rig Veda, who was previously a pupil of Bashkáli.

PANTHEISM—The identification of God and the Universe. This is a principle which the Puráṇas most unequivocally and resolutely maintain. Vishṇu, Śiva, or Sakti, whatever individual they undertake to glorify, is not only the remote and efficient, but the proximate and substantial cause of the world. Thus in the Linga Puráṇa, Brahmá addresses Śiva, 'Glory to thee whose form is the universe.' In the Vishṇu Puráṇa, 'This world was produced from Vishṇu; it exists in him; he is the cause of its continuance and cessation, he is the world.' In the Kalika Puráṇa, the goddess Kalí is said to be identical with the universe, as well as distinct from it; and in the Brahmá Vaivartta, even Rádhá is eulogised as the mother of the world; and the world itself; as one with primæval nature—with universal nature, and with all created forms; with all cause and with all effect.' Expressions of this tenor occur in every page of the Puráṇas; and although something may be ascribed to the exaggerations of panegyric, and the obscurities of mysticism, yet the declarations are too positive and reiterated to admit of reasonable doubt. And it cannot be questioned that these writers confound the creature with the Creator, and expose themselves justly to the imputation of gross materialism.

Little doubt can be entertained that the materialism of the Puráṇas derives some countenance from the Vedas. Universality is there predicated of the Supreme Being directly, without the intervention of any one of his hypostasia. Thus it is said, 'This whole is Brahmá, from Brahmá to a clod of earth. Brahmá is both the efficient and the material cause of the world. He is the potter by whom the fictive vase is formed; he is the clay of which it is fabricated. Everything proceeds from him without waste or diminution of the source, as light radiates from the sun. Everything merges into him again, as bubbles bursting mingle with the air, as rivers fall into the ocean, and lose their identity in its waters. 'Everything proceeds from and returns to him, as the web of the spider is emitted from and retracted into itself.'* These and similar illustrations speak the language of materialism too plainly to be misunderstood, although it may be possible that the full extent of their signification was not intended; that these comparisons are not to be interpreted too literally; that they purpose no more than to assert the origin of all things from the same first cause; that the authors of the texts may have been in the same predicament as the author of the 'Essay on Man,' and inculcated materialism without being aware of it.† (* *Trans. R. As. Society*, 111, 413. † Wilson, *Works*, II, 94, 95.)

PAPA-PURUSA—'Man of sin.' A personification of all wickedness in a human form, of which all the members are great sins. The head is brāhmaṇicide, the arm cow killing, the woman-murder, &c.

PAPA—The name of one of the Narakas.

PARA OR PARA—A river in Malwa, the Párvatí.

PARADAS—A barbarous people dwelling in the north-west. Manu says they were kṣatriyas degraded to be śūdras.

PARAMANU—A measure of time, equal to one Anu.

PARAMARSIS—(Parama-ṛṣis). The great *ṛṣis*. (*see* ṚṢI)

PARAMATMA—A name of Vishṇu, meaning 'supreme

spirit.'

PARAMATMAN—The supreme soul of the universe.

PARAMESTHIN—**(1)** 'Who stands in the highest place.' A title applied to any superior god and to some distinguished mortals. A name used in the Vedas for a son or a creation of Prajāpati. **(2)** The son of Indrayumna, a descendant of Bharata.

PARAMIKSHA—A son of Anu.

PARAM—The duration of Brahmá's life, consisting of a hundred of his years.

PARANDALA—(Parándalá), a local name of Vishṇu.

PARAN—The heavenly one, in Tamil. It corresponds with Brahm, or Para Brahm of the Upanishads. In the South there has been a controversy whether Vishṇu or Śiva is Paran, or the Supreme Being.

PARARDDHAM—**(1)** Half of the duration of Brahmá's life; **(2)** That number, which occurs in the eighteenth place of figures, enumerated according to the rule of decimal notation.

PARAS—A class of deities, consisting of twelve, to appear in the ninth Manwantara.

PARASARA PURANA—(*see* PURĀṆA)

PARASARA—A Vedic *ṛṣi* to whom some hymns of the *Ṛgveda* are attributed. He was a disciple of Kapila, and he received the *Viṣṇu Purāṇa* from Pulastya and taught it to Maitreya. He was also a writer on Dharmaśāstra, and texts of his are often cited in books on law. Speculations as to his era differ widely, from 575 BC to 1391 BC, and cannot be trusted. By an amour with Satyavatī he was father of Kṛṣṇa Dvaipāyana, the Vyāsa or arranger of the Vedas. According to the *Nirukta*, he was son of Visiṣtha, but the *Mahābhārata* and the *Viṣṇu Purāṇa* make him the son of Śaktri and grandson of Vasiṣtha. The legend of his birth, as given in the *Mahābhārata*, is that King Kalmāṣapāda met with Śaktri in a narrow path, and desired him to get out of the way. The sage refused, and the *rājā* struck him with his whip. Thereupon the sage cursed the *rājā so* that he became a man-eating *rākṣasa*. In this state he ate up Śaktri, whose wife, Adṛśyantī, afterwards gave birth to Parāśara. When this child grew up and heard the particulars of his father's death, he instituted a sacrifice for the destruction of all the *rākṣasas*, but was dissuaded from its completion by Vasiṣtha and other sages. As he desisted, he scattered the remaining sacrificial fire upon the northern face of the Himālaya, where it still blazes forth at the phases of the moon, consuming *rākṣasas*, forests, and mountains.

A great sage, the son of Śakti, and grandson of Vaṣishtha. In order to avenge the death of his father, who had been devoured by a Rákshas, he commenced a sacrifice to effect the destruction of all the Rákshasas, but was dissuaded from it by his grandsire; who allowed him that his father's death was the work of destiny. Pulastya taught him the Vishṇu Purána, which he related to Maitareya, to convey the truths that the world was produced from Vishṇu; that it exists in him; that he is the cause of its continuance and cessation; that he is the world. Paráṣara was also the Vyása of the twenty-sixth Dwápara, and a teacher of a branch of the Rig-Veda, and of the Sáma Veda.

Buchanan has noticed the incompatibility of Paráṣara's genealogy with his being, as it is stated, contemporary with Śántanu, king of Hastinápur, that prince being the 44th in descent from Atri, who *is* contemporary with Vaṣishtha, who again is but three generations anterior to Paráṣara; he supposes therefore that many generations in the line of Vaṣishtha must have been omitted. It is not necessary, however, to attempt to reconcile these incongruities, for the coetaneous existence of Atri and Vaṣishtha is less chronological than mythological, or perhaps, as they are both enumerated amongst the stars of the great bear, astronomical; it extends throughout the Manwantara, their immediate successors, who hold a sacred character, enjoy a like longevity, and are similarly contemporary, at any period, with their ancestry and posterity; if we consider them as mere mortals we must suppose that Paráṣara preceded the great war by three generations, Krishṇa Dwaipáyana Vyása, his son, being the father of Dhritaráshtra, Páṇḍu, and Vidura, by the widows of Vichitravírya. Vyása was, however, contemporary with his grandson and their descendants, agreeably to the above system of saintly immortality. Mr. Bentley places Parásara, about 575, B.C., (*Hindu Astronomy*); Buchanan, about 1300, B.C., (*Genealogies of the Hindus*); and Wilford, 1391, B.C., (*As. Res.* IX. 87); Wilson's *Works*, III, 123. **(2)** A second Paráṣara is the author of a celebrated code of laws; he is mentioned by Yajnavalka in his standard work, and often quoted by the commentaries; **(3)** There is a third of the same name the reputed author of a Tantra; and, **(4)** A fourth, the author of an astronomical work.

PARASIKAS—Pārśikas or Fārsikas, *i.e.*, Persians. The people of Pars.

PARA—Supreme, infinite; and Pára, the farther bank or limit, the point that is to be attained by crossing a river or sea, or figuratively the world or existence. Vishṇu, then, is Pára, that which nothing surpasses; and Pára, the end or object of existence; he is Apára pára, the farthest bound of that which is illimitable, or space and time: he is Param parabhyah, above or beyond the highest being, beyond or superior to all the elements: he is Paramartha rúpí, or identical with final truth, or knowledge of soul: he is Brahmá pára, the object or essence of spiritual wisdom. Parapárabhuta is said to imply the farther limit (Pára) of rudimental matter. See Wilson's *Notes* to Vishṇu Purána, 113.

PARASURAMA—'Rāma with the axe.' The first Rāma and the sixth *avatāra* of Viṣṇu. He was a brāhmaṇa, the fifth son of Jamadagni and Reṇukā. By his father's side he descended from Bhṛgu, and was, *par excellence*, the Bhārgava; by his mother's side he belonged to the royal race of the Kuśikas. He became manifest in the world at the beginning of the *tretā yuga*, for the purpose of repressing the tyranny of the kṣatriya or regal caste. His story is told in the *Mahābhārata* and in the Purāṇas. He also appears in the *Rāmāyaṇa*, but chiefly as an opponent of Rāmacandra. According to the *Mahābhārata*, he instructed Arjuna in the use of arms, and had a combat with Bhīṣma, in which both suffered equally. He is also represented as being present at the great war council of the Kaurava princes. This Paraśurāma, the sixth *avatāra* of Viṣṇu, appeared in the world before Rāma or Rāmacandra, the seventh *avatāra*, but they were both living at the same time, and the elder incarnation showed some jealousy of the younger. The *Mahābhārata* represents Paraśurāma as being struck senseless by Ramacandra, and the *Rāmāyaṇa* relates how Paraśurāma, who was a follower of Śiva, felt aggrieved by Rāma's breaking the bow of Śiva, and challenged him to a trial of strength. This ended in his defeat, and in some way led to his being "excluded from a seat in the celestial world". In early life Paraśurāma was under the protection of Śiva, who instructed him in the use of arms, and gave him the *paraśu*, or axe, from which he is named. The first act recorded of him by the *Mahābhārata is* that, by command of his father, he cut off the head of his mother, Reṇukā. She had incensed her husband by entertaining impure thoughts, and he called upon each of his sons in succession to kill her. Paraśurāma alone obeyed, and his readiness so pleased his father that he told him to ask a boon. He begged that his mother might be restored pure to life, and, for himself, that he might be invincible in single combat and enjoy length of days. Paraśurāma's hostility to the kṣatriyas evidently indicates a severe struggle for the supremacy between them and the brāhmaṇas. He is said to have cleared the earth of the kṣatriyas twenty-one times, and to have given the earth to the brāhmaṇas. The origin of his hostility to the kṣatriyas is thus related: Kārtavīrya, a kṣatriya, and king of the Haihayas had a thousand arms. This king paid a visit to the hermitage of Jamadagni in the absence of that sage, and was hospitably entertained by his wife, but when he departed he carried off a sacrificial calf belonging to their host. This act so enraged Paraśurāma that he pursued Kārtavīrya, cut off his thousand arms and killed him. In retaliation the sons of Kārtavīrya killed Jamadagni, and for that murder Paraśurāma vowed vengeance against them and the whole kṣatriya race. "Thrice seven times did he clear the earth of the kṣatriya caste, and he filled with their blood the five large lakes of Samantapañcaka." He then gave the earth to Kaśyapa, and retired to the Mahendra mountains, where he was visited by Arjuna. Tradition ascribes the origin of the country of Malabar to Paraśurāma. According to one account he received it as a gift from Varuṇa and according to another he drove back the ocean and cut fissures in the *ghāṭs* with blows of his axe. He is said to have brought brāhmaṇas into this country from the north, and to have bestowed the land upon them in expiation of the slaughter of the kṣatriyas. He bears the appellations *khaṇḍaparaśu*, 'who strikes with the axe', and *nyakṣa*, 'inferior'

PARA—The son of Anga, a descendant of Anu; also a son of Prithusena, a descendant of Hastin; and of Samara, in the same line.

PARAVASU—(*see* RAIBHYA and YAVAKRĪTA)

PARAVATAS—A class of deities of the Second Manwantara.

PARAVRIJ—An outcast mentioned in the Rig-Veda who was blind and lame, but restored to sight and the power of walking by the Aṣvins. *O.S.T.*, V, 246.

PARAVRIT—A prince, the son of Rukmakavacha, and father of Jyámagha.

PÁRIJAT TREE—A celestial tree, produced at the churning of the ocean, from the whirlpool of the deep, the delight of the nymphs of heaven, perfuming the world with its blossoms. Krishṇa, at the desire of his wife Satyabháma carried off this tree from the gardens of Indra. Śachí excited Indra to prevent its removal. A conflict ensued between the gods and Krishṇa, which is narrated at great length in the *Harivamsa*, and with some variations in the Vishṇu Purána. Krishṇa was victorious, and took the tree to Dwáraka where it was planted in Satyabháma's garden. When Krishṇa abandoned his mortal body the tree proceeded to heaven again along with the Sudharman palace.

PARIKSHIT—Son of Abhimanyu by his wife Uttarā, grandson of Arjuna, and father of Janamejaya. After the destruction of the Kurus the child (Paríkshit) was killed in die womb of his mother Uttará, by the magic Brahmá weapon hurled by Aswattháman, but restored to life again by Krishṇa. When the Pándava princes determined to renounce the world and retire into the forest, the Rájah Yudhishthira gave the Ráj of Hastinápur to Paríkshit. The commencement of the Kali age is placed at the beginning of the reign of Paríkshit, though according to the usual notions it commenced from the death of Krishṇa. The Vyása, who arranged or compiled the Puránas, flourished during the reign of Paríkshit. The prince himself died of the bite of a snake, according to the Mahabhárata, and it is said the Bhágavata Purána was related to him between the bite and its fatal effect. The king had incurred the imprecation of a hermit by which he was sentenced to die of the bite of a venomous snake, at the expiration of seven days; and in preparation for this event, he repaired to the banks of the Ganges; thither also went the gods and sages to witness his death. Amongst the latter was Suka the son of Vyása; and it was in reply to Parikshit's question "what should a man do who is about to die" that he narrated the Bhágavata, as he had heard it from Vyása; believing that nothing secures final happiness so certainly as to die while the thoughts are wholly engrossed by Vishṇu. *V.P.*

PARINAMIN—That which may be modified, one of the definitions of Pradhána, *q.v.*

PARIPATRA—**(1)** The northern part of the Vindhya range of mountains. According to the *Harivaṁśa*, it was the scene of the combat between Kṛṣṇa and Indra, and its heights sank down under the pressure of Kṛṣṇa's feet. Also called Pāriyātra. **(2)** A prince, the son of Ahínagu, a descendant of Kusa.

PARIPLAVA—A prince, the son of Sukhibala, or Sukhinala, of the race of Puru.

PARISAD—A college or community of brāhmaṇas associated for the study of the Vedas.

PARIVATSARA—One of the five Cyclic years, or Yugas, *q.v.*

PARIVRAJAKA—A religious mendicant. A brāhmaṇa in the fourth stage of his religious life. (*see* Brāhmaṇa)

PARIYATRA—A mountain range, to the west of Meru, called in the Vishṇu Puráṇa the limitative mountains in the west. It is said in Wilson's notes to be the same as Paripátra, the northern and western portion of the Vindhya.

PARJANYA—**(1)** The thundering rain god. There are several hymns in the Rig Veda which celebrate Parjanya, as the procreative and stimulating fructifier. "The winds blow, the lightning falls, the plants shoot up; the heaven fructifies; food is produced for all created things, when Parjanya, thundering, replenishes the earth with moisture." Parjanya forms the subject of two papers by Dr. G. Bühler, containing a comparison of Parjanya with the Lithuanian god Perkunas, the god of thunder. Dr. Bühler holds Parjanya to have been decidedly distinct from Indra. "Taking a review of the whole, we find that Parjanya is a god who presides over the lightning, the thunder, the rain, and the procreation of plants and living creatures. But it is by no means clear whether he is originally a god of the rain or a god of the thunder." He inclines, however, to think that from the etymology of his name, and the analogy between him and Perkunas, he was originally the thunder god. In his German essay, his conclusion is that Parjanya is "the god of thunderstorms and rain, the generator and nourisher of plants and living creatures."—Muir, *O.S.T.*, V, 142.

Parjanya is also represented as the brother of Aditi, and husband of Prithivi, the Earth. He is also described as the father of Soma, and the protector of the Soma plant. **(2)** A Lókapála, the regent of the north and king of clouds; **(3)** The wife of Maríchí, whose son became a Lókapála. **(4)** One of the Ādityas

PARNA—One of the fifteen teachers of the White Yajush.

PARSADA—Any treatise on the Vedas produced in a Pariṣad or Vedic college.

PARSHATA—(Párshata), son of Prishaia, the patronymic of Rája Drupada.

PARSWANATHA—The twenty-third of the Tírthankaras, or deified saints of the Jainas in the present era. He and Mahávíra the twenty-fourth, are regarded with the greatest veneration throughout Hindustan. At Belupura, near Benares, there is a temple honoured as the birthplace of Páraswanátha.

PARTHA—A son of Pṛthā or Kuntī. A title applicable to the three elder Pāṇḍavas, but especially used for Arjuna.

PARVANA SRADDHAS—Ancestral oblations, or the worship of progenitors, at certain lunar periods.

PARVASA—Called also Sarvagas the son of Paurnamása, and brother of Kaṣyapa.

PARVAS—Day of periodical impurity when a wise man must desist from the study of the Vedas.

PARVASI—The wife of Parvasa, and mother of Yajnaváma and Kaṣyata, who were both founders of Gotras or families.

PARVATHI—(Párvathi), a divine Rishi, of whom little is known except that he is called a son of Kaṣyapa. He is usually named together with Nárada.

PARVATI—The daughter of Himálaya and spouse of Mahádeva. Her name was changed to Durgá (*q.v.*); she is also called Deví, Uma, &c. Dr. Muir quotes various passages to show the dignity to which this goddess has eventually been elevated in the estimation of her worshippers; and that she has now attained a far higher rank in the Indian pantheon than was originally enjoyed by the daughter of Daksha and Himavat. *O.S.T.*, IV, 372.

PARVATIYAS—A designation of many of the aboriginal tribes of India, meaning "dwellers in mountains," from Parvati, mountain.

PASUMEDHRA—(Paṣumedhra), a disciple of Visvámitra, who visited the princes, Ráma and Lakshmana when they were residing in the forest of Daṇḍaka.

PASUPATI—'Lord of creatures.' A name of Rudra or one of his manifestations, (*see* RUDRA) There is a treatise on the Páṣupata worship, or worship of Śiva by Páṣupati. One of the eight Rudras, the one who has the place of fire.

PASUYAJNA—One of the five great sacrificial ceremonies; the sacrifice of a horse or animal. See Aṣwamedha.

PATALA—The infernal regions, inhabited by *nāgas* (serpents), *daityas*, *dānavas*,*yakṣas*, and others. They are seven in number, and their names, according to the *Viṣṇu Purāṇa*, are Atala, Vitala, Nitala, Gabhastimat, Mahātala, Sutala, and Pātāla, but these names vary in different authorities. The *Padma Purāṇa* gives the names of the seven regions and their respective rulers as follows: (1) Atala, subject to Mahāmāyā; (2) Vitala, ruled by a form of Śiva called Hātakeśvara; (3) Sutála, ruled by Bāli; (4) Talātala, ruled by Māya; (5) Mahātala, where reside the great serpents; (6) Rasātala, where the *daityas* and *dānavas* dwell; (7) Pātāla, the lowermost, in which Vāsuki reigns over the chief Nāgas or snake-gods. In the *Śiva Purāṇa* there are eight: Pātāla, Tala, Atala, Vitala, Tāla, Vidhipātāla, Sarkarābhūmi, and Vijaya. The sage Nārada paid a visit to these regions, and on his return to the skies gave a glowing account of them, declaring them to be far more delightful than Indra's heaven, and abounding with every kind of luxury and sensual gratification.

PATAÑJALA—The Yoga philosophy, (*see* DARŚANA)

PATAÑJALI—The founder of the Yoga philosophy, (*see* Darśana) The author of the *Mahābhāṣya*, a celebrated commentary on the Grammar of Pāṇini, and a defence of that work against the criticisms of Kātyāyana. He is supposed to have written about 200 B.C. Rām Kṛṣṇa Gopāl Bhaṇḍārkar, a late inquirer, says, "He probably wrote the third chapter of his *bhāṣya* between 144 and 142 B.C." Weber, however, makes his date to be AD 25. He is also called Gonardīya and Goṇikāputra. A legend accounting for his name represents that he fell as a small snake from heaven into the palm of Pāṇini (*pata*, 'fallen'; *añjali*, 'palm')

Is the name of two celebrated authors of ancient India, who are generally looked upon as the same personage, but apparently for no other reason than that they bear the same name. The one is the author of the system of philosophy called Yoga, the other the great critic of Kátyáyana and Pánini. Of the former nothing is known beyond his work—*see* YOGA. The few historical facts relating to the latter, as at present ascertained, may be gathered from his great work the Mahábháshya, or the great Commentary. The name of his mother was Goṇika; his birthplace was Gonarda, situated in the east of India, and he resided temporarily in Kashmir, where his work was especially patronised. From circumstantial evidence Professor Goldstücker has, moreover, proved that he wrote between 140 and 120 B. C. (*Pánini, his place in Sanskrit Literature.*) The Mahábháshya of Patanjali is not a full commentary on Páṇini, but with a few exceptions, only a commentary on the Várttikas, or critical remarks of Kátyáyana on Páṇini. Patanjali being the third of the grammatical triad of India, and his work therefore having the advantage of profiting by the scholarship of his predecessors, he is looked upon as a paramount authority in all matters relating to classical Sanskrit Grammar; and very justly so, for as to learning, ingenuity, and conscientiousness, there is no grammatical author of India who can be held superior to him.—Chambers' *Encyclopœdia*.

PATHA—'Reading.' There are three forms, called *pāṭhas*, in which the Vedic text is read and written: (1) Saṁhitā-pāṭha, the ordinary form, in which the words coalesce according to the rules of *sandhi*; (2) Pādapāṭha, in which each word stands separate and independent; (3) Krama-pāṭha, in which each word is given twice, first joined with the word preceding and then with the word following.

PATHYA—A teacher of the Sáma Veda.

PATTANA—'City.' Several great places have been known as Pattan or 'the city". Somanāthawas Pattan; Anhalwāra is still known as Pattan, and there is also Patna.

PATUMAT—One of the Andhra kings of Magadha, the son of Meghaswáti.

PATUMITRA—One of the kings of Mekalá, a country in the Narhada. Vishṇu Purána, p. 479.

PAULOMAS—Kaśyapa by his wife Puloma had many thousand "distinguished *dānavas* called Paulomas, who were powerful, ferocious, and cruel". They were killed by Arjuna.

PAUNDRA, PAUṆḌRAKA Belonging to the country of Puṇḍra. The conch-shell of Bhīṣma.

PAUNDRAKA—A Vasudeva, who assumed the insignia and style of Krishṇa, and was supported by his friend and ally the king of Kásí. Krishṇa marched against them and destroyed them both. The son of the king of Kásí then sent a magical being against Krishṇa; but the discus, Sudarsana, speedily destroyed it, with the army of Kásí, and the demi-gods attendant upon Śiva: the discus afterwards set on fire the city of Benares consuming it and its inhabitants. In this legend, says Professor Wilson, we have a contest between the followers of Vishṇu and Śiva intimated, as, besides the assistance given by the latter to Paundraka, Benares has been from all time, as it is at present, the high place of the Saiva worship.

PAUNDRAS—The inhabitants of Pundra, a western province of Bengal.

PAURAS—A race of kings whose dynasty continued three hundred years. *Vishṇu Purána*, p. 477.

PAURAVAS—Descendants of Puru of the Lunar race. (*see* PURU)

PAURAVI—A title, attached to the second Rohini, wife of Vasudeva, to distinguish her from the first, the mother of Balaráma.

PAURNAMASA—The son of Maríchí and Sambhúti.

PAURNAMASI—The day of full moon one of the seasons when gifts are meritorious.

PAUSHA—The name of one of the lunar months, corresponding to December.

PAUSHINJI—A teacher of the Sáma Veda.

PAVAKA, PAVAMANA—Two of the brilliant sons of Agni. According to the Váyu Purána Pauvamána is the fire produced by friction, or Nirmathaya; and Pávaka is electric or Vaidyata fire. The Bhágavata makes these two fires the sons of Antarddhána. When dominion over different provinces of creation was assigned to different beings, Pávaka was made chief of the Vásus.

PAVANA—'Wind.' The god of the wind. (*see* VĀYU)

PAVITRAS—One of the five classes of deities of the fourteenth Manwantars.

PAYOSHNI—A river that the Vishṇu Purána says rises from the Riksha mountains; but the Váyu and Kúrna bring it from the Vindhya range. There are several indications of its position in the Mahábhárata, but none very precise. Its source appears to be near that of the Krishna; it flows near the beginning of the Dandaka forest, which should place it rather new to the sources of the Godáverí; it passes through Vidarbha or Berar, and Yudhishthira having bathed in it, comes to the Vaidúrya mountain and the Narbadá river. These circumstances make it likely that the Payín Ganga is the river in question.

PERUMAL TIRUMAL—This is a festival in honour of Vishṇu celebrated by the Vishṇubhaktis. It lasts eleven days or longer, Vishṇu and his consort being daily carried about the streets with great pomp—in the first two days in a palanquin; on the third day in his vehicle Garuda; on the fourth on the monkey Hanumán; on the fifth on a lion; on the sixth under a small arch or bow of metal called Tiruvasi; on the seventh under a large Tiruvasi; on the eighth on a horse; and on the ninth on a large car; at these processions the idols are followed by many Vaishṇava Brahmans, beating cymbals and chanting the praises of Vishṇu; on the tenth day—the great day of the feast, Vishṇu is for the last time carried about early in the morning; and in the evening of the eleventh day, which is called Dhar-ba-tirumal, he and his consort Lakshmí are seated on a couch of Dharba-grass, placed on a raft in a tank; and Brahmans, musicians and dancing girls, having entered on the name raft, it is floated from one end of the tank to the other, thrice, in the sight of a multitude of people standing on the banks, which are studded with many lights and adorned with many flowers.—Metzger's *Ziegenbalg*.

PHALGUNA—(1) A name of Arjuna. **(2)** Name of a month. A lunar month corresponding nearly to January.

PILGRIMAGE—Pilgrimages have been customary in India for many centuries. In various parts of the country there are celebrated temples or places of reputed sanctity, at which great numbers of people annually assemble for professedly religious purposes. "The name of Jagannáth still draws the faithful from a hundred provinces of India to the Puri sands. This yearning after holy places seems, indeed, to form part of the universal religion of mankind. To gaze upon the scenes amid which the deity has dwelt, to bathe in the rivers that once laved his mystical incarnate frame, to halt at noon-day under hoary trees beneath which the divine presence has reposed, to pray upon the mountain hallowed by his lonely communings, and to behold in the everlasting rock the foot-prints of the god, are longings which have, at one period or another, filled the imagination and stirred the innermost heart of all noble races. From that ancient night on which the ladder was let down from heaven, and the angels ascended and descended before the sleeper on the pillow of stones at Bethel, till the time when the true cross began to give *of* its inexhaustible splinters to the Christian world, and thence down to the present hour, a strip of sand and rock has been regarded with passionate tenderness by the august dynasty of religions to which our own belongs.

"This longing after shrines forms a very important feature in the national character of the Hindus. Day and night throughout every month of the year, troops of devotees arrive at Puri, and for three hundred miles along the great Orissa road, every village has its pilgrim encampment. The parties consist of from 20 to 300 persons. At the time of the great festivals these bands follow so close as to touch each other; and a continuous train of pilgrims, many miles long, may often be seen in the Puri high road. They march in orderly procession, each party under its spiritual leader.

At least five-sixths, and often nine-tenths of them, are females. Now a straggling band of slender, diminutive women, clothed in white muslin, and limping sadly along, announces a pilgrim company from lower Bengal; then a joyous retinue, with flowing garments, of bright red or blue, trudging stoutly forward, their noses pierced with elaborate rings, their faces tattooed, and their hands encumbered with bundles of very dirty cloth, proclaims the stalwart female peasantry of Northern Hindustan. Ninety-five out of a hundred are on foot. Mixed with the throng are devotees of various sorts, almost naked.

The great spiritual army that thus marches its hundreds, and sometimes its thousands of miles, along burning roads, across unbridged rivers, and through pestilent regions of jungle and swamp, is annually recruited with as much tact and regularity as is bestowed on any military force. Attached to the temple is a body of emissaries, called pilgrim hunters, or pilgrim guides, according as a friendly or hostile view is taken of their functions, numbering about 3,000 men, who visit every province and district of India in search of devotees. They wander about from village to village within their allotted beats, preaching pilgrimage as the liberation from sin, and sometimes using arguments as worldly and drawing pictures as overstrained, as those by which the flagging devotion of Europe was lashed into zeal during the later Crusades.

The arrival of a pilgrim hunter is a memorable event in the still life of an Indian village. There is no mistaking the man ... He waits till the men have gone out to the fields, and then makes a round of visits to the women. Skilled in every artifice of persuasion, he works upon the religious fears and the worldly hopes of the female mind; and by the time the unsuspecting husbands come home from their work every house has its fair apostle of pilgrimage...The shut-up aimless life of Indian women gives a peculiar charm to the enterprise. The arrival of a pilgrim-hunter sends a flutter through the whole zenanas of the district. The great majority of pilgrims are always females. Many of them die on the road. Those who reach the end of their journey have their bleeding feet bound up in rags.

During their stay in Puri they are badly lodged and miserably fed. The scenes of agony and suffocation that take place in the putrid dens in which they lodge baffle description. On the return journey, the misery of the pilgrims reaches its climax. The rapacity of the Puri priests and lodging housekeepers has passed into a proverb. When the stripped and half-starved pilgrims leave the holy city hundreds of them have nothing left to pay for being ferried over the net work of rivers in the Delta. The numbers that perish annually are computed at from 10,000 to 50,000.

It has been absolutely established that cholera is exclusively propagated in India, and that every outbreak of the disease beyond the confines of British India may be traced back to Hindustan. America, Europe, and the greater part of Asia, may justly blame India for all they have suffered from cholera, and India can blame Puri for annually subjecting whole provinces to the chance of the epidemic. These over-crowded pest-haunted dens around Jagannáth may become at any moment the centre from which the disease radiates to the great manufacturing towns of France and England. One of man's most deadly enemies has his lair in this remote comer of Orissa, ever ready to rush out upon the world, to devastate households, to sack cities, and to mark its line of march by a broad black track across three continents. (Abridged from Hunter's *Orissa.*)

PINDARAKA—A Tírtha. A village in Gujarat, still held in reverence from the following legend connected with it. The three sages Viswamitra, Kanwa, and Nárada were here observed by some boys who determined to play a trick upon them. They accordingly took a boy named Sámba, and having dressed him as a damsel, conducted him to the sages, and with deep respect enquired, what child will this female, the wife of Babhra, who is anxious to have a son give birth to. The sages, knowing what was done, replied, "She will bring forth a club that shall crush the whole of the Yádava race." The boys related all that had occurred to Ugrasena; and as foretold a club was produced from the belly of Sámba. Ugrasena had the club which was of iron, ground to dust, and thrown into the sea; but the particles of dust there became rushes; one part, which could not be broken, was swallowed by a fish; the fish was caught, the iron spike was extracted from its belly, and was taken by a hunter named Jará. This hunter afterwards shot Krishṇa with an arrow tipped with the iron spike. So was it determined by fate. *V.P.*

PINDAS—Balls of food, offered at Sráddas. They are made of boiled rice, sesamum seeds, honey and butter; various kinds of fruit of pulse, and of grain, water, frankincense, sugar and milk, are also mixed up in them at times; the size differs from that of a fowl's egg to that of a coconut; but the Piṇḍa is usually of such a magnitude as to be conveniently held in the hand.

PINGALA—**(1)** The great authority on the *chandas* or Prosody of the Vedas. He is supposed to have written about the second century B.C. **(2)** Name of one of the serpent kings sometimes identified with the foregoing. **(3)** One of the eleven Rudras, according to the enumeration in the Matsya Purána.

PIPAL TREE—*Ficus religiosa*: the one in Vipula mountain, on the west of Meru, is said in . the Vishṇu Purána to spread over eleven hundred yójanás.

PIPPALADA—A school of the *Atharvaveda*, founded by a sage of that name.

PIPPALA—The name of one portion of Jambu-dwípa, according to the Mahábhárata; the other portion is called Sása; the two are reflected in the lunar orb as in a mirror.

PIPRU—One of the demons of drought, represented in the Rig Veda as one of the malevolent powers in the atmosphere, to encounter whom Indra marches forth accompanied by the Maruts, and sometimes attended by Vishṇu. The dreadful battles that are described are evidently personifications of the storms that occur at the bursting of the monsoons in India.

PISACHA MARRIAGE—A marriage in which a damsel is neither purchased, nor seduced, nor carried away captive, but simply taken at a disadvantage; an outrage, says Mr. Wheeler, "far more likely to be committed amongst a peaceful community than amongst a race of chivalrous warriors, like the Kshatriyas." "If a damsel found herself likely to become a mother, without being able to furnish a satisfactory reason for her maternity, she would naturally plead that she had been victimised by a Pisácha; and probably from this circumstance the term came to be applied to all cases in which a damsel had been taken at a disadvantage by a mortal lover." In modern times the belief is still common in the rural districts of India that such events occur.

PISACHA—A daughter of Daksba, and wife of Kaṣyapa.

PISACHA-LOKA—(*see* Loka)

PISACHAS (mas.), **PIŚĀCĪ** (fem.)—Fiends, evil spirits, placed by the Vedas as lower than *rākṣasas.* The vilest and most malignant order of malevolent beings. Accounts differ as to their origin. The Brāhmaṇa and the *Mahābhārata* say that they were created by

Brahmā, together with the asuras and *rākṣasas*, from the stray drops of water which fell apart from the drops out of which god, men, *gandharvas*, &c., had been produced. According to Manu they sprang from the Prajāpatis. In the Purāṇas they are represented as the offspring of Kaśyapa by his wife Krodhavaśā, or Piśācā, or Kapiśā.

PISACHIKA—A river that has its rise on the Riksha mountains.

PISITASANAS, PIŚITĀŚINS—Carnivorous and cannibal imps descended from Nikaṣā.

PITAMAHA—A paternal grandfather. A name of Brahmā as the great father of all.

PITAMBARA—'Clothed in yellow garments.' A name of Viṣṇu.

PITHA-STHANA—'Seat', or lit. 'place of a seat'. "Fifty-one places where, according to the Tantras, the limbs of Satī fell when scattered by her husband Śiva, as he bore her dead body about and tore it to pieces after she had put an end to her existence at Dakṣa's sacrifice. This part of the legend seems to be an addition to the original fable, made by the Tantras, as it is not in the Purāṇas. (*see* Dakṣa) It bears some analogy to the Egyptian fable of Isis and Osiris. At the Pīṭhasthānas, however, of Jvālāmukhī, Vindhyavāsinī, Kālīghāṭ, and others, temples are erected to the different forms of Devī or Satī, not to the phallic emblem of Mahādeva, which, if present, is there as an accessory, not as a principal; and the chief object of worship is a figure of the goddess—a circumstance in which there is an essential difference between the temples of Durgā and the shrines of Osiris."—*Wilson.*

PITRAYAJÑA—Obsequial rites; or libations to the manes; one of the great obligations or sacrifices.

PITRI-LOKA—One of the seven spheres above the earth, the heaven of Pitris and Brahmans.

PITṚ-LOKA—(*see* LOKA)

PITṚ-PATI—'The lord of the Manes.' Yama, judge of the dead.

PITRS—Patres; the fathers; the Manes. This name is applied to three different classes of beings: **(1)** The Maneṣ of departed forefathers, to whom *piṇdas* (balls of rice and flour) and water are offered at stated periods. **(2)** The ten Prajāpatis or mythical progenitors of the human race. **(3)** "According to a legend in the *Harivaṁśa* and in the *Vāyu Purāṇa*, the first *pitṛs* were the sons of the gods. The gods having offended Brahmā by neglecting to worship him, were cursed by him to become fools; but, upon their repentance, he directed them to apply to their sons for instruction. Being taught accordingly the rites of expiation and penance by their sons, they addressed them as fathers; whence the sons of the gods were the first *pitṛs*." The account given of the *pitṛs* is much the same in all the Purāṇas. "They agree in distinguishing them into seven classes, three of which are without form, or composed of intellectual, not elementary substance, and assuming what forms they please; and four are corporeal. When the Purāṇas come to the enumeration of the particular classes, they somewhat differ, and the accounts in all the works are singularly imperfect." The incorporeal *pitṛs*, according to one enumeration, are the Vairājas, Agniṣvāttas, and Barhiṣads. The first of these seem also to be called Subhāsvars, Somasads, and Saumyas. The corporeal are the Sukālas or Sukālins, Āṅgirasas, Susvadhas and Somapas. The Sukālas are also called Mānasas; the Somapas are also called Uṣmapas; the Āṅgirasas seem also to be called Haviṣmats, Havirbhūjas, and Upahutas; and the Susvadhas are apparently the same as the Ājyapas and Kāvyas or Kavyas. The Vairājas are the Manes of great ascetices and anchorites, the Agniṣvāttas are the *pitṛs* of the gods, the Barhiṣads of demons, the Somapas of brāhmaṇas, the Haviṣmats of kṣatriyas, the Ājyapas of vaiśyas, and the Sukālins of the śūdras; but one authority, the *Harivaṁśa*, makes the Somapas belong to the Śūras, and the Sukālins to the brāhmaṇas, and there appears to be good reason for this. Other names are given by Dr. F. Hall from various authorities (*Viṣṇu Purāṇa*, III. 339): Raśmipas, Phenapas, Sudhāvats, Gārhapatyas, Ekaśṛṅgas, Caturvedas, and Kālas. Besides these there are the Vyāmas, 'fumes', the *pitṛs* of the barbarians. The *Ṛgveda* and Manu make two independent classes, the Agnidagdhas and the Anagnidagdhas, those 'who when alive kept up (or did not keep up) the household flame', and presented (or did not present) oblations with fire. The VISTIU *Purāṇa* makes the Barhiṣads identical with the former, and the Agniṣvāttas with the latter. Yama, god of the dead, is king of the *pitṛs*, and Svadhā, 'oblation', is sometimes said to be their mother, at others their wife.—Wilson, *Viṣṇu*, *Purāṇa* III. 157, 339. (*see* Manu, III. 192).

PIVARI of Vedaṣir—The wife as; they had many children, who constituted the family, or Brahmanical tribe of Bhārgavas, sons of Bhrigu.

PIYADASI, or PIYADASANO—An Indian king identified both by name and circumstances, with Aṣóka. There are many inscriptions on columns and rocks, by a Buddhist prince, in an ancient form of letter and the Pálí language, found in India; and many of these are attributed to Aṣóka. Their purport agrees with his character, and their wide diffusion with the traditionary report of the number of his monuments. His date is near that of Antiochus the Great. See Wilson's Notes to Vishṇu Purána, p. 470.

PLAKSHA—One of the seven Dwípas, or great insular continents; surrounded with a sea of sugar cane juice or Ikshu; the king was named Medhatithe; the Dwípa was divided amongst his seven sons, and each division was named after the prince to whom it was subject. The several kingdoms were bounded by as many ranges of mountains, in which the sinless inhabitants ever dwell, along with celestial spirits and gods; in them are many holy places; and the people there live for a long period, exempt from care and pain, and enjoying uninterrupted felicity. There are also in the seven divisions of Plaksha seven rivers flowing to the sea, whose names alone are sufficient to take away sin; the people who drink of their waters are always contented and happy; and there is neither decrease nor increase amongst them. Vishṇu Purána, p.197.

PLYADASI—(*see* AŚOKA)

POETRY—The classical literature of India is all poetical. The two great poems are the Ramáyaṇa and Mahábhárata; the Puráṇas are all in metre. ''Tender attachment to natural objects is one of the most pleasing features in the poetical compositions of the Hindus. It is very frequently expressed, and perhaps in few places with more beauty than in the drama of Śakuntalá, where upon departing from the bower of her foster father, she bids adieu to the plants she had carefully tended, and the orphan fawn she bad reared. The whole of this scene must be read with pleasure; and may be classed with the departure of Goldsmith's village family from Auburn, and the farewell of Eve to the bowers of Paradise."—*Wilson*.

PONGAL, or SANKRANTI—The Pongāl is the greatest of the unsectarian festivals of the Hindus. It is celebrated at their astronomical new year when the sun enters Capricorn about the 11th of January; and lasts three days; during which the Hindus employ themselves in mutual visits and compliments, something in the same manner as the Europeans do on the first day of the year. The feast of the Pongāl is a season of rejoicing for two special reasons. The first is, that the month of Magha, *i.e.*, December–January, every day in which is unlucky, is now over; and the other, that it is succeeded by a month, each day of which is lucky.

For the purpose of averting the evil effect of the baleful month of Magha, about four o'clock in the morning, a sort of Sannyásis, *i.e.*, penitents, go from door to door of every house, beating on a plate of iron or copper, which produces a piercing sound. All who sleep, being thus roused, are counselled to take wise precautions, and to guard against the evil presages of the month, by expiatory offerings, and sacrifices to Śiva, who presides over it. With this view, every morning, the women scour a space of about two feet square before the door of the house, upon which they draw several white lines with flowers; and upon these they place several little balls of cow-dung, sticking in each a citron blossom. These little balls are probably designed to represent Vighnéṣvara, the remover of obstacles, whom they desire to propitiate with the flower. Each day these little lumps of cow-dung, with their flowers, are picked up and preserved in a private place, till the last day of the month Magha; and when that comes, the women, who are alone charged with this ceremony, put the whole in a basket, and march from the house, with musical instruments before them, clapping their hands, till they reach some waste place where they dispose of the relics.

Then, with the first day of the new month begins the festival, the first day of which is called Bhōgi Pongāl, *i.e.*, Indra's Pongāl, and it is kept by inviting the near relations to an entertainment, which passes off with hilarity and mirth.

The second day is called Sūrya Pongāl, *i.e.* Pongāl of the sun, because it is set apart in honour of the sun. Married women, after purifying themselves by bathing, which they perform by plunging into the water without taking off their clothes, and coming out all wet, set about boiling rice with milk, in the open air, and not under any cover; and when it begins to simmer, they make a loud cry, all at once, repeating the words: Pongāl, Pongāl ! The vessel is then lifted off the fire, and set before the idol of Vighnéṣvara, which is placed close by, and after having been offered to the image, part of the rice is given to the cow; and the remainder distributed among the people.

This is the great day of visits among the Hindus. The salutation begins with the question, "has the milk boiled ?" to which the answer is, "it has boiled;" and from this the festival takes its name "Pongāl" *i.e.* "boiling."

The third day is called the Pongāl of cows. On it they mix in a great vessel filled with water, some saffron, cotton seeds, and leaves of the Margona tree: and then going several times round all the cows and oxen belonging to the house, they sprinkle them with the water, as they turn to the four cardinal points; and make the Sáshtānga, or prostration of the eight members, before them four times. The men perform this ceremony only. Next the cows are fell dressed out, their horns being painted with various colours, and garlands of flowers and foliage put round their necks and over their backs. They likewise add strings of coconuts and other fruits, which are soon shaken off by the brisk motion of the animals, which these trappings occasion, and are picked up by children and others, who follow the cattle on purpose, and greedily eat what they gather, as something sacred. The cattle then, being driven in herds through the villages, and made to scamper about from side to side by the jarring note of many sounding instruments, are, during the remainder of the day, allowed to feed at large without a keeper; and whatever trespasses they commit are suffered to pass without notice or restraint.

At the conclusion of the festival they take the idols from the temples, and carry them in pomp to the place where the cattle have been again collected. The girls of pleasure, named *Devadasis*, who are found at all ceremonies, are also not wanting here. *Abbé Dubois.*

PRABHA—The daughter of Swarbhána, and wife of Namuchi; according to the Matsya Purána she was the wife of the sun, by whom he had Prabhata; according to the Bhágavata she was the wife of Kalpa, who had by her Pratáh, (dawn) Madhyadina, (noon) and Sáya, (evening.)

PRABHAKARA—A Rishi of the house of Atri, who married the ten daughters of Raudráswa, a descendant of Puru.

PRABHASA—(Light.) **(1)** One of the deities called Vásas, because they are always present in light, or luminous irradiation; **(2)** A place of pilgrimage in the west of India on the coast of Guzerat, near the temple of Sómanath, and town of Pattan Sómanath. In the Mahábhárata it Is placed near Dwáraka. It was visited by Arjuna, and afterwards by Balaráma during the great war. Before the destruction of Dwáraka Krishṇa issued a proclamation that all the people of the city should go to the seashore at Prabhása and pay their devotions to the deity of Dwáraka.

PRABHATA—A son of Vivaswat, the Sun, by his wife Prabhá.

PRABHAVATI—Wife of Pradyumna (*q.v.*).

PRABODHA-CANDRODAYA—'The rise of the moon of knowledge.' A philosophical drama by Kṛṣṇa Miśra, who is supposed to have lived about the twelfth century. It has been translated into English by Dr. Taylor, and into German by Rosenkranz and Hirzel.

PRACANDA-PANDAVA—'The incensed Pāṇḍavas.' A drama in two acts by Rāja Śekhara, the main incident in which is the outrage of Draupadī by the assembled Kaurava princes.

PRACETAS—**(1)** One of the Prajāpatis. **(2)** An ancient sage and law-giver. **(3)** The ten Pracetasas were sons of Prācinabarhis and great-grandsons of Pṛthu, and, according to the *Viṣṇu Purāṇa*, they passed ten thousand years in the great ocean, deep in meditation upon Viṣṇu, and obtained from him the boon of becoming the progenitors of mankind. They took to wife Māriṣā, daughter of Kaṇḍu, and Dakṣa was their son. (*see* DAKṢA)

PRACHETAS—**(1)** A deity who presides over the tongue; **(2)** A son of Duryáman, a descendant of Druhya;

PRACHETASAS—The ten sons of Práchínaverhis, who, instructed by their father, plunged into the depths of the ocean, and with minds wholly devoted to Náráyana, the sovereign of the universe, were engrossed by religious austerity for ten thousand years: on which, Vishṇu, being pleased with them, appeared to them amidst the waters, of the complexion of the full-blown lotus leaf. Beholding him mounted on the king of birds, Garuda, the Prachetásas bowed down their heads in devout homage; when Vishṇu said to them, "Receive the boon you have desired; for I, the giver of good, am content with you, and am present." The Prachetásas replied to him with reverence, and told him that the cause of their devotions was the command of their father to effect the multiplication of mankind. The god, having accordingly granted to them. the object of their prayers, disappeared, and they came up from the water.

The Prachetásas took to wife Márishá, (*q.v.*) and from her was born the eminent patriarch Daksha, who had in a former life been born as a son of Brahmá. Vishṇu Purána.

PRACHINAVERHIS—The eldest of the six cons of Havirdhána; he was a great prince and patriarch by whom mankind was multiplied after the death of Havirdhana; he was called Prachínaverhis from his placing upon the earth the sacred grass, pointing to the east. He married Savarṇá, the daughter of the ocean, who was the mother of ten sons, styled Prachetásas, who were in the sea for ten thousand years. Vishṇu Purána.

PRACHINVAT—A prince, the son of Janamejaya, and grandson of Puru.

PRACYAS—The people of the east; those east of the Ganges; the Prasii of the Greeks.

PRADARSANAS—A class of deities of the third Manwantara.

PRADHANA—Primary or crude matter; a form of Vishṇu; it is also designated Prakriti, Nature; it comprehends both causes and effects; it is durable, self-sustained, undecaying; the mother of the world; without beginning; and that into which all that is produced is resolved. Pradhána, when unmodified, is according to the Sankhyas and Pauránics, nothing more than the three qualities in equilibrium, or goodness, foulness, and darkness neutralising each other. *Sankhya Karika*, p. 52.

PRADHANATMA—A name of Vishṇu, meaning, one with crude nature, or Viswabhávana.

PRADOSHA—A son of Kalpa, and Doshá. Pradosha had two brothers Niṣítha and Vyushta; the three names mean the beginning, middle and end of night.

PRADYOTA—A king of Magadha, son of the minister Simika, who having killed his sovereign placed his son Pradyóta on the throne; the dynasty lasted one hundred and thirty-eight years.

PRADYUMANA-VIJAYA—'Pradyumna victorious.' A drama in seven acts upon the victory of Pradyumna over the *daitya* Vajranābha, written by Śaṅkara Dīkṣita about the middle of the last century. "The play is the work of a Paṇḍit, not of a poet."—*Wilson.*

PRADYUMNA—The son of Krishṇa and Rukminí—the incarnate Indian Cupid. He is called in the South Manmatha (the co-founder of the mind) and in the North of India, Káma (Desire.) He is said to be the mental son of Vishṇu, and to have become incarnate in Pradyumna, the first bore of the 108,000 sons of Krishṇa. His history is thus related in the Vishṇu Purána.

"When Pradyumna vas but six days old, he was stolen from the lying-in chamber by Sambara, terrible as death; for the demon foreknew that Pradyumna, if he lived, would be his destroyer. Taking away the boy, Sambara cast him into the ocean, swarming with monsters, into a whirlpool of roaring waves, the haunt of the huge creatures of the deep. A large fish swallowed the child, but he died not, and was born anew from its belly: for that fish, with others, was caught by the fishermen, and delivered by them to the great Ásura Sambara. His wife Máyádeví, the mistress of his household, superintended the operations of the cooks, and saw, when the fish was cut open, a beautiful child, looking like a now shoot of the blighted tree of love. Whilst wondering who this should be, and how he could have got into the belly of the fish, Nárada came to satisfy her curiosity, and said to the graceful dame, "This is the son of him by whom the whole world is created arid destroyed, the son of Vishṇu, who was stolen by Sambara from the lying-in chamber, and tossed by him into the sea, where he was swallowed by the fish. He is now in thy power; do thou, beautiful woman, tenderly rear this jewel of mankind." Thus counselled by Nárada, Máyádeví took charge of the boy, and carefully reared him from childhood, being fascinated by the beauty of his person. Her affection became still more impassioned when he was decorated with the bloom of adolescence. The gracefully moving Máyávatí then, fixing her heart and eyes upon the light-minded Pradyumna, gave him, whom she regarded as herself, all her magic (and illusive) powers.

Observing these marks of passionate affection, the son of Krishṇa said to the lotus-eyed Máyádeví, "Why do you indulge in feelings so unbecoming the character of a mother ?" To which she replied, "Thou art not a son of mine; thou art the son of Vishṇu, whom Kála Sambara carried away, and threw into the sea: thou wast swallowed by a fish, but wast rescued by me from its belly. Thy fond mother, O beloved, is still weeping for thee." When the valiant Pradyumna beard this he was filled with wrath, and defied Sambara to battle. In the conflict that ensued, the son of Mádhava slew the whole host of Sambara. Seven times he foiled the delusions of the enchanter, and making himself master of the eighth, turned it against Sambara, and killed him. By the same faculty he ascended into the air, and proceeded to his father's house, where he alighted, along with Máyávatí, in the inner apartments. When the women beheld Pradyumna, they thought it was Krishṇa himself. Rukminí, her eyes dimmed with tears, spoke tenderly to him, and said, "Happy is she who has a son like this, in the bloom of youth. Such would be the age of my son Pradyumna, if he was alive. Who is the fortunate mother adorned by thee ? and yet from thy appearance, and from the affection I feel for thee, thou art assuredly the son of Hari."

At this moment Krishṇa accompanied by Nárada, arrived; and the latter said to the delighted Rukminí, "This is thine own SON, who has come hither after killing Sambara, by whom, when an infant, he was stolen from the lying-in chamber. This is the virtuous Máyávatí, his wife, and not the wife of Sambara. Hear the reason. When Manmatha, the deity of love, had perished,* the goddess of beauty, desirous to secure his revival, assumed a delusive form, and by her charms fascinated the demon Sambara, and exhibited herself to him in various illusory enjoyments. This thy son is the descended Káma; and this is the goddess Ratí, his wife.' There is no occasion for any uncertainty: this is thy daughter-in-law." Then Rukmini was glad, and Keśava also; the whole city resounded with exclamations of joy, and all the people of Dwáraká were surprised at Rukminí's recovering a son who had so long been lost.

Pradyumna is represented as a man, with a crown on his head; and his ears, neck, breast, arms, hands, feet, and the remaining part of his body, are adorned with various ornaments of pearls, precious stones, gold and silver. On his shoulders he wears a Bāhupattai, *i. e.*, a shoulder girdle. In one of his hands he holds a bow of sugar cane, with a string of insects; and in the other an arrow, ready for discharge. On his back he carries a quiver, with five sorts of arrows, consisting of five kinds of flowers. His standard is a fish; his vehicle, a parrot; and the color of his body, yellow. Ratí his wife, is represented as a female with long black hair, braided into a pigtail that reaches to the ground. Like her husband, she wears also a crown, and is on the whole adorned and equipped similar to him. (*When he was reduced to ashes by a fiery glance from Siva, in resentment of his inflaming him with passion for Uma.)

PRAGHASA—A distinguished warrior of Rávana's, who attacked Hanumán armed with an axe. The intrepid Simian, stained by blood, arrows everywhere quivering in his colossal frame, seized a huge rock which he hurled at his adversary with a shout of fury, and the warrior disappeared beneath the whelming mass.

PRAGJYOTISA—A city situated in the east, in Kāmarūpa on the borders of Assam, (*see* NARAKA)

PRAHASANA—A farcical or comic satire, that might be thought to have originated, like the old comedy, from the Phallic Hymn. Unlike the aristophanic comedy, however, it is not levelled at the many-headed mob, but in general at the sanctified and privileged orders of the community, as Ascetics, Brahmans, men of rank and wealth, and princes. The vices satirised in the two latter are those which emanate from an abuse of riches rather than of power, and are those of low luxury, not tyrannic despotism; the objects of satire in the former are sensuality and hypocrisy. It is in their extreme indelicacy that they resemble, although perhaps they scarcely equal, the Greek comedy; but they have not its redeeming properties; exuberant gaiety and brilliant imagination: they have some causticity and humour, but they are deficient in the high merits of poetry and wit. The *Prahasana* is generally a drama in one act, intended to excite laughter. The story is fictitious, and the hero an ascetic, a brahman, a king, or a rogue. The dramatis personæ are courtiers, menials, mendicants, knaves, and harlots; the inferior persons speak low Prákṛit, or a local dialect.—Wilson, *Works*, *XI*, p. xxxi.

PRAHASTA—A general in the army of the Rákshasas, who reported to Rávaṇa the arrival of Ráma; informing him that though the sea was terrible and rough, with a line of huge breakers on all sides, yet Ráma had crossed it like a mere cow's track, and having encamped his army on Suvelá occupied in person the outskirts of the city.

PRAHLADA, PRAHRĀDA—A *daitya*, son of Hiraṇyakaśipu and father of Bali. Hiraṇyakaśipu, in his wars with the gods, had wrested the sovereignty of heaven from Indra and dwelt there in luxury. His son Prahlāda, while yet a boy, became an ardent devotee of Viṣṇu, which so enraged his father that he ordered the boy to be killed; but not the weapons of the *daityas*, the fangs of the serpents, the tusks of the celestial elephants, nor the flames of fire took any effect, and his father was constrained to send him back to his preceptor, where he continued so earnest in performing and promoting the worship of Viṣṇu that he eventually obtained final exemption from existence. According to some accounts, it was to avenge Prahlāda, as well as to vindicate his own insulted majesty, that Viṣṇu became incarnate as the Narasiṁha, 'man-lion', and slew Hiraṇyakaśipu. After the death of his father, Prahlāda became king of the *daityas* and dwelt in Pātāla; but, according to the *Padma Purāṇa*, he was raised to the rank of Indra for life, and finally united with Viṣṇu. The *Padma Purāṇa* carries the story farther back to a previous birth. In this previous existence Prahlāda was a brāhmaṇa named Somaśarmān, fifth son of Śivaśarman, His four brothers died and obtained union with Viṣṇu, and he desired to follow them. To accomplish this he engaged in profound meditation, but he allowed himself to be disturbed by an alarm of the *daityas*, and so was born again as one of them. He took the part of his race in the war between them and the gods, and was killed by the discus of Viṣṇu, after which he was again born as son of Hiraṇyakaśipu.

PRAJANI—A prince, the son of Pransa, descendant of Nedishta.

PRAJAPATI—'Lord of creatures', a progenitor, creator. In the Veda the term is applied to Indra, Savitṛ, Soma, Hiraṇyagarbha, and other deities. In Manu the term is applied to Brahmā as the active creator and supporter of the universe; so Brahmā is the Prajāpati. It is also given to Manu Svāyambhuva himself, as the son of Brahmā and as the secondary creator of the ten *ṛṣis*, or "mind-born sons" of Brahmā, from whom mankind has descended. It is to these ten sages, as fathers of the human race, that the name Prajāpati most commonly is given. They are Marīci, Atri, Aṅgiras, Pulastya, Pulaha, Kratu, Vasiṣṭha, Pracetas or Dakṣa, Bhṛgu, and Nārada, According to some authorities the Prajāpatis are only seven in number, being identical with seven great *ṛṣis*. (*see* Ṛṣɪ) The number and names of the Prajāpatis vary in different authorities: the *Mahābhārata* makes twenty-one.

PRAJAPATI-YAJNA—Propagation of offspring; a recent addition to the five great obligations of Manu.

PRAJAPATYA—**(1)** A particular sacrifice performed before appointing a daughter to raise issue in default of male heirs; **(2)** A sort of penance, eating once a day for three days in the mornings, once in the night for three nights, subsisting three days on food given as alms, and fasting three days more.

PRAJNA—A synonym of Mahat. That by which the properties of things are known.

PRAKARANA—A second species of *Rúpaka* or dramatic composition, which agrees in all respects with the *Nátaka*, (*q.v.*) except that it takes a rather less elevated range. The fable is to be a pure fiction drawn from real life in a reputable class of society, and the most appropriate subject is love. The hero may be of ministerial rank, or a brahman, or a merchant of respectability. The heroine may be a maid of family or a courtesan. In the former case the Prakaraṇa is termed Suddha, or pure, in the latter Sankírna, or mixed.—Wilson, *Works*, xɪ, p. xxviii.

PRAKASAS—Messengers of Viṣṇu, also called Viṣṇudūtas.

PRAKRITA—Primary Creation: Elemental Dissolution: Nature. The general resolution of the elements into their primitive source. Prakrita is generally translated Nature. See Pʀᴀᴅʜáɴᴀ.

PRAKRIT (PRAKṚTA)—The name of the early vernaculars of India; a form of speech used in ancient Indian dramas by the inferior castes and by women, while kings and brahmans are made to speak Sanskrit; the Prákṛit differs both from Sanskrit and from the existing vernacular tongues. The Prákṛit Grammar of Vararuchi is considered by Lassen to have been composed about eighteen hundred years ago.

It is clear from an examination of the Indian dramas, and of the examples furnished by the grammarians who treat of the dramatic dialects, that the words which we find in Prákṛit are in great part identical with those of Sanskrit, but more or less modified in their forms, and that these modifications are, in numerous instances, intermediate between the original Sanskrit words and the still more corrupted forms which we discover in the languages descended from the Prákṛits, the modem vernacular dialects.

But, while the majority of Prákṛit words can, by the application of proper methods, be traced back to a Sanskrit source, there are some others which refuse to yield to the action of even the most powerful tests which criticism can employ, and successfully assert their claim to an origin independent of classical Sanskrit, and which we must therefore conclude either to belong to the vernacular Áryan speech, or to be of non-Áryan derivation.—*Muir*, ɪɪ, 26.

PRAKRTI—Nature; matter as opposed to spirit. The personified will of the Supreme in the creation, and the prototype of the female sex, identified with *māyā* or illusion. The Śakti or female energy of any deity.

PRALAMBA—An *asura* killed by Kṛṣṇa, according to the *Mahābhārata*. His story as told in the *Viṣṇu Purāṇa is*, that he was an *asura* and a dependant of Kaṁśa. With the object of devouring the boys Kṛṣṇa and Balarāma, he joined them and their playmates in jumping. Pralambā was beaten by his opponent Balarāma, and by the rules of the game had to carry the victor back on his shoulders to the starting-place. He took up Balarāma and then expanded his form, and was making off with his rider when Balarāma called upon Kṛṣṇa for assistance. Kṛṣṇa made a long speech, and ended by telling him to suspend awhile his mortal character and do what was right. Balarāma laughed, squeezed Pralamba with his knees, and beat him on the head with his fists till his eyes were knocked out and his brain forced through his skull, so that he fell to the ground and expired.

PRALAYA—"Dissolution." The dissolution of all things is of four kinds: Naimittaka, occasional; Prakrittika, elemental; Atyantika, absolute; Nitya, perpetual. 1, The first occurs when the sovereign of the world reclines in sleep; 2, In the second the mundane egg resolves into the primary element from whence it was derived; 3, Absolute non-existence of the world is the absorption of the sage through knowledge, into the supreme spirit; 4, Perpetual destruction is the constant disappearance, day and night, of all that are born. Vishṇu Purána.

Professor Wilson states, "the first is called Naimittaka, 'occasional' or 'incidental,' or Bráhmya, as occasioned by the intervals of Brahmá's days; the destruction of creatures, though not of the substance of the world, occurring during his night. The general resolution of the elements into their primitive source, or Prakriti, is the Prákritika destruction, and occurs at the end of Brahmá's life. The third, the Absolute or final, is individual annihilation; Móksha; exemption forever from future existence. The Bhágavata here notices the fourth kind, Nitya, or constant dissolution; explaining it to be the imperceptible change that all things suffer, in the various stages of growth and decay, life and death. The various conditions of beings subject to change are occasioned by that constant dissolution of life which is rapidly produced by the resistless stream of time, taking everything perpetually away."

PRAMATHAS—A class of demi-gods or fiends attendant upon Śiva.

PRAMLOCA—A celestial nymph sent by Indra to beguile the sage Kaṇḍu from his devotion and austerities. She lived with him for some hundreds of years, which were but as a day to the sage. When he awoke from his delusion he drove the nymph from his presence. The child with whom she was pregnant by him came forth from her body in drops of perspiration, which she left upon the leaves of the trees. These drops congealed and became eventually the lovely nymph Māriṣā. (*q.v.*).

PRAMODA—Pleasure. A son of Brahmá. The virtues and vices are enumerated as the progeny of Brahmá.

PRANA—'Breath or life.' In the *Atharvaveda* it is personified and a hymn is addressed to it.

PRANA—**(1)** A measure of time equal to a respiration, six respirations make one vikála; **(2)** A son of Dhátri and Ayati; **(3)** One of the seven Rishis of the third Manwantara.

PRANAYAMA—Suppression of breathing. It is performed by three modifications of breathing: the first act is expiration, which is performed through the right nostril, whilst the left is closed with the fingers of the right hand: this is called Rechakas, the thumb is then placed upon the right nostril, and the fingers raised from the left, through which breath is inhaled; this is called Púraka: in the third act both nostrils are closed, and breathing suspended; this is Kumbhaka: and a succession of these operations is the practice of Práṇayáma.

PRANSU—**(1)** One of the ten sons of the Manu Vaivaswata; **(2)** The son of Vatsapri.

PRAPTI—One of the wives of Kansa.

PRASADA—(Favour) one of the sons of Dharma.

PRASANNA-RAGHAVA—A drama by Jayadeva in seven acts. It has been printed at Benares.

PRASENAJIT—**(1)** A prince, the son of Kuśáśwa, **(2)** The son of Susandhi, of the family of Ikshváku.

> "Susandhi fortunate and wise.
> Two noble sons had he, to wit
> Dhruvasandhi and Prasenajit."

Professor Wilson places this prince, the twenty-fourth of the line of Ikshváku, in the sixth century before Christ.

PRASENA—The son of Nighana and brother, of Satrájit. It was to Satrájit the Sun presented the Syamantaka gem which he wore ON his neck. Satrájit, fearing that Krishṇa would ask him for the jewel transferred it to his brother Prasena. But though the jewel was an inexhaustible source of good to a virtuous person, if a man of bad character wore it would cause his death. Prasena having taken the gem, and hung it about his neck, mounted his horse and went to the woods to hunt. In the chase a lion killed him. The precious gem afterwards came into the possession of Akrúra.

PRAŚNA—Name of an Upaniṣad (*q.v.*).

PRASRAYA—(Affection.) One of the allegorical sons of Dharma (moral and religious duty.)

PRASTARA—A prince, the son of Udgítha, a descendant of Bharata.

PRASTUTAS—A class of deities of the sixth Manwantara.

PRASUSRAKA—A prince, the son of Maru, a descendant of Kuṣa. In the Vishṇu Purána it is said that Maru is still living in the village called Kalápa.

PRASUTI—One of the daughters of the Manu Swáyambhuva, who was married to Daksha; they had twenty-four daughters, all plainly allegorical, being personifications of intelligence and virtues and religious rites.

PRATAH—(Dawn.) The son of Kalpa and Prabhah.

PRATARDDANA—The son of Divodása, (king of Benares) so named from destroying the race of Bhadraṣrenya. He had various other appellations, as Satrájit, 'the victor over his foes,' from having vanquished all his enemies: Vatsa, or 'child,' from his father's frequently calling him by that name; Ritadhwaja, 'he whose emblem is truth,' being a great observer of veracity; and Kuvalayáṣwa, because he had a horse called Kuvalaya. Vishṇu Purána, p. 408. In the notes it is said that from the scanty and ill-digested notices in other Puránas it appears that Divodása, on being expelled from Benares, took some city and district on the Gomati, from the family of Bhadraṣrenya; that Durdama recovered the country; and that Pratarddana again conquered it from his descendants.

PRATIBANDHAKA—A king of Mithila, the son of Maru, of the family of Janaka.

PRATIBHASIKA—Being, merely seeming—that belonging to what presents itself in dreams, &c., illusions rather than realities.

PRATIBIMBA—'Reflection' a form of Brahmá. *V.P.*, p. 40, note 15.

PRATIHARA—A prince, the son of Parameshtín, of the race of Bharata.

PRATIHARTTA—The son of Pratihára, and father of Bhava, of the race of Bharata.

PRATIKSHATRA—**(1)** A king of Kási, the son of Kshatravriddha; **(2)** A son of Saíma, of the Yadava race.

PRATIPA—The son of Dilípa, a descendant of Kuru.

PRATISAKHYAS—Treatises on the phonetic laws of the language of the Vedas, dealing with the euphonic combination of letters and the peculiarities of their pronunciation as they prevailed in the different Śākhās or Vedic schools. These treatises are very ancient, but they are considerably later than the hymns, for the idiom of the hymns must have become obscure and obsolete before these treatises were necessary. Four such treatises are known:

Ṛgveda.—One which is considered to belong to the Śākhalāśākhā of this Veda, and is ascribed to Śaunaka. It has been edited and translated into German by Max Müller, and into French by M. Regnier.

Yajurveda.—Taittirīya-prātiśākhya, belonging to the Black Yajur, printed in the *Bibliotheca Indica* and also in the *Journal of the American Oriental Society*, with a translation by Professor Whitney.

Vājasaneyī-prātiśākhya.—Belonging to the White *Yajur.* It is attributed to Kātyāyana, and has been edited and translated by Weber.

Atharvaveda.—The Śaunaklya Caturādhyāyika, *i.e.*, Śaunaka's treatise in four chapters. Edited and translated into English by Whitney.

No Prātiśākhya of the *Sāmaveda* has been discovered.

PRATISARGA—Secondary creation—that which took place at the commencement of the present Kalpa; water, and even the earth, being in existence, and consequently having been preceded by the creation of Mahat and the elements.

PRATISHTHANA—The capital city of Sudyumna; situated on the eastern side of the confluence of the Ganges and Jumna, opposite to the modern Allāhābād; the country between which rivers was the territory of the direct male descendants of Vaivaswata. In consequence of his having been a female formerly, Sudyumna was excluded from any share in his paternal dominions; but his father, at the suggestion of Vaṣishtha, bestowed upon him the city Pratishthána, and be gave it to Pnrúravas.

PRATISUKYA—A short section of the Vedas; or more strictly, a collection of phonetic rules, peculiar to one of the different branches of the four Vedas.—Müller,

A.S.L., p. 119.

PRATIVAHU—The youngest son of Swaphalka.

PRATIVINDYA—One of the sons of Yudhishthira by Draupadi.

PRATIVYOMAN—A prince, the son of Vatsavyuha, of the family of Ikshváku.

PRATYAHARA—Restraining the organs of sense from susceptibility to outward impressions, and directing them entirely to mental perceptions. This is one of the means for effecting the entire subjugation of the senses; and if they are not completely controlled the sage cannot accomplish his devotions.

PRATYAYA SARGA—Intellectual creation of the Sánkhya philosophy; the creation of which we have a notion, or to which we give assent; in contradistinction to organic creation, or that existence of which we have no sensible perception. In its specific sub-divisions it is the notion of certain inseparable properties in the four different orders of beings: obstruction, or solidity in inanimate things; inability or imperfection in animals; perfectibility in man; and acquiescence or tranquil enjoyment in gods. *V.P.*, Notes. 37.

PRATYUSHA—(Daybreak.) One of the deities called Vásus.

PRAUDHA-BRAHMANA—One of the eight *Brāhmaṇas* of the *Sāmaveda.* It contains twenty-five sections, and is therefore also called *Pañcaviṁś'a.*

PRAVAHA—The name of one of the winds; so termed because it bears along the planets, which turn round, like a disc of fire, driven by the aerial wheel.

PRAVA—One of the daughters of Daksha who was married to. Kaṣyapa.

PRAVILASENA—One of the kings of Andhra, the son of Tálaka.

PRAVIRA—**(1)** The son of Prachinvat, or according to the Mahábhárata the son of Puru; **(2)** One of the sons of Hariyaṣwa, a descendant of Hastin.

PRAYAGA—The modern Allāhābād. The place where the Ganges, Jumnā, and the fabled subterranean Sarasvatī unite, called also Triveṇī, 'the triple braid'. It has always been a celebrated place of pilgrimage.

PRAYASCHITA—Penance; expiation. The ceremony of general cleansing or general expiation, performed when a Brahman is at the point of death, is termed Práyaschita. This is accomplished, after the administration of the Panchakarya (*q.v.*) by the Purohita and chief mourner, going up to the dying man and making him recite within himself, if he cannot articulate, the proper Mantras; by the efficacy of which he is delivered from all his sins. This is followed by another ceremony which the Abbé Dubois remarks can scarcely be described with gravity.

"A cow is introduced with her calf. Her horns are decorated with rings of gold or brass, and her neck with garlands of flowers. A clean cloth is laid over her body; and thus bedecked she is led up to the sick man, who takes hold of her tail. Mantras in the meantime are recited or sung, the prayer of which is that the cow would conduct him by a blessed path to the next world. He then makes a gift of the cow to a Brahman, on whose hand a little water is poured while he accepts the present; which is the ordinary ratification of a gift."

When the soul leaves the body for the abode of Yama it has to pass a river of fire, and those who have presented a cow to a Brahman, as above, are met on the banks by a cow sent from Yama, and by her enabled to cross the fiery stream without injury.

"It is fitting that a Brahman should die on the ground, not on a bed, nor even on a mat; and the reason is this; his soul being disengaged from his body must enter another which will carry it to the world that is destined for it. And if he should die on his bed or on a mat, he must carry these movables wherever he goes, which would be very tormenting."* (* Abbé Dubois, *D.P.I.*)

PRAYASCHITTA—'Expiation' or 'sacred philosophy,' created from the eastern mouth of Brahmá.

PREKSHAGARA—House of seeing; a sort of theatre; a place made for seeing the sacrifice; a sort of stockade used as a place where spectacles could be witnessed.

PRETA—A ghost; an evil spirit animating a dead carcass, and haunting cemeteries and other places.

PRETA-RAT—The Lord of the dead; a name of Yama, the Hindu Pluto.

PRISHADASWA—A prince, the son of Anaraṇya.

PRISHADHRA—One of the sons of the Manu Vaivaswata, who, in consequence of the crime of killing a cow was degraded to the condition of a Súdra. This story, says Professor Wilson, has been modified apparently at different periods, according to a progressive horror of the crime. The Vishṇu Purána simply states the fact. The Váyu says he was hungry, and not only killed, but also ate the cow of his spiritual preceptor Chyavana. In the Markaṇḍeya he is described as being out a hunting, and killing the cow of the father of Babhravya, mistaking it for a Gavaya or Gayal. The Bhágavata, as usual, improves upon the story, and says that Prishadhra was appointed by his Guru Vasishtha to protect his cattle. In the night a tiger made his way into the fold, and the prince in his haste, and in the dark, killed the cow upon which he had fastened, instead of the tiger. In all the authorities the effect is the same, and the imprecation of the offended sage degraded Prishadhra to the caste of a Súdra. According to the Bhágavata, the prince led a life of devotion, and perishing in the flame of a forest, obtained final liberation. The obvious purport of this legend, and of some that follow, is to account for the origin of the different castes from one common ancestor.

PRISHATA—The youngest of the hundred sons of Somaka.

PRISHTAJA—One of the sons of Kumára.

PRISISTA—A supplement or appendix. A series of works called *pariśiṣṭas* belong to the Vedic period, but they are the last of the series, and indicate a transition state. They "supply information on theological or ceremonial points which had been passed over in the *sūtras*, and they treat everything in a popular and superficial manner, as if the time was gone when students would spend ten or twenty years of their lives in fathoming the mysteries and mastering the intricacies of the Brāhmaṇa literature."—*Max Müller.*

PRISNI—A prince, the son of Anamitra.

PRITHA, OR KUNTI—The daughter of Súra, and wife of Pándu. For her history see KUNTI; also KARNA.

PRITHIVI—Earth personified as a goddess. The Vishṇu Purána contains a hymn of adoration addressed by the goddess to Náráyana when he was incarnate as a boar, and descended to the subterrene regions. When Prithu took up his divine bow Ajagava, and marched forth to assail the Earth, the latter, assuming the figure of a cow, fled hastily from him, and traversed, through fear of the king, the regions of Brahmá and the heavenly spheres; but wherever went the supporter of living things, there she beheld Vaiṇya with uplifted weapons; overcome with apprehension the goddess Earth addressed Prithu, who. made Swáyambhuva Manu, a calf to milk the Earth for the benefit of mankind. By granting life to the Earth, Prithu was as her father, and she thence derived the patronymic Prithivi (the daughter of Prithu). There are many mystifications in the Puránas of the original simple allegory, which typified the Earth as a cow who yielded to every class of beings the milk they desired, or the object of their wishes. *V.P.*, Notes. *See* DYAUS.

PRITHIVI—Earth, as one of the elements in Hindu philosophy, where it is said to be produced from the rudiment of smell. The waters becoming productive, engendered the rudiment of smell; whence an aggregate (earth) originates, of which smell is the property. *V.P.*, p. 16.

PRITHU—**(1)** The most distinguished individual of this name was the son of Veṇa (*q.v.*) engendered by friction from the right arm of his dead father (*V.P.*, 101.) He was resplendent in person as if the blazing deity of Fire had been manifested. At the birth of Prithu all living creatures rejoiced: and Veṇa, delivered by his birth from the hell named Put, ascended to the realms above. The mighty Prithu was invested by the gods with universal dominion, and soon removed the grievances of the people whom his father had oppressed. They complained of the want of edible fruits and plants, and said they were suffering from famine. On hearing this Prithu took up his divine bow, Ajagava, and soon extorted a promise from the Earth to supply mankind with all that was necessary for their sustenance. The legend of Prithu occurs in most of the Puránas, and all the versions are essentially the same. See *Vishṇu Purána*, p. 104. **(2)** A prince, the son of Prastára. **(3)** A prince, the son of Anenas, and grandson of Kakutsha. **(4)** A prince, the son of Para, a descendant of Hastin. **(5)** A prince, the son of Anaraṇya, and father of Triśanku of the line of Ikshváku.

> "Anaraṇya, strong to fight,
> His son was Prithu, glorious name,
> From him the wise Trisanku came."

PRITHUDANA, PRITHUJAYA, PRITHUKARMAN, PRITHUKIRTTI, PRITHYASAS—Six princes, the most renowned of the million sons of Saṣavindu.

PRITHUGAS—A class of deities of the sixth Manwantara.

PRITHULOKSHA—A prince, the son of Chaturanga, a descendant of Anu.

PRITHURUKMAN—The brother of Jayámagha, and son of Parávrit, a descendant of Sasavindu.

PRITI—'Affection'—One of the daughters of Daksha

who was married to the sage Pulastya.

PRIYA—A princess in the city of Kapila, who was seized with white leprosy and taken to a distant jungle, and placed in a large cave where she was supplied with fire, fuel, and all kinds of food. At the same time, Ráma, Rája of Benares, was seized with the same disorder, and abandoned his Ráj, retiring to the same jungle. Subsequently he found a remedy in the root, leaves, fruit, and bark of a certain tree, and his body became pure as gold. Ultimately he fell in with Priya, cured her leprosy, and married her; and they resided in the city of Koli. Wheeler's Notes to the Mahábhárata.

PRIYADARŚI—(*see* AŚOKA)

PRIYAMITRA—After Triprishta. (*q.v.*), had been born as a lion, and had migrated through various forms, he became the Chakravartti Priyamitra in the division of the world Mahavideha. After a victorious reign of eighty-four lakhs of years he became an ascetic for a further period of a hundred lakhs, and was then translated to one of the higher heavens.—*Wilson*, I, 292.

PRIYAMVADA—A Vidyādhara, son of the king of the Gandharvas.

PRIYAVRATA—The eldest son of the divine Manu Swáyambhuva. He married Kámya the daughter of the patriarch Kardama, and had by her two daughters, Samrat and Kukshi, and ten sons, wise, valiant, modest and dutiful, named Agnídhra, Agnibáhu, Vapushmat, Dyutimat, Medha, Medhatithi, Bhavya, Savala, Putra, and the tenth was Jyotishmat, illustrious by nature as by name. These were the sons of Priyavrata, famous for strength and prowess. Of these, three, or Medha, Putra, and Agnibáhu, adopted a religious life: remembering the occurrences of a prior existence, they did not covet dominion, but diligently practiced the rites of devotion in due season, wholly disinterested, and looking for no reward. *V.P.*

Priyavrata having divided the earth into seven continents, gave them respectively to his other seven sons. According to the Bhágavata, he drove his chariot seven times round the earth, and the ruts left by the wheels became the beds of the oceans, separating it into seven Dwípas. To Agnídhra he gave Jambu-dwípa; to Medhatithi he gave Plaksha-dwípa: he installed Vapushmat in the sovereignty over the Dwípa of Sálmali; and made Jyotishmat king of Kuśa-dwípa: he appointed Dyutimat to rule over Krauncha-dwípa; Bhavya to reign over Sáka-dwípa: and Savala he nominated the monarch of the Dwípa of Pushkara.

PRSADHRA—A son of Manu Vaivasvata, who, according to the *Harivaṁśa* and the Purāṇas, became a sudra because he killed the cow of his religious preceptor.

PṚSATA—Drupada's father.

PṚSHAKAS, PṚOSHTAS—Inhabitors of valleys, a designation of some aboriginal tribes.

PṚSINI—In the Vedas and Purāṇas, the earth, the mother of the Maruts. The name is used in the Vedas also for a cow. There were several females of this name, and one of them is said to have been a new birth of Devakī.

PṚTHA—A name of Kuntī.

PUṆḌARĪKĀKṢA—'The lotus-eyed'; a name of Viṣṇu.

PUṆḌRA—A country corresponding "to Bengal proper, with part of South Bihār and the Jungle Mahals". A fabulous city between the Himavat and Hemakūṭa.

PUṆYA-ŚLOKA (mas.), **PUṆYA-ŚLOKĀ** (fem.). 'Hymned in holy verse.' An appellation applied to Kṛṣṇa, Yudhiṣṭhira, and Nala, also to Draupadī and Sītā.

PUDKALAI—One of the two wives of the gramadevata Ayanár.

PUJARI—An inferior priest who officiates in the pagodas, offering sacrifices, and receiving those offerings, which are brought by the people in fulfillment of, vows.

PUJA—Adoration of the deity; worship of the gods with various ceremonies and offerings: the term is also applied to the respect or homage paid to superiors.

PUKU—The sixth king of the Lunar race, youngest son of Yayāti and Sarmiṣṭhā. He and his brother Yadu were founders of two great branches of the Lunar race. The descendants of Puru were called Pauravas, and of this race came the Kauravas and Pāṇḍavas. Among the Yādavas or descendants of Yadu was Kṛṣṇa. (*see* Yayāti)

PULAHA—Name of one of the Prajāpatis and great *ṛṣis.* His wife was Kṣamā, and he had three sons, Kardama, Arvarīvat, and Sahiṣṇu. A *gandharva* (*q.v.*).

PULASTYA—Another Prajápati who was also one of the mind-born sons of Brahmá. It was he who appeared to Paráṣara, and communicated to him the Vishṇu Purána, as a summary or compendium of Puranic traditions. Pulastya was married to Príti, (Affection) one of the daughters of Daksha. In the Vishṇu Purána it is said their son, now known as the sage Agastya, was called in a former birth, or in the Swáyambhuva Manwantara, Dattoli. The Váyu specifies three sons of Pulastya Dattoli, Vedabāhu, and Viníta; also a daughter, Sadwati, married to Agni. Pulastya is considered as the ancestor of the Rákshasas, as he is the father of Visravas, the father of Rávana and his brethren.

PULIMAT—One of the Andhra kings, the son of Gomatiputra: he reigned twenty-eight years.

PULINDAKA—One of the ten Sungas, who reigned at Magadha for a hundred and ten years after the Mauryan dynasty. Pulindaka was the son of Ardraka, and only reigned three years.

PULINDAS—A name applied to any wild or barbarous tribe; in the Vishṇu Purána it refers to the people of the deserts along the Indus: but Pulindas are met with in many other positions, especially in the mountains and forests across Central India, the haunts of the Bhíls and Gonds. Ptolemy places the Pulindai along the banks of the Narmada. Notes to Vishṇu Purána, 186.

PULOMAN—**(1)** A Dánava; one of the distinguished sons of Kaṣyapa and Danu; **(2)** A son of Viprachitti, and father of Sáchí the wife of Indra.

PULOMA—One of the daughters of Vaiswánara; the other was named Kálika; both were married to Kaṣyapa, and became the mothers of sixty thousand distinguished Dánavas, who were powerful, ferocious, and cruel.

PULOMARCHISH—The last of the Andhrabhritya kings; the Vishṇu Purána states that there were thirty of them whose united reigns amounted to four hundred and fifty-six years.

PULOMAVIT—One of the Andhra kings, the son of Swátikarna: he reigned thirty-six years.

PUMAN—Incorporated spirit; the same as Purusha. In the Notes to the Vishṇu Puráua it is said the meaning is that Vishṇu is any form of spiritual being that is acknowledged by different philosophical systems; or that he is the Brahmá of the Vedánta, the Iswara of the Pátanjala, and the Purusha of the Sánkhya school.

PUNARVASU—**(1)** A lunar mansion in Airávati, in the Northern Avashthána; **(2)** A Yádava chief, the son of Abhijit.

PUNDARIKA—(Pundaríká.) **(1)** A daughter of Vaṣishtha, and wife of Práṇa; **(2)** One of the Apsaras.

PUNDARIKA—**(1)** One of the serpent-kings, of the progeny of Kádru; **(2)** A prince, the son of Nabhas, a descendant of Kúṣa.

PUNDARIKAKSHA—A name of Vishṇu, occurring in the first line of the Vishṇu Purána; it means having eyes like a lotus, or heart pervading; or Pundaríka is explained, 'supreme glory,' and Aksha imperishable.

PUNDRA—**(1)** A prince, one of the sons of Bali a descendant of Anu; **(2)** The name of a fabulous city between the Himavat and Hemakúta mountains.

PUNDRAS—The inhabitants of the western provinces of Bengal; sometimes the term designates the provinces themselves, and includes the districts of Dinájpur, Rangpur, Bírbhúm, Burdwan, Midnapur, the jungle Mehats, &c.

PUNJAKASTHALI—The daughter of Varuna, in the Puranic mythology.

PUNUL—The Tamil name of the sacred thread worn by the Brahmáns, Kshatriyas and Vaisyas.

PUNYA—**(1)** (Merit) A daughter of the sage Kratu, according to the Váyu list; **(2)** A river in Behar, now termed Pun-pun.

PUNYAJANAS—A class of Rákshasas, who destroyed Kuṣasthali, the capital of Kakudmin, surnamed Raivata, whilst he was on a visit to the region of Brahmá.

PUṢKARA—A blue lotus. A celebrated tank about five miles from Ajmer. One of the seven Dvīpas. (*see* Dvīpa) The name of several persons. Of the brother of Nala to whom Nala lost his kingdom and all that he possessed in gambling. Of a son of Bharata and nephew of Rāmacandra, who reigned over the Gāndhāras.

PURAHOTIA—A prince, the son of Anuratha, one of the descendants of Jyámagha.

PURAKA—A modification of breathing so termed; the act is performed as follows: the thumb is placed in the right nostril, and the fingers raised from the left, through which breath is inhaled.

PURANAI—One of the two wives of the gramadevata Ayanár.

PURANAS—There are eighteen large treatises so designated. The following is a list of them:—

1. Brahmá Purána.
2. Pádma Purána.
3. Vishṇu Purána.
4. Vayavíya Purána.
5. Sri Bhágavata.

6. Nárada, or Náradíya Purána.
7. Markaṇḍa, or Markaṇḍeya Purána.
8. Agni Purána.
9. Bhavishya Purána.
10. Brahmá Vaivartta Purána.
11. Linga Purána.
12. Varáha Purána.
13. Skanda Purána.
14. Vámana Purána,
15. Kúrma Purána
16. Matsya Purána.
17. Gáruda Purána.
18. Brahmáṇḍa Purána.

A brief account of the contents of each of the above will be found under (heir separate titles. The Preface to the Vishṇu Purána by Dr. Wilson contains the following excellent remarks ON their general character.

"The different works known by the name of Puránas are evidently derived from the same religious system as the Rámáyana and Mahábhárata, or from the mytho-heroic stage of Hindu belief. They present, however, peculiarities which designate their belonging to & later period, and to an important modification in the progress of opinion. They repeat the theoretical cosmogony of the two great poems , they expand and systematize the chronological computations; and they give a more definite and connected representation of the mythological fictions, and the historical traditions. But besides these and other particulars, which may be derivable from an old, if not from a primitive era, they offer characteristic peculiarities of a more modern description, in the paramount importance which they assign to individual divinities, in the variety and purport of the rites and observances addressed to them, and in the invention of new legends illustrative of the power and graciousness of those deities, and of the efficacy of implicit devotion to them. Śiva and Vishṇu, under one or other form, are almost the sole objects that claim the homage of the Hindus in the Puránas; departing from the domestic and elemental ritual of the Vedas, and exhibiting a sectarial fervour and exclusiveness not traceable in the Rámáyana, and only to a qualified extent in the Mahábhárata. They are no longer authorities for Hindu belief as a whole; they are special guides for separate and sometimes conflicting branches of it, compiled for the evident purpose of promoting the preferential, or in some cases the sole worship of Vishṇu or of Śiva.

"That the Puránas always bore the character here given of them, may admit of reasonable doubt; that it correctly applies to them as they now are met with, the following pages will irrefragably substantiate. It is possible, however, that there may have been an earlier class of Puránas, of which those we now have are but the partial and adulterated representatives. The identity of the legends in many of them, and still more the identity of the words—for in several of them long passages are literally the same—is a sufficient proof that in all such cases they must be copied either from some other similar work, or from a common and prior original. It is not unusual also for a fact to be stated upon the authority of an 'old stanza,' which is cited accordingly; showing the existence of an earlier source of information: and in very many instances legends are alluded to, not told; evincing acquaintance with their prior narration somewhere else. The name itself, Purána, which implies 'old,' indicates the object of the compilation to be the preservation of ancient traditions, a purpose is the present condition of the Puránas very imperfectly fulfilled. Whatever weight may be attached to these considerations, there is no disputing evidence to the like effect afforded by other and unquestionable authority. The description given by Mr. Colebrooke of the contents of a Purána is taken from Sanskrit writers. The Lexicon of Amara Sinha gives as a synonym of Purána, Pancha-lakshanam, 'that which has five characteristic topics:' and there is no difference of opinion amongst the scholiasts as to what these are. They are, as Mr. Colebrooke mentions; (1) Primary creation, or cosmogony; (2) Secondary creation, or the destruction and renovation of worlds, including chronology; (3) Genealogy of gods and patriarchs; (4) Reigns of the Manus, or periods called Manwantaras; and (5) History, or such particulars as have been preserved of the princes of the solar and lunar races, and of their descendants to modern times. Such, at any rate, were the constituent and characteristic portions of a Purána in the days of Amara Sinha, fifty-six years before the Christian era; and if the Puránas had undergone no change since his time, such we should expect to find them still. Do they conform to this description? Not exactly in any one instance; to some of them it is utterly inapplicable; to others it only partially applies. There is not one to which it belongs so entirely as to the Vishṇu Purána, and it is one of the circumstances which gives to tins work a more authentic character than most of its fellows can pretend to. Yet even in this instance we have a book upon the institutes of society and obsequial rites interposed between the Manwantaras and the genealogies of princes, and a life of Krishṇa separating the latter from an account of the end of the world, besides the insertion of various legends of a manifestly popular and sectarial character. No doubt many of the Purános, as they now are, correspond with the view which Col. Vans Kennedy takes of their purport. "I cannot discover in them," he remarks, "any other object than that of religious instruction." The description of the earth and of the planetary system, and the lists of royal races which occur in them, he asserts to be "evidently extraneous, and not essential circumstances, as they are entirely omitted in some Purános, and very concisely illustrated in others; while, on the contrary, in all the Purános some or other of the leading principles, rites, and observances of the Hindu religion are fully dwelt upon, and illus-trated either by suitable legends or by prescribing the ceremonies to be practiced, and the prayers and invocations to be employed, in the worship of different deities." Now, however accurate this description may be of the Purános as they are, it is clear that it does not apply to what they were when they were synonymously designated as Pancha-lakshanas, or 'treatises on five topics;' not one of which five is ever specified by text or comment to be "religious instruction." In the knowledge of Amara Sinha the lists of princes were not extraneous and unessential, and their being now so considered by a writer so well acquainted with the contents of the Purános as Col. Vans Kennedy, is a decisive proof that since the days of the lexicographer they have undergone some material alteration, and that we have not at present the same works in all respects that were current under the denomination of Purános in the century prior to Christianity..

"The inference deduced from the discrepancy between the actual form and the older definition of a Purána, unfavourable to the antiquity of the extant works generally, is converted into certainty when we come to examine them in detail; for although they have no dates attached to them, yet circumstances are sometimes mentioned or alluded to, or references to authorities are made, or legends are narrated, or places are particularized, of which the comparatively recent date is indisputable, and which enforce a corresponding reduction of the antiquity of the work in which they are discovered. At the same time they may be acquitted of subservience to any but sectarial imposture. They were pious frauds for temporary purposes: they never emanated from any impossible combination of the Brahmans to fabricate for the antiquity of the entire Hindu system any claims which it cannot fully support A very great portion of the contents of many, some portion of the contents of all, is genuine and old. The sectarial interpolation or embellishment is always sufficiently palpable to be set aside, without injury to the more authentic and primitive material; and the Purános, although they belong especially to that stage of the Hindu religion in which faith in some one divinity was the prevailing principle, are also a valuable record of the form of Hindu belief which came next in order to that of the Vedas; which grafted hero-worship upon the simpler ritual of the latter; and which had been adopted, and was extensively, perhaps universally, established in India at the time of the Greek invasion. The Hercules of the Greek writers was undoughtedly the Balaráma of the Hindus; and their notices of Mathurá on the Jumna, and of the kingdom of the Suraseni and the Pandæan country, evidence the prior currency of the traditions which constitute the argument of the Mahábhárata, and which are constantly repeated in the Purános, relating to the Paṇḍava and Yádava races, to Krishṇa and his contemporary heroes, and to the dynasties of the solar and lunar kings.

"The theogony and cosmogony of the Purános may probably be traced to the Vedas. They are not, as for as is yet known, described in detail in those works, but they are frequently alluded to in a strain more or less mystical and obscure, which indicates acquaintance with their existence, and which seems to have supplied the Purános with the groundwork of their systems. The scheme of primary or elementary creation they borrow from the Sáṅkhya philosophy, which is probably one of the oldest forms of speculation on man and nature amongst the Hindus. Agreeably, however, to that part of the Pauráṇik character that there is reason to suspect of later origin, their inculcation of the worship of a favourite deity, they combine the interposition of a creator with the independent evolution of matter, in a somewhat contradictory and unintelligible style. It is evident too that their accounts of secondary creation, or the development of the existing forms of things, and the disposition of the universe, are derived from several and different sources; and it appears very likely that they are to be accused of some of the incongruities and absurdities by which the narrative is disfigured, in consequence of having attempted to assign reality and significance to what was merely metaphor or mysticism. There is, however, amidst the unnecessary complexity of the description, a general agreement amongst them as to the origin of things, and their final distribution; and in many of the circumstances there is a striking concurrence with the ideas which seem to have pervaded the whole of the ancient world, and which we may therefore believe to be faithfully represented in the Puránas.

"The Pantheism of the Puránas in one of their invariable characteristics, although the particular divinity, who is all things, from whom all things proceed, and to whom all things return, be diversified according to their individual sectarial bias. They seem to have derived the notion from the Vedas: but in them the one universal Being is of a higher order than a personification of attributes or elements, and, however imperfectly conceived, or unworthy described, is God. In the Puránas the one only Supreme Being is supposed to be manifest in the person of Śiva or Vishṇu, either in the way of illusion or in sport; and one or other of these divinities is therefore also the cause of all that is, is himself all that exists. The identity of God and nature is not a new notion; it was very general in the speculations of antiquity, but it assumed a new vigour in the early ages of Christianity, and was carried to an equal pitch of extravagance by the Platonic Christians as by the Saiva or Vaishṇava Hindus. It seems not impossible that there was some communication between them. We know that there was an active communication between India and the Red Sea in the early ages of the Christian era, and that doctrines, as well as articles of merchandise, were brought to Alexandria from the former. Epiphanius and Eusebius accuse Scythianus of having imported from India, in the second century, books on magic, and heretical notions leading to Manichæism, and it was at the same period that Ammonius instituted the sect of the new Platonists at Alexandria. The basis of his heresy was, that true philosophy derived its origin from the eastern nations: his doctrine of the identity of God and the universe is that of the Vedas and Puránas; and the practices he enjoined, as well as their object, were precisely those described in several of the Puránas under the name of Yóga. His disciples were taught "to extenuate by mortification and contemplation the bodily restraints upon the immortal spirit, so that in his life they might enjoy communion with the Supreme Being, and ascend after death to the universal parent." That these are Hindu tenets the following pages will testify; and by the admission of their Alexandrian teacher, they originated in India. The importation was perhaps not wholly unrequited; the loan may not have been left unpaid. It is not impossible that the Hindu doctrines received fresh animation from their adoption by the successors of Ammonius, and especially by the mystics, who may have prompted, as well as employed, the expressions of the Puránas. Anquetil du Perron has given, in the introduction to his translation of the 'Oupnekhat,' several hymns by Synesius, a bishop of the beginning of the fifth century, which may serve as parallels to many of the hymns and prayers addressed to Vishṇu in the Vishṇu Purána.

"But the ascription to individual and personal deities of the attributes of the one universal and spiritual Supreme Being, is an indication of a later date than the Vedas certainly, and apparently also than the Rámáyana, where Ráma, although an incarnation of Vishṇu, commonly appears in his human character alone. There is something of the kind in the Mahábhárata in respect to Krishṇa, especially in the philosophical episode known as the Bhagavat Gíta. In other places the divine nature of Krishṇa is less decidedly affirmed; in some it is disputed or denied; and in most of the situations in which he is exhibited in action, it is as a prince and warrior, not as a divinity. He exercises no superhuman faculties in the defence of himself or his friends, or in the defeat and destruction of his foes. The Mahábhárata, however, is evidently a work of various periods, and requires to be read throughout carefully and critically before its weight as an authority can be accurately appreciated. As it is now in type—thanks to the public spirit of the Asiatic Society of Bengal, and their Secretary, Mr. J. Prinsep—it will not be long before the Sanskrit scholars of the continent will accurately appreciate its value.

"The Puránas are also works of evidently different ages, and have been compiled under different circumstances, the precise nature of which we can imperfectly conjecture from internal evidence, and from what we know of the history of religious opinion in India. It is highly probable, that of the present popular forms of the Hindu religion, none assumed their actual state earlier than the time of Śankara Áchárya, the great Śaiva reformer, who flourished, in all likelihood, in the eighth or ninth century. Of the Vaishnava teachers, Rámánuja dates in the twelfth century, Madhwácharya in the thirteenth, and Vallabha in the sixteenth; and the Purāṇas seem to have accompanied or followed their innovations, being obviously intended to advocate the doctrines they taught. This is to assign to some of them a very modern date, it is true; but I cannot think that a higher can with justice be ascribed to them. This, however, applies to some only out of the number, as I shall presently proceed to specify.

"Another evidence of a. comparatively modem date must be admitted in those chapters of the Puráṇas which, assuming a prophetic tone, foretell what dynasties of kings will reign in the Kalí age. These chapters, it is true, are found but in four of the Puráṇas, but they are conclusive in bringing down the date of those four to a period considerably subsequent to Christianity. It is also to be remarked, that the Váyu, Vishṇu, Bhágavata, and Matsya Puráṇas, in which these particulars are foretold, have in all other respects the character of as great antiquity as any works of their class.

"The invariable form of the Puráṇas is that of a dialogue, in which some person relates its contents in reply to the inquiries of another. This dialogue is interwoven with others, which are repeated as having been held on other occasions between different individuals, in consequence of similar questions having been asked. The immediate narrator is commonly, though not constantly, Lomaharshaṇa or Romaharshana, the disciple of Vyása, who is supposed to communicate what was imparted to him by his preceptor, as be had heard it from some other sage. Vyása, as will be seen in the body of the work, is a generic title, meaning an 'arranger' or 'compiler.' It is in this age applied to Krishṇa Dwaipáyana, the son of Parásara, who is said to have taught the Vedas and Puránas to various disciples, but who appears to have been the head of a college or school, under whom various learned men gave to the sacred literature of the Hindus the form in which it now presents itself. In this task the disciples, as they are termed, of Vyása were rather his colleagues and coadjutors, for they were already conversant with what he is fabled to have taught them; and amongst them, Lomaharshaṇa represents the class of persons who were especially charged with the record of political and temporal events. He is called Súta, as if it was a proper name; but it is more correctly a title; and Lomaharshaṇa was 'a Súta,' that is, a bard or panegyrist, who was created, according to the text, to celebrate the exploits of princes; and who, according to the Váyu and Pádma Puráṇas, has a right by birth and profession to nanate the Puráṇas, in preference even to the Brahmans. It is not unlikely therefore that we are to understand, by his being represented as the disciple of Vyása, the institution of some attempt, made under the direction of the latter, to collect from the heralds and annalists of his day the scattered traditions which they had imperfectly preserved; and hence the consequent appropriation of the Puráṇas, in a great measure, to the genealogies of regal dynasties, and descriptions of the universe. However this may be, the machinery has been but loosely adhered to, and many of the Puráṇas, like the Vishṇu, are referred to a different narrator." *Preface to V.P.*

"The Puráṇas are uniformly stated to be eighteen in number. It is said that there are also eighteen Upa-Puráṇas, or minor Puránas, but many of them are not now procurable. The following eighteen are specified in the Deví Bhagavata:—

1. Sanatkumára.	10. Kálika.
2. Nárasimha.	11. Sámba.
3. Naradiya.	12. Nandi.
4. Śiva.	13. Saura.
5. Durvasasa.	14. Páráṣara.
6. Kapila.	15. Áditya.
7. Manava.	16. Máheṣwara.
8. Ausanaṣa.	17. Bhargava.
9. Varuṇa.	18. Vasishtha.

Of the contents of these books very little is known. There are many local legends of particular temples that are sometimes designated Upa-Puráṇas. Many ancient notions and traditions are preserved in the Puráṇas, but they have been so much mixed up with sectarian views, intended to favour the popularity of particular forms of worship, or articles of faith, that they cannot be received as authorities for the mythological religion of the Hindus at any remote period."

'Old', hence an ancient legend or tale of olden times. The Purāṇas succeed the Itihāsas or epic poems, but at a considerable distance of time, and must be distinguished from them. The epics treat of the legendary actions of heroes as mortal men; the Purāṇas celebrate the powers and works of positive gods, and represent a later and more extravagant development of Hinduism, of which they are in fact the Scriptures. These are the *pañcalakṣṇas* or distinguishing marks, but no one of the Purāṇas answers exactly to the description; some show a partial conformity with it, others depart from it very widely. The *Viṣṇu Purāṇa* is the one which best accords with the title. Wilson says, "A very great portion of the contents of many is genuine and old. The sectarial interpolation or embellishment is always sufficiently palpable to be set aside without injury to the more authentic and primitive material; and the Purāṇas, although they belong especially to that stage of the Hindu religion in which faith in some one divinity was the prevailing principle, are also a valuable record of the form of Hindu belief which came next in order to that of the Vedas, which grafted hero-worship upon the simpler ritual of the latter, and which had been adopted, and was extensively, perhaps universally, established in India at the time of the Greek invasion." According to the same authority, Pantheism "is one of their invariable characteristics", and underlies their whole teaching, "although the particular divinity who is all things, from whom all things proceed, and to whom all things return, is diversified according to their individual sectarian bias". The Purāṇas are all written in verse, and their invariable form is that of a dialogue between an exponent and an inquirer, interspersed with the dialogues and observations of other individuals. Thus, Pulastya received the *Viṣṇu Purāṇa* from Brahmā; he made it known to Parāśra, and Parāśara narrated it to his disciple Maitreya. The Purāṇas are eighteen in number, and in addition to these there are eighteen Upa Purāṇas or subordinate works. The Purāṇas are classified in three categories, according to the prevalence in them of the qualities of purity, gloom, and passion. Those in which the qualities of sattva or purity prevail are—(1) *Viṣṇu*, (2) *Nāradīya*, (3) *Bhāgavata*, (4) *Garuḍa*, (5) *Padma*, and (6) *Varāha*. These are Vaiṣṇava Purāṇas, in which the god Viṣṇu holds the pre-eminence. The Purāṇas in which *tamas*, the quality of gloom or ignorance, predominates are—(1) *Matsya*, (2) *Kūrma*, (3) *Liṅga*, (4) *Śiva*, (5) *Skanda*, (6) *Agni*. These are devoted to the god Śiva. Those in which *rajas* or passion prevails relate chiefly to the god Brahmā. They are—(1) *Brahmā*, (2) *Brahmāṇḍa*, (3) *Brahmā vaivarta*, (4) *Mārkaṇḍeya*, (5) *Bhaviṣya*, and (6) *Vāmana*. The works themselves do not fully justify this classification. None of them are devoted exclusively to one god, but Viṣṇu and his incarnations fill the largest space. One called the *Vāyu Purāṇa* is in some of the Purāṇas substituted for the Agni, and in others for the Śiva. This *Vāyu* is apparently the oldest of them, and may date as far back as the sixth century, and it is considered that some of the others may be as late as the thirteenth or even the sixteenth century. One fact appears certain: they must all have received a supplementary revision, because each one of them enumerates the whole eighteen. The *Mārkaṇḍeya* is the least sectarian of the Purāṇas; and the *Bhāgavata*, which deals at length with the incarnations of *Viṣṇu*, and particularly with his form Kṛṣṇa, is the most popular. The most perfect and the best known is the *Viṣṇu*, which has been entirely translated into English by Professor Wilson, and a second edition, with many valuable notes, has been edited by Dr. F.E. Hall. The text of the *Agni* and *Mārkaṇḍeya Purāṇas* has been published in the *Bibliotheca Indica*.

The Purāṇas vary greatly in length. Some of them specify the number of couplets that each of the eighteen contains. According to the *Bhāgavata*, the sum total of couplets in the whole eighteen is 400,000; the Skanda is the longest, with 81,000 the *Brahmā* and the *Vāmana* the shortest, with 10,000 couplets each.

The Upa Purāṇas are named—(l) *Sanatkumāra*, (2) *Narasiṁha* or *Nṛsiṁha*, (3) *Nāradīya* or *Vṛhan* (old) *Nāradīya*, (4) *Śiva*, (5) *Durvāsas*, (6) *Kāpila*, (7) *Mānava*, (8) *Anśanasa*, (9) *Vāruṇa*, (10) *Kālikā*, (11) *Śāmba*, (12) *Nandī*, (13) *Saura*, (14) *Pārāśara*, (15) *Āditya*, (16) *Māheśvara*, (17) *Bhāgavata*, (18) *Vāsiṣṭha*. These works are not common. Other modern works exist to which the term *Purāṇa* has been applied.

An account of each of the eighteen great Purāṇas is given under its own name.

PURANDARA—The Indra of the seventh (the present) Manwantara.

PURAÑJAYA—**(1)** 'City-conqueror.' A prince of the Solar race, son of Vikukṣi. His story, as told in the *Viṣṇu Purāṇa*, is that in the *tretā* age there was war between the gods and the asuras, in which the former were worsted. They had recourse to Viṣṇu for assistance, and he directed them to obtain the aid of Purañjaya, into whose person he promised to infuse a portion of himself. The prince complied with their wishes, and asked that their chief, Indra, would assume the form of a bull and carry him, the prince, upon his hump. This was done, and thus seated Purañjaya destroyed all the enemies of the gods. As he rode on the hump he obtained the cognomen of Kakutstha. In explanation of his title Purañjaya, the *Bhāgavata Purāṇa* says that he took the city of the *daityas* situated in the west. **(2)** A king of Ayodhya, son of Vikukshi, whose reign preceded that of Ikshváku. Puranjaya assisted the gods in their contest with the Asuras. As he destroyed the demon host whilst seated on the hump of a bull, he obtained the appellation Kakutstha, *q.v.*; 3, A prince, the son of Srinjaya; 4, A

Yavana chief, the son of Vindhyaṣakti.

PURAVAS—Descendants of Puru.

PURAVATI—A river not identified.

PURNASA—(Parnasa). A river that rises in the Páripátra mountain.

PURNOTSANGA—One of the thirty Andhrabhritya kings, the son of Sri Sátakarni; his reign lasted eighteen years.

PUROCANA—The emissary of Duryodhana who attempted to bum the Pāṇḍavas in their house and was burnt in his own house by Bhima. (*see* MAHĀBHĀRATA)

PUROHITA—A family priest, or chaplain. "The most ancient name for a priest by profession," says Prof. Max Müller "is Puróhita, which means *prepositus* or *prœsesi.* The Puróhita, however, was more than a priest. He was the friend and counsellor of the chief, the minister of the king, and his companion in peace and war. The original occupation of the Puróhita may have consisted in the performance of the usual sacrifices; but, with the ambitious policy of the Brahmans, it soon became a stepping stone to political power."

The office of a Puróhita now-a-days is, in the words of the Abbé Dubois, to prognosticate what are good and what are evil days for beginning any affair, or for putting it off; to avert, by Mantras or prayers, the pernicious effects of maledictions or the influence of malign constellations; to assign names to new born children and calculate their nativity; to bless new houses, wells, or tanks; to purify temples and consecrate them; to imbibe idols with the divine essence: all these ceremonies, and many others of smaller importance, are the province of the Brahmans called Puróhitas.

The most important of the ceremonies over which they preside are those of marriages and burials. They are so complex that an ordinary Brahman would be found incapable of performing them. A regular study is necessary for the exactness and precision that they require; and Mantras are requisite of which the greater part are ignorant. The Puróhitas alone are accomplished in the management of these rites, the detail of which they have in writing, in certain formularies, which they permit nobody to see, not even the other Brahmans. Indeed the principal Mantras that are used are not reduced into writing, from the fear that some other Brahmans might acquire them, and so become their rivals, to the diminution of their exclusive profits. The father teaches them to his son, and thus they pass from generation to generation in one family. This shows that it is self-interest rather than superstition which occasions this reserve. By hindering the other Brahmans from learning these ceremonies and the corresponding Mantras, the Puróhitas render themselves more necessary to the people, and to the Brahmans themselves, who cannot dispense with their services on many occasions.

One of the highest privileges attached to the profession of the Puróhita is the exclusive right of publishing the Hindu Almanac. There are but few who are found capable of making the calculations; perhaps one or two only in a district. It is not upon a knowledge of the motions of the heavenly bodies that the Hindu Almanac is compiled, but upon the approximation and agreement of numerous tables and formulæ of great antiquity, and therefore the calculation is very complicated, and much time, attention, and labour is required to arrive at exact conclusions.

On the first day of the year, the Puróhita assembles the principal inhabitants of the place where be lives. In their presence he announces, by sound of trumpet, who is to be supreme over the stars. He determines also the quantity of rain and of drought, and foretells, in short, whether it is to be a year of health or of disease; whether the deaths or the births shall predominate, and many other contingencies of equal importance.

The Puróhita is essentially a family priest and a religious preceptor. Amongst the poorer classes he may officiate for very many families, in which case he employs assistants, and gives them a stipulated share of the gifts and other perquisites which he may receive. But amongst the richer classes, the duties of a Puróhita are confined to a single family, and under such circumstances his influence becomes paramount in the household. He performs all the necessary religious rites and ceremonies for the members of the family, and imparts religious instruction from the sacred books. At the same time, he is the repository of all the family secrets, and the confidential and authoritative counsellor in all times of doubt and difficulty. He is also frequently engaged in more secular matters, such as the settlement of disputes; and in modern times a Hindu Zemindar or Rája has occasionally employed his Puróhita as an ambassador or envoy.

PUR—One of the synonyms of Mahat, defined in the Vishṇu Purána to be "that by which the concurrence of nature occupies and fills all bodies."

PURU—**(1)** One of the sons of the Manu Chakshusha; **(2)** the youngest son of king Yayáti, who consented to give his youth and vigour to his father, and receive in exchange Yayáti's infirmities. After Yayáti had had a thousand years experience of the vanity of sensual pleasures, he restored his youth to Puru, and installed him in the sovereignty of Pratishtháná. The descendants of Puru were numerous and celebrated; and included the Páṇḍavas and Kauravas.

PURUJANU—One of the kings of Kámpilya, the son of Suṣánti.

PURUKUTSA—A son of Māndhātṛ, into whose person Viṣṇu entered for the purpose of destroying the subterranean *gandharvas*, called Mauneyas. He reigned on the banks of the Narmadā, and that river personified as one of the Nāgas was his wife. By her he had a son, Trasadasyu. The *Viṣṇu Purāṇa* is said to have been narrated to him by "Dakṣa and other venerable sages".

PURUMIDHA—One of the sons of Hastin, the founder of Hastinápur.

PURUṢA-SŪKTA—A hymn of the *Ṛgveda* in which the four castes are first mentioned. It is considered to be one of the latest in date. See Muir's *Texts*, I, p.7.

PURURAVAS—The son of Budha and Sudyumna (Ila.) He was a prince renowned for liberality, devotion, magnificence, love of truth, and for personal beauty. Urvaśí having incurred the imprecation of Mitra and Varuṇa, determined to take up her abode in the world of mortals; and descending accordingly, beheld Purúravas. As soon as she saw him she forgot all reserve, and disregarding the delights of Swarga, became deeply enamoured of the prince. Beholding her infinitely superior to all other females in grace, elegance, symmetry, delicacy, and beauty, Purúravas was equally fascinated by Urvaśí: both were inspired by similar sentiments, and mutually feeling that each was every thing to the other, thought no more of any other object. Confiding in his merits, Purúravas addressed the nymph, and said, "Fair creature, I love you; have compassion on me, and return my affection." Urvaśí, half averting her face through modesty, replied, "I will do so, if you will observe the conditions I have to propose." "What are they ?" inquired the prince; "declare them." "I have two rams," said the nymph, "which I love as children; they must be kept near my bedside, and never suffered to be carried away: you must also take care never to be seen by me undressed; and clarified butter alone must be my food." To these terms the king readily gave assent.

After this, Purúravas and Urvaśí dwelt together in Alaká, sporting amidst the groves and lotus-crowned lakes of Chaitraratha, and the other forests there situated, for sixty-one thousand years. The love of Purúravas for his bride increased every day of its duration; and the affection of Urvaśí augmenting equally in fervour, she never called to recollection residence amongst the immortals. Not so with the attendant spirits at the court of Indra; and nymphs, genii, and quiristers, found heaven itself but dull whilst Urvaśí was away. Knowing the agreement that Urvaśí had made with the king, Viswavasu was appointed by the Gandharvas to effect its violation; and he, coming by night to the chamber where they slept, carried off' one of the rams. Urvaśí was awakened by its cries, and exclaimed, "Ah me ! who has stolen one of my children ? Had I a husband, this would not have happened ! To whom shall I apply for aid ?" The Rája overheard her lamentation, but recollecting that he was undressed, and that Urvaśí might see him in that state, did not move from the couch. Then the Gandharvas came and stole the other ram; and Urvaśí, hearing it blent, cried out that a woman had no protector who was the bride of a prince so dastardly as to submit to this outrage. This incensed Purúravas highly, and trusting that the nymph would not see his person, as it was dark, he rose, and took his sword, and pursued the robbers, calling upon them to stop, and receive their punishment. At that moment the Gandharvas caused a flash of brilliant lightning to play upon the chamber, and Urvaśí beheld the king undressed: the compact was violated, and the nymph immediately disappeared. The Gandharvas, abandoning the rams, departed to the region of the gods.

Having recovered the animals, the king returned delighted to his couch, but there he beheld no Urvaśí; and not finding her anywhere, he wandered naked over the world, like one insane. At length coming to Kurukshetra, he saw Urvaśí sporting with four other nymphs of heaven in a lake beautified with lotuses, and he ran to her, and called her his wife, and wildly implored her to return. "Mighty monarch," said the nymph, "refrain from this extravagance. I am now pregnant: depart at present, and come-hither again at the end of a year, when I will deliver to you a son, and remain with you for one night." Purúravas, thus comforted, returned to his capital. Urvaśí said to her companions, "This prince is a most excellent mortal: I lived with him long and affectionately united." "It was well done of you," they replied; "he is indeed of comely appearance, and one with whom we could live happily for ever,"

When the year had expired, Urvaṣí and the monarch met at Kurukshetra, and she consigned to him his first-born Áyus; and these annual interviews were repeated, until she had borne to him five sons. She then said to Purúravas, "Through regard for me, all the Gandharvas have expressed their joint purpose to bestow upon my lord their benediction: let him therefore demand a boon." The Rája replied, "My enemies are all destroyed, my faculties are all entire; I have friends and kindred, armies and treasures: there is nothing which I may not attain except living in the same region with my Urvaṣí. My only desire therefore is, to pass my life with her." When he had thus spoken, the Gandharvas brought to Purúravas a vessel with fire, and said to him, "Take this fire, and, according to the precepts of the Vedas, divide it into three fires; then fixing your mind upon the idea of living with Urvaṣí, offer oblations, and you shall assuredly obtain your wishes." The Rája took the brasier, and departed, and came to a forest. Then he began to reflect that he had committed a great folly in bringing away the vessel of fire instead of his bride; and leaving the vessel in the wood, he went disconsolate to his palace. In the middle of the night he awoke, and considered that the Gandharvas had given him the brasier to enable him to obtain the felicity of living with Urvaṣí, and that it was absurd in him to have left it by the way. Resolving therefore to recover it, he rose, and went to the place where he had deposited the vessel; but it was gone. In its stead he saw a young Áṣwattha tree growing out of a Śami plant, and he reasoned with himself, and said, "I left in this spot a vessel of fire, and now behold a young Áṣwattha tree growing out of a Śami plant. Verily I will take these types of fire to my capital, and there, having engendered fire by their attrition, I will worship it." *V.P.*

Having thus determined, he took the plants to his city, and prepared their wood for attrition, with pieces of as many inches long as there are syllables in the Gáyatrí; he recited that holy verse, and rubbed together sticks of as many inches as he recited syllables in the Gáyatrí. Having thence elicited fire, he made it threefold, according to the injunctions of the Vedas, and offered oblations with it, proposing as the end of the ceremony reunion with Urvaṣí. In this way, celebrating many sacrifices agreeably to the form in which offerings are presented with fire, Purúravas obtained a seat in the sphere of the Gandharvas, and was no more separated from his beloved. Thus fire, that was at first but one, was made threefold in the present Manwantara by the son of Ilá."

Purúravas is also called Vikrama; and the legend forms the subject of Kálidása's drama. "Vikrama and Urvaṣí; or the Hero and Nymph." The legend as related in the Satapatha Brahmana differs from the above in several particulars. An explanation of the myth is given by Max Müller in his *Comparative Mythology*,* (*Chips from a German Workshop*, Vol. II, p. 101.) "One of the myths of the Veda which expresses this correlation of the Dawn and the Sun, this love between the mortal and the immortal, and the identity of the morning dawn and the evening twilight, is the story of Urvaṣí Purúravas...Urvaṣí was originally an appellation and meant dawn." Another explanation is that Purúravas personifies the sun; while Urvaṣí is the morning mist. Urvaṣí is an Apsaras; and the Apsaras are "personifications of the vapours which are attracted by the sun, and form into mists or clouds." Dr. Goldstücker holds therefore that the legend represents the absorption by the sun of the vapour floating in the air. When Purúravas becomes distinctly visible, Urvaṣí vanishes; because when the sun shines forth, the mist is absorbed.

In a recent paper read before the Philological Society, "On Nomina Numina in its Two Phases." Professor Goldstücker said its object was to illustrate the influence which in ancient times, the mistaken etymology of words exercised on the formation of religious ideas and myths, and in modern times the mistaken interpretation of myths on the formation of wrong etymologies. In adverting to Max Müller's view of the supposed original import of Daphne in Greek, and of Urvaṣí in Hindu mythology, Professor Goldstücker observed that the common feature of the Greek and Hindu legends of Daphne and Urvaṣí, was the transformation of these beings—of Urvaṣí into a bird or vine, and of Daphne into a laurel tree. Moreover in the Hindu legend, Urvaṣí disappears in the lightning of the Gandharvas who steal her rams, and Purúravas establishes a new ceremony, which consists in producing fire by means of the attrition of two pieces of wood. And finally in all legendary accounts Urvaṣí is represented as an Apsaras, or as the name indicates (from *ap* water, and *saras*, arising,) from a water-born being; while Daphne as we are told by the Greek mythonomists, is the daughter of a river. Not any one of these *essential* features of the legend receives any light from the assumption that Daphne or Urvaṣí is the Dawn. Professor Goldstücker therefore proposed to read the legend thus: the sky is clouded (the ram being the symbol of the cloud) and the atmosphere charged with electricity. Lightning flashing through the cloud disperses them (the Gandharvas,) under lightning, steal the rams of Urvaṣí; the sun comes forth and absorbs the vapours that had enveloped the scene, when the objects hidden until then become visible. Again the effect of the tropical sun may be a conflagration of the dry forest wood; or as the legend says, Purúravas is the institution of the ceremony by which fire is produced through natural heat.

PURUSA—'Man.' **(1)** The original eternal man, the Supreme Being, and soul of the universe. **(2)** A name of Brahmā.

PURUSA-NARAYANA—The original male. The divine creator Brahmā.

PURUSHA—Spirit. The first form of Vishṇu. Mahat is also called Purusha from its abiding within the body.

PURUSOTTAMA—Literally 'best of men'; but the word *puruṣa* is here used in its mythic sense of soul of the universe, and so the compound means the "supreme soul" It is a title of Viṣṇu, and asserts his right to be considered the Supreme God. So the *Harivaṁśa* says, "Puruṣottama is whatever is declared to be the highest, Puruṣa the sacrifice, and everything else which is known by the name of Puruṣa."

PURUSOTTAMA-KSETRA—The sacred territory round about the temple of Jagnnātha in Orissa.

PURVA-BHADRAPADA—A lunar mansion in Vaiswánarí, in the Southern Avashthána.

PURVACHITTI—One of the Apsaras; of the Daivika or divine class.

PURVAJA—An appellation of Vishṇu, meaning produced or appearing before creation.

PURVA-MIMAMSA—A school of philosophy, (*see* DARŚANA)

PURVAPHALGUNI—A lunar mansion in Arshabhi, in the Central Avashthána.

PURVASHADA—A lunar mansion in Ajávíthi, in the Southern Avashthána.

PUSAN—A deity frequently mentioned in the Vedas, but he is not of a distinctly defined character. Many hymns are addressed to him. The word comes from the root *puṣ*, and the primary idea is that of "nourisher" or providence. So the *Taittirīya Brāhmaṇa* says, "When Prajāpati formed living creatures Pūṣan nourished them." The account given in Böhtlingk and Roth's Dictionary, and adopted by Dr. Muir, is as follows: "Pūṣan is a protector and multiplier of cattle and of human possessions in general. As a cowherd he carries an ox-goad, and he is drawn by goats. In the character of a Solar deity, he beholds the entire universe, and is a guide on roads and journeys and to the other world. He is called the lover of his sister Sūryā. He aids in the revolution of day and night, and shares with Soma the guardianship of living creatures. He is invoked along with the most various deities, but most frequently with Indra and Bhaga." He is a patron of conjurors, especially of those who discover stolen goods, and he is connected with the marriage ceremonial, being besought to take the bride's hand and bless her. (*see* Muir's *Texts*, V, p. 171)

In the *Nirukta*, and in works of later date, Pūṣan is identified with sun. He is also called the brother of Indra, and is enumerated among the twelve Ādityas. Pūṣan is toothless, and feeds upon a kind of gruel, and the cooked oblations offered to him are of ground materials, hence, he is called Karambhād. The cause of his being toothless is variously explained. According to the *Taittirīya Saṁhitā*, the deity Rudra, being excluded from a certain sacrifice, shot an arrow at the offering and pierced it. A portion of this sacrifice was presented to Pūṣan, and it broke his teeth. In the *Mahābhārata* and in the Purāṇas the legend takes a more definite shape. "Rudra (Śiva), of dreadful power, ran up to the gods present at Dakṣa's sacrifice, and in his rage knocked out the eyes of Bhaga with a blow, and, incensed, assaulted Pūṣan with his foot, and knocked out his teeth as he was eating the *puroḍāśa* offering." In the Purāṇas it is not Śiva himself, but his manifestation the Rudras, who disturbed the sacrifice of the gods and knocked Pūṣan's teeth down his throat. Pūṣan is called Āghṛni, 'splendid'; Dasra, Dasma, and Dasmavarcas, 'of wonderful appearance of power', and Kapardin (*q.v.*).

PUSHKALAS—The designation of Kshatriyas in Krauncha Dwípa.

PUSHKARA—**(1)** The brother of Nala, who engaged him in the gambling match that cost him his kingdom. When Nala was dispossessed of Kali, and received king Rituparna'a skill in dice, he won back his kingdom, gold, jewels, and all his treasures, but treated Pushkara kindly and gave him a city to dwell in. **(2)**

One of the sons of Bharata; he was king of Gandhára, residing at Pushkaravati; **(3)** The designation of brahmans in Krauncha Dwípa. Last of the seven great insular continents, or Dwípas, encompassing the sea of milk, and being itself surrounded by a sea of fresh water. Pushkara is represented as a terrestrial paradise; where all the inhabitants are happy, and rejoice in total exemption from sickness and decay. They live a thousand years undisturbed by anger or affection. There is neither virtue nor vice, killer nor slain: there is no jealousy, envy, fear, hatred, covetousness, nor any moral defect; neither is there truth or falsehood. *V.P.* 201. **(4)** A blue lotus. A celebrated tank about five miles from Ajmer.

PUSHKARAVARTTAKAS—A designation of the class of clouds Pakshaja; so termed from their including water in their vortices; they are the largest and most formidable of all, and are those which, at the end of the Yugas and Kalpas, pour down the waters of the deluge.

PUSHKARIN—A prince the son of Urukshaya, a descendant of Bharata.

PUSHKARINI—The daughter of the patriarch Anaranya, and mother of the Manu Chákshusha.

PUSHPADANTA—One of Śiva's principal attendants. "On the summit of Kailása, a lofty peak of the Himálaya range, resided the mighty deity Maheṣwara, attended by innumerable spirits and genii, and worshipped even by the superior divinities. The daughter of the mountain monarch, and the spouse of Mahadeva, propitiated her lord by her celestial strains; and, being pleased by her adulations, he proffered her whatever boon she might request. Her only demand was to receive instruction from his lips, and to hear from him such narrations as were yet unknown to the immortals or herself. Śiva, giving orders that no person should be admitted, proceeded to reveal to the goddess those narratives which illustrate the felicity of the gods, the troubles of mankind, and the intermediate and varying conditions of the spirits of earth and heaven.

It happened that Pushpadanta came to the palace gate and was refused admission by the warder. As he was a great favourite with his master and had always ready access to his person, the refusal excited his astonishment and curiosity; and, rendering himself invisible, he passed in, determined to ascertain why entrance was so rigorously barred. In this manner having come to where Śiva and Bhaváni were seated, he overheard all the marvellous stories repeated by the deity. When these were concluded, he retired as he had entered, unobserved, and going home communicated the narrative to his wife Jayá, it being impossible to keep wealth or secrets from a woman. Jayá, equally unable to preserve silence, communicated what she had heard to her fellow attendants on Párvatí: and the affair soon became known to the goddess and her lord. As the punishment of impertinence, Pushpadanta was condemned to a human birth, and his friend Málvavan, who presumed to intercede for him, was sentenced to a like fate. Being, however, subdued by the distress of Jayá, the offended goddess fixed a term to their degradation, and thus spoke. 'When Pushpadanta, encountering a Yaksha, who has been doomed by Kubera to haunt the Vindhya mountains as a goblin, shall recollect his original condition, and shall repeat the tales he has rashly over-heard, the curse shall no more prevail.' So saying, she ceased, and the two culprits, instantly, like a flash of lightning, blazed and disappeared.

After a due interval Pushpadanta was born at Kauṣámbí as Vararuchi, and when arrived at years of discretion found the goblin, and recollecting his origin, repeated to him the seven great narratives of Śiva, each comprehending a hundred thousand verses.—Wilson's *Works, III*, 160-163.

PUSHPADANTHA—One of the serpent kings; of the progeny of Kadru. (2) One of the guardian elephants, (*see* Lokapāla)

PUSHPAGIRI—The mountain of flowers; the residence of Varuṇa in the more recent mythology.

PUSHPAKA—The name of Ráma's aerial vehicle which he kept after defeating Ravana, the demon king of Lanka. The description of this vehicle and its flying prowess and seating capacity has often led to unbelief, which is quite misplaced. The readers wishing to inquire more on this matter can refer to my detailed work, titled *Ancient Indian Sciences* (pub. 2002, in 3 vols.), which has a few detailed chapters devoted to this aspect and describes the ancient Indian technology of flying and space. It would interest the readers to know that there existed a seperate work, titled the *Vimana Shastra*, only a few fragments of which are available in India in the custody of the Indian Air Force. The bulk of the technical treatise is believed to be in the possessions of the Germans. The reading of the few fragments available is enough to convince that the ancient Indians possessed a very advanced knowledge of flying and manufacturing flying crafts.

Kubera obtained it by gift from Brahmā, but it was carried off by Rāvaṇa, his half-brother, and constantly used by him. After Rāmacandra had slain Rāvaṇa, he made use of this capacious car to convey himself and Sītā, with Lakṣmaṇa, Hanuman and all his allies, back to Ayodhyā; after that he returned it to its owner, Kubera. It is also called Ratnavarṣaka, "that rains jewels".

PUSHPAMITRA—A king of Pátaliputra, who obtained the throne about 178 B.C. The Matsya Purána assigns him a reign of 36 years, from 178 B.C. to 142 B.C. It was during this reign that Patanjali lived and wrote his commentary on Pánini. He probably wrote the third chapter of his Bhashya between 144 and 142 B.C. And this agrees with the conclusion drawn by Professor Goldstücker, that the author, of the Mahabhashya nourished after the Maurya dynasty was extinct. This date of Patanjali may be regarded as trustworthy, and in the history of Sanskrit Literature it is of great importance. See *Ind. Antiq.*, Sept. 1873.

PUSHPATMITRA—The first king of the Sunga Dynasty; he reigned at Mekala, a country on the Narmada; he was the general of the last Maurya prince, whom he put to death, and ascended the throne himself; the dynasty lasted a hundred and twelve years.

PUSHPAVAT—A prince, the son of Rishabha.

PUSHPOTKATA—One of the wives of the patriarch Pulastya and the mother of the great giant Rávaṇa.

PUSHPOTTARA—One of the heavens of the Jainas. When Priyamitra returned to the earth in the Bhárata division as Nandana, after an existence of twenty-five lakhs of years, he was raised to the dignity of king of the gods in the Pushpottara heaven, in which capacity he preserved his ancient faith, offering flowers to, and bathing daily, the hundred and eighty images of the Arhats. Such exalted piety was now to meet with its reward, and the pains of existence were to be terminated in the person of the Tírthankara Mahávíra or Varddhamana.—*Wilson, I*, 293.

PUSHTI—'Thriving'; **(1)** A daughter of Daksha and wife of Dharma; **(2)** A daughter of Paurṇamása.

PUSHYA—**(1)** A prince, the son of the saintly king Yajñavalkya; **(2)** The eighth lunar mansion; in Airávata, in the Northern Avashthana.

> "The morning dawned with cloudless ray
> On Pushya's high auspicious day,
> And Cancer with benignant power
> Looked down on Ráma's natal hour."

PUSKARAVATI A city of the Gāndhāras not far from the Indus. It is the Pousekielofati of Hiuen-Tsang.

PUSKOLA—The palm leaf upon which the native books are written in Ceylon.

PUSPAKARANDINI—A name of Ujjayinī.

PUSPAMITRA—The first of the Śuṅga kings, who succeeded the Mauryas, and reigned at Pāṭaliputra. In his time the grammarian Patañjali is supposed to have lived.

PUSPOTKATA—A *rākṣasī*, the wife of Viśravas and mother of Rāvaṇa and Kumbhakarṇa.

PUT—A hell to which childless men are said to be condemned. "A name invented to explain the word *puttra*, son (hell-saver)."

PUTANA—A female fiend or Asura, the daughter of Bali; she was known as a child killer, and attempted the life of Krishṇa when he was an infant, but was killed herself in the act.

PUTRA—One of the three sons of Priyavrata who adopted a religions life; remembering the occurrences of a prior existence, he did not covet dominion, but diligently practiced the rites of devotion.

PUTRAKA—The founder and sovereign of Pátali-putra; his history will be found under that Heading.

RADHA—One of Krishṇa's favourite mistresses, while he lived as Gopala among the cowherds of Vrindavan. She was wife of Ayanaghoṣa, a cowherd. Considered by some to be an incarnation of Lakṣmī, and worshipped accordingly. Some have discovered a mystical character in Rādhā, and consider her as the type of the human soul drawn to the ineffable god, Kṛṣṇa, or as that pure divine love to which the fickle lover returns. The Gíta Govinda is a poem on their attachment to each other. The poet opens the first interview of Krishṇa and Rádha with an animated description of a night in the rainy season, in which Krishṇa is represented as a wanderer, and Rádha, daughter of the shepherd Naṇda, is sent to offer him shelter in their cottage. Naṇda thus speaks to Rádha "The firmament is obscured by clouds; the woodlands are black with Tamála trees; that youth who roves in the forest will be fearful in the gloom of night; go, my daughter, bring the wanderer to my rustic mansion." Such was the command of Naṇda the herdsman, and hence arose the love of Rádha and Madhava. (Tod's *Rajasthan*, Vol. I, p. 540)

RADHA—(Rádhá), the wife of the charioteer of Duryodhana, who bred Karna as her son, after he was exposed on the banks of the Yamuna by her own mother Pṛtha.

RADHEYA—A metronymic of Karṇa.

RADHIKA—A diminutive and endearing form of the name Rādhā.

RAGA (mas.), **RĀGINĪ** (fem.)—**(1)** The *rāgas* are the musical modes or melodies personified, six or more in number, and the *rāginis* are their consorts. **(2)** Love. One of "the five afflictions" in the Patanjala philosophy; the other four are Avidya, Asmitá, Dwesha, and Abhinivesa.

RAGHAVA—Descendant of Raghu, a name of Rāma.

RAGHAVA-PANDAVIYA—A modern poem by Kavi Rāja, which is in high repute. It is an artificial work, which exhibits extraordinary ingenuity in the employment of words. As its name implies, the poem celebrates the actions of Rāghava, *i.e.*, Rāma, the descendant of Raghu, and also those of the Pāṇḍava princes. It thus recounts at once in the same words the story of the *Rāmāyaṇa* and that of the *Mahābhārata*; and the composition is so managed that the words may be understood as applying either to Rāma or the Pāṇḍavas. It has been printed.

RAGHAVA-VILASA A poem on the life of Rāma by Viśvanātha, the author of the *Sāhityadarpaṇa*.

RAGHU—**(1)** A distinguished mythical Mahárája of the solar race, the son of Dilípa, and sovereign of Ayodhya, celebrated for his learning, his riches, his bravery, and his uniform success. The Raghuvansa narrates his wonderful achievements and varied conquests, and concludes with the following legend. A brahman named Koutsya, a disciple of the great Rishi Varatanta, having completed his course of studies, asked his guru what acknowledgment he should make to show his gratitude. The tutor professed himself satisfied with the services the disciple had rendered; the latter, however, insisting on bestowing a gift, the guru asked for fourteen crores of rupees. For this enormous sum Koutsya applied to Mahárája Raghu, who having just emptied his treasury by the performance of the sacrifice termed Visvajit-yajna, determined to conquer Kubera (the god of riches), who was so alarmed at the prospect that he at once sent innumerable crores to the Mahárája. The money was then given to the brahman, who in return blessed the king with the promise of a good son, and in due course the illustrious *Aja* was born. **(2)** One of the sons of Yadu, the founder of the Yádava race.

RAGHUPATI—(*see* RAGHU)

RAGHUVAMSA—'The race of Raghu.' The name of a celebrated poem in nineteen cantos by Kālidāsa on the ancestry and life of Rāma. It has been translated into Latin by Stenzler, and into English by Griffiths. There are other translations and many editions of the text.

RAGHUVAMSHA TILAKA—The glory of the house of Raghu; a name of Ráma, the son of Dasaratha, who was grandson of Raghu.

RĀHU—Rāhu and Ketu are in astronomy the ascending and descending nodes. Rāhu is the cause of eclipses, and the term is used to designate the eclipse itself. He is also considered as one of the planets, as king of meteors, and as guardian of the south-west quarter. Mythologially Rāhu is a *daitya* who is supposed to seize the sun and moon and swallow them, thus obscuring their rays and causing eclipses. He was son of Vipracitti and Siṁhikā, and is called by his metronymic Saiṁhikeya. He had four arms, and his lower part ended in a tail. He was a great mischief-maker, and when the gods had produced the *amṛta* by churning the ocean, he assumed a disguise, and insinuating himself amongst them, drank some of it. The sun and moon detected him and informed Viṣṇu, who cut off his head and two of his arms, but, as he had secured immortality, his body was placed in the stellar sphere, the upper parts, represented by a dragon's head, being the ascending node, and the lower parts, represented by a dragon's tail, being Ketu the descending node. Rāhu wreaks his vengeance on the sun and moon by occasionally swallowing them. The *Viṣṇu Purāṇa* says, "Eight black horses draw the dusky chariot of Rāhu, and once harnessed are attached to it for ever. On the Parvans (nodes, or lunar and solar eclipses) Rāhu directs his course from the sun to the moon, and back again from the moon to the sun. The eight horses of the chariot of Ketu, swift as the wind, are of the dusky red colour of lac, or of the smoke of burning straw." Rāhu is called *Abhrapiśāca*, 'the demon of the *sky*'; Bharaṇībhū, 'born from the asterism

Bharaṇī'; Graha, 'the seizer'; Kabandha, 'the headless'.

RAHULA—A prince, the son of Sákya. A name, says Dr. Wilson, of considerable chronological interest; for Sákya is the name of the author or reviver of Buddhism, whose birth appears to have occurred in the seventh, and death in the sixth century before Christ (B. C. 621-543.) Sákya, as the twenty-second of the line of Ikshváku is contemporary with Ripunjaya, the last of the kings of Magadha. The chronology is not easily adjusted, but it is not altogether incompatible. The Buddhists always consider their teacher Sákya to be descended from Ikshváku. In Tibet, where several sects of Buddhists are found, some of them profess themselves to be followers of Ráhula.

RAIBHYA—A sage who was the friend of Bharadvāja. He had two sons, Arvāvasu and Parāvasu. The latter, under the curse of Bharadvāja, killed his father, mistaking him for an antelope, as he was walking about at night covered with an antelope's skin. Arvāvasu retired into the forest to obtain by devotion a remission of his brother's guilt. When he returned, Parāvasu charged him with the crime, and he again retired to his devotions. These so pleased the gods that they drove away Parāvasu and restored Raibhya to life. (*see* YAVAKRĪTA)

RAIVATA—**(1)** One of the sons of Priyavrata according to the Bhágavata list, and the Manu of the fifth Manwantara. Four Manus were descended from Priyavrata, who in consequence of propitiating Vishṇu by his devotions, obtained these rulerships of the Manwantara, for his posterity. The Markaṇḍeya contains a legend of the birth of Raivata, as the son of king Durgama, by the nymph Revatí, sprung from the constellation Revatí. **(2)** An appellation of one of the eleven Rudras. **(3)** A name of Kakudmin (*q.v.*) the eldest of the sons of Revatí; he visited Brahmá, Anil gave his daughter in marriage to Balaráma. **(4)** The name of a mountain.

RAJA—A prince, the son of Vnája a descendant of Bharata. Rája is derived from Ráj, to shine or be splendid.

RAJADHIDEVI—A daughter of Súra, who was married to Jayasena, king of Avantí.

RAJAGAHA—A city near Benares, celebrated as the residence of Gautama Buddha, and the place where he died.

RAJAGRHA—The capital of Magadha. Its site is still traceable in the hills between Patna and Gayā.

RAJANYA—A Vedic designation of the kṣatriya caste.

RAJARSI—(Rāja-ṛṣi). A *ṛṣi* or saint of the regal caste; a kṣatriya who, through pure and holy life on earth, has been raised as a saint or demigod to Indra's heaven, as Viśvāmitra, Purūravas, &c.

RAJASEKHARA—A dramatist who was the author of the dramas *Viddha-Śālabhañjikā* and *Pracaṇḍa-Pāṇḍava*. He was also the writer of *Karpūra Mañjarī*, a drama entirely in Prākṛt. Another play, *Bāla Rāmāyaṇa*, is attributed to him. He appears to have been the minister of some Rājput, and to have lived about the beginning of the twelfth century.

RAJASUYA—'A royal sacrifice.' A great sacrifice performed at the installation of a king, religious in its nature but political in its operation, because it implied that he who instituted the sacrifice was a supreme lord, a king over kings, and his tributary princes were required to be present at the rite.

RAJA-TARANGINI—A Sanskṛt metrical history of Kaśmīr by Kalhaṇa Paṇḍit. It commences with the days of fable and comes down to year AD 1027. The author probably lived about AD 1148. This is the only known work in Sanskṛt which deserves the name of a history. The text has been printed in Calcutta. Troyer published the text with a French translation. Wilson and Lassen have analysed it, and Dr. Bühler has lately reviewed the work in the *Indian Antiquary*.

RAJI—A son of Āyus and father of 500 sons of great valour. In one of the chronic wars between the gods and the *asuras* it was declared by Brahmā that the victory should be gained by that side which Raji joined. The *asuras* first sought him, and he undertook to aid them if they promised to make him their king on their victory being secured. They declined. The heavenly hosts repaired to him and undertook to make him their Indra. After the *asuras* were defeated he became king of the gods, and Indra paid him homage. When he returned to his own city, he left Indra as his deputy in heaven. On Raji's death Indra refused to acknowledge the succession of his son, and by the help of Bṛhaspati, who led them astray and effected their ruin, Indra recovered his sovereignty.

RAJYAVARDDHANA—A prince, the son of Dama, a descendant of Marutta.

RAKA—**(1)** A *rākṣasī* wife of Viśravas and mother of Kharaand Śurpanakhā. **(2)** One of the phases of the moon, represented as one of the four daughters of

Angiras; **(3)** The day when the moon is quite round.

RAKHI—A bracelet used as an armlet, or preservative against evil (Ráksha) consisting of a piece of thread or silk or some more costly material, bound round the wrist or arm, with an appropriate prayer. Besides its application to children to avert the effects of evil eyes, or to protect them against Demons or witches, there is one day in the year, the Rákhí Purnimá, or full moon in the month of Sravan (July-August) when it is bound upon the wrists of adults, by friendly or kindred brahmins, with a short prayer or benediction. The Rákhí is also sent sometimes by persons of distinction, and especially by females, to members of a different family or race to intimate a sort of brotherly or sisterly adoption., Colonel Tod received the bracelet from three queens in Rajasthan, and after he returned to his own country set a high value on these testimonies of friendly regard.—*Wilson.*

In his *Annals* he says, "The festival of the Rákhí is in spring, and whatever its origin it is one of the few when an intercourse of gallantry of the most delicate nature is established between the fair sex and the cavaliers of Rajasthan. Though the bracelet may be sent by maidens, it is only on occasion of urgent necessity or danger. The Rájput dame bestows with the Rákhí the title of adopted brother; and while its acceptance secures to her all the protection of a '*cavaliere serventé,*' scandal itself never suggests any other tie to his devotion. He may hazard his life in her cause, and yet never receive a smile in reward, for he cannot even see the fair object who, as the brother of her adoption, has constituted him her defender. But there is a charm in the mystery of such connections, never endangered by close observation, and the loyal to the fair may well attach a value to the public recognition of being the Rákhí-bund Bháe, the 'bracelet-bound-brother' of a princess. The intrinsic value of such pledge is never looked to, nor is it requisite it should be costly, though it varies with the means and rank of the donor, and may be of flock silk and spangles, or gilt chains and gems. The acceptance of the pledge and its return, is by the *kalchli* or corset of simple silk, or satin, or gold brocade and pearls. In shape or application there is nothing similar in Europe, and as defending the most delicate part of the structure of the fair, it is peculiarly appropriate as an emblem of devotion.

The emperor Humáyún was so pleased with this courteous delicacy in the customs of Rajasthan, on receiving the bracelet of the princess Kurnavati, which invested him with the title of her brother, and uncle and protector to her infant, that he pledged himself to her service. He proved himself a true knight, and abandoned his conquests in Bengal when called on to redeem his pledge. Many romantic tales are founded on the gift of the Rákhí. See Tod's *Rajasthan*, I, 312.

RĀKṢASA-LOKA—(*see* LOKA)

RĀKṢASAS—Goblins or evil spirits. They are not all equally bad, but have been classified as of three sorts—one as a set of beings like the *yakṣas*, another as a sort of Titans or enemies of the gods, and lastly, in the common acceptation of the term, demons and fiends who haunt cemeteries, disturb sacrifices, harass devout men, animate dead bodies, devour human beings, and vex and afflict mankind in all sorts of ways. These last are the *rākṣasas* of whom Rāvaṇa was chief, and according to some authorities, they are descended, like Ravaṇa himself, from the sage Pulastya. According to other authorities, they sprang from Brahmā's foot. The *Viṣṇu Purāṇa* also makes them descendants of Kaśyapa and Khaśā, a daughter of Dakṣa, through their son Rākṣas; and the *Rāmāyaṇa* states that when Brahmā created the waters, he formed certain beings to guard them who were called *rākṣasas* (from the root *rakṣ*, to guard, but the derivation from this root may have suggested the explanation), and the *Viṣṇu Purāṇa* gives a somewhat similar derivation. It is thought that the *rākṣasas* of the epic poems were the rude barbarian races of India who were subdued by the Āryans.

When Hanumān entered the city of Laṅkā to reconnoitre in the form of a cat, he saw that "the *rākṣasas* sleeping in the houses were of every shape and form. Some of them disgusted the eye, while some were beautiful to look upon. Some had long arms and frightful shapes; some were very fat and some were very lean: some were mere dwarfs and some were prodigiously tall. Some had only one eye and others only one ear. Some had monstrous bellies, hanging breasts, long projecting teeth, and crooked thighs; whilst others were exceedingly beautiful to behold and clothed in great splendour. Some had two legs, some three legs, and some four legs. Some had the heads of serpents, some the heads of donkeys, some the heads of horses, and some the heads of elephants."—(*Rāmāyaṇa.*)

The *rākṣasas* have a great many epithets descriptive of their characters and actions. They are called

Anuśaras, Aśaras, and Hanūṣas, 'killers or hurters'; Iṣṭipacas, 'stealers of offerings'; Sandhyābalas, 'strong in twilight'; Kṣapāṭas, Naktancaras, Rātricaras, and Śamanīṣadas, 'night-walkers'; Nṛjagdhas or Nṛcakṣas, 'cannibals'; Palalas, Palādas, Palankaṣas, Kravyāds, 'carnivorous'; Asrapas, Asṛkpas, Kaunapas, Kīlālapas, and Raktapas, 'blood-drinkers'; Dandaśukas, 'biters'; Praghasas, 'gluttons'; Malinamukhas, 'black-faced'; Karbūras, &c. But many of these epithets are not reserved exclusively for *rākṣasas.*

Giants. They are said in the Vishṇu Purána to be the descendants of Pulastya, through Rákshas. They are also represented in the same work as having proceeded .from Brahmá; beings of hideous aspect, and with long beards. They hastened to the deity; such of them as exclaimed "Oh ! preserve us," were thence called Rákshasas (from Raksha to preserve); others who cried out, "let us eat," were denominated Yakslias from (yaksha to eat.)

"In their earliest conception," says Mr. J. C. Thomson, "they seem to be those unknown creatures of darkness, to which the superstition of all ages and races has attributed the evils that attend this life, and a malignant desire to injure mankind. In the Epic period they seem to be personifications of the aborigines of India, presented under the terrible aspect of vampires flying through the air, sucking blood, &c., in order to heighten the triumphs of the Aryan heroes who subdued them. In this character they play a very prominent part on the Rámáyaṇa, the beautiful epic of Válmíki. Here they are led by Rávaṇa, the king of Lanka, which is supposed to be the island of Ceylon and its capital, and they are subdued by Dasaratha Ráma the hero of the poem. In the Puránic period they are infernal giants, the children of the Rishi Pulastya, and enemies of the gods. They are then divided into three classes:—

(1) The slaves of Kubera the god of wealth, and guardians of his treasures.
(2) Malevolent imps whose chief delight is to disturb the pious in their devotions.
(3) Giants of enormous proportions, inhabiting Naraka, or hell, and hostile to the gods. In the second Manwantara they are the sons of Kaṣyapa and Khasá."

The most celebrated Rákshakas are Rávaṇa, and his brothers Kumbhakarna and Vibhíshana, an account of whom will be found under their respective names.

RĀKṢASA-RITUAL—By violence. Manu says, the seizure of a maiden by force, whilst she weeps and calls for assistance, after her kinsmen and friends have been slain in battle or wounded, and their houses broken open, is the marriage called Rákshasa.

RAKTAVIJA—A demon who had a sort of charmed life, but was ultimately slain by Deví. The contest took place after the goddess had killed Chanda and Munda. "Each drop of blood shed from his body had the singular virtue of producing hundreds of demons like himself. The strokes of the goddess's weapons began, therefore, to harass her own self more than her malignant enemy, and that exactly in proportion to her success. The demons produced by the Asura's blood infested the whole universe. The gods were quite afraid. Seeing them frightened, the goddess struck Raktavíja with her spear and received his blood into her mouth; and ate up the other demons produced from the blood previously shed. Thus fell Raktavíja the great Asura, on the earth, wounded by various weapons, his blood drunk up by Chámuṇḍá. (*Markandeya Purana*, by K. M. Bannerjea.)

RAMA, RĀMACANDRA—Eldest son of Daśaratha, a king of the Solar race, reigning at Ayodhyā. This Rāma is the seventh incarnation of the god Viṣṇu, and made his appearance in the world at the end of the *tretā* or second age. His story is briefly told in the Vana Parva of the *Mahābhārata*, but it is given in full length as the grand subject of the *Rāmāyaṇa.* King Daśaratha was childless, and performed the *aśvamedha* sacrifice with scrupulous care, in the hope of obtaining offspring. The gods accepted his devotion, and he received the promise of four sons. At this time the gods were in great terror and alarm at the deeds and menaces of Ravaṇa, the *rākṣasa* king of Laṅkā, who had obtained extraordinary power, in virtue of severe penance and austere devotion to Brahmā. In their terror the gods appealed to Viṣṇu for deliverance, and he resolved to become manifest in the world with Daśaratha as his human father. Daśaratha was performing a sacrifice when Viṣṇu appeared to him as a glorious being from out of the sacrificial fire, and gave to him a pot of nectar for his wives to drink. Daśaratha gave half of the nectar to Kauśalyā, who brought forth Rāma with a half of the divine essence, a quarter to Kaikeyī, whose son Bharata was endowed with a quarter of the deity, and the fourth part to Sumitrā, who brought forth two sons, Lakṣmaṇa and Śatrughna, each having an eighth part of the divine essence. The brothers were all attached to each other, but Lakṣmaṇa was more especially devoted to Rāma and Śatrughna to

Bharata.

[The two sons of Sumitrā and the pairing off of the brothers have not passed without notice. The version of the *Rāmāyaṇa* given by Mr. Wheeler endeavours to account for these circumstances. It says that Daśaratha divided the divine nectar between his senior wives, Kauśalya and Kaikeyī, and that when the younger, Sumitrā, asked for some, Daśaratha desired them to share their portions with her. Each gave her half, so Sumitrā received two quarters and gave birth to two sons: "from the quarter which she received from Kauśalyā she gave birth to Lakṣmaṇa, who became the ever-faithful friend of Rāma, and from the quarter she received from Kaikeyī she gave birth to Śatrughna, who became the ever-faithful friend of Bharata". This account is silent as to the superior divinity of Rāma, and according to it all four brothers must have been equals as manifestations of the deity.]

The four brothers grew up together at Ayodhyā, but while they were yet striplings, the sage Viśvāmitra sought the aid of Rāma to protect him from the *rākṣasas.* Daśaratha, though very unwilling, was constrained to consent to the sage's request. Rāma and Lakṣmaṇa then went to the hermitage of Viśvāmitra, and there Rāma killed the female demon Tārakā, but it required a good deal of persuasion from the sage before he was induced to kill a female. Viśvāmitra supplied Rāma with celestial arms, and exercised a considerable influence over his actions. Viśvāmitra afterwards took Rāma and his brothers to Mithilā to the court of Janaka king of Videha. This king had a lovely daughter named Sītā, whom he offered in marriage to anyone who could bend the wonderful bow that had once belonged to Śiva. Rāma not only bent the bow but also broke it, and thus won the hand of the princess, who became a most virtuous and devoted wife. Rāma's three brothers also were married to a sister and two cousins of Sītā.

This breaking of the bow of Śiva brought about a very curious incident, which is probably an interpolation of a later date, introduced for a sectarian purpose. Paraśurāma, the sixth incarnation of Viṣṇu, the brāhmaṇa exterminator of the kṣatriyas, was still living upon earth. He was a follower of Śiva, and was offended at the breaking of that deity's bow. Notwithstanding that he and Rāma were both incarnations of Viṣṇu, he challenged Rāma to a trial of strength and was discomfited, but Rāma spared his life because he was a brāhmaṇa.

Preparations were made at Ayodhyā for the inauguration of Rāma as successor to the throne. Kaikeyī, the second wife of Daśaratha, and mother of Bharata, was her husband's favourite. She was kind to Rāma in childhood and youth, but she had a spiteful humpbacked female slave named Mantharā. This woman worked upon the maternal affection of her mistress until she aroused a strong feeling of jealousy against Rāma. Kaikeyī had a quarrel and a long struggle with her husband, but he at length consented to install Bharata and to send Rāma into exile for fourteen years. Rāma departed with his wife Sītā and his brother Lakṣmaṇa, and travelling southwards, he took up this abode at Citrakūṭa, in the Daṇḍaka forest, between the Yamunā and Godāvarī. Soon after the departure of Rāma, his father Daśaratha died, and Bharata was called upon to ascend the throne. He declined, and set out for the forest with an army to bring Rāma back. When the brothers met there was a long contention. Rāma refused to return until the term of his father's sentence was completed, and Bharata declined to ascend the throne. At length it was arranged that Bharata should return and act as his brother's vicegerent. As a sign of Rāma's supremacy Bharata carried back with him a pair of Rāma's shoes, and these were always brought out ceremoniously when business had to be transacted. Rāma passed ten years of his banishment moving from one hermitage to another, and went at length to the hermitage of the sage Agastya, near the Vindhya mountains. This holy man recommended Rāma to take up his abode at Pañcavaṭī, on the river Godāvarī, and the party accordingly proceeded thither. This district was infested with *rākṣasas,* and one of them named Śūrpanakhā, a sister of Rāvaṇa, saw Rāma and fell in love with him. He repelled her advances, and in her jealousy she attacked Sītā This so enraged Lakṣmaṇa that he cut off her ears and nose. She brought her brothers Khara and Dūṣaṇa with an army *of rākṣasas to* avenge her wrongs, but they were all destroyed. Smarting under her mutilation and with *spretae injuria formae*, she repaired to her brother Rāvaṇa in Laṅkā, and inspired him by her description with a fierce passion for Sītā. Rāvaṇa proceeded to Rāma's residence in an aerial car, and his accomplice Mārīca having lured Rāma from home, Rāvaṇa assumed the form of a religious mendicant and lulled Sītā's apprehensions until he found an opportunity to declare himself and carry her off by force to Laṅkā. Rāma's despair and rage at the loss of his faithful wife were terrible. He and Lakṣmaṇa went in pursuit and tracked the ravisher. On their way they killed Kabandha, a headless monster, whose disembodied spirit counselled Rāma to seek the aid of Sugrīva, king of the monkeys. The two brothers accordingly went on their way to Sugrīva, and after overcoming some obstacles and assisting Sugrīva to recover Kiṣkindhā, his capital, from his usurping brother Bālin, they entered into a firm alliance with him. Through this connection Rāma got the appellations of Kapiprabhu and Kapiratha. He received not only the support of all the forces of Sugrīva and his allies, but the active aid of Hanumān, son of the wind, minister and general of Sugrīva. Hanumān's extraordinary powers of leaping and flying enabled him to do all the work of reconnoitering. By superhuman efforts their armies were transported to Ceylon by "Rāma's bridge", and after many fiercely contested battles the city of Laṅkā was taken, Rāvaṇa was killed and Sītā rescued. The recovery of his wife filled Rāma with joy, but he was jealous of her honour, received her coldly, and refused to take her back. She asserted her purity in touching and dignified language, and determined to prove her innocence by the ordeal of fire. She entered the flames in the presence of men and gods, and Agni, god of fire, led her forth and placed her in Rāma's arms unhurt. Rāma then returned, taking with him his chief allies to Ayodhyā. Reunited with his three brothers, he was solemnly crowned and began a glorious reign, Lakṣmaṇa being associated with him in the government. The sixth section of the *Rāmāyaṇa* here concludes; the remainder of the story is told in the Uttara Kāṇḍa, a subsequent addition. The treatment, which Sità received in captivity, was better than might have been expected at the hands of a *rākṣasa.* She had asserted and proved her purity, and Rāma believed her; but jealous thoughts would cross his sensitive mind, and when his subjects blamed him for taking back his wife, he resolved, although she was pregnant, to send her to spend the rest of her life at the hermitage of Vālmīki. There she was delivered other twin sons Kuśa and Lava, who bore upon their persons the marks of their high paternity. When they were about fifteen-year-old they wandered accidentally to Ayodhyā and were recognised by their father, who acknowledged them, and recalled Sītā to attest her innocence. She returned, and in a public assembly declared her purity, and called upon the earth to verify her words. It did so. The ground opened and received "the daughter of the furrow", and Rāma lost his beloved and only wife. Unable to endure life without her, he' resolved to follow, and the gods favoured his determination. Time appeared to him in the form of an ascetic and told him that he must stay on earth or ascend to heaven and rule over the gods. Lakṣmaṇa with devoted fraternal affection endeavoured to save his brother from what he deemed the baleful visit of Time. He incurred a sentence of death for his interference, and was conveyed bodily to Indra's heaven. Rāma with great state and ceremony went to the river Sarayū, and walking into the water was hailed by Brahmā's voice of welcome from heaven, and entered "into the glory of Viṣṇu".

The conclusion of the story as told in the version of the *Rāmāyaṇa* used by Mr. Wheeler differs materially. It represents that Sītā remained in exile until her sons were fifteen or sixteen years of age. Rāma had resolved upon performing the *aśvamedha* sacrifice; the horse was turned loose, and Śatrughna followed it with an army. Kuśa and Lava took the horse and defeated and wounded Śatrughna. Rāma then sent Lakṣmaṇa to recover the horse, but he was defeated and left for dead. Next Bharata was sent with Hanumān, but they were also defeated. Rāma then set out himself to repair his reverses. When the father and sons came into each other's presence, nature spoke out, and Rāma acknowledged his sons. Sītā also, after receiving an admonition from Vālmīki, agreed to forgive her husband. They returned to Ayodhyā. Rāma performed the *aśvamedha*, and they passed the remainder of their lives in peace and joy.

The incidents of the first six *kāṇḍas* of the *Rāmāyaṇa* supply the plot of Bhavabhūti's drama *Mahāvīracarita.* The Uttara Kāṇḍa is the basis of this *Uttara-rāma-carita.* This describes Rāma's jealousy, the banishment of Sītā, and the birth of her sons; but the subsequent action is more human and affecting than in the poem. Rāma repents of his unjust treatment of his wife, and goes forth to seek her. The course of his wanderings is depicted with great poetic beauty, and his meeting with his sons and his reconciliation with Sītā are described with exquisite pathos and tenderness. The drama closes when "All conspires to make their happiness complete.

The worship of Rāma still holds its ground, particularly in Oude and Bihār, and he has numerous worshippers. "It is noteworthy," says Professor Williams, "that the Rāma legends have always retained their purity, and unlike those of Brahmā, Kṛṣṇa, Śiva, and Durgā, have never been mixed up with indecencies and licentiousness. In fact, the worship of Rāma has never degenerated to the same extent as that of some of these other deities." This is true; but it may be observed that Rāma and his wife were pure; there was nothing in their characters suggestive of license; and if "the husband of one wife' and the devoted and affectionate wife had come to be associated with impure ideas, they must have lost all that gave them a title to veneration. The name of Rāma, as 'Rām! Rām!' is a common form of salutation.

RAMA—There are three Rāmas: Paraśurāma, Rāmacandra, and Balarāma; but it is to the second of these that the name is specially applied.

RAMAGIRI—'The hill of Rāma'. It stands a short distance north of Nāgpur.

RAMANAKA—One of the eight islands enumerated in the Bhágavata, as peopled by Mlechchhas, who worship Hindu divinities.

RAMANUJA—A celebrated Vaishnava teacher, who lived some time in the twelfth century. He was a native of the South of India, and according to the legendary narratives of his life which are current there, be was an incarnation of the serpent Śesha, while his chief companions and disciples were the embodied Discus, Mace, Lotus, and other insignia of Vishṇu. In a Kanara account of his life called the Divya charitra, he is said to have been the son of Śrí Keṣava Acharya and Bhúmi Devi; and, as before, an incarnation of Śesha. He was born at Perambur and studied at Conjeveram, where also he taught his system of the Vaishnava faith. He afterwards resided at Śrí Ranga, worshipping Vishṇu as Śrí Ranga Nátha, and there composed his principal works; he then visited various parts of India, disputing with the professors of different creeds, overcoming them of course, and reclaiming various shrines, then in possession of the Śhaivas, for the worshippers of Vishṇu, particularly the celebrated temple of Tripety.

On his return to Śrí Ranga the disputes between the Vaishnava and Śaiva religions, became exceedingly violent, and the Chola monarch commanded all the Brahmans in his dominions to Men an acknowledgment of the supremacy of Śiva. Rámánuja was impracticable, and the king sent armed men to seize him. With the assistance of his disciples he effected his escape and found refuge with the Jain sovereign of Mysore. In consequence of rendering medical service to the daughter of this prince, or in the terms of the legend, expelling an evil spirit by whom she was possessed, he obtained the monarch's grateful regard, and finally converted him to the Vaishnava faith. Rámánuja remained several years in Mysore at a temple in Yádava Giri, now known as Mélkóté.—Wilson, *Works*, *I*, 37.

RAMANUJIYAS—(Rámánujiyas), the followers of Rámánuja, a numerous sect who are distinguished by some peculiar rites and observances which will be found described under the article Vaishnavas.

RAMA-SETU—'Rāma's bridge', constructed for him by his general, Nala, son of Viśvakarmā, at the time of his invasion of Ceylon. This name is given to the line of rocks in the channel between the continent and Ceylon, called in maps "Adam's bridge".

RAMATAPANIYOPANISAD—An Upaniṣad of the *Atharvaveda*, in which Rāma is worshipped as the supreme god and the sage Yājñavalkya is his glorifier. It has been printed and translated by Weber in his *Indische Studien*, vol. IX.

RAMAYANA—One of the great Epic poems of the Hindus, the other being the Mahábhárata. It is perhaps impossible to fix the exact period at which either of thorn was composed; though it is evident from internal evidence that both are productions of a *post-vedic* age. The Rámáyaṇa was the more ancient of the two Indian Epics. Probably neither it nor the Mahábhárata, nor any of the productions of antecedent ages, were committed to writing till long after their original composition. In the fourth chapter of the first book of the Rámáyana, we meet with special reference to the ministrels and reciters, by whom the ancient Hindu poems; previous to the invention of writing in India, were preserved and transmitted from age to age.

The word Rámáyaṇa means the adventures of Ráma, who was one of the incarnations of Vishṇu, the Preserver, and is still a favourite deity in most parts of India, more especially in the districts of Oude and Bahár, where Krishṇa has not supplanted him. There were three Rámas in Hindu mythology, *viz.*, Parasu-Ráma, Ráma-Chandra, and Bala-Rama, all avatars (or incarnations) of Vishṇu. The last is the Indian Hercules, and as the elder brother of Krishṇa, appears frequently in the Mahábhárata. Parasu-Ráma, as the son of the sage Jamadagni, is the type of Brahmanism, arrayed in opposition to the Kshatriyas, or military caste. He is introduced once into the Rámáyaṇa, but only to exhibit his inferiority to the real hero of the work, *viz.*, Ráma-Chandra, who, as the son of Dasaratha, a prince of the solar dynasty, typifies the conquering Kshatriyas, advancing towards the south, and subjugating the barbarous aborigines, who are represented by Rávaṇa and his followers.

There are many poems bearing the name of Rámáyaṇa—all relating to the same hero—but by far the most complete and famous is the lengthy epic, the authorship of which is attributed to *Vâlmiki.*

It narrates the banishment of Ráma, under the surname of Chandra (the moon,) a prince belonging to the dynasty of the kings of Ayodhya; his wanderings through the southern peninsula; the seizure of his wife, Sítá, by the giant ruler of Ceylon (Rávaṇa); the miraculous conquest of this island by Ráma, aided by Sugríva, king of the monkeys (or foresters—the word *bandar* meaning both,) or *Rákshasas* as they are also called, and by Vibhíshaṇa, the brother of Rávaṇa; the slaying of the ravishing demon by Ráma, and recovering of Sítá; and the restoration, of Ráma-Chandra to the empire of his ancestors at Ayodhya.

No mention is made of Ráma in the Vedas, but he may be regarded as the first real Kshatriya hero of the *post-vedic* age; and looking to the great simplicity of the style of the Rámáyaṇa, the absence of any reliable allusion to Buddhism as an established fact, and to the practices known to have prevailed in India as early as the fourth century before Christ, as well as from other considerations, "we cannot," says Monier Williams (*Essay on Indian Epic Poetry,*) "be far wrong is asserting that a great portion, if not the whole, of the Rámáyaṇa, as we have now it, must have been current in India as early as the fifth century before Christ."

Válmílki's work consists of 24,000 ṣlokas (or distichs,) divided into seven books, which are again sub-divided into chapters. It may be divided into three principal parts, or periods, corresponding to the three chief epochs in the life of Ráma. (I.) The account of his youthful days; his education and residence at the court of his father Dasarath, king of Ayodhya; his happy marriage to Sítá; and his inauguration as heir-apparent or Crown Prince. (II.) The circumstances that led to his banishment; the description of his exile and residence in the forests of Central India. (III.) His war with the giants or demons of the south for the recovery of his wife Sítá, who had been carried off by their chief Rávaṇa; his conquest and destruction of Rávaṇa, and his restoration to the throne of his father.

In the first two sections of the poem, there is little of extravagant fiction; but in the third, the poet mars the beauty of the descriptions by the wildest exaggeration and hyperbole

The poem seems to be founded on historical fact; and the traditions of the south of India uniformly ascribe its civilization, the subjugation, or dispersion of its forest tribes of barbarians, and the settlement of civilized Hindus, to the conquest of Lanká (Ceylon) by Ráma.

[A good analysis of the Rámáyaṇa will be found in Monier Williams' Indian Epic Poetry, 1863. An abridged English translation has been published by Mr. Talboys Wheeler, forming the second volume of his History of India, 1869. The first English translation was made by Carey and Marshman, at Serampore, when they printed the first volume containing the first book of the poem, in 1806.

An excellent translation, into English verse, of the First and Second Books has just been published (1870-71) by Mr. R. T. Griffiths, M. A., the then Principal of the Benares College, already favorably known by his *Idylls from the Sanskrit.*]

Professor Weber, of Berlin, in a recent dissertation on the sources of the Rámáyana, gives it as his opinion that the rape of Helen and the siege of Troy have served as a model for the corresponding incidents in the poem of Válmíki. "I do not imagine that he had himself studied Homer, or even that he must have been aware of the existence of the Homeric poems. Nor am I inclined to go so far as to attach importance to the apparent analogies between Agamemnon and Sugríva, Patroklos and Lakshmana, Nestor and Jámbavat, Odysseus and Hanumán, Hektor and Indrajit,—analogies which have led Hippolyte Fauche, who has translated the Rámáyana into French, to adopt the converse theory that Homer has borrowed the materials of his work from that of Valmíki ! I pass over the coincidences, noticed by Monier Williams,*—the consoling of the forsaken Síta by means of a dream; the surveying and enumerating of the hostile troops from the battlements of Lanka; and the appearing of Síta before the army. Nor do I wish to disease the very wide and far-reaching question, 'In how far an acquaintance with the Greek epic may have exercised an influence on the development of the Indian one ?' I content myself rather with the simple assumption that in consequence of the mutual relations, which Alexander's expedition into India brought about, between that country and the Greeks, some kind of knowledge of the substance of Homeric story found its way to India."—*Indian Antiquary*, June 1872. (* *Indian Epic Poetry.*)

RAMBHA—(1) An apsaras or nymph produced at the churning of the ocean, and popularly the type of female beauty. She was sent by Indra to seduce Viśvamitra, but was cursed by that sage to become a stone, and remain so for a thousand years. According to the *Rāmāyaṇa*, she was seen by Rāvaṇa when he went to Kailāsa, and he was so smitten by her charms that he ravished her, although she told him that she was the wife of Nalakūbera, son of his brother Kubera. **(2)** One of the five sons of Áyus.

RAMESVARA—'Lord of Rāma.' Name of one of the twelve great *lingas* set up, as is said, by Rāma at Rāmeśvaram or Rāmisvaram or Rāmisseram, which is a celebrated place of pilgrimage, and contains a most magnificent temple.

RAMOPAKHYANA—'The story of Rāma', as told in the Vana Parva of the *Mahābhārata*. It relates many, but far from all, of the incidents celebrated in the *Rāmāyaṇa*; it makes no mention of Vālmīki, the author of that poem, and it represents Rāma as a human being and a great hero, but not a deity.

RAMYAKA—A district to the north of Meru, extending from the Níla or blue mountains to the Sweta or white mountains.

RAMYA—One of the nine sons of king Agnídhra, and who became king of the countries situated between mount Meru and the Níla mountain.

RANANJAYA—A prince, the son of Kritanjaya, of the family of Ikshváku.

RANTIDEVA—A pious and benevolent king of the Lunar race, sixth in descent from Bharata. He is mentioned in the *Mahābhārata* and Purāṇas as being enormously rich, very religious, and charitable and profuse in his sacrifices. The former authority says that he had 200,000 cooks, that he had 2000 head of cattle and as many other animals slaughtered daily for use in his kitchen, and that he fed innumerable beggars daily with beef.

RANTINARA—A prince, the son of Riteya, descendant of Puru.

RASA DANCE—A fabled dance of Krishṇa with the Gopis, in which it is said the circle of the dance could not be constructed, as each of the Gopis attempted to keep in one place, close to the side of Krishṇa; he therefore took each by the hand, and when their eyelids were shut, by the effects of such touch, the circle was formed. Professor Wilson says, Krishṇa, in order to form the circle takes each damsel by the hand and leads her to her place; there he quits her; but the effect of the contact is such that it deprives her of the power of perception, and she contentedly takes the hand of her female neighbour, thinking it to be Krishṇa's. The Bhágavata is bolder and asserts that Krishṇa multiplied himself, and actually stood between each pair of damsels.

RASA YATRA—An animal festival celebrated in various parts of India, in the month of Kártika, upon the sun's entrance into Libra, by nocturnal dances, and representations of the sports of Krishṇa. Some of the earliest labourers in the field of Hindu mythology have thought this circular dance to typify the dance of the planets round the sun, (Maurice) but there seems to be no foundation for such a notion. See Wilson'a Notes to Vishṇu Purána, 534.

RASALOMA—The wife of one of the eleven Rudras, Mahinasa.

RASATALA—One of the divisions of Pátáḷa, as enumerated in the Bhágavata, Pádma Purána and Váyu.

RASAYANA—One of the eight branches of medical science, that which treats of alchemical therapeutics.

RASHTRAPALA—One of the sons of Ugrasena.

RASHTRAPALI—A daughter of Ugrasena.

RASOLLASA—The spontaneous or prompt evolution of the juices of the body, independently of nutriment from without; this is termed one of the eight perfections or Siddhis.

RATHACHITRA—A river mentioned in the Puránas but not yet identified.

RATHAKRIT—One of the Yakshas, or guardians of the sun for the month of Sukra.

RATHANTARA—(1) A teacher of the Rig Veda and pupil of Satyasri; **(2)** The portion of the Sáma Veda which proceeded from the eastern mouth of Brahmá.

RATHINARA—One of the Angirasas, or warrior priests, a Kshatriya by both parents, who became a brahman by profession.

RATI—'Love, desire.' The Venus of the Hindus, the goddess of sexual pleasures, wife of Kāma, the god of love, and daughter of Dakṣa. She is also called Revā, Kāmi, Prīti, Kāmapatni, 'wife of Kāma'; Kāmakalā, 'part of Kāma'; Kāmapriyā, 'beloved of Kāma';

Rāgalaṭā, 'vine of love'; Māyāvatī, 'deceiver'; Kelikilā, 'wanton'; Śubhāṅgī 'fair-limbed'.

RATNAGARBHA—A commentator on the Vishṇu Purána. His book is entitled Vaishnavakúta Chandriká, 'the moon-light of devotion to Vishṇu;' but his date has not been ascertained.

RATNAGIR—The modern name of the mountain called in the Mahábhárata Yaráha, (*q.v.*)

RATNAVALI, or THE NECKLACE—The title of a Sanskrit Drama that has been translated by Professor Wilson; who states, that considered under a purely literary point of view it marks a change in the principles of dramatic composition, as well as in those of social organization. Besides the want of passion, and the substitution of intrigue, there is in it no poetic spirit, no gleam of inspiration. The only poetry of the play is in fact mechanical. The structure of the original language is eminently elegant, particularly in the Prákrit. This dialect appears to equal advantage in no other drama; the Sanskrit style is also very smooth and beautiful, without being painfully elaborate. The play is indeed especially interesting in this account, that whilst both in thought and expression there is little fire or genius, a generally correct and delicate taste regulates the composition, and avoids those absurdities which writers of more pretension than judgment, the writers of more recent periods, invariably commit. The play must have been written between A.D. 1113 and 1125.

RATRI—Night. One of the forms of Brahmá. Prof. Wilson says "the notions of night, day, twilight, and moon-light, being derived from Brahmá, seem to have originated with the Vedas. All the authorities place night before day, and the Asuras or Titans before the gods, in the order of appearance as did Hesiod, and other ancient theogonists."

RATULA—A prince, the son of Suddhodana of the family of Ikshváku.

RAUCHYA—The Manu of the thirteenth Manwantara, and son of the Prajápati Ruchi by the nymph Mániní. According to the Matsya and Pádma, the ninth Manu was named Rauchya. (*see* MANU)

RAUDRA—A descendant of Rudra. A name of Kārttikeya, the god of war.

RAURAVA—One of the Narakas, that in which falsehood and perjury are punished.

RAVANA—The demon king of Laṅkā or Ceylon from which he expelled his half-brother Kubera. He was son of Viśravas by his wife Nikaṣā, daughter of the *rākṣasa* Sumāli. He was half-brother of Kubera, and grandson of the *ṛṣi* Pulastya; and as Kubera is king of the *yakṣas*, Rāvaṇa is king of the demons called *rākṣasas*. Pulastya is said to be the progenitor, not only of Ravaṇa, but also of the whole race of *rākṣasas*. By penance and devotion to Brahmā, Rāvaṇa was made invulnerable against gods and demons, but he was doomed to die through a woman. He was also enabled to assume any form he pleased. All *rākṣasas* are malignant and terrible, but Rāvaṇa as their chief attained the utmost degree of wickedness, and was a very incarnation of evil. He is described in the *Rāmāyaṇa* as having "ten heads (hence his names Daśakaṇṭha, and Paṇktigrīva), twenty arms, and copper-coloured eyes, and bright teeth like the young moon. His form was as a thick cloud or a mountain, or the god of death with open mouth. He had all the marks of royalty, but his body bore the impress of wounds inflicted by all the divine arms in his warfare with the gods. It was scarred by the thunderbolt of Indra, by the tusks of Indra's elephant Airāvata, and by the discus of Viṣṇu. His strength was so great that he could agitate the seas and split the tops of mountains. He was a breaker of all laws and a ravisher of other men's wives.... Tall as a mountain peak, he stopped with his arms the sun and moon in their course, and prevented their rising." The terror he inspires is such that where he is "the sun does not give out its heat, the winds do not blow, and the ocean becomes motionless". His evil deeds cried aloud for vengeance, and the cry reached heaven. Viṣṇu declared that, as Rāvaṇa had been too proud to seek protection against men and beasts, he should fall under their attacks, so Viṣṇu became incarnate as Rāmacandra for the express purpose of destroying Rāvaṇa, and vast numbers of monkeys and bears were created to aid in the enterprise. Rāma's wars against the *rākṣasas* inflicted such losses upon them as greatly to incense Rāvaṇa. Burning with rage, and excited by a passion for Sītā, the wife of Rāma, he left his island abode, repaired to Rāma's dwelling, assumed the appearance of a religious mendicant, and carried off Sītā to Laṅkā. Rāvaṇa urged Sītā to become his wife, and threatened to kill and eat her if she refused. Sītā persistently resisted, and was saved from death by the interposition of one of Rāvaṇa's wives. Rāma called to his assistance his allies Sugrīva and Hanumān, with their hosts of monkeys and bears. They built Rāma's bridge, by which they passed over into Lanka, and after many battles and wholesale slaughter Rāvaṇa was brought to bay at the city of Lanka. Rāma and Rāvaṇa fought together on equal terms for a long while, victory sometimes inclining to one sometimes to the other. Rāma with a sharp arrow cut off one of Rāvaṇa's heads, "but no sooner did the head fall on the ground than another sprang up in its room". Rāma then took an arrow which had been made by Brahmā, and discharged it at his foe. It entered his breast, came out of his back, went to the ocean, and then returned clean to the quiver of Rāma. "Rāvaṇa fell to the ground and expired, and the gods sounded celestial music in the heavens, and assembled in the sky and praised Rāma as Viṣṇu, in that he had slain that Rāvaṇa who would otherwise have caused their destruction." Rāvaṇa, though he was chief among *rākṣasas*, was a brāhmaṇa on his father's side; he was well versed in Sanskṛt, used the Vedic ritual, and his body was burnt with Brāhmaṇical rites. There is a story that Rāvaṇa made each of the gods perform some menial office in his household: thus Agni was his cook, Varuṇa supplied water, Kubera furnished money, Vāyu swept the house, &c. The *Viṣṇu Purāṇa* relates that Rāvaṇa, "elevated with wine, came on his tour of triumph to the city of Mahiṣmatī, but there he was taken prisoner by King Kārtavīrya, and confined like a beast in a comer of his capital". The same authority states that, in another birth, Rāvaṇa was Śiśupāla. Rāvaṇa's chief wife was Mandodarī, but he had many others, and they were burnt at his obsequies. His sons were Meghanāda, also called Indrajīt, Rāvaṇi, and Akṣa; Triśikha or Triśiras, Devāntaka, Narāntaka and Atikāya. (*see* NANDĪŚA)

RAVI—The sun. (*see* SŪRYA)

RAYANANIYA—The son of Lokákshi, a distinguished teacher of the Sáma-veda, and author of a Sanhita still extant.

RAYA—The name of one of the six sons of Purúravas, according to the list in the Bhágavata.

RBHAVAS—(*see* ṚIBHUS)

REBHA—A Rishi who had been hidden by malignant demons, bound, overwhelmed in the waters, (a well, according to the commentator,) for ten nights and nine days, and abandoned until he was nearly if not entirely dead; the Aṣvins drew him up as soma juice is raised with a ladle.—*O.S.T.*, v, 245.

RECHAKA—One of the three modifications of breathing in the practice of Pránáyáma: the first act is expiration, which is performed through the right nostril whilst the left is closed with the fingers of the right hand; this is called Rechaka.

RENUKA—Daughter of King Prasenajit or Renu, wife of Jamadagni, and mother of Paraśurāma. A sight of the connubial endearments of King Citraratha and his wife inspired her with impure thoughts, and her husband, perceiving that she had "fallen from perfection", desired her sons to kill her. Rumaṇvat, Suṣena, and Vasu, the three seniors, declined, and their father cursed them so that they became idiots. Paraśurāma, the fourth son, cut off her head, which act so gratified his father that Jamadagni promised him whatever blessings he desired. Among other things, Paraśurāma asked that his mother might be brought back to life in ignorance of her death and in perfect purity He also desired that his brothers might be restored to their senses. All this Jamadagani bestowed. She was also called Konkanā.

REVA—**(1)** Wife of Karṇa. **(2)** A name of Rati. **(3)** The Narmadā river.

REVALI—The daughter of Raivata, whose loveliness was such that no one could be found on earth worthy of her hand. Her father therefore repaired with her to Brahmá, to consult the god where a fit bridegroom was to be met with. When they arrived the quiristers Háhá, Húhú, and others, were singing before Brahmá; and Raivata, waiting till they had finished, imagined the ages that elapsed during their performance, to be but as a moment. At the end of their singing Raivata prostrated himself before Brahmá and explained his errand He was informed that many successions of ages had passed away while he had been listening to the heavenly songsters; that a portion of Vishṇu was then reigning on earth in the person of Balaráma at Dwáraka which had formerly been his own capital of Kusasthali. Raivata returned with his daughter to earth, where he found the race of men dwindled in stature, reduced in vigour, and enfeebled in intellect. He bestowed his unequalled daughter on Balaráma, who beholding the damsel of excessively lofty height, shortened her with the end of his ploughshare and she became his wife. The object of this legend, says Professor Wilson, is obviously to account for the anachronism of making Balaráma contemporary with Raivata; the one early in the Treta age, and the other at the close of the Dwápara. *V.P.*

REVANTA—In the Vishṇu Purána Revanta is said to be a son of the sun by his wife Sanjna; according to other accounts he was the son of Vivaswat and Rajni.

REVATA—The son of Ánartta, king of the country called after his father Anartta, who dwelt at the capital denominated *Kusa-sthali*—in Gujarat.

REVATI—Daughter of King Raivata and wife of Balarāma. She was so beautiful that her father, thinking no one upon earth worthy other, repaired to the god Brahmā to consult him about a husband. Brahmā delivered a long discourse on the glories of Viṣṇu, and directed Raivata to proceed to Dvārakā, where a portion of Viṣṇu was incarnate in the person of Balarāma. Ages had elapsed while Raivata was in heaven without his knowledge. When he returned to earth, "he found the race of men dwindled in stature, reduced in vigour, and enfeebled in intellect". He went to Balarāma and gave him Revatī, but that hero, "beholding the damsel of excessively lofty height, he shortened her with the end of his ploughshare, and she became his wife". She had two sons. Revatī is said to have taken part with her husband in his drinking bouts.

RIBHU—**(1)** 'Clever, skilful.' An epithet used for Indra, Agni, and the Ādityas. An ancient vedic deity, not now worshipped. "The practical portion of the Vedas consists of little else than detached prayers addressed with a few exceptions to divinities no longer worshipped, some of whom are even unknown. There is one for instance named Ribhu, of whose history, office, or even name, a person might ask in vain from one end of India to the other."—Wilson's *Works*, Vol. II, p. 48. **(2)** One of the mind-born sons of Brahmá; of the ninth or Kaumára creation; these, declining to create progeny, remained, as the name of the first implies, ever boys, Kumáras; that is, ever pure and innocent; whence their creation is called the Kaumára. Ribhu, being a son of the supreme Brahmá was of a holy character and acquainted with true wisdom. Nidágha, the son of Pulastya, was his disciple, and to him Ribhu communicated perfect knowledge. The residence of Pulastya was at Víranagara, a large handsome city on the banks of the Devíka river. Nidágha lived in a grove adjoining to the stream. When a thousand years had elapsed, Ribhu went to the city of Pulastya to visit his disciple; and after having fully explained to him the principles of unity departed. After the expiration of another thousand years Ribhu returned to his disciple and perfected him in divine knowledge.

RIBHUS—The sons of Sudhanvau, who on account of their artistic skill attained to immortality and divine honours. They are said to have made Indra's chariot and horses, restored their own parents to youth, &c. They are represented as *fabricating* hymns also. "These Ribhus are said to have made into four a single new sacrificial cup which Tvashṭri had formed. This exhibition of skill was performed by command of the gods, and in consequence of a promise that its accomplishment should be rewarded by exaltation to divine honours. Tvashṭri is represented as becoming ashamed, and hiding himself among the goddesses, when he saw this alteration of his work, and as resenting this change in his own manufacture as a slight to himself, and as having in consequence sought to slay his rivals. In another place, on the contrary, ho is said to have applauded their design, and admired the brilliant results of their skill."—Muir, *O.S.T., Vol. V, p.* 227.

"It was part of the Vedic creed that holy men, as in the case of *Ribhus*, might attain the condition of gods. These intimations, however, are incidental and vague, and all that we can positively conclude from them is that the Vedas recognised after the dissolution of the body, the life of the soul which animated it, and its continued existence in some heavenly sphere."—*Wilson*, v, 345.

RIBHUKṢAN—The first of the three Ṛibhus. In the plural, the three Ṛibhus.

RICHAS—The hymns of the Rig Veda, which were recited by the priests termed Hotri,

RICHIKA—A sage, of the descendants of Bhrigu, who demanded in marriage Śatyavatí, the daughter of king Gádhi. The king was very unwilling to give his daughter to a peevish old brahman, and demanded of him as the nuptial present, a thousand fleet horses, whose colour should be white, with one black ear. Richíka, having propitiated Varuṇa, the god of ocean, obtained from him, at the holy place called Áswatírtha, a thousand such steeds; and giving them to the king espoused his daughter. See Jamadagni, also Satyavati.

RIDDHI—'Prosperity.' The wife of Kubera, god of wealth. The name is also used for Pārvatī, the wife of Śiva.

RIG VEDA—The oldest and most important of the four Vedas. "As long as man continues to take an interest in the history of his race, and as long as we collect in libraries and museums the relics of former ages, the first place in that long row of books which contains the records of the Áryan branch of mankind, will belong for ever to the Rig Veda."* The hymns of the Rig Veda are amongst the oldest writings known to mankind, they are generally short, and are addressed to the great powers of nature, to Indra, the god of the firmament; to Fire, to the Sun, to the Moon; and as regards the latter, they are more especially devoted to the praise of the Sóma, or Moon plant, the juice of which plays a prominent part in many of the Vedic hymns. This juice was probably fermented, and formed into an exhilarating or intoxicating beverage, which was held in very high esteem.

"The total number of hymns in the Rig Veda is about 1,020. Their composition was doubtless the work of many men and of long periods of time. They bear evident marks of having been handed down by tradition, and although they were collected and arranged in their present forms about ten centuries before the Christian era, a long time must have passed before they were brought together by the sage, who from his performance of this work is called Vyása, the arranger.

"The language of the hymns, besides being archaic, is very involved and elliptical, abounding with epithets of which it is difficult to see the force, and with metaphors and comparisons which are by no means obvious. It 'teems with words which require a justification,' The hymns consequently demand, as Mr. Müller observes, a similar treatment to that bestowed upon the interpretation of ancient inscriptions; a careful collection of all grammatical forms, and a thorough comparison of all passages in which the same word occurs. The metre of the hymns is a very important guide to the correct reading of the text, but this presents so many apparent anomalies that its rules are variously explained. The hymns of the Rig Veda contain very little poetry of an agreeable or elevated order. The chief desires expressed are for riches, victory, and various temporal blessings. Moral sentiments rarely occur; the hymns addressed to Varuna contain the most.

Often passages among the Mantras of the Veda are in the form of a dialogue, and in such cases, the discoursers were alternately considered as Rishi and Devata.

Mr. Müller after working for more than twenty years at his translation of the Rig Veda, thus writes:—"My work is a mere contribution towards a better understanding of the Vedic hymns, and though I hope it may give in the main, a right rendering of the sense of the Vedic poets, I feel that in many points my translation is liable to correction, and will sooner or later be replaced by a more satisfactory one."

The following hymn, addressed to Agni the god of fire, and the Maruts, or the Storm-gods, is one of the most readable in the present volume:—

1. Thou art called forth to this fair sacrifice for a draught of milk; with the Maruts come hither O Agni!
2. No god indeed, no mortal, is beyond the might of thee, the mighty one; with the Maruts, &c., &c.
3. They who know of the great sky, the Visva Devas without guile; with the Maruts, &c.
4. The wild ones who sing their song, unconquerable by force; with the Maruts, *&c.*
5. They who are brilliant, of awful shape, powerful, and devourers of foes; with the Maruts, &c.
6. They who in heaven are enthroned as gods, in the light of the firmament; with the Maruts, &c.
7. They who toss the clouds across the surging sea; with the Maruts come hither, &c.
8. They who shoot with their darts across the sea with might; with the Maruts, &c.
9. I pour out to thee for the early draught the sweet juice of Soma; with the Maruts. &c."—*Sat. Review*, 1869.

RIGVIDHANA—Writings which treat of the mystic and magic efficacy of the recitation of hymns of the *Ṛgveda*, or even of single verses. Some of them are attributed to Śaunaka, but probably belong only to the time of the Purāṇas.—*Weber.*

RIJISWAN—A king mentioned in the Rig Veda, the friend of Indra, and who conquered the Dasyu Krishṇa on the banks of the Ansumatí.

RIJRASVA—A person mentioned in the Rig Veda, who had been made blind .by his cruel father, for slaughtering one hundred and one sheep, and giving them to a she-wolf to eat: the wolf having supplicated the Aṣvins on behalf of her blind benefactor, they restored sight to Rijráṣva.—*O.S.T., V*, 245.

RIJUDESA—A son of Vasudeva by his wife Devakí.

RIKSHA—(1) A descendant of Bhrigu, the Vyása of the twenty-fourth Dwápara, sometimes called also Valmíka. **(2)** A prince, the son of Ajamídha. **(3)** A prince, the son of Akrodhána, a descendant of Kuru. **(4)** A chain of mountains .in Gondwána.

RINA—A Vyása in the eighteenth Dwápara.

RIPU, RIPUNJAYA—Two of the sons of Slishti and Suchcháya, grandsons of Dhruva.

RISHABHA—(1) The son of king Nabhi by his queen

Meru. Rishabha had a hundred sons, the eldest of whom was Bharata; having ruled with equity and wisdom and celebrated many sacrificial rites, he resigned the sovereignty of the earth to the heroic Bharata, and, retiring to the hermitage of Pulastya, adopted the life of an anchorite, practicing religious penance, and performing all prescribed ceremonies, until, emaciated by his austerities so as to be but a collection of skin and fibers, be put a pebble in his mouth and naked went the way of all flesh. *V.P.* In a note Wilson adds 'the great road' 'the road of heroes.' The pebble was intended either to compel perpetual silence, or to prevent his eating. The Bhágavata adverts to the same circumstances, and gives more details of Rishabha's devotion, and connects him with the spread of Jain doctrines in the western parts of the peninsula. Rishabha is the name of the first Tirthankara, or Jain saint of the present era. **(2)** One of the seven Rishis of the second Manwantara; **(3)** A prince, the son of Kuṣágra; **(4)** A mountain on the north of Meru. **(5)** One of the generals in Ráma's army at the siege of Lanka; he was severely wounded by the magical Weapons of Indrajit, and left apparently dead on the battle field; but was restored to life by the healing plants brought by Hanuman from the golden hill called Rishabha. **(6)** The name of a golden hill on the very crest of Kailása; on which grew four medicinal herbs, by virtue of which the dead and wounded might be restored to life.

RISHIKA, RISHIKALYA—A river that rises in the Mahendra mountain and flows into the sea near Ganjam.

RISHIKAS—A people placed by the Rámáyana both in the north and in the south; Arjuna visits the former and exacts from them eight horses.

RISHIS (ṚṢIS)—Great Sages. Seven are enumerated; they are the same as the Prajápatis, *q.v.* One of the Rishis is an attendant on the sun in each mouth of the year, along with one of the Ádityas, Gandharvhas, Apsaras, Yakshas, etc. The Vishnu Purána says there are three kinds of Rishis, or inspired sages; royal Rishis, or princes who have adopted a life of devotion, as Viswámitra; divine Rishis, or sages who are demi-gods also, as Nárada; and Brahman Rishis, or sages who are the sons of Brahmá, or Brahmans, as Vasishtha and others. J.C.Thomson writes "in the Epic period Rishi is merely a name for historical personages, distinguished for their piety and wisdom, either by their acts or their writings. In the Puránic period the Rishis, *par excellence*, are seven primeval personages, born of Brahmá's mind, and presiding, under different forms, over each Manwantara." The word Rishi is derived from rish, an old vedic root meaning 'to see.'

The constellation of the Great Bear. For an account of its revolutions see the Vishṇu Purána, p. 485, and Wilson's learned notes on the subject.

An inspired poet or sage. The inspired persons to whom the hymns of the Vedas were revealed, and under whose names they stand. "The seven *ṛṣis*" (*saptarṣi*), or the Prajāpatis, "the mind born sons" of Brahmā, are often referred to. In the *Śatapatha Brāhmaṇa* their names are given as Gautama, Bharadvāja, Viśvāmitra, Jamadagni, Vasiṣtha, Kaśyapa, and Atri. The *Mahābhārata* gives them as Marīci, Atri, Aṅgiras, Pulaha, Kratu, Pulastya, and Vasiṣtha. The *Vāyu Purāṇa* adds Bhṛgu to this list, making eight, although it still calls them "seven". The *Viṣṇu Purāṇa*, more consistently, adds Bhṛgu and Dakṣa, and calls them the nine Brahmārṣis (*brahma-ṛṣi*). The names of Gautama, Kaṇva, Vālmīki, Vyāsa, Manu and Vibhāṇḍaka are also enumerated among the great *ṛṣis* by different authorities. Besides these great *ṛṣis* there are many *ṛṣis*. The seven *ṛṣis* are represented in the sky by the seven stars of the Great Bear, and as such are called Ṛkṣa and Citraśikhaṇḍinas, 'having bright crests'.

RSIBRAHMANA—An old Anukramaṇī, or Index of the *Sāmaveda*.

RISHYAMUKHA—A well-wooded mountain near the river Pampa. In this wood there dwelt a Prince of the Simian tribe, the august monkey king Sugríva, who had been banished from the city by his brother Bálin. As he was walking on the banks of the river early one morning he saw Rávaṇa the king of Rákshasas, sailing overhead; and struggling in his swarthy arms a lovely young woman, whose garments seemed woven out of sunbeams. This was Síta, who called out for help, and dropped a golden anklet and a scarf. These were carefully preserved by Sugríva, and shown to Ráma, when he and Lakshmana visited the wood. This mountainous region comprised of course the whole of the tract about the sources of the Pampa; but in the Rámáyana, Ráma passes them before he comes to the dwelling of the monkey chief.

RISHYA-SRINGA—A horned sage, celebrated in the first book of the Rámáyana.

He was the son of Vibháṇḍak, a Rishi descended from Kaṣyapa.

"Bred with the deer that round him roam,

The wood shall be that hermit's home.
To him no mortal shall be known
Except his holy sire alone."

He was thus brought up in the forest with his father and saw no other human being until he attained early manhood. At a season of great drought, Somapád, king of Anga, enquired what should be done to cause rain, when the brahmans said,

"By every art O monarch try
Hither to bring Vibháṇḍak's child,
Persuaded, captured or beguiled,
And when the boy is hither led
To him thy daughter duly wed."

After much deliberation as to the way in which the "wondrous boy" should be induced to leave his father's home, the poem proceeds,

"Then this shall be the plan agreed,
That damsels shall be sent,
Attired in holy hermit's weed
And skilled in blandishment,
That they the hermit may beguile
With every art and amorous wile,
Whose use they know so well,
And by their witcheries seduce
The unsuspecting young recluse
To leave his father's cell.

Then when the boy with willing feet
Shall wander from his calm retreat,
And in that city stand,
The troubles of the king shall end
And streams of blessed rain descend
Upon the thirsty land.

Thus shall the holy Rishyaṣring
To Somapád the mighty king
By wedlock be allied;
For Śántá, fairest of the fair,
In mind and grace beyond compare,
Shall be his royal bride."

All this took place accordingly.

"In ships with wondrous art prepared
Away the lovely women fared,
And soon beneath the shade they stood
Of the wild lonely dreary wood.
And there the leafy cot they found
Where dwelt the devotee
And looked with eager eyes around
The hermit's son to see.

* * *

Forth came the hermit's son to view
The wondrous sight to him so new,
And gazed in rapt surprise,
For from his natal hour till then
On woman or the sons of men
He ne'er had cast his eyes.

The scheme was successful. On the following day when his father went as usual to the forest, Rishyaṣring eagerly sought his charming visitants and accompanied them to their "lovely, home."

Vibháṇḍak returned to his cottage in the evening to learn the will of fate—

"A stately ship, at early morn,
The hermit's son away had borne.
Loud roared the clouds as on he sped,
The sky grew blacker overhead;
Till as he reached the royal town,
A mighty flood of rain came down,
By the great rain the monarch's mind
The coming of his guest divined.
To meet the honoured youth he went,
And low to earth his head he bent.
And sought, with all who dwelt within
The city walls, his grace to win.
He fed him with the daintiest fare,
He served him with unceasing care,
And gave to be the Brahman's bride
His own fair daughter, lotus-eyed.
Thus loved and honoured by the king,
The glorious Brahman Rishyaṣring
Passed in that royal town his life
With Śántá his beloved wife."

—Griffiths' *Rámáyana*

According to the *Rāmāyaṇa* and *Mahābhārata* he was born of a doe and had a small horn on his forehead.

RITADHAMAN—The Manu of the thirteenth Manwantara, according to the list in the Pádma and Matsya Puránas.

RITADHWAJA—**(1)** One of the eleven Rudras, according to the enumeration in the Bhágavata; **(2)** One of the designations of Pratarddana, meaning he whose emblem was truth, being a great observer of veracity.

RITA—**(1)** Truth. The son of Dharma, by one of the daughters of Daksha; **(2)** A king of Mithila, the son of Vijaya.

RITEYA—A prince, the eldest of the ten sons of Raudraṣwa, a descendant of Puru.

RITUDHAMAN—The Indra of the twelfth Manwantara.

RITUJIT—One of the kings of Mithila, the son of Anjana.

RITUPARNA—A king of Ayódhyá, a monarch celebrated for his skill in dice. He determined to be present at the second Svayamvara of Damayanti, but could only be so by the help of his charioteer Váhuka whose skill in horsemanship enabled him to drive from Ayódhya to Vidarbha in one day. On the road Naḷa, disguised as Váhuka, agreed to impart to Rituparṇa his knowledge of horsemanship in return for that monarch's skill in dice. They made the exchange, and, arriving at Ayódhya, Naḷa re-assumed his own form and was restored to his wife. Returning with her to Nishadha he sought Pushkara, renewed the game and won back his kingdom.

ṚTU-SAMHARA—'The round of the seasons.' A poem attributed to Kālidāsa. W. Jones published this poem, and was the first Sanskṛt work ever printed. There are other editions. It has been translated into Latin by Bohlen.

RODHA—One of the Narakas; that for the punishment of the crimes of causing abortion, killing a cow, plundering, &c.

ROHINI—**(1)** Daughter of Kaśyapa and Surabhi, and mother of horned cattle, including Kāmadhenu, the cow which grants desires. **(2)** Daughter of Dakṣa and fourth of the lunar asterisms, the favourite wife of the moon. **(3)** One of the wives of Vasudeva, the father of Kṛṣṇa, and mother of Balarāma. She was burned with her husband's corpse at Dvārakā. **(4)** Kṛṣṇa himself also had a wife so-called, and the name is common.

ROHITA—'Red.' A red horse; a horse of the sun or of fire. **(1)** A deity celebrated in the *Atharvaveda*, probably a form of fire or the sun. **(2)** Son of King Hariścandra. He is also called Rohitāśva. The fort of Rohtas is said to derive its name from him. (*see* HARIŚCANDRA)

ROMAHARSHANA—A disciple of Vyása, and the narrator of the Puránas. See SÚTA.

ROMANAS, ROPANAS—A people mentioned in the Puránas; it has been conjectured that the Romans may be meant.

ROMAPADA—**(1)** A son of Vidarbha and the princess rescued by Jyámagha, (*q.v.*); **(2)** A prince, the son of Chitraratha.

RUCHI—One of the Prajápatis or mind-born sons of Brahmá. He was married to Akúti, who bore him twins, Yajna and Dakshina, who afterwards became husband and wife, and had twelve sons, the deities called Yámas, in the Manwantara of Swáyambhuva.

RUCHIRADHI—A prince, the son of Sankrite, of the race of Bharata.

RUCHIRASWA—A prince, the son of Senajit, descendant of Hastin.

RUDHIRANDHA—One of the Narakas, designed for incendiaries, treacherous friends, soothsayers, &c.

RUDRA—'A howler or roarer; terrible.' In the Vedas Rudra has many attributes and many names. He is the howling terrible god, the god of storms, the father of the Rudras or Maruts, and is sometimes identified with the god of fire. On the one hand he is a destructive deity who brings diseases upon men and cattle, and upon the other he is a beneficent deity supposed to have a healing influence. These are the germs which afterwards developed the god Śiva. It is worthy of note that Rudra is first called Mahādeva in the White *Yajurveda.* As applied to the god Śiva, the name of Rudra generally designates him in his destructive character. In the *Bṛhadāraṇyaka Upaniṣad* the Rudras are "ten vital breaths (*prāṇa*) with the heart (*manas*) as eleventh". In the *Viṣṇu Purāṇa* the god Rudra is said to have sprung from the forehead of Brahmā, and at the command of that god to have separated his nature into male and female, then to have multiplied each of these into eleven persons, some of which were white and gentle, others black and furious. Elsewhere it is said that the eleven Rudras were sons of Kaśyapa and Surabhi, and in another chapter of the same Purāṇa it is represented that Brahmā desired to create a son, and that Rudra came into existence as a youth. He wept and asked for a name. Brahmā gave him the name of Rudra; but he wept seven times more, and so he obtained seven other names: Bhava, Śarva, Īsāna, Paśupati, Bhīma, Ugra, and Mahā-deva. Other of the Purāṇas agree in this nomenclature. These names are sometimes used for Rudra or Śiva himself, and at others for the seven manifestations of him, sometimes called his sons. The names of the eleven Rudras vary considerably in different books.

An agent in creation; who sprang from the forehead of Brahmá, radiant as the noontide sun, fierce, and of vast bulk, and of a figure which was half-male, half-female. At the command of Brahmá, Rudra became two-folds disjoining his male and female natures. His male being he again divided into eleven persons, of whom some were agreeable, some hideous, some fierce, some mild: and he multiplied his female nature manifold, of complexions black or white. This is considered by Professor Wilson to be the primitive form of the legend.

The Vishṇu Purána gives another account, as follows:

> In the beginning of the Kalpa, as Brahmá purposed to create a son, who should be like himself, a youth of a purple complexion appeared, crying with a low cry, and running about. Brahmá, when he beheld him thus afflicted, said to him, "Why dost thou weep ?" "Give me a name," replied the boy. "Rudra be thy name," rejoined the great father of all creatures: "be composed; desist from tears." But, thus addressed, the boy still wept seven times, and Brahmá therefore gave to him seven other denominations; and to these eight persons regions and wives and posterity belong. The eight manifestations, then, are named Rudra, Bhava, Sarva, Iṣána, Paṣupati, Bhíma, Ugra, and Mahádeva, which were given to them by their great progenitor. He also assigned to them their respective stations, the sun, water, earth, air, fire, ether, the ministrant Brahman, and the moon; for these are their several forms.

The Váyu details the application of each name severally. These eight Rudras are therefore but one, under as many appellations, and in as many types. The Pádma, Márkaṇḍeya, Kúrma, Linga, and Váyu agree with the *V.P.*, in the nomenclature of the Rudras, and their types, their wives, and progeny.

In the Vedic period, Rudra was the god of the tempest. The Maruta are called the sons of Rudra. As their father he is very often mentioned; as a divinity with independent attributes he is of much rarer occurrence; hymns addressed to him alone are but few. He is, as might be expected, a terrible god: he carries a great bow from which he hurls a sharp missile at the earth; he is called the slayer of men; his wrath is deprecated, and he is besought not to harm his worshipper; if not in the Rik, at least in the Atharva and Bráhmanas, he is styled 'lord of the animals,' as the unhoused beasts of the field are especially at the mercy of the pitiless storm. At the same time, he is to propitiate him, addressed as master of a thousand remedies, best of physicians, protector from harm; this may have its ground, too, partly in the beneficial effects of the tempest in freshening the atmosphere of that sultry clime. Rudra's chief interest consists in the circumstance that he forms the point of connection between the Vedic religion and the later Śiva worship. Śiva is a god unknown to the Vedas; his name is a word of not infrequent occurrence in the hymns, but means simply propitious; not even in the Atharva is it the epithet of a particular divinity, or distinguished by its usage from any other adjective. As given to him, whose title it has since become, it .seems one of those euphemisms so frequent in the Indian religion, applied as a soothing and flattering address to the most terrible god in the whole pantheon. The precise relation between Śiva and Rudra is not yet satisfactorily traced out. The introduction of an entirely new divinity from the mountains of the north has been supposed, who was grafted in upon the ancient religion by being identified with Rudra; or again, a blending of some of Agni's attributes with those of Rudra to originate a new development: perhaps neither of these may be necessary: Śiva may be a local form of Rudra, arisen under the influence of peculiar climatic relations in the districts from which he made his way into Hindustan proper; introduced among, and readily accepted by, a people which, as the Atharva shows, was strongly tending towards a terrorism in its religion."—Whitney, as quoted in *O.S.T.*, IV, 337.

RUDRAKÁLI—A form of Uma, in which she accompanied Vírabhadra when he was sent by Siva to spoil the sacrifice of Daksha.

RUDRÁKSHA—A rosary, or string of beads, the fruit of the *eleocarpus*, resembling in form, size, and colour, the nutmeg, but with a rough surface. The meaning of the word is Rudra's (*i.e.* Śiva's) eye, and then also tear. It is said that Śiva once, in a war with the Asúras, having burned three cities, wept at the loss of lives involved, and a tears falling to the ground, sprung up as shrubs, producing berries, which were thence celled Rudráksha.

RUDRA-LOKA—The heaven above Brahmá-loka.

RUDRANI—The wife of the Rudra Dhritavrata.

RUDRA-SAVARNA—The twelfth Manu. (*see* MANU)

RUKMINI—Daughter of Bhīshmaka. king of Vidarbha. According to the *Harivaṁśa* she was sought in marriage by Kṛṣṇa, with whom she fell in love. But her brother Rukmin was a friend of Kaṁsa, whom Kṛṣṇa had killed. He, therefore, opposed him and thwarted the match. Rukmiṇī was then betrothed to Śiśupāla, king of Cedi, but on her wedding day, as she was going to the temple, "Kṛṣṇa saw her, took her by the hand, and carried her away in his chariot". They were pursued by her intended husband and by her brother Rukmin, but Kṛṣṇa defeated them both, and took her safe to Dvārakā, where he married her. She was his principal wife and bore him a son, Pradyumna (*q.v.*). By him also she had nine other sons and one daughter. "These other sons were Cārudeṣṇa, Sudeṣṇa, Cārudeha, Suṣena, Cārugupta, Bhadracāru, Cāruvinda, Sucāru, and the very mighty Cāru; also one daughter, Cārumatī". At Kṛṣṇa's death she and seven other of his wives immolated on his funeral pile.

RUKMIN—The son of Bhishmaka, king of Vidarbha. He had a beautiful sister named Rukmini, with whom Krishṇa fell in love and selected in marriage; but her brother, who hated Krishṇa, would not assent to the espousals. The father then affianced Rukminí to Siṣupála. In other to celebrate the nuptials, Jarásandha and other princes, the friends of Siṣupála, assembled in Kundina, the capital of Vidarbha; and Krishṇa, attended by Balaráma and many other Yádavas, also went to witness the wedding. When there Krishna contrived to carry off the princess, leaving Ráma and his kinsmen to sustain the weight of his enemies. The sovereigns who had assembled to be present at the marriage, indignant at the insult, exerted themselves to kill Krishṇa; and Rukmin, vowing that he would never enter Kundina until he had slain him in fight, pursued and overtook him. In the combat that ensued Krishṇa destroyed with his discus the whole host of Rukmin, and would have put him to death, but was withheld by the entreaties of Rukminí. Rukmin, thus spared, built the city Bhojakata, and in pursuance of his vow, ever after dwelt therein. He was ultimately killed by Balaráma in a quarrel that occurred at a game of dice.

RUMA—Wife of the monkey king Sugrīva.

RUMANWAT—The general-in-chief of king Vatsa in the play of Ratnávalí.

RUPAKA—The general term for all dramatic compositions, from *rúpa*, form; it being their chief object to embody characters and feelings, and to exhibit the natural indications of passion. A play is also deemed a Poem that is to be seen, or Poem that is to be seen and heard. Dramatic writings are arranged in two classes, the Rúpakas, properly so termed, and the Uparúpakas, the minor or inferior Rúpakas, "le théâtre du second ordre," although not precisely in the same sense. There are ten species of the former, and eighteen of the latter class.—WILSON.

RUPAVAHIKAS, RUPAVASIKAS—People mentioned in the Puránas as Southern tribes, probably in the vicinity of the Rupa river.

RUSHADRA—The son of Swáhi, and grandfather of Sasavinda.

S

SABALASVAS—Sons of Dakṣa, one thousand in number, brought forth after the loss of the Haryaśvas. Like their predecessors, they were dissuaded by Nārada from begetting offspring, and "scattered themselves through the regions" never to return.

SABHANARA—One of the sons of Anu.

SABHIKA—A person who presides at houses where assemblies are held for purposes of gambling, and who provides the dice and all other materials.

SACI—Wife of Indra. (*see* INDRAṆĪ)

SADACHARAS—Fixed observances; the institutions or observances of the pious; the perpetual obligations of a householder, consisting of daily purifications, ablutions, libations, and oblations; hospitality, obsequial rites, ceremonies to be observed at meals, at morning and evening worship, and on going to rest.

SADAKANTA, SADANIRA—Puránic rivers, the latter is said to flow from Páripátra.

SADASWA—A prince, the son of Samara.

SADHUS—Saints; just or pious men; those who are free from all defects.

SADHYA—A daughter of Daksha and one of the wives of Dharma.

SADHYAS—A *gaṇa* or class of inferior deities; the personified rites and prayers of the Vedas who dwell with the gods or in the intermediate region between heaven and earth. Their number is twelve according to one authority, and seventeen according to another, and the Purāṇas make them sons of Dharma and Sādhyā, daughter of Dakṣa.

SADNOVA—The youngest son of the Rája of Chitapur, who was thrown into a cauldron of boiling oil for delaying to join his father in an expedition against Arjuna. Sadnova prayed to God, and the oil became quite cold. Sadnova came out unhurt and went with the army to fight against Arjuna, but he and all his brethren were slain.

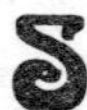

SADWATI—The daughter of Pulastya and wife of Agni.

SAGANKA—"Fawn-spotted," a name of the god Soma or Cháṇḍra. He is also called *Sasin*; from a fancied resemblance of the spots of the moon to a leveret.

SAGARA—The son of Báhu or Báhuka. His birth is thus narrated in the Vishṇu Purána. Báhu was vanquished by the tribes of Haihayas and Tálajanghas, and his country overrun by them; in consequence of which he fled into the forests with his wives. One of these was pregnant, and being an object of jealousy to a rival queen, the latter gave her poison to prevent her delivery. The poison had the effect of confining the child in the womb for seven years. Báhu, having waxed old, died in the neighbourhood of the residence of the Muni Aurva. His queen having constructed his pile, ascended it with the determination of accompanying him in death; but the sage Aurva, who knew all things, past, present, and to come, issued forth from his hermitage, and forbade her, saying, "Hold! hold! this is unrighteous; a valiant prince, the monarch of many realms, the offerer of many sacrifices, the destroyer of his foes, a universal emperor, is in thy womb; think not of committing so desperate an act!" Accordingly, in obedience to his injunctions, she relinquished her intention, The sage then conducted her to his abode, and after some time a very splendid boy was there born. Along with him the poison that had been given to his mother was expelled; and Aurva, after performing the ceremonies required at birth, gave him on that account the name of Sagara (from *Sa*, 'with,' and *Gara*, 'poison.') The same holy sage celebrated his investure with the cord of his class, instructed him fully in the Vedas, and taught him the use of arms, especially those of fire, called after Bhárgava.

When the boy had grown up, and was capable of reflection, he said to his mother one day, "Why are we dwelling in this hermitage ? where is my father ? and who is he ?" His mother, in reply, related to him all that had happened. Upon hearing which he was highly incensed, and vowed to recover his patrimonial kingdom, and exterminate the Haihayas and Tálajanghas, by whom it had been overrun. Accordingly when he became a man be put nearly the whole of the Haihayas to death, and would have also destroyed the Śakas, the Yavanas, Kámbojas, Páradas, and Pahnavas, but that they applied to Vaṣiṣhtha, the family priest of Sagara, for protection. Vasiṣhṭha regarding them as annihilated (or deprived of power), though living, thus spoke to Sagara: "Enough, enough, my son, pursue no farther these objects of your wrath, whom you may look upon as no more. In order to fulfil your vow I have separated them from affinity to the regenerate tribes, and from the duties of their castes." Sagara, in compliance with the injunctions of his spiritual guide, contented himself therefore with imposing upon the vanquished nations peculiar distinguishing marks. He made the Yavanas shave their heads entirely: the Śakas he compelled to shave (the upper) half of their heads; the Páradas wore their hair long; and the Pahnavas let their beards grow, in obedience to his commands. Them also, and other Kshatriya races, he deprived of the established usage of oblations to fire and the study of the Vedas; and thus separated from religious rites, and abandoned by the Brahmans, these different tribes became Mlechchhas. Sagara, after the recovery of his kingdom, reigned over the seven-zoned earth with undisputed dominion.

Sumati the daughter of Kaṣyapa, and Keṣiní the daughter of Rája Viderbha, were the two wives of Sagara. Being without progeny, the king solicited the aid of the sage Aurva with great earnestness, and the Muni pronounced this boon, that one wife should bear one son, the upholder of his race, and the other should give birth to sixty thousand sons; and he left it to them to make their election. Keṣiní chose to have the single son; Sumati the multitude: and it came to pass in a short time that the former bore Asamanjas, a prince through whom the dynasty continued; and the daughter of Vinatá (Sumati) had sixty thousand sons.

"The elder consort bare
A son called Asamanj, the heir.
Then Sumati, the younger, gave
Birth to a gourd,* O, hero brave,
Whose rind, when burst and cleft in two,
Gave sixty thousand babes to view."

The son of Asamanjas was Ansumat.

Asamanjas was from his boyhood of very irregular conduct. His father hoped that as he grew up to manhood he would reform; but finding that he continued guilty of the same immorality, Sagara abandoned him. The sixty thousand sons of Sagara followed the example of their brother Asamanjas. The path of virtue and piety being obstructed in the world by the sons of Sagara, the gods repaired to the Muni Kapila, who was a portion of Vishṇu, free from fault, and endowed with all true wisdom. Having approached him with respect, they said, "O Lord, what will become of the world, if these sons of Sagara are permitted to go on in the evil ways which they have learned from Asamanjas ! Do thou, then, assume a visible form, for the protection of the afflicted universe." "Be satisfied," replied the sage, "in a brief time the sons of Sagara shall be all destroyed."

At that period Sagara commenced the performance of the solemn sacrifice of a horse, which was guarded by his own sons: nevertheless some one stole the animal, and carried it off into a chasm in the earth. Sagara commanded his sons to search for the steed; and they, tracing him by the impressions of his hoofs, followed his course with perseverance, until coming to the chasm where he had entered, they proceeded to enlarge it, and dug downwards each for a league. Coming to Pátáḷa, they beheld the horse wandering freely about, and at no great distance from him they saw the Rishi Kapila sitting, with his head declined in meditation, and illuminating the surrounding space with radiance as bright as the splendours of the autumnal sun, shining in an unclouded sky. Exclaiming, "This is the villain who has maliciously interrupted our sacrifice, and stolen the horse! kill him 'kill him!" they ran towards him with uplifted weapons. The Muni slowly raised his eyes, and for an instant looked upon them, and they were reduced to ashes by the sacred flame that darted from his person.

"Then all the princes lofty souled,
Of wondrous vigour, strong and bold,
Saw Vásudeva standing there
In Kapil's form he loved to wear,
And near the everlasting God,
The victim charger cropped the sod.
They saw with joy and eager eyes
The fancied robber and the prize,
And on him rushed the furious band
Crying aloud, stand, villain ! stand !'
Avaunt ! avaunt! great Kapil cried,
His bosom flushed with passion's tide;
Then by his might that proud array
All scorched to heaps of ashes lay." '**

When Sagara learned that his sons, whom he had sent in pursuit of the sacrificial steed, had been destroyed by the might of the great Rishi Kapila, he dispatched Anṣumat, the son of Asamanjas, to effect the animal's recovery. The youth, proceeding by the deep path which the princes had dug, arrived where Kapila was, and bowing respectfully, prayed to him, and so propitiated him, that the saint said, 'Go, my son, deliver the horse to your grandfather; and demand a boon; thy grandson shall bring down the river of heaven on the earth." Anṣumat requested as a boon that his uncles, who had perished through the sage's displeasure, might, although unworthy of it, he raised to heaven through his favour. "I have told you," replied Kapila, "that your grandson shall bring down upon earth the Ganges of the gods; and when her waters shall wash the bones and ashes of thy grandfather's sons, they shall be raised to Swarga. Such is the efficacy of the stream that flows from the toe of Vishṇu, that it confers heaven upon all who bathe in it designedly, or who even become accidentally immersed in it: those even shall obtain Swarga, whose bones, skin, fibers, hair or any other part, shall be left after death upon the earth which is contiguous to the Ganges." Having acknowledged reverentially the kindness of the sage, Anṣumat returned, to his grandfather, and delivered to him the horse. Sagara, on recovering the steed, completed his sacrifice; and in affectionate memory of his sons, denominated Sagara the chasm which, they had dug.

Sagara is still the name of the ocean, and especially of the Bay of Bengal, at the mouth of the Ganges. *V.P.*

* Ikshváku, the name of a king of Ayodhyá, who is regarded as the founder of the solar race, means also a *gourd.* Hence perhaps the myth.—*Griffiths.*

** It appears to me that this my third story has reference to the volcanic phenomena of nature. Kapil may very possibly be that hidden fiery force which suddenly unprisons itself and bursts forth in volcanic effects. Kapil is, moreover, one of the names of Agni, the god of Fire.—*Gorresio.*

SAHADEVA—(1) The fifth and youngest son of Páṇḍu by his wife Madri, but mystically begotten by Dasra, the younger of the two Aswinis. He is considered as the *beau ideal* of masculine beauty. He was taught Astronomy and the use of the sword by Droṇa. When the Paṇḍavas applied for service to the Rája Viráta, Sahadeva was made master of the cattle, and caster of nativities and teller of fortunes; (*see* MAHĀBHĀRATA) He had a son named Suhotra by his wife Vijayā. **(2)** A prince, the son of Srinjaya; **(3)** The son of Harshavarddhana; **(4)** A son of Sudása; **(5)** A son of Jarásandha; **(6)** The son of Divákara, of the family of Ikshváku.

SAHAJANYA—A divine nymph; one of the ten in the class termed Daivika.

SAHANJI—A prince, the son of Kuntí.

SAHARAKSHA—The fire of the Asuras; the

Bhágavata explains the different fires to be so many appellations of fire employed in the invocations with which different oblations to fire are offered in the ritual of the Vedas.

SAHAS, SAHASYA—The names of two of the months, occurring in the Vedas and belonging to a system now obsolete.

SAHASRABALA—A prince, a descendant of Kusa, according to the lists in the Matysa, Linga, &c.

SAHASRAJIT—**(1)** The eldest son of Yadu; **(2)** One of the sons of Bhajamána.

SAHASRAKSA—'Thousand-eyed.' An epithet of Indra.

SAHASRANIKA—The son of Śatáníka, (*q.v.*) The fate of his father naturally interested Indra for the young prince, and he not infrequently conveyed him to visit the regions of the skies. On one of these occasions he incurred the displeasure of Tilottamá, a nymph of paradise, and she denounced an imprecation on his future fortune, sentencing him to the pangs of separation from his beloved. Sahasráníka was married to Mṛigávatí, daughter of Kṛipavarmá, king of Oude. During her pregnancy she was seized with a strange fancy, inspired, in fact, by the influence of the imprecation, to bathe in human blood. When the king found compliance with her longing was unavoidable, he deceived her by substituting an infusion of the Lac-dye, in which the queen contentedly performed her ablutions. The crimson tint left upon her person by the effect of the immersion, deceived one of the gigantic brood of Garuḍa, as he pursued his flight through the air. Thinking her to be a lump of flesh, he pounced upon the queen, and carried her off to the mountain Udya, where, finding her alive, he abandoned her to her destiny, having thus been the unconscious instrument of separating Śahaṣráníka from his bride.

In this helpless condition the queen, overcome with terror and affliction, sought alone for death to terminate her distress. With this view she threw herself in the way of the wild elephants and the vast serpents, with which the thickets were peopled; but in vain—an unseen spirit of the air protected her, and guided her unharmed amidst the ferocious monsters of the forest, until she was encountered by a holy hermit, Jamadagni, who resided on the mountain, and who led her to his cell, where he Consoled her with assurances, that she would in time be re-united to her lord. Mṛigávatí was here delivered of a son, whom, in allusion to the place of his nativity, she named Udáyana, and who was trained in letters and arms, and in the duties of his regal birth, by his venerable guardian.—*Wilson*, iii, 192.

SAHISHNA—**(1)** One of the sons of the patriarch Pulaka; **(2)** A son of Vanakapívat, and father of Kámadeva.

SAHITYA-DARPAṆA—'The mirror of composition.' A celebrated work on poetry and rhetoric by Viśvanātha Kavi Rāja, written about the fifteenth century. It has been translated into English for the *Bibliotheca Indica*. There are several editions of the text.

SAHYA—One of the seven principal chains of mountains in Bharata: the northern portions of the Western Ghauts, the mountains of the Konkan.

SAIBYA—Wife of Hariścandra (*q.v.*); wife of Jyāmagha (*q.v.*); wife of Śatadhanu (*q.v.*).

SAINDHAVA, OR SAINDHAVAYANA—A teacher of the Atharva Veda, and founder of a school of brahmans.

SAINDHAVAS—**(1)** The people of Sindhu or Sindh, of the country between the Indus and the Jhelam; **(2)** A school of brahmans.

SAINEYAS—The descendants of Siní, a branch of the Yádavas.

SAINHIKEYAS—A class of Dánavas, the sons of Viprachitti and Sinbiká.

SAISIKATAS—Inhabitants of mountainous regions and sandy deserts.

SAISIRI—A teacher of the White Yajush. *V.P.*, 281.

SAISIRIYA—A teacher of the Rig Veda, a disciple of Vedamitra, called also Sákalya.

SAISUNAGA—A king of Magadha, and founder of the dynasty of that name, consisting of ten kings. He relinquished Benares to his son and established himself at Girivraja in Beliar, where he is said to have reigned forty years.

SAIVA PURANA—Same as *Śiva Purāṇa.*

SAIVA PURANA—The fourth Purána in the enumeration given in the Vishṇu Purána. In some lists it is omitted, and when that is the case it is replaced by the Váyu, or Vayuvíya. When the Saiva is specified, as in the Bhágavata, then the Váyu is omitted; intimating the possible identity of these two works. This Purána contains the genealogies of the patriarchs, a description of the universe, and the incidents of the first six Manwantaras; intermixed with legends and praises of Śiva. A long account of the Pitris or progenitors is also peculiar to this Purána; as are stories of some of the most celebrated Rishis, who were engaged in the distribution of the Vedas. See VÁYU PURÁNA.

SAIVYA—(1) The wife of Hariṣchandra, (*q.v.*) whose heroic fortitude was shown in her patient endurance of the long series of severe trials to which she and her husband were subjected by Viṣvámitra.

"According to the Markaṇḍeya Purána, Hariṣchandra gave up his whole country, and sold his wife and son, and finally himself, in satisfaction of Viṣvámitra's demands for money. The sufferings of Hariṣchandra, his wife, and son, are very pathetically depicted, and the effect of the various incidents is heightened with great artistic skill. The story, in fact, appears to me one of the most touching to be found in Indian literature. Hariṣchandra, the Purána tells us, was a royal Rishi who lived in the Tretá age, and was renowned for his virtues, and the universal prosperity, moral and physical, which prevailed during his reign. On one occasion, when hunting, the king heard a sound of female lamentation which proceeded, it appears, from the sciences who were becoming mastered by the austerely fervid sage Viṣvámitra, in a way they bad never been before by any one else; and were consequently crying out in alarm at his superiority. In fulfillment of his duly as a Kshattriya to defend the weak, and inspired by the god Ganeṣa, who had entered into him, Hariṣchandra exclaimed "'What sinner is this who is binding fire in the hem of his garment, while I, his lord, am present, resplendent with force and fiery vigour ?' He shall to-day eater on his long sleep, pierced in all his limbs by arrows, which, by their discharge from my bow, illuminate all the quarters of the firmament." Viṣvámitra was provoked by this address. In consequence of his wrath the sciences instantly perished, and Hariṣchandra, trembling like the leaf of an aṣvattha tree, submissively represented that he had merely done his duty as a king, which he defined as consisting in the bestowal of gifts on eminent Brahmans and other persons of slender means, the protection of the timid, and war against enemies. Viṣvámitra hereupon demands a gift as a Brahman intent upon receiving one. The king offers him whatever he may ask: Gold, his own son, wife, body, life, kingdom, and good fortune. The saint first requires the present for the Rájasúya sacrifice. On this being promised, and still more offered, he asks for the empire of the whole earth, including everything but Hariṣchandra himself, his wife and son, and his virtue which follows its possessor whereve[r] he goes.* Hariṣchandra joyfully agrees. Viṣvámitra the[n] requires him to strip off all his ornaments, to cloth[e] himself in the bark of trees, and to quit the kingdo[m] with his wife Saivyá and his son. When he is depart[-]ing the sage stops him and demands payment of hi[s] yet unpaid sacrificial fee. The king replies that he ha[s] only the persons of his wife, his son, and himsel[f] left. Viṣvámitra insists that he mast nevertheless pay and that "unfulfilled promises of gifts to Brahman[s] bring destruction." The unfortunate prince, after be[-]ing threatened with a curse, engages to make the pay[-]ment in a month; and commences his journey with [a] wife unused to such fatigues, amid the universal lam[-]entations of his subjects. While he lingers, listening t[o] their affectionate remonstrances against his desertio[n] of his kingdom, Viṣvámitra comes up, and being in[-]censed at the delay and the king's apparent hesita[-]tion, strikes the queen with his staff, as she is dragge[d] on by her husband. All this Hariṣchandra endures wit[h] patience, uttering no complaint. Then the fiv[e] Viṣvedevas, merciful gods, exclaimed, "'To what world[s] shall this sinner Viṣvámitra go, who has thrust dow[n] this most excellent of sacrifices from the royal dig[-]nity ? Whose faith shall now sanctify the soma-juic[e] poured out with recitation of texts at the great sacri[-]fice, that we may drink it, and become exhilarated' [?] "Viṣvámitra heard what they said, and by a curs[e] doomed them to become men; he relented, however so far as to exempt them from having offspring, an[d] from other family ties and human weaknesses, an[d] promised that they should eventually be restored t[o] their pristine position as gods.

(* Compare Manu's very striking verses, which ma[y] be freely rendered as follows:—

"Our virtue is the only friend that follow us i[n]
death;
All other ties and friendships and with our
departing breath.
Nor father, mother, wife, nor son beside us then
can stay,
Nor kinsfolk:—virtue is the one companion of
our way.
Alone each creature sons the light, alone the
world he leaves;
Alone of actions, wrong or right, the recom-
pense receives.
Like log or clod, beneath the sod their lifeless
kinsman laid,
His friends turn round and quit the ground; but
virtue tends the dead.
Be then a hoard of virtue stored, to help in day

of doom;
By virtue led, we crow the dread, immeasurable
gloom."

They in consequence became partially incarnate as the five Páṇḍus, the sons of Draupadí. Resuming the story of Hariṣchandra, the writer tells us that he then proceeded with his wife and little son to Benares, imagining that this divine city, as the special property of Śiva, could not be possessed by any mortal. Here be found the relentless Viṣvámitra waiting for him, and ready to press his demand for the payment of his sacrificial gift, even before the expiration of the full period of grace. In this extremity Saivyá the queen suggests with a sobbing voice that her husband should sell her. On hearing this proposal Hariṣchandra swoons, then recovers, utters lamentations, and swoons again, and his wife, seeing his sad condition, swoons also. While they are in a state of unconsciousness, their famished child exclaims in distress, "O father, father, give me bread; O mother, mother, give me food: hunger overpowers me; and my tongue is parched." At this moment Viṣvámitra returns, and after recalling Hariṣchandra to consciousness by sprinkling water over him, again urges payment of the present. The king again swoons, and is again restored. The sage threatens to curse him if his engagement is not fulfilled by sunset. Being now pressed by his wife, the king agrees to sell her, adding, however, "If my voice can utter such a wicked word, I do what the most inhuman wretches cannot perpetrate." He then goes into the city, and in self-accusing language offers his queen for sale as a slave. A rich old Brahman offers to buy her at a price corresponding to her value, to do his household work. Hariṣchandra's heart was torn, and he could make no reply. The Brahman paid down the money, and was dragging away the queen by the hair of her head, when her little son Rohitáṣva, seeing his mother about to be taken away from him, began to cry, and laid hold of her skirts. The mother then exclaims: "'Let me go, let me go, venerable sir, till I look upon my son. I shall hardly ever behold him again. Come, my darling, see thy mother now become a slave. Touch me. not, young prince; I may no longer be handled by thee.' Seeing his mother dragged away, the child ran after her, his eyes dimmed with tears, and crying 'mother.' The Brahman purchaser kicked him when he came up; but he would not let his mother go, and continued crying "mother, mother.' The queen then said to the Brahman, 'Be so kind, my master, as to buy also this child, as without him I shall prove to thee but a useless purchase. Be thus merciful to me in my wretchedness; unite me with my son, like a cow to her calf.' The Brahman agrees: 'Take this money and give me the boy.'" When his wife and son were being carried away, Hariṣchandra broke out into lamentations: "'She, my spouse, whom neither air, nor sun, nor moon, nor stranger had beheld, is now gone into slavery. This my son, a scion of the solar race, with his delicate hands and fingers, has been sold. Woe to me, wicked wretch that I am.'"—*O.S.T.*, Vol. I, pp. 379-383. **(2)** Saivyá, was the name of the wife of king Jyámagha. Her history will be found in the account of her husband. [JYÁMAGHA.]

SAIVYA—A celebrated legendary king of ancient India, of whom an affecting story is related of a hawk and a dove.

"Saivya, a king whom earth obeyed,
Once to a hawk a promise made,
Gave to the bird his flesh and bone
And by his truth made heaven his own."

"Learn from that tale, the Hawk and Dove,
How strong for truth was Saivya's love
Pledged by his word the monarch gave
His flesh the suppliant bird to save."

"The following is a free version of this very ancient story, which occurs more than once in the Mahábhárata.

THE SUPPLIANT DOVE.

Chased by a hawk there came a dove
With worn and weary wing,
And took her stand upon the hand
Of Káśí's mighty king.

The monarch smoothed her ruffled plumes
And laid her on his breast,
And cried, 'No fear shall vex thee here,
Best, pretty egg-born, rest !

Fair Káśí's realm is rich and wide,
With golden harvests gay,
But all that's mine will I resign
Ere I my guest betray.'

But panting for his half-won spoil
The hawk was close behind;
And with wild cry and eager eye
Came swooping down the wind:

'This bird,' he cried, my destined prize,
'Tis not for thee to shield:
'Tis mine by right and toilsome flight
O'er hill and dale and field.

Hunger and thirst oppress me sore,
And I am faint with toil:
Thou shouldst not stay a bird of prey

Who claims his rightful spoil.

'They say thou art a glorious king,
And justice is thy care:
Then justly reign in thy domain,
Nor rob the birds of air.'

Then cried the king: 'A cow or deer
For thee shall straightway bleed,
Or let a ram or tender lamb
Be slain, for thee to feed.

Mine oath forbids me to betray
My little twice-born guest:
See how she clings with trembling wings
To her protector's breast.'

'No flesh of lambs,' the hawk replied,
'No blood of deer for me;
The falcon loves to feed on doves,
And such is Heaven's decree.

But if affection for the dove
Thy pitying heart has stirred,
Let thine own flesh my maw refresh,
Weighed down against the bird.'

He carved the flesh from off his side,
And threw it in the scale,
While women's cries smote on the skies
With loud lament and wail.

He hacked the flesh from side and arm,
From chest and back and thigh,
But still above the little dove
The monarch's scale stood high.

He heaped the scale with piles of flesh,
With sinews, blood, and skin,
And when alone was left him bone
He threw himself therein.

Then thundered voices through the air;
The sky grew black as night;
And fever took the earth that shook
To see that wondrous sight.

The blessed Gods, from every sphere,
By Indra led, came nigh;
While drum and flute and shell and lute
Made music in the sky.

They rained immortal chaplets down,
Which hands celestial twine,
And softly shed upon his head
Pure Amrit, drink divine.

Then God and Seraph, Bard and Nymph
Their heavenly voices raised,
And a glad throng with dance and song
The glorious monarch praised.

They set him on a golden car
That blazed with many a gem;
Then swiftly through the air they flew,
And bore him home with them.

Thus Káśí's lord, by noble deed,
Won heaven and deathless fame;
And when the weak protection seek
From thee, do thou the same.

—Griffiths. *Scences from the Rámáyan, &c.*

SAIVYA—The wife of king Satadhanu, and a woman of great virtue. The legend of her life is peculiar to the Vishṇu Purána and is thus narrated. She was devoted to her husband, benevolent, sincere, pure, adorned with every female excellence, with humility, and discretion. The Rája and his wife daily worshipped the god of gods, Janárdana, with pious meditations, oblations to fire, prayers, gifts, fasting, and every other mark of entire faith, and exclusive devotion. On one occasion when they had fasted on the full moon of Kártika, and had bathed in the Bhagirathí, they beheld, as they came up from the water, a heretic approach them, who was the friend of the Rája's military preceptor. The Rája, out of respect to the latter, entered into conversation with the heretic; but not so did the princess; reflecting that she was observing a fast, she turned from him, and cast her eyes up to the sun. On their arrival at home, the husband and wife, as usual, performed the worship of Vishṇu, agreeably to the ritual. After a time the Rája, triumphant over his enemies, died; and the princess ascended the funeral pile of her husband.

In consequence of the fault committed by Satadhanu, by speaking to an infidel when he was engaged in a solemn fast, he was born again as a dog. His wife was born as the daughter of the Rája of Káṣí, with the knowledge of the events of her preexistence, accomplished in every science, and endowed with every virtue. Her father was anxious to give her in marriage to some suitable husband, but she constantly opposed his design, and she prevented the king from accomplishing her nuptials. With the eye of divine intelligence she knew that her own husband had been regenerate as a dog, and going once to the city of Vaidiṣá, she saw the dog, and recognised her former lord in him. Knowing that the animal was her husband, she placed upon his neck the bridal garland, accompanying it with the marriage rites and prayers: but he, eating the delicate food presented to him, expressed his delight after the fashion of his species; at which she was much ashamed, and, bowing reverently to him, thus spoke to her degraded spouse: "Recall to memory, illustrious prince, the ill-timed politeness on account of which you have been born as a dog, and are now fawning upon me. In consequence of speaking to a heretic, after bathing in a sacred river, you have been condemned to this abject birth. Do you not remember it ?" Thus reminded, the Rája recollected his former condition, and was lost in thought, and felt deep humiliation. With a broken spirit he went .forth from the city, and falling dead in the desert, was born anew as a jackal. In the course of the following year the princess knew what had happened, and went to the mountain Koláhala to seek for her husband. Finding him there, the lovely daughter of the king of the earth said to her lord, thus disguised as a jackal, "Dost thou not remember, oh king, the circumstance of conversing with a heretic, which I called to thy recollection when thou wast a dog ?" The Rája, thus addressed, knew that what the princess had spoken was true, and thereupon desisted from food, and died. He then became a wolf; but his blameless wife knew it, and came to him in the lonely forest, and awakened his remembrance of his original state. "No wolf art thou," she said, "but the illustrious sovereign Satadhanu. Thou wast then a dog, then a jackal, and art now a wolf." Upon this, recollecting himself, the prince abandoned his life, and became a vulture; in which form his lovely queen still found him, and aroused him to a knowledge of the past. "Prince," she exclaimed, "recollect yourself: away with this uncouth form. to which the sin of conversing with a heretic has condemned you !" The Rája was next born as a crow; when the princess, who through her mystical powers was aware of it, said to him, "Thou art now thyself the eater of tributary grain, to whom, in a prior existence, all the kings of the earth paid tribute." Having abandoned his body, in consequence of the recollections excited by these words, the king next became a peacock, which the princess took to herself, and petted, and fed constantly with such food as is agreeable to birds of its class. The king of Káṣí instituted at that time the solemn sacrifice of a horse. In the ablutions with which it terminated tike princess caused her peacock to be bathed, bathing also herself; and she then reminded Satadhanu how he had been successively born as various animals. On recollecting this, he resigned his life. He was then born as the son of a person of distinction; and the princess now assenting to the wishes of her father to see her wedded, the king of Káṣí caused it to be made known that she would elect a bridegroom from those who should present themselves as suitors for her hand. When the election took place, the princess made choice of her former lord, who appeared amongst the candidates, and again invested him with the character of her husband. They lived happily together, and upon her father's decease, Satadhanu ruled over the country of Videha. He offered many sacrifices, and gave away many gifts, and begot SONS, and subdued his enemies in war; and having duly exercised the sovereign power, and cherished benignantly the earth, he died, as became his warrior birth, in battle. His queen again followed him in death, and, conformably to sacred precepts, once more mounted cheerfully his funeral pile. The king then, along with his princess, ascended beyond the sphere of Indra to the regions where all desires are for ever gratified, obtaining ever-during and unequalled happiness in heaven, the perfect felicity that is the rarely realised reward of conjugal fidelity."

SAKA—An era commencing AD 78, and called the era of Śālivāhana. Cunningham supposes its epoch to be connected with a defeat of the Śakas by Śālivāhana.

SAKA—One of the seven Dwípas, or great insular continents; it is surrounded with a sea of milk. In this Dwípa there are seven mountains and seven sacred rivers. There grows a large Saka (teak) tree, frequented by the Siddhas and Gandharvas, the wind from which, as produced by its fluttering leaves, diffuses delight. The inhabitants are described as sinless and happy.

SAKALA—The city of the Bāhīkas or Madras, in the Panjāb. It has been identified with the Sagala of Ptolemy on the Hyphasis (Byās), south-west of Lahore. Cunningham says it is the Saṁgala of Alexander.

SAKALYA—A teacher of the Rig Veda. An old grammarian and expositor of the Vedas who lived before the time of Yāska. He is said in the Vishṇu Purána to have divided the Sanhita, or collection of hymns, given to him, into five Sanhitas, which he distributed amongst as many disciples, who became founders of schools for teaching the truths of the Veda. He was also called Vedamitra and Devamitra.

SAKAPUNI, ŚĀKAPŪRṆI—(Called also Rathantara.) A teacher of the Rig Veda, who divided the original Sanhita into three portions, and added a glossary (Nirukta) constituting a fourth. See Vishṇu Purána, 277. He lived before the time of Yāska.

SAKAS—A northern people, usually associated with the Yavanas. Wilson says, "These people, the Sakai and Sacae of classical writers, the Indo-Scythians of Ptolemy, extended. about the commencement of our era, along the West of India, from the Hindu Koh to the mouths of the Indus." They were probably Turk or Tatar tribes, and were among those recorded as conquered by King Sagara, who compelled them to shave the upper half of their heads. They seem to have been encountered and kept back by King Vikramāditya of Ujjayinī, who was called Śakāri, 'foe of the Śakas'. Professor Wilson thinks they were not improbably connected with Saxon forefathers. Sixteen kings of this race are mentioned in the Vishṇu Purána which also mentions their conquest by Sagara, along with the Yavanas and Kambojas.

SAKATAYANA—An ancient grammarian anterior to Yāska and Pāṇini. Part of his work is said to have been lately discovered by Dr. Bühler.

SAKHA—'Branch, sect' (*i.e.*, of the Veda considered as a tree); The *śākhas* of the Vedas are the different recensions of the same text as taught and handed down traditionally by different schools and teachers, showing some slight variations, the effect of long-continued oral tradition, (*see* VEDA) A Sákhá generally comprised a Sanhita and a Bráhmaṇa.

SAKHA—One of the sons of Kumára, and grandson of Agni.

SAKINIS—Female demons attendant on Durgā.

SAKRA—**(1)** A name of Indra, (*q.v.*); **(2)** One of the twelve Ádityas.

SAKRANI—Wife of Indra. (*see* INDRĀṆĪ)

SAKRAPRASTHA—Same as Indraprastha.

SAKTAS—The worshippers of the ŚAKTI, the power or energy of the divine nature in action, are exceedingly numerous amongst all classes of Hindus. This active energy is, agreeably to the spirit of the mythological system, personified, and the form with which it is invested, considered as the especial object of veneration, depends upon the bias entertained by the individuals towards the adoration of VISHNU or ŚIVA. In the former case the personified Śakti is termed LAKSHMÍ, or MAHÁ LAKSHMÍ, and in the latter, PARVATÍ, Bhaváni, or DURGÁ. Even SARASYATÍ enjoys some portion of homage, much more than her lord, BRAHMÁ, whilst a vast variety of inferior beings of malevolent character and formidable aspect receive the worship of the multitude. The bride of Śiva, however, in one or other of her many and varied forms, is by far the most popular emblem in Bengal and along the Ganges.

The worship of the female principle, as distinct from the divinity, appears to have originated in the literal interpretation of the metaphorical language of the *Vedas*, in which the *will or purpose to create* the universe is represented as originating from the creator, and co-existent with him as his bride, and part of himself. Thus in the *Rig Veda* it is said, "That divine spirit breathed without afflation, single with (*Svadhá*) her who is sustained within him; other than him nothing existed. First desire was formed in his mind, and that became the original productive seed," and the *Sáma Veda*, speaking of the divine cause of creation, says, "He felt not delight, being alone. He wished another, and instantly became such. He caused his own self to fall in twain, and thus became husband and wife. He approached her, and thus were human beings produced." In these passages it is not unlikely that reference is made to the primitive tradition of the origin of mankind, but there is also a figurative representation of the first indication of *wish* or *will* in the Supreme Being. Being devoid of all qualities whatever, he was alone, until he permitted the wish to be multiplied, to be generated within himself. This wish being put into action, it is said, became united with its parent, and then created beings were produced. Thus this first manifestation of divine power is termed *Ichchhárúpa*, personified desire, and the creator is designated as *Svechchhámaya*, united with his own will, whilst in the *Vedánta* philosophy, and the popular sects, such as that of KABÍR, and others, in which all created things are held to be illusory, the Śakti, or active will of the deity, is always designated and spoken of as *Máyá* or *Mahá-máyá*, original deceit or illusion.

Another set of notions of some antiquity which contributed to form the character of the Śakti, whether general or particular, were derived from the *Sánkhya* philosophy. In this system nature, Prakṛiti, or *Múla Prakriti*, is defined to be of eternal existence and independent origin, distinct from the supreme spirit, productive though no production, and the plastic origin of all things, including even the gods. Hence *Prakriti* has come to be regarded as the mother of gods and men, whilst as one with matter, the source of error, it is again identified with *Máya*, or delusion, and as co-existent with the supreme as his Śakti, his personified energy, or his bride.

These mythological fancies have been principally disseminated by the *Puránas*, in all which *Prakriti*, or *Máya* bears a prominent part. The aggregate of the whole is given in the *Brahmá Vaivartta Purána*, one section of which, the Prakṛiti *Khanda*, is devoted to ne subject, and in which the legends relating to the rincipal modifications of the female principle are narrated.—*Wilson.*

AKTI, SAKTRI—A celebrated sage, the son of Vaṣiṣhtha. King Kalmáshapáda, one day met Śakti, in narrow path in a thicket and desired him to stand ut of his way. The sage refused; on which the rája eat him with his whip, and Śakti cursed him to become a Rakshas, or cannibal. The Rája in this transformation killed and ate its author, Sakti, and all the ther sons of Vaṣiṣhtha. Paráṣara was a posthumous on of Śakti. In the twenty-fifth Dwápara Sakti was he Vyása.

SAKTI—Energy. Potency. Mythologically the word neans consort of a deity. Parvati is the Śakti of Śiva. Sarasvati the Sakti of Brahmá. The Sakti is said to ave originated in God, the Supreme Being. From the first Śakti nine others are derived who are called Navasakti. They for their arrogance, were banished from heaven to earth; and when here obtained the office of protecting mankind from demons; hence temples are erected and festivals celebrated in their honour. They are in fact the Grámadevatas so often mentioned. The Śakti is worshipped in the pagodas under the form of the Śivalinga. There are many special forms of Sakti-worship, some of them accompanied with the grossest obscenities. The Abbé Dubois terms one of them an "occult sacrifice, secret and abominable." The Śakti worship is to a certain extent sanctioned by the Puránas, but it is especially prescribed in certain works called Tantras. The female forms of Rudra, white and black, are termed in the Vishṇu Purána, Śaktis. (*see* DEVĪ and TANTRA)

SAKUNI—**(1)** The son of the Rája of Gandhára, who conducted his sister Gandhárí to the city of Hastinápur to be married to Rája Dritaráshtra. He was very skilful in throwing dice, and in playing with dice that were loaded; so that he always won the game. At the celebrated gambling match when Yudhishthira lost all his property, himself, his brothers and his wife, it was Sakuni who threw the dice and won every game, and obliged the Pándavas to go into exile. Sakuni plotted with Duryodhana to seize Krishṇa, when the latter revealed his divinity and disconcerted the whole. He also was known by the patronymic Saubala, from Subala, his father. **(2)** A Daitya of great prowess, one of the sons of Hiraṇyáksha.

SAKUNI—A female fiend or Asura, the daughter of Bali, and sister of Pútaná.

SAKUNTALA—A nymph who was the daughter of Viśvāmitra by the nymph Menakā. She was born and left in a forest, where she was nourished by birds until found by the sage Kaṇva. She was brought up by this sage in his hermitage as his daughter, and is often called his daughter. The loves, marriage, separation, and re-union of Śakuntalā and King Duṣyanta are the subject of the celebrated drama *Śakuntalā.* She was mother of Bharata, the head of a long race of kings, who has given his name to India (Bhāratavarṣa), and the wars of whose descendants are sung in the *Mahābhārata.* The story of the loves of Duṣyanta and Śakuntalā is, that while she was living in the hermitage of Kaṇva she was seen in the forest by King Duṣyanta, who fell in love with her. He induced her to contact with him a Gandharva marriage, that is, a simple declaration of mutual acceptance. On leaving her to return to his city, he gave her a ring as a pledge of his love. When the nymph went back to the hermitage, she was so engrossed with thoughts of her husband that she heeded not the approach of the Sage Durvāsas, who had come to visit Kaṇva, so that choleric saint cursed her to be forgotten by her beloved. He afterwards relented, and promised that the curse should be removed as soon as Duṣyanta should see the ring. Śakuntalā, finding herself with child, set off to her husband; but on her way she bathed in a sacred pool, and there lost the ring. On reaching the palace, the king did not recognise her and would not own her, so she was taken by her mother to the forest, where she gave birth to Bharata. Then it happened that a fisherman caught a large fish and in it found a ring that he carried to Duṣyanta. The king recognised his own ring, and he soon afterwards accepted Śakuntalā and her son Bharata. Kālidāsa's drama of *Śakuntalā* was the first translation made from Sanskṛt into English. It excited great curiosity and gained much admiration when it appeared. There are several recensions of the text extant. The text has been often printed, and there are many translations into the languages of Europe. Professor Williams has published a beautifully illustrated translation.

SAKWALA—A mundane system; being the space to which the light of a sun extends, each sakwala, of which there is a great number, including a heaven, earth, hells, &c.

SAKYA, or SAKYAMUNI—The author or reviver of Buddhism, whose birth appears to have occurred in the seventh, and death in the sixth century before

Christ (B.C. 621-543). He was the son of Suddhodana, king of Kapila-vastu, or of Magadha (Behar.) See Buddha and Gautama.

SALAGRAMA—A holy place of pilgrimage, often mentioned, but the locality is unknown. The kings Agnídhra, Bharata, and others, are said to have retired thither to a life of penance. The term Sálagráma is usually applied to a stone, an ammonite, which is supposed to be a type of Vishṇu, and of which the worship is enjoined in some books. Ammonites are found chiefly in the Gandak river, and Professor Wilson thinks that the Sálagráma Tírtha was probably at the source of that stream, or at its confluence with the Ganges. He adds that its sanctity, and that of the stone, are probably of comparatively modern origin.

SALAKA—One of the eight branches of medical science; that which treats of external organic affections; this and Salya constitute surgery.

SALA—One of the sons of Báhlíka, of the family of Kuru.

SALIGOTRA—A teacher of the Sáma-veda; he was the son of Lángali and established six schools.

SALIN—One of the fifteen teachers of the white Yájush.

SALISUKA—A king of Magadha, of the Maurya dynasty, the son of Sangata.

SALIVAHANA—A celebrated king of the south of India, who was the enemy of Vikramāditya, and whose era, the Śaka, dates from AD 78. His capital was Pratiṣṭhāna on the Godāvarī, He was killed in battle at Kārūr.

A Hindu king who reigned in Magadha. He instituted an era that bears his name and is still commonly used in the Dekkan. It commenced when 3179 years of the Kali-Yuga, or the present mundane age, had expired; that is 78 years after the beginning of the Christian era. This era is called Sáliváhana Śáka, or simply Śáka. Thus 1871 of the Christian era would be tantamount to 1793 of the Śáka era. The Śáka year is the same as and begins with the common solar year.

SALIYA—A disciple of Vedamítra and teacher of the Rig Veda.

SALMALI—One of the Dwípas or seven great insular continents into which the Puránas divide the world. In this Dwípa there are seven mountain ranges abounding in precious gems and medicinal herbs. There are seven rivers whose waters wash away sins. A large Sálmalí (silk cotton) tree grows in this Dwípa and gives it its name. The Dwípa is surrounded by the Súra sea (sea of wine) of the same extent as itself.

SALWAS, OR SALYAS—Are placed by the Váyu and Matsya amongst the central nations, and seem to have occupied part of Rájasthan, a Sálwa Rája being described in the Vishṇu Purána as engaging in hostilities with the people of Dwáraka in Guzerat.

SALYA—**(1)** King of the Madra, and brother of Mādrī, second wife of Pāṇḍu. He was Rája of one of the mountain tribes occupying the southern slopes of the Himálayas. In the great war he left the side of the Pāṇḍavas and went over to the Kauravas. He acted as charioteer of Karṇa in the great battle. At the death of Karṇa he succeeded him as general, and commanded the army on the last day of the battle, when he was slain by Yudhiṣṭhira. **(2)** A Danava, the son of Viprachittí renowned for great strength.

SALYA—The first of the eight branches of medical science, that which treats of the extraction of extraneous bodies. Śalya and Saláka constitute surgery.

SAMADHI—The result of meditation; or that state of mind when there is an absence of all idea of individuality, when the meditator, the meditation, and the thing or object meditated upon, are all considered to be but one. According to the text of Patanjali: 'Restraint of the body, retention of the mind, and meditation, which thence is exclusively confined to one object is Dhyána; the idea of identification with the object of such meditation, so as if devoid of individual nature, is Samádhi. The word is sometimes used to express the power that enables its possessor to exercise an entire control over all his faculties, and keep them in perfect restraint.

SAMANERA—The novice of Buddhism, from sranana, an ascetic. He must be at least eight years of age, and must have received the consent of his parents to his abandonment of the world. The vows of the Sámanéra are not in any case irrevocable, and there are many circumstances that make his yoke less onerous than that of the stricter communities among the western celibates,

SAMANODAKAS—People who are related or connected only by presentations of water. *V.P.*, p. 316.

SAMAN—The name of the third Veda. See SAMA-VEDA.

SAMARA—The eldest of the hundred sons of Nípa, and king of Kampilya in the Doab. The Matsya makes

Samara the son of Káṣya.

SAMARAVIRA—A king in Bharatakshetra, whose daughter Yaṣodá was married to prince Varddhamána, who afterwards became the distinguished Jaina saint Mahávíra.

SAMAVAT, SAṀVATSARA—'Year.' The era of Vikrāmaditya, dating from 57 B.C.

SAMA-VEDA—Sáman is the name of third Veda, which in the Bhágavat Gíta is called the best of the three. It appears to be little more than a recast of the Rich, (see Rig Veda) consisting chiefly of the same hymns, broken up and arranged so as to be chanted daring the various expiatory ceremonies. Thus, while the Rich is said to be in regular metre to be recited aloud; and the Yájush consists chiefly of prose to be inaudibly muttered, the Sáman contains a certain rhythm, or mode, which was sung to music, and the name is also generally employed to designate a hymn.

The principal part of the Sáma-veda is that entitled Árchika. It comprises prayers arranged in six chapters; sub-divided into half chapters and into sections, ten in each chapter, and usually containing exactly ten verses each. The same collection of prayers, in the same order, but prepared for chanting, is distributed in seventeen chapters, under the title of *Grámageya gána.* Another portion of the Sáma-veda, arranged for chanting, bears the title of Aranya-gana, and is sub-divided in the same manner as the Árchika. There are four Bráhmanas of this Veda, received by four different schools. One is denominated *Shadvinsa*, probably from its containing twenty-six chapters. Another is called the *Adbhuta Bráhmana.* But the best known is that entitled the Tandya, and an exposition of it by Sáyanácharya. Its principal Upanishad is the Chhandogya, divided into eight chapters. Another is called the *Kena Upanishad.* These works are disquisitions on abtruse and mystical theology. The *Kena* has been translated by Rammohan Roy.—Small, *H.S.L.*

SAMAVIDHANA BRAHMANA—The third *Brāhmaṇa* of the *Sāmaveda*. It has been edited and translated by Burnell.

SAMAYACARIKA SUTRAS—Rules for the usage and practices of everyday life. (*see* SŪTRAS)

SAMBA—A son of Kṛṣṇa by Jāmbavatī, but the *Liṅga Purāṇa* names Rukmiṇī as his mother. At the *svayaṁvara* of Draupadī he carried off that princess, but he was pursued by Duryodhana and his friends and made prisoner. Balarāma undertook to obtain his release, and when that hero thrust his ploughshare under the ramparts of Hastināpura and threatened it with ruin, the Kauravas gave up their prisoner and Balarāma took him to Dvārakā. There he lived a dissolute life and scoffed at sacred things. The devotions of the three great sages Viśvāmitra, Durvāsas, and Nārada, excited the ridicule of Śāmba and his boon companions. They dressed Śāmba up to represent a woman with child and took him to the sages, inquiring whether he would give birth to a boy or a girl. The sage answered, "This is not a woman, but the son of Kṛṣṇa, and he shall bring forth an iron club which shall destroy the whole race of Yadu, ... and you and all your people shall perish by that club." Śāmba accordingly brought forth an iron club, which Ugrasena caused to be pounded and cast into the sea. These ashes produced rushes, and the rushes when gathered turned into clubs, or into reeds which were used as swords. One piece could not be crushed. This was subsequently found in the belly of a fish, and was used to tip an arrow, which arrow was used by the hunter Jaras, who with it unintentionally killed Kṛṣṇa. Under the curse of Durvāsas, Śāmba became a leper and retired to the Panjāb, where by fasting, penance, and prayer he obtained the favour of Sūrya (the sun), and was cured of his leprosy. He built a temple to the sun on the banks of the Candrabhāgā (Cināb), and introduced the worship of that luminary.

SAMBA-PURANA—(*see* PURĀṆA)

SAMBARA—In the Vedas, a demon, also called a *dasyu*, who fought against King Divodāsa, but was defeated and had his many castles destroyed by Indra. He appears to be a mythical personification of drought, of a kindred character to Vṛtra, or identical with him. In the Purāṇas a *daitya* who carried off Pradyumna and threw him into the sea, but was subsequently slain by him. (*see* PRADYUMNA) He was also employed by Hiraṇyakaśipu to destroy Prahlāda.

SAMBARA—(1) An ancient aboriginal king mentioned in the Rig Veda as a black-skinned enemy, who dwelt forty years on the mountains and possessed a hundred impregnable cities. These cities were coveted by one of Indra's white-complexioned friends, the 'hospitable Divodása.' Divodása was repulsed, and obliged to hide himself in the water; but Indra to give him pleasure, struck off the bead of Sambara. Sambara lived in Udavraja, "a country into which the waters flow." He believed himself invulnerable: but Indra discovered him when issuing from the mountain, and scattered the hundreds and thousands of his hosts. For the mighty Divodása, Indra, who dances with delight in battle, destroyed ninety cities. Indra hurled Sambara from the mountain; ninety-nine cities he destroyed; the hundredth he gave to Divo-dása.—Wilson's *Rig Veda.* **(2)** A great Asura or demon, 'terrible as death,' who knowing that Pradyumna, if he lived, would be his destroyer, carried off the infant and threw him into the ocean. Pradyumna was preserved by a fish and rescued. When he reached manhood and heard, what Sambara had done; he challenged the demon, and after a terrible conflict, killed him. *V.P.* **(3)** One of the demons who personify drought; they are described in the Rig Veda as shutting up the watery treasures in the clouds, until Indra attacks them and after severe contests overcomes them, and the clouds discharge their imprisoned waters on the thirsty earth.

"And now the clouds disperse, the blue
Of heaven once more comes forth to view.
The sun shines out, all nature smiles,
Redeemed from Vrittra's powers and wiles;
The gods, with gratulations meet,
And loud acclaim, the victor greet;
While Indra's mortal votaries sing
The praises of their friend and king."

—*O.S.T.*, Vol. v, p. 135.

SAMBHALA—A village celebrated as the birthplace of the sage Kalki, who was endowed with eight superhuman faculties.

SAMBHU—**(1)** A name of Śiva;

Thy journey next o'er Kanakhala bends,
Where Jahnu's daughter from the hills descends;
Whose sacred waters to Bhagírath given,
Conveyed the sons of Sagara to heaven.
She who with smiling waves disportive strayed
Through Śambha's locks, and with his tresses played;
Unheeding, as she flowed delighted down,
The gathering storm of Gauri's jealous frown.

(2) One of the eleven Rudras; **(3)** The wife of Dhruva. **(4)** The king of the Daityas, who slew the rishi Kusadhvaja, the father of Vedavati.

SAMBHUTA—A prince, the son of Trasadasyu.

SAMBHUTI—'Fitness.' A daughter of Daksha and wife of Marichi.

SAMBUKA—A śūdra, mentioned in the *Raghuvaṁśā*, who performed religious austerities and penance improper for a man of his caste, and was consequently killed by Rāmacandra.

SAMHITA—That portion of a Veda that comprises the hymns. (*see* VEDA)

SAMHITOPANISAD—The eighth *Brāhmaṇa* of the *Sāmaveda.* The text with a commentary has been published by Burnell.

SAMI—The *Acacia suma*, the wood of which is used for obtaining fire by friction. So Agni, or fire, is called Śamīgarbha, 'having the Śamī for its womb'. It is sometimes personified and worshipped as a goddess, Śamīdevī.

SAMIKA—One of the sons of Súra and brother of Vasudeva.

SAMMADA—The name of the fish that lived in the pond where the sage Saubhari was immersed for twelve years.

SAMPADVASA—One of the seven principal solar rays—the one which supplies heat to the planet Mars.

SAMPARA—A prince, the son of Samara.

SAMPARAYANA—One of the fifteen teachers of the White Yojush, who founded various new schools.

SAMPATI—A mythical bird who appears in the *Rāmāyaṇa* as son of Viṣṇu's bird Garuḍa, and brother of Jaṭāyus. According to another account he was son of Aruṇa and Śyenī. He was the ally of Rāma. It was he who informed Hanumán that Rávaṇa had carried Síta to Lanka.

SAMRAT—**(1)** The Manu of any particular period; **(2)** One of the daughters of Priyavrata, by his wife Kámya.

SAMUDRA—The daughter of Samudrá by his wife Velá. Samudrá was married to Prachínavarshish, and became the mother of the ten Prachetasas.

SAMUDRA—The king of rivers.

SAMVARA—A son of Kaṣyapa and Danu, and one of the most celebrated Daityas. He is called in the Vishṇu Puráṇa the mightiest of enchanters, to whom Hiranyakaṣipu had recourse, when he was himself unable to influence or destroy his son Prahláda. Samvara undertook to effect his destruction, but all his schemes were frustrated.

SAMVARANA—Son of Ṛkṣa, fourth in descent from Ikṣvāku, and father of Kuru. According to the *Mahābhārata* he was driven from Hastināpura by the Pāñcālas, who forced to take refuge among the thickets of the Indus. When the sage Vasiṣtha joined his people and became the Rājā's family priest, they recovered their country under Kuru.

SAMVARTA—Writer of a Dharmaśāstra or code of law bearing his name.

SAMVATSARA—**(1)** The name of the first of the five Cycles or Yugas, consisting of twelve years; **(2)** The lord of times and seasons.

SAMVIT—That in which all things are found or known, and which is found or known in all things. A synonym of Mahat.

SAMYA—An original property of man. One of the eight perfections or Siddhis, defined in the notes to the Vishṇu Purána as sameness of degree.

SAMYATI—A son of Prachinvat or Bahugava, of the race of Puru.

SAMYOGA—The union of contiguity, in opposition to that of identification or perfect unity—*Tadaikyam.*

SANAISCHARA, SATURN—'Slow-moving.' The son of Rudra and Suvarchalá. Saturn is also represented in the Vishṇu Purána, as the son of the sun and his handmaid Chháya, and is said to move slowly along in a car drawn by piebald steeds.

SANAKA, SANĀTANA, SANAT-KUMĀRA—The four Kumāras or mind-born sons of Brahmā. Some specify seven. Sanatkumāra (or Sanatsujāta) was the most prominent of them. They are also called by the patronymic Vaidhātra. (*see* KUMĀRA)

Sons of Rudra, who declining to create progeny, remained, as the name of the last implies, ever-boys, kumarás, that is, ever pure and innocent, whence their creation is called the Káumara.

SANAKADI, SAMPRADAYIS—One of the *Vaishnava* sects among the Hindus. They worship *Krishna* and *Radha* conjointly, and are distinguished from other sects by a circular black mark in the centre of the ordinary double streak of white earth; and also by the use of the necklace and rosary of the stem of *Tulasi.* The members of this sect are scattered throughout the whole of Upper India. They are very numerous about Mathura, and they are also among the most numerous of the Vaishnava sects in Bengal.

SANAT-KUMARA PURANA—(*see* PURĀṆA)

SANDANSA—One of the Narakas, the hell of pincers; into which falls the violator of a vow, and one who breaks the rules of his order.

SANDASA—A prince, the son of Sudása; named also Mitrasaha, to which the reader is referred for the legend of his life.

SANDHYA—Twilight; a form of Brahmá; also the name of the period preceding a Yuga. In the Vishṇu Purána it is said, "The night is called Ushá, and the day is denominated Vyush'ta, and the interval between them is called Sandhyá. On the occurrence of the awful Sandhyá, the terrific fiends termed Mandehas, attempt to devour the sun; for Brahmá denounced this curse upon them, that, without the power to perish, they should die every day (and revive by night), and therefore a fierce content occurs daily between them and the sun. At this season pious Brahman scatter water, purified by the mystical Omkára, and consecrated by the Gáyatri, and by this water, as by a thunderbolt, the foul fiends are consumed When the first oblation is offered with solemn invocations in the morning rite, the thousand-rayed deity shines forth with unclouded splendour. Omkára is Vishṇu the mighty, the substance of the three Vedas, 'he lord of speech; and by its enunciation those Rákshasas are destroyed. The sun is a principal part of Vishṇu, and light is his immutable essence, the active manifestation of which is excited by the mystic syllable Om. Light effused by the utterance of Omkára becomes radiant, and burnt up entirely the Rákshas called Mandehas. The performance of the Sandhyá (the morning) sacrifice must never therefore be delayed, for he who neglects it is guilty of the murder of the sun. Protected thus by the Brahmans and the pigmy sages called Bálakhilvas, the sun goes on Ins course to give light to the world.

SANDHYA-BALA—'Strong in twilight.' *Rakśasas* and other demons, supposed to be most powerful at twilight.

SANDHYANSA—The name of the period succeeding a Yuga.

SANDILYA—A descendant of Śaṇḍila. A particular sage who was connected with the *Chāndogya Upaniṣad*; one who wrote a book of *sutras*, one who wrote upon law, and one who was the author of the *Bhāgavata* heresy: two or more of these may be one and the same person. The *sūtras* or aphorisms have been published in the *Bibliotheca Indica.*

A celebrated teacher of whom Mr. Max Müller says, "It was an epoch in the history of the human mind when the identity of the masculine self and the neutral Brahmá was for the first time perceived, and the name of the discoverer has not been forgotten. It was Sándilya who declared that the self within our heart is Brahmá, and this tenet, somewhat amplified, is quoted as Sándilya'a wisdom." The age in which he lived is not given.—*A.S.L*, p. 323.

SANDIPANI—The tutor of Krishṇa and Balaráma; who was so astonished at their rapid progress that he thought the sun and moon had become his scholars. When they had acquired all that he could teach and enquired what fee he demanded, he requested them to give him his dead son drowned in the sea of Prabhása. The sea said, 'I have not killed the son of Sándípani; a demon named Panchajana, who lives in the form of a conch shell, seized the boy: he is still under my waters.' Krishṇa then plunged into the sea; and having slain the demon, took the conch shell as his horn; the boy was also restored to life and given to his father.

SANDRACOTTUS—*See* CHANDRAGUPTA.

SANGATA—One of the ten Mauryas, descendants of Chandragupta, whose dynasty at Mithila lasted a hundred and thirty-seven years.

SANGHA DISESA—A class of priestly misdemeanours.

SANGHA—An assembly or chapter of Buddhist priests.

SANGHA-BHEDA—The causing of a division among the priesthood.

SANGHAMITTA—A princess, the daughter of the grandson of Chandragupta, who on being left by her husband became a priestess, and was the first who visited Ceylon.

SANGITA-RATNĀKARA—A work on singing, dancing, and pantomime, written by Śāgī Deva.

SANGRAMAJIT—One of the sons of Krishṇa, by his wife Saivya or Mitravinda.

SANHATASWA—A prince, the son of Nikumbha.

SANHITAS—Collections of Hymns. By a Sanhita is generally understood a collection or compilation. The Sanhitas of the Vedas are collections of hymns and prayers belonging to them, arranged according to the judgment of some individual sage who is therefore regarded as the originator and teacher of each. The Vishṇu Purána mentions the names of the principal teachers of the Sanhitas of the Vedas and of their disciples and the schools founded by them.

SANHLADA—The youngest of the four sons of Hiraṇyakasipu, distinguished for his heroism, and termed the augmentor of the Daitya race.

SANI—The planet Saturn. The regent of that planet, represented as a black man in black garments. Śani was a son of the sun and Chāyā, but another statement is that he was. the offspring of Balarāma and Revatī. He is also known as Āra, Koṇa, and Kroda and by the patronymic Śaura. His influence is evil, hence, he is called Krūradṛś and Krūralocana, 'the evil-eyed one'. He is also Manda, 'the slow'; Paṅgu, 'the lame'; Sanaiścara, 'slow-moving'; Saptārcī, 'seven-rayed'; and Asita, 'the dark'.

SANJAYA—**(1)** The minister and charioteer of Maharája Dhritaráshtra. He was sent on an embassy to the Páṇḍavas, and is, says Mr. Wheeler, evidently the type of an ancient diplomatist. His object was to induce the Páṇḍavas to return to Hastinápur, without giving them any distinct pledge that their Ráj would be restored to them. He was surprised at the greatness of their preparations for war. The Páṇḍavas received him in Council, and he delivered the message of the Maháraja; to which Yudhishthira replied that whoever is wise would never give his consent to a war on trivial grounds; but that when war seemed to be inevitable it would be useless in them to humiliate themselves to the dust for the sake of concord. "He, however, who is intent upon a war of malice is always in a fever, and the fever burns stronger and stronger in his heart day by day, until he can feel no pleasure in the ordinary gratifications of the world." As for Dhritaráshtra we acknowledge him to be our Maháraja, and we know that he is kind and benevolent, and averse to doing evil; but for the sake of humouring his son Duryodhana, and keeping on good terms with him, the Maháraja stoops to act deceitfully towards us, and would entrap us into his presence by mere offers of protection." Krishṇa spoke to the same effect, Yudhishthira then gave costly presents to the envoy Saṇjaya, both for himself and some of his old friends, to whom he sent kind messages. The mission however was a fruitless one, and when the war broke out, Sanjaya was employed to inform the blind Maháraja of every event that transpired during its progress. It was Sanjaya who recited the Bhagavat Gíta; **(2)** A prince, the son of Supárṣwa; **(3)** the son of Pratikshatra; **(4)** A prince of the family of Ikshváku, son of Ranaṇjaya. **(5)** A King of Ujjayinī and father of Vāsavadattā.

SANJNA—The daughter of Viṣvakarman, was the wife of the sun and bore him three children, the Manu (Vaivaswata), Yama, and the goddess Yamí (or the Yamuná river). Unable to endure the fervours of her lord, Sanjná gave him Chháya his handmaid, and repaired to the forests to practice devout exercises. The sun, supposing Chháyá to be his wife Sanjná, begot by her three other children, Sanaiṣchara (Saturn), another Manu (Sávarṇi), and a daughter Tapatí (the Tapti River). Chháyá, upon one occasion, being offended with Yama, the son of Sanjna, denounced an imprecation upon him, and thereby revealed to Yama and to the sun that she was not in truth Sanjná, the mother of the former. Being further informed by Chháyá that his wife had gone to the wilderness, the sun beheld her by the eye of meditation engaged in austerities, in the figure of a mare (in the region of Uttara Kuru.) Metamorphosing himself into a horse, he rejoined his wife, and begot three other children, the two Áṣvins and Revanta, and then brought Sanjná back to his own dwelling. To diminish his intensity, Viṣvakarman placed the luminary on his lathe, to grind off some of his effulgence; and in this manner reduced it an eighth, for more than that was inseparable. The parts of the divine Vaishṇava splendour, residing in the sun, that were filed off by Viṣwakarman, fell blazing down upon the earth, and the artist constructed of them the discus of Vishṇu, the trident of Śiva, the weapon of the god of wealth, the lance of Kártikeya, and the weapons of the other gods: all these Viṣvakarman fabricated from the superfluous rays of the sun. *V.P.*

SANKALPA—(1) One of the prajápatis, according to the Kúrma list; **(2)** A daughter of Daksha and wife of Dharma.

SANKANA—A prince, the son of Kalmáshapáda according to the Rámáyana.

SANKARACHARYA—(Śaṅkara+ācārya) The great Saiva Reformer, who flourished, it is supposed, in the eighth or ninth century; Professor Wilson is of opinion that of the present popular forms of the Hindu religion, some assumed their actual state earlier than the above date. Sankara Achárya was a distinguished professor of the Vedanta and Advaita system. He was a native of Kérala or Malabar, of the tribe of Nambúri brahmans, and in the mythological language of the sect an incarnation of Śiva.

"In Malabar, he is said to have divided the four original tribes into seventy-two, or eighteen sub-divisions each, and to have assigned them their respective rites and duties. Notwithstanding this, he seems to have met with particular disrespect, either on account of his opinions, or his origin, or his wandering life. On his return home, on one occasion, his mother died, and he had to perform the funeral rites, for which his relations refused to supply him with fire, and at which all the Brahmans declined to assist. Sankara then produced fire from his arm and burnt the corpse in the court-yard of the house, denouncing imprecations to the effect, that the Brahmans there should not study the Vedas, that religious mendicants should never obtain alms, and that the dead should always be burnt close to the houses in which they had resided—a custom which is said to have survived him.

"All accounts concur in representing Sankara as leading an erratic life, and engaging in successful controversy with various sects, whether Saiva, or Vaishṇava, or of less orthodox opinions as the Buddhists and Jainas. In the course of his peregrinations, he established several Maths, or convents, under the presidencies of his disciples, particularly one, still flourishing at Sringeri, or Sríngiri, on the Western Ghats, near the sources of the Tungabadra. Towards the close of his life, he repaired as far as Kashmir, and seated himself, after triumphing over various Opponents, on the throne of Sarasvati. He next went to Badarikásrama, and finally to Kedarnáth, in the Himálaya, where he died at the early age of thirty-two. The events of his last days are confirmed by local traditions, and the Pítha, or throne of Sarasvati, on which Sankara sat, is still shown in Kashmir; whilst at the temple of Śiva at Badari, a Malabar Brahman, of the Nambúri tribe, has always been the officiating priest.

"The influence exercised by Sankara in person, has been perpetuated by his writings, the most eminent of which are his Bhashvas, or commentaries on the Sútras or Aphorisms of Vyása. A commentary on the Bhagavat Gíta, is also ascribed to him, as is one on the Nrisinha Tapaníya Upanishad, and a cento of verses in praise of Durga. The Saundarya Lahari is likewise said to be his composition." See VÉDÁNTA.

SANKARA—(1) 'Auspicious.' A name of Śiva in his creative character or as chief of the Rudras; **(2)** A renowned Dánava, son of Kaṣyapa and Danu.

SANKARA-VIJAYA—'The triumph of Śaṅkara.' A biography of Śaṅkarācārya relating his controversies with heretical sects and his refutation of their doctrines and superstitions. There is more than one work bearing this name; one by Ānanda Giri, which is published in the *Bibliotheca Indica*; another by Mādhavācārya; the latter is distinguished as the Sankṣepa *Śaṅkara-vijaya.* The work of Ānanda Giri has been critically examined by Kaśināth Trimbak Telang in the *Indian Antiquary*, vol. v.

SANKARSHANA—A name of Balaráma, given to him in consequence of his being extracted from his mother's womb to be transferred to that of Rohiṇí.

SANKASYA—A country in the Doab, near Mainpuri.

SANKHA—Writer of a Dharmaś āstra or law-book bearing his name. He is often coupled with Likhita, and the two seem to have worked together.

SANKHA—**(1)** A powerful many-headed serpent, one of the progeny of Kadru; **(2)** one of the minor Dwípas, peopled by Mlechhas who worship Hindu deities; **(3)** A conch shell, one of the principal weapons of Vishṇu.

SANKHAKUTA—One of the mountain ridges on the north of Meru.

SANKHANATA—A prince, the son of Vajranábha, a descendant of Ráma.

SANKHAPADA—One of the eight Lokapálas, and son of the patriarch Kardama by Sruti. He is the regent of the south.

SANKHAYANA—**(1)** Name of a writer who was the author of the *Sānkhāyana Brāhmaṇa* of the *Ṛgveda*, and of certain Śrautasūtras also called by his name. **(2)** He is the oldest known writer on the Ars Erotica, and is author of the work called Sānkhāyana *Kāmasūtra.*

SANKHYA—One of the six Śastras properly so called. It is ascribed to the Muni Kapila. It is the principal of the six philosophical schools of India. This system say some, is an attempt to account for the existence of the universe without the deity, by asserting the principle of duality, or in other words, the co-existence of spirit and matter. Dr. Ballantyne gives the following outline of the system. "The Sánkhya makes a step in advance of the Nyáya by reducing the external from the category of *substance* to that of *quality. Souls alone* are, in the Sánkhya, regarded as *substances*; whatever *affects* the soul being arranged under the head of a quality—(1) pleasing; 2, displeasing; or 3, indifferent. This mode of viewing the universe may be designated the emotional view of things.

The word Sánkhya means "*numeral, rational or discriminative.*" The system promises beatitude as the reward of that discrimination which rightly distinguishes between soul and nature. The meaning to be attached to these two words will be explained presently.

The *Sánkhya* system was delivered by *Kapila* in a set of aphorisms no less concise than those of the *Nyáya were*, He begins by defining the *chief end of Man*. His first aphorism is as follows:—"Now th complete (or highest) end of man." By the three kin of pain are meant—1, diseases, griefs, &c., which a intrinsic or inherent in the sufferer; 2, injuries fro ordinary external things; and 3, injuries from thing supernatural or meteorological. In his nineteenth apho rism, he declares that the bondage (*bandha*) under whic the. soul, or individual man (purusha), groans, is du to its conjunction with nature (prakṛiti); and this bon age is merely *seeming*, because soul is "ever essen tially a pure and free intelligence."

In his fifty-ninth aphorism, he says again of th soul's bondage—"It is merely verbal, and not a real ity, since it resides in [the soul's organ] the *mind* [an not in the soul or self];" on which the Hindu com mentator remarks,—"That is to say, since bondag &c., resides only in the mind (*chitta*), all this, as fa as concerns the soul *[purusha}*, is merely *verbal*, be cause, it is merely a *reflection*, like the redness of [pellucid] crystal [when a China rose is near it], bu not a *reality*, with no false imputation like the rednes of the China rose itself."

Of *nature*, which thus, by conjunction, make the soul *seem* to be in bondage when it is really *not* he gives, in his sixty-second aphorism, the followin account:—"Nature (prakṛiti) is the state of equipois of goodness (*sattwa*), passion (*rajas*), and darknes (*tamas*); from nature [proceeds] intellect (*mahat*), fron intellect self-consciousness (*ahankára*), from self-con sciousness the five subtle elements (*taumátra*), an both sets [external and internal] of organs (*indriya*) and from the subtle elements the gross elements (*sthúla-bhâla*), [then, besides, there is] soul (*purusha*); such is the class of twenty-five."

We may add further, that, in aphorism 105, we are told that "experience (*bhoga*) [whether of pleasure or pain, liberation from both of which is desiderated], *ends with* [the discrimination of] *though* [*i. e.*, soul as contra-distinguished from nature];" tha *a plurality of souls* is asserted (in opposition to the *Vedánta*) in another aphorism (150), *viz.*: "From the diverse allotment of birth, &c., the plurality of souls [is to be inferred];" and, finally, that the *Sánkhya* system explicitly repudiates the charge *of annihilation*, aphorism 47 declaring that, "In neither way [whether as a means or as an end] is this [*viz.*, annihilation], the soul's aim."

Mr. J. C. Thomson writes, "The Sánkhya is divided into three classes:—

1. The pure Sánkhya, which, if it admits, does not mention, a deity or Supreme Being, but considers the material essence as the plastic principle of all things, and is therefore called *nirishwara or* atheistic. Its text-books are the 'Sánkhya-pravachana,' and the 'Tattwa Samása,' both attributed to Kapila himself, and the 'Sánkhya-kárika,' to his disciple Ishwara Krishṇa. Asuri and Panchashika are also mentioned as the earliest followers of this system;

2. The Yoga system, called *seshwara*, or theistical, founded by Patanjali, whose Yoga-sútras are its text book, and followed by the author of the Bhágavat Gíta;

3. The Puránic school, a corrupt mixture of the other two. (Lit., 'rational,' from *Sânkhya*, 'reasoning, computation.')

SANKHYA-DARŚANA—Kapila's aphorisms on the Sāṁkhya philosophy. They have been printed.

SANKHYA-KARIKA—A work on the Sāṃkhya philosophy, written by Īśvara Kṛṣṇa; translated by Colebrooke and Wilson.

SANKHYA-PRAVACANA—A textbook of the Sāṁkhya philosophy, said to have been written by Kapila himself. Printed in the *Bibliotheca Indica.*

SANKHYA-SĀRA—A work on the Sāṁkhya philosophy by Vijnāna Bhikṣu. Edited by Hall in the *Bibliotheca Indica.*

SANKHYAYANA—A teacher of the Rig Veda.

SANKRANTA—The beginning of the year or a month, and the name of the festival that is commonly called Pongal, (*q.v.*)

SANKRITI—(1) A prince, the son of Sankriti; **(2)** The son of Nara, descendant of Bharata.

SANKRSANA—A name of Balarāma.

SANKU—One of the sons of Ugrasena.

SANKUSIRAS—A powerful Dánava—one of the sons of Kaṣyapa and Danu.

SANMUKHA—A name of Kartikeya, the war-god.

SANNATI—-Humility; one of the daughters of the patriarch Daksha, who was married to the Muni Kratu.

SANNATIMAT—A prince, the son of Sumati,

SANNYASI—An ascetic; the last of the four conditions of life prescribed for brahmans. These four conditions are: 1, That of the Brahmachári or bachelor, who, from the time of .his investment with the sacred cord, is required to tend the sacred fires and to follow his studies under, or in the presence of, his preceptor; 2, That of the Grihasta or householder, who, from his marriage, must strictly observe his religious duties, maintain the sacred fires, and liberally practice hospitality for the support of the other three orders; 3, That of the Vánaprastha or recluse, who, with or without his wife, relinquishes domestic life, retires to the desert, feeding on leaves, roots and fruits, or on the hospitality of the second order, and continues to perform his daily rites; 4, That of the Sannyási or ascetic, who performs no rite whatever, and appears sometimes in a state of nudity; who has renounced social life, with all its enjoyments and attachments, and subjected his passions; who lives on what is given him unasked, and remains in a village only one day, in a town not more than three days, and in a city only five; lest his mind become secularized.

SANSAPAYANA—A teacher of the Puránas, and composer of a "fundamental Sanhita," the substance of which is included in the Vishṇu Purána.

SANSKARAS—The ten essential ceremonies of Hindus of the first three castes; *viz.*, three before birth; then, "At the birth of a child the father should feed two brahmans, seated with their faces to the east; and according to his means offer sacrifices to the gods and progenitors. Let him present to the manes balls of meat mixed with curds, barley, and jujubes, with the part of his hand sacred to the gods, or with that sacred to Prajápati. Let a brahman perform such a Śraddha, with all its offerings and circumambulations, on every occasion of good fortune."

"Next, upon the tenth day (after birth), let the father give a name to his child,—the first term of which shall be the appellation of a god; the second, of a man; as Śarman. or Varman; the former being the appropriate designation of a brahman; the latter, of a warrior; whilst Gupta and Dása are best fitted for the names of Vaiṣyas and Śúdras. A name should not be void of meaning; it should not be indecent, nor absurd, nor ill-omened, nor fearful; it should consist of an even number of syllables; it should not be too long, nor too short, nor too full of long vowels, but contain a proportion of short vowels, and be easily articulated. After this and the succeeding initiatory rites, the purified youth is to acquire religious knowledge, in the mode that has been described, in the dwelling of his spiritual guide."

SANTA—Daughter of Daśaratha, son of Aja, but

adopted by Lomapāda or Romapāda, king of Aṅga. She was married to Ṛsyaśṛṅga.

SANTANA—Mercury. The son of the Rudra Ugra.

SANTANU—A king of the lunar race, the thirteenth in descent from Kuru, the prince who gives the designation to Duryodhana and his brothers, thence called Kauravas, their cousins, and the sons of Páṇḍu being termed Páṇḍavas. Śántanu had four sons, Bhíshma, Chitrángada, Vichitravírya and Vyása. Of these the eldest and youngest both lived unmarried, the other two Chitrángada and Vichitravírya both died without issue; on which, to prevent the extinction of the family, and in accordance with the ancient Hindu law, Vyása begot offspring on his brother's widows. The sons were Dhritaráshtra and Páṇḍu. Dhritaráshtra had a hundred sons by Gandhárí, the princess of Gaudhára, of whom Duryodhana was the eldest. Páṇḍu had five sons, the celebrated princes Yudhishtnira, Bhíma, Arjuna, and the twin brothers Nakula and Sahadeva. Of these the first was remarkable for his piety and integrity; the second for his gigantic bulk and strength. Arjuna was eminent for his valour, and was the particular friend of Krishṇa—*Wilson*, Vol. III, p. 291. *See* VIDURA. (*see* MAHĀBHĀRATA) He was called Satyavāc, 'truth-speaker', and was remarkable for his "devotion and charity, modesty, constancy, and resolution".

SANTARDDANA—A prince, the son of Dhrishtaketu, rája of Kaikeya, or according to the Pádma, king of Kashmír.

SANTATEYU—A prince, the son of Randraswa, of the house of Puru.

SANTATI—The son of Alarka, who became king and succeeded his father as sovereign of Benares, but whose reign was only that of an ordinary mortal, though his father is said to have reigned as a youthful monarch for sixty thousand and sixty hundred years.

SANTI—**(1)** Placidity, a property of sensible objects, according to the Sánkhya philosophy; **(2)** The Indra of the tenth Manwantara; **(3)** A brahman, pupil of Angiras, who having suffered the holy fire to go out in his master's absence, prayed to Agni, and so propitiated him, that be not only relighted the flame but desired Sánti to demand a further boon; **(4)** A prince, the son of Níla; **(5)** A daughter of Daksha, 'Expiation,' and wife

SANTIDEVA—A daughter of Devaka, who was married to Vasudeva.

SANTI-ŚATAKA—A century of verses on peace of mind. A poem of repute written by Śri Śihiana.

SANTOSHA—Content. The son of Dharma by his wife Tushti, (Resignation) one of the daughters of Dharma.

SAPEIJON—A teacher of the white Yajus and founder of several schools.

SAPINDANA—An ancestral Śráddha, performed at the expiration of twelve months after the death of a person. The practices of this rite are the same as those of the monthly obsequies, but a lustration is made with four vessels of water, perfumes, and sesamum; one of these vessels is considered as dedicated to the deceased, the other three to the progenitors in general; and the contents of the former are *to* be transferred to the other three, by which the deceased becomes included in the class of ancestors to whom worship is to be addressed with all the ceremonies of the Sráddha.

SAPINDAS—Relations connected by offerings of cakes to common ancestors; they extend to seven degrees, ascending or descending.

SAPTADASA—A collection of hymns created from the western mouth of Brahmá, along with the Sáma Veda, &c.

SAPTARSI—(Sapta-ṛṣi). The seven great *ṛṣis*. (*see* ṚṢI)

SAPTASATI—A poem of 700 verses on the triumphs of Durgā. It is also called *Devimāhātmya.*

SAPTA-SINDHAVA—'The seven rivers.' The term frequently occurs in the Vedas, and has been widely known and somewhat differently applied. It was apparently known to the Romans in the days of Augustus, for Virgil says:—

"Ceu septem surgens sedatis amnibus altus Per tacitum Ganges."—*Eneid*, IX.30.

They appear in Zend as the Hapta-heando, and the early Muhammadan travellers have translated the term. But their Saba' Sīn, 'seven rivers', according to Bīrūnī, applies to the rivers which flow northwards from the mountains of the Hindu Koh, and "uniting near Turmuz, form the river of Balkh (the Oxus)". The hymn in which the names of the rivers have been given has the following description: "Each set of seven (streams) has followed a threefold course. The Sindhu surpasses the other rivers in impetuosity ... Receive favourably this my hymn, O Gaṅgā, Yamunā, Sarasvati, Śutudri, Paruṣṇi; hear, O Marudvṛdhā, with the Asiknī and Vitastā, and thou, Ārjīkīyā, with the Suṣomā. Unite first in thy course with the Triṣṭāmā, the Susartū, the Rasā, and the Svetī; thou meetest with the Gomatī, and the Krumu with the Kubhā and the Mehatnū." According to this, the "seven rivers" are—(1) Gaṅgā (Ganges); (2)Yamunā (Jumnā); (3) Sarasvatī (Sarsuti); (4) Śutudri (Satluj); (5) Paruṣṇi; (6) Marudvṛdhā; (7) Ārjīkīyā (the Vipāśā, Hyphasis, Byās). Wilson says "the Paruṣṇi is identified with the Irāvati" (Hydraotes, Rāvī), but in this hymn it is the Marudvṛdhā which would seem to be the Irāvatī, because it is said to unite with the Asiknī (Akesines, Candrabhāgā, Cināb) and the Vitastā (Hydaspes or Jhelam). This would leave the Paruṣṇi unsettled. The other names, with the exception of the Gomatī (Gūmtī), are not identified. Suṣomā has been said to be the Sindhu, but in this hymn the Sindhu is clearly distinct. In the *Mahābhārata* the seven rivers are named in one place Vaśvokasārā, Nalinī, Pāvanī, Gaṅgā, Sītā, Sindhu, and Jambūnadī; and in another, Gaṅgā, Yamunā, Plakṣagā, Rathasthā, Saryu (Sarju), Gomatī and Gaṇḍakī (Gaṇḍak). In the *Rāmāyaṇa* and the Purāṇas the seven rivers are the seven streams into which the Ganges divided after falling from the brow of Śiva, the Nalinī, Hlādinī, and Pāvanī going east, the Cakṣu, Sītā, and Sindhu to the west, while the Ganges proper, the Bhāgīrathī flowed to the south. The term is also used for the seven great oceans of the world, and for the country of the seven rivers.

SAPTAVADHRI—A Vedic *ṛṣi*. In a hymn he says, "Aśvins, by your devices under the wickerwork for the liberation of the terrified, imploring *ṛṣi* Saptavadhri." Concerning this the following old story is told. Saptavadhri had seven brothers who determined to prevent his having intercourse with his wife. So they shut him up every night in a large basket, which they locked and sealed, and in the morning they let him out. He prayed to the Aśvins, who enabled him to get out of his cage during the night and to return to it at daybreak.

SARABHA—(L) A fabulous animal represented as having eight legs and as dwelling in the Himālayas. It is called also Utpādaka and Kuñjarārāti. **(2)** One of Rāma's monkey allies.

SARABHANGA—A celebrated devotee described in the Rámáyana. He was visited by Indra and invited to return with him to heaven; and when asked afterwards by Ráma the reason of Indra's coming to his hermitage, Sarabhanga, replied, "O Ráma, the sovereign of the gods or demons came to take me to the heaven of Brahmá, which I have gained by my severe austerities; but knowing that you were not far off I would not depart to heaven until I had seen you." Sarabhanga then said, "Behold, now while I put off this body, as a serpent pasts its slough !" Then the sage prepared a fire, offered ghee, and entered the flame; the fire consumed his body; and a youth, bright as the fire, was instantly produced; and in this shape, Sarabhanga sought the heaven of the sages who had devoted their lives to religious austerities, and passing by the heaven of the gods, he ascended to the heaven of Brahmá.

SARADA-TILAKA—(1) A mystic poem by Lakṣmaṇa. **(2)** A dramatic monologue by Śaṅkara, not earlier than the twelfth century. **(3)** Name of a Tantra.

SARADVAT—A *ṛṣi* said to be the father of Kṛpā. He is also called Gautama, (*see* KṚPĀ)

SARADWAT—The husband of Ahalya and father of Satyadhriti.

SARAGU OR SARJU—A river, commonly identified with the Devá; but though identical through greet part of their course, they rise as different streams, and again divide and enter the Ganges by distinct branches.

SARAMA—(1) In the *Ṛgveda* the dog of Indra and mother of the two dogs called, after their mother, Sārameyas, who each had four eyes, and were the watchdogs of Yama. Saramā is said to have pursued and recovered the cows stolen by the Paṇis, a myth which has been supposed to mean that Saramā is the same as Uṣas, the dawn, and that the cows represent the rays of the sun carried away by night. **(2)** The wife of Vibhīṣaṇa, who attended upon Sītā, and showed her great kindness when she was in captivity with Rāvaṇa. **(3)** In the *Bhāgavata Purāṇa*, Saramā is one of the daughter of Daksha and wife of Kaṣyapa; she is said to be the mother of canine animals. Vishṇu Purána, 122

SARAMEYAS—The two children of Saramā, Indra's watchdog; they were the watchdogs of Yama, and each had four eyes. They have been compared with the Greek Hermes.

SARANU—(1) One of the ministers of Rávaṇa, who was sent with Súka to spy out the army of Ráma, and obtain information of the chief heroes and counsellors. *See* SÚKA. **(2)** One of the sons of Vaṣudeva, by his wife Rohiní.

SARANYU—'The fleet runner.' A daughter of Tvaṣṭṛ.

She has been identified with the Greek Erinnys. The beginning of this myth is in a hymn of the *Ṛgveda*, which says—"(1) Tvaṣṭṛ makes a wedding for his daughter. (Hearing) this, the whole world assembles. The mother of Yama, the wedded wife of the great Vivasvat (the sun), disappeared. (2) They concealed the immortal (bride) from mortals. Making (another) of like appearance, they gave her to Vivasvat. Saraṇyū bore the two Aśvins, and when she had done so she deserted the two twins." In the *Nirukta* the story is expanded as follows: "Saraṇyū, the daughter of Tvaṣṭṛ, bore twins to Vivasvat, the son of Aditi. She then substituted for herself another female of similar appearance, and fled in the form of a mare. Vivasvat in like manner assumed the shape of a horse and followed her. From their intercourse sprang two Aśvins, while Manu was the offspring of Savarṇā (or the female of like appearance)." The *Bṛhaddevatā* has another version of the same story: "Tvaṣṭṛ had twin children, (a daughter) Saranyū and (a son) Triśiras. He gave Saraṇyū in marriage to Vivasvat, to whom she bore Yama and Yamī, who also were twins. Creating a female like herself without her husband's knowledge, and making the twins over in charge to her, Saraṇyū took the form of a mare and departed. Vivasvat, in ignorance, begot on the female who was left Manu, a royal *ṛṣi*, who resembled his father in glory; but discovering that the real Saraṇyū, Tvaṣṭṛ's daughter, had gone away, Vivasvat followed her quickly, taking the shape of a horse of the same species as she. Recognising him in that form, she approached him with the desire of sexual connection, which he gratified. In their haste his seed fell on the ground, and she, being desirous of offspring, smelled it. From this act sprang the two Kumāras (youths), Nāsatya and Basra, who were lauded as Aśvins (sprung from a horse)."—Muir's *Texts*, v. 227. see the Purāṇic version under "Samjña".

SARASVAT—A river god, the consort of Sarasvati, who rolls along his fertilizing waters, and is invoked by the worshippers who are seeking for wives and offspring, as well as for plenty and protection.—*O.S.T.*, v, 340.

SARASVATA—**(1)** In the *Mahābhārata* the *ṛṣi* Sārasvata is represented as being the son of the personified river Sarasvatī. In a time of great drought he was fed with fish by his mother, and so was enabled to keep up his knowledge of the Vedas, while other brāhmaṇas were reduced to such straits for the means of subsistence that study was neglected and the Vedas were lost. When the drought was over, the brāhmaṇas flocked to him for instruction, and 60,000 acquired knowledge of the Vedas from him. "This legend," says Wilson, "appears to indicate the revival, or, more probably, the introduction of the Hindu ritual by the race of brāhmaṇas, or the people called Sārasvata", who dwelt near the Sarasvatī river. Sārasvata brāhmaṇas still dwell in the Panjāb, and are met with in many other parts. **(2)** The country about the Sarasvatī river. **(3)** A great national division of the brāhmaṇa caste. **(4)** A sage who related the Vishṇu Purána to Paráṣara; **(5)** A Vyása in the ninth Dwápara age. In the notes to the Vishṇu Purána, a legend is given from the Mahábhárata in which it is said "that during a great drought the Brahmans, engrossed by the care of subsistence, neglected the study of the sacred books, and the Vedas were lost. The Rishi Sárasvata alone, being fed with fish by his mother Sarasvatí, the personified river so named, kept up his studies, and preserved the Hindu scriptures. At the end of the famine the Brahmans repaired to him to be taught, and sixty thousand disciples again acquired knowledge of the Vedas from Sárasvata. This legend appears to indicate the revival, or more probably the introduction, of the Hindu ritual by the race of Brahmans, or the *people* called Sárasvata; for according to the Hindu geographers, it was the name of a nation, as it still is the appellation of a class of Brahmans who chiefly inhabit the Panjab. The Sárasvata Brahmans are met with in many parts of India, and are usually fair-complexioned, tall, and handsome men. They are classed in the Játi málás, or popular lists of castes, amongst the five Gaura Brahmans, and are divided into ten tribes: they are said also to be especially the Purohits or family priests of the Kshatriya or military castes: circumstances in harmony with the purport of the legend, and confirmatory of the Sárasvatas of the Panjab having been prominent agents in the establishment of the Hindu religion in India. The Holy Land of the Hindus, or the primary seat, perhaps, of Brahmanism, has for one of its boundaries the Sarasvatí river." *V.P.*, 285.

SARASVATA—A dialect of Sanscrit; the term is employed by Mr. Colebrooke to designate that modification of Sanscrit, which is generally termed Prakṛit.

SARASVATAS—A tribe of brahmans, which occupied the banks of the river Sarasvati. See above, under Sarasvata.

SARASVATI—'Watery, elegant.' In the Vedas, Sarasvatī is primarily a river, but is celebrated in the hymns both as a river and a deity. The Sarasvatī river was one boundary of Brahmāvartta, the home of the early Āryans, and was to them, in all likelihood, a sacred river, as the Ganges has long been to their descendants. As a river goddess, Sarasvatī is lauded for the fertilising and purifying powers of her waters, and as the bestower of fertility, fatness, and wealth. Her position as Vac, the goddess of speech, finds no mention in the *Ṛgveda*, but is recognised by the *Brāhmaṇas* and the *Mahābhārata*. Dr. Muir endeavours to account for her acquisition of this character. He say, "When once the river had acquired a divine character, it was quite natural that she should be regarded as the patroness of the ceremonies which were celebrated on the margin of her holy waters, and that her direction and blessing should be invoked as essential to their proper performance and success. The connection into which she was thus brought with sacred rites may have led to the further step of imagining her to have an influence on the composition of the hymns which formed so important a part of the proceedings, and of identifying her with Vāc, the goddess of speech." In later times Sarasvatī is the wife of Brahmā, the goddess of speech and learning, inventress of the Sanskṛt language and Devanāgarī letters, and patroness of the arts and sciences. "She is represented as of a white colour, without any superfluity of limbs, and not unfrequently of a graceful figure, wearing a slender crescent on her brow and sitting on a lotus."—*Wilson.*

The same authority states that "the Vaiṣṇavas of Bengal have a popular legend that she was the wife of Viṣṇu, as were also Lakṣmī and Gaṅgā. The ladies disagreed; Sarasvatī like the other prototype of learned ladies, Minerva, being something of a termagant, and Viṣṇu finding that one wife was as much as he could manage, transferred Sarasvatī to Brahmā and Gaṅgā to Śiva, and contented himself with Lakṣmī alone, (*see* Vāc) Other names of Sarasvatī are Bhāraṭi, Brāhmī, Pūtkārī, Śāradā, Vāgīśvarī. The river is now called Sarsuti. It falls from the Himālayas and is lost in the sands of the desert. In ancient times it flowed on to the sea. A passage in the *Ṛgveda* says of it, "She who goes on pure from the mountains as far as the sea."—Max Müller, *Veda*, 45. According to the *Mahābhārata* it was dried up by the curse of the sage Utathya (*q.v.*). (*see* SAPTA-SINDHAVA)

The consort of Brahmá, and the goddess of wisdom, knowledge, science, art, learning and eloquence, the patroness of music and inventor of the Sanscrit language and Devanagari letters. 'She is represented as a young female, of their complexion, with four arms and hands. In one of the two right hands she holds a flower, which she offers to her husband, by whose side she is continually standing, and in the other a book of palm leaves, indicating that she is fond of learning, and imparts knowledge to those who study. In one of her two left hands she holds a string of pearls, called Sivamála, which serve her as a rosary, and in the other a damaru, or small drum. An annual festival is celebrated in her honour. She dwells among men, but her special abode is Brahmá lóka, with Brahmá, her husband.'

The name Sarasvati means flowing, and is applied to a celebrated river as well as to the goddess of speech. The river rises in the mountains north-east of Delhi. Sarasvati was also the name of one of the daughters of Daksha who was married to Dhárma.

"Sarasvati, by the standard mythological authorities, is the wife of Brahmá, and the goddess presiding over letters and arts. The Vaishṇavas of Bengal have a popular legend that she was the wife of Vishṇu, as were also Lakshmí and Gangá. The ladies disagreed; Sarasvati, like the other prototype of learned ladies, Minerva, being something of a termagant, and Vishṇu, finding that one wife was as much as even a god could manage, transferred Sarasvati to Brahmá, and Gangá, to Śiva, and contented himself with Lakshmí alone. It is worthy of remark that Sarasvati is represented as of a white colour, without any superfluity of limbs, and not unfrequently of a graceful figure, wearing a slender crescent on her brow, and sitting on a lotus."—Wilson's *Works*, Vol. II, pp. 187-8.

"Sarasvati is a goddess or some, though not of very great importance, in the Rig Veda. As observed by Yáska, she is celebrated both as a river and a deity. She was no doubt primarily a river deity, as her name, "the watery," clearly denotes, and in this capacity she is celebrated in a few separate passages. Allusion is made in the hymns and in the Brahmanas to sacrifices performed on the banks of this river, and the adjoining Dhrishdavati: and the Sarasvati in particular seems to have been associated with the reputation for sanctity which was ascribed to the whole region, called Brahmavartta, lying between those two small streams, and situated immediately to the westward of the Jumna. The Sarasvati thus appears to have been to the early Indians what the Ganges (which is only twice named in the Rig-Veda) became to their descendants. When once the river had acquired a divine character, it was quite natural that she should be regarded as the patroness of the ceremonies which were celebrated on the margin of her holy waters, and that her direction and blessing should be invoked as essential to their proper performance and success. The connection into which she was thus brought with sacred rites may have led to the further step of imagining her to have an influence on the composition of the hymns which formed so important a part of the proceedings, and of identifying her with Vách, the goddess of speech. At least, I have no other explanation to offer of this double character and identification.

Sarasvati is frequently invited to the sacrifices along with other goddesses Ilá, Mahí, Varutrí, who however were not like her, river nymphs, but personifications of some department of religious worship or sacred science.

In many of the passages where Sarasvati is celebrated, her original character is distinctly preserved. Thus in two places she is mentioned along with rivers, or fertilizing waters. She is spoken of as having seven sisters, as one of seven rivers, and as the mother of streams. In another place she is said to pour on her fertilizing waters, to surpass till other rivers, and to flow pure from the mountains to the sea. She is called the best of mothers, of rivers, and of goddesses.

In the later mythology, as is well known, Sarasvati was identified with Vách, and became, under different names, the spouse of Brahmá., and the goddess of wisdom and eloquence, and is invoked as a Muse. In the Mahábhárata she is called the mother of the Vedas, and the same is said of Vách in the Taitt. Br. In the Sántiparva it is related that when the Brahmarshis were performing austerities, prior to the creation of the universe, "a voice derived from Brahmá entered into the ears of them all; the celestial Sarasvatí was then produced from the heavens,"—*O.S.T.*, v, 337-343.

SARASVATI KAṆṬHĀBHARAṆA—A treatise on poetical and rhetorical composition generally ascribed to Bhoja Rāja.

SARAYU—The Sarju river or Gogra.

SARDHAWA—Confidence. One of the Charitas, or vistes of mind, which the Buddhist priest is taught to cultivate. The priest who has attained this condition is known by his being always cheerful; by the pleasure he has in hearing the sacred writings, and by the general excellence of his conduct.

SARMAJAYA—A prince, the son of Swaphalka.

SARMAN—An appropriate name for a brahman, affixed to the appellation of a god; both to be given by the father the tenth day after the birth of the child. Vishṇu Purána, 297.

SARMISHTA—The daughter of Vrishaparvan, and one of the wives of king Yayáti. She was the mother of Puru, who gave his youth to his father, receiving in exchange Yayáti's infirmities. (*see* DEVAYĀṆĪ)

SARNGA—The bow of Kṛṣṇa.

SARPA—The name of one of the eleven Rúdras according to the Váyu list.

SARPI—The wife of the Rudra Śiva, whose place is the air.

SARU—One of the sons of Vaṣudeva by his wife Rohini.

SARVA, ŚARVA—A Vedic deity; the destroyer. Afterwards a name of Śiva and of one of the Rudras. (*see* Rudra).

SARVABHAUMA—A prince, the son of Vidúratha, a descendant of Kuru.

SARVA-DARŚANA SAṀGRAHA—A work by Mādhavācārya which gives an account of the Darśanas or schools of philosophy, whether orthodox or heretical. It has been printed.

SARVAGA—**(1)** A son of the sage Paurnamása, of the race of Maríchi; **(2)** one of the Páṇḍava princes, the son of Bhíma.

SARVA—One of the eight modifications or manifestations of Rudra; the one whose station is the earth. *Vishṇu Purána*, 58.

SARVARI—A woman of low caste, who was very devout and looked for the coming of Rāma until she had grown old. In reward other piety a sage raised her from her low caste, and when she had seen Rāma she burnt herself on a funeral pile. She ascended from the pile in a chariot to the heaven of Viṣṇu.

SARVASARA—Name of an Upaniṣad.

SARVE'SVARA—One of the names of the Supreme Being, meaning "The Lord of all." Ziegenbalg writes, "When the Hindus speak of the highest Divine being as altogether spiritual and immaterial, they talk quite reasonably. They take for unquestionable truth all that Christians believe of God's nature and attributes, saying that there is, but one God, who is purely spiritual, incomprehensible, eternal, almighty, omniscient, all-wise, holy, true, just, gracious, and merciful; who creates, upholds, and governs all; who has pleasure in dwelling with mankind and making them happy, both in this world and the world to come; wherefore to serve him is happiness. The names they give to this Divine Being are altogether expressive of divine attributes."

SARYATAS—Sons of Sáryátas, descendant of Raivata, who through fear of the Rákshasas took refuge in forests and mountains, and afterwards, according to the legends, became renowned in all regions.

SARYATI—(1) One of the sons of the great Manu Vaivaswata; **(2)** A son of Nahusha, according to the list in the Linga Purána.

SASA—A portion of Jambu-dwípa, reflected in the lunar orb as in a mirror.

SASADA—(1) The son of Ikshváku, who on the death of his father succeeded to the sovereignty of Ayodhya, or as the Vishṇu Purána has it, to the dominion of the earth. **(2)** 'Hare-eater.' A name given to Vikukṣi (*q.v.*).

SASADHARMAN—One of the Mauryan kings, or descendants of Chandragupta, king of Magadhá.

SASAVINDA—A prince, the son of Chitrarathra; celebrated as the lord of the fourteen great gems; or articles the best of their kind, seven animate and seven inanimate; a wife, a priest, a general, a charioteer, a horse, an elephant, and a body of foot soldiers; or instead of the last three, an executioner, an encomiast, a reader of the Vedas: and a chariot, an umbrella, a jewel, a sword, a shield, a banner, and a treasure. The Vishṇu Purána states that he had a hundred thousand wives and a million of sons !

SASI, ŚAŚIN—The moon, so-called from the marks on the moon being considered to resemble hare (*śaśa*).

SASTRA—'A rule, book, treatise,' Any book of divine or recognised authority, but more especially the law-books.

SASTRA-DEVATAS—Gods of the divine weapons; a hundred are enumerated in the Rámáyana, and they are there termed the sons of Kriaswa by Jaya and Vijaya, daughters of the Prajápati, that is, of Daksha.

SASWATA—One of the kings of Mithila, the son of Sruta.

SATA SANKHYAS—A class of deities in the tenth Manwantara.

SATABALI—A distinguished general in the army of the monkey king Sugríva.

SATABHISHA—A lunar mansion in Mrigavithi in. the southern Avashthána.

SATADHANU—(1) A king who had a virtuous and discreet wife named Śaibyā. They were both worshippers of Viṣṇu. One day they met a heretic, with whom Śatadhanu conversed; but the wife "turned away from him and cast her eyes up to the sun." After a time Śatadhanu died and his wife ascended his funeral pile. The wife was born again as a princess with a knowledge of her previous existence, but the husband received the form of a dog. She recognised him in this form and placed the bridal garland on his neck. Then she reminded him of his previous existence and of the fault which had caused his degradation. He was greatly humiliated and died from a broken spirit. After that, he was born successively as a jackal, a wolf, a crow, and a peacock. In each form his wife recognised him, reminded him of his sin, and urged him to make efforts for restoration to his former dignity. At length "he was born as the son of a person of distinction", and Śaibyā then elected him as her bridegroom; and having "again invested him with the character of her husband, they lived happily together". When he died she again followed him in death, and both "ascended beyond the sphere of Indra to the regions where all desires are for ever gratified". "The legend," says Wilson, "is peculiar to the *Viṣṇu Purāṇa*, although the doctrine it inculcates is to be found elsewhere. **(2)** One of the sons of Hridika, of the Yádava race.

SATADHANVAN, ŚATADHANUS—'Having a hundred bows.' A Yādava and son of Hṛdika. He killed Satrājit, father of Satyabhāmā, the wife of Kṛṣṇa, in his sleep, and was himself killed in revenge by Kṛṣṇa, who struck off his head with his discus.

SATADRU—'Flowing in a hundred (channels).' The name of the river Sutlej, the Zaradrus of Ptolemy, the Hesudrus of Pliny.

SATADYUNMA—(1) One of the ten sons of the Manu Chákshusha; **(2)** One of the kings of Mithila, the son of Bhánumat.

SATAGHNI—'Slaying hundreds.' A missile weapon used by Kṛṣṇa. It is described in the *Mahābhārata* as a stone set round with iron spikes, but many have supposed it to be a rocket or other fiery weapon.

SATAJIT—(1) One of the kings of Bhárata, the son of Rája; **(2)** A son of Sahasrajit of the Yádava race; **(3)** One of the sons of Bhajamána.

SATAKARNI—The name or title of several Andhra princes.

SATANANDA—The son of Gautama by Ahalya According to the Rámáyaṇa, Satánanda was the family priest of Janaka, the father of Síta.

SATANIKA—**(1)** One of the Páṇḍava princes, the son of Nakula; **(2)** The son of Janamejaya and grandson of Paríkshit. He was killed in battle with the Titans, having gone to the assistance of Indra, and was succeeded in his throne by Śahaṣráníka.; **(3)** The son of Vasudána, of the race of Puru.

SATAPATHA-BRAHMANA—An appendix to the White Yajur Veda, which describes a variety of solemn sacrifices in which the juice of the Soma plant is the chief ingredient. It also contains various theories of creation and wild legends that show that "the old Sanskrit philosophers found it extremely difficult to determine the difference between gods and men."

"Considered religiously the Satapatha-Brahmana appears to offer a thorough type of scepticism. Man makes gods, god makes a chief god, the chief god (Prajápati) maltes the world and gods. But the gods were mortal. Rites and austerities were invented which insure immortality. Death becomes alarmed. Death is promised that only without the body shall gods or men become immortal. But after the gods have become immortal, they are unable to determine which among them shall be greatest."*

The contents of the Satapatha-Brahmana are somewhat heterogeneous, and amongst other curious stories there is one relating to the Deluge, which has been already given under the article MANU. (* Mrs. Manning. *A. and M. I.*)

SATARUPA—The female portion of Brahmá who, after detaching from himself the property of anger, in the form of Rúdra, converted himself into two persons, the first male, or the Manu Swáyambhuva, and the first woman, or Satarúpa: Professor Wilson says, "The division of Brahmá into two halves, designates, as is very evident from the passage in the Vedas given by Mr. Colebrooke, the distinction of corporeal substance into two sexes;

> Viráj being all male animals, Satarúpa, all female animals. Sata-rúpa, the bride of Brahmá, of Viráj, or of Manu, is nothing more than beings of varied or manifold forms, from Sata, 'a hundred,' and rúpa, 'form'; explained by the annotator in the Hari Vansa by Anantarúpa, of infinite shape, and Vividharúpa, of diversified shape, being as he states, the same as Máyá 'illusion,' or the power of multiform metamorphosis." Vishṇu Purána, 53.

SATATAPA—An old writer on law.

SATAVAHANA—A name by which Śālivāhana is sometimes called.

SATAVALAKA—A pupil of Sakapurni and teacher of the Rig Veda.

SATAYUS—One of the six sons of Purúravas.

SATI—Truth; one of the daughters of Daksha, and wife of Bhairava *i.e.*, Śiva. The Vishṇu Purána says she abandoned her corporeal existence in consequence of the displeasure of Daksha: and was afterwards the daughter of Himavan by Mená; and in that character, as the only Umá, the mighty Bhava again married her. Urged by her Mahéswara went to the sacrifice of Daksha; the different Puránas furnish contradictory accounts of her share in the transaction and of the way in which she met her death. (*see* PĪṬHASTHĀNA)

SATPURA—'The sixfold city', or 'the six cities' granted by Brahmā to the *asuras*, and of which Nikumbha was king. It was taken by Kṛṣṇa and given to Brahmādatta, a brāhma.—*Harivaṁśa.*

SATRAJIT, SATRAJITA—The son of Nighna and friend of the divine Áditya, the Sun. The Vishṇu Purána relates the following legend respecting him:—"On one occasion, Satrájit, whilst walking along the sea-shore, addressed his mind to Súrya, and hymned his praises; on which, the divinity appeared and stood before him. Beholding him in an indistinct shape, Satrájit said to the Sun: "I have beheld thee, lord, in the ḥeavens, as a globe of fire. Now do thou show favour unto me, that I may see thee in thy proper form." On this, the Sun, taking the jewel called Syamantaka from off his neck, placed it apart; and Satrájit beheld him of a dwarfish stature, with a body like burnished copper, and with slightly reddish eyes. Having offered his adorations, the Sun desired him to demand a boon; and he requested that the jewel might become his. The Sun presented it to him, and then resumed his place in the sky. Having obtained the spotless gem of gems, Satrájit wore it on his neck; and, becoming as brilliant, thereby, as the Sun himself, irradiating all the regions with his splendour, he returned to Dwáraka. The inhabitants of that city, beholding him approach, repaired to the eternal male, Purushottama,—who, to sustain the burden of the earth, had assumed a mortal form (as Krishṇa),—and said to him: "Lord, assuredly the (divine) Sun is coming to visit you." But Krishṇa smiled, and said: "It is not the divine Sun, but Satrájit, to whom Áditya has presented the Syamantaka gem; and he now wears it. Go and behold him without apprehension." Accordingly, they departed. Satrájit, having gone to his house, there deposited the jewel, which yielded, daily, eight loads of gold, and, through its marvelous virtue, dispelled all fear of portents, wild beasts, fire, robbers, and famine. Satrájit was ultimately killed by Satadhanwan in order to obtain possession of the jewel.

SATRUGHNA—'Foe destroyer.' Twin-brother of Lakṣmaṇa and half-brother of Rāma, in whom an eighth part of the divinity of Viṣṇu was incarnate. His wife was Śrutakīrtti, cousin of Sītā. He fought on the side of Rāma and killed the *rākṣasa* chief Lavaṇa and took possession of his capital Mathura. (*see* Daśaratha and Rāma)

SATVA-DEVI—**(1)** A name of Párvati; **(2)** The name of a nurse to the children of the giant Rávaṇa.

SATWATA—A prince of the Yádava race, whose descendants were termed Satwatas.

SATYABHAMA—The daughter of Satrájit and one of the wives of Krishṇa. In consequence of some aspersions cast on the character of Krishṇa relating to the disappearance of the Syamantaka gem, Satrájit reflected that he had been their cause, and to conciliate Krishṇa gave him to wife his daughter Satyabháma. When the jewel was recovered, Balabhadra claimed it as his property jointly with Krishṇa, while Satyabhháma demanded it as her right, as it had originally belonged to her father. She afterwards desired to possess the Parijáta tree, which Krishṇa accordingly removed from heaven to Dwáraka, though strongly opposed by Indra and the other gods. She had ten sons, Bhānu, Subhānu, Svarbhānu, Prabhānu, Bhānumat, Candrabhānu, Bṛhadbhānu, Atibhānu, Śribhānu, and Pratibhānu. Kṛṣṇa took her with him to Indra's heaven, and she induced him to bring away the *pārijāta* tree.

SATYADHRITA—**(1)** A prince, the son of Pushpavat. Sataydhriti. (1) One of the kings of Mithila, the son of Mahávírya; **(2)** The son of Sarana; **(3)** The son of Dhritimat; **(4)** The son of Satánanda: and a proficient in military science. Being enamoured of the nymph Urvaṣí, Satyadhriti was the parent of two children, a boy and a girl; who were found exposed in a clump of long Sara grass, by the Rája Santana whilst out hunting.

SATYADHRTI—Son of Śaradvat and grandson of the sage Gautama. According to the *Viṣṇu Purāṇa* he was father by the nymph Urvaśī of Kṛpa and Kṛpī.

SATYADHWAJA—A prince, the son of Urjjavaha, king of Mithila.

SATYAHITA—A teacher of the Rig Veda.

SATYAJIT—One of the kings of Mágadha, the son of Sanhita.

SATYAKA—A prince, the son of Sini.

SATYAKARMAN—One of the kings of Anga, the son of Dhritavrata.

SATYAKETU—A king of Káṣí, the son of Sukamara, a descendant of Alarka.

SATYAKI—A kinsman of Kṛṣṇa, who fought on the side of the Pāṇḍavas, and was Kṛṣṇa's charioteer. He assassinated Kṛtavarma in a drinking bout at Dvārakā, and was himself cut down by the friends of his victim. He is also called Dāruka and Yuyudhāna; and Śaineya from his father, Śini.

SATYALOKA—The world of infinite wisdom and truth, the inhabitants of which never again know death. It is said in the Vishṇu Purána to be situated one hundred and twenty millions of leagues above Dhruva. (*see* LOKA)

SATYARATHA—One of the kings of Mithila, the son of Mína-ratha.

SATYARATHI—The son and successor of the above.

SATYAS—A class of deities in the third Manwantara. (See JAYAS.)

SATYASRAVAS—A teacher of the Rig Veda.

SATYA—The quality of goodness, or purity, knowledge, quiescence. An incarnation of Vishṇu in the third Manwantara.

SATYAVAK—One of the noble sons of the Manu Chákshusha.

SATAVAHANA—The son and successor of Dípakarni, (*q.v.*) Dípakarní, in obedience to Śiva's commands, repaired to a certain forest to hunt; and whilst thus employed, met, as he had been forewarned, a lovely boy riding upon a monstrous lion. Still acting as he had been enjoined, the king aimed an arrow at the beast, and he fell as dead. Immediately, however, up rose from the carcase a celestial form, who thus addressed the astonished monarch. 'Dismiss your apprehension; I am a Yaksha, Sáta by name. It was my chance to see and love the beautiful daughter of a holy sage; my passion was returned; and this boy whom you behold, is our son. When the secret of our union was discovered, the angry sire condemned us both to wear the forms of brutes during the remainder of our earthly career. My bride was liberated from the effects of the curse in giving birth to her son; and your shaft has rendered me the same kind office. I am now at liberty; but ere I depart to the region of the gods, I bequeath to you this child, to be cherished by you as your own.' So saying, he vanished, leaving the boy with the king, who gladly received him, and gave him the name Sátaváhana, in reference to the appellation of his father and the váhana, or vehicle, on which the king had first beheld the infant mounted. Upon the death of his adoptive father Sátaváhana succeeded to the throne and became a mighty monarch.—Wilson's *Works*, III, 183.

SATYAVAN—The son of a blind old king who had been driven from his throne and was living in the forest as a hermit, when Savitrí, the lovely daughter of king Aswapati saw Satyaván and loved him. She was warned by a seer to overcome her attachment as Satyaván was a doomed man having only one year to live. But Savitrí replies:—

> Whether his years be few or many, be he gifted with all grace
> Or graceless, him my heart hath chosen, and it chooseth not again

They are therefore married and the bride strives to forget the ominous prophecy; out as the last day of the year approaches, her anxiety becomes irrepressible. She accompanied her husband to the forest on the fatal morning with a heavy heart, while he was cutting wood a thrill of agony suddenly shot through his temples, and he called out to his wife to support him—

> Then she received her fainting husband in her arms, and sate herself
> On the cold ground, and gently laid his drooping head upon her lap;
> Sorrowing she called to mind the sage's prophecy, and reckoned up
> The days and hour;. All in an instant she beheld an awful shape
> Standing before her, dressed in blood-red garments, with a glittering crown
> Upon his head: his form, though glowing like the iron, was yet obscure,
> And eyes he had like flames, a noose depended from his hand, and he
> Was terrible to look upon, as by her husband's side he stood
> And glanced upon him with a fiery glance. Shuddering she started up
> And laid her dying Satyavan upon the ground, and with her hands
> Joined reverently, she thus with beating heart addressed the shape;
> Surely thou art a god, such form as thine must men than mortal be,
> Tell me, thou god-like being, who thou art, and wherefore thou art here ?

After binding the spirit, Yama proceeds with it towards his own quarter, the South. The faithful wife follows him closely. Yama bids her go home and prepare her husband's funeral rites; but she persists in following, till Yama, pleased with her devotion, grants her any boon she pleases *except* the life of her husband. She chooses that her husband's father, who is blind, may recover his sight. Yama consents, and bids her now return home. Still she persists in following. At last, overcome by her constancy, Yama grants a boon without exception. The delighted Savitrí exclaims—

> Nought, mlgh'ty king, this time hast thou excepted: let my husband live:
> Without him I desire not happiness, nor even heaven itself:
> Without him I most die.' 'So be it, faithful wife,' replied the king of death,
> 'Thus I release him; and with that he loosed the cord that bound his soul." —*See* SAVITRÍ.

SATYAVANA—Name of a brāhmaṇa.

SATYAVATI—(1) Daughter of Uparicara, king of Cedi, by an apsara named Adrikā, who was condemned to live on earth in the form of a fish. She was mother of Vyāsa by the *ṛṣi* Parāśara, and she was also wife of King Śāntanu, mother of Vicitravīrya and Citrāṅgadā, and grandmother of the Kauravas and Pāṇḍavas, the rivals in the great war. The sage Parāśara met her as she was crossing the river Yamunā when she was quite a girl, and the offspring of their illicit intercourse was brought forth on an island (*dvīpa*) in that river, and was hence called Dvaipāyana. (*see* VYĀSA) She was also called Gandhakālī, Gandhavatī, and Kālāngnī; and as her mother lived in the form of a fish, she is called Dāsanandinī, Dāseyī, Jhajhodarī, and Matsyodarī, 'fish-born'. **(2)** The daughter of king Gádhí, who was demanded in marriage by an elderly brahmin name Richíka. The king would only consent to give his daughter on the condition that the sage should give him as the nuptial present, a thousand fleet horses whose colour should be white with one black ear. Richíka, having propitiated Varuṇa, the god of the ocean, obtained from him, at (the holy place called) Aṣwatírtha, a thousand such steeds, and, giving them to the king, espoused his daughter.

In order to effect the birth of a son, Richíka prepared a dish of rice, barley, and pulse, with butter and milk, for his wife to eat; and, at her request, he consecrated a similar mixture for her mother, by partaking of which, she should give birth to a prince of martial prowess. Leaving both dishes with his wife,—after describing, particularly, which was intended for her, and which for her mother,—the sage went forth to the forests. When the time arrived for the food to be eaten, the queen said to Satyavatí: "Daughter, all persons wish their children to be possessed of excellent qualities, and would be mortified to see them surpassed by the merits of their mother's brother. It will be desirable for you, therefore, to give me the mess your husband has set apart for you, and to eat of that intended for me; for the son which it is to procure me is destined to be the monarch of the whole world, whilst that which your dish would give you must be a brahman, alike devoid of affluence, valour, and power." Satyavatí agreed to her mother's proposal; and they exchanged messes.

When Richíka returned home, and beheld Satyavatí, he said to her: "Sinful woman, what hast thou done ? I view thy body of a fearful appearance. Of a surety, thou hast eaten the consecrated food which was prepared for thy mother: thou hast done wrong. In that food I had infused the properties of power, and strength, and heroism; in thine, the qualities suited to a brahman,—gentleness, knowledge, and resignation. In consequence of having reversed my plans, thy son shall follow a warrior's propensities, and use weapons, and fight, and slay. Thy mother's son shall be born with the inclinations of a brahman, and be addicted to peace and piety." Satyavatí, hearing this, fell at her husband's feet, and said: "My lord, I have done this thing through ignorance. Have compassion on me: let me not have a son such as thou hast foretold. If such there must be, let it be my grandson, not my son." The Muni, relenting at her distress, replied: "So let it be." Accordingly, in due season, she gave birth to Jamadagni; and her mother brought forth Viṣvámitra. Satyavatí afterwards became the Kauṣikí river. *V.P.*

SATYAVRATA—(1) Name of the seventh Manu. (*see* MANU) **(2)** A king of the Solar race, descended from Ikṣvāku. He was father of Hariścandra, and is also named Vedhas and Triśaṅku. According to the *Rāmāyaṇa* he was a pious king, and was desirous of performing a sacrifice in virtue of which he might ascend bodily to heaven. Vasiṣṭha, his priest, declined to perform it, declaring it impossible. He then applied to Vasiṣṭha's sons, and they condemned him to become a cāṇḍāla for his presumption. In his distress and degradation he applied to Viśvāmitra, who promised to raise him in that form to heaven, Viśvāmitra's intended sacrifice was strongly resisted by the sons of Vasiṣṭha, but he reduced them to ashes, and condemned them to be born again as outcasts for seven hundred births. The wrathful sage bore down all other opposition, and Triśaṅku ascended to heaven. Here his entry was opposed by Indra and the gods, but Viśvāmitra in a fury declared that he would create "another Indra, or the world should have no Indra at all". The gods were obliged to yield, and it was agreed that Triśaṅku, an immortal, should hang with his head downwards, and shine among some stars newly called into being by Viśvāmitra.

The *Viṣṇu Purāṇa* gives a simpler version. While Satyavrata was a cāṇḍāla, and the famine was raging, he supported Viśvāmitra's family by hanging deer's flesh on a tree on the bank of the Ganges, so that they might obtain food without the degradation of receiving it from a cāṇḍāla: for this charity Viśvāmitra raised him to heaven.

The story is differently told in the *Harivaṁśa*. Satyavrata or Triśaṅku, when a prince, attempted to carry off the wife of a citizen, in consequence of which his father drove him from home, nor did Vasiṣṭha, the family priest, endeavour to soften the father's decision. The period of his exile was a time of famine, and he greatly succoured the wife and family of Viśvāmitra, who were in deep distress while the sage was absent far away. He completed his twelve years' exile and penance, and being hungry one day, and having no flesh to eat, he killed Vasiṣṭha's wondrous cow, the Kāmadhenu, and ate thereof himself, and gave some to the sons of Viśvāmitra. In his rage Vasiṣṭha gave him the name Triśaṅku, as being guilty of three great sins. Viśvāmitra was gratified by the assistance which Satyavrata had rendered to his family; "he installed him in his father's kingdom,...and, in spite of the resistance of the gods and of Vasiṣṭha, exalted the king alive to heaven"

The Bhágavata has no allusion to this legend, saying that Trişanku is still visible in heaven. The Váyu furnishes some further information from an older source: Both my copies have a blank, where it is marked; and a similar passage does not elsewhere occur: but the word should probably be *nisha*, and the whole may be thus rendered: "Men acquainted with the Puránas recite these two stanzas: 'By the favour of Vişvámitra, the illustrious Trişanku shines in heaven, along with the gods, through the kindness of that sage. Slowly passes the lovely night in winter, embellished by the moon, decorated with three watches, and ornamented with the constellation Trişanku.'" This legend is, therefore, clearly astronomical, and alludes, possibly, to some reformation of the sphere by Vişvámitra, under the patronage of Trişanku, and in opposition to a more ancient system advocated by the school of Vaşişhtha. It might be no very rash conjecture, perhaps, to identify Trişanku with Orion, the three bright stars of whose belt may have suggested the three Sankus (stakes or pins) which from his name.

"The seven ancient rishis or saints, as has been said before, were the seven stars of Ursa Major. The seven other new saints which are here said to have been created by Vişvámitra, should be seven new southern stars, a sort of new Ursa. Von Schlegel thinks that this mythical fiction of new stars created by Vişvámitra may signify that these southern stars, unknown to the Indians as long as they remained in the neighbourhood of the Ganges, became known to them at a later date when they colonised the southern regions of India."—*Gorresio*.

SATYAYAJÑA—The observance of truth; one of the great obligations of brahmans.

SATYA-YAUVANA—A certain Vidyādhara.

SAUBHA—A magical city, apparently first mentioned, in the *Yajurveda.* An aerial city belonging to Hariścandra, and according to popular belief still visible occasionally. It is called also Khapura, Pratimārgaka, and Traṅga. In the *Mahābhārata* an aerial or self-supporting city belonging to the *daityas*, on the shore of the ocean, protected by the Śālva king.

SAUBHARI—A devout sage, learned in the Vedas, of whom the following extraordinary legend is narrated. He spent twelve years immersed in a lake, the sovereign of the fish in which, named Sammada, had a very numerous progeny. His children and his grandchildren were wont to frolic around him, in all directions; and he lived amongst them happily, playing with them night and day. Saubhari, the sage, being disturbed, in his devotions, by their sports, contemplated the patriarchal felicity of the monarch of the lake, and reflected: "How enviable is this creature, who, although born in a degraded state of being, is ever thus sporting cheerfully amongst his offspring and their young ! Of a truth, he awakens, in my mind, the wish to taste such pleasure; and I, also, will make merry amidst my children." Having thus resolved, the Muni came up, hastily, from the water, and, desirous of entering upon the condition of a householder, went to Mándhátṛi, to demand one of his daughters as his wife. As soon as he was informed of the arrival of the sage, the king rose up from his throne, offered him the customary libation, and treated him with the most profound respect. Having taken a seat, Saubhari said to the Rája: "I have determined to marry. Do you, king, give me one of your daughters, as a wife ? Disappoint not my affection. It is not the practice of the princes of the race of Kakutstha to turn away from compliance with the wishes .of those who come to them for succour. There are, O monarch, other kings of the earth to whom daughters have been born; but your family is, above all, renowned for observance of liberality in your donations to those who ask your bounty. You have, O prince, fifty daughters. Give one of them to me; that so I may be relieved from the anxiety I suffer through fear that my suit may be denied."

When Mándhátṛi heard this request, and looked upon the person of the sage, emaciated by (austerity and) old age, he felt disposed to refuse his consent: but, dreading to incur the anger and imprecation of the holy man, he was much perplexed, and, declining his head, was lost awhile in thought. The Rishi, observing his hesitation, said: "On what, O Rája, do you meditate ? I have asked for nothing that may not be readily accorded. And what is there that shall be unattainable to you, if my desires be gratified by the damsel whom you must needs give unto me ?" To this, the king, apprehensive of his displeasure, answered and said: "Grave sir, it is the established usage of our house to wed our daughters to such persons only as they shall, themselves, select from suitors of fitting rank; and, since this your request is not yet made known to my maidens, it is impossible to say whether it may be equally agreeably to them as it is to me. This is the occasion of my perplexity; and I am at a loss what to do." This answer of the king was fully understood by the Rishi, who said to himself: "This is merely a device of the Rája, to evade compliance with my suit. He has reflected that I am an old man, having no attractions for women, and not likely to be accepted by any of his daughters. Even be it so: I will be a match for him." And he then spoke aloud, and said: "Since such is the custom, mighty prince, give orders that I be admitted into the interior of the palace. Should any of the maidens, your daughters, be willing to take me for a bridegroom, I will have her for my bride. If no one be willing, then let the blame attach alone to the years that I have numbered." Having thus spoken, he was silent.

Mándhátṛi, unwilling to provoke the indignation of the Muni, was accordingly, obliged to command the eunuch to lead the sage into the inner chambers; who, as he entered the apartments, put on a form and features of beauty far exceeding the personal charms of mortals, or even of heavenly spirits. His conductor, addressing the princesses, said to them: "Your father, young ladies, sends you this pious sage, who has demanded of him a bride; and the Rája has promised him, that he will not refuse him any one of you who shall choose him for her husband." When the damsels heard this, and looked upon the person of the Rishi, they were equally inspired with passion and desire, and, like a troop of female elephants disputing the favours of the master of the herd, they all contended for the choice. "Away, away, sister!" said each to the other: "this is my election; he is my choice; he is not a meet bridegroom for you; he has been created, by Brahmá, on purpose for me, as I have been created in order to become his wife; he has been chosen, by me, before you; you have no right to prevent his becoming my husband." In this way arose a violent quarrel amongst the daughters of the king, each insisting upon the exclusive election of the Rishi; and, as the blameless sage was thus contended for by the rival princesses, the superintendent of the inner apartments, with a downcast look, reported to the king what had occurred. Perplexed, more than ever, by this information, the Rája exclaimed: "What is all this ? And what am I to do now ? What is it that I have said ? And, at last, although with extreme reluctance, he was obliged to agree that the Rishi should marry all his daughters.

Having then wedded, agreeably to law, all the princesses, the sage took them home to his habitation, where he employed the chief of architects, Visvakarman,—equal, in taste and skill, to Brahmá, himself,—to construct separate palaces for each of his wives: he ordered him to provide each building with elegant couches, and seats, and furniture, and to attach to them gardens and groves, with reservoirs of water, where the wild-duck and the swan should sport amidst beds of lotus flowers. The divine artist obeyed his injunctions, and constructed splendid apartments for the wives of the Rishi; in which, by command of Saubhari, the inexhaustible and divine treasure called Nanda took up his permanent abode; and the princesses entertained all their guests and dependants with abundant viands of every description and the choicest quality.

After some period had elapsed, the heart of king Mándhátṛi yearned for his daughters; and he felt solicitous to know whether they were happily circumstanced. Setting off, therefore, on a visit to the hermitage of Saubhari, he beheld, upon his arrival, a row of. beautiful crystal palaces, shining as brilliantly as the rays of the sun, and situated amidst lovely gardens and reservoirs of pellucid water. Entering into one of these magnificent palaces, he found and embraced a daughter, and said to her, as the tears of affection and delight trembled in his eyes: "Dear child, tell me how it is with you. Are you happy here, or not ? Does the great sage treat you with tenderness ? Or do you revert, with regret, to your early home':"' The princess replied: "You behold, my father, how delightful a mansion I inhabit,—surrounded by lovely gardens and lakes, where the lotus blooms, and the wild swans murmur. Here I have delicious viands, fragrant unguents, costly ornaments, splendid raiment, soft beds, and every enjoyment that affluence can procure. Why, then, should I call to memory the place of my birth ? To your favour am I indebted for all that I possess. I have only one cause of anxiety, which is this: my husband is never absent from my dwelling; solely attached to me, he is always at my side; he never goes near my sisters; and I am concerned to think that they must feel mortified by his neglect: this is the only circumstance that gives me uneasiness."

Proceeding to visit another of his daughters, the king, after embracing her, and sitting down, made the same inquiry, and received the same account of the enjoyments with which the princess was provided. There was, also the same complaint, that the Rishi was wholly devoted to her, and paid no attention to her sisters. In every palace, Mándhátṛi heard the same story, from each of his daughters, in reply to his questions; and, with a heart overflowing with wonder and delight, he repaired to the wise Saubhari, whom he found alone, and after paying homage to him, thus addressed him: "Holy sage, I have witnessed this thy marvellous power. The like miraculous faculties I have never known any other to possess. How great is the reward of thy devout austerities !" Having thus saluted the sage, and been received by him, with respect, the Rája resided with him for some time, partaking of the pleasures of the place, and then returned to his capital.

In the course of time, the daughters of Mándhátṛi bore to Saubhari a hundred and fifty sons; and, day by day, his affection for his children became more intense, and his heart was wholly occupied with the sentiment of self. "These my sons," he loved to think, "will charm me with their infant prattle; then they will learn to walk; they will, then, grow up to youth, and to manhood; I shall see them married, and they will have children; and I may behold the children of those children." By these and similar reflections, however, he perceived that his anticipations every day outstripped the course of time; and, at last, he exclaimed: "What exceeding folly is mine ! There is no end to my desires. Though all I hope should come to pass for ten thousand or a hundred thousand years, still new wishes would spring up. When I have seen my infants walk; when I have beheld their youth, their manhood, their marriage, their progeny; still my expectations are unsatisfied, and my soul yearns to behold the descendants of their descendants. Shall I even see them, some other wish will be engendered; and, when that is accomplished, how is the birth of fresh desires to be prevented ? I have at last, discovered, that there is no end to hope, until it terminates in death; and that the rapid that is perpetually engrossed by expectation can never be attached to the supreme spirit. My mental devotions, whilst immersed in water, were interrupted by attachment to my friend the fish. The result of that connection was my marriage; and insatiable desires are the consequences of my married life. The pain attendant upon the birth of my single body is now augmented by the cares attached to fifty others, and is further multiplied by the numerous children whom the princesses have borne to me. The sources of affliction will be repeatedly renewed by their children, and by their espousals, and by their progeny, and will be infinitely increased: a married life is a mine of individual anxiety. My devotions, first disturbed by the fish of the pool, have since been obstructed by temporal indulgence; and I have been beguiled by that desire for progeny which was communicated to me by association with Sammada. Separation from the world is the only path of the sage to final liberation: from commerce with mankind innumerable errors proceed. The ascetic who has accomplished a coarse of self-denial falls from perfection, by contracting worldly attachments. How much more likely should one so fall, whose observances we incomplete ! My intellect has been a prey to the desire of married happiness: but I will, now, so exert myself, for the salvation of my soul, that exempt from human imperfections, I may be exonerated from human sufferings. To that end, I will propitiate, by arduous penance, Vishṇu, the creator of the universe, whose form is inscrutable, who is smaller than the smallest, larger than the largest, the source of darkness and of light, the sovereign god of gods. On his everlasting body, which is both discrete and indiscrete substance, illimitably mighty, and identical with the universe, may my mind, wholly free from sin, be ever steadily intent, so that I may be born no more ! To him I fly for refuge; to that Vishṇu who is the teacher of teachers, who is one with all beings, the pure eternal lord of all, without beginning, middle, or end, and besides whom is nothing." *V.P.*

SAUDASA—Son of King Sudās. Their descendants are all Saudāsas. (*see* KALMĀṢAPĀDA)

SAUMITRI—A teacher of the Sáma Veda.

SAUMYA—A division of the Varsha of Bhárata.

SAUNAHOTRA—A Rishi, the son of Sunahotra. On one occasion Indra himself went to a sacrifice of the Rishi in order to please him. The great Asuras, thinking that Indra was above, and wishing to take him, surrounded the sacrificial enclosure. Indra, however, perceived it, and taking the guise of the Rishi, he went away. The Asuras, seeing the sacrificer again, seized Saunahotra, taking him for Indra. He pointed out India to them and was released by the Asuras.—*A.S.L.*, 231.

SAUNAKA—(1) A sage, the son of Śunaka and grandson of Gṛtsamada. He was the author of the *Bṛhaddevatā*, an *Anukramaṇī*, and other works, and he was a teacher of the *Atharvaveda*. His pupil was Āśvalāyana. There was a family of the name, and the works attributed to Śaunaka are probably the productions of more than one person. It was Saunaka who established the distinctions of the four castes. See *A.S.L.*, 232-36. **(2)** A teacher of the Atharva Veda

SAUNANDA—A club shaped like a pestle, which was one of the weapons of Balarāma.

SAURA PURANA—(*see* PURĀṆA)

SAURASHTRAS—The people of Surat; the Surastrene of Ptolemy.

SAURASRAS—The people of Surāṣṭra.

SAUTI—Name of the sage who repeated the *Mahābhārata* to the *ṛṣis* in the Naimiṣa forest.

SAUVIRAI—The nations of Sindh, and Western Rájputána.

SAUVIRAS—A people connected with the Saindhavas or people of Sindh, and probably inhabitants of the western and southern parts of the Panjāb. Cunningham says that Sauvīra was the plain country.

SAVALA—One of the sons of Priyavrata, who was nominated by his father to be the monarch of the Dwípa of Pushkara.

SAVALASWAS—Daksha, at the command of Brahmá, is said to have created various living creatures. His first four thousand sons, termed Haryaswas, were dissuaded by Nárada from propagating offspring, and dispersed themselves throughout the universe. Daksha then created a thousand other sons, named Savaláswas, who were desirous of engendering posterity, but were dissuaded by Nárada, in a similar manner. They said to one another "what the sage has observed is perfectly just." We must follow the path that our brothers have travelled, and when we have ascertained the extent of the universe, we will multiply our race. Accordingly they scattered themselves through the regions, and, like rivers flowing into the sea, they returned cot again.

SAVANA—One of the seven sons of the Muni Vaṣiṣhtha.

SAVARNA, SĀVARṆI—The eighth Manu. The name is used either alone or in combination for all the succeeding Manus to the fourteenth and last. (*see* MANU)

SAVARNA—Wife of the sun. "The female of like appearance", whom Saraṇyū, wife of Vivasvat, substituted for herself when she fled (*see* SARAṆYŪ) Manu was the offspring of Savarṇā. This is the version given in the *Nirukta*. In the *Viṣṇu Purāṇa*, Savarṇā is daughter of the ocean, wife of Prācīnabarhis, and mother of the ten Pracetasas.

SAVARNI—A Manu, the son of the sun by his maid Chhāya. He is to be the Manu of the eighth Manwantara.

SAVIBHASA—One of the seven suns into which the solar rays dilate at the end of the day of Brahmá, when the world is destroyed.

SAVITR—'Generator'. **(1)** A name used in the Vedas for the sun. Many hymns are addressed to him, and he is sometimes distinguished from that deity. **(2)** One of the Ādityas.

SAVITRI—**(1)** The holy verse of the Veda, commonly called Gāyatrī. **(2)** A name of Śatarūpā, the daughter and wife of Brahmā, who is sometimes regarded as a personification of the holy verse. **(3)** Daughter of King Aśvapati, and lover of Satyavān, whom she insisted on marrying, although she was warned by a seer that he had only one year to live. When the fatal day arrived, Satyavān went out to cut wood, and she followed him. There he fell, dying, to the earth, and she, as she supported him, saw a figure, who told her that he was Yama, king of the dead, and that he had come for her husband's spirit. Yama carried off the spirit towards the shades, but Sāvitrī followed him. Her devotion pleased Yama, and he offered her any boon except the life of her husband. She extorted three such boons from Yama, but still she followed him, and he was finally constrained to restore her husband to life.

"A king, named Aswapati, sighed for offspring, and after praying in vain for eighteen years, the gods of heaven sent him a daughter, who grew up so "bright in her beauty," that she appeared like a child of the Immortals; and the princes around were so dazzled, that none dared to ask for her as a bride.

"So passing fair the young Sávitri grew
That all adored her but none thought to woo.
No lovelier nymph e'er left her native skies
To dazzle mortals with her heavenly eyes;
And how might e'en the proudest chieftain dare,
To woo a Princess so divinely fair."

This distressed her father, and he said that she must go now and make choice herself.

"Meekly bowed the modert maiden, with her eyes upon the ground,
And departed, as be bade her, with attendants troop'd around.
Many a hermitage she travers'd, riding in a gold-bright car;
Many a wilderness and forest, holy places near and far."

"When she came back she told of a blind old king, driven from his throne by a ruthless kinsman, living with his beloved wife in a grove; and his brave son, Satyaván, her heart has chosen. "Satyaván," she says, "has all my love."

At this announcement a Rishi, who happened to be present, exclaims, in distress, that she would choose care and grief, in choosing Satyaván. He is

"Learned as the gods' own teacher,—glorious as the sun is he;
With the eartb'e untiring patience, and great Indra's bravery."
He is noble,
"True, and great of soul,
Bountiful is he, and modest,—every sense does he control.
Gentle, brave, all creatures love him,—keeping in the righteous way,
Number'd with the holy hermits,—pure and virtuous as they."

But alas! in a year, counting from this day, "Satyaván will die." On hearing this, the king considers a marriage out of the question, and says: "Go, then, my dearest child, and choose again." But his daughter replies:

'Be he virtuous or worthless,—many he his days, or few,—
Once for all I choose my husband: to than choice will I be true."

The sage and her father give way to her decided wishes: and in due time the young couple are married, and live in great happiness with the hermits in the grove. Sâvitrî, the bride, put aside her jewels, and wore the coarse raiment usually adopted by hermits; and, by her meekness and affection, won the hearts of all with whom she dwelt.

"Sadly, sadly as she counted, day by day flew swiftly by,
And the fated time came nearer when her Satyavan must die.
Yet three days and he must perish, sadly thought the loving wife,
And she vowed to fast, unresting, for his last three days of life."

Her husband's father feared that the trial would be too great for her, but she answered: "'Firm resolve has made me vow it; firm resolve will give me strength." She kept her vow, and maintained her fast; and when the third day dawned, and the fire of worship was kindled and the morning rites performed, she reverently saluted the aged Brâhmans and her husband's honoured parents, but still refused food. Presently, her husband takes his axe upon his shoulder to perform his daily task of felling trees. She begs him to let her go also; he replies:

"All unknown to thee the forest; rough the part and weary thou:
How, then, will thy feet support thee, fainting from thy fasting vow?"
"Nay, I sink not from my tasting, and no weakness fell today;
I have set my heart on going: oh I forbid me not, I pray !"

Sâvitrî has always kept her sad secret from her husband; and he has, therefore, no idea of her real reason for wishing to accompany him. He, however, consents, and calls her attention to the lovely woods, stately peacocks, and flowers of brilliant hue; but she can look only upon him, and mourn for him as one about to die. She gathers cooling fruits, and he makes the woods resound with the strokes of hie hatchet. But, soon a thrilling agony shoots through his temple ... She sits down upon the ground, and he rests his head upon her breast, and sleeps. But,—

"Sudden, to! before Sâvitrî stood a great and awful One;
Red as blood was his apparel, bright and glowing as the sun.
In his hand a noose was hanging; he to Satyavan stood high,
And upon the weary sleeper fix'd his fearful, glittering eye."

This awful apparition was Yama, god of Death, come to bind and take the spirit of Satyavan. Having done this, he moved towards the south, Sâvitrî closely following. Yama tries to persuade her to go back; but she says, no: wherever her husband goes, there she will go also. Yama praises her sweet speech, and offers her any boon except the life of Satyavan; and she begs that the blind king, her father-in-law, may be restored to sight, but without relinquishing her first request. Yama tries again and again to get rid of her, and says she will faint.

"Can I faint when near my husband ? where he goes my path shall be.
I will follow where thou leadest;—listen once again to me."

Nothing can induce her to return without Satyavan; and at length "love conquers death." Yama relents; the happy wife hastens to where her husband's dead body lay, and, leaning upon her faithful bosom he awakes again to sense and life. A very touching conversation follows, during which he gradually recovers his recollection; but his wife, avoiding any full explanation of what had been occurring, says:

> "Night's dark shadows round us tall:
> When the morrow's light reterneth, dearest ! I will tell thee all.
> Up, then, and away, I pray thee,—come unto thy parents, love !
> See! the sun long time has vanish'd, and the night grows black above."

And accordingly they return to the hermitage, when Satyavan finds his father no longer blind; and every kind of happiness awaits them."—*See* SATYATAN.

SAVITRI—**(1)** One of the twelve Ádityas, the sun. "Savitri has established the earth by supports; Savitri has fixed the sky in unsupported space: Savitri has milked the atmosphere, restless (or noisy) as a hoi'se [or, Savitri has extracted from the atmosphere the ocean, &c., restless as a horse;]—the ocean fastened on the unpassable expanse. Savitri, son of the waters, knows the place where the ocean supported, issued forth. From him the earth, from him the atmosphere, arose; from him the heaven and earth extended." The sun also whose place is on the sky is called Savitṛi.

Súrya and Savitṛi are exact personifications of the sun. It is under these two different appellations that the sun is chiefly celebrated in the Rig Veda. Savitṛi is permanently the golden deity; being hiraṇyáksha, golden-eyed; *hiranya-hasta*, golden-handed, &c. Luminous in his aspect, he ascends a golden car, drawn by radiant, brown, white-footed horses; and beholding all creatures he pursues an ascending and descending path. Surrounded by a golden lustre, he illuminates the atmosphere and all the regions of the earth. His robust and golden arms, which he stretches out 10 bless, and infuse energy into all creatures, reach to the utmost ends of heaven. In one place, however, he is called *ayohanu*, the iron-jawed, though even. there the commentator says that *ayas*, which ordinarily means iron, is to be rendered by gold. His ancient paths in the sky are said to be free from dust. He is called (like Varuṇa and others of the gods) *asura*, a divine spirit. His will and independent authority cannot be resisted by Indra, Varuṇa, Mitra, Aryaman, Rudra, or by any other being. The other gods follow his lead. The waters and the wind obey his ordinance. His praises are celebrated by the Vasus, by Aditi, by the royal Varuṇa, by Mitra, and by Aryaman. He is lord of all desirable things, and sends blessings from the sky, from the atmosphere, and from the earth. He impels the car of the Aṣvins before the dawn. He is *Prajápati*, the lord of all creatures, the supporter of the sky and of the world, and is supplicated to hasten to his worshippers with the same eagerness as cattle to a village, as warriors to their horses, as a cow to give milk to a calf, as a husband to his wife. He is called viṣvadeva, "in all attributes a god." He measured (or fashioned) the terrestrial regions. He bestows immortality on the gods, as he did on the Ribhus, who by the greatness of their merits attained to his abode. He is prayed to convey the departed spirit to the abode of the righteous. He is supplicated to deliver his worshippers from sin.

Savitṛi is sometimes called *apamnapat*, son of the waters, an epithet which is more commonly applied to Agni.

The word Savitṛi is not always a proper name; but is sometimes used as an epithet.—*O.S.T.*, v, 164. **(2)** The "Vyása of the fifth Dwápara age.

SAVYASACIN—'Who pulls a bow with either hand.' A title of Arjuna.

SAYANA—Sāyaṇācārya, the celebrated commentator on the *Ṛgveda*. "He was brother of Mādhavācārya, the Prime Minister of Vīra Bukka Rāya, Rājā of Vijayanagara, in the fourteenth century, a munificent patron of Hindu literature Both the brothers are celebrated as scholars, and many important works are attributed to them; not only scholia on the Saṁhitās and Brāhmaṇas of the Vedas, but original works on grammar and law; the fact, no doubt, being that they availed themselves of those means which their situation and influence secured them, and employed the most learned brāhmaṇas they could attract to Vijayanagara upon the works which bear their name, and to which they also contributed their own labour and learning; their works were, therefore, compiled under peculiar advantages, and are deservedly held in the highest estimation."—*Wilson.*

SCMAPAS—A class of Pitris, "drinkers of the acid juice."

SENA or SEIN—Sometimes written Gandharva-Sena, or Gundrusein, a Gandharba who was condemned for an affront to Indra, to be born on earth in the shape of an ass, but on entreaty the sentence was mitigated, and he was allowed at night to re-assume the form and functions of a man. This incarnation took place at Ujein, in the reign of Rája Sundersein, Whose daughter was demanded in marriage by the ass; and his consent was obtained on learning the divine origin of his intended son-in-law, confirmed, as he witnessed, by certain prodigies. All day he lived in the stables like an ass; at night, secretly slipping out of his skin, and assuming the appearance of a handsome and accomplished young prince, he repaired to the palace and enjoyed the conversation of his beauteous bride.

In due time the princess became pregnant; and her chastity being suspected, she revealed to her father the mystery of her husband's happy nocturnal metamorphosis; which the Rája, being conveniently concealed, himself beheld; and unwilling that his son should return to his uncouth disguise, set fire to, and consumed, the vacant ass's skin.

Although rejoiced at his release, the Gandharba foresaw the resentment of Indra, disappointed of his vengeance; and warned his wife to quit the city, about to be overwhelmed with a shower of earth. She fled to a village at a safe distance, and brought forth a son, the celebrated *Vikramaditya*; and a shower of cold earth, poured down by Indra, buried the city and its inhabitants.—*As. Res.*, Vol. VI.

This legend gives a date to the catastrophe; for the prince, so renowned in his origin and birth, was not less so as a monarch and an astronomer; and his name marks an era much used all over India, commencing fifty-six years before our era.—Moor, *H.P.*, *p.* 262.

This story is supposed to be the original form of the 'Golden Ass' of Apuleius, which is in fact the story of Beauty and the Beast.

SENAJIT—One of the kings of Hastinápur, the son of Viswajit.

SENANI—One of the eleven Rudras according to the enumeration in the Matsya Purána.

SERPENTS—These are represented in the Vishṇu Purána as the progeny of Kadru, they are described as powerful and many-headed; and some as fierce and venomous. The chiefs are mentioned by name.

SESHA, SESA, ŚEṢA-NĀGA—Eternal matter in which Vishṇu reposes during the night of Bramhá when the destructive power only is in operation. It is represented as an immense snake, forming by its many coils, a bed on which Vishṇu sleeps, and with its thousand heads erect, to form a canopy over Vishṇu's head, and to present the idea of defence against any invasion of the sleeper's repose. *Sésha* is also said to support the eight elephants which support the world and sometimes as upholding the seven *pātālas* or hells.. The name Sésha is considered by Sir William Jones and others to designate abstract eternity, but the emblem does not altogether correspond with the Egyptian hieroglyphic used for this purpose. The literal meaning is primal serpent, and many of the Hindu legends introduce this snake. In the Puránas there is an account of a dispute between it and *Váyu*, regent of the wind. The latter blew with all his strength against the thousand peaks of Mount Meru, and Sásha covered every one of the peaks, each by one of his thousand heads. The sanctity of Tripiti, a hill in the north of Mysore is derived from a traditionally version of this legend. Váyu is said to have ceased blowing for a time when Sésha lifted up one head to ascertain the cause, and Váyu suddenly blew off the exposed peak, which was carried through the air and fell at Tripiti, conferring on the place the sanctity of Mount Meru. At the Seven Pagodas, near Madras, there is a good sculpture of Sésha in one of the hill caves. The subject is a favorite one with the Vaishnavas. Sir C. Wilkins thus describes one in the north of India, the rock of Ichangiri in the province of Behar. Among the images carved in relief in the surface of the rock, is one of *Hari*, (a title of Vishṇu) of gigantic dimensions, recumbent upon a coiled serpent, whose heads, which are numerous, the artist has contrived to spread into a kind of canopy over the sleeping god; and from each of its mouths issues a forked tongue, seeming to threaten instant death to any whom rashness might prompt to disturb him. The whole lies almost clear of the block on which it is hewn. It is finely imagined and is executed with great skill. The Hindus believe that at the end of every kalpa (creation) all things are absorbed in the deity, and that in the interval of another creation he reposeth himself upon the serpent Sésha (duration), who is also called *Ananta*, (endless), *q.v.*

"Sésha, worshipped by all the gods, supports the whole region of the earth like a diadem, and is the foundation of Pátáḷa. The Siddhantas, or scientific astronomical works of India, however, maintain that the earth is unsupported."—*O.S.T.*, Vol. IV, p. 96.

SESHA—One of the Prajápatis.

SETU-BANDHA—'Rāma's bridge.' The line of rocks between the continent and Ceylon called in maps "Adam's bridge". It is also know as Samudrāru. There is a poem called *Setubandha* or *Setu-kāvya* on the subject of the building of the bridge by Rāma's allies.

SIDDHANTA KAUMUDI—A modern and simplified form of Pāṇini's Grammar by Bhaṭṭojī Dīkṣita. It is in print.

SIDDHANTA, Any scientific work on astronomy or mathematics.

SIDDHANTASIROMANI. A work on astronomy by Bhāskarācārya. It has been printed, and has been translated for the *Bibliotheca Indica.*

SIDDHARTHA—A prince of the family of Ikshváku. He was king of Parana in Bharatakshetra when by supernatural agency he was made the father of the great Tírthankara Mahávíra, *q.v.*

SIDDHAS—Pure and holy beings, exempt from covetousness and concupiscence, love and hatred, taking no part in the procreation of living beings, and detecting the unreality of the properties of elementary matter. The Vishṇu Purána states that eighty-eight thousand of these chaste beings tenant the regions of the sky, north of the sun, until the destruction of the universe.

SIDDHI—Perfection; One of the daughters of Daksha, married to Dharma.

SIDDHIS—The eight perfections; 1, *Rasollása*, the spontaneous or prompt evolution of the juices of the body, independently of nutriment from without; 2, Tṛipti, mental satisfaction, or freedom from sensual desire; 3, Sámya, sameness of degree; 4, Tulyatá, similarity of life, form, and feature; 5, Viṣoká, exemption alike from infirmity or grief; 6, Consummation of penance and meditation, by attainment of true knowledge; 7, The power of going everywhere at will; 8, The faculty of reposing at any time or in any place. These attributes are alluded to, though obscurely, in the Váyu, and are partly specified in the Márkaṇḍeya Purána.

SIGHRA—A prince, the son of Agnivara, descendant of Kuṣa; Also a river.

SIKHANDIN, ŚIKHAṆḌINĪ—Śikhaṇḍinī is said to have been the daughter of Rājā Drupada, but according to another statement she was one of the two wives whom Bhīṣma obtained for his brother Vicitravīrya. "She (the widow) perished in the jungle, but before her death she had been assured by Paraśurāma that she should become a man in a future birth, and cause the death of Bhīṣma, who had been the author of her misfortunes." Accordingly she was born again as Śikhaṇḍin, son of Drupada. Bhīṣma fell in battle pierced all over by the arrows of Arjuna, but according to this story the fatal shaft came from the hands of Śikhaṇḍin. (*see* AMBĀ)

SIKHANDINI—The wife of Antarddhána, descendant of Prithu.

SIKSA—Phonetics; one of the Vedāṅgas. The science which teaches the proper pronunciation and manner of reciting the Vedas. There are many treatises on this subject.

SILPA-SASTRA—The science of mechanics; it includes architecture. Any book or treatise on this science.

SIMHALA, SIṀALA-DVĪPA—Ceylon. (now Sri Lanka)

SIMHASANA DVATRIMSAT—The thirty-two stories told by the images which supported the throne of King Vikramāditya. It is the *Singhāsan Battīsī* in Hindustānī, and is current in most of the languages of India.

SIMHIKA—**(1)** A daughter of Dakṣa and wife of Kaśyapa; also a daughter of Kaśyapa and wife of Vipracitti. **(2)** A *rākṣasi* who tried to swallow Hanumān and make a meal of him. He allowed her to do so and then rent her body to pieces and departed. Her habit was to seize the shadow of the object she wished to devour and so drag the prey into her jaws.

SINDHU—**(1)** The river Indus; also the country along that river and the people dwelling in it. From *Sindhu* came the *Hind* of the Arabs, the *Hindoi* or *Indoi* of the Greeks, and our *India.* **(2)** A river in Mālwa. There are others of the name. (*see* Saptasindhava) **(3)** A country near the forest of Káma. It was the Rája of Sindhu, Jayadrath, who visited Draupadi, in the absence of her husbands, and attempted to carry her away.

SINDHUDWIPA—One of the kings of Ayodhya, the son of Ambarísha.

SINHIKA—One of the daughters of Kaṣyapa, and wife of Vipra-chitti. She was the sister of the celebrated Danava Hiraṇyakaṣipu.

SINI—One of the Bhoja princes of Mrittikávati, the son of Sumitra.

SINIVALI—**(1)** The name of the day when the new moon is first visible; **(2)** One of the daughters of Angiras.

SIPRA—The river on which the city of Ujjayini stands.

SIPRAKA—The first Andhra king; and founder of the Andhra-bhritya dynasty. He had previously been minister to Suşarman, the last of the Kaṇwa kings of Magadha, against whom Siprak conspired, and assumed the sovereignty himself.

SIRADHVAJA—'He of the plough-banner.' An epithet for Janaka. king of Mithila, celebrated as the father of Síta.

SISIRA—A teacher of the Rig Veda.

SISUMARA—'A porpoise.' The planetary sphere, which, as explained by the *Viṣṇu Purāṇa*, has the shape of a porpoise, Viṣṇu being seated in its heart, and Dhruva or the pole star in its tail. "As Dhruva revolves, it causes the sun, moon, and other planets to turn round also; and the lunar asterisms follow in its circular path, for all the celestial luminaries are, in fact, bound to the polar star by aerial cords."

SISUNAGA—One of the kings of Magadha, who relinquished Benares to his son, and established himself at Girivraja, in Behar.

SISUPALA—The son of Damaghosha, king of Chedí. This prince was in a former existence the unrighteous but valiant monarch of the Daityas, Hiraṇyakaṣipu, who was killed by the divine guardian of the creation (in the man-lion Avatara.) He was next the ten-headed sovereign Rávaṇa, whose unequalled prowess, strength, and power, were overcome by the lord of the three worlds Ráma; when born again as Siṣupála, he renewed with greater inveteracy than ever, his hostile hatred towards the god surnamed Puṇdaríkáksha, a portion of the Supreme Being who had descended to lighten the burden of the earth, and was in consequence slain by him: but because his thoughts were constantly engrossed by the Supreme Being, Siṣupála was united with him after death; *V.P.* The death of Siṣupála is thus related in the Mahábhárata: "now the custom was at the beginning of a Rájasúya to declare who was the greatest and strongest of all the Rájas there assembled, in order that the Argha might be given to him; and Bhíshma, as ruler of the feast, declared that the honour was due to Krishṇa, who was the greatest and strongest of them all. But Siṣupála, the Rája of Chedí, was exceedingly wroth with Krishṇa, for when he was betrothed to the beautiful Rukminí, Krishṇa had carried her away and made her his own wife. So Siṣupala arose and threw the whole assembly into an uproar, and he said with a loud voice:—"If the honour be due to age, it; should have been given to Vaṣudeva; if it be due to him who has the greatest Raj, it should have be given to Rája Drupada; if it be due to the youth of loftiest mind, it should have been given to Rája Duryodhana; if it be due to the greatest preceptor, it should have been given to Drona; and if it be due to the greatest saint, it should have been given to Vyása: but shame be upon this assembly, who hath given that honour to a cowherd, who was the murderer of his own Rája." Having thus spoken, Siṣupála and his friends who were with him made a great tumult. Yudhishthira and Bhíshrna then reasoned with Siṣupála, but he would not heed their words, and drew his sword, and threatened to slay all the guests and spoil the sacrifice. Yudhishthira and his brethren then rose to fight against Siṣupála, but Bhíshma withheld them; and Siṣupála in his rage abused Bhíshma and Krishṇa in such opprobrious terms that the whole assembly was alarmed.. At last Krishṇa said:—"I have hitherto restrained my hand, because this man is my own kinsman, but I can bear with his words no longer." And thus speaking he whirled his chakra furiously at Siṣupála, and severed his head from his body; and Siṣupála fell dead upon the ground, and his sons carried away his body and burnt it upon the funeral pile. Thus Krishṇa saved the Rájasúya of Yudhishthira by the slaughter of Siṣupála; for had Rája Yudhishthira been set at defiance by a Rája who had not been conquered, the Rájasúya would have been imperfect and of no avail."

SISUPALA-VADHA—'The death of Siśupāla', an epic poem by Māgha, in twenty cantos. It has been often printed, and has been translated into French by Fauche.

SITA—'A furrow.' In the Veda, Sītā is the furrow, or husbandry personified, and worshipped as a deity presiding over agriculture and fruits. In the *Rāmāyaṇa* and later works she is daughter of .Janaka, king of Videha, and wife of Rāma. The old Vedic idea still adhered to her, for she sprang from a furrow. In the *Rāmāyaṇa* her father Janaka says, "As I was ploughing my field, there sprang from the plough a girl, obtained by me while cleansing my field, and known by name as Sītā (the furrow). This girl sprung from the earth grew up as my daughter." Hence, she is styled Ayonijā, 'not born from the womb'. She is said to have lived before in the *kṛta* age as Vedāvatī, and to be in reality the goddess Lakṣmī in human form, born in the world for bringing about the destruction of Rāvaṇa, the *rākṣasa* king of Laṅkā, who was invulnerable to ordinary means, but doomed to die on account of a woman. Sītā became the wife of Rāma, who won her by bending the great bow of Śiva. She was his only wife, and was the embodiment of purity, tenderness, and conjugal affection. She accompanied her husband in his exile, but was carried off from him by Rāvaṇa and kept in his palace at Laṅkā. There he made many efforts to win her to his will, but she continued firm against all persuasions, threats and terrors, and maintained a dignified serenity throughout. When Rāma had slain the ravisher and recovered his wife, he received her coldly, and refused to take her back, for it was hard to believe it possible that she had retained her honour. She asserted her purity in touching language, and resolved to establish it by the ordeal of fire. The pile was raised and she entered the flames in the presence of gods and men, but she remained unhurt, and the god of fire brought her forth and placed her in her husband's arms. Notwithstanding this proof of her innocence, jealous thoughts passed through the mind of Rāma, and after he had ascended his ancestral throne at Ayodhyā, his people blamed him for taking back a wife who had been in the power of a licentious ravisher. So, although she was pregnant, he banished her and sent her to the hermitage of Vālmīki, where she gave birth to twin sons, Kuśa and Lava. There she lived till the boys were about fifteen years old. One day they strayed to their father's capital. He recognised and acknowledged them and then recalled Sītā. She returned and publicly declared her innocence. But her heart was deeply wounded. She called upon her mother earth to attest her purity, and it did so. The ground opened, and she was taken back into the source from which she had sprung. Rāma was now disconsolate and resolved to quit this mortal life. (*see* Rāma) Sītā had the appellations of Bhūmijā, Dharaṇīsutā, and Pārthivī, all meaning 'daughter of the earth'.—*John Dowson*.

The daughter of Janaka, king of Mithila, (Síradhwaja.) She is called earth-born, as having been turned up from the soil by a plough, as Janaka was ploughing a spot to prepare for a sacrifice. She was promised in marriage to the Rája who could bend the great bow of Śiva; many distinguished Rájas attempted the feat, but could not succeed; "now when Ráma saw the bow he lifted it with one hand from the ground playfully, while a great multitude looked on in amazement. Then Ráma bent the bow till it broke in the midst, and the noise was like the crash of a falling mountain, so that the bystanders were stunned and fell down. After this Sítá was married to Ráma. The story of their honeymoon in the Rámáyana, is supposed to be an interpolation of recent date. When Ráma had to go into exile Sítá avowed her determination to accompany him to the jungle. Ráma objected to this, but at length yielded to her earnest entreaties. They met with many adventures in their jungle life which are described in great detail in the Rámáyana. They rested in the cave of the sage Atri, whose wife Anásúya gave Sítá an ointment to render her young and "beautiful for ever." On one occasion. she besought Ráma to pursue a beautiful deer, his brother Lakshmana remaining behind for her protection. Sounds of distress were heard as if proceeding from Ráma, and Sítá taunted Lakshmana with unconcern for his brother until he left her. Then Rávaṇa, by whose contrivance all this had come about, entered the hut as a brahman mendicant, assumed his true form, and addressed Sítá, who replied to him with anger, and Rávaṇa carried her off by force to Lanka, where she *was* discovered by Hanumán in the Asóka garden. While being carried by Rávaṇa through the air, which she filled with cries and lamentations, she saw five monkeys sitting in the mountain named Rishamukhá, and throws down her ornaments amongst them in the hope that they might find their way to Ráma. They were found by Sugríva and by him shown to. Ráma. Sítá wrathfully refused to receive the addresses of Rávaṇa, who threatened to slay her. She had an interview with Hanumán, and was finally rescued by Ráma; but had to pass through a severe ordeal before she was received as pure after being imprisoned in the palace of Rávaṇa. She entered the fire and the god Agni attested her purity. She was then installed as Rání with great splendour. She had two children Lava, and Kuṣa.—*John Garrett*.

SITEYUS—A prince, the son of Uṣanas, (*q.v.*).

SIVA—The name Śiva is unknown to the Vedas, but Rudra, another name of this deity, and almost equally common, occurs in the Veda both in the singular and plural, and from these the great deity Śiva and his manifestations, the Rudras, have been developed. In the *Ṛgveda* the word Rudra is used for Agni, and the Maruts are called his sons. In other passages he is distinct from Agni. He is lauded as "the lord of songs, the lord of sacrifices, who heals remedies, is brilliant as the sun, the best and most bountiful of gods, who grants prosperity and welfare to horses and sheep, men, women, and cows; the lord of nourishment, who drives away diseases, dispenses remedies, and removes sin; but, on the other hand he is the wielder of the thunderbolt, the bearer of bow and arrows, and mounted on his chariot is terrible as a wild beast, destructive and fierce." In the *Yajurveda* there is a long prayer called Śatarudriya which is addressed to him and appeals to him under a great variety of epithets. He is "auspicious, not terrible"; "the deliverer, the first divine physician"; he is "blue-necked and red-coloured, who has a thousand eyes and bears a thousand quivers"; and in another hymn he is called "Tryambaka, the sweet-scented enhancer of prosperity"; "a medicine for kine and horses, a medicine for men, and a (source of) ease to rams and ewes". In the *Atharvaveda* he is still the protector of cattle, but his character is fiercer. He is "dark, black, destroying, terrible". He is the "fierce god", who is besought to betake himself elsewhere, "and not to assail mankind with consumption, poison, or celestial fire". The Brāhmaṇas tell that when Rudra was born he wept, and his father, Prajāpati, asked the reason, and on being told that he wept because he had not received a name, his father gave him the name of Rudra (from the root *rud* 'weep'). They also relate that at the request of the gods he pierced Prajāpati because of his incestuous intercourse with his daughter. In another place he is said to have applied to his father eight successive times for a name, and that he received in succession the names Bhava, Sarva, Paśupati, Ugradeva, Mahādeva, Rudra, Īśāna, and Aśani. In the Upaniṣads his character is further developed. He declares to the inquiring gods, "I alone was before (all things), and I exist and I shall be. No other transcends me. I am eternal and not eternal, discernible and undiscernible, I am Brahma and I am not Brahma." Again it is said, "He is the only Rudra, he is Īśāna, he is divine, he is Maheśvara, he is Mahādeva." "There is only one Rudra, there is no place for a second. He rules this fourth world, controlling and productive; living beings abide with him, united with him. At the time of the end he annihilates all worlds, the protector." "He is without beginning, middle, or end; the one, the pervading, the spiritual and blessed, the wonderful, the consort of Umā, the supreme lord, the three-eyed, the blue-throated, the tranquil ... He is Brahmā, he is Śiva, he is Indra; he is undecaying, supreme, self -resplendent; he is Viṣṇu, he is breath, he is the spirit, the supreme lord; he is all that had been or that shall be, eternal. Knowing him, a man overpasses death. There is no other way to liberation". In the *Rāmāyaṇa* Śiva is a great god, but the references to him have more of the idea of a personal god than of a supreme divinity. He is represented as fighting with Viṣṇu, and as receiving worship with Brahmā, Viṣṇu, and Indra, but he acknowledges the divinity of Rama, and holds a less exalted position than Viṣṇu. The *Mahābhārata* also gives Viṣṇu or Kṛṣṇa the highest honour upon the whole. But it has many passages in which Śiva occupies the supreme place, and receives the homage and worship of Viṣṇu and Kṛṣṇa. "Mahādeva," it says, "is an all-pervading god yet is nowhere seen; he is the creator and the lord of Brahmā, Viṣṇu, and Indra, whom the gods, from Brahmā to the Piśācas, worship." The rival claims of Śiva and Viṣṇu to supremacy are clearly displayed in this poem; and many of those powers and attributes are ascribed to them which were afterwards so widely developed in the Purāṇas. Attempts also are made to reconcile their conflicting claims by representing Śiva and Viṣṇu, Śiva and Kṛṣṇa, to be one, or, as it is expressed at a later time in the *Harivaṁśa*, there is "no difference between Śiva who exists in the form of Viṣṇu, and Viṣṇu who exists in the form of Śiva".

The Purāṇas distinctly assert the supremacy of their particular divinity, whether it be Śiva or whether it be Viṣṇu, and they have developed and amplified the myths and allusions of the older writings into numberless legends and stories for the glorification and honour of their favourite god.

The Rudra of the Vedas has developed in the course of ages into the great and powerful god Śiva, the third deity of the Hindu triad, and the supreme god of his votaries. He is shortly described as the destroying principle, but his powers and attributes are more numerous and much wider. Under the name of Rudra or Mahākāla, he is the great destroying and dissolving power. But destruction in Hindu belief implies reproduction; so as Śiva or Śaṅkara, 'the auspicious', he is the reproductive power which is perpetually restoring that which has been dissolved, and hence he is regarded as Īśvara, the supreme lord, and Mahādeva, the great god. Under this character of restorer he is represented by his symbol the *liṅga*, or phallus, typical of reproduction; and it is under this form alone, or combined with the yoni, or female organ, the representative of his Śakti, or female energy, that he is everywhere worshipped. Thirdly, he is the *mahāyogī*, the great ascetic, in whom is centered the highest perfection of austere penance and abstract meditation, by which the most unlimited powers are attained, marvels and miracles are worked, the highest spiritual knowledge is acquired, and union with the great spirit of the universe is eventually gained. In this character he is the naked ascetic Digambara, 'clothed with the elements', of Dhūrjaṭi, 'loaded with matted hair', and his body smeared with ashes. His first or destructive character is sometimes intensified, and he becomes Bhairava, 'the terrible destroyer', who takes a pleasure in destruction. He is also Bhūteśvara, the lord of ghosts and goblins. In these characters he haunts cemeteries and places of cremation, wearing serpents round his head and skulls for a necklace, attended by troops of imps and trampling on rebellious demons. He sometimes indulges in revelry, and, heated with drink, dances furiously with his wife Devī the dance called *tāṇḍava*, while troops of drunken imps caper around them. Possessed of so many powers and attributes, he has a great number of names, and is represented under a variety of forms. One authority enumerates a thousand and eight names, but most of these are descriptive epithets, as Trilocana, 'the three-eyed', Nīlakaṇṭha, 'the blue-throated', and Pañcānana, 'the five-faced'. Śiva is a fair man with five faces and four arms. He is commonly represented seated in profound thought, with a third eye in the middle of his forehead, contained in or surmounted by the moon's crescent; his matted locks are gathered up into a coil like a horn, which bears upon it a symbol of the river Ganges, which he caught as it fell from heaven; a necklace of skulls (*muṇḍamālā*), hangs round his neck, and serpents twine about his neck as a collar (*nāga-kauṇḍala*); his neck is blue from drinking the deadly poison which would have destroyed the world, and in his hand he holds a *triśūla* or trident called Pināka. His garment is the skin of a tiger, a deer, or an elephant, hence, he is called Kṛttivāsas; sometimes he is clothed in a skin and seated upon a tiger-skin, and he holds a deer in his hand. His bull Nandì generally accompanies him. He also carries the bow Ajagava, a drum (*ḍamaru*) in the shape of an hourglass, the *khaṭvāṅga* or club with a skull at the end, or a cord (*pāśa*) for binding refractory offenders. His Pramathas or attendants are numerous, and are imps and demons of various kinds. His third eye has been very destructive. With it he reduced to ashes Kāma, the god of love, for daring to inspire amorous thoughts of his consort Pārvatī while he was engaged in penance; and the gods and all created beings were destroyed by its glance at one of the periodical destruction of the universe. He is represented to have cut off one of the heads of Brahmā for speaking disrespectfully, so that Brahmā has only four heads instead of five. Śiva is the great object of worship at Benares under the name of Viśveśvara. His heaven is on Mount Kailāsa.

There are various legends respecting Śiva's garments and weapons. It is said that "he once visited a forest in the form of a religious mendicant and the wives of the *ṛṣis* residing there fell in love with his great beauty, which the *ṛṣis*, perceiving, resented; in order, therefore, to overpower him, they first dug a pit, and by magical arts caused a tiger to rush out of it, which he slew, and taking his skin wore it as a garment; they next caused a deer to spring out upon him, which he took up in his left hand and ever after retained there. They then produced a red-hot iron, but this too he took up and kept in his hand as a weapon...The elephant's skin belonged to an *asura* named Gaya, who acquired such power that he would have conquered the gods, and would have destroyed the *munis* had they not fled to Benares and taken refuge in a temple of Śiva, who then destroyed the *asura*, and ripping up his body, stripped off the (elephant) hide, which he cast over his shoulders for a cloak."—*Williams.*

Other names or epithets of Śiva are Aghora, 'horrible; Babhru, Bhagavat, 'divine'; Candraśekhara, 'moon-crested'; Gaṅgādhara, 'bearer of the Ganges'; Giriśa, 'mountain lord'; Hara, 'seizer'; Īśāna, 'ruler'; Jaṭādhara, 'wearing matted hair'; Jala-mūrti, 'whose form is water'; Kāla, 'time'; Kālañjara; Kapālamālin, 'wearing a garland of skulls'; Mahākāla, 'great time'; Maheśa, 'great lord'; Mṛtyuñjaya, 'vanquisher of death'; Paśupati, 'lord of animals'; Śaṅkara, Śarva, Sadāśiva or Śambhu, 'the auspicious'; Śthānu, 'the firm'; Tryambaka, 'three-eyed'; Ugra, 'fierce'; Virūpākṣa, 'of misformed eyes'; Viśvanātha, 'lord of all'.

The third deity in the Hindu triad. Wilson says that Śiva is the same as Vishṇu in the character of destroyer of creation. He also personifies reproduction, as Hindu philosophy excludes the idea of total annihilation without subsequent regeneration. Hence he is sometimes identified with Brahmá the first person in the triad.

Śiva is the particular god of the Tantrikas, or followers of the books called Tantras. His worshippers are termed Saivas, and although not so numerous as the Vaiṣhnavas, exalt their god to the highest place in the heavens, and combine in him many of the attributes which properly belong to the other deities. According to them, Śiva is Time, Justice, Fire, Water, the Sun, the Destroyer and Creator. As presiding over generation, his type is the Linga, or Phallus, the origin probably of the Phallic emblem of Egypt and Greece. As the god of generation and of justice, which latter character he shares with the god Yama, he is represented riding a white bull. His own colour, as well as that of the bull, is generally white, referring probably to the unsullied purity of justice. His throat is dark-blue; his hair of a light reddish colours, and thickly matted together, and gathered above his head like the hair of an ascetic. He is sometimes seen with two hands, sometimes with four, eight, or ten, and with five faces. He has three eyes, one being in the centre of his forehead, pointing up and down. These are said to denote his view of the three divisions of time, past, present, and future. He holds a trident in his hand to denote, as some say, his relationship to water, or according to others, to show that the three great attributes of Creator, Destroyer, and Regenerator are combined in him. His loins are enveloped in a tiger's skin. In his character of Time, he not only presides over its extinction, but also its astronomical regulation. A crescent or half-moon on his forehead indicates the measure of time by the phases of the moon; a serpent forms one of his necklaces to denote the measure of time by years, and a second necklace of human skulls marks the lapse and revolution of ages, and the extinction and succession of the generations of mankind. He is often represented as entirely covered with serpents, which are the emblems of immortality. They are bound in his hair, round his neck, wrists, waist, arms, and legs; they serve as rings for his fingers, and earrings for his ears, and are his constant companions. Śiva has more than a thousand names, which are detailed at length in the sixty-ninth chapter of the Śiva Purána. The following list of the principal of these will give the best idea of his character and attributes. The auspicious one. The Lord of the Universe. The Destroyer, a personification of time that destroys all things. The Reproducer, the Conqueror of life and death, and Cause of life and being. The Disperser of the Tears of mortals."—*Williams.*

SIVA PURANA—(*see* PURĀṆA)

SIVA-UPA-PURANA—The Śiva Upa-puráṇa contains about six thousand stanzas, distributed into two parts. Sanatkumára relates it to Vyása and the Rishis at Naimisháraṇya; and its character may be judged of from the questions to which it is a reply. "Teach us," said the Rishis, "the rules of worshipping the Linga, and of the god of gods adored under that type: describe to us his various forms, the places sanctified by him, and the prayers with which he is to be addressed." In answer, Sanat-kumára repeats the Śiva Purána, containing the birth of Vishṇu and Brahmá; the creation and divisions of the universe; the origin of all things from the Linga; the rules of worshipping it and Śiva; the sanctity of times, places, and things, dedicated to him; the delusion of Brahmá and Vishṇu by the Linga; the rewards of offering flowers and the like to a Linga; rules for various observances in honour of Mahádeva; the mode of practicing the Yoga; the glory of Benares and other Saiva Tirthas; and the perfection of the objects of life by union with Maheswara. These objects are illustrated, in the first part, with very few legends; but the second is made up, almost wholly, of Saiva stories, as the defeat of Tripurásura; the sacrifice of Daksha; the births of Kárttikeya and Gaṇesa, (the sons of Śiva), and Nandi and Bhṛingaríti (his attendants) and others; together with descriptions of Benares and other places of pilgrimage, and rules for observing such festivals as the Śivarátri. This work is a Saiva manual, not a Purána.—*Wilson.*

SIVA—**(1)** The wife of the Rudra Iṣána; **(2)** The wife of Anila, (Wind.)

SIVAS—A class of deities in the third Manwantara.

SIVASKANDHA—One of the Andhra kings, the son of Sivasri Satakarni.

SIVASTI—Another of the Andhra kings.

SIVI—**(1)** Son of Uśīnara, and king of the country also called Uśīnara, near Gāndhāra. The great charity and devotion of Śivi are extolled in the *Mahābhārata* by the sage Mārkaṇḍeya. Agni having assumed the form of a pigeon, was pursued by Indra in the shape of a falcon. The pigeon took refuge in the bosom of Śivi, and the falcon would accept nothing from Śivi instead of the pigeon but an equal weight of the king's own flesh. Śivi cut a piece of flesh from his right thigh and placed it in the balance, but the bird was the heavier. He cut again and again, and still the pigeon drew the scale, until the king placed his whole body in the balance. This outweighed the pigeon and the falcon flew away. On another occasion Viṣṇu went to Śivi in the form of a brāhmaṇa and demanded food, but would accept no food but Śivi's own son Vṛhadgarbha, whom he required Śivi to kill and cook. The king did so, and placed the food before the brāhmaṇa, who then told him to eat it himself. Śivi took up the head and prepared to eat. The brāhmaṇa then stayed his hand, commended his devotion, and restoring the son to life, vanished from sight. **(2)** A Daitya, the son of Sanhráda; **(3)** The Indra of the fourth Manwantara.

SKAMBHA—The Supporter or Upholder; an appellation of the Supreme Being, In a hymn of the Atharva Veda, Skambha is considered like Purusha, as a vast embodied being co-extensive with the universe, and comprehending, in his several members, not only the different parts of the material world, but a variety of abstract conceptions, such as austere fervour (*tapas*,) faith,, truth, and the divisions of time. He is distinct from, and superior to, Prajápati, who founds the worlds upon him. The thirty-three gods are comprehended in him, and arose out of nonentity, which forms his highest member, and, as well as entity, is embraced within him. The gods who form part of him, as branches of a tree, do him homage, and bring him tribute. He is identified with Indra; and perhaps also with the highest Brahmá, who is mentioned in verses 32-34, 36, and in the first verse of the next hymn, x. 8, 1. In verse 36, however, this Brahmá is represented as being born (or, perhaps, developed) from toil and *tapas*, whilst in x. 8, 1, the attributes of the Supreme Deity are assigned to him. In compositions of this age, however, we are not to expect very accurate or rigorous thinking, or perfect consistency:—

> In Skambha are contained the worlds, austere fervour, and the ceremonial. Skambha, I clearly know thee to be contained entire in Indra. In Indra are contained the worlds, austere fervour, and the ceremonial. Indra, I clearly know thee to be contained entire in Skambha. When the Unborn first sprang into being, he attained to that independent dominion, than that which nothing higher has ever been. Reverence be to that greatest Brahmá, of whom the earth is the basis, the atmosphere the belly, who made the sky his head, of whom the sun and the ever-renewed moon are the eye; who made Agni his mouth, of whom the wind formed two of the vital airs, and the Angiras the eye, who made the regions his organs of sense. Skambha established both these [worlds], earth and sky, the wide atmosphere, and the six vast regions; Skambha pervaded this entire universe. Reverence to that greatest Brahmá, who, born from toil and austere fervour (*tapas*,) penetrated all the worlds, who made soma for himself alone. How is it that the wind does not rest ? How is not the soul quiescent ? Why do not the waters, seeking after truth, ever repose ? The great being [is] absorbed in austere fervour in the midst of the world, on the surface of the waters. To him all the gods are joined, as the branches around the trunk of a tree. Say who is that Skambha to whom the gods, with hands, feet, voice, ear, eye, present continually an unlimited tribute ? He dispels darkness; he is free from evil; in him are all the three luminaries that reside in Prajápati. He who knows the golden reed standing in the waters is the mysterious Prajápati.

Professor Goldstücker adds that Skambha "seems to mean the fulcrum of the whole world, in all its physical, religious, and other aspects. The object of the hymn being to inquire what this fulcrum is, from the answer given to the various questions it seems to follow that it is there imagined to be the primitive deity, or the *primitive* Veda, the word *brahman* in the neuter implying both. From this *primitive* Veda, not visibly but really (*sat*) existing, not only all the gods, worlds, religious rites, &c. were derived, but also the existing three Vedas and the Atharvan were 'fashioned.'"—*O.S.T.*, v, 384.

SKANDA—(1) A name of Kartikeya, the son of Śiva and Párvati, and the *Mars* of Hindu mythology. For the legend of his birth, son Kartikeya. In a note to the Megha Dúte, Professor Wilson writes, "Several instances of the solitary production of offspring occur in the Hindu as well as in the Grecian mythology. Thus as Pallas sprang from the brow of Jupiter, we have Skanda generated solely by the deity Śiva: Gangá, springs from the head of the same deity, and Ganesa is the self-born son of the goddess Párvati. The miraculous birth of the warrior deity, Skanda, was for the purpose of destroying Táraka, an Asura or demon, who, by the performance of continued and severe austerities, had acquired powers formidable to the gods. The exceubric genius of Southey has rendered it unnecessary, by his poem 'The curse of Kehâma,' for me to explain the nature or results of these acts of devotion. The germ of Skanda was cast by Śiva into the flame of Agni, the god of fire; who, being unable to sustain the increasing burden, transferred it to the goddess Gangá: she accordingly was delivered of the deity. Skanda; who was afterwards received and reared, among thickets of the Sara reed (Saccharum Sara), by the six daughters of a king, named Krittiká; or according to other legends, by the wives of seven great Rishis or Saints, In either case, they form in astronomy the asterism of the Pleisdes. Upon his coming to maturity, Skanda encountered and killed the demon, who had filled the reign of Indra with dismay:—

> *Emissumque imâ de sede Typhoëa terrâ,*

Cœlitibus fecisse metum.—Works IV, 353.

(2) The son of the Rudra Paṣupati, by his wife Swáha.

SKANDA PURANA—"The Skánda Purána is that in which the six-faced deity (Skánda) has related the events of the Tatpurusha Kalpa, enlarged with many tales, and subservient to the duties taught by Maheṣwara. It is said to contain eighty-one thousand one hundred stanzas: so it is asserted amongst mankind."

'It is uniformly agreed that the Skánda Purána, in a collective form, has no existence; and the fragments, in the shape of Sanhitás, Kháṇḍas, and Máhátmyas, which are affirmed, in various parts of India, to be portions of the Purána, present a much more formidable mass of stanzas than even the immense number of which it is said to consist. The most celebrated of these portions, in Hindustan, is the Háśí Kháṇḍa, a very minute description of the temples of Śiva in or adjacent to Benares, mixed with directions for worshipping Maheṣwara, and a great variety of legends explanatory of its merits and of the holiness of Káśí. Many of them are puerile and uninteresting; but some are of a higher character. The story of Agastya records, probably in a legendary style, the propagation of Hinduism in the south of India; and, in the history of Divodása, king of Káśí, we have an embellished tradition of the temporary depression of the worship of Śiva, even in its metropolis, before the ascendancy of the followers of Buddha. There is every reason to believe the greater part of the contents of the Káśí Kháṇḍa anterior to the first attack upon Benares by Mahmud of Ghizni. The Káśí Kháṇḍa alone contains fifteen thousand stanzas.—*Wilson.*

SLISHTI—One of the sons of the great sage Dhruva, by his wife Śambhu.

SMARTA—Appertaining to the Smṛti. The *Smārta-sūtras.* (*see* SŪTRAS)

SMAYA—Wonder. A son of Dharma.

SMIRTI—**(1)** 'What was remembered.' Inspiration, as distinguished from Śruti, or direct revelation. What has been remembered and handed down by tradition. In its widest application, the term includes the Vedāṅgas, the Sūtras, the *Rāmāyaṇa*, the *Mahābhārata*, the Purāṇas, the Dharmaśāstras, especially the works of Manu, Yājñavalkya, and other inspired law-givers, and the Nītiśāstras or ethics, but its ordinary application is to the Dharmaśāstras; as Manu says, "By Śruti is meant the Veda, and by Smṛti the institutes of law", II. 10. **(2)** One of the daughters of Daksha, married to the Muni Angiras; **(3)** The faculty of recognising all things, past, present, or to come.—*Wilson's* Notes to *Vishnu Purána.*

SMRITI-CANDRIKA—A treatise on law, according to the Drāviḍian or Southern school, by Devana Bhaṭṭa.

SMRITI—Tradition, as distinguished from Sruti, revelation. The Veda is regarded as revelation , and what is called the whole body of the law is regarded as tradition. "This distinction may be of some importance as an illustration of the national belief in inspiration; and it may throw some light on that era in the history of Sanskrit literature when inspiration was supposed to end and tradition to begin."* Mr. Max Müller makes a similar remark, and discusses the subject in his *History of Sanskrit Literature.* (* Talboys Wheeler)

SOKA—Sorrow: one of the children of Mritya (Death.)

SOMA—The juice of a milky climbing plant (*Asclepias acida*), extracted and fermented, forming a beverage offered in libations to the deities, and drunk by the brāhmaṇas. Its exhilarating qualities were grateful to the priests, and the gods were represented as being equally found of it. This sown juice occupies a large space in the *Ṛgveda*; one Maṇḍala is almost wholly devoted to its praise and uses. It was raised to the position of a deity, and represented to be primeval, all-powerful, healing all diseases, bestower of riches, lord of other gods, and even identified with the Supreme Being. As a personification, Soma was the god who represented and animated the *soma* juice, an Indian Dionysus or Bacchus.

The simple-minded Arian people, whose whole religion was a worship of the wonderful powers and phenomena of nature, had no sooner perceived that this liquid had power to elevate the spirits and produce a temporary frenzy, under the influence of which the individual was prompted to, and capable of, deeds beyond his natural powers, than they found in it something divine: it was to their apprehension a god, endowing those into whom it entered with godlike powers; the plant which afforded it became to them the king of plants; the process of preparing it was a holy sacrifice; the instruments used therefor were sacred. The high antiquity of this cult is attested by the references to it found occurring in the Persian Avesta; it seems, however, to have received a new impulse on

Indian Territory.—*Whitney.*

In later times, the name was appropriated to the moon, and some of the qualities of the *soma* juice have been transferred to the luminary, who is Oṣadhipati, or lord of herbs. So Soma is considered the guardian of sacrifices and penance, asterisms and healing herbs.

In the Puranic mythology Soma, as the moon, is commonly said to be the son of the *ṛṣi* Atri by his wife Anasūyā, but the authorities are not agreed. One makes him son of Dharma; another gives his paternity to Prabhākara, of the race of Atri; and he is also said to have been produced from the churning of the ocean in another *manvantara.* In the *Viṣṇu Purāṇa* he is called "the monarch of Brahmāns"; but the *Bṛhadāraṇyaka*, an older work, makes him a kṣatriya. He married twenty-seven daughters of the *ṛṣi* Dakṣa, who are really personifications of the twenty-seven lunar asterisms; but keeping up the personality, he paid such attention to Rohiṇī. the fourth of them, that the rest became jealous, and appealed to their father. Dakṣa's interference was fruitless, and he cursed his son-in-law, so that he remained childless, and became affected with consumption. This moved the pity of his wives, and they interceded with their father for him. He could not recall his curse, but he modified it so that the decay should be periodical, not permanent. Hence, the wane and increase of the moon. He performed the *rājasūya* sacrifice, and became in consequence so arrogant and licentious that he carried off Tārā, the wife of Bṛhaspati, and refused to give her up either on the entreaties of her husband or at the command of Brahmā. This gave rise to a widespread quarrel. The sage Uśanas, out of enmity to Bṛhaspati, sided with Soma, and he was supported by the *dānavas*, the *daityas*, and other foes of the gods. Indra and the gods in general sided with Bṛhaspati. There ensued a fierce contest, and "the earth was shaken to her centre". Soma had his body cut in two by Śiva's trident, and hence he is called Bhagnātmā. At length Brahmā interposed and stopped the fight, compelling Soma to restore Tārā to her husband. The result of this intrigue was the birth of a child, whom Tārā, after great persuasion, declared to be the son of Soma, and to whom the name of Budha was given: from him the Lunar race sprung.

According to the Purāṇas, the chariot of Soma has three wheels, and is drawn by ten horses of the whiteness of the jasmine, five on the right half of the yoke, and five on the left.

The moon has many names and descriptive epithets, as Candra, Indu, Śaśī, 'marked like a hare'; Niśākara, 'maker of night'; Nakṣatranātha, 'lord of the constellations'; Śītamārīci, 'having cool rays'; Sītānśu, 'havingwhite rays'; Mṛgāṅka, 'marked like a deer'; Śiva-śekhara, 'the crest of Śiva'; Kumudapati, 'lord of the lotus'; Śvetavājī, 'drawn by white horses'.

Reference has been already made to the important share which the exhilarating juice of the soma-plant assumes in bracing Indra for his conflict with the hostile powers in the atmosphere, and in the eagerness of all the gods to partake in this beverage.

Soma is the god who represents and animates this juice, an intoxicating draught which plays a conspicuous part in the sacrifices of the Vedic age. He is, or rather was in former times, the Indian Dionysus or Bacchus. Not only are the whole of the hymns in the ninth book of the Rig Veda, one hundred and fourteen in number, besides a few in other places, dedicated to his honour, but constant references to the juice of the Soma occur in a large proportion of the other hymns. It is clear therefore, as remarked by Prof. Whitney, that his worship must at one time, have attained a remarkable popularity. 'The simple-minded Arian people, whose whole religion was a worship of the wonderful powers and phenomena of nature, had no sooner perceived that this liquid had power to elevate the spirits, and produce a temporary frenzy, under the influence of which the individual was prompted to, and capable of, deeds beyond his natural powers, than they found in it something divine; it was to their apprehension a god endowing those into whom it entered with god-like powers; the plant which afforded it became to them the king of plants; the process of preparing it was a holy sacrifice; the instruments used therefore were sacred.'

With the decline of the Vedic worship however, and the introduction of new deities and new ceremonies, the popularity of Soma gradually decreased, and has long since passed away; and his name is now familiar to those few Brahmans only. who still maintain in a few places the early Vedic observances.

A great variety of divine attributes and operations are ascribed to Soma. 'He is addressed as a god in the highest strains of adulation and veneration; all powers belong to him; all blessings are besought of him as his to bestow.* In a passage where the joys of paradise are more distinctly anticipated and more fervently implored then in most other parts of the Rig

Veda, Soma is addressed AS the god from whom the gift of future felicity is expected.

Soma exhilarates Varuṇa, Mitra, Indra, Vishṇu, the Maruts, the other gods, Váyu, Heaven and Earth. Both gods and men resort to him saying that his juice is sweet, by him the Adityas are strong and the earth vast. He is the friend, helper, and soul of Indra, whom he succours in his conflicts with Vrittra. He rides in the same chariot with Indra, but has winged mares of his own and a team-like Váyu.—*O.S.T.*, v, 258-67.

In the post-Vedic age the name Soma came to be commonly applied to the moon and its regent, who is represented as the son of Atri; the monarch of the stars and planets, of brahmans and of plants, of sacrifices and of penance. The Vishṇu Purána has the following legend: Soma celebrated the Rájasúya (sacrifice); and, from the glory thence acquired, and the extensive dominion with which he had been invested, he became arrogant (and licentious,) and carried off Tárá, the wife of Bṛihaspati, the preceptor of the gods. In. vain Bṛihaspati sought to recover his bride; in vain Brahmá commanded, and the holy sages remonstrated: Soma refused to relinquish her. Uṣanas, out of enmity to Bṛihaspati, took part with Soma. Rudra, who had studied under Angiras, (the father of Bṛihaspati,) befriended his fellow-student. In consequence of Uṣanas, their preceptor, joining Soma, Jambha, Kujambha, and all the Daityas, Dánavas, and other foes of the gods, came also to his assistance; whilst Indra and all the gods were the allies of Bṛihaspati.

Then there ensued a fierce contest, which, being on account of Táraká (or Tárá,) was termed the Tárakámaya or Táraká war. In this, the gods, led by Rudra, hurled their missiles on the enemy; and the Daityas with equal determination assailed the gods. Earth, shaken to her centre by the struggle between such foes, had recourse to Brahmá, for protection; on which be interposed, and, commanding Uṣanas, with the demons, and Rudra, with the deities, to desist from strife, compelled Soma to restore Tárá to her husband. Finding that she was pregnant, Bṛihaspati desired her no longer to retain her burden; and, in obedience to his orders, she was delivered of a son, whom she deposited in a clump of long Munja-grass. The child, from the moment of its birth was endued with a splendour that dimmed the radiance of every other divinity; and both Bṛihaspati and Soma, fascinated by his beauty, claimed him as their child. The gods, in order to settle the dispute, appealed to Tárá; but she was ashamed, and would make no answer. As she still continued mute to their repeated applications, the child (became incensed, and) was about to curse her, saying:." Unless, vile woman, you immediately declare who is my father, I will sentence you to such a fate as shall deter every female, in future, from hesitating to speak the truth." On this, Brahmá again interfered, and pacified the child, and then, addressing Tárá, said: "Tell me, daughter, is this the child of Bṛihaspati or of Soma ?" "Of Soma," said Tárá, blushing. As soon as she had spoken, the lord of the constellations—his countenance bright, and expanding with rapture,—embraced his son, and said: "Well done, my boy ! Verily, thou art wise." And, hence, his name was Budha.

'He who knows.' Much erroneous speculation has originated in confounding this Budha, the son of Soma, and regent of the planet Mercury,—'he who knows,' 'the intelligent,'—with Buddha, any defied mortal, or 'he by whom truth is known;' or as individually applicable, Gautama or Śákya, son of Rája Śuddho-dana, by whom, the Buddhists themselves aver, their doctrines were first promulgated. The two characters have nothing in common; and the names are identical, only when one or other is misspelt. This Budha was the founder of the lunar race. The Brahmá Purána and Harivansa have a legend of the birth of Soma, the moon, from the Rishi Prabhákara of the race of Atri.—*Wilson.*

SOMA-PLANT—A plant constantly mentioned in the Vedic ritual, and corresponding to the Homa of the Zendavesta, but it is uncertain what plant was originally intended by the name. "It is described as 'a creeper, of a dark colour, sour, without leaves, milky, and pulpy externally; it causes phlegm and vomiting, and is a favourite food of goats,' see Müller, Zeitscher, d. D. M. G. ix. It is said to come from the north, and to be bought of barbarian tribes; but the soma of the 'Veda' is no longer known in India. Dr. Haug says that 'the plant at present used by the sacrificial priests of the Dekkhan is not the soma of the Vedas, but appears to belong to the same order. It grows on hills in the neighbourhood of Poona, to the height of about four or five feet, and forms a kind of bush, consisting of a certain number of shoots, all coming from the same root; their stem is solid like wood, the bark greyish, they are without leaves, the sap appears whitish, has a very stringent taste, is bitter but not sour; it is a very nasty drink, but has some intoxicating effect.' (*Ait. Br.*, Vol. II., p. 489). "The ceremonial writers allow the plant *putika*, Guilandina Bondue, to be used as a substitute for the soma. The Parsees of Bombay use the branches of a particular tree, obtained from Persia in a dried state."

In the Rig Veda the soma plant is said to have been brought to the earth by a falcon. In another passage it is declared to have been brought by the daughter of the Sun from the place where it had been nourished by Parjanya, the rain-god, when the Gandharvas took it and infused into it sap.

SOMADATTA—A king of Vaiṣálí, the son of Kriṣaswa. He is famed for his having celebrated ten times the sacrifice of a horse.

SOMADEVA BHAṬṬA—The writer or compiler of the collection of stories called *Kathā-sarit-sāgara.*

SOMAKA—(1) Grandfather of Drupada, who transmitted his name to his descendants. **(2)** One of the kings of Magadha, the son of Sahadeva.

SOMA-LOKA—(*see* LOKA)

SOMANATHA, SOMEŚVARA—'Lord of the moon.' The name of a celebrated *liṅgam* or emblem of Śiva at the city of Somnāthpattan in Gujarat. It was destroyed by Mahmūd of Ghaznī.

SOMA—One of the deities called Vasus, because they are always present in luminous irradiation.

SOMAPAS—'Soma-drinkers.' A class of *pitṛs* or manes who drink the *soma* juice, (*see* PITṚIS)

SOMASARMMAN—One of the Mauryan kings of Magadha.

SOMASUSHMAPANA—The Vyása of the twenty-third Dwápara age.

SOMA-TIRTHA—A place of pilgrimage in the west of India, on the coast of Guzerat, near the celebrated temple of Somanath, and town of Pattau Somanath. Its name is derived from the legend that Soma the moon, was there cured of the consumption brought upon him by the imprecation of Daksha, his father-in-law. The place is also called Prabhása.

SOMAVAMSA—(*see* CANDRAVAŚA)

SOMAYAJNA—Offerings and libations of the juice of the acid asclepias.

SONA—The Sone river rising in Mainíka or Amarakantak, and flowing east to the Ganges.

SONITAPURA—The city of Báṇa, considered to be the modern Devicotta in the Carnatic.

SRADDHA—(1) Faith, personified in the Vedas and lauded in a few hymns. **(2)** Daughter of the sage Dakṣa, wife of the god Dharma, and reputed mother of Kāmadeva, the god of love.

SRADDHA—An obsequial or funeral sacrifice; but it also implies offerings to the progenitors of an individual and of mankind, and always forms part of a religious ceremony on an occasion of rejoicing or an occasion of prosperity, this being termed the Abhyudaya or Vriddhi Sráddha.

"The offerings of the Hindus to the Pitris partake of the character of those of the Romans to the lares and manes, but bear a more conspicuous part in their ritual. They are said indeed by Manu to be of more moment than the worship of the gods. These ceremonies are not to be regarded as merely obsequial; for independently of the rites addressed to a recently deceased relative,—and, in connection with him, to remote ancestors, and to the progenitors of all beings,—which are of a strictly obsequial or funeral description, offerings to deceased ancestors, and the Pitris in general, form an essential ceremony, on a great variety of festive and domestic occasions. The Nirṇaya Sindhu, in a passage referred to by Mr. Colebrooks* specifies the following Sráddhas; 1, The Nitya, or perpetual; daily offerings to ancestors in general; 2, The Naimittika, or occasional; as the Ekoddishta, or obsequial offerings on account of a kinsman recently deceased; 3, The Kámya, voluntary: performed for the accomplishment of a special design; 4, The Vṛiddhi; performed on occasions of rejoicing or prosperity; 5, The Sapiṇḍana; offerings to all individual and to general ancestors; 6, The Párvaṇa Sráddha; offerings to the manes, on certain lunar days called Párvans, or day of full-moon and new-moon, and the eighth and fourteenth days of the lunar fortnight; 7, The Goshṭhí; for the advantage of a number of learned persons, or of an assembly of Brahmans, invited for the purpose; 8, The Śuddhi; one performed to purify a person from some defilement,—an expiatory Sráddha; 9, The Karmánga; one forming part of the initiatory ceremonies, or Samskáras. observed at conception, birth, tonsure, &c.; 10, The Daivika; to which the gods are invited; 11, The Yátrá Sráddha; held by a person going a journey; and, 12, The Pushṭi Sráddha; one performed to promote health and wealth. Of these, the four which are considered the most solemn are the rite performed for a parent, or near relative, lately deceased; that which is performed for kindred, collectively; that observed on certain lunar days; and that celebrated on occasions of rejoicing.

The following extract from Talboys Wheeler's *History of India*, Vol. II, gives a very complete view of this subject.

"The Sráddha, or feast of the dead, is perhaps one of the most primitive, as it certainly is one of the most simple, of all the Vedic rites that have been handed down from a period of remote antiquity to the present day. It originated in the crude idea already indicated, that the spirit or ghost had a separate existence after death, and that it might be gratified or propitiated with offerings of food. This idea certainly involved a belief in the prolonged existence of the spirit in a future state of being; but in its origin it had no connection with the doctrine of future rewards and punishments. It is rather to be traced to the old world belief, which has existed in all ages, and which still lingers in the imagination of even a philosophic and material generation, that the spirits of the departed hover at times near those persons and places which were associated with their earthly careers, and are gratified by any tribute of respect which may be paid to their memory.

The Sráddha, or feast of the dead, was thus in its earliest form a pleasing expression of natural religion, which long preceded the advent of a priestly caste, or the introduction of a systematic ritual. But, like every other popular ceremonial which has been handed down amongst the Hindus from the Vedic period, it has been recast in a Brahmanical mould; and it is in this latter form that the institution appears in the Epics as well as in the laws of Manu. It consists of three distinct rites:—

1st—The daily Sráddha, to be performed in propitiation of the Pitris, or ghosts of remote ancestors.

2nd—The monthly Sráddha, to be performed in propitiation of the more immediate paternal ancestors.

3rd—The funeral Sráddha, to be performed within a certain period after death, or the hearing of the death, of a near kinsman.

It should also be remarked that Sráddhas are likewise performed on other occasions, and notably at the celebration of any marriage ceremony.

The daily Sráddha was au offering either of boiled rice, or of milk, roots, and fruit, or of water only, to the Pitris, or remote ancestors. This ceremonial has been already described, and it will be only necessary to add that in modern practice it is considered sufficient to pour water out of a particular vessel every day as a drink offering to the Pitris.

The monthly Sráddha may be considered under four separate heads:—

1st—Ceremonies to be performed at a monthly Sráddha.

2nd—Persons to be entertained at the monthly Sráddha.

3rd—Persons to be excluded from the monthly Sráddha.

4th—Relative merits of the different kinds of victuals which may be offered at a monthly Sráddha.

The ceremonies at the monthly Sráddha, as described in the Institutes of Manu, are of a very intelligible character; and seem to have been laid down for the purpose of converting the old Vedic offering of food and water into a great feast to the Brahmans, The monthly Sráddha was performed on the dark day of the moon, that is, when the sun and moon are in conjunction. A sequestered spot was selected, such as was supposed to be pleasing to the ghosts; and then the invited Brahmans were conducted to their allotted seats, which had been purified with kusa grass, and were presented with garlands of flowers and sweet perfumes. The officiating Brahman then satisfied the three Vedic deities,—Agni, Soma, and Yama,—by pouring an oblation of ghee upon the sacred fire. He then proceeded to satisfy the ancestors of the giver of the Sráddha. He first sprinkled water on the ground with his right hand, and then formed three balls or cakes of boiled rice, which are called piṇḍas. One of these cakes is presented to each of the three immediate paternal ancestors, namely, the father, the grandfather, and the great-grandfather. The offering of piṇḍas, however, is said to be extended to the fourth, fifth, and sixth degrees of paternal ancestors in the ascending line, by the simple process of wiping the hand with kusa grass after offering the piṇḍas to the ancestors of the first, second, and third degree. This ceremony was followed by a great feast to the Brahmans, consisting of vessels filled with rice, together with broths, pot herbs, milk and curds, ghee, spiced puddings, milky messes of various sorts, roots of herbs, ripe fruits, and savoury meats; and during the feast, passages were read from the Sástras. The remains of the cakes were to be eaten by a cow, a Brahman, or a kid; or to be cast into water or fire; but the wife of the householder was to eat the middle of the three cakes, in order that she might become the mother of a son, who should be long-lived, famous, strong-minded, wealthy, and the father of many sons. When the Brahmans had duly feasted, the householder gave a feast to the kinsmen of his father, and afterwards to the kinsmen of his mother. In cases of poverty, however, the offering of water seems to be considered a sufficient satisfaction of the spirits of the six paternal ancestors.

As regards the persons to be invited to the monthly Sráddha, great stress is laid by the code upon the entertainment of learned Brahmans, and the exclusion of ignorant ones from the Sráddha; but it is added that if such learned Brahmans cannot be found, certain relatives may be entertained. This last expression is somewhat obscure, and may possibly imply that the Sráddha was originally eaten by the kinsmen, and that the introduction of learned Brahmans was a later idea.

Manu's catalogue of the persons who were to be excluded from a monthly Sráddha is of a very miscellaneous character; and is chiefly valuable from the illustrations which it furnishes of the Brahmánical notion of impure or immoral characters. The catalogue may be re-distributed under four general heads, according to the four different grounds upon which the individuals specified have been respectively excluded, namely, moral, religious, physical and professional.

The persons to be excluded from a Sráddha on moral grounds, are:—

"A Brahmachári who has not read the Veda; a Brahmán who has committed theft; one who opposes his preceptor; a younger brother married before the elder; an elder brother not married before the younger; one who subsists by the wealth of many relatives; the husband of a Súdra; the son of a twice-married woman; a husband in whose house an adulterer dwells; one who teaches the Veda for wages; one who gives wages to such a teacher; the pupil of a Súdra; the Súdra preceptor; a rude speaker; the son of an adulteress born either before or after the death of her husband; a forsaker of his mother, father, or preceptor without just cause; a man who forms a connection with great sinners; a house-burner; a giver of poison; an eater of food offered by the son of an adulterer; a suborner of perjury; a wrangler with his father; a drinker of intoxicating spirits; one of evil repute; a cheat; the husband of a younger sister married before the elder; an injurer of his friend; a father instructed in the Veda by his own son; one who diverts watercourses; a seducer of damsels; a man who delights in mischief; a Brahman living as a Súdra; one who observes neither approved customs nor prescribed duties; a constant and importunate asker of favours; one who is despised by the virtuous; the husband of a twice-married woman; a Brahman of bad manners; and an ignorant Brahman."

The persons to be excluded front a Sráddha on religious grounds, are:—

"Those who profess to disbelieve in a future state; a Brahman who has performed many sacrifices for other men; those who worship images for gain; one who deserts the sacred fire; one who omits the five great sacraments; a contemner of Brahmans; a despiser of scripture; and one who sacrifices only to the inferior gods.

SRADDHA-DEVA, ŚRĀDDHA-DEVA—Manu is called by the former name in the *Brāhmaṇas*, and by the latter in the *Mahābhārata*. The latter is commonly applied to Yama.

SRAUTA-SUTRA—(*see* Sūtra and Vedāṅgas)

SRAVASTI—An ancient city which seems to have stood near Faizābād in Oude.

SRI BHAGAVATA—(*see* Bhāgavata Purāṇa)

SRI HARSA—A great sceptical philosopher, and author of the poem called *Naiṣadha* or *Naiṣadhīya.* There were several kings of the name.

SRI HARSADEVA—A king who was author of the drama *Ratnāvalī.*

SRI—'Fortune, prosperity.' **(1)** The wife of Viṣṇu. (*see* Lakṣmī) **(2)** An honorific prefix to the names of gods, kings, heroes, and men and books of high estimation.

SRIDAMA CARITRA—A modern drama in five acts by Sāma Rāja Dīkṣita, on the sudden elevation to affluence of Śrī Dāman, a friend of Kṛṣṇa. It is not a good play, "but there is some vivacity in the thoughts and much melody in the style".—*Wilson.*

SRIDHARA SWAMI—Author of several commentaries of repute on the *Bhagavad Gītā, Viṣṇu Purāṇa*, &c.

SRI-SAILA The mountain of Śri, the goddess of fortune. It is a holy place in the Dakhin, near the Kṛṣṇa, and was formerly a place of great splendour. It retains its sanctity but has lost its grandeur. Also called Śrī-parvata.

SRIVATSA—A particular mark, said to be a curl of hair on the breast of Viṣṇu or Kṛṣṇa.

SṚNGA-GIRI—A hill on the edge of the Western Ghāṭs in Mysore, where there is a *maṭh* or monastic establishment of brāhmaṇs, said to have been founded by Śaṅkarācārya.

SṚNGARA TILAKA—'The mark of love.' A work by Rudra Bhaṭṭa on the sentiments and emotions of lovers as exhibited in poetry and the drama.

SṚNGAVERA—The modern Sungroor, a town on the left bank of the Ganges and on the frontier of Kosala and the Bhīl country. The country around was inhabited by Niṣādas or wild tribes, and Guha, the friend of Rāma, was their chief.

SṚUTA-BODHA—A work on metres attributed to Kālidāsa. It has been edited and translated into French by Lancereau.

SṚUTAKIRTTI—Cousin of Sītā and wife of Śatrughna.

SṚUTA ṚṢI—A *Ṛṣi* who did not receive the Śruti (revelation) direct, but obtained it at second-hand from the Vedic *ṛṣis*.

SṚUTI—'What was heard.' The revealed word. The *mantras* and *Brāhmaṇas* of the Vedas are always included in the term, and the Upaniṣads are generally classed with them.

SṚUTA—Belonging to the Śruti. (*see* ŚRUTI and SŪTRA)

STAYANETRA—A sage, one of the sons of Atri, according to the series in the Váyu.

STHALI-DEVATAS, DEVATĀS—Gods or goddesses of the soil, local deities.

STHANU—A name of Śiva.

STHĀPATYAVEDA—The science of architecture, one of the Upavedas.

STHUNA, STHUṆĀ-KARṆA—A *yakṣa* who is represented in the *Mahābhārata* to have changed sexes for a while with Śikhaṇḍinī, daughter of Drupada.

SUBAHU—'Five-armed'. **(1)** A son of Dhṛtarāṣṭra and king of Cedi. **(2)** A son of Śatrughna and king of Mathurā.

SUBALA—**(1)** A king of Gāndhāra, father of Gāndhārī, wife of Dhṛtarāṣṭra. **(2)** A mountain in Laṅkā on which Hanumān alighted after leaping over the channel.

SUBHADRA—Daughter of Vasudeva, sister of Kṛṣṇa and wife of Arjuna. Balarāma, her elder brother, wished to give her to Duryodhana, but Arjuna carried her off from Dvārakā at Kṛṣṇa's suggestion, and Balarāma subsequently acquiesced in their union. She was mother of Abhimanyu. She appears especially as sister of Kṛṣṇa in his form Jagannātha, and according to tradition there was an incestuous intimacy between them. When the car of Jagannātha is brought out the images of Subhadrā and Balarāma accompany the idol, and the intimacy of Jagannātha and Subhadrā is said to provoke taunts and reproaches.

SUBHANGI—'Fair-limbed.' An epithet of Rati, wife of Kāma, and of Yakṣi, wife of Kubera.

SUBHANU—Son of Kṛṣṇa and Satyabhāmā.

SUBODHINI—A commentary by Viśveśvara Bhaṭṭa on the law-book called Mitākṣarā.

SUBRAHMANYA—A name of Kārttikeya, god of war, used especially in the South, (*see* KĀRTTIKEYA)

SUCARU—A son of Kṛṣṇa and Rukmiṇī.

SUDARSANA—A son of Kṛṣṇa's *cakra* or discus weapon, (*see* VAJRANĀBHA)

SUDAS—A king who frequently appears in the *Ṛgveda*, and at whose court the rival *ṛṣis* Vasiṣṭha and Viśvāmitra are represented as living. He was famous for his sacrifices.

SUDESNA—'Good-looking.' **(1)** Wife of the Rājā of Virāṭa, the patron of the disguised Pāṇḍavas, and mistress of Draupadī; **(2)** Also the wife of Bālin.

SUDESNA—Son of Kṛṣṇa and Rukmiṇī.

SUDHARMA, SUDHAKMAN—The hall of Indra, "the unrivalled gem of princely courts", which Kṛṣṇa commanded Indra to resign to Ugrasena, for the assemblage of the race of Yadu. After the death of Kṛṣṇa it returned to Indra's heaven.

SUDRA—The fourth or servile caste. (*see* VARṆA)

SUDRAKA—A king who wrote the play called *Mṛcchakaṭi*, 'the toycart', in ten acts.

SUDYUMNA—Son of the Manu Vaivasvata. At his birth he was a female, Ilā, but was afterwards changed into a male and called Sudyumna. Under the curse of Śiva he again became Ilā, who married Budha or Mercury, and was mother of Purūravas. By favour of Viṣṇu the male form was again recovered, and Sudyumna became the father of three sons. This legend evidently has reference to the origin of the Lunar race of kings.

SUGRIVA, 'Handsome neck.' A monkey king who was dethroned by his brother Bālin, but after the latter had been killed, Sugrīva was re-installed by Rāma as king at Kiṣkindhā. He, with his adviser Hanumān and their army of monkeys, were the allies of Rāma in his war against Ravaṇa, in which he was wounded. He is said to have been son of the sun, and from his paternity he is called Ravinandana and by other similar names. He is described as being grateful, active in aiding his friends, and able to change his form at will. His wife's name was Rūmā.

The monkey chieftain in the Rishya-mukha mountain, who received Ráma and Lakshmana when they were trying to discover Síta, and showed her ornaments, which she had purposely dropped in her flight, to Ráma. He then related the story of his grievances against his brother Báli, and solicited Ráma's aid, Ráma had afforded evidence of his superhuman strength and skill.

"Then high Sugríva's spirit rose,
Assured of conquest o'er his foes.
With his new champion by his side,
To vast Kishkindhyá's cave he hied.
Then summoned by his awful shout.
King Báli came in fury out,
First comforted his trembling wife,
sought Sugríva in the strife.
One shaft from Ráma's deadly bow,
The monarch in the dust laid low.
Then Ráma bade Sugríva reign
place of royal Báli slain." —*Griffiths.*

When Báli was dying he acknowledged his fault, and asked his brother's forgiveness, commending his son Anga and his wife Tára to Sugríva's care. The latter, when reinstated on the throne at Kishkindhya invited Ráma and Lakshmana to live with him there. This invitation Ráma was unable to accept on account of his vow; but after the rainy season, Sugríva summoned his armies to assist Ráma in conquering the Rákshasas and recovering Síta. He marshalled his troops in four great divisions. The first he sent north under Vinata. The second, south, under various generals, especially Hanumán, and Jámbavat. The third, west, under Susheṇa. The fourth, east, under Sátabali,

When Hanumán returned with tidings that Síta was a prisoner in Lanka, Sugríva set forth at the head of his army to aid in effecting her deliverance. Sugríva was wounded by Rávaṇa, and afterwards suffered greatly from the wounds inflicted by the magical weapons of Indrajit, the brave son of Rávaṇa. Sugríva was restored by the medicinal herbs brought by Hanumán from Kailása. After the death of Rávaṇa, Sugríva accompanied Ráma and Lakshmana on their return to Ayodhya on the self-moving car Pushpaka (q.v.).

SUHMA—A country said to be east of Bengal.

SUKASAPTATI—'The seventy (tales) of a parrot.' This is the original of the Tūtīnāmaḥ of the Persian, from which the Hindustānī *Totā-kahānī* was translated.

SUKRA—The planet Venus and its regent. Śukra was son of Bhṛgu and priest of Bali and the *daityas* (*daitya-guru}*. He is also called the son of Ravi. His wife's name was Śuśumā or Śataparvā. His daughter Devayāṇī married Yayāti of the lunar race, and her husband's infidelity induced Śukra to curse him. Śukra is identified with Uśanas, and is author of a code of law. The *Harivaṁśa* relates that he went to Śiva and asked for means of protecting the *asuras* against the gods, and for obtaining his object he performed "a painful rite, imbibing the smoke of chaff with his head downwards for a thousand years". In his absence the gods attacked the *asuras* and Viṣṇu killed his mother, for which deed Śukra cursed him "to be born seven times in the world of men". Śukra restored his mother to life, and the gods being alarmed lest Śukra's penance should be accomplished, Indra sent his daughter Jayantī to lure him from it. She waited upon him and soothed him, but he accomplished his penance and afterwards married her. Śukra is known by his patronymic Bhārgava, and also as Bhṛgu. He is also Kavi or Kāvya, 'the poet'. The planet is called Āsphujit, Maghābhava, 'son of Maghā'; Ṣoḍasāṁśu, 'having sixteen rays'; and Sveta, 'the white'.

SUKTA—A Vedic hymn.

SU-MANTRA—The chief counsellor of Rājā Daśaratha and friend of Rāma.

SUMANTU—The collector of the hymns of the *Atharvaveda*; he is said to have been a pupil of Veda Vyāsa, and to have acted under his guidance.

SUMBHA and **NIŚUMBHA**—Two *asuras*, brothers, who were killed by Durgā. These brothers, as related in the *Mārkaṇḍeya Purāṇa*, were votaries of Śiva, and performed severe penance for 5000 years in order to obtain immortality. Śiva refused the boon, and they continued their devotions with such increased intensity for 800 years more, that the gods trembled for their power. By advice of Indra, the god of love, Kāma, went to them with two celestial nymphs, Rambhā and Tilottamā, and they succeeded in seducing the two *asuras* and holding them in the toils of sensuality for 5000 years. On recovering from their voluptuous aberration they drove the nymphs back to paradise and recommenced their penance. At the end of 1000 years Śiva blessed them "that in riches and strength they should excel the gods". In their exaltation they warred against the gods, who, in despair, appealed in succession to Brahmā, Viṣṇu, and Śiva, but in vain. The latter advised them to apply to Durgā, and they did so. She contrived to engage the *asuras* in war, defeated their forces, slew their commanders, Caṇḍa and Muṇḍa, and finally killed them. (*see* SUNDA)

SUMERU—The mountain Meru, actual or personified.

SUMITRĀ—Wife of Daśaratha and mother of Lakṣmaṇa and Śatrughna. (*see* DAŚARATHA)

SUMUKHA—'Handsome face.' This epithet is used for Garuḍa and for the son of Garuḍa.

SUNAHSEPHAS—The legend of Śunaḥśephas, as told in the *Aitareya Brāhmaṇa*, is as follows: King Hariścandra, of the race of Ikṣvāku, being childless, made avow that if he obtained a son he would sacrifice him to Varuṇa. A son was born who received the name of Rohita, but the father postponed, under various pretexts, the fulfillment of his vow. When at length he resolved to perform the sacrifice, Rohita refused to be the victim, and went out into the forest, where he lived for six years. He then met a poor brāhmaṇa *ṛṣi* called Ajīgartta, who had three sons, and Rohita purchased from Ajīgartta, for a hundred cows, the second son, named Śunaḥśephas, to be the substitute for himself in the sacrifice. Varuṇa approved of the substitute, and the sacrifice was about to be performed, the father receiving another hundred cows for binding his son to the sacrificial post, and a third hundred for agreeing to slaughter him. Śunaḥśephas saved himself by reciting verses in honour of different deities, and was received into the family of Viśvāmitra, who was one of the officiating priests. The Rāmāyaṇa gives a different version of the legend. Ambarīṣa, king of Ayodhyā, was performing a sacrifice when Indra carried off the victim. The officiating priest represented that this loss could be atoned for only by the sacrifice of a human victim. The king, after a long search, found a brāhmaṇa *ṛṣi* named Ṛcīka, who had two sons, and the younger, Śunaḥśephas, was then sold by his own consent for a hundred thousand cows, ten millions of gold pieces and heaps of jewels. Śunaḥśephas met with his maternal uncle, Viśvāmitra, who taught him two divine verses which he was to repeat when about to be sacrificed. As he was bound at the stake to be immolated, he celebrated the two gods Indra and Viṣṇu with the excellent verses, and Indra, being pleased, bestowed upon him long life. He was afterwards called Devarāta, and is said to have become son of Viśvāmitra. The *Mahābhārata* and the Purāṇas show some few variations. A series of seven hymns in the *Ṛgveda* is attributed to Sunaḥśephas. (*see* Muir's *Texts*, I. 355, 407, 413; *Viṣṇu Purāṇa*, IV. 25; Müller's *Sanskrit Literature*, 408; Wilson's *Ṛgveda*, 1.60.)

SUNAMAN—Son of Ugrasena and brother of Kaṁsa. He was king of the Śūrasenas. When Kaṁsa was overpowered in battle by Kṛṣṇa, Sunāman went to succour him, but was encountered and slain by Balarāma.

SUNANDA—A princess of Cedi who befriended Damayantī when she was deserted by her husband.

SUNDA—Sunda and Upasunda, of the *Mahābhārata*, were two *daityas*, sons of Nisunda, for whose destruction the *apsaras* Tilottamā was sent down from heaven. They quarrelled for her, and killed each other, (*see* Śumbha)

SUPARNAS—'Fine-winged'. "Beings of superhuman character, as Garuḍa, and other birds of equally fanciful description; one of those classes first created by the Brahmādikas, and included in the daily presentation of water to deceased ancestors, &c."—*Wilson.*

SUPARSVA—A fabulous bird in the *Rāmāyaṇa.* He was son of Sampāti and nephew of Jaṭāyus.

SUPRIYA—'Very dear.' Chief of the *gandharvas.*

SURA—A Yādava king who ruled over the Śūrasenas at Mathurā; he was father of Vasudeva and Kuntī, and grandfather of Kṛṣṇa.

SURA—Wine or spirituous liquor, personified as Surādevī, a goddess or nymph produced at the churning of the ocean.

SURABHI—The 'cow of plenty', produced at the churning of the ocean, who granted every desire, and is reverenced as "the fountain of milk and curds", (*see* Kāmadhenu and Nandinī)

SURAS—In the Vedas, a class of beings connected with Sūrya, the sun. The inferior deities who inhabit *svarga*; a god in general. According to some, the word is allied to *svar*, 'heaven'; others think it to have sprung from the derivation assigned to *asura*, and as *asura* is said to signify 'not a god', sura has come to mean 'god'.

SURASA—A *rākṣasī*, mother of the Nāgas. When Hanumān was on his flight to Laṅkā against Rāvaṇa, she tried to save her relative by swallowing Hanumān bodily. To avoid this Hanumān distended his body and continued to do so, while she stretched her mouth till it was a hundred leagues wide. Then he suddenly shrank up to the size of a thumb, darted through her, and came out at her right ear.

SURASENAS—Name of a people, the Śūraseni of Arrian. Their capital was Mathurā on the Yamunā, which Manu calls Śūrasena.

SURPANAKHA—'Having nails like winnowing-fans.' Sister of Rāvaṇa. This *rākṣasī* admired the beauty of Rāma and fell in love with him. When she made advances to Rāma he referred her to Lakṣmaṇa, and Lakṣmaṇa in like manner sent her back to Rāma. Enraged at this double rejection, she fell upon Sītā, and Rāma was obliged to interfere forcibly for the protection of his wife. He called out to Lakṣmaṇa to disfigure the violent *rākṣasī*, and Lakṣmaṇa cut off her nose and ears. She flew to her brothers for revenge, and this brought on the war between Rāma and Rāvaṇa. She descanted to Rāvaṇa on the beauty of Sītā, and instigated his carrying her off, and finally she cursed him just before the engagement in which he was killed.

SURYA SINDDHĀNTA—A celebrated work on astronomy, said to have been revealed by the sun (Sūrya). It has been edited in the *Bibliotheca Indica* by Hall, and there are other editions. It has been translated by Whitney and Burgess.

SURYA—The sun or its deity. He is one of the three chief deities in the Vedas, as the great source of light and warmth, but the references to him are more poetical than precise. Sometimes he is identical with Savitṛ and Āditya, sometimes he is distinct. "Sometimes he is called son of Dyaus, sometimes of Aditi. In one passage, Uṣas, the dawn, is his wife, in another he is called the child of the dawns; he moves through the sky in a chariot drawn by seven ruddy horses or mares." Sūrya has several wives, but, according to later legends, his twin sons the Aśvins, who are ever young and handsome and ride in a golden car as precursors of Uṣas, the dawn, were born of a nymph called Aśvinī, from her having concealed herself in the form of a mare. the In *Rāmāyaṇa* and Purāṇas, Sūrya is said to be the son of Kaśyapa and Aditi, but in the *Rāmāyaṇa* he is otherwise referred to as a son of Brahmā. His wife was Saṁjñā, daughter of Viśvakarmā, and by her he had three children, the Manu Vaivasvata, Yama, and the goddess Yamī, or the Yamunā river. His effulgence was so overpowering that his wife gave him Chāyā (shade) for a handmaid, and retired into the forest to devote herself to religion. While thus engaged, and in the form of a mare, the sun saw her and approached her in the form of a horse. Hence, sprang the two Aśvins and Revanta. Sūrya brought back his wife Saṁjñā to his home, and her father, the sage Viśvakarmā, placed the luminary on his lathe and cut away an eighth of his effulgence, trimming him in every part except the feet. The fragments that were cut off fell blazing to the earth, and from Viśvakarmā formed the discus of Viṣṇu, the trident of Śiva, the weapon of Kubera, the lance of Kārttikeya, and the weapons of the other gods. According to the *Mahābhārata*, Karṇa was his illegitimate son by Kuntī. He is also fabled to be the father of Śani and the monkey chief Sugrīva. The Manu Vaivasvata was father of Ikṣvāku, and from him, the grandson of the sun, the Sūryavaṁśa, or Solar race of kings, draws its origin. In the form of a horse Sūrya communicated the White *Yajurveda* to Yājñavalkya, and it was he who bestowed on Satrājit the *syamantaka* gem. A set of terrific *rākṣasas* called Mandehas made an attack upon him and sought to devour him, but were dispersed by his light. According to *Viṣṇu Purāṇa* he was seen by Satrājit in "his proper form", "of dwarfish stature, with a body like burnished copper, and with slightly reddish eyes". Sūrya is represented in a chariot drawn by seven horses, or a horse with seven heads, surrounded with rays. His charioteer is Aruna or Vivasvat, and his city Vivasvatī or Bhāsvatī. There are temples of the sun, and he receives worship. The names and epithets of the sun are numberless. He is Savitṛ, 'the nourisher'; Vivasvat, 'the brilliant'; Bhāskara, 'light-maker'; Dinakara, 'day-maker'; Arhapati, 'lord of day'; Lokacakṣuh, 'eye of the world'; Karmasākṣī, 'witness of the deeds (of men)'; Graharāja, 'king of the constellations'; Gabhastimān, 'possessed of rays'; Sahasrakiraṇa, 'having a thousand rays'; Vikarttana, 'shorn of his beams' (by Viśvakarmā); Mārtaṇḍa, 'descended from Mṛtaṇḍa'; &c. Sūrya's wives are called Savarṇā, Swātī, and Mahāvīryā.

The mythical ancestor of the Rájas of Koṣala, This deity seems, "under different names to have always held a high place amongst the primitive gods of every nation, by virtue of its prominence in the heavens and the extent to which its influence is felt upon earth. Its daily course and its annual course, its welcome rising in the morning, and its glorious setting in the evening, must all have excited the keenest curiosity amongst a child-like and inquisitive people; and at the same time, the imagination was left to account for the existence of phenomena which in a non-scientific age, are altogether beyond human ken. Thus it seems extremely probable that one of the earliest efforts of poetical genius was to personify the sun as the deity of light, travelling through the blue ether in a golden chariot which all men might see, drawn however by steeds which were invisible to the outward eye, but which were easily assumed to be white, resplendent, and beautiful beyond expression. In the Vedas the attributes of this deity are frequently the same as those of Agni, especially that of originating and diffusing light; but still the sun stands forward as a deity altogether distinct; from Fire, when described as journeying through the firmament in an upward and downward course, and especially in his character of measuring days and nights. This god is apparently addressed under a variety of names—but in the Epics he is chiefly known by the name of Súrya, and was regarded as the great ancestor of the solar race who appear in the Rámáyana."—*Wheeler.*

1. By lustrous heralds led on high,
The omniscient Sun ascends the sky,
His glory drawing every eye.
2. All-seeing Sun, the stars so bright,
Which gleamed throughout the sombre night,
Now scared, like thieves, slink fast away,
Quenched by the splendour of thy ray.
3. Thy beams to men thy presence shew;
Like blazing fires they seem to glow.
4. Conspicuous, rapid, source of light,
Thou makest all the welkin bright.
5. In sight of gods, and mortal eyes,
In sight of heaven thou scal'st the skies.
6. Bright god, thou scann'st with searching ken
The doings all of busy men.
7. Thou stridest o'er the sky; thy rays
Create, and measure out, our days;
Thine eye all living things surveys.
8. Seven lucid mares thy chariot bear,
Self-yoked athwart the fields of air,
Bright Súrya, god with flaming hair.
10. That glow above the darkness we
Beholding, upward soar to thee,
For there among the gods thy light
Supreme is seen, divinely bright.

—*O.S.T.*, v. 160.

SURYA-KĀNTA—'The sun-gem.' A crystal supposed to be formed of condensed rays of sun, and though cool to the touch, to give out heat in the sun's rays. There is a similar moonstone. It is also called Dahanopala. (*see* CANDRAKĀNTA)

SURYAVAMSA—The Solar race. A race or lineage of kṣatriyas which sprang from Ikṣvāku, grandson of the sun. Rāma was of this race, and so were many other great kings and heroes. Many Rājpūts claim descent from this and the other great lineage, the Lunar race. The Rāṇā of Udaypur claims to be of the Sūryavaṁśa, and the Jhārejas of Cutch and Sindh assert a descent from the Candravaṁśa. There were two dynasties of the Solar race. The elder branch, which reigned at Ayodhyā, descended from Ikṣvāku through his eldest son, Vikukṣ.. The other dynasty, reigning at Mithilā, descended from another of Ikṣvāku's sons, named Nimi. The lists of these two dynasties on the opposite page are taken from the *Viṣṇu Purāṇa*. The lists given by other authorities show some discrepancies, but they agree in general as to the chief names.

SUSANDHI—A prince, the son of Prasuṣruta, a descendant of Kusa.

SU-SARMAN—The Rája of Trigarta. He proposed to the Kauravas to invade the kingdom of Viráta. After the plan of the campaign had been decided on, he challenged the Rája Viráta to single combat, defeated and captured him. Susannas was afterwards taken prisoner himself by Bhíma. In the great war he and his four brothers challenged Arjuna to battle in the first day of Drona's command. The five brothers were vanquished by Arjuna; on the following day Susarman sent a second challenge to Arjuna to fight in the southern quarter of the plain; Arjuna accepted the challenge, and it was during his absence on this occasion that his son, the young and heroic Abhimanyu was slain.

SUSENA—**(1)** One of the sons of Vasudeva, who was killed by Kansa; **(2)** The son of Vrishṇimat, of the race of Puru; **(3)** One of the sons of Krishṇa by his wife Rukminí; **(4)** A distinguished physician in the Rámáyana, who restored the dead monkeys to life by herbs brought from the Himálaya mountains.

SUSHNA—A name of Vrittra, the demon who personifies drought, and is also called Ahi.

"The lightnings then began to flash,
The direful thunderbolts to crash,
By Indra proudly hurled.
The gods themselves with awe were stilled
And stood aghast; and terror filled
The universal world.

* * *

Now bound by Šushça's spell no more,
The clouds discharge their liquid store;
And long by torrid sunbeams baked,
The plains by copious showers are slaked;
The rivers swell and sea-wards sweep
Their turbid torrents broad and deep.
The peasant views with deep delight,
And thankful heart, the auspicious sight,
His leafless fields so sere and sad,
Will soon with waving crops be clad,
And mother earth now brown and bare,
A robe of brilliant green will wear."

—*O.S.T.*, Vol. v, p. 135

SUSENA—An asura mentioned in the *Ṛgveda* as killed by Indra.

SUSHUMNA—One of the seven principal rays of the sun; that which supplies heat to the moon.

SUSRAVAS—One of the Prajápatis, according to the enumeration in the Váyu Purána.

SUSRUTA—A medical writer whose date is uncertain, but his work was translated into Arabic before the end of the eighth century. The book has been printed at Calcutta. There is a Latin translation by Hepler and one in German by Vullers.

SUTA—'Charioteer.' A title given to Karṇa. A generic term for chroniclers and bards. The bard and herald of the Hindus, being attached to the state of all men of rack to chant their praises, celebrate their actions, and commemorate their ancestry. Also the name of a celebrated pupil of Vyása, from whom he learned many historical and legendary traditions. It was to Súta that the great Muni communicated the Puránas. Súta bad himself six scholars who acquired distinction.

SUTALA—One of the seven divisions of Pátáḷa, that with a stony soil, but embellished with magnificent palaces.

SUTANU——One of the five daughters of Ugrasena.

SUTAPAS—One of the seven pure sages according to the enumeration in the Vishṇu Pnrána, sons of the great sage Vaíahtha.

SUTAPAS—A class of deities of the eighth Manwantara.

SUTARA—The daughter of Swaphalka.

SUSTI—A goddess, who is propitiated with offerings when children are troublesome. When the infant Ráma cried for the moon and could not be quieted, it was said the goddess Sustí was unpropitious.

SUTIKSNA—An ascetic who figures in the Rámáyana, as of extraordinary merit on account of his austerities. When Ráma and Síta visited him in his hermitage in the forest they found him covered with mud, and his head covered with matted hair; his body reduced to bones and skin. He was absorbed in profound forgetfulness of all things earthly; but when Ráma paid his respects the sage at once embraced him, and bestowed his blessings on him.

SUTODHANA—'Fair fighter,' A name of Duryodhana.

SUTRA—"(From the Sanscrit *siv, to* sew, literally, therefore, a thread or string) is, in Sanscrit Literature, the technical name of aphoristic rules, and of works consisting of such rules. The importance of the term will be understood from the fact, that the *groundworks* of the whole ritual, grammatical, metrical, and philosophical literature of India are written in such aphorisms, which therefore constitute one of the peculiarities of Hindu authorship. The object of the Sútras is extreme brevity; and, especially in the oldest works of this class, this brevity is carried to such an excess, that even the most experienced would find it extremely difficult, and sometimes impossible, to understand these aphorisms without the aid of commentaries, which, however, are fortunately never wanting, wherever a work is written in this style. Though there is no positive evidence as to the cause or causes which gave rise to this peculiarity of Hindu composition, the method of teaching in ancient India—an account of which is afforded is some of the oldest works—renders it highly probable that these Sútras were intended as memorial sentences which the pupil had to learn by heart, in order better to retain the fuller oral explanation which his teacher appended to them. But it is likewise probable that this method of instruction itself originated in the scarcity or awkwardness of the writing material used, and in the necessity, therefore, of economising this material as much as possible; for that writing was known and practiced at the remotest period of Hindu antiquity, is now placed beyond a doubt, though a startling theory was propounded, some years ago, to the effect that writing was unknown in India, even at the time of the great grammarian Paṇini. The manner, however, in which up to this day, the Hindus are in the habit of keeping the leaves of their books together, seems to throw some light on (he name given to this aphoristic literature. The leaves—generally narrow, and even at the present time often being dried palm leaves, on which the words are either written with ink or scratched with a style—are piled up, and, according to the length of the leaves, pierced in one or two places, when, through the hole or holes, one or two long *strings* are passed to keep them together. The name of Sútra was probably, therefore, applied to works, not because they represent a thread or string of rules, but on account of the manner in which these works were rendered fit for practical use; just as in German a volume is called *Band*, from its being 'bound.' That a habit deeply rooted outlives necessity, is probably also shewn of these Sútra works; for while the oldest works of this class may be called Sútras by necessity, there are others which convey the suspicion that they merely imitated the Sútra style after the necessity had passed away, more especially as they do not adhere to the original brevity of the oldest Sútras; and the Sútras of the Buddhists, conspicuous for their prolixity, could scarcely lay claim to the term, if compared with the Sútra of the Brahmánical literature."—*Goldstücker.*

The Sútra period of Sanscrit literature is fixed by Max Müller at from 600 to 200, B. C., the characteristic of the period is that the Brahmánical writers used very curt and dry sentences, or Sútras, for expressing their thoughts. Numerous Sútra works by different authors are still extant, among which the Vyákarna Sútras of Pâṇini, and the Vedánta Sútras of Vyása, occupy a prominent place.

There are *sūtras* upon almost every subject, but "the *sūtras*" generally signify those which are connected with the Vedas, *viz.*, the *Kalpa sūtras*, relating to ritual; the *Gṛhya Sūtras*, to domestic rites; and the *Sāmayacārika Sūtras*, to conventional usages. The *Kalpa Sūtras*, having especial reference to the Veda or Śruti, are called Śrauta; the others are classed as Smārta, being derived from the Smṛti. The *sūtras* generally are anterior to Manu, and are probably as old as the sixth century B.C. Several have been published in the *Bibliotheca Indica.*

SUTTEE—"(An English corruption from the Sanscrit *sail*, a virtuous wife) means the practice which prevailed in India, of a wife burning herself on the funeral pile, either with the body of her husband, or separably, if he died at a distance.

The practice of Suttee is based by the orthodox Hindus on the injunctions of their Sástras, or sacred books, and there can be no doubt that various passages in their Puránas (*q.v.*,) and codes of law *countenance* the belief which they entertain of its meritori-ous-ness and efficacy. Thus, the *Brahmá-Purána* says: 'No other way is known for a virtuous woman after the death of her husband; the separate cremation of her husband would be lost (to all religious intents). If her lord die in another country, let the faithful wife place his sandals on her breast, and, pure, enter the fire. The faithful widow is pronounced no suicide by the recited text of the Rig Veda.' Or the code of *Vyâsa*; 'Learn the power of that widow who, learning that her husband has deceased, and been burned in another region, speedily casts herself into the fire,' &e. Or the code of *Angiras:* 'That woman, who, on the death of her husband, ascends the same burning pile with him, is exalted to heaven, as equal in virtue to Arundhati (the wife of Vaṣishtha). She who follows her husband (to another world) shall dwell in a region of joy for so many years as there are hairs on the human body, or 35 millions. As a serpent-catcher forcibly draws a sneke from his hole, thus drawing her lord (from a region of torment), she enjoys delight together with him. The woman who follows her husband to the pile expiates the sins of three generations on the paternal and maternal side of that family to which she was given as a virgin—No other effectual duty is known for virtuous women, at any time after the death of their lords, except casting themselves into the same fire. As long as a woman (*in.* her successive transmigrations) shall decline burning herself, like a faithful wife on the same fire with her deceased lord, so long shall she be not exempted from springing again to life in the body of some female animal. When their lords have departed at the fated time of attaining heaven, no other way but entering the same fire is known for women whose virtuous conduct and whose thoughts have been devoted to their husbands, and who fear the dangers of separation.' But however emphatically these and similar passages recommend a wife to burn herself together with her deceased husband, it should, in the first place, be observed, that *Manu*, who, among legislators of ancient India, occupies the foremost rank, contains no words which enjoin, or even would seem to countenance, this cruel practice; and, secondly, that no injunction of any religious work is admitted by the orthodox Hindus as authoritative, unless it can show that it is taken from, or based on, the revealed books, the. Vedas. An attempt has of late years been made by Rája Râdhâkant Deb, to show that, in a text belonging to a particular school of the Black Yajurveda, there is really a passage which would justify the practice of suttee; but in the controversy which ensued on. this subject between him and the late Professor H. H.

Wilson, it clearly transpired that the text cited by the learned Rája is of any thing but indubitable canonicity; moreover, that there is a verse in the Rig Veda which, if properly read, would enjoin a widow not to burn herself, but, after having attended the funeral ceremonies of her husband, to return to her home, and to fulfil her domestic duties; and it seems, at the same time, that merely from a misreading of a single word of this verse from the Rig Veda, that interpretation, arose which ultimately led to a belief and an injunction so disastrous in their results. That an immense number of widows have fallen victims to this erroneous interpretation of the oldest Vedic text, is but too true. Some thirty years ago, however, the East India Company took energetic measures to suppress a practice which it was perfectly justified in looking upon as revolting to all human feelings, and which it would have likewise been entitled to consider as contrary to the spirit of the Vedic religion. This practice may now be said to have been successfully stopped; for though, from habit and superstition, even now-a-days cases of suttee occur, they are extremely rare; and all reports agree that the enlightened natives everywhere, except, perhaps, in certain native states, support the action of government to repress this evil of bygone times.—Chambers' *Encyclopedia.*

SUTUDRI—The river Satluj. (*see* ŠATADRU)

SUVAHU—A *ràksasa*, son of Tàrakà. He was killed by Ràma.

SUVALA—A king of Magadha, the son of Sumati.

SUVAMA—The beautiful river; identified by Wilford with the Ram-gangá.

SUVARNA—A prince, the son of Antaríksha, of the family of Ikshváku.

SUVÀRNAROMAN—One of the kings of Mithila, the son of Maharoman.

SUVELA—One of the three peaks of the mountain Trikùta, on the midmost of which the city of Lankà was built.

SUVIBHU—One of the Kasya princes, the sixth in descent from Alàrka, rája of Benares.

SUVIRA—**(1)** One of the sons of Sivi; **(2)** One of the Kaurava princes, the son of Kshemya.

SUVRATA-SUYASAS—One of the kings of A king of Magadha, whose reign is said to have lasted 60 years: he was the son of Rája Kshemya. Magadha, son of the Buddhist king Asokavarddhana, (*q.v.*)

SUYODHANA—A name sometimes given (euphemistically) to Duryodhana, the eldest of the hundred sons of Dhritaráshtra, and who as the representative of the others is painted in the darkest colours, and embodies all their bad qualities. Many Hindus regard him as the visible type of vice, or the evil principle in human nature, forever doing battle with Virtue, or the good and divine principle, symbolised by the five sons of Páçœu. At Duryodhana's birth various evil omens of the usual hackneyed description occurred; jackals yelled, donkeys brayed, whirlwinds blew, and the sky seemed on fire. Dhritaráshtra alarmed, called his ministers together, who recommended him to abandon the child, but could not persuade him to do so.

SVADHA—'Oblation'. Daughter of Daksa and Prasùti according to one statement, and of Agni according to another. She is connected with the *pitrs* or Manes, and is represented as wife of Kavi or of one class of *pitrs*, and as mother of others.

SVAR—(*see* VYÀHÛTI)

SVASTIKA—A mystical religious mark placed upon persons, or things. It is in the form of a Greek cross with the ends bent round

SVETAŠVATARA—An Upanisad attached to the *Yajurveda.* It is one of the most modem. Translated by Dr. Roer for the *Bibliotheca Indica.*

SVETKETU—A sage who, according to the *Mahàbhàrata*, put a stop to the practice of married women consorting with other men, especially with bràhmanas. His indignation was aroused at seeing a bràhmana take his mother by the hand and invite her to go away with him. The husband saw this, and told his son that there was no ground of offence, for the practice had prevailed from time immemorial. Švetaketu would not tolerate it, and introduced the rule by which a wife is forbidden to have intercourse with another man unless specially appointed by her husband to raise up seed to him.

SWABHAVAS—The characteristics, or inherent properties, of the Gunas (or qualities) by which they act, as soothing, terrifying, stupifying, &c.

SWABHOJANA—One of the Narakas; that for the punishment of the religious student who sleeps in the day; and for those who though mature, have to be instructed in sacred literature by their children.

SWADHA—**(1)** Oblation: one of the daughters of Dakaha, and wife of the Pitris; **(2)** One of the wives of Angiras; **(3)** The wife of one of the eleven Rudras.

SWAHA—(1) Offering: one of the daughters of Daksha, who was married to Agni; **(2)** The wife of the Rudra Pasupati.

SWAHI—One of the Kroshtri princes, son of Vrijinívat, and grandson of Yadu.

SWAMABHAK—One of the seven suns, into which the seven solar rays dilate at the end of the day of Brahmá.

SWAPHALKA—A sage of great sanctity; wherever he dwelt, there famine, plague, dearth, and other visitations were unknown; wherever rain was wanted his presence secured the blessing. He was married to the daughter of Kásirája, named Gándiní, (*q.v.*), whose remarkable birth has already been related. Gándiní, as long .as she lived, gave a cow to the brahmans every day. Akrúra was their son; and his birth therefore proceeded from a. combination of uncommon excellence. *V.P.*, 432.

SWARAJ—One of the seven principal solar rays, that which supplies heat to the planet Saturn.

SWARAT—Brahmá, the Creator.

SWARBHANU—(1) A renowned Dánava, son of Kaya; **(2)** One of equal celebrity, the son of Viprachitti.

SWARGA—(1) The son of Rudra Bhíma; **(2)** Paradise, on Mount Meru, the seat of the righteous, and where the wicked do not arrive even after a hundred births. The heaven of Indra, the abode of the inferior gods and of beatified mortals, supposed to be situated on Mount Meru. It is called also Sairibha, Mišrakàvana, Tàvisa, Tridivam, Tripistapam, and *Ùrdhva-loka.* Names of heaven or paradise in general are also used for it.

SWAR-LOKA—The planetary sphere, extending from the sun to Dhruva, explained in the Puránas to be heaven.

SWARNAPRASTHA—One of the eight minor Dwípas situated beyond those sited by Miecchas, but who worship Hindu divinities.

SWAROCHISHA—The Manu of the second Manwantara; so named from the splendour of his appearance when born. He was the son of the nymph Varnthiní by the Gandharva *'Káll.* The seven Rishis of the period were the Manu's sons.

SWASTYATREYAS—A race of brahmans, celebrated for their sanctity; a branch of the lunar race.

SWATI—A lunar mánsion in Govithi, in the Central Avashthána.

SWAYAMBHU—(1) Brahmá; a synonym of Mahat, so termed from its being ungenerated; **(2)** the Vyása of the first Dwápara.

SWAYAMBHOJA—A Yádava chief, the son of Pratikshatra.

SWAYAMBHUVA—The Manu, born of and one with Brahmá; Brahmá converted himself into two persons, the first male, or the Manu Swayambhuva, and the first woman or Satarúpa.

SWAYAMVARA—Self-choice. The public choice of a husband. The most popular of all the forms of marriage which prevailed amongst the Vedic Aryans. The Swayamvara, says Mr. Wheller was evidently an institution of the Kshatriyas, resembling in a remarkable degree the tournaments of the age of chivalry.

The man who gained the day became the husband of the damsel. The Mahábhárata contains a long narrative of the Swayanvara of Draupadi. The Swayamvara emphatically belongs to the old Vedic period, and is distinctly recognised in the hymns of the Rig Veda. The institution is an exaggerated expression of the age of chivalry.—*Wheeler.*

"The Swayamvara, the free, or self-election of a husband, was a not uncommon practice amongst the Hindus, and forms the subject of frequent description both in ancient and modern poetry: the Princes being assembled in a public place with appropriate ceremonies, the Princess performed the tour of the circle, and signified her preference by throwing a garland of flowers upon the neck of the successful competitor; the marriage rite was subsequently performed as usual. It may be easily supposed that the preference was not always the suggestion of the moment, and grew out of previous acquaintance: thus Damayanti adopted this mode of choosing Nala in concert with her lover; Tarávati chose Chandrase by the guidance of her nurse; and the Princess of Kanoj invited Pritha Rai to her Swayamvara. The consequences may also be easily conjectured, and mortified vanity, or disappointed expectation must often have engendered personal hostility: the result may not infrequently have been long and widely felt; and though neither the Swayamvaras of Draupadi or Damayanti may have been attended with any remarkable events, the choice of the Princess of Kanoj was less innocuous: for the animosity which it excited between her father and her lord, laid India bare to Mohammedan aggression, and paved the way for European ascendancy."—Wilson's *Works*, III, 324.

SWETA—**(1)** A serpent king, one of the progeny of Kadru; **(2)** A range of mountains north of Meru.

SWETA-DWIPA—The white or silver island, the abode of Vishnu. Colonel Wilford bestowed great pains on the verification of these fictitious Dwípas, which lie imagined to represent actual divisions of the globe. The white or silver island, or island of the moon, was the island of Great Britain, according to him. Still, says Wilson, his essays on these subjects, contain much curious and interesting matter.

SYADVADIS—"Assertors of probabilities, or of what may be;" a designation of the Jainas.

SYALA—'A brother-in-law.' A Yàdava prince who insulted the sage Gàrgya, and was the cause of his becoming the father of Kàla-yavana, a great foe of Krisna and the Yàdava family. See KÁLAYAVANA.

SYAMA—'The black.' A name of Šiva's consort, (*see* Devì)

SYAMANTAKA GEM—A jewel of great celebrity that insured its possessor, if a good man, safety, prosperity and happiness. It was presented by the Sun to Satrájit who wore it on his neck, and became thereby as brilliant as the sun himself. Satrájit, fearing that Krishça would him for the jewel, transferred it to his brother Prasena; and as Prasena's character was bad it caused his death; he being killed by a lion when hunting. The lion taking the jewel in his mouth was about to depart, when he was killed by Jámbavat, the king of the bears, who carried off the gem to his cave and gave it to his son Sukumára to play with. Krishna was suspected of having murdered Prasena to get possession of the jewel. To clear himself Krishna tracked the jewel to the bear's cave, and after a conflict with Jámbavat that lasted twenty-one days, recovered the jewel. Jámbavat then recognised Krishna's divinity, and gave him his daughter Jambavatí in marriage. The jewel was again restored to Satrájit, who was killed by Satadhanwan for the sake of it. Krishna resolved that Satadhanwan should relinquish the prize, pursued him, put him to death, but found not the jewel, as it had been given to Akrúra to keep. Balabhadra thought Krishna's deceiving him and quarrelled with his brother on account of it.

Akrúra retained the precious jewel fifty-two years, and in consequence enjoyed immunity from all kinds of evil, the whole country partaking of the benefit. This led Krishça to conjecture that Akrúra had the gem in his possession; and in a full assembly Akrúra owned to it and offered it to Krishça; but it was decided that it should remain with Akrúra, who wore it publicly ever after as a garland of light. *V.P.*

SYAMA—One of the sons of Súra.

SYAMAYANI—A teacher of the Yajur Veda, and chief of the northern class.

SYAVASVA—Son of Arcanànas. Both were Vedic *rsis*. In a hymn he says, "Šašiyasi has given me cattle, comprising horses and cows and hundreds of sheeps". The story told in explanation is that Arcanànas, having seen the daughter of Ràjà Rathavìti, asked her in marriage for his son Šyàvàšva. The king was inclined to consent, but the queen objected that no daughter of their house had ever been given to any one less saintly than a *ṛsi*. To qualify himself Šyàvàšva engaged in austerities and begged alms. Among others, he begged of Šašiyasì wife of Ràjà Taranta. She took him to her husband, with whose permission she gave him a herd of cattle and costly ornaments. The Ràjà also gave him whatever he asked for, and sent him on to his younger brother, Purumìlha. On his way he met the Maruts, and lauded them in a hymn, for which they made him a *ṛsi*. He then returned to Rathavìti, and received his daughter to wife.

SYENI—A daughter of Kasyapa, and the parent of hawks.

TABLA—A small drum with only one opening, which is covered with a thin skin, the part opposite to this being round and made of wood. The drum rests upon the ground, the covered opening being uppermost, and is struck rapidly and sharply by the fingers. Sometimes two such dramas are played by the right and left hands together.

TADAIKYAM—Union; perfect union; or identification of one with another. "The mind of man is the cause both of his bondage and his liberation: its addiction to the objects of sense is the means of his bondage; its separation from objects of sense is the means of his freedom. The sage who is capable of discriminative knowledge must therefore restrain his mind from all the objects of sense, and therewith meditate upon the Supreme Being, who is one with spirit, in order to attain liberation; for that supreme spirit attracts to itself him who meditates upon it, and who is of the same nature, as the loadstone attracts the iron by the virtue which is common to itself and its products. Yet the union that takes place is only that of contiguity, (Samyoga) not that of identification or unity, Tadaikyam. *Vishṇu Purána* and note.

TADAKA—(*see* TĀRAKĀ)

TAITTIRIYA—This term is applied to the Saṁhitā of the Black *Yajurveda.* (*see* VEDA) It is also applied to a Brāhmaṇa, to an Āraṇyaka, to an Upaniṣad, and a Prātiśākhya of the same Veda. All these are printed in the *Bibliotheca Indica*, and of the last there is a translation in that serial.

TAKSA, TAKṢAKA—Son of Bharat, and nephew of Rāmacandra. The sovereign of Gāndhāra, who resided at and probably founded Takṣaśilā or Taxila, in the Panjāb.

TAKSAKA—'One who cuts off; a carpenter.' A name of Viśvakarmā. A serpent, son of Kadru, and chief of snakes.

TAKSASILA, TAXILA—A city of the Gāndhāras, situated in the Panjāb. It was the residence of Takṣa, son of Bharata and nephew of Rāmachandra, and perhaps took its name from him. It is the Taxila of Ptolemy and other classical writers. Arrian describes it as "a large and wealthy city, and the most populous between the Indus and Hydaspes." It was three days' journey east of the Indus, and General Cunningham has found its remains at Sāhhdharī, one-mile northeast of Kalakīsarāī.

TAKSHAKA—The younger brother of the Ádityas, and ruler of snakes.—Wilson, *Works*, XI, 219.

TAKSHA—The son of Bhárata; he was Rája of Gandhára, residing at Takshaṣila.

TALAJANGHA—A prince of the Yádava race, Son of Jayadhvaja, king of Avantī; the father of a hundred sons, who were called Tálajanghas: they conquered Bahu, but were afterwards subdued by Sagara. They were a branch of the Haihayas.

TALAKA—One of the Andhra kings, the son of Hala.

TALAKETU—'Palm-banner.' An appellation of Bhiṣma, also of an enemy killed by Kṛṣṇa. Balarāma had the synonymous Tāladhvaja.

TALAM—The throne of Durgā.

TALA—One of the Narakas—that for the punishment of adultery, murder, &c.

TALATALA—The fourth of the seven regions of Pátála: Máya reigns over Talátala, having been raised to that dignity after the destruction of his three cities by Śiva.

TALAVAKARA—A name of the *Kena Upaniṣad.*

TAMAS—**(1)** The quality of darkness, ignorance, inertia. Ignorance is said to be five-fold; in this definition Tamas, or obscurity, is the first thing of which it consists; **(2)** One of the Narakas; **(3)** A Yádava prince, the son of Prithuṣravas.

TAMASA—The fourth Manu. (*see* MANU)

TAMASA—**(1)** A Manu, the son of Priyavrata; the Manu of the fourth *Manwantara*; **(2)** A river, the Touse. It was on the banks of *this river that Ráma* halted the first night of his exile; when the Máháràja had been carried back to Ayodhya, and the people would keep with the chariot of Ráma. They all spent the night on the banks of the river Tamasa, and at early morning Ráma rose from his bed of leaves, and with Síta and Lakshmana left before the people awoke.

TAMISRA—Gloom: the fourth quality of Ignorance in the definition that makes it five-fold.

TAMRA—**(1)** One of the daughters of Daksa, married to Kaṣyapa; **(2)** A river.

TAMRALIPTA—The country immediately west of the Bhāgīrathī; Tamlook, Hijjali, and Midnapore. Its inhabitants are called Tāmraliptakas.

TAMRAPAKSHI—A son of Krishṇa by his wife Rohiní.

TAMRA-PARNA, TÀMRA-PARNÌ—**(1)** Ceylon, the ancient Taprobane. There was a town in the island called Tàmraparçì, from which the whole island has been called by that name. **(2)** A river in Tinnevelly, which rises at the southern extremity of the Western Ghats.

TAMRAVARNA—One of the nine portions of the Varsha of Bhárata.

TAMRAYANI—A teacher of the white Yájus, and founder of a school.

TANDRI—Sloth; a form of Brahmá.

TANDU—One of Śiva's attendants, whom the god instructed in a new style of dancing, hence termed

Táṇḍava, and which is reckoned one of the modes of dramatic performance.

TANDYA, TĀṆḌAKA—The most important of the eight *Brāhmaṇas* of the *Sāmaveda*. It has been published in the *Bibliotheca Indica*.

TANMATRA—The rudiment or type of an element; the characteristic property of an element.

TANSU—A prince, the son of Rantináru, a descendant of Puru; called also Tansurodha.

TANTRA—'Rule, ritual.' The title of a numerous class of religious and magical works, generally of later date than the Purāṇas, and representing a later development of religion, although the worship of the female energy had its origin at an earlier period. The chief peculiarity of the Tantras is the prominence they give to the female energy of the deity, his active nature being personified in the person of his Śakti, or wife. There are a few Tantras which make Viṣṇu's wife or Rādhā the object of devotion, but the great majority of them are devoted to one of the manifold forms of Devī, the Śakti of Śiva, and they are commonly written in the form of a dialogue between these two deities. Devī, as the Śakti of Śiva, is the especial energy concerned with sexuality and magical powers, and these are the leading topics of the Tantras. There are five requisites for Tantra worship, the five *makāras* or five *m*'s—(1) *Madya*, wine; (2) *Māṁsa*, flesh; (3) *Matsya*, fish; (4) *Mudrā*, parched grain and mystic gesticulations; (5) *Maithuna*, sexual intercourse. Each Śakti has a twofold nature, white and black, gentle and ferocious. Thus Umā and Gaurī are gentle forms of the Śakti of Śiva, while Durgā and Kālī are fierce forms. The Śāktas or worshippers of the Śaktis are divided into two classes, Dakṣinācārīs and Vāmācārīs, the right-handed and the left-handed. The worship of the right-hand Śāktas is comparatively decent, but that of the left hand is addressed to the fierce forms of the Śaktis, and is most licentious. The female principle is worshipped, not only symbolically, but also in the actual woman, and promiscuous intercourse forms part of the rituals. Tantra worship prevails chiefly in Bengal and the Eastern provinces.

A religious textbook: the principal rites and formulae connected with the adoration of *Prakriti* or *Sakti* are derived from the works known by the collective term of Tantras. The followers of the Tantras profess to consider them as a fifth *Veda*, and attribute to them equal antiquity and superior authority. "The Tantras are a class of books of which little is known in Europe, but which, until English education began in India, were the creed of a large proportion of Hindus. Old Pandits in Bengal will still maintain that the Tantric was the grandest religion of all, only it was beyond human nature to carry it out; for it is based on the idea that we should practice every kind of excess to the utmost, and yet carry a mind fixed on the Supreme Being in the midst of it all. He who worshipped God with purity of life was but a *pásu*, a mere beast; while he who worshipped him in orgies of drunkenness and licentiousness was a víra, a hero. The Tantric rites were not long ago very prevalent in Bengal, and though, as western culture and the study of English spread, such ideas and rites retreat into obscurity, the Tantras were but the lowest step of that progressive degradation which we traced from the simple and elevated nature-worship of the Rig Veda."* The observances they prescribe have indeed, in Bengal, almost superseded the original ritual. The question of their date is involved in considerable obscurity. From the practices described in some of the Puránas, particularly that of the *Diksha, or* rite of initiation, in the Agni Purána, from the specification of formulae comprising the mystic monosyllables of the Tantras in that and other similar compilations, and from the citation of some of them by name in different Pauranic works, we must conclude that some of the Tantras are prior to those authorities. It may be inferred that the system originated at some period in the early centuries of Christianity, being founded in the previous worship of the female principle, and the practices of the *Yoga* with the *Mantras*, or mystical formula of the Vedas. It is equally certain that the observances of the Tantras have been carried to more exceptionable extremes in comparatively modern times; and that many of the works themselves are of recent composition. They appear also to have been written chiefly in Bengal and the eastern districts, many of them being unknown in the west and south of India; and the rites they teach having failed to set aside the ceremonies of the Vedas, although they are not without an important influence upon the belief and the practices of the people.

The Tantras are too numerous to admit in this place of their specifications, but the principal are the *Syáma Rahasya*, *Rudra*, *Yámala*, *Mantra Mahodadhi*, *Sárada Tilaka*, and *Kaliká Tantra*; whilst the Kula Chúdámani, Kularnava, and similar works, are the chief authorities of one portion of the Sáktas; the sect being *divided* into two leading branches, the Dakahinácháris and Vámácháris, or followers of the right-hand and left-hand ritual. Works of *H. H. Wilson*, Vol., I. p. 250. (* *Quarterly Review*, July 1870. (Also see *Encyclopaedia of Tantra* by Santideva. It includes very interesting material).

TANTRAVARTTIKA—(Tantravárttika), a celebrated Mimansa treatise by Kumarila Bhatta, forming a commentary on the Jaimini-sutras. Mr. Burnell states that it contains the earliest known mention in Sanskrit of the Dravidian languages.* Kumarila Bhatta lived at the end of the seventh century, A.D., and "it is interesting to remark that the words he mentions are still good current Tamil words."† Bhatta regarded the Dravidian dialects as *Mlechchka* or unbrahmanic, uncivilized languages, he does not say so expressly, but his words imply that he thought so, "It is not to assume too much therefore if we infer that about 700 A. D., brahmanical civilization had but little penetrated the South of India."‡ (* *Indian Antiquary*, September 1872. † *Ibid.* ‡ *Ibid.)*

TAPAAIYAS—Brahmáns of a branch of the Yájus.

TAPA-LOKA, TAPAR-LOKA, TAPO-LOKA—The sphere or world of the seven Rishis. The sphere of penance, inhabited by the deities called Vaibhrájas, who are unconsumable by fire. (*see* LOKA)

TAPAS, TAPAAYA—The names of two of the months occurring in the Vedas, and belonging to a system now obsolete.

TAPASWIN—One of the sons of the Manu Cháks-husha.

TAPATI—The river Tapī personified as a daughter of the Sun by Chāyā. She was mother of Kuru by Samvaraṇa.

TAPTAKHNMBA—One of the Narakas, that in which murder and incest are punished.

TAPTALOKA—The red-hot iron Naraka, for jailers, horse-dealers and deserters.

TARA—The wife of Báli, the elder brother of Sugríva. She attempted to dissuade Báli from fighting with his brother, but was unable to do so, and Báli was killed. When she was grieving for her loss, Ráma consoled her, and she was afterwards married to Sugríva.

TARA—The wife of Vrihaspati, the preceptor of the gods; she was carried off by Soma, who refused to give her up even at the command of Brahmá. A fierce contest ensued between the gods and the *asuras*, termed the Tára-kamaya war. It was brought to a close by the interference of Brahmá, who compelled Soma to restore Tárá to her husband. Her son Budha was born shortly after. See BUDHA. SOMA.

TARAKA—A female *daitya*, daughter of the *yakṣa* Suketu or of the demon Sunda, and mother of Mārīca. She was changed into a *rākṣasī* by Agastya, and lived in a forest called by her name on the Ganges, opposite the confluence of the Sarju, and she ravaged all the country round. Viśvāmitra desired Rāmacandra to kill her, but he was reluctant to kill a woman. He resolved to deprive her of the power of doing harm, and cut off her two arms. Lakṣmaṇa cut off her nose and ears. She, by the power of sorcery, assailed Rāma and Lakṣmaṇa with a fearful shower of stones, and at the earnest command of Viśvāmitra, the former killed her with an arrow.—*Rāmāyaṇa*.

TARAKA—Son of Vajrānaka. A *daitya* whose austerities made him formidable to the gods, and for whose destruction Skanda, the god of war, was miraculously born.

TARAKA—(1) A Daitya of great prowess, the son of Hiranyaksha; **(2)** A Danava son of Kaṣyapa by Danu.

TARAKA—A star; *Kshinapunya Táraka*, the stars that have lost their virtue. The Hindu notion is that the stars are individuals raised to that honour for a time proportioned to the sum of their merits; this being exhausted they descend to earth, often visibly, as in the case of shooting stars.—WILSON.

TARAKA-MAYA—The war which arose in consequence of Soma, the moon, having carried off Tārā, the wife of Bṛhaspati.

TARAPIDA—A prince, the son of Chandrávaloka, one of the rájas of Ayodhya before the great war.

TARKSYA—An ancient mythological personification of the sun in the form of a horse or bird. In later times the name is applied to Garuḍa.

TAROBA—A lake in the Chāṇḍa district of the Central Provinces; it is situated east of Segaon, in a basin of the Chimur hills at a considerable height above the plain, and is believed by the natives of the surrounding country to owe its origin to enchantment. It is far from any village, and though artificially embanked at one point has all the appearance of a natural lake. The legend connected with it is as follows: In the early ages a marriage procession was passing through these hills from the west. Hot and thirsty they sought for water but found none, when a strange-looking old man suggested that the bride and bridegroom should join in digging for a spring. Laughingly they consented, and with the removal of a few spadesful of earth a clear fountain leapt to the surface. While all were delightedly drinking, the freed waters rose and spread into a wide lake, overwhelming bride, bridegroom, and procession, but fairy hands soon constructed a temple in the depths, where the spirits of the drowned are supposed still to dwell. Afterwards on the lake aide a palm tree grew up, which only appeared during the day, sinking into the earth at twilight. One morning a rash pilgrim seated himself upon the treetop, and was borne into the skies where the flames of the sun consumed him. The palm-tree then shriveled into dust, and in its place appeared an image of the spirit of the lake, which is worshipped under the name of Taroba. Formerly at the call of pilgrims, all necessary vessels rose from the lake, and after being used were washed and returned to the waters. But at last one evil-minded man took those he had received to his home; they quickly vanished, and from that day the mystic provision wholly ceased. In quiet nights the country-folk still hear faint sounds of drum and trumpet passing round the lake

"She is not dead, she has no grave,
She lives beneath Lough Ullin's water,
And in the murmur of each wave,
Methinks I catch the songs I taught her."

The old men say that in one dry year when the waters sank low, golden pinnacles of the fairy temple were seen glittering in the depths—

"On Lough Neagh's banks as the fisherman strays,
On a cold calm eve's declining,
He sees the round towers of other days
In the waves beneath him shining."

The lake is much visited, especially during the months of December and January; and a Gond performs the rites of the god. Wives seek its waters for their supposed virtue in causing fertility, and sick persons for health. Fish in the lake grow to a large size, the skeleton of one which was stranded some years ago measuring eight feet in length.* (* *Indian Antiquary*, Jane 1872.)

TATAKA—(Tátaká), a terrible Rákshasí, the daughter of Suketu, wife of Sundágara, and mother of Marícha. She was killed by Ráma, after his scruples about taking the life of a female who had been overcome by the reasoning of Viṣvámitra.

TATVA SAMASA—A textbook of the Saṁkhya philosophy attributed to Kapila himself.

TEJAS—Light or fire, the element; said to be produced from the rudiment of form or colour; while itself is the producer of that of taste. *V.P.*

TELINGA—The Telugu country, stretching along the coast from Orissa to Madras.

THARU—The Thárus are one of the aboriginal races of India, now in a depressed and abject condition, yet formerly of considerable influence and power. They claim to have been originally Rájputs; and state that their ancestors lost their caste by taking to intoxicating liquors and rearing fowls; but this is very doubtful. The Thárus keep their residences scrupulously clean.—*Sherring.*

TIGMA—A prince, the son of Mridu, of the race of Puru.

TÍLAKA—A mark on the forehead and between the eye brows, either as an ornament or a sectarian distinction.—WILSON.

TILLOTAMA—A celestial nymph or Apsarasa, of die Laukíka class. Tillotamá is described as having been originally a Brahmán female, who in consequence of being born in the month of Mágha, dwelt four thousand ages in Vaikuntha, and was then born as the Apsaras Tillotamá, for the purpose of causing the mutual destruction of Sunda and Upasnnda, an incident taken from the Mahábhárát.—Wilson's Works, Vol. III, p. 55.

TIMI—A daughter of Daksa, who was married to Kaṣyapa, and became the mother of fishes.

TIMIN, TIMIṄGILA—The Timin is a large fabulous fish. The Timiṅgila, 'swallower of the Timin', is a still larger one; and there is one yet larger, the Timiṅgilagila or Timi-timiṅgila, 'swallower of the Timiṅgila'. *Cf.* the Arabic Tinnin, sea serpent. It is also called Samudrāru.

TINAVINDA—**(1)** The Vyása of the twenty-third Dwápara age; **(2)** A prince, the son of Budha, of whom the celestial nymph Alambusha became enamoured.

TIRTHA—A holy shrine or sacred place; in the Pádma Purána, persons are also considered as Tírthas, as a guru, a father, a wife, a son; and in illustration of this, Vishṇu recited several stories to king Veṇa.

TIRTHANKARA—A Jain saint of the present era, of whom twenty-four are enumerated.

1. Rishaba.
2. Ajita.

13. Vimala.
14. Ananta.

3. Sambhava.
4. Abhinandana.
5. Sumati.
6. Padmaprabhu.
7. Suparsva.
8. Chandraprabhu.
9. Pushpadhanta.
10. Sitála.
11. Sreyánsa.
12. Vasu pujya.
15. Dharma.
16. Tánti.
17. Kunthu.
18. Ara.
19. Malli.
20. Manisuvrata.
21. Nami.
22. Nemi.
23. Parsva.
24. Mahávíra or Vardhamani-svami.

Colossal statues of these Tirthankaras are often placed in the courtyards of the Jain temples. There is a remarkably fine one at Sravana Bella Gola, near Chenraipatam, in Mysore. Its height is seventy feet three inches. The Duke of Wellington, who visited the place in 1801, was of opinion that the rock had been cut until nothing but the image remained.

TIRUKALYANA—This is a festival in commemoration of the marriage of Śiva and Párvati. It is celebrated by various ceremonies performed by Brahmans, and usually lasts nine or ten days, during which daily offerings are made, and images of the gods carried about in the streets in the morning and evening. Multitudes of people assemble on these occasions, when musicians and dancing girls are always present.

TIRUVALLAVA—The author of the celebrated Dravidian poem "The Kural." He lived about the third century of the Christian era. His parents were Bhagavan and Adiyal, an eminent Brahman and a beautiful pariah; the condition on which they lived together was that every child born should he at once abandoned. A girl was first born named Avveyar, (*q.v.*) The mother longed to keep the child; but Bhagavan replied in words that are still often quoted—

Is that God dead who wrote upon our brow
The things that are to be ? Can deepest pain
Be more than he can bear? Doth not he know
Thou hast a child ? Let not thy fear complain.

Four other children were born, two girls and two boys, all of whom were similarly forsaken, the mother being comforted on each occasion by a verse on the goodness of God, composed by Bhagavan. Mr. Gover says these verses are now most sacred and are always quoted with deep reverence. He thinks they are probably quotations from some larger work on the Providence of God which has been lost during the many centuries that have passed since the days of Tiruvallava.

"Bhagavan and Adi came towards Madras, and at Mylapore, one of its present suburbs, Tiruvallava was born. For the last time the poor mother cried out against the hard lot which compelled her to abandon her child." Bhagavan gave her the usual consolation by reminding her of the God whose care protects all living things and the infant was left under the branches of a tree, the Bassi Longifolia. The wife of a cultivator found and adopted the child, calling it Tiruvallava, or the holy pariah. He left his adoptive parents at an early age, and was educated by some ascetics in the hill country.

When Tiruvallava was grown up a fearful monster invaded the plains, for the destruction of which a rich landowner offered immense rewards. Tiruvallava succeeded in killing the monster and restoring peace and prosperity to the country. The grateful landowner gave all that he had promised, and added the hand of his daughter Vasukí, whom Tiruvallava married. "She proved almost a miracle of goodness, and the songs in the Kural describing the excellence and value of a good wife, were confessedly drawn from her life."

"Tiruvallava was now wealthy, but he thought it wrong for any man merely to live without producing some share of that which he consumed. After careful thought therefore he became a weaver. His good wife and he toiled hard at their work, living the while in the performance of every public and private duty. He now gathered many disciples, instructing them in all that concerned holy living. As his disciples increased they desired that he should make a book in his own name, so that the entire world might know how best to live, both in this life and those that were to come. In reply to this repeated request he sung the Cural in thirteen hundred and thirty verses. He divided it into three parts, treating respectively of virtue, wealth, and physical pleasure.

"Strip the story of its brahmanical element and we learn that Tiruvallava was a member of a low Dravidian caste, that he attained great celebrity as a poet and as a noble man, that he owed nothing and gave nothing to the sacerdotal caste, and that he was but one of many great Tamil poets who lived about the same time. He probably flourished about the third century of our era."—Gover's *Folk Songs*, 217.

TIRYAKSROTAS—The name given to the animal creation at their first "manifestation," from their nutriment following a winding course. *V.P.*

TISYA—The *kali yuga* or fourth age.

TITIKSHA—A prince, the son of Mahámanas, a descendant of Yayátí.

TITIKSHA—Patience; a daughter of Daksa, married to Dharma; one of the allegorical unions.

TITTIRI—'A partridge.' An ancient sage who was the pupil of Yāska, and is an authority referred to by Pāṇini. Some attribute the *Taittirīya Saṁhitā* of the *Yajurveda* to him. (*see* VEDA)

TOSALAKA—An athlete and boxer who was killed by Kṛṣṇa in the public arena in the presence of Kaṁsa.

TRAIGARTTAS—The people of Trigartta (*q.v.*).

TRANSMIGRATION—"Or the passing from one place, state, or condition into another, means, in the theological acceptation of the term, the supposed transition of the soul after death into another substance or body than that which it occupied before. The belief in such a transition is one of the most important phases in the religions of mankind. It was common to the most uncivilised and the most civilised nations of the earth, it was the object of fantastical superstition, as well as that of philosophical speculation, and it is the property of both ancient and modem times. Its basis being the assumption that the human soul does not perish together with the body, it could belong to those nations only which had already conceived an idea of the immortality of the soul; but in proportion as such an idea is crude or developed, as it is founded merely on a vague fear of death, and a craving for material life, or on ethical grounds, and a supposed casual connection between this and a future life, the belief in transmigration assumes various forms, and influences more or less the actions of men.

At the time when in *India* the dogma of transmigration became an integral part of the Brahmánic religion, the Hindus believed that the human souls emanated from a Supreme Being, which, as it were, in a state of bewilderment or forgetfulness, allowed them to become separate existences, and to be born on earth. The soul, thus severed from the real source of its life, is bound to return to it, or to become merged again into that divine substance with which it was originally one; but as its nature becomes contaminated with sin through its earthly career, it must, so long as it remains in this world, endeavor to free itself from all guilt, and thus to become fit for its ultimate destiny. Religion teaches that this is done by the observance of religious rites, and a life in conformity with the precepts of the sacred books; philosophy, that the soul will be re-united with Brahmán, if it *understands* the true nature of the divine essence whence it comes. So long, therefore, as the soul has not attained this condition of purity, it must be born again, after the dissolution of the body to which it was allied; and the degree of its impurity at one of these various deaths, determines the existence which it will assume in a subsequent life.

Since there can be no proof of the soul's migrations, the detail in which these are described in the religious works of the Hindus, is merely fantastical, and interesting only so far as it affords a kind of standard by which, at various epochs, and by different writers, the moral merit or demerit of human actions was measured in India. Thus, Manu (in the 12th book of his Code of Laws) teaches:

'The slayer of a Bráhmaṇa—according to the degree of his guilt—is reborn as a dog, a boar, an ass, a camel, a bull, a goat, a sheep, a stag, a bird, a Chânḍâla, or a Pukkaṣa. A Bráhmaṇa, who drinks spirituous liquor, will migrate into the bodies of a worm, an insect, a grasshopper, a fly feeding on ordure, or some mischievous animal. A twice born who steals (the gold of a Bráhmaṇa,) will pass a thousand times into the bodies of spiders, snakes, and chameleons, of aquatic monsters, or of murderous bloodthirsty demons. He who violates the bed of his guru, will a hundred times migrate into the forms of grasses, of shrubs, and of creeping plants, of carnivorous animals and beasts with long teeth, or of cruel brutes. Those who inflict injury (on sentient beings,) become flesh-eaters; and those who eat forbidden things, worms. Thieves become devourers of each other; and those who embrace women of the lowest castes, become ghosts...If a man, through covetousness, has stolen gems, pearl, or coral, or whatever belongs to the precious substances, be is reborn in the tribe of goldsmiths; if he has stolen grain, he becomes a rat; if kámsya (a composition of zinc and copper,) a *hamsa* bird; if water, a diver; if honey, a gadfly; if milk, a crow; if juice (of the sugarcane or the like,) a dog; if clarified butter, an ichneumon; if flesh, a vulture; if fat, a shag; if oil, a cockroach; if salt, a cricket; if curds, the crane, called Valáká;' Ac. A more general doctrine of the migration of souls is based by Hindu philosophers on the assumption of the three cosmic qualities of *sattwa*, *i.e.*; purity or goodness; rajas, *i.e.*; troubleness or passion; and *tamas*, *i.e.*; darkness or sin, with which the human soul may become endued. And on this doctrine, again, Manu and other writers build an elaborate theory of the various births to which the soul may become subject. Manu, for instance, teaches that 'souls endued with the quality of *sattwa*, attain the condition of deities; those having the quality of *rajas*, the condition of men; and those having the quality of *tamas*, the condition of beasts.' Each of these conditions, he continues, is, according to the acts or knowledge of the soul, threefold: the lowest, the middle, and the highest. 'The lowest embodiment of the quality *tamas* is inanimate objects, worms, insects, fish, serpents, tortoises, tame and wild beasts: the middle state, to which the same quality leads, is (the state of) an elephant, a horse, a Súdra, a Mleccha or barbarian, a lion, a tiger, and a boar: the highest, that of a public performer, a bird, a cheat, a demon called *Rakshas*, and a vampire-demon. The lowest condition to which the soul imbued with the quality *rajas* arrives is that of a cudgel-player, a boxer, a public dancer, a man who lives on the use of weapons, and one addicted to gambling and drinking; the middle condition, that of a king, a man of the Kshattriya or military caste, a house-priest of a king, and a man fond of learned controversy; the highest, that of a Gandharva or musician in Indra's heaven, a Guhyaka or Yaksha (two kinds of attendants on the god of riches,) or another attendant on another god, or an Apsaras or heavenly nymph in Indra's heaven. The lowest state procured by the quality of *sattwa* is that of a Vánaprastha—or a hermit of the third order of life—a religious mendicant, a Bráhmaṇa, or one of the demigods travelling about in palace-like cars, one of (the genii presiding over) the lunar mansions, or an offspring of Diti. The middle state, procured by the same quality, is that of a sacrificer, a Rishi (*q.v.*), a god of the lower heaven (a deity personating one of the) Vedas, (a deity presiding over one of) the luminaries or years, one of the manes or progenitors of mankind, and of the demigods called Sádhya. The highest condition to which the quality of *sattwa* leads is that of the god Brahmá, that of a creator of the world (as *Maríchi*, or another patriarch of the same rank,) that of the genius of Dharma (virtue or right), of *Mahat*, or the intellectual principle of creation, and of *Prakriti*, or matter.'

It is not necessary here to show that this detail regarding the migrations of the souls is more or less differently given by other authors at other periods of Hindu religion, according to the views which they entertained of right and wrong, of the value and rank of imaginary or created beings, and of the social conditions of men. For, since all orthodox Hindu writers agree in principle with Manu, the quotations alleged from his work suffice to illustrate the imaginary positiveness with which the doctrine of transmigration was propounded, and to establish the conclusion that this doctrine rested in India on ethical grounds.

It has been already pointed out that the belief in the soul's life after the death of the body roust precede the doctrine of transmigration, As such a belief, however, may be traced in some hymns of the *Rig Veda*, it has been supposed that this doctrine, too, is as old as this Veda. But apart from the uncertainty which still exists regarding not only the age, but even the relative age at which the different hymns of the *Rig Veda* were composed, and setting aside the fallacy which therefore attaches to speaking of this Veda as a contemporaneous whole, it is necessary to observe that the only passage which has been adduced in proof of this important discovery does not bear it out. It is the 32nd verse of the hymn I, 164, and according to the translation of Professor Wilson (Vol. IL pp. 137, 138,) runs as follows: 'He who has made (this state of things) does not comprehend it; he who has beheld it, has it also verily hidden (from him); he, whilst yet enveloped in his mother's womb, *it subject to many births*, and has entered upon evil.' But the word of the text, *bahuprajáh*, rendered by Wilson, according to the commentator,' is subject to many births,' may, according to the same commentator, also mean, 'has many offspring,' or 'has many children;' and as the latter sense is the more literal and usual sense of the word, whereas the former is artificial, no conclusion whatever regarding the doctrine of transmigration can safely be founded on it.

The Buddhist belief in transmigration is derived from that of the Brahmánic Hindus; it agrees with the latter in principle, though it differs from it in the imaginary detail in which it was worked out.

Like the Brahmanic Hindus, the Buddhists believe that all souls have existed from the beginning; like them, they believe in the unreality and sinfulness of the world in the necessity of the soul's freeing itself from the bondage of this world, and in the causal connection between the actions of man in this, and his condition in a subsequent, life. Like the Brahmánic Hindus, they hold, therefore, that sin is the cause of transmigration, and that by a total expiation of sin, the soul ceases to be reborn, and attains its final resting-place- But since this resting-piece is to the Buddhists Nirvána (*q.v.,*) or Non-entity, whereas to Brahmanism it is Brahmán, or the principle of Entity; since they reject the institution of caste, which is the social foundation of Brahmánic life; since they do not acknowledge the authority of the Vedas, and the codes based on it, and therefore consider as morally wrong much that the Brahmáni Śastras enjoin as morally right, the standard according to which the life of a Buddhist is regulated must differ in many respects from that which governs the conduct of a Brahmánic Hindu; and his ideas of reward and punishment, therefore, as reflected by his ideas of the mode of transmigration, likewise' differ from those of the Brahmánic believer. To enlarge here on this difference is not necessary, for, after the illustrations already afforded from Manu, it is easy to conceive that the *detail* of the Buddhistic doctrine of transmigration is as fanciful as that of the Brahmánic doctrine; that it is therefore partly devoid of interest, and partly intelligible only if taken in connection with the detail of Buddhistic religion and literature. Yet it is not superfluous to point out one great difference which separates the notions of one class of Buddhists from (hose of the rest, as well as from those of the Brahmánic Hindus. According to the latter, and the great mass of Buddhists, it is always the same soul which ever from its first birth reappears in its subsequent births, until it is finally liberated from transmigration. But among the southern Buddhists, another idea has also taken root. In their belief, the succession of existences of a being *w.* also a succession of souls; and each such soul, though the result of its predecessor, is not identical with it. According to this view, the body dies, and with it the soul, too, is 'extinguished,' leaving behind only the good and bad acts, which it has performed during its life. The result of these acts now becomes the seed of a new life, and the soul of this new life is therefore the necessary product of the soul of the former life. Thus all the succeeding souls have to labour at the solution of the same problem, which began when their first ancestor entered this world, but no succeeding birth is animated by the same soul. This dogma is illustrated in their works by various similes. One lamp, they say, for instance, is kindled at another; the light f the former is not identical with that of the latter, but nevertheless, without this, the other light could not have originated. Or, a tree produces fruit; from the fruit, another tree arises, and so on; the last tree is therefore not the same as the first, though the fruit is the necessary cause of the last."—*Goldstucker*.

TRASADASYU—"The Terrifier of thieves." **(1)** A name given in the Bhágavata to Mándhátri; **(2)** A royal sage and author of hymns. According to Sāyaṇa, he was son of Purukutsa. When Purukutsa was a prisoner, "his queen propitiated the seven *ṛṣis* to obtain a son who might take his father's place. They advised her to worship Indra and Varuṇa, in consequence of which Trasadasyu was born." He was renowned for his generosity. According to the *Bhāgavata Purāṇa* he was father of Purukutsa.

TRASARENU—A measure of time, consisting of three Anus.

TRAYYARUNA—**(L)** The Vyása of the fifteenth Dwápara age; **(2)** A. contributor to the Rig-Veda, be was a prince, the son of Tridhanwau; **(3)** Another prince, the son of Uruksaya, a descendant of Bharata.

TRETA YUGA—The second age of the world, a period of 1,296,000 years, (*see* YUGA)

TRETAGNI—(Tretágni), the triad of sacred fires, in opposition to the Laukika or merely temporal ones. The sacred fire of the Hindus, originally one, was made three-fold by Pururavas. The three fires are 1st *Gárhapatya*, perpetual household fire; 2nd, *Dakshina*, a fire for sacrifices; and 3rd, *Ahavaniya*, a fire for oblations. See FIRE SACRIFICIAL.

TRIAHYAS—The designation of Sudras in Krauncha Dwipa.

TRIAMBAKA—The three-eyed, a name of Śiva, derived from *tri*, three, and ambaka, eye.

TRIBHUVANA, TRILOKA—The three worlds, *svarga bhūmi*, *pātāla*—heaven, earth, and hell.

TRIDASA—'Three times ten, thirty.' In round numbers, the thirty-three deities—twelve Ādityas, eight Vasus, eleven Rudras, and two Aśvins.

TRIDHAMAN—The Vyása of the tenth Dwápara age.

TRIDHANWAN—An ancient Rája of the solar line, the son of Sumanas.

TRIGARTTA—'The country of the three strongholds', lately identified with the northern hill state of Kotoch, which is still called by the people "the country of Traigart".—*Wilson.* General Cunningham, however, clearly identifies it with the Jalandhar Doāb and Kāngrā.

TRIJATA—An amiable *rākṣasī* who befriended Sītā when she was the captive of Rāvaṇa in Ceylon. She is also called Dharmajñā.

TRIKĀṆḌA ŚEṢA—A Sanskrit vocabulary in three

chapters, composed as a supplement to the *Amarakosa.* It has been printed in India.

TRIKUTA—'Three peaks.' **(1)** The mountain on which the city of Laṅkā was built. **(2)** A mountain range running south from Meru.

TRILOCANA—'Three-eyed', *i.e.*, Śiva. The *Mahābhārata* relates that the third eye burst from Śiva's forehead with a great flame when his wife playfully placed her hands over his eyes after he had been engaged in austerities in the Himālaya. This eye has been very destructive. It reduced Kāma, the god of love, to ashes.

TRIMADHU—A class of Brahmáns so denominated from the particular part of the Vedas they study and recite. Three Anuvákas of the Yajur Veda begin Madhuváta, &c.

TRIMURTI—(From the Sanskrit *tri*, three, and *múrti*, form) 'Triple form.' The Hindu triad. This was foreshadowed in the Vedic association of the three gods Agni, Vāyu, and Sūrya. The triad consists of gods Brahmā, Śiva, and Viṣṇu, the representatives of the creative, destructive and preservative principles. Brahmā is the embodiment "of the Rajoguṇa, the quality of passion or desire, by which the world was called into being; Śiva is the embodied Tamoguna, the attribute of darkness or wrath, and the destructive fire by which the earth is annihilated; and Viṣṇu is the embodied Satvaguṇa or property of mercy and goodness by which the world is preserved. The three exist in one and one in three, as the Veda is divided into three and is yet but one; and they are all Āśrita, or comprehended within that one being who is Parama or 'supreme', Guhya or 'secret', and Sarvātmā, 'the soul of all things'."—*Wilson.*

The *Padma Purāṇa*, which is a Vaiṣṇava work and gives the supremacy to Viṣṇu, says, "In the beginning of creation, the great Viṣṇu, desirous of creating the whole world, became threefold: creator, preserver, and destroyer. In order to create this world, the supreme spirit produced from the right side of his body himself as Brahmā; then in order to preserve the world he produced from the left side of his body Viṣṇu; and in order to destroy the world he produced from the middle of his body the eternal Śiva. Some worship Brahmā, others Viṣṇu, other Śiva; but Viṣṇu, one yet threefold, creates, preserves, and destroys, therefore let the pious make no difference between the three." The representation of the Trimūrti is one body with three heads: in the middle Brahmā, on the right Viṣṇu, and on the left Śiva. The worship of Brahmā is almost extinct, but Viṣṇu and Śiva receive unbounded adoration from their respective followers, and each is elevated to the dignity of Supreme Being.

TRINA—A prince, the son Uṣinnara, descendant of Yayáti.

TRINACHIKETA—A class of Brahmáns so called from studying or reciting the Rathaka branch of the Yajur Veda, commencing with the term Trinachiketa.

TRINAVINDU—There is a third Triṇavindu who was amongst the brahmans and ascetics who followed the Páṇḍavas into exile, He was originally a king but became a Rishi.

TRIPADA—'Three-footed.' Fever personified as having three feet, symbolising the three stages of fever—heat, cold, and sweat.

TRIPATI or TIRUPATI—A sacred hill in the Arcot district, about eighty miles from Madras, celebrated as the scene of a minor incarnation of Vishṇu, in whose honour a splendid temple has been erected and richly endowed. There is an image of Vishnu, seven feet in height, with four arms, and having in three of his hands, the Chakra, the Chank, and the lotus. The temple, which is of great antiquity, is built of stone, and covered with plates of gilt copper. It stands in a valley in the centre of a range of hills. "Pilgrimages are made to Tripati from all parts of India, especially from Gujarat, the trading inhabitants of which province are in the habit of presenting five or ten per cent of their annual profits to this temple, whose deity appears to be the tutelary patron of traffic; rich gifts and votive offerings are likewise received from other quarters. Princes send their vakíls or ambassadors to present their offerings to the shrine; and the poor peasant wraps up some petty oblation in a piece of wax cloth. These offerings are made generally from personal motives, and comprise the widest possible range of articles. The writer has seen the long hair cut from the head of a respectable young Hindu female, given up by her in compliance with a vow made by her parent in infancy, and taken as an offering to the idol. Coleman says that a man who is lame presents a silver leg; if blind, a gold or silver eye. The reason of all these offerings is said to be to enable a rája to repay to Kubera the money lent by him ages ago, when the idol was married to the daughter of a neighbouring rája.

TRIPRISHTHA—Mahávíra in one of his births was a Vásudeva, named Triprishtha, from having three back bones: his uncle and foe in a former life, Visabhánandi, was born as his Protagonist or Prativásudeva, named Aṣvagriva or Hayagriva, and was in the course of events destroyed by the Vásudeva, a palpable adaptation of the Panranic legend of Vishṇu and Hayagriva. Triprishtha having put his chamberlain cruelly to death was condemned to hell, and again born as a lion.

TRIPTI—One of the Siddhis, or eight perfections of man. Tripti is the second and means mental satisfaction, or freedom from sensual desire.

TRIPURA—Triple city.' **(1)** According to the *Harivaṁśa* it was aerial, and was burnt in a war with the gods. **(2)** A name of the demon Bāṇa, because he received in gift three cities from Śiva, Brahmā, and Viṣṇu. He was killed by Śiva. His name at full length is Tripurāsura. The name is also applied to Śiva.

TRIPURARDANA or TRIPURANTAKA—A name of Śiva, from his having destroyed Tripura an Asura.

TRIPURARI—The capital city of the Cedis, now traceable in the insignificant village of Tewar, on the banks of the Narmadā.

TRISALA—The wife of Siddhártha, king of Pavana, and mother of the celebrated Tirthankara Mahávíra.

TRISANKU—A king of the solar line, who loved justice and truth and governed his dominions wisely. One fault marred the perfection of his character; and that was an overweening love for his body. The thought that death would deprive him of it, and that it would be reduced to ashes upon the funeral pile, was very grievous to him. He sought out the sage Vasishtha, and wished him to offer a solemn asvamedha to obtain from heaven permission to retain his cherished body. The Brahman, however, refused his request, as did also the hundred sons of Vasishtha to whom he next applied. 'Farewell' then, he said haughtily, 'I shall seek no more counsel from you or Vasishtha. It is clear to me that you are unable to obtain my petition.' 'We will give thee a proof of our power,' said they, 'may this precious body thou thinkest so beautiful, assume the degraded form of a Chandála!' The curse took immediate effect, and the unhappy monarch dared not return to his palace. But having heard of the astounding self-macerations of Visvámitra he sought out that elephant among men.* When the royal ascetic saw the condition of Trisanku, he was filled with compassion, and asked who had dared to reduce him to such a condition. The sons of Vasishtha, answered Trisanku; and then related the circumstances. Visvámitra was very indignant, and vowed to obtain the vow that Trisanku wished for. He proclaimed a great asvamédha and sent messengers far and near to summon to it all who devoted their lives to prayer. Those who disregarded the summons were punished in various ways. But when the asvamédha was celebrated, the gods themselves paid no heed to the sacrifice. Then this Tiger amongst kings in a rage exclaimed, listen noble Trisanku. By virtue of my severe penances I myself will perform this deed. Mount up into heaven with the body thou lovest. I, Visvámitra, in the hearing of gods and men, command it.' Then like a bubble of air through the water, Trisanku began to ascend, conquering the waves of space; but when his head struck against the celestial azure, Indra, looking over, said Fall, Trisanku! And the luckless monarch began to fall, but was arrested by the powerful voice of Visvámitra, the indomitable Lion among ascetics, when half-way between heaven and earth, where the body of the monarch still remains, and is supposed by the uninformed to be merely an astral constellation.—*Iliad of the East*, *p.* 70. (* "Such expressions are frequent in the Rámáyana. We meet with 'Lion among kings,' 'Tiger of men,' 'bull among penitents,' when we should say the most excellent of anchorites, the most eminent of men, the noblest of kings, &c.")—*Fauche.*

TRISHNA—" Greediness;" one of the children of Mrityu, 'death.'

TRISHTNBH—The name of the metre, created along with the Yajur Veda, &e., from the southern mouth of Brahmá.

TRISIRAS—'Tree-headed.' **(1)** In the Vedas, a son of Tvaṣṭṛ; also called Viśvarūpa; he is twice mentioned in the Rig Veda under this name. He is said to have had three heads and six eyes, and three mouths; one of his mouths was the soma drinker, the second the wine drinker and the third were destined for consuming other things. Indra hated this Viṣvarupa and cut off his three heads.—Muir, *O.S.T.*, Vol. V., p. 228-232. **(2)** Fever personified as a demon with three heads, typical of the three stages of heat, cold, and sweating. **(3)** Kubera, god of wealth. **(4)** An *asura* killed by Viṣṇu. **(5)** A son or a friend of Ravāṇa killed by Rāma.

TRISULA—(Trisúla), the trident of Śiva. It is considered to be in continual motion over the face of the universe to guard and preserve its creatures. To oppose its course would be to incur instant death. Its motion is regular but varying according to the days of the week. Thus it is. imagined that it is unlucky to proceed towards the westward on Sundays and Fridays, to the northward on Tuesdays and Wednesdays, to the eastward on Saturdays and Mondays and to the southward on Thursdays.

TRITA, TRITA, TĀPTYA—A minor deity mentioned occasionally in the *Ṛgveda*, and generally in some relation to Indra. Thus "Indra broke through the defenses of Vala, as did Trita through the coverings (of the well)."In explanation of this and similar allusions, a legend is told by the commentator to the effect, that Ekata, Dvita, and Trita (first, second, and third), were three men produced in water by Agni, for the purpose of rubbing off the remains of an oblation of clarified butter. Agni threw the cinders of the offerings into water, and from them sprang the three brothers, who, from their origin in water (*āp*), were called Āptyas. Trita went one day to draw water from a well and fell into it. The *asuras* then heaped coverings over the mouth of it to prevent his getting out, but he broke through them with ease. The *Nītimañjarī* tells the story differently. Ekata, Dvita, and Trita were travelling in a desert and suffered from thirst. They came to a well from which Trita drew water and gave it to his brothers. In order to appropriate his property the two brothers threw him into the well, placed a cartwheel over it, and there left him. Trita prayed earnestly to the gods, and with their help he escaped.

TRIVENA—Three plaited locks; indicating the mystical union of the three sacred rivers, the Ganga, Yamuna, and Sarasvati, severally the consorts or energies of the three great Powers; Trivena is regarded as symbolical of a female Triad, like the Trimurti of male powers. The Ganges and Yamina unite near Allahabad, and the Sarasvati, which is also supposed to join the other two under-ground. A person dying near the imagined confluence of the three streams is supposed to attain immediate beatitude.

TRIVIKRAMA—A name of Viṣṇu used in the *Ṛgveda*, and referring to three steps or paces which he is represented as taking. These steps, according to the opinion of a commentator, are "the three periods of the sun's course,—his rising, culminating, and setting". An old commentator says, "Viṣṇu stepped by separate strides over the whole universe. In three places he planted his step, one step on the earth, a second in the atmosphere, and a third in the sky, in the successive forms of Agni, Vāyu, and Sūrya." The great commentator Sāyaṇa, a comparatively modern writer, understands these steps as being the three steps of Viṣṇu in the Vāmana or dwarf incarnation, and no doubt they were the origin of this fiction.—(*Wilson*) "Vishṇu is the sun. How! Because he says 'thrice he planted his foot.' Where did he do so? On the earth, in the firmament, and in the heaven, says Sákapúni."—(*Muir*, II, 204.)

TRIVRISHAN—The Vyása of the eleventh Dwápara age.

TRIVRIT—A collection of hymns created along with the Rig Veda from the eastern mouth of Brahmá.

TRNAVARTTA—A demon that assumed the form of a whirlwind and carried off the infant Kṛṣṇa, but was overpowered and killed by the child.

TRNTI—A measure of time, consisting of three Tresarenns.

TRTSUS—A people frequently mentioned in the Veda. Sāyaṇa says they were "priests who were Vasiṣṭha's disciples". Vasiṣṭha himself is said to have belonged to the tribe.

TRYAMBAKA—'Three-eyed', or 'Having three wives or sisters'. **(1)** A name of Śiva. **(2)** One of the Rudras. **(3)** Name of one of the twelve great *liṅgas*. (*see* LIṄGA)

TRYARUNA—Aking, son of Trivṛsan, of the race of Ikṣvāku. He was riding in a chariot which Vṛśa, his *purohita* or family priest, was driving. The vehicle passed over and killed a brāhmaṇa boy, and a question arose as to who was responsible for the death. The question was referred to an assembly of the Ikṣvākus, and they decided it against Vṛśa. The *purohita* by his prayers then restored the boy to life, and being very angry with them for what he deemed partiality, "fire henceforth ceased to perform its functions in their dwellings, and the cooking of their food and other offices ceased". The Ikṣvākus appeased him, and upon his prayers the use of fire was restored to them. This story is told by Sāyaṇa in elucidation of a Vedic allusion, and he quotes the *Śāṭyāyana Brāhmaṇa* as the authority.

TUKHARAS—A northern tribe from whom Tukhāristān obtained its name. They are probably the tribe of Śakas, by whom Bactria was taken from Greeks. They are also called Tuṣāras.

TULADHA—A trading vaiśya mentioned in the *Mahābhārata* as very virtuous and learned, to whom Jājali, an arrogant brāhmaṇa, was sent by a voice from the sky to learn wisdom.

TULASI PLANT—A tree sacred to Krishṇa, said to have been produced at the churning of the ocean; but considered by Wilson to be a sectarial addition to the articles originally specified.

TULUNGA—Tuluva, or the country where the Tulu language is spoken, on the western coast below Goa.

TULYATA—One of the Siddhis, the fourth, meaning similarity of life, form, and feature.

TUMBURU—A Gandharvas, who resides in the sun's car as one of its seven guardians in the month of Madha or Chaitra. (*see* VIRĀDHA)

TUNDA—A fierce demon mentioned in the Pádma Purána, which has a long narrative of the destruction of the demon by Nahusha the son of Áyus. He had a son named Vituṇḍa, who was killed by Bhagavatī (Durgā).

TUNDIKERAS—One of the great divisions of the Haihaya tribe.

TUNGAPRASTHA—A mountain to the east of Ramghur.

TUNGA—The son of Atri, who having propitiated Náráyana by penance, obtained a son equal to Indra; this son was Veṇa, who was made by the Rishis the first king of the earth.

TUNI—One of the Saineya princes, the son of Asanga.

TURANGA-VAKTRA—'Horse-faced people.' (*see* KINNARAS)

TURUSKAS—Turks; the people of Turkistan. The Indo-Scythians, who, under Kaniṣka tind other kings of the race, held northern India.

TURVASA, TURVAŚU—Son of Yayāti by Devayāṇī. He refused to bear the curse of premature decrepitude passed upon his father, and so his father cursed him that his posterity should "not possess dominion". His father gave him a part of his kingdom, but after some generations, his line merged into that of his brother Puru, who bore for a time the curse passed upon his father.

TURVASN—One of the sons of Yayáti, to whom his father made over the southeast districts of his kingdom, to govern as viceroy under his younger brother Puru. Turvasu refused to take his father's infirmities on him, in consequence of which his line soon failed and became merged in that of Puru.

TUSHARAS—**(1)** A people, called also Tukháraa, probably the Tochari, or tribe of the Sakas, by whom Bactria, was taken from the Greeks, and from whom Tocharistan derives the name it still bears; **(2)** A race of princes; the dynasty consisted of fourteen, and the Váyu Purána states that their united reigns lasted 500 years.

TUSHITAS—A class of deities, thirty-six in number, but sometimes reduced to twelve, of the second Manwantara; and who were called the Adityas in the Manwantara of Vaivaswata. According to the Váyu the Tushitas were the sons of Kratu. The deities of each period are those to whom offerings of the soma juice, &c., are presented collectively.

TUSHTI—**(1)** Resignation; a daughter of Daksa who became the wife of Dharma; **(2)** A daughter of Pauruamáṣa.

TUSHTIMAT—One of the sons of Ugrasena and Devaka.

TVAHTRI—This god, who in the later mythology is regarded as one of the Adityas, but does not bear that character in the Rig Veda, is the Hephaistos or Vnlcau, of the Indian Pantheon, the ideal artist, the divine artizan, the most skilful of workmen, who is versed in all wonderful and admirable contrivance. He sharpens the iron axe of Brahmáṇaspati, and forges the thunderbolts of Indra, which are described as golden, or of iron, with a thousand points and a hundred edges. He is styled the beautiful, or skilful-handed, the skilful worker, the omniform, or archetype of all forms, and *Savitri*, the vivifier He imparts generative power and bestows offspring. He develops the seminal germ in the womb, and is the shaper of all forms, human and animal. He has produced and nourishes a great variety of creatures; all worlds (or beings) are his, and are known to him; he has given to heaven and earth and to all things their forms. He bestows long life. He puts speed into the legs of a horse. He is said to be skilled in all Sáma texts, and to have created Brahmáṇaspati above all creatures; and is said, along with heaven and earth, the waters, and the Bhrigus, to have generated Agni. He is master of the universe, a first-born protector and leader. He is a companion of the Angirases and knows the region of the gods. He is supplicated to nourish the worshipper and protect his sacrifice. He is the bestower of blessings and possessed of abundant wealth; and is asked, like other gods, to take pleasure in the hymns of his worshippers, and to grant them riches.

Tvashtri is in several passages connected with the Ribhus, who, like him, are celebrated as skilful workmen, and are called his pupils. An exhibition of their skill is mentioned; they are said to have made into four a single new sacrificial cup which Tvashtri had formed, and when be saw this alteration of his work, he is represented as becoming ashamed and hiding himself among the goddesses. In one place he is said to have resented this change in his own workmanship, while in another he is made to applaud their design and admire the superior products of their skill.

Tvashtri had twin children, (a daughter) Saraṇyú, and (a son) Triṣiras. He is represented as having for his most frequent attendants the wives of the gods whom Professor Roth considers to refer to the principal sphere of his creative action, as the bestower of offspring.

Indra sometimes appears to be in a state of hostility with Tvashtri and his son; and at last a quarrel occurs in which Indra slays him. In the Márkaṇḍeya Purána Tvashtri is identified with Visvakarman and Prajápati. See Muir's *Orig. Sans. Texts*, Vol. V, pp. 224-233, where the authorities are quoted for all the preceding statements.

TWISHA—A daughter of Paurnamása.

UCCHAIHSRAVAS—The model horse. The white horse of Indra, produced at the churning of the ocean. It is fed on ambrosia, and is held to be the king of horses.

UCCHISTA The remains of a sacrifice, to which divine powers are ascribed by the *Rgveda*.

UDAKSENA—A king of Hastinápnra, the son of Viswaksena.

UDARADHI—The son of Pushti, and grandson of Dhruva.

UDAVASU—A king of Mithila, the son of Janaka, (*q.v.*)

UDAVRAJA—A country mentioned in the Rig Veda as one "into which the waters flow," the residence of the black-skinned aboriginal king Sambara, who possessed one hundred ancient impregnable cities.

UDAYAGIRI PARVATA The eastern mountain from behind which the sun rises.

UDAYAGIR—The modern name of the hill called in the Mahábhárata Rishígiri. See VARAHA.

UDAYANA—**(1)** A prince of the lunar race, and son of Sahasrānīka, who is the hero of a popular story. He was king of Vatsa, and is commonly called Vatsarāja. His capital was Kauśāmbī. Vāsavadattā, princess of Ujjayinī, saw him in a dream and fell in love with him. He was decoyed to that city, and there kept in captivity by the king, Caṇḍasena; but when the minister set him at liberty, he carried off Vāsavadattā from her father and a rival suitor. **(2)** A name of Agastya.

UDAYASWA—A king of Magadha, the son of Dharbaka.

UDAYIN—One of the sons of Vasudeva, by his wife Devakí

UDDALIN—One of the fifteen teachers of the White Yájus.

UDDHAVA The friend and counsellor of Kṛṣṇa. According to some he was Kṛṣṇa's cousin, being son of Devabhāga, the brother of Vasudeva. He was also called Pavanavyādhi. A sage, versed in the Yoga doctrine, foreseeing the destruction of the Yádavas, applied to Krishṇa for advice, and was seat to Badarikaṣrama to practice penance and prepare for heaven.

UDGATRI—The title of the priest who chants the prayers and hymns in the administratioṇ of sacrificial rites from the *Sāmaveda*.

UDGITHA—One of the kings of Bhárata Varsha, the son of Bhava.

UDRANKA—Hariścandra's aerial, (*see* SAUBHA)

UGRA, UGRARITAS—Two of the eleven Rudras. A name of Rudra, or of one of his manifestations, (*see* RUDRA)

UGRADEVA—The name of a deceased ancestor conceived of as still existing in another world, and invoked in one of the hymns of the Rig Veda, along with the souls of other deceased ancestors; they are thus called on, "Let not the gods injure us here, nor our early Fathers who know the realms! 'May the Fathers protect me in my invocation to the gods.'"

UGRAJIT, UGRAMPASYA—Two Apsaras, who are invoked in the Atharva Veda, and asked to remit sins committed while gambling. There are many verses which show that the Apsaras were intimately connected with gambling. Dr. Muir translates the following:—"I invoke hither the skillfully playing Apsaras who cuts up and conquers and gets gains in the game of dice. I invoke hither the skillfully playing Apsaras who collects and scatters, and receives gains in the game of dice. May she who dances about with the dice, when she wins by gaming, grant gain to us, and obtain success through her skill. May she come to us with abundance of food. Let them not conquer this money of ours. I invoke hither the joyful and exulting Apsaras—those [goddesses] who delight in dice, and who cherish grief and anger. In another verse they are said to be "fond of dice," and soul-bewitching."

UGRASENA—(1) The Rája of Mathura, who was deposed by his son Kansa and kept in confinement. The Rája Kansa was afterwards killed by Krishṇa in a severe contest. Krishṇa then restored Ugrasena to the throne, and sent to Indra for his royal hall Sudharman, which was conveyed from heaven by Váyu, and used by the Yádava chiefs. Ugrasena is then described as reigning wisely and well for a long period at Mathura; but when the death of Krishṇa took place, Ugrasena and his wives committed themselves to the flames; **(2)** One of the sons of Paríkṣhit.

UGRAYUDHA—A Kaurava prince, the son of Krita; by whose prowess the Nipa race of Kshatriyas was destroyed. Ugráyudha was slain by Bhíshma in consequence of demanding in marriage the widow of Sántana.

UJJAYANI—The ancient Avanti; a city of great antiquity, that is considered the first meridian by Hindu geographers and astronomers. Modem Oujein or Ujjain. It was the capital of Vikramāditya and one of the seven sacred cities. The ancient city was about a mile further south, and now lies buried in the earth, to the depth of from fifteen to eighteen feet: on digging, its walls are said to be found entire, pillars unbroken, &c. Whatever may have been the real cause of this catastrophe, Hindu fancy has attributed it to the intervention of the gods. Hindu geographers calculate their longitude from it, making it their first meridian.

UKTHA—(1) The name of a portion of the Sáma Veda, created from the southern mouth of Brahmá;' **(2)** A prince, the son of Chhala, descendant of Kusa.

ULJJAVAHA—A king of Mithila, the son of Suchi.

ULMUKA—One of the sons of Balabhadra by his wife Revatí.

ULNKI—The parent of owls. *V.P*, 148.

ULUKA 'An owl.' Son of Kitava. He was king of a country and people of the same name. He was an ally of the Kauravas, and acted as their envoy to the Pāṇḍavas.

ULUPI—A daughter of Kauravya, Rāja of the Nāgas, with whom Arjuna contracted a kind of marriage. She was nurse to her stepson, Babhruvāhana, and had great influence over him. According to the *Viṣṇu Purāṇa* she had a son named Irāvat.

ULWANA—One of the seven Rishis of the third Manwantara; they were sons of Vasishṭha.

UMAPATI—'Husband of Umā', that is to say, Śiva.

UMA—'Light.' A name of the consort of Śiva. The earliest known mention of the name is in the *Kena Upaniṣad*, where she appears as a mediatrix between Brahmā and the other gods, and seems to be identified with Vāc. (*see* DEVĪ)

The Harivansa gives the following history of Umá, which differs in some points from that of the Rámáyana, as it assigns three daughters to Himavat and Mená, among whom the Ganga is not included. 'Their (the Pitṛis') mental daughter was Mená, the eminent wife of the great mountain Himavat. The king of the mountains begot three daughters upon Mená,—*viz.*, Aparṇá, Ekaparṇá, and Ekapáṭala. These three, performing very great austerity, such as could not be performed by gods or Danavas, distressed with alarm both the stationary and moving worlds. Ekaparṇá (one leaf) fed upon one leaf. Ekapáṭalá took only one páṭalá (Bignonia) for her food. One (Aparṇá) took no sustenance, but her mother, distressed through maternal affection, forbade her, dissuading her with the words, *u ma* (O don't). The beautiful goddess, performing arduous austerity, having been thus addressed by tier mother on that occasion, became known hi the three-worlds as Umá. In this manner the contemplative goddess became renowned under that name. But this world shall remain distinguished by having these three maids... Umá was the eldest and most excellent among the three. Distinguished by the force derived from deep contemplation she obtained Mahadeva for her husband.—*O.S.T.*, Vol. IV, p. 367.

The first work in which the name of Umá occurs is the Talava-kára, or Kena Upanishad. In his remarks on a passage in this work, relating a victory gained by Brahmá for the gods, Weber supplies an ingenious contribution to the mythological history of Umá. He says: "The representation in Sections 3 and 4 indicates that the Kena Upanishad was produced at a time when,—in place of the three principal gods, Agni,

Váyu, and Súrya, who had come to be regarded as the representatives of the divine principle oil earth, in the atmosphere, and in heaven,—Agni, Váyu, and Indra were regarded as such. These are properly only two, since Indra is essentially identical with Váyu. Though I have found numerous examples of the first triad, especially in the two Yajur-vedas, I have noticed only one other of the second' triad, which is properly one a duad, *viz.*, in the Rik-text of the Purusha Sukta (R. V., x. 99, 13). Nor am I able to give a satisfactory explanation of it. On the other hand, the totality of the divine was already comprehended in Brahmá (neuter), and it is the object of the legend here to make clear and to enforce the supremacy of Brahmá, over all temporary divine manifestations, and even over the triad of such.

"But how shall we explain the position of Umá Haimavatí, who comes forward as mediatrix between the eternal Brahmá, and the gods? According to Sánkara, she is Vidyá (knowledge) who appears Umá rupini (in the form of Uma) to Indra. The same explanation is found in Sāyana, who (on *Taitt. Ar.* x, 1, 150) when interpreting the word *soma*, cites this passage, and remarks:

"Since Gauri, the daughter of Himavat, is the impersonation of divine knowledge, the word Umá, which denotes Gaurí, indicates divine knowledge. Hence in the Talavakára Upanishad, in the passage on the impersonation of divine knowledge, the impersonation of divine knowledge is introduced in these words: 'He said to the very resplendent Umá Haimavati.'

There are, however, some additional points that seem to place the original signification of Umá in quite a different light First of all, why is she called Haimavatí? What has she to do with Himavat ? Is it that the *brahmd-vidya* (divine knowledge) came originally from the Himavat to the Aryans dwelling in Madhya-déṣa (the central region of Hindustan)? We have learnt from the Haushítáki Bráhmana (*Ind. Stud.* i, 153) that the north of India was distinguished by greater purity of speech, and the students travelled thither to learn the language (*vácham sixitum*) and on their return thence enjoyed great consideration and authority. Now it would have been quite natural if this state of things had not been confined to language, but had become extended to speculation also, and if the knowledge of the one, eternal Brahmá, had been sooner attained in the peaceful valleys of the Himálaya, than was possible for men living in Madhyadéṣa, where their minds were more occupied by the practical concerns of life." Such a view of Umá, Haimavatí appears to me, however, to be very hazardous.

For,—not to say that in our explanations of the ancient Indian deities we act wisely when we attach greater importance to the physical than to the speculative element,—we are by no means certain that Umá actually does signify divine knowledge (*brahmá vidyá*); and moreover, her subsequent position as Rudra's wife (in the *Taitt. Ar.*) would thus be quite inexplicable. Now there is among the epithets of this latter goddess a similar one, *viz.*, Párvatí, which would lead us in interpreting the word Haimavatí, to place the emphasis not upon the *Himavat*, but upon the mountain (*parvata*): and with this I might connect the epithets of Rudra which we have learnt from the Sátarudriya, *Girisa*, *Giri-sa.nta*, *Girisaya*, *Giritra*, in which we recognize the germ of the conception of Śiva's dwelling on Kailása. He is the tempest, which rages in the mountains, and his wife is therefore properly called Párvatí, Haimavatí, "the mountaineer," 'the daughter of Himavat.' At the same time, it is not clear what we have to understand by his wife; and further she is perhaps, originally not his wife, but his sister, for Umá and Ambiká are at a later period evidently identical, and Ambiká is Rudra's sister (*Ind. Stud.* I, 183). Besides, this identification of Umá with Ambiká leads us to a new etymology of the former. For as Ambiká, 'mother,' appears to be merely an euphemistic and flattering epithet, employed to propitiate the cruel goddess, in the same way it appears that we must derive Umá from the root *u*, *av*, 'to protect.'*

As the consort of Śiva, the goddess has various names; as Durga, Devi, Káli, Párvati, Bhavani, &c. Some of these names have in the Vedic writings a different import from those assigned in the later mythology, as Śiva was not a deity of the Vedic period, or not of the whole of it. "Though this double character of the consort of Śiva is not always discernible in the myths which are connected with special designations of hers, and though at a late period the popular creed looked upon her far more as the type of destruction than as that of divine wisdom, yet the works devoted to her praise never fail to extol her also as the personification of the highest knowledge." Various myths relating to this goddess are to be found scattered over nearly the whole range of Hindu literature.

Some of those have already been narrated in the

articles given under her other names in this volume- In a previous existence she is said to have been Sati, the daughter of Daksha, who abandoned her mortal life because she was slighted by her father when he performed his great sacrifice and neglected to invite Śiva to partake of it. As Uma she was the mother of Ganeṣa and Karttikeya, (*q.v.*)

"According to the Harívansa she was, in another life, born as the daughter of Yaṣoda, and exchanged for Vishṇu, when in his incarnation as Krishṇa he was born as a son of Devaki. On that occasion Kansa killed her, but as soon as he bad dashed her to the ground, she rose to the sky, leaving behind her corporeal frame, and became a divine virgin to whom the gods addressed their praises. Hence her names Kanyá, Kumari, &c., the virgin. This connection between the legendary history of Umá and Vishṇu, is also briefly referred to in the Devimahátmya, though this work is chiefly concerned in the narrative of the martial exploits of the goddess. The latter consisted in the destruction by her of two demons, Madhu and Kaiṭabha, who had endangered the existence of the god Brahmá; and of the demon Mahisha or Mahishasura, who, having conquered all the gods, had expelled them from heaven, and who met Umá, assisted only by her lion, with a numberless host of demon; moreover in her defeating the army of Cháṇḍa and Muṇḍa, two demon servants of Śumhha and Nisumbha; in her killing the demon Raktavija, who had a sort of charmed life, each drop of his blood, when shed, producing hundreds of demons like himself; and ultimately in her destroying the demons Śumbha and Nisumbha themselves.

"In commemoration of her victory over Mahishasura, a festival celled the Durgápújá is annually celebrated in Bengal. The goddess is there represented with ten arms trampling upon the demon, which is also attacked by her lion, and wounds! in the chest by her spear. She has also laid hold of him by the hair, and is about to chop off his head."—*Goldstucker*. (* Muir, *O.S.T.*, Vol. IV, p. 360.

UNMADA—Insanity; a form of Brahmá.

UNNATI—Elevation; one of the allegorical daughters of Daksha, married to Dharma.

UPADANAVI—The daughter of Vrishaparvan the Daitya, and wife of Hiranyaksha.

UPADEVA—**(1)** One of the sons of Akrúra; **(2)** A son of Devaka.

UPADEVA—A daughter of Devaka.

UPAGU—A king of Mithila, the son of Satyaratbi.

UPAKOSA—The wife of Vararuchi, (*q.v.*) During her husband's absence she attracted the notice and desires of several suitors, whom she succeeded in exposing and punishing in a very ludicrous manner. See Wilson's Works, III, 170.

UPAMADGU—A prince, one of the sons of Swaphalka by Gandini.

UPANANDA, UPANIDHI—Two sons of Vasudeva, by his wives Madira and Bhadrá, respectively.

UPANISHAD—" Is the name of those Sanskrit works belonging to the Vedic literature which contain the mystical doctrine of the Hindus on the nature of a supreme being, its relation to the human soul, and the process of creation. The word (derived from the Sankrit prefixes *upa*, 'beneath' or 'near,' and ni, 'in,' combined with the radical *sad*, 'sit') is explained by the great theologian *Sankara* (*q.v.*), and others after him, as meaning the 'science of Brahmá,' or 'the understanding of the identity of Brahmá and the soul,' because • in those devoted to it, this science *sets to rest* (or destroys) the world, together with (ignorance) its cause;' or in other words, because it shows to them that the world has, besides Brahmán, no reality. Grammatical commentators explain its etymology as implying that' eternal bliss *reposes on. it* (*upani-shidati sreyo 'syam*);' and Professor Max Müller has surmised that the word 'Upanishad meant originally the act of sitting down near a teacher, of submissively listening to him,' whence it came to mean' implicit faith, and at last truth or divine revelation.' But apart from the artificialness of all these interpretations, it deserves notice that the earliest sense of the word appears to be that of 'secret' or 'mystery' (literally, that which *sits* or rests *beneath.* ') In this sense, it' is mentioned by the grammarian Paṇini; and as it is very probable that, in his tirco, the works bearing the name of Upanishads were not yet in existence, it may be assumed that these works derived their name from the mysteriousness of the doctrine contained in them: and perhaps also from the mystical manner in which they propounded it.

In order to understand the origin and purport of the Upanishads, as well as the relation in which they stand to the Vedas, properly so called, it must be borne in mind that, though the Vedic hymns are based on the worship of the elementary powers, and the Bráhmaṇa portion connected with them is chiefly concerned in legendary and ritual matter relating to that worship, yet in both these portions of the Vedas, and especially in the Bráhmanas, the beginning of a period become already visible when the poets raised the questions as to the origin of the world and the true nature of the gods. A first attempt at a systematic answer to these questions was made in works which bear an intimate relation to the Bráhmaṇas; and so great was the awe in which, on this account, these works were held, that they bad to be read in the solitude, where the mind. could ponder in perfect calmness over the mysterious problems in which they are engaged. These are the Áraṇyakas (from *aranya*, a forest.) But as the style and contents of the Áraṇyakas are extremely obscure, and as, through the close alliance of these works to the Bráhmaṇas, of which some of them form part, the theological questions of which they treat are much overlaid with ritual and other matters which properly belong to the Bráhmaṇas, a further progress made in the came direction, led to the composition of works and treatises, the diction of which is somewhat clearer, and less entangled with subjects extraneous to the problems they intend to solve. Such works and treatises are the *Upanishads.* Their object, like that of the Áraṇyakas, is to impress the mind with the belief in one Supreme Spirit (*Brahmá*, as a neuter, and different, therefore, from the same word as a masculine, which is the name of the first god of the *Trimúrti*, *q.v.*)—to show that this Supreme Spirit is the creator of the world; that the world has no reality if thought of besides Brahmá, and that the human soul is identical in nature with that same spirit whence it emanates. The reward the Upanishads hold out to the believer, who understands their doctrine, and firmly follow it, is freedom from Transmigration (*q.v.*) and consequent eternal bliss. The object and aim of the Upanishads are therefore the same as those propounded in the philosophical systems; and the Upanishads may therefore be looked upon as the forerunners of these systems themselves—those Upanishads, at least, which we may call the older Upanishads; for as to the more recent ones, and those which bear the stamp of sectarian character, their claim to be ranked among the Vedic writings is extremely doubtful, if at all admissible.

Though agreeing in the main points of their doctrine, it is easily understood that works of this nature, ranging over different periods of Hindu religion, will also differ from one another both in the manner and detail in which they deliver their subject-matter, and in the degree of completeness with which they treat of it. Thus, in some, the legendary narrative, and even ritual detail, are still considerably blended with the theosophical speculation—and these stand nearest, therefore, the Áraṇyakas, probably also in time; *in* others, more philosophical, the nature of Brahmá and the human soul is the only subject of inquiry; in others, the process of creation is also enlarged upon, with detail which harmonises more or less either with the ulterior views of the Vedanta (*q.v.*) or those of the Śámkhya (*q.v.*) philosophy; some Upanishads, again, especially emphasise the inefficiency, for the attainment of eternal bliss, of the performing religious acts and of worldly studies—the knowledge of Brahmá being the only means that leads to this end; others, on the contrary, in conformity with the Yoga (*q.v.*) doctrine, assign a prominent place to the exterior means, by using which the soul would quality itself for union with the Supreme Spirit; while the sectarian Upanishads, which identify this spirit with Vishṇu and Śiva, have, besides, the tendency of reconciling the popular with the philosophical creed.

Of the older Upanishads, a typical instance is furnished in the Chhándogya Upanishad of the Sámaveda, the framework of which is legendary throughout, and its contents allegories! and mystical. Other shorter Upanishads, freer from narratives and allusions to the mysterious import of ritual acts, aim at a more intelligible exposition of the doctrine of the Soul. Of their mode of treatment, the following passage from the Káṭhaka Upanishads will serve as an example: *Nachiketas*, the son of Vájaṣravas, having come to the abode of Yama, the judge of the dead, and obtained from him the grant of three boons, asks of him, for his third boon, an answer to the following question: 'There is this doubt: some say that (the soul) exists after the death of a man (in connection with another body than this); others say that it does not. This I should like to know, instructed by thee.' And Yama, after some hesitation, explains to him that the *soul* and Brahmá are one, but that a man attains immortality only by understanding this unity, and that, to arrive at this understanding, he must free his mind from sensual desires, and get a correct knowledge both of the nature of Brahmá and of the soul. 'Know the soul as the rider, and the body as the car; know intellect as the charioteer, and *manas* (the organ of volition) as the rein. The senses, they say, are the horses, the objects (their) roads; and the enjoyer (*i.e.*, the rider) is (the soul') endowed with body, senses, and manas. Thus say the wise. If he (the charioteer) is unwise, and his manas is always unbridled, his senses are uncontrolled like vicious horses; but if he is wise, and his manas is always bridled, his senses are controlled like good horses. He who, always impure, is unwise, and whose manas is unbridled, does not attain that abode (of immortality,) but comes to the world (of birth and death); he, however, who, always pure, is wise, and whose manas is bridled, he attains *that* abode whence he is not born again. The man who has a wise charioteer, and whose manas is bridled, reaches the other shore of the road (of the world,) the highest abode of Vishṇu. Higher, (*i.e.*, subtler,) indeed, than the objects are the senses; higher than the senses is manas; higher than manas, intellect; and higher than intellect, the great one, the soul. Higher than the great one is that which is unmanifested, and higher than the unmanifested is Purusha, the Supreme Spirit. But higher than Purusha there is nothing; he is the goal, the highest resort. The highest spirit is the soul hidden in all created beings; it is not manifest, but is beheld by those who can see what is subtle with an attentive, subtle intellect.' The coincidence between the allegory, in the foregoing passage, and that in Plato's *Phadrus*, imparts an additional interest to this Upanishad, which is valuable, moreover, on account of the evidence it affords as to points of agreement and difference between its views of the development of the world and those expounded in the Sánkhya (*q.v.*) The Muṇḍaka Upanishad is important for the relative position which it assigns to the teaching of the Vedas, and the doctrine of the Upanishads. 'Two sciences,' it says, the knowers of Brahmá tell us, 'must be known, the higher and the inferior. The inferior is (the knowledge of) the Rig Veda, the Yajurveda, the Sámaveda, and the Atharvaveda, the knowledge of pronunciation, the ritual, grammar, explanation of Vedic texts, prosody, and astronomy. But the higher knowledge is that by which that imperishable Brahmá is comprehended. That which is invisible, unseizable, without descent (or origin,) without either colour, eye, or ear, without hand or foot, eternal, manifold (in creation,) all-pervading, very subtle, undecaying—the wise behold it as the cause of created beings.' And in another place, the performers of the sacrificial rites ordained by the Veda are said to attain, indeed, to Indra's heaven in virtue of their pious work; but this state of bliss is declared to be unstable and perishable, and these 'fools ... drop (from their heaven) as soon-as this heaven (the reward of their acts) has faded away. Fancying that pious acts, ordained by the Vedas and codes of law, are the highest (object of man,) these ignorant people do not know that there is something else which leads to eternal bliss. Having enjoyed (the reward of their deeds) on the happy summit of paradise, they enter again this world, or one that is (even) lower. Those, on the contrary,—who practice penance and faith, and, with subdued desire, live in the forest, under the vow of a religious mendicant, they, free from sin, enter through the sun to that abode where resides that immortal spirit, that spirit, indeed, of undecaying nature.'

The *Talavakdra, or Kena*, Upanishad, which, being one of the shortest, is in form one of the most philosophical treatises of this kind, puts in clearer language, perhaps, than any other Upanishad, the doctrine that the true knowledge of the Supreme Spirit consists in the consciousness which man acquires of his *incapacity* to understand it, since the human mind being capable only to comprehend finite objects, cannot have a knowledge of what is infinite.

The Upanishads are not supposed to have been revealed in the same manner as the Vedic hymns. Nevertheless, with- the exception of a few confessedly modern Upanishad, they are not assigned to human authorship, but looked upon as inspired writings, to which the term Śruti (*q.v.*) applies. In several Upanishads, no special mention is made of their divine origin; in some, however, this is done. Thus the *Chhándogya* Upanishad, in the concluding section, relates: 'This (knowledge of the soul) Brahmá (the god of the Trimúrti) imparted to Prajápati (a lord of creation—the patriarch Kaşyapa, as Śankara explains); Prajápati imparted it to Manu, and Manu to mankind;' the Brihaḍáraṇyaka Upanishad, which on three occasions gives long list of teachers who handed it down to their pupils, always ascribes itself, in the but instance, to the authorship of 'the self-existent Brahma (the Supreme Spirit);' and in a similar manner the Muṇḍak Upanishad says that it was Brahmá, (the god of the Trimúrti,) the creator of the universe, who first taught the science of the Supreme Spirit to his eldest son, Atharvan. As in the case of most ancient works of Sanskrit literature, the date of the Upanishads also still remains quite uncertain, and, wherever given, is purely conjectural. According to the native system, they are classified as belonging to one or the other of the four Vedas, with which they are held to stand in immediate connection. There are Upanishads, consequently, of the Rig-, Yajur-, Sáma-, and Atharva-veda. But this classification has no reference whatever to chronology."—Chambers' *Encyclopedia*

'Esoteric doctrine.' The third division of the Vedas attached to the *Brāhmaṇa* portion, and forming part of the Śruti or revealed word. The Upaniṣads are generally written in prose with interspersed verses, but some are wholly in verse. There are about 150 of these works, probably even more. They are of later date than the *Brāhmaṇas*, but it is thought that the oldest may date as far back as the sixth century B.C. The object of these treatises is to ascertain the mystic sense of the text of the Veda, and so they enter into such abstruse questions as the origin of the universe, the nature of the deity, the nature of soul, and the connection of mind and matter. Thus they contain the beginnings of that metaphysical inquiry which ended in the full development of Hindu Philosophy. The Upaniṣads have "one remarkable peculiarity, the total absence of any Brahmāṇical exclusiveness in their doctrine. They are evidently later than the older Saṁhitās and *Brāhmaṇas* but they breathe an entirely different spirit, a freedom of thought unknown in any earlier work except the *Ṛgveda* hymns themselves. The great teachers of the higher knowledge and brāhmaṇas are continually represented as going to kṣatriya kings to become their pupils."—*Professor Cowell.*

The *Ṛgveda* has the Upaniṣad called *Aitareya* attached to the *Aitareya Brāhmaṇa.* The *Taittirīya Saṁhitā* of the *Yajur* has an Upaniṣad of the same name. The *Vājasaneyī Saṁhitā* has the *Īśa*, and attached to the *Śatapatha Brāhmaṇa* it has the *Bṛhadāraṇyaka*, which is the most important of them. The *Sāmaveda* has the *Kena* and *Chāndogya.* All these have been translated into English. The *Atharvaveda* has the *Kaṭha*, *Praśna*, *Muṇḍaka*, *Māṇḍūkya*, and others, altogether fifty-two in number. These are the most important of the Upaniṣads. Many of the Upaniṣads have been printed, and several of them translated in the *Bibliotheca Indica*, and by Poley. There is a catalogue by Müller in the *Zeitschrift des D.M.G.*, vol. XIX..

UPAPLAVYA—Matsya, the capital of the king of Virāta.

UPA-PURANAS—Minor Puránas, of which there are said to be eighteen; "but the names of only a few of these are specified in the least exceptionable authorities, and the greater number of the works is not procurable." (*Wilton.*) The Matsya enumerates but four, but the Devi Bhagavata specifies eighteen. The Devi Khanda has a different list but enumerates eighteen. "Of the Upa Puránas few are to be procured. Those in my possession are the Śiva, considered as distinct from the Váyu; the Kálika, and perhaps one of the Naradíyas."—*Wilson.*

UPARICARA—A Vasu or demigod, who, according to the *Mahābhārata*, became king of Cedi by command of Indra. He had five sons by his wife; and by an apsaras, named Adrikā, condemned to live on earth in the form of a fish, he had a son named Matsya (fish), and a daughter, Satyavatī, who was the mother of Vyāsa.

UPASRUTI—A supernatural voice which is heard at night revealing the secrets of the future.

UPASUNDA—A *daitya*, son of Nisunda, brother of Sunda, and father of Múka.

UPA-VEDAS—Subordinate or inferior Vedas. These are sciences which have no connection whatever with the Śruti or revealed Veda. They are four in number—(1) *Āyurveda*, medicine; (2) *Gāndharvaveda*, music and dancing; (3) *Dhanurveda*, archery, military science; (4) *Sthāpatyaveda*, architecture.

UPAYAJA—A brahman of eminent learning and sanctity, to whom king Drupada applied in his anxiety to procure a son, promising a million of cows if he enabled him to obtain the son he desired. Upayája however declined the task, and referred him to his elder brother Yája. (*q.v.*)

UPENDRA—(1) A title given to Kṛṣṇa by Indra; **(2)** The divinity who presides over the feet.

URAGAS—The Nāgas or serpents inhabiting *pātāla.*

URDDHABAHN—One of the seven pure sages, of the first and third Manwantara, the eons of *Vasishâha* by his wife Urjja.

URDDHABAHUS—"Personal privation and torture being of great efficacy in the creed of the Hindus, various individuals, some influenced by credulity, and some by knavery, have adopted modes of distorting their limbs, and forcing them out of their natural position, until they can no longér resume their ordinary directions.

The Uraddhábahus extend one or both hands above their heads, till they remain of themselves thus elevated. They also close the fist, and the nails being necessarily suffered to grow *make* then-way between the metacarpal bones, and completely perforate the hand. The *Urddhabahus* are solitary mandicants, as are all of this description, and never have any fixed abode: they subsist upon alms; many of them go naked, but some wear a wrapper stained with ochre; they usually assume the *Saiva* marks, and twist their hair so as to project from the forehead, in imitation of the Játa of *Śiva.—Wilson*, Vol. I.

URJA—**(1)** One of the seven Rishis of the second Manwantara; **(2)** An obsolete name of a month.

URJASWATI—**(1)** A daughter of Daksha who was married to Dharma; **(2)** The daughter of Priyavrata.

URJJA—Energy; A daughter of Dakahs who was married to Vasishṭha.

URMILA—(Urmilá), a daughter of king Janaka, and sister of Síta. She was given in marriage by her father king Janaka to Lakshmana, the brother of Ráma.

URMILA—Daughter of Janaka, sister of Sītā, wife of Lakṣmaṇa and mother of Gandharvī Somadā.

URUASHAYA—A prince, the son of Mahavírya, a descendant of Bharata.

URU—One of the ten noble sons of the Manu Chakshusha.

URVA—Father of Ṛcika and grandfather of Jamadagni.

URVASI—A celestial nymph, mentioned first in the *Ṛgveda.* The sight of her beauty is said to have caused the generation, in a peculiar way, of the sages Agastya and Vasiṣṭha by Mitra and Varuṇa. A verse says, "And thou, O Vasiṣṭha, art a son of Mitra and Varuṇa." She roused the anger of these ṭwo deities and incurred their curse, through which she came to live upon the earth, and became the wife or mistress of Purūravas. The story of her amour. with Purūravas is first told in the *Śatapatha Brāhmaṇa.* The loves of Purūravas, the Vikram or hero, and of Urvaśī, the nymph, are the subjects of Kālidāsa's drama called *Vikramorvaśī.* (*see* PURŪRAVAS).

USANAS—**(1)** The planet Venus or its regent, also called Śukra (*q.v.*). **(2)** Author of a Dharmaśāstra or law-book. **(3)** The preceptor of the Daityas, one of the Brah-manical tribe of Bhárgavas, sons of Bhrigu; **(4)** The Vyása of the third Dwápara age; **(5)** A prince, the son of Támas, who celebrated a hundred sacrifices of the horse.

USHA—**(1)** The wife of the Rudra Bhava; **(2)** The daughter of Báṇa, who saw Aniruddha in a dream and became enamoured of him. She related this to Chitrlekha, a female confidante, who advised the employment of a portrait painter to take likenesses of all the young princes in the neighbourhood. On seeing the portrait of Aniruddha, grandson of Krishṇa, Usha recognised the youth-she had seen in her dream. The same confidante now offered her services; and by her means Aniruddha held clandestine meetings with Usha; and at length was secreted in her private apartments. Báṇa discovered this, and made Aniruddha a prisoner.' Krishṇa then interfered, and after a terrible fight Aniruddha was released; both parents agreed to a marriage, which was publicly celebrated at Dwáiaka. See ANIRUDDHA. She is called also Prītijuṣā.

USHAS—The Dawn. The Aurora of Hindu mythology. "This goddess, who corresponds to the 'Hue of the Greeks and to the Aurora of the Latins, is a favourite object of celebration with the poets of the Rig Veda, and the hymns addressed to her are among the most beautiful—if not the most beautiful—in the entire collection."*

Ushas is continually described as the daughter of the Sky. She is called the sister of Bhaga, and the kinswoman of Varuṇa. She is also the sister of Night, who is also the daughter of the Sky. Ushas is also frequently brought into connection with the Sun. He is called her lover and is said to follow her track; and she is represented as leading on the beautiful white hone the Sun. She is declared to be the mistress of the world and the wife of the Sun. Ushas and Agni are also frequently brought into conjunction, fire being always kindled for sacrificial purposes at dawn. He is called her lover and is said to appear with or before the dawn. Ushas is also often connected with the Aṣvins, the time of whose manifestation is regarded by Yáska as being between midnight and sunrise. They are said to associate with her, and she is called their friend.* In one place the moon is said to be born again and again, ever new, and to go before Ushas as the herald of the day. Indra is said to have created, or lighted up, Ushas. He is however sometimes represented as assuming a hostile attitude towards her, and is said to have crushed her chariot with his thunderbolt.

The Nighaṇṭu gives sixteen names of Ushas, which seem to be almost entirely epithets, *viz.*, the resplendent,' the beautiful, the shining, the flowing, the possessor of brilliant riches, the white, the bringer of food, the giver of joy, the bright, the fair-coloured, the ruddy, the utterer of pleasant voices. Some of these epithets are of frequent occurrence in the hymns, and there are also many others to be found there, such as the magnificent, the righteous, the immortal, the gold-hued, &c., &c.

Ushas is borne onward on a shining chariot, of massive construction, richly decorated and spontaneously yoked, drawn by ruddy horses, or by cows or bulls of the same colour, traversing rapidly a distance of thirty yojanas. Like a beautiful young woman dressed by her mother, a richly-decked dancing girl, a gaily attired wife appearing before her husband, or a female rising resplendent out of the bath, smiling and confiding in the irresistible power of her attractions, she unveils her bosom to the gaze of the beholder. She dispels the darkness, *disclosing* the treasures it had concealed: she illuminates the world, revealing its most distant extremities. She is the life and breath of all things, causing the birds to fly forth from their nests, visiting every house, and like an active housewife arousing her household, awakening the five races of men, yea gods generally are described as waking with Ushas.†

Dr. Muir gives the following metrical sketch of Ushas as represented in the hymns of the Rig Veda.

Hail, Ushas, daughter of the sky,
Who, borne upon thy shining car

By ruddy all creatures, as if from death, and sending men forth to the pursuit of their several occupations; and rendering good service to the gods by causing all worshippers to awake, and the sacrificial fires to be kindled. She is however entreated to arouse only the devout and liberal worshipper, and to leave the ungodly niggard to sleep on in unconsciousness. She is young, being born anew every day, and yet she is old, nay immortal, and wears out the lives of successive generations, which disappear one after another, while she continues undecaying.*

The worshippers however sometimes venture to take the credit of being more alert than Ushas, and of awaking her instead of being awakened by her: and in one place she is solicited to make no delay that the sun may not scorch her as like a thief or an enemy. She is prayed to bring the gods to drink the libations of Soma. Agni and the steeds from realms afar,

And ever lightening, drawest nigh:—
Thou sweetly smilest, goddess fair,
Disclosing all thy youthful grace,
Thy bosom bright, thy radiant face,
And lustre of thy golden hair:
(So shines a fond and winning bride,
Who robes her form in brilliant guise,
And to her lord's admiring eyes
Displays her charms with conscious pride:—
Or virgin by her mother decked,
Who, glorying in her beauty, shows
In every glance, her power she knows
All eyes to fix, all hearts subject:
Or actress, who by skill in song
And dance, and graceful gestures light,
And many-coloured vestures bright,
Enchants the eager, gazing throng:—
Or maid who, wont her limbs to lave
In some cool stream among the woods,
Where never vulgar eye intrudes,
Emerges fairer from the wave):—
But closely by the amorous sun
Pursued, and vanquished in the race,
Thou soon art locked in his embrace,
And with him blendest into one.
Fair Ushas, though through years untold
Thou hast lived on, yet thou art born
Anew on each succeeding morn,
And so thou art both young and old.
As in thy fated ceaseless course
Thou risest on us day by day,
Thou wearest all our lives away
With silent, ever-wasting, force.
Their round our generations run:
The old depart, and in their place
Springs ever up a younger race,
Whilst thou, immortal, lookest on.
All those who watched for thee of old
Are gone, and now 't is we who gaze
On thy approach; in future days
Shall other men thy beams behold.
But't is not thoughts so grave and sad
Alone that thou dost with thee bring,
A shadow o'er our hearts to fling;—
Thy beams returning make us glad.
Thy sister, sad and sombre Night
With stars that in the blue expanse
Like sleepless eyes mysterious glance,
At thy approach is quenched in light:—
And earthly forms, till now concealed
Behind her veil of dusky hue,
Once more come sharply out to view,
By thine illuming glow revealed.
Thou art the life of all that lives,
The breath of all that breathes; the sight
Of thee makes every countenance bright,
New strength to every spirit gives.
When thou dost pierce the musky gloom,
Birds flutter forth from every brake,
All sleepers as from death awake,
And men their myriad tasks resume.
Some prosperous, wake in listless mood,
And others every nerve to strain
The goal of power or wealth to gain,
Or what they deem the highest good.
But some to holier thoughts aspire,
In hymns the race celestial praise,
And light, on human hearths to blaze,

The heaven-born sacrificial fire.
And not alone do bard and priest
Awake;—the gods thy power confess
By starting into consciousness
When thy first rays suffuse the east:
And basting downward from the sky,
They visit men devout and good,
Consume their consecrated food,
And all their longings satisfy.
Bright goddess, let thy genial rays
To us bring stores of envied wealth
In kine and steeds, and sons, with health,
And joy of heart, and length of days.

* Muir, *O.S.T*, Vol. v, p. 181. ** *Ibid.* † *Ibid.*

USIJ—Mentioned in the *Ṛgveda* as the mother of Kakṣīvat. A female servant of the queen of the Kaliṅga Rāja. The king desired his queen to submit to the embraces of the sage Dīrghatamas, in order that he might beget a son. The queen substituted her bondmaid Uśij. The sage, cognisant of the deception, sanctified Uśij, and begot upon her a son, Kakṣivat, who, through his affiliation by the king, was a kṣatriya, but, as the son of Dīrghatamas, was a brāhmaṇa. This story is told in the *Mahābhārata* and some of the Purāṇas.

USMAPAS—The *pitṛs* or a class of *pitṛs* (*q.v.*).

UTATHYA—A brāhmaṇa of the race of Aṅgiras, who married Bhadrā, daughter of Soma, a woman of great beauty. The god Varuṇa, who had formerly been enamoured of her, carried her off from Utathya's hermitage, and would not give her up to Nārada, who was sent to bring her back. Utathya, greatly enraged, drank up all the sea, still Varuṇa would not let her go. At the desire of Utathya, the lake of Varuṇa was then dried up and the ocean swept away. The saint then addressed himself to the countries and to the river: "Sarasvatī, disappear into the deserts, and let this land, deserted by thee, become impure." "After the country had become dried up, Varuṇa submitted himself to Utathya and brought back Bhadrā. The sage was pleased to get back his wife, and released both the world and Varuṇa from their sufferings."

UTKALA—The modern Orissa. It gives its name to one of the five northern nations of brāhmaṇas. (*see* BRĀHMAṆA) One of the sons of Sudyumna after his transformation.

UTTAMA—**(1)** The son of Uttanápada and grandson of the Manu Swáyambhuva. **(2)** A Manu, the son of Priyavrata. **(3)** The Manu of the third Manwantara. **(4)** The Vyása of the twenty-first Dwápara age.

UTTAMAUJAS—A warrior of great strength, and an ally of the Pāṇḍavas.

UTTANAPAD—'Outstretched, supine.' In the Vedas, a peculiar creative source from which the earth sprang. Supposed to refer to the posture of a woman in parturition.

UTTANAPADA—A son of Manu and Śatarūpa. By his wife Sunṛtā he had four sons, Dhruva, Kirtimān, Ayuṣmān, and Vasu. Some of the Purāṇas gave him another wife, Suruci, and a son, Uttama. (*see* DHRUVA)

The son of the Manu Swáyambhuva. The Vishṇu Purána describes him as heroic and pious, but gives no particulars of his history,

UTTARA. (mas.), **UTTARĀ** (fem.)—A son and daughter of the Rājā of Virāṭa. Uttara was killed in battle by Śalya. The daughter married Abhimanyu, son of Arjuna.

UTTARA-BHADRAPADA—A lunar mansion in Vaiswánari in the Southern Avashthána.

UTTARA-KURU—A region lying far to the north, (*see* JAMBUDVĪPA) (Plural) The inhabitants of this region. A varsha or country beyond the Sringi range of mountains, south of Meru.

UTTARA-MIMANSA—A school of philosophy, (*see* DARŚANA)

UTTARA-NAIṢADA-CAMTA—A poem on the life of Nala, king of Niṣada, written about the year AD 1000 by Śrī Harṣa, a celebrated skeptical philosopher. It has been printed in the *Bibliotheca Indica.*

UTTARA-PHALGUNI—A lunar mansion in Arshabhí, in the Central Avashthána.

UTTARA-RĀMA-CARITA—'The later chronicle of Rāma. A drama by Bhavabhūti on the latter part of Rāma's life. The second part of King Rāma, as the *Mahāvīra-carita* is the first. The drama is based on the Uttara Kaṇḍa of the *Rāmāyaṇa*, and quotes two or three verses from that poem. It was probably written about the beginning of the eighth century. It has been translated in blank verse by Wilson, and more literally by Professor C.H.Tawney. There are several editions of the text.

UTTARASHADHA—A lunar mansion in Ajavithi, in the Southern Avashthana.

UTTARAYANA—The winter solstice. The festival which in the South of India is termed the Pongal, is celebrated in Upper India as the Uttaráyaṇa or Makara Sankránti, or sun's entrance into the sign Capricornus. The observances enjoined on this occasion are partly of a private, partly of a public character. The first consists of offerings to the Pitṛis, or progenitors, whether general, as of all mankind; or special, as of the family of the worshipper; to the "Vástu devas, the Dii Lares, or domestic genii; the guardians of the dwelling, or the site on which it is erected; and to the Viswa devas or universal gods. The ceremonies addressed to all these are performed within the abode of the householder, and are conducted by the family priest. The principal article of the offering is tila or sesamum seeds, either separately or mixed with molasses, or the saccharine juice of the fruit of the date tree, and made up into a kind of sweetmeat, called Tilüá. Pishtakas, or cakes, also are offered, composed of ground rice, mixed with sugar and ghee; whence the festival has the denomination of Tilüá Sankránti and Pishtaka Sankránti, the solar conjunction of the sweetmeat in the cake.

The good things prepared on this occasion are not intended exclusively for those imaginary beings that are unable to eat them. They are presented merely for the purpose of consecration, and that they may be eaten with greater zest by the householder and his family; nor is that all, for a portion of them is sent to friends and relations, as memorials of regard, enclosed in fine linen, silk or velvet, according to the means of the presenter, and the station of those to whom they are presented.

In many places in Bengal a curious practice is observed, called Báwana bandhana, particularly by the females of the family. In the evening one of the women takes a wisp of straw, and from the bundle picks out separate straws, which she ties singly to every article of furniture in the house, exclaiming 'Bawanna pauti,' implying 'may the measure of corn be increased fifty-two fold,' pauti denoting a measure of grain. In the villages similar straws are attached to the Golas, or thatched granaries, in which the grain of the preceding harvest has been stored.

All the Uttaráyaṇa bathing at the confluence of the Ganges with the ocean is particularly meritorious, and accordingly a vast concourse of people is annually assembled at; Gangá Ságar, or the mouth of the Hoogly branch of the Ganges; and as usual in all such assemblages, objects of a secular nature are blended with those of devotion; and the Melá, which originates in purposes of pilgrimage, becomes equally a meeting of itinerant merchants, or a fair.

On the first day bathing in the sea is to be performed; and many of those whose parents are recently deceased celebrate their ṣraddha, or obsequial ceremonies, on the seashore. After ablution the pilgrims repair to the temple of Kapila, (*q.v.*) Vishnu became incarnate in the person of Kapila for the destruction of the sixty thousand wicked sons of king Sagara. He is said to have stationed himself at this place which was then on the brink of a vast chasm leading to the infernal regions. The temple is under the alternate charge of a Bairági and Sannyási, mendicants of the Vaishnava and Śaiva sects; they exact a fee of four annas from each person who comes to the temple. * (* Wilson, *Works*, II, pp. 158-168.)

UTTATAHYA—A sage, the son of Angiras, and husband of Mamata.

VA—A name of Varuṇa; also name of his dwelling.

VAC—'Speech.' In the *Ṛgveda* Vāc appears to be the personification of speech by whom knowledge was communicated to man. Thus she is said to have "entered into the *ṛṣis*", and to make whom she loves terrible and intelligent, a priest and a *ṛṣi.* She was "generated by the gods", and is called "the divine Vāc", "queen of the gods", and she is described as "the melodious cow who milked forth sustenance and water", "who yields us nourishment and sustenance". The Brāhmaṇas associate her with Prajāpati in the work of creation. In the *Taittirīya Brāhmaṇa* she is called "the mother of the Vedas", and "the wife of Indra, who contains within herself all worlds". In the *Śatapatha Brāhmaṇa* she is represented as entering into a sexual connection with Prajāpati, who "being desirous of creating, connected himself with various spouses", and among them, "through his mind, with Vāc," from whom "he created the waters"; or, this last sentence is differently translated. "He created the waters from the world [in the form] of speech (Vāc)." In the *Kāṭhaka Upaniṣad* this idea is more distinctly formulated: "Prajāpati was this universe. Vāc was a second to him. He associated sexually with her; she became pregnant; she departed from him; she produced these creatures; she again entered into Prajāpati."

The *Aitareya Brāhmaṇa* and the *Śatapatha Brāhmaṇa* have a story of the *gandharvas* having stolen the *soma* juice, or, as one calls it, "King Soma", and that as the *gandharvas* were fond of women. Vāc was, at her own suggestion, "turned into a female" by the gods and *ṛṣis* and went to recover it from them.

In the *Atharvaveda* she is identified with Viraj, and is the daughter of Kāma (desire). "That daughter of thine, O Kāma, is called the cow, she whom sages denominate Vāc-Virāj."

The *Mahābhārata* also calls her "the mother of the Vedas", and says, "A voice derived from Brahmā entered into the ears of them all; the celestial Sarasvatī was then produced from the heavens." Here and "in the later mythology, Sarasvatī was identified with Vac, and became under different names the spouse of Brahmā and the goddess of wisdom and eloquence, and is invoked as a muse," generally under the name of Sarasvatī, but sometimes as Vāc.

The *Bhāgavata Purāṇa* recognises her as "the slender and enchanting daughter" of Brahmā, for whom he had a passion, and from whom mankind was produced, that is the female Virāj. (*see* VIRĀJ and ŚATARŪPĀ) Sarasvatī, as wife of Brahmā and goddess of wisdom, represents perhaps the union of power and intelligence that was supposed to operate in the work of creation. According to the *Padma Purāṇa*, Vāc was daughter of Dakṣa, wife of Kaśyapa, and mother of the *gandharvas* and apsaras.

Vách is represented as the wife of Prajápati, and as pervading all that exists. She is termed the mother of the Vedas. Vách is also designated as a cow. "Let a man worship the cow Vách. She has four udders, the formulæ, *svaha*, *vashat*, *hauta*, and s*vadha*. The gods live upon her two udders, *svaha* and *vashat*; men upon *hauta*; and the fathers upon *svadha*. Breath is her bull; the mind, her calf."—*O.S.T.*, II, 256.

VADAVA, VĀḌAVĀNALA—The submarine fire which "devours the water of the ocean", causing it to throw off the vapours which are condensed into rain and snow. The word is also written Vadava and Baḍava. (*see* Aurva)

VADHRIMATI—The wise female to whose invocation the Asvina listened and gave her a son called Hiranyahasta.—*O.S.T.*, v, 247.

VAHANA—'A vehicle.' Most of the gods are represented as having animals as their *vāhanas*. Brahmā has the Haṁsa, swan or goose; Viṣṇu has Garuḍa, half eagle, half man; Śiva, the bull Nandi; Indra, an elephant; Yama, a buffalo; Kārttikeya, a peacock; Kāmadeva, the marine monster Makara, or a parrot; Agni, a ram; Varuṇa, a fish; Gaṇeśā, a rat; Vayu, an antelope; Śani, or Saturn, a vulture; Durgā, a tiger. and the other goddesses, the vahans of their respective lords. The vahan of Brahmá, Hamsa, or Hans, sometimes Hansi, Major Moor tells us, is precisely the name that in Suffolk, is commonly given to the heron, that Saraswati rides on. The swan or goose, the eagle, and the bull, are the vehicles respectively allotted to the three great powers. The terrestrial sluggish nature of the first, is an apt type of matter, personified in the creative power, and a contrast to Vishṇu, or spirit, the preserving power, appropriately mounted on a buoyant eagle, the celestial Garuda. Śiva, the destructive energy of the Deity, is Time or Justice; and the Hindus, deem the bull also its type, and give it to Śiva as his vahan, or modes of conveyance. These vehicles are supposed by Mr. Paterson (*As. Res.* Vol. VII, p. 48,) to have allusion to Purity, Truth, and Justice: the first, he says, typified by the swan, which, clothed with unspotted whiteness, swims, amidst the waters, as it were, distinct from, and unsullied by, them; as the truly pure mind remains untainted amidst the surrounding temptations of the world. Garuda, brother to Aruna, is remarkable for strength and swiftness; and the latter is described as imperfect, and, on account of his defects, destined to act as charioteer to the Sun, he being the dawn, the twilight preceding the sun. Garuda is perfect light; the dazzling full blaze of day; the type of Truth; the celestial vahan of Vishṇu. Perhaps the Hindus may, like western observers, have noticed the strong optic nerves of the eagle tribe; and have heard of the fable of the parents destroying such of their brood as are unable to look steadily on the sun; the eagle in western poetry is called bird of the sun, as well as bird of Jove; in both of which characters Vishṇu particularly appears. Justice, typified in the sacred bull, is the vahan of Śiva: the bull, whose body is Paramesvara, and whose every joint is a virtue; whose three horns are the three Vedas; whose tail ends where adharma, or injustice, begins.—*Coleman*, *Moor.* "The creatures here named, alone suffice to indicate the northern origin of the people who believe in them, and the readiness with which they have accommodated themselves to change. There is no swan nor eagle in Southern India, so far as we know, nor is the buffalo or brahmany-kite known in the highlands of Central Asia."—*Balfour*.

VAHNI—Fire. (*see* AGNI)

VAHNIJWALA—One of the Narakas that for shepherds and potters.

VAHUKA—A name and office assumed by Nala in his time of disguise.

VAHUKA—'Charioteer.' The name of Nala when he was disguised, and employed as the charioteer of Mahárája Ritupurna, king of Ayódhya. Vahuka drove his royal master in one day from Ayódhya to far Vidarbha, when Damayantí, as a means of recovering her lost Nala, proclaimed that her Svayamvara was to be held. It was during this journey that Nala was dispossessed of Kali, and only then wanted his proper form.

VAIBHOJAS—The *Mahābhārata* says, "The descendants of Druhyu are the Vaibhojas." "A people unacquainted with the use of cars or beasts of burden, and who travel on rafts; they have no kings."—*Wilson.*

VAIBHRAJA—A celestial grove; the grove of the gods on mount Supārsva, west of Meru.

VAIDARBHA—Belonging to the country of Vidarbha or Berār. The people of that country.

VAIDEHA—"The son of the bodiless;" a name of Rája Janaka, Belonging to the country of Videha or Tirhoot, &c. The king or the people of the country. Janaka was called Vaideha and Sītā was Vaidehī,

VAIDEHI—A name of Síta, who was princess of Vaidehá and Mithila.

VAIDEYHA—One of the fifteen teachers of the White Yajush.

VAIDIKA—The designation of a class of Brahmans who never follow any worldly occupation, or mix themselves up with the public service; their pursuits are exclusively religious, and they are supported by the charitable contributions of others. The Brahmans who are employed in public offices are termed Laukíka, or men engaged in the business of the world. Many of the Vaidíka class now engage in tuition and often make excellent schoolmasters.

VAIDURYA—One of the principal mountain ridges which project from the base of Meru, on the western side.

VAIDYANATHA—'Lord of physicians.' A title of Śiva. Name of one of the twelve great *liṅgas.* (*see* LIṄGA)

VAIHARA—(Vaihára), a mountain mentioned in the Mahábhárata, now identified as one of the five mountains of Rájgir, in Magadha; it is called Mount Baibhar, and is a rocky hill running three or four miles northwest, and terminating at its eastern side in the hot wells of Rájgir. Here the valley is entered by a narrow ravine through the midst of which the Sarasvatí rivulet forces its way into the low country to the north of the hills.—*I.A.*, p. 70.

VAIJAYANTA The palace or the banner of Indra.

VAIJAYANTI—**(1)** The necklace of Viṣṇu, composed of five precious gems, pearl, ruby, emerald, sapphire, and diamond; it "is the aggregate of the five elemental rudiments". **(2)** A law-book current in the south. It is a commentary by Nanda Paṇḍita on the *Viṣṇu Smṛti.*

VAIKANKA—A similar ridge in the eastern side.

VAIKARTTANA—A name of Karṇa from his putative father, Vikarttana, the sun.

VAIKRITA—Secondary or instrumental creation.

VAIKUNTHA—The paradise of Viṣṇu, sometimes described as on mount Meru, and at others as in the Northern Ocean. It is also called Vaibhra. Viṣṇu himself is sometimes designated by this term. This is considered by Wilson to be a sectarian addition to the seven Lokas or spheres above the earth. Vaikuntha is also the name of an incarnation of Vishṇu in the seventh Manwantara.

VAIKUNTHAS—A class of deities of the sixth Manwantara.

VAIMANIKAS—The deities who travel in Vimánas, 'heavenly cars,' or rather 'moving spheres.'

VAINAHOTRA—One of the Rájas of Kási, the son of Hrishtaketu.

VAINATEYA—A name of Viṣṇu's bird Garuḍa.

VAIRAJ—Manu the son of Virāj.

VAIRAJA—**(1)** Part of the Sama Veda created from the northern mouth of Brahmá; **(2)** A name of the first Manu.

VAIRAJAS—Semi-divine beings or Manes unconsumable by fire, who dwell in *Tapoloka*, but are capable of translation to *Satyaloka.* The Kāśi Khaṇḍa explains this term as the Manes of "ascetics, mendicants, anchorites, and penitents, who have completed a course of rigorous austerities." (*see* PITṚS)

VAIROCHANA—A name of Bali, the son of Prahláda, the son of Hiraṇyakaṣipu, all eminent princes of the Daitya or Titanic family. *See* BALI.

VAIRUA—The name of a portion of the Sama Veda

created from the western mouth of Brahmá.

VAISAKHA—An obsolete name of one of the months.

VAISAKHI, VAISLAI—Two of the wives of Vasudeva.

VAISALI—A city founded by Viśāla, son of Tṛnabindu. This is "a city of considerable renown in Indian tradition, but its site is a subject of some uncertainty." It was a celebrated place among the Buddhists, and would seem to have been situated on the left bank of the Ganges. General Cunningham places it about 27 miles north of Patna. It is frequently confounded with Viśala, *i.e.*, Ujjayini.

VAISAMPAYANA—A celebrated sage who was the original teacher of the Black *Yajurveda.* He was a pupil of the great Vyāsa, from whom he learned the *Mahābhārata*, which he afterwards recited to King Janamejaya at a festival. "It seems probable that the tradition is true that records the first establishment of a school, of which the Vyása was the head, and the other persons named were the teachers." Vaisampáyana was the teacher of the Yajur Veda. There is a legend that Rája Janamejaya killed a brahman and in order to expiate this dreadful crime he listened to a recitation of the whole of the Mahábhárata, which was performed by Vaisampáyana. Accordingly the Mahábhárata, which is said to have been originally composed by Vyása, is supposed to be written as Vaisampáyana recited it. The *Harivaṁsa is* also represented as having been communicated by him.

VAISESHIKA—"Is the name of one of the two great divisions of the Nyáya (*q.v.*). The Atomic school of Hindu philosophy, and probably a later development of the Nyáya itself, properly so called, with which it agrees in its analytical method of treating the subjects of human research, but from which it differs in the arrangement of its topics, and more especially by its doctrine of atomic individualities, or *viseshas*—whence its name is derived." The reputed founder of the Vaiseshika is Kanáda, of whose history or date, however, nothing is known.

Kanáda taught that the visible form of God was light; that when the desire of creation arose in the divine mind, he first gave existence to water, and then to innumerable worlds, floating on the waters like the mundane egg; that in these primeval eggs water was contained, on which lay Vishṇu, and from whose navel issued a lotus, in which Brahmá was born; that Brahmá, receiving instructions from God, created the world, first from his mind, and then with the primary atoms; that spirit and animal life were separate substances.

To him are attributed the *Vaiseshika-Sutras*, which contain about 550 aphorisms, or sentences. These relate to seven subjects (*padarthas*,) under the following distinct heads, *viz.*;—1, *Things*; 2, *Qualities*; 3, *Actions*; 4, *Genus*; 5, *Spirits*; 6, The inseparable *Connection of Constituent Parts*; and 7, *non-entity.*

After a long discussion of the different subjects included in this arrangement, Kanáda discourses on religion, riches, happiness, and final liberation. Having first explained the nature of religion, he then arranges the component parts of the universe, and, lastly, gives a discourse on the divine nature, which he divides into three heads: (1) that God is essentially possessed of wisdom (which, however, does not comprise the whole of his nature or character); (2) that He is the ever blessed and supremely happy; and (3) that in all His works and His will He is irresistible and omnipotent. Emancipation from matter he held to be inseparably connected with complete deliverance from sorrow, and the enjoyment of final bliss.

Several commentaries have been written, and are extant on the Sútras of Kanáda, of which the principal are a large one called the *Bháshya*, and a smaller one entitled the *Vaisesheka Sútrapushkara:* but the only work now read in Bengal which has any relation to the Vaiseshika Philosophy is that of Visva Nátha Siddhánta, which merely treats of the logical terms of this system, and of the Nyáya school. In the Nyáya Colleges of Bengal the students read that part of this work that relates to the Vaiseshika system, and then proceed to study the Nyáya system itself.—Goldstucker, in Chambers' *Encyclopædia.*

VAISHNAVAS—Is the name of one of the great divisions of Hindu sects. The word, derived from Vishṇu (*q.v.*,) designates the worshippers of this deity, and comprises a great variety of sects; but this variety itself differs according to the different periods of the medieval history of India, old divisions becoming extinct, and new ones taking their place. Thus, the account of the Vaishnavas, as given in a celebrated work of *Anandagiri*, the *Sankaradig-vijaya*, *or* the victory of the great theologian Śankara over his religious adversaries, would no longer apply in detail to the present condition of the Vaishnavas; and even some of those varieties mentioned by the late Professor Wilson in his *Sketch of the Religious Sects of the Hindus*, written in 1832, would seem to have disappeared already in our days. The common link of all the sects comprised under the name of Vaishnavas, is their belief in the supremacy of Vishṇu over the other gods of the Trimúrti (*q.v.*) Their difference consists in the character that they assign to this supremacy, and to the god Vishṇu himself, in the religious and other practices founded on the nature of their belief, and in their sectarian marks. The following .sects belonging to this category may especially be noticed here.

1. The Rámánujas, or Sri Vaishnavas, or Sri-Sampradáyins. They derive their origin from *Rámánuja*, a celebrated reformer, who was born at Perumbur, in the south of India, about the middle of the twelfth century, and is considered by his followers as an incarnation of *Sesha* (*q.v.*,) the serpent of Vishṇu. He studied at Conjeveram, resided afterwards at Sríranga, and then traveled over different parts of India, where he was especially engaged in combating the professors of different creeds, particularly the Saivas. On his return to Sríranga, he was seized by the king Kerikála Chola, but effected his escape, and found refuge with the Jain king of Mysore, Vitála Deva, whom he converted to the Vaishṇava faith. For twelve years he then remained at Mysore; but at the death of the Chola Sting, returned to Sríranga, where he spent the remainder of his life in religious seclusion. The Rámánujas address their worship to Vishṇu and his consort, Laksmí (*q.v.*,) and their respective incarnations, either singly or conjointly. Hence their sect consists of corresponding sub-divisions, according as Nárāyaṇa or Laksmí, or Laksmí-Nárāyana, or Ráma, or Sítá or Sítá-Ráma, or any other incarnation of these deities, is the preferential object of the veneration of the votary. Their most striking peculiarity is the preparation and the scrupulous privacy of their meals; for should the meal during its preparation, or while they are eating, attract even the looks of a stranger, the operation is instantly stopped, and the viands buried in the ground. The marks by which they distinguish themselves from other sects are two perpendicular white lines, drawn with a white earth, *Gopíchandana*, from the root of the hair to the commencement of each eyebrow, and a transverse streak connecting them across the root of the nose; in the centre is a perpendicular streak of red, made with red sanders, or a preparation of turmeric and lime; other marks, representing several of the attributes of Vishṇu, they have either painted or impressed on the breast and each upper arm; and, besides, they wear a necklace of the wood of the Tulasí (holy basil,) and carry a rosary of the seeds of the same plant, or of the lotus. The sacred formula with which a member of this sect is initiated into it consists merely of the words *Om rámáya namah*, 'Om, salutation to Ráma.' Their principal religious tenet is the belief that Vishṇu is the cause and creator of all worlds; that he and the universe are one, though lie is of a two-fold form: the supreme spirit or cause, and the gross one, the effect or matter. In distinction from the Vedánta, with which their doctrine has otherwise many points of contact, they regard their supreme deity as endowed with qualities, all of which are of course excellent; and teach that the universe consists of *chit*, thinking or spirit, *achit*, unthinking or matter, íṣwara, or god; the relation of which is that of enjoyer, the thing enjoyed, and the ruler of both. The deity, they assume, is or has been visibly present in five modifications: in the objects of worship, as images, &c.; in the incarnations; in certain forms called Vyúhas, *viz.*, Vásudeva or Krishṇa; Balaráma, Pradyumna, and Aniruddha; and in the subtle form which comprises six qualities—absence of passion, immortality, exemption from pain or care, absence of natural wants, love, and practice of truth—and the human soul; all of which have to be worshipped seriatim, as the votary ascends in the scale of perfection. It is in the south that the followers of Rámánuja, and their temples and establishments, are still numerous; in the north of India, where they are better known as *Sri Vaishnavas*, they are not of frequent occurrence.

2. The Rámánandas, or Rámávats. They are by far the most numerous class of sectaries in Gangetic India: in the district of Agra, they alone constitute seven-tenths of the ascetic population. They belong chiefly to the poorer and inferior classes, with the exception of the Rajputs and military Brahmáns. The founder of this sect was *Rámánanda*, who, by some, is considered to have been the immediate disciple of Rámánuja; by others, the fifth in descent from that teacher, when he would have lived about the end of the thirteenth century; but other more reliable accounts place him toward the end of the fourteenth, or the beginning of the fifteenth century. According to common tradition, Rámánanda seceded from the Rámánujas, to where he originally belonged, because, having spent some time in travelling through various parts of India, and, in consequence, having been suspected by his fellow-disciples not to have conformed to the rule of the Rámánujas in taking his meals, he was condemned to feed in a place apart from the rest of them, but did not acquiesce in *the* affront thus offered him. His residence was at Benares, at the Pancha Gangá Ghát, where a *Math*, or monastery, of his followers is said to have existed. The especial object of their worship is Vishṇu, in his incarnation as *Rámachandra*, and his consort *Sítá*, and, as amongst the Rámánujas, these deities either singly or jointly. Some members of this sect also pay adoration to other forms of Vishṇu; and the religious mendicants of the sect consider all form of adoration superfluous, being content with the incessant invocation of Krishṇa and Rama. Their practices are less precise than those of the Rámánujas; but the most important difference between them consists in the fact, that Rámánanda abolished the distinction of caste amongst the religious orders, and taught that a *Vairágin*, or one who quitted the ties of nature and society, shook off at the same time all personal distinction. The initiatory formula of a Rámánanda is *Srí Ráma*, or 'blessed Rama.' Their sectarian marks are the same as those of the Rámánujas; except that the red perpendicular streak on the forehead is varied in shape and extent, and generally narrower than that of the Rámánujas. There are various sub-divisions of this sect, believed to have been founded by several eminent disciples of Rámánanda. Their doctrines vary often from that of the latter, but they maintain an amicable intercourse with the Rámánujas and with each other.

Besides these Vaishnava sects there are others of less importance who are sometimes included, on the ground of paying more respect to Vishṇu than to any other god of the Trimúrti, (*q.v.*)—Chambers' *Encyclopœdia.*

VAISHNAVI, VARAHI—(Vaishnaví, Varáhí), two of the Śaktis, or eight goddesses so termed, all of them attend on Śiva when he appears as the terrific and destructive deity, Bhairava, who is propitiated by offerings of wine and blood.

VAISRAVANA—Patronymic of Kubera. The eldest son of Pulastya, who deserted his father and went to Brahmá, who as a reward made him immortal, and appointed him the god of riches, with Lanka for his capital and the car Pushpaka for his vehicle. He was afterwards expelled from Lanka by his younger brother Rávaṇa, and retired to Gandhamádana [KUBERA].

VAISVANARA—A name by which Agni is occasionally known in the *Ṛgveda.*

VAISWADEVA—A ceremony in the observance of a Śraddha, which comprehends offerings to both paternal and maternal ancestors, and to ancestors in general.

VAISWANARA—**(1)** A Danava, the father of Puloma and Kálíká; **(2)** The Southern Avashthâma.

VAISWANARI—A division of the lunar mansions, comprising the last three in the Southern Avasthánam

VAISYAS—The third of the regenerate caste—said to have been born from the thighs of Brahmá. The occupations of commerce and agriculture, the feeding of flocks and herds, are the duties of the Vaisyas. No opposition seems ever to have arisen between the Vaisyas and the other two castes, like that, which broke out between the Brahmáns and the Kshatriyas. Indeed the wealth of the Vaisyas rendered them at a later period of considerable influence, inasmuch as they employed Brahmáns to perform sacrifices, and took Kshatriyas into their pay as soldiers and guards.—*Wheeler.*

VAITABANI—'(The river) to be crossed', that is, the river of hell, which must be crossed before the infernal regions can be entered. This river is described as being filled with blood, ordure and all sorts of filth, and to run with great impetuosity. A second river stated by the *Mahābhārata* to be in the country of the Kaliṅgas; it must be the river of the same name (vulg. "Byetumee") somewhat higher up in Cuttack.

VAITALAKI—A teacher of the Rig Veda.

VAITALIKA—A poetical watchman or crier or bellman—one who announces in verse the change of the seasons and the hours of the day—when not retained for the purpose he is a public singer.—*Wilson.*

VAITANA SUTRA—The ritual of the *Atharvaveda.* The text has been published by Dr. Garbe.

VAITANDYA—The eldest son of the Vasu Apa.

VAITARANI—**(1)** A sacred river at Tripishtapa in the country of the Kalingas. It is connected with the worship of Śiva, and the act of bathing there and worshipping the god who wields the trident and whose ensign is the bull, (Mahádeva) is said to ensure purification from all sin and the attainment of the highest felicity.—*O.S.T.*, IV, 241. **(2)** One of the Narakas, that for the punishment, of the man who destroys a beehive or pillages a hamlet.

VAIVASVATA—**(1)** Name of the seventh Manu; he was son of Sūrya and father of Ikṣvāku, the founder of the Solar race of kings. **(2)** Also an appellation of one of the Rudras.

VAJASANEYI—A portion of the Yajur Veda.

VAJASANEYISAMHITA—The body of hymns forming the White *Yajurveda*. (*see* VEDA)

VAJIN—A priest of the White *Yajurveda*.

VAJINS—Students of the white Yajush; this Veda was revealed by the sun in the form of a horse, (vaji) hence the name applied to the brahmans.

VAJRA—(1) The thunderbolt of Indra, said to have been made of the bones of the *ṛsi* Dadhīci. It is a circular weapon, with a hole in the centre, according to some, but others represent it as consisting of two transverse bars. It has many names; Aśani, Abhrottha, 'sky-born'; Bahudāra much cleaving"; Bhidira or Chidaka, 'the splitter'; Dambholi and Jasuri, 'destructive'; Hrādin, 'roaring'; Kuliśa, 'axe'; Pavi, 'pointed'; Phenavāhin, 'foam-bearing'; Ṣaṭkoṇa, 'hexagon'; Śambha and Śvaru. **(2)** Son of Aniruddha. His mother is sometimes said to be Aniruddha's wife Subhadrà, and at others the *daitya* princess Ūṣā. Kṛṣṇa just before his death made him king over the Yàdavas at Indraprastha.

VAJRAMITRA—One of the ten Sunga princes, the son of Ghoshavasu.

VAJRA-NABHA—The celebrated *cakra* (discus) of Kṛṣṇa. According to the *Mahābhārata* Agni gave it to him for his assistance in defeating Indra and burning the Khāṇḍava forest.

VAJRANABHA—A prince, the son of Uktha, of the line of Kúsa.

VAKA—'A crane.' A great *asura* who lived near the city of Eka-cakrā, and forced the Rājā of the place to send him daily a large quantity of provisions, which he devoured, and not only the provisions, but the men who carried them. Under the directions of Kuntī, her son Bhīma took the provisions, and when the demon struck him, a terrific combat followed; each one tore up trees by the roots and belaboured the other, till Bhīma seized the demon by the legs and tore him asunder. Kubera is sometimes called by this name.

VAKTRAYODHI—An eminent Danava, one of the sons of Vipra-chitti.

VALAKA—A teacher of the Rig Veda, and disciple of Sákapurni.

VALAKASWA—A prince, the son of Ajaka, descendant of Purúravas.

VALA-KHILYAS—**(1)** Eleven hymns of an apocryphal or peculiar character interpolated in the *Ṛgveda*. **(2)** "Pigmy sages no bigger than a joint of the thumb, chaste, pious, resplendent as the rays of the sun." So described by the *Viṣṇu Purāṇa*, which says that they were brought forth by Sammati (humility), wife of Kratu, and were 60,000 in number. They are able to fly swifter than birds. The *Ṛgveda* says that they sprang from the hairs of Prajāpati (Brahmā). They are the guards of the chariot of the sun. They are also called Kharvas.

VALKALA—A garment of bark worn by anchorites in the desert.

VALLABHA—A celebrated Vaishnava teacher who lived in the sixteenth century.

VALLABHACHARYAS—(Vallabhácháryas), a numerous sect in Western and Central India; the chief book of authority to the sect is the Bhágavata Purāṇa, and after it the works of Vallabha, the founder of the sect. The object of their adoration is Vishṇu in his incarnation as Krishṇa, whose residence is Goloka, far above the three worlds. There he originally lived alone, but in meditating on the works of creation, created a female form, which became the primary agent in creation; this was Máya. He then produced crude matter, the five elements and all the divine beings; the Trimúrti, their female consorts, and 300 millions of Gopis, or cowherdesses, who are the special attendants on Krishṇa." (Goldstucker in Chambers' *Encyclopædia*.)

VALLABHAS—A people mentioned in the Purānas, and supposed to be inhabitants of Vallabhí in Rajputana. See Tod's *Rajasthan*.

VALMIKI—A sage, famous as the author of the Rámáyana; he lived at Chitrakuta, a celebrated hill in Bundlekund, to the south of the river Yamuna. He was surrounded by a band of Brahmán disciples, who led the ideal life of austerity, sacrifice and devotion, so frequently described and recommended, by Brahmánical writers. It was in this hill, that Ráma, with his wife and brother, took up their abode, when exiled from Ayodhya. According to the Rámáyana they spent some pleasant years there. The locality is said to have abounded in game, fruit, honey, and other products of the jungle, which were suitable for food. Long after, when Rama and Sítá had returned in triumph to Koṣala, and Sitá was about to become a mother, she was repudiated by Rama, though she had passed the ordeal of fire and been declared innocent; she was conveyed to the jungle by Lakshmana, who left her in a panic of surprise and fear, near the hill Chitra Kúta; in this state she was found by Valmíkí, who had been the brahman preceptor of her father Janaka. he took her to his own house and placed her in charge of his wife and female servants. It was then that Sitá's two sons, were born; Valmíkí gave them the names of Lava and Kúsa, and brought them up, and educated them with the greatest care. It is said he taught his poem, the Rámáyana, to them. There are however many chronological difficulties connected with the history of Valmíkí, though it seems certain he was a real person.

VALMIKI—The Vyása of the twenty-fourth Dwapara age, called also Reksha, a descendant of Bhrigu.

VAMACARIS—Followers of the left-hand sect. (*see* TANTRA)

VAMA-DEVA—**(1)** A Vedic *ṛṣi*, author of many hymns. In one of his hymns he represents himself as speaking before his birth, saying, "Let me not come forth by this path, for it is difficult (of issue): let me come forth obliquely from the side." Sāyaṇa, the commentator, says in explanation, "The *ṛṣi* Vāmadeva, whilst yet in the womb, was reluctant to be born in the usual manner, and resolved to come into the world through his mother's side. Aware of his purpose, the mother prayed to Aditi, who thereupon came with her son Indra to expostulate with the *ṛṣi*." [This story accords with that told by the Buddhists of the birth of Buddha.] In the same hymn Vāmadeva says, "In extreme destitution I have cooked the entrails of a dog", and Manu cites this to show that a man is not rendered impure even by eating the flesh of dogs for the preservation of his life. In another hymn he says, "As a hawk I came forth with speed"; and a commentator explains, "Having assumed the form of a hawk, he came forth from the womb by the power of Yoga, for he is considered to have been endowed with divine knowledge from the period of his conception." **(2)** A Vedic sage mentioned in the *Mahābhārata* as possessor of two horses of marvelous speed called Vāmyas. **(3)** A name of Śiva; also of one of the Rudras.

VAMANA PURANA—"That in which the four-faced Brahmà taught the three objects of existence as subservient to the greatness of Trivikrama (Visnu), which treats also of the Šiva kalpa, and which consists of 10,000 stanzas, is called the Vàmana Puràna." This contains an account of the dwarf incarnation of Vishṇu: Wilson thinks its contents scarcely establish its claim to the character of a Purána.

"There is little or no order in the subjects which this work recapitulates, and which arise out of replies made by Pulastya to questions put, abruptly and unconnectedly, by Nárada. The greater part of them relate to the worship of the Linga; a rather strange topic for a Vaishnava Purána, but engrossing the principal part of the compilation. They are, however, subservient to the object of illustrating the sanctity of certain holy places; so that the Vámana Purána is little else than a succession of Máhátmyas. Thus, in the opening, almost, of the work, occurs the story of Daksha's sacrifice, the object of which is to send Śiva to Pápamochana Tírtha, at Benares, where he is released from the sin of Brahmánicide. Next comes the story of the burning of Kámadeva, for the purpose of illustrating the holiness of a Śiva-linga at Kedárnath in the Himalaya, and of Badarikáṣrama. The larger part of the work consists of the Saro-máhátmya, or legendary exemplification of the holiness of Stháṇu Tirtha; that is, of the sanctity of various Lingas and certain pools, at Thanesar and Kurukshetra, the country northwest from Delhi. There are some stories, also, relating to the holiness of the Godávarí river: but the general site of the legends is in Hindusthán. In the course of these accounts, we have a long narrative of the marriage of Śiva with Umá, and the birth of Kárttikeya. There are a few brief allusions to creation and the Manwantaras; but they are merely incidental: and all the five characteristics of a Purána are deficient.

In noticing the Swárochisha Manwantra, towards the end of the book, the elevation of Bali as monarch of the Daityas, and his subjugation of the universe, the gods included, are described; and this leads to the narration that gives its title to the Purana, the birth of Vishṇu as a dwarf, for the purpose of humiliating Bali by fraud, as he was invincible by force. The story is told as usual; but the scene is laid at Kurukshetra.

A more minute examination of this work than that which has been given to it, might, perhaps, discover some hint from which to conjecture its date. It is of a more tolerant character than the Puránas, and divides its homage between Śiva and Vishṇu with tolerable impartiality. It is not connected, therefore, with any sectarial principles, and may have preceded their introduction. It has not, however, the air of any antiquity; and its compilation may have amused the leisure of some Brahmán of Benares three or four centuries ago."—*Wilson.*

VAMANA—Vishṇu, at the request of the deities, was

born as a dwarf, Vámana, the son of Aditi by Kaṣyapa; when Vámana applied to Rája Balí, the monarch of the Daityas, for alms, he was promised by the Raja whatever he might demand, notwithstanding Sukra, the preceptor of the Daityas, apprised him whom he had to deal with. The dwarf demanded as much space as he could step over at three steps; and upon the assent of Bali, enlarged himself to such dimensions as to stride with one pace over the earth, with a second over the intermediate space (the atmosphere), and with a third over the sky, thus leaving for Bali only the subterranean regions, which he assigned him for his future abode. "The demons endeavored to frustrate this result, after Vishṇu had taken his first two strides, but they were overcome by the followers of Vishnu; and Bali, when resigning himself to his fate, in reply to a reproach addressed to him by the dwarf for trying to break his promise, uttered—according to the Bhágavata-Purána—the following words, which may serve as one of many instances to show how sacred a promise was held by the Hindus when once given, and even though artfully obtained: 'If, renowned chief of the gods, you consider the word which I uttered to be deceitful, I now do what is sincere, and can be no deception—place your third step on my head. Fallen from my position, I fear not the infernal regions, or binding in bonds, or misfortune difficult to escape, or loss of wealth, or your restraint, so much as I am afflicted by a bad name.' (See J. Muir's *Original Sanskrit Texts*, Vol. iv, p. 128.)

For his righteousness, he was then rewarded by Vishṇu with the promise, that after a temporary residence in one of the most delightful places of Pátála (*q.v.*), he should be born as the Indra, in the reign of the eighth Manu. In this incarnation as dwarf, Vishṇu is considered to have been a son of the same Kaṣyapa who is also the father of Hiraṇyakaṣipu and Hiraṇyáksha; but while their mother is Diti, the dwarfs mother is Aditi (space); and since she previously had brought forth Indra, Vishṇu is sometimes called Upendra, or the younger or later Indra. As a son of Aditi, Vishṇu becomes one of the Ádityas (see before).—The Vedic conception of the three strides of Vishṇu, is doubtless the basis of the idea whence this Avatar arose."—*Goldstücker.*

VAMA—One of the eleven Rudras, according to the list in the Bhágavata.

VAMSA—A race or family. Lists of the *ṛṣis* or successive teachers of the Vedas which are found attached to some of the *Brāhmaṇas* are called Vaṁśas.

VAMSA-BRAHMAṆA—The eighth *Brāhmaṇa* of the *Sāmaveda.* It has been edited by Burnell.

VANACARAS (mas.), **VANECARĪS** (fem.). Wanderers of the woods. Fauns, Dryads, or sylvan guardians.

VANA-DEVATAS and STHALA-DEVATAS—(Sthaḷa-devatas), genii of the soil and forest, who are often invoked and supplicated; like the Fauns and Dryads of European literature, who preside over the mountain and wood.

VANAKAPIVAT—The son of the patriarch Pulaka.

VĀNAPRASTHA—Hermit. The third stage of Brahmánical life. "When the householder, after performing the acts incumbent on his condition, arrives at the decline of life, let him consign his wife to the care of his sons, and go, himself, to the forests. Let him there subsist upon leaves, roots, and fruit; and suffer his hair and beard to grow, and braid the former upon his brows; and sleep upon the ground. His dress must be made of skin, or of Káṣa or Kuṣa grasses; and he must bathe thrice a day; and he must offer oblations to the gods and to fire, and treat all that come to him with hospitality. He must beg alms, and present food to all creatures; he must anoint himself with such unguents as the woods afford; and, in his devotional exercises, he must be endurant of heat and cold. The sage who diligently follows these rules, and leads the life of the hermit (or Vánaprastha,) consumes, like fire, all imperfections, and conquers, for himself, the mansions of eternity." *V.P.*

VĀNARAS—(Vánaras), monkeys; the term applied in the Rámáyana to designate the savage tribes occupying the Vindhya and its neighbourhood. They differed from the Áryas in race, language, colour, and features, but must, in the opinion of Signor Gorresio, have shown a disposition to receive the Aryan civilization; since they entered into league with Ráma, and joined in his expedition against the black tribes further south. The greater part of the tribes south of the Vindhya submitted to the institutions of the Áryas. "The woodland inhabitants of India south of the Vindhya range are called in the Rámáyana monkeys in contempt, I conceive, of their savage condition, and also, perhaps, because they were little known at that time. In the same way Homer related fabulous stories about the races that in his age were unknown to the Greeks. The occupants of the Dekhan differed from the Sanskrit speaking Indians in origin, worship, and language."—*Gorresio*, quoted by Muir, II, p., 417.

VANECHARI—A female forest-goer; the *Dryad* under whose protection the wood, or any part of it, may be.

VANEYU—One of the ten sons of Raudraṣwa, a descendant of Puru.

VANGRIDA—(Vangṛida), a prince who had under his rule a hundred cities. He is mentioned in the Rig-Veda as having been subdued by Indra who 'broke down the hundred cities that had been blockaded by Rejiṣvan.'

VAPU—Body; a daughter of Daksa, married to Dharma.

VAPRA—The Vyása of the fourteenth Dwápara age.

VAPUSHMAT—One of the sons of Priyavrata and Kámya; lie was installed by his father in the sovereignty over the Dwípa of Salmali, (*q.v.*) He had seven SONS, whose names gave designations to seven varshas or divisions.

A man who killed King Marutta of the Solar race. Dama, son or grandson of Marutta, in retaliation killed Vapuṣmat. With his blood he made the funeral offerings to the Manes of Marutta, and with the flesh he fed the brāhmaṇas who were of *rākṣasa* descent.

VARADA—'Bestower of boons.' A name of Devī, also of Sarasvatī.

VARAHA KALPA—The present *kalpa* or year of Brahmā, (*see* KALPA)

VARAHA PURANA—"That in which the glory of the great Varāha is predominant, as it was revealed to Earth by Viṣṇu, in connection, wise Munis, with the Mānava *kalpa*, and which contains 24,000 verses, is called the *Varāha Purāṇa*"; but this description differs so from the Purāṇa which bears the name in the present-day, that Wilson doubts its applying to it. The known work "is narrated by Viṣṇu as Varāha, or in the boar incarnation, to the personified Earth. Its extent, however, is not half that specified, little exceeding 10,000 stanzas. It furnishes also itself evidence of the prior currency of some other work similarly denominated." "It may perhaps be referred to the early part of the twelfth century."

VARAHA—(Varáha), one of the five mountains of Rájgir, in Magadha, now called Mount Vipula, on the eastern side of the Sarasvatí; it is a lofty mountain, and a branch of it runs as far as Giryak, a distance of six miles. Hardly a quarter of a mile from the western side of the hill it is joined at right angles by a third mountain running from the north called Ratnagir;—the Vrishába of the Mahábhárata. This hill is of inconsiderable length and terminates in a narrow ravine branching away to the west. On the opposite side of this ravine rises Mount Udayagír, (the old Rishigiri) a less important hill, running due south, and terminating in the ancient wall and fort of Bángangá, the southern gate of the ancient capital of Magadha.—*I.A.*, p. 70.

VARAHA—A boar. The Varáha Avatar is the third incarnation of Vishṇu in the shape of a boar. It is supposed to have taken place when, at the period of creation, the earth was immersed in water, and Vishṇu, in order to raise it up, assumed the form of a gigantic boar. The boar is said to be a type of the ritual of the Vedas. "The elevation of the earth from beneath the ocean, in this form, was therefore, probably, at first, an allegorical representation of the extrication of the world from a deluge of iniquity, by the rites of religion. Geologists may perhaps suspect, in the original and unmystified tradition, an allusion to a geological fact, or the existence of lacustrine mammalia in the early periods of the earth."—*Wilson*.

The boar is described as the sacrifice personified; his feet being the Vedas; his tusks the sacrificial posts to which the victim is tied; his teeth, the sacrificial offerings; his mouth, the altar; his tongue, the fire; his hairs, the sacrificial grass; his eyes, day and night; his head, the place of Brahmá; his mane, the hymns of the Vedas; his nostrils, all the oblations; his snout, the ladle of oblation; his voice, the chanting of the Sáma-veda; his body, the hall of sacrifice; his joints, the different ceremonies; and his ears as having the properties of voluntary and obligatory rites.

According to a legend in the Bhágavata Purána, Jaya and Vijaya, two doorkeepers of Vishṇu, once offended some Munis who claimed admission to the paradise of Vishṇu, and in consequence were doomed to lose their position in heaven, and to be reborn on earth. They became thus the sons of Kasyapa and Diti, under the names of Hiranyakasipu and Hiranyaksha. The former subdued the three worlds, and the latter went straight to heaven to conquer the gods also. The gods implored the assistance of Vishṇu, who at that period was the mysterious boar and slew Hiranyáksha. A similar contest between Vishṇu and numerous demons, the progeny of Diti, always ending in the defeat of the latter, is also described, showing that the boar-avatara had gradually lost its original character, and assumed that common to the remaining avatars.

VARAHA—One of the six minor Dwípas, peopled by Mlcchas who worship Hindu deities.

VARAHAMIHIRA—A celebrated astronomer and astrologer, born at Ujjein A. D. 530 and died in 587. Dr. Kern observes that "he was in the awkward position of a man who has to reconcile the exigencies of science with the decrees, deemed infallible, of the Ri.shis;" for curious examples of which he refers to the *Brihat-Sanhita*, chapters v and ix. * With a strong taste for astrology, and falling into errors which Aryabhata had exposed, Varahamihira made some remarkable observations on the moon and on eclipses thus

"One-half of the moon whose orbit lies between the sun and the earth, is always bright by the sun's rays; the other half is dark, by its own shadow; like the two sides of a pot standing in the sunshine."

After alluding to the popular notion of Ráhu as the demon that causes eclipse by devouring part of the sun or moon, he says

"The true explanation of the phenomena is this: in an eclipse of the moon he enters into the earth's shadow; in a solar eclipse the same things happen to the sun. Hence the commencement of a lunar eclipse does not take place from the west side, nor that of a solar eclipse from the east." *Brihat Sanhita*, quoted in *A. and M. I*, Vol. I, p. 371. (* A work which Dr. Kern edited and published at Calcutta in 1865, and is understood to be now translating into English.)

VARANCHI—A celebrated brahman, the son of Somadatta, distinguished for a wonderful memory, which enabled him to recite perfectly any discourse he had once heard. He instructed Vyadi, and both of them were writers of note on philological topics. They were contemporaries of Nanda who reigned at Pataliputra—a fact that Professor Wilson regards as of considerable interest in the literary history of the Hindus. Vararuchi is also called Katyáyana (*q.v.*) who is one of the earliest communicators of Pánini (*q.v.*) Nanda is the predecessor or one of the predecessors of Chandragupta; and consequently the chief institutes of Sanskrit Grammar are thus dated from the fourth century before the Christian era.—*Wilson*, III, 166.

VARANASI—The sacred city of Benares; also called Kāśī.

VARANA—The ninth division in Bhárata Varsha.

VARANAVATA—The modern Allahabad, "the sacred city at the junction of the Ganges and Jumna, and one of the most famous places of pilgrimage in Hindustan. It is said to have been celebrated for gold and jewels. The visit of the Pandava princes to this city as related in the Mahabharata is considered by Mr. Wheeler to be a later interpolation for the sole purpose of associating the Páṇḍavas with the famous city of Váranávrta.

VARARUCI—A grammarian who is generally supposed to be one with Kātyāyana (*q.v.*). There was another Vararuci who was one of "the nine gems" at the court of Vikramāditya.

VARCHAS—Light; the son of Vasu Soma, and father of Varchaswi, Radiance.

VARDDHAKSATRI—A patronymic of Jayadratha.

VARENYA——Most Excellent; a name of Vishṇu, said to be the same as supreme felicity.

VARHADRATHAS—A dynasty of kings of Magadha, who according to the Vishṇu Purána were to reign for a thousand years.

VARHASPATYAS—Heretics; followers of Vrihaspatti, who seem to have been numerous and bold at some period anterior to the fourteenth century.—*Wilson*.

VARISHADS—A class of Pitris, identified by some with the months. They are formless or incorporeal Pitris, sons of Atri, and Pitris of the demons.

VARISHMATI—The wife of Priyavrata, according to the Bhágavata, which states that she was the daughter of Visvakarman.

VARIYAS—One of the sons of the patriarch Pulaha, according to the Bhágavata.

VARKSHI—Daughter of a sage, who is instanced in the *Mahābhārata* as being a virtuous woman and wife often husbands.

VARMAN—This designation is said in the Visnu Purána to be an appropriate name for a Kshatriya.

VARNA—'Class or caste.' The *Caturvarṇa*, *or* four castes, as found established in the code of Manu, are

1. Brāhmaṇa: The sacerdotal and learned class, the members of which may be, but not necessarily priests.
2. Kṣatriya: The regal and warrior caste.
3. Vaiśya: Trading and agricultural caste.
4. Śūdra: Servile caste, whose duty is to serve the other three.

The first three castes were called *dvija*, "twice

born regenerate", from their being entitled to investiture with the sacred thread which effects a second birth. The brāhmaṇas maintain that their caste alone remains, that the other three have been lost or degraded, and it is generally believed that there are no pure kṣatriyas or vaiśyas now existing. The numerous castes which have sprung up from the intercourse of people of different castes or from other causes are called *varṇaśaṅkara*, 'mixed castes'.

VARNAM—Colour. *See* CASTE.

VARNAVATA—The city in which the Pāṇḍavas dwelt in exile.

VARṢA—A region. Nine *varṣas* are enumerated as situated between the great mountain ranges of the earth: (1) Bhāratavarṣa, India; (2) Kimpuruṣa or Kinnara; (3) Hari; (4) Ramyaka; (5) Hiraṇmaya; (6) Uttarakuru; (7) Ilāvṛta; (8) Bhadrāśva; (9) Ketumāla.

VARSHAS—Countries; a term applied to the divisions in Jambu Dwípa.

VARSNEYA—A name of Kṛṣṇa as a descendant of Vrsni. Name of King Nala's charioteer.

VARTTIKAS—Supplementary rules or notes to the grammar of Pāṇini by later grammarians, as Kātyāyana, Patañjali, &c. Kātyāyana is the chief of these annotators, and is called *vārttikakāra*, 'the annotator'.

VARUDA CHATURTHI—(Varudá Chaturthí), a festival that occurs in the fourth lunar day of the light half of Magha (30th Jany.–1st Feby.) The name implies a goddess, the giver of boons, who in some of the Purāṇas is identified with Gauri, or with Umá, the bride of Śiva. She is on this day to be worshipped with offering of flowers, of incense, or of lights, with platters of sugar and ginger, or milk or salt, with scarlet or saffron-tinted strings and golden bracelets. She is to be worshipped by both sexes, but especially by women; and women themselves are to be treated with peculiar homage. The due observance of this festival is said to secure a flourishing progeny. The worship of Gauri at this season is popular in the South of India.

VARUNANI, VARUṆĪ—Wife of Varuṇa and goddess of wine. She is said to have sprung from the churning of the ocean. The goddess of wine is also called Madā and Surā.

VARUNA—The Neptune of Hindu mythology. The god of ocean, the god of rain and clouds. He is distinctly termed the god of Ocean in the Vishṇu Purána, and Wilson in noticing the circumstance that it was Varuna who supplied the sage Richíka with a thousand fleet horses, remarks that the agency of the god of ocean in procuring horses is a rather curious additional coincidence between Varuṇa and Neptune. The Vedic Áryans were evidently acquainted with the sea, for the hymns contain allusions to merchants, to sea voyages, and to ships with a hundred oars. Professor Max Müller in his History of Sanskrit Literature has translated a beautiful hymn to Varuṇa in which this deity is addressed in the two-fold character of controlling tempests and punishing sin.

"The grandest cosmical functions are ascribed to Varuṇa-Possessed of illimitable resources (or knowledge), this divine being has meted out, (or fashioned), and upholds, heaven and earth; he dwells in all worlds as sovereign ruler, indeed, the three worlds are embraced within him; he made the golden and revolving sun to shine in the firmament. The wind which resounds through the atmosphere is his breath. He has opened boundless paths for the sun, and has hollowed out channels for the rivers, which flow, by his command. By this wonderful contrivance the rivers pour their waters into the one ocean, but never fill it. His ordinances are fixed and unassailable. They rest on him, unshaken, as upon a mountain; through their operation, the moon walks in brightness, and the stars which appear in the nightly sky mysteriously vanish in daylight. Neither the birds flying in the air, nor the rivers in their sleepless flow, can attain knowledge of his power or his wrath. His messengers behold both worlds. He knows the flight of birds in the sky, the path of ships on the ocean, the course of the far-travelling wind, and beholds all the secret things that have been, or shall be done. No creature can even wink without him. He witnesses men's truth and falsehood. He instructs the rishi Vasishṭha in mysteries. But his secrets and those of Mitra are not to be revealed to the foolish."

In the sixteenth hymn of the fourth book of the Atharva-veda, his power and omniscience are thus celebrated:—

"1, The great one who rules over these worlds beholds as if he were close at hand. When any man thinks he is doing aught by stealth, the gods know it all; 2, (and they perceive) every one who stands, or walks, or glides along secretly, or withdraws into his house, or into any lurking-place. Whatever two persons, sitting together, devise, Varuṇa the king knows it, (being present there as) a third; 3, This earth, too, belongs to the king Varuṇa, and that vast sky whose ends are so remote. The two oceans [the aerial and terrestrial] are Varuṇa's stomachs; he resides in this small pool of water; 4, He, who should flee far beyond the sky, would not there escape from Varuṇa the king. His messengers, descending from heaven, traverse this world; thousand-eyed, they look across the whole earth; 5, King Varuṇa perceives all that exists within heaven and earth and all that is beyond. The winking of men's eyes are all numbered by him. He handles (all) these (things) as a gamester throws his dice; 6, May thy destructive nooses, O Varuṇa, which are cast seven-fold, and three-fold, ensnare the man who speaks lies, and pass by him who speaks truth."

The mighty Lord on high, our deeds, as if at hand, espies:

The gods know all men do, though men would fain their deeds disguise.
Whoever stands, whoever movet, or steals from place to place,
Or hides him in his secret cell,—the gods his movements trace,
Wherever two together plot, and deem they are a!one,
King Varnna ia there, a third, and all their schemes ape known.
This earth *is* his, to him belong those vast and boundless skies;
Bot'i seas within him rest, and yet in that small pool he lies.
Whoever far beyond the sky should think his way to wing,
He could not there elude the graap of Varuna the king.
His pies descending from the skies glide all this world around,
Their thousand eyes all-scanning sweep to earth's remotest bound.
Whnte'er exists in heaven and earth, whate'er beyond the skies,
Before the eyes of Vanma, the king, unfolded lies.
The ceaseless winkings all he counts of every mortal's eyes:
He wields this universal frame, as gamester throws his dice.
Those knotted nooses which thou fling'st, O god, the bad to mare,—
All liars let them overtake, but all the truthful spare."

Varuṇa is represented as having unlimited control over the destinies of mankind. He is said to have a hundred, a thousand remedies, and is supplicated to shew his wide and deep benevolence, and drive away evil and sin; to untie like a rope, and remove sin; he is entreated not to steal away, but to prolong, life; and to spare the supplicant who daily transgresses his laws. In many places mention is made of the bonds, or nooses, with which he seizes and punishes transgressors. Mitra and Varuṇa conjointly are spoken of in one passage as being barriers against falsehood, furnished with many nooses, which the hostile mortal cannot surmount; and in another place Indra and Varuṇa are described as binding with bonds not formed of rope. On the other hand, Varuṇa is said to be gracious even to him who has committed sin. He is the wise guardian of immortality, and a hope is held out that he and Yama reigning in blessedness shall be beheld in the next world by the righteous.

"The attributes and functions ascribed to Varuṇa impart to his character a moral elevation and sanctity for surpassing that attributed to any other Vedic deity. This appears not only from the passages to which I have 'already referred, but also from the two hymns translated by Professor Müller in his *Anc. Sansk. Lit*; pp. 540*f.*, and *Chips*, *I*, 39*jf*; in which the rishi, who is said to be Vasishṭha, while palliating his sins, implores the god's forgiveness, and entreats that his life may be spared. I shall quote a part of the first and the whole of the second:

"Seeking to perceive that sin, O Varuṇa, I inquire; I resort to the wise to ask. The sages all tell me the same; it is Varuna who is angry with thee. 4. What great sin is it, Varuṇa, for which thou seekest to slay thy worshipper and friend ? Tell me, O unassailable and self-dependent god; and, freed from sin, I shall speedily come to thee with adoration; 5, Release us from the sins of our fathers, and from those which we have committed in our own persons. O king, release Vasishṭha like a robber who has fed upon cattle; release him like a calf from its tether; 6, It was not our will, Varuṇa, but some seduction, which led us astray,—wine, anger, dice, or thoughtlessness. The stronger perverts the weaker. Even sleep occasions sin."

"Let me not, O king Varuṇa, go to the house of earth. Be gracious, O mighty god, be gracious; 2, Go along, O thunderer, quivering like an inflated skin; be gracious, &c.; 3, O bright and mighty god, I have transgressed through want of power, be gracious, &c. 4.

Thirst has overwhelmed thy worshipper when standing even in the midst of the waters; be gracious, &c.; 5, Whatever offence this be, O Varuṇa, that we mortals commit against the people of the sky (the gods): in whatever way we have broken thy laws by thoughtlessness, be gracious, O mighty god, be gracious."

In another place the same rishi alludes to his previous friendship with Varuṇa, and to the favours the god had formerly conferred upon him, and enquires why they had now ceased:

"Varuṇa placed Vasishṭha on his boat: by his power the wise and mighty deity made him a rishi to offer praise in an auspicious period of his life, that his days and dawns might be prolonged; 5, Where are those friendships of us two? Let us seek the harmony winch (we enjoyed) of old. I have gone, O self-sustaining Varuṇa, to thy vast and spacious house with a thousand gates; 6, He who was thy friend, intimate, thine own, and beloved, has committed offences against thee. Let not us who are guilty reap the, fruits of our sin. Do thou, a wise god, grant protection to him who praises thee."

The same or nearly the same functions and attributes as are ascribed to Varuṇa are also attributed to him and Mitra conjointly. They uphold and rule over the earth and sky, the shining and the terrestrial regions, and place the sun in the heavens.

In his paper on "the highest gods of the Arian races," Professor Roth has the following ingenious and interesting observations on Mitra and Varuṇa: "Within the circle of the Adityas there subsists the closest connection between Mitra and Varuna, who are invoked more frequently together than Varuṇa is invoked singly. We find only one hymn in which Mitra is invoked by himself.

The essential character of the two gods, as distinguished from one another, is nowhere distinctly expressed in the hymns, and was in fact originally one which could not be defined with intellectual precision. But the stage of religious culture which lies before us in the Rig Veda, enables us to distinguish this difference as one already existing, *viz.*; that Mitra is the celestial light in its manifestation by day, while Varuṇa, though the lord of light and of all time, yet rules especially over the nightly heaven. A hymn of Vasishṭha: 'One of you (Varuṇa) is the lord, and unassailable guide, and lie who is called Mitra, (*i.e*; the friend) calls men to activity.' Here so much at least is declared (and the same thing is expressed in nearly the same words in other places), that the light of day, which awakens life, and brings joy and activity into the world, is the narrower sphere of Mitra's power; though, however, Varuṇa is not thereby relegated to the night alone, for he continues to be the lord and the first.

"Though therefore such representations as are expressed in Indian exegesis, (as for instance, when Sayana says on *R.V.*, vii. 87, 1, that Varuna is the setting sun), are far too narrow and one-sided, they still contain some truth; and we may guess by what process they arc to be developed. If Varuna is, as his name shows, that one among the lucid Ádityas whose seat and sphere of authority is the bright heaven, ill whose bosom is embraced all that lives, and therefore also the remotest boundary, beyond which human thought seeks nothing further, then is he also one who can scarcely be attained either by the eye or by the imagination. By day the power of vision cannot discover this remotest limit, the bright heaven presents to it no resting-place. But at night, this veil of the world, in which Varuṇa is enthroned, appears to approach nearer, and becomes perceptible, for the eye finds a limit. Varuṇa is closer to men. Besides, the other divine forms which, in the clouds, the atmosphere, the rays of light, filled the space between the earth and yonder immeasurable outermost sphere, have disappeared: no other god now stands between Varuna and the mortal who gazes at him."—*O.S.T.*, Vol. V, p. 70.

Varuṇa is also called Pracetas, Amburāja, Jalapati, Keśa, 'lord of the waters'; Uddāma, 'the surrounder'; Pāśabhṛt, 'the noose-carrier'; Viloma, Vāriloma, 'watery hair'; Yādaḥpati, 'king of aquatic animals'. His son is named Agasti.

VASANTA. Spring and its deified personification.

VASANTAKA—The confidential companion of king Vatsa in the Ratnavali.

VASANTASENA—The heroine of the drama called *Mṛcchakaṭī*, 'the toy cart'.

VASANTOTSAVA—(Vasantótsava), the feast of Vasanta, or Spring. See HOLI.

VASAVADATTA—(Vasavadattá), the queen of Vatsa, (Udáyana), king of Kausambí.

A princess of Ujjayinī, who is the heroine of a popular story by Subandhu. The work has been printed by Dr. F. Hall in the *Bibliotheca Indica*. He considers it to have been written early in the seventh century, (*see* Udayana).

VASAVA—Váyu, a name of the god of the winds.

VASHATKARA—Deified oblation; one of the thirty-three divinities who are born again at the end of a thousand ages, according to their own pleasure.

VASHKALA—A Daitya, the son of Sanhráda, or Prahláda, according to the Pádma Purána.

VASISTHA—'Most wealthy.' A celebrated Vedic sage to whom many hymns are ascribed. According to Manu he was one of the seven great *ṛṣis* and of the ten Prajāpatis. There was a special rivalry between him and the sage Viśvāmitra, who raised himself from the kṣatriya to the brāhmaṇa caste. Vasiṣṭha was the possessor of a "cow of plenty", called Nandinī, who had the power of granting him all things (*vastu*) he desired, hence his name. A law-book is attributed to him, or to another of the same name. Though Vasiṣṭha is classed among the Prajāpatis who sprang from Brahmā, a hymn in the *Ṛgveda* and the commentaries thereon assign him a different origin, or rather a second birth, and represent him and the sage Agastya to have sprung from Mitra and Varuṇa. The hymn says, "Thou, O Vasiṣṭha, art a son of Mitra and Varuṇa, born a brāhmaṇa from the soul of Urvaśi. All the gods placed in the vessel thee the drop which had fallen through divine contemplation." The comment on this hymn says, "When these two Ādityas (Mitra and Varuṇa) beheld the apsaras Urvaśi at a sacrifice their seed fell from them...It fell on many places, into a jar, into water, and on the ground. The *muni* Vasiṣṭha was produced on the ground, while Agastya was born in the jar."

There is a peculiar hymn attributed to Vasiṣṭha in the *Ṛgveda* (*Wilson*, IV. 121), beginning "Protector of the dwelling", which the commentators explain as having been addressed by him to a house-dog which barked as he entered the house of Varuṇa by night to obtain food after a three days' fast. By it the dog was appeased and put to sleep, "wherefore these verses are to be recited on similar occasions by thieves and burglars."

In the same Veda and in the *Aitareya Brāhmaṇa*, Vasiṣṭha appears as the family priest of King Sudās, a position to which his rival Viśvāmitra aspired. This is amplified in the *Mahābhārata*, where he is not the priest of Sudās but of his son Kalmāṣapāda, who bore the patronymic Saudāsa. It is said that his rival Viśvāmitra was jealous, and wished to have this office for himself, but the king preferred Vasiṣṭha. Vasiṣṭha had a hundred sons, the eldest of whom was named Śaktri. He, meeting the king in the road, was ordered to get out of the way; but he civilly replied that the path was his, for by the law a king must cede the way to a brāhmaṇa. The king struck him with a whip, and he retorted by cursing the king to become a man-eater. Viśvāmitra was present, but invisible, and he maliciously commanded a man-devouring *rākṣasa* to enter the king. So the king became a man-eater, and his first victim was Śaktri. The same fate befell all the hundred sons, and Vasiṣṭha's grief was boundless. He endeavoured to destroy himself in various ways. He cast himself from the top of mount Meru, but the rocks he fell upon were like cotton. He passed through a burning forest without harm. He threw himself into the sea with a heavy stone tied to his neck, but the waves cast him on dry land. He plunged into a river swollen by rain, but although he had bound his arms with cords, the stream loosened his bonds and landed him unbound (*vipāsa*) on its banks. From this the river received the name of Vipāśa (Byās). He threw himself into another river full of alligators, but the river rushed away in hundred directions, and was consequently called Śatadru (Sutlej). Finding that he could not kill himself, he returned to his hermitage, and was met in the wood by King Kalmāṣapāda, who was about to devour him, but Vasiṣṭha exorcised him and delivered him from the curse he had borne for twelve years. The sage then directed the king to return to his kingdom and pay due respect to brāhmaṇas. Kamāṣapāda begged Vasiṣṭha to give him offspring. He promised to do so, and "being solicited by the king to beget an heir to the throne, the queen became pregnant by him and brought forth a son at the end of twelve years".

Another legend in the *Mahābhārata* represents Viśvāmitra as commanding the river Sarasvatī to bring Vasiṣṭha, so that he might kill him. By direction of Vasiṣṭha the river obeyed the command, but on approaching Viśvāmitra, who stood ready armed, it promptly carried away Vasiṣṭha in another direction.

The enmity of Vasiṣṭha and Viśvāmitra comes out very strongly in the *Rāmāyaṇa*. Viśvāmitra ruled the earth for many thousand years as king, but he coveted the wondrous cow of plenty that he had seen at Vasiṣṭha's hermitage, and attempted to take her away by force. A great battle followed between the hosts of King Viśvāmitra and the warriors produced by the cow to support her master. A hundred of Viśvāmitra's sons were reduced to ashes by the blast of Vasiṣṭha's mouth, and Viśvāmitra being utterly defeated, he abdicated and retired to the Himalaya. The two met again after an interval and fought in single combat. Viśvāmitra was again worsted by the Brahmāṇical power, and "resolved to work out his own elevation to the Brahmāṇical order" so as to be upon equality with his rival. He accomplished his object and became a priest, and Vasiṣṭha suffered from his power. The hundred sons of Vasiṣṭha denounced Viśvāmitra for presuming though a ksatriya, to act as a priest. This so incensed Viśvāmitra that he "by a curse doomed the sons of Vasiṣṭha to be reduced to ashes and reborn as degraded outcasts for seven hundred births". Eventually, "Vasiṣṭha, being propitiated by the gods, became reconciled to Viśvāmitra, and recognised his claim to all the prerogatives of a brāhmaṇa *ṛsi*, and Viśvāmitra paid all honour to Vasiṣṭha". A legend in the *Viṣṇu Purāṇa* represents Vasiṣṭha as being requested by Nimi, a son of Ikṣvāku, to officiate at a sacrifice which was to last for a thousand years. The sage pleaded a prior engagement to Indra for five hundred years, but offered to come at the end of that period. The king made no remark, and Vasiṣṭha, taking silence as assent, returned as he had proposed. He then found that Nimi had engaged the *ṛsi* Gautama to perform the sacrifice, and this so angered him that he cursed the king to lose his corporeal form. Nimi retorted the curse, and in consequence "the vigour of Vasiṣṭha entered into the vigour of Mitra and Varuṇa. Vasiṣṭha, however, received from them another body when their seed had fallen from them at the sight of Urvaśī."

In the *Mārkaṇḍeya Purāṇa* he appears as the family priest of Hariścandra. He was so incensed at the treatment shown to that monarch by Viśvāmitra, that he cursed that sage to be transformed into a crane. His adversary retorted by dooming him to become another bird, and in the forms of two monstrous birds they fought so furiously that the course of the universe was disturbed, and many creatures perished. Brahmā at length put an end to the conflict by restoring them to their natural forms and compelling them to be reconciled.

According to the *Viṣṇu Purāṇa*, Vasiṣṭha had for wife Ūrjā, one of the daughters of Dakṣa, and by her he had seven sons. The *Bhāgavata Purāṇa* gives him Arundhati for wife. The *Viṣṇu Purāṇa* also makes him the family priest "of the house of Ikṣvāku"; and he was not only contemporary with Ikṣvāku himself, but with his descendants down to the sixty-first generation. "Vasiṣṭha, according to all accounts (says Dr. Muir), must have been possessed of a vitality altogether superhuman", for it appears that the name Vasiṣṭha is "used not to denote merely a person belonging to a family so-called, but to represent the founder of the family himself as taking part in the transactions of many successive ages."

"It is clear that Vasiṣṭha, although he is frequently designated in post-Vedic writings as a brāhmaṇa, was, according to some authorities, not really such in any proper sense of the word, as in the accounts which are given of his birth he is declared to have been either a mind-born son of Brahmā, or the son of Mitra and Varuṇa and the Apsaras Urvaśī, or to have had some other supernatural origin" (*Muir*, I. 337). Vasiṣṭha's descendants are called Vasiṣṭhas and Vāṣkalas.

VASTOSPATI—'House protector.' One of the later gods of the Veda, represented as springing from Brahmā's alliance with his daughter. He was the protector of sacred rites and guardian of houses.

VASU—The Vasus are a class of deities, eight in number, chiefly known as attendants upon Indra, so called because they are always present in light, or luminous radiation: or according to the Vishṇu Purana, because preceded by fire they abound in splendour and might. They seem to have been in Vedic times personifications of natural phenomena. They are Āpa (water), Dhruva (pole-star), Soma (moon), Dharā (earth), Anila (wind), Anala (fire), Prabhāsa (dawn), and Pratyūsa (light). According to the *Rāmāyaṇa* they were children of Aditi. **(2)** A daughter of Daksha who was married to Dharma; **(3)** One of the sons of Kúsa.

VASUBHATI—(Vasubhúti), the ambassador of the king of Śimhala, or Ceylon, in the drama of the Ratnávalí.

VASUBHRIDYANA—One of the sons of Vasishṭha, who was devoured by Rája Kalmashápada.

VASUDEVA—A name of Vishṇu: it means, says the Vishṇu Purana, that all beings abide in that supreme being, and that he abides in all beings. "The form or sensible type of Vasudeva is here considered to be the monosyllable Om, and which is one with the three mystical words Bhuh, Bhuvar, Swar, and with the Vadas: consequently the Vyáhritis and the Vedas are also forms of Vásudeva, diversified as to their typical character, but essentially one and the same."—*Wilson*.

A name of Kṛṣṇa, derived from that of his father, Vasudeva; but as that is incompatible with his claims to divinity, the *Mahābhārata* explains that he is so-called "from his dwelling (*vasanāt*) in all beings, from his issuing as a Vasu from a divine womb". The name was assumed by an impostor named Pauṇḍraka, who was killed by Kṛṣṇa. (*see* PAUṆḌRAKA)

VASUDEVA—Son of Śura, of the Yādava branch of the Lunar race. He was father of Kṛṣṇa, and Kuntī, the mother of the Pāṇḍava princes, was his sister. He married seven daughters of Āhuka, and the youngest of them, Devakī, was the mother of Kṛṣṇa. After the death of Kṛṣṇa and Balarāma he also died, and four of his wives burnt themselves with his corpse. So says the *Mahābhārata*, but according to the *Viṣṇu Purāṇa* he and Devakī and Rohinī burnt themselves at Dwārakā. He received the additional name of Ānakadundubhi, because the gods, conscious that he was to be the putative father of the divine Kṛṣṇa, sounded the drums of heaven at his birth. He was also called Bhūkaśyapa and Dundu, 'drum'. **(2)** The first prince of the Kanwa dynasty. *V.P*

VASUKI—King of the Nāgas or serpents who live in *pātāla*. One of the progeny of Kadru; a powerful many-headed snake; he was the snake king according to some authorities: but chiefly celebrated from having been used as a cord or rope, around Mount Mandara as a churn, when the gods and Asuras churned the ocean for the Amrita.

VASUMITRA—One of the ten Sunga princes.

VASUSENA—A name of Karṇa.

VATA—'Wind.' Generally the same as Vāyu, but the name is sometimes combined in the Veda with that of Parjanya, and Parjanyavātā and Vāyu are then mentioned distinctively.

VATAPI—Vātāpi and Ilvala, two *rākṣasas*, sons either of Hrāda or Vipracitti. They are mentioned in the *Rāmāyaṇa* as dwelling in the Daṇḍaka forest. Vātāpi assumed the form of a ram that was offered in sacrifice and afterwards eaten by brāhmaṇas. Ilvala then called upon him to come forth, and accordingly he tore his way out of the stomachs of the brāhmaṇas. He tried the same trick upon Agastya, but that austere sage ate and digested him. Dvala, as before, called his brother to come forth, and assaulted the sage, who told him that his brother would never return. Then Ilvala was burnt up by fire from the eyes of Agastya. The *Mahābhārata*'s story varies slightly. **(2)** A cruel Rákshasa, a devourer of brahmans; he lived in the forest near the Vindhya mountains, and was himself eaten, according to the Rámáyan, by the sage Agastya.

VÁTA-TREE—The Ficus Indica; the enormous tree which is fabled to grow in the mountain Supárṣwa, to the south of Mera, and described aś spreading over eleven hundred yojanas, is a Váta tree.

VATA-VASIN—'Dwelling in fig-trees' (*vaṭa*). *Yakṣas*.

VATSA, VATSA-RĀJA—King of Vatsa, the capital of which was Kauśāmbī. A title of the prince Udayana. There are many persons named Vatsa.

VATSA—A celebrated character in Hindu fiction. He was the son of Sahasráṇikn, (*q.v.*) and king of Kausaṃbi. Vatsa was named Udáyana, from being educated on the Udya mountain, by the sage Jamadagni. When arrived at maturity he was decoyed into captivity by the king of Ujjain. On his escape he carried off Vasavadatta, the daughter of his captor. Vatsa is the hero of the Ratnávali.—See *Wilson*, XII, 264.

VATSABALAKA—A son of Súra and brother of Vasudeva.

VATSABHUMI—A prince, the eighth in descent from Alarka.

VATSA—Child; a name of Pratarddana, from his father's frequently calling him by that name.

VATSAPRI—A celebrated prince of the solar race. the son of Bhalandana.

VATSARA—**(1)** One of the sons of Dhruva; **(2)** The fifth cyclic year.

VATSAVYUHA—An ancient Rája of the solar race, the son of Vatsa.

VATSYA—**(1)** A teacher of the Rig Veda; **(2)** One of the fifteen teachers of the White Yajur.

VATSYAYANA—A sage who wrote upon erotic subjects, and was author of the *Kāma-sūtras* and *Nyāya-bhāṣa*. He is also called Mallanāga.

VAVRIDDHAS—A class of deities in the fourteenth Manwantara.

VAYU—The god of wind; the Æolus of Hindu mythology, while the Maruts are the breezes who attended upon Indra. Váyu was the mythical father of Bhíma, and of Hanumán. It was Váyu who testified to the fidelity of Damayanti; who conveyed the palace of Indra to the earth, &c.

In the Vedic mythology of the Hindus, Váyu is a deity who originally seems to have held an equal rank with Indra, but much more rarely occupies the imagination of the poets than this god, or Agni, or the Sun; for though, according to Yâska, ancient commentators of the Vedas hold that there are only three great deities—*viz.*, Agni, fire, whose place is on earth; Surya;

the sun, whose place is in heaven; and Váyu, or Indra, whose place is in the intermediate sphere—only a few hymns, comparatively speaking, are dedicated to Váyu, whereas the other deities named are the subject of manifold praise. The description given by the Rig Veda the greatness of Váyu nevertheless answers the position that those ancient commentators assign to him.

Váyu, is said to be the son-in-law of Tvashtri. He moves in a shining car, drawn by a pair of red or purple horses. His team is often said to consist of ninety-nine, of a hundred, or even of a thousand horses, yoked by his will. Váyu, like the ether gods is drinker of soma. In fact, he alone, or in conjunction with Indra, was, by the admission of (he other gods, entitled to the first draught of this libation. It is remarkable that Váyu is but rarely connected with the Maruts or deities of die storm; but in one place he is said to have begotten them from the rivers of heaven; and in another place to be attended by Pushan, the Maruts and the Viṣva devas.

The following hymns are addressed to Váta (another name of the god of the wind). The imagery in the first is highly poetical.

I, (I celebrate) the glory of Váta's chariot; its noise comes rending and resounding. Touching the sky, he moves onward, making all things ruddy: and he comes propelling the dust of the earth; 2, The gusts (?) of the air rush after him, and congregate in him as women in an assembly. Sitting along with them on the same car, the god, who is king of this universe, is borne along; 3, Hasting forward, by paths in the atmosphere, he never rests on any day. Friend of the waters, first-born, holy, in what place was he born? Whence has he sprung? 4, Soul of the gods, source of the universe, this deity moves as he lists. His sounds have been heard, but his form is not (seen): this Váta let us worship with an oblation."

1, Let Váta, the wind, waft to us healing, salutary, and auspicious, to our heart: may he prolong our lives; 2, And, Váta, thou art our father, our brother, and our friend: cause us to. live; 3, From the treasure of immortality, which is deposited yonder in thy house, O Váta,—give us to live."

Here the same property is ascribed to Váta which is elsewhere ascribed to Rudra, that of bringing healing.*

There are not many hymns addressed to him. According to the *Nirukta* there are three gods specially connected with each other. "Agni, whose place is on earth; Vāyu or Indra, whose place is in the air; and Sūrya, whose place is in the heaven." In the hymn Puruṣasūkta Vāyu is said to have sprung from the breath of Puruṣa, and in another hymn he is called the son-in-law of Tvaṣṭṛ. He is regent of the northwest quarter, where he dwells.

According to the *Viṣṇu Purāṇa* he is king of the *gandharvas.* The *Bhāgavata Parāṇa* relates that the sage Nārada incited the wind to break down the summit of mount Meru. He raised a terrible storm which lasted for a year, but Viṣṇu's bird, Garuḍa shielded the mountain with his wings, and all the blasts of the wind-god were in vain. Nārada then told him to attack the mountain in Garuḍa's absence. He did so, and breaking off the summit of the mountain, he hurled it into the sea, where it became the island of Laṅkā (Ceylon).

Other names of Vāyu (wind) are Anila, Marut, Pavana, Vāta, Gandhavaha, 'bearer of perfumes'; Jalakāntara, 'whose garden is water'; Sadāgata, Satataga, 'ever moving', &c. (* Dr. Muir, *O.S.T.*, Vol. v, p. 146.)

VAYUKA—A sage, one of the sons of Kriṣáṣwa; the Rámáyana terms the sons of Kriṣáṣwa the Sastra devatas, or gods of the divine weapons.

VÁYU-PURÁNA—The Váyu Purána is narrated, by Súta, to the Rishis at Nairnisháraṇya, as Váyu formerly told it, at the same place, to similar persons; a repetition of circumstances not uncharacteristic of the inartificial style of this Purána. It is divided into four Pádas, termed, severally, Prakriya, Upodghita, Anushanga, and Upasamhára; a classification peculiar to this work. These are preceded by an index, or heads of chapters, in the manner of the Mahábhárata and Rámáyana—another peculiarity.

The Prakriyá portion contains but a few chapters, and treats, chiefly, of elemental creation, and the first evolutions of beings, to the same purport as the Vishṇu, but in a more obscure and unmethodical style. The Upodghata then continues the subject of creation, and describes the various *Kalpas* or periods during which the world has existed; a greater number of which is specified by the Saiva, than by the Vaishnáva Puránas. Thirty-three are here described, the last of which is the Śweta or 'white' Kalpa, from Śiva's being born in it, of a white complexion. The genealogies of the patriarchs, the description of the universe, and the incidents of the first six Manwantaras are all treated of in this part of the work; but they are intermixed with legends and praises of Śiva, as the sacrifice of Daksha, the Maheṣwara Máhatmya, the Nilakaṇṭha Stotra, and others. The genealogies, although, in the main, the same as those in the Vaishnáva Puránas, present some variations. A long account of the Pitris or progenitors is also peculiar to this Purana; as are stories of some of the most celebrated Rishis who were engaged in the distribution of the Vedas.

The third division commences with an account of the seven Rishis and their descendants, and describes the origin of the different classes of creatures from the daughters of Daksa, with as profuse copiousness of nomenclature, not found in any other Purána. With the exception of the greater minuteness of detail, the particulars agree with those of the Vishṇu Purána. A chapter then occurs on the worship of the Pitris; another, on Tirthas or places sacred to them; and several, on the performance of Śráddhas, constituting the Śráddha Kalpa. After this comes a full account of the solar and lunar dynasties, forming a parallel to that in the Vishṇu Purana, with this difference, that it is, throughout, in verse, whilst that of our text, as noticed in its place, is, chiefly, in prose. It is extended, also, by the insertion of detailed accounts of various incidents, briefly noticed in the Vishṇu, though derived, apparently, from a common original. The section terminates with similar accounts of future kings, and the same chronological calculations that are found in the Vishṇu.

The last portion, the Upasamhára, describes briefly the future Manwantaras, the measures of space and time, the end of the world, the efficacy of Yoga, and the glories of Śivapura, or the dwelling of Śiva, with whom the Yogin is to be united. The manuscript concludes with a different history of the successive teachers of the Váyu Purána, tracing them from Brahmá to Váyu, from Váyu to Bṛihaspati, and from him, through various deities and sages, to Dwaipáyana and Súta.—*Wilson*.

VEṆA—A Chakkravartti, or universal emperor, the son of Anga or Tunga. When he was inaugurated by the Rishis monarch of the earth he caused it to be everywhere proclaimed that no worship should be performed, no oblations offered, no gifts bestowed upon the Brahmáns. "I, the king 'said he' I am the lord of sacrifice; for who but I, am entitled to the oblations," The Rishis remonstrated without effect; and then says the Vishṇu Purána, "these pious Munis were filled with wrath, and said let this wicked wretch be slain: and they fell upon the king, and beat him with blades of holy grass, consecrated by prayer, and slew him who had first been destroyed by his impiety toward God,"

According to the Pádma Purána, Veṇa commenced his reign auspiciously, but lapsing into the Jain heresy, the sages deposed him, and pummelled him until the Nishâda, or progenitor of the wild races, was extracted from his left thigh, and Prithu from his right arm. Being freed from sin by the birth of the Nishâda, Veṇa retired to the banks of the Narmadá, where he performed penance in honour of Vishṇu, who appeared to him and read him a lecture on the merit of gifts of various kinds, especially at different holy places or Tírthas. After this Vishṇu desired Veṇa to demand a boon, and he solicited that he might be incorporated with the deity; Vishṇu told him first to celebrate an Aṣwamedha, after which the king should become one with himself, and he then disappeared. Prithu enabled his father Veṇa to consummate the sacrifice by which he was united to Vishṇu, and this incident is said to illustrate the efficacy of a son considered as a Tírtha.—Wilson's *Works*, III, 38.

VEDA—Root, *vid*, 'know'. 'Divine knowledge.' The Vedas are the holy books that are the foundation of the Hindu religion. They consist of hymns written in an old form of Sanskṛt and according to the most generally received opinion they were composed between 1500 and 1000 B.C. But there is no direct avidence as to their age, and opinions about it vary considerably. Some scholars have thought that the oldest of the hymns may be carried back a thousand years farther. It seems likely that some of the hymns were composed before the arrival of the Āryan immigrants in India, and there is no doubt that the hymns vary greatly in age and spread over a very considerable period.

There are various statements as to the origin of the Vedas. One is that the hymns emanated like breath from Brahmā, the soul of the universe. It is agreed that they were revealed orally to the ṛṣis or sages whose names they bear; and, hence, the whole body of the Veda is known as Śruti, 'what was heard'.

The Vedas are now four in number: (1) *Ṛg*, (2) *Yajur*, (3) *Sāma*, (4) *Atharva*; but the *Atharva is* of comparatively modern origin. The other three are spoken of by Manu as the "three Vedas", and are said by him to have been "milked out as it were", from fire, air, and the sun. In reality the *Ṛgveda* is the Veda, the original work for the *Yajur* and the *Sāma* are merely different arrangements of its hymns for special purposes.

Each Veda is divided into two parts, *Mantra* and *Brāhmaṇa*. The *Mantra*, or 'instrument of conveying thought', consists of prayer and praise embodied in the metrical hymns. The *Brāhmaṇa*, a collective term for the treatises called *Brāhmaṇas*, *is* of later date than the *Mantra*. It is written in prose, and contains liturgical and ritualistic glosses, explanations, and applications of the hymns illustrated by numerous legends. To the *Brāhmaṇas* are added the Āraṇyakas and Upaniṣads, mystical treatises in prose and verse, which speculate upon the nature of spirit and of God, and exhibit a freedom of thought and speculation which was the beginning of Hindu philosophy. All the Vedic writings are classified in two great divisions, exoteric and esoteric: the Karma-kāṇḍa, 'department of works', the ceremonial; and the Jñāna-kāṇḍa, 'department of knowledge'. The hymns and prayers of the *Mantra* come under the first, the philosophical speculations of the *Brāhmaṇas*, and especially of the Upaniṣads, under the second division. All are alike Śruti or revelation, (*see* Brāhmaṇa, Upaniṣad, &c.)

The *Mantra* or metrical portion is the most ancient, and the book or books in which the hymns are collected are called Saṁhitās. The *Ṛgveda* and the *Sāmaveda* have each one *Saṁhitā*; the *Yajurveda* has two Saṁhitās.

As before stated, the *Ṛgveda* is the original Veda from which the *Yajur* and *Sāman* are almost exclusively derived. It consists of 1017 *sūktas* or hymns, or with eleven additional hymns called Vālakhilyasofan apocryphal character, 1028. These are arranged in eight *aṣṭakas*, 'octaves', or *khaṇḍas*, 'sections', which are again subdivided into as many *adhyāyas*, 'chapters', 2006 *vargas* or 'classes', 10,417 *ṛks* or 'verses', and 153,826 *padas* or 'words'. There is another division, which runs on concurrently with this division, in ten *maṇḍalas*, 'circles' or 'classes', and 85 *anuvākas* or 'sections'. The total number of hymns is the same in both arrangements. It is a generally received opinion that the hymns of the tenth *maṇḍala* are later in date than the others.

A few hymns of the *Ṛgveda*, more especially some of the later hymns in the tenth *maṇḍala*, appear to contain some vague, hazy conception of one Supreme Being; but as a whole they are addressed directly to certain personifications of the powers of nature, which personifications were worshipped as deities having those physical powers under their control. From these powers the Vedic poets invoked prosperity on themselves and their flocks; they extolled the prowess of these elemental powers in the struggles between light and darkness, warmth and cold, and they offered up joyous praise and thanksgiving for the fruits of the earth and personal protection. Chief among the deities so praised and worshipped were Agni, Indra, and Sūrya. More hymns are addressed to Agni (Ignis), 'fire', than to any other deity and chiefly in its sacrificial character, though it receives honour also for its domestic uses. Indra was honoured as the god of the atmosphere, who controlled the rains and the dew, so all-important to an agricultural people. Sūrya, 'the sun', was 'the source of heat', but he shared this honour with Agni, the sun being considered a celestial fire. Among the most ancient of the myths was that of Dyaus-pitar, 'heavenly father', the regent of the sky. Others were Aditi, 'the finite expanse'; Varuṇa, 'the investing sky', afterwards god of the waters; Uṣas, 'the dawn', daughter of the sky; the two Aśvins, 'twin sons of the sun', ever young and handsome, and riding in a golden car as precursors of the dawn. Pṛthivī, 'the broad one', as the earth was called, received honour as the mother of all beings. There were also the Maruts or storm-gods, personifications of the wind, the especial foes of Vṛtra, the spirit of drought and ungenial weather, who was in constant conflict with Indra; Rudra, the howling, furious god, who ruled the tempest and the storm; Yama, the god of the dead and judge of departed spirits, also received his meed of reverence: last, though apparently not least in the estimation of the Āryan worshippers, was Soma, the personification of the fermented juice of the plant so named. This exhilarating liquid was alike acceptable to the gods and their worshippers, and many hymns are addressed to it as a deity.

To each hymn of the *Ṛgveda* there is prefixed the name of the *ṛsi* to whom it was revealed, as Vasiṣṭha, Viśvāmitra, Bhraradvāja, and many others; and these sages are frequently spoken of as authors of the hymns bearing their names. It is quite unknown when the hymns were first committed to writing. They were transmitted orally from generation to generation, and continued to be so handed down even after they had been collected and arranged by Kṛṣṇa Dvaipāyana, 'the arranger'. The oral teaching of the Vedas produced what are called the *sākhas* or 'schools' of the

Vedas. Different learned men, or bodies of men, became famous for their particular versions of the text, and taught these versions to their respective pupils. These different versions constitute the *śākhās*, they present, as might be expected, many verbal variations, but no very material discrepancies.

"The poetry of the *Ṛgveda*," says Professor Cowell, "is remarkably deficient in that simplicity and natural pathos or sublimity which we naturally look for in the songs of an early period of civilisation. The language and style of most of the hymns is singularly artificial...Occasionally we meet with fine outbursts of poetry, especially in the hymns addressed to the dawn, but these are never long sustained; and as a rule we find few grand similes or metaphors." Professor Williams, who finds them "to abound more in puerile ideas than in striking thoughts and lofty conceptions", expresses a similar opinion.

The *Yajur or* second Veda is composed almost exclusively of hymns taken the *Ṛg*, but it contains some prose passages which are new. Many of the hymns show considerable deviations from the original text of the *Ṛg*. These differences may perhaps be attributable either to an original difference of the traditional text or to modifications required by the ritualistic uses of the *Yajur.* The *Yajurveda is* the priests' office-book, arranged in a liturgical form for the performance of sacrifices. As the manual of the priesthood, it became the great subject of study, and it has a great number of different *sākhās* or schools. It has two Saṁhitās, one called the *Taittirya Sanhita*, the other *Vajasaneyī Saṁhitā*, commonly known as the Black and White *Yajur.* Of these, the former is the more ancient, and seems to have been known in the third century B.C. These Saṁhitās contain upon the whole the same matter, but the arrangement is different. The White *Yajur* is the more orderly and systematic, and it contains some texts which are not in the Black.

The Saṁhitā of the *Taittirīya* or Black *Yajur is* arranged in 7 *kāṇḍas* or books, 44 *praśnas*, or chapters, 651 *anuuākas* or section, and 2198 *kaṇḍikās* or pieces, "fifty words as a rule forming a *kaṇḍikā*". The Saṁhitā of the *Vājasaneyī* or White *Yajur* is in 40 *adhyāyas or* chapters, 303 *anuvākas*, and 1975 *kaṇḍikās*.

How the separation into two Saṁhitās arose has not been ascertained. It probably originated in a schism led by the sage Yājñavalkya; but if it did not, it produced one, and the adherents of the two divisions were hostile to each other and quarreled like men of different creeds. In later days a legend was invented to account for the division, which is thus given by the *Viṣṇu* and *Vāyu Purāṇas:* Vaisampàyana taught The Yajurveda, in twenty-seven branches (sàkhàs) to his disciple Yājñavalkyas. Vaiśampāyana had the misfortune to kill his sister's child by an accidental kick, and he then called upon his disciples to perform the appropriate expiatory penance. Yājñavalkya refused to join the "miserable inefficient brāhmaṇas", and a quarrel ensured. The teacher called upon the disciple to give up all that he had learnt from him; and the disciple, with the same quick temper, vomited forth the *Yajur* texts which he had acquired, and they fell upon the ground stained with blood. The other pupils were turned into partridges (Tittiri), and they picked up the disgorged texts; hence the part of the Veda which was thus acquired was called *Taittirīya* and Black. Yājñavalkya sorrowfully departed, and by the performance of severe penance induced the Sun to impart to him those *Yajur* texts which his master had not possessed. The Sun then assumed the form of a horse (Vājin), and communicated to him the desired texts. The priests of this portion of the Veda were called Vājins, while the Saṁhitā itself was called Vājasaneyī, and also White (or bright), because it was revealed by the sun. The statement that Yājñavalkya received this Veda from the sun is, however, earlier than the Purāṇas, for the grammarian Kàtyàyana mentions it. A more reasonable and intelligible explanation is, that Vājasaneyī is a patronymic of Yājñavalkya, the offspring of Vājsani, and that *Taittirīya* is derived from Tittiri, the name of a pupil of Yāska's. Weber, the man best acquainted with this Veda, says, "However absurd this legend (of the Purāṇas) may be, a certain amount of sense lurks beneath its surface. The Black *Yajur* is, in fact, a motley undigested jumble of different pieces; and I am myself more inclined to derive the name *Taittirīya* from the variegated partridge (*Tittiri*) than from the *ṛṣi* Tittiri." Goldstücker's view is, that the "motely character of the Black *Yajurveda* arises from the circumstance that the distinction between the *Mantra* and *Brāhmaṇa* portions is not so clearly established in it as in the other Vedas, hymns and matter properly belonging to the *Brāhmaṇas* being there intermixed. This defect is remedied in the White *Yajurveda*, and it points, therefore, to a period when the material of the old *Yajur* was brought into a system consonant with prevalent theories, literary and ritualistic."

The *Sāmaveda Saṁhitā* is wholly metrical. It contains 1549 verses, only seventy-eight of which have not been traced to the *Ṛgveda.* The readings of the text in this Veda frequently differ, like those of the *Yajur*, from the text as found in the *Ṛg*, and Weber considers that the verses "occurring in the *Sāma Saṁhitā* generally stamp themselves as older and more original by the greater antiquity of their grammatical forms". But this opinion is disputed. The verses of the *Sāma* have been selected and arranged for the purpose of being chanted at the sacrifices or offerings of the Soma. Many of the invocations are addressed to Soma, some to Agni, and some to Indra. The *mantra* or metrical part of the *Sāma* is poor in literary and historical interest, but its *Brāhmaṇas* and the other literature belonging to it are full and important.

There were different sets of priests for each of the three Vedas. Those whose duty it was to recite the *Ṛgveda* were called Hotṛs or Bahvṛcas, and they were required to know the whole Veda. The priests of the *Yajur*, who muttered its formulas in a peculiar manner at sacrifices, were called Adhvaryus, and the chanters of the verses of the *Sāman* were called Udgātṛs.

The *Atharvaveda*, the fourth Veda, is of later origin than the others. This is acknowledged by the brāhmaṇas, and is proved by the internal evidence of the book itself. It is supposed to date from about the same period as the tenth *maṇḍala* of the *Ṛgveda*, and as Manu speaks of only "the three Vedas", the *Atharva* could hardly have been acknowledged in his time. Professor Whitney thinks its contents may be later than even the tenth *maṇḍala* of the *Ṛg*, although these two "stand nearly connected in import and origin". There are reasons for supposing it to have had its origin among the Saindhavas on the banks of the Indus. One-sixth of the whole work is not metrical, "and about one-sixth (of the hymns) is also found among the hymns of the *Ṛgveda*, and mostly in the tenth book of the latter; the rest is peculiar to the *Atharva*". The number of the hymns is about 760, and of the verses about 6000. Professor Whitney, the editor of the *Atharva*, speaks of it thus: "As to the internal character of the *Atharva* hymns, it may be said of them, as of the tenth of the *Ṛg*, that they are productions of another and a later period, and the expressions of a different spirit from that of the earlier hymns in the other Vedas. In the latter, the gods are approached with reverential awe indeed, but with love and confidence also; a worship is paid them that exalts the offerer of it; the demons embraced under the general name *rākṣasa* are objects of horror whom the gods ward off and destroy; the divinities of the *Atharva* are regarded rather with a kind of cringing fear, as powers whose wrath is to be deprecated and whose favour curried, for it knows a whole host of imps and hobgoblins, in ranks and classes, and addresses itself to them directly, offering them homage to induce them to abstain from doing harm. The *mantra* prayer, which in the older Veda is the instrument of devotion, is here rather the tool of superstition; it wrings from the unwilling hands of the gods the favours which of old their goodwill to men induced them to grant, or by simple magical power obtains the fulfillment of the utterer's wishes. The most prominent characteristic feature of the *Atharva* is the multitude of incantations which it contains; these are pronounced either by the person who is himself to be benefited, or more often by the sorcerer for him, and are directed to the procuring of the greatest variety of desirable ends; most frequently perhaps long life or recovery from grievous sickness is the object sought; then a talisman, such as a necklace, is sometimes given or in very numerous cases some plant endowed with marvelous virtues is to be the immediate external means of the cure; further, the attainment of wealth or power is aimed at, the downfall of enemies, success in love or in play, the removal of petty pests, and so on, even down to the growth of hair on a bald pate. There are hymns, too, in which a single rite or ceremony is taken up and exalted, somewhat in the same strain as the Soma in the Pāvamanya hymns of the *Ṛg*. Others of a speculative mystical character are not wanting; yet their number is not so great as might naturally be expected, considering the development which the Hindu religion received in the periods following that of the primitive Veda. It seems in the main that the *Atharva* is of popular rather than of priestly origin; that in making the transition from the Vedic to modem times, it forms an intermediate step rather to gross idolatries and superstitions of the ignorant mass than to the sublimated Pantheism of the brāhmaṇas." Such is the general character of the fourth Veda, but Max Müller has translated a hymn-in his *Ancient Sanskrit Literature*, of which Professor Wilson said in the *Edinburgh Review*, "We know of no passage in Vedic literature which approaches its simple sublimity." This hymn is addressed to Varuṇa, "the great one who rules over these worlds, and beholds all as if he were close by; who sees all that is within and beyond heaven and earth," &c.

This Veda is also called the brāhmaṇa Veda, "because it claims to be the Veda for the chief sacrificial priest, the brāhmaṇa". It has a *Brāhmaṇa* called Gopatha and many Upaniṣads. An entirely new recension of this Veda has lately been found in Kaśmīr. It is in the hands of Professor Roth, and is believed to show many important variations.

The whole of the *Ṛgveda*, with the commentary of Sāyaṇa, has been magnificently printed in six large quarto volumes under the editorship of Max Müller, at the expense of the Government of India. Editions of the text separately in the Saṁhitā and in the *pada* forms have been published by him; also another edition with the Samhitā and pada texts in opposite pages. There is also a complete edition of the text in Roman characters by Aufrecht, and a portion of the text was published by Roer in the *Bibliotheca Indica.* Dr. Rosen published the first *aṣṭaka* of the text, with a Latin translation, in 1838. Seven volumes of Wilson's translation have appeared. There is a French translation by Langlois, and Max Müller has printed a critical translation of twelve hymns to the Maruts. There are other translations of portions. Translations by Ludwig and by Grassmann have also lately appeared. The text, with an English and Marāṭhī translation, has appeared in monthly parts in Bombay.

The Saṁhitā of the Black *Yajurveda* has been published by Roer and Cowell in the *Bibliotheca Indica.* The White has been printed by Weber, and another edition has been published in Calcutta.

Of the *Sāma Saṁhitā*, the text and a translation have been published by Dr. Stevenson. Benfey has also published the text with a German translation and a glossary; and an edition with the commentary of Sāyaṇa has come out in the *Bibliothica Indica* (vol. I).

The text of the *Atharvaveda Saṁhitā* has been printed by Roth and Whitney, and a part of it also by Aufrecht.

"The Veda has a two-fold interest; it belongs to the history of the world and to the history of India. In the history of the world the Veda fills a gap which no literary work in any other language could fill. It carries us back to times of which we have no records anywhere, and gives us the very words of a generation of men of whom otherwise we could form but the vaguest estimate by means of conjectures and inferences.

"It is difficult no doubt to believe that the most ancient literary work of the Áryan race, a work more ancient than the Zendavesta and Homer, should, after a lapse of at least three thousand years, have been discovered, and for the first time published, in its entirety, not in one of the Parishads on the borders of the Ganges, but in one of the Colleges of an English University. It is difficult to believe that sufficient MSS. should have been preserved, in spite of the perishable nature of the material on which they are written, to enable an editor to publish the collection of the Vedic hymns in exactly that form in which they existed at least 800 years before the Christian era; and, still more, that this collection, which was completed at the time of Lykurgos, should contain the poetical relics of a pre-Homeric age; an age in which the names of the Greek gods and heroes had not yet lost their original sense, and in which the simple worship of the Divine powers of nature was not yet supplanted by a worship of personal gods. It is difficult to believe this and we have a right to be skeptical. But it is likewise our duty to inquire into the value of what has been preserved for us in so extraordinary a manner, and to extract from it those lessons which the study of mankind was intended to teach to man."*

"The religion of the Vedas, as far as we are acquainted with it, differs in many very material points, from that of the present day. The worship they prescribe is, with a few exceptions, domestic, consisting of oblations to fire, and invocations of the deities of fire, of the firmament, of the winds, the seasons, the moon, the sun; who are invited by the sacrificer, if a brahman, or by his family priest if he is not a brahman, to be present and accept the offering, either oiled butter or the juice of the soma, a species of asclepias, which are poured upon the sacrificial fire, in return for which they are supplicated to confer temporal blessings upon the worshipper, riches, life, posterity; the short-sighted vanities of human desire, which constituted the sum of heathen prayer in all heathen countries.

The titles and functions of the deities commonly addressed on these invocations give to the religion of the Vedas the character of the worship of the elements, and it is not unlikely that it was so in its earliest and rudest condition. It is declared in some texts that the deities are only three; whose places are earth, the middle region between heaven and earth, and the heaven; namely, fire, air, the sun. Upon this however seems to have been grafted some loftier speculation, and the elements came to be regarded as types and emblems of divine power, as there can be no doubt that the fundamental doctrine of the Vedas is monotheism.** "There is in truth," say repeated texts, "but one deity, the Supreme Spirit." "He from whom the universal world proceeds, who is Lord of the universe, and whose work is the universe, is the Supreme Being." Injunctions also repeatedly occur to worship Him, and Him only. "Adore God alone, know God alone, give up all other discourse;" and the Vedanta says, "it is found in the Vedas that none but the Supreme Being is to be worshipped, nothing excepting Him should be adored by a wise man."—Wilson's *Works*, Vol. II, pp. 50-52.

"The simple patriarchal life of the Aryans is indicated in the Vedic hymns, precisely as it is depicted in the main tradition of the Mahábhárata. They were a people partly pastoral and partly agricultural; keeping cows for the sake of their milk, butter, and curds, and sowing the land with grain. They also seem to have had some acquaintance with the manufacture of weapons and coats of mail, and to have sometimes undertaken sea-voyages for the sake of gain. These people prayed to their gods, as such a people might be expected to pray, for plenty of rain, abundant harvests, and prolific cattle; for bodily vigour, long life, numerous progeny, and protection against all foes and robbers, such as the cattle lifting aborigines. Their gods appear to have been mere abstractions; personifications of those powers of nature on whom they relied for good harvests. They wanted seasonable rain, warmth, and fresh breezes. Accordingly, they prayed to the god of rain, the god of fire and light, and the god of wind. But from the very first, there appears to have been some confusion in these personifications, which led both to a multiplicity of deities, and the confounding together of different deities. Thus the conception of the god of rain was Indra, and he was identified with the firmament as well as with the unseen power which smote the rain-cloud and brought down the waters; and so important was the acquisition of rain in due season, that Indra is regarded as the sovereign of the gods, and subsequently became a type of sovereignty. But rain and water are frequently different things, and thus there was another, and perchance an older, deity, named Varuṇa, who was particularly worshipped as the god of the waters, and deity of the ocean. Again, the conception of the god of fire was Agni, and Agni was not only the flame which burns upon the hearth or alter, but also the lightning which manifests itself in the clouds, and even the light of the sun, moon, and stars. Yet both the sun and moon appear as separate and individual deities, the latter under the name of Soma or Chandra. Again, there seems to have been a striking difference as regards wind. The god of wind, or air, was Váyu , but the different breezes which bring on or accompany the rain, are called Maruts, and are represented as the attendants of Indra. Thus, whilst there is a Pantheon of separate and individual deities, the conception of one deity frequently overlapped the conceptions of other deities; and whilst the more prominent powers of nature, such as water, fire, and wind, were separately individualized, a monotheistic tendency was always at work, ascribing the attributes of every deity to each one in turn. Of these deities, the following appear to be the most important:—

Rain.
Indra, god of the firmament.
Varuça, god of the waters.
Fire.
Agni, god of fire.
Súrya, the sun.
Soma, or Chandra, the moon.
Air.
Váyu, the god of wind.
Maruts, the breezes who attended upon Indra.

To these must be added a god of death, or judge of the dead who was known as Yama. The characteristics of Yama as a Vedic deity would open up a large field of inquiry; but the subject at present is vague and speculative. In the Epics, Yama appears distinctly as a judge of the dead; and men who are about to die are frequently said to be about to go to the mansions of Yama."

"In the Vedic period the Brahmáns were scarcely known as a separate community; the caste system had not been introduced. And the gods who were worshipped were subsequently superseded by deities of other names and other forms."† (*Max Müller, *Hist. Sans. Lit.*; **Colebrooke's *Essays*, I, p. 12; Max Müller, *History of Ancient Sans. Lit.*, pp. 558-71; †Talboys Wheeler *History of India*, Vol. I, pp. 8-11.)

VEDABAHU—A son of the patriarch Pulastya.

VEDAMATṚ—'Mother of the Vedas.' The Gāyatrī.

VEDAMITRA—A teacher of the Rig Veda; who divided his Sanhita into five, which he distributed to as many disciples.

VEDANA—Fortune; a daughter of Anrita (falsehood,)

married to Naraka (hell).

VEDANGA—From Veda and *anga*, limb; hence, literally, 'the limb of (the body of) the Veda'—is the name of six Sanskrit works, the object of which is to teach how to read and understand correctly the Vedic texts, and how to apply them correctly to sacrificial purposes. Whether the number of these works was originally the same as it now is, and already was at the time of the Upanishads, may be doubtful. Tradition mentions the following Vedángas: 1, Śikshá, or the science of proper pronunciation. It is represented by a short treatise of 35, or, in another recension, of 59 verses, which explains the nature of letters, accent, and pronunciation, and is ascribed to *Panini*; 2, *Chhandas*, or (a work on) metre, which is ascribed to *Pingala*; 3, Vyákarana, or grammar, by which native authorities understand the celebrated work of Páṇini; but never those short books, especially concerned in Vedic peculiarities, called Prátiṣákhyas, the existing representatives of which, in all probability, are posterior to Paṇini; 4, *Nirukta*; 5, *Jyotisha*, or astronomy. 'Its chief object is to convey such knowledge of the heavenly bodies as is necessary for fixing the days and hours of the Vadic sacrifices;' 6, *Kalpa*, or works on the Vedic ceremonial, winch systematise the ritual taught by the Bralimana portion of the Veda, omitting, however, all legendary or mystical detail. They are composed in the Sútra style. The Kalpa, or Śranta, Sútras belonging to the Rig Veda are the Aṣwaláyana-, *Sánkháyana*, and Saunaka *Sútras*; those relating to the Sámaveda, the Masaka-, *Látyáyana*-, and Dráhyayaṇa Sútras; those of the Black Yajur-veda, the Apastamba-, *Baudháyana*; Satyasháḍha-, Hiranyakesin-, *Mdnava*-, *Bhdradvája*-, *Vddkúna*-, Vaikhánasa-, *Laugákshi*-, *Maitra*-, Kaṭha-, and *Váráha, Sútras*. The White Yajurveda has only one Kalpa, or Śranta, Sútras connected with it, the *Kátyáyana* Sútra, and the Atharvaveda likewise only one, the *Kusika Sútra*.

At a later period, these works were supplemented by a similar class of works, which, however, merely describe the domestic ceremonies, *viz*., the marriage rite, the rites to be performed at the conception of a child, at various periods before his birth, at the time of his birth, the ceremony of naming the child, of carrying him out to see the sun, of feeding him, of cutting his hair, and lastly, of investing him as a student, and handing him to a guru, under whose care he is to study the sacred writings.' Works of this kind are called Gṛihya-Sútras (from *griha*, house), and to these, again, were added the *Sámayáichárika-Sútras* (from *samayáchára*, conventional practice), which treat of customs sanctioned by the practice of pious men, but not enjoined or expressly stated in the Grihya-Sútras. The two last classes of Sútras, which are not comprised amongst the Kalpa works, then grew into the Dharma-ṣástras, or law-books, of which that of Manu is the chief representative.—*Chambers' Encyclopedia.*

VEDANTA—(From the Sanskrit *veda*, and *anta*, end; hence, literally, "the end or ultimate aim of the Vedas") is the second great division of the Mimamsa school of Hindu philosophy. It is chiefly concerned in the investigation of *Brahmán* (neuter) or the Supreme Spirit, and the relation in which the universe, and especially the human soul, stands to it; and in contradistinction from the Púrvamímánsa, or the investigation (*mímánsá*) of the former (*púrva*) part of the Vedas—*viz*., the Sanhitá, and especially the Bráhmaṇas—which contain the *dharma*, or religious law, it is also called *Uttara-mímánsá*, or the investigation (*mimamsa*) of the latter (*uttara*) part of the Vedas—*viz*., Áraṇyakás and *Upanishads* which treat of (the neuter) *Brahmán*, or the Supreme Spirit [not to be confounded with (the masculine) *Brahmán*, or the god of the mythological *Trimúrti*). Sometimes, the name given to it is *Sáríraka-mímánsá*, or the investigation of the soul (Sáríraka). In its method, the Vedánta differs from the Nyáya by endeavouring to explain the universe as a successive development from one ultimate source or principle—whereas the Nyáya, in both its divisions, treats of the object of human knowledge of which the universe is composed, under different topics, unconcerned about their mutual relation of effect and cause; and from the *Sánkhya*, it is distinct, inasmuch as that system is based on the assumption of a duality of principles whence the universe derives its origin.

The subject-matter of the Vedánta is the proof that the universe emanates in a successive development from a Supreme Spirit or soul, which is called *Brahmán*, or *paramátman*; that the human soul is therefore identical in origin with Brahmán; that the worldly existence of the human soul is merely the result of its ignorance of this sameness between itself and the Supreme Spirit; and that its final liberation or freedom from Transmigration is attained by removal of this ignorance, that is, by a proper understanding of the truth of the Vedánta doctrine.

According to this doctrine. *Brahmán* (neuter) is both the efficient and material cause of the world, creator and creation, doer and deed. It is one, self-existent, supreme, as truth, wisdom, intelligence, and happiness; devoid of the three qualities, in the sense in which created beings possess them; and at the consummation of all things, the whole universe is resolved or absorbed into it. From Brahmán individual souls emanate, as innumerable sparks issue from a blazing fire. The soul, therefore, is neither born, nor does it die; it is of divine substance, and as such, infinite, immortal, intelligent, sentient, true. Its separate existence, as distinct from Brahmán, is the cause of its ignorance; and this ignorance, which consists in regarding the world as a reality capable of subsisting without Brahmán, has a double power—that of enveloping and projecting. By means of the former, it makes the soul liable to mundane vicissitudes, as to the sensations of pleasure, pain, &c. The projective power of ignorance, when encompassing the soul in its fourth condition, or that of pure intellect (its other conditions are: waking, dreaming, and dreamless sleep) produces out of the darkness which then prevails the five subtle elements—*viz.*, *ether*, which is the substratum of the quality sound; *air*, which arises from ether, the substratum of touch; from air, *fire or light*, the substratum of colour; from light, *water*, the substratum of savour; and from water, *earth*, the substratum of smell. From these subtle elements are then produced seventeen subtle bodies and the five gross elements. The former, also called lingaṣaríra, because they are bodies (ṣarira) which impart to existing beings their individual character (*linga*), are *the five organs of perception*—*viz.*, the organs of hearing, touch, sight, taste, and smell, which arise severally from the *pure* or inactive particles of each of the subtle elements; further, *two intellectual organs*, which are produced from the *mingled pure*, or inactive particles of the subtle elements—*viz.*, *buddhi*, understanding, the function of which is to arrive at a certainty or conclusion, and *manas* (an organ of volition and imagination), the function of which consists in willing and doubting—thinking and referring the external objects to one's own self, being two functions common to both of them; lastly, *the five organs of action*—*viz.*, the voice, the hands, the feet, the organ of excretion and that of generation, which are severally produced from the *foul* or *active* particles of each of the subtle elements; and *the five vital airs*, which are produced from the *mingled foul*, or *active* particles of the subtle elements—*viz.*, the air breathed forth, which has its place in the fore-part of the nose; the air breathed downwards, which has its place in the lower intestines; the air which circulates through the whole body; the ascending air, which has its place in the throat, and the descending air in the middle of the body, which causes assimilation and digestion of food, produces semen, excrements, &c. (Later Vedantists assume ten such vital airs—*viz.*, besides the foregoing, the airs which severally cause retching, winking, hunger, yawning,' and fattening.) The five *gross elements* are the five subtle elements, when, according to a theory derived from a scriptural text, they have become so divided and combined that each of them retains a preponderating portion of itself, and consequently of the quality of which it is the substratum as ether of sound, &c.—and besides smaller portions of the other subtle elements, and the qualities of which they are the substrata. From these gross elements then arise the various (mythological) worlds, and this world too, with bodies which are distinguished as viviparous, or those produced from a womb, as men, beasts, &c.; oviparous, or those produced from an egg, as birds, snakes, &c.; those generated by 'sweat' OR hot moisture, as lice, gnats, &c.; and those germinating, as creepers, trees, &c. The soul, when existing in the body, is encased in a succession of 'sheaths.' The first or interior 'sheath' consists of *buddhi*, associated with the organs of perception; the second, of *manas*, associated with the organs of action; and the third, of the vital airs together with the organs of action. These three 'sheaths' constitute the subtle body of the soul, which attends the soul in its transmigration; and the collective totality of such subtle bodies is the supreme soul, as regarded in its relation to the world; when it is also called 'the soul which is the thread,' or passes like the thread through the universe, or Hiraṇyagarbha, or life. The fourth and exterior 'sheath' of the soul is composed of the gross elements; and the collective aggregate of such gross bodies is the gross body of the deity. This whole development being the result of ignorance, the soul frees itself from its error by understanding that the different stages in which this development appears, do not represent real or absolute truth; and when its error has completely vanished, it ceases to be re-born, and becomes re-united with Brahmán, whence it emanated. But since the means of arriving at a final deliverance can only be the complete mastery of the truths of the Vedánta, other means, such as the performance of sacrifices or other religious acts enjoined by the

Vedas, or the practice of the Yoga, cannot lead to the same result. They may be meritorious, and are even recommended as such, but can effect only an apparent liberation. Of this, there are two kinds: one liberation which is effected in lifetime, and enables a man to perform supernatural actions or wonders, as the evocation of the shades of progenitors, going anywhere at will, and similar feats; and another which takes place after death, and enables the soul, not divested of its subtle body, to reside in heaven; but after a time its effect ceases, and the soul has to renew its mundane existence. In order to fit the mind for meditating on these truths, various moral duties are enjoined, and various practices are recommended, especially by later Vedánta writers. Thus, the student of the Vedánta is told not to hurt a sentient being, to speak the truth, not to steal, to practice continence, and not to accept gifts; to remain pure and content, to do penance, and to study the Vedas; also to remain in certain postures, to practice various modes of suppressing his breath, and the like. These injunctions, however, are extraneous to the doctrine itself, and appear to be a compromise with the old orthodox faith, which requires the performance of religious acts, and a later stage of it, which favours such austere practices as are especially known by the name of Yoga. The doctrine of *bhakti*, or faith, *'does* not belong to the older Vedánta; it is, however, an interesting feature of the later periods of this philosophy; and the same observation applies to the doctrine *of Máyá*, or illusion, according to which the world has no reality whatever, but is merely the product of imagination; for the older Vedánta, as will have been seen, merely teaches that the world is not *the truth*, but does not deny its material reality." (* The late Dr. J.R.Ballantyne published an able Lecture on the Vedánta, embracing the Text of the Vedánta Sara. Allahabad, 1850. There is an excellent article on the Ontology of the Vedánta, in the *Benares Magazine* for December 1851, written by Dr. F. E. Hall.)

VEDANTA-PARIBHASA—A modern textbook on the Vedānta philosophy.

VEDANTA-SARA—'Essence of the Vedānta'. A short popular work on the Vedānta philosophy. It has been translated by Ballantyne, and also by Böhtlingk, Roer, and Frank.

VEDANTA-SUTRA—The aphorisms of Bādarāyaṇa on the Vedānta philosophy. They are commonly called *Brahmāsūtras*, and a translation under that name by the K.M. Banerjee has been published in the *Bibliotheca Indica*. There is a French translation by Poley.

VEDARTHA-PRAKASA—'Elucidation of the meaning on the Veda.' This is the name of Sāyaṇa's great commentary on the *Ṛgveda*. Also of a commentary on the *Taittirīya Saṁhitā* by Mādhavacārya.

VEDASIRAS—A sage, the son of Márkáṇdya: he married Pivarí, and had many children, who constituted the family, or brahmanical tribe, of Bhárgavas, sons of Bhrigu. The most celebrated of those was Uṣanas, the preceptor of the Daityas.

VEDAVATI—The vocal daughter of the Rishi Kuṣadhvaja, sprung from him during his constant study of the Veda. She was a damsel of brilliant beauty, but dressed in ascetic garb, and lived in forests on the Himálaya. It was there she was seen by the giant Rávaṇa, in the course of his progress through the world, and he at once became enamoured of her. He enquired who she was, and told her that such an austere life was unsuited to her youth and attractions. As a reason for leading each an ascetic existence she said the gods, gandharvas, &c., wished that she should choose a husband, but her father would give her to no one else than to Vishṇu, the lord of the world, whom he desired for his son-in-law. This resolution provoked Sambhu, king of the Daityas, who slew her father, Kuṣadhvaja, while sleeping, on which her mother (whose name is not given) after embracing his body, entered into the fire. Vedavati then proceeds "In order that I may fulfil this desire of my father in respect of Náráyana, I wed him with my heart. Having entered into this engagement, I practice great austerity. Náráyana, and no other than he, Purushottama, is my husband. From the desire of obtaining him, I resort to this severe observance." Rávaṇa's passion is not in the least diminished by this explanation, and he urges that it is the old alone who should seek to become distinguished by accumulating merit through austerity; prays that she who is so young and beautiful, shall become his bride; and boasts that he is superior to Vishṇu. She rejoins that no one but he would thus contemn that deity. On receiving this reply, he touches the hair of her head with the tip of his finger. She is greatly incensed, and forthwith cuts off her hair, and tells him that as he has so insulted her, she cannot continue to live, but will enter into the fire before his eyes. She goes on: "'Since I have been insulted in the forest by thee who art wicked-hearted, I shall be born again for thy destruction. For a man of evil design cannot be slain by a woman; and the merit of my austerity would be lost if I were to launch a curse against thee. But if I have performed, or bestowed, or sacrificed, aught, may I be born the virtuous daughter, not produced from the womb, of a righteous man.' Having thus spoken, she entered the blazing fire. Then a shower of celestial flowers fell from every part of the sky. It is she, lord, who (having seen Vedavati in the Kritá age, has been burn in the Treta age) as the daughter of the king of the Janakas and [has become] thy bride, for thou art the eternal Vishṇu. The mountain-like enemy who was [virtually] destroyed before by her wrath, has now been slain by her, having recourse to thy superhuman energy." On this the commentator remarks: "By this it is signified that Sítá was the principal cause of Rávaṇa's death; but the function of destroying him is ascribed to Ráma." On the words "thou art Vishṇu," in the preceding verse the same commentator remarks "By this it is clearly affirmed that Sítá was Lakshṃi. This is what Parásara says. In the god's life as Ráma, she became Sítá, and in his birth as Krishṇa [she became] Rukminí."—*O.S.T.*, IV., 392.

VEDA-VYASA—Arrangers of the Vedas: "In every Dwápara (or third) age, Vishṇu, in the person of Vyása, in order to promote the good of mankind, divides the Veda, which is properly but one, into many portions: observing the limited perseverance, energy, and application of mortals, he makes the Veda fourfold, to adapt it to their capacities; and the bodily form which he assumes in order to effect that classification, is known by the name of Veda-vyása."—*Vishṇu Purána.*

VEDDAH—A wild semi-savage race, residing in the interior of Ceylon. *The forest Veddahs* dwell in hollow trees or caves, subsist on game which they kill with rudery formed bows and arrows, wandering from jungle to jungle, as the game becomes scarce. They will not hold the slightest intercourse with any natives but those of their own tribe, and their language is said to be unintelligible to all others. The village Veddahs dwell in certain districts, hold but slight intercourse with the other inhabitants of the island will not intermarry nor mix with them. They can make themselves understood to the Singhalese. Their sole clothing is a strip of cloth that hangs down in front, and is fastened by a coir cord, which passes round their loins. Their hair, beards and whiskers are never shorn or cleansed, but hang down in matted masses. The forest Veddahs are dexterous hunters, and especially skilful in snaring the wild elephants. The two tribes do not intermarry, as they mutually distrust each other. The Veddahs generally deposit their dead in the jungle to be devoured by wild animals. They seem to worship the planets? Evil spirits, and spirits of their deceased ancestors. They have their own headmen whom they elect and obey. They use bows and arrows and clubs of ironwood.—Sirr's *Ceylon*, Vol. II, p. 216.

They occupy a district about 90 miles long and 45 broad in the southeastern side of Ceylon, lying between the sea and the base of the Badulla and Oovah hills. They are a remnant of the Yakkos, the aboriginal inhabitants of Ceylon, who, 2000 years ago, after the conquest of the island by Wijayo and his followers, returned into the wilds as the Kulis in Guzerat, the Bhíls in Malwa, the Putu in Cuttack, the Konds in Gondwana, and the

Bedas in Mysore, retired before conquerors. The Bisadæ, or Besadæ, which in mediæval Greek is called Vesadæ, are alluded to In the tract of Palladius de Moribus Brachmanorum, written about A. D. 400, and the same name is applied by Ptolemy to a similar race inhabiting northern India. A forest tribe of Mysore, known by the name of Vedas or Redas, formed part of the army of Tippu Sultan. The Veddahs live by hunting and use the bow, in drawing which they employ their hands and their feet. They are omniverous, and eat carrion and vermin, roots, grain, fruit, birds, bats, crows, owls, kites, but refuse the bear, elephant and buffalo. Their language is a dialect of Singhalese, free from Sanskrit or Pali, but the vocabulary is very limited and they have recourse to gestures and signs. They have no knowledge of God, nor of a future state, and have no temples, idols, altars, prayers or charms, but have a devil worship. They do not bury but cover their dead with leaves in the jungle. They are regarded by the Singhalese as of high descent.—*J. E. Tennant.*

VEDHA—A measure of time; 100 Trutis.

VEDHAKA—One of the Narakas; that for the makers of arrows.

VEDODAYA—'Source of the Veda.' An epithet of the sun as the source of the *Sāmaveda.*

VEGAVAT—'Swift.' **(1)** A son of Kṛṣṇa; **(2)** A *dānava* who fought on the side of the Śālvas against Kṛṣṇa, and was killed by Śamba. **(3)** An ancient prince of the solar race; the son of Bandhumat.

VELA—The daughter of Meru and wife of Samudra.

VENA—Son of Aṅga, and a descendant of Manu

Svāyambhuva. When he became king he issued this proclamation: "Men must not sacrifice or give gifts or present oblations. Who else but myself is the enjoyer of sacrifices? I am for ever the lord of offerings." The sages remonstrated respectfully with him, but in vain; they admonished him in stranger terms; but when nothing availed, they slew him with blades of consecrated grass. After his death the sages beheld clouds of dust, and on inquiry found that they arose from bands of men who had taken to plundering because the country was left without a king. As Veṇa was childless, the sages, after consultation, rubbed the thigh (or, according to the *Harivaṁśa*, the right arm) of the dead king to produce a son. From it there came forth "a man like a charred log, with flat face, and extremely short". The sages told him to sit down (Niṣīda). He did so, and thus bacame a Nisāda, from whom, "sprang the Niṣādas dwelling in the Vindhya Mountains, distinguished by their wicked deeds". The brāhmaṇas then rubbed the right hand of Veṇa, and from it "sprang the majestic Pṛthu, Veṇa's son, resplendent in body, glowing like the manifested Agni". The above is the story as told, with little variation, in the *Mahābhārata*, the *Viṣṇu* and *Bhāgavata Purāṇas*, and the *Harivaṁśa*. The *Padma Purāṇa* says that Veṇa began his reign well, but fell into the Jaina heresy. For this the sages pummelled him until the first of the Niṣāda came forth from his thigh and Pṛthu from his right arm. Being freed from sin by the birth of the Niṣāda, he retired to a hermitage on the Narmadā, where he engaged in penance. Viṣṇu was thus conciliated, and granted him the boon of becoming one with himself, (*see* PṚTHI)

VENI-SAMHARA—'The binding of the braid.' A drama by Bhaṭṭa Nārāyaṇa. The plot is taken from the *Mahābhārata.* Draupadī, the wife of the Pāṇḍu princes, was dragged by the hair other head into the hall of the Kauravas by Duḥśāsana, and she vowed that it should remain dishevelled until the insult was avenged. After the death of the Kauravas she again braided her hair. Wilson has given an analysis of the drama. There are several editions of the text.

VENKATA, VENKAṬĀDRI—A hill which was a seat of the worship of Viṣṇu. It is the modern Tripati.

VENU—A Yádava prince, the son of Satajit.

VETALA—A ghost or goblin; a sprite who haunts cemeteries and animates dead bodies.

VETALA-PAÑCHAVIMSATI—The twenty-five stories of the Vetāla. It is the *BaitāīPacīsī* of Hindustāni, and has been translated into all the languages of India. The work is ascribed to an author named Jambaladatta.

VETAL—The demon-god of the outcaste helot races; the circle of large stones, which may be observed outside almost every village, is sacred to this god; the superstition has for ages held, and still holds, its ground against all Bralimanical innovations. The stones remind the traveller of the Druid circles of the northern nations. Sir *B.Frere.** (* *Introduction to Old Deccan Days*.)

VETRAVATI--The river Betvā, which rises in the Vindhyas and falls into the Jumnā below Kalpi.

VHAJA—A pastoral district about Āgrā and Mathurā, where Kṛṣṇa passed his boyhood with the cowherds.

VIAVACHI—One of the Daiviki Apsaras, or divine nymphs who engage in the interruption of the penance of holy sages.

VIBHANDAKA—(Vibhaṇḍaka), a sage who retired from the world to the deepest shades of the forest, with his heart full of bitterness and morose hatred for men, because amongst them he had found crime and folly. He despised pleasure too and scorned beauty; for once he had been deceived by both. Taking with him his infant son, Rishya-sringa, he chose a cave, in the glen of the wood, to be this young child's nursery.

'I give thee, my son,' he said, the savage beasts of prey for comrades; from them thou wilt learn less cruelty and wickedness than from thy fellows! Thou shalt hear the parrot shriek, the jackal how!, the lynx mewl, and the hyæna screech, but thou shalt be spared the discordant voice of man ! Here, amid reptiles and venomous insects, thou shall yet live in ignorance of what is most vile and loathsome in Nature! Exposed to the caprices of heaven, a thousand dangers attending thy every footstep, thy life a series of hardships, afflictions, and perils, thou shalt know more peace and security than in the crowded city. Grow then; and, if it be possible, lose the base nature Brahm has laid on thee; and ignore that thou art a vile and miserable creature,—a man! *See* RISHYASRINGA.

VIBHÍSHAṆA—The younger brother of the giant Rávaṇa; when he and his brothers had practiced rigid austerities for a long series of years, Brahmá appeared to offer them boons: Vibhíshaṇa asked that he might never meditate any unrighteousness. When his elder brother Vaisravana (Kubera) was expelled from Lanka, Vibhíshaṇa followed him to Gandhamádana, where he is said to have dwelt with a white umbrella and white garlands, on the Śvetaparvata or white mountain, attended by his four counsellors, and apart from his disreputable brothers Kumbhakarṇa, &c., who, naked, with disheveled hair and red garlands, frequented the south.

When Hanumán was taken before Rávaṇa, and announced himself as the ambassador of Sugríva, warning the ravisher of Sítá that nothing could save him from the vengeance of Ráma, Rávaṇa, infuriated, ordered him to be put to death; but Vibhíshaṇa reminded his brother that the life of ambassadors was sacred. On another occasion, after a long altercation, Rávaṇa was so enraged with Vibhíshaṇa for persisting in urging the restoration of Sítá, that he rose in a fury and kicked him from his seat. Smarting under this outrage, Vibhíshaṇa left Lanka and flew through the air to Kailása to the court of his brother Kuvera, where Śiva also at that time happened to be present. The latter made known to Vibhíshaṇa the divine character of Ráma, and directed him to desert Rávaṇa and join Ráma's standard, which

Vibhíshaṇa accordingly did. He was at first taken for a spy, but afterwards Ráma accepted him as an ally and embraced him. On the death of Rávaṇa, Vibhíshaṇa was installed as Rája of Lanka; he afterwards accompanied Ráma and Lakshmana to Ayodhya.—*I.E.P.*, 80-83.

VIBHRATRA—A king of Hastinápura, the son of Sukriti.

VIBHU—**(1)** The Indra of the fifth Manwantara; **(2)** A prince, the grandson of Alarka.

VIBHUTI—(Vibhúti), a grayish-white coloured powder made of the ashes of burnt cow-dung; Śiva is represented with his person sprinkled or smeared with this powder; and it is used in a similar way by all the Śaiva and many of the Vaishnava ascetics.

VIBUDHA—A king of Mithila, the son of Krita.

VICHITRA-VIRYA—A prince, the son of Śántanu, rája of Hastinápur: "he married Ambá and Ambalika, the daughter of the rája of Kásí; and indulging too freely in connubial rites, fell into a consumption of which he died. (Vishṇu Purána.) See Śántanu. The legend as related in the Mahábhárata is slightly different. Vichitravirya's half brother Bhíshma is there said to have gone to Kásí for the purpose of seeing the Rája's daughters, and finding them very beautiful he did not wait for the day of the Swayamvara, but seizing the three damsels, placed them in his own chariot, and challenged every Rája present to do him battle. Thus did Bhíshma win the daughters of the Rája of Kásí and carry them away in triumph to the city of Hastinápur, that they might become the wives of Vichitra-virya. The widows of Vichitra-virya were afterwards the mothers of Dhritaráshtra and Páṇḍu.

VIDAGDHA-MADHAVA—A drama in seven acts by Rūpa on the loves of Kṛṣṇa and Rādhā, written in AD 1533. "It is weak as a drama, and its literary merits are small."

VIDARBHA—**(1)** Berar, and probably including with it the adjoining district of Beder, which name is apparently a corruption of Vidarbha. The capital was Kuṇḍinapura, the modern "Kundapur", about forty miles east of Amarāvatī. **(2)** The only son of Jyámagha and Saivya; he was married to the damsel the father had brought home before his birth. See Jayámagha.

VIDDHASALABHAÑJIKA—'The statue.' A comedy of domestic intrigue by Rājaśekhara. It was probably written earlier than the tenth century.

VIDEHA—An ancient country, of which the capital was Mithilā. It corresponds with the modern Tirhut or North Bihar.

VIDHATṚ—'Creator.' A name of Brahmā, of Viṣṇu, and of Viśvakarmā.

VIDHATRI—A son of the demi-god Bhrigu, married to Niryati.

VIDMISARA—A king of Magadha, the son of Kshatranjas.

VIDURA—A mountain in Ceylon, probably Adam's Peak.

VIDURATHA—**(1)** A prince; the son of Bhajamána and father of Súra; **(2)** The son of Suratha, a descendant of Kuru.

VIDURA—The brother of Dhṛitaráshtra and Páṇḍu. "Soma, the moon, the progenitor of the lunar race, who reigned at Hastinápur, was the child of the Rishi Atri, and father of Budha, who married Ilá, or Iḍá, daughter of the solar prince Ikshváku, and had by her a son Aila or Purúravas. The latter had a son by Urvaṣi named Áyus, from whom came Nahusha, the father of Yayáti. The latter had two sons, Puru and Yadu, from whom proceeded the two branches of the lunar line. In the line of Yadu we need only mention the last three princes. Sura, Vasudeva, and Krishṇa, with his brother Balaráma. Fifteenth in the other line—that of Puru—came Dushyanta, father of the great Bharata.

Ninth from Bharata came Kuru, and fourteenth from him Śántanu, this Śántanu had by his wife Satyavatí, a son named Vichitra-vírya. Bhíshma who renounced the right of succession and took the vow of perpetual celibacy, was the son of Śántanu by a former wife, the goddess Gangá, whence one of his names is Gángeya. Satyavati also had, before her marriage with Sántanu, borne Vyása to the sage Paráșara; so that Vichitra-vírya, Bhíshma and Vyása were half-brothers: and Vyása, though he retired into the wilderness to live a life of contemplation, promised his mother that he would place himself at her disposal whenever she required his services. Satyavatí had recourse to. him when her son Vichtra-vírya died childless, and requested him to pay his addresses to Vichitra-vírya's two widows, named Ambiká and Ambáliká. He consented, and had by them respectively two children, Dhṛitaráshtra who was born blind, and Paṇḍu, who was born with a pale complexion. When Satyavati begged Vyása to become the father of a third son (who should be without any defect) the elder wife, terrified by Vyása's austere appearance, sent him one of her slave girls, dressed in her own clothes; and this girl was the mother of Vidura. Vyása was so much pleased with this slave-girl that he pronounced her free, and declared that her child Vidura should be eminently wise and good.

Dhṛitaráshtra, Páṇḍu and Vidura, were thus brothers, the sons of Vyása, the supposed author or compiler of the Mahábhárata. "Vidura is one of the best characters in the Mahábhárata, always ready with good advice both for the Páṇḍavas and for his brother Dhṛitaráshtra. His disposition leads him always to take the part of the Páṇḍu princes, and warn them of the evil designs of their cousins." Bhíshma promoted the marriage of Vidura with a beautiful slave girl belonging to king Devaka. *I.E.P.*

VIDUSHAKA—(Vidúshaka), the buffoon in the theatre of the Hindus. He is the humble companion, not the servant, of a prince, or man of rank; and it is a curious peculiarity that he is always a Brahman. He bears more affinity to Sancho Panza, perhaps, than any other character in western fiction, imitating him in his combination of shrewdness and simplicity, his fondness of good living, and his love of ease. This character is always lively, and sometimes almost witty, although in general his facetiousness does not take a very lofty flight. According to the technical definition of his attributes he is to excite mirth by being ridiculous in person, age, and attire.—*Wilson*, XI, p. xlvii.

VIDVAN-MODA-TARANGINI—'Fountain of pleasure to the learned.' A philosophical work by Rāma-deva, translated into English by Rāja Kālī Kṛṣṇa.

VIDYADHABA (mas.), **VĪDYĀDHARĪ** (fem.). 'Possessors of knowledge.' A class of inferior deities inhabiting the regions between the earth and sky, and generally of benevolent disposition. They are attendants upon Indra, but they have chiefs and kings of their own, and are represented as intermarrying and having much intercourse with men. They are also called Kāmarūpin, 'taking shapes at will'; Khecara and Nabhaścara, 'moving in the air'; Priyamvada, 'sweet-spoken'.

VIDYADHARAS—(Vidyádharas), in Buddhist mythology are the bards of heaven, or celestial musicians, demigods or angels, corresponding to the Gandharvas of Hinduism.

VIDYARANYA, VIDYĀRAṆYASWĀMĪ—'Forest of learning.' A title of Mādhavācārya, as patron of the city of Vidyānagara, afterwards altered to Vijayanagara, the capital of the last great Hindu dynasty of the Dakhin.

VIDYUJJIHVA—A magician in the service of Rávaṇa; when the latter wished to persuade Síta that Ráma had been killed in battle, he called the magician, who produced by illusion a head bearing a resemblance to the noble countenance of Ráma; this was thrown down on the floor near to Síta, along with a mighty bow which seemed the one Visvámitra had given to Ráma.

VIGNESVARA—(Vigneșvara), a name of Ganésa, the remover of difficulties.

VIGNESWARA—A name of Ganeșa (*q.v.*).

VIHANGHAMAS—A class of deities of the eleventh Manwantara.

VIHARA—(Vihara), a convent of Bauddha ascetics. The word also means taking exercise, or walking about for pleasure.

VIJAGANITA—A work on algebra, translated by Colebrooke and by Strachey. It is a chapter of the work called *Siddhānta-śiromaṇi*, written by Bhāskarācārya. There are several editions of the text.

VIJAYA—**(1)** A prince, the son of Chunchu; **(2)** A king of Mithila, the son of Jaya; **(3)** The son of Sanjaya, of the race of Áyus; **(4)** A son of Jayadratha; **(5)** One of the Andhra princes.

VIJAYA—A daughter of the patriarch Daksha, married to Kriașwa.

VIJITASWA—The eldest son of Prithu, called also Antarddhána, in consequence of having obtained from Indra the power of ma king himself invisible.

VIJNAÑESVARA—Author of the law-book called Mitākṣarā.

VIKALA—A measure of time, six Práṇas.

VIKARNA—A son of Dhṛtarāṣṭra.

VIKATA—(Vikatá), the bow-legged; one of the Rákshasí guardians of Síta when in captivity in Lanka; she proposed to devour Síta for not yielding to Rávaṇa's wishes.

VIKESI—The wife of the Rudra Sarva.

VIKRAMADITYA—A celebrated Hindu king of Malwa, whose reign began fifty-six years before the Christian era. The ancient city of Ujjein was his capital. Vikramaditya had no estate assigned him by his father, and lived for a considerable time with his illegitimate brother Bhurtri at Ujjein, of which Bhurtri was governor. A quarrel having occurred between the brothers Vikramaditya left Ujjein and travelled in great poverty over Guzerat and other parts of India. On his return to Malwa he found that his brother had resigned all worldly concerns and become a religious mendicant; he therefore assumed charge of the province, and from that period commenced a career which led to the establishment of his power over the greatest part of India. He is said to have restored the Hindu monarchy to that splendor which it had lost through a succession of weak sovereigns, whose character had encouraged the governors of distant provinces to rebel, and to form the territories committed to their charge into independent states.*

Vikramaditya is described as the greatest monarch of his age, of which there is the most satisfactory proof in the fact that his era is still current throughout Hindustan. He encouraged literature beyond all former examples. He invited learned brahmans from every part of India, and rewarded them with magnificent presents; and they have repaid him by investing him with immortality. They have exhausted the resources of flattery in their attempt to describe the magnitude of his power, and have assured us that without his permission the loadstone had no power over iron, or amber on the chaff of the field. So exemplary was his temperance, that while in the enjoyment of supreme power, he constantly slept on a mat, which, with a water-pot replenished from the spring, formed the whole furniture of his chamber. It is stated that while he extended his patronage to the worship of the gods and goddesses then rising into popularity, he himself continued to profess the old creed, and adored the one infinite and invisible God.† (*Malcolm's *Memoir of Central India*, I, 24; † Marshman's *History of India*, I, 20.)

VIKRAMORVASI—'The hero and the nymph.' A celebrated drama by Kālidāsa, translated in Wilson's *Hindu Theatre.* There are many editions and translations, (*see* PURŪRAVAS)

VIKRANTA—One of the Prajápatis.

VIKRITA—The second of the Prajápatis, who was married to one of the daughters of Daksha.

VIKRITI—A king of Chedi, the son of Jímúta.

VIKUKSHI—One of the hundred sons of Ikshváku: The *V.P.* has the following legend of this prince:—On one of the days of Ashtaka, Ikshváku being desirous of celebrating ancestral obsequies, ordered Vikukshi to bring him flesh suitable for the offering. The prince accordingly went into the forest and killed many deer and other wild animals for the celebration. Being weary with the chase and hungry, he sat down and ate a hare; after which being refreshed, he carried the rest of the game to his father. Vasishṭha, the family priest, was summoned to consecrate the food; but he declared that it was impure in consequence of Vikukshi's having eaten a hare from amongst it, (making it thus, as it were, the residue of his meal.) Vikukshi was therefore abandoned by his offended father, and the epithet Sasáda, hare-eater, was affixed to him by the Guru. But on the death of Ikshváku, the sovereignty of Ayodhya descended to Vikukshi. The Matsya Purána says that Indra was born as Vikukshi, and that Ikshváku had a hundred and fourteen other sons who were kings of the countries south of Meru; and as many who reigned north of that mountain. Wilson says that it seems very probable that by these sons of Ikshváku we are to understand colonies or settlers in various parts of India.

VILOMAN—A Yádava chief, the son of Kapotaroman.

VIMADA—**(1)** In the *Ṛgveda* it is said the Aśvins gave a bride to the youthful Vimada, and the commentator explains that Vimada had won his bride at a *svayaṁvara*, but was stopped on the way home by his unsuccessful competitors. The Aśvins came to his succour, repulsed the assailants, placed the bride in their chariot, and carried her to the home of the prince. **(2)** A Rishi mentioned in the Rig Veda as on very friendly terms with Indra; **(3)** A young prince to whom the Aṣvins brought in a car a bride named Kamadyú, who seems to have been the beautiful wife of Purumitra.—*O.S.T.*, v., 244.

VIMALA—One of the sons of Sudyumna after his transformation.

VIMOHANA—One of the Narakas; the place of bewildering; for the punishment of the thief and the condemner of prescribed observances.

VINATA—**(1)** A daughter of Dakṣa, one of the wives of Kaśyapa, and mother of Garuḍa. According to the *Bhāgavata Purāna* she was the wife of Tārkṣya or Garuḍa. **(2)** The crooked one; one of the Rákshasí guardians of Síta when a captive in Lanka. She represented Rávaṇa as a consort to be proud of, and tried to persuade Síta to yield.

VINA—The Hindu lute; an instrument of much sweetness and compass, but little power. It is a fretted instrument of the guitar kind, usually having seven wires or strings, and a large gourd at each end of the fingerboard. The extent of the instrument is two octaves. It is supposed to be the invention of Nárada, the son of Brahmá, and has many varieties, enumerated according to the number of strings, &c.

VINAYA—Good behavior; a son of Dharma by Lajja, modesty, daughter of Daksha, obviously allegorical.

VINAYAKA—(Vináyaka), one of the names of Ganesa or Vigneṣvara, the god of obstacles; the deity is supposed capable of either causing or removing difficulties or impediments.

VINDA—Vinda and Anuvinda were joint kings of Avantī, and fought in the great war.

VINDHYA—The mountains that stretch across India, and divide what Manu calls the Madhyadeśa or 'middle land', the land of the Hindus, from the south, that is, they divide Hindustān from the Dakhin. The mountain is personified, and according to a legend he was jealous of the Himālaya, and called upon the sun to revolve round him as he did round Meru. When the sun refused the mountain began to raise its head to obstruct that luminary, and to tower above Himālaya and Meru. The gods invoked the aid of Agastya, the spiritual guide of Vindhya. That sage called upon the mountain to bow down before him, and afford him an easy passage to and from the south. It obeyed, and Agastya passed over. But he never returned, and so the mountain remains in its humbled condition, far inferior to the Himālaya.

VINDHYASAKTI—The chief of the Kailakila Yavana kings; a warrior of a mixed race, sprung from a Brahmán father and a Kshatriya mother. Kailakila was a city in the Mahratta country. Wilson is of opinion that the Puránas refer to a time when the Greek princes, or their Indo-Scythic successors, following the course of the Indus, spread to the upper part of the western coast of the peninsula.

VINDHYA—The chain of mountains which divides Hindustan from the Dekhan or South country. These mountains, usually called Bindh, hold an important position both in the mythology and geography of India. According to some authorities they are called Bindhya, because they appear to obstruct the progress of the sun. The course of the Narmadá river, indicates the direction of the principal range; but the mountainous tract spreads much more widely; it meets the Ganges in several places towards the North; and the Godáveri is held to be its Southern limit.

The vast extent of this mountainous tract, contrasted with the small elevation of these hills, viewed from the plains of Hindustan, has furnished grounds for a legend to which the mythological writings of the Hindus often allude. Vindhya having once prostrated himself before his spiritual guide, Agastya, still remains in that posture by command of the holy personage. This humiliation is the punishment of his presumption in emulating the lofty height of Himálaya and Meru.

The Vindhya mountains are divided into three parts, of which the first, or eastern part, extends from the Bay of Bengal to the source of the Narmada and Sone. The western portion extends from thence to the Gulf of Cambay. The third, or Southern, lies on the south of the Narmada and Sone, and gives rise to the Tapti, and the Vaitarani or Cattack river.

VINDHYAVALI—The wife of Bali the *asura*.

VINDHYA-VASINI—'The dweller in the Vindhyas.' The wife of Śiva. (*see* DEVĪ) An ancient and still celebrated shrine of Durgá, a short distance from Mirzapur.

VINDUMATI—The wife of the Rája Mándhátri.

VINDUSARA—The son and successor of Chandragupta.

VINITA—One of the sons of the sage Pulastya.

VIPAS, VIPĀŚĀ—The river Byās, the Hyphasis or Bibasis of the classical writers. A legend relates that it obtained its name through the sage Vasiṣtha, who wishing to commit suicide, bound his limbs with cords and threw himself into the water. The river, declining to drown him, cast him unbound (*vipāśa*) on its bank.

VIPASCHIT—The Indra of the second Manwantara.

VIPRA—(1) One of the sons of Dhruva; **(2)** A king of Magadha, the son of Srutanjaya.

VIPRACHITTI—The king of the Dánavas, he was the son of Kaṣyapa and Danu, and the hero of many legends. He was one of the leaders in the contest between the gods and demons that took place after the churning of the ocean.

VIPRITHA—A prince of the solar race, the son of Chitrika.

VIPULA—A mountain in Ilávrita, forming the western buttress to Meru. The modern name of the mountain termed in the Mahábhárata Varáha (*q.v.*).

VIRABHADRA—A formidable being created from the mouth of Śiva, for the purpose of spoiling the sacrifice of Daksha. He is thus described in the Váyu Purána.

"A divine being, with a thousand heads, a thousand eyes, a thousand feet; wielding a thousand clubs, a thousand shafts; holding the shell, the discus, the mace, and bearing a blazing bow and battle-axe; fierce and terrific, shining with dreadful splendour, and decorated with the crescent moon; clothed in a tiger's skin dripping with blood, having a capacious stomach, and a vast mouth armed with formidable tusks. His ears were erect; his lips were pendulous; his tongue was lightning; his hand brandished the thunderbolt; flames streamed from his hair; a necklace of pearls wound round his neck; a garland of flame descended on his breast. Radiant with lustre, he looked like the final fire that consumes the world. Four tremendous tusks projected from a mouth which extended from ear to ear. He was of vast bulk, vast strength, a mighty male and lord, the destroyer of the universe, and like a large fig-tree in circumference; shining like a hundred moons at once; fierce as the fire of love; having four heads, sharp white teeth, and of mighty fierceness, vigour, activity, and courage; glowing with the blaze of a thousand fiery suns at the end of the world; like a thousand undimmed moons; in bulk, like Himádri, Kailása, or Sumeru, or Mandara, with all its gleaming herbs; bright as the sun of destruction at the end of ages; of irresistible prowess and beautiful aspect; irascible, with lowering eyes, and a countenance burning like fire; clothed in the hide of the elephant and lion, and girt round with snakes; wearing a turban on his head, a moon on his brow; sometimes savage, sometimes mild; having a chaplet of many flowers on his head, anointed with various unguents, adorned with different ornaments and many sorts of jewels, wearing a garland of heavenly Karṇikar- flowers, and rolling his eyes with rage. Sometimes he danced; sometimes he laughed aloud; sometimes he stood rapt in meditation; sometimes he trampled upon the earth; sometimes he sang; sometimes he wept repeatedly. And he was endowed with the faculties of wisdom, dispassion, power, penance, truth, endurance, fortitude, dominion, and self-knowledge."

VIRACARITA—A book of tales by Ananta, which describes the feuds between the descendants of Vikramāditya and Śālivāhana.

VIRADHA—A horrible man-eating *rākṣasa*, son of Kāla and Śatahṛdā. By penance he had obtained from Brahmā the boon of invulnerability. He is described as "being like a mountain peak, a man-eater, loud-voiced, hollow-eyed, large-mouthed, huge-bellied, horrible, rude, long, deformed, of dreadful aspect, wearing a tiger's skin, dripping with fat, wetted with blood, terrific to all creatures, like death with open mouth, bearing three lions, four tigers, two wolves, ten deer, and the great head of an elephant with the tusks, and smeared with fat, on the point of an iron pike, shouting with a loud voice." Rāma, with Lakṣmaṇa and Sītā, encountered him in, the Daṇḍaka forest, when he foully abused and taunted the brothers, and seized upon Sītā. The brothers proved with their arrows that he was not invulnerable, but he caught them, threw them over his shoulders, and ran off with them as if they had been children. They broke both his arms, threw him down, beat him with their fists, and dashed him to the earth, but they could not kill him, so they dug a deep hole and buried him alive. After his burial there arose from the earth a beautiful person, who said that he was *a gandharva* who had been condemned by Kubera to assume the shape of a *rākṣasa*, from which Rāma had enabled him to escape. He was also called Tumburu.

VIRAJ—A person of a mythical or mystical character. Manu says "Having divided his own substance, the mighty power of Brahmá became half-male, half-female: and from that female he produced Viráj. Know me to be that person whom the male Viráj produced by himself." The Linga and Váyu Purána describe the origin of Viráj and Satarúpá from Brahmá; in the first instance, and in the second, with Manu, who is termed Vairája, is the son of Viráj. It is also explained allegorically; Viráj being all male animals, Satarúpá all female animals. (*see* MANU) One passage in the *Ṛgveda* says, "From him (Puruṣa) sprang Virāj, and from Virāj (sprang) Puruṣa" (Muir's *Texts*, V. 50, 369), like as Aditi is said to have sprung from Dakṣa, and Dakṣa from Aditi. Viraj, the male half of Brahmā, is supposed to typify all male creatures; and Śatarūpā, the female half, all female forms.

VIRAJA—One of the Rájas of India in the Swayambhuva or first Manwantara: he was the son of Tvashtri.

VIRAJAS—**(1)** A son of the sage Paurnamása; **(2)** A son of the sage Vasishṭha.

VIRA-MITRODAYA—A law-book by Mitramiśra, of authority in the Benares School. It is in the form of a commentary on the Mitākṣarā. The text has been printed.

VIRANA—**(1)** A sage, the father of Viraní and Asikní; **(2)** A teacher of the White Yajush.

VIRANI—The daughter of the above, and mother of the Manu Chákshusa.

VIRAT—**(1)** One of the Rájas of India in the first Manwantara; the son of Nará; **(2)** The material universe—Brahmáṇda.

VIRATA—A country in the vicinity of the modern Jaipur. The present town of Bairaṭ is 105 miles south of Delhi. Its king was called Rājā of Virāṭa or Rājā Virāṭa. It was at his court that the Pāṇḍava princes and Draupadī lived in disguise. They rendered him great services against his enemies, and he fought on their side in the great war and was killed by Droṇa. (*see* MATSYA)

VIRATA—The fourth book of the Mahábharata is called Viráta-Parva, as it recounts the adventures of the Páṇḍavas, when, being obliged to live incognito, they journeyed to the court of king Viráta, and entered his service in various disguises. Viráta's capital was called Matsya, (or sometimes Upaplavya.) There, four months after the arrival of the Páṇḍavas, a great festival was held, at which a number of wrestlers exhibited their prowess. Bhíma then astonished Viráta by dashing to the ground and killing the strongest of the wrestlers named Jimúta.

When Suṣarman, king of Trigarta, made a raid into Viráta's territory for the sake of plunder and carried off his cattle, Viráta, accompanied by all the Páṇḍavas except Arjuna, invaded Trigarta to recover the property. A great battle was fought and Viráta was taken prisoner by Suṣarman. Bhíma, as usual, tore up a tree and prepared to rescue him; but Yudhisbthira advised him not to display his strength too conspicuously, lest he should be recognised. He then took a bow, pursued Suṣarman, defeated him, released Viráta, and recovered the cattle.

VIROCANA—A *dānava*, son of Prahlāda, and father of Bali. He is also called Dṛśana. When the earth was milked, Virocana acted as the calf of the *asuras*. (*see* PṚTHI)

VIRUDDHAS—A class of deities in the tenth Manwantara.

VIRUPA—An ancient rája who reigned somewhere on the banks of the Yamuná, he was the son of Ambarísha.

VIRUPAKSA—**(1)** 'Deformed as to the eyes.' A name of Śiva, who has three eyes. Also one of the Rudras. Also a *dānava*, son of Kaśyapa. **(2)** A renowned warrior who was sent by Rávaṇa to fight with Hanumán. He rushed on the gallant Ape with upraised club and mallet, but the vigorous Hanumán tore up a lofty palm tree with which he speedily felled his adversary to the ground lifeless.—*I.E.*, p. 232.

VIRUPAKSHA—One of the eleven Rudras.

VIRUPAKSHA—**(1)** One of the four elephants by whom the earth is sustained, with its forests and mountains, its cities and villages. If in momentary weariness the monstrous elephant stir his head, then the world quakes and its inhabitants are alarmed. The lordly Virupáksha is at the Northern quarter. At the Southern quarter another colossal elephant, the magnanimous Mahapadma, stands. In the West the robust Saumanas, and in the East the sublime Himapándura. These are the four supports of the world.—*I.E.* **(2)** A name of Śiva; the god with deformed (*virupa*) eyes, (*akshi*); Śiva being usually represented with a third eye in the middle of his forehead.

VISAKADATTA—(Viṣákadatta), a prince, the son of Mahárája Prithu, and author of the drama Mudrá-Rákshasa. Wilson calls him the MASSINGER of the Hindus; and says that he was not a poet of the sphere of Bhavabhúti or Kálidása. His imagination rises not to their level, and there is scarcely a brilliant or beautiful thought in 'The Signet of the Minister.' As some equivalent for the want of imagination, he has a vigorous perception of character, and a manly strain ef sentiment, that are inferior only to elevated conception and delicate feeling.—Wilson, *Works*, XII, 254.

VISAKHA—**(1)** A lunar mansion in Járadghavi, in the Central Avashthána; **(2)** A sage, one of the sons of Kumára.

VISAKHADATTA—Author of the drama *Mudrārākṣasa.* He is said to be of royal descent, but his family has not been identified.

VISAKHAYUPA—A king of Magadha, the son of Pálaka.

VISALA—**(1)** A name of the city Ujjayinī. **(2)** The founder and king of the city of Vaisálí; he was the sun of Trinavinda, by the celestial nymph Alambusha.

VISASANA—One of the Narakas, for the punishment of the maker of swords, lances and other weapons.

VISHṆU-LOKA—Vaikuntha, the lofty world of Vishṇu.

VISHṆU-PURANA—This Purāṇa generally stands third in the lists, and is described as "that in which Parāśara, beginning with the events of the Varāha *kalpa*, expounds all duties, is called the Vaiṣṇava, and the learned know its extent to be 23,000 stanzas." The actual number of stanzas does not amount to 7000, and there is no appearance of any part being wanting. "The Vishṇu-Purána most closely conforms to the definition of a Pancha-lakshaṇa Purána, or one which treats of five specified topics. It comprehends them all; and, although it has infused a portion of extraneous and sectarial matter, it has done so with sobriety and with judgment, and has not suffered the fervour of its religious zeal to transport it into very wide deviations from the prescribed path. The legendary tales which it has inserted are few, and are conveniently arranged, so that they do not distract the attention of the compiler from objects of more permanent interest and importance.

The first book of the six, into which the work is divided, is occupied chiefly with the details of creation, primary (Sarga) and secondary (Pratisarga); the first explaining how the universe. proceeds from Prakṛiti or eternal crude matter; the second, in what manner the forms of things are developed from the elementary substances previously evolved, or how they reappear after their temporary destruction. Both these creations are periodical; but the termination of the first occurs only at the end of the life of Brahmá, when not only all the gods and all other forms are annihilated, but the elements are again merged into primary substance, besides which, one only spiritual being exists. The latter takes place at the end of every Kalpa or day of Brahmá, and affects only the forms of inferior creatures, and lower worlds; leaving the substance of the universe entire, and sages and gods unharmed. The explanation of these events involves a description of the periods of time upon which they depend, and which are, accordingly, detailed. Their character has been a source of very unnecessary perplexity to European writers; as they belong to a scheme of chronology wholly mythological, having no reference to any real or supposed history of the Hindus, but applicable, according to their system, to the infinite and eternal revolutions of the universe. In these notions, and in that of the co-eternity of spirit and matter, the theogony and cosmogony of the Puránas, as they appear in the Vishṇu Purána, belong to and illustrate systems of high antiquity, of which we have only fragmentary traces in the records of other nations.

The course of the elementary creation is, in the Vishṇu, as in other Puránas, taken from the Sánkhya philosophy; but the agency that operates upon passive matter is confusedly exhibited, in consequence of a partial adoption of the illusory theory of the Vedánta philosophy, and the prevalence of the Pauráṇik doctrine of pantheism. However incompatible with the independent existence of Pradhána or crude matter, and however incongruous with the separate condition of pure spirit or Purusha, it is declared, repeatedly, that Visunu, as one with the supreme being, is not only spirit, but crude matter, and not only the latter, but all visible substance, and Time. He is Purusha, 'spirit;' Pradhána, 'crude matter;' Vyakta, 'visible form;' and Kála, 'time.' This cannot but be regarded as a departure from the primitive dogmas of the Hindus, in which the distinctness of the Deity and his works was enunciated; in which, upon his willing the world to be, it was; and in which his interposition in creation, held to be inconsistent with the quiescence of perfection, was explained away by the personification of attributes in action, which afterwards came to be considered as real divinities, Brahmá, Vishṇu, and Śiva, charged, severally, for a given season, with the creation, preservation, and temporary annihilation of material forms. These divinities are declared to be no other than Vishṇu. In Śaiva Puránas, they are, in like manner, identified with Śiva; the Puránas thus displaying and explaining the seeming incompatibility, of which there are traces in other ancient mythologies, between three distinct hypostases of one superior deity, and the identification of one or other of those hypostases with their common and separate original.

After the world has been fitted for the reception of living creatures, it is peopled by the will-engendered sons of Brahmá, the Prajápatis or patriarchs, and their posterity. It would seem as if a primitive tradition of the descent of mankind from seven holy personages had at first prevailed, but that, in the course of time, it had been expanded into complicated, and not always consistent, amplification. How could these Rishis or patriarchs have posterity ? It was necessary to provide them with wives. In order to account for their existence, the Manu Swáyambhuva and his wife Satarúpá, were added to the scheme; or Brahmá becomes twofold, male and female; and daughters are then begotten, who are married to the Prajápatis. Upon this basis various legends of Brahmá's double nature, come, no doubt, as old as the Vedas, have been constructed. But, although they may have been derived, in some degree, from the authentic tradition of the origin of mankind from a single pair, yet the circumstances intended to give more interest and precision to the story are, evidently, of an allegorical or mystical description, and conduced, in apparently later times, to a coarseness of realization which was neither the letter nor spirit of the original legend. Swáyambhuva, the son of the self-born or uncreated, and his wife Satarúpá, the hundred-formed or multiform, are, themselves, allegories; and their female descendants, who become the wives of the Rishis, are Faith, Devotion, Content, Intelligence, Tradition, and the like; whilst, amongst their posterity, we have the different phases of the moon and the sacrificial fires. In another creation, the chief source of creatures is the patriarch Daksha (ability,) whose daughters—Virtues, or Passions, or Astronomical Phenomena—are the. mothers of all existing things. These legends, perplexed as they appear to be, seem to admit of allowable solution, in the conjecture that the Prajápatis and Rishis were real personages, the authors of the Hindu system of social, moral, and religious obligations, and the first observers of the heavens, and teachers of astronomical science.

The regal personages of the Swáyambhuva Manwantara are but few; but they are described, in the outset, as governing the earth in the dawn of society, and as introducing agriculture and civilization. How much of their story rests upon a traditional remembrance of their actions, it would be useless to conjecture; although there is no extravagance in supposing that the legends relate to a period prior to the full establishment, in India, of the Brahmánical institutions. The legends of Dhruva and Prahláda, which are intermingled with these particulars, are, in all probability, ancient; but they are amplified, in a strain conformable to the Vaishṇava purport of this Purána, by doctrines and prayers asserting the identity of Vishṇu wilh the Supreme. It is clear that the stories do not originate with this Purána. In that of Prahláda, particularly, circumstances essential to the completeness of the story are only alluded to, not recounted , showing, indisputably, the writer's having availed himself of some prior authority for his narration.

The second book opens with a continuation of the kings of the first Manwantara; amongst whom, Bharata is said to have given a name to India, called, after him, Bhárata-varsha. This leads to a detail of the geographical system of the Puránas, with mount Meru, the seven circular continents, and their surrounding oceans, to the limits of the world; all of which are mythological fictions, in which there is little reason to imagine that any topographical truths are concealed. With regard to Bhárata or India, the case is different. The mountains and rivers which are named are readily verifiable; and the cities and nations that are particularized may, also, in many instances, be proved to have had a real existence. The list is not a very long one, in the Vishṇu Purána, and is, probably, abridged from some more ample detail, like that which the Mahábhárata affords, and which, in the hope of supplying information with respect to a subject yet imperfectly investigated, the ancient political condition of India, I have inserted and elucidated.

The description which this book also contains of the planetary and other spheres, is equally mythological, although occasionally presenting practical details and notions in which there is an approach to accuracy. The concluding legend of Bharata—in his former life, the king so named, but now a Brahmán, who acquires true wisdom, and thereby attains liberation—is, palpably, an invention of the compiler, and is peculiar to this Purána.

The arrangement of the Vedas and other writings considered sacred by the Hindus,—being, in fact, the authorities of their religious rites and belief,—which is described in the beginning of the third book, is of much importance to the history of Hindu literature and of the Hindu religion. The sage Vyása is here represented, not us the author, but the arranger or compiler of the Vedas, the Itihásas, and Puránas. His name denotes his character, meaning the 'arranger' or 'distributor;' and the recurrence of many Vyásas, many individuals who new-modelled the Hindu scriptures, has nothing, in it, that is improbable, except the fabulous intervals by which their labours are separated. The re-arranging, the refashioniug, of old materials is nothing more than the progress of time would be likely to render necessary. The last recognized compilation is that of Krishṇa Dwaipáyana, assisted by Brahmáns who were already conversant with the subjects respectively assigned to them. They were the members of a college, or school, supposed, by the Hindus, to have flourished in a period more remote, no doubt, than the truth, but not at all unlikely to have been instituted at some time prior to the accounts of India, which we owe to Greek writers, and in which we see enough of the system to justify our inferring that it was then entire. That there have been other Vyásas and other schools since that date, that Brahmáns unknown to fame have remodelled some of the Hindu scriptures, and especially, the Puránas, cannot reasonably be contested, after dispassionately weighing the strong internal evidence, which all of them afford, of the intermixture of unauthorized and comparatively modern ingredients. But the same internal testimony furnishes proof, equally decisive, of the anterior existence of ancient materials; and it is, therefore, as idle as it is irrational, to dispute the antiquity or authenticity of the greater portion of the contents of the Puránas, in the face of abundant positive and circumstantial evidence of the prevalence of the doctrines which they teach, the currency of the legends which they narrate, and the integrity of the institutting which they describe, at least three centuries before the Christian era. But the origin aud development of their doctrines, traditions, and institutions were not the work of a day; and the testimony that establishes their existence three centuries before Christianity, carries it back to a much more remote antiquity, to an antiquity that is, probably, not surpassed by any of the prevailing fictions, institutions, or beliefs, of the ancient world.

The remainder of the third book describes the leading institutions of the Hindus, the duties of castes, the obligations of different stages of life, and the celebration of obsequial rites, in a short but primitive strain, and in harmony with the laws of Manu. It is a distinguishing feature of the Vishṇu Purána, and it is characteristic of its being the work of an earlier period than most of the Puranas, that it enjoins no sectarial or other acts of supererogation; no Vratas, occasional self-imposed observances; no holydays, no birthdays of Krishṇa, no nights dedicated to Lakshmí; no sacrifices or modes of worship other than those conformable to the ritual of the Vedas. It contains no Máhátmyas or golden legends, even of the temples in which Vishṇu is adored.

The fourth book contains all that the Hindus have of their ancient history. It is a tolerably comprehensive list of dynasties and individuals; it is a barren record of events. It can scarcely be doubted, however, that much of it is a genuine chronicle of persons, if not of occurrences. That it is discredited by palpable absurdities in regard to the longevity of the princes of the earlier dynasties, must be granted; and the particulars preserved of some of them are trivial and fabulous. Still, there is an innartificial simplicity and consistency in the succession of persons, and a possibility and probability in some of the transactions, which give to these traditions the semblance of authenticity, and render it likely, that they are not altogether without foundation. At any rate, in the absence of all other sources of information, the record, such as it is, deserves not to be altogether set aside. It is not essential to its credibility, or its usefulness, that any exact chronological adjustment of the different reigns should be attempted. Their distribution amongst the several Yugas, undertaken by Sir William Jones, or his Pandits, finds no countenance from the original texts, further than an incidental notice of the age in which a particular monarch ruled, or the general fact that the dynasties prior to Krishṇa precede the time of the Great War and the beginning of the Káli age; both which events we are not obliged, with the Hindus, to place five thousand years ago. To that age the solar dynasty of princes offers ninety-three descents, the lunar, but forty-five; though they both commence at the same time. Some names may have been added to the former list, some omitted in the latter; and it seems most likely, that, notwithstanding their synchronous beginning, the princes of the lunar race were Subsequent to those of the solar dynasty. They avowedly branched off from the solar line; and the legend of Sudyumna, that explains the connexion, has every appearance of having been contrived for the purpose of referring it to a period more remote than the truth.

Deducting, however, from the larger number of princes a considerable proportion, there is nothing to shock probability in supposing, that the Hindu dynasties and their ramifications were spread through an interval of about twelve centuries anterior to the war of the Mahábhárata, and, conjecturing that event to have happened about fourteen centuries before Christianity, thus carrying the commencement of the regal dynasties of India to about two thousand six hundred years before that date. This may, or may not, be too remote; but it is sufficient, in a subject where precision is impossible, to be satisfied with the general impression, that, in the dynasties of kings detailed in the Puránas, we have a record which, although it cannot fail to have suffered detriment from age, and may have been injured by careless or injudicious compilation, preserves an account, not wholly undeserving of confidence, of the establishment and succession of regular monarchies, amongst the Hindus, from as early an era, and for as continuous a duration, as any in the credible annals of mankind.

After the date of the great war, the Vishṇu Purána, in common with those Puránas which contain similar lists, specifies kings and dynasties with greater precision, and offers political and chronological particulars to which, on the score of probability, .there is nothing to object. In truth, their general accuracy has been incontrovertibly established. Inscriptions on columns of stone, on rocks, on coins, deciphered only of late years, through the extraordinary ingenuity and perseverance of Mr. James Prinsep, have verified the names of races and titles of princes—the Gupta and Andhra Rájas, mentioned in the Puránas—and have placed beyond dispute the identity of Chandragupta and Sandrocoptus; thus giving us a fixed point from which to compute the date of other persons and events. Thus, the Vishṇu Purána specifies the interval between Chandragupta and the Great War to be eleven hundred years; and the occurrence of the latter little more than fourteen centuries B. C., remarkably concurs with inferences of the like date from different premises. The historical notices that then follow are considerably confused; but they probably afford an accurate picture of the political distractions of India at the time when they were written: and much of the perplexity arises from the corrupt state of the manuscripts, the obscure brevity of the record, and our total want of the means of collateral illustration.

The fifth book of the Vishṇu Purána is exclusively occupied with the life of Krishṇa. This is one of the distinguishing characteristics of the Purána, and is one argument against its antiquity. It is possible, though not yet proved, that Krishṇa, as an Avatára of Vishṇu, is mentioned in an indisputably genuine text of the Vedas. He is conspicuously prominent in the Mahábhárata, but very contradictorily described there. The part that he usually performs is that of a mere mortal; although the passages are numerous that attach divinity to his person. There are, however, no descriptions, in the Mahábhárata, of his juvenile frolics, of his sports in Vṛindávana, his pastimes with the cow-boys, or even his destruction of the Asuras sent to kill him. These stories have, all, a modern complexion; they do not harmonize with the tone of the ancient legends, which is, generally, grave, and, sometimes, majestic. They are the creations of a puerile taste and grovelling imagination. These chapters of the Vishṇu Purána offer some difficulties as to their originality. They are the same as those on the same subject in the Brahmá Purána: they are not very dissimilar to those of the Bhágavata. The latter has some incidents which the Vishṇu has not, and may, therefore, be thought to have improved upon the prior narrative of the latter. On the other hand, abridgment is equally a proof of posteriority as amplification. The simpler style of the Vishṇu Purána is, however, in favour of its priority; and the miscellaneous composition of the Brahmá Purána renders it likely to have borrowed these chapters from the Vishṇu. The life of Krishṇa in the Hari Vamṣa and the Brahmá Vaivarta are, indisputably, of later date.

The last book contains an account of the dissolution of the world, in both its major and minor cataclysms; and, in the particulars of the end of all things by fire and water, as well as in the principle of their perpetual renovation, presents a faithful exhibition of opinions that were general in the ancient world. The metaphysical annihilation of the universe, by the release of the spirit from bodily existence, offers, as already remarked, other analogies to doctrines and practices taught by Pythagoras and Plate, and by the Platonic Christians of later days.

The Vishṇu Purána has kept very clear of particulars from which an approximation of its date may be conjectured. No place is described of which the sacredness has any known limit, nor any work cited of probable recent composition. The Vedas, the Puránas, other works forming the body of Sanskrit literature, are named; and so is the Mahábhárata, to which, therefore, it is subsequent. Both Bauddhas and

Jainas are adverted to. It was, therefore, written before the former had disappeared. But they existed, in some parts of India, as late as the twelfth century, at least; and it is probable that the Purána was compiled before that period. The Gupta kings reigned in the seventh century. The historical record of the Purána which mentions them was, therefore, later; and there seems little doubt that the same alludes to itie first incursions of the Mohammedans, which took place in the eighth century; which brings it still lower. In describing the latter dynasties, some, if not all, of which were, no doubt, contemporary, they are described as reigning, altogether, one thousand seven hundred and ninety-six years. Why this duration should have been chosen does not appear; unless, in conjunction with the number of years which are said to have elapsed between the Great War and the last of the Andhra dynasty, which preceded these different races, and which amounted to two thousand three hundred and fifty, the compiler was influenced by the actual date at which he wrote. The aggregate of the two periods would be the Kálí year 4146, equivalent to A. D. 1045. There are some variety and indistinctness in the enumeration of the periods which compose this total: but the date which results from it is not unlikely to be an approximation to that of the Vishṇu Purána."—Wilson's *Works*, Vol. VI, 102-112.

VISHṆU—The second person of the mythological Hindu triad, and now the most celebrated and popular of all the gods of India. But it appears from the Rig-Veda that Indra at that time was regarded as superior to Vishṇu, who is there classed with Varuṇa, the Maruts, Rndra, Váyu, the luminous deities called Ádityas, and, others. "There is no trace of Vishṇu, or anything relating to him in the Institutes of Manu, although the allusions to idolaters and the worship of inferior gods might possibly have some reference to him also." "In the Mahábhárata, Vishṇu is often identified with the supreme spirit; but while in some portions of this poem—the different parts of which belong to different epochs of Hindu antiquity—he is thus regarded as the most exalted deity; he is again, in others, represented as paying homage to Śiva (*q.v.*), the third person of the Trimúrti, and as acknowledging the superiority of this god over himself. Taking, therefore, the Mahábhárata as a whole, he does not occupy, in this epos, the exclusive supremacy which is assigned to him in the Rámáyana, and still more in those Puránas especially devoted to his praise.

"The large circle of myths relating to Vishṇu, in the epic poems and Puránas, is distinguished by a feature which, though not quite absent from the mythological history of Śiva, especially characterises that of Vishṇu. It arose from the idea, that whenever a great disorder, physical or moral, disturbed the world, Vishṇu descended 'in a small portion of his essence' to set it right, to restore the law, and thus to preserve creation. Such descents of the god are called his *Avatáras* (from *ava* and *tri*, descend); and they consist in Vishṇu's being supposed to have either Assumed the form of some wonderful animal or superhuman being, or to have been born of human parents, in a human form, always, of course, possessed of miraculous properties. Some of these Avatáras are of an entirely cosmical character; others, however, are probably based on historical events, the leading personage of which was gradually endowed with divine attributes, until he was regarded as the incarnation of the deity itself. With the exception of the last, all these Avatáras belong to the past; the last, however, is yet to come."

Viṣṇu's preserving and restoring power has been manifested to the world in a variety of forms called *avatāras*, literally 'descents', but more intelligibly 'incarnations', in which a portion of his divine essence was embodied in a human or supernatural form possessed of superhuman powers. All these *avatāras* bacame manifest for correcting some great evil or effecting some great good in the world. The *avatāras* are ten in number, but the *Bhāgavata Purāṇa* increases them to twenty-two, and adds that in reality they are innumerable. All the ten *avatāras* are honoured, but the seventh, and eighth, Rāma and Kṛṣṇa, are honoured as great mortal heroes and receive worship as great gods. Kṛṣṇa is more especially looked upon as a full manifestation of Viṣṇu, and as one with Viṣṇu himself, and he is the object of a widely extended and very popular worship, (*see* AVATĀRA)

"His ten avatáras are: '1, The *Matsya*, or fish. In this avatár, Vishṇu descended in the form of a fish to save the pious king Satyavrata, who with the seven Rishis and their wives had taken refuge in the ark to escape the deluge which then destroyed the earth; 2, The *Kúrma*, or Tortoise. In this he descended in the form of a tortoise, for the purpose of restoring to man some of the comforts lost during the flood. To this end he stationed himself at the bottom of the ocean, and allowed the point of the great mountain Mandara to be placed upon his back, which served as a hard axis, whereon the gods and demons, with the serpent Vásuki twisted round the mountain for a rope, churned the waters for the recovery of the amrita or nectar, and fourteen other sacred things; 3. The *Varáha*, or Boar. In this he descended in the form of a boar to rescue the earth from the power of a demon called 'golden-eyed' Hiraṇyáksha. This demon had seized on the earth and carried it with him into the depths of the ocean. Vishṇu dived into the abyss, and after a contest of a thousand years slew the monster; 4. The *Narasimha*, or Man-lion. In this terrific shape of a creature half-man, half-lion, Vishṇu delivered the earth from the tyranny of an insolent demon called Hiraṇyakaśipu; 5, *Vámana*, or Dwarf. This avatár happened in the second age of the Hindus or Tretáyug, the four preceding are said to have occurred in the first or Satyayug; the object of this avatár was to trick Bali out of the dominion of the three worlds. Assuming the form of a dwarf he appeared before the king and asked, as a boon, as much land as he could pace in three steps. This was granted; and Vishṇu immediately expanding himself till he filled the world, deprived Báli at two steps of heaven and earth, but in consideration of some merit, left Pátála still in his dominion; 6, Parasurámá; 7, Rámachandra; 8, Krishṇa, or according to some Balaráma; 9, Buddha. In this avatár, Vishṇu descended in the form of a sage for the purpose of making some reform in the religion of the Brahmáns, and especially to reclaim them from their proneness to animal sacrifice. Many of the Hindus will not allow this to have been an incarnation of their favourite god; 10, *Kalki*, or White Horse. This is yet to come. Vishṇu mounted on a white horse, with a drawn scimitar, blazing like a comet, will, according to prophecy, end this present age, *viz.*, the fourth or Kaliyug, by destroying the world, and then renovating creation by an age of purity."*

"This number and enumeration of Avatáras, however, was not at all times the same. The Mahábhárata, though also mentioning ten, names successively the Hansa-, tortoise-, fish-, boar-, man-lion-, dwarf-, Paraṣu-Ráma-, Ráma-, Sátvata-, and Kalkin- Avatáras. The Bhágavata-Purána speaks of twenty-two Avatáras of Vishṇu, which, for instance, also comprise Prithu, (*q.v.*), Dhanvantari, the god of medicine; and Kapila, the reputed founder of the Sánkhya (*q.v.*) philosophy. Other works have twenty-four Avatáras, or even call them numberless; but the generally-received Avatáras, are those ten mentioned before."†

The holy river Ganges is said to spring from the feet of Viṣṇu.

As preserver and restorer, Viṣṇu is a very popular deity, and the worship paid to him is of a joyous character. He has a thousand names (*sahasranāma*), the repetition of which is a meritorious act of devotion. His wife is Lakṣmī or Śrī, the goddess of fortune, his heaven is Vaikuṇṭha, and his vehicle is the bird Garuḍa. He is represented as a comely youth of a dark-blue colour, and dressed like an ancient king. He has four hands. One holds the Pañcajanya (*q.v.*), a *śarikha* or conch-shell; another the *Sudarś ana* or Vajranābha, a *cakra* or quoit weapon; the third, a *gadā* or club called Kaumodakī; and the fourth, *apadma* or lotus. He has a bow called *śārṅga*, and a sword called Nandaka. On his breast are the peculiar mark or curl called *śrīvatsa* and the jewel *kaustubha*, and on his wrist is the jewel *syamantaka.* He is sometimes represented seated on a lotus with Lakṣmī beside him, or reclining on a leaf of that plant. Sometimes he is portrayed reclining on the serpent Śeṣa, and at others as riding on his gigantic bird Garuḍa.

Of the thousand names of Viṣnu the following are some of the most common: Acyuta, 'unfallen, imperishable'; Ananta, 'the 'endless'; Anantaśayana, 'who sleeps on the serpent Ananta'; Caturbhuja, 'four-armed'; Dāmodara, 'bound round the belly with a rope', as Kṛṣṇa; Govinda or Gopāla, 'the cowkeeper' (Kṛṣṇa); Hari; Hṛsikeśa, 'lord of the organs of sense'; Jalaśāyin, 'who sleeps on the waters'; Janārdana, 'whom men worship'; Keśava, 'the hairy, the radiant'; Kirīṭin, 'wearing a tiara'; Lakṣmīpati, 'lord of Lakṣmī'; Madusūdana, 'destroyer of Madhu'; Mādhava, 'descendant of Madhu'; Mukunda, 'deliverer'; Murāri, 'the foe of Mura'; Nara, 'the man'; Nārāyana, 'who moves in the waters'; Pañcāyudha, 'armed with five weapons'; Padmanābha, 'lotus-navel'; Pītāmbara, 'clothed in yellow garments'; Puruṣa, 'the man, the spirit'; Puruṣottama, 'the highest of men, the supreme spirit'; Sārngin or Śārṅgipāṇi, 'carrying the bow *Śārṅga*'; Vāsudeva, Kṛṣṇa, son of Vasudeva; Vārṣaṇeya, 'descendant of Vṛsni'; Vaikuṇṭhanātha, 'lord of Vaikuṇṭha (paradise)'; Yajñeśa, Yajñeśvara, 'lord of sacrifice'. (* Williams' *English Sanskrit Dictionary.*)

VISHNAPU—In the legends regarding various persons delivered or favoured by the Aṣvins, it is said "they restored Vishṇápú, like a lost animal, to the sight of Viṣvaka, son of Krishṇa, their worshipper. The names both of Viṣvaka and Vishṇápú occur in the Rig Veda."—*O.S.T.*, v., p. 244.

VISISHTA ADVAITA—The Brahmans of Southern

India are divided into three great sects—those who believe there is but one soul, in short that everything is God, (ADVAITA. *q.v.*)—those who believe there are two souls. God and man, (Dwaita)—aud those who take a medium course, and believe there is but one soul, which in man and created things is somewhat different from the divine soul, (Visishta Adwaita). To those who are not Brahmans these philosophical distinctions are almost unknown, and men worship a being to whom they give the puranic names of Vishṇu and Śiva, Krishṇa and Hanumán. While so many names are given and acknowledged by every Hindu, as if each referred to a separate deity, each person acknowledges but one as his own. God, and ascribes to him all the attributes of the godhead.

It will be seen however that while the philosophy of the Schools is unknown to the crowd, the strong tendency of the popular mind is towards monotheism of a character not unlike that of the Visishta Advaita School. Vishṇu and Śiva according to books, members of a triad of equal Gods, but in popular theology the worshipper of either scorns the others. In social life and act the worshipper of Vishṇu acknowledges but one God. He speaks of Vishnu as if there were no other God. So with the devotee of Śiva even in a greater degree. He transposes the name into the neuter Sivam; and expresses thus his belief that his deity is the one great essence, without sex or corporeal shape.

VISMAPANA—'Astounding.' The aerial city of the *gandharvas*, which appears and disappears at intervals.

VISNU—Author of a Dharmaśātra or law book.

VISOKA—One of the eight original properties or perfections of man, called Siddhis; it means exemption alike from infirmity or grief.

VISRAVAS—Son of the Prajāpati Pulastya, or according to a statement of the *Mahābhārata*, a reproduction of half Pulastya himself. By a brāhmaṇī wife, daughter of the sage Bharadvāja, named Iḍaviḍā or Ilāviḍā, he had a son, Kubera, the god of wealth. By a *rākṣasī* named Nikaṣā or Kaikasī, daughter of Sumāli, he had three sons, Rāvaṇa, Kumbhakarṇa, and Vibhīṣana and a daughter named Śūrpanakhā. The *Viṣṇu Purāṇa* substitutes Keśinī for Nikaṣā. The account given by the *Mahābhārata* is that Pulastya, being offended with Kubera for his adulation of Brahmā, reproduced half of himself as Viśravas, and Kubera to recover his favour gave him three *rākṣasī* handmaids: Puṣpotkaṭā, the mother of Rāvaṇa and Kumbhakarṇa; Mālini, the mother of Vibhīṣaṇa; and Rākā, the mother of Khara and Śūrpanakhā.

VISRUTAVAT—A distinguished prince of the family of Ikshváku; he was the son of Mahaswat; and took part in the great war.

VISVA—A daughter of the patriarch Daksha, who was married to Dharma and became the mother of the Visvadevas.

VISVABHAVANA—A name of Vishṇu, as creator of the universe; meaning one with crude nature.

VISVA-DEVAS, VIŚVE-DEVAS—'All the gods.' In the Vedas they form a class nine in number. All the deities of inferior order. They are addressed in the Veda as "preservers of men, bestowers of rewards". In later times, a class of deities particularly interested in exequial offerings. The accounts of them are rather vague. They are generally said to be ten in number, but the lists vary, both as to the number and the names. The following is one list: (1) Vasu, (2) Satya, (3) Kratu, (4) Dakṣa, (5) Kāla, (6) Kāma, (7) Dhṛti, (8) Kuru, (9) Purūravas, (10) Mādravas. Two others are sometimes added, Rocaka or Locana and Dhuri or Dhvani. See *Viṣṇu Purāṇa*, Hall's edition, vol. III. pp. 178, 188,189.

VISVAGASWA—An ancient rája of the solar line—the son of Prithu.

VISVAGJYOTISH—The eldest of the hundred sons of Satajit, who reigned in India in the first Manwantara.

VISVAJIT—**(1)** A king of Hastinápura, the son of Jayadratha; **(2)** A king of Magadha, the son of Satyajit.

VISVAKARMA, VIŚVAKARMAN—'Omnificent.' This name seems to have been originally an epithet of any powerful god, as of Indra and Sūrya, but in course of time it came to designate a personification of the creative power. In this character Viśvakarmā was the great architect of the universe, and is described in two hymns of the *Ṛgveda* as the one "all-seeing god, who has on every side eyes, faces, arms and feet, who, when producing heaven and earth, blows them forth (or shapes them) with his arms and wings; the father, generator, disposer, who knows all worlds, gives the gods their names, and is beyond the comprehension of mortals". In these hymns also he is said to sacrifice himself or to himself, and the *Nirukta* explains this by a legend which represents that "Viśvakarmā, son of Bhuvana, first of all offered up all worlds in a Sarvamedha (general sacrifice), and ended by sacrificial himself."

In the Epic and Purāṇic periods Viśvakarmā is invested with the powers and offices of the Vedic Tvaṣṭṛ, and is sometimes so-called. He is not only the great architect, but the general artificer of the gods and maker of their weapons. It was he who made the Āgneyāstra or "fiery weapon", and it was he who revealed the *Sthāpatyaveda*, or science of architecture and mechanics. The *Mahābhārata* describes him as "the lord of the arts, executor of a thousand handicrafts, the carpenter of the gods, the fashioner of all ornaments, the most eminent of artisans, who formed the celestial chariots of the deities, on whose craft men subsist, and whom, a great and immortal god, they continually worship."

In the *Rāmāyaṇa*, Viśvakarmā is represented as having built the city of Laṅkā for the *rākṣasa*, and as having generated the ape Nala, who constructed Rāma's bridge from the continent to Ceylon.

The Purāṇas make Viśvakarmā the son of Prabhāsa, the eighth Vasu, by his wife "the lovely virtuous Yogasiddhā". His daughter Saṁjñā was married to Sūrya, the sun; but as she was unable to endure his effulgence, Viśvakarmā placed the sun upon his lathe and cut away an eighth part of his brightness. The fragments fell to the earth, and from these Viśvakarmā formed "the discus of Viṣṇu, the trident of Śiva, the weapon of Kubera the god of wealth, the lance of Kārttikeya god of war, and the weapons of the other gods". Viśvakarmā is also represented as having made the great image of Jagannātha.

In his creative capacity he is sometimes designated Prajāpati. He also has the appellations Kāru, 'workman'; Takṣaka, 'woodcutter'; Devavardhika, 'the builder of the gods'; Sudhanvan, 'having a good bow'.

VISVAKARMAN, VISVAKARYA—Two of the seven principal solar rays.

VISVAKENA—(1) The Manu of the fourteenth Manwantara according to the lists in the Matsya and Pádma Puránas; (2) A king of Hastinápura, the son of Brahmádatta.

VISVÁMITRA—A celebrated Rishi. According to the Rámáyana he had originally been a Kshatriya and a great warrior, but subsequently practised so may religious austerities in the Himálaya mountains that he ultimately became a brahman. His character is therefore somewhat anomalous. Max Müller considers that he opposed the ambition of the brahmans, and would not submit to their exclusive claims. He at length succeeded in gaining for himself and family the rights for which he struggled, and which the Brahmáns had previously withheld from all but their own caste. Visvámitra, however, was reconciled as soon as he was allowed to share in the profits of the priestly power, and became a favourite hero in Brahmánical tradition.

When Mahárája Dasaratha was one day discussing with his Councillors the subject of his son Ráma's marriage, Visvámitra arrived at the gate of the palace, and desired the doorkeeper to go within and tell the Maháraja that Visvámitra the son of Gadhi, was there. The Maháraja on hearing the message rose up with his two priests and went out to meet the sage, whom he received with every honour, saying, "Your coming, O great sage, is as grateful to me as amrita, as the fall of rain in the proper season, as the birth of a son to a childless father, as the recovery of lost treasure, as the dawning of a great joy." Visvámitra then stated the object of his visit—that Ráma should accompany him back to his hermitage to destroy the Rákshasas; an arrangement to which the Maháraja reluctantly consented. He then acted as Guru to Ráma and commanded him to slay Táraká; removing his objections about killing a woman, and providing him with divine weapons and mantras. After the marriage of Ráma, Visvámitra retired to the Himálaya mountains. During a twelve years' famine, Triṣanku provided food for Visvámitra and his family, and the sage being highly pleased, elevated him in his living body to heaven. This legend Wilson thinks is astronomical, and alludes possibly to some reformation of the sphere by Visvámitra under the patronage of Triṣankn, and in opposition to a more ancient system advocated by the school of Vasishṭha, *q.v.* The fact of Visvámitra having been both a rishi and an officiating priest, is undoubted. If we look to the number of Vedic hymns ascribed to him and to his family, to the long devotion to sacerdotal functions which this fact implies, and to the apparent improbability that a person who had himself stood in the position of a king should afterwards have become a professional priest, we may find it difficult to believe that although (as he certainly was) a scion of royal stock, he had ever himself exercised royal functions.—*O.S.T.*, I, 364.

"A kind of consecutive biography of Visvámitra is given in the first book of the Rámáyana, of which it forms one of the most interesting episodes. Its substance is as follows:—Once, when roaming over the earth with his armies, Visvámitra came to the hermitage of Vasishṭha, and was there received by the saint in the most sumptuous style. Vasishṭha could afford to entertain the king in this manner because he possessed a fabulous cow of plenty that yielded him everything he desired. Visvámitra becoming aware of the source of Vasishṭha's wealth, strongly wished to possess the cow, and asked Vasishṭha to sell her to him. The saint however refusing this offer, the king seized her, intending to carry her off by force. But the cow resisted and ultimately displayed her supernatural powers in producing from different parts of her body numerous peoples, and by them destroying the armies of Visvámitra. The king then had recourse to the magical weapons he possessed, but they were defeated by those of Vasishṭha, and to the humiliation thus inflicted on him he then gave rent in exclaiming: 'Contemptible is the might of a Kshatriya; a Brahmán's might alone is might.' And reflecting what he should do in this emergency, he resolved to practise austerities in order to attain the rank of a Brahmán. In consequence he went to the south, and performed severe penance during a thousand years; when at the end of this period the god Brahmá appeared to him, and announced that he had become a Rajarshi, or Royal Rishi. But Visvámitra was not satisfied with this degree of promotion, and continued his austerities for another such period. During that time, king Triṣanku of Ayodhya, of the family of Ikshváku, had determined to perform a sacrifice that would enable him to proceed bodily to heaven, and solicited for this purpose the assistance of Vasishṭha, who was the family priest of "all the Ikshvákus." This saint, however, having declared the scheme of the king impossible, and his sons also having refused to act in tlieir father's place, Triṣanku told them he would resort to another priest. He applied to Visvámitra, who showed his power by performing the sacrifice so much desired by Triṣanku, and accomplishing his object in spite of the resistance of Vasishṭha and his sons, and that of the gods themselves.

This event having caused a serious interruption in the austerities of Visvámitra, he proceeded to the forest Pushkara in the west, to remain undisturbed. It was then the tragic incident related under HARISCHANDRA occurred. It was in the forest that Sunaṣepha saw his uncle Visvámitra, and implored him to come to nis rescue. Visvámitra first commanded fifty of his own sons to offer themselves up as a ransom for their cousin. And on their refusing to do so, cursed them to become outcastes but afterwards taught Sunaṣepha two hymns, which if sung by him at the sacrifice would save his life. The liberation of Sunaṣepha having been effected, and Visvámitra having continued his penance for another thousand years, Brahmá conferred on him the dignity of a Rishi. But not satisfied with this distinction he went on practising still fiercer austerities than ever. These the gods interrupted by sending a heavenly nymph Menaka, who excited his worldly passions; still in the end he attained the rank of a Maharshi, or great Rishi. And after two thousand years of still more rigorous penance which for a time was again interrupted by the allurements of a nymph Rambha, the gods headed by Brahmá, came to acknowledge that he had now become a Brahmárshi, or Brahmán Rishi; and Vasishṭha himself was compelled to express acquiescence in the result he had achieved.

The above three paragraphs are abridged from Goldstücker's article in Chambers's Encyclopædia. Many other legends are given in Muir's *O.S.T.*, Vol. I. Visvámitra's cruel treatment of Harischandra and his family has already been quoted. (See SAIVYA). Various versions are given of the legend of Trisanku; and of the conflicts between Vasishṭha and Visvámitra. Professor Lassen, who quotes the stories, makes the following remarks on their import:

"The legend of the struggle between Vasishṭha and Visvámitra embraces two distinct points; one is the contest between the priests and warriors for the highest rank; the other is the temporary alienation of the Ikshvákus from their family priests. Vasishṭha is represented as the exemplar of such a priest; and the story of Kalmáshapáda is related for the express purpose of showing by an example that the Ikshvákus, after they had retained him, were victorious; in his capacity of priest he continued to live on, and is the representative of his whole race. We may conclude from the legend that his descendants had acquired the position of family priests to the Ikshvákus, though neither he himself nor his son Śaktri belonged to their number. Trisanku is the first prince who forsook them, and had recourse to Visvámitra. His successor Ambarísha received support from that personage, as well as from Richíka, one of the Bhrigus;—a family whose connection with the Kuṣikas appears also in the story of Paruṣaráma. The hostility between the Ikshvákus and the family of Vasishstha continued down to Kalmáshapáda. Visvámitra is represented as having intentionally fostered the alienation; while Vasishṭha is represented as forbearing (though he had the power) to annihilate his rival.

The conflict between the two rivals, with its motives and machinery, is described in the forms peculiar to the fully-developed epos. To this style of poetry is to be referred the wonder-working cow, which supplies all objects of desire. There is no ground for believing in any actual war with weapons between the contending parties; or in any participation of degraded Kshatriyas, or aboriginal tribes, in the contest; for all these things are mere poetical creations. Besides, the proper victory of Vasishṭha was not gained by arms, but by his rod. The legend represents the superiority of the Brahmáns as complete, since Visvámitra is forced to acknowledge the insufficiency of a warrior's power; and acquires his position as a Brahmán by purely Brahmánical methods.

Viśvāmitra's relationship to Jamadagni naturally places him in a prominent position in the *Rāmāyaṇa*. Here the old animosity between him and Vasiṣṭha again appears. He as a king paid visit to Vasiṣṭha's hermitage, and was most hospitably entertained; but he wished to obtain Vasiṣṭha's wondrous cow, the Kāmadhenu, which had furnished all the dainties of the feast. His offers were immense, but were all declined. The cow resisted and broke away when he attempted to take her by force, and when he battled for her, his armies were defeated by the hosts summoned up by the cow, and his "hundred sons were reduced to ashes in a moment by the blast of Vasiṣṭha's mouth". A long and fierce combat followed between Vasiṣṭha and Viśvāmitra, in which the latter was defeated; the kṣatriya had to submit to the humiliation of acknowledging his inferiority to the brāhmaṇa, and he therefore resolved to work out his own elevation to the Brāhmaṇical order.

While he was engaged in austerities for accomplishing his object of becoming a brāhmaṇa he became connected with King Triśaṅku. This monarch was a descendant of King Ikṣvāku, and desired to perform a sacrifice in virtue of which he might ascend bodily to heaven. His priest, Vasiṣṭha, declared it to be impossible, and that priest's hundred sons, on being applied to, refused to undertake what their father had declined. When the king told them that he would seek some other means of accomplishing his object, they condemnedhim to become a cāṇḍāla. In this condition he had resort to Viśvāmitra, and he, taking pity on him, raised him to heaven in his bodily form, notwithstanding the opposition of the sons of Vasiṣṭha. The *Harivaṁśa* version of this story is different. Triśaṅku, also called Satyavrata, had attempted the abduction of the young wife of a citizen. For this his father banished him, and condemned him to "the performance of a silent penance for twelve years". During his exile there was a famine, and Triśaṅku succoured and supported the wife and family of Viśvāmitra, who were reduced to the direst extemity in that sage's absence. Vasiṣṭha, the family priest, had done nothing to assuage the wrath of the aggrieved father, and this offended Triśaṅku. At the end of his penance, being in want of meat, he killed Vasiṣṭha's wonder-working cow and partook of her flesh; for this act Vasiṣṭha gave him the name of Triśaṅku, 'guilty of three sins'. Viśvāmitra was grateful for the assistance rendered by Triśaṅku and gave him the choice of a boon. He begged that he might ascend bodily to heaven. Viśvāmitra then installed Triśaṅku in his father's kingdom, "and in spite of the resistance of the gods and of Vasiṣṭha he exalted the king alive to heaven".

The *Mahābhārata* and the *Rāmāyaṇa* tell the story of Viśvāmitra's amour with Menakā. His austerities had so alarmed the gods that Indra sent this apsaras to seduce Viśvāmitra "by the display of her charms and the exercise of all her allurements". She succeded, and the result was the birth of Śakuntalā. Viśvāmitra at length became ashamed of his passion, and "dismissing the nymph with gentle accents, he retired to the northern mountains, where he practised severe austerities for a thousand years". He is said also to have had an amour with the nymph Rambhā.

The result of the struggle between Vasiṣṭha and Viśvāmitra is thus told in the *Rāmāyaṇa:* "Vasiṣṭha, being propitiated by the gods, became reconciled to Viśvāmitra, and recognised his claim to all the prerogatives of a brāhmaṇa *ṛṣi* ... Viśvāmitra, too, having attained the Brāhmaṇical rank, paid all honour to Vasiṣṭha."

The *Rāmāyaṇa* gives many particulars of Viśvāmitra's connection with Rāma. It was Viśvāmitra who prevailed upon King Daśaratha to send his son Rāma for the protection of the brāhmaṇas against the attacks of Rāvaṇa and his *rākṣasas*. He acted as his *guru*, and returned with Rāma to Ayodhyā, where the prince obtained the hand of Sītā.

In the *Mārkaṇḍeya* and other Purāṇas the story is told of Viśvāmitra's implacable presecution of King Hariścandra (*see* HARIŚCANDRA), one result of which was that Vasiṣṭha and Viśvāmitra cursed each other so that they were turned into birds, and fought together most furiously till Brahmā put an end to the conflict, restored them to their natural forms, and compelled them to be reconciled.

From Visvámitra are derived many of the sacerdotal families which bear the common name of Kauṣika, and to which many rishis, famous in tradition belong. As there were also kings in this family, we have here an example of the fact that one of the old vedic races became divided, and in later times belonged to both of the two higher castes. It appears impossible that any of the aboriginal tribes should have been among the descendants of Visvámitra's sons, as the legend represents; and the meaning of this account may therefore be that some of his sons and their descendants accepted the position of priests among these tribes, and are in consequence described as accursed."—*O.S.T., I*, 426.

VISVÁMITRAS—The Visvámitras are known as Kúṣikas or Kauṣikas; that is, they came from Kush, to this day the name of a river near the Asia Palus, where M. Ferrier found the ruins of a large place called Kussan. The Kushan, he tells us, were a famous Scythian race, who held Balkh in remote antiquity. Sir II. Rawlinson found their bricks, with cuneiform Scythic legends at Susa and in the Persian Gulf. Kush is largely used in a local nomenclature in Central Asia. The Caspian Sea, Cashgar, Kashmere, Khas-Saks, (Sacæ or Cossaks) Caucas-as (Khas-mountain) Coasæ or Cisü in Persia, the Bal-kash lake and the Kush, and these are but a mere sample, and it is supposed that the Scythians did not come to the Cushites, but that the Cushites colonized Mongolia as they colonized Arabia, Ethiopia and the N. coast of the Indian Ocean. Indra himself is called a son of Kuṣika. Fire and Indra-worship seem to have been introduced by the Visvámitras and to have supplanted a previous sun-worship of earlier immigrants.—*Calcutta Review.*

VISVARUPA—**(1)** A name of Vishṇu; who is both Bhúteṣa, 'lord of created tilings;' and Visvarúpa, 'universal substance;' he is therefore as one with sensible things subject to his own control; **(2)** A name of one of the Rudras.

VISVASAHA—**(1)** A king of Mithila, the son of Ilavila;

(2) Another king of Mithila, the son of Abhyutthitaṣwa, descendant of Ráma.

VISVASPHATIKA—A Rája of Magadha, who is said to have extirpated the Kshatryas and elevated fishermen, barbarians, Brahmáns, and other castes, to power. His name is sometimes made Viṣwasphurtti,

VISVAVASA—One of the sons of Purúravas.

VISVAVASU—**(1)** (Visvávasu), in Buddhist mythology the king of the Siddhas, and father of Malayavati, the heroine of the Nága-nanda, **(2)** One of the chief of the Gandharvas, or singers and musicians in the Court of Indra.

VISVAVASU—A chief of the *gandharvas* in Indra's heaven.

VISVESA—A daughter of Daksha married to Dharma.

VISVESVARA—'Lord of all.' A name of Śiva. The celebrated *liṅga* or emblem of Śiva at Benares, (*see* LIṄGA)

VITA—A character in the Hindu drama not very easily understood. It is necessary that he should be accomplished in the lighter arts, particularly poetry, music, and singing; and he appears indiscriminately as the companion of a man or woman, although in the latter case the female is the courtesan. He is generally represented on familiar and easy, and yet dependent, terms, with his associate, and evinces something of the Parasite of the Greek comedy, but that he is never rendered contemptible. In lexicons the person indicated by the Viṭa is a despicable being of whose character no vestiges occur in the theatrical picture.

VITAHAVYA—A king of the Haihayas. His sons attacked and slew all the family of Divodāsa, king of Kāśī. A son, named Pratardana (*q.v.*), was subsequently born to Divodāsa, and he attacked the Haihayas and compelled Vītahavya to fly to the sage Bhṛgu for protection. Pratardana pursued him, and demanded that he should be given up. Then "Vītahavya, by the mere word of Bhṛgu, became a brāhmaṇa *ṛṣi* and an utterer of the Veda" (*Mahābhārata*). His son, Gṛtsamada, was a highly honoured *ṛṣi*, and author of several hymns in the *Ṛgveda.* He was the founder of the tribe of Haihayas called Vītahavyas.

VITAHAVYA—A king of Mithila, the son of Sunaya.

VITALA—The second of the seven divisions of Pátáÿa; whose soil is black.

VITASTA—The classic Hydaspes, the Behat of later days, and the modern Jhelam.

VITATHA—Unprofitable; a name given to Rája Bharatwája, who was a sage as well as king.

VITHI—(Víthi), a play something similar to the Bhāṇa; it is in one act and may be performed by one actor, though the Daṣa Rúpaka admits of two. In either case it is a love-story, carried on in comic dialogue, consisting of equivoque, evasion, enigma, quibble, jest, repartee, wilful misconstruction and misapplication, ironical praise, extravagant endearment, and jocose abuse. It is not very different, perhaps, in character from the *Fabulæ Attellanæ* of the Tuscans.—WILSON.

VITHI—A division of the planetary sphere.

VITHOBA—A deified sage, very popular, and extensively worshipped in the Poona Deccan.

VITIHOTRA—**(1)** The ninth son of Priyavrata, according to the Bhágavata; he is called Putra in the other Puránas, and adopted a religious life; **(2)** The eldest son of Tálajangha, a Yádava chief.

VITIHOTRAS—A branch of the Haihaya tribe.

VITTORA—The name of Vishṇu in one of his minor Avatars, as related in some of the Puránas. He is represented as retaining on his breast an indelible mark of Bhrigu'a foot, with which the following legend is connected. In a divine assembly Bhrigu was asked who, of the gods, was the most mighty; he said he would proceed to inquire, and first went to Brahmá, in approaching whom it was usual to pay very respectful obeisance, which on this occasion, Bhrigu purposely omitted, and experienced in consequence severe reprehension, including copious abuse, (for the Hindu gods, like Homer's, are very abusive,) from Brahmá, who however became pacified by seasonable apologies. Bhrigu next proceeded to Śiva, and omitted, as before, the usual tokens of adoration on entering the divine presence; Śiva was still more enraged than Brahmá, but was in like manner pacified by Bhrigu's apologies. He then repaired to Vaikuntha, the celestial residence of Vishṇu, whom he found asleep, with Lakshmi shampooing his feet. Bhrigu knew that the mere omission of respect would not be sufficient to move the gentle god to auger, and to make a trial of his temper he boldly gave the recumbent deity a severe kick on his breast. Vishṇu awoke, and seeing Bhrigu arose, and in place of anger, expressed apprehensions that he must have hurt his foot by striking it against his (Vishṇu's) breast, and proceeded to lament it and to rub and chafe Bhrigu's foot to remove any consequent pain. 'This, said Bhrigu, is the mightiest god; he overpowers by the most potent of all arms, affability and generosity ?' See Moor's *Hindu Pantheon*, p. 418.—This is a favourite story amongst the Brahmáns of the south.

VITUNDA—A demon, the son of Tuṇḍa; the Pádma Purána contains an account of its destruction by Bhágavati.

VIVADA-BHANGARNAVA—A code of Hindu law according to the Bengal school, composed by Jagannātha Tarkālaṅkāra at the end of last century. It has been translated by Colebrooke, and is commonly known as Colebrooke's *Digest*.

VIVADA-CANDRA—A law-book of the Benares school by Lakhimā Devī, a learned lady.

VIVADA-CINTAMANI—A law-book of the Mithilā school by Vācaspati Miśra. The text has been printed.

VIVADA-RATNAKARA A law-book of the Benares school by Chandeśvara who iived about AD 1314.

VIVADA-TANDAVA—A law-book of the Benares school by Ratnākara.

VIVASWAT—**(1)** A Prajápati; **(2)** One of the twelve Ádityas; **(3)** 'The bright one.'The Sun, and father of Vaivaswata Manu. (*see* SŪRYA) Used sometimes perhaps for the firmament.

VIVINDHAYA—A *dānva* killed in battle by Cārudeṣṇa, son of Kṛṣṇa. (*see* Mahābhārata)

VIVINSATI—A prince of the solar dynasty, the son of Vinsa.

VLTAYANAGARA—The capital of the last great Hindu dynasty of the south. It was originally called Vidyānagara, 'city of learning', after the great scholar and minister Mādhavācārya, entitled Vidyāraṇya, 'forest of learning'. But in the days of its glory the Vidyā was altered to Vijaya, 'victory'.

VOPA-DEVA—A grammarian of great repute, who lived about the thirteenth century AD at Devagiri, and wrote the *Mugdhabodha*.

VRAJA—One of the sons of Havirdhána and uncle of the Prachetasas.

VRATA—An occasional self-imposed observance or ceremony.

VRATYA—"Persons whom the twice-bom beget on women of their own classes, butwho omit the prescribed rites andhave abandoned the Gāyatrī, are to be designated as Vrātyas."

VṚDDHA—'Old.' An epithet frequently found prefixed to the books of ancient writers, and evidently implying that there are one or more versions or recensions—as Vṛddha Manu, Vṛddha Hārīta. (*see* DHARMA-ŚĀSTRA)

VRHAN NARADIYA PURANA—An Upapurāṇa. (*see* Purāṇa).

VRHAT-KATHA—'Great story.' A large collection of tales from which the *Kathā-sarit-sāgara* was drawn. There is a critical examination of this work by Dr. Bühler in the *Indian Antiquary*, vol. I.

VRHAT-SAMHITA—The astronomical work of Varāhamihira.

VRIHADASWA—A Rája of Bhárata, the father of the celebrated Kuvalayaswa, *q.v.*, a sage who related to king Yudhishthira the story of Nala. This was done for the purpose of consoling the Páṇḍava princes in exile, after Yudhishthira had lost all his possessions in a game of hazard.

VRIHADBALA—A prince of the solar race, the son of Visrutavat; he was slain in the great war by Abhimanyu, the son of Arjuna.

VRIHADBHANU—A Rája of Bhárata, the son of Vrihatkarman.

VRIHADISHA—**(1)** A king of Hastinápura, the son of Ajamídha; **(2)** One of the five sons of Haryyaṣwa, termed the Panchálas.

VRIHADRATHA—**(1)** A Rája of Bhárata, the son of Bhadraratba; **(2)** A son of Uparichara the Vasu; **(3)** A son of Tigma of the race of Puru; **(4)** The last of the ten Mauryan kings of Magadha, the son of Sasadharman.

VRIHANNARADIYA PURÁNA—A modern compilation, erroneously termed a Purána, containing paneygrical prayers addressed to Vishṇu, and injunctions to observe various rites and keep holy certain seasons in honour of him.

VRIHASPATI—**(1)** A sage, the son of Angiras, the priest and preceptor of the Devatas; a teacher of the science of government. He had a handsome wife named Tárá, who was carried off by Soma (the moon), which led to a fierce contest termed the Táraká war. The Daityas, Danavas, and other foes of the gods took part with Soma; whilst Indra and all the gods were the allies of Vrihaspati. Peace was not restored till Brahmá interposed and compelled Soma to restore Tárá ta her husband. Vrihaspati was Vyása of the fourth Manwantara. **(2)** The planet Jupiter; described in the *V.P.* as having a golden car drawn by eight pale-coloured horses.

VRIHATKARMAN—**(1)** A prince, the son of the Rája of Bhárata, Bhadraratha; **(2)** A king of Hastinápur, son of Vrihadvasu; **(3)** A king of Magadha, son of Sukshatra.

VRIHATKSHATRA—A prince of Bhárata, the son of Bhavanmanya.

VRIHAT-SAMA—A portion of the Sáma Veda, created from the southern mouth of Brahmá.

VRIHATSHANA—A Rája of the solar race after the great war. His father Vribadhala, was killed by Abhimanyu.

VRIJINIVAT—A Yádava prince, the son of Kroshtri.

VRIKA—**(1)** One of the sons of Prithu, according to the Bhágavata; **(2)** The son of Rája Ruruka; **(3)** A son of Krishṇa.

VRIKADEVA—One of the daughters of Devaka, who was married to Vasudeva.

VRIKALA, VRIKATEJAS—Two sons of Slishtí, and grandsons of Dhruva.

VRIKODARA—(Vṛikodara), 'wolf-stomached;' a name of Bhíma, the second of the Páṇḍavas; in allusion to his voracious appetite; from *vrika*, (a wolf,) and *udara*, (belly.) In the Mahábhárata we read, that at the daily meals of the five brothers half of the whole food provided had to be given to Bhíma.—(*Ádi-Parva*, 7161.)*
(*Cover. *Folk Songs of Southern India*.)

VRISHA—**(1)** The Indra of the eleventh Manwantara; **(2)** A Yádava chief, the son of Vítihotra.

VRISHADARBHA—A Rája of the solar race, the son of Sivi.

VRISHAKAPI—An appellation of one of the eleven Rudras.

VRISHANA—One of the hundred sons of the Mahárája Karttavirya.

VRISHAPARVAN—A powerful Dánava chief, the son of Kaṣyapa and Danu.

VRISHASENA—One of the Anga kings, the son of Karṇa.

VRISHNI—**(1)** A Yádava chief, the eldest son of Madhu; **(2)** Another Yádava chief, the son of Kunti or Kumbhi; **(3)** A son of Satwata, a Rája of Mrittikavatí; **(4)** A cousin of the above, the son of Bhajamána.

VRISHNIMAT—A Rája of the solar race, the son of Chitraratha.

VRISHOTSARGA—(*Vrisha*, a bull, and *utsarga* forsaking, or offering). The Hindus are accustomed at marriages and other ceremonials to let loose a bull, who thenceforward rambies about at will without an owner. No person would presume to appropriate a stray animal of this kind, and many think it a merit to feed him. In large towns, where these bulls are most abundant, they are generally in good case, and numerous enough to be very much in the way, although they are rarely mischievous. They seem to know their privileged character, and haunt the market places and shops with an air of independence. At Benares they are prover-bially abundant, and that city is famed for its *ránrh*, *sanrh*, and *sirhi*, or widows, bulls, and landing places.—Wilson, *Works*, XI, 20.

VRITRA—The demon who personifies drought; the cloud enemy of Indra, who imprisons the rain in the storm-clord. He is represented as false and treacherous as he is malignant. He is termed the thief who hides away the rain-clouds. He constantly appears as the enemy of Indra, who is called Vritrahan; the Vritra-slayer, Vritra became a name applied to any enemy. "The Vrittra of the Vrittras denoted the most malignant of adversaries. So again Vrittra the thief is also called Ahi, the throttling snake, or dragon with three heads."*

"Who is that, without alarm,
Defies the might of Indra's arm;
That stands and sees without dismay
The approachmg Maruts' dread array;
That does not shun in wild affright,
The terrors of the deadly fight ?
'Tis Vrittra, he whose magic powers
From earth withhold the genial showers,
Of mortal men the foe malign,
And rival of the race divine
Whose demon hosts from age to age,
With Indra war unceasing wage,
Who, times unnumbered, crushed and slain,
Is ever newly born again,
And evermore renew the strife
In which again he forfeits life.
Perched on a steep aerial height,
Shone Vṛittra's stately fortress bright.
Upon the wall, in martial mood,
The bold gigantic demon stood,
Confiding in his magic arts,
And armed with store of fiery darts.
And then was seen a dreadful sight,
When god and demon met in fight.
His sharpest missiles Vṛittra shot,
His thunderbolts and lightnings hot
He hurled as thick as rain.

* * * * * *

And soon the knell of Vṛittra's doom
Was sounded by the clang and boom
Of Indra's iron shower;
Pierced, cloven, crushed, with horrid yell,
The dying demon headlong fell
Down from his cloud-built tower."**

(* Cox, *Mythölogy of the Aryan Nations*; ** Muir, *O.S.T.*, V, 133-5.)

VṚKODARA—'Wolf belly.' An epithet of Bhīma.

VṚNDAVANA—A wood in the district of Mathurā where Kṛṣṇa passed his youth, under the name of Gopāla, amongthe cowherds.

VṚSNI—A descendant of Yadu, and the ancestor from whom Kṛṣṇa got the name Vārṣṇeya.

VṚSNIS, VṚṢṆAYAS—The descendants of Vṛṣṇi, son of Madhu, whose ancestor was the eldest son of Yadu. Kṛṣṇa belonged to this branch of the Lunar race.

VṚTRA—In the Vedas he is the demon of drought and ungenial weather, with whom Indra, the god of the firmament, is constantly at war, and whom he is constantly overpowering and releasing the rain. Sometimes called Vṛtrāsura.

VṚTRA-HAN—The slayer of Vṛtra. A title of Indra.

VYADHI—An old grammarian and lexicographer, somewhat latter in time than Pāṇini. A story in the *Vṛhatkathā* represents him as contemporary with Vararuci.

VYADHI—Disease; Represented as the son of Mritya, (Death.)

VYADI—A brahman who stopped at the dwelling of Vararuchi on one occasion and solicited hospitality, as a stranger weary with long travel. He then became acquainted with Vararuchi's wonderful powers of memory—was instructed by him, and became a writer of note on philological topics.—*Wilson*, III, 165.

VYAHRITIS—The three mystical words, Bhúh, Bhuvar, Swar; which, with the monosyllable Om, and the Vedas, are considered as forms of Vásudeva (Brahmá,) diversified as to their typical character, but essentially one and the same. The daily prayers of the Brahmán commence with the formula, Om bhúh, bhuvar, swar; Om earth, sky, heaven; these three mystical terms called Vyáhritis, are scarcely of less sanctity than the Praṇava itself. Their efficacy, and the order of their repetition preceding the Gáyatri, are fully detailed in Manu, II, 76-81. In the Mitákshara they are directed to be twice repeated mentally, with Om prefixed to each; Om bhúh, Om bhuvah, Om swar; the breath being suppressed by closing the lips and nostrils.—Wilson's *Notes to Vishṇu Purána*.

VYAHRTIS—Three mystical words said by Manu to have been milked from the Vedas by Prajāpati—the word *bhūr*, from the *Ṛgveda*; the word *bhuvaḥ*, from the *Yajurveda*; and the word *svar*, from the *Sāmaveda* (*Manu*, 11.76). The *Śatapata Brāhmaṇa* defines them as "three luminous essences" which Prajāpati produced from the Vedas by heating them. "He uttered the word *bhūr*, which became this earth; *bhuvaḥ*, which became this firmament; and the *svar*, which became that sky." A fourth word, *mahar*, *is* sometimes added, and is probably intended to represent the *Atharvaveda*. (*see* Loka)

VYAKARANA—Grammar; an Anga of the Vedas. That a scientific study of Grammar was cultivated at a very early period of Hindu literature is borne out by the testimony of the oldest glossator on the Vedas, Yaska (*q.v.*) The oldest extant work, however, on Sanskrit Grammar is posterior to the work of Yaska; it is the Grammar of Pánini (*q.v.*) which was criticised by Kátgáya, in the Várṭṭikas, these again being commented on the criticised by Patanjali in the *Mahábhásya*. (See PÁNINI, WHERE some of the principal later works connected with his system are mentioned.)—Goldstucker.

VYAKTA—Visible substance; a form of Vishṇu.

VYANSA—A powerful Dáuava, the eldest son of Viprachitti.

VYAPTI—Universal; the inherent and essential presence of any one thing or property in another, as the deity in the universe, &c. In the Nyáya system of Gautama a Vyápti means a pervading rule. It is thus explained by Professor Max Müller: knowledge is a quality of the Self, in the same manner as colour is of light. It is inseparably connected with it, and is explained as the cause of every conception that is expressed in language. Knowledge is either remembrance or perception. Perception is two-fold, right or wrong. Right perception represents the thing such as it is, silver as silver. Wrong perception represents the thing as the thing is not, mother o'pearl as silver. Right perception is four-fold, sensuous, conclusive, comparative, and authoritative. It is produced by the senses, by inferring, by comparing, and by revealed authority.

The different kinds of sensuous perception arise from the different ways in which the organs of sense are brought into contact with their objects, which objects may be either substantial matter, or qualities and actions, as inherent in substance, or the Genus as inherent in substances, qualities and actions.

After sensuous knowledge comes conclusive knowledge, which is gained by means of inferring. Conclusive knowledge is for instance. "This mountain is a volcano," whereas our sensuous perception is only that the mountain smokes. In order to arrive from this at the conclusion that it, is a volcano, we must be in possession of what is called a pervading rule or a Vyápti. This smoke is inseparably connected with fire, or as the Hindu calls it, that smokiuess is pervaded by fieriness, that wherever there is smoke there is fire. If we possess this Vyápti, which we may remember by such instances as a culinary hearth, &c., then in order to arrive at conclusive knowledge we only require consideration, (parámarsa) in order to find out in any sensuous impressiop something which can be pervaded, something which can make the mountain the member of a Vyápti this something being in our case the smoke. If we know that the smoke which we perceive is qualified to become part of a Vyápti (this Vyápti being 'wherever there is smoke there is fire'), then we know conclusively that this mountain is fiery because it smokes.

The conditions under which it is allowed to form a Vyápti, that is to say to form Universals, have occupied the attention or Hindu philosophers more than any other point in Logic. They distinctly exclude the mere accumulation of observations. For things they say may be together a hundred times and may still not be mutually inherent. They make exceptions for practical purposes. Their repeated observations may be turned into a general rule, but not in philosophical discussions. Volumes after volumes have been written on this subject, and though I do not believe they will throw new light on the question of the origin of Universals, yet they would furnish a curious parallel to the history of the European intellect. (*Indian Logic. Outline of the necessary Laws of Thought*, by Archbishop of York, 286-90.)

VYÁSA—A great brahman sage who lived in the forest, and by a long course of religious penances had become emaciated and hideous in appearance. He is described as the son of Paráṣara and a fish girl named Matsya, who was employed as a furry woman in one of the many small rivers which intersect eastern Bengal, and flow into the Brahmáputra. His original name was Krishṇa Dwaipáyana, but having become famous as the compiler of the Mahábhárata, and the Vedas, he is generally known by the name of Vyása, or "the arranger." Among all the Brahmán sages of antiquity famous for their learning, their austerities, and their miracles few can be compared with the Rishi Vyása. The following legend is related to show that he was the direct aucestor of the Kauravas and Páṇḍavas who fought in the great war; but is considered by Mr. Wheeler to be open to the gravest suspicion. After the death of Rája Vichítravírya (*q.v.*) his widows were filled with sorrow, because they had no son to perpetuate the race of Bharata. The custom was that when a man died without issue, his brother or near kinsman should marry his widows. The Ráni Satyavati therefore applied to Bhíshma, who refused on account of his vow. Slie then requested the sage Vyása to take his place. He proceeded to the palace of Hastinápur and fulfilled the wishes of the Ráni; but his presence filled the widows with terror. The first shut her eyes when she beheld him, and she gave birth to a son who was blind, and who was named Dhritaráshtra; and the second widow was so white with fear that she gave birth to a son who was pale, and who was named Páṇḍu. Then Satyavati requested Vyása to become the father of a third son who should be without blemish; and the first widow would not go to him, but arrayed her maid servant in garments of her own, and sent her to the sage in her stead; and the servant gave birth to a third son who was named Vidura. Thus were born three sons to the royal house at Hastinápur; viz: Dhritaráshtra the blind; Páṇḍu, the pale; and Vidura, the slave-born.

VYÁSAS—Arrangers of the Vedas in every Dwapara age: twenty-eight, are enumerated: The following is the list contained in Vishṇu Purána:—

"Twenty-eight times have the Vedas been arranged by the great Rishis in the Vaivaswata Manwantara in the Dwápara age; and, consequently, eight and twenty Vyásas have passed away; by whom, in their respective periods, the Veda has been divided into four. In the first Dwápara age, the distribution was made by Swayambhú (Brahmá) himself; in the second, the arranger of the Veda (Vedavyása) wis Prajápati (or Manu); in the third, Uṣanas; in the fourth, Brihaspati; in the fifth, Savitṛi in the sixth, Mrityu (Death, or Yama); in the seventh, Indra; in the eighth, Vasishṭha; in the ninth, Saraswara in the tenth, Tridháman; in the eleventh, Trivrishan in the twelfth Bharadwája; in the thirteenth, Antariksha; in the fourteenth Vaprívan; in the fifteenth, Trayyáruna; in the sixteenth, Dhananjaya; in the seventeenth, Kritanjaya; in the eighteenth Riṇajaya, in the nineteenth, Bharadwája; in the twenteeth, Gautama; in the twenty-first, Uttama, also called Harvatman; in the twenty-second, Veṇa, who is name Rájasravas; in the twenty-third, Saumaṣushmáyana, also the twenty-fourth, Riksha, the descendant of Bhrigu who is known also by the name Válmiki; in the twenty-fifth, my father, Sakti, was the Vyása; I was the Vyása of the twenty-sixth Dwápara, and was succeeded by Játúkarna; the Vyása of the twenty-eighth, who followed him, was Krishṇa Dwaipayana. These are the twenty-eight elder Vyásas, by whom, in the preceding Dwápara ages, the Veda has been divided into four. In the next Dwápara, Drauṇi (the son of Droṇa) will be the Vyása, when my son, the Muni Krishṇa Dwaipáyana, who is the actual Vyása, shall cease to be (in that character)."

"A similar list is given in the Kúrma and Váyu Puránas. Many of the individuals appear as authors of different hymns and prayers in the Vedas; and it is very possible that the greater portion, if not all of them, had a real existence, being the framers or teachers of the religion of the Hindus before a complete ritual was compiled."—*Wilson's Notes to V.P.*

VYAVAHARA-CINTĀMAṆI—A law-book of the Benares school by Vācaspati Miśra.

VYAVAHARA-MAYŪKHA—A law-book of the Mahratta school by Nīlakaṇṭha Bhaṭṭa. Translated by Borrodaile.

VYAVAHARA-TATVA—A modem work on law accrording to the Bengal school by Raghunandana, who is also called Smārta-Bhaṭṭācārya.

VYAVASAYA—Perseverance. One of the allegorical sons of Dharma.

VYAYA—A name of Pradhána—meaning "that which may be expended."

VYOMAN—A Rája of the solar race, the son of Dasárha.

VYUSHTA—A name of Day: night is called Usha, and the interval between them, Sandhya.

Y

YADAVAS—The descendants of Yadu, the eldest son of Yayáti and Devayáni. A nomad race that grazed cattle and made butter, and occasionally migrated to different places accompanied by their cows and waggons. The time and circumstances under which they first entered Hindustan are alike unknown. At the birth of Krishṇa they appear to have settled in the neighborhood of the city of Mathurá, the modern Muttra, on the banks of the river Jumna, and about a hundred and twenty miles to the south of the site of the ancient city of Hastinápur. They dwelt on both sides of the river, in the village of Vrindávana on the western bank, and in the country of Gokul on the opposite shore. They afterwards migrated to Dwáraka, on the western coast of the peninsula of Guzerat, above seven hundred miles from Hastinápur.

Krishṇa belonged to this tribe; and many mythical details seem to have been connected with its history for the purpose of exalting the tribe from which the favourite deity sprung. It is plain that great violence and disorder prevailed wherever the Yádavas settled. They were induced by Krishṇa to renounce the worship of Indra and substitute the mountain Govarddhana in his place; an incident which Mr. Wheeler thinks seems to imply a conflict between a low Fetische worship, and the worship of the Vedic deities.

The Puránas describe the destruction of the whole tribe in a drunken affray at Prabhása. The Mahábhárata says that all the Yádavas were slaughtered by the curse of the three Rishis, and all the sons and grandsons of Krishṇa were among the slain.

"The Rájas of Vijayanagar, who in the 15th century of the Christian era maintained a supremacy over the whole of the country south of the Krishṇa river, and thus possessed the last great Hindu empire which was established in India, claimed to be descendants of the Yádava tribe; and it is a curious fact that it was from one of the decayed chieftains of this fallen dynasty that the East India Company obtained, in the first half of the 17th century, the grant of land on the coast of Coromandel on which stands the modern city of Madras. The original grant on a gold plate appears to have been preserved for more than a century; but was finally lost in 1746 when Madras was captured by the French under Labourdonnais."—*Wheeler.*

YADU—Son of King Yayāti of the Lunar race, and founder of the line of the Yādavas in which Kṛṣṇa was born. He refused to bear the curse of decrepitude passed upon his father by the sage Śukra, and in consequence he incurred the paternal curse, "Your posterity shall not possess dominion." Still he received from his father the southern districts of his kingdom, and his posterity prospered.

YADUGIRI—A celebrated place of pilgrimage in Mysore, now called Mélkóté. Vaishṇava brahmans still congregate there in numbers. The Puráṇas assign a great antiquity to the locality and connect many legends with it.

YAJA—A brahman of distinguished attainments to whom king Drupada was referred when he was seeking to obtain a son. The king promised Yája ten million of kine; and with much reluctance Yája undertook to direct a sacrificial ceremony by which the king should obtain offspring and called his younger brother to his assistance. When the rite had reached the proper period, the queen was invited to partake of it, but she had not completed her toilet and begged the brahmans to delay the ceremony. It was too late, and the sacrifice proceeding without her, the children were born independent of her participation. His "altar-born" children, Dhṛṣtadyumna and Draupadī, came forth from the sacrificial fire.—*Wilson*, III. 326.

YAJÑA, Sacrifice personified in the Purāṇas as son of Ruci and husband of Dakṣiṇā. He had the head of a deer, and was killed by Vīrabhadra at Dakṣa's sacrifice. According to the *Harivaṁśa* he was raised to the planetary sphere by Brahmā, and made into the constellation Mṛgaśiras (deer-head).

YAJÑABAHU—The name of one of the sons of Priyavrata, as given in the Bhágavata. See AGNIBÁHU.

YAJÑADATTA-VADHA—'The death of Yajñadatta.' An episode of the *Rāmāyaṇa.* It has been translated into French by Chézy.

YAJNAHA—(Yajnahá), a name of Śiva; from his having disturbed the sacrifice of Daksha, his father-in-law, who had omitted to invite him to the ceremony. Śiva sent Vírabhadra and a host of attendants to Daksha's sacrifice, where they overturned and defiled the altars, and beat and mutilated the sages and gods who had been invited. The occurrence is a favourite subject of sculpture in the cave temples of the South of India.—*F. Johnson*.

YAJÑA-PARIBHASA—A *sūtra* work by Āpastambha.

YAJÑA—Sacrifice; the character of Brahmánical sacrifice is thus expressed by Dr. Haug, in the Introduction to the *Aitareya Brahmána*.* "The sacrifice is regarded as the means for obtaining power over this and the other world, over visible as well as invisible beings, animate as well as inanimate creatures. Who knows its proper application, and has it duly performed, is in fact looked upon as the real master of the world: for any desire he may entertain, even if it be the most ambitious, can be gratified; any object he has in view can be obtained by means of it. The *Yajña* taken as a whole is conceived to be a kind of machinery, in which every piece must tally with the other; or a sort of large chain in which no link is allowed to be wanting; or a staircase by which one may ascend to heaven; or as a personage, endowed with all the characteristics of the human body. It exists from eternity and proceeded from the Supreme Being, (Prajápati or Brahmá *neuter*) along with the *Traividya*, *i.e.*, the three-fold science. The creation of the world was even regarded as the fruit of a sacrifice performed by the Supreme Being. The Yajña exists as an invisible thing at all times. It is like the latent power of electricity in an electrifying machine, requiring only the operation of a suitable apparatus in order to be elicited. It is supposed to extend, when unrolled from the Áhavaníya or sacrificial fire, (into which all oblations are thrown,) to heaven, forming thus a bridge or ladder, by means of which the sacrifice can communicate with the world of gods and spirits, and even ascend when alone to their abodes."—* *Wilson*, Vol. I, p. 73.

YAJÑASENA—A name of Drupada.

YAJÑÁS—Five are enumerated, which are translated great sacrifices, or great obligations: Brahmáyajna, sacred study; Pitriyajna, libations to the manes; Devayajna, burnt offerings to the gods; Baliyajna, offerings to all creatures; Nriyajna, hospitality.

The Prajápatiyajna, propagation of offspring, and Satyayajna, observance of truth, are apparently later additions.—*Wilson's Notes to V.P.*

YAJÑASRI—One of the Andhrabhritya rájas: the son of Swaskandha.

YĀJÑAVALKYA—A celebrated sage, to whom is attributed the White *Yajurveda*, the Śatapatha Brāhmaṇa, the *Bṛhadāraṇyaka*, and the code of law called *Yājñavalkya-smṛti*. He lived before the grammarian Kātyāyana, and was probably later than Manu; at any rate, the code bearing his name is posterior to that of Manu. He was a disciple of Bāṣkali, and more particularly of Vaiśampāyana. The *Mahābhārata* makes him present at the *rājasūya* sacrifice performed by Yushiṣṭhira; and according to the *Śatapatha Brāhmaṇa* he flourished at the court of Janaka, king of Videha and father of Sītā. Janaka had long contentions with the brāhmaṇas, in which he was supported, and probably prompted, by Yājñavalkya. This sage was a dissenter from the religious teaching and practices of his time, and is represented as contending with the silencing brāhmaṇas at the court of his patron. A brāhmaṇa named Vidagdha Śākalya was his especial adversary, but he vanquished him and cursed him, so that "his head dropped off, and his bones were stolen by robbers". Yājñavalkya also is represented as inculcating the duty and necessity of religious retirement and meditation, so he is considered as having been the originator of the Yoga doctrine, and to have helped in preparing the world for the preaching of Buddha. He had two wives, Maitreyī and Kātyāyanī, and he instructed the former in his philosophical doctrine. Max Müller quotes a dialogue between them from the *Śatapatha Brāhmaṇa* (*Ancient Sanskrit Literature*, p. 22), in which the sage sets forth his views. Professor Max Müller observes "that it would be a mistake to call Yajnawalkya the author, in our sense of the word of the Vájasaneya Sanhita and the Satapatha Brahmána. But we have no reason to doubt that it was Yájnawalkya who brought the ancient Mantras and Brahmánas into their present form." *A.S.L.*

The White *Yajurveda* originated in a schism, of which Yājñavalkya was a leader, if not the author. He was the originator and compiler of this Veda, and according to some it was called *Vājasaneya Saṁhitā*, from his surname Vājasaneya. (*see* VEDA)

What share Yājñavalkya had in the production of the *Śatapatha Brāhmaṇa* and *Bṛhadāraṇyaka* is very doubtful. Some part of them may, perhaps, have sprung directly from him, and they were probably compiled under his superintendence; but it may be, as some think, that they are so-called because they treat of him and embody his teaching. One portion of the *Bṛhadāraṇyaka*, called the *Yājñavalkīya Kāṇḍa*, cannot have been his composition, for it is devoted to his glorification and honour, and was probably written after his death.

The Smṛti, or code of law that bears the name of Yājñavalkya, is posterior to that of Manu, and is more precise and stringent in its provisions. Its authority is inferior only to that of Manu, and as explained and developed by the celebrated commentary *Mitākṣarā*, it is in force all over India except in Bengal proper, but even there the original textbook is received. The second century AD has been named as the earliest date of this work. Like Manu, it has two recensions, the Bṛhad and Vṛddha, perhaps more. The text has been printed in Calcutta, and has been translated into German by Stenzler and into English by Roer and Montriou. .

"Yajñavalkya Vajasaneya was evidently a man of great influence, a leader of public opinion in his day; and one longs to know when he lived. But this is a subject still requiring much elucidation, as may be seen in the Introduction to Professor Goldstücker's Pánini."—Mrs. Manning, *A. & M. I.*

YAJUR OR YAJUṢ—The second Veda. (*see* VEDA)

YAJUR VEDA—"The history of the Yajur Veda differs in so far from that of the other Vedas, as it is marked by a dissension between its own schools, far more important than the differences which separated the schools of each other Veda. It is known by the distinction between a Yajur Veda, called the *Black-*, and another, called the *White-Yajur Veda.* Tradition, especially that of the Puránas, records a legend to account for it. Vaisampáyana, it says, the disciple of Vyása, who had received from him the Yajur Veda, once having committed an offence, desired his disciples to assist him in the performing of some expiatory act. One of these, however, *Yájnavalkya*, proposed that he should alone perform the whole rite; upon which, Vaiṣampáyana, enraged at what he considered to be the arrogance of Yájnavalkya, uttered a curse on him, the effect of which was, that Yájnavalkya disgorged all the Yajus texts he had learned from Vaiṣampáyana. The other disciples, having meanwhile been transformed into partridges (*tittiri*), picked up these tainted texts, and retained them. Hence these texts are called *Taittiríyas.* But Yájñavalkya, desirous of obtaining other Yajus texts, devoutly prayed to the Sun, and had granted to him his wish—'to possess such texts as were not known to his teacher.' And because the Sun on that occasion appeared to Yájnavalkya in the shape of a horse (*vája*), those who studied these texts were called. *Vájins.* That part of this legend was invented merely to account for the name of the *Taittiríyas*, after whom a Sanhitá and Bráhmana of the Black Yajur Veda, and for that of the *Vájasaneyins*, after whom the Sanhitá of the White Yajur Veda is named is clear enough. Nor is greater faith to be placed on it when it implies that the origin of this dissension ascended to the very oldest period of the Yajur Veda; for there is strong reason to assume that the division took place even after the time of the grammarian Páṇiní, (*q.v.*). But so much in it is consistent with truth—that the Black Yajur Veda is the older of the two; that the White Yajur Veda contains texts which are not in the Black; and that, compared to the motley character of the former, it looks 'white,' or orderly. This motley character of the Black Yajur Veda, however, arises from the circumstance, that the distinction between a Mantra and Bráhmaṇa portion, is not so clearly established in it as the other Vedas; hymns and matter properly belonging to the Bráhmaṇas there being intermixed. This defect is remedied in the White Yajur Veda; and it points, therefore, to a period when the material of the old Yajus was brought into a system consonant with prevalent theories, literary and ritual.

The contents of both divisions of the Yajur Veda are similar in many respects. Two of the principal sacrifices of which they treat are the Darṣapúrṇamása, or the sacrifice to be performed at new and full moon, and the Aṣwamedha, or the horse-sacrifice, at the performance of which 609 animals of various descriptions, domestic and wild, were tied to 21 sacrificial posts. A *Purushamedha*, or man-sacrifice, unknown to the other Vedas, is also mentioned in it; its character, however, is symbolical.

The text of the Black Yajur Veda is extant in the recension of two schools—that of *Apastamba*, to which the *Taittiríya Sanhitá* belongs, and that of *Charaka.* The former, which is in course of publication—the first volume and part of the second having been already published, with the commentary of Mádhavácharya (Sáyaṇa), by Dr. E. Roer and E. B. Cowell in the *Bibliotheca Indica* (Calcutta, 1860-1864)—consists of seven Káṇḍa, or books, which comprise 44 Prapáṭhaka, or chapters sub-divided into 651 Anuváka, or sections, and containing 2,198 Káṇḍikás, or portions.

The *Vájasaneyi-Sanhitá*, or the Sanhitá of the White Yajur Veda, exists in the recension of the *Mádhyandina* and Káṇva School. In the former—the text of which, apparently also with the commentary of *Mahidkara*, has been edited by Professor A. Weber (Berlin, 1852)—this Sanhitá has 40 *Adhyáyas*, or books, sub-divided into 303 *Anuvákas*, with 1,975 Káṇḍikás.

The principal Bráhmaṇa of the Black Yajur Veda is the *Taittiríya*-Bráhmaṇa, which, with the commentary of (Mádhava) Sáyaṇa, is in the course of publication by Rajendralála Mitra—the first volume and part of the second having already appeared in print (Calcutta, 1860-1865) in the *Bibliotheca Indica.* That of the White Yajur Veda is the Śatapatha-Brahmána, the most complete and systematic of all Bráhmaṇas. Its text, with a semblance of the commentary of Sáyaṇa, has been edited by Professor A. Weber (Berlin, 1855).—Chambers' *Encyclopœdia*, Vol. IX, p. 727.

YAJUSH—The Yajur Veda.

YAKSAS—A class of supernatural beings attendant on Kubera, the god of wealth. Authorities differ as to their origin. They have no very special attributes, but they are generally considered as inoffensive, and so are called Puṇyajanas, 'good people', but they occasionally appear as imps of evil. It is a *yakṣa* in whose mouth Kālidāsa placed his poem *Meghadūta* (cloud messenger).

YAKSA-LOKA—(*see* LOKA)

YAKSHA—The son of Khasá and parent of the Yakshas, as his brother Rákshas was of the Rákshasas.

YAKSHINIS—Female Yakshas; Kálidása, in the Megha Dúta, describes the toilet of the Yakshiṇis through the six seasons of the year by mentioning as the selected flowers those peculiar to each period. Thus the Lotus blooms in Surat, or the sultry season, two months of our autumn; the Kunda (jasmine) in Śiṣira or the Dewy season; the Lodh (Symplocos racemosa) is in blossom in Hemanta or winter; the Kuruvaka (crimson amaranth) in Vasanta, or spring; the Śirísha (Mimosa) in the hot months, or Gríshma; and the Nípa or Kadamba, at the setting in of the rains. While the sole occupation of the goddesses is said to be pleasure and dress, we cannot help being pleased with the simplicity and propriety of taste which gives to the graceful ornaments of nature so prominent a part in the decoration of feminine beauty.—*Wilson*.

YAMA—**(1)** One of the minor Dwípas; **(2)** A watch of the day or night.

YAMA-GITA—The song of Yama; a name given to the seventh chapter of the third book of the Vishṇu Purána.

YAMAS—Moral duties; five acts of restraint: absence of cruelty or violence, (Ahinsa), honesty (Asteya), truth (Satya), chastity (Bramácháryya), disinterestedness (Aparigraha).

YAMAS—Twelve deities, sons of Yajna and Dakshiṇa.

YAMA—The first of the eight stages of Yoga, being self-government, of which five kinds are specified:—1. Freedom from any wish to injure others. 2. Truth in reference to words and thoughts. 3. Freedom from appropriation of others' property in thought, word or deed. 4. The subjection of one's members in order to overcome desire. 5. Renunciation of all indulgence of pleasure.

Yama is also one of the Lokapalas, or guardians of the world; his district is the South.

YAMA—The monarch of the Pitris and judge of the dead—the Pluto of Hindu mythology. Indeed he combines the offices of Pluto and Rhadamanthus. He is represented to be the son of the Sun.

"Yama is the son of Vivasvat (the sun), and of Saraṇyú, the, immortal daughter of Tvashtri, (the Sun), and had a twin-sister named Yamī or Yamunā. He is elsewhere said to have been one of the original pair of human beings, and to have sprung from the Gandharva, a deity of the atmosphere, and his wife. In the same hymn he is said to have resisted the solicitations of his twin sister Yamí to form a sexual union with her for the continuation of the species. He was the first of mortals who died, and discovered the way to the other world; he guides other men thither, and assembles them in a home that is secured to them forever. In one place he is represented as carousing with the gods under a leafy tree. He is a king and dwells in celestial light, in the innermost sanctuary of heaven, where the departed behold him associated in blessedness with Varuṇa. He grants luminous abodes in heaven to the pious, which dwell with him in festive enjoyment.

"In the Rig Veda Yama is nowhere represented (as he is in the later Indian Mythology,) as having anything to do with the punishment of the wicked. Nevertheless, Yama is still, to some extent, an object of terror. He is represented as having two insatiable dogs, with four eyes and wide nostrils, which guard the road to his abode, and which the departed are advised to hurry past with all possible speed. These dogs are said to wander about among men as his messengers, for the purpose of summoning men to the presence of their master, who is in another place identified with death, and is described as sending a bird as the herald of doom. Again, death is said to be the messenger of Yama, who conveys the spirits of men to the abode of their forefathers.

"To great king Yama homage pay,
Who was the first of men that died,
That crossed the mighty gulf, and spied
For mortals out the heavenly way.
No power can ever close the road
Which he to us laid open then,
By which in long succession, men
Ascend to his sublime abode.
By it our fathers all have passed;
And that same path we too shall trace,
And every new succeeding race
Of mortal men, w'hile time shall last.
The god assembles round his throne
A growing throng, the good and wise
All those whom, scanned with searching eyes,
He recognizes as his own.
Departed mortal, speed from earth
By those old ways thy sires have trod;
Ascend, behold the expectant god,
Who calls thee to a higher birth.
First must each several element
That joined to form thy living frame
Flit to the region whence it came,
And with its parent source be blent.
Thine eye shall seek the solar orb,
Thy life-breath to the wind shall fly,
Thy part ethereal to the sky;
Thine earthy part shall earth absorb.
Thine unborn part shall Agni bright
With his benignest rays illume;
And guide it through the trackless gloom
To yonder sphere of life and light.
All imperfections leave behind;
Assume thine ancient form once more,
Each limb and sense thou hadst before,
From every earthly taint refined.
And now with heavenly glory bright,
With life intenser, nobler, blest,
With large capacity to taste
A fuller measure of delight.
Thou there once more each well known face
Shalt see of those thou lovedst here;
Thy parents, wife, and children dear,
With rapture shall thou soon embrace.
The good which thou on earth hast wrought,
Each sacrifice, each pious deed,
Shall there receive its ample meed;
No worthy act shall be forgot.
In those fair realms of cloudless day
Where Yama every joy supplies,
And every longing satisfies
Thy bliss shall never know decay."

—Muir, *O.S.T.*, v, 329.

Yama is still to some extent an object of terror. He is represented as having two insatiable dogs with four eyes and wide nostrils, which guard the road to his abode, and which the departed are advised to hurry past with all possible speed. These dogs are said to wander about among men as his messengers, no doubt for the purpose of summoning them to their master, who is in another place identified with death, and is described as sending a bird as the herald of doom."

In the epic poems Yama is the son of the Sun by Saṁjña (conscience), and brother of Vaivasvata (Manu). Mythologically he was the father of Yudhiṣṭhira. He is the god of departed spirits and judge of the dead. A soul when it quits its mortal form repairs to his abode in the lower regions; there the recorder Citragupta, reads out his account from the great register called Agrasandhānī, and a just sentence follows, when the soul either ascends to the abodes of the *pitṛs* (manes), or is sent to one of the twenty-one hells according to its guilt, or it is born again on earth in another form. Yama is regent of the south quarter, and as such is called Dakṣiṇāśāpati. He is represented as of a green colour and clothed with red. He rides upon a buffalo, and is armed with a ponderous mace and a noose to secure his victims.

In the Purāṇas a legend is told of Yama having shifted his foot to kick Chāyā, the handmaid of his father. She cursed him to have his leg affected with sores and worms, but his father gave him a cock which picked off the worms and cured the discharge. Through this incident he is called Śīrṇapāda, 'shriveled foot'.

Yama had several wives, as Hemamālā, Suśilā, and Vijayā. He dwells in the lower world, in his city Yamapura. There, in his palace called Kālīcī, he sits upon his throne of judgement, Vicārabhū. He is assisted by his recorder and councilor, Chitragupta, and waited upon by his two chief attendants and custodians, Chanda or Mahāchanda, and Kālapuruṣa. His messengers, *yamadūtas*, bring in the souls of the dead, and the door of his judgement-hall is kept by his porter, Vaidhyata.

Yama has many names descriptive of his office. He is Mṛtyu, Kāla, and Antaka, 'death'; Kṛtānta, 'the finisher'; 'Śamana, the settler'; Daṇḍī or Daṇḍadhara, 'the rod-bearer'; 'Bhīmaśāsana, 'of terrible decrees'; Pāśī, 'the noose-carrier'; Pitṛpati, 'lord of the manes';

Pretarāja, 'king of the ghosts'; Śrāddhadeva, 'god of the exequial offerings'; and especially Dharmarāja, 'king of justice'. He is Audumbara, from Udumbara, the fig tree', and from his parentage he is Vaivasvata. There is a Dharmaśāstra which bears the name of Yama.

YAMA-VAIVAŚVATA—Yama as son of Vivasvat.

YAMI—**(1)** A daughter of Daksha aud wife of Dharma; **(2)** A daughter of the sun, the twin sister of Yama; she became the Yamuna river.

YAMUNA—The river which rises in a mountain, called Kalinda (Sun). His wife Saôjñà personifies the river Yamunà as the daughter of the Sun. So she was sister of Yama. Balarāma, in a state of inebriety, called upon her to come to him that he might bathe, and as she did not heed, he, in a great rage, seized his ploughshare-weapon, dragged her to him and compelled her to follow him whithersoever he wandered through the wood. The river then assumed a human form and besought his forgiveness, but it was some time before she could appease him. Wilson thinks that "the legend probably alludes to the construction of canals from the Jumnā for the purposes of irrigation". The river is also called Kālindī, from the place of its source, Sūryajā, from her father, and Triyāmā.

YASAS—A son of Dharma.

YASKA—A predecessor of Páṇini (*q.v.*) and author of Nirukta, explaining different Vedic words. Yáska was also the author of a Commentary which bears the name of Nirukta. "Besides the great importance which Yáksha's Nirukta possesses for a proper understanding of the Vedic texts; it is valuable also on account of several discussions which it raises on grammatical and other questions; and on account of the insight it affords us into the scientific and religious condition of its time."—GOLDSTUCKER.

YASODA—Wife of the cowherd Nanda, and foster-mother of Kṛṣṇa, who was conveyed at his birth to the bed of Yaṣodá, by his father Vasudevs, and her own new born infant Yoganidrá, removed to the bed of Devakí, and destroyed by Kansa.

YASODA—The daughter of king Samoravira, who was married to Varddhamána, who afterwards became the twenty-fourth Tirthankara of the Jains, Mahávira.

YASODHARA—The wife of Sahishnu and mother of Kámadeva.

YATI—One of the sons of Nahusha and brother of Yayáti.

YATUDHANAS, YATUS—A designation given in the Rig-Veda to a class like the Dasyus and Rákshasas, all of whom are described as destitute of or averse to religious ceremonies, practicing different rites, haters of prayer, inhuman, godless, ferocious-looking or with fierce eyes; as flesh-eaters of human and of horse-flesh, as monstrous in form, and possessed of magical or super-human powers.—*Muir*, II, 418.

Yet Vasishtha himself, the very type of the Aryan brahman, when in feud with Viṣvámitra, is called not only an enemy, but a Yátudhána, and other names, which in common parlance, are only bestowed on barbarian savages and evil spirits,—II, 389. In the Rig-Veda we read 'the Yátudhánas who gloat on the bloody flesh of men or horses, and steal the milk of the cow, O Agni, cut off their heads with thy fiery sword.'—*Ib.* 391.

YAUDHEYA—The wife of Yudhishthira and mother of Devaka.

YAUGANDHARAYANA—(Yaugandharáyana), the chief minister of king Vatsa.

YAVAKRI, YAVAKRĪTA—'Bought with barley.' Son of the sage Bharadvāja. He performed great penance in order to obtain knowledge of the Vedas without study, and having obtained this and other boons from Indra, he became arrogant and treated other sages with disrespect. He made love to the wife of Parāvasu, son of his father's friend, Raibhya. That sage in his anger performed a sacrifice which brought into being a fearful *rākṣasa* who killed Yavakṛta at his father's chapel. Bharadvāja, in grief for his son, burnt himself upon the funeral pile. Before his death he cursed Parāvasu to be the death of his father, Raibhya, and the son killed his father in mistake for an antelope. All three were restored to life by the gods in recompense of the great devotions of Arvāvasu, the other son of Raibhya (*q.v.*).—*Mahābhārata.*

YAVANAS—The Yavans of the Hebrew. The term is found in Pāṇini, who speaks of the writing of the Yavanas. The Purāṇas represent them to be descendants of Turvasu, but they are always associated with the tribes of the northwest frontier, and there can be no doubt that the Macedonian or Bactrian Greeks are the people most usually intended by the term. In the Bactrian Pāli inscription of King Priyadarśī the word is contracted to Yona, and the term Yonarāja "is associated with the name of Antiochus, probably Antiochus the Great, the ally of the Indian prince Sophagasenas, about 210 B.C." The Purāṇas characterise them as "wise and eminently brave". They were among the races conquered by King Sagara, and "he made them shave their heads entirely'. In a later age they were encountered on the Indus by Puṣpamitra, a Mauryan general, who dethroned his master and took the throne. In modern times the term has been applied to the Muhammadans. They are placed by the *V.P.* in the west of Bhárata.

YAVINARA—A king of Hastinápura, the son of Dwinudha and grandson of Hastin.

YAVISTHA—The ever young; a name of Agni.

YAYATI—The son of Rája Nahusha. He had two wives, Devayání, the daughter of Uṣanas, and Sarmiṣhthá, the daughter of Vṛishaparvan; of whom this genealogical verse is recited: "Devayání bore two sons, Yadu and Turvasu. Sarmiṣhthá, the daughter of Vṛishaparvan, had three sons, Druhyu, Anu, and Púru." Through the curse of Uṣanas, Yayáti became old and infirm before his time; but, having appeased his father-in-law, he obtained permission to transfer his decrepitude to any one who would consent to take it. He first applied to his eldest son, Yadu, and said: "Your maternal grandfather has brought this premature decay upon me. By his permission, however, I may transfer it to you for a thousand years. I am not yet satiate with worldly enjoyments, and wish to partake of them through the means of your youth. Do not refuse compliance with my request." Yadu, however, was not willing to take upon him his father's decay; on which, his father denounced an imprecation upon him, and said: "Your posterity shall not possess dominion." He then applied, successively, to Druhyu, Turvasu, and Anu, and demanded of them their juvenile vigour. They all refused, and were, in consequence, cursed by the king. Lastly, he made the same request of Sarmishtha's youngest son Púru, who bowed to his father, and readily consented to give him his youth, and receive, in exchange. Yayáti's infirmities, saying that his father had conferred upon him a great favour.

The king Yayáti being, thus, endowed with renovated youth, conducted the affairs of State for the good of his people, enjoying such pleasures as were suited to his age and strength, and were not incompatible with virtue. He formed a connexion with the celestial nymph Viṣwáchí, and was wholly attached to her, and conceived no end to his desires. The more they were gratified, the more ardent they became; as it is said in this verse: "Desire is not appeased by enjoyment: fire fed with sacrificial oil becomes but the more intense. No one has ever more than enough of rice, or barley, or gold, or cattle, or women. Abandon, therefore, inordinate desire. When a mind finds neither good nor ill in all objects, but looks on all with an equal eye, then everything yields it pleasure. The wise man is filled with happiness, who escapes from desire, which the feeble-minded can with difficulty relinquish, and which grows not old with the aged. The hair becomes gray, the teeth fall out, as man advances in years; but the love of wealth, the love of life, are not impaired by age." "A thousand years have passed," reflected Yayáti, "and my mind is still devoted to pleasure: every day my desires are awakened by new objects. I will, therefore, now renounce all sensual enjoyment, and fix my mind upon spiritual truth. Unaffected by the alternatives of pleasure and pain, and having nothing I may call my own, I will, henceforth, roam the forests with the deer."

Having made this determination, Yayáti restored his youth to Púru, resumed his own decrepitude, installed his youngest son in the sovereignty, and departed to the wood of penance (Tapovana). To Turvasu he consigned the south-east districts of his kingdom; the west, to Druhyu; the south, to Yadu; and the north, to Anu; to govern, as viceroys, under their younger brother Púru, who he appointed supreme monarch of the earth." *V.P.*

A different account is given in the Pádma Purána. It is there said that Yayáti was invited by Indra to heaven, and conveyed on the way thither by Mátali, Indra's charioteer. For the conversation that took place between them, see MÁTALI; the result was that Yayáti returned to earth, where, by his virtuous administration he rendered all his subjects exempt from passion and decay: Yama complained that men had ceased to die, and Indra sent Kámadeva and his daughter Aṣruvindumati to endeavour to excite passion in the breast of Yayáti; they succeeded, and it was then the aged king asked his sons to give him their youth in exchange for his decrepitude. As related above they all refused except Púru, the youngest. Not long after Yayáti proceeded with his subjects to Indra and ultimately to the abode of Vishṇu.—*Wilson*, III, 37.

YAYATI-CARITRA—A drama in seven acts on the life of Yayāti. It is attributed to Rudradeva. The subject is Yayāti's intrigue with Sarmiṣṭhā.

YEDILLIAN—The wife of Ladurlad. It was on the latter that Southey makes the terrible curse of Kehama to rest. Ladurlad was at this time a widower, but his beloved daughter Kaliyal was miraculously preserved to him, and afforded him some solace amidst his wanderings and sufferings, so well depicted in Southey's poem. When at length by the descent of the Ganges to the earth the father and daughter are enabled to escape to Mount Meru and find a place of rest beyond the influence of Kehama's Curse, and then the long-lost Yedillian returns to him in the bower of bliss to complete his happiness. The scene is so affectingly described that the whole passage may be quoted:

Three happy beings are there here,
The Sire, the Maid, the Glendoveer;
A fourth approaches, ...who is this
That enters in the Bower of Bliss ?
No form so fair might painter find
Among the daughters of mankind;
For death her beauties hath refined,
And unto her a form hath given
Framed of the elements of Heaven;
Pure dwelling place for perfect mind.
She stood and gazed on Sire and Child;
Her tongue not yet had power to speak,
The tears were streaming down her cheek;
And when those tears her sight beguiled,
And still her faltering accents fail'd,
The Spirit, mute ard motionless,
Spread out her aims for the caress.
Made still and silent witli excess
Of love and painful happiness.
The Maid that lovely form survey'd;
Wistful she gazed, and knew her not,
But Nature to her heart convey'd
A sudden thrill, a startling thought,
A feeling many a year forgot,
Now like a dream anew recurring,
As if again in every vein
Her mother's milk was stirring.
With straining neck and earnest eye
She stretched her hands imploringly,
As if she fain would have her nigh,
Yet fear'd to meet the wish'd embrace,
At once with love and awe opprest.
Not so Ladurlad; he could trace,
Though brighten'd with angelic grace,
His own Yedillian's earthly face;
He ran and held her to his breast !
Oh joy above all joys of Heaven,
By Death alone to others given,
This moment hath to him restored
The early-lost, the long-deplored.
They sin who tell us Love can die,
With life all other passions fly,
All others are but vanity.
In Heaven Ambition cannot dwell,
Nor Avarice in the vaults of Hell;
Earthly these passions of the Earth,
They perish where they have their birth;
But Love is indestructible.
Its holy flame for ever burneth,
From Heaven it came, to Heaven returneth;
Too oft on Earth a troubled guest,
At times deceived, at times oppress,
It here is tried and purified,
Then hath in Heaven its perfect rest:
It soweth here with toil and care,
But the harvest time of Love is there.
Oh ! when a Mother meets on high
The Babe she lost in infancy,
Hath she not then, for pains and fears,
The day of woe, the watchful night,
For all her sorrow, all her tears,
An over-payment of delight ?

YOGA—Union, junction; in a spiritual sense it denotes union of separated with universal soul; and with some latitude of expression it conies to signify the means by which such union is effected. In the Bhágavat Gítá it is variously applied, but ordinarily denotes the performance of religious ceremonies as a duty, and not for interested purposes. The word has accordingly been rendered 'devotion' by Wilkins [and by Mr. J. C. Thomson] and 'devotion' by Schlegel, in their translations of the Gítá. In the Vishṇu Purána it is used in a less general sense, and signifies reunion with spirit, through the exercises necessary to perfect abstraction as they are taught and practiced by the followers of Patanjaii.

A school of philosophy, (*see* DARŚANA and YAJÑAVALKYA)

YOGANIDRA—Personified delusion: the great illusory energy of Vishṇu, by whom, as utter ignorance, the whole world is beguiled. Yoganidrá is the sleep of devotion or abstraction, the active principle of illusion, personified, and also termed Máya and Mahamáyá, also Avidya or ignorance. In the Markáṇḍeya Purána she appears as Devi or Durgá, the Sakti or bride of Śiva; but in the Vishṇu Purána as Vaishṇavi, or the Sakti of Vishṇu.

YOGASIDDHA—The lovely and virtuous daughter of Váchaspati who pervades the whole world without being devoted to it, was the wife of Prabhása, the eighth of the Vasus, and bore to him the patriarch Visvakarma, the architect and mechanist of the gods.

YOGINI—A sorceress. The Yoginīs are eight female demons attendant on Durgā. Their names are Mārjanī, Karpūratilakā, Malayagandhinī, Kaumudikā, Bheruṇḍā, Mātālī, Nāyakī, and Jayā or Śubhācāra; Sulakṣaṇā,

Sunandā.

YOGI-YOGIN—A devotee seeking the attainment of Yóga; he has to pass through four principal stages: 1. He learns the rules of Yóga. 2. He acquires perfect knowledge .3. He employs this knowledge practically and overcomes the material influence of the primary elements. 4. He destroys all consciousness of personality and individuality, (*ahankára*); and the soul thus becomes free from matter.

Thus by the prescribed methods, he has attained the state termed Yóga, the union of the living with the supreme soul; the identity of the living with the supreme spirit; of the Jívátma, with Brahmá; the identity of the contemplator with the object contemplated.

YONI—The female organ. Alone, or in combination with the *liṅga*, it is an object of worship by the followers of the Śaktis.

YUDAMUSHTI—One of the sons of the Yádava chief Ugrasena.

YUDHAJIT—**(1)** A prince, the son of Asvapati, rája of Kekaya, and uncle of Bharata.

Then Bharat for the road prepared,
And with Satrughna forth he fared.
First to his sire he bade adieu,
Brave Ráma, and his mothers too.
Lord Yudhájit with joyful pride
Went forth, the brothers by his side,
And reached the city where he dwelt:
And mighty joy his father felt.

(2) A prince, the second son of Vrishni, rája of Mrittikávati.

YUDHISHTHIRA—The eldest of the Páṇḍu princes. "The characters of the five brothers in the Mahábhárata are drawn with an individuality which is very unusual in Oriental Poetry. They each have their distinguishing traits, which are often painted with much discrimination and even delicacy of touch in the lighter shades; and yet there evidently runs a family likeness through them all. To the European reader, Arjuna, the third brother is the most interesting, and approaches the nearest to our ideal of chivalry; many of his exploits remind us of Arthur's knights, or Charlemagne's paladins; and it is he who wins Draupadi as his wife in a tournament, where her father had offered her hand as the conqueror's prize. With the Hindus, however, Yudhishthira, the eldest, is the favourite; his cold passionless heroism is with them the *beau ideal* of humanity; and he moves through the poem in a calm majesty of self-possession, as if far above all the weaknesses of man, while the sorrows and joys which chequer his life.

Viennent tonjours glisser sur son étre insensible,
Commes de gouttes déan sur un marbre poli.'*

Yudhishthira, as we have already seen, [PANDAVAS] was taught the use of the spear by Droṇa, but became more distinguished by wisdom and goodness than for military exploits. His uncle Dhritaráshtra decided that Yudhishthira had the best right to succeed him, and he was installed as Yuvarája. This excited the jealousy of his cousin Duryodhana, who expostulated with the old Mahárája until he agreed to divide the kingdom between them, when Yudhishthira and his brethren took leave of the Mahárája, and of all their kinsmen, and departed with their mother Kunti to the city of Váranávati. Before their departure they were cautioned by their uncle Vidura to beware of fire; and soon after their arrival they discovered a wicked plot that had been devised by Duryodhana and his' friends for their destruction. A trusty retainer of Duryodhana's, named Purochana, had been sent on to prepare a handsome house in the city of Váranávati for the sons of Páṇḍu: and Purochana had built the walls of the house with lac or resin, mingled with hemp; so that some night when the Páṇḍavas were asleep, the doors might be fastened in the outside and the house set on fire, and all within it be consumed in the flames. Accordingly Purochana heartily welcomed the Páṇḍavas; and after having conducted them to the college of devotees, lie led them to the house prepared for their reception, and set before them a collation of fruit, &c. Shortly after a man came from their uncle saying, "Vidura has sent me to dig an underground passage from your house, to deliver you from it, should it be set on fire." When the passage was completed Bhima resolved that Purochana should fall into the scare be had laid for them. One day Kunti invited all the poor people of the city and gave them a feast; among her guests were a Bhil woman and her five sons, who according to the practice of their tribe drank a large quantity of strong liquor, and then lay down and slept heavily. The same night a violent wind arose, and Bhíma stole out through the passage, and strongly barricaded the house of Purochna and set it on fire; and the flames speedily destroyed the building and reached the house of the Páṇḍavas; then Bhíma conducted his mother and brethren through the passage underground and hurried them away into the jungle. Next morning the people of the city saw that both houses were destroyed by fire, and believed that all the inmates had perished; for they discovered the blackened remains of Purochana and his servants, and also those of the Bhil woman and her five sons, whom they took to be those of Kunti and the Páṇḍavas. The tidings now reached the city of Hastinápur, and the Kauravas greatly rejoiced at the supposed death of their enemies the Páṇḍavas; but Bhíshma, Droṇa, and Dritaráshtra were affected even unto tears.

The Páṇḍavas having escaped into the jungle met with many adventures there. Once when the party, overcome with fatigue were all asleep except Bhíma, who stood by to guard them, an Ásura named Hidimba attacked him, but after a severe fight, Bhíma slew the cannibal. The sister of the Asúra then set up a terrible cry, but afterwards followed Bhíma and his party. She was ultimately married to him. They all afterwards dwelt in the city of Ekachakra, (*q.v.*). The next event of importance was the marriage of the five brothers to Draupadí, the beautiful daughter of Drupada, the Rája of Pánchála. At her Swayamvara the Kauravas and many distinguished Rájas assembled; but all failed to bend the bow, when Arjuna disguised as a brahman, accomplished the feat, and shot the arrow in the eye of the golden fish, having first gone through the whirling Chakra below the fish. Draupadi then threw the garland round Arjuna's neck and accompanied him to the house of his mother. Afterwards by the advice of the sage Vyása she was married to all the five brothers. They then returned to Hastinápur on the invitation of Bhíshma, and were given the sovereignty of Khaṇdava-prastha, as their half of the Ráj.

When the Páṇḍavas were settled in tins new country, they built at first at Indra-prastha, cleared the jungle of Khaṇdava, and drove out the Scythian tribe known as the Nágas. When they had thus established a supremacy over every bordering enemy, and proved to the satisfaction of their new subject; that they could protect cattle and harvests, they invited all their kinsmen and neighbours to a Rájasúya, and in the presence of all the people solemnly inaugurated their elder brother Yudhishthira as Rája of Khándaprastha. The ceremonies performed at the sacrifice were these: a number of priests marked out the spot, and strewed the place with the sacred kusa grass, kindled the sacrificial fire and chanted the Vedic hymns. The so-called Rájas who attended, were probably a rude company of half-naked warriors who feasted boisterously beneath the shade of trees.†

The Rájasúya excited the jealous anger of Duryodhana, who arranged for his cousin's visit to a great gambling match at Hastinápur. Yudhishthira reluctantly consented to go from a sense of obligation to obey the Mahárája, and accept a challenge, Through the fraudulent contrivances of Duryodhana he lost the whole of the Ráj; staked his brothers as slaves and lost them; lost himself; then Draupadí; then went into exile.

After thirteen years of exile in which they had many adventures, negotiations were opened for the return of the Páṇḍavas. These all-failing, preparations were made for the great war which forms the chief event in the Mahábhárata, *q.v.* See also PANDAVAS, &c.

The closing scene of the Mahábhárata, describing the last days of Yudhishthira, is considered the very finest specimen of the heroic poetry' of India. "We know of no episode even in the Homeric poems, which can surpass its mournful grandeur, or raise a more solemn dirge over the desolation of the fallen heart of man! Yudhishthira has won the throne, and his enemies are all fallen; and an inferior poet would have concluded the story with a pæan upon his happiness. But the Hindu bard bad a far deeper insight into man's nature, and his genius would, not content itself with any such commonplace catastrophe; he knew well that the human soul was born for the infinite, and that no finite line could fathom the depths of its longings! It was no idle fiction in Grecian mythology that Ulysses after his return to Ithaca, wandered forth again with his hungry heart into the world.

'For all experience is an arch, where thro' Gleams that untraversed laud, whose margin fades, For ever and for ever as we move.'

"And Ulysses had found that the Ithaca, which had lured him on through ten years of war, and ten more of wandering, changed, upon his arrival, into a bleak barren rock, and his restless soul stretched out her hands once more towards the untrodden beyond. Just in the same way, and with the same deep significance, Yudhishthira learns, after his victory, that the throne for which he had suffered so much leaves him unsatisfied and hungry as before. The friends of his youth are fallen, and the excitement of contest is over; and he learns in sorrow that kings are but men, and that the Fall has overshadowed the throne as much as the poorest cottage! In gloomy disappointment Yudhishthira resigns his crown, and he and his brothers and Draupadí set out in a forlorn journey to Mount

Meru, where Indra's heaven lies amongst the wilds of the Himâlayas,‡ there to find that rest which seemed denied to their search upon earth. We present a literal prose version of their pilgrimage arid with it close our extracts.

I.

Having heard Yudhishthira's resolve, and seen the destruction of Krishṇa,

The five brothers set forth, and Draupadi, and the seventh was a dog that followed them,

Yudhishthira himself was the last that quitted Hastinápura;

And all the citizens and the court followed them on their way,

But none felt able to say unto him 'return;'

And at length they all went back unto the city,

Then the high-souled sons of Pándu, and far-tamed Draupadi,

Pursued their way, fasting, and with their faces turned towards the east,

Resolved upon separation from earth, and longing for release from its laws;

They roamed onward over many regions, and to many a river and sea.

Yudhishthira went before, and Bhíma followed next behind him,

And Arjuna came after him, and then the twin sons of Madri,

And sixth, after them, came Draupadi, with her fair face and lotus eyes.

And last of all followed the dog, as they wandered on till they came to the ocean.

For my purpose holds '"To sail unto the West until I die.

It may be that the gulfs will wash us down, It may be we shall reach the blessed isles;

And see the great Achilles whom we knew"'

But Arjuna left not hold of his heavenly bow, Lured by the splendour of its gems, nor of those two heavenly arrows;

And suddenly they saw Agni standing like a mountain before them, Standing in gigantic form and stopping up their path;

And thus to them spoke the god,—'O sons of Pándu, do yon know me not?' O Yudhishthira, mighty hero, knowest thou not my voice! I am Agni, who gave that bow unto Arjuna;

Let him leave it here and go, for none other is worthy to bear it:

For Arjuna's lake I stole that bow of Varuna, the ocean god,

Let Gandhiva, that best of bows, be given back to ocean again !'

Then the brothers all besought Arjuna to obey,

And he flung the bow into the sea, and he flung those immortal arrows:

And lo ! as they tell into the sea. Agni vanished before them.

And once more the sons of Pándu set forth, with their faces turned to the south.

And then by the upper shore of the briny sea,

They turned toward the south-west, and went on their way;

And as they journeyed onwards, and came unto the west,

There they beheld the old city of Krishṇa, now washed over by the ocean tide,

Again they turned to the north, and still they went on in their way,

Circumambulating round the continent to find separation from earth.

II.

Then with their senses subdued, the heroes having reached the north,

Beheld, with their heaven-desiring eyes, the lofty mountain Himavat,

And having crossed its height they beheld the sea of sand,

And next they saw rocky Meru, the king of mountains.

But while they were thus faring onwards. In eager search for separation,

Draupadi lost hold of her hope, and tell on the face of the earth;

And Bhíma the mighty having beheld her fall,

Spoke to the king of justice,† looking back to her as there she lay,

'No act of evil hath she done, that faultless daughter of a king.

Wherefore then, O conqueror, hath she fallen thus low on the ground ?'

And thus to him answered Yudhishthira 'too great was her love for Arjuna,'

And the fruit thereof, Oh Bhíma, hath she gathered here this day.

Thus speaking, Bharata's glorious descendant, went onwards, not looking back,

Gathering up his soul in himself in his unstooping wisdom and justice.

Next the fair Sahadeva fell upon the face of the earth.

And Bhíma, beholding him fall, thus spoke to the king;

'Oh Yudhishthira, *he* the greatest, the least froward and wilful of us all,

He the son of fair Madri,—wherefore hath he fallen

on the ground ?'

And him thus answered Yudhishthira, 'He esteemed none equal to himself,

This was his fault, and therefore hath the prince fallen this day.'

Thus speaking, he left Sahadeva, and went on;

Yudhishthira, king of justice, and his brothers, and the dog.

But when Nakula saw the fall of Draupadi and his brother,

The hero, full of love for his kindred, in his grief tell down like them to the earth.

And when Nakula, the fair-faced, had thus fallen like the others,

Once more, in his wonder, spoke Bhíma unto the king:—

'What ! *he* the undeviating in virtue, ever true to his honour and faith.

Unequalled for beauty in the world, hath he too fallen on the ground?' And him thus answered Yudhishthira,' Ever was the thought in his heart, There it none equal in beauty to me, and I am superior unto all!' Therefore hath Nakula fallen; come Bhíma, and follow my steps;

'Whatsoever each hath done, assuredly he cateth thereof.' And when Arjuna beheld them thus fallen behind him, He too, the great conqueror, tell, with his soul pierced through with sorrow:

And when he, the lion-hearted, was fallen, like Indra himself in majesty, When he, the invincible, was dead, once more Bhíma spoke unto the king:

'No act of evil do I remember in all that Arjuna hath done;

Wherefore then is this change, add why hath he too fallen on the ground ?'

And him thus answered Yudhishthira, 'In one day I could destroy all my enemies.'

Such was Arjuna's boast, and he falls, for he fulfilled it not!

And he ever desplsed all warriors beside himself,

This he ought not to have done, and therefore hath he fallen to-day.

Thus speaking, the king went on, and then Bhíma hinnelt next fell to the earth.

And, as he fell, he cried with a loud voice unto Yudhishthira,

'Oh king of justice look back, I—I thy dear brother am fallen,

What la the cause of my fall. Oh tell it to me it thou knowest?'

Once more him answered Yudhishthira,' When thou gazed'st on thy foe,

Thou hast cursed him with thy breath, therefore thou too tallest to-day !'

Thus having spoken, the mighty king, not looking back, went on,

And still, as ever, behind him, went following that dog alone !

III.

'Lo ! suddenly, with a sound that ran through heaven and earth

Indra came riding on his chariot, and he cried to the king 'ascend.'

Then indeed did the lord of justice look back to his fallen brothers,

And thus unto India he spoke with a sorrowful heart,

'Let my brothers who yonder lie fallen, go with me,

Not even into thy heaven would I enter it they were not there:

And yon fair-faced daughter of a king, Draupadi, the all-deserving;

Let her too enter with us? Oh Indra, approve my prayer !'

Indra.

In heaven thou shall find thy brothers, they are already there before thee, There are they all with Draupadi; weep not then. Oh son of Bharata! Thither are they entered, prince, having thrown away their mortal weeds, But thou alone shalt enter, still wearing thy body of flesh.

Yudhishthira.

Oh Indra and what of this dog? It hath faithfully followed me through;

Let it go with me into heaven, for my soul is full of compassion.

Indra.

Immortality and fellowship with me, and the height of joy and felicity, All these hast thou reached today; leave then the dog behind thee.

Yudhishthira.

The good may oft act an evil part, but never a part like this;

Away then with that felicity, whose price is to abandon the faithful.

Indra.

My heaven hath no place for dogs; they steal away our offerings on earth, Leave then thy dog behind thee, nor think in thy heart that it is cruel.

Yudhishthira.

To abandon the faithful and devoted is an endless crime, like the murder of a Brahmán,

Never therefore, come weal or woe, will I abandon yon faithful dog,

Yon poor creature, in tear and distress, hath trusted in my power to save it;

Not therefore, for even life itself, will I break my plighted word.

Indra.

If a dog but beholds a sacrifice, men esteem it unholy and void;

Forsake then the dog, O hero, and heaven is thine own as a reward.

Already thou hast borne to forsake thy fondly-loved brothers and Draupadi,

Why then forsakest thou not the dog ? wherefore now falls thy heart ?

Yudhishthira.

Mortals, when they are dead, are dead to love or hate, so runs the world's belief, I could not bring them back to life, but while they lived I never left them;

To oppress the suppliant, to kill a wife, to spoil a Brahmán, and to betray one's friends, These are the four great crimes; and to forsake a dependent, I count equal unto them.

* * *

Yudhishthira then enters heaven; but one more trial awaits him. He finds there Duryodhana and the other sons of Dhritaráshtrá, but he looks in vain for his own brothers. He refuses to stay in the Swarga without them, and a messenger is sent to bring him where they are. He descends to the Indian hell and finds them there; and he proudly resolves to stay with them and share their sorrows, rather than dwell in heaven without them. But the whole scene was only a *máyá* or illusion, to prove his virtue; the sorrows suddenly vanish, the surrounding hell changes into heaven where Yudhishthira and his brothers dwell with Indra in full content of heart for ever.

Thus closes the Mahábhárata, the new mythic world, which a modern Columbus has opened."‡‡

Yudhishthira is also called Dharmarája, Dharmaputra and sometimes simply Rájan.

(* *Westminster Review*, Vol. I, p. 53; † *Wheeler*, I,167.

†† This is in fact a precise counterpart to the legend of Ulysses, as Tennyson describes it in his poem,—the most epicean fragment since Milton's days; ‡The god of Fire from whom Arjuna had obtained the bow Gandhiva. † The usual title of Yudhishthira; ‡‡ *Westminster Review*, Vol. L, p. 61.)

YUGAS—An age of the world. Each of these ages is preceded by a period called its Sandhyā or twilight, and is followed by another period of equal length called Sandhyāṁśa, 'portion of twilight', each being equal to one-tenth of the *yuga*. The *yugas* are four in number, and their duration is first computed by years of the gods:

Thus	Kṛita Yuga	4,000	
	Sandhya	400	
	Sandhyásana	400	
			=4,800
	—Tretá Yuga	3,000	
	Sandhya	300	
	Sandhyásana	300	
			=3,600
	—Dwápara Yuga	2,000	
	Sandhya	200	
	Sandhyásana	200	
			=2,400
		Carried over	10,800
		Brought over	10,800
	—Kálí Yuga	1,000	
	Sandhya	100	
	Sandhyásana	100	
			=1,200
		Total	=12,000

—See *V.P.* and Notes.

To estimate the length of each it is necessary to remember that six months form an Ayana (the period of the sun's progress north or south of the ecliptic); and two Ayanas compose a year. The southern Ayana is a night, and the northern a day, of the gods. Twelve thousand divine years, each composed of three hundred and sixty such days, constitute the period of the four Yugas or ages. They are thus distributed; the Kṛita age has four thousand divine years; the Tretá, three thousand; the Dwápara, two thousand; and the Kálí age, one thousand. The period that precedes a Yuga is called a Sandhya, and it is of as many hundred years as there are thousands in the Yuga; and the period that follows a Yuga, termed the Sandhyásana, is of similar duration.

This elaborate and practically boundless system of chronology was invented between the age of the *Ṛgveda* and that of the *Mahābhārata.* No traces of it are to be found in the hymns of the *Ṛg*, but it was fully established in the days of the great epic. In this work the four ages are described at length by Hanūmat, the learned monkey chief, and from that description the following account has been abridged:

The *kṛta* is the age in which righteousness is eternal, when duties did not languish nor people decline. Men made no efforts, the fruit of the earth was obtained by their mere wish. There was no malice, weeping, pride, or deceit; no contention, no hatred, cruelty, fear, affliction, jealousy, or envy. The castes alike in their functions fulfilled their duties, were unceasingly devoted to one deity, and used one formula, one rule, and one rite. Though they had separate duties, they had but one Veda and practiced one duty.

In the *tretā yuga* sacrifice commenced, righteousness decreased by one-fourth; men adhered to truth, and were devoted to a righteousness dependent on ceremonies. Sacrifices prevailed with holy acts and a variety of rites. Men acted with an object in view, seeking after reward for their rites and their gifts, and were no longer disposed to austerities and to liberality from a simple feeling of duty.

In the *dvāpara yuga* righteousness was diminished by a half. The Veda became fourfold. Some men studied four Vedas, others three, others two, others one and some none at all. Ceremonies were celebrated in a great variety of ways. From the decline of goodness only few men adhered to truth. When men had fallen away from goodness, many diseases, desires, and calamities, caused by destiny, assailed them, by which they were severely afflicted and driven to practice austerities. Others desiring heavenly bliss offered sacrifices. Thus men declined through unrighteousness.

In the *kali yuga* righteousness remained to the extent of one-fourth only. Practices enjoined by the Vedas, works of righteousness, and rites of sacrifice ceased. Calamities, diseases, fatigue, faults, such as anger, &c., distresses, hunger, and fear prevailed. As the ages revolve righteousness declines, and the people also decline. When they decay their motives grow weak, and the general decline frustrates their aims.—*Muir*, I. 144

In the *kṛta yuga* the duration of life was four thousand years, in the *tretā* three thousand, in the *dvāpara* two thousand. In the *kali yuga* there is no fixed measure. Other passages of the *Mahābhārata* indicate "that the *kṛta yuga* was regarded as an age in which brāhmaṇas alone existed, and that ksatriyas only began to be born in the *tretā*".

YUGA—A cycle of five years. The years are called severally Samvatsara, Parivatsara, Idvatsara, Anuvatsara, and Vatsara. There are four kinds of months: 1, the Saura, or Solar-sidereal, consisting of the sun's passage through a sign of the zodiac; 2, the Saumya or Chánḍra or lunar mouth, comprehending thirty lunations or Tithis, and reckoned most usually from new moon to new moon, though sometimes from full moon to full moon; 3, the Savana, or solar month, containing thirty days of sunrise and sunset; and 4, the Nakshatra or lunar asterismal month, which is the moon's revolution through the twenty-eight lunar mansions. The five years forming the Yuga differ only in denomination, being composed of the months just described, with such Malamásas or intercalary months, as may be necessary to complete the period, according to Vriddha Garga. The cycle comprehends therefore sixty solar-sidereal months of 1,800 days: sixty-one solar months or 1,830 days; sixty-two lunar months, or 1,860 lunations; and sixty-seven lunar-asterismal months, or 1,809 such days.

YUGADYA—(Yugádyá), full moon of Mághu (14th February). Bathing and feasting, and the offering of sesamum seeds to the manes, are enjoined on the full moon of Mágha, and it is also held in additional honour as the anniversary of the commencement of the Kali Yug, or present age of the world, the age of impurity.

YUGANDHARA—A city in the Panjāb. A people dwelling there and in the vicinity.

YUPAKHYA—(Yupákhya), one of the five warriors whom Rávaṇa sent against Hanumán; but the Hanuman assuming gigantic form tore up a lofty palm tree and beat down his weapons and then himself, so that he was soon in Yama's world.—*I.E.*

YUPAKSHA—(Yupaksha), one of Rávaṇa's nobles; the first who spoke to Kumbhakarna after they had succeeded in awaking the bull-brained giant.

YUVANASWA—**(1)** A prince, the son of Ardra; **(2)** the son of Prasenajit, and father of Mandhatra, *q.v.* A legend represents this son as being conceived by and born of his father; **(3)** the son of Ambarísha.

YUVARAJ—'Young king.' The heir apparent to a throne.

YUYUDHANA—The son of Satyaka, and grandson of Siní.

YUYUTSU—A youngest son of Dhṛtarāṣṭra by a vaiśya handmaid. On the eve of the great battle he left the side of the Kauravas and joined the Pāṇḍavas. When Yudiṣṭhira retired from the world he established Yuyutsu in the kingdom of Indraprastha.